The Wiley Handbook on the Theories, Assessment, and Treatment of Sexual Offending

The Wiley Handbook on the Theories, Assessment, and Treatment of Sexual Offending

Editor-in-Chief

Douglas P. Boer

Volume II: Assessment

Edited by

Leam A. Craig and Martin Rettenberger

WILEY Blackwell

This edition first published 2017
© 2017 John Wiley & Sons, Ltd.

Registered Office
John Wiley & Sons Ltd, The Atrium, Southern Gate, Chichester, West Sussex,
PO19 8SQ, UK

Editorial Offices
350 Main Street, Malden, MA 02148-5020, USA
9600 Garsington Road, Oxford, OX4 2DQ, UK
The Atrium, Southern Gate, Chichester, West Sussex, PO19 8SQ, UK

For details of our global editorial offices, for customer services, and for information about
how to apply for permission to reuse the copyright material in this book please see our website
at www.wiley.com/wiley-blackwell.

The right of Douglas P. Boer to be identified as the author of the editorial material in this
work has been asserted in accordance with the UK Copyright, Designs and Patents Act 1988.

Library of Congress Cataloging-in-Publication Data

Names: Boer, Douglas Peter, 1956- editor.
Title: The Wiley handbook on the theories, assessment, and treatment of sexual offending /
    edited by Douglas P. Boer.
Other titles: Wiley handbook on the theories, assessment, and treatment of sexual offending
    2016. | Includes bibliographical references and index.
Identifiers: LCCN 2016023969 | ISBN 9781118572665 (hardback)
Subjects: LCSH: Sex offenders–Rehabilitation. | Psychosexual disorders–Diagnosis. |
    BISAC: PSYCHOLOGY / Forensic Psychology.
Classification: LCC RC560.S47 W55 2016 | DDC 616.85/83–dc23 LC record available at
    https://lccn.loc.gov/2016023969

A catalogue record for this book is available from the British Library.

Cover image: © sl_photo / Shutterstock

Set in Galliard 10/12.5 by SPi Global, Chennai, India
Printed and bound in Singapore by Markono Print Media Pte Ltd

1   2017

Contents

Volume I: Theories

Volume II: Assessment

Volume III: Treatment

About the Editors

Editor-in-Chief

Douglas P. Boer began working at the University of Canberra in September 2012 after working for 7 years at the University of Waikato, Hamilton, New Zealand. Prior to 2006 he worked for the Correctional Service of Canada for 15 years in a variety of contexts including sex offender therapist and treatment programme supervisor. Professor Boer's research interests include offender rehabilitation and the integration of modern theories of offending with practical intervention strategies to try and help effective reintegration. His primary area of clinical work is currently that of working with offenders with an intellectual disability and other complicating mental health issues. He has published approximately 75 articles and book chapters as well as several structured clinical assessment manuals in regard to sexual offenders, most notably helping to co-author the Sexual Violence Risk – 20 (the SVR-20) and the Assessment of Risk and Manageability for Individuals with Developmental and Intellectual Limitations who Offend – Sexually (the ARMIDILO-S). Professor Boer is also a clinical associate of the Forensic Department Brøset, St. Olav's Hospital, Trondheim, Norway.

Editors Volume II

Leam A. Craig, BA (Hons), MSc, PhD, MAE, CSci, C.Psychol, FBPsS, EuroPsy, is a Consultant Forensic and Clinical Psychologist and Partner at Forensic Psychology Practice Ltd. He is Professor (Hon) of Forensic Psychology at the Centre for Forensic and Criminological Psychology, University of Birmingham, UK, and Visiting Professor of Forensic Clinical Psychology at the School of Social Sciences, Birmingham City University, UK. In 2013 he was appointed Fellow of the British Psychological Society. He is a Chartered and Registered [Forensic and Clinical] Psychologist, a Chartered Scientist, and holder of the European Certificate in Psychology, permitting practice throughout the European Union, and an Accredited Member of The Academy of Experts. His current practice includes direct services to forensic adult mental health and learning disability hospitals and consultancy to prison and probation services throughout England and Wales and Northern Ireland. He acts as an expert witness to civil and criminal courts in the assessment of sexual and violent offenders and he has previously been instructed by the Catholic and Church of England Dioceses, South African Police Service and the United States Air Force as an expert witness. He has published over 80 research articles and chapters in a range of research and professional journals including 10 books. He is a Series Editor for the *What Works in Offender Rehabilitation* book series for Wiley. In 2013 he was the recipient of the Senior Academic Award by the Division of Forensic Psychology for distinguished contributions to academic knowledge in forensic psychology. His research interests include sexual and violent offenders, personality disorder and forensic risk assessment, and the use of expert witnesses in civil and criminal courts. He sits on the Editorial Boards of several international journals.

Martin Rettenberger, MA, Dipl. -Psych., Dr. biol. hum., is Director of the Centre for Criminology (Kriminologische Zentralstelle – KrimZ) in Wiesbaden, Germany, and was between 2013 and 2015 an Associate Professor for Forensic Psychology at the Department of Psychology at the Johannes Gutenberg University Mainz (JGU), Germany. He previously worked at the Federal Evaluation Centre for Violent and Sexual Offenders (FECVSO) in the Austrian Prison System in Vienna, Austria, and at the Institute of Sex Research and Forensic Psychiatry at the University Medical Centre Hamburg-Eppendorf, Germany. Since 2012, he has served as Secretary Vice General of the International Association for the Treatment of Sexual Offenders (IATSO) and as co-editor of the IATSO e-journal *Sexual Offender Treatment.*

Contributors to Volume II

A. Scott Aylwin, PhD, completed undergraduate studies in Criminology in 1992 and began working with adolescent sex offenders in a residential treatment facility. Working primarily as a group therapist, Scott began work at the Alberta Hospital Edmonton's Phoenix Program in 1997. This program employed several theoretical orientations, but primarily offered inpatient treatment to adult male sex offenders utilizing here-and-now process groups with psychodynamic and existential leanings. CBT was utilized in some content-specific groups. Obtaining a PhD from the University of Alberta in Psychiatry (Psychotherapy Research), Scott's dissertation was a prospective examination of the therapeutic alliance in sex offender treatment, and also examined the affective experience of therapists working with this population over time. Scott's most recent post in a forensic setting was Program Manager of the Northern Alberta Forensic Psychiatry Service. Currently, Scott is Senior Director Operations, Addiction and Mental Health for Covenant Health.

Ross M. Bartels, PhD, is a Lecturer in Psychology and member of the Forensic and Clinical Research Group at the University of Lincoln, UK. He is also an associate editor of *nextgenforensic*, an online blog for the NextGen working in the field of sexual offending research and treatment. Ross' research interests focus on adapting indirect measures and sociocognitive paradigms to gain new insights into the processes underlying and associated with deviant sexual cognition, thoughts, and fantasies.

Anthony R. Beech, DPhil, FBPsS, CPsychol, is Head of the Centre for Forensic and Criminological Psychology at the University of Birmingham, UK. He has authored over 180 peer-reviewed articles and 50 book chapters and has authored/edited seven books in the area of forensic science/criminal justice. His particular areas of research interests are improving risk assessment, exploring the neurobiological bases of offending, reducing online exploitation of children, and increasing psychotherapeutic effectiveness of the treatment given to offenders. In 2009 he received the Significant Achievement Award from the Association for the Treatment of Sexual Abusers in Dallas, Texas, and the Senior Award from the Division of Forensic Psychology, British Psychological Society, for recognition of his work in this area.

Astrid Birgden, PhD, is a Consultant Forensic Psychologist (Just Forensic) and an adjunct Clinical Associate Professor (Deakin University) in Australia. For over 25 years, she has designed policy, developed services, and managed service delivery to serious offenders, including to sexual offenders, to offenders with an intellectual disability, and as a warden of a compulsory drug treatment prison. She is published in offender rehabilitation, law–psychology intersections, and human rights.

Douglas P. Boer, PhD, RClinPsych, is Professor of Clinical Psychology at the University of Canberra, Australia. His research interests include risk assessment instrument development (e.g., SVR-20, ARMIDILO-S), theory, and intervention with various groups of sexual offenders, including child exploitation material (CEM) offenders, intellectually disabled sexual offenders, as well as male and female sex offenders with and without mental illness.

Johann Brink, MB ChB, FCPsych (SA), FRCPC, is a Clinical Professor and Head, Division of Forensic Psychiatry at the University of British Columbia. He is a Founding Member of the Canadian Royal College of Physicians and Surgeons Forensic Psychiatry subspecialty and is Vice President, Medical Affairs and Research, for the Forensic Psychiatric Services Commission in British Columbia, an agency of BC Mental Health and Addiction Services. He is President of the Canadian Academy of Psychiatry and the Law (CAPL) and is the Co-Chair of the Canadian Forensic Mental Health Network. He completed his medical undergraduate and postgraduate training in psychiatry in South Africa, and also obtained a BA Honours degree in philosophy, before moving to Canada in 1992. Dr Brink has authored and co-authored more than 100 academic papers, books, and book chapters in forensic mental health.

Karen Chu is a researcher at the Forensic Psychiatric Services Commission, an agency of the Mental Health and Substance Use Services, Provincial Health Services Authority in British Columbia, Canada. She received her Bachelor of Arts in Criminology from Simon Fraser University. Her current research interests include persons with mental illness who are, or are at risk of being, in conflict with the law, and on risk assessments that facilitate the safe transportation of psychiatric patients in air ambulance transports.

Franca Cortoni, PhD, is a clinical and forensic psychologist and is an Associate Professor at the School of Criminology of the Université de Montréal and Research Fellow at the International Centre of Comparative Criminology. Since 1989, she has worked with and conducted research on male and female sexual offenders. Dr Cortoni has published extensively and made numerous presentations at national and international conferences on sexual offender issues. Among others, she has co-edited a book on female sexual offenders and a book on criminal violence (published in French). She is also a member of the Editorial Boards of *Sexual Abuse: A Journal of Research and Treatment* and of the *Journal of Sexual Aggression*.

Leam A. Craig, BA (Hons), MSc, PhD, MAE, FBPsS, CSci, CPsychol, EuroPsy, is a Consultant Forensic and Clinical Psychologist and Partner at Forensic Psychology Practice Ltd. He is Professor (Hon) of Forensic Psychology at the Centre for Forensic and Criminological Psychology, University of Birmingham, and Visiting Professor of Forensic Clinical Psychology at Birmingham City University, UK. He is a Fellow of the British Psychological Society. His current practice includes direct services to forensic adult mental health and learning disability hospitals and consultancy to prison and probation services throughout England and Wales and Northern Ireland. He has published over 80 research articles and chapters in a range of research and professional journals including 10 books. He is a Series Editor for the *What Works in Offender Rehabilitation* book series for Wiley. In 2013, he was the recipient of the Senior Academic Award by the Division of Forensic Psychology for distinguished contributions to academic knowledge in forensic psychology. His research interests include sexual and violent offenders, personality disorder and forensic risk assessment, and the use of expert witnesses in civil and criminal courts.

Deirdre M. D'Orazio, PhD, is a clinical psychologist in private practice as the CEO of Central Coast Clinical and Forensic Psychology Services in California. She also works as a consultant to the CA Department of State Hospitals, where she has worked in various capacities for about 15 years, including as the Director of Evaluation and Development Services, overseeing the treatment programme and forensic services for the Sexually Violent Predator programme. Dr D'Orazio has extensive experience in the sexual offender arena, providing treatment, clinical assessment, expert forensic assessment and court services, professional training, and programme consultation, outcome evaluation, and programme development services. She is on the Board of Directors for the California Coalition on Sexual Offending (CCOSO) as the Chairperson of the Civil Commitment Committee and the lead author of the CCOSO paper on the California SVP system and an author on the Adult Treatment Standards paper. Dr D'Orazio has particular interest and published papers, professional presentations and research projects in the areas of sexual risk assessment, diagnosis, offender treatment, programme evaluation, psychopathy, and clinical supervision.

Kevin S. Douglas, PhD, is Professor and Associate Chair, Department of Psychology, Simon Fraser University; Senior Research Advisor at the University of Oslo; and Threat Assessment Specialist at Protect International Risk and Safety Services Inc. Dr Douglas received his law degree in 2000 from the University of British Columbia, and his PhD in Clinical (forensic) Psychology from Simon Fraser University in 2002. He was awarded the Saleem Shah Award for Early Career Excellence in Psychology and Law (2005) by the American Psychology-Law Society and the American Academy of Forensic Psychology. His research interests include violence risk assessment and management, the association between mental and personality disorders and violence, and dynamic risk factors. Dr Douglas has authored over 150 journal articles, books, and book chapters, including the Historical-Clinical-Risk Management-20 (HCR-20) violence risk assessment guide.

Reinhard Eher, MD, is an Associate Professor of Forensic Psychiatry at the Medical Centre of the University of Ulm, Germany. He is Head of the Federal Evaluation Centre for Violent and Sexual Offenders (FECVSO) in the Austrian Prison System in Vienna, Austria. He serves as Secretary General of the International Association for the Treatment of Sexual Offenders (IATSO) and as co-editor of the IATSO e-journal *Sexual Offender Treatment.*

Allen Frances, MD, is a psychiatrist and Professor Emeritus, Duke University, Durham, NC, USA. He was the DSM-IV Task Force Chair.

Peter Fromberger, PhD, works as a research assistant at the Department for Forensic Psychiatry and Psychotherapy at the Georg-August-University Göttingen, Germany. He previously worked at the Asklepios Clinic for Forensic Psychiatry and Psychotherapy Göttingen. In 2011 he won the Eberhard Schorsch Prize of the German Society for Sexual Research (DGfS) and 2012 the Award for Empirical Research in Forensic Psychiatry of the German Association for Psychiatry and Psychotherapy (DGPPN) for his work on eye movements in paedophiles. His main research interests are paedophilia, assessment of sexual interest, application of virtual reality in forensic psychiatry, neurobiology and psychotherapy of forensic-relevant disorders.

Theresa A. Gannon, DPhil, CPsychol (Forensic), is Director of the Centre for Research and Education in Forensic Psychology (CORE-FP), and Professor of Forensic Psychology at the University of Kent, UK. Theresa also works as a Consultant Forensic Psychologist specializing in sexual offenders and firesetters for Kent Forensic Psychiatry Service, UK. Theresa has published over 100 chapters, articles, books and other scholarly works in the areas of male- and female-perpetrated sexual offending and firesetting. She is particularly interested in research relating to both the treatment needs and overall supervision of sexual offenders. This includes offence-related cognition and emotion, rehabilitation models (i.e., the Good Lives Model), offence-process models of offending behaviour, polygraph-assisted supervision and truth facilitation, and attitudes towards offenders. Theresa is lead editor of several books, including *Aggressive Offenders' Cognition: Theory, Research, and Treatment* (Wiley) along with Professor Tony Ward, Professor Anthony Beech and Dr Dawn Fisher, and *Female Sexual Offenders: Theory, Assessment and Treatment* (Wiley) along with Dr Franca Cortoni. Theresa is also co-editor of several books that discuss or integrate sexual offending with other forensic topics and psychological factors, including *Public Opinion and Criminal Justice* (Willan) along with Dr Jane Wood, *Crime and Crime Reduction: The Importance of Group Processes* (Routledge) along with Dr Wood, and *What Works in Offender Rehabilitation: An Evidence-Based Approach to Assessment and Treatment* (Wiley) along with Professor Leam Craig and Dr Louise Dixon. Theresa serves on the Editorial Boards of several journals, including *Aggression and Violent Behavior, British Journal of Forensic Practice, International Journal of Offender Therapy and Comparative Criminology*, and *Sexual Abuse: A Journal of Research and Treatment*. Theresa is also Editor of *Psychology Crime and Law* and Associate Editor of *Journal of Sexual Aggression*.

Nicola S. Gray, PhD, is Head of Psychology for Pastoral Healthcare and an Honorary Professor in the School of Medicine, Swansea University, UK. She also is the Director at the Wales Applied Risk Research Network (WARRN). She received a PhD and MSc from the Institute of Psychiatry, University of London. Her major interests are in the assessment of aggression, self-harm and sexual aggression in patients with a mental disorder.

Laura S. Guy, PhD, obtained her PhD in Clinical (Forensic) Psychology at Simon Fraser University in 2008. She completed a two-year post-doctoral fellowship in forensic psychology at the University of Massachusetts Medical School (UMMS) in the USA. She is a Threat Assessment Specialist at Protect International Risk and Safety Services Inc. and is a part-time psychologist with the Forensic Psychiatric Services Commission of British Columbia. She has Board Certification in Forensic Psychology from the American Board of Professional Psychology and is licensed to practice psychology in Canada and the United States. She was on faculty in the Department of Psychiatry at UMMS from 2009 to 2015 and currently is Adjunct Professor at Simon Fraser University. Laura has extensive experience conducting threat and violence risk assessments in various settings, including workplaces, post secondary institutions, forensic psychiatric hospitals, and prisons. She also is active in research, having received research grants from federal agencies and private foundations in the USA and Canada and is the (co) author of over 150 articles, chapters, reports, manuals, and presentations.

Benedikt Habermeyer, MD, is a senior physician at the University Hospital of Psychiatry Zurich, Switzerland. His main research interests are functional imaging in psychiatry, clinical neuropsychiatry, and social psychiatry.

Elmar Habermeyer, MD, is Head of the Department for Forensic Psychiatry at the University Hospital of Psychiatry Zurich, Switzerland. He is also a Professor in the Department of Medicine at the University of Zurich. His primary research interests are antisocial personality disorder, forensic risk assessment, and the quality of psychiatric expert evidence.

Stephen D. Hart, PhD, obtained his PhD in Clinical Psychology at the University of British Columbia in 1993. He currently holds positions as Professor in the Department of Psychology at Simon Fraser University, Visiting Professor in the Faculty of Psychology at the University of Bergen, and Threat Assessment Specialist at Protect International Risk and Safety Services Inc. His expertise is in the field of clinical–forensic psychology, with a special focus on the assessment of violence risk and psychopathic personality disorder. He has served as Editor of the *International Journal of Forensic Mental Health* and the *Journal of Threat Assessment and Management* and as President of the American Psychology-Law Society (Division 41 of the American Psychological Association) and the International Association of Forensic Mental Health Services.

Todd E. Hogue, PhD, is Professor of Forensic Psychology at the University of Lincoln, UK, and a registered forensic and clinical psychologist who has worked in prison and secure healthcare settings mainly developing treatment services for personality disorder offenders and those who commit sexual offences. Currently his research interests include the impact of attitudes on judgements and decision-making, the assessment of sexual interest using implicit measures and new technologies (eye-tracking/tablet technology), and the use of structured professional judgement systems to guide risk-related decision-making in forensic and non-forensic settings.

Stephen J. Hucker, MD, is a Professor of Psychiatry with the Forensic Psychiatric Program, University of Toronto, Canada. Dr Hucker has been working in the field of forensic psychiatry for over 35 years, based in Academic Health Science Centres in Toronto, Hamilton, and Kingston, Ontario, Canada. He has conducted numerous assessments of sex offenders, including sexual sadists, for courts, lawyers, and correctional facilities across Canada and elsewhere and has testified in court many times.

Kirsten Jordan, PD, works as a research assistant at the Department for Forensic Psychiatry and Psychotherapy at the Georg-August-University Göttingen, Germany. She previously worked at the Leibniz-Institute for Neurobiology in Magdeburg, at the Department of Psychology at the Otto-von-Guericke University Magdeburg, and at the Department of Medical Psychology at the University of Göttingen. Her main research interests are the neurobiology of sexuality and paedophilia, endocrinological aspects of forensic-relevant disorders, and spatial cognition.

Kevin J. Kerr, PhD, is a registered forensic psychologist and currently works at Ashworth High Secure Hospital. He completed his Bachelor's degree in psychology at the University of Newcastle and then a Master's degree in forensic psychology at the University of Surrey. He completed his PhD at Birmingham University, which focused on the offence of sexual homicide in mentally disordered offenders. Dr Kerr has worked for over 10 years in a number of forensic psychiatric settings with a range of client groups. As well as the area of sexual offending, he has an interest in the study of risk assessment, personality disorder, and psychopathy.

Drew A. Kingston, PhD, CPsych, received his doctorate in clinical psychology at the University of Ottawa and completed his residency at the Royal Ottawa Health Care Group. He is a registered psychologist in the province of Ontario and is currently the Director of Groups and Program Evaluation at the St. Lawrence Valley Correctional and Treatment Centre, a secure treatment unit for incarcerated mentally disordered offenders. Dr Kingston is also a clinical professor of Psychology, and cross-appointed to the Department of Psychiatry, at the University of Ottawa. Dr Kingston is on the editorial boards of the *Archives of Sexual Behavior and Sexual Abuse: A Journal of Research and Treatment* and serves as an ad-hoc reviewer for several journals. He has published a number of articles and book chapters in the areas of serious mental illness, hypersexuality, paraphilic disorders, the impact of pornography on sexual aggression, and the sexual offence cycle.

Calvin M. Langton, PhD, CPsych, is a clinical and forensic psychologist who has been involved since 1997 in assessment, treatment, and research with adolescents and adults who sexually offend. In addition to maintaining his clinical practice, Dr Langton is on faculty at the University of Windsor. He is also an associate faculty member at the University of Toronto and a Senior Fellow at the University of Nottingham, UK. He serves on the Editorial Boards of *Sexual Abuse: A Journal of Research and Treatment* and *Criminal Justice and Behavior*.

William R. Lindsay, PhD, FBPsS, FIASSID, FAcSS, is a Consultant Clinical and Forensic Psychologist and Clinical Director in Scotland for Danshell Healthcare. He is Professor of Learning Disabilities at the University of West of Scotland (UWS), Paisley, UK, and Honorary Professor at Deakin University, Melbourne, Australia. He has published over 300 research articles and book chapters, published five books, held around £2 million in research grants, and given many presentations and workshops on cognitive therapy and the assessment and treatment of offenders with intellectual disability. His current research and clinical interests are in dynamic risk assessment, sex offenders, personality disorder, alcohol-related violence, and CBT, all in relation to intellectual disability.

Jan Looman, PhD, CPsych, completed his PhD in Clinical/Forensic psychology at Queen's University in Kingston, Ontario, in 2000. He is currently a psychologist on the Forensic Unit at Providence Care Mental Health Services in Kingston, ON. He has been working on the assessment and treatment of sexual offenders since 1987 and was the Program Director of the High intensity Sexual Offender Treatment Program at the Regional Treatment Centre (Ontario) from 1997 to 2011, when that program was discontinued. Dr Looman's research interests include risk assessment, treatment outcome and psychopathy in sexual offender populations. He has published over 30 articles in peer-reviewed journals on these topics.

William L. (Bill) Marshall, OC, PhD, FRSC, was the Director of Rockwood Psychological Services for 45 years. Rockwood provided treatment to sex offenders in various Canadian federal prisons, as well as at an institution for mentally disordered offenders, and in a community outpatient centre. He has been on the Editorial Boards of 17 international journals and has over 400 publications, including 21 books. Bill's work has been recognized by several awards; most particularly he was elected a Fellow of the Royal Society of Canada in 2003 and was appointed an Officer of the Order of Canada in 2006.

Danielle Matsuo is the Director, Statewide Programs, Corrective Services New South Wales, Australia. She has worked as a forensic psychologist for the past 15 years, primarily in risk assessment and treatment planning for serious sexual and violent offenders.

Andreas Mokros, PhD, studied Psychology at the University of Bochum (Dipl-Psych), the University of Liverpool (MSc, Investigative Psychology) and the University of Wuppertal (PhD). Dr Mokros is a research psychologist in the Department for Forensic Psychiatry at the University Hospital of Psychiatry Zurich, Switzerland. He is also a Senior Lecturer (Privatdozent) in the Department of Psychology at the University of Regensburg, Germany. The main focus of his research is on indirect cognitive measures for the assessment of sexual preference disorders. Further interests include the aetiology and the assessment of psychopathy as well as quantitative methods.

Jürgen L. Müller, PhD, is the Head of the Department for Forensic Psychiatry and Psychotherapy at the Georg-August-University Göttingen and Chief of the Asklepios Clinic for Forensic Psychiatry and Psychotherapy, Göttingen, Germany. Some of his previous appointments were at the Department of Psychiatry and Psychotherapy at the University Regensburg, the Clinic for Forensic Psychiatry at the Bezirksklinikum Regensburg, and the University of Bern. He is a member of the board of the DGPPN. Until 2014 he was the speaker of the DGPPN Section of Forensic Psychiatry. (Deutsche Gesellschaft für Psychiatrie, Psychotherapie, Psychosomatik und Neurologie; German Association for Psychiatry, Psychotherapy and Psychosomatics and Neurology). His main research interests are the neurobiological underpinnings of criminal behaviour and sexual-related disorders, psychopathy, and preventive detention.

Joachim Nitschke, MD, is the Head of the Clinic of Forensic Psychiatry, Ansbach District Hospital, Germany. Dr Nitschke is a trained neurologist, psychiatrist, and psychotherapist who specializes in the field of forensic psychiatry. In 2010, he became Head of the Clinic of Forensic Psychiatry of Ansbach District Hospital. His special research interests are in the field of paraphilias, psychopathy and schizophrenia, and violence.

Mark E. Olver, PhD, is Associate Professor, Registered Doctoral Psychologist (Saskatchewan, Canada) and Director of Clinical Psychology Training at the University of Saskatchewan, where he is involved in programme administration, graduate and undergraduate teaching, research, and clinical training. Prior to his academic appointment, Mark worked as a clinical psychologist in various capacities, including providing assessment, treatment, and consultation services to young offenders in the Saskatoon Health Region and with adult federal inmates in the Correctional Service of Canada. Mark's research interests include sexual offender risk assessment and treatment, young offenders, psychopathy, and the evaluation of therapeutic change.

Derek Perkins, PhD, is a Registered Consultant Clinical and Forensic Psychologist and Associate Fellow of the British Psychological Society. He has worked in sex offender assessment and treatment in prison, the community, and forensic mental health, including at Broadmoor Hospital. He is Visiting Professor of Forensic Psychology at the University of Surrey and Royal Holloway University of London, is co-lead (with Dr Hannah Merdian, University of Lincoln) of the onlinePROTECT research group on Internet-related sexual offending and is a Trustee of the Lucy Faithfull Foundation.

Ethel Quayle, PhD, is Reader in Clinical Psychology in the School of Health in Social Science at the University of Edinburgh, Scotland, and Director of COPINE research, which until September 2008 was based at University College Cork, Ireland. She is a clinical psychologist and as a practitioner worked with both sex offenders and their victims. For the last 17 years she has been conducting research in the area of technology-mediated crimes, collaborating internationally with government and non-government agencies in the context of research, policy, and practice. Her most recent book, with Kurt Ribsl of the Univeristy of North Carolina, was published in 2012, entitled *Internet Child Pornography: Understanding and Preventing On-line Child Abuse*, published by Routledge/Taylor & Francis. In addition to academic research activities, she plays an active role in a number of government and non-government organizations.

John R. Reddon, PhD, received Bachelor of Arts, Bachelor of Commerce and Master of Science degrees from the University of Alberta and then received a Doctor of Philosophy from the University of Western Ontario. At the PhD level, work was conducted in psychometrics, methodology, and assessment. Since 1983, he has been ensconced at Alberta Hospital Edmonton (a psychiatric and forensic facility). Initially his work was largely methodological, but over time included a more substantive focus. In 1983 he commenced his tenure at Alberta Hospital in the Department of Neuropsychology and Research, in 1992 he transitioned to the Clinical Diagnostics and Research Centre and from 2008 until the present he has been in Forensic Psychiatry. Since 1995, he has also been an Adjunct Professor of Psychology at the University of Alberta. Briefly, his focus has been applied research, programme evaluation, and training in support of assessment and treatment programmes in the forensic and mental health areas with children, adults, and the elderly. To date he has published around 130 papers and book chapters.

Martin Rettenberger, Dipl-Psych, MA, Dr biol hum, is Director of the Centre for Criminology (Kriminologische Zentralstelle – KrimZ) in Wiesbaden, Germany, and was between 2013 and 2015 an Associate Professor of Forensic Psychology at the Department of Psychology at the Johannes Gutenberg University Mainz (JGU), Germany. He previously worked at the Federal Evaluation Centre for Violent and Sexual Offenders (FECVSO) in the Austrian Prison System in Vienna, Austria, and at the Institute of Sex Research and Forensic Psychiatry at the University Medical Center Hamburg-Eppendorf, Germany. Since 2012, he has served as Secretary Vice General of the International Association for the Treatment of Sexual Offenders (IATSO) and as co-editor of the IATSO e-journal *Sexual Offender Treatment*.

Jeffrey C. Singer, PhD, is a psychologist in private practice as an Associate at Morris Psychological Group, PA, in Parsippany, NJ, USA. There he maintains a comprehensive forensic and clinical practice, with the ultimate goal of meeting each client's unique needs. He is a Past President of the New Jersey Psychological Association (NJPA). Since 1995, he has treated sexual offenders. Dr Singer has expertise in evaluating sexual offenders, addressing such complex issues as child pornography, community notification, risk assessment, and involuntary civil commitment proceedings under 'sexually dangerous person' or 'sexually violent predator' statutes. He regularly testifies as an expert witness in State and Federal Courts. Aside from being active in various professional organizations, Dr Singer has been an adjunct instructor, teaching graduate-level courses in forensic ethics and also abnormal psychology. He serves on the Editorial Boards of *Open Access Journal of Forensic Psychology* (OAJFP) and *Sexual Abuse in Australia and New Zealand: An Interdisciplinary Journal* (SAANZ). Dr Singer has also given numerous educational presentations and workshops.

Robert J. Snowden, PhD, is a Professor at Cardiff University, UK. He received a PhD from Cambridge University and did post-doctoral work at MIT. He has many research interests, including forensic and clinical psychology and visual perception.

Armon J. Tamatea, PhD, PGDipPsych(Clin), is a clinical psychologist of Maori (Rongowhakaata; Te Aitanga-A-Maahaki) and English descent who was a senior psychologist and research advisor for the Department of Corrections (New Zealand) before being appointed Senior Lecturer in Psychology at the University of Waikato. His involvement with sexual offenders ranges from assessment, rehabilitation, and research to contributing to culturally informed approaches to offender management. He is also the New Zealand editor for *Sexual Abuse in Australia and New Zealand: An Interdisciplinary Journal*.

Jo Thakker, PhD, is a Senior Lecturer in Psychology at the University of Waikato in Hamilton, New Zealand. She received her PhD in Psychology from Canterbury University in New Zealand in 1997 and has since worked in both clinical and university settings. Most of her clinical work has been with offenders in prisons in Australia and New Zealand. Her key research areas include cultural psychology, substance use and abuse, and sexual offenders. She also has a background in theoretical research.

David Thornton, PhD, is currently Research Director for the Wisconsin Chapter 980 programme in the USA. This forensic mental health programme provides services for high-risk mentally disordered sexual offenders. He also works part time as a Professor in the Department of Clinical Psychology at the University of Bergen in Norway. He previously worked as Treatment Director for the Wisconsin Chapter 980 programme (2001 until July 2013) and earlier led the Offending Behaviour Programmes Unit in Her Majesty's Prison Service HQ in the UK. His primary research interests are the assessment and treatment of sexual and violent offenders.

Tony Ward, PhD, DipClinPsyc, is Professor of Clinical Psychology at Victoria University of Wellington, New Zealand. He was Director of the Kia Marama Treatment Centre for Sex Offenders in Christchurch, New Zealand, and has taught clinical and forensic psychology at the Universities of Canterbury, Victoria, Melbourne and Deakin. Professor Ward's current research interests include offender rehabilitation and desistance, restorative justice and ethical issues in forensic psychology, theoretical psychopathology, and cognition in offenders. He is the creator of the Good Lives Model of offender rehabilitation and gives numerous workshops, keynote addresses, and consultations around the world on this model. He has published over 355 academic articles and is an Adjunct Professor at the Universities of Birmingham and Kent, UK.

Jayson Ware, is the Group Director, Offender Services & Programs, Corrective Services New South Wales, Australia. He has worked with sexual offenders for the past 20 years and has authored over 30 journal articles and book chapters, primarily relating to the treatment of sexual offenders. He has particular interests in sex offender denial, group therapy and enhancing treatment effectiveness.

Charlotte Wesson, BSc, is a PhD candidate at the University of Lincoln, UK, where she has undertaken sexuality research using eye-tracking and is now developing a new tablet-based method to investigate sexuality and inappropriate sexual interest drawing on existing implicit and explicit measures.

Robin J. Wilson, PhD, ABPP, is a researcher, educator, and board-certified clinical psychologist who has worked with sexual and other offenders in hospital, correctional, and private practice settings for more than 30 years. He currently maintains an international practice in consulting psychology based in Sarasota, Florida, and is an Assistant Clinical Professor (Adjunct) of Psychiatry and Behavioural Neurosciences at McMaster University in Hamilton, Ontario. Robin's current interests are focused on collaborative models of risk management and restoration as persons of risk are transitioned from institutional to community settings. He has published and presented internationally on the diagnosis and treatment of social and sexual psychopathology, in addition to being a member of the Editorial Boards of *Sexual Abuse: A Journal of Research & Treatment*, the *Journal of Sexual Aggression* and the *Howard Journal of Criminal Justice*.

Richard Wollert, PhD, is a licensed clinical psychologist and was tenured full Professor at the University of Saskatchewan and Lewis & Clark College. He has evaluated and treated sex offenders since 1978.

Stephen C. P. Wong, PhD, is a forensic psychologist and currently Honorary Professor at the University of Nottingham, UK, and Adjunct Professor at the Department of Psychology, University of Saskatchewan, Canada, and at Swinburne University of Technology, Melbourne, Australia. He is a member of the Correctional Services Advisory and Accreditation Panel, Ministry of Justice, UK, and Fellow of the Canadian Psychological Association. He and his colleagues developed the Violence Risk Scale, the Violence Risk Scale: Sexual Offender Version, and the Violence Reduction Programme that are now used internationally in the assessment and rehabilitation of high-risk and violence-prone forensic clients, including psychopathic offenders. He has received a number of honours from the Canadian Federal and Provincial Governments and the Criminal Justice Section of the Canadian Psychological Association in recognition of his professional practice.

James R. Worling, PhD, CPsych, is a clinical and forensic psychologist who has worked extensively since 1988 with adolescents who sexually offend, and their families. During this time, he has presented many workshops internationally, and he has written a number of articles and book chapters regarding the aetiology, assessment and treatment of adolescent sexual aggression. In addition to his full-time consulting and clinical practice, he serves as an Associate Editor for *Sexual Abuse: A Journal of Research & Treatment*.

Section I
Introduction

27

Overview and Structure of the Book

Leam A. Craig

Forensic Psychology Practice Ltd, University of Birmingham,
and Birmingham City University, United Kingdom

Martin Rettenberger

Centre for Criminology (Kriminologische Zentralstelle - KrimZ), Wiesbaden, and
Johannes Gutenberg University Mainz (JGU), Germany

Introduction

The accurate assessment of treatment need and recidivism risk is the cornerstone of effective practice in treating and managing sexual offenders. Over the last 30 years, sexual offender assessment and treatment protocols have developed beyond recognition. Thanks to advanced meta-analytical research techniques and theories of offending behaviour, more is known of offender characteristics, criminogenic factors, assessment and understanding of the aetiology of sexual deviance, treatment needs, and the assessment of risk of future sexual offence recidivism.

The assessment of sexual offenders is predominantly driven by the need to establish the likelihood of future occurrences of sexual offending behaviour and to reduce the likelihood of the behaviour reoccurring through treatment and risk management interventions. The assessment of risk of recidivism and the identification of treatment needs often go hand in hand.

Risk has been defined as '… a compound estimate of the likelihood and severity of an undesirable outcome' (Yates & Stone, 1992). The *risk approach* can be seen as a management strategy for the flexible and rational distribution of limited resources to best effect (Browne & Herbert, 1997, p. 20). Therefore, *risk assessments* are useful in the planning and management of sexual offenders both in the community and in prison, and are most applicable when a sexual offender returns to a community. Resources and services that are required to monitor, manage, and supervise the activities of convicted sexual offenders in the community can then be targeted to those who are most dangerous and who are highly likely to commit a violent and/or sexual

The Wiley Handbook on the Theories, Assessment, and Treatment of Sexual Offending.
Edited by Douglas P. Boer. Volume II: Assessment, edited by Leam A. Craig and Martin Rettenberger.
© 2017 John Wiley & Sons, Ltd. Published 2017 by John Wiley & Sons, Ltd.

offence, if left to their own devices. Thus, the maximal utilization of resources by risk management ensures the safety of children and vulnerable adults.

In North America, Western Europe, and Australasia, professionals concerned with the safety and protection of women, children, and other vulnerable adults were the first to develop new initiatives in the identification of criminogenic factors, assessment of treatment need, and assessment of risk potential. It was realized that responding to the needs of individuals who commit sex offences is a more effective way of protecting vulnerable individuals in the community. Comprehensive diagnostic, treatment, and risk assessment protocols have been developed from grounded theoretical models greatly advancing our understanding of sexually abusive behaviour.

It is widely accepted that, without treatment, *all* offenders are more likely to reoffend. When imprisoning sexual offenders in isolation with other sexual offenders (for their safety), their fantasies and cognitive distortions are rarely challenged and, indeed, may be shared with others, which may reinforce cognitive distortions and make the chances of reoffending on release higher. By identifying psychologically meaningful risk factors (Mann, Hanson, & Thornton, 2010) associated with sexual offending behaviour and working with offenders, the number of victims may potentially be reduced. Although some incidence studies are beginning to indicate that this may indeed be the case (Jones, Finkelhor, & Kopiec, 2001), researchers caution that the decline in reported sexual abuse cases in the 1990s may be a result of multiple factors (Finkelhor & Jones, 2004). Nevertheless, further work is required in determining those who respond to the interventions available and reduce their risk of recidivism, as opposed to those who do not respond to interventions and remain at high risk of reoffending.

There are three main assessment strategies that are broadly used in the assessment of risk and treatment need in sexual offenders (Craig & Beech, 2010). The first strategy is *functional analysis*, a clinical tool used to investigate the antecedents, behaviours, and consequences of the offence (Ireland & Craig, 2011). This type of analysis is an important first step to ascertaining the type of goals and strategies that a sexual offender has towards offending (Craig, Browne, & Beech, 2008).

A recent direction in sexual offender assessment is towards combining actuarial, dynamic, and detailed formulation together as a manner of clearly understanding risk and what may be unique to the offender (see Ireland & Craig, 2011). Such an assessment aims to draw together a detailed understanding as to what led the individual to commit the offence(s), potential future triggers and destabilizers, what may be maintaining the unhelpful behaviours, and an understanding of potential protective factors for the individual. Information on developmental influences, cognitive capacity, and neurobiology are included to establish a development pathway or trajectory in explaining offending behaviour. This approach attempts to tell the offender's story, from developmental influences to clinical presentation, and where clear areas of treatment can then be identified to support individuals in managing their risk and to enhance their potential for a life that is offence free.

The second strategy is *actuarial risk assessment*. This assessment consists of the completion of an empirically established scale that codifies the presence or absence of static (historical) risk factors. Actuarial scales provide estimates or probabilities of risk based on the total score obtained on the scale. Several such scales have been developed specifically to assess the risk of sexual recidivism, including the Static-99 (Hanson & Thornton, 2000; for Static-99R, see Helmus, Thornton, Hanson, & Babchishin, 2012), the Sexual Offender Risk Appraisal Guide (SORAG) (Quinsey et al., 2006), Static-2002 (Hanson & Thornton, 2003; for Static-2002R, see Helmus et al., 2012), and the Risk-Matrix 2000 (RM2000) (Thornton et al., 2003), which are arguably the most commonly used actuarial risk assessment instruments (ARAIs). These scales provide superior predictive utility to unstructured clinical judgements based on traditional models of psychopathology or clinical experience (Hanson & Bussière, 1998; Hanson & Morton-Bourgon, 2009; Quinsey et al., 2006; Rettenberger, Matthes, Boer, & Eher, 2010).

Finally, dynamic (enduring but amenable to change) risk assessment is where research meets clinical perceptions. Within this strategy, the *stable and acute dynamic risk factors* are assessed. Several dynamic frameworks have been developed, including the Structured Assessment of Risk and Need (SARN) (Thornton, 2002; Webster et al., 2006) and the STABLE-2007 and ACUTE-2007 (Eher, Matthes, Schilling, Haubner-MacLean, & Rettenberger, 2012; Hanson, Harris, Scott, & Helmus, 2007).

Recent advances have been primarily driven by detailed theoretical models of offending. New theories have been developed that seek to explain sexual offending behaviour (see Marshall, Marshall, Serran, & O'Brien, 2013; Ward, Polaschek, & Beech, 2006), and also theories of risk assessment (Beech & Ward, 2004).

Continuing their work in redefining risk assessment, Ward and Beech (2015) argue that relatively little attention has been paid to theoretical issues related to risk and its conceptualization and they suggest alternative ways of understanding dynamic risk factors and their utility in theory construction and case formulation. Until recently, dynamic risk factors have received little theoretical attention and development. Ward and Beech (2015) suggest that dynamic risk factors are complex clinical constructs with multiple, sometimes contradictory, conceptual strands and one should separate out the symptom-like or descriptive aspects of dynamic risk factors from their causal components, and use the nascent causal strands of dynamic risk factors to construct explanatory theories – in essence, developing a clinical theoretical understanding of the symptoms, or cluster of symptoms, that manifest in psychological vulnerabilities, which have until now been vaguely referred to as dynamic risk factors. One example often cited in various theories of sexual offending (Ward & Beech, 2015) is that of isolation and poor association with society. Lack of interpersonal skills through adolescence and young adulthood may result in some men avoiding social situations and increasing their personal isolation. Time alone with little or inadequate association may allow deviant sexual fantasies and maladaptive sexual schemas to foster, which increase the possibility of a sexual offence.

This volume brings together behavioural, cognitive, physiological, and neurological aspects of sexual offender assessment. One hopes that with the continued advances in theory and assessment technologies, greater accuracy in assessing risk of recidivism and the identification of treatment needs in individuals who commit sexual offences will ultimately result in more effective practice and safer communities.

Structure of the Book

This volume is divided into seven sections, as follows.

Section I: Introduction

In the second chapter of the introductory section of this volume, Calvin Langton and James Worling provide an overview of assessment practices with adolescents and adults who have committed sexual offences. They offer a comprehensive review of a number of assessment methodologies, including interviewing schedules, the use of self-report questionnaires, psychophysiological technologies, specifically phallometry, polygraphy, and measures of cognitive processing and the assessment of risk for recidivism. Although great advances have been made in the areas of assessment of risk and treatment need, they highlight that research into protective or strength-based factors has not kept pace and some assessments with adolescents and adults who have sexually offended are without a firm empirical basis. They conclude by pointing to work in the cognitive and neurosciences, the technologies and methods of which are not yet routinely incorporated in assessment practices but which may provide further insights into individuals who have sexually offended.

Section II: Assessing Risk of Sexual Recidivism

In the first chapter of the second section, Martin Rettenberger and Leam Craig provide a comprehensive overview about the above-mentioned actuarial approach to risk assessment, which is usually discussed in terms of the value of actuarial risk assessment instruments (ARAIs). First, they describe the most important characteristics of ARAIs: they are highly structured, consist of empirically derived risk factors, use explicit methods of combining these risk factors, and the total score is linked to an empirically derived probability figure. Based on Meehl's (1954) seminal work, it is an undisputed result of psychological assessment research that ARAIs yield usually better predictive accuracy than alternative prognostic approaches. The chapter gives an overview of the internationally most important ARAIs for sexual offenders and of the current state of research on ARAIs, and discusses their strengths and opportunities in addition to potential problems in the application of the ARAIs. Furthermore, the implications of ARAIs for the implementation of effective and successful rehabilitation and treatment programmes following the risk–need–responsivity (RNR) model about the effectiveness of offender rehabilitation programmes (Andrews & Bonta, 2006; Hanson, Bourgon, Helmus, & Hodgson, 2009) are discussed.

This is followed by Chapter 30, in which Stephen Hart, Kevin Douglas, and Laura Guy introduce an alternative approach to risk assessment, the so-called Structured Professional Judgement (SPJ) approach. The main aim of this chapter is to provide a comprehensive overview and summary about the origins, nature, and potential and possible advances of the SPJ approach for the assessment of violence risk in general and for sexual offenders in particular. The authors mention the most important SPJ instruments specifically developed for sexual offenders, such as the Sexual Violence Risk-20 (SVR-20) (Boer, Hart, Kropp, & Webster, 1997) and the Risk for Sexual Violence

Protocol (RSVP) (Hart et al., 2003), and discuss possible differences between these clinical guidelines and the ARAIs discussed before. One of the major advantages of SPJ guidelines is the individualized (or idiographic) prognostic procedure, which allows the formulation of an explanatory model of the causality and the reasons relevant in each individual case. The authors explain the theoretical, conceptual, and clinical background of the case formulation approach and the scenario planning part, which are core features of the SPJ guidelines but still too often ignored in clinical practice and research (Rettenberger, Boer, & Eher, 2011).

In Chapter 31, David Thornton and Deirdre D'Orazio explore the nature and role of psychological factors in assessing the risk presented by sexual offenders. It is argued that it is incumbent upon those tasked with assessing risk to conduct a comprehensive assessment of psychological factors as an essential aspect of effective sexual offender risk assessment. Not only do instruments that provide comprehensive assessment of psychological risk factors afford a similar level of predictive accuracy to that afforded by traditional static actuarial instruments, but also the combination of static and psychological risk factors leads to even better prediction than either alone. Moreover, the predictive properties of the static actuarial instruments become unstable if either the density of psychological risk factors or the degree of external control prevailing in the release environment varies. Psychological risk factors have both enduring and more actively dynamic aspects and assessors are cautioned not to overweight recent functioning in rendering risk predictions. The chapter articulates a model of these temporal aspects of risk factors and their interaction. Risk reduction is understood in terms of managing long-term vulnerabilities through improved self-regulation and the development of resources supportive of prosocial goals.

In Chapter 32, Jeffrey Singer, Martin Rettenberger, and Douglas Boer propose ideas about a convergent approach to sexual offender risk assessment, which tries to bring together the two above-mentioned risk assessment 'camps', in order to utilize the advantages and potentials of both the ARAIs and the SPJ approach. However, they suggest that a simple anchoring strategy as recommended by some other authors is probably not the method of choice. From a methodological and statistical point of view, the examination of the incremental validity seems to be of particular research interest, in order to analyse the independent contributions of different approaches developed to do the same (or a similar) job.

Section III: Assessing Treatment Need

In the first chapter in this section, Jayson Ware and Danielle Matsuo discuss how the information gained from the assessment process can be used in treatment planning. They argue that (risk) assessment should be based on a thorough examination of both static and dynamic risk factors, through the use of any of the validated risk measures mentioned in Section II. In accordance with the RNR model (Andrews & Bonta, 2006; Hanson et al., 2009), static or historical risk factors will provide a valid predictor of long-term risk and could serve as useful markers of long-term psychological issues. These factors assist the treatment provider to plan for how much treatment will be required and who should be prioritized into treatment when resources are scarce. On the other hand, dynamic or changeable risk factors are essentially the targets of treatment. The authors explain the different types of dynamic risk measures and their usefulness for treatment planning and also the importance of an individualized case formulation. At the end of the chapter, they conclude that treatment providers should ensure that they are treating the dynamic risk factors with the strongest empirical relationship to sexual recidivism.

This is followed by Jo Thakker, who provides a detailed review of the process of case formulation. She suggests that case formulation is a cornerstone of contemporary psychology and should be based on accepted and established theory and practices. It is argued that a case formulation is in essence a hypothesis or a working theory generated to explain what is going on and to assist the clinician in identifying the best treatment for the client. Thakker describes the process of case formulation within the forensic field and specifically in relation to sexual offenders, which includes a formulation of risk as well as positive and protective factors. The final part of the chapter discusses formulation-based treatment versus manual-based treatment. Although it is often argued that the two are mutually exclusive, Thakker highlights that some programmes have been successful in combining traditional cognitive–behavioural methods and client-specific formulations.

In Chapter 35, Andreas Mokros, Benedikt Habermeyer, and Elmar Habermeyer discuss the neurophysiological findings on the sexual arousal response and review studies on brain functioning and structure associated with deviant sexual interest, arousal, and behaviour. Electrophysiological and neuroimaging studies are discussed, in addition to findings from neuropsychology and neuroendocrinology. They discuss the brain activation patterns associated with sexual arousal before considering the evidence base for event-related brain potentials (ERPs), electroencephalogram (EEG), magnetic resonance imaging (MRI), functional magnetic resonance imaging (fMRI), and positron emission tomography (PET) in measuring deviant arousal. Although some differences were observed, these were small, and they suggest that one should be cautious not to overinterpret neuroimaging data as necessarily implying defect, disturbance, or disorder. They go on to discuss genetic, connatal, and hormonal peculiarities that can be associated with a greater risk of sexual offending.

In Chapter 36, Mark Olver and Stephen Wong discuss the diagnostic and prognostic opportunities of the assessment of change in sexual offenders by using standardized risk assessment instruments. After examining relevant conceptual, methodological, and statistical issues in the evaluation of treatment change in general, the authors review the international sexual offender treatment change literature with regard to psychometric batteries, on the one hand, and to standardized risk assessment instruments (of the third generation; see Harris & Hanson, 2010), on the other. One of the internationally most important instrument is the Violence Risk Scale–Sexual Offender version (VRS-SO) (Wong, Olver, Nicholaichuk, & Gordon, 2003), a comprehensive and well-researched risk assessment instrument, which is based on the more general Violence Risk Scale (VRS) (Wong & Gordon, 2006) and which was developed and intensively researched by the chapter authors. Olver and Wong conclude that the currently available scientific evidence provides support for the dynamism of sexual violence risk and underscores the clinical importance of incorporating dynamic risk assessment instruments into the general diagnostic and therapeutic process. They recommend a systematic approach that involves the use of static and dynamic risk assessment instruments, and claim to refrain from unsystematic, unstandardized, and/or unstructured assessment or adjustments to ARAIs.

Section IV: Diagnostic Assessment and Sexual Interest

In the first chapter of this section, Jan Looman discusses the clinical assessment of sexual deviance, and how such an assessment can be situated in a case formulation that is linked to treatment. Looman provides a detailed discussion on the criminogenic factors when conducting assessments of sexual offenders for clinical purposes, in addition to considering factors related to responsivity issues associated with treatment. This discussion focuses on the process of case formulations, a process that describes how each of the enumerated factors is related to risk for reoffence.

In the next chapter, Robin Wilson gives a comprehensive overview of the use of phallometric testing in the diagnosis, treatment, and risk management of male adults who have sexually offended. First, he reviews extensively the history of this technology, which is also known as the penile plethysmograph (or PPG). In the opinion of the author, the PPG is currently perhaps the only objective measure of differential sexual arousal available to researchers and practitioners concerned with paraphilic interests and preferences. However, although the method has been the subject of many empirical investigations, questions still remain about its reliability and validity, which are discussed in detail. At the end of the chapter, he concludes that the sexual arousal measured by PPG could serve as a proxy variable for sexual preference; however, at the same time one must concede that this is still an open question. Furthermore, Wilson draws attention to the fact that the use of PPG in the evaluation of treatment efficacy seems to be still scientifically unsupported and clinically unwise.

This is followed by William Marshall, Stephen Hucker, Joachim Nitschke, and Andreas Mokros, who consider the key developments of the concept of sexual sadism. They discuss the four main approaches to the assessment of sexual sadism (psychiatric diagnoses, phallometric evaluations, utilization of crime scene data, and a measure based on a variety of data) and argue for the use of a rating scale that can be used categorically to provide a diagnosis and also dimensionality to identify the degree of sadism. They present empirical support for the rating scale in discriminating sadists from other sexual offenders. They argue that although further empirical support is needed, clinician-rated scales allow estimates along a dimension of the degree of sadistic motivation that would contribute more valuable information and might allow treatment providers to estimate offenders' success in reducing their problems.

In Chapter 40, Reinhard Eher considers the forensic relevance of the diagnosis of paedophilia in the assessment of child molesters. His starting point is the empirical findings about the lack of reliability and validity of the diagnostic criteria for paedophilia, which is, in his opinion, a serious contrast to the putative relevance of the diagnosis in the clinical and psycholegal decision-making process. He reviews the current state of research on the discriminant and predictive validity of paedophilia and concludes that the currently available scientific data are ambiguous and do not provide clear evidence for concrete clinical use and legal interpretation of the paedophilia diagnosis in convicted child molesters. Therefore, Eher suggests that the diagnosis of paedophilia has little forensic value. Instead of relying on DSM data alone, it seems to be crucial for risk assessment purposes in child molesters to incorporate additional clinical, psychological, and criminological factors relevant for this offender subgroup.

This is followed by Drew Kingston, who discusses the assessment of paraphilic and non-paraphilic rapists. The chapter begins with a review of the characteristics of rapists followed by the psychological assessment of rapists, including nosological diagnoses (sadism, paraphilic rape, arousal to non-consent), the risk to reoffending, and the identification of treatment need. Kingston highlights the versatility of rapists' criminal histories along with studies that have shown rapists to present with various types of antisocial traits that are similar to those of offenders without any known sexual offence histories. He considers offender needs that may be important to consider for sexual offenders in general and rapists in particular, and discusses a multidimensional assessment of sex and aggression and also additional psychometric measures. The chapter goes on to look at the assessment benefits of physiological assessment and also attentional measures of sexual interest. The author draws attention to the limitations in nosological systems and argues that wider assessment domains may be more clinically useful than considering specific DSM diagnostic categories.

Continuing with the discussion on nosological systems, Richard Wollert and Allen Frances consider the use of the DSM-5 taxonomy of paraphilias in sexually violent predator (SVP) evaluations. They provide a historical context by describing SVP laws and discussing events leading to the adoption of the taxonomy of paraphilias as a vehicle for pursuing SVP convictions. They discuss recent changes in DSM-5 relevant for evaluations of paraphilia and summarize practice issues with using residual labels in SVP evaluations. They highlight that the value of a source taxonomy for determining a person's location in a target taxonomy depends on the quality of the alignment between the taxonomies and the reliability and validity of the source taxonomy. They provide helpful suggestions to evaluators when assessing paraphilias and the limitations of the taxonomy of paraphilias and the residual paraphilias.

In the next chapter, Kirsten Jordan, Peter Fromberger, and Jürgen Müller give a comprehensive overview of structural and functional magnetic resonance imaging techniques in assessing sexual preference in general and sexual offenders in particular. First, they review the current knowledge about the measurement of sexual arousal and sexual preference in healthy humans and also in paraphilic patients using functional brain imaging methods. After a description of the most common methods and experimental designs, studies with healthy persons are discussed, showing a relatively clear network evoked by sexual arousing stimuli. The authors then describe neurobiological models of paraphilia – especially of paedophilia – and analyse different findings about structural brain abnormalities in paraphilic patients. Furthermore, methods and results of functional brain imaging studies are discussed, which address the question of the underlying neuronal basis of sexual preference in paraphilic subjects. Finally, they discuss critically the potential benefits and limitations of the assessment of (deviant) sexual preference in the field of forensic psychology and psychiatry.

Ross Bartels, Nicola Gray, and Robert Snowden discuss the merits of indirect measures of deviant sexual interest in Chapter 44. They provide a comprehensive overview of latency and accuracy-based indirect measures useful for both clinicians and researchers. They compare and contrast several techniques, including viewing time, implicit association test, emotional stroop, choice reaction time, and rapid serial visual presentation to determine the presence and degree of deviant sexual interests. They argue that viewing time and the implicit association test have received the most empirical attention in discriminating sexual offenders from controls. However, they highlight that no one measure will provide a clear-cut indication of deviant sexual interests and a multimethod approach will likely be more accurate.

Continuing the theme of visual-based assessment of deviant sexual interest, Todd Hogue, Charlotte Wesson, and Derek Perkins discuss how eye-tracking technology has been used to infer underlying cognitive processes related to observed behaviour in clinical, offending, and non-offending samples. They begin by providing a detailed summary of the history and development of eye-tracking research before considering its application in sexual offender samples. They highlight a number of important challenges to this work, such as selecting an appropriate range of imagery that will be effective in differentiating between (a) offenders and non-offenders and (b) different typologies of sexual aggressors (e.g., compensatory versus sadistic rapists). Although this area of research is relatively new, studies have found that child sexual offenders demonstrate significantly more fixations to the upper body of 10-year-old girls and offenders showed significantly different viewing patterns of child males and females compared with non-offenders viewing adult figures. The authors argue that the growing body of research demonstrates that eye-tracking technology can be used to understand sexual behaviour and sexually inappropriate and sexually aggressive behaviour.

Section V: Special Populations

In the first chapter of this section on special populations, Franca Cortoni and Theresa Gannon discuss the assessment of female sexual offenders. They provide a review of the latest theoretical and empirical knowledge when assessing risk of recidivism in this client group contrasted with those of male sexual offenders. They examine the recidivism rates of female sexual offenders and the associated risk factors and highlight the implications for risk assessment. Throughout the chapter, they emphasize the importance of understanding the gender-specific nature of female sexual offending for assessment and treatment planning, and conclude by offering helpful suggestions for gender-informed assessment practices to evaluators working in the field.

In the next chapter, Ethel Quayle discusses the historical development of typologies of Internet sexual offenders and frameworks for measuring both their behaviour and the risk posed for future offending. As Quayle points out, the debate, which dominates the research on Internet offenders, is whether they are similar to, or different from, existing offender groups and one of escalation in offending. She provides a detailed review of the literature and psychological profiles of Internet, contact, and mixed Internet/contact sexual offenders to distinguish subtle differences in offence-supportive attitudes and empathic concern. This is followed by a discussion on typologies of offenders, including grooming typologies, with the second half of the chapter dealing with risk assessment in this client group. Quayle highlights that although there are indications that the risk of future (or past) offending posed by these individuals is low, this is likely to be challenged by polygraph studies, which suggest that these people are essentially good at avoiding detection.

Continuing the theme of special populations, William Lindsay discusses offence-related issues, quality of life, and risk in sexual offenders with intellectual disability. Lindsay notes that there have been great advances in the assessment of cognitions that support offending, assessment of victim awareness, emotion including anger, anxiety, and depression, behaviour, quality of life, and relationships and in the understanding of dynamic or immediate risk with factors emerging that have strong relationships with offending within this client group. Lindsay provides a comprehensive review of the assessment of offence-related issues often seen in mainstream client groups such as socioaffective functioning, assessment of attitudes, cognitions and beliefs, self-management and self-regulation, and sexual preference and sexual drive in terms of distinguishing characteristics and areas of intervention. Emphasis is placed on the importance of developing good quality of life and relationships in the rehabilitation in this client group.

In Chapter 49, Johann Brink and Karen Chu discuss the assessment of sexual offenders who suffer from major mental illness. Sexual offenders with mental illness and co-occurring mental disorders often present in a complex manner that renders difficult the task of distinguishing the respective contributions to offending behaviour. The authors begin by examining the literature on the co-occurrence of major mental illness and sexual offending and also autism spectrum and traumatic brain disorders. In discussing the prevalence rate of sexual offenders suffering from major mental illness, they compare and contrast definitions of mental illness and other mental disorders between DSM-IV-TR (American Psychiatric Association, 2000) and DSM-5 (American Psychiatric Association, 2013) and comment on the co-morbidity of mental illness with paraphilias and personality disorders. For sexual offenders who suffer from major mental illness, the authors provide useful case examples to illustrate a classification model first proposed by Craig and Giotakos (2011), which organizes sexual offending behaviour in those suffering from mental illness into four groups. They go on to discuss the assessment of treatment need in this client group and highlight that any assessment requires careful elucidation of psychiatric symptoms that could be indicative of a major mental illness or organic brain conditions. Helpfully, the authors outline recovery-oriented treatment targets that may be considered in the assessment of treatment needs for sexual offenders with mental illness. They comment on the use of static and dynamic frameworks before concluding by discussing public policy that seeks to marginalize those with mental illness in conflict with criminal justice and those who have committed a sex offence.

In the next chapter, James Worling and Calvin Langton review the scientific literature on the assessment of adolescents who show sexually harmful, deviant, and/or offending behaviour. The authors are convinced that the heterogeneity of this population requires a highly individualized assessment procedure, which should include a number of different domains of the adolescents' resources, risks, and needs. They describe the different methods and approaches to gather diagnostic and prognostic data in adolescents who have sexually offended and discuss potential challenges that might be especially relevant for this group of sexual offenders. As a final recommendation, Worling and Langton conclude that it is necessary to gather and interpret information from multiple sources. However, at the same time, they warn against the uncritical use of physiological assessment tools, such as phallometry, polygraph, and indirect or implicit measures such as viewing time, because there is currently still a clear need for more research before it can be established that these tools are reliable and valid measures of sexually deviant interests and recidivism risk. Similarly, they recommend that risk assessors and evaluators should act with caution when using standardized risk assessment instruments even when they are specifically developed for adolescents.

In Chapter 51, Scott Aylwin and John Reddon discuss the assessment of incest offenders. The chapter begins with providing a detailed account of the history of incest and prevalence of offending before considering issues around classification. They challenge the view that incest offenders have a lesser likelihood of reoffending than extra-familial offenders and raise concern that perceptions of lower prevalence rates (and deviant arousal) are being misinterpreted as meaning less dangerous. They argue that clinicians should put only limited emphasis on the fact that an individual presents as an incest offender and that it is likely they will have committed other sexual offences against other victims. They suggest that owing to the absence of differences between incest and child molester groups, specific assessment protocols are not needed and the assessment is best focused on known factors for any given (sexual) offender. They emphasize the importance of understanding the meaning, development, and trajectory of behaviours that resulted in offending behaviour. In terms of treatment, they highlight that most patients have never been exposed to a therapeutic experience and many have longstanding interpersonal difficulties originating in the family of origin and extending into adulthood. Many offenders only come to see the merit of therapy once they have witnessed the positive results displayed by other group members.

In the final chapter of this section, Kevin Kerr and Anthony Beech report the key areas that are relevant to the assessment of sexual murderers. Even though they state initially that sexual homicide in general is a relatively poorly understood phenomenon, they were able to find studies from a number of different assessment areas, including psychosocial development, psychopathology, anger, cognition, neurology, and genetics. Finally, they provide a clinical and theoretical framework based on their own clinical experience of working with sexual homicide offenders in secure psychiatric services in England.

Section VI: Ethics and Rights

In the first chapter of this section, Tony Ward and Astrid Birgden discuss the rights in relation to risk assessment in sexual offenders. Ward and Birgden begin by discussing the ethical problems and dilemmas that frequently arise in the context of sexual offender risk assessment and risk management – to balance competing interests between offenders and others, and ascertaining which (and how) interests should be prioritized. They highlight key areas of clusters of ethical conflict in risk assessment, vague terminology or conceptualization of risk, the science or technological (in)accuracy of risk assessment, and the value-laden nature of risk assessment which informs policy. Following a discussion on the conflict often seen within correctional services, one of punishment, community protection, and how best to resolve the problem of conflicting professional roles, they suggest ways in which some of the ethical pitfalls that are pervasive in the field can be avoided. They advocate adopting a human rights framework when working with offenders for overall balance of interests at stake in specific assessment situations, and to take note of each person's obligations and entitlements.

In Chapter 54, Armon Tamatea and Douglas Boer discuss issues around cultural sensitivity and risk assessment. They state that sexual offending – like every other human behaviour – is occurring always within a certain cultural context, which must be kept in mind when evaluations and (risk) assessment reports are written about an individual offender. This is especially relevant when this individual offender is from an indigenous, a non-dominant, and/or a marginalized community because this information could be a key aspect in the understanding of the offending behaviour. In general, the chapter provides an analysis of some of the most relevant diversity issues that are involved in the research and practice of assessing risk with sexual offenders who are culturally different.

Section VII: Conclusions

In the final chapter, we draw together the advances in assessing risk and treatment need in sexual offenders. We consider the development of actuarial risk assessment instruments and structured dynamic frameworks and describe approaches used to assess treatment targets and areas of intervention currently used in England and Wales and North America. What appears consistent throughout the research is that objective and structured assessment protocols, incorporating those criminogenic factors considered to be relevant to sexual offending behaviour, produce the most promising results in differentiating levels of risk and treatment deficits in sexual offenders. Developments in the structured assessment of dynamic risk and treatment need to emphasize the inclusion of protective factors, responsivity issues, and factors of desistance as part of a more balanced assessment framework. We highlight emerging evidence that static and dynamic factors may be functionally linked and represent manifestations of the same behaviour measured and presented in different forms. Future research into the assessment of risk and treatment need may look to redefine our understanding of dynamic risk factors as part of a more theoretically coherent approach to understanding the 'symptoms' (psychological problems) associated with sexual offending behaviour.

References

American Psychiatric Association. (2000). *Diagnostic and statistical manual of mental disorders* (4th ed., text revision) (DSM-IV-TR). Washington, DC: Author.

American Psychiatric Association. (2013). *Diagnostic and statistical manual of mental disorders* (5th ed.) (DSM-5). Arlington, VA: American Psychiatric Publishing.

Andrews, D. A., & Bonta, J. (2006). *The psychology of criminal conduct* (4th ed.). Cincinnati, OH: Anderson.

Beech, A. R., & Ward, T. (2004). The integration of etiology and risk in sex offenders: A theoretical model. *Aggression and Violent Behavior*, *10*, 31–63.

Boer, D. P., Hart, S. D., Kropp, P. R., & Webster, C. D. (1997). *Sexual Violence Risk-20*. Burnaby, Canada: Mental Health, Law, and Policy Institute, Simon Fraser University.

Browne, K. D., & Herbert, M. (1997). *Preventing family violence*. Chichester, England: John Wiley & Sons, Ltd.

Craig, L. A., & Beech, A. R. (2010). Towards a best practice in conducting actuarial risk assessments with adult sexual offenders. *Aggression and Violent Behavior, 15,* 278–293.

Craig, L. A., Browne, K. D., & Beech, A. R. (2008). *Assessing risk in sex offenders: A practitioner's guide.* Chichester, England: John Wiley & Sons, Ltd.

Craig, L. A., & Giotakos, O. (2011). Sexual offending in psychotic patients. In D. P. Boer, R. Eher, L. A. Craig, M. H. Miner, & F. Pffaffin (Eds.), *International perspectives on the assessment and treatment of sexual offenders: Theory, practice, and research* (pp. 463–478). Chichester, England: John Wiley & Sons, Ltd.

Eher, R., Matthes, A., Schilling, F. Haubner-MacLean, T., & Rettenberger, M. (2012). Dynamic risk assessment in sexual offenders using STABLE-2000 and the STABLE-2007: An investigation of predictive and incremental validity. *Sexual Abuse: A Journal of Research and Treatment, 24,* 5–28.

Finkelhor, D., & Jones, L. M. (2004). Explanations for the decline in child sexual abuse cases *(Juvenile Justice Bulletin, January, pp. 1–12).* Washington, DC: US Department of Justice, Office of Justice Programs, Office of Juvenile Justice and Delinquency Prevention. Retrieved from https://www.ncjrs.gov/pdffiles1/ojjdp/199298.pdf

Hanson, R. K., Bourgon, G., Helmus, L., & Hodgson, S. (2009). The principles of effective correctional treatment also apply to sexual offenders: A meta-analysis. *Criminal Justice and Behavior, 36,* 865–891.

Hanson, R. K., & Bussière, M. T. (1998). Predicting relapse: A meta-analysis of sexual offender recidivism studies. *Journal of Consulting and Clinical Psychology, 66,* 348–362.

Hanson, R. K., Harris, A. J. R., Scott, T. L., & Helmus, T. (2007). Assessing the risk of sexual offenders on community supervision: The Dynamic Supervision Project *(User Report 2007-05).* Ottawa, Canada: Corrections Research, Public Safety Canada. Retrieved from www.static99.org/pdfdocs/hansonharrisscottandhelmus2007.pdf

Hanson, R. K., & Morton-Bourgon, K. E. (2009). The accuracy of recidivism risk assessments for sexual offenders: A meta-analysis. *Psychological Assessment, 21,* 1–21.

Hanson, R. K., & Thornton, D. (2000). Improving risk assessments for sex offenders: A comparison of three actuarial scales. *Law and Human Behavior, 24,* 119–136.

Hanson, R. K., & Thornton, D. (2003). Notes on the development of a Static-2002 *(Corrections Research User Report 2003-01).*Ottawa, Canada: Department of the Solicitor General of Canada. Retrieved from http://www.publicsafety.gc.ca/cnt/rsrcs/pblctns/nts-dvlpmnt-sttc/index-en.aspx

Harris, A. J. R., & Hanson, R. K. (2010). Clinical, actuarial, and dynamic risk assessment of sexual offenders: Why do things keep changing? *Journal of Sexual Aggression, 16,* 296–310.

Hart, S. D., Kropp, P. R., Laws, D. R., Klaver, J., Logan, C., & Watt, K. A. (2003). *The Risk for Sexual Violence Protocol (RSVP): Structured professional guidelines for assessing risk of sexual violence.* Burnaby, Canada: Mental Health, Law, and Policy Institute, Simon Fraser University.

Helmus, L., Thornton, D., Hanson, R. K., & Babchishin, K. M. (2012). Improving the predictive accuracy of Static-99 and Static-2002 with older sex offenders: Revised age weights. *Sexual Abuse: A Journal of Research and Treatment, 24,* 64–101.

Ireland, C. A., & Craig, L. A. (2011). Adult sexual offender assessment. In D. P. Boer (Sr. Ed.), R. Eher, L. A. Craig, M. H. Miner, & F. Pfäfflin (Eds.), *International perspectives on the assessment and treatment of sexual offenders: Theory, practice and research* (pp. 13–34). Chichester, England: John Wiley & Sons, Ltd.

Jones, L.M., Finkelhor, D., & Kopiec, K. (2001). Why is sexual abuse declining? A survey of state child protection administrators. *Child Abuse & Neglect, 25,* 1139–1158.

Mann, R. E., Hanson, R. K., & Thornton, D. (2010). Assessing risk for sexual recidivism: Some proposals on the nature of psychologically meaningful risk factors. *Sexual Abuse: A Journal of Research and Treatment, 22*, 191–217.

Marshall, W. L., Marshall, L. E., Serran, G. A., & O'Brien, M. D. (2011). *Rehabilitating sexual offenders: A strength-based approach*. Washington, DC: American Psychological Association.

Meehl, P. E. (1954). *Clinical versus statistical prediction: A theoretical analysis and a review of the evidence*. Minneapolis, MN: University of Minnesota.

Quinsey, V. L., Harris, G. T., Rice, M. E., & Cormier, C. A. (2006). *Violent offenders: Appraising and managing risk* (2nd ed.). Washington, DC: American Psychological Association.

Rettenberger, M., Boer, D. P., & Eher, R. (2011). The predictive accuracy of risk factors in the Sexual Violence Risk-20 (SVR-20). *Criminal Justice and Behavior, 38*, 1009–1027.

Rettenberger, M., Matthes, A., Boer, D. P., & Eher, R. (2010). Actuarial recidivism risk assessment and sexual delinquency: A comparison of five risk assessment tools in different sexual offender subtypes. *International Journal of Offender Therapy and Comparative Criminology, 54*, 169–186.

Thornton, D. (2002). Constructing and testing a framework for dynamic risk assessment. *Sexual Abuse: A Journal of Research and Treatment, 14*, 137–151.

Thornton, D., Mann, R., Webster, S., Blud, L., Travers, R, Friendship, C., & Erikson, M. (2003). Distinguishing and combining risks for sexual and violent recidivism. *Annals of the New York Academy of Sciences, 989*, 225–235.

Ward, T., & Beech, A. R. (2015). Dynamic risk factors: A theoretical dead-end? *Psychology, Crime and Law, 21*, 100–113.

Ward, T., Polaschek, D. L. L., & Beech, A. R. (2006). *Theories of sexual offending*. Chichester, England: John Wiley & Sons, Ltd.

Webster, S. D., Mann, R. E., Carter, A. J., Long, J., Milner, R. J., O'Brien, M. D., ... Ray, N. L. (2006). Inter-rater reliability of dynamic risk assessment with sexual offenders. *Psychology, Crime and Law, 12*, 439–452.

Wong, S. C. P., & Gordon, A. E. (2006). The validity and reliability of the Violence Risk Scale: A treatment-friendly violence risk assessment tool. *Psychology, Public Policy, and Law, 12*, 279–309.

Wong, S., Olver, M. E., Nicholaichuk, T. P., & Gordon, A. (2003). *The Violence Risk Scale: Sexual Offender version (VRS-SO)*. Saskatoon, Canada: Regional Psychiatric Centre and University of Saskatchewan.

Yates, J. F., & Stone, E. (1992). The risk construct. In J. F. Yates (Ed.), *Risk-taking behavior* (pp. 1–25). Chichester, England: John Wiley & Sons, Ltd.

28

Trends Over Time in Clinical Assessment Practices with Individuals Who Have Sexually Offended

Calvin M. Langton

University of Windsor and University of Toronto, Canada

James R. Worling

Private Practice, Toronto, Canada

Introduction

During the past three decades and longer, there have been many publications in which various assessment purposes and practices with adolescent and adult males who have sexually offended have been critically discussed and recommendations for practice given (e.g., American Academy of Child and Adolescent Psychiatry, 1999; American Psychiatric Association Task Force, 1999; Association for the Treatment of Sexual Abusers, 2005; Barbaree & Seto, 1997; Camilleri & Quinsey, 2008; Groth, 1979; Leversee, 2010; Miner et al., 2006; National Adolescent Perpetrator Network, 1993; Quinsey & Lalumière, 2001; Rich, 2011; Salter, 1988; Seto, Abramowitz, & Barbaree, 2008; Thakker, Collie, Gannon, & Ward, 2008; Ward, McCormack, Hudson, & Polaschek, 1997; see also other contributions to this volume). The assessment literature with females who have sexually abused others has only recently begun to expand on the basis of emerging empirical evidence (see, for example, Cortoni, 2010; Ford & Cortoni, 2008; Hunter & Matthews, 1997) so, in the discussion of trends in assessment practices that follows, we concentrate principally on the literature concerning males.

The Wiley Handbook on the Theories, Assessment, and Treatment of Sexual Offending.
Edited by Douglas P. Boer. Volume II: Assessment, edited by Leam A. Craig and Martin Rettenberger.
© 2017 John Wiley & Sons, Ltd. Published 2017 by John Wiley & Sons, Ltd.

Assessment Domains and Methodologies

In terms of foci for assessment (perhaps most clearly for treatment planning), this literature is characterized by remarkable consistency over time in what has generally been regarded as important. As a rather simple but illustrative exercise, one can start with the list of types of information that Salter (1988) recommended be obtained in her influential early guide to assessment and treatment of individuals who have sexually harmed others. Looking at the domains identified as central to assessment work with these individuals in authoritative sources that followed over one-quarter of a century, the overlap can be seen to be substantial.

In Table 28.1, Salter's list is in the first column, followed by columns for each of a number of reviews and guidelines that we consider to be key sources. The operationalizations of constructs and assessment methodologies recommended certainly vary, but the consistencies over time are more striking. Listed in the last column are the core treatment targets commonly endorsed by North American service providers in the most recent iteration of the largest, longest running survey project of its kind of which we are aware, the Safer Society Foundation (SSF) surveys, which began in 1986 (McGrath, Cumming, Burchard, Zeoli, & Ellerby, 2010). We provide introductory comments about these surveys and then draw extensively on the assessment practices data reported in them in the sections that follow. Although our intention here is not to suggest that trends in North American practices are the only ones meriting attention, space limitations restrict our focus to the SSF surveys, which are optimal for the purpose of considering trends in assessment practices over time.

Of note, the core treatment targets are, as McGrath et al. observe, 'commonly identified in the practice guidelines of several professional groups for adult male sexual abusers (Association for the Treatment of Sexual Abusers, 2005; Correctional Service of Canada, 2000; Home Office Communication Directorate, 2000), as well as for adolescent male sexual abusers (American Academy of Child and Adolescent Psychiatry, 1999; National Adolescent Perpetrator Network, 1993)' (p. 64). The correspondence between the columns in Table 28.1 is noteworthy. To the extent that current treatment is focusing on what represents state-of-the-art knowledge about clinically relevant targets (at least for male adults and adolescents), it appears that many of the appropriate foci for assessment practices have been known for some time. Assessment work should inform treatment planning and monitoring and treatment evaluation work also, purposes that are pertinent to the evidence-based assessment framework we consider shortly. Importantly, the point here is that there has been little substantial change in the key domains in decades.

To be sure, additional domains or clinical foci have been identified in the assessment literature, and some of those in Table 28.1 have been revisited in the light of further theoretical work and also empirical research. Despite the heterogeneity that characterizes subgroups within the population, whether determined by age of the perpetrator, age of the victim, or specifics of the sexual offence (Knight & Prentky, 1990; Worling, 1995), meta-analyses attest to the progress that has been made in identifying characteristics that differentiate those who sexually offend from others (e.g., Seto & Lalumière, 2010) and also that predict sexual recidivism (e.g., Hanson & Bussière, 1998). Understandably, the field has placed significant importance on the demonstrated associations

Table 28.1 Correspondence between assessment domains identified in selected reviews from 1988 onwards and commonly endorsed core treatment targets from the Safer Society 2009 North American survey

Assessment domains Salter (1988)	National Adolescent Perpetrator Network (1993)[a]	Beckett (1994)[b]	Ward et al. (1997)[c]	Lane (1997)[a]	Quinsey & Lalumière (2001)[b]	Calder (2001)[a]	ATSA (2005)[c]	Thakker et al. (2008)[c]	Core treatment targets McGrath et al. (2010)
Sexual history (sexual behaviours and fantasies)	×	×	×	×	×	×	×	×	
Sexual arousal	×	×	×	×	×	×	×	×	Arousal control
Attitudes and knowledge regarding sexuality			×	×	×	×	×	×	
Offence-specific information and offence chain	×	×	×	×	×	×	×	×	Self-monitoring
Cognitive distortions	×	×	×		×	×		×	Offence-supportive attitudes

(continued overleaf)

Table 28.1 (*Continued*)

Assessment domains	National Adolescent Perpetrator Network (1993)[a]	Beckett (1994)[b]	Ward et al. (1997)[c]	Lane (1997)[a]	Quinsey & Lalumière (2001)[b]	Calder (2001)[a]	ATSA (2005)[c]	Thakker et al. (2008)[c]	Core treatment targets
Salter (1988)									McGrath et al. (2010)
Degree of denial	X		X	X	X	X	X		Offence responsibility
Degree of empathy for victim	X	X	X	X	X	X		X	Victim-awareness and empathy
Degree of antisocial behaviour		X	X	X	X	X	X		
Attitudes towards women			X					X	Offence-supportive attitudes
Social skills	X	X	X	X	X	X			Social skills training and problem solving
Assertiveness	X	X	X	X		X			Social skills training
Aggressiveness	X	X	X	X	X	X	X	X	Self-monitoring and emotion regulation

Strength and problems in marriage	×				×
Family problems	×	×	×		×
Personal/developmental history	×	×	×	×	×
Alcohol use/abuse	×	×	×	×	
Personality traits correlated with sexual abuse	×	×	×	×	×
Intimacy/relationship skills					
Family support networks					

ATSA, Association for the Treatment of Sexual Abusers.

[a]Focused on adolescents who have sexually abused others.

[b]Focused on adults who have sexually abused children.

[c]Focused on adults who have sexually abused adult females.

between various constructs (operationalized and measured in various ways) and reoffending behaviour because of the potential implications for policy and intervention work. However, not all such constructs, at least as operationalized to date, are associated with sexual recidivism (Hanson & Morton-Bourgon, 2005), calling into question the focus on some of the assessment domains and treatment targets in Table 28.1 (and, in applied assessment work, requires explicit reasoning).

Of course, a construct (whether a characteristic of individuals or of their environment) might represent an important clinical consideration because it affects engagement in interventions intended to lower the likelihood of recidivism rather than because it has a direct relationship with recidivism. In the terminology of the highly influential Risk–Needs–Responsivity (RNR) model (Andrews & Bonta, 2010; Andrews, Bonta, & Hoge, 1990; Bonta & Wormith, 2013), the latter are criminogenic needs while the former would be considered responsivity factors. We return to criminogenic needs in the context of risk assessment further on. Here, we note that the field has made much less progress in clearly identifying responsivity factors and how they exert an influence.

As just one example, denial and minimization are clinical constructs that may predict recidivism in at least certain subsets of adult males convicted of sexual offences (Langton et al., 2008; Nunes et al., 2007), may prevent meaningful engagement in at least some components of treatment (Levenson & Macgowan, 2004) and so moderate treatment effects, or possibly function as both risk factors and responsivity factors – it simply is not clear yet on the basis of limited empirical evidence. The relative dearth of scientifically supported theory renders the assessor's task in selecting measures and methods for use in an individual case that much more difficult and underscores the importance of providing explicit clinical rationales about the grounds on which a construct (such as denial or minimization) is being assessed, the purpose of assessing it, and the appropriateness of how it is assessed and how the results are interpreted.

Space limitations here preclude consideration of how each of the domains in Table 28.1 have been assessed over time and the extent to which assessment work with reference to each could be considered evidence based. It must suffice here to note that these domains have been assessed using one or more commonly employed formats, including clinical interviewing (Lambie & McCarthy, 2004; McGrath, 1990) and paper-and-pencil or computer administration of questionnaire measures, of which a large number, from single-construct scales to multiscale inventories, have been used over the years. Some of these questionnaire measures are intended for adults who have sexually offended (Abel et al., 1989; Nichols & Molinder, 1984). Other measures have been used on the basis of their perceived clinical relevance as part of the comprehensive assessment process (Center for Sex Offender Management, 2007; National Adolescent Perpetrator Network, 1993). With few exceptions, developmentally sensitive measures intended for adolescents have been notable by their absence until the past decade or so (Becker, 1998) even as treatment efforts began to be tailored to the specific developmental characteristics and needs of adolescents who sexually offended from the 1980s onwards (Marshall & Laws, 2003). Although the use of such self-report measures has had a place in assessment practice historically and does so currently (Craig & Beech, 2009; Groth, 1979; Olver, Nicholaichuk, & Wong, 2014), the relative lack of systematic evaluation research to determine their psychometric properties has been an often expressed concern (Grady, Brodersen, & Abramson, 2011; Hanson, Cox, & Woszczyna, 1991).

Interviews with individuals with sexual offences have been core to research efforts for many decades (e.g., Gebhard, Gagnon, Pomeroy, & Christenson, 1965). In applied work, the emphasis has shifted considerably over time from a confrontational and shame-based orientation to one that is more invitational and strength based. During the 1980s and early 1990s, for example, it was common for authors to recommend that interviewers adopt a confrontational style to extract truthful information (e.g., Goocher, 1994; Salter, 1988) and ensure that clients are uncomfortable, so as to be caught off guard (e.g., Ross & Loss, 1988). This has changed as a result of the recognition that aggressive confrontation and shame-inducing approaches actually impede the process and interfere with the formation of a strong therapeutic alliance (Bumby, Marshall, & Langton, 1999; Marshall, et al., 2003). This change in our field was also influenced by the work of Prochaska, Norocross, and DiClimente (1994), which demonstrated that clients can be at different stages of readiness to address their concerns, and that of Miller and Rollnick (2002), which demonstrated that a more invitational and encouraging approach is actually more efficacious.

However, both interviewing and questionnaires require clear definitions and standardized operationalizations to afford reliability and validity and, unfortunately, definitional issues regarding sexual deviance have persisted over time. As a prime example, the diagnosis of paraphilias has been plagued by problems such as unknown reliability and also the vagueness of certain criteria and arbitrariness of other criteria (Laws & O'Donohue, 2008; Marshall, 2006; O'Donohue, Regev, & Hagstrom, 2000).

Furthermore, clinical interviewing and questionnaire measures are vulnerable to dissimulation, something that should be considered in the light of the nature and purposes of assessments with those who have sexually abused others. Some questionnaire measures include validity scales that can be clinically useful in this regard, but reviews over the past three decades suggest that detection of dissimulation has been a consistent concern and remains so in assessment work with these individuals (Langevin, 1988; Lanyon & Thomas, 2008; Sewell & Salekin, 1997).

As such, both historically and currently, a heavy emphasis has been placed on the use of psychophysiological assessment technologies, principally phallometry (e.g., Groth, 1979; Seto et al., 2008) and polygraphy (Groth, 1979; Grubin, 2010), because these methods have been perceived by many (but not all) to be less susceptible to dissimulation. Given the special relevance that they have been ascribed in assessment work with individuals who have sexually offended, we discuss trends over time in their use in a later section.

This emphasis on psychophysiological approaches also likely reflects, in part, the significant emphasis that was historically placed on the assessment and treatment of sexual deviance. Although a brief perusal of Table 28.1 suggests that the foci of assessment have always been fairly comprehensive, assessments were typically concentrated on sexual deviance and the specific details regarding past sexual offending behaviours (e.g., Becker & Kaplan, 1988; Maletzky, 1991; Steen & Monnette, 1989). Over the last two decades, however, the field has shifted such that assessments are arguably more balanced with respect to the attention now paid to issues such as affective functioning and regulation, social relationships, impact of potentially traumatic events, and sociocultural context, for example (e.g., Marshall, Marshall, Serran, & O'Brien, 2011; Rich, 2009).

Another area to which we devote closer attention in this chapter is the use of risk of reoffence assessment tools completed by assessors, which we argue represent one of the most significant developments in assessment practices in recent years. The limited data currently available on trends in their use certainly affirm the growing importance being ascribed to them in practice. But before we turn to trends, it is worth framing our discussion in terms of the evidence base that should ground assessment practices, which is perhaps the most important trend to which we can draw attention in this chapter (Laws & O'Donohue, 2008).

Criteria for Evidence-Based Assessment

Scholarly discussion has, for some time, made clear the kinds of evidence that should be considered in determining the suitability and strengths of methods and measures in assessment work (Anastasi & Urbina, 1997). Even so, more recent work to operationalize criteria that would underpin an evidence-based approach to assessment has great potential to inform assessment development/evaluation research programmes and to guide decision-making in practice (Hunsley & Mash, 2008). Efforts over the years to develop and evaluate tools specifically for use with those who have offended sexually span a continuum from extensive and systematic (including independent replications in the peer-reviewed literature) to single-source offerings without empirical data (but perhaps perceived clinical value). The same can be said of efforts to evaluate the appropriateness of tools with this population that were actually developed for other populations and/or for problems not specific to sexually abusive behaviours. Given that assessing these individuals is a challenging task (Campbell, 2007; see also Chapter 50), having to rely on an assessment literature based on such variable empirical foundations is highly problematic. As Hunsley and Mash (2008, p. 3) observed:

> In this era of evidence-based health-care practices, the need for scientifically sound assessment methods and instruments is greater than ever (Barlow, 2005). Assessment is the key to the accurate identification of patients' problems and strengths. Whether construed as individual patient monitoring, ongoing quality assurance efforts, or program evaluation, assessment is central to efforts to gauge the impact of health-care services provided to ameliorate these problems.

Hunsley and Mash (2008) identify three defining aspects that they deem critical to evidence-based assessment (EBA). The first is that the concepts to be assessed and the process of assessment itself should be determined with reference to scientifically supported theories and research evidence concerning normal human development and psychopathology. Hunsley and Mash advocate that this work be problem specific, which they note should allow closer integration of EBA with evidence-based treatments. With this in mind, it is a concern that understanding of the development of human sexual interests and behaviours, particularly what might inform definitions of 'normal', remains an ongoing endeavour in the field (Bancroft, 2006). In particular, the field has historically lacked normative data for common assessment practices and arguably this remains the case, particularly norms for those who have sexually offended.

This is not to say that the field is without theoretical foundations to inform clinical work with those who sexually offend against children or adults. From early influential work such as by McGuire, Carlisle, and Young (1965) through to comprehensive efforts (e.g., Hall & Hirschman, 1991; Lalumière, Harris, Quinsey, & Rice, 2005; Marshall & Barbaree, 1990; Seto, 2008; Ward & Beech, 2008; Ward, Polaschek, & Beech, 2006), there has been much to ground and focus assessment practices. However, empirical support for these theories has generally been limited. For example, in their brief history of behavioural and cognitive–behavioural approaches with this population, Laws and Marshall (2003) discussed McGuire et al.'s (1965) work and the sexual preference hypothesis. In particular, they noted that this hypothesis required treatment focus on eliminating deviant sexual preferences (and, indeed, this remains a core treatment target in current practice; McGrath et al., 2010). But, importantly, Laws and Marshall concluded that it has been anecdotal evidence rather than empirical support that appears to have maintained it over time.

The second aspect of the EBA framework emphasizes the necessarily strong psychometric properties of measures to be used. It is this second aspect that perhaps is most familiar to researchers and practitioners but which critical reviews of commonly used assessment tools in our field generally indicate remains inadequate. Hunsley and Mash (2008) point to the need for evidence of reliability (such as internal consistency, interrater reliability, and test–retest reliability), validity (including content validity, predictive validity, concurrent validity, and convergent and discriminant validity), and clinical utility (in essence, 'brief, clear, clinically feasible and good enough to get the job done', p. 5, which might be demonstrated by improvements in clinical decision-making and patients' service-related outcomes).

Importantly, Hunsley and Mash (2008) note that the psychometric characteristics are properties of the measure when used with a specific sample and for a specific purpose. Examples include screening and diagnosis, prognosis and other prediction questions, case conceptualization and formulation, treatment design and planning, and also treatment monitoring and evaluation. (Concerning assessments for the purpose of establishing guilt or innocence regarding sexual offending behaviour, in our field there has been a consensus over time with regard to the inappropriateness of any of the available assessment technologies; Association for the Treatment of Sexual Abusers, 2005; Langevin, 1988; Lanyon & Thomas, 2008; Sewell & Salekin, 1997). Hunsley and Mash also note that certain properties will be more important for some purposes than others. They give the example of assessments for the purposes of screening, diagnosis, and prognosis, which should have high indices for validity statistics such as specificity, sensitivity, and positive and negative predictive power, whereas sensitivity to change would be an important psychometric feature for assessments used for treatment monitoring or evaluation.

More generally, they indicate that EBAs should be sensitive to characteristics such as age, gender, ethnicity, and culture, and have appropriate norms (if norm referencing is to be undertaken), in addition to specific criterion-related cut-off scores in order to facilitate accurate interpretation in individual cases. Despite the aforementioned general lack of normative data, nomothetic measures, which are intended to facilitate comparisons on assessed constructs across groups, have for many years been an integral component of assessment work with individuals who have sexually abused others (as described in the sources cited above). Similarly, idiographic instruments, which can be designed to assess unique aspects of an individual's experience or performance and, therefore, can be especially suitable for evaluating change over time, have been another component relied upon in our field (Worling, 2012).

Hunsley and Mash's (2008) third aspect of EBA emphasizes the decision-making nature of the assessment process, involving iterative formulation and testing of hypotheses through integration of the data. The usefulness of the assessment process is determined in part by its associated costs, the implications of errors in measurement, synthesis, and interpretation, and its impact on real-world outcomes. Arguably, with regard to this third aspect, our field is lacking a notable body of critical thinking and empirical evidence. It represents a challenging but potentially rewarding avenue for future attention, as do further efforts with regard to the first two EBA aspects.

Trends in Assessment Practices Over Time

There are very few comprehensive surveys of service providers' assessment practices in the literature. The best example is the SSF series. Beginning with the efforts of Fay Honey Knopp and her colleagues (Knopp, Rosenberg, & Stevenson, 1986), the SSF has published nine surveys of North American providers of services to adults and adolescents with sexual offences (we are not aware of comparable surveys over such a long period in other geographical locations). The surveys, conducted in 1986, 1988, 1990, 1992, 1994, 1996, 2000, 2002, and 2009, allow discernment of trends over time in what Knopp and Stevenson (1989) referred to as the 'developing specialized sex-offender assessment and treatment discipline' (p. 5). Indeed, in the 2009 survey, McGrath et al. (2010) explicitly included the monitoring of trends in common practices among the purposes of the work. Importantly, they observe that 'what is common practice is not always evidence based or best practice' (p. 2), which is why, of course, diligent scrutiny of the empirical evidence and adherence to professional guidelines in clinical contexts concerning assessment methodologies are required.

It is the important work by McGrath et al. (2010) for the most recent of the SSF surveys that we draw upon, in large part, here. Responses from programmes to the 2009 survey totalled 1379, representing all 50 states and the District of Columbia in the United States and nine Canadian provinces. Of perhaps greater interest, McGrath and colleagues tabulated much of the available data on assessment (and treatment) practices across all nine surveys in their report. The assessment data in the subsections and figures that follow are taken from those tables. Caution is warranted when considering these data, however, for a number of reasons. As McGrath et al. note, the representativeness of the samples for the surveys is not known, the scope of distribution of the surveys has varied over time, as have the numbers of respondents, and the survey methodology and questions have changed over time.

Data on the use of assessment methods *other* than the penile plethysmograph (PPG) and polygraph technology were collected only in the two most recent surveys (2002 and 2009). Having the results of only two surveys does allow comments about assessment methodology over time, albeit of a limited nature only, and we turn to those data shortly. Data on PPG use were collected from the 1986 survey onwards, whereas data on the use of polygraph technology were collected from 1992 onwards. It is to psychophysiological assessment methods, including these two, that we turn first.

Psychophysiological Assessment Methods

Phallometry

Phallometric measurement of sexual arousal involves the monitoring of a male's sexual arousal by measuring his penile responses using change in either volume or circumference during visual or auditory presentation of stimuli of sexual and non-sexual content. The heavy emphasis both historically and currently in the field on sexual deviance in assessment and treatment work with those who sexually abuse others (Barbaree & Langton, 2006) is reflected in the considerable literature on the PPG. Laws and Marshall (2003) provided a brief history of the development of this technology, which was introduced by Kurt Freund in Czechoslovakia in the 1950s, noting that 'The penile plethysmographic (phallometric) procedure was accepted because it did not seem to be overly influenced by the participant's voluntary control, and was thought to provide a more objective, and thereby more accurate description of the client's sexual preferences than self-report. Thus measures of erectile response quickly became the standard in establishing the degree of deviance in [adult] clients and evaluating the effectiveness of behavioral interventions' (p. 84).

It can be seen in Figure 28.1a that the use of PPG technology has remained fairly consistent since 1986, at a little less than 30%, in community programmes for adult males. A similar pattern is evident for residential programmes in the United States between 1986 and 1996, with an overall increase then evident across the three surveys in the 2000s. The pattern in the same period for both community and residential programmes in the United States for adolescent males is bell-shaped, with percentages roughly doubling from 13 and 8%, respectively, in 1986 to highs of 24 and 19%, respectively, in the early 1990s, and then decreasing to about the same levels in 2009 as found in the 1986 survey, 10 and 9%, respectively (see Figure 28.1b).

Assessment methods in the domain of sexual interest/arousal have been the subject of a focused application of the EBA framework (Seto et al., 2008). On the basis of their review, Seto and colleagues recommended the use of the PPG for diagnostic purposes and also for treatment monitoring and outcome evaluation. Of particular note, meta-analytic findings attest to its predictive validity in terms of sexual recidivism, primarily with adult male samples (Hanson & Bussière, 1998). Yet the lack of standardization, absence of norms, and an extensive but contradictory body of empirical evidence concerning reliability and validity issues with the PPG have been debated for decades (see, for example, Camilleri & Quinsey, 2008; Lalumière et al., 2005; Laws, 2003; Marshall & Fernandez, 2000; Murphy & Barbaree, 1994; O'Donohue & Letourneau, 1992;

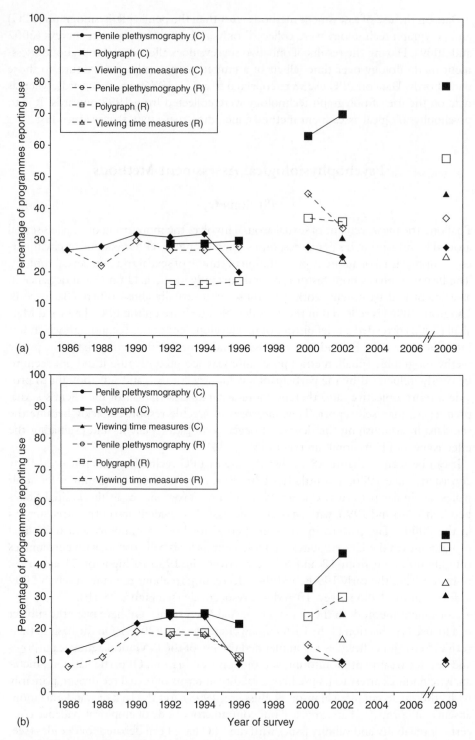

Figure 28.1 Percentage of programmes in the United States using surveyed sexual interest measures in community (C in legend) and residential (R in legend) settings with adults (a, top) and adolescents (b, bottom) by Safer Society survey year. Data from McGrath et al. (2010).

Worling, 2012). It is noteworthy that there have been far fewer empirical investigations of the PPG with adolescent males who sexually offended than with their adult counterparts, but its clinical use with adolescents is advocated by some (Rice, Harris, Lang, & Chaplin, 2012). Given what we view as the significant scientific and ethical concerns regarding the use of the PPG with adolescents (Fanniff & Becker, 2006; Worling, 2012), we see the downward trend over time in its reported use in North American programmes for adolescents as positive. Future survey work should determine which alternative assessment methodologies are being used to assess sexual interest.

Cognitive-Processing Measures

In the light of the scientific and ethical concerns regarding the PPG, several cognitive-processing measures have been developed in an effort to assess sexual interests. These measures are based on the assumption that the cognitive processing of sexually appealing stimuli will be affected in a measurable way relative to the cognitive process of sexually unappealing or neutral stimuli. The most widely studied of these methodologies is unobtrusively measured viewing time (VT). Clients view photographs of males and females in different age groups via a computer, and they are asked to rate the sexual attractiveness of the models. In addition to these ratings, the time that the individual takes to rate each photograph is also unobtrusively recorded, and the assumption with this methodology is that longer viewing times will be indicative of sexual interests.

Employing participants who had offended sexually, some researchers have reported support for the premise that VT can provide information regarding the sexual interests of both adults (e.g., Gray & Plaud, 2005; Letourneau, 2002) and adolescents (e.g., Abel et al., 2004; Worling, 2006). On the other hand, however, there have also been significant questions raised regarding the reliability and validity of these tools (e.g., Mokros et al., 2013; Smith & Fisher, 1999).

Several additional cognitive-processing measures have been investigated. For example, the attentional blink phenomenon (Raymond, Shapiro, & Arnell, 1992) has been employed in research with adult males who have sexually offended, and preliminary findings indicate that this approach could provide useful information regarding sexual interests (Beech et al., 2008). Likewise, some researchers have reported that an implicit association task can differentiate men who have sexually offended against children from controls (e.g., Banse, Schmidt, & Clarbour, 2010; Nunes, Firestone, & Baldwin, 2007). As in the case of VT measures, however, it is clear that much more research is needed to establish any of the cognitive-processing approaches as reliable and valid measures of sexual interests.

Given the relatively recent emergence of cognitive-processing measures, it is perhaps not surprising that data on the use of VT were collected in only the two most recent SSF surveys. Other cognitive-processing measures are not widely utilized in the field at this point, and they were not included in the survey. As is evident in Figure 28.1a, the use of VT has increased among community programmes in the United States for adults, from 31% in 2002 to 45% in 2009, but remained steady at 24 and 25% in residential programmes. Among programmes for adolescents, use increased in residential programmes, from 17 to 35%, and in community programmes, from 25 to 31% (see Figure 28.1b). But, as noted above, VT is an emerging technology for the field and, with further development and evaluation work still needed, it remains to be seen whether the general increase becomes an established trend when future survey data are reported.

Polygraph

McGrath et al. (2010) noted that, 'Typically, programmes employ the polygraph post-conviction to motivate abusers to be truthful about their sexual offending history, to follow treatment and supervision rules, and to verify that they have complied with those rules' (p. 56). According to the 2009 SSF survey, the use of polygraph technology is much more widespread in the United States than is the use of the PPG. Of particular interest in terms of trends over time, the reported use of polygraph technology in community programmes in the United States for adults increased in each of the six SSF surveys for which these data were collected (see Figure 28.1a). The percentage of US community programmes for adults reporting usage in 2009 was nearly three times higher than the percentage reporting usage in 1992, and the percentage was 3.5 times higher in 2009 than it was in 1992 for residential programmes. Among programmes for adolescents, a similarly large increase over time was evident, with twice as many community programmes reporting the use of polygraph technology in 2009 compared with 1992 and nearly 2.5 times as many residential programmes in 2009 compared with 1992 (see Figure 28.1b).

Despite its widespread use (according to Faigman, Fienberg, and Stern, 2003, more than 30 US states actually require its use for monitoring purposes with those with sexual offences), there has been considerable debate over time about the evidence base for the polygraph in general (National Research Council, 2003) and specifically with those who have sexually offended (e.g., Abrams & Abrams, 1993; Branaman & Gallagher, 2005; Gannon, Beech, & Ward, 2008; Grubin, 2010; Heil, Simons, & Burton, 2010; Rosky, 2013; Vess, 2011). Authors of studies with individuals who sexually offended have found that those subjected to polygraph examinations do report higher rates of past sexual offending (e.g., Ahlmeyer, Heil, McKee, & English, 2000) and engagement in high-risk behaviours while under supervision (Grubin, Madsen, Parsons, Sosnowski, & Warberg, 2004). In addition, such disclosures appear to influence supervision practices (Gannon et al., 2014). What has not been established is whether there is a significant deterrence effect (Rosky, 2013), nor has the impact of the use of the polygraph on the therapeutic alliance been determined (McGrath et al., 2010). In the only study to have examined its association with reoffences, rates of sexual recidivism did not differ between those subjected to polygraph examination and those not (McGrath, Cumming, Hoke, & Bonn-Miller, 2007).

Given the trend in the use of this technology in the United States (and the possibility that programmes outside North America followed suit), an accompanying trend in the evidence base is urgently needed in order for the field to move beyond reliance on a literature characterized by methodological shortcomings, which preclude strong conclusions about the polygraph's reliability, validity, and utility with this population. In addition to our concerns about the evidence base more generally, we share Chaffin's (2011) and Prescott's (2012) concerns regarding the ethics of its use with adolescents who have sexually offended. In particular, we are concerned that the polygraph is a potentially coercive tool that could impact negatively on a positive therapeutic alliance and result in faulty 'disclosures' because of the fear and anxiety caused by the process.

Risk Assessment Tools for Criminal Recidivism Outcomes

Sexual Recidivism

One of the most important developments for the field over the past two decades and longer has been in the area of assessing risk of sexual recidivism in addition to future violence and other types of criminal recidivism (Barbaree, Langton, Gopnik-Lewinski, & Beach, 2013; Craig, Browne, & Beech, 2008). Indeed, this area has seen rapid change and progress that is expected to continue in the next few years (Becker & Murphy, 1998; Hanson, Morton, & Harris, 2003; Harris & Hanson, 2010). Preceding this, the pessimism about the ability of mental health professionals to predict future violence was well founded, given the empirical evidence up to the early 1990s (Monahan, 1981, 1996; Quinsey, Harris, Rice, & Cormier, 2006), but the influential work of various researchers (for example, Hanson, 1997; Hanson & Thornton, 2000; Harris, Rice, & Quinsey, 1993; Monahan et al., 2001; Prentky, Harris, Frizzell, & Righthand, 2000; Webster, Douglas, Eaves, & Hart, 1997; Worling & Curwen, 2001) proved to be a watershed. Since the early 1990s, there has been a proliferation of such tools for use with adults with sexual offences and also with adolescents who have sexually harmed others. Findings for some of these tools, principally concerning interrater reliability and predictive validity in addition to concordant and concurrent validity, have been replicated in cross-validation and independent samples.

It is noteworthy that the most extensively evaluated of these tools for adults who have offended sexually are comprised exclusively or principally of static risk factors. Static factors would not be expected to change over time, at least not in the direction of decreasing risk of recidivism. For example, *criminal history*, generally a strong predictor of criminal recidivism, might include variables tapping frequency and diversity. An individual's scores on such items would increase if new offences are committed, resulting in an increased level of risk of recidivism in later assessments. As another example, the variable *any sexual offending against a stranger victim*, a strong predictor of sexual recidivism, could change if an individual with a history of offending only against known individuals goes on to sexually assault a stranger, resulting in an increase in risk of recidivism but, once present, it cannot change (and so is considered a static predictor). This insensitivity to intervention-related decreases in risk of recidivism renders such tools of limited use in terms of treatment planning, and of no practical use in monitoring progress during interventions.

However, some of the most widely used of these tools do have moderate predictive validity (Hanson & Morton-Bourgon, 2009). As such, they also have potential value in treatment evaluation work, providing an index of risk that may moderate the association between treatment and recidivism outcomes (for a general discussion of the incorporation of risk of recidivism as a moderator in treatment evaluation designs with forensic populations, including those who have sexually offended, see Langton, 2007, and Langton & Barbaree, 2006). Testing for moderating effects has yet to become a common design feature in individual sexual offence treatment evaluation studies, although meta-analytic findings indicate larger effect sizes for those programmes that adhere to Andrews and Bonta's (2010) RNR model *Risk Principle*, which holds that the intensity of services should be matched with level of assessed risk of reoffence (Hanson, Bourgon, Helmus, & Hodgson, 2009).

Although other risk assessment tools for adults are available and widely used elsewhere – for example, in the United Kingdom the Risk Matrix 2000 (Thornton et al., 2003) and the Structured Risk Assessment (SRA) (Thornton, 2002) which is also known as the Structured Assessment of Risk and Need (SARN) framework – the 2002 and 2009 SSF surveys both enquired about use of the following five: the Vermont Assessment of Sex-Offender Risk (VASOR) (McGrath & Hoke, 2001); the Rapid Risk Assessment for Sex Offense Recidivism (RRASOR) (Hanson, 1997); the Static-99 (Hanson & Thornton, 2000); the Minnesota Sex Offender Screening Tool – Revised (MnSOST-R) (Epperson, Kaul, & Heselton, 1999); and the Sexual Violent Risk – 20 (SVR-20) (Boer, Hart, Kropp, & Webster, 1997); McGrath et al. (2010) reported a number of statistical comparisons between the two sets of data. Most encouraging, given the general empirical support for these tools, about 87% of community and residential programmes for adult males in the United States responding to the 2009 survey reported use of one or more of them, a statistically significant increase over the 63.3% of community programmes and 55.9% of residential programmes reporting use of one or more in 2002. Canadian data were given only for the 2009 survey, with 93 and 100% of community and residential programmes using one or more, respectively.

Looking at the individual tools (see Figure 28.2a), the use of the VASOR, an empirically informed risk assessment tool, roughly doubled between 2002 and 2009, although in absolute terms its use remained limited (with a high of nearly 12% of US community programmes using it in 2009, up from 5.8% in 2002). This increase is curious in the light of the fact that although this tool, the first of these to be developed for the purpose of assessing risk of sexual recidivism, appeared in 1994, no empirical work by independent researchers was reported until the efforts of Langton and colleagues (Langton, Barbaree, & Seto, 2002), and no further evaluations followed during the period between 2002 and 2009. More recently, McGrath, Lasher, Cumming, Langton, and Hoke (2014) have reported encouraging data across multiple samples regarding the VASOR and, importantly, its revision (McGrath, Hoke, & Lasher, 2013). Use of this revision might be expected to surpass the use of the original VASOR in the next few years, but clearly additional research replicating those findings beyond samples from Vermont and Ontario would be desirable.

Use of the RRASOR remained essentially unchanged between 2002 and 2009 at about one-third of all such programmes in the United States. It is interesting that the RRASOR was even this widely used during the period (although this is likely due in part to it being one of the early actuarial risk assessment tools for use with those with sexual offences, with only four items that are reasonably straightforward to score); we would expect that the use of the RRASOR will decrease over time given that the Static-99, another actuarial risk assessment tool, was intended as its replacement (Hanson & Thornton, 2000; cf., Babchishin, Hanson, & Helmus, 2012). Certainly, the Static-99 is by far the most commonly used sexual recidivism risk assessment tool in North

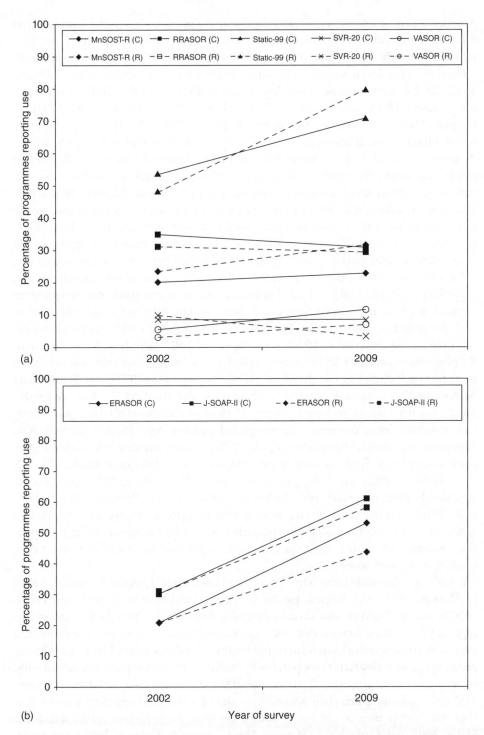

Figure 28.2 Percentage of programmes in the United States using surveyed tools to assess risk of sexual recidivism in community (C in legend) and residential (R in legend) settings with adults (a, top) and adolescents (b, bottom) by Safer Society survey year. Data from McGrath et al. (2010).

America. In the 2009 survey, 71.2% of community programmes in the United States for adult males and 80% of residential programmes reported its use, both representing statistically significant increases over the 2002 numbers of 54% and 48.4%, respectively.

Hanson and colleagues have published analyses with a large number of Static-99 and Static-2002 datasets obtained from researchers around the world which support their use (Hanson, Helmus, & Thornton, 2010; Hanson & Morton-Bourgon, 2009; cf., Helmus, Hanson, Thornton, Babchishin, & Harris, 2012). Furthermore, the 2002 revision has the added advantage of being conceptually coherent, with clearly distinct domains associated with risk for sexual recidivism (Hanson & Thornton, 2000) that can inform treatment planning also. Indeed, there is preliminary evidence of concurrent validity for these domains (Langton, Barbaree, Hansen, Harkins, & Peacock, 2007). So, in addition to anticipating that the RRASOR will drop out of use, we are interested to see if the use of the Static-2002 increases over time to levels currently reported for the Static-99. In the 2009 survey, 22.1% of community programmes and 16.5% of residential programmes for adult males in the United States reported its use.

A small increase in the use of the MnSOST-R, another actuarial risk assessment tool, was evident between 2002 and 2009 in both community and residential programmes for adult males in the United States, with between one-fifth and nearly one-third of such programmes employing it. The SVR-20, a structured clinical judgement tool, was used by less than one in 10 US programmes in 2002, with only 3.5% of residential programmes in 2009. In the next few years, however, we expect that use of both of these tools will diminish. For the MnSOST-R, this decrease will likely be in large part because another revision within this family of tools, the MnSOST-3 (Duwe & Freske, 2012), has been shown to have moderate levels of predictive validity and good inter-rater reliability by its developers (although independent replication is needed). Also important from an EBA perspective, the MnSOST-3 is not vulnerable to the same criticisms as have been expressed about the development and validation of the MnSOST-R (e.g., Wollert, 2002). Similarly, a revision of the SVR-20 (Boer, 2011) and another structured clinical judgment tool, the Risk for Sexual Violence Protocol (RSVP) (Hart et al., 2003), will likely also receive more clinical attention and empirical investigation in the coming years. The RSVP is particularly noteworthy because it explicitly emphasizes dynamic risk factors and a risk management purpose for assessment rather than prediction accuracy alone.

It was the influential research by Quinsey and colleagues (Quinsey, Coleman, Jones, & Altrows, 1997) with forensic psychiatric patients and then by Hanson and Harris (2000) with individuals who sexually offended that moved the field forward in this regard. Unlike static factors, dynamic risk factors are changeable and, therefore, can inform intervention work intended to reduce the risk of recidivism. Hence tools incorporating dynamic risk factors are potentially useful for treatment planning, monitoring of progress, and treatment evaluation. The 2009 SSF survey collected data on the use of three, confirming that their adoption as part of assessment practices is under way (but trends over time in the use of such tools must await further survey data): the Stable-2007 and Acute-2007 (Hanson, Harris, Scott, & Helmus, 2007), the Structured Risk Assessment (SRA) (Thornton, 2002), and the Sex Offender Treatment Needs and Progress Scale (TPS) McGrath & Cumming, 2003).

Of these, the Stable-2007 and Acute-2007 are by far the most widely used in the United States, with roughly one-third of both residential and community programmes reporting their use. The TPS is used in nearly one-fifth of community programmes in the United States but only 2.4% of residential programmes. The SRA is used in less than 10% of community programmes in the United States and only 12.9% of residential programmes.

These tools have been developed only relatively recently, and there are far fewer empirical investigations of these from which to draw conclusions about the current evidence base. In addition to the short period for which they have been available, the dearth of research may be due to some extent to methodological challenges. We suspect that difficulties in reliably coding many of these dynamic risk factors (which often require specific types of information not always found in older assessment reports) from archived case file materials has limited the number of evaluations published to date. The use of archival case files to code static factors at a single point in time, blind to criminal recidivism outcomes but often years after the sample has been released or otherwise had opportunity to reoffend, has been a common design in risk assessment research. The information required to code such items is often readily available from basic demographic information, criminal records, and descriptions of offences and victims in case files.

In contrast, demonstrating associations between scores on a dynamic risk tool at the time of assessment (or changes in scores over repeated assessments) and recidivism perhaps years later is difficult, given that these dynamic factors may have changed over time with or without formal intervention (Langton & Barbaree, 2001). If participants in a study sample reoffend sexually while under supervision (during which regular assessments of dynamic risk have been undertaken), associations with recidivism may be found in a study with sufficient statistical power because of the temporal proximity of the assessment and the reoffence. However, such prospective evaluations of risk assessment tools are considerably fewer in number than are the many studies that employed archival case coding. Notable examples with adults include those by Hanson et al. (2007) and McGrath, Lasher, and Cumming (2012). Evidence for interrater reliability and also predictive and incremental validity for the Stable has been independently reported (Eher, Matthes, Schilling, Haubner-MacLean, & Rettenberger, 2012), as also has preliminary evidence of concurrent validity (Nunes & Babchishin, 2012). Predictive validity of the SARN framework is also accumulating (Craig, Thornton, Beech, & Browne, 2007; Wakeling, Beech, & Freemantle, 2013).

Except in archival designs for which very comprehensive and complete case files are available, we expect that it will be through prospective designs that the field will progress further in terms of dynamic factors, particularly in assessing change over time and establishing associations between these changes and recidivism outcomes (see, for example, Wakeling et al., 2013). Indeed, the field may take some time before research into dynamic risk factors affords an evidence base with the depth and breadth comparable to those for tools comprised of static risk factors.

Whether the use of one or other of the tools mentioned above, further revisions of these, or new dynamic risk tools become widespread (which, in the case of the Stable-2007 and Acute-2007 in Canada, for example, has already happened; McGrath et al.,

2010), the value of linking assessing domains that can be addressed through interventions in order to lower an individual's risk of sexual recidivism should be clear: such assessments afford a means to link purposefully assessment with treatment planning, monitoring of progress, and programme evaluation work also. Clearly, there is great promise of clinical utility here. However, the field is in need of further research that guides how assessments of dynamic risk should be used in conjunction with current static risk assessment tools – at present the evidence base in this regard is limited.

Consistent with other aspects of clinical work with adolescents who have sexually harmed others, assessment of risk for sexual recidivism with this distinct population has encompassed direct application of work with adults. Although the Static-99 is intended for use with individuals aged 18 years and older, authors have reported moderate levels of predictive accuracy with adolescent samples, despite some of the items lacking a clear developmentally appropriate corollary for adolescents (Viljoen, Mordell, & Beneteau, 2012). Efforts at developing tools specifically for use with adolescents have resulted in several with growing evidence bases. We limit our comments here to the tools identified in the SSF as those most commonly used in North America (see Figure 28.2b): the Estimate of Risk of Adolescent Sexual Offense Recidivism (ERASOR) (Worling & Curwen, 2001), the Juvenile Sex Offender Assessment Protocol-II (J-SOAP-II) (Prentky & Righthand, 2003), and the Juvenile Sexual Offense Recidivism Risk Assessment Tool-II (J-SORRAT-II) (Epperson, Ralston, Fowers, DeWitt, & Gore, 2006) (see Figure 28.2b; the J-SORRAT-II was not available in 2002 and so its use is not plotted).

Again, McGrath et al. (2010) reported a number of statistical comparisons between the 2002 and 2009 survey data. As with the tools for use with adults, large and statistically significant increases in the number of programmes using at least one or more of the tools were found (with slightly more than three-quarters of community and residential programmes in 2009 for adolescent males in the United States compared with roughly 40% of such programmes in 2002). These data are encouraging given the accumulating empirical evidence of interrater reliability and moderate predictive validity of these tools (e.g., Viljoen et al., 2012; Worling, Bookalam, & Litteljohn, 2012), although the evidence base is far from comprehensive or conclusive (e.g., Fanniff & Letourneau, 2012; Vitacco, Caldwell, Ryba, Malesky, & Kurus, 2009).

Looking at each of them individually, between 2002 and 2009, use of the ERASOR, a structured clinical judgment tool, in the United States increased significantly (in the community, from 21% of 477 programmes to 53.1% of 275 programmes, and in residential settings, from 20.9% of 187 programmes to 43.8% of 98 programmes). Similarly, the use of the J-SOAP-II, an empirically informed assessment tool, in the United States increased significantly (in the community, from 30.4 to 61.1%, and in residential settings, from 31.0 to 58.2%). Use of the more recently developed J-SORRAT-II, an actuarial tool, was only surveyed for the 2009 report, with roughly 18% of programmes in both settings using it.

Of particular interest is the fact that, of these three, the ERASOR and the J-SOAP-II include items that are dynamic in nature and, therefore, as discussed above, are potentially suitable for assessing change in risk over time. To date, no research in the peer-reviewed literature has yet been reported that links change over time in scores on these tools with recidivism outcomes. This represents an important avenue of research if these tools are to have demonstrated utility in treatment planning monitoring, and evaluation. Survey data on whether these tools are already being used for these purposes are also needed.

General Criminal Recidivism

Evidence shows that rates of criminal recidivism among adults and adolescents who have sexually offended against others are higher for offences of a non-sexual nature than for sexual reoffences (Hanson & Morton-Bourgon, 2005; Reitzel & Carbonell, 2006). It makes sense, therefore, to consider the risk of non-sexual offending in assessment work with these populations. McGrath et al. (2010) tabulated US data on the use of three tools for use with adults developed for this purpose from the 2002 and 2009 surveys: the Level of Service Inventory-Revised (LSI-R) (Andrews & Bonta, 1995), the Sex Offender Risk Appraisal Guide (SORAG) (Quinsey et al., 2006), and the Violence Risk Appraisal Guide (VRAG) (Quinsey et al., 2006). Percentages of programmes for adult males in the United States reporting use of these tools over time is plotted in Figure 28.3.

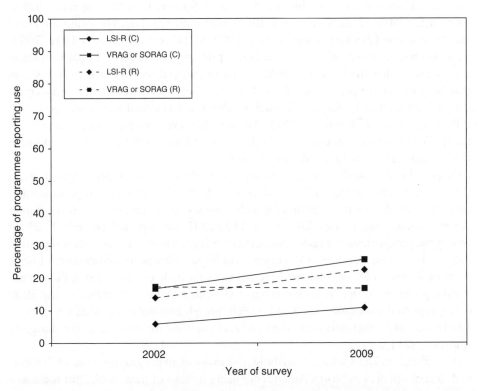

Figure 28.3 Percentage of programmes in the United States using surveyed tools to assess risk of non-sexual recidivism in community (C in legend) and residential (R in legend) settings with adult males by Safer Society survey year. Data from McGrath et al. (2010).

Among community programmes in the United States for adult males, the percentage using the LSI-R doubled between 2002 and 2009, from 5.8 to 10.9%, with an increase of similar size, from 13.9 to 22.4%, in residential programmes. Community programmes for adult males reporting the use of either the VRAG or SORAG increased from 16.9 to 25.5% in the same period, but use in residential programmes remained essentially unchanged, decreasing from 17.2 to 16.5%. It is worth noting that, although these increases in the use of these well-researched tools are large, in absolute terms these percentages are small – despite independent replications demonstrating interrater reliability and predictive validity for all three appearing in the literature in the decade preceding the 2002 survey (e.g., Barbaree, Seto, Langton, & Peacock, 2001; Simourd & Malcolm, 1998). Hence one important question that arises from these data concerns what, if anything, the majority of the programmes participating in these surveys are employing to assess risk of non-sexual recidivism. In the case of the LSI-R, it is worth noting also that it is explicitly intended to guide intervention planning in addition to monitoring progress over time through its inclusion of dynamic risk factors.

The use of tools for assessing risk of non-sexual recidivism among adolescents was surveyed in only the most recent of the SSF reports, so again, discernment of trends over time in the use of such tools must await further survey data. Data for a single general risk assessment tool, the Youth Level of Service/Case Management Inventory (YLS/CMI) (Hoge & Andrews, 2002) were reported. Data regarding the use of the Psychopathy Checklist: Youth Version (PCL:YV) (Forth, Kosson, & Hare, 2003) were also reported, but this is a tool designed primarily to assess psychopathic traits in adolescence rather than as a tool to assess risk of criminal recidivism. Research shows that both tools have predictive validity for recidivism among adolescents with criminal (including sexual) offences, although neither predicts sexual recidivism specifically (Olver, Stockdale, & Wormith, 2009). Of note, however, are various concerns about the application of the concept of psychopathy with adolescents (Edens, Skeem, Cruise, & Cauffman, 2001; Seagrave & Grisso, 2002).

Despite the meta-analytic findings in support of their use as risk assessment tools, in the United States, the PCL:YV is used in only 10.9% of community programmes and even fewer residential programmes for male adolescents. Rates are even lower among US residential programmes. Use of the YLS/CMI was reported by only 12.2% of residential programmes for male adolescents, with community programmes reporting roughly half those numbers. Conversely, and highly disconcerting (although low in absolute terms), 6.7% of residential programmes for male children and 2.4% of community programmes for male children in the United States responding to the 2009 survey reported use of the YLS/CMI – even though the tool is intended for use with 12–18-year-olds, and normative data are available only for this age range (Hoge & Andrews, 2011).

It is difficult to know what, if anything, the majority of programmes for adolescents with sexual offences in North America are using instead of these tools, but these low rates are surprising, not just because the tools have predictive validity but also, in the case of the YLS/CMI, because of the potential utility for intervention planning and use in monitoring intervention progress and risk of recidivism over time and treatment evaluation. Such utility raises the additional question of why the percentage of residential programmes in the United States using the tool is twice that of the community programmes, where arguably many of the challenges of risk management are more immediate. It remains to be seen if these patterns for types of programme reverses over the next decade as survey data accumulate.

Apart from the YLS/CMI and the PCL:YV, there are general recidivism risk assessment tools that have been developed and validated for use in specific jurisdictions (see, for example, Barnoski, 2004). This can have the noteworthy advantages of established reliability and validity indices for the population specific to that jurisdiction as well as appropriate norms. Whether such tools or others for assessing risk of criminal behaviour or violence that have received notable empirical attention in the past decade (such as the Structured Assessment of Violence Risk in Youth; Borum, Bartel, & Forth, 2006) are employed in many programmes not using the YLS/CMI or PCL:YV should be addressed in future survey work. We hope that the trend over the next decade will be towards the widespread use of tools that include risk factors demonstrated to be dynamic, which research shows to predict accurately specific types of recidivism. In the next decade, it will be important to establish whether such tools have clinical utility in terms of planning interventions and monitoring progress. Furthermore, assessment of children's continued involvement in interpersonal aggression and/or sexually inappropriate behaviour requires a developmental perspective and purpose-developed tools for that age range rather than the use of tools intended for adolescents (see, for example, Calder, 2001; Grant & Lundeberg, 2009).

Looking forward, we note the increasing attention being paid to desistance from sexual offending (Laws & Ward, 2011). Among the various principles underpinning Andrews and Bonta's RNR model is the *Strengths Principle*, which requires that personal strengths be assessed and integrated into intervention plans for those who offend (Andrews, Bonta, & Wormith, 2011). In clinical practice, it is important to assess for the presence and action of static or dynamic variables within the intrapersonal, interpersonal/social, and environmental domains that might ameliorate the effects of risk factors (Rogers, 2000). As already mentioned, the field has seen considerable progress in the development, validation, and incorporation of risk assessment practices in work with adolescents and adults who have sexually offended (Hanson & Morton-Bourgon, 2005; McGrath et al., 2010; Rich, 2009; Viljoen et al., 2012). However, efforts to identify factors which in the wider literature have been described as enhancing personal competencies, serving a stabilizing function, or ameliorating specific risks (e.g., Luthar, Cicchetti, & Becker, 2000), have not kept pace. Despite longstanding reference to the importance of strengths in assessment work with those who have sexually offended (Association for the Treatment of Sexual Abusers, 2005; National Adolescent Perpetrator Network, 1993) and also promising early work (e.g., Bremer, 1998; Gilgun, 1999), and continued attention (e.g., de Vries Robbé, de Vogel, & Douglas, 2013; Spice, Viljoen, Latzman, Scalora, & Ullman, 2012; Worling, 2013), currently assessments with adolescents and adults who have sexually offended are without a firm empirical basis in this regard. As such, the field awaits the replication and extension of recent efforts to establish an evidence base for the assessment of factors associated with desistence with these individuals (see, for example, Langton & Worling, 2015).

Conclusion

Arguably, the field has much still to do in order to establish the evidence base for its assessment practices, as per the criteria described by Hunsley and Mash (2008). Trends evident in North American survey data provide focus points in terms of the domains assessed and technologies widely used on which further research is required. Assessment practices that are being increasingly adopted across programmes are not all accompanied by comprehensive and systemic bodies of empirical evidence, despite the need for such a basis for the various purposes for which these assessment practices are being put and the various groups with which they are being used. The field is also in need of survey work on assessment practices elsewhere in the world, particularly over time, in order to obtain a complete picture of what is being done, how, and with whom. In addition to the speculative comments we have offered about the trends discussed above, we close by pointing to work in the cognitive and neurosciences (see, for example, Joyal, Black, & Dassylva, 2007; Snowden, Craig, & Gray, 2011) which could, over time, afford important insights through technologies and methods that are not yet routinely incorporated in assessment practices with individuals who have sexually offended. It will be some time before trends in their use will be discernible, but further improvement in the design, provision, and evaluation of services depends, in part, on such work.

References

Abel, G. G., Gore, D. K., Holland, C. L., Camp, N., Becker, J. V., & Rathner, J. (1989). The measurement of the cognitive distortions of child molesters. *Annals of Sex Research*, 2, 135–153.

Abel, G. G., Jordan, A., Rouleau, J. L., Emerick, R., Barboza-Whitehead, S., & Osborn, C. (2004). Use of visual reaction time to assess male adolescents who molest children. *Sexual Abuse: A Journal of Research and Treatment*, 16, 255–265.

Abrams, S., & Abrams, J. (1993). *Polygraph testing of the pedophile*. Portland, OR: Ryan Gwinner Press.

Ahlmeyer, S., Heil, P., McKee, B., & English, K. (2000). The impact of polygraph on admissions of victims and offences in adult sex offenders. *Sexual Abuse: A Journal of Research and Treatment*, 12, 123–138.

American Academy of Child and Adolescent Psychiatry (1999). Practice parameters for the assessment and treatment of children and adolescents who are sexually abusive to others. *Journal of American Academy of Child and Adolescent Psychiatry*, 38 (12, Suppl.), 55S–76S.

American Psychiatric Association Task Force (1999). *Dangerous sex offenders: A task force report of the American Psychiatric Association*. Washington, DC: American Psychiatric Association.

Anastasi, A., & Urbina, S. (1997). *Psychological testing* (7th ed.). Upper Saddle River, NJ: Prentice Hall.

Andrews, D. A., & Bonta, J. (1995). *The level of service inventory – revised manual*. North Tonawanda, NY: Multi-Health Systems.

Andrews, D. A., & Bonta, J. (2010). *The psychology of criminal conduct* (5th ed. New Providence, NJ: LexisNexis.

Andrews, D. A., Bonta, J., & Hoge, R. D. (1990). Classification for effective rehabilitation: Rediscovering psychology. *Criminal Justice and Behavior, 17*, 19–52.

Andrews, D. A., Bonta, J., & Wormith, J. S. (2011). The Risk–Need–Responsivity model: Does adding the Good Lives model contribute to effective crime prevention? *Criminal Justice and Behavior, 38*, 735–755.

Association for the Treatment of Sexual Abusers (2005). *Practice standards and guidelines for the evaluation, treatment, and management of adult male sexual offenders*. Beaverton, OR: Author.

Babchishin, K. M., Hanson, R. K., & Helmus, L. (2012). Even highly correlated measures can add incrementally to predicting recidivism among sex offenders. *Assessment, 19*, 442–461.

Bancroft, J. (2006). Normal sexual development. In H. E. Barbaree & W. L. Marshall (Eds.), *The juvenile sex offender* (pp. 19–57). New York, NY: Guilford Press.

Banse, R., Schmidt, A. F., & Clarbour, J. (2010). Indirect measures of sexual interest in child sex offenders: A multimethod approach. *Criminal Justice and Behavior, 37*, 319–335.

Barbaree, H. E., & Langton, C. M. (2006). Deviant sexual behavior. In D. A. Wolfe & E. J. Mash (Eds.), *Behavioral and emotional disorders in adolescents* (pp. 589–617). New York, NY: Guilford Press.

Barbaree, H. E., Langton, C. M., Gopnik-Lewinski, A., & Beach, C. (2013). Sex offender risk assessment. In H. Bloom & R. D. Schneider (Eds.), *Law and mental disorder: A comprehensive and practical approach*. Toronto, Canada: Irwin Law.

Barbaree, H. E., & Seto, M. C. (1997). Pedophilia: Assessment and treatment. In D. R. Laws & W. O'Donohue (Eds.), *Sexual deviance: Theory, assessment, and treatment* (pp. 175–193). New York, NY: Guilford Press.

Barbaree, H. E., Seto, M. C., Langton, C. M., & Peacock, E. J. (2001). Evaluating the predictive accuracy of six risk assessment instruments for adult sex offenders. *Criminal Justice and Behavior, 28*, 490–521.

Barlow, D. H. (2005). What's new about evidence-based assessment? *Psychological Assessment, 17*, 308–311.

Barnoski, R. (2004). *Assessing risk for re-offense: Validating the Washington state juvenile court assessment*. Olympia, WA: Washington State Institute for Public Policy.

Becker, J. V. (1998). The assessment of adolescent perpetrators of childhood sexual abuse. *The Irish Journal of Psychology, 19*, 68–81.

Becker, J. V., & Kaplan, M. S. (1988). Assessment and treatment of the male sex offender. In D. H. Schetky & A. H. Green (Eds.), *Child sexual abuse: A handbook for health care and legal professionals* (pp. 136–149). New York, NY: Brunner/Mazel.

Becker, J. V., & Murphy, W. D. (1998). What we know and do not know about assessing and treating sex offenders. *Psychology, Public Policy, and Law, 4*, 116–137.

Beech, A. R., Kalmus, E., Tipper, S. P., Baudouin, J., Flak, V., & Humphreys, G. W. (2008). Children induce an enhanced attentional blink in child molesters. *Psychological Assessment, 20*, 397–402.

Boer, D. P. (2011, October). *SVR-20 Version 2: Item descriptions*. Paper presented at the New Directions in Sex Offender Practice Conference, University of Birmingham, England.

Boer, D. P., Hart, S. D., Kropp, R. P., & Webster, C. D. (1997). *Manual for the Sexual Violence Risk − 20*. Vancouver, Canada: British Columbia Institute Against Family Violence.

Bonta, J., & Wormith, J. S. (2013). Applying the Risk–Need–Responsivity principles to offender assessment. In L. A. Craig, L. Dixon, & T. A. Gannon (Eds.), *What works in offender rehabilitation: An evidence-based approach to assessment and treatment* (pp. 71–93). Chichester, England: John Wiley & Sons, Ltd.

Borum, R., Bartel, P., & Forth, A. (2006). *SAVRY Structured Assessment of Violence Risk in Youth: Professional manual*. Lutz, FL: Psychological Assessment Resources, Inc.

Branaman, T. F., & Gallagher, S. N. (2005). Polygraph testing in sex offender treatment: A review of limitations. *American Journal of Forensic Psychology, 23*, 45–64.

Bremer, J. F. (1998). Challenges in the assessment and treatment of sexually abusive adolescents. *Irish Journal of Psychology, 19*, 82–92.

Bumby, K. M., Marshall, W. L., & Langton, C. M. (1999). A theoretical model of the influences of shame and guilt on sexual offending. In B. K. Schwartz (Ed.), *The sex offender: Theoretical advances, treating special populations and legal developments* (Vol. III, pp. 5-1–5-12). Kingston, NJ: Civic Research Institute.

Calder, M. C. (2001). *Juveniles and children who sexually abuse: Frameworks for assessment.* Lyme Regis, England: Russell House.

Camilleri, J. A., & Quinsey, V. L. (2008). Pedophilia: Assessment and treatment. In D. R. Laws & W. T. O'Donohue (Eds.), *Sexual deviance: Theory, assessment, and treatment* (2nd ed., pp. 183–212). New York, NY: Guilford Press.

Campbell, T. W. (2007). *Assessing sex offenders: Problems and pitfalls* (2nd ed.). Springfield, IL: Charles C. Thomas.

Center for Sex Offender Management (2007). *The comprehensive assessment protocol: A systemwide review of adult and juvenile sex offender management strategies.* Retrieved from http://www.csom.org/pubs/cap/index.html

Chaffin, M. (2011). The case of juvenile polygraphy as a clinical ethics dilemma. *Sexual Abuse: A Journal of Research and Treatment, 23*, 314–328.

Correctional Service of Canada (2000). *Standards for the provision of assessment and treatment services to sex offenders.* Ottawa, Canada: Author.

Cortoni, F. (2010). The assessment of female sexual offenders. In T. A. Gannon & F. Cortoni (Eds.), *Female sexual offenders: Theory, assessment and treatment* (pp. 87–100). Chichester, England: John Wiley & Sons, Ltd.

Craig, L. A., & Beech, A. R. (2009). Psychometric assessment of sexual deviance. In A. R. Beech, L. A. Craig, & K. D. Browne (Eds.), *Assessment and treatment of sex offenders: A handbook* (pp. 89–107). Chichester, England: John Wiley & Sons, Ltd.

Craig, L. A., Browne, K. D., & Beech, A. R. (2008). *Assessing risk in sex offenders: A practitioner's guide.* Chichester, England: John Wiley & Sons, Ltd.

Craig, L. A., Thornton, D., Beech, A., & Browne, K. D. (2007). The relationship of statistical and psychological risk markers to sexual reconviction in child molesters. *Criminal Justice and Behavior, 34*, 314–329.

de Vries Robbé, M., de Vogel, V., & Douglas, K. S. (2013). Risk factors and protective factors: A two-sided dynamic approach to violence risk assessment. *Journal of Forensic Psychiatry & Psychology, 24*, 440–457.

Duwe, G., & Freske, P. J. (2012). Using logistic regression modeling to predict sexual recidivism: The Minnesota Sex Offender Screening Tool-3 (MnSOST-3). *Sexual Abuse: A Journal of Research and Treatment, 24*, 350–377.

Edens, J. F., Skeem, J. L., Cruise, K. R., & Cauffman, E. (2001). Assessment of 'juvenile psychopathy' and its association with violence: A critical review. *Behavioral Sciences and Law, 19*, 53–80.

Eher, R., Matthes, A., Schilling, F., Haubner-MacLean, T., & Rettenberger, M. (2012). Dynamic risk assessment in sexual offenders using the STABLE-2000 and the STABLE-2007: An investigation of predictive and incremental validity. *Sexual Abuse: A Journal of Research and Treatment, 24*, 5–28.

Epperson, D. L., Kaul, J. D., & Heselton, D. (1999). *Minnesota Sex Offender Screening Tool – Revised (MnSOST-R): Development, performance, and recommended risk level cut scores.* Unpublished manuscript, Iowa State University, Ames. IA.

Epperson, D. L., Ralston, C. A., Fowers, D., DeWitt, J., & Gore, K. A. (2006). Actuarial risk assessment with juveniles who offend sexually: Development of the Juvenile Sexual Offense Recidivism Risk Assessment Tool-II (JSORRAT-II). In D. Prescott (Ed.), *Risk assessment of youth who have sexually abused: Theory, controversy, and emerging strategies* (pp. 118–169). Oklahoma City, OK: Wood & Barnes.

Faigman, D. L., Fienberg, S. E., & Stern, P. C. (2003). The limits of the polygraph. *Issues in Science and Technology, 20*, 40–48.

Fanniff, A. M., & Becker, J. V. (2006). Specialized assessment and treatment of adolescent sex offenders. *Aggression and Violent Behavior, 11*, 265–282.

Fanniff, A. M., & Letourneau, E. J. (2012). Another piece of the puzzle: Psychometric properties of the J-SOAP-II. *Sexual Abuse: A Journal of Research and Treatment, 24*, 378–408.

Ford, H., & Cortoni, F. (2008). Sexual deviance in females: Assessment and treatment. In D. R. Laws & W. T. O'Donohue (Eds.), *Sexual deviance: Theory, assessment, and treatment* (2nd ed., pp. 508–526). New York, NY: Guilford Press.

Forth, A. E., Kosson, D. S., & Hare, R. D. (2003). *Psychopathy checklist: Youth version*. Toronto, Canada: Multi-Health Systems.

Gannon, T. A., Beech, A. R., & Ward, T. (2008). Does the polygraph lead to better risk prediction for sexual offenders? *Aggression and Violent Behavior, 13*, 29–44.

Gannon, T. A., Wood, J. L., Pina, A., Tyler, N., Barnoux, M. F. L., & Vasquez, E. A. (2014). An evaluation of mandatory polygraph testing for sexual offenders in the United Kingdom. *Sexual Abuse: A Journal of Research and Treatment, 26*, 178–203.

Gebhard, P. H., Gagnon, J. H., Pomeroy, W. B., & Christenson, C. V. (1965). *Sex offenders: An analysis of types*. New York, NY: Harper and Row.

Gilgun, J. F. (1999). CASPARS: Clinical assessment instruments that measure strengths and risks in children and families. In M. C. Calder (Ed.), *Working with young people who sexually abuse: New pieces of the jigsaw puzzle* (pp. 49–58). Lyme Regis, England: Russell House.

Goocher, B. E. (1994). Some comments on the residential treatment of juvenile sex offenders. *Child & Youth Care Forum, 23*, 243–250.

Grady, M. D., Brodersen, M., & Abramson, J. M. (2011). The state of psychological measures for adult sexual offenders. *Aggression and Violent Behavior, 16*, 227–240.

Grant, R. K., & Lundeberg, L. H. (2009). *Interventions for children with sexual behavior problems: Research, theory, and treatment*. Kingston, NJ: Civic Research Institute.

Gray, S. R., & Plaud, J. J. (2005). A comparison of the Abel Assessment for Sexual Interest and penile plethysmography in an outpatient sample of sexual offenders. *Journal of Sexual Offender Civil Commitment: Science and the Law, 1*, 1–10.

Groth, A. N. (1979). *Men who rape: The psychology of the offender*. New York, NY: Plenum.

Grubin, D. (2010). The polygraph and forensic psychiatry. *The Journal of the American Academy of Psychiatry and the Law, 38*, 446–451.

Grubin, D., Madsen, L., Parsons, S., Sosnowski, D., & Warberg, B. (2004). A prospective study of the impact of polygraphy on high-risk behaviors in adult sex offenders. *Sexual Abuse: A Journal of Research and Treatment, 16*, 209–222.

Hall, G. C. N., & Hirschman, R. (1991). Toward a theory of sexual aggression: A quadripartite model. *Journal of Consulting and Clinical Psychology, 59*, 662–669.

Hanson, R. K. (1997). The development of a brief actuarial risk scale for sexual offense recidivism *(User Report 1997-04)*. Ottawa, Canada: Solicitor General of Canada.

Hanson, R. K., Bourgon, G., Helmus, L., & Hodgson, L. (2009). The principles of effective correctional treatment also apply to sexual offenders: A metaanalysis. *Criminal Justice and Behavior, 36*, 865–891.

Hanson, R. K., & Bussière, M. T. (1998). Predicting relapse: A meta-analysis of sexual offender recidivism studies. *Journal of Consulting and Clinical Psychology, 66*, 348–362.

Hanson, R. K., Cox, B. C., & Woszczyna, C. (1991). Assessing treatment outcome for sexual offenders. *Annals of Sex Research, 4,* 177–208.

Hanson, R. K., & Harris, A. J. R. (2000). Where should we intervene? Dynamic predictors of sexual offense recidivism. *Criminal Justice and Behavior, 27,* 6–35.

Hanson, R. K., Harris, A. J. R., Scott, T., & Helmus, L. (2007). *Assessing the risk of sexual offenders on community supervision: The dynamic supervision project.* Ottawa, Canada: Public Safety and Emergency Preparedness Canada.

Hanson, R. K., Helmus, L, & Thornton, D. (2010). Predicting recidivism amongst sexual offenders: A multi-site study of Static-2002. *Law and Human Behavior, 34,* 198–211.

Hanson, R. K., & Morton-Bourgon, K. (2005). The characteristics of persistent sexual offenders: A meta-analysis of recidivism studies. *Journal of Consulting and Clinical Psychology, 73,* 1154–1163.

Hanson, R. K., & Morton-Bourgon, K. E. (2009). The accuracy of recidivism risk assessments for sexual offenders: A meta-analysis of 118 prediction studies. *Psychological Assessment, 21,* 1–21.

Hanson, R. K., Morton, K. E., & Harris, A. J. R. (2003). Sexual offender recidivism risk: What we know and what we need to know. *Annals of the New York Academy of Sciences, 989,* 154–166.

Hanson, R. K., & Thornton, D. (2000). Improving risk assessments for sex offenders: A comparison of three actuarial scales. *Law and Human Behavior, 24,* 119–136.

Harris, A. J. R., & Hanson, R. K. (2010). Clinical, actuarial and dynamic risk assessment of sexual offenders: Why do things keep changing? *Journal of Sexual Aggression, 16,* 296–310.

Harris, G. T., Rice, M. E., & Quinsey, V. L. (1993). Violent recidivism of mentally disordered offenders: The development of a statistical prediction instrument. *Criminal Justice and Behavior, 20,* 315–335.

Hart, S. D., Kropp, P. R., Laws, D. R., Klaver, J., Long, C., & Watt, K. A. (2003). *The Risk for Sexual Violence Protocol (RSVP): Structured professional guidelines for assessing risk of sexual violence.* Burnaby, Canada: Simon Fraser University, Mental Health Law and Policy Institute.

Heil, P., Simons, D., & Burton, D. (2010). Using the polygraph with female sexual offenders. In T. A. Gannon & F. Cortoni (Eds.), *Female sexual offenders: Theory, assessment and treatment* (pp. 143–160). Chichester, England: John Wiley & Sons, Ltd.

Helmus, L., Hanson, R. K., Thornton, D., Babchishin, K. M., & Harris, A. J. R. (2012). Absolute recidivism rates predicted by Static-99R and Static-2002R sex offender assessment tools vary across samples. *Criminal Justice and Behavior, 39,* 1148–1171.

Hoge, R. D., & Andrews, D. A. (2002). *Youth Level of Service/Case Management Inventory.* North Tonawanda, NY: Multi-Health Systems.

Hoge, R. D., & Andrews, D. A. (2011). *Youth Level of Service/Case Management Inventory 2.0 (YLS/CMI 2.0) user's manual.* Toronto, Canada: Multi-Health Systems.

Home Office Communication Directorate (2000). *What works: First report from the Joint Prison/Probation Accreditation Panel.* London, England: Author.

Hunsley, J., & Mash, E. J. (2008). Developing criteria for evidence-based assessment: An introduction to assessments that work. In J. Hunsley & E. J. Mash (Eds.), *A guide to assessments that work* (pp. 3–14). New York, NY: Oxford University Press.

Hunter, J. A., & Mathews, R. (1997). Sexual deviance in females. In D. R. Laws & W. O'Donohue (Eds.), *Sexual deviance: Theory, assessment, and treatment* (pp. 465–480). New York, NY: Guilford Press.

Joyal, C. C., Black, D. N., & Dassylva, B. (2007). The neuropsychology and neurology of sexual deviance: A review and pilot study. *Sexual Abuse: A Journal of Research and Treatment, 19,* 155–173.

Knight, R. A., & Prentky, R. A. (1990). Classifying sexual offenders: The development and cor-roboration of taxonomic models. In W. L. Marshall, D. R. Laws, & H. E. Barbaree (Eds.), *Handbook of sexual assault: Issues, theories, and treatment of the offender* (pp. 23–52). New York, NY: Plenum.

Knopp, F. H., Rosenberg, J., & Stevenson, W. (1986). *Report on nationwide survey of juvenile and adult sex-offender treatment programs and providers: 1986.* Brandon, VT: Safer Society Press.

Knopp, F. H., & Stevenson, W. F. (1989). *Nationwide survey of juvenile and adult sex-offender treatment programs and models, 1988.* Brandon, VT: Safer Society Press.

Lalumière, M. L., Harris, G. T., Quinsey, V. L., & Rice, M. E. (2005). *The causes of rape: Understanding individual differences in male propensity for sexual aggression.* Washington, DC: American Psychological Association.

Lambie, I., & McCarthy, J. (2004). Interviewing strategies with sexually abusive youth. *Journal of Child Sexual Abuse, 13,* 107–123.

Lane, S. (1997). Assessment of sexually abusive youth. In G. Ryan & S. Lane (Eds.), *Juvenile sexual offending: Causes, consequences, and corrections* (pp. 219–263). San Francisco, CA: Jossey-Bass.

Langevin, R. (1988). Defensiveness in sex offenders. In R. Rogers (Ed.), *Clinical assessment of malingering and deception* (pp. 269–290). New York, NY: Guilford Press.

Langton, C. M. (2007). Assessment implications of 'What Works' research for Dangerous and Severe Personality Disorder (DSPD) service evaluation. *Psychology, Crime & Law, 13,* 97–111.

Langton, C. M., & Barbaree, H. E. (2001, July). Implications of study design for research on risk factors. *Paper presented at the 26th International Congress on Law and Mental Health,* Montreal, Canada.

Langton, C. M., & Barbaree, H. E. (2006). Conceptual issues in treatment evaluation research with juvenile sexual offenders. In H. E. Barbaree & W. L. Marshall (Eds.), *The juvenile sex offender* (2nd ed., pp. 248–274). New York, NY: Guilford Press.

Langton, C. M., Barbaree, H. E., & Seto, M. C. (2002). *Evaluating the predictive valid-ity of seven risk assessment instruments for sexual offenders.* Paper presented at the 21st Annual Research and Treatment Conference of the Association for the Treatment of Sex-ual Abusers, Montreal, Canada.

Langton, C. M., Barbaree, H. E., Hansen, K. T., Harkins, L., & Peacock, E. J. (2007). Reliabil-ity and validity of the Static-2002 among adult sex offenders with reference to treatment status. *Criminal Justice and Behavior, 34,* 616–640.

Langton, C. M., Barbaree, H. E., Harkins, L., Arenovich, T., McNamee, J., Peacock, E. J., … Marcon, H. (2008). Denial and minimization among sexual offenders: Post-treatment presentation and association with sexual recidivism. *Criminal Justice and Behavior, 35,* 69–98.

Langton, C. M., & Worling, J. R. (2015). Introduction to the special issue on factors positively associated with desistance for adolescents and adults who have sexually offended. *Sexual Abuse: A Journal of Research and Treatment, 27,* 3–15.

Lanyon, R. I., & Thomas, M. L. (2008). Detecting deception in sex offender assessment. In R. Rogers (Ed.), *Clinical assessment of malingering and deception* (3rd ed., pp. 285–300). New York, NY: Guilford Press.

Laws, D. R. (2003). Penile plethysmography: Will we ever get it right? In T. Ward, D. R. Laws, & S. M. Hudson (Eds.), *Sexual deviance: Issues and controversies* (pp. 82–102). Thousand Oaks, CA: Sage.

Laws, D. R., & Marshall, W. L. (2003). A brief history of behavioral and cognitive behavioral approaches to sexual offenders: Part 1. Early developments. *Sexual Abuse: A Journal of Research and Treatment, 15,* 75–92.

Laws, D. R., & O'Donohue, W. T. (2008). Introduction. In D. R. Laws & W. T. O'Donohue (Eds.), *Sexual deviance: Theory, assessment, and treatment* (2nd ed., pp. 1–20). New York, NY: Guilford Press.

Laws, D. R., & Ward, T. (2011). *Desistence from sex offending: Alternatives to throwing away the keys.* New York, NY: Guilford Press.

Letourneau, E. J. (2002). A comparison of objective measures of sexual arousal and interest: Visual reaction time and penile plethysmography. *Sexual Abuse: A Journal of Research and Treatment, 14,* 207–223.

Levenson, J. S., & Macgowan, M. J. (2004). Engagement, denial, and treatment progress among sex offenders in group therapy. *Sexual Abuse: A Journal of Research and Treatment, 16,* 49–63.

Leversee, T. (2010). Comprehensive and individualized evaluation and ongoing assessment. In G. Ryan, T. Leversee, & S. Lane (Eds.), *Juvenile sexual offending* (3rd ed., pp. 201–223). Hoboken, NJ: John Wiley & Sons, Inc.

Luthar, S. S., Cicchetti, D., & Becker, B. (2000). The construct of resilience: A critical evaluation and guidelines for future work. *Child Development, 71,* 543–562.

Maletzky, B. M. (1991). *Treating the sexual offender.* Thousand Oaks, CA: Sage.

Marshall, W. L. (2006). Diagnostic problems with sexual offenders. In W. L. Marshall, Y. M. Fernandez, L. E. Marshall, & G. A. Serran (Eds.), *Sexual offender treatment: Controversial issues* (pp. 33–43). Chichester, England: John Wiley & Sons, Ltd.

Marshall, W. L., & Barbaree, H. E. (1990). An integrated theory of the etiology of sexual offending. In W. L. Marshall, D. R. Laws, & H. E. Barbaree (Eds.), *Handbook of sexual assault: Issues, theories, and treatment of the offender* (pp. 257–275). New York, NY: Plenum.

Marshall, W. L., & Fernandez, Y. M. (2000). Phallometric testing with sexual offenders: Limits to its value. *Clinical Psychology Review, 20,* 807–822.

Marshall, W. L., Fernandez, Y. M., Serran, G. A., Mulloy, R., Thornton, D., Mann, R. E., & Anderson, D. (2003). Process variables in the treatment of sexual offenders: A review of the relevant literature. *Aggression and Violent Behavior, 8,* 205–234.

Marshall, W. L., & Laws, D. R. (2003). A brief history of behavioral and cognitive behavioral approaches to sexual offenders: Part 2. The modern era. *Sexual Abuse: A Journal of Research and Treatment, 15,* 93–120.

Marshall, W. L., Marshall, L. E., Serran, G. A., & O'Brien, M. D. (2011). *Rehabilitating sexual offenders: A strength-based approach.* Washington, DC: American Psychological Association.

McGrath, R. J. (1990). Assessment of sexual aggressors: Practical clinical interviewing strategies. *Journal of Interpersonal Violence, 5,* 507–519.

McGrath, R. J., & Cumming, G. (2003). *Sex offender treatment needs and progress scale manual.* Middlebury, VT: Authors.

McGrath, R. J., Cumming, G. F., Burchard, B. L., Zeoli, S., & Ellerby, L. (2010). *Current practices and emerging trends in sexual abuser management: The Safer Society 2009 North American Survey.* Brandon, VT: Safer Society Press.

McGrath, R. J., Cumming, G. F., Hoke, S. E., & Bonn-Miller, M. O. (2007). Outcomes in a community sex offender treatment program: A comparison between polygraphed and matched non-polygraphed offenders. *Sexual Abuse: A Journal of Research and Treatment, 19,* 381–393.

McGrath, R. J., & Hoke, S. E. (2001). *Vermont Assessment of Sex Offender Risk manual*. Middlebury, VT: Authors (original work published 1994).

McGrath, R. J., Hoke, S. E., & Lasher, M. P. (2013). *Vermont Assessment of Sex Offender Risk-2 (VASOR-2) manual*. Middlebury, VT: Authors.

McGrath, R. J., Lasher, M. P., & Cumming, G. F. (2012). The Sex Offender Treatment Intervention and Progress Scale (SOTIPS): Psychometric properties and incremental predictive validity with Static-99R. *Sexual Abuse: A Journal of Research and Treatment, 24*, 431–458.

McGrath, R. J., Lasher, M. P., Cumming, G. F., Langton, C. M., & Hoke, S. E. (2014). Development of Vermont Assessment of Sex Offender Risk-2 (VASOR-2) reoffense risk scale. *Sexual Abuse: A Journal of Research and Treatment, 26*, 271–290.

McGuire, R. J., Carlisle, J. M., & Young, B. G. (1965). Sexual deviation as a conditioned response: A hypothesis. *Behavior Research and Therapy, 2*, 185–190.

Miller, W. R., & Rollnick, S. (2002). *Motivational interviewing: Preparing people for change* (2nd ed.). New York, NY: Guilford Press.

Miner, M., Borduin, C., Prescott, D., Bovensmann, H., Schepker, R., Du Bois, R., ... Pfäfflin, F. (2006). Standards of care for juvenile sexual offenders of the International Association for the Treatment of Sexual Offenders. *Sexual Offender Treatment, 1*(3), 1–7.

Mokros, A., Gebhard, M., Heinz, V., Marschall, R. W., Nitschke, J., Glasgow, D. V., Gress, C. L. Z., & Laws, D. R. (2013). Computerized assessment of pedophilic sexual interest through self-report and viewing time: Reliability, validity, and classification accuracy of the Affinity Program. *Sexual Abuse: A Journal of Research and Treatment, 25*, 230–258.

Monahan, J. (1981). *Predicting violent behavior: An assessment of clinical techniques*. Beverly Hills, CA: Sage.

Monahan, J. (1996). Violence prediction: The past twenty years and the next twenty years. *Criminal Justice and Behavior, 23*, 107–120.

Monahan, J., Steadman, H. J., Silver, E., Appelbaum, P. S., Robbins, P. C., Mulvey, E. P., ... Banks, S. (2001). *Rethinking risk assessment: The MacArthur Study of Mental Disorder and Violence*. New York, NY: Oxford University Press.

Murphy, W. D., & Barbaree, H. E. (1994). *Assessment of sex offenders by measures of erectile response: Psychometric properties and decision making*. Brandon, VT: Safer Society Press.

National Adolescent Perpetrator Network (1993). The revised report from the National Task Force on Juvenile Sexual Offending 1993 of the National Adolescent Perpetrator Network. *Juvenile and Family Court Journal, 44*, 1–120.

National Research Council (2003). *The polygraph and lie detection*. Washington, DC: National Academies Press.

Nichols, H. R., & Molinder, I. (1984). *Multiphasic sex inventory*. Fircrest, WA: Nichols and Molinder Assessments.

Nunes, K. L., & Babchishin, K. M. (2012). Construct validity of Stable-2000 and Stable-2007 scores. *Sexual Abuse: A Journal Of Research & Treatment, 24*, 29–45.

Nunes, K. L., Firestone, P., & Baldwin, M. W. (2007). Indirect assessment of cognitions of child sexual abusers with the implicit association test. *Criminal Justice and Behavior, 34*, 454–475.

Nunes, K. L., Hanson, R. K., Firestone, P., Moulden, H. M., Greenberg, D. M., & Bradford, J. M. (2007). Denial predicts recidivism for some sexual offenders. *Sexual Abuse: A Journal of Research and Treatment, 19*, 91–105.

O'Donohue, W., & Letourneau, E. (1992). The psychometric properties of the penile tumescence assessment of child molesters. *Journal of Psychopathology and Behavioral Assessment, 14*, 123–174.

O'Donohue, W. T., Regev, L., & Hagstrom, A. (2000). Problems with the DSM-IV diagnosis of pedophilia. *Sexual Abuse: A Journal of Research and Treatment, 12,* 95–105.

Olver, M. E., Nicholaichuk, T. P., & Wong, S. C. P. (2014). The predictive and convergent validity of a psychometric battery used to assess sexual offenders in a treatment programme: An 18-year follow-up. *Journal of Sexual Aggression, 20,* 216–239.

Olver, M. E., Stockdale, K. C., & Wormith, J. S. (2009). Risk assessment with young offenders: A meta-analysis of three assessment measures. *Criminal Justice and Behavior, 36,* 329–353.

Prentky, R., Harris, B., Frizzell, K., & Righthand, S. (2000). An actuarial procedure for assessing risk with juvenile sex offenders. *Sexual Abuse: A Journal of Research and Treatment, 12,* 71–93.

Prentky, R., & Righthand, S. (2003). *Juvenile Sex Offender Assessment Protocol-II: Manual.* Unpublished manuscript. Retrieved from http://www.csom.org/pubs/jsoap.pdf

Prescott, D. S. (2012). What do young people learn from coercion? Polygraph examinations with youth who have sexually abused. *ATSA Forum, 24,* 2.

Prochaska, J. O., Norocross, J. C., & DiClemente, C. C. (1994). *Changing for good: A revolutionary six-stage program for overcoming bad habits and moving your life positively forward.* New York, NY: HarperCollins.

Quinsey, V. L., Coleman, G., Jones, B., & Altrows, I. F. (1997). Proximal antecedents of eloping and reoffending among supervised mentally disordered offenders. *Journal of Interpersonal Violence, 12,* 794–813.

Quinsey, V. L., Harris, G. T., Rice, M. E., & Cormier, C. A. (2006). *Violent offenders: Appraising and managing risk* (2nd ed.). Washington, DC: American Psychological Association.

Quinsey, V. L., & Lalumière, M. (2001). *Assessment of sexual offenders against children* (2nd ed.). Thousand Oaks, CA: Sage.

Raymond, J. E., Shapiro, K. L., & Arnell, K. M. (1992). Temporary suppression of visual processing in an RSVP task: An attentional blink? *Journal of Experimental Psychology: Human Perception & Performance, 18,* 849–860.

Reitzel, L. R., & Carbonell, J. L. (2006). The effectiveness of sex offender treatment for juveniles as measured by recidivism. *Sexual Abuse: A Journal of Research and Treatment, 18,* 401–421.

Rice, M. E., Harris, G. T., Lang, C., & Chaplin, T. C. (2012). Adolescents who have sexually offended: Is phallometry valid? *Sexual Abuse: A Journal of Research and Treatment, 24,* 133–152.

Rich, P. (2009). *Juvenile sexual offenders: A comprehensive guide to risk evaluation.* Hoboken, NJ: John Wiley & Sons, Inc.

Rich, P. (2011). *Understanding, assessing, and rehabilitating juvenile sex offenders* (2nd ed.). Hoboken, NJ: John Wiley & Sons, Inc.

Rogers, R. (2000). The uncritical assessment of risk assessment in forensic practice. *Law and Human Behavior, 24,* 595–605.

Rosky, J. W. (2013). The (f)utility of post-conviction polygraph testing. *Sexual Abuse: A Journal of Research and Treatment, 25,* 259–281.

Ross, J. E., & Loss, P. (1988). *Risk assessment/interviewing protocol for adolescent sex offenders.* Mystic, CT: Authors.

Salter, A. C. (1988). *Treating child sexual offenders and victims: A practical guide.* Newbury Park, CA: Sage.

Seagrave, D., & Grisso, T. (2002). Adolescent development and the measurement of juvenile psychopathy. *Law and Human Behavior, 26,* 219–239.

Seto, M. C. (2008). *Pedophilia and sexual offending against children.* Washington, DC: American Psychological Association.

Seto, M. C., Abramowitz, C. S., & Barbaree, H. E. (2008). Paraphilias. In J. Hunsley & E. J. Mash (Eds.), *A guide to assessments that work* (pp. 488–512). New York, NY: Oxford University Press.

Seto, M. C., & Lalumière, M. L. (2010). What is so special about male adolescent sexual offending? A review and test of explanations through meta-analysis. *Psychological Bulletin, 136,* 526–575.

Sewell, K. W., & Salekin, R. T. (1997). Understanding and detecting dissimulation in sex offenders. In R. Rogers (Ed.), *Clinical assessment of malingering and deception* (2nd ed., pp. 328–350). New York, NY: Guilford Press.

Simourd, D. J., & Malcolm, P. B. (1998). Reliability and validity of the Level of Service Inventory – Revised among federally incarcerated sex offenders. *Journal of Interpersonal Violence, 13,* 261–274.

Smith, G., & Fischer, L. (1999). Assessment of juvenile sexual offenders: Reliability and validity of the Abel assessment for interest in paraphilias. *Sexual Abuse: A Journal of Research and Treatment, 11,* 207–216.

Snowden, R. J., Craig, R. L., & Gray, N. S. (2011). Indirect behavioral measures of cognition among sexual offenders. *Journal of Sex Research, 48,* 192–217.

Spice, A., Viljoen, J. L., Latzman, N. E., Scalora, M. J., & Ullman, D. (2012). Risk and protective factors for recidivism among juveniles who have offended sexually. *Sexual Abuse: A Journal of Research and Treatment, 25,* 347–369.

Steen, C., & Monnette, B. (1989). *Treating adolescent sex offenders in the community.* Springfield, IL: Charles C. Thomas.

Thakker, J., Collie, R. M., Gannon, T. A., & Ward, T. (2008). Rape: Assessment and treatment. In D. R. Laws & W. T. O'Donohue (Eds.), *Sexual deviance: Theory, assessment, and treatment* (2nd ed., pp. 356–383). New York, NY: Guilford Press.

Thornton, D. (2002). Constructing and testing a framework for dynamic risk assessment. *Sexual Abuse: A Journal of Research and Treatment, 14,* 139–153.

Thornton, D., Mann, R., Webster, S., Blud, L., Travers, R., Friendship, C., & Erikson, M. (2003). Distinguishing and combining risks for sexual and violent recidivism. *Annals of the New York Academy of Sciences, 989,* 225–235; discussion, 236–246.

Vess, J. (2011). Ethical practice in sex offender assessment: Consideration of actuarial and polygraph methods. *Sexual Abuse: A Journal of Research and Treatment, 23,* 381–396.

Viljoen, J. L., Mordell, S., & Beneteau, J. (2012). Prediction of adolescent sexual reoffending: A meta-analysis of the J-SOAP-II, ERASOR, J-SORRAT-II, and Static-99. *Law and Human Behavior, 36,* 423–438.

Vitacco, M. J., Caldwell, M., Ryba, N. L., Malesky, A., & Kurus, S. J. (2009). Assessing risk in adolescent sexual offenders: Recommendations for clinical practice. *Behavioral Sciences and the Law, 27,* 929–940.

Wakeling, H., Beech, A. R., & Freemantle, N. (2013). Investigating treatment change and its relationship to recidivism in a sample of 3773 sex offenders in the UK. *Psychology, Crime & Law, 19,* 233–252.

Ward, T., & Beech, A. R. (2008). An integrated theory of sexual offending. In D. R. Laws & W. T. O'Donohue (Eds.), *Sexual deviance: Theory, assessment, and treatment* (2nd ed., pp. 21–36). New York, NY: Guilford Press.

Ward, T., McCormack, J., Hudson, S. M., & Polaschek, D. (1997). Rape: Assessment and treatment. In D. R. Laws & W. O'Donohue (Eds.), *Sexual deviance: Theory, assessment, and treatment* (pp. 356–393). New York, NY: Guilford Press.

Ward, T., Polaschek, D. L. L., & Beech, A. R. (2006). *Theories of sexual offending.* Chichester, England: John Wiley and Sons, Ltd.

Webster, C. D., Douglas, K. S., Eaves, D., & Hart, S. D. (1997). *HCR-20: Assessing risk for violence. Version 2.* Burnaby, BC: Mental Health, Law, and Policy Institute, Simon Fraser University.

Wollert, R. (2002). The importance of cross-validation in actuarial test construction: Shrinkage in the risk estimates for the Minnesota Sex Offender Screening Tool – Revised. *Journal of Threat Assessment, 2,* 87–102.

Worling, J. R. (1995). Sexual abuse histories of adolescent male sex offenders: Differences based on the age and gender of their victims. *Journal of Abnormal Psychology, 104,* 610–613.

Worling, J. R. (2006). Assessing sexual arousal with adolescent males who have offended sexually: Self-report and unobtrusively measured viewing time. *Sexual Abuse: A Journal of Research and Treatment, 18,* 383–400.

Worling, J. (2012). The assessment and treatment of deviant sexual arousal with adolescents who have offended sexually. *Journal of Sexual Aggression, 18,* 36–63.

Worling, J. R. (2013). *Desistence for Adolescents who Sexually Harm (DASH-13).* Unpublished document.

Worling, J. R., Bookalam, D., & Litteljohn, A. (2012). Prospective validity of the Estimate of Risk of Adolescent Sexual Offense Recidivism (ERASOR). *Sexual Abuse: A Journal of Research and Treatment, 24,* 203–223.

Worling, J. R., & Curwen, T. (2001). Estimate of Risk of Adolescent Sexual Offense Recidivism (ERASOR; Version 2.0). In M. C. Calder (Ed.), *Juveniles and children who sexually abuse: Frameworks for assessment* (pp. 372–397). Lyme Regis, England: Russell House. Retrieved from at www.erasor.org.

Section II
Assessing Risk of Sexual Recidivism

29

Actuarial Risk Assessment of Sexual Offenders

Martin Rettenberger

Centre for Criminology (Kriminologische Zentralstelle - KrimZ), Wiesbaden, and
Johannes Gutenberg University Mainz (JGU), Germany

Leam A. Craig

Forensic Psychology Practice Ltd, University of Birmingham,
and Birmingham City University, United Kingdom

The Methodology of Actuarial Risk Assessment

In modern forensic psychology, there are basically three different methodological approaches to risk assessment (e.g., Boer & Hart, 2009; Craig, Browne, & Beech, 2008; Hanson, 2009): unstructured clinical judgement (UCJ), actuarial risk assessment instruments (ARAIs), and structured professional judgement (SPJ). Intuitively made UCJs – even if done by experienced clinicians – should no longer be taken into account in professional risk assessment settings (Boer & Hart, 2009) because they cannot be regarded as a scientific procedure and, therefore, should not even be named 'professional' (Hanson, 2009). By far the most important reason for neglecting UCJ is that – as in other areas of psychological prediction research – empirical results indicate that structured and standardized risk assessment approaches such as ARAIs and SPJ instruments are more accurate in predicting recidivism than unstructured prediction methods (e.g., Bonta, Law, & Hanson, 1998; Dawes, Faust, & Meehl, 1989; Grove & Meehl, 1996; Grove, Zald, Lebow, Snitz, & Nelson, 2000). Meta-analytic research has shown that this is also true for sexual offenders (Hanson & Morton-Bourgon, 2009). SPJ instruments such as the Sexual Violence Risk-20 (SVR-20) (Boer, Hart, Kropp, & Webster, 1997) consist of an empirically derived list of risk and protective factors, whereas scoring is typically based on professional considerations about which items apply best to an individual case. The final risk judgement in SPJ procedures – for example, if an offender has to be classified as low, moderate, or high risk – is based

The Wiley Handbook on the Theories, Assessment, and Treatment of Sexual Offending.
Edited by Douglas P. Boer. Volume II: Assessment, edited by Leam A. Craig and Martin Rettenberger.
© 2017 John Wiley & Sons, Ltd. Published 2017 by John Wiley & Sons, Ltd.

primarily on the professional's judgement using clinical experience, and the professional's theoretical and empirical knowledge about (re)offending behaviour.

ARAIs represent highly structured risk assessment scales using combinations of empirically determined and thoroughly operationalized predictor variables (e.g., Craig et al., 2008; Hanson & Morton-Bourgon, 2009; Quinsey, Harris, Rice, & Cormier, 2006). Based on Meehl's (1954) seminal work on the comparison between actuarial and clinical prediction methods, two core variables of ARAIs are that they use explicit methods of combining the risk factors, and that the total score, which resulted usually from adding up the individual item scores to give a total sum score, is linked to an empirically derived probability figure (Dawes et al., 1989; Hanson & Morton-Bourgon, 2009). Referring to Sawyer (1966), Hanson and Morton-Bourgon (2007) differentiated risk assessment into one of the four following categories depending whether the risk factors are empirically or conceptually derived, and whether the final judgement is determined by an SPJ-related procedure or by an explicit algorithm: empirical actuarial, conceptual actuarial, SPJ, and unstructured. The empirical actuarial approach proposed by Hanson and Morton-Bourgon (2007) is most comparable to the above-mentioned historical definition of actuarial assessment by Meehl (1954). In this approach, the items are selected based on the observed relationship with outcome (i.e., recidivism risk), and explicit rules are provided for combining the items into an overall risk judgement (e.g., the Sex Offender Risk Appraisal Guide [SORAG], Quinsey et al., 2006; or the Static-99, Hanson & Thornton, 2000). In the conceptual actuarial approach, the final judgement is determined by explicit rules, but the items are selected based on theory, or on a combination of theory and empiricism. Popular examples of conceptual actuarial risk assessment instruments for sexual offenders are the Structure Risk Assessment (SRA) (Thornton, 2002) and the Violence Risk Scale – Sex Offender Version (VRS-SO) (Wong, Olver, Nicholaichuk, & Gordon, 2003).

In their updated meta-analysis, Hanson and Morton-Bourgon (2009) proposed two further categories of standardized risk assessment instruments that could be more or less actuarial in terms of Meehl (1954): mechanical and adjusted actuarial. Mechanical risk assessment tools have explicit item rules in addition to clear definitions for combining the item scores into a total score. However, they did not provide a table that linked the total scores to empirically derived recidivism probabilities, which was a core feature of Meehl's (1954) definition of an actuarial risk assessment procedure. Furthermore, mechanical instruments selected their items based primarily on theory or literature reviews instead of empirical investigations on the relationships between predictors and outcome (Hanson & Morton-Bourgon, 2009). SPJ instruments such as the SVR-20 could become mechanical risk assessment tools in this sense if if – which is not uncommon in clinical practice – the user omits the SPJ-related final risk judgement and instead simply adds up the single item scores to obtain a total score (Hanson & Morton-Bourgon, 2007; Rettenberger, Boer, & Eher, 2011). Another example is the Juvenile Sex Offender Assessment Protocol (J-SOAP) (Prentky, Harris, Frizzell, & Righthand, 2000), which is specifically designed for juvenile sex offenders and is, therefore, not applicable for adult sex offender assessment purposes.

The adjusted actuarial risk assessment method is based on the total scores of actuarial or mechanical tools but provides the additional judgement option of a so-called 'clinical override'. In this case, the evaluator is allowed to overrule the actuarially derived final judgement by external factors that are usually not specified in advance. Furthermore, the method of combining the external factors with the results of the actuarial tool are also not predetermined (Hanson & Morton-Bourgon, 2009). The clinical override is one core feature of most SPJ instruments (Boer & Hart, 2009) and is also included in the VRS-SO (Wong et al., 2003). However, care must be taken when using clinical override in SPJ, and in particular with ARAIs, as any deviation from the empirically approved methodology runs the risk of invalidating the scale (Craig & Beech, 2010).

The Different Generations of Risk Assessment and the RNR Model of Offender Rehabilitation

Another kind of categorization of (actuarial) risk assessment methods is based on the influential work of Andrews and Bonta (2006) on their Psychology of Criminal Conduct (PCC), which is related not just to sexual or violent offences but to all kinds of delinquent or criminal behaviour. The focus on the conceptualization of different 'generations' of risk assessment is that risk assessment should provide not only as much as possible predictive accuracy but also information about the opportunities of risk management, i.e., about the potential risk-reducing influence of (therapeutic) interventions and sanctions (Boer & Hart, 2009; Hanson & Morton-Bourgon, 2007, 2009; Wong et al., 2003). Andrews and Bonta (2006) proposed three (subsequently four) generations of risk assessment: first, unstructured-intuitive clinical/professional judgement; second, actuarial (i.e., empirically derived) risk assessment methods based on predominantly or exclusively static/historical/biographical risk factors; and third, actuarial risk assessment methods based on dynamic factors or criminogenic needs (Harris & Hanson, 2010; Mann, Hanson, & Thornton, 2010). The fourth generation of risk assessment tools are intended to integrate more systematically data about the intervention and monitoring process with a comprehensive, permanently up-to-date assessment, a procedure that is usually called 'case management' in non-forensic settings (Andrews, Bonta, & Wormith, 2006).

Currently, probably the most prominent example of a fourth-generation risk assessment instrument is the Level of Service/Case Management Inventory (LS/CMI) (Andrews, Bonta, & Wormith, 2004). However, so far there have been very few empirical studies of the utility of fourth-generation risk assessment instruments such as the LS/CMI in sexual offenders, so it remains unclear whether the value of risk assessment has actually increased from the third to the fourth generation. In a more recent study, Wormith, Hogg, and Guzzo (2012) investigated the clinical utility and predictive validity of the LS/CMI in a large Canadian sexual offender sample ($n = 1905$) released from the Canadian prison system in the province of Ontario. The instrument showed good predictive accuracy[1] for the prediction of general, violent, and sexual recidivism (area under the curve [AUC] = 0.77, 0.74,

---

[1] Referring to Cohen (1992), Rice and Harris (2005) formulated the following interpretation criteria for AUC values: results of 0.71 or above are classified as 'good' and results between 0.64 and 0.71 are classified as 'moderate'. Significant AUC values that are below 0.64 are classified as 'small'.

and 0.74, respectively), which was comparable to the predictive accuracy reported for non-sexual offenders. However, the so-called clinical (or professional) override, a core feature of the application of the LS/CMI compared with, for example, most of the second- and third-generation actuarial instruments, reduced the predictive validity of the instrument and, therefore, challenged the additional clinical value of this feature (Wormith et al., 2012). Similarly, Hanson and Morton-Bourgon (2009) reported in a meta-analytic review that at that time only three investigations of clinical or professional adjustments and overrides of numerically derived final risk judgements could have been identified (Gore, 2007; Hanson, 2007; Vrana, Sroga, & Guzzo, 2008), and in each study, the clinical and professional adjustments decreased the predictive accuracy of the instruments. In other words, every clinical add-on deteriorates the actuarial–statistical–nomothetical–empirical result of a risk assessment tool – a well-known but obviously difficult to accept finding in the psychological assessment literature (Grove & Meehl, 1996). The reasons for this deterioration of predictive accuracy are still not fully understood but, as Hanson and Morton-Bourgon (2009) suggested, 'the simplest interpretation is that the overrides simply added noise' (p. 9) to the risk assessment result yielded by the instrument alone, i.e., the clinical interpretation reduces the reliability of the total assessment process. This assumption was confirmed by findings about the interrater reliability for the clinical override, which was not above the chance level in the Hanson (2007) study (intraclass correlation [ICC]^2 = 0.14).

The proliferation of the second-generation and the subsequent development of third- and fourth-generation risk assessment instruments were strongly influenced and supported by the Risk–Need–Responsivity (RNR) model of offender rehabilitation (Andrews & Bonta, 2006; Bonta & Andrews, 2007; Bonta & Wormith, 2013; Harris & Hanson, 2010). Andrews and Bonta (2006) suggested that an effective intervention has to focus on risk (i.e., the risk potential of the single offender for committing new offences), need (i.e., consideration of empirically proven criminogenic needs in terms of particular treatment goals), and responsivity (i.e., the use of intervention techniques and treatment programmes to which the individual offender's abilities, learning style, motivation, and strengths respond). Today, the RNR model is regarded as probably the most influential model for the assessment and treatment of offenders (Bonta & Andrews, 2007; Ward, Mesler, & Yates, 2007) and was also successfully proven for sexual offenders (Hanson, Bourgon, Helmus, & Hodgson, 2009). In the last named study, Hanson et al. (2009) reported that treatment programmes that adhered to the RNR principles showed the best results in reducing recidivism in sexual offenders. Because of the consistency of these findings with the general offender rehabilitation literature (Andrews & Bonta, 2006; Bonta & Andrews, 2007), the authors suggested that the RNR model should be the most relevant aspect in the design and implementation of interventions for sexual offenders (Hanson et al., 2009). Obviously, the use of actuarial risk assessment could, therefore, be able to improve the risk-reducing results of treatment programmes by measuring accurately the individual level of risk with second-generation risk assessment instruments and

---

[2] Hart and Boer (2010) used, according to Fleiss (1981), the following critical values for single-measure ICC: ICC < 0.39 = poor, ICC = 0.40–0.59 = fair, ICC = 0.60–0.74 = good, and ICC > 0.75 = excellent.

by defining treatment targets in terms of criminogenic needs with third-(or fourth-) generation risk assessment instruments.

Overall, the current state of research indicated that actuarially based instruments are today the best available instruments for the prediction of recidivism risk in sexual offenders (Grove & Meehl, 1996; Hanson & Morton-Bourgon, 2009). Furthermore, the use of these instruments has to be regarded as a necessary precondition for the implementation and application of effective treatment programmes for sexual offenders (Andrews & Bonta, 2006; Bonta & Andrews, 2007; Hanson et al., 2009). In the following sections, we introduce briefly the internationally most commonly used second- and third-generation actuarial risk assessment instruments for sexual offenders. Because of the currently already overwhelming and continually increasing state of empirical knowledge about actuarial risk assessment instruments, it is certainly not possible here to give a complete review of all existing validation studies of every instrument. Rather, the aim of the following overview is to give an insight into the most important instruments and their scientific and empirical foundation.

Second-Generation Actuarial Risk Assessment Instruments

Validation studies for second-generation ARAIs have consistently demonstrated predictive accuracy across samples and countries, including Australia (Allan, Dawson, & Allan, 2006), Austria (Rettenberger, Matthes, Boer, & Eher, 2010), Belgium (Ducro & Pham, 2006), Brazil (Baltieri & de Andrade, 2008), Canada (Kingston, Yates, Firestone, Babchishin, & Bradford, 2008), Denmark (Bengtson, 2008), Germany (Stadtland et al., 2005), New Zealand (Skelton, Riley, Wales, & Vess, 2006), and the United Kingdom (Craig, Beech, & Browne, 2006). In North America and the United Kingdom, ARAIs have permeated the entire criminal justice system when assessing potential future risk of sexual recidivism in either civil commitment or parole board assessments (Craig & Beech, 2010). Below, we offer a brief summary of the most commonly used ARAIs.

Rapid Risk Assessment for Sexual Offense Recidivism (RRASOR)

The Rapid Risk Assessment for Sexual Offense Recidivism (RRASOR) (Hanson, 1997) was developed for the prediction of sexual recidivism of convicted sexual offenders and consists of four items (Hanson, 1997): prior sex offences, age when exposed to risk, victim gender, and relationship to victim. In a meta-analytic review, Hanson and Bussière (1996) found that indicators of deviant sexual interests (e.g., the number of prior sex offences) consistently predicted sexual recidivism. Drawing from these results, Hanson (1997) selected variables with a minimum correlation of 0.10 with sexual recidivism and developed the RRASOR as a brief actuarial measure of sexual deviance related directly to recidivism risk in sexual offenders. The first focus of the examination of the psychometric properties of a risk assessment instrument is usually the reliability of the measure, which, in psychological measurement theory, is usually defined as the extent to which the observed scores can be directly linked to the construct of interest rather than to measurement error (Anderson & Hanson, 2010).

There are several different indicators of the reliability of a psychological assessment tool (e.g., the internal consistency or the test–retest reliability), but in the area of risk assessment instruments, the interrater reliability or rater agreement is the most popular method. As one might expect, the interrater reliability for second-generation ARAIs such as the RRASOR is usually excellent, given the static and relatively easy to score nature of the items. Consequently, an empirical investigation of the interrater reliability indicated a high intraclass correlation (ICC = 0.90, single measure) (Rettenberger et al., 2010). Across six development samples and one validation sample, comprising a total of $n = 2592$ sexual offenders, Hanson (1997) found that the RRASOR had an average correlation of $r = 0.27$ and an average AUC of 0.71 with sexual recidivism. The predictive accuracy of the RRASOR in the independent validation sample ($n = 303$) was $r = 0.25$ and AUC = 0.67. In an independent Canadian validation study by Barbaree, Seto, Langton, and Peacock (2001) with a mixed sample of $n = 215$ child molesters and rapists assessed for a prison-based treatment programme, the RRASOR exhibited good concurrent and predictive accuracy (AUC = 0.77) concerning sexual recidivism, moderate predictive accuracy (AUC = 0.65) for serious recidivism, and low but still significant predictive accuracy (AUC = 0.60) for any recidivism. The authors evaluated the predictive accuracy of six different risk assessment tools and the RRASOR achieved the highest AUC value of all included instruments for the prediction of sexual recidivism (Barbaree et al., 2001).

In a large cross-validation sample of $n = 1400$ sexual offenders followed for an average of 3.7 years in Sweden, Sjöstedt and Långstrom (2001) found that the RRA-SOR had a correlation of $r = 0.22$ and AUC = 0.72 with sexual recidivism. In the first cross-validation study from Austria (Rettenberger & Eher, 2006), the instrument showed moderate predictive accuracy for an average follow-up time of 7.7 years for general (AUC = 0.66), sexual (AUC = 0.68), and violent (AUC = 0.67) recidivism using a sample of adult male sexual offenders ($n = 81$). In a second cross-validation study with five different risk assessment instruments using another independent sample from the Austrian prison system (Rettenberger et al., 2010), the RRASOR again yielded good concurrent and predictive validity using a larger sample size ($n = 394$) and a prospective-longitudinal research design: for the prediction of sexual offenders, the predictive validity for the total sample was AUC = 0.74, and for the prediction of violent and general criminal recidivism, AUC = 0.66. However, conducting further subsample analyses separately for rapists, extra-familial child molesters and incest offenders, the RRASOR – and also the other included instruments – failed to demonstrate predictive validity for sexual recidivism because there were too few reoffences in these categories (Rettenberger et al., 2010; for a recently published general discussion about the low base rates for sexual offender recidivism, see, for example, Rettenberger, Briken, Turner, & Eher, 2015).

Static-99: The International Gold Standard of Actuarial Risk Assessment

The Static-99, developed by R. Karl Hanson and David Thornton (Hanson & Thornton, 2000), is today the actuarial risk assessment instrument most commonly used and best validated for sexual offenders (e.g., Anderson & Hanson, 2010; Archer, Buffington-Vollum, Stredny, & Handel, 2006; Hanson & Morton-Bourgon, 2009;

Helmus, Hanson, & Morton-Bourgon, 2011). The instrument was derived from a fusion of two previously developed risk assessment instruments, the above-mentioned RRASOR and a brief version of the Structured Anchored Clinical Judgment (SACJ-Min) (Grubin, 1998), and consists of 10 predominantly static risk factors that can organized into four broad categories associated with increased likelihood of committing further sexual offences: sexual deviance measured by whether the offender has offended against males, ever been married, and has committed a non-contact sexual offence; range of potential victim measured by whether the offender offended against an unrelated or stranger victim; persistent sexual offending measured by the number of previous sexual convictions; and antisociality as measured by current or previous non-sexual violence or four or more previous criminal convictions, and under 25 years of age (for further information, see Harris, Phenix, Hanson, & Thornton, 2003). The individual risk factors for a sexual offender add up to a maximum total score of 12, assigning the offender to one of the four risk categories and also to relative and absolute risk estimates (Eher, Schilling, Haubner-MacLean, Jahn, & Rettenberger, 2012; Helmus, Hanson, Thornton, Babchishin, & Harris, 2012; Phenix, Helmus, & Hanson, 2012; for further information, see also http://www.static99.org).

A number of different studies have investigated the interrater reliability of the Static-99 and usually obtained excellent results (Anderson & Hanson, 2010). For example, Barbaree et al. (2001), Harris et al. (2003), Looman (2006), and Rettenberger et al. (2010) all reported reliability indices of ICC ≥ 0.87. Furthermore, the reliability was also tested and confirmed by using scores of practitioners and clinicians: Hanson, Harris, Scott, and Helmus (2007) reported excellent rater agreement values for trained probation officers in their influential prospective-longitudinal Dynamic Supervision Project (DSP) (ICC = 0.91). In a further Static-99 field trial, Storey, Watt, Jackson, and Hart (2012) compared the Static-99 ratings of clinicians with those of researchers in a sample of $n = 100$ adult males who completed an outpatient sex offender treatment programme. The results showed good agreement between the ratings of clinicians and researchers for total scores on the Static-99 (ICC = 0.92), and also for most individual items (median ICC = 0.77). The lowest agreement was for Item 3, 'index nonsexual violence' (ICC = 0.56), and the highest agreement was for item 5, 'prior sex offences' (ICC = 0.89). In general, the ratings made by clinicians tended to be slightly lower than those made by researchers (Storey et al., 2012).

In the developmental study, Hanson and Thornton (2000) investigated the predictive accuracy of the Static-99 using four different datasets of $n = 1301$ sexual offenders in Canada and the United Kingdom. Datasets included child molesters and rapists from prison and high-security forensic psychiatric settings. The Static-99 showed moderate to good predictive accuracy for sexual recidivism (AUC = 0.71) and for any violent (including sexual) recidivism (AUC = 0.69). In the following years, a large number of further cross-validation studies were published (for overviews see, for example, Anderson & Hanson, 2010; Hanson & Morton-Bourgon, 2009), including studies with Canadian (Barbaree et al., 2001), Dutch (de Vogel, de Ruiter, van Beek, & Mead, 2004), Belgian (Ducro & Pham, 2006), Austrian (Rettenberger et al., 2010), Swedish (Sjöstedt & Långstrom, 2001), and UK (Craig et al., 2006; Craig, Browne, & Stringer, 2004; Craig, Thornton, Beech & Browne, 2007) sexual offender samples. For sexual recidivism, the predictive accuracy values ranged in these studies from moderate (AUC = 0.66) (Ducro & Pham, 2006) to good validity indices (up to AUC = 0.91) (Thornton & Beech, 2002). Furthermore, more recent research findings indicated that the Static-99 is a useful tool for the prediction of long-term recidivism in sexual offenders (Swinburne Romine, Miner, Poulin, Dwyer, & Berg, 2012) and in a sample of Catholic clergy sexual offenders (Montana et al., 2012), and provided promising first results when applied to child molesters who had worked with children (Turner, Rettenberger, Lohmann, Eher, & Briken, 2014).

Another frequently discussed concern about the validity of the Static-99 relates to the stability or variability of the recidivism rates which are linked to every total score (Anderson & Hanson, 2010; Eher, Rettenberger, Schilling, & Pfäfflin, 2008). Considering the fact that most data included in previous studies that have reported recidivism rates for the Static-99 are based on data sources that have their origins in the 1960s–1980s (e.g., Hanson & Thornton, 2000; Harris, Phenix et al., 2003), it seems to be a relevant question for forensic practice and research whether recidivism rates have changed in the last few decades. Given the broad cultural changes during the past 40 years, Helmus, Hanson, and Thornton (2009) concluded that 'it is important to consider whether the recidivism rates of sexual offenders have remained the same during that time' (p. 38). The authors further reported that crime rates peaked in the early 1990s and have in general been declining since then. The phenomenon of declining base rates has been documented for property, violent, and sexual offences using both official crime data (e.g., Public Safety Canada, 2007) and victimization surveys (e.g., Finkelhor & Jones, 2006).

The reasons for this phenomenon are still not fully understood, but Helmus et al. (2009) provided a few possible explanations: first, demographic factors (e.g., ageing population, increased obesity, reliance on medications such as Prozac or other serotonin-affecting agents); second, cultural factors (e.g., changing morals regarding sexuality, increased awareness about sexual assault leading to greater vigilance and supervision of children); and, third, criminal justice system factors (e.g., offender treatment, increased supervision, deterrent and incapacitating effects of longer sentences) (for further information see Finkelhor & Jones, 2006). They concluded that there are at least two research implications: on the one hand, criminologists and forensic scientists would like to know more about the causes of changing crime rates, and on the other hand, one may know how these changes affect best practices in offender assessment, management, and supervision because – even without understanding the reasons for the change – the evidence of change may force evaluators to adjust their practice. Recent empirical evidence has provided further support that substantial changes in sexual offender recidivism base rates have occurred, which must inevitably lead to the development of up-to-date norm tables (Rettenberger et al., 2015).

Actuarial risk assessment instruments provide several types of information that could be of value to decision-makers (Hanson, Babchishin, Helmus, & Thornton, 2013). The most prominent and traditional measure of risk is a recidivism rate estimate linked to every single total score of an instrument. On the other hand, relative risk measures provide information about a particular offender's risk relative to other offenders (i.e., to the population to which he/she belongs) and can be quantified by, for example, so-called relative risk ratios or percentile ranks (Hanson, Lloyd, Helmus, & Thornton, 2012). Given the above-mentioned changes in recidivism-related norms and rates, comprehensive empirical investigations on the stability of the relative and absolute risk estimates derived from the Static-99 have recently been conducted and published: whereas a recently published meta-analytical review suggested that absolute recidivism rates predicted by the Static-99 varied substantially across samples (Helmus et al., 2012), the relative risk estimates are relatively stable over time and for different settings and jurisdictions (Hanson et al., 2013).

The Impact of Age and the Development of the Age-Revised Static-99R

One of the most important features of the actuarial paradigm of risk assessment is the sole reliance on empirically derived relations between data and the event of interest. Therefore, it is necessary to investigate regularly whether revisions of the instrument or specific risk factors are needed. A very intense discussion about the imperative of a revision of the Static-99 and other second-generation ARAIs referred to the question of the risk-related influence of age on the recidivism risk estimates of sexual offenders (Helmus, Thornton, Hanson, & Babchishin, 2012; Prentky, Janus, Barbaree, Schwartz, & Kafka, 2006; Rettenberger, Haubner-MacLean, & Eher, 2013; Rettenberger et al., 2015; Wollert, 2006). Although there is usually a broad consensus regarding the inclusion of age items in actuarial risk scales, the questions still remain of which age variable should be used (e.g., age at first offence, age at index offence, or age at release from custody), and what weighting method would perform best in the prediction of recidivism (for a review of the effect of age on sexual recidivism see, for example, Craig, 2008; Rice & Harris, 2014).

The general relationship between age and criminal behaviour is one of the most robust findings in the field of forensic psychology and criminology (e.g., Barbaree, Langton, Blanchard, & Cantor, 2009; Hirschi & Gottfredson, 1983; Sampson & Laub, 2003; Wollert, 2006). The so-called 'age effect' describes the age-related reduction in crime rates or in simple terms: the older the offender, the lower the probability of criminal behaviour. Hirschi and Gottfredson (1983) pointed out that the age effect can be observed in different centuries, different countries, and different offender populations. The age effect has also been described for sexual offenders. A large body of evidence indicates that the risk of recidivism in sexual offenders decreases as their age increases (Barbaree & Blanchard, 2008; Hanson, 2002, 2006; Prentky & Lee, 2007; Rettenberger et al., 2015; Thornton, 2006). Some researchers have proposed an alternative expression of the relationship between age and recidivism and have postulated that the age of onset of criminal behaviour is an indicator of the general level of antisociality that is much more important than the actual or current age of an offender (Doren, 2006; Harris & Rice, 2003, 2007). To conclude, the most important information for risk assessment would be the age of onset of antisocial behaviour rather than the age of the offender at some other distinct point in time (Rice & Harris, 2014).[3]

---

[3]The fact that Thornton (2006), Craig (2011), and Rettenberger et al. (2015) reported a non-linear relationship between age and sexual recidivism risk seems to support a more comprehensive model (than simple linear assumptions) for the age-related change process in the recidivism risk of sexual offenders. Both Thornton (2006) and Rettenberger et al. (2015) used representative prison-released samples and

Assessing Risk of Sexual Recidivism

In order to consider the age-related influence on the Static-99-based risk assessment appropriately, Helmus, Thornton et al. (2012), however, argued that the 'age at release' variable in the Static-99 should be weighted more heavily, which led to the development of a revised version of the Static-99, the Static-99R. They examined the relationship between Static-99 scores, age, and reoffence rates. Using a large dataset with approximately $n = 8400$ sexual offenders from 24 different samples, the offender's age at release was found to add incremental predictive validity above the Static-99 score. Therefore, they presented a revised version of the instrument with new age weights, called the Static-99R. In the original Static-99 version, offenders aged between 18 and 24 years at the time of release from prison received one additional point on their total score, whereas offenders aged 25 years and older received no additional points on their total score (Harris, Phenix et al., 2003). In the new Static-99R version, offenders younger than 35 years of age receive one additional point and offenders aged between 35 and 39 years receive zero additional point. One point is subtracted from the Static-99R total scores of offenders between the ages of 40 and 59 years, and three points are subtracted from the total scores of offenders aged 60 years and older. Using a validation sample of approximately $n = 2400$ subjects, the Static-99R showed a slight but non-significant improvement in predictive validity compared with the Static-99 for sexual and violent recidivism (Helmus, Thornton et al., 2012); e.g., for 5-year sexual recidivism the predictive accuracy of the Static-99R was AUC $= 0.72$, compared with AUC $= 0.71$ for the Static-99).

In an independent cross-validation study of this newly developed revised version, Rettenberger et al. (2013) examined the influence of several age-related variables on the predictive accuracy of the German version of the Static-99. Furthermore, the predictive accuracy of the original Static-99 and the new Static-99R were compared using a population-based sample of prison-released sexual offenders ($n = 1077$). The results indicated that the original Static-99 (AUC $= 0.73$) performed better than the age-corrected Static-99R (AUC $= 0.71$) for sexual recidivism using the total sample. Whereas Helmus, Thornton et al. (2012) recommended switching to the revised age weights when using the Static-99 in applied risk assessment settings, Rettenberger et al. (2013) concluded that their results indicated that – at least for the German version – the original Static-99 yields better predictive accuracy than the age-corrected Static-99R for the prediction of sexual recidivism and, therefore, supported the use of the original version of the instrument.

Another way to deal with the aspect of age-related variations in recidivism risk of sexual offenders suggested by Wollert, Cramer, Waggoner, Skelton, and Vess (2010), was by calculating 'age-stratified' actuarial tables. Using a large sample of $n = 9305$ sexual offenders, they developed age-stratified tables of sexual recidivism rates for the Static-99 and called their approach the Multi-Sample Age-Stratified Table of Sexual Recidivism Rates (MATS-1). The MATS-1 purports to compensate the so-called 'age invariance effect' (i.e., the above-mentioned age effect) and indicated that age-restricted tables underestimate risk for younger offenders and overestimate risk for older offenders. Therefore, the authors concluded that risk assessors should use the

reported a significant cubic trend (i.e., the graph describing the relationship between age and recidivism changed slope twice) rather than simplistic linear relationships.

MATS-1 when reporting recidivism rates for sexual offenders, particularly when evaluating relatively old sexual offenders (Wollert et al., 2010). However, Helmus and Thornton (2014) recently raised concerns about the development of the MATS-1 and conducted a cross-validation of the tool using a combined sexual offender sample of $n = 3510$. They differentiated their concerns regarding the MATS-1 into three categories: first, the approximations lead to a loss of precision; second, the absence of an appropriate statistical test; and third, the use of inappropriate statistical techniques. Furthermore, the predictive validity of the MATS-1 (AUC = 0.66) was significantly lower than the corresponding validity index of the Static-99R (AUC = 0.71). Because the MATS-1 also significantly underestimated recidivism for some offenders, and both relative and absolute risk estimates of the MATS-1 showed a substantial variability across the individual samples included in their study, the authors concluded that the MATS-1 is not an appropriate tool for applied risk assessment settings (Helmus & Thornton, 2014).

Further Members of the Static Family: The Static-2002 and the Static-2002R

The Static-2002 was developed shortly after the Static-99, in order to increase the conceptual clarity and coherence of the Static-99 and to improve the scoring criteria and the predictive accuracy (Hanson & Thornton, 2003). The Static-2002 also assesses the sexual and violent recidivism risk of adult male sexual offenders. Even though it was developed as a separate instrument from the Static-99 (Cortoni et al., 2010), the Static-2002 shares some items with its predecessor. The Static-2002 consisted of 14 items grouped into five domains: age (one item examining the age at the time of release), persistence of sexual offending (prior sentencing occasions for sexual offences, any juvenile arrest for a sexual offence and convicted as an adult, and rate of sexual offending), deviant sexual interests (any sentencing occasion for non-contact sex offences, any male victim, and young and unrelated victims), relationship to victims (any unrelated victim and any stranger victim), and general criminality (any prior involvement with the criminal justice system, prior sentencing occasions for anything, any community supervision violation, years free prior to index sexual offence, and any prior non-sexual violence sentencing occasion). Hanson and Thornton (2003) used multiple datasets (10 independent samples with a total size of $n = 4596$ offenders) in order to develop the Static-2002. To design the subscales, content areas were identified and the univariate relationships between sexual recidivism and different potential predictor variables were calculated. After extracting the risk factors for each dimension, the incremental contribution of the subscales was examined. In the first validation study, the Static-2002 yielded good predictive accuracy for sexual recidivism (AUC = 0.71, $n = 2142$) and for violent recidivism (AUC = 0.71, $n = 2143$). Although the Static-2002 showed significantly better results for violent recidivism than the Static-99, no significant differences for sexual recidivism could be examined (Hanson & Thornton, 2003).

One of the first cross-validation studies was published by Langton et al. (2007), who reported that the Static-2002 ($n = 476$) showed medium effect sizes for the prediction of general criminal, sexual, and violent recidivism that were substantially higher than for the Static-99 (AUC = 0.69 versus 0.65, AUC = 0.71 versus 0.64, AUC = 0.70

versus 0.64, respectively). A study in Denmark (Bengtson, 2008) analysed the predictive accuracy of the Static-2002 ($n = 445$) and reported similar results, insofar that the Static-2002 showed moderate results for the prediction of sexual and violent recidivism (AUC = 0.67 and 0.69, respectively). Although the Static-2002 showed generally higher AUC values than the Static-99 (AUC = 0.64 and 0.67), these differences again did not reach statistical significance. In a Canadian study, Helmus and Hanson (2007) reported after a mean follow-up period of 3 years ($n = 702$) that the Static-99 and Static-2002 were equally accurate in predicting sexual recidivism (AUC = 0.76 for both instruments). Similar results were recently published by Martens, Rettenberger, and Eher (2015) using an Austrian sample of sexual offenders ($n = 452$): The Static-2002 yielded slightly better results (AUC > 0.74) than the Static-99 (AUC > 0.71) for different recidivism criteria. However, the Static-2002 showed higher predictive accuracy than the Static-99 for the prediction of violent and general criminal recidivism. Three years later, Hanson, Helmus, and Thornton (2010) published a multisite study using the Static-2002 with eight different sexual offenders samples (five Canadian, one US, one UK, and one Danish; $n = 3034$). The Static-2002 showed moderate to good predictive power for sexual, violent, and general criminal recidivism (AUC = 0.68, 0.71, and 0.70, respectively), and was more accurate than the Static-99. Therefore, the authors concluded that their findings support the use of Static-2002 in applied risk assessment settings (Hanson et al., 2010). The above-mentioned discussion about the relationship between age and recidivism risk assessment by second-generation ARAIs also led subsequently to a revised version of the Static-2002 with modified age weights, called Static-2002R (Helmus, Thornton et al., 2012).

Studies of the incremental validity of different sexual offender risk assessment instruments have generally only rarely been conducted and published (Singer, Boer, & Rettenberger, 2013; for an often-cited exception see, for example, Seto, 2005). Babchishin, Hanson, and Helmus (2012) analysed whether the RRASOR, the Static-99R, and the Static-2002R added incremental predictive validity to each other using multiple samples from different jurisdictions ($n = 7491$) for different recidivism criteria. The results showed that the Static-99R and the Static-2002R outperformed the RRASOR in predicting general criminal, violent, and sexual recidivism, and no significant differences were found between the Static-99R and the Static-2002R. However, the authors showed that even highly correlated risk measures such as the Static-99R and the Static-2002R showed incremental validity to one another (Babchishin et al., 2012).

The Risk Matrix 2000 – Sex and Violence Versions

The Risk Matrix 2000 – Sex/Violence (Thornton et al., 2003) is today probably the most frequently used second-generation ARAI in the United Kingdom (Cortoni, Craig, & Beech, 2010; Craig et al., 2008) and is also based on the Structured Anchored Clinical Judgment Scale (SACJ) (Grubin, 1998; see also the development of the Static-99 as described in Hanson & Thornton, 2000) and on the meta-analytic findings of Hanson and Bussière (1998). The instrument consists of two separate scales, one for measuring the risk of sexual recidivism, the Risk Matrix 2000/Sex (RM2000/S), and the other measuring the risk of non-sexual violent recidivism, the

Risk Matrix 2000/Violence (RM2000/V). Both subscales were specifically developed for use with sexual offenders, i.e. the RM2000/V also has to be regarded as a second-generation ARAI for sexual offenders. Additionally, both scale scores can be combined to assess the composite risk for sexual and non-sexual violent reoffence, which is called the Risk Matrix 2000/Combined (RM2000/C). The individual risk level, which is indicated by four separate risk categories (low, medium, high, and very high), is determined by a two-stage risk assessment process in which the first stage involves three items (age, previous sexual and previous general criminal offences) and the second consists of four items (male victim, stranger victim, non-contact sexual offences, and no long-term relationship).

In the developmental study, Thornton et al. (2003) examined the predictive accuracy of the RM2000/S on a treated ($n = 647$) and an untreated ($n = 429$) sexual offender sample and obtained good AUC values (AUC = 0.77 for the treated and 0.75 for the untreated sample, respectively), and the RM2000/V gave even higher validity indices (AUC > 0.78) for the prediction of non-sexual violent recidivism in different long-term samples. Conducting a series of cross-validation studies with different UK samples Craig and colleagues reported varying results for the predictive accuracy of the RM2000 scales (Craig et al., 2004, 2006). On the one hand, the tools yielded impressive validity indices up to AUC = 0.86 for the prediction of violent including sexual recidivism by the RM2000/V (Craig et al., 2006). On the other hand, in other analyses the predictive accuracy was hardly better than chance (e.g., as indicated by AUC = 0.56 for the prediction of sexual recidivism by the RM2000/S as described in Craig et al., 2004).

In a recently published meta-analysis, Helmus, Babchishin, and Hanson (2013) integrated the findings for 16 unique samples (derived from 14 studies) that had examined the extent to which the RM2000 scales are able to discriminate between recidivists and non-recidivists. The major results of the study were that all three RM2000 scales (RM2000/S, RM2000/V, and RM2000/C) provided significant predictive power for all recidivism types that were investigated in this meta-analysis (i.e., sexual, non-sexual violent, any violent, non-violent, and any recidivism). The RM2000/S yielded the best predictive accuracy for sexual recidivism (Cohen's $d = 0.74$[4]). The RM2000/V and the RM2000/C predicted non-sexual violent recidivism and any violent recidivism with similarly large effect sizes. An interesting finding was that the effect sizes were significantly higher in investigations using samples from the United Kingdom compared with studies with samples from other countries. Furthermore, the predictive accuracy was fairly low in sexual offender samples preselected as high risk or high need. Overall, the authors concluded that these results support the use of the Risk Matrix in applied risk assessment settings (Helmus, Babchishin, & Hanson, 2013).

The Sex Offender Risk Appraisal Guide (SORAG)

The Sex Offender Risk Appraisal Guide (SORAG) (Quinsey et al., 2006) is another second-generation actuarial risk assessment tool for sexual offenders, which was developed by the Canadian research group headed by Vernon L. Quinsey, Marnie E. Rice,

---

[4]Cohen (1988) suggested for interpretation purposes the following guidelines: a value of $d = 0.20$ can be regarded as a small, $d = 0.50$ as a moderate, and $d = 0.80$ as a large effect.

and Grant T. Harris. Together with the Static-99, the SORAG can be regarded as the internationally most frequently used and best validated instrument (for an overview see, for example, Rice, Harris, & Hilton, 2010). It is a modification of the Violence Risk Appraisal Guide (VRAG) (Quinsey et al., 2006), which was developed to predict violent (including sexual hands-on) recidivism among adult male offenders. Therefore, 10 of the 14 items of the SORAG are the same as in the VRAG. The SORAG is conceptualized for sexual offenders to assess violent recidivism risk, which includes sexual offences involving physical contact with the victim. The instrument consists of the following 14 weighted items: lived with biological parents up to age 16 years, elementary school maladjustment, history of alcohol problems, marital status, criminal history of non-violent offences, criminal history of violent offences, previous convictions for sexual offences, sexual offences against girls under the age of 14 only, failure on prior conditional releases, age at index offence, *Diagnostic and Statistical Manual of Mental Disorders*, 3rd edition (DSM-III) (American Psychiatric Association, 1980) criteria for any personality disorder, DSM-III criteria for schizophrenia, phallometric test results indicating paedophilia or sexual sadism, and PCL-R score. Based on the total score, the risk assessor can allocate the offender to one of nine risk categories. By means of these risk categories, it is possible to infer empirically calculated probabilities of violent (including sexual) recidivism after 7 and 10 years at risk. Furthermore, evaluators can use relative risk ratios in terms of percentile ranks (Quinsey et al., 2006).

Although the majority of the validation studies were completed in Anglo-American countries, there have also been cross-validation studies in several European countries (e.g., Belgium, Austria, Switzerland, and Sweden; for details see, for example, Harris, Rice, & Quinsey, 2010; Rice et al., 2010). Harris et al. (2003) concluded that at that time, the existing research in several North American studies (e.g., Barbaree et al., 2001; Nunes, Firestone, Bradford, Greenberg, & Broom, 2002; Rice & Harris, 1995) showed the SORAG to have high accuracy in the prediction of violent (including sexual) recidivism and moderate accuracy in predicting sexual offences. For the prediction of violent (including sexual) recidivism, they calculated a median AUC value of 0.75. With regard to European samples, Ducro and Pham (2006), for example, evaluated the predictive accuracy of the SORAG on Belgian sexual offenders committed to a forensic facility. For the total sample ($n = 147$), the instrument showed strong predictive validity for general (AUC = 0.70) and violent (AUC = 0.72) recidivism and moderate predictive validity for sexual recidivism (AUC = 0.64). Rettenberger and Eher (2007) also found good predictive validity values of a German version of the SORAG for general (AUC = 0.73), violent (AUC = 0.76), and sexual (AUC = 0.73) recidivism. More recent overviews of the reliability and validity of the SORAG reported more than 50 empirical investigations (Harris et al., 2010; Rice et al., 2010) and the meta-analysis published by Hanson and Morton-Bourgon (2009) indicated that the SORAG was one of the instruments with the strongest predictive power.

Despite the large number of empirical studies that provide strong scientific support for the clinical use of the SORAG, there still remain a few frequently discussed or unresolved research questions. For example, some authors have called the stability of the absolute and relative risk indices into question (Rossegger, Gerth, Singh, & Endrass, 2013), whereas other papers picked the so-called allegiance effect out as the central theme of controversy about the usefulness of actuarial risk assessment instruments such as the VRAG and the SORAG (Blair, Marcus, & Boccaccini, 2008; Harris et al., 2010). Allegiance in this context describes an effect well known in psychological assessment research that studies conducted by researchers who have developed a particular test or instrument usually report substantially better results (i.e., higher predictive validity indices) than are reported in independent cross-validation studies. However, the underlying reasons for these results – that is, for example, whether actually allegiance or rather fidelity to the predefined and validated procedures is responsible for this effect – remain unknown (Harris et al., 2010). Furthermore, the allegiance effect clearly refers to all kinds of diagnostic and prognostic instruments and is certainly not an aspect specifically relevant for the SORAG or ARAIs in general.

Another often-discussed research topic is the question of the differential validity of ARAIs in general and the SORAG in particular. Bartosh, Garby, Lewis, and Gray (2003), for example, showed that the SORAG significantly predicted sexual, violent, and overall recidivism for extra-familial child molesters (AUC values ranged from 0.70 to 0.93) and for incest offenders (AUCs ranged from 0.72 to 0.91). However, the SORAG showed much less predictive power (AUCs ranged from 0.46 to 0.71) for rapists and hands-off offenders. In the Belgian validation study of the SORAG, the AUC values ranged from 0.64 (sexual recidivism in the rapist subgroup) to 0.77 (violent recidivism in the rapist subgroup), demonstrating strong variations depending on offender subgroup and recidivism criterion (Ducro & Pham, 2006). In the Austrian cross-validation study, the ability to predict recidivism also varied strongly depending on offender type and reoffence category. AUC values ranged from 0.56 (violent non-sexual recidivism in the rapist subgroup) to 0.95 (any recidivism in the incest offender subgroup; Rettenberger & Eher, 2007). These results provide, on the one hand, evidence of good predictive validity of the SORAG and, on the other hand, emphasize the importance of looking at the different performances of risk prediction tools depending on sexual offender subgroups and recidivism criteria (Rettenberger et al., 2010).

The Minnesota Sex Offender Screening Tool (MnSOST) and Its Revision (MnSOST-R)

The Minnesota Sex Offender Screening Tool (MnSOST) and its revised version, the Minnesota Sex Offender Screening Tool – Revised (MnSOST-R) (Epperson, Kaul, & Hesselton, 1998; Epperson et al., 2000), were developed by the Minnesota Department of Corrections for the recidivism risk assessment of male adult sexual offenders. The MnSOST consists of the following 16 items (Craig et al., 2008): number of sexual convictions, length of sexual offending history, sexual offending while under supervision, sexual offence committed in a public place, use of threat or force, multiple acts on a single victim, different age groups of victims, offences against a 13- to 15-year-old and being at least 5 years older than the victim, stranger victims, antisocial behaviour during adolescence, substance abuse, employment history, institutional misconduct (one item refers to behavioural misconduct, another to the use of illicit substances while incarcerated), participation in sexual offender treatment programmes during incarceration, and age at the time of release. A later revised version of the MnSOST consists of 17 items and showed good predictive accuracy (AUC = 0.77) for the prediction of sexual recidivism using 6-year follow-up data ($n = 274$) (Craig et al., 2008).

However, Barbaree et al. (2001) reported a clearly lower predictive validity (AUC = 0.65) using an independent Canadian sample. Further empirical studies using the MnSOST and the revised version, the MnSOST-R, yielded mixed results, ranging from poor predictive performance (Bartosh et al., 2003) up to moderate to good predictive accuracy (Craig et al., 2008; Epperson et al., 2000; Langton, Barbaree, Harkins, Seto, & Peacock, 2002). Integrating the status of research at that time, Hanson and Morton-Bourgon (2009) reported in their meta-analysis that the MnSOST was one of the best instruments for the prediction of sexual recidivism. However, the MnSOST and the MnSOST-R have so far been predominantly used in North American jurisdictions, especially in the United States, so the international relevance of the instrument is still limited.

Third-Generation Actuarial Risk Assessment Instruments

Stable and Acute Dynamic Risk Factors: The Stable-2007 and Acute-2007

Dynamic risk factors – sometimes also called criminogenic needs or psychologically meaningful risk factors (Mann et al., 2010) – are the core construct of third-generation instruments (Harris & Hanson, 2010). The central difference between static risk factors captured in the second-generation ARAIs and these third-generation dynamic risk factors is that they are amenable to changes based on interventions that can lead to risk-related changes in the individual offender. Therefore, dynamic risk factors play a major role in treatment planning and in the monitoring of treatment process and success, and have to be regarded today as a cornerstone of effective treatment programme implementation (Hanson et al., 2009).

One of the first and so far still one of the most influential research projects on dynamic risk factors in sexual offenders was the Dynamic Predictors Project (DPP) headed by Karl Hanson and Andrew Harris (e.g., Hanson & Harris, 2000; Harris & Hanson, 2010). In the DPP, Hanson and Harris (2000) investigated the differences between two approximately equally large samples of sexual offenders known to have reoffended sexually while under community supervision ($n = 208$) and of sexual offenders who had not reoffended ($n = 201$). With a focus specifically on the risk factors that could have changed in the periods preceding the reoffence, Hanson and Harris (2000) identified two separate types of dynamic risk factors: on the one hand, relatively stable enduring traits (e.g., attitudes, cognitive distortions, self-regulation deficits) and, on the other hand, temporally rapidly changeable acute risk factors located rather in the environment and situational context. Finally, the DPP research led to the development of the Sex Offender Risk Assessment Rating (SONAR) (Hanson & Harris, 2001), which consisted of five stable dynamic risk factors (intimacy deficits, social influences, attitudes, general and sexual self-regulation) and four acute dynamic risk factors (substance abuse, negative mood, anger/hostility, and opportunities for victim access).

Because of important conceptual and clinical concerns about the SONAR, Hanson and colleagues started to develop the Acute-2000 and Stable-2000 as two separate measures of dynamic risk factors (Harris & Hanson, 2000). Primarily influenced by

Beech's (1998) work on the measurement of psychological deviance, by Thornton's (2002) Initial Deviancy Assessment derived from his Structured Risk Assessment, the concept of Dynamic Antisociality by Quinsey, Coleman, Jones, and Altrows (1997), Cortoni's and Marshall's (2001) concept of sexualized coping, and Wilson's (1999) clinical observation of child molesters' emotional identification with children, the number of items in the new tools was higher and the items themselves were more theoretically and conceptually established. Furthermore, a manual was developed that provided clear operationalizations and definitions of all important constructs and rating details. The Stable-2000 consisted of 16 items divided into six subsections: significant social influences (one item), intimacy deficits (five items: lovers/intimate partners, emotional identification with children, hostility towards women, general social rejection/loneliness, and lack of concern for others), sexual self-regulation (three items: sex drive/preoccupation, sex as coping, and deviant sexual interests), general self-regulation (three items: impulsive acts, poor cognitive problem solving, and negative emotionality/hostility), cooperation with supervision (one item), and attitudes supportive of sexual offending (three items: sexual entitlement, rape attitudes, and child molester attitudes). The Acute-2000 contains of the following eight items: victim access, hostility, sexual preoccupation, rejection of supervision, emotional collapse, collapse of social support, substance abuse, and a unique risk factor relevant in the individual case.

Around 1999, Hanson and colleagues initiated the Dynamic Supervision Project (DSP), a prospective-longitudinal field trial of the reliability, validity, and clinical utility of the Acute-2000 and Stable-2000 (Hanson et al., 2007). For the DSP, parole and probation officers from every Canadian province and from the US states of Alaska and Iowa were trained in the application of the Static-99 (which should be used once at the beginning of the supervision process), the Stable-2000 (which should be assessed every 6 months), and the Acute-2000 (which should be used at every supervisory meeting). A total of 156 parole and probation officers completed these static, stable, and acute risk assessments on $n = 997$ sexual offenders across 16 jurisdictions. After an average follow-up of 3 years, the predictive accuracy of the Static-99 for the prediction of sexual recidivism was expectably high (AUC = 0.74). The same was true for the Acute-2000 (AUC = 0.74), whereas the AUC value of the Stable-2000 was considerably lower (AUC = 0.64). Further problems with the Stable-2000 were that, first, not all risk factors showed the hypothesized linear relationship with recidivism, and second, the instrument showed no incremental predictive accuracy above the Static-99. Therefore, the authors made a few minor rating and operationalization changes for some items (deviant sexual interests, lovers/intimate partners, and emotional identification with children) and dropped the three attitude items owing to a lack of prognostic relevance. This revised version of the instrument, called the Stable-2007, showed higher predictive accuracy (AUC = 0.67) and incremental predictive power for the prediction of sexual recidivism than that captured by the Static-99 alone (Hanson et al., 2007).

One major result for the Acute-2000 was that only a subset of the included risk factors was significantly related to all outcome measures used in the DSP (sexual, violent, and general criminal recidivism). This result led to a revision of the risk tool, called Acute-2007, and to the separation of two different factors: one consisting of acute risk factors relevant for the prediction of violent and sexual recidivism (victim access, hostility, sexual preoccupation, and rejection of supervision) and the other a general criminality factor that contains all seven of the above-mentioned specified risk factors. The option of an eighth unspecified unique risk factor was dropped in the revised Acute-2007 version because, first, this option was generally only rarely used, and second, if it was used it had no relationship with recidivism (Harris & Hanson, 2010). This result fits again with the above-mentioned research findings that additionally included clinical or professional individual risk factors and adjustments usually provide no incremental predictive validity (Hanson & Morton-Bourgon, 2009; Wormith et al., 2012). Another interesting and, especially for policy-makers in applied risk assessment settings, relevant finding was that the Static-99/Stable-2007 risk prediction system showed higher predictive accuracy (up to AUC = 0.84) when used by 'conscientious' officers who were defined by the fact that they had submitted complete data sets without missing data (Hanson et al., 2007).

So far, there have been only a few independent cross-validation studies of the Stable-2007, and for the Acute-2007 independent validation data are still lacking. Nunes and Babchishin (2012) conducted a construct validity study of the Stable-2000 and the Stable-2007 by examining correlations between selected items of the risk tools and validated independent measures of relevant constructs. They concluded that the results generally supported the construct validity of the stable risk measures but the degree of convergence was lower than expected (Nunes & Babchishin, 2012). Eher, Matthes, Schilling, Haubner-MacLean, and Rettenberger (2012) investigated the predictive and incremental validity of the Stable-2000 and the Stable-2007 in a prison-released sample of sexual offenders in Austria ($n = 263$) by using a prospective-longitudinal research design. After an average follow-up period of 6.4 years, the Stable-2007 was significantly related to all outcomes (AUC = $0.67–0.71$), whereas the Stable-2000 showed only weak predictive accuracy for the prediction of sexual recidivism (AUC = 0.62). Furthermore, the study provided additional evidence for the incremental validity of the Stable-2007 beyond the second-generation static risk factors (Eher, Matthes, et al., 2012). In a further cross-validation study in Austria, Eher et al. (2013) investigated the predictive accuracy of the Static-99 and the Stable-2007 in a sample ($n = 96$) of released male forensic patients hospitalized under mandatory treatment who committed sexually motivated offences. The Static-99 (AUC = 0.86) and the Stable-2007 (AUC = 0.71) were significantly related to sexual reoffending after an average follow-up period of approximately 7 years. Again, the Stable-2007 provided evidence for incremental predictive validity beyond the Static-99 alone (Eher, Matthes et al., 2013). In a recent German study, Briken and Müller (2014) examined the utility of risk assessment instruments such as the Stable-2007 for assessing the criminal responsibility and the necessity for placement in a forensic psychiatric hospital according to the German penal code. They concluded that specific items of the Stable-2007 (e.g., deviant sexual interests, sexual preoccupation, or relationship deficits) and of the Acute-2007 (e.g., sexual preoccupation, emotional collapse, or collapse of social support) could be used as empirically well-established proxy variables beyond and additionally to formal diagnosis according to the *International Classification of Diseases* (ICD) and the *Diagnostic and Statistical Manual of Mental Diseases* (DSM) criteria, in order to assess the severity of paraphilic disorders (Briken & Müller, 2014).

The Structured Assessment of Risk and Need Framework (SARN)

The Structured Assessment of Risk and Need Framework (SARN) (Thornton, 2002; Webster et al., 2006) is not an actuarial risk instrument in a strict methodological sense (Dawes et al., 1989; Meehl, 1954). However, owing to its rigorously empirical orientation it could be regarded as a conceptual actuarial risk tool (Hanson & Morton-Bourgon, 2007; Sawyer, 1966). Thornton (2002) proposed the Structured Risk Assessment (SRA) as a process for evaluating the risk presented by sexual offenders. The SRA consisted of four subsystems: the first is called Static Assessment and is based on unchangeable, static risk factors, the second is called the Initial Deviance Assessment and is based on potentially changeable but relatively stable risk factors, the third is called the Evaluation of Progress and is based on the offender's response to treatment, and the fourth is called the Risk Management and is based on offence-related, environmental, and other acute risk factors. Furthermore, Thornton (2002) postulated that the main dynamic risk factors fall into four domains: sexual interests, distorted attitudes, socioaffective functioning, and self-management. Within SRA, the term deviance is defined by the extent to which the offender's functioning is dominated by the psychological factors that contribute to his offending. High deviance is defined as an individual showing problems within at least three domains, moderate deviance means that dynamic risk factors are present in one or two domains, and low deviance is defined by the absence of any dynamic risk factor in these domains (Cortoni et al., 2010).

The Structured Assessment of Risk and Need Framework (SARN) was developed based on Thornton's SRA approach and consisted of 16 items allocated to one of the above-mentioned dynamic risk domains (Craig et al., 2008; Webster et al., 2006): the sexual interests domain contains four subdomains (sexual preoccupation, sexual preference for children, sexualized violence, and other offence-related sexual interests), the distorted attitudes domain has five items (adversarial sexual attitudes, child abuse-supportive beliefs, sexual entitlement, rape-supportive beliefs, and women are deceitful beliefs), the socioaffective functioning domain exhibited four specified risk factors (grievance thinking, inadequacy, lack of emotional intimacy, and distorted intimacy balance), and the self-management domain consisted of three items (lifestyle impulsiveness, poor problem solving, and poor emotional control). The SARN is regularly applied in the English and Welsh Prison System and in the National Offender Management System (NOMS) in the United Kingdom (Craig et al., 2008).

As for the other third-generation instruments, the number of empirical studies using the SARN and its derivatives is still relatively small (for a more detailed description of the development of SARN, its derivatives, and the current status of research, see, for example, Craig et al., 2007, 2008; see also Chapter 55). Webster et al. (2006) examined the interrater reliability of the SARN and concluded that their study provided support for the reliability of the instrument. Thornton (2002) tested the construct validity of three SARN domains (distorted attitudes, socioaffective functioning, and self-management) and showed that various measures of these domains are able to discriminate effectively between first-time offenders and repeat offenders. In subsequent studies, Thornton and Beech (2002) and Craig et al. (2007) provided evidence for the incremental validity of the SARN beyond second-generation ARAIs such as the

Static-99. Furthermore, Wakeling, Beech, and Freemantle (2013) reported data on the importance and utility of the SARN for repeated evaluation of the treatment process, indicating again that structured assessment methods have to be regarded as a precondition for the implementation of effective (i.e., sustainably risk-reducing) sexual offender treatment programmes (Hanson et al., 2009). Recently, Thornton and Knight (2015) developed the Structured Risk Assessment – Forensic Version (SRA-FV), which is based on the previous research on the SRA. They reported that the SRA-FV significantly predicted sexual recidivism for child molesters and rapists and had better incremental predictive accuracy than two widely used second-generation ARAIs, the Static-99R and the RM2000/S (Thornton & Knight, 2015).

The Violence Risk Scale – Sexual Offender Version (VRS-SO)

The Violence Risk Scale – Sexual Offender Version (VRS-SO) (Olver, Wong, Nicholaichuk, & Gordon, 2007; Wong et al., 2003) is a conceptual actuarial third-generation risk assessment instrument (Hanson & Morton-Bourgon, 2007; Wong & Olver, 2010) and is based predominantly on the Violence Risk Scale (VRS) (Wong & Gordon, 2006), which was developed for the prediction of general (rather than only sexual) violence. The major theoretical and conceptual underpinnings of the VRS and the VRS-SO were the Psychology of Criminal Conduct (PCC) (Andrews & Bonta, 2006) and the RNR model of effective treatment implementation (Bonta & Andrews, 2007; Hanson et al., 2009). The VRS-SO was specifically developed to assess the risk of sexual violence for forensic patients who are considered for release into the community after attending a treatment programme (Wong et al., 2003). The instrument consists of seven static items (age at release, age at first sexual offence, offender type, prior sexual offences, unrelated victims, victim gender, and prior sentencing dates) and 17 dynamic items (sexually deviant lifestyle, sexual compulsivity, offence planning, criminal personality, cognitive distortions, interpersonal aggression, emotional control, insight, substance abuse, community support, release to high-risk situation, sexual offending cycle, impulsivity, compliance with community supervision, treatment compliance, deviant sexual preference, and intimacy deficits).

Both the static and the dynamic items are used to determine the recidivism risk of an individual offender (i.e., to fulfil the risk principle), whereas the dynamic variables were developed to identify treatment targets and to measure treatment-induced changes in recidivism risk (i.e., to fulfil the need principle; Wong & Olver, 2010). The static and dynamic factors are all rated on a four-point Likert scale to reflect the extent of the problems identified by the factors (Wong et al., 2003). The total score represents the individual's current (or pretreatment) risk and can be differentiated into four risk categories: low (total scores from 0 to 20), moderate–low (21–30), moderate–high (31–40), and high (41–72). Despite this opportunity of using categories, the authors recommend linking the scores of the instrument directly to recidivism risk tables because the meaning of labels such as 'high risk' or 'low risk' could vary substantially between different users (Hilton, Carter, Harris, & Sharpe, 2008; Wong & Gordon, 2006; Wong & Olver, 2010). The dynamic factors with high ratings are potential treatment targets and should be worked on during therapy. Both the VRS and the VRS-SO provide the opportunity for a clinical override, in order to adjust the actuarially derived result under exceptional circumstances (Wong & Olver, 2010). However, as already noted above, this option might also for these risk tools provide more measurement problems than potential (Hanson & Morton-Bourgon, 2009; Wormith et al., 2012).

The theoretical basis for the measurement of treatment-related changes in sexual offenders is the so-called Stages of Change Model or Transtheoretical Model of Change (Prochaska, DeClemente, & Norcross, 1992). This model provides a useful heuristic to conceptualize the change process and differentiates the change process into the following distinct stages (Wong et al., 2003): the precontemplation stage (i.e., the individual has no awareness of his/her problems and has no intention of changing in the near future), the contemplation stage (i.e., a person is able to recognize his/her problems and wants to cope with them but relevant behavioural changes are not yet evident), the preparation stage (i.e., behavioural indications of change related to the individual's problem areas are now evident but lapses occur frequently or regularly), the action stage (i.e., an individual is actively modifying his/her behaviour, in order to cope with his/her problems for an extended period of time), and the maintenance stage (i.e., in this last stage relapse prevention techniques are used to prevent relapse and to consolidate the gains and efforts made in the previous stages). At the end of a treatment programme, for all identified (pre)treatment targets, the respective post-treatment score has to be rated according to the Stages of Change: the more treatment-induced changes, the higher the risk reduction in the VRS-SO post-treatment total score.

The first studies on the psychometric properties of the VRS-SO provided evidence for the construct validity (e.g., due to high correlations between the Static-99 and the VRS-SO static items) and indicated a three-factor solution, denoted Sexual Deviance, Criminality, and Treatment Responsivity (Olver et al., 2007). Furthermore, the internal consistency ($\alpha = 0.81$ for the dynamic items score and $\alpha = 0.84$ for the total VRS-SO score) (Olver et al., 2007) and the interrater reliability were good to excellent, even for the more complex dynamic items (ICC = 0.74–0.95) (Beggs & Grace, 2010; Beyko & Wong, 2005; Olver et al., 2007). The predictive validity of the VRS-SO was examined by Olver et al. (2007) in a sample of $n = 321$ sexual offenders with an average follow-up period of 10 years. For the prediction of sexual recidivism, both the VRS-SO static and the VRS-SO dynamic total subscale scores showed significant AUC values (AUC = 0.74 for the static and 0.67 for the dynamic items). Furthermore, the dynamic items provided a greater incremental predictive contribution than the static items. The VRS-SO total had AUC = 0.72, a predictive accuracy that could be regarded as a large effect size (Rice & Harris, 2005). Interestingly, the predictive accuracy for non-sexual violent recidivism was substantially lower than that for sexual recidivism, particularly because of a negative predictability of the Sexual Deviance subscale of the VRS-SO dynamic part (Olver et al., 2007). Beggs and Grace (2010) investigated the predictive accuracy of the VRS-SO in an independent cross-validation study by using a sample of $n = 218$ child molesters and an average follow-up period of about 4.5 years. In this study, especially the dynamic items of the VRS-SO obtained a high AUC value (0.80), which was considerably higher than for the static items (AUC = 0.67) and again showed a greater incremental predictive contribution than the static items (Beggs & Grace, 2010). A recently published study from Austria confirmed the promising results of the VRS-SO (Eher et al., 2015).

Although some researchers have argued that dynamic variables are useful if they have greater incremental predictive validity than static variables (e.g., Harris, Rice et al., 2003), the developers of the VRS-SO argued that dynamic variables do not necessarily have to outperform the predictive accuracy of static variables to be useful (Wong & Gordon, 2006). In a nutshell, the authors proposed that there is more to dynamic variables than simply recidivism prediction because their utility in treatment and risk reduction is at least equally important (Olver et al., 2007). Much more relevant than incremental predictive accuracy is whether or not the amount of change is related to recidivism – ideally beyond the static and dynamic pretreatment assessment scores (Wong & Olver, 2010). Considering the overall current state of research, the VRS-SO could be regarded as the best validated dynamic tool because in the meantime some different studies have found that risk-related changes in dynamic areas of the VRS-SO were associated with reductions in sexual and violent recidivism in sexual offenders (e.g., Beggs & Grace, 2011; Olver et al., 2007). In a recent study using a combined international sample of $n = 539$ sexual offenders followed up for an average of 15.5 years post-release, Olver, Beggs Christofferson, Grace, and Wong (2014) reported that VRS-SO change scores were significantly associated with decreases in different recidivism criteria after controlling for pretreatment risk and individual differences in follow-up time. In a prospective multisite study with a Canadian sample of $n = 676$ treated sexual offenders followed up for an average of 6.3 years post-release (Olver, Nicholaichuk, Kingston, & Wong, 2014), again the VRS-SO dynamic factors demonstrated moderate predictive accuracy for sexual, violent, and general recidivism (AUC = 0.66–0.68) and there were significant pre–post-treatment changes in the dynamic factors ranging from small to moderate in magnitude ($d = 0.22–0.62$) across different intensity programmes. Furthermore, the study showed again that the changes in scores were systematically associated with decreases in recidivism and provided an additional explanatory value over and above the pretreatment information (Olver, Nicholaichuk et al., 2014).

Conclusions

The development and promulgation of the actuarial risk assessment methodology is certainly one of the most important advances in forensic and criminological psychology in the last few decades. Based on the seminal work of Paul E. Meehl (Meehl, 1954), we are now able to provide reliable and valid prognoses about the recidivism risk of sexual offenders by using comparably easy to score and scientifically sound actuarial instruments. Furthermore, the third-generation instruments provide information about the most relevant and promising (in terms of sustainably risk-reducing) therapeutic aims in sexual offender treatment settings. Overall, actuarial risk assessment instruments should be an integral part of every clinical or correctional institution that has to diagnose, assess, and/or treat sexual offenders.

Despite these important advances in research and clinical practice, there are still a number of unresolved issues and unanswered questions. First, different special populations exist where we do not know as much as we do about male adult sexual offenders. For example, there is little knowledge about the utility of ARAIs for female sexual offenders (Cortoni, Hanson, & Choache, 2010), even though we have some evidence that they will work with general criminal and violent females (e.g., Eisenbarth, Osterheider, Nedopil, & Stadtland, 2012). For other subgroups, some evidence exists that ARAIs could be helpful, but much more research would be necessary and desirable: among others, initial studies have been published about the use of ARAIs with sexual murderers (Hill et al., 2012), sexually motivated domestic violent offenders (Rettenberger & Eher, 2013), and developmentally delayed sexual offenders (Hanson, Sheahan, & van Zuylen, 2013). All of this research poses the question of the differential validity of the ARAIs, i.e., whether the psychometric properties vary between different subgroups of sexual offenders – a question that will certainly accompany us over the next few years. Another important question refers to the incremental validity and the additional benefit of integrating different ARAIs into the risk assessment process for one individual case (Babchishin et al., 2012; Lehmann et al., 2013; Seto, 2005; Singer et al., 2013). Further interesting research topics include the influence of age (e.g., Helmus, Thornton, et al., 2012; Rettenberger et al., 2013) and offence-free time in the community (Hanson, Harris, Helmus, & Thornton, 2014) on actuarial risk prediction.

In addition to the above-mentioned future tasks and topics within the field of forensic prediction research, researchers and clinicians should also try to apply findings beyond their own noses, i.e., from other domains of psychological science (e.g., cognitive, clinical, or social psychology). One of the most promising research approaches considers the multiple bias sources that could play an important role in forensic mental health assessment (Kahneman, 2011; Neal & Grisso, 2014). For example, Murrie, Boccaccini, Guarnera, and Rufino (2013) investigated evidence for a so-called 'allegiance effect' in risk assessment procedures where experts tend to interpret risk assessment data in a way that supports the mandating position. Another aspect for future research will be the different opportunities to communicate the results provided by ARAIs. Scurich and John (2011), for example, reported interesting data about how easily forensic decision-makers can be influenced by the risk communication format. Despite these open questions, it is obvious from the research findings reviewed for the present chapter that research on actuarial risk assessment methods is one of the most prolific and impressive fields in forensic and criminological psychology.

References

Allan, A., Dawson, D., & Allan, M. M. (2006). Prediction of the risk of male sexual reoffending in Australia. *Australian Psychologist, 41*, 60–68. doi:10.1080/00050060500391886

American Psychiatric Association (1980). *Diagnostic and statistical manual of mental disorders* (3rd ed.) (DSM-III). Washington, DC: Author.

Anderson, D., & Hanson, R. K. (2010). Static-99: An actuarial tool to assess risk of sexual and violent recidivism among sexual offenders. In R. K. Otto & K. S. Douglas (Eds.), *Handbook of violence risk assessment* (pp. 251–267). Abingdon, England: Routledge.

Andrews, D. A., & Bonta, J. (2006). *The psychology of criminal conduct* (4th ed.). Cincinnati, OH: Anderson.

Andrews, D. A., Bonta, J., & Wormith, S. J. (2004). *The Level of Service/Case Management Inventory (LS/CMI).* Toronto, Canada: Multi-Health Systems.

Andrews, D. A., Bonta, J., & Wormith, S. J. (2006). The recent past and near future of risk and/or need assessment. *Crime and Delinquency, 52,* 7–27. doi:10.1177/0011128705281756

Archer, R. P., Buffington-Vollum, J. K., Stredny, R. V., & Handel, R. W. (2006). A survey of psychological test use patterns among forensic psychologists. *Journal of Personality Assessment, 87,* 84–94. doi:10.1207/s15327752jpa8701_07

Babchishin, K. M, Hanson, R. K., & Helmus, L. (2012). Even highly correlated measures can add incrementally to predicting recidivism among sex offenders. *Assessment, 19,* 442–461. doi:10.1177/1073191112458312

Baltieri, D. A., & de Andrade, A. G. (2008). Comparing serial and nonserial sexual offenders: Alcohol and street drug consumption, impulsiveness and history of sexual abuse. *Revista Brasileira de Psiquiatria, 30,* 25–31. doi:10.1590/S1516-44462006005000067

Barbaree, H. E., & Blanchard, R. (2008). Sexual deviance over the lifespan: Reductions in deviant sexual behavior in the aging sex offender. In D. R. Laws & W. O'Donohue (Eds.), *Sexual deviance: Theory, assessment, and treatment* (2nd ed., pp. 37–60). New York, NY: Guilford Press.

Barbaree, H. E., Langton, C. M., Blanchard, R., & Cantor, J. M. (2009). Aging versus stable enduring traits as explanatory constructs in sex offender recidivism: Partitioning actuarial prediction into conceptually meaningful components. *Criminal Justice and Behavior, 36,* 443–465. doi:10.1177/0093854809332283

Barbaree, H. E., Seto, M. C., Langton, C. M., & Peacock, E. J. (2001). Evaluating the predictive accuracy of six risk assessment instruments for adult sex offenders. *Criminal Justice and Behavior, 28,* 490–521. doi:10.1177/009385480102800406

Bartosh, D. L., Garby, T., Lewis, D., & Gray, S. (2003). Differences in the predictive validity of actuarial risk assessments in relation to sex offender type. *International Journal of Offender Therapy and Comparative Criminology, 47,* 422–438. doi:10.1177/0306624X03253850

Beech, A. R. (1998). A psychometric typology of child abusers. *International Journal of Offender Therapy and Comparative Criminology, 42,* 319–339. doi:10.1177/0306624X9804200405

Beggs, S. M., & Grace, R. C. (2010). Assessment of dynamic risk factors: An independent validation study of the Violence Risk Scale: Sexual Offender Version. *Sexual Abuse: A Journal of Research and Treatment, 22,* 234–251. doi:10.1177/1079063210369014

Beggs, S. M., & Grace, R. C. (2011). Treatment gains for sexual offenders against children predicts reduced recidivism: A comparative validity study. *Journal of Consulting and Clinical Psychology, 79,* 182–192. doi:10.1037/a0022900

Bengtson, S. (2008). Is new better? A cross-validation of the Static-2002 and the Risk Matrix 2000 in a Danish sample of sexual offenders. *Psychology, Crime & Law, 14,* 85–106. doi:10.1080/10683160701483104.

Beyko, M. J., & Wong, S. C. P. (2005). Predictors of treatment attrition as indicators for program improvement not offender shortcomings: A study of sex offender treatment attrition. *Sexual Abuse: A Journal of Research and Treatment, 17,* 375–389. doi:10.1177/107906320501700403

Blair, P. R., Marcus, D. K., & Boccaccini, M. T. (2008). Is there an allegiance effect for assessment instruments? Actuarial risk assessment as an exemplar. *Clinical Psychology Science and Practice, 15,* 346–360. doi:10.1111/j.1468-2850.2008.00147.x

Boer, D. P., & Hart, S. D. (2009). Sex offender risk assessment: Research, evaluation, 'best-practice' recommendations and future directions. In J. L. Ireland, C. A. Ireland, & P. Birch (Eds.), *Violent and sexual offenders. Assessment, treatment and management* (pp. 27–42). Cullompton, England: Willan.

Boer, D. P., Hart, S. D., Kropp, P. R., & Webster, C. D. (1997). *Manual for the Sexual Violence Risk-20: Professional guidelines for assessing risk of sexual violence.* Vancouver, Canada: Mental Health, Law and Policy Institute.

Bonta, J., & Andrews, D. A. (2007). *Risk–Need–Responsivity model for offender assessment and rehabilitation* (User Report 2007-06). Ottawa, Canada: Public Safety Canada. Retrieved from http://www.publicsafety.gc.ca/cnt/rsrcs/pblctns/rsk-nd-rspnsvty/index-eng.aspx

Bonta, J., Law, M., & Hanson, R. K. (1998). The prediction of criminal and violent recidivism among mentally disordered offenders: A meta-analysis. *Psychological Bulletin, 123,* 123–142. doi:10.1037/0033-2909.123.2.123

Bonta, J., & Wormith, J. S. (2013). Applying the risk–need–responsivity principles to offender assessment. In L. A. Craig., L. Dixon., & T. A. Gannon (Eds.), *What works in offender rehabilitation: An evidence based approach to assessment and treatment* (pp. 71–93). Chichester, England: John Wiley & Sons, Ltd.

Briken, P., & Müller, J. L. (2014). Beurteilung der Schuldfähigkeit bei paraphiler Störung. Kann der Schweregrad der Störung mithilfe von Kriterien aus Prognoseinstrumenten erfasst werden? [Assessment of criminal responsibility in paraphilic disorder. Can the severity of the disorder be assessed with items of standardized prognostic instruments?]. *Nervenarzt, 85,* 304–311. doi:10.1007/s00115-013-3901-x

Cohen, J. (1988). *Statistical power analysis for the behavioral sciences* (2nd ed.). Hillsdale, NJ: Erlbaum.

Cohen, J. (1992). A power primer. *Psychological Bulletin, 112,* 155–159. doi:10.1037/0033-2909.112.1.155

Cortoni, F., Craig, L., & Beech, A. R. (2010). Risk assessment of sexual offenders. In M. Herzog-Evans (Ed.), *Transnational criminology manual* (Vol. 3, pp. 503–527). Nijmegen, The Netherlands: Wolf Legal.

Cortoni, F., Hanson, R. K., & Choache, M.-E. (2010). The recidivism rates of female sexual offenders are low: A meta-analysis. *Sexual Abuse: A Journal of Research and Treatment, 22,* 387–401. doi:10.1177/1079063210372142

Cortoni, F., & Marshall, W. L. (2001). Sex as a coping strategy and its relationship to juvenile sexual history and intimacy in sexual offenders. *Sexual Abuse: A Journal of Research and Treatment, 13,* 27–43. doi:10.1177/107906320101300104

Craig, L. A. (2008). How should we understand the effect of age on sexual reconviction? *Journal of Sexual Aggression, 14,* 185–198. doi:10.1080/13552600802073132

Craig, L. A. (2011). The effect of age on sexual and violent reconviction. *International Journal of Offender Therapy and Comparative Criminology, 55,* 1, 75–97. doi:10.1177/0306624X09353290

Craig, L. A., & Beech, A. R. (2010). Towards a guide to best practice in conducting actuarial risk assessments with sex offenders. *Aggression and Violent Behavior, 15,* 278–293. doi:10.1016/j.avb.2010.01.007

Craig, L. A., Beech, A. R., & Browne, K. D. (2006). Cross-validation of the Risk Matrix 2000 Sexual and Violent scales. *Journal of Interpersonal Violence, 21,* 612–633. doi:10.1177/0886260506286876

Craig, L. A., Browne, K. D., & Beech, A. R. (2008). *Assessing risk in sex offenders: A practitioner's guide.* Chichester, England: John Wiley & Sons, Ltd.

Craig, L. A., Browne, K. D., & Stringer, I. (2004). Comparing sex offender risk assessment measures on a UK sample. *International Journal of Offender Therapy and Comparative Criminology*, *48*, 7–27. doi:10.1177/0306624X03257243

Craig, L. A., Thornton, D., Beech, A. R., & Browne, K. D. (2007). The relationship of statistical and psychological risk markers to sexual reconviction. *Criminal Justice and Behavior*, *34*, 314–329. doi:10.1177/0093854806291416

Dawes, R. M., Faust, D., & Meehl, P. E. (1989). Clinical versus actuarial judgement. *Science*, *243*, 1668–1674. doi:10.1126/science.2648573

de Vogel, V., de Ruiter, C., van Beek, D., & Mead, G. (2004). Predictive validity of the SVR-20 and Static-99 in a Dutch sample of treated sex offenders. *Law and Human Behavior*, *28*, 235–251. doi:10.1023/B:LAHU.0000029137.41974.eb

Doren, D. M. (2006). What do we know about the effect of aging on recidivism risk for sexual offenders. *Sexual Abuse: A Journal of Research and Treatment*, *18*, 137–157. doi:10.1177/107906320601800203

Ducro, C., & Pham, T. (2006). Evaluation of the SORAG and the Static-99 on Belgian sex offenders committed to a forensic facility. *Sexual Abuse: A Journal of Research and Treatment*, *18*, 15–26. doi:10.1177/107906320601800102

Eher, R., Matthes, A., Schilling, F. Haubner-MacLean, T., & Rettenberger, M. (2012). Dynamic risk assessment in sexual offenders using STABLE-2000 and the STABLE-2007: An investigation of predictive and incremental validity. *Sexual Abuse: A Journal of Research and Treatment*, *24*, 5–28. doi:10.1177/1079063211403164

Eher, R., Olver, M., Heurix, I., Schilling, F., & Rettenberger, M. (2015). Predicting reoffense in pedophilic child molesters by clinical diagnoses and risk assessment. *Law and Human Behavior*, *39*, 571–580. doi:10.1037/lhb0000144

Eher, R., Rettenberger, M., Gaunersdorfer, K., Haubner-MacLean, T., Matthes, A., Schilling, F., & Mokros, A. (2013). Über die Treffsicherheit der standardisierten Risikoeinschätzungsverahren Static-99 und Stable-2007 bei aus einer Sicherungsmaßnahme entlassenen Sexualstraftätern [On the accuracy of the standardardized risk assessment procedures Static-99 and Stable-2007 for sexual offenders released from detention]. *Forensische Psychiatrie, Psychologie, Kriminologie*, *7*, 264–272. doi:10.1007/s11757-013-0212-9

Eher, R., Rettenberger, M., Schilling, F., & Pfäfflin, F. (2008). Failure of Static-99 and SORAG to predict relevant reoffense categories in relevant sexual offender subtypes: A prospective study. *Sexual Offender Treatment*, *3*(1), 1–14. Retrieved from http://www.sexual-offender-treatment.org/1-2008_02.html

Eher, R., Schilling, F., Haubner-MacLean, T., Jahn, T., & Rettenberger, M. (2012). Ermittlung des relativen und absoluten Rückfallrisikos mithilfe des Static-99 in einer deutschsprachigen Population entlassener Sexualstraftäter [Assessment of the relative and absolute risk of recidivism using Static-99 in a German-speaking population of released sexual offenders]. *Forensische Psychiatrie, Psychologie, Kriminologie*, *6*, 32–40. doi:10.1007/s11757-011-0146-z

Eisenbarth, H., Osterheider, M., Nedopil, N., & Stadtland, C. (2012). Recidivism in female offenders: PCL-R lifestyle factor and VRAG show predictive validity in a German sample. *Behavioral Sciences and the Law*, *30*, 575–584. doi:10.1002/bsl.2013

Epperson, D. L., Kaul, J. D., Huot, S. J., Hesselton, D., Alexander, W., & Goldman, R. (2000, November). *Cross-validation of the Minnesota Sex Offender Screening Tool – Revised*. Paper presented at the 19th Annual Research and Treatment Conference of the Association for the Treatment of Sexual Abusers, San Diego, CA.

Epperson, D. L., Kaul, J. D., & Hesselton, D. (1998, October). *Final report on the development of the Minnesota Sex Offender Screening Tool – Revised*. Paper presented at the 17th

Annual Research and Treatment Conference of the Association for the Treatment of Sexual Abusers, Vancouver, Canada.

Finkelhor, D., & Jones, L. (2006). Why have child maltreatment and child victimization declined? *Journal of Social Issues*, *62*, 685–716. doi:10.1111/j.1540-4560.2006.00483.x

Fleiss, J. L. (1981). *Statistical methods for rates and proportions* (2nd ed.). New York, NY: John Wiley & Sons, Inc.

Gore, K. S. (2007). Adjusted actuarial assessment of sex offenders: The impact of clinical overrides on predictive accuracy. *Dissertation Abstracts International*, *68*(07), 4824B (UMI No. 3274898).

Grove, W. M., & Meehl, P. E. (1996). Comparative efficiency of informal (subjective, impressionistic) and formal (mechanical, algorithmic) prediction procedures: The clinical–statistical controversy. *Psychology, Public Policy, and Law*, *2*, 293–323. doi:10.1037/1076-8971.2.2.293

Grove, W. M., Zald, D. H., Lebow, B. S., Snitz, B. E., & Nelson, C. (2000). Clinical versus mechanical prediction: A meta-analysis. *Psychological Assessment*, *12*, 19–30. doi:10.1037/1040-3590.12.1.19

Grubin, D. (1998). *Sex offending against children: Understanding the risk* (Police Research Series, Paper 99). London, England: Home Office.

Hanson, R. K. (1997). *The development of a brief actuarial risk scale for sexual offense recidivism* (User Report 1997-04). Ottawa, Canada: Department of the Solicitor General of Canada.

Hanson, R. K. (2002). Recidivism and age: Follow-up data on 4,673 sexual offenders. *Journal of Interpersonal Violence*, *17*, 1046–1062. doi:10.1177/088626002236659

Hanson, R. K. (2006). Does Static-99 predict recidivism among older sexual offenders? *Sexual Abuse: A Journal of Research and Treatment*, *18*, 343–355. doi:10.1007/s11194-006-9027-y

Hanson, R. K. (2007, March). *How should risk assessments for sexual offenders be conducted?* Paper presented at the Fourth Annual Forensic Psychiatry Conference, Victoria, Canada.

Hanson, R. K. (2009). The psychological assessment of risk for crime and violence. *Canadian Psychology*, *50*, 172–182. doi:10.1037/a0015726

Hanson, R. K., Babchishin, K. M., Helmus, L., & Thornton, D. (2013). Quantifying the relative risk of sex offenders: Risk ratios for Static-99R. *Sexual Abuse: A Journal of Research and Treatment*, *24*, 482–515. doi:10.1177/1079063212469060

Hanson, R. K., Bourgon, G., Helmus, L., & Hodgson, S. (2009). The principles of effective correctional treatment also apply to sexual offenders: A meta-analysis. *Criminal Justice and Behavior*, *36*, 865–891. doi:10.1177/0093854809338545

Hanson, R. K., & Bussière, M. T. (1996). *Predictors of sexual offender recidivism: A meta-analysis* (User Report 1996-04). Ottawa, Canada: Department of the Solicitor General of Canada.

Hanson, R. K., & Bussière, M. T. (1998). Predicting relapse: A meta-analysis of sexual offender recidivism studies. *Journal of Consulting and Clinical Psychology*, *66*, 348–362. doi:10.1037//0022-006X.66.2.348

Hanson, R. K., & Harris, A. J. R. (2000). Where should we intervene? Dynamic predictors of sexual offence recidivism. *Criminal Justice and Behavior*, *27*, 6–35. doi:10.1177/0093854800027001002

Hanson, R. K., & Harris, A. J. R. (2001). A structured approach to evaluating change among sexual offenders. *Sexual Abuse: A Journal of Research and Treatment*, *13*, 105–122. doi:10.1177/107906320101300204

Hanson, R. K., Harris, A. J. R., Helmus, L., & Thornton, D. (2014). High-risk sex offenders may not be high risk forever. *Journal of Interpersonal Violence*, *29*, 2792–2813. doi:10.1177/0886260514526062

Hanson, R. K., Harris, A. J. R, Scott, T. L., & Helmus, L. (2007). *Assessing the risk of sexual offenders on community supervision: The Dynamic Supervision Project* (Corrections research User Report 2007-05). Ottawa, Canada: Public Safety Canada. Retrieved from www.static99.org/pdfdocs/hansonharrisscottandhelmus2007.pdf

Hanson, R. K., Helmus, L., & Thornton, D. (2010). Predicting recidivism among sexual offenders: A multi-site study of Static-2002. *Law and Human Behavior, 34*, 198–211. doi:10.1007/s10979-009-9180-1.

Hanson, R. K., Lloyd, C. D., Helmus, L., & Thornton, D. (2012). Developing non-arbitrary metrics for risk communication: Percentile ranks for the Static-99/R and Static-2002/R sexual offender risk tools. *International Journal of Forensic Mental Health, 11*, 9–23. doi:10.1080/14999013.2012.667511

Hanson, R. K., & Morton-Bourgon, K. (2007). *The accuracy of recidivism risk assessment for sexual offenders: A meta-analysis* (Corrections Research User Report 2007-01). Ottawa, Canada: Public Safety Canada.

Hanson, R. K., & Morton-Bourgon, K. (2009). The accuracy of recidivism risk assessments for sexual offenders: A meta-analysis of 118 prediction studies. *Psychological Assessment, 21*, 1–21. doi:10.1037/a0014421

Hanson, R. K., Sheahan, C. L., & van Zuylen, H. (2013). STATIC-99 and RRASOR predict recidivism among developmentally delayed sexual offenders: A cumulative meta-analysis. *Sexual Offender Treatment, 8*(1), 1–14. Retrieved from http://www.sexual-offender-treatment.org/index.php?id=119&type=123

Hanson, R. K., & Thornton, D. (2000). Improving risk assessment for sex offenders: A comparison of three actuarial scales. *Law and Human Behavior, 24*, 119–136. doi:10.1023/A:1005482921333

Hanson, R. K., & Thornton, D. (2003). *Notes on the development of Static-2002* (Corrections Research User Report 2003-01). Ottawa, Canada: Department of the Solicitor General of Canada. Retrieved from http://www.publicsafety.gc.ca/cnt/rsrcs/pblctns/nts-dvlpmnt-sttc/nts-dvlpmnt-sttc-eng.pdf

Harris, A. J. R., & Hanson, R. K. (2010). Clinical, actuarial, and dynamic risk assessment of sexual offenders: Why do things keep changing? *Journal of Sexual Aggression, 16*, 296–310. doi:10.1080/13552600.2010.494772

Harris, A. J. R., Phenix, A., Hanson, R. K., & Thornton, D. (2003). *Static-99 coding rules revised – 2003*. Ottawa, Canada: Department of the Solicitor General of Canada. Retrieved from http://www.static99.org/pdfdocs/static-99-coding-rules_e.pdf

Harris, G. T., & Rice, M. E. (2003). Actuarial assessment of risk among sex offenders. *Annals of the New York Academy of Sciences, 989*, 198–210.

Harris, G. T., & Rice, M. E. (2007). Adjusting actuarial violence risk assessments based on aging or the passage of time. *Criminal Justice and Behavior, 34*, 297–313. doi:10.1177/0093854806293486

Harris, G. T., Rice, M. E., & Quinsey, V. L. (2010). Allegiance or fidelity? A clarifying reply. *Clinical Psychology: Science and Practice, 17*, 82–89. doi:10.1111/j.1468-2850.2009.01197.x

Harris, G. T., Rice, M. E., Quinsey, V. L., Lalumière, M. L., Boer, D., & Lang, C. (2003). A multisite comparison of actuarial risk instruments for sex offenders. *Psychological Assessment, 15*, 413–425. doi:10.1037/1040-3590.15.3.413

Hart, S. D., & Boer, D. P. (2010). Structured professional judgment guidelines for sexual violence risk assessment: The Sexual Violence Risk-20 (SVR-20) and Risk for Sexual Violence Protocol (RSVP). In R. K. Otto & K. S. Douglas (Eds.), *Handbook of violence risk assessment* (pp. 269–294). New York, NY: Routledge.

Helmus, L., Babchishin, K. M., & Hanson, R. K. (2013). The predictive accuracy of the Risk Matrix 2000: A meta-analysis. *Sexual Offender Treatment, 8*(2), 1–20. Retrieved from http://www.sexual-offender-treatment.org/index.php?id=125&type=123

Helmus, L., & Hanson, R. K., (2007). Predictive validity of the Static-99 and Static-2002 for sex offenders on community supervision. *Sexual Offender Treatment, 2*(2), 1–14. Retrieved from http://www.sexual-offender-treatment.org/index.php?id=60&type=123

Helmus, L., Hanson, R. K., & Morton-Bourgon, K. E. (2011). International comparisons of the validity of actuarial risk tools for sexual offenders, with a focus on Static-99. In D. P. Boer, L. A. Craig, R. Eher, M. H. Miner, & F. Pfäfflin (Eds.), *International perspectives on the assessment and treatment of sexual offenders: Theory, practice, and research* (pp. 57–84). Chichester, England: John Wiley & Sons, Ltd.

Helmus, L., Hanson, R. K., & Thornton, D. (2009). Reporting Static-99 in light of new research on recidivism norms. *The Forum, 21*, 38–45. Retrieved from http://static99.org/pdfdocs/forum_article_feb2009.pdf

Helmus, L., Hanson, R. K., Thornton, D., Babchishin, K. M., & Harris, A. J. R. (2012). Absolute recidivism rates predicted by Static-99R and Static-2002R sex offender risk assessment tools vary across samples: A meta-analysis. *Criminal Justice and Behavior, 33*, 1148–1171. doi:10.1177/0093854812443648

Helmus, L., & Thornton, D. (2014). The MATS-1 risk assessment scale: Summary of methodological concerns and an empirical validation. *Sexual Abuse: A Journal of Research and Treatment, 28*, 160–186. doi:10.1177/1079063214529801

Helmus, L., Thornton, D., Hanson, R. K., & Babchishin, K. M. (2012). Improving the predictive accuracy of Static-99 and Static-2002 with older sex offenders: Revised age weights. *Sexual Abuse: A Journal of Research and Treatment, 24*, 64–101. doi:10.1177/1079063211409951

Hill, A., Rettenberger, M., Habermann, N., Berner, W., Eher, R., & Briken, P. (2012). The utility of risk assessment instruments for the prediction of recidivism in sexual homicide perpetrators. *Journal of Interpersonal Violence, 27*, 3553–3578. doi:10.1177/0886260512447570

Hilton, N. Z., Carter, A. M., Harris, G. T., & Sharpe, A. J. B. (2008). Does using nonnumerical terms to describe risk aid violence risk communication? Clinician agreement and decision making. *Journal of Interpersonal Violence, 23*, 171–188. doi:10.1177/0886260507309337

Hirschi, T., & Gottfredson, M. R. (1983). Age and the explanation of crime. *American Journal of Sociology, 89*, 552–584.

Kahneman, D. (2011). *Thinking, fast and slow*. New York, NY: Farrar, Straus and Giroux.

Kingston, D. A., Yates, P. M., Firestone, P., Babchishin, K., & Bradford, J. (2008). Long term predictive validity of the Risk Matrix 2000: A comparison with the Static-99 and the Sex Offender Risk Appraisal Guide. *Sexual Abuse: A Journal of Research and Treatment, 20*, 466–484. doi:10.1177/1079063208325206

Langton, C. M., Barbaree, H. E., Harkins, L., Seto, M. C., & Peacock, E. J. (2002, October). *Evaluating the predictive validity of seven risk assessment instruments for sexual offenders*. Paper presented at the 21st Annual Research and Treatment Conference of the Association for the Treatment of Sexual Abusers, Montreal, Canada.

Langton, C. M., Barbaree, H. E., Seto, M. C., Peacock, E. J., Harkins, L., & Hansen, K. T. (2007). Actuarial assessment of risk for reoffense among adult sex offenders: Evaluating the predictive accuracy of the Static-2002 and five other instruments. *Criminal Justice and Behavior, 34*, 37–59. doi:10.1177/0093854806291157.

Lehmann, R. J. B., Hanson, R. K., Babchishin, K. M., Gallasch-Nemitz, F., Biedermann, J., & Dahle, K.-P. (2013). Interpreting multiple risk scales for sex offenders: Evidence for averaging. *Psychological Assessment*, 25, 1019–1024. doi:10.1037/a0033098

Looman, J. A. (2006). Comparison of two risk assessment instruments for sexual offenders. *Sexual Abuse: A Journal of Research and Treatment*, 18, 193–206. doi:10.1177/107906320601800206

Mann, R. E., Hanson, R. K., & Thornton, D. (2010). Assessing risk for sexual recidivism: Some proposals on the nature of psychologically meaningful risk factors. *Sexual Abuse: A Journal of Research and Treatment*, 22, 191–217. doi:10.1177/1079063210366039

Martens, R., Rettenberger, M., & Eher, R. (2015). The predictive and incremental validity of the German adaptation of the Static-2002 in a sexual offender sample released from the prison system. *Legal and Criminological Psychology*. Advance online publication. doi:10.1111/lcrp.12080

Meehl, P. E. (1954). *Clinical versus statistical prediction: A theoretical analysis and a review of the evidence*. Minneapolis, MN: University of Minnesota Press.

Montana, S., Thompson, G., Ellsworth, P., Lagan, H., Helmus, L., & Rhoades, C. J. (2012). Predicting relapse for Catholic clergy sex offenders: The use of the Static-99. *Sexual Abuse: A Journal of Research and Treatment*, 24, 575–590. doi:10.1177/1079063212445570

Murrie, D. C., Boccaccini, M. T., Guarnera, L. A., & Rufino, K. (2013). Are forensic experts biased by the side that retained them? *Psychological Science*, 24, 1889–1897. doi:10.1177/0956797613481812

Neal, T. M. S., & Grisso, T. (2014). The cognitive underpinnings of bias in forensic mental health evaluations. *Psychology, Public Policy, and Law*, 20, 200–211. doi:10.1037/a0035824

Nunes, K. L., & Babchishin, K. M. (2012). Construct validity of Stable-2000 and Stable-2007 scores. *Sexual Abuse: A Journal of Research and Treatment*, 24, 29–45. doi:10.1177/1079063211404921

Nunes, K. L., Firestone, P., Bradford, J. M., Greenberg, D. M., & Broom, I. (2002). A comparison of modified versions of the Static-99 and the Sex Offender Risk Appraisal Guide (SORAG). *Sexual Abuse: A Journal of Research and Treatment*, 14, 253–269. doi:10.1177/107906320201400305

Olver, M. E., Beggs Christofferson, S. M., Grace, R. C., & Wong, S. C. P. (2014). Incorporating change information into sexual offender risk assessments using the Violence Risk Scale–Sexual Offender Version. *Sexual Abuse: A Journal of Research and Treatment*, 26, 472–499. doi:10.1177/1079063213502679

Olver, M. E., Nicholaichuk, T. P., Kingston, D. A., & Wong, S. C. P. (2014). A multisite examination of sexual violence risk and therapeutic change. *Journal of Consulting and Clinical Psychology*, 82, 312–324. doi:10.1037/a0035340

Olver, M. E., Wong, S. C. P., Nicholaichuk, T., & Gordon, A. (2007). The validity and reliability of the Violence Risk Scale–Sexual Offender version: Assessing sex offender risk and evaluating therapeutic change. *Psychological Assessment*, 19, 318–329. doi:10.1037/1040-3590.19.3.318

Phenix, A., Helmus, L., & Hanson, R. K. (2012). *Static-99R. Evaluators' workbook*. Unpublished document. Retrieved from http://www.static99.org/pdfdocs/st-99rworkbookwithsamplesandsummaries.pdf

Prentky, R., Harris, B., Frizzell, K., & Righthand, S. (2000). An actuarial procedure for assessing risk with juvenile sex offenders. *Sexual Abuse: A Journal of Research and Treatment*, 12, 71–93. doi:10.1177/107906320001200201

Prentky, R. A., Janus, E., Barbaree, H. E., Schwartz, B. K., & Kafka, M. P. (2006). Sexually violent predators in the courtroom: Science on trial. *Psychology, Public Policy, and Law, 12*, 357–393. doi:10.1037/1076-8971.12.4.357

Prentky, R. A., & Lee, A. F. S. (2007). Effect of age-at-release on long-term sexual re-offense rates in civilly committed sexual offenders. *Sexual Abuse: A Journal of Research and Treatment, 19*, 43–59. doi:10.1177/107906320701900105

Prochaska, J. O., DiClemente, C. C., & Norcross, J. C. (1992). In search of how people change: Applications to the addictive behaviors. *American Psychologist, 47*, 1102–1114. doi:10.1037/0003-066X.47.9.1102

Public Safety Canada (2007). *Corrections and conditional release statistical overview: Annual report 2007*. Ottawa, Canada: Author. Retrieved from http://www.publicsafety.gc.ca/res/cor/rep/_fl/CCRSO_2007-eng.pdf

Quinsey, V. L., Coleman, G., Jones, B., & Altrows, I. (1997). Proximal antecedents of eloping and reoffending among supervised mentally disordered offenders. *Journal of Interpersonal Violence, 12*, 794–813. doi:10.1177/088626097012006002

Quinsey, V. L., Harris, G. T., Rice, M. E., & Cormier, C. (2006). *Violent offenders: Appraising and managing risk* (2nd ed.). Washington, DC: American Psychological Association.

Rettenberger, M., Boer, D. P., & Eher, R. (2011). The predictive accuracy of risk factors in the Sexual Violence Risk-20 (SVR-20). *Criminal Justice and Behavior, 38*, 1009–1027. doi:10.1177/0093854811416908

Rettenberger, M., Briken, P., Turner, D., & Eher, R. (2015). Sexual offender recidivism among a population-based prison sample. *International Journal of Offender Therapy and Comparative Criminology, 59*, 424–444. doi:10.1177/0306624X13516732

Rettenberger, M., & Eher, R. (2006). Actuarial assessment of sex offender recidivism risk: A validation of the German version of the Static-99. *Sexual Offender Treatment, 1*(3), 1–11. Retrieved from http://www.sexual-offender-treatment.org/51.html

Rettenberger, M., & Eher, R. (2007). Predicting reoffense in sexual offender subtypes: A prospective validation study of the German version of the sexual offender risk appraisal guide (SORAG). *Sexual Offender Treatment, 2*(2), 1–12. Retrieved from http://www.sexual-offender-treatment.org/index.php?id=62&type=123

Rettenberger, M., & Eher, R. (2013). Actuarial risk assessment in sexually motivated intimate-partner violence. *Law and Human Behavior, 37*, 75–86. doi:10.1037/b0000001

Rettenberger, M., Haubner-MacLean, T., & Eher, R. (2013). The contribution of age to the Static-99 risk assessment in a population-based prison sample of sexual offenders. *Criminal Justice and Behavior, 40*, 1413–1433. doi:10.1177/0093854813492518

Rettenberger, M., Matthes, A., Boer, D. P., & Eher, R. (2010). Actuarial recidivism risk assessment and sexual delinquency: A comparison of five risk assessment tools in different sexual offender subtypes. *International Journal of Offender Therapy and Comparative Criminology, 54*, 169–186. doi:10.1177/0306624X08328755

Rice, M. E., & Harris, G. T. (1995). Violent recidivism: Assessing predictive validity. *Journal of Consulting and Clinical Psychology, 63*, 737–748. doi:10.1037/0022-006X.63.5.737

Rice, M. E., & Harris, G. T. (2005). Comparing effect sizes in follow-up studies: ROC, Cohen's *d*, and *r. Law and Human Behavior, 29*, 615–620. doi:10.1007/s10979-005-6832-7

Rice, M. E., & Harris, G. T. (2014). What does it mean when age is related to recidivism among sex offenders? *Law and Human Behavior, 38*, 151–161. doi:10.1037/lhb0000052

Rice, M. E., Harris, G. T., & Hilton, N. Z. (2010). The Violence Risk Appraisal Guide and Sex Offender Risk Appraisal Guide for violence risk assessment and the Ontario Domestic Assault Risk Assessment and Domestic Violence Risk Appraisal Guide for wife assault risk assessment. In R. K. Otto & K. S. Douglas (Eds.), *Handbook of violence risk assessment tools* (pp. 99–120). Abingdon, England: Routledge.

Rossegger, A., Gerth, J., Singh, J. P., & Endrass, J. (2013). Examining the predictive validity of the SORAG in Switzerland. *Sexual Offender Treatment*, 8(2), 1–12. Retrieved from http://www.sexual-offender-treatment.org/index.php?id=123&type=123

Sampson, R. J., & Laub, J. H. (2003). Life-course desisters? Trajectories of crime among delinquent boys followed to age 70. *Criminology*, 41, 555–592. doi:10.1111/j.1745-9125.2003.tb00997.x

Sawyer, J. (1966). Measurement and prediction: Clinical and statistical. *Psychological Bulletin*, 66, 178–200. doi:10.1037/h0023624

Scurich, N., & John, R. S. (2011). The effect of framing actuarial risk probabilities on involuntary civil commitment decisions. *Law and Human Behavior*, 35, 83–91. doi:10.1007/s10979-010-9218-4

Seto, M. C. (2005). Is more better? Combining actuarial risk scales to predict recidivism among adult sex offenders. *Psychological Assessment*, 17, 156–167. doi:10.1037/1040-3590.17.2.156.

Singer, J. C., Boer, D. P., & Rettenberger, M. (2013). A convergent approach to sex offender risk assessment. In K. Harrison & B. Rainey (Eds.), *The Wiley-Blackwell handbook of legal and ethical aspects of sex offender treatment and management* (pp. 341–355). Chichester, England: John Wiley & Sons, Ltd.

Sjöstedt, G., & Långstrom, N. (2001). Actuarial assessment of sex offender recidivism risk: A cross-validation of the RRASOR and the Static-99 in Sweden. *Law and Human Behavior*, 25, 629–645. doi:10.1023/A:1012758307983

Skelton, A., Riley, D., Wales, D., & Vess, J. (2006). Assessing risk for sexual offenders in New Zealand: Development and validation of a computer-scored risk measure. *Journal of Sexual Aggression*, 12, 277–286. doi:10.1080/13552600601100326

Stadtland, C., Hollweg, M., Kleindienst, N., Dietl, J., Reich, U., & Nedopil, N. (2005). Risk assessment and prediction of violent and sexual recidivism in sex offenders: Long-term predictive validity of four risk assessment instruments. *Journal of Forensic Psychiatry and Psychology*, 16, 92–108. doi:10.1080/1478994042000270247

Storey, J. E., Watt, K. A., Jackson, K. J., & Hart, S. D. (2012). Utilization and implications of the Static-99 in practice. *Sexual Abuse: A Journal of Research and Treatment*, 24, 289–302. doi:10.1177/1079063211423943

Swinburne Romine, R. E., Miner, M. H., Poulin, D., Dwyer, S. M., & Berg, D. (2012). Predicting reoffense for community-based sexual offenders: An analysis of 30 years of data. *Sexual Abuse: A Journal of Research and Treatment*, 24, 501–514. doi:10.1177/1079063212446514

Thornton, D. (2002). Constructing and testing a framework for dynamic risk assessment. *Sexual Abuse: A Journal of Research and Treatment*, 14, 139–153. doi:10.1177/107906320201400205

Thornton, D. (2006). Age and sexual recidivism: A variable connection. *Sexual Abuse: A Journal of Research and Treatment*, 18, 123–135. doi:10.1177/107906320601800202

Thornton, D., & Beech, A. R. (2002, October). *Integrating statistical and psychological factors through the Structured Risk Assessment model*. Paper presented at the 21st Annual Research and Treatment Conference of the Association for the Treatment of Sexual Abusers, Montreal, Canada.

Thornton, D., & Knight, R. A. (2015). Construction and validation of SRA-FV need assessment. *Sexual Abuse: A Journal of Research and Treatment*, 27, 360–375. doi:10.1177/1079063213511120

Thornton, D., Mann, R., Webster, S., Blud, L., Travers, R., Friendship, C., & Erikson, M. (2003). Distinguishing and combining risks for sexual and violent recidivism. *Annals of the New York Academy of Sciences*, 989, 225–235.

Turner, D., Rettenberger, M., Lohmann, L., Eher, R., & Briken, P. (2014). Pedophilic sexual interests and psychopathy in child sexual abusers working with children. *Child Abuse & Neglect, 38*, 326–335. doi:10.1016/j.chiabu.2013.07.019

Vrana, G. C., Sroga, M., & Guzzo, L. (2008). *Predictive validity of the LSI–OR among a sample of adult male sexual assaulters.* Unpublished manuscript, Nipissing University, North Bay, Canada.

Wakeling, H., Beech, A. R., & Freemantle, N. (2013). Investigating treatment change and its relationship to recidivism in a sample of 3773 sex offenders in the UK. *Psychology, Crime and Law, 19*, 233–252. doi:10.1080/1068316X.2011.626413

Ward, T., Mesler, J., & Yates, P. (2007). Reconstructing the Risk–Need–Responsivity model: A theoretical elaboration and evaluation. *Aggression and Violent Behavior, 12*, 208–228. doi:10.1016/j.avb.2006.07.001

Webster, S. D., Mann, R. E., Carter, A. J., Long, J., Milner, R. J., O'Brien, M. D., Wakeling, H. C., & Ray, N. L. (2006). Inter-rater reliability of dynamic risk assessment with sexual offenders. *Psychology, Crime & Law, 12*, 439–452. doi:10.1080/10683160500036889

Wilson, R. J. (1999). Emotional congruence in sexual offenders against children. *Sexual Abuse: A Journal of Research and Treatment, 11*, 33–47. doi:10.1177/107906329901100104

Wollert, R. (2006). Low base rates limit expert certainty when current actuarials are used to identify sexually violent predators: An application of Bayes's theorem. *Psychology, Public Policy, and Law, 12*, 56–85. doi:10.1037/1076-8971.12.1.56

Wollert, R., Cramer, E., Waggoner, J., Skelton, A., & Vess, J. (2010). Recent research (N = 9,305) underscores the importance of using age-stratified actuarial tables in sex offender risk assessments. *Sexual Abuse: A Journal of Research and Treatment, 22*, 471–490. doi:10.1177/1079063210384633

Wong, S. C. P., & Gordon, A. E. (2006). The validity and reliability of the Violence Risk Scale: A treatment-friendly violence risk assessment tool. *Psychology, Public Policy, and Law, 12*, 279–309. doi:10.1037/1076-8971.12.3.279

Wong, S. C. P., & Olver, M. E. (2010). Two treatment- and change-oriented risk assessment tools: The Violence Risk Scale and the Violence Risk Scale–Sexual Offender Version. In R. K. Otto & K. S. Douglas (Eds.), *Handbook of violence risk assessment tools* (pp. 121–146). Abingdon, England: Routledge.

Wong, S. C. P., Olver, M. E., Nicholaichuk, T. P., & Gordon, A. (2003). *The Violence Risk Scale: Sexual Offender version (VRS-SO).* Saskatoon, Canada: Regional Psychiatric Centre and University of Saskatchewan.

Wormith, S. J., Hogg, S., & Guzzo, L. (2012). The predictive validity of a general risk/needs assessment inventory on sexual offender recidivism and an exploration of the professional override. *Criminal Justice and Behavior, 39*, 1511–1538. doi:10.1177/0093854812455741

30

The Structured Professional Judgement Approach to Violence Risk Assessment

Origins, Nature, and Advances

Stephen D. Hart

Simon Fraser University, Canada; University of Bergen, Norway; Protect International
Risk and Safety Services Inc., Canada

Kevin S. Douglas

Simon Fraser University, Canada; Protect International Risk and Safety Services Inc.,
Canada

Laura S. Guy

Protect International Risk and Safety Services Inc., Canada; Simon Fraser University,
Canada

Introduction

The *Structured Professional Judgement (SPJ) approach* is an analytical method used to understand and mitigate the risk for interpersonal violence posed by individual people that is discretionary in essence but relies on evidence-based guidelines to systematize the exercise of discretion (Guy, Douglas, & Hart, 2015). *SPJ guidelines* are specific evaluative devices or procedures developed according to the SPJ approach that are intended to assess and manage risk for specific forms of violence or in specific contexts. SPJ guidelines developed specifically to assess risk for sexual violence in adults include the *Sexual Violence Risk-20* (SVR-20) (Boer, Hart, Kropp, & Webster, 1997, 2015) and the *Risk for Sexual Violence Protocol* (RSVP) (Hart et al., 2003).

The Wiley Handbook on the Theories, Assessment, and Treatment of Sexual Offending.
Edited by Douglas P. Boer. Volume II: Assessment, edited by Leam A. Craig and Martin Rettenberger.
© 2017 John Wiley & Sons, Ltd. Published 2017 by John Wiley & Sons, Ltd.

The birth of the SPJ approach can be dated to 1994, which was the year that the first set of SPJ guidelines – the *Spousal Assault Risk Assessment Guide* (SARA) (Kropp, Hart, Webster, & Eaves, 1994) – was published. The SARA survived through a second and, most recently, a third edition (Kropp, Hart, Webster, & Eaves, 1995, 2015). The second set of SPJ guidelines – the Historical, Clinical, Risk Management-20 (Webster, Eaves, Douglas, & Wintrup, 1995) – was published shortly thereafter, on 1 January 1995. The HCR-20 also survived through second and third editions (Webster, Douglas, Eaves, & Hart, 1997; Douglas, Hart, Webster, & Belfrage, 2013). Many sets of SPJ guidelines have been developed to assess risk for different kinds of violence in different contexts (Guy et al., 2015; Webster, Hucker, & Bloom, 2002), and a number of them have been rapidly and readily adopted in practice by healthcare and criminal justice agencies around the world.

Of course, birth is preceded by conception, and the conception of SPJ can be dated to 1993. In several important respects, 1993 was a critical year for the field of violence risk assessment – the year everything changed. Prior to that time, violence risk assessment relied almost exclusively on 'pure' discretion, now referred to as the *unstructured clinical judgement (UCJ) approach*, one that is informal and relies on intuition or instinct. There were some attempts over the years (discussed below) to replace UCJ with approaches that incorporated some degree of systematization or structure. These attempts included the development of a non-discretionary approach, which attempted to minimize or avoid altogether reliance on judgement, as reflected in various evaluative devices or procedures known as *actuarial* violence risk assessment instruments. These attempts all met with little success.

But 1993 saw the publication of the first of a new generation of actuarial instruments, the *Violence Risk Assessment Guide*, later renamed the *Violence Risk Appraisal Guide* (VRAG) (Harris, Rice, & Quinsey, 1993; see also Quinsey, Harris, Rice, & Cormier, 1998, 2006; Harris, Rice, Quinsey, & Cormier, 2016). The VRAG was influential in two very different ways. First, given its strong correlation with subsequent violence in the calibration sample, it was met with enthusiasm by many, and among them spurred the development of a host of similar evaluative devices. Second, it was met with scepticism and dissatisfaction by others, and among them planted the seed out of which grew the SPJ approach – an attempt to formalize the exercise of discretion. In short, the SPJ approach evolved out of a repudiation of (in direct reaction to) the explosion of actuarial instruments that began with the VRAG in 1993. The history of violence risk assessment since 1993 is really the story of the schism of the field into two opposing camps: those who support the non-discretionary approach as reflected in actuarial instruments, and those who support the SPJ approach as reflected in SPJ guidelines.

This chapter was written at the end of 2014 and beginning of 2015, which was the 20th anniversary of the birth of the SPJ approach and the beginning of the schism in violence risk assessment. It is a suitable time for retrospection and reflection. In this chapter, we:

- discuss the task of violence risk assessment;
- compare and contrast three major approaches to violence risk assessment, including their hallmarks;

- discuss important milestones in the evolution of the SPJ approach, including recent advances;
- evaluate the current status of SPJ compared with alternative approaches to violence risk assessment; and
- set out plans for the future of the SPJ approach.

The Task of Violence Risk Assessment

It is impossible to appreciate fully why the various approaches to violence risk assessment developed, or how they evolved into their present forms, without considering the task of violence risk assessment. Below, we outline the nature of this task, and also the different groups of people involved in or affected by the task and the different goals people seek to achieve through the task.

Nature

In a conceptual or theoretical sense, violence risk assessment may be described as comprising two phases (Guy et al., 2015; Heilbrun, 1997). The first phase involves forecasting or prediction in the most general sense of those terms – that is, thinking about possible futures. More specifically, evaluators analyse a wide range of factors to gain a detailed understanding of a person's potential for violence, including such things as what kinds of violence the person might perpetrate, against which victims, for what reasons, at what times, and in what places, and also what events or occurrences might exacerbate or mitigate the person's violence potential. The second phase involves planning or management. Evaluators analyse specific interventions to identify those steps that should be undertaken to prevent violence in the light of both the person's potential for violence and any relevant legal, situational, and practical constraints on possible interventions. These constraints include the person's likely living circumstances with and without intervention. Although the two phases may be conceptually distinct, it is questionable whether they can be separated in practice. Good forecasting would appear to be impossible without some sort of consideration of what could be done to manage risks, and, contrariwise, good planning would appear to be impossible without some sort of consideration of what kinds of violence the person might perpetrate. The association between these two phases is recursive and bidirectional: each informs and influences the other.

In a procedural sense, violence risk assessment may be described as a series of stages of activity. Several models of these stages have been proposed over the years (e.g., Hart, 2001; Monahan, 1981/1995; Webster, Müller-Isberner, & Fransson, 2002). They often include steps such as clarifying the purpose of the evaluation and the psycholegal decisions that it is intended to assist; gathering and synthesizing relevant information; analysing the information to determine the presence of relevant risk factors; weighting and combining risk factors to characterize violence potential; planning a preferred course of action to prevent violence; and communicating findings and opinions about violence risk. Evaluators may proceed through the stages in an iterative as opposed to linear manner; rather, at any stage, an evaluator may decide to go backwards and start the process again from a previous stage.

The key implication here is that evaluative devices or procedures should be judged based on, inter alia, the extent to which they assist the entire process of violence risk assessment – that is, both phases, or all steps, of the process. An evaluative device or procedure that assists only one phase or one part of the process is problematic.

Stakeholders

Different groups of people play a role in or are affected by violence risk assessment (Hart, 2001, 2009). One group is the people whose violence risk is being assessed. A second is the professionals whose responsibility is to conduct assessments. A third is the administrators who oversee the professionals and are responsible for ensuring the quality of assessments. A fourth is the courts, tribunals, review boards, and other bodies who are, or ultimately may be, responsible for making legal decisions based in part on assessments. A fifth is the public, whose health and safety may be threatened by violence and whose representatives determine law and policy regarding the assessment and management of violence risk.

The key implication here is that evaluative devices or procedures should be judged based on, inter alia, the extent to which they satisfy the needs of all stakeholders. An evaluative device or procedure that is deemed unsatisfactory or unacceptable by any group of stakeholders is problematic.

Goals

The ultimate goal or objective of violence risk assessment is to prevent violence (Guy et al., 2015). However, given the diverse stakeholders involved, violence risk assessment also involves a number of proximal or penultimate goals. For example, it should assist decision-making about what can or should be done to manage violence risk – it must guide action. It should also enhance accountability, protect the rights of patients and offenders, and minimize professionals' exposure to liability by ensuring transparency and consistency (Hart, 2001, 2009).

The key implication here is that evaluative devices or procedures should be judged based on, inter alia, the extent to which they achieve both the ultimate and penultimate goals identified above. An evaluative device or procedure that is deemed unsatisfactory or unacceptable by any group of stakeholders is problematic.

Summary

Violence risk assessment is a complex and continuous process that involves multiple phases and steps, involves multiple stakeholders, and strives to achieve multiple goals. Violence risk assessment is perhaps more accurately viewed as an enterprise – a difficult, intricate undertaking that requires coordination of activities by multiple people over time.

Approaches to Violence Risk Assessment

In the Introduction, we identified three general approaches to the task of violence risk assessment: UCJ, non-discretionary, and SPJ. In this section, we discuss the differences between the three approaches in more detail, specifically with respect to how they view and execute the task of violence risk assessment. Our description of the approaches is based primarily on the work of Monahan (1981/1995), Hart (2001), Otto (2000), and Guy et al. (2015).

The Unstructured Clinical Judgement Approach

The UCJ approach is defined by the absence of formal (i.e., explicit) procedures or rules for making decisions regarding violence risk. The UCJ approach is actually a 'non-approach' – that is, the absence of any systematic approach. This may sound unfair, as practitioners over the years have offered useful advice concerning the analysis of a person's history of violence. This is sometimes referred to as *anamnestic* violence risk assessment. Yet a naïve observer would be unable to differentiate between a practitioner conducting a violence risk assessment using 'pure' UCJ and another conducting an anamnestic assessment.

The rationale underlying UCJ is that the complexity of violence risk assessment is best dealt with by relying solely on an expert evaluator. The lack of a priori guidance concerning what information to gather, which risk factors to consider, how to define or operationalize risk factors, and how to combine risk factors to yield decisions regarding risk means that the practice of an evaluator is guided solely by professional discretion, itself a reflection of the evaluator's education, training, experience, and intuition. Put another way, the UCJ approach relies on charismatic authority: if one trusts a professional's education, training, experience, and intuition, then one trusts the outcome of that professional's violence risk assessment. It is difficult to impeach or critique a violence risk assessment conducted using the UCJ approach without introducing an opposing risk assessment conducted using the same approach – presumably by a second professional whose education, training, experience, or intuition is, at least arguably and in some respects, superior to those of the first.

The UCJ approach to decision-making generally and violence risk assessment more specifically has several strengths (e.g., Hart, 2001; Otto, 2000), including individualization (strong idiographic focus) and flexibility (adaptability to new problems and contexts). However, its limitations are serious. The problems with UCJ as applied to risk for general criminality (in corrections, penology, and applied criminology) were identified and discussed in detail in the first half of the 20th century, primarily by people such as the Gluecks and others (e.g., Glueck & Glueck, 1950), and in the last half of the 20th century, primarily by people such as by the Gottfredsons (e.g., Gottfredson & Gottfredson, 1988; Gottfredson & Moriarty, 2006), Andrews, Bonta, and colleagues (e.g., Andrews, Bonta, & Hoge, 1990), and others. The problems with UCJ as applied to decision-making by mental health professionals were discussed in detail during the last half of the 20th century, primarily by people such as Meehl and others (e.g., Meehl, 1954; Faust & Ziskin, 1988). The problems with UCJ specifically as it applies to violence risk assessment were discussed in the second half of the 20th century, primarily by Monahan, Webster, and others (e.g., Monahan, 1981/1995; Grove & Meehl, 1996; Webster, Menzies, & Hart, 1995). The chief limitations identified included a lack of transparency, low reliability (consistency, reproducibility), and low predictive validity (accuracy).

The Non-Discretionary Approach

The non-discretionary approach is defined by the use of fixed and explicit rules, established a priori, to minimize reliance on the judgement of evaluators when making decisions. The rules are algorithms, such as mathematical formulae or decision trees, that specify exactly which information elements shall be considered and how they shall be combined. The identification of information elements and the development of combinatoric algorithms are often (but not necessarily) guided by empirical research in the form of statistical profiles, also known as *experience tables*. The same empirical research may be used to transform the outcome of the combinatoric algorithm into a probabilistic prediction or quantitative statement regarding the likelihood of future violence. More precisely, this is a 'postdiction' – a summary statement about the observed frequency of violence in a previously studied reference group that, following the rules of inductive logic (i.e., reasoning by analogy), may be relevant to the case at hand.

The rationale underlying the non-discretionary approach is that the complexity of violence risk assessment is a tractable problem, one that stems from the limited cognitive abilities and resources of human evaluators and can be solved through simplification and automation of the assessment process. Those who advocate the non-discretionary approach often cite in support of their views research on cognitive biases and heuristics, and also research that (in their view) demonstrates the superiority of simple algorithms to human judges when making decisions of all sorts (e.g., Dawes, Faust, & Meehl, 1989; Grove & Meehl, 1996; Quinsey et al., 1998). Thus, the non-discretionary approach relies on what might be called *scientific* or *statistical authority*.

The non-discretionary approach is typically associated with the use of specialized evaluative devices, known as actuarial risk assessment instruments (ARAIs). ARAIs are developed specifically to assess risk, that is, to categorize people according to risk or estimate the probability or absolute likelihood of some outcome. However, it is also possible to use tests that were developed for some other purpose in an actuarial manner. An example is the actuarial use of the *Hare Psychopathy Checklist – Revised* (PCL-R) (Hare, 1991, 2003). The PCL-R is a quantitative psychological test (in technical terms, an expert observer rating scale) developed to assess the lifetime presence of features of psychopathic personality disorder. The PCL-R has been used in many studies on violence risk, and it is often included in reviews of violence risk assessment instruments. By definition, one could use the PCL-R in an actuarial manner by applying specific cut-off scores to identify people as, say, low versus high risk for violence; one could even estimate the probability or absolute likelihood of violence given a specific score on the PCL-R. However, in reality, it would be logically, ethically, and legally questionable to rely on a single test to 'predict' violence – especially when the test was designed for another purpose altogether, the test's developer explicitly advises against this, and research suggests that the test has serious limitations when used on its own to predict violence. In our opinion, ARAIs are legitimate instantiations of the non-discretionary approach, whereas the actuarial use of a single test designed for some other purpose is not; we will therefore focus on the former and ignore the latter.

The non-discretionary approach to decision-making, and more specifically the development of ARAIs, is certainly not a new phenomenon. In corrections, ARAIs can be traced back to the early to middle 20th century, and many modern correction agencies rely in part on ARAIs to assess risk for general criminality (for a helpful historical review, see Harcourt, 2007). However, as we noted in the Introduction, ARAIs never really caught on as a way of assessing violence risk prior to 1993, despite several valiant attempts by groups at the RAND Corporation (Chaiken & Chaiken, 1982; Greenwood, 1982), METFORS (Menzies, Webster, & Sepejak, 1985), and elsewhere. The success of the VRAG and ARAIs developed due to improved construction methods, such as the identification and inclusion of risk factors with good validity, and to improved validation methods, such as the use of large samples and careful follow-ups.

The strengths and limitations of the non-discretionary approach are directly opposite to those of UCJ. The non-discretionary approach yields violence risk assessments that have high transparency, moderate to high reliability, and moderate predictive validity, but at the same time, its reliance on fixed and restricted sets of risk factors means that it may be judged incomplete or inadequate for clinical and legal decision-making. In addition, its combinatoric algorithms are optimized for use in specific outcomes and in specific settings. This results in two major problems. First, the combinatoric algorithm is designed to work as well as possible 'on average' (i.e., across subjects) in the validation or construction sample. This means that it suffers in terms of individualization and flexibility. The algorithm cannot be changed or adapted to recognize the diversity or uniqueness of populations and settings, or people within populations or settings. Second, because they are optimized in their validation or construction samples, combinatoric algorithms are by definition non-optimal when used in new samples. This is sometimes referred to as 'shrinkage' upon cross-validation or calibration. Shrinkage is a problem that affects all optimized mathematical models. It has been discussed at length in the psychological literature more generally since the 1950s (see especially the classic review by Wiggins, 1973), and discussed more specifically with respect to violence risk since the 1980s (see especially Gottfredson & Gottfredson, 1988, and Gottfredson & Moriarty, 2006; for some illustrative empirical research, see Blair, Marcus, & Boccaccini, 2008).

This last point is worth discussing in more detail. Let us focus on ARAIs such as the VRAG as the primary instantiation of the non-discretionary approach to violence risk assessment. Regardless of whether they are developed using logic, experience tables, statistics, or some combination of the three, ARAIs make two strong assumptions. First, ARAIs assume that the individual risk factors included in the tests are individually necessary and jointly sufficient to make a good decision. A test that includes invalid factors or excludes valid factors is a fundamentally misspecified statistical model or representation of reality. Second, ARAIs assume that their combinatoric algorithms are stationary and ergodic – that is, consistent or generalizable across populations, settings, and time. Put differently, they assume that importance of and interaction among risk factors are unvarying. This is especially true for ARAIs that estimate the probability or absolute likelihood of future violence. Any violation of these assumptions means that ARAIs will yield results that are, at best, non-optimal, and, at worst, simply invalid.

Unfortunately, these two assumptions are clearly violated. Even those who develop or use ARAIs acknowledge that the tests are not comprehensive in content, and also that the risk factors and combinatoric algorithms change over time or across populations and settings. For example, the VRAG – the test responsible for the surge of interest in ARAIs that started in 1993 – recently underwent a major revision (Rice, Harris, & Lang, 2013). Cross-validation research in a large sample indicated that the predictive validity of the VRAG risk factors changed over time and, as a consequence, the original combinatoric algorithm was no longer optimal and the original estimates of the probability of future violence were no longer accurate. The developers therefore constructed a revised VRAG, or VRAG-R. The VRAG-R retains only six of the 12 items from the original VRAG, adds six new items, uses a completely new combinatoric algorithm, and makes completely different estimates of the probability of future violence. This is despite the fact that the VRAG-R was developed using a sample that incorporated the entire sample used to construct the original VRAG.

This revision raises some troubling questions. If we assume that the combinatoric algorithms that form the basis of ARAIs capture some important aspect of nature itself, as opposed to flawed human understanding of nature, then was the original VRAG simply 'wrong'? Is the new VRAG-R wrong? Or are both wrong? Did the world change sometime between the development of the original and revised versions? How long have evaluators been using the VRAG to make incorrect violence risk estimates, and thus how long have decision-makers relied unknowingly on incorrect information provided by evaluators? Should we review every case previously assessed using the VRAG to see if opinions regarding risk would change substantially using the VRAG-R? If the operating characteristics of the VRAG changed over time, will not the same be true for the VRAG-R? How will we reassure decision-makers that the information that we are giving them is correct, or at least useful even if not correct? When should work begin on a revised VRAG-R (VRAG-R-R)?

The problems with the VRAG and VRAG-R also plague other ARAIs. One of the first ARAIs developed specifically to assess risk for sexual violence was the four-item *Rapid Risk Assessment for Sexual Offense Recidivism* (RRASOR) (Hanson, 1997). Only 2 years later, the RRASOR's developer decided that the test was not optimal and joined forces with another ARAI author to publish a new hybrid test, the 10-item *Static-99* (Hanson & Thornton, 1999). However, the new test was also found to be problematic in some respects, resulting in some relatively minor elaboration and revision to the coding rules (Harris, Phenix, Hanson, & Thornton, 2003). This was followed by the publication of a major revision, the *Static-99R* (Hanson, Phenix, & Helmus, 2009), which also was subject to series of corrections, elaborations, and minor revisions (Phenix, Helmus, & Hanson, 2009, 2012a, 2012b). In parallel, the same group developed an alternative to the *Static-99* and *Static-99R*, called the *Static-2002* (Hanson & Thornton, 2003), but this was followed quickly by the publication of a major revision, the *Static-2002R* (Hanson et al., 2009) and another series of corrections, elaborations, and minor revisions (Phenix et al., 2009, 2012a, 2012b).

Even more changes are in the pipeline. Quite obviously, the RRASOR and its progeny (*Static-99, Static-99R, Static-2002, Static-2002R*) cannot be considered 'stationary', which makes the name 'Static' rather ironic.

The Structured Professional Judgement Approach

As discussed earlier, the SPJ approach is defined by the use of guidelines to systematize the exercise of discretion by evaluators. The guidelines may be considered evidence based because they are founded on a careful review of the relevant clinical, scientific, and legal literature. The guidelines may be considered comprehensive because they provide recommendations regarding the entire process of violence risk assessment – from how to collect information, to identifying the presence and relevance of risk factors, to developing plans and communicating final opinions. Finally, the guidelines may be considered management oriented because they include a strong focus on prevention of violence via planning.

The rationale underlying SPJ is that the complexity of violence risk assessment is best dealt with by developing decision-making aids to assist an expert evaluator. The decision-making aids are SPJ guidelines. They acknowledge that good practice must build on existing knowledge (theory, research, and opinion), yet at the same time they recognize the existing knowledge is inchoate, incomplete, and imperfect for making decisions about individual cases. SPJ guidelines provide some structure and systematization, while at the same time helping to tailor the assessment to the characteristics and context of the case at hand. SPJ guidelines are intended to support and build on the evaluator's education, training, experience, and intuition, rather than to replace the latter or minimize their role in violence risk assessments. Given their strong emphasis on systemic review of the scientific, professional, and legal literature to develop guidelines, the SPJ approach may be characterized as relying on *rational-legal authority*. In more contemporary terms, the SPJ approach to decision-making is *evidence based*, per the original and classic definitions by Sackett and colleagues (Sackett, Rosenberg, Gray, Haynes, & Richardson, 1996). In contrast, the actuarial approach, with its reliance on fixed algorithms and statistical profiles, is *empirically validated*. More extensive discussions of the distinction between evidence-based and empirically validated decision-making with respect to violence risk assessment can be found elsewhere (Hart, 2009; Hart & Logan, 2011).

SPJ guidelines may sound imposing, but they are designed to be succinct rather than encyclopaedic. They typically are published as a manual or small book, often with coil binding, something that is meant to be consulted frequently. To assist their day-to-day use, tools such as worksheets, rating sheets, and even software applications have been developed for use with them. These tools facilitate good documentation and communication. The English language versions of most SPJ guidelines are about 50–150 letter-sized pages in length, inclusive of table of contents, preface, references, samples of worksheets or rating sheets, and sample cases. This translates into about 15,000–40,000 words in the main body of the text, which provides an introduction to the guidelines, an overview of the development, an outline of the administration procedures, a definition of the basic risk factors, and, in some cases, a review of or referral to empirical evaluations. Many ARAIs are equivalent in length and complexity to corresponding SPJ guidelines, despite the fact that ARAIs generally include only half the number of risk factors and do not need to discuss topics such as determining the relevance of risk factors and formulation of violence risk or management plans. For example, the instructions for completing the Static-99-R and Static-2002-R are longer and more complex than those for the SVR-20 or RSVP.

The SPJ approach was developed to embody the best features and curb the excesses of both the UCJ and non-discretionary approaches. SPJ guidelines provide an organizational scheme that increases the transparency, reliability, and predictive validity of violence risk assessments without sacrificing their individualization and flexibility. But, the SPJ approach still has limitations, of course. First, like the UCJ approach, the SPJ approach assumes that evaluators have some basic level of competence. Merely giving evaluators a set of SPJ guidelines cannot overcome limitations in their knowledge, skill, or experience. Second, like the non-discretionary approach, the SPJ approach assumes that the content of evaluative devices (i.e., the procedural details, and most importantly the risk factors included) is optimal. Changes in knowledge about risk, and also changes in society itself, may require revisions to evaluative devices. As such, in contrast to ARAIs, revisions to SPJ guidelines occur primarily when the scientific research base indicates a revision is timely or warranted.

The SPJ approach to violence risk assessment was inspired by the work of Andrews, Bonta, and colleagues on the assessment of risk for general criminality (Andrews, 2012; Andrews & Bonta, 2006; Andrews et al., 1990). One of the most influential outcomes of that work was the development of a structured assessment tool, the *Level of Supervision Inventory* (Andrews, 1982), which has been renamed and revised over the years (e.g., Andrews & Bonta, 1995). In its most recent iteration, the *Level of Service – Case Management Inventory* (LS-CMI) (Andrews, Bonta, & Wormith, 2004) comprises 11 sections. Section 1 is the core of the LS-CMI. It contains 43 items that are summed to yield a numerical score reflecting risk for general criminality. The items were selected rationally, based on the Psychology of Criminal Conduct, also known as the General Personality and Cognitive Social Learning theoretical framework (PCC/GPCSL) (Andrews & Bonta, 2006). Sections 2–5 contain additional items that reflect factors relevant to risk assessment and management. Sections 6 and 7 are devoted to the interpretation of numerical scores from Section 1, using cut-off scores followed by discretionary adjustment. Sections 8–11 are used to recommend, implement, evaluate, and document case management strategies. Clearly, the LS-CMI is not a simple ARAI: Section 1 yields numerical scores, but these are interpreted and incorporated in decision-making in a manner that relies fundamentally on the evaluator's professional judgement.

Although inspired by the work of Andrews and colleagues, the SPJ approach differs from it in some important respects. The first is that SPJ guidelines conceptualize risk factors differently than does the LS-CMI. SPJ guidelines consider all information elements relevant to risk assessment and management to be risk factors, whereas the LS-CMI (following PCC/GPCSL) distinguishes (somewhat idiosyncratically) among risk, need, and responsivity factors. Second, various SPJ guidelines contain more factors related to specific forms of violence and to mental disorder associated with violence than does the LS-CMI. Third, SPJ guidelines do not include a procedural step in which risk factors are combined numerically for the purpose of interpretation, unlike the LS-CMI. Following Meehl, the SPJ approach assumes that it does not make much sense to calculate an actuarial estimate of risk and then adjust it using discretion, as the end result is pseudo-actuarial UCJ masquerading as an ARAI. These differences are the consequence of the fact that SPJ guidelines define risk more broadly than does the LS-CMI (i.e., not only in terms of the probability of violence, but also in terms of the nature, seriousness, imminence, and frequency of future violence, which are difficult to conceptualize in numerical terms), in addition to the fact that the SPJ approach focuses specifically on violence, rather than on general criminality, and therefore is not based explicitly on the PCC/GPCSL theoretical framework.

Advances in the SPJ Approach

In the early years, most of the effort in developing SPJ guidelines focused on identifying general principles for gathering information, a set of risk factors whose presence was to be determined based on the information gathered, and a simple scheme for making summary ratings of overall risk. Most of the effort in drafting the guidelines was devoted to the definition of the risk factors and a summary of the justification for their inclusion. Most of the effort in training evaluators to use the guidelines was devoted to convincing them that systematic consideration of risk factors would provide a solid foundation for the exercise of professional discretion, and would not limit their ability to consider, weight, and incorporate additional information. Most of the effort in writing the guidelines was devoted to the definition of the risk factors and a summary of the justification for their inclusion. Most of the effort in validating guidelines was devoted to evaluating the extent to which risk factors and overall judgements of risk could be coded reliably and were predictive of future violence, including the extent to which changes in risk factors are associated with changes in the likelihood of future violence. Things have changed considerably since that time.

Development of SPJ Guidelines

As we discussed previously, violence risk assessment may be conceptualized as comprising a number of steps: gathering information, identifying the presence of risk factors, considering the relevance of risk factors that are present, developing a formulation of violence risk based on the relevant risk factors, identifying scenarios of future violence based on formulation of violence risk, developing plans for risk management based on scenarios, and then communicating summary judgements of violence risk. However, the structure in early SPJ guidelines was limited primarily to the first two steps and the last step. The middle steps were a kind of 'black box' that evaluators had to figure out on their own.

Why ignore the middle steps? There were two major reasons. First, some evaluators were sceptical of imposing any structure on the process of violence risk assessment. It was difficult to convince them even to consider routinely the presence of a set of basic risk factors. Introducing too much structure, too quickly, might have resulted in complete rejection of SPJ guidelines. Second, it was not clear how best to structure the middle steps. Although systematic review of the scientific, professional, and legal literature provided a good means of identifying basic risk factors, it did not help to make sense of the black box.

After some years of experience in the use of SPJ guidelines and their implementation in various applied settings around the world, developers turned their attention to the middle steps. Starting in the late 1990s, we began to consider the difficulties inherent in and experiment with ways of integrating complex information about individual cases to make decisions about future action. This involved a task analysis of violence risk assessment – reflection about and discussion of what evaluators typically do in practice. It also involved a review of research on decision-making and planning more generally. The end result was the incorporation of methods for formulation (case conceptualization) of violence risk from the literature on abductive reasoning, and also methods for developing case management strategies based on the scenario planning literature. The formulation and scenario planning methods were retrofitted to existing SPJ guidelines via 'add-on' worksheets, starting with the HCR-20 Version 2 in 1998, and incorporated explicitly into new SPJ guidelines, starting with the RSVP in 2003. Most SPJ guidelines published since 2003 incorporate at least some elements of formulation and scenario planning.

Formulation. There are many different techniques that can be used for the formulation of violence risk. They can be grouped loosely into two categories. Naïve or atheoretical techniques do not make a priori assumptions about causal mechanisms underlying violence or the causal roles played by risk factors. Instead of imposing meaning on the case, evaluators let the meaning emerge from their analysis of the case. This may be done using a graphical technique, in which risk factors are written on a whiteboard, grouped into conceptual clusters, and then linked using arrows whose heads indicate the direction of causal influences among clusters. This approach was inspired by the graphical approach to modelling and analysing causality developed by Pearl (2009). Alternatively, evaluators may use an abbreviated version of Root Cause Analysis, in which proximal causes are traced back to distal causes. Root Cause Analysis is widely used in fields such as accident investigation, engineering, and medicine to help understand the origin of problems in individual cases.

Theoretical techniques can also be used for formulation. This involves analysing the case with a particular conceptual model or lens. A number of such models or lenses exist, including the General Personality Cognitive and Social Learning model, Offence Paralleling Behaviour, Good Lives, biopsychosocial, psychodynamic, and so forth (for a review and discussion, see Hart & Logan, 2011). One model that is particularly well suited to the SPJ approach is Decision Theory or Action Theory. According to this model, violence, like all other voluntary behaviour, is the result of a decision-making process that involves movement from goal to intent to action. Action Theory assumes that people are agents who make rational choices – but rational only in the limited sense of involving thought, not as in the sense of being logically correct. Indeed, Action Theory assumes that a variety of factors impinge on or influence a person's decision-making processes, often resulting in bad choices (i.e., those with non-optimal or maladaptive outcomes) or choices made badly (i.e., in a disorganized or incoherent manner). The foundations of Action Theory are well accepted in fields such as philosophy, law, economics, and cognitive neuroscience; in psychology and criminology, it has given birth to a number of variants, such as the Theories of Reasoned Action and Planned Behaviour, Control Theory, Strain Theory, Situational Action Theory, Routine Activity Theory, and I3 Theory.

Viewed through the lens of Action Theory, violence risk assessment is the process of understanding risk factors that motivated, disinhibited, or destabilized decisions about violence. Motivators increase the likelihood that people will consider violence as a potential response in a given situation, or increase the perceived potential benefits or positive consequences of violence. Disinhibitors decrease the likelihood that people will inhibit or self-censor thoughts of violence as a potential response in a given situation, or decrease the perceived potential costs or negative consequences of violence. Destabilizers generally disrupt, disturb, or disorganize the decision-making process, making it difficult for people accurately to perceive and appreciate situational dues, consider alternatives, or weigh potential costs and benefits. Further discussion of formulation using Action Theory can be found elsewhere (e.g., Hart & Logan, 2011).

Both atheoretical and theoretical approaches to formulation have their strengths and weaknesses. The former can sometimes feel more liberating, unencumbered by theoretical baggage, but at the same time can be inefficient or leave the evaluator feeling lost. The latter can feel more simple and straightforward, although it can also feel Procrustean or restrictive.

Scenario planning. Formulation is focused on the past, and then uses any insights gained to understand possible futures. Scenario planning, in contrast, is focused squarely on the future, although mindful of the past.

Scenario planning is a method of planning that was designed for use in situations of unbounded uncertainty, situations in which 'unknown unknowns' abound. Originally developed by military planners, it was subsequently adapted and adopted for use in areas as diverse as business, emergency preparedness, and public safety. It is based on the assumption that plausible scenarios – brief accounts of possible futures, informed or educated by knowledge and experience – are essential to developing sensible and detailed plans to achieve desired outcomes and avoid undesired outcomes. Put simply, the stories that we construct about how violence might occur are the same stories that will help us prevent violence. But we cannot figure out how best to prevent it – that is, the future violence that a person might perpetrate – unless we know what 'it' is.

It is common in scenario planning to develop a reasonably brief set of scenarios, perhaps two or three up to about five or six, that seem realistic and represent a range of outcomes, including both 'best-case' and 'worst-case' scenarios. This helps to avoid tunnel vision. Implausible scenarios, those that are unrealistic, are 'pruned' and not considered further. The plausible scenarios are detailed and used for planning. In the context of violence risk assessment, we have recommended that evaluators consider, at a minimum, repeat, escalation, twist, and desistence scenarios. Repeat scenarios are those in which people commit any of the kinds of violence they perpetrated in the past. Escalation scenarios are those in which people's violence escalates in severity to lethal or life-threatening harm. Twist scenarios are those in which people's violence changes in nature – for example, their motivation, modus operandi, or victim selection changes. Finally, desistence scenarios are those in which people stop perpetrating violence. This is, in many respects, the most important scenario, as it is the ultimate goal of violence risk assessment and management: effective prevention of violence. It is what we are trying to accomplish. The other scenarios are reasonably foreseeable obstacles to achieving desistence, adverse outcomes that must be avoided if we wish to reach our preferred future.

Each scenario that we entertain must be outlined in some detail. We must ask ourselves, what kind of violence am I worried that the person might commit? What will he do, to whom, and why? What might be the psychological or physical harm suffered by others? Where and when is he likely to perpetrate such violence? Is the risk acute in nature, limited to certain times or situations, or is it chronic? How certain or confident am I that this kind of violence might actually occur? The process of answering these questions allows us to use narrative cognition to evaluate the plausibility of the scenario in the light of what we know about violence and people in general, and more specifically about the person we are evaluating and his or her history of violence. We must remember that all scenarios, as stories of a future that has not yet and may never occur, are fictional. The goal is not to predict what will happen, but rather to consider systematically what might happen. For evaluators, scenario planning may be considered a form of thought experiment or *Gedankenspiel* about what kinds of violence a person might perpetrate in the future, a way to do one's mental 'due diligence' with respect to violence risk.

Practised in this way, scenario planning relies heavily on affective risk analysis. It mines the instincts or intuitions of evaluators. Some of our concerns are so vague or unrealistic that plausible scenarios cannot be constructed for them, and they become irrelevant for developing risk management plans. However, other concerns are highly plausible and realistic, and they become the primary focus of our plans. Put simply, when we try to put our fears into words, some cannot withstand scrutiny and are easily put aside, whereas others survive and are transformed from fears into practical, potentially soluble problems.

There is an art to developing scenarios. For example, they should not be too specific or detailed. We should ask, could this type of violence occur in a different way, or with a different outcome, or under different circumstances? If so, we can broaden one scenario to encompass several variations on a single theme. Also, we should avoid generating too many scenarios, else case management planning is cumbersome. We start by considering our greatest fear or concern, then consider the next largest, and so forth. At some point, the remaining fears or concerns are relatively minor and, in this respect, more or less indistinguishable. There is no need to proceed further. Good plans are focused on primary hazards; it is impossible to develop plans that take into account every possible outcome. Although artful, scenarios developed in this way should not be perceived by others as fantasy or wild speculation, but rather as descriptions of negative outcomes that are plausible or reasonable in the light of general knowledge, professional experience, and the facts of the case at hand.

The development of risk management plans is facilitated greatly by the formulation of violence risk and the identification of plausible, optimally detailed scenarios. Evaluators use them, together with their understanding of local circumstances, to identify potentially effective management strategies. These strategies can be grouped into four major categories. *Monitoring* strategies are intended to provide feedback about the status of critical risk factors and the effectiveness of the management plans. *Supervision* strategies are intended to make it more difficult for people to commit violence by restricting their rights and freedoms (e.g., of residence, association, movement, activity, and so forth). *Treatment* strategies are intended to remediate deficits in people's psychological or social functioning that may be functionally related to risk. *Victim safety planning* strategies are intended to enhance the internal and external security resources of identifiable potential targets of violence, helping them better to avoid or withstand violence. The strategies in each of these categories should be targeted at critical risk factors (i.e., those that figure prominently in formulating violence risk); each critical risk factor should be addressed by one or more strategies, and each strategy should address one or critical risk factors.

But, identifying potential effective strategies is only the start of developing good plans. Next, strategies must be translated into tactics, specific activities to achieve objectives. Finally, tactics must be supported by logistics – activities that support the implementation and coordination of tactics.

For example, a strategy for managing a sexual offender's risk might be, 'sex offender treatment programming to change negative attitudes toward women'. From a tactical perspective, the next step is to identify treatment programmes that are available, accessible, appropriate, affordable, and acceptable. From a logistical perspective, the final step is to determine whether any of these treatment programmes has a space available and is willing to accept the person in question, how to ensure that the person is able to get to and from the treatment programme safely, and so forth. Evaluators should keep in mind that every strategy with the potential to reduce risk also has the potential to enhance risk, if implemented thoughtlessly. Medicine administered improperly may become a poison.

Implementation. Another major advance in the SPJ approach to risk assessment is with respect to implementation. It is one thing to create SPJ guidelines and demonstrate that they can be used reliably and validly under controlled conditions, but it is quite another to make sure they can be done so in routine practice. This is the critical distinction between effectiveness and efficacy.

SPJ guidelines are all constructed for use in field settings by diverse professionals. Not surprisingly, then, considerable efforts were made to ensure that they are acceptable to and easily used by professionals, and research has evaluated the extent to which these efforts yielded success. The research has taken many different forms: surveys and focus groups to evaluate usage and consumer satisfaction (e.g., Crocker et al., 2011); small- to large-scale empirical studies to evaluate interrater reliability (e.g., Douglas & Belfrage, 2014; Vincent, Guy, Fusco, & Gershenson, 2011), content validity, concurrent validity, and predictive validity (see Douglas et al., 2014); case studies to evaluate practical relevance (e.g., Guy, Packer, & Warnken, 2012); and empirical studies to evaluate the extent to which training improves buy-in and adoption (e.g., Vincent, Guy, Gershenson, & McCabe 2012), administration and interpretation (e.g., Storey, Gibas, Reeves, & Hart, 2011), and development of individualized risk management plans (e.g., Belfrage et al., 2012).

It is tempting to summarize the results of this research as 'promising' insofar as most of it dictates that SPJ guidelines can and are used effectively in a wide range of field settings. It is perhaps more important, however, to emphasize that research of this sort is crucial for any tool. It is the detailed findings, not the simple summaries, that are most important and will help both developers and users to maximize the efficacy of SPJ guidelines.

Current Status of the SPJ Approach

International surveys of practitioners (Singh et al., 2014; Viljoen, McLachlan, & Vincent, 2010) and reviews of case law in Canada and the United States (Storey, Campbell, & Hart, 2013; Vitacco, Erickson, Kurus, & Apple, 2012) indicate that SPJ guidelines are used widely and accepted routinely in evidence in courts of law and quasi-judicial proceedings. Indeed, the categorical, contextual manner in which information about future risk is communicated using the SPJ approach is well received by judges and other triers of fact, and typically is preferred to absolute, numeric, probabilistic estimates (Kwartner, Lyons, & Boccaccini, 2006). Formal workshops on the SPJ approach and various SPJ guidelines have been delivered on every continent except Antarctica.

A solid empirical foundation underlies this widespread application of the SPJ model. Well over 400 evaluations of SPJ guidelines have been published or otherwise disseminated, including research showing good interrater reliability and predictive validity (Otto & Douglas, 2010).

Research has compared the SPJ approach with the alternative, actuarial, approach. Meta-analyses examining effect sizes for actuarial measures and SPJ guidelines indicate that, on average, the predictive validity for the two approaches is similar and of moderate magnitude, even when SPJ tools are used numerically (for a recent review, see Guy et al., 2015). Meta-analysis of a subset of studies in which an actuarial and a SPJ measure were evaluated using the same sample confirmed this finding (Guy, 2008).

Although the HCR-20 is the best researched of the SPJ guidelines, the association between summary risk ratings and violence has been investigated for many other SPJ guidelines. Among the 34 published disseminations in which this question was posed, comprising samples from Europe, the United Kingdom, and North America, strong support for the predictive validity of the tool was reported in approximately 90% of cases. Moreover, in almost all studies in which the predictive validity of the summary risk rating was compared with a numeric use of the tool (by applying numbers to items' categorical ratings and summing to yield a total score), incremental predicative validity for the former was observed relative to the latter (see Douglas, Hart, Groscup, & Litwack, 2013).

Relatively less research has been undertaken on the newer additions to the SPJ approach: ratings of the individual relevance of items, formulation, scenario planning, and risk management activities. For example, relevance ratings are intended to bridge the divide between nomothetic and idiographic approaches to and applications of risk assessment. Preliminary evaluation of the validity of relevance ratings using HCR-20[V3] showed incremental postdictive validity over presence ratings (Blanchard & Douglas, 2011), although in a subsequent prospective study relevance ratings did not add incrementally to presence ratings (Strub, Douglas, & Nicholls, 2014). In two studies in which the reliability of relevance ratings was examined (Douglas & Belfrage, 2014;

Hart et al., 2003), agreement overall was good using the using the RSVP and HCR-20^{V3}. Although respectable reliability should be demonstrated for relevance ratings, in general we expect agreement indices to be relatively lower than those for presence ratings, which are intended to reflect an objective summary of the information available about a risk factor. In contrast, because relevance ratings are intended to inform formulation, scenario planning, and risk management, they purposefully allow for a greater degree of subjectivity. For instance, evaluators may place different weights on certain risk factors depending on the theoretical and conceptual model of formulation they follow. Or, reflecting an equifinal process, two root cause analyses may identify a similar root cause but place different weights or relevance on risk factors operating in the problem fault sequence.

Researchers only recently have begun to evaluate the influence of using an SPJ guideline on the quality of risk management plans and their impact on recidivism. For example, studying the development of case plans for juvenile probationers, office-wide adoption of the *Structured Assessment of Violence Risk in Youth* (SAVRY) (Borum, Bartel, & Forth, 2006) was related to inclusion of a greater number of relevant risk factors compared with practice prior to its adoption, and youth at relatively higher risk received more service referrals than youth rated as being at lower risk for violence (Vincent et al., 2012). In a study of police in Sweden, adoption of the *Brief Spousal Assault Form for the Evaluation of Risk* (B-SAFER) (Kropp, Hart, & Belfrage, 2005, 2010) was associated with the use of a greater number of protective actions with high-risk intimate partner offenders, including high-level actions such as initiating a no-contact order or personal alarm system; the reduction in recidivism was relatively greater among individuals rated as being at high risk compared with those at lower risk for intimate partner violence (Belfrage & Strand, 2012).

Research on formulation and scenario planning is nascent, but attracting considerable interest. Three studies using the RSVP have yielded preliminary support for the utility of these steps (Darjee et al., 2016; Sutherland et al., 2012; Wilson, 2013). These are just two of the many cutting-edge topics that will dominate the upcoming SPJ research agenda, even further advancing the utility of the approach for violence prevention fieldwork. It is towards such exciting prospects that we turn next.

The Future of SPJ

Technology

From the inception of the SPJ model, violence risk assessment guidelines were intended to be integrated into existing professional practice. Innovations in technology, increasing demands on scare resources, and expectations for data-driven performance benchmarks in larger organizations have changed expectations regarding the ways in which those practices can or should occur. Electronic systems that will dramatically enhance the 'user experience' of SPJ guidelines are in development. Fillable worksheets for many guidelines exist already in Portable Document Format. In the near future, evaluators will be able to use an electronic interface on a computer, tablet, or smartphone to collate data pertinent to individual risk assessments. The software will provide prompts to evaluators regarding questions or issues they ought to have considered with respect to formulation, scenario planning, and risk management recommendations. The technology will aid the development of risk management plans that are comprehensive in terms of their consideration of strategies, tactics, and logistics by, for example, integrating with a data system that provides information about locally available interventions categorized by the risk domain they address and intensity of service provision. Report-writing aides will be facilitated by integration with the case-specific data to ensure that all vital components of a report are included, individualized for that particular evaluee.

In addition to the use of technology to improve the procedures followed for assessing and managing risk, other benefits offered by the use of such technology include ease of data collection to facilitate programme evaluation to, for example, monitor risk profiles of the population served, monitor changes in risk profiles for individuals or groups as a function of risk management activities, identify gaps in available services for frequently identified risk domains, and so on. Of course, data collection of this sort also would facilitate research endeavours.

Research

The horizon is wide with respect to the scope of research needed to advance the SPJ approach further. As noted above, research on the 'middle steps' in the administration process – formulation and scenario planning – is needed. What approaches to formulation are most fruitful, and under what circumstances for which types of professionals? Do formulations add value in terms of the quality and effectiveness of risk management, compared with the absence of formulation? Do they result in a reduction of risk? What types of scenarios – repeat, twist, escalation, or desistance – are most commonly relied upon? To what extent and in what ways are such scenarios valid, in that they are more likely to occur in the future relative to scenarios that were not identified? Do scenarios facilitate the development of risk management planning? Research on formulation and scenario planning should extend beyond reliability and validity, but also acceptability of these practices among practitioners engaging in them and consumers receiving them, such as judges and other triers of fact, administrators of agencies, and other end users of risk assessment reports.

Consideration of individual strengths or factors has long been part of the SPJ approach, with some guidelines such as the SAVRY, *Structured Assessment of Protective Factors* (SAPROF) (de Vogel, de Ruiter, Bouman, & de Vries Robbé, 2012), and *Short-Term Assessment of Risk and Treatability* (START) (Webster, Martin, Brink, Nicholls, & Desmarais, 2009) incorporating them explicitly into ratings schemes, and others such as the HCR-20^{V3} incorporating them less explicitly into presence ratings of risk factors and in the formulation, scenario planning, and risk management stages. Research generally supports the association between the presence of protective factors and reduced violence (e.g., Desmarais, Nicholls, Wilson, & Brink, 2012), but much work remains to be done on this important topic in terms of clarifying how protective factors are conceptualized generally and defined specifically in guidelines. For instance, do protective factors lie on a continuum with risk factors? Or are they separate constructs? Should they exert a main effect or an interaction effect, and does that matter for assessment and management?

Although some empirical investigation of the impact on the quality of risk management plans following implementation of SPJ guidelines has been undertaken (e.g., Storey, Kropp, Hart, Belfrage & Strand, 2014), more is needed to understand better the critical link between assessment of violence risk and management of that risk. Do the guidelines increase the quality of risk management plans, both in terms of appropriate coverage of risk domains relevant for the particular person, in addition to being commensurate with the assessed level of risk? Further research on the important concept of 'dynamic' validity is relevant here. Are changes (hopefully reductions) in the evaluee's level of risk, perhaps resulting from intervention or merely the passage of time, associated with changes in subsequent violence?

Most SPJ guidelines include several types of summary risk ratings (SRR) to facilitate risk communication, and more evaluation of them is needed. What is the reliability and validity of these more sophisticated types of global ratings that address, for example, lethal or near-lethal versus less severe acts of violence, imminent versus longer-term violence, etc.? As reviewed above, research has shown that basic SRRs add incremental predictive validity over the numeric use of guidelines. However, exactly *why* this is so remains unknown. Research investigating, for example, the role of relevance ratings and the degree to which the structure provided by the guidelines may facilitate idiographic optimization of nomothetic data needs further inquiry.

Development of SPJ Guidelines for Adolescents and Young Adults

Several SPJ guidelines have been developed to evaluate risk for violence among children, such as the *Early Assessment Risk List* tools (see Augimeri, Koegl, Webster, & Levene, 2001; Levene et al., 2001), and teenagers, such as the *Estimate of Risk Adolescent Sexual Offense Recidivism* (ERASOR) (Worling & Curwen, 2001), *SAVRY*, and *Short-Term Assessment of Risk and Treatability: Adolescent Version* (START:AV) (Viljoen, Nicholls, Cruise, Desmarais, & Webster, 2014). Given the peak in perpetration of crime and violence among older teenagers and people in their early 20s, and also the unique developmental influences at play during these ages compared with adults (e.g., Steinberg, 2009), guidelines for assessing and managing risk among this 'transition age' population are in development. The need for the development of guidelines to assess specific forms of violence (stalking, bullying, domestic violence, etc.) among adolescents is also being explored.

References

Andrews, D. A. (1982). *The Level of Supervision Inventory (LSI): The first follow-up*. Toronto, Canada: Ontario Ministry of Correctional Services.

Andrews, D. A. (2012). The risk–need–responsivity (RNR) model of correctional assessment and treatment. In J. A. Dvoskin, J. L. Skeem, R. W. Novaco, & K. S. Douglas (Eds.), *Using social science to reduce violent offending* (pp. 127–156). New York, NY: Oxford University Press.

Andrews, D. A., & Bonta, J. (1995). *Level of Service Inventory – Revised*. Toronto, Canada: Multi-Health Systems.

Andrews, D. A., & Bonta, J. (2006). *The psychology of criminal conduct* (4th ed.). Cincinnati, OH: Anderson.

Andrews, D. A., Bonta, J., & Hoge, R. D. (1990). Classification for effective rehabilitation: Rediscovering psychology. *Criminal Justice and Behavior, 17*, 19–52.

Andrews, D. A., Bonta, J., & Wormith, S. J. (2004). *The Level of Service/Case Management Inventory (LS/CMI)*. Toronto, Canada: Multi-Health Systems.

Augimeri, L. K., Koegl, C. J., Webster, C. D., & Levene, K. S. (2001). *Early Assessment Risk Lists for Boys: Version 2*. Toronto, Canada: Earlscourt Child and Family Centre.

Belfrage, H., & Strand, S. (2012). Measuring the outcome of structured spousal violence risk assessments using the B-SAFER : Risk in relation to recidivism and intervention. *Behavioral Sciences & the Law, 30*, 420–430.

Belfrage, H., Strand, S., Storey, J. E., Gibas, A. L., Kropp, P. R., & Hart, S. D. (2012). Assessment and management of risk for intimate partner violence by police officers using the Spousal Assault Risk Assessment Guide. *Law and Human Behavior, 36*, 60–67.

Blair, P. R., Marcus, D. K., & Boccaccini, M. T. (2008). Is there an allegiance effect for assessment instruments? Actuarial risk assessment as an exemplar. *Clinical Psychology: Science and Practice, 15*, 346–360.

Blanchard, A. J. E., & Douglas, K. S. (2011). *The Historical, Clinical, Risk-Management Version 3: The inclusion of idiographic relevance ratings in violence risk assessment*. Poster presented at the Annual Conference of the American Psychology-Law Society, Miami, FL.

Boer, D. P., Hart, S. D., Kropp, P. R., & Webster, C. D. (1997). *Sexual Violence Risk-20*. Burnaby, Canada: Mental Health, Law, & Policy Institute, Simon Fraser University.

Boer, D. P., Hart, S. D., Kropp, P. R., & Webster, C. D. (2015). *Sexual Violence Risk-20, Version 2*. Burnaby, Canada: Mental Health, Law, & Policy Institute, Simon Fraser University.

Borum, R., Bartel, P., & Forth, A. (2006). *Manual for the Structured Assessment of Violence Risk in Youth (SAVRY)*. Tampa, FL: University of South Florida, Louis de la Parte Florida Mental Health Institute.

Chaiken, J. M., & Chaiken, M. R. (1982). *Varieties of criminal behavior*, R-2814-NIJ. Santa Monica, CA: Rand.

Crocker, A. G., Braithwaite, E., Laferrière, D., Gagnon, D., Venegas, C., & Jenkins, T. (2011). START changing practice: Implementing a risk assessment and management tool in a civil psychiatric setting. *The International Journal of Forensic Mental Health, 10*, 13–28. doi:10.1080/14999013.2011.553146

Darjee, R., Russell, K., Forrest, L., Milton, E., Savoie, V., Baron, E., Kirkland, J., & Stobie, S. (2016). A real world study of the reliability, validity and utility of a structured professional judgement instrument in the assessment and management of sexual offenders in South East Scotland. Paisley, Scotland: Risk Management Authority. Available at: http://www.rmascotland.gov.uk/files/7814/5311/6043/Risk_for_Sexual_Violence_Protocol_-_RSVP.pdf.

Dawes, R. M., Faust, D., & Meehl, P. E. (1989). Clinical versus actuarial judgment. *Science, 243*, 1668–1674.

de Vogel, V., de Ruiter, C., Bouman, Y., & de Vries Robbé, M. (2012). *SAPROF. Guidelines for the assessment of protective factors for violence risk* (2nd ed.). Utrecht, The Netherlands: Forum Educatief.

Desmarais, S. L., Nicholls, T., Wilson, C. M., & Brink, J. (2012). Reliability and validity of the Short-Term Assessment of Risk and Treatability (START) in assessing risk for inpatient aggression. *Psychological Assessment, 24*, 685–700.

Douglas, K. S., & Belfrage, H. (2014). Interrater reliability and concurrent validity of the HCR-20 Version 3. *International Journal of Forensic Mental Health, 13*, 130–139.

Douglas, K. S., Hart, S. D., Groscup, J. L., & Litwack, T. R. (2013). Assessing violence risk. In I. B. Weiner & R. K. Otto (Eds.), *The handbook of forensic psychology* (4th ed., pp. 385–442). Hoboken, NJ: John Wiley & Sons, Inc.

Douglas, K. S., Hart, S. D., Webster, C. D., & Belfrage, H. (2013). *HCR-20 Version 3: Assessing risk of violence – User guide*. Burnaby, Canada: Mental Health, Law, and Policy Institute, Simon Fraser University.

Douglas, K. S., Shaffer, C., Blanchard, A., Guy, L. S., Reeves, K., & Weir, J. (2014). *HCR-20 violence risk assessment scheme: Overview and annotated bibliography*. HCR-20 Violence Risk Assessment White Paper Series, No. 1. Burnaby, Canada: Mental Health, Law, and Policy Institute, Simon Fraser University. Retrieved from http://kdouglas.files.wordpress.com/2014/01/hcr-20-annotated-bibliography-version-12-january-20142.pdf

Faust, D., & Ziskin, J. (1988). The expert witness in psychology and psychiatry. *Science, 241*, 31–35.

Glueck, S., & Glueck, A. (1950). *Unraveling juvenile justice*. Cambridge, MA: Harvard University Press.

Gottfredson, S. D., & Gottfredson, D. M. (1988). Violence prediction methods: Statistical and clinical strategies. *Violence and Victims, 3*, 303–324.

Gottfredson, S. D., & Moriarty, L. J. (2006). Statistical risk assessment: Old problems and new applications. *Crime & Delinquency, 52*, 178–200.

Greenwood, P. W. (1982). *Selective incapacitation*. Santa Monica, CA: Rand.

Grove, W. M., & Meehl, P. E. (1996). Comparative efficiency of informal (subjective, impressionistic) and formal (mechanical, algorithmic) prediction procedures: The clinical–statistical controversy. *Psychology, Public Policy, and Law, 2*, 293–323.

Guy, L. S. (2008). *Performance indicators of the structured professional judgement approach for assessing risk for violence to others: A meta-analytic survey* (Unpublished doctoral dissertation). Department of Psychology, Simon Fraser University, Burnaby, Canada.

Guy, L. S., Douglas, K. S., & Hart, S. D. (2015). Risk assessment and communication. In B. Cutler & P. Zapf (Eds.), *APA handbook of forensic psychology: Vol. 1. Individual and situational influences in criminal and civil contexts* (pp. 35–86). Washington, DC: American Psychological Association.

Guy, L. S., Packer, I. K., & Warnken, W. (2012). Assessing risk of violence using structured professional guidelines, *Journal of Forensic Psychology Practice, 12*, 270–283.

Hanson, R. K. (1997). *The development of a brief actuarial scale for sexual offense recidivism* (User Report 1997-04). Ottawa, Canada: Department of the Solicitor General of Canada.

Hanson, R. K., & Thornton, D. (1999). *Static-99: Improving actuarial risk assessments for sex offenders* (User Report 1999-02). Ottawa, Canada: Department of the Solicitor General of Canada.

Hanson, R. K., & Thornton, D. (2003). *Notes on the development of Static-2002* (User Report 2003-01). Ottawa, Canada: Department of the Solicitor General of Canada.

Hanson, R. K., Phenix, A., & Helmus, L. (2009, September). *Static-99(R) and Static-2002(R): How to interpret and report in light of recent research*. Paper presented at the 28th Annual Research and Treatment Conference of the Association for the Treatment of Sexual Abusers, Dallas, TX.

Harcourt, B. E. (2007). *Against prediction: Punishing and policing in an actuarial age*. Chicago, IL: University of Chicago Press.

Hare, R. (1991). *The Hare Psychopathy Checklist – Revised*. Toronto, Canada: Multi-Health Systems.

Hare, R. D. (2003). *The Revised Psychopathy Checklist*. Toronto, Canada: Multi-Health Systems.

Harris, A. J. R., Phenix, A., Hanson, R. K., & Thornton, D. (2003). *Static-99 coding rules: Revised 2003*. Ottawa, Canada: Solicitor General Canada.

Harris, G., Rice, M., & Quinsey, V. (1993). Violent recidivism of mentally disordered offenders: The development of a statistical prediction instrument. *Criminal Justice and Behavior, 20,* 315–335.

Harris, G. T., Rice, M. E., Quinsey, V. L., & Cormier, C. A. (2016). *Violent offenders: Appraising and managing risk* (3rd ed.). Washington, DC: American Psychological Association.

Hart, S. D. (2001). Assessing and managing violence risk. In K. Douglas, C. Webster, S. Hart, D. Eaves, & J. Ogloff (Eds.), *HCR-20 violence risk management companion guide* (pp. 13–25). Burnaby, Canada: Mental Health, Law, & Policy Institute, Simon Fraser University, and Tampa, FL: Department of Mental Health Law and Policy, Florida Mental Health Institute, University of South Florida.

Hart, S. D. (2009). Evidence-based assessment of risk for sexual violence. *Chapman Journal of Criminal Justice, 1,* 143–165.

Hart, S. D., Kropp, P. R., Laws, D. R., Klaver, J., Logan, C., & Watt, K. A. (2003). *The Risk for Sexual Violence Protocol (RSVP): Structured professional guidelines for assessing risk of sexual violence.* Burnaby, Canada: Mental Health, Law, and Policy Institute, Simon Fraser University.

Hart, S. D., & Logan, C. (2011). Formulation of violence risk using evidence-based assessments: The structured professional judgment approach. In P. Sturmey & M. McMurran (Eds.), *Forensic case formulation* (pp. 83–106). Chichester, England: John Wiley & Sons, Ltd.

Heilbrun, K. (1997). Prediction versus management models relevant to risk assessment: The importance of legal decision-making context. *Law and Human Behavior, 21,* 347–359.

Kropp, P. R., Hart, S. D., & Belfrage, H. (2005). *Brief Spousal Assault Form for the Evaluation of Risk (B-SAFER): User manual.* Vancouver, Canada: ProActive ReSolutions.

Kropp, P. R., Hart, S. D., & Belfrage, H. (2010). *Brief Spousal Assault Form for the Evaluation of Risk (B-SAFER): User manual, Version 2.* Vancouver, Canada: ProActive ReSolutions.

Kropp, P. R., Hart, S. D., Webster, C. D., & Eaves, D. (1994). *Manual for the Spousal Assault Risk Assessment Guide.* Vancouver, Canada: British Columbia Institute on Family Violence.

Kropp, P. R., Hart, S. D., Webster, C. D., & Eaves, D. (1995). *Manual for the Spousal Assault Risk Assessment Guide* (2nd ed.). Vancouver, Canada: British Columbia Institute on Family Violence.

Kropp, P. R., Hart, S. D., Webster, C. D., & Eaves, D. (2015). *Manual for the Spousal Assault Risk Assessment Guide* (3rd ed.). Vancouver, Canada: ProActive ReSolutions Inc.

Kwartner, P. P., Lyons, P. M., &, Boccaccini, M. T. (2006). Judges' risk communication preferences in risk for future violence cases. *International Journal of Forensic Mental Health, 5,* 185–194.

Levene, K. S., Augimeri, L. K., Pepler, D., Walsh, M. M., Webster, C. D., & Koegl, C. J. (2001). *Early Assessment Risk Lists for Girls: Consultation Version.* Toronto, Canada: Earlscourt Child and Family Centre.

Meehl, P. E. (1954). *Clinical versus statistical prediction: A theoretical analysis and review of the evidence.* Minneapolis, MN: University of Minneapolis Press.

Menzies, R., Webster, C. D., & Hart, S. D. (1995). Observations on the rise of risk in psychology and law. In B. Gillies & G. James (Eds.), *Proceedings of the Fifth Symposium on Violence and Aggression* (pp. 91–107). Saskatoon, Canada: University Extension Press, University of Saskatchewan.

Menzies, R. J., Webster, C. D., & Sepejak, D. S. (1985). The dimensions of dangerousness: Evaluating the accuracy of psychometric predictions of violence among forensic patients. *Law and Human Behavior, 9,* 49–70.

Monahan, J. (1995). *The clinical prediction of violent behavior.* Northvale, NJ: Jason Aronson. (Original work published 1981).

Otto, R. K. (2000). Assessing and managing violence risk in outpatient settings. *Journal of Clinical Psychology, 56,* 1239–1262.

Otto, R. K., & K. S. Douglas (Eds.), (2010). *Handbook of violence risk assessment.* Milton Park, UK: Routledge.

Pearl, J. (2009). *Causality: Models, reasoning, and inference* (2nd ed.). Cambridge, England: Cambridge University Press.

Phenix, A., Helmus, L., & Hanson, R. K. (2009). *Static-99R evaluator's workbook.* Retrieved from http://www.static99.org

Phenix, A., Helmus, L., & Hanson, R. K. (2012a). *Static-99R and Static-2002R evaluators' workbook.* Retrieved from http://www.static99.org

Phenix, A., Helmus, L., & Hanson, R. K. (2012b). *Static-99R and Static-2002R evaluators' workbook, revised.* Retrieved from http://www.static99.org

Quinsey, V., Harris, G., Rice, M., & Cormier, C. (1998). *Violent offenders: Appraising and managing risk.* Washington, DC: American Psychological Association.

Quinsey, V., Harris, G., Rice, M., & Cormier, C. (2006). *Violent offenders: Appraising and managing risk* (2nd ed.). Washington, DC: American Psychological Association.

Rice, M. E., Harris, G. T., & Lang, C. (2013). Validation of and revision to the VRAG and SORAG: The Violence Risk Appraisal Guide – Revised (VRAG-R). *Psychological Assessment, 3,* 951–965.

Sackett, D. L., Rosenberg, W. M., Gray, J. A., Haynes, R. B., & Richardson, W. S. (1996). Evidence based medicine: What it is and what it isn't. *British Medical Journal, 312,* 71–72.

Singh, J. P., Desmarais, S., Hurducas, C., Arbach-Lucioni, K., Condemarin, C., Dean, K., ... Otto, R. K. (2014). International perspectives on the practical application of violence risk assessment: A global survey of 44 countries. *International Journal of Forensic Mental Health, 13,* 193–206.

Steinberg, L. (2009). Adolescent development and juvenile justice. *The Annual Review of Clinical Psychology, 5,* 47–73.

Storey, J. S., Campbell, V. J., & Hart, S. D. (2013). Expert evidence about violence risk assessment: A study of Canadian legal decisions. *International Journal of Forensic Mental Health, 12,* 287–296.

Storey, J., Gibas, A. L., Reeves, K. A., & Hart, S. D. (2011). Evaluation of a violence risk (threat) assessment training program for police and other criminal justice professionals. *Criminal Justice and Behavior, 38,* 554–564.

Storey, J., Kropp, P. R., Hart, D. S., Belfrage, H., & Strand, S. (2014). Assessment and management of risk for intimate partner violence by police officers using the Brief Spousal Assault Form for the Evaluation of Risk (B-SAFER). *Criminal Justice and Behavior, 41,* 256–271.

Strub, D. S., Douglas, K. S., & Nicholls, T. L. (2014). The validity of Version 3 of the HCR-20 violence risk assessment scheme amongst offenders and civil psychiatric patients. *International Journal of Forensic Mental Health, 13,* 148–159. doi:10.1080/14999013.2014.911785

Sutherland, A. A., Johnstone, L., Davidson, K. M., Hart, S. D., Cooke, D. J., Kropp, P. R., Logan, C., Michie, C., & Stocks, R. (2012). Sexual violence risk assessment: An investigation of the interrater reliability of professional judgments made using the Risk for Sexual Violence Protocol. *International Journal of Forensic Mental Health, 11,* 119–133.

Viljoen, J. L., McLachlan, K., & Vincent, G. M. (2010). Assessing violence risk and psychopathy in juvenile and adult offenders: A survey of clinical practices. *Assessment, 17,* 377–395.

Viljoen, J. L., Nicholls, T. L., Cruise, K. R., Desmarais, S. L., & Webster, C. D. (2014). *Short-Term Assessment of Risk and Treatability: Adolescent Version (START:AV), user guide.* Burnaby, Canada: Mental Health, Law, and Policy Institute, Simon Fraser University.

Vincent, G. M., Guy, L. S., Fusco, S., & Gershenson, B. S. (2011). Field reliability of the SAVRY with juvenile probation officers: Implications for training. *Law and Human Behavior, 36,* 225–236.

Vincent, G. M., Guy, L. S., Gershenson, B.G., & McCabe, P. (2012). Does risk assessment make a difference? Results of implementing the SAVRY in juvenile probation. *Behavioral Sciences and the Law, 30,* 384–405.

Vitacco, M. J., Erickson, S. K., Kurus, S., & Apple, B. N. (2012). The role of the Violence Risk Appraisal Guide and the Historical, Clinical, Risk-20 in US Courts: A case law survey. *Psychology, Public Policy, and Law, 18,* 361–391. doi:10.1037/a0025834

Webster, C. D., Douglas, K., Eaves, D., & Hart, S. (1997). *HCR-20: Assessing risk for violence, Version 2.* Burnaby, Canada: Simon Fraser University.

Webster, C. D., Eaves, D., Douglas, K. S., & Wintrup, A. (1995). *The HCR-20 scheme: The assessment of dangerousness and risk.* Burnaby, Canada: Simon Fraser University and British Columbia Forensic Psychiatric Services Commission.

Webster, C. D., Hucker, S. J., & Bloom, H. (2002). Transcending the actuarial versus clinical polemic in assessing risk for violence. *Criminal Justice and Behavior, 29,* 659–665.

Webster, C. D., Martin, M. L., Brink, J., Nicholls, T. L., & Desmarais, S. L. (2009). *Manual for the Short-Term Assessment of Risk and Treatability (START) (Version 1.1).* Coquitlam, Canada: British Columbia Mental Health and Addiction Services.

Webster, C. D., Menzies, R. J., & Hart, S. D. (1995). Dangerousness and risk. In R. Bull & D. Carson (Eds.), *Handbook of psychology in legal contexts* (pp. 465–479). Chichester, England: John Wiley & Sons, Ltd.

Webster, C. D., Müller-Isberner, R., & Fransson, G. (2002). Violence risk assessment: Using structured clinical guides professionally. *International Journal of Forensic Mental Health, 1,* 185–193.

Wiggins, J. S. (1973). *Personality and prediction: Principles of personality assessment.* Reading, MA: Addison-Wesley.

Wilson, C. M. (2013). *Reliability and consistency of risk formulations in assessments of sexual violence risk. Unpublished doctoral dissertation.* Burnaby, Canada: Department of Psychology, Simon Fraser University.

Worling, J. R., & Curwen, T. (2001). *Estimate of Risk Adolescent Sexual Offense Recidivism (ERASOR) Version 2.0.* Toronto, Canada: SAFE-T Program, Thistletown Regional Centre, Ontario Ministry of Community and Social Services.

31

Advancing the Evolution of Sexual Offender Risk Assessment

The Relevance of Psychological Risk Factors

David Thornton

Sand Ridge Secure Treatment Center, United States

Deirdre M. D'Orazio

Central Coast Clinical and Forensic Psychology Services, United States

Introduction: The Historical Context of Sexual Offender Risk Assessment

The problem of sexual abuse has been documented since biblical times. For example, King David's son lured his half-sister under false pretences and forced sexual intercourse upon her (2 Samuel 13:11–14). Even though its documented existence dates back thousands of years, it was not until the late 1970s that 'Sexual Abuse' became validated as a bona fide societal concern (Conte, 1994). Sexual abuse awareness came alongside feminist movements of this era that sought to equalize legal rights and protections for women as had existed for men (D'Orazio, 2013). Emerging from the shadows of sociopolitical systems that had perceived women and children as the property of men, the seriousness of the problem of maltreatment of women and children by men was illuminated. Pioneering this era of increased knowledge about the prevalence of sexual abuse, the research of Finkelhor (1979) revealed that one in four females and one in five males were sexually victimized before the age of 18 years. The tables slowly turned through the 1980s and early 1990s, revealing vast suppression of the reporting, arrest, and sanctioning of male sexual offenders and the illusion that sexual abuse was a scarcely prevalent social malady.

The Wiley Handbook on the Theories, Assessment, and Treatment of Sexual Offending.
Edited by Douglas P. Boer. Volume II: Assessment, edited by Leam A. Craig and Martin Rettenberger.
© 2017 John Wiley & Sons, Ltd. Published 2017 by John Wiley & Sons, Ltd.

The final years of the 20th century saw a formidable response to society's new awareness of the seriousness of the problem of sexual abuse, including longer punishments, post-incarceration civil detainment, registration and more intensive supervision, and mandated rehabilitative programmes for detected sexual offenders. Equally impacting the proliferation of treatment programmes for sexual offenders were advancements in media technology and sensational media coverage of the most extreme cases of violent sexual offending perpetrated by repeat sexual offenders. Such extreme examples ignited strong emotional reactions from the public, which in turn influenced legislators to increase criminal justice sanctions for sexual offence perpetrators and promoted a misperception that all sexual offenders are highly predatory and likely to reoffend.

Emanating from this sociopolitical context, contemporary prisons, forensic hospitals, and outpatient treatment programmes are faced with the challenge of implementing and expanding sexual offender treatment programmes to treat rapidly increasing numbers of sexual offenders. The explosive propagation of criminal justice responses to the problem of sexual offending, however, is not without fiduciary consequence. Indeed, alongside the global economic recession, the early years of this century have led to serious reconsideration of resource expenditure towards sexual recidivism prevention. Contemporary programmes are faced with reduced budgets and increased fiduciary scrutiny regarding resource allocation.

The field of assessing risk for sexual reoffence was born out of the need for well-reasoned decision-making regarding important questions such as: how should limited resources be assigned to a large population of sexual offenders?; which sexual offenders need treatment the most?; how much treatment is needed for a given offender?; and is this offender so dangerous that he must be removed from society? The desire to anchor such decisions upon an empirical research base as opposed to mere unstructured professional judgement motivated the field to develop risk assessment instruments. As these questions are more salient than ever in contemporary times, a rigorous focus on the development and understanding of risk assessment tools is an essential feature of the field of sexual offender treatment.

The Evolution of Risk Assessment

Up to the 1970s, the prevailing risk assessment methodology was for the evaluator to render reasonable speculations about the dangerousness of a given offender based upon familiarity with the case at hand and the evaluator's experience with other cases. This early method of unstructured clinical judgement is commonly described as the first generation of risk assessment (Andrews, Bonta, & Wormith, 2006). In the 1990s, research fuelled a professional consensus that research-based instruments lead to better predictions about reoffence behaviour than unstructured clinical judgement, a method demonstrated to be not much better at prediction than tossing a coin (Menzies, Webster, McMain, Staley, & Scaglione, 1994). This ushered in a booming era of developing risk assessment instruments. Such instruments indeed predict substantially better than unstructured clinical judgement (Andrews et al., 2006). Across the four generations of risk assessment, the available methodology to make risk predictions has become nuanced, complex, and substantially improved, providing not only information about reoffence likelihood but also the factors that can be addressed to reduce such likelihood (Andrews & Bonta, 2006).

Modern methods for assessing sexual offence risk developed from two distinct approaches: the statistical approach and the structured professional judgement approach.

The Statistical Approach

In the statistical approach, also called the actuarial approach, statistical correlates of sexual reoffending are identified based upon large-scale recidivism studies. Numerical scores are assigned for each indicator based upon specified coding rules. These numerical scores are then combined through a specified algebraic formula (for example, summing or averaging item scores) to provide a total risk score. The meaning of this total risk score is then investigated by examining the score's relationship to recidivism in large samples of released offenders for whom recidivism outcomes are known. An individual is characterized in terms of the statistical properties of the group of individuals having the same total risk score, for example, 'Thirty percent of the sexual offenders with the same score on the instrument as Mark recidivated over a 10 year-period. This rate is three times the recidivism rate observed for offenders that have average scores on this instrument. Mark scores at the 90th percentile compared to other sexual offenders.' The statistical method allows offenders to be assigned to broad risk groups that differ in their average rate of sexual recidivism but does not ensure that all persons with the same risk score will present the same risk since factors influencing risk that are not measured by a statistical instrument may vary.

The statistical approach has been used to create a number of specific instruments to aid professionals in evaluating the dangerousness of sexual offenders. Widely used instruments that were developed around 2000 include the original Static-99 (Hanson & Thornton, 2000) and the Risk Matrix 2000 (Thornton et al., 2003).

A commonality of these statistical sexual offence risk assessment instruments is that they rely heavily on assessing three underlying kinds of statistical risk indicators. These primary risk indicators are prior sexual criminal behaviour, prior general criminal behaviour, and youth. As statistical research has developed, the way in which these underlying dimensions are assessed or weighted by individual instruments has been revised (e.g., Helmus, Thornton, Hanson, & Babchishin, 2011: Static-99R; Duwe & Freske, 2012: MnSOST-3), but no major additional prediction dimensions have been introduced.

The dependence of statistical risk assessment instruments on large samples for their creation and validation generally means that the statistical risk indicators they contain were derived from easily available facts from offenders' official records, and consequently, as noted above, largely reflect the age and prior general and sexual criminality of the offender. Statistical risk instrument developers such as Hanson and Thornton (2000) caution that the resulting instruments would consequently present only an incomplete picture of an individual's risk since this focus on easily available and measured items meant that other potentially important factors were not included in the instruments. To summarize, the shortcomings of statistical risk assessment instruments are that they include an incomplete sample of known risk factors; owing to their atheoretical nature they are not able to inform the selection of treatment targets; they tend to over-focus on historical static factors and do not adequately reflect the influence of either enduring or fluctuating psychological risk factors, and they are not designed to measure the impact of treatment. These kinds of instruments born out of the statistical approach are considered representative of the second generation of risk assessment.

The Structured Professional Judgement Approach

Like the statistical approach, the Structured Professional Judgement (SPJ) approach to risk assessment attempts to avoid the weaknesses of unstructured clinical judgement. The SPJ approach also endeavours to avoid some of the limitations of the statistical approach. SPJ instruments contain theoretically meaningful risk factors identified on the basis of empirically supported theory, review of the empirical prediction literature, and professional consensus regarding good practice. SPJ instruments provide raters with a summary of relevant research and a conceptual definition of each factor. The evaluator is expected to make a professional judgement about the applicability of each factor to the individual being assessed and then encouraged to make a thoughtful professional judgement regarding the overall level of risk presented by the individual, taking into account the individual relevance of the factors they have identified as present. Particularly in later versions of the tradition, raters are encouraged to integrate factors through a qualitative case formulation and to envision what potential reoffence scenarios would look like so that appropriate risk management strategies can be developed (e.g., Douglas et al., 2014; Logan, 2014). SPJ is a non-numerical approach to risk assessment and the resulting Low/Medium/High ratings are probably better understood as expressing the level of risk management that is required rather than any quantitative specification of probability of offending. SPJ instruments have been particularly well developed for predicting non-sexual violence (e.g., the HCR-20: Webster et al., 1995, 1997; the SARA: Kropp, Hart, Webster, & Eaves, 1994; the SAVRY: Borum et al., 2002). SPJ instruments designed to assess sexual recidivism have also been developed (the SVR-20: Boer, Hart, Kropp, & Webster, 1997; the RSVP: Boer et al., 1997; the ARMIDILO: Blacker et al., 2011; and the SAPROF: de Vogel, de Ruiter, Bouman, & de Vries Robbé, 2009).

There are some similarities between statistical and SPJ instruments: both kinds of instruments use a predetermined list of items with instructions to guide raters in scoring the items. The approaches differ in three important ways: the statistical risk indicators included in statistical instruments are typically defined and scored without regard to their psychological meaning whereas SPJ factors are defined conceptually and their psychological meaning is the primary determinant in scoring them; items are included in statistical instruments only when it has been possible to score them all together in large-scale prediction studies analyses whereas SPJ instruments can incorporate a more comprehensive range of factors, and in statistical instruments, overall risk score is calculated through some algebraic rule whereas for SPJ instruments the overall assessment of risk is based on a qualitative, non-numerical integration of the relevance to the individual's functioning of the factors identified by the instrument that are judged to apply.

These differences mean that SPJ instruments are in some ways more advanced than statistical instruments. For example, SPJ instruments incorporated psychological risk factors, assessment of change, and even aspects of the release environment into their assessments, long before statistical instruments sought to do so. These features align SPJ instruments with the third generation of risk assessment (Andrews et al., 2006). The downside of the SPJ approach is that it is able to do this only because it requires less evidence to incorporate a factor into an assessment scheme and sometimes as a result a particular factor may turn out to have been mistakenly incorporated.

The contrasting strengths and weaknesses of the approaches seem to have resulted in markedly different ways of doing risk assessment that nevertheless yield similar overall levels of predictive accuracy (Singh et al., 2011).

Researchers working within the statistical approach have responded to the limitations of earlier statistical instruments by developing instruments in which atheoretical statistical risk indicators are replaced by more psychologically meaningful risk factors. Examples of statistical instruments of this third-generation type include the Violence Risk Scale – Sex Offender Version (VRS-SO) (Olver, Wong, Nicholaichuk, & Gordon, 2007), STABLE-2007 (Hanson, Harris, Scott, & Helmus, 2007), Structured Risk Assessment – Forensic Version (SRA-FV) (Knight & Thornton, 2007; Thornton & Knight, 2015), and SOTIPS (McGrath, Lasher, & Cumming, 2012).

In some respects, this development represents statistical instruments catching up with SPJ instruments in the scope of the factors covered. This has been achieved in part by borrowing the kind of conceptually meaningful definition of risk factors that SPJ instruments use. However, the two traditions are still distinct in that total scores are determined algebraically in statistical instruments and through case formulation-based professional judgement in the SPJ approach.

The Role of Psychological Risk Factors in Effective Treatment

Out of the increased societal response to the problem of sexual abuse of the 1980s, the field of sexual offender treatment emerged as a specialization distinct from general offender treatment (D'Orazio, 2013). Over the past four decades, the supporting body of research has flourished, as exemplified by the fact that by the end of the first decade of the 21st century the field averaged 176 risk assessment papers yearly compared with just 32 in the 1990s (Harris & Hanson, 2010). Earlier attempts at the treatment of sexual offenders had limited success, but by about 2000 the field had evolved more effective treatment paradigms (Hanson et al., 2002). Over the past decade, our knowledge has been refined by the finding that the degree to which treatment interventions reduce sexual recidivism depends on the degree to which they follow the Risk–Need–Responsivity (RNR) model (Hanson, Bourgon, Helmus, & Hodgson, 2009). There are still, however, insufficient well-controlled trials of modern treatment methods to allow definitive precise statements about the degree to which treatment is effective.

The RNR model describes consistent patterns found in hundreds of evaluations of offender treatment programmes in terms of three guiding principles (Andrews & Bonta, 2006). Programmes that do not target any of the three principles have been found either to have no effect on recidivism or to increase it, whereas those that target all three have the most positive impact upon recidivism rates. The available body of research clearly indicates that sexual offender interventions should be grounded in RNR principles to maximize efficacy. These principles can be described as follows.

1.   The Risk Principle instructs to match the intensity of treatment to the offender's risk to reoffend. In short, it speaks to the issue of 'who' should be treated. This means that higher risk offenders should receive more intensive interventions than lower risk sexual offenders. Programmes that target high-risk offenders produce substantially greater reductions in recidivism than those that treat low-risk offenders.
2.   The Need Principle speaks to the issue of 'what' should be treated. It instructs that treatment should target social or psychological factors that are linked to offending. These are referred to as 'Criminogenic Needs', since they are the factors that need to be treated to reduce recidivism.
3.   The Responsivity Principle speaks to the issue of 'how' treatment should be delivered. It advocates for intentionally engaging the motivation of participating offenders so that they become partners in the treatment process rather than someone that treatment is 'done to'. It focuses on maximizing offenders' response to treatment by tailoring it to the learning style, personality, motivation, abilities, and skills of the offender client.

In the literature, the terms 'Criminogenic Needs', 'dynamic risk factors', and 'psychological risk factors' are used in almost interchangeable ways. We prefer the phrase 'psychological risk factors', intended to refer both to internal psychological characteristics and to characteristic patterns of the offender's interaction with the environment, and to include factors that are relatively enduring in addition to those that may change rapidly.

Assessment of psychological risk factors is key to following the RNR model. It is most apparently central to following the Need principle but it can also allow more accurate application of the Risk principle than can determining risk level based solely on static actuarial instruments.

What Are the Psychological Factors Most Related to Sexual Reoffence?

Thornton (2002) proposed a general framework known as Structured Risk Assessment (SRA) for psychological factors related to sexual recidivism. Subsequent statistical research (Mann, Hanson, & Thornton, 2010) has largely confirmed the relevance of the kinds of factors indicated by this framework. Accordingly, the current version of SRA is summarized below with an emphasis on those factors for which there is greater empirical support.

Psychological factors that have been studied and for which there is evidence that they are associated with sexual recidivism can be conceptualized as falling into four broad domains: (1) Sexual Interests; (2) Offence-Supportive Attitudes; (3) Relational Style; and (4) Self-Management. These factors are discussed below.

Sexual Interests

One domain of psychological risk factors empirically associated with sexual reoffence involves the direction and strength of sexual interests. The two major subdomains of sexual interests are problems with sexual self-regulation and offence-related sexual interests.

Problems with sexual self-regulation (sexual preoccupation/hypersexuality) include such things as (1) internal functioning is excessively dominated by sexual fantasies, sexual urges, or planning sexual behaviour; (2) excessive involvement in impersonal sexual activity; (3) engaging in sexual fantasies, experiencing sexual urges, planning or engaging in sexual behaviour in response to negative internal moods or stressful external events; (4) impulsive sexual functioning – where little effort is made to regulate the expression of sexual urges; (5) compulsive sexual functioning – where sexual fantasies, sexual urges, or sexual behaviour are experienced as hard to control; and (6) questing through multiple kinds of sexual outlets.

Offence-related sexual interests are interests that are hard to satisfy through legal sexual behaviour. The two that have been most clearly identified as related to sexual recidivism are a sexual interest in young children and sexual interest in violence. Both of these interest patterns are best conceptualized as dimensions: the age dimension and the agonistic dimension. Preference for prepubescent children denotes the most extreme version of the sexual interest in children factor with preference for children in the early stages of puberty being a related but less extreme form of the interest (see Blanchard et al., 2012, for the dimensional structure of age/gender preferences). Sexual interest in violence can be understood (following Knight, Sims-Knight, & Guay, 2013) as having a sexual interest in choking, killing, and beating at the extreme, sexual interest in humiliating, frightening, and hurting as a less extreme form, and sexual preference for coercion as the mildest form of this sexual interest.

Offence-Supportive Attitudes

A second domain of psychological risk factors empirically associated with sexual reoffence involves beliefs supportive of sexual offending. Specific factors within this domain that have been studied and determined to be associated with sexual reoffence are general offence-supportive attitudes (may involve those regarding children, or rape of women), hostile beliefs about women (seeing women as malicious or deceptive towards men), and Machiavellianism (viewing others as weak, easily manipulated, and deserving of being taken advantage of). Relevance of the attitude to the particular kind of offending in which the individual is interested seems to improve prediction and external rating of the attitude appears to be more predictive than self-report, except when self-report is obtained under research conditions (Helmus, Hanson, Babchishin, & Mann, 2013). Thus, for example, pro-child-molesting attitudes seem to be primarily predictive when held by persons who already have a history of molesting children as compared with those with sexual offences against adults only.

Offence-supportive attitudes are a domain that requires clarification through further research. Past conceptualizations of the domain have focused on beliefs that permit some kind of moral rationalization of offending. There are several alternative perspectives that may offer more promising ways of understanding the connection between attitudes and offending. Namely, it appears that attitudes have traditionally been conceptualized in an overly narrow way. In contrast, social psychological models of attitudes towards a behaviour emphasize the person's overall evaluation of the behaviour, beyond simply their ability to rationalize it morally. The Reasoned Action Approach (Fishbein & Ajzen, 2010), for example, emphasizes how personally attractive the consequences that come to mind when thinking about engaging in a specific behaviour are to the person choosing whether or not to act. While thoughts about potential harm to victims or moral culpability may be one aspect of these consequences, other, more selfish kinds of beliefs, likely play a central role in one forming the kind of positive (or negative) attitude towards offending that influences offending behaviour.

This Reasoned Action interpretation of attitude applied towards offending makes it more similar to the person's stage of change in relation to offending and sees purposive striving to avoid future offending (for example, by completing a treatment programme) as a natural expression of an attitude negative to offending, while dropping out of treatment is a natural expression of a pro-offending attitude. Support for this way of conceptualizing the attitudes domain of psychological risk factors can be found in factor analyses of the VRS-SO, for example, where negative attitudes towards treatment are loaded with the same factor as expressions of traditional cognitive distortions (Beggs & Grace, 2010; Olver et al., 2007).

Another possible elaboration of the attitudes domain is to conceptualize 'belief' as the way in which cognitive contents are associated in implicit cognitive structures. We know, for example, that the idea of 'child' is implicitly associated with the idea of 'sex' in the cognitive structures of child molesters (e.g., Gray, Brown, MacCulloch, Smith, & Snowden, 2005; Nunes, Firestone, & Baldwin, 2007). This kind of abnormal cognitive structure means that when the idea of child comes to mind, ideas about sex will automatically occur, and similarly, if the idea of sex comes to mind, thoughts about children will automatically occur. Similarly, there is evidence that sexual offenders have abnormal associations between power/dominance and sex (Kamphuis, De Ruiter, Janssen, & Spiering, 2005). These kinds of cognitive structures seem liable to influence behaviour in a way that is quite different from moral rationalizing, although Mihailides, Devilly, and Ward (2004) argued that they are closely related to the implicit theories that Ward and Keenan (1999) proposed underlie common cognitive distortions.

A practical difficulty with risk factors from the attitudes domain is that they are relatively easy for an offender to conceal. As such, they are hard to identify accurately, except possibly under research conditions.

Relational Style

A third domain of psychological risk factors empirically associated with sexual reoffence involves the manner in which the offender relates to others. Factors of this kind can be grouped into three subdomains: (1) an inadequate relational style in which the offender has a sense of inadequacy as an adult and finds it easier to satisfy needs for friendship, validation, and romance with children; (2) an aggressive relational style, which can involve hostility, a sense of grievance, and callous or angry aggression; (3) difficulty making and sustaining emotionally close marital-type relationships.

Self-Management Deficits

A fourth domain of psychological risk factors empirically associated with sexual reoffence involves the degree to which the individual manages his immediate impulses and lifestyle in general in the service of longer term interests. This domain includes early-onset oppositional reactions to rules and supervision, spending time with antisocial associates, poor self-control, and impulsive/reckless responding to the problems of daily living cumulatively resulting in a chaotic self-defeating criminal lifestyle.

The Value of Comprehensive Assessment of Psychological Risk Factors

The Mann et al. (2010) meta-analysis demonstrated that a range of psychological risk factors is predictive of sexual recidivism but no factor, considered by itself, demonstrated even a moderate predictive value. Hence there is a need for a comprehensive structured assessment of psychological risk factors if the value of assessing them is to be judged. The SRA model holds that credible assessment of psychological factors from at least three of the four domains is required for an acceptably comprehensive assessment of psychological risk factors (e.g., Thornton & Knight, 2015).

Rating scales such as SRA-FV, STABLE-2007, and the VRS-SO meet this criterion for a comprehensive structured assessment of psychological risk factors although they differ in how they assess the particular domains. Similarly, self-report batteries have been devised that also meet the criterion for comprehensiveness according to the SRA framework. For example, Thornton's (2002) battery administered prior to a prison treatment programme or Beech's battery (Beech, Fisher, & Beckett, 1998) administered as part of a programme evaluation have both been deliberately employed to operationalize the SRA framework while retrospective analysis of the battery used with the Kia Marama programme in New Zealand showed that it too mapped into the SRA domains (Allan, Grace, Rutherford, & Hudson, 2007). Table 31.1 summarizes AUC (area under the curve) statistics for studies examining how well these various comprehensive assessments of psychological risk factors predicted sexual recidivism. All of these AUCs show statistically significant prediction of sexual recidivism with the median AUC being in the low 0.7s. This is comparable to average AUCs normally found for traditional statistical risk assessment instruments that do not incorporate psychological risk factors. For example, Static-99R is reported to have an average AUC of around 0.71–0.72 (Helmus et al., 2011).

Thus, although psychological factors only have limited predictive value when individually considered, when they are combined into a more comprehensive assessment they provide a moderate level of accuracy in predicting sexual reoffence.

Table 31.1 Predictive value of comprehensive assessment of psychological risk factors

Authors	Instrument	AUC
Helmus & Hanson, 2012	STABLE-2007	0.64
Eher et al., 2013: inmates	STABLE-2007	0.71
Eher et al., 2013: detainees	STABLE-2007	0.71
Looman & Abracen, 2012	STABLE-2007	0.73
Olver et al., 2007	VRS-SO Initial Dynamic	0.66
Beggs & Grace, 2010	VRS-SO Initial Dynamic	0.78
Thornton & Knight, 2015	SRA-FV	0.73
Thornton, 2002	Early prison Q-battery	0.78
Craig, Thornton, Beech, & Browne, 2007	Reduced Beech Q-battery	0.69
Allan et al., 2007	New Zealand Q-battery	0.76
Harkins, Beech, & Thornton, 2009	Full Beech Q-battery	0.79

Another important question to consider is whether psychological risk factor assessment adds some prediction beyond that provided by simpler methods of statistical risk assessment that are based on easily available more or less static variables such as criminal history, sexual offence history, and age. One might argue that psychological risk assessment expresses the sources of risk in a more meaningful way, regardless of whether it adds predictive value – put simply, that the underlying psychological factors are what drives the individual's risk to reoffend, whereas the static factors are superficial markers for those underlying factors. However, it turns out that comprehensive assessments of psychological risk factors generally are incrementally predictive beyond standard static actuarial instruments. Statistically significant incremental prediction was found in almost all the studies summarized in Table 31.1.

The Temporal Dimension of Risk Factors: Stability and Change

The purpose of this section is to elaborate a useful theoretical model of the temporal aspects of psychological factors. For example, what aspects are more stable, what aspects are more rapidly dynamic, and what is the interplay of enduring and dynamic features? Here we attempt to further our work in this area (Thornton & D'Orazio, 2011). It is in the tradition of the related model articulated by Beech and Ward (2004).

The Long-Term Vulnerability Construct

Psychological risk factors are best conceptualized as enduring propensities (Mann et al., 2010) fuelled by long-term vulnerabilities (Thornton & Knight, 2015) within the individual. A long-term vulnerability (LTV) is a way of functioning that has become sufficiently persistent and generalized that it is expected to reoccur even if it is not active at the moment. LTVs may be dormant, persistently active, or activated episodically in response to the meaning given either to some internally generated experience or to some transaction with the environment. When active, LTVs transform the person's functioning in a criminogenic way, changing what is noticed, how cognitions and feeling states arise from experience, and what is attractive or unattractive.

Classic examples of LTVs are sexual interest in children or hostile beliefs about women. These examples are elaborated to clarify further the construct of long-term vulnerability.

It is proposed that once a man has laid down sufficient vivid erotic memories of children, these memories remain as a potential erotic trigger for the man. He may go for many months without showing any behavioural sign of an interest in children, but the potential for this interest to be reignited remains. Hanson et al.'s (2007) description of the construction of STABLE-2007 illustrates this LTV nature of child sexual interest. Ratings of the deviant sexual interests risk factor based on recent behaviour in the community turned out to have marginal predictive value, but the variable became predictive when the coding instructions were changed to force the assignment of a deviant sexual interest based on a history of relevant offending. Thus, the child sexual interest need not be consistently or even currently active to signify risk.

Somewhat similarly, through his earlier experiences a man may form a schema in which women are depicted as malicious and deceptive. Later in life, when calm, he may cognitively 'know' that women and men are heterogeneous in these traits, with some being more benign than others. However, when he has an emotionally activating negative interaction with a woman an old schema may reactivate, leading him to demonize women again.

Evidence for the predictive significance of LTVs is detailed in Table 31.1. It is noted that the AUCs from almost all the studies listed refer to pretreatment ratings of the psychological risk factors and as such are consistent with an LTV way of conceptualizing risk factors. Further evidence of the relevance of the enduring aspect of risk factors is that when scores based upon assessments of recent functioning are compared with scores derived from assessments based upon long-term functioning, the latter provide more robust and longer term prediction (Thornton & D'Orazio, 2011).

LTVs can change, but the time scale for change in most circumstances is multiple years, and can even require decades.

Behavioural Intentions

Whereas LTVs are remarkably enduring, at the other extreme are behavioural intentions, which can change rapidly, for example over a period of seconds or minutes.

Here the phrase 'behavioural intention' is used in a way that is fairly close to its use in the work of Fishbein and Ajzen in what they have at different times have referred to as the theory of reasoned action, the theory of planned behaviour, and the reasoned action approach. A behavioural intention is an intention to engage in a specific action in relation to a specific target, in a particular context, at a particular time. It involves a motivated readiness to engage in both the immediate behaviour and associated preparatory behaviours. Although intentions can be vague, what we are concerned with here are behavioural intentions that are sufficiently specific in terms of actions, target, context, and time that they, in essence, are a behavioural script.

Fishbein and Ajzen's work stretches back over many years and has been particularly developed in the context of understanding and predicting health behaviours. An excellent review of their theoretical concepts and supporting evidence can be found in Fishbein and Ajzen (2010). Their work has identified three primary determinants of behavioural intentions: (i) how the person values the outcomes of the behaviour that come to mind when the person thinks about engaging in the behaviour; (ii) what the person supposes that other people whose opinions they value would think of them engaging in the behaviour; and (iii) whether the person thinks they can successfully carry out the behaviour. Behavioural intentions are highly predictable from these three variables and while intentions are sustained they strongly determine behaviour (Fishbein & Ajzen, 2010).

One of the primary ways in which LTVs can be expected to influence behaviour is that when activated, they influence these more proximate variables that determine the formation of behavioural intentions. That is, activation of LTVs can change which behavioural outcomes are salient and how they are valued, how the opinions of important others are attended to and valued, and whether the person believes they can successfully complete the behaviour. However, these proximate influences on behavioural intentions are also very influenced by events and situations: subtle features of the stimulus environment can change the cognitive availability of different outcomes or of approving or disapproving others (and motivation to comply with their views), and as a consequence, although behavioural intentions can sometimes be enduring, they can also change rapidly.

Since these concepts are somewhat abstract, an example is given involving a non-offending behaviour. This example involves the struggles of a middle-aged professional to improve his fitness. An insightful self-description might go something like this:

> At the beginning of last week, I planned to go to the gym on Thursday evening (*formation of behavioural intention*) when I expected to have a break in my schedule. When making this plan, I was thinking about the benefits of keeping fit, thinking that I will live longer if I exercise and that I usually feel more energetic in weeks when I exercise (*positive salient behavioural outcomes*). I also recalled that my wife commented negatively on my waistline and that she regularly goes to a yoga class, so I thought she would approve of my going to the gym (*favourable opinion of valued other*). However, on Thursday, my wife remarked that the children had reduced the house to chaos again and that me going out that night meant that she would be stuck trying to tidy the house and look after our children by herself (*opinion of valued other now negative*). I then recalled how arduous a session at the gym felt the last time I went and I remembered just how much time going to the gym really takes – pretty well absorbing a whole evening (*negative behavioural outcomes now more salient*). And as my motivation started to wane, I began to doubt whether I was really the kind of person who will exercise persistently enough to get any real benefits (*subjective behavioural control reduced*). So I decided to stay home that night (*change in behavioural intention*).

As illustrated above, the proximate influences on behavioural intentions can be impacted by immediate situational variables and events. They are also potentially the subject of clinical intervention. For example, Motivational Interviewing, a brief clinical intervention that has been shown to influence many behaviours effectively

(Miller & Rollnick, 2013), can be seen as primarily working to change these three proximal influences on behavioural intentions.

Resources

Intermediate in stability between LTVs and behavioural intentions are the resources that people have to draw on to support their intentions. Resources include skills and knowledge relevant to carrying out intentions such as self-regulation capacities, the ability to recognize rapidly opportunities to enact the behaviour, a network of other people who are supportive of the behaviour, and an identity that is congruent with the behaviour.

Resources can be prosocial or antisocial. For example, resources supportive of child molestation might include (1) the skills and knowledge relevant to grooming a child and the child's potential protectors; (2) the ability to recognize rapidly vulnerable children who may be more easily molested and to locate circumstances in which they will be less protected; (3) a social network that includes persons who speak about children in sexualized ways or who minimize the harm that molestation may cause; (4) thinking of himself as 'a paedophile' for whom struggling against sexual urges directed toward children is just hopeless.

Antisocial resources such as those illustrated above tend to be accumulated by persons who repeatedly form the behavioural intention to molest children and who work to overcome obstacles to offending. Essentially, they become 'expert' offenders for whom offending is a skilled performance. Because of their expertise, they anticipate easily creating offence experiences that are exciting and pleasurable. Thus, well-developed antisocial resources influence some of the proximate determinants of forming a behavioural intention to offend while repeated offending builds up these resources.

Corresponding prosocial resources support intentions to obtain life satisfaction through non-offending behaviours while avoiding situations that create a high risk for reoffending. Essentially, prosocial resources are resources that support intentions to achieve the kinds of experience necessary for the person to have a sufficiently satisfying life without offending. Such experiences include such things as being able to acquire and obtain value through work, being able to acquire safe, non-stressful accommodation, being able to find reward in available and safe leisure activities, and being able to form non-abusive and satisfying friendships and romantic relationships. A more elaborate typology of the different kinds of experience that can lead to life satisfaction has been developed by Ward (e.g., Ward & Stewart, 2003).

Prosocial resources therefore include the ability to recognize opportunities for rewarding non-offending activities, a social network that facilitates and supports these activities, the ability to regulate affect and cognition that might interfere with pursuing these goals, and an identity that supports the plausibility of transforming life in a prosocial direction.

Just as repeatedly forming antisocial intentions and engaging in sexual offending can build up antisocial resources, so persistently forming prosocial intentions and acting on them can build up the range of prosocial resources described above.

Building up prosocial resources is something that should be facilitated during the course of treatment or community management of a person who is at risk for future sexual offending. Some assessment instruments are beginning to capture aspects of this buildup of prosocial resources. The VRS-SO Change score captures the self-regulation aspect whereas some of the community social protective factors (employment, residence, and social network) are captured by the SOTIPS. Both of these instruments have shown a relationship between change and reduced recidivism (McGrath et al., 2012; Olver, Beggs Christofferson, Grace, & Wong, 2014). Arguably, the instrument that best captures this notion of the development of prosocial resources is the SAPROF (Structured Assessment of Protective Factors for Violence Risk) (de Vogel et al., 2009), and here again an increase in prosocial resources (labelled protective factors in the SAPROF) has been associated with reduced sexual and violent recidivism (de Vries Robbé, de Vogel, & Douglas, 2013).

External Support and Control

Another changeable influence on likelihood of reoffence is the interaction between external protective factors of support and control provided in the release environment with the individual's motivation and ability to benefit from these external protective factors. As an example of this interaction, consider an individual with a major mental illness whose regulation of his sexual preoccupation tends to fail when his psychotic symptoms become more acute. External support in the form of antipsychotic medication may reduce his risk, but only if his mental illness is responsive to the medication and he is motivated (or compelled) to take it.

Statistical research has barely begun to measure, and integrate with other influences, the effects of different kinds and degrees of external support and control on behavioural outcome. One exception is studies of the impact of being released to intensive and long-lasting supervision that is now more common in the United States. Two studies have compared men released with versus without this intensive parole/probation supervision. Both found that even when other risk factors are controlled for, being released with supervision is associated with significantly lower sexual recidivism rates (Boccaccini, Murrie, Caperton, & Hawes, 2009; Duwe & Freske, 2012). The Duwe and Freske study is of particular relevance since it was carried out in Minnesota, where the intensity of modern supervision is well documented (Minnesota Department of Corrections, 2007). The effect of being released to supervision was large: it reduced recidivism to about one-quarter of what it would be for comparable cases released without supervision.

Base Rate Variability and the Need to Incorporate Psychological Factors into Risk Assessment

So far, this chapter has discussed the temporal domain of psychological risk factors, that is, the more enduring and more changeable aspects, and the impact of the release environment upon their expression. In consideration of this discussion, we advocate that a nuanced assessment of the interaction of psychological factors should be an essential aspect of assessing risk for sexual recidivism. In response to this proposition, a sceptic might argue that because widely used statistical risk instruments that use criminal history and age as risk indicators are much simpler to administer, they should be used alone without considering assessment of psychological factors. The sceptic might concede that the more comprehensive assessment might be better, but question whether it allows a sufficient improvement to justify the time and effort involved.

Only a decade ago, such a sceptic's position might have seemed plausible. Since then, however, there have been developments in research that make it increasingly difficult to sustain this sceptical position. To understand this, we have to take a detour into studies of sexual recidivism base rates.

The documentation accompanying statistical risk assessment instruments commonly includes tables that associate recidivism rates with scores on the instrument. These kinds of tables implicitly contain two kinds of information: information about the average rate of sexual recidivism in the sample(s) comprising the table (known as the base rate) and information about how the sexual recidivism rate of offenders with a particular score compare with the base rate (their relative risk). Researchers who create statistical risk assessment instruments have always known that the base rate (average rate of recidivism) might vary between jurisdictions or within jurisdictions over time. Indeed, at the same time that now widely used statistical risk assessment instruments were first introduced (Hanson & Thornton, 2000; Thornton et al., 2003), Friendship and Thornton (2001) documented that the sexual recidivism base rate for sexual offenders released from prison in England and Wales had halved between 1980 and the early 1990s. Hence, right from the beginning it was known that, although the relative risk associated with statistical risk scores might be expected to be relatively stable (i.e., more who score 6 recidivate than those who score 5), there was a very real possibility that the absolute recidivism rates associated with scores would change in response to changes in prevailing base rates.

Furthermore, there were good grounds for expecting base rates to reduce as during the late 1990s and early 2000s societal efforts to manage sex offenders became increasingly aggressive. In the United States, one form that this took was drastic changes in how sex offenders were supervised by Departments of Corrections and another form was the advent of civil commitment programmes. For example, in 1990 in the Minnesota Department of Corrections (DOC), sexual offender releases from the DOC were supervised for an average of 13 months but by 2002 the average length of supervision was 63 months. Similarly, prior to 1997, very few sex offenders were released to intensive supervision but by 2005 over half of Minnesota DOC sexual offender releases were to intensive supervision (Minnesota Department of Corrections, 2007). This kind of change in supervision practices, which has occurred across many US states, typically leads to a large proportion of sexual offenders being revoked for reasons other than a new sexual offence. Likewise, in the mid-1990s, only a small handful of states in the United States had civil commitment programmes for sexual offenders, but by 2010, 20 states plus the District of Columbia (US Federal Government) had such programmes (Thornton & D'Orazio, 2013). Higher revocation rates and civil commitment surely reduce observed recidivism rates for the offenders subjected to these conditions during the confinement period, as their removal from the community essentially eliminates the opportunity to reoffend. Further, longer supervision sentences along with concomitant increased revoking in response to non-compliance may in effect interrupt pre-offence behaviour before it can lead to actual offence.

It is worth emphasizing here that there is nothing internal to instruments such as Static-99 that allows the user to know whether the base rate in some unresearched era or setting is similar to that in eras or settings that have been researched. This can only be investigated by examining average recidivism rates in these new eras or settings. By the mid-2000s, there was good reason to suggest that base rates might be changing. In response to this, researchers periodically monitored sexual recidivism base rates to see if changes sufficient to alter significantly the recidivism rates associated with risk scores had taken place.

Doren (2004) reported an initial examination of base rate variability. He found that the recidivism rates associated with Static-99 scores were reasonably well replicated in 2638 sexual offenders drawn from new samples in that average observed rates were fairly close to those in the initial Static-99 samples. However, the rates for the new samples were consistently slightly lower than the initial rates published with the instrument, reflecting a base rate (average rate for the new samples) that had declined from 18% (initial Static-99 instrument samples) to 13% (new samples) for an approximate 5-year follow-up. Furthermore, Doren noted what appeared to be meaningful variation in base rates between samples and went on to try to explore how base rate variation affected the recidivism rates associated with higher Static-99 scores.

Further evidence of lower base rates came from data for releases from various US correctional agencies mainly during the early 2000s. These were subsequently summarized by Wollert and Waggoner (2009), who reported the average sexual recidivism base rate for a follow-up of about 5 years to be 6.5%. These results were later confirmed by Zgoba et al. (2012), who found that the average 5-year sexual recidivism base rate for prison releases from four US states was 5.1%. These average rates of recidivism for prison samples are significantly lower then the rates found in the original Static-99 normative samples.

Additional support for these concerns surfaced when, working in 2006 and 2007 with a small collection of Static-99 replication samples, Helmus (2007) found evidence that the observed rates associated with Static-99 scores were lower than expected. This led to a project collating results from a much larger number of samples. By 2008, a definitive need for new norms was identified (Harris, Helmus, Hanson, & Thornton, 2008).

By itself, a change in base rates can be responded to fairly straightforwardly by developing recidivism norms that correspond to the new base rates. However, as results from an increasing number studies were collated and meta-analysed, a more concerning finding emerged. Although there was evidence that overall base rates were different from those that applied in the original Static-99 normative samples, what was more striking was the substantial variation in base rates between the new samples (i.e., scores of 4 in one sample had a different mean recidivism rate than scores of 4 in another sample). This was significantly larger than could be expected to arise by chance (Helmus, 2009; Helmus, Hanson, Thornton, Babchishin, & and Harris, 2012) and it held even when a revised version of Static-99 (Helmus et al., 2011) was used that better accounted for the effect of age upon recidivism rates. This finding of base rate variability was much more problematic than a mere change in base rates to a new consistent level: if base rates vary in an unpredictable way, then no specific recidivism rate can be associated with a given risk score.

In response to this concern, potential influences on base rates were tested to see if they could explain between-sample base rate variation (Helmus, 2009). Overwhelmingly, the most powerful influence on base rates appeared to be how the sample had been selected, with samples that appeared to the researchers to have been selected for risk (i.e., selected through administrators making some decision in response to an unusual concern about the level of risk presented by the offenders involved) tending to have higher recidivism rates at any given Static-99R score than unselected samples. Thornton, Hanson, and Helmus (2009) proposed that this can be understood in terms of risk-related sample selection simultaneously selecting for bad criminal history and for psychological risk factors. Such a selection process would mean that in samples selected for risk, not only would the average Static-99R score be higher, but also a higher level of psychological risk factors would typically accompany any given Static-99R score compared with unselected samples. Since psychological factors have an effect on recidivism that is incremental to that of age and bad criminal history, this leads to correspondingly higher recidivism rates at any given Static-99R score. Hanson and Thornton (2012) subsequently substantiated the claim that risk-selected samples tend to have higher levels of psychological risk factors.

An important conclusion can be drawn from this review of research related to sexual recidivism base rates. The prediction properties of statistical predictors such as Static-99R become unstable unless external factors such as the overall density of psychological risk factors and the nature of the release environment are accounted for. Thus, considering these factors is not an optional and expensive extra – assessing psychological risk factors is a necessity if statistical predictors are to have a reliable meaning.

Models for Integrating Different Kinds of Risk Factors

Statistical risk prediction instruments are generally based on age and criminal history. The Static-99R and Risk Matrix 2000 are undoubtedly among the best researched statistical risk assessment instruments currently available to evaluators, but it is essential to integrate their results with consideration of the density of psychological risk factors, the nature of the release environment, and, where relevant, assessment of change. Unfortunately, existing statistical research is not sufficient to support a fully rule-defined method of integrating these different kinds of factors, but there are a number of methods that are consistent with available research findings. In this section, these are illustrated in relation to Static-99R, but they could also be applied with other well-researched statistical risk prediction instruments.

To those who are interested in rendering state-of-the-art assessments of reoffence likelihood, we recommend an integrated approach. This approach has three steps: (1) estimating long-term sexual recidivism rates associated with the combined effect of Static-99R and psychological risk factors; (2) allowing for the development of internal protective factors; and (3) allowing for the release environment. There are different ways in which each of these steps can be accomplished.

The first step in this approach is to estimate the long-term recidivism rate associated with the combination of Static-99R score and psychological risk factors that apply to the individual after the index sex offence and prior to participation in subsequent meaningful treatment. This recidivism estimate will relate to the average offence behaviour of untreated offenders similar in assessed risk features to the individual being assessed in the release environments that prevailed for samples used to estimate recidivism rates.

Estimating Long-Term Sexual Recidivism Rates Associated with Static-99R and Psychological Risk

There are at least four methods for the first step of conducting an integrated risk assessment. These methods are consistent with the research findings discussed previously in this chapter and are summarized as follows: differences in recidivism base rates between samples selected in risk-related ways and unselected samples reflect differences in the average density of psychological risk factors resulting from this selection process. Some of the strengths and limitations of the different methods are now discussed.

1. *Match referral process to sample selection process*

Where separate recidivism norms have been produced for different sample-selection processes, the evaluator should choose the recidivism norms generated by a sample-selection process that most closely resembles the process through which the individual being assessed was referred to the evaluator. For example, if all sexual offenders sentenced in a given district are routinely referred to an evaluator for assessment, then this evaluator should use recidivism norms from unselected samples. On the other hand, if only individuals whose presentation involves unusual and worrying features are referred to the evaluator, then recidivism norms from samples that were selected in a risk-related way are a better match.

The main two advantages of this selection matching method are that in some circumstances it is uncomplicated to apply and it takes into account implicit selection on unmeasured risk factors. There are two corresponding and serious disadvantages that make this, in our opinion, the method of last choice. First, the method is often complicated to apply since the nature of the referral process may be poorly understood or may not match any of the kinds of sample-selection processes of the normative samples. Second, even though samples selected in risk-related ways may on average show higher densities of psychological risk factors, this does not mean that every person selected in that way will show the same density of psychological risk factors. Some will show higher densities than are usual for that type of sample and others will show lower densities, and their risk can be expected to vary accordingly. Attempting to match the selection process will inevitably result in associating the offender's density of psychological risk factors to the average for the sample, which will be incorrect in many cases.

2. *Match the individual's density of psychological risk factors to the average density of psychological risk factors found in a given kind of normative sample.*

Phenix and Hanson (2013) gave recommended score thresholds on three instruments assessing density of psychological risk factors which instructs selecting the higher risk static instrument recidivism norms. These recidivism norms are used if these thresholds are met and otherwise norms from unselected (i.e., the norms from samples not preselected for risk) samples can be used.

Compared with the sample matching approach, the merit of this approach is that it offers a more objective way of selecting recidivism norms that is also likely to be more accurate. It does have two significant disadvantages. First, it in effect treats offenders as if they have only two different levels of psychological risk factors (the level associated with samples selected on a risk-related basis and the level associated with unselected samples), whereas in reality the density of psychological risk factors varies in a continuous way. As a consequence, this method significantly over-simplifies the influence of psychological risk factors upon risk. Second, because the research into any specific measure of psychological risk factors is limited, the statistical properties are not known precisely, and it is not clear how reliably clinicians can score them under adversarial conditions.

3. *Use equations that directly estimate the joint effect of Static-99R and specific measures of psychological risk factors*

Any of the studies that demonstrated the incremental predictive validity of psychological risk factors could be used to generate a prediction equation showing expected reconviction rates for any particular combination of psychological risk factors and Static-99R score. Equations of this kind have been calculated for SRA-FV, the VRS-SO (although using its own static measure rather than Static-99R), and STABLE-2007. For ease of use, the equations are sometimes simplified into tables that show the effect of three or four levels of psychological risk factors. These equations are available from the authors of the various scales and sometimes have been published (e.g., Thornton & Knight, 2015). This method represents an ideal yet early state-of-the-art of the field where risk assessment directly incorporates the influence of psychological and static risk factors.

This method has the advantage that it allows the joint effect upon recidivism of Static-99R and degree of psychological risk to be directly calculated in a much more precise way. It has the disadvantage that the equations have been estimated from fairly limited sample sizes at present, especially compared with the very large data sets supporting the Static-99 instruments. It is unclear how well the results from these early studies of the direct combined influence of psychological risk factors on risk will generalize across populations other than the limited range of specific ones studied. Although there is some support for thinking that these equations are reasonably good approximations because the level of prediction from different measures of psychological risk factors appears to be fairly similar over fairly diverse samples, a particular concern is that sample-specific factors may have influenced the base rates in the samples used to generate the prediction equations.

4.   *Use of prediction equations to adjust Static-99R scores within routine samples*

This methodology requires information about the relationship between density of psychological risk factors and scores on Static-99R in typical samples unselected for risk (routine samples). For any given Static-99R score, this information should tell us what the expected density of psychological risk factors is. The density of psychological risk factors shown by the individual can then be compared with the density expected, given his Static-99R score. If the density shown by the individual is unusually high or unusually low relative to this expectation, then prediction equations expressing the incremental predictive value of psychological risk factors over and above Static-99R can be used to adjust the risk estimate quantitatively.

In some ways, similarly to the third method described, this fourth method has the added advantage that the base rate is anchored in data from a more representative selection of routine samples than are used to estimate the prediction equations. Only the incremental slope parameter is used from the samples used to estimate equations, which means that no assumptions about the representativeness of the base rate in the samples used to estimate the equations is required.

The main limitation of this fourth method is that we do not currently have good data on the relation between psychological risk factors and Static-99R scores in routine samples; almost all of the data of this kind are from either samples preselected for treatment or samples selected for risk. In principle, of course, one might develop recidivism norms for samples selected for treatment or for risk, but these kinds of samples are less well defined than routine, unselected samples and so in the long run may provide a less satisfactory foundation.

The third and fourth methods also require a higher level of mathematical sophistication (use of equations, etc.) than most practising evaluators are comfortable with. This may only be a limitation in the short term, however, since equations can be implemented in spreadsheets so that the evaluator who wishes to use equation-based methods might simply pull up the relevant spreadsheet (perhaps from a website) and enter numbers representing Static-99R scores and the density of psychological risk factors.

Assessing for the Development of Internal Protective Factors

Having obtained an estimate of pretreatment risk, the second step in an integrated risk assessment is to assess for the development of internal protective factors that may have occurred in response to treatment. Arguably, this step might be omitted if the individual has not participated in a treatment programme since the only evidence we have of change leading to reduced recidivism has been from studies of treatment participants, but of course it is possible in principle that internal protective factors might develop in other ways. Currently the most credible work regarding the impact of protective factors is with the VRS-SO, where there are statistically convincing data over several samples, including different treatment programmes, showing that the VRS-SO Change score has incremental predictive value over pretreatment assessments of static risk factors and long-term vulnerabilities (Olver et al., 2013). For this instrument, prediction equations are available that allow a recidivism estimate to be based on the joint effect of static statistical risk factors, density of initial psychological risk factors, and change. This is essentially an extension of the third method described above.

The VRS-SO prediction model is a good fit for assessing offenders in treatment programmes that last up to 2 years and that occur within a few years of both sentencing and release. These constraints reflect the nature of samples from which the equations were estimated. Whether the model applies to materially different contexts is not yet known. Additionally, there are conceptual difficulties in applying this prediction model to individuals who have spent more than a decade in custody and who may have participated in multiple intensive treatment programmes over the years, with these programmes themselves lasting multiple years. The evaluator has to make a decision on where to place the point in time to assess pretreatment function (before the first treatment programme in the current sentence versus before the start of the most recent programme, etc.), and the assessment results obtained may be different depending on what decision the evaluator makes.

The other assessment scheme currently available that credibly measures the development of protective factors is the SAPROF (de Vogel et al., 2009). The primary available research with this instrument includes a mixture of sexually and non-sexually violent offenders and focuses on overall violence as an outcome measure. These analyses demonstrate that where high levels of predominantly internal protective factors are developed recidivism rates are much lower than those shown by individuals with the same risk factors but who had not developed this level of protective factors (de Vries Robbé et al., 2013). The magnitude of this effect is fairly substantial. For high-risk offenders, rated on the SAPROF as having developed at least moderate levels of protective factors, the recidivism rate was at least halved at all follow-up periods compared with those with low levels of protective factors. These results suggest that it is reasonable to halve expected recidivism rates based on pretreatment levels of risk factors for those who develop at least moderate levels of protective factors according to this instrument. de Vries Robbé (2014) has expanded these analyses to show that the incremental predictive value of protective factors defined by the SAPROF is reasonably similar regardless of whether the outcome is general violence or sexual violence, and regardless of whether those involved are sexual offenders or violent offenders.

The reader should note that the reliance of the above discussion of the effects of change on a very small number of samples, sometimes of limited sample size, is a reflection of the limited amount of research currently available regarding the predictive meaning of change. In short, the magnitude of the effect of developing protective factors upon the mitigation of likelihood of sexual reoffence is not known with precision.

Allowing for the Release Environment

Having obtained a pretreatment risk estimate and, where appropriate, having adjusted this risk estimate for the development of protective factors during treatment, a further adjustment must be made that takes into account the nature of the release environment. In this third step of integrated risk assessment, the evaluator compares the release environment that the individual being assessed is expected to return to with the release environment that was typical for the offenders in the samples used to generate the recidivism estimate in step one. If they differ significantly, the evaluator will want to review how sexual recidivism base rates differ between samples drawn from the different kinds of release environment. This comparison can then be used as a basis for adjusting the recidivism rate that would be expected for persons like the individual being assessed.

The Need for Professional Judgement in integrating different kinds of Influence

It is apparent from the above discussion that although risk assessment can be informed by statistical research, the complexity of the interacting influences on risk of recidivism is such that we urgently need research that systematically examines their combined influences within a single model. Until this is available, evaluators will need to use professional judgement in combining the different classes of influence in a way that is most relevant to the individual being assessed. A helpful perspective here is to think of statistical risk indicators and psychological risk factors as sources of risk for sexual reoffence and the development of protective factors, including controls in the external environment, as ways of mitigating the concern presented by these risks.

Summary and Conclusions

There are several valuable conclusions that can be drawn from this summary of the literature on psychological risk factors and their role in sexual reoffence. In an effort to advance the evolution of sexual offender risk assessment, we highlight the following:

1. Comprehensive assessment of psychological risk factors alone allows risk predictions that have about the same level of accuracy as those afforded by statistical prediction instruments based on simple demographics and criminal history.
2. The overall density of psychological risk factors has incremental predictive value beyond that afforded by static predictors.
3. The predictive properties of conventional statistical instruments such as Static-99R become unstable if the density of psychological risk factors is not assessed and taken into account.
4. Models for integrating static statistical risk indicators and psychological risk factors exist but are technically complicated and in need of further development. Nonetheless, those who wish to employ a risk assessment approach that is supported by contemporary research must employ a method of incorporating psychological risk factors into risk assessment.
5. Psychological risk factors and their contribution to risk vary in the temporal domain.
6. Enduring aspects of psychological risk factors can be conceptualized as long-term vulnerabilities.
7. More actively dynamic aspects of psychological risk factors can be understood in terms of behavioural intentions, their proximate determinants, and accumulation of internal and external resources supportive of those intentions.

8. Resources enabling self-regulation of long-term vulnerabilities and the accumulation of resources supportive of prosocial intentions can be understood as protective factors and make appropriate targets in treatment.
9. The development of internal protective factors can significantly reduce level of risk even for individuals with high levels of statistical and psychological risk factors. This is best documented in the context of offenders participating in treatment programmes.
10. Risk may be further reduced by the development of external protective factors through intensive community risk management.
11. Truly high levels of risk apply when high levels of statistical and psychological risk indicators are present, protective factors have not been developed, and intensive community risk management is not available.

References

Allan, M., Grace, R. C., Rutherford, B., & Hudson, S. M. (2007). Psychometric assessment of dynamic risk factors for child molesters. *Sexual Abuse: A Journal of Research and Treatment*, *19*, 347–367.

Andrews, D. A., & Bonta, J. (2006). *The psychology of criminal conduct* (4th ed.). Newark, NJ: LexisNexis.

Andrews, D. A., Bonta, J., & Wormith, S. J. (2006). The recent past and near future of risk and/or need assessment. *Crime and Delinquency*, *52*, 7–27.

Bartleby.com (1999). *Holy Bible, King James Version*. New York, NY: American Bible Society. Retrieved from www.bartleby.com/108/

Beech, A. R., Fisher, D. D., & Beckett, R. (1998). *Step 3: An evaluation of the Prison Sex Offender Treatment Programme. A report for the Home Office by the STEP team*. London: Home Office.

Beech, A. R., and Ward, T. (2004). The integration of etiology and risk in sexual offenders: A theoretical framework. *Aggression and Violent Behavior*, *10*, 31–63.

Beggs, S. M., & Grace, R. C. (2010). Assessment of dynamic risk factors: An independent validation study of the Violence Risk Scale: Sexual Offender Version. *Sexual Abuse: A Journal of Research and Treatment*, *22*, 234–251.

Blacker, J., Beech, A. R., Wilcox, D. T., & Boer, D. P. (2011). The assessment of dynamic risk and recidivism in a sample of special needs sex offenders. *Psychology, Crime & Law*, *17*, 75–92.

Blanchard, R., Kuban, M. E., Blak, T., Klassen, P. E. Dickey, R., & Cantor, J. M. (2012). Sexual attraction to others: A comparison of two models of alloerotic responding in men. *Archives of Sexual Behavior*, *41*, 13–29.

Boccaccini, M. T., Murrie, D. C., Caperton, J. D., & Hawes, S. W. (2009). Field validity of the Static-99 and MnSOST-R among sex offenders evaluated for civil commitment as sexually violent predators. *Psychology, Public Policy and Law*, *15*, 278–314.

Boer, D. P., Hart, S. D., Kropp, P. R., & Webster, C. D. (1997). *Manual for the Sexual Violence Risk-20: Professional guidelines for assessing risk of sexual violence*. Vancouver, Canada: British Columbia Institute Against Family Violence.

Borum, R., Bartel, P., & Forth, A. (2003). *Manual for the structured assessment of violence risk in youth (SAVRY), version 1.1*. Tampa, FL: University of South Florida.

Conte, J. (1994). Child sexual abuse: Awareness and backlash. *The Future of Children*, *4*, 224–232.

Craig, L. A., Thornton, D., Beech, A., & Browne, K. D. (2007). The relationship of statistical and psychological risk marker to sexual reconviction in child molesters. *Criminal Justice and Behavior*, *34*, 314–329.

de Vogel, V., de Ruiter, C., Bouman, Y., & de Vries Robbé, M. (2009). *SAPROF. Guidelines for the assessment of protective factors for violence risk*. Utrecht, The Netherlands: Forum Educatief.

de Vries Robbé, M. (2014). *Protective factors: Validation of the structured assessment of protective factors for violence risk in forensic psychiatry* (PhD thesis, Van der Hoeven Kliniek, Utrecht, The Netherlands).

de Vries Robbé, M., de Vogel, V., & Douglas, K. S. (2013). Risk factors and protective factors: A two-sided dynamic approach to violence risk assessment. *Journal of Forensic Psychiatry & Psychology*, *24*, 440–457.

D'Orazio, D. M. (2013). Lessons learned from history and experience: Five simple ways to improve the efficacy of sexual offender treatment. *International Journal of Behavioral Consultation and Therapy*, *8*, 3–4.

Doren, D. M. (2004). Stability of the interpretative risk percentages for the RRASOR and Static-99. *Sexual Abuse: A Journal of Research and Treatment*, *16*, 25–36.

Douglas, K. S., Hart, S. D., Webster, C. D., Belfrage, H., Guy, L., & Wilson, C. M. (2014). Historical-Clinical-Risk Management-20, Version 3 (HCR-20^{V3}): Development and overview. *International Journal of Forensic Mental Health*, *13*, 93–108. Retrieved from http://tinyurl.com/orvyj2a

Duwe, G., & Freske, P. J. (2012). Using logistic regression modeling to predict sexual recidivism: The Minnesota Sex Offender Screening Tool-3 (MnSOST-3). *Sexual Abuse: A Journal of Research and Treatment*, *24*, 350–377. doi:10.1177/1079063211429470

Eher, R., Rettenberger, M., Gaunersdorfer, K., Haubner-MacLean, T., Matthes, A., Schilling, F., & Mokros, A. (2013). Über die Treffsicherheit standardisierter Risikoeinschätzungsverfahren bei aus der Maßregel entlassenen Sexualstraftätern [On the accuracy of standardized risk assessment procedures for the evaluation of discharged sex offenders]. *Forensische Psychiatrie, Psychologie, Kriminologie*, *7*, 264–272.

Finkelhor, D. (1979). *Sexually victimized children*. New York, NY: Free Press.

Fishbein, M., & Ajzen, I. (2010). *Predicting and changing behavior*. New York, NY: Psychology Press.

Friendship, C., & Thornton, D. (2001). Sexual reconviction for sexual offenders discharged from prison in England and Wales: Implications for evaluating treatment. *British Journal of Criminology*, *41*, 285–292.

Gray, N. S., Brown, A. S., MacCulloch, M. J., Smith, J., & Snowden, R. J. (2005). An implicit test of the associations between children and sex in paedophiles. *Journal of Abnormal Psychology*, *114*, 304–308.

Hanson, R. K., Bourgon, G., Helmus, L., & Hodgson, S. (2009). The principles of effective correctional treatment also apply to sexual offenders: A meta-analysis. *Criminal Justice and Behavior*, *36*, 865–891.

Hanson, R. K., Gordon, A., Harris, A. J. R., Marques, J. K., Murphey, W., Quinsey, V. L., & Seto, M. C. (2002). First report of the collaborative outcome data project on the effectiveness of psychological treatment for sex offenders. *Sexual Abuse: A Journal of Research and Treatment*, *14*, 169–194.

Hanson, R. K., Harris, A. J. R., Scott, T.-L., & Helmus, L. (2007). *Assessing the risk of sexual offenders on community supervision: The Dynamic Supervision Project (User Report Corrections Research)*. Ottawa, Canada: Public Safety Canada.

Hanson, R.K., & Thornton, D. (2000). Static-99: Improving risk assessments for sex offenders: A comparison of three actuarial scales. *Law and Human Behavior*, *24*, 119–136.

Hanson, R. K., & Thornton, D. (2012, October). Preselection effects can explain group differences in sexual recidivism base rates in Static-99R Validation studies. Paper presented at the Association for the Treatment of Sexual Abusers Annual Research and Treatment Conference, Denver, CO.

Harkins, L., Beech, A., & Thornton, D. (2009, October). *The use of dynamic risk domains assessed using psychometric measures to revise relative risk assessment using RM 2000 and Static 2002.* Paper presented at the 28th Annual Research and Treatment Conference of the Association for the Treatment of Sexual Abusers, Dallas, TX.

Harris, A., & Hanson, R. K. (2010). Clinical, actuarial and dynamic risk assessment of sexual offenders: Why do things keep changing?. *Journal of Sexual Aggression, 16*(3), 296–310.

Harris, A. J. R., Helmus, L., Hanson, R. K., & Thornton, D. (2008, October). Are new norms needed for Static-99? Workshop presented at the ATSA 27th Annual Research and Treatment Conference on October 23, 2008, Atlanta, GA. Retrieved from http://www.static99.org/pdfdocs/arenewnormsneededforstatic-99october2008.pdf

Helmus, L. (2007). *A multi-site comparison of the validity and utility of the Static-99 and Static-2002 for risk assessment with sexual offenders* (Unpublished honours thesis). Carleton University, Ottawa, Canada.

Helmus, L. (2009). *Re-norming Static-99 recidivism estimates: Exploring base rate variability across sex offender samples* (Unpublished master's thesis). Carleton University, Ottawa, Canada.

Helmus, L., & Hanson, R. K. (2012, October). Dynamic risk assessment using STABLE-2007: Updated follow up and new findings from the Dynamic Supervision Project. Paper presented at the ATSA Conference, Denver CO.

Helmus, L., Hanson, R. K., Babchishin, K. M., & Mann, R. E. (2013) Attitudes supportive of sexual offending predict recidivism: A meta-analysis. *Trauma, Violence and Abuse, 14,* 34–53.

Helmus, L., Hanson, R. K., Thornton, D., Babchishin, K. M., & and Harris, A. J. R. (2012). Absolute recidivism rates predicted by Static-99R and Static-2002R sex offender risk assessment tools vary across samples: A meta-analysis. *Criminal Justice and Behavior, 39,* 1148–1171.

Helmus, L., Thornton, D., Hanson, R. K., & Babchishin, K. M. (2011). Improving the predictive accuracy of Static-99 and Static-2002 with older sex offenders: Revised age weights. *Sexual Abuse: A Journal of Research and Treatment, 24,* 64–101. doi:10.1177/1079063211409951

Kamphuis, J. H., De Ruiter, C., Janssen, B., & Spiering, M. (2005). Preliminary evidence for an automatic link between sex and power among men who molest children. *Journal of Interpersonal Violence, 20,* 1351–1365.

Knight, R. A., Sims-Knight, J., & Guay, J. (2013). Is a separate diagnostic category defensible for paraphilic coercion? *Journal of Criminal Justice, 41,* 90–99.

Knight, R. A., & Thornton, D. (2007). Evaluating and improving risk assessment schemes for sexual recidivism: A long term follow up of convicted sexual offenders (Final Report: US Department of Justice, Award No. 2003-WG-BX-1002). Retrieved from http://www.ncjrs.gov/pdffiles1/nij/grants/217618.pdf

Kropp, P. R., Hart, S. D., Webster, C. D., & Eaves, D. (1994). *Manual for the Spousal Assault Risk Assessment guide.* Vancouver, Canada: British Columbia Institute on Family Violence.

Logan, C. (2014). The HCR-20 Version 3: A case study in risk formulation. *International Journal of Forensic Mental Health, 13,* 172–180. Retrieved from http://tinyurl.com/p3lnknv

Looman, J., & Abracen, J. (2012, October). Long-term follow-up of two groups of sex offenders. Paper presented at the Annual Research and Treatment Conference of the Association for the Treatment of Sexual Abusers, Denver, CO.

Mann, R. E., Hanson, R. K., & Thornton, D. T. (2010). Assessing risk for sexual recidivism: Some proposals on the nature of psychologically meaningful risk factors. *Sexual Abuse: A Journal of Research and treatment, 22,* 191–217.

McGrath, R. J., Lasher, M. P., & Cumming, G. F. (2012). The sex offender treatment intervention and progress scale (SOTIPS): Psychometric properties and incremental predictive validity with Static-99R. *Sexual Abuse: A Journal of Research and Treatment, 24,* 431–458.

Menzies, R. J., Webster, C. D., McMain, S., Staley, S., & Scaglione, R. (1994). The dimensions of dangerousness revisited: Assessing forensic predictions about criminality and violence. *Law and Human Behaviour, 18,* 695–700.

Mihailides, S., Devilly, G. J., & Ward, T. (2004). Implicit cognitive distortions and sexual offending. *Sexual Abuse: A Journal of Research and Treatment, 16,* 333–350.

Miller, W., & Rollnick, S. (2013). *Motivational interviewing: Helping people change* (3rd ed.). New York, NY: Guilford Press.

Minnesota Department of Corrections (2007). *Sex offender recidivism in Minnesota.* St. Paul, MN: Author.

Nunes, K. L., Firestone, P., & Baldwin, M. W. (2007). Indirect assessment of cognitions of child sexual abusers with the implicit association test. *Criminal Justice and Behavior, 34,* 454–474.

Olver, M.E., Beggs Christofferson, S. M., Grace, R. C., & Wong, S. P. C. (2014). Incorporating change information into sexual offender risk assessments using the Violence Risk Scale – Sexual Offender Version. *Sex Abuse: A Journal of Research and Treatment, 26,* 472–499.

Olver, M. E., Wong, S. C. P., Nicholaichuk, T., & Gordon, A. (2007). The validity and reliability of the Violence Risk Scale – Sexual Offender Version: Assessing sex offender risk and evaluating therapeutic change. *Psychological Assessment, 19,* 318–329.

Phenix, A., & Hanson, R. K. (2013, October). Issues in report writing and court testimony: Static-99R and Static-2002R. Paper presented at the Association for the Treatment of Sexual Abusers Annual Research and Treatment Conference, Chicago, IL.

Singh, J. P., Grann, M., & Fazel, S. (2011). A comparative study of risk assessment tools: A systematic review and metaregression analysis of 68 studies involving 25,980 participants. *Clinical Psychology Review, 31,* 499–513. doi:10.1016/j.cpr.2010.11.00931

Thornton, D. (2002). Constructing and testing a framework for dynamic risk assessment. *Sexual Abuse: A Journal of Research and Treatment, 14,* 137–151.

Thornton, D., & D'Orazio, D. (2011, June). *Elaborating the long-term vulnerability model of criminogenic needs.* Paper presented at the International Association of Forensic Mental Health Services Annual Conference, Barcelona, Spain.

Thornton, D., & D'Orazio, D. (2013). Best practice in SVP treatment programs. In L. C. Craig, L. Dixon, & T. Gannon (Eds.), *What works in offender rehabilitation: An evidenced based approach to assessment and treatment.* Chichester, England, John Wiley & Sons, Ltd.

Thornton, D., Hanson, R. K., & Helmus, L. (2009). *Moving beyond the standard model of actuarial assessment for sex offenders.* Perspectives: Quarterly Newsletter of the California Coalition on Sexual Offending, 1–4.

Thornton, D., & Knight, R. A. (2015). Construction and validation of SRA-FV need assessment. *Sex Abuse, A Journal of Research and Treatment, 27,* 360–375.

Thornton, D., Mann, R., Webster, S., Blud, L., Travers, R., Friendship, C., & Erickson, M. (2003). Distinguishing and combining risks for sexual and violent recidivism. *Annals of the New York Academy of Sciences, 989,* 225–235; Discussion, 236–246.

Ward, T., & Keenan, T. (1999). Child molesters' implicit theories. *Journal of Interpersonal Violence, 14*, 821–838.

Ward, T., & Stewart, C. A. (2003). Good lives and the rehabilitation of sexual offenders. In T. Ward, D. R. Laws, & S. M. Hudson (Eds.), *Sexual deviance: Issues and controversies* (pp. 21–44). Thousand Oaks, CA, Sage.

Webster, C. D., Douglas, K. S., Eaves, D., & Hart, S. D. (1997). *HCR-20: Assessing risk for violence (version 2).* Burnaby, Canada: Simon Fraser University, Mental Health, Law, and Policy Institute.

Webster, C. D., Eaves, D., Douglas, K. S., & Wintrup, A. (1995). *The HCR-20 scheme: The assessment of dangerousness and risk.* Burnaby, Canada: Simon Fraser University, Mental Health, Law, and Policy Institute, and Forensic Psychiatric Services Commission of British Columbia.

Wollert, R., & Waggoner, J. (2009). Bayesian computations protect sexually violent predator evaluations from the degrading effects of confirmation bias and illusions of certainty: A reply to Doren and Levenson (2009). *Sexual Offender Treatment, 4*(1), 1–23.

Zgoba, K. M., Miner, M., Knight, R., Letourneau, E., Levinson, J., & Thornton, D. (2012). A multi-state recidivism study using Static-99R and Static-2002 risk scores and tier guidelines from the Adam Walsh Act (End of Grant Report: US Department of Justice Award No. 2008-MU-MU-0001). Retrieved from https://www.ncjrs.gov/pdffiles1/nij/grants/240099.pdf

32

Further Support for a Convergent Approach to Sex Offender Risk Assessment

Jeffrey C. Singer

Private Practice, Morris Psychological Group, United States

Martin Rettenberger

Centre for Criminology (Kriminologische Zentralstelle – KrimZ), Wiesbaden, and
Johannes Gutenberg University Mainz (JGU), Germany

Douglas P. Boer

University of Canberra, Australia

Introduction

As we noted in an earlier book chapter on this topic,[1] Lanyon (2001) provided a useful framework for conducting psychological evaluations with sex offenders. However, there is more than one general method or approach to conducting sex offender risk evaluations. These approaches can be broadly defined as either actuarial risk assessment or structured professional judgement of risk. Some other terms have been used to describe hybrid methods, such as conceptual actuarial and empirical actuarial (Hanson & Morton-Bourgon, 2007). According to some authors, 'risk assessment procedures for sexual offenders over the last 15 years have evolved at a "dizzying pace"' (Harris & Hanson, 2010, p. 296). Yet it appears that Boer's (2006) conclusion that there was no convergence of opinion regarding the best method for risk assessment of sex offenders is still the case today, a finding strongly supported by several authoritative meta-analyses from the violence and sexual violence risk assessment measurement literature (Coid et al., 2011; Fazel, Sungh, Doll, & Grann, 2012; Singh, Grann, & Fazel,

---

[1] The present chapter is an updated and revised version of a previously published chapter by the current authors, with permission of the publisher (Singer, Boer, & Rettenberger, 2013).

The Wiley Handbook on the Theories, Assessment, and Treatment of Sexual Offending.
Edited by Douglas P. Boer. Volume II: Assessment, edited by Leam A. Craig and Martin Rettenberger.
© 2017 John Wiley & Sons, Ltd. Published 2017 by John Wiley & Sons, Ltd.

2011; Smid, Kamphuis, Wever, & Van Beek, 2014, Tully, Chou, & Browne, 2013; Yang, Wong, & Coid, 2010). Nonetheless, it is possible we as a field are approaching another developmental phase of risk assessment sophistication.

Skeem and Monahan (2011) stated, 'The violence risk assessment field may be reaching a point of diminishing returns in instrument development. … specific structured techniques seem to account for very little of the variance in predictive accuracy' (p. 41). Simultaneously, Lussier and Davies (2011) proposed implementing 'a person-oriented approach', while questioning the utility of the current state of risk assessment, dominated by the 'variable-oriented perspective' (p. 530). According to Lussier and Davies (2011), the current 'variable-oriented perspective' is too simplistic as it is 'based on the assumption that the risk of reoffending is linear, additive, and relatively stable over time' (p. 530). The 'person-oriented approach' that they proposed is more in line with prior criminological life course scholarship (Moffitt, 1993; Sampson & Laub, 2005), rather than emphasizing the unique, historical, static risk factors that seem to dominate the field today. Finally, commenting on the current state of risk assessment, Haque and Webster (2013) succinctly stated, 'asymptote has, it seems, been reached – at least for the time being' (p. 242).

Regardless of which side of the actuarial versus structured professional judgement debate one lands on (Dvoskin & Heilbrun, 2001; Sjöstedt & Grann, 2002), there is consensus that unguided clinical judgement (UCJ) is no longer a viable approach to risk assessment. UCJ has been aptly referred to as 'subjective and impressionistic' (Grove & Meehl, 1996), 'intuitive' and 'experiential' (Hart, 2008), and 'unrestrained' (Wollert, 2007). UCJ occurs when the evaluator formulates a clinical hypothesis using idiosyncratic and unverifiable criteria for drawing risk conclusions. Such practice typically occurs with a review of records and an unstructured clinical interview, but could include the use of tests that are potentially unrelated to risk (e.g., most personality tests). Sometimes UCJ is offered without the articulation of rationale. UCJ has the advantage of convenience and feels intuitively good, relying on basic common sense.

Evaluators relying on UCJ often produce reports that contain material similar to the following: He was unempathic and showed no remorse; his answers were too rehearsed or not rehearsed enough; too emotional or not emotional enough; didn't know his crime cycle or knew his crime cycle by rote; wore a T-shirt with the slogan 'Anarchy' on it and is therefore violent; has stared at female therapists and therefore has 'rapism'; had group sex and is therefore deviant; minimized, denied, and blamed others; sees self as a victim of the system, and the best of the worst UCJ behaviour to emit to assess risk to sexually reoffend: he walked out of the interview. Other examples of UCJ errors include noting that inconsistency, prevaricating, having access to willing partners yet sexually offending, not having partners to have sex with and therefore sexual offending to gratify his sexual needs, having insufficient treatment, needing treatment, being antisocial, being angry, having intimacy deficits, having cognitive distortions, and substance abuse have all been viewed by assessors as indicative of high sexual reoffence risk. The aforementioned variables are greatly dependent on the evaluation circumstance context. Research has either not supported the above factors as being directly associated with sexual reoffence, or suggests they are indicative of being merely a typical recidivist (e.g., antisocial), or the constructs are so vague that they are unfalsifiable, meaning untestable.

Bad ideas apparently die very slowly, perhaps in part due to the availability cascade heuristic, which posits that if something is said enough times, it must be true (Kuran & Sunstein, 1999), and debiasing in general (Hansen, Gerbasi, Todorov, Kruse, & Pronin, 2014; Lewandowsky, Ecker, Seifert, Schwarz, & Cook, 2012). Yet as far back as 1986, Meehl concluded that when compared with a mechanical algorithmic assessment approach, unaided clinical judgement is inferior. Meehl concluded, 'There is no controversy in social science that shows such a large body of qualitatively diverse studies coming out so uniformly in the same direction as this one' (Meehl, 1986, pp. 373–374). For the past 50 years, unstructured, or unguided, clinical judgement has been shown to be an inaccurate method to make diagnoses or judgements and typically creates false-positive results (Janus & Meehl, 1997). A false positive means concluding that a condition exists when it does not. Such approaches are vulnerable to numerous sources of error, including the Fundamental Attribution Error (Ross, 1977), and various forms of cognitive heuristics (Kanheman, 2003, 2011; Kahneman & Tversky, 1973, 1984, 1996; Neal & Grisso, 2014; Tversky & Kahneman, 1974, 1983), i.e., the tendency to use thinking short cuts when faced with complex tasks. Aside from being an inaccurate method, not surprisingly, UCJ has poor interrater reliability (Grove, Zald, Lebow, Snitz, & Nelson, 2000; Monahan & Steadman, 1994), yet continues to be used even in basic clinical practice (Vrieze & Grove, 2009).

The problems with UCJ came into sharp focus with the landmark ruling of the Supreme Court of the United States in *Barefoot v. Estelle*, 463 U.S. 880 (1983), noting 'that psychiatrists are always wrong with respect to future dangerousness, only most of the time'. In that case, one of the experts cited Monahan's (1981) classic book *Predicting Violent Behaviour: An Assessment of Clinical Techniques*, highlighting that the '"best" clinical research currently in existence indicates that psychiatrists and psychologists are accurate in no more than one out of three predictions of violent behavior over a several-year period among institutionalized populations that had both committed violence in the past … and who were diagnosed as mentally ill' (p. 77). Yet Monahan (1981) began his monograph by highlighting, 'there may be circumstances in which prediction is both empirically possible and ethically appropriate' (p. 19). During the same period, much research on the prediction of violence was being done in the maximum-security treatment programme in the Oak Ridge Division of the Mental Health Centre in Penetanguishene, Ontario, Canada. The aggregate of this important work can be found in *Violent Offenders: Appraising and Managing Risk* (Quinsey, Harris, Rice, & Cormier, 1998). These events helped herald in the second generation of risk assessment measures (Monahan, 1984; Otto 1992), driven by enthusiasm over actuarial, static factor assessment.

Actuarial Risk Assessment

The allure of actuarial assessment is understandable. This approach considers a small number of variables with the application of explicit statistical rules for combining and weighing a few variables into a total risk tally (Meehl, 1954). In addition to empirically based norms, true actuarial assessment eliminates the potential error and bias of human judgement (Dawes, Faust, & Meehl, 1989). The elimination of human error is enhanced by the focus in actuarial assessment on static, or historical, variables that cannot be altered. Sexual recidivism actuarial risk assessment instruments (Janus & Prentky, 2003; Prentky et al., 2006), also called actuarial risk assessment instruments (ARAIs) (Vrieze & Grove, 2008), are also based on regression equations between predictor and outcome variables, decision trees, or arithmetic algorithms and have explicit rules for scoring (Hanson & Morton-Bourgon, 2009; Quinsey et al., 1998). Actuarial tests are based on the idea that practitioners can tally the number of predefined risk factors and see the observed rate of sexual recidivism with other sexual recidivists who share the same historical predetermined risk factors. The clear advantage of actuarial risk assessment is the elimination of subjective human judgement. Actuarial tests yield ranges of risk such as low, medium, and high, with percentages of those sexual recidivists who share the common historical risk characteristics. A highly recognized sexual recidivism actuarial risk assessment instrument is the Static-99R (www.static99 .org) (Helmus, Thornton, Hanson, & Babchishin, 2012; Rettenberger, Haubner-MacLean, & Eher, 2013), based on the Static-99 (Hanson & Thornton, 1999). Also recently revised is the Sex Offender Risk Appraisal Guide (SORAG) (Quinsey et al., 1998; Rice, Harris, & Lang, 2013).

Assuming that the empirical validation studies of actuarial tests are psychometrically sound, actuarial risk assessment can potentially be a relevant source of information regarding risk assessment (e.g., Barbaree, Seto, Langton, & Peacock, 2001; Rettenberger, Matthes, Boer, & Eher, 2010). However, actuarial risk assessment instruments do not usually yield information regarding recognized diagnoses of any form of psychopathology, mental disorders, mental conditions, personality disorders, or mental illnesses. Nor do such instruments provide any information on risk-relevant symptomology of the client being assessed. The use of actuarial risk assessment instruments under diagnostic conditions can be likened to a cardiologist applying a life insurance actuarial table to make a diagnosis of cardiac disease.[2] However, since one might argue that actuarial results can be a proxy to impaired sexual behavioural control, several issues regarding actuarial assessment need to be addressed.

All forms of assessment require an understanding of the base rate issue. The base rate is simply the frequency with which any event of interest occurs. For example, if 0.5% of the general public were ophthalmologists and 99.5% of the public were not ophthalmologists, then the base rate of being an ophthalmologist is simply 0.5%. A difficult concept to accept is that sexual reoffence rates among convicted sex offenders are low (Rettenberger, Briken, Turner, & Eher, 2015; Sandler, Freeman, & Socia, 2008; Wollert & Waggoner, 2009) and subsequent analyses by the Static-99 research shows that the recidivism rates are decreasing, resulting in reduced percentage risk levels (Helmus, Hanson, & Thornton, 2009) and reduced certainty in assessed risk levels (Wollert, 2006). Hence the question, considering the low base rate of sexual reoffence, becomes: are actuarial tests able to detect a counterintuitively low-frequency event without creating too many false positives?

---

[2]The more recently proposed third generation of actuarial risk assessment methods, which are based on dynamic factors or criminogenic needs (Harris & Hanson, 2010; Mann, Hanson, & Thornton, 2010), provide a possible solution for some of the methodological and clinical problems and shortcomings discussed in the present section (Eher, Matthes, Schilling, Haubner-MacLean, & Rettenberger, 2012; Hanson, Harris, Scott, & Helmus, 2007).

Another problem with actuarial assessment is the applicability of nomothetic data to the individual case. The analogy between actuarial risk assessments in the insurance industry and this type of assessment clouds an important difference between the two situations. The insurance actuary has no interest in when a particular death will occur but only how to maximize profits based on group data. The current circumstance does not call for an aggregate norm but case-specific information. The authors of the Static-99 echo this caution: 'The recidivism estimates provided by the Static-99 are group estimates based upon reconvictions and were derived from groups of individuals with these characteristics. As such, these estimates do not directly correspond to the recidivism risk of an individual offender' (www.static99.org, Static-99 coding rules 2003, Appendix 7, p. 71). Mossman (2006, 2008) and Mossman and Sellke (2007) have published a series of articles noting that this issue can be overcome, but not surprisingly, some others disagree (Cooke & Michie, 2010; Hart & Cooke, 2013; Hart, Michie, & Cooke, 2007; Vrieze & Grove, 2008) and some offer advice on how to overcome this challenge (e.g., Donaldson & Abbott, 2011). Nonetheless, there is no shortage of criticisms regarding the use of actuarial instruments in sex offence evaluations, and these issues are beyond the scope of this chapter (e.g., Cooke, 2010; Hart, 2008; Waggoner, Wollert, & Cramer, 2008).

The accuracy issue of the Static-99 was noted by its authors: 'In applying these actuarial (risk assessment) instruments, there are, however, a number of important points that practitioners must keep in mind. First, the prediction level of all the instruments is low. Such levels do not warrant high confidence in decisions. Second, typically the instruments are applied to situations in which the base rate of recidivism is low, making it difficult to increase the overall hit rate over simply using the base rates' (Knight & Thornton, 2007, p. 83).

In spite of the relatively recent introduction of the Static-99R with the hope of increased actuarial accuracy, problems remain (Rettenberger et al., 2013). Currently, scoring the Static-99R now requires human judgement to choose one of four reference groups, obviating one of the distinct advantages of actuarial risk assessment. Furthermore, the properties of reference groups themselves have been questioned (Abbott, 2009, 2011; Donaldson & Abbott, 2011; Campbell & DeClue, 2010a,2010b), with recent research attempting to address these substantive issues (Hanson, Thornton, Helmus, & Babchishin, 2015). In addition, the scoring norms have changed several times, most recently with the publication of the 1 January 2015 version of the Evaluator's Workbook on the www.static99.org website (Phenix, Helmus, & Hansen, 2015). Parenthetically, an interesting timeline, replete with references to the entire Static-99R evolution, is provided at Karen Franklin's oft-cited forensic psychology blog by using the search term 'Static-99: A bumpy developmental path'.

Static-99R troubles notwithstanding, reviews of the performance of actuarial risk assessment instruments to assess risk of sexual recidivism have been mediocre (Eher, Rettenberger, Schilling, & Pfäfflin, 2008; Kroner, Mills, & Reddon, 2005; Langton et al., 2007; Mokros, Stadtland, Osterheider, & Nedopil, 2010; Rettenberger et al., 2010; Vrieze & Grove, 2010; Yang et al., 2010), except to rule out risk of sexual reoffence given the low base rates of such events (Campbell, 2011).

Another assessment approach with an intuitive appeal combines actuarial with clinical judgement, commonly referred to as the 'adjusted-actuarial approach' (AAA)

(Petrila & Otto, 2001). Using AAA, an evaluator finds an actuarial tool's estimate of recidivism risk and then adjusts, either higher or lower, the actuarial result, purportedly relying on risk factors that have empirical support to go 'beyond the actuarial scheme' (Doren, 2002, pp. 156–158). Research by Hanson and Morton-Bourgon (2009) has borne out that this is not an acceptable method as it creates error from the mixing of two completely different approaches of assessment. The effects of anchoring, a cognitive heuristic (thinking short cut), further compounds the error rate with the AAA and is addressed more comprehensively in the following section. Research examining clinical overrides with the outdated Static-99 highlights this error in assessment practice (Storey, Watt, Jackson, & Hart, 2012). Basically, Storey et al. (2012) found that when clinicians used their discretion to override risk ratings derived using the Static-99, the accuracy of risk ratings decreased. Further, Campbell and DeClue (2010a) highlighted the substantial pitfalls associated with adjusting actuarial scores. In addition to the informative history of actuarial assessment provided, DeClue (2013) concluded, especially in reference to sexually violent predator civil commitment hearings in the United States, 'Available research does not support the use of professional judgment to adjust or override actuarial-based risk assessment of sexual recidivism' (p. 23).

Structured Professional Judgement

The other major method is called structured professional judgement (SPJ) (Douglas & Skeem, 2005), which has also been called guided professional judgement (Lieberman, Krauss, & Kyger, 2007). SPJ appears to be enjoying a recent resurgence of interest across a broad set of domains (Belfrage et al., 2012; Douglas et al., 2014; Falzer, 2013; Guy, Packer, & Warnken, 2012; Haque & Webster, 2013; Pedersen, Rasmussen, & Elsass, 2010). SPJ can be broadly defined as 'decision(s) made without fixed and explicit rules but based at least in part on consideration of a standardized information base' (Kropp & Hart, 2000, p. 103, footnote 4). SPJ instruments assess risk factors and symptom variables that have been found repeatedly in the extant empirical literature to be associated with sexual reoffence risk and diagnostic accuracy. SPJ allows the examiner to integrate and synthesize a multitude of variables in a structured manner with the goal of deciphering the empirically supported relevant diagnostic or risk factors along the continuums of frequency, intensity, duration, likelihood, imminence, and salience. This approach is more flexible than an actuarial approach and allows for the consideration of case-specific considerations. The relevant risk factor variables are combined accordingly in the present, to make a systematic, professional opinion about the respondents' diagnosis and/or risk depending on the referral question.

The Sexual Violence Risk-20 (SVR-20) (Boer, Hart, Kropp, & Webster, 1997) is a structured clinical guideline designed for the risk assessment of sexual violence in sex offenders. The authors of SVR-20 refer to it as an 'aide memoire' or a means to structure one's clinical thinking about the case at hand. This procedure reflects the application of what was called an empirically guided approach, or guided professional judgement, and is presently referred to as SPJ. The items are based on sexual

offence recidivism risk factors gathered from reviews of the extant empirical literature. The final risk judgement can be indicated in terms of low, moderate, or high in
terms of need for treatment, level of supervision intensity, and level of need for a risk
management plan.

Limitations to using this approach are the absence of actual empirically derived
scoring norms and cut-off scores, the presumption that more risk factors present automatically means greater risk, and methodological and clinical problems in the communication process of risk-relevant information (Hilton, Carter, Harris, & Sharpe, 2008),
the assumption that the list is exhaustive, and that this type of risk assessment approach
leaves the weighting of each risk factor to each individual examiner. It is also worth
noting that seeing a large number of risk factors can unduly bias the perception of risk
just as easily as seeing a small number of risk factors as an artifact of cognitive heuristics
(i.e., availability and representativeness heuristics; Neal & Grisso, 2014).

Among the strengths of SPJ risk assessment is that the risk items have an empirical basis for consideration and that 'case-specific' factors can be considered, which
in such evaluations seems prudent. In the meantime, there exist a number of independent cross-validation studies that indicated moderate to good predictive accuracy
comparable to the above-mentioned actuarial risk assessment instruments (e.g., de
Vogel, de Ruiter, van Beek, & Mead, 2004; Rettenberger, Boer, & Eher, 2011; Rettenberger et al., 2010). The SVR-20 also helps organize the myriad of variables in
such evaluations. While this approach allows for the consideration of either higher,
or lower, sexual recidivism risk than fixed actuarial scoring rules allow, merely tallying
SVR-20 factors to adjust an actuarial score is not acceptable practice: it would be the
haphazard, i.e., untested, mixing of two assessment models plus the error created by
anchoring effects.

Anchoring

The issue of anchoring deserves some special attention in this chapter as it is seen
as one possible means of providing a risk assessment that incorporates actuarial data
with either SPJ data or, more loosely termed, 'psychologically meaningful risk factors'
(Mann et al., 2010). The term 'risk assessment' was defined by Boer et al. (1997) as
'the process of evaluating individuals to (1) characterize the risk that they will commit
violence in the future, and (2) develop interventions to manage or reduce that risk'
(p. 1). Given that such risk characterizations would be different for each individual,
risk assessment necessarily occurs under conditions of uncertainty.

When people are tasked with making decisions under conditions of uncertainty,
Tversky and Kahneman (1974) demonstrated that people would resort to thinking
short cuts, also called 'cognitive heuristics'. Despite the function of cognitive heuristics to economize complex judgements, these short cuts can lead to systematic and
substantial severe errors. One reliable heuristic occurs when people are given identical
information in various orders and make significantly different judgements when an initial estimate is adjusted as new information is added. Tversky and Kahneman (1974)
noted, 'different starting points yield different estimates, which are biased toward the
initial values' (p. 1128). In other words, when people are tasked to make judgements

under conditions of uncertainty, such as risk assessments, they are greatly influenced, or 'anchored' by, their starting point in the analysis. That the anchoring bias was still being discussed over 35 years later (Kahneman, 2011, pp. 119–128) highlights the importance of this bias.

Adjusting actuarial results within any type of assessment method appears to be an exemplar of the anchoring bias. For example, regarding pure actuarial results:

> This strategy is not that of taking an actuarial estimate as an additional piece of information to combine with a clinical appraisal of dangerousness, but rather to *anchor* [italics added] clinical judgment by having the clinician start with an actuarial estimate of risk and then to alter it by examining dynamic variables, such as treatment outcome, treatment intensity, and supervision quality. (Quinsey, Rice, & Harris, 1995, p. 100)

That advice defines the anchoring bias. In a well-known article on risk communication, actuarial data are again laden with this term: 'Actuarial data to *anchor* [italics added] clinical risk assessments have been reported both for inpatient violence (McNiel & Binder, 1994) and for violence in the open community (Harris, Rice, & Quinsey, 1993)' (Monahan & Steadman, 1996, p. 931). Adjusting actuarial data causes inaccurate findings not only as a result of the anchoring heuristic, but also from the compounding error variance created from data that covary. Whatever accurate yield has been already gleaned will be diminished by either double counting information already accounted for within the variables of the actuarial itself, or from error variance from the imposition of an untested, entirely different method of assessment. In concordance with the previously cited research on the pitfalls of AAA, we clearly do not see adjusting actuarial test data using SPJ information, however conceived, as a valid approach to risk assessment.

Incremental Validity

From a methodological point of view, the issue of convergent risk assessment refers to the question of whether a combination of two or more risk assessment instruments yields a better (i.e., higher predictive accuracy and/or higher clinical utility) result than one instrument alone. In other words, the empirical question is whether the combination of the Static-99 and the SVR-20 or the Stable-2007 (Hanson, Harris, Scott, & Helmus, 2007) provides more and better risk assessment information than the Static-99 alone. If true, than these results might serve as a psychometric basis for a convergent approach to risk assessment. In the field of psychological assessment, the term 'incremental validity' is usually used for the description of this research question and is conceptually defined as the degree to which a measure explains or predicts a phenomenon of interest, relative to other measures (Haynes & Lench, 2003). In a more comprehensive manner, Hunsley (2003) noted various ways of defining incremental validity, including psychological measures to improve base rate measures, increasing predictive efficiency, and improving predictions in comparison with other sources of data. Despite the high potential for psychological research and clinical practice, until now there has been only little systematic effort in most areas of applied psychology to evaluate the incremental validity of measures and assessment procedures (Hunsley & Meyer, 2003).[3]

In forensic psychology, the concept of incremental validity has become relevant to the field of risk assessment, research, and practice. In simple words, the issue of incremental validity raises the question of whether a particular risk assessment instrument adds to the prediction of recidivism beyond what is captured by other risk assessment instruments alone (Rettenberger & Eher, 2013).

The concept of incremental validity is of interest for both forensic prediction research and practice for several reasons. First, surveys of forensic clinicians involved in sexual offender risk assessment and civil commitment proceedings demonstrated that most evaluators use different kinds of clinical and predictive data sources (Archer, Buffington-Vollum, Stredny, & Handel, 2006; Seto, 2005). Second, if used independently of each other, different risk assessment methods reach satisfactory predictive validity indices (Hanson & Morton-Bourgon, 2009; Rettenberger et al., 2010). For instance, Hanson and Morton-Bourgon (2009) showed that actuarial tests and also SPJ methods yielded effect sizes that were classified as moderate to good for the prediction of violent and sexual recidivism for different sexual offender populations. Third, even if different risk assessment instruments showed independently predictive validity, upon closer inspection of the results, different risk assessment instruments for sexual offenders could produce different risk rankings and the risk judgements derived from different instruments could also differ significantly (Barbaree, Langton, & Peacock, 2006a, 2006b; Craig, Browne, Stringer, & Beech, 2004). Therefore, studies about the incremental validity of forensic risk assessment instruments could help to guide the selection, application, and combination of different risk prediction measures for sexual offenders.

Although these findings from previous studies indicate the need for research on incremental validity, so far only a few exist.[4] One promising approach is the development and promulgation of so-called third-generation actuarial risk assessment instruments, which include exclusively or predominantly dynamic risk factors (sometimes also called criminogenic needs or psychologically meaningful risk factors; Harris & Hanson, 2010; Mann, Hanson, & Thornton, 2010). These instruments consist of risk factors that are amenable to changes based on interventions and therefore provide already conceptually incremental validity from a clinical point of view. Such instruments include the Stable-2007 (Hanson et al., 2007), Violence Risk Scale: Sex Offender Version (VRS:SO) (Wong, Olver, Nicholaichuk, & Gordon, 2003), and the Structured Assessment of Risk and Need – Treatment Needs Analysis (SARN-TNA; formerly the SRA as cited in Tully, Brown, & Craig, 2015), which could provide diagnostic and prognostic information over and above second-generation actuarial

---

[3] Therefore, in 2003, the journal *Psychological Assessment* addressed the problem of incremental validity in a special section on incremental validity and utility in clinical assessment (Hunsley, 2003).

[4] An exception is the concept of psychopathy defined by Hare (2003) and his Psychopathy Checklist-Revised (PCL-R). Originally conceptualized as a personality disorder, the PCL-R is mostly used as a risk assessment instrument. However, probably because of the fact that the PCL-R has its seeds in general personality research, a few studies exist on the incremental (predictive) validity of the PCL-R (Garb, 2003; Quinsey et al., 1998; Rettenberger & Eher, 2013).

risk assessment instruments such as the Static-99 and the SORAG, and could be used as a scientifically based guide for treatment planning and for monitoring of the treatment process (Hanson et al., 2009). However, even this approach could have unexpected findings (Tully et al., 2015). In the meantime, there have been a number of studies that also provide support for the incremental predictive accuracy of dynamic risk factors beyond the static ones (e.g., Beggs & Grace, 2010, 2011; Eher et al., 2012; Hanson et al., 2007; Olver, Nicholaichuk, Kingston, & Wong, 2014; Olver, Wong, Nicholaichuk, & Gordon, 2007).

For SPJ instruments such as the SVR-20, this kind of statistical evidence for incremental predictive validity still remains unknown. However, from a clinical point of view, SPJ instruments have an incremental value over actuarial tools because they are also able to provide treatment planning and monitoring information (Boer & Hart, 2009). Taking into account the existing research on incremental validity in forensic risk assessment instruments, there are at least two reasons to assume that SPJ instruments are incrementally valid beyond the second-generation actuarial risk assessment instruments such as Static-99 and SORAG. First, the above-mentioned research papers indicated that risk assessment instruments that contain predominantly dynamic risk factors show a significant improvement in predictive accuracy beyond the static risk factors as captured by, for instance, Static-99 or SORAG (e.g., Beggs & Grace, 2010, 2011; Eher et al., 2011; Hanson et al., 2007; Olver et al., 2007, 2014). Given the fact that SPJ instruments usually consist of a substantial amount of dynamic items, one could further assume that SPJ instruments are also incrementally valid. Second, the incremental validity cannot be assessed only by predictive accuracy but has also considered other issues of risk assessment and management, underscoring SPJ's dynamic, flexible approach to assessing risk. SPJ instruments have a clear focus not only on risk prediction per se but also on strategies that would most effectively manage this risk (Hart & Boer, 2009). Therefore, one of the most important 'incremental' improvements of SPJ instruments beyond ARAIs could be the consideration of the characteristics of each individual case in order to prevent future violence in the most effective way. However, so far there have been only very few studies of the incremental validity of SPJ instruments, so at present the concept of incremental validity provides hypotheses for future research rather than clear empirical evidence.

Another remaining question refers to situations and cases where conceptually similar instruments – for example, two or more second-generation actuarial risk assessment instruments – provide different information (Barbaree et al., 2006b). Whereas the initial research on this topic indicated that combining multiple actuarial risk tools did not provide a consistent advantage over the predictive accuracy of the best single scale (Seto, 2005), more recent studies indicated that even highly correlated measures could be able to have an incremental predictive effect (Babchishin, Hanson, & Helmus, 2012; Lehmann et al., 2013).

The previously mentioned studies show that the concept of incremental validity could be especially relevant for the discussion about a convergent risk assessment approach, because if someone is able to examine the additional value of a particular measure (e.g., a risk assessment instrument that is measuring clinical, therapeutic relevant, and dynamic risk factors) beyond what is captured by another measure (e.g., an actuarial tool that is using only static and historical risk factors in order to estimate the base rate for recidivism), one could argue that the best practice recommendation is to use both measures and to combine the results in a convergent approach (Boer, 2006).

Conclusions and Recommendations

The idea of a 'convergent' approach to risk is not to be confused with anchoring actuarial findings with SPJ findings or complementing actuarial findings with 'psychologically meaningful risk factors' (Mann et al., 2010). Nor is the use of actuarial test data as an anchor for SPJ findings or other risk factors a valid approach. There are no data that provide any empirical support for either approach, and such idiosyncratic approaches appear akin to unstructured clinical judgement, in our opinion. Indeed, even if some empirical validation were to be found showing the incremental validity of using both actuarial and SPJ strategies, the end result might have better predictive accuracy, but probably be no more useful than using the two types of tests independently.

The convergent approach simply means using a variety of tests that 'converge' on the issue at hand. Medical doctors, when diagnosing an illness, often order blood tests (or other physical tests), take the patient's temperature and blood pressure, plus observe the patient, to come to an initial hypothesis of what might be ailing the patient.[5] Some of these data are actuarial, others more SPJ in nature, all leading to or converging on a potential diagnosis, summary risk rating, and treatment or management plan, depending on the referral question. The value of the diagnosis could be to provide a starting point for treatment or to answer a psycho-legal question. The analogy with risk assessment and risk management is clear: we do a variety of tests to find out the risk issues and levels to intervene and manage risk appropriately.

Actuarial tests are valuable in that such instruments give us an idea of the person's risk from a group perspective – the characteristics that the evaluee shares in common with a validation group – and gives us a baseline idea of the risk present within certain time frames (provided that the validation study is from a relevant population). SPJs provide an individualized case analysis of risk issues that are unique to that individual. The combination of the findings is not to be done in any numerical fashion, but reported separately initially, and then discussed in combination. Thus, Mr Doe was assessed using the Static-99R (for example), indicating a risk level of X. He was also assessed with the SVR-20 (for example), indicating a risk level of Y. If these risk levels are similar (e.g., both high), it is a matter of prescribing risk management measures appropriate to his risk level. If the risk levels were different, then an explanation as to why this might be the case would be useful. For example, if the Static-99 finding of risk was lower than the SVR-20 finding, the dynamic nature of SVR-20 assessment may provide the explanation for the discrepant findings.

In sum, we recommend the independent reporting of findings from risk assessment tests and the integration of these findings in the discussion section of risk assessment

---

[5] These ideas may even evoke the multitrait–multimethod matrix examining construct validity (Campbell & Fiske, 1959).

reports. As noted by Skeem and Monahan (2011), there is still a lack of evidence for the supremacy of one sort of test over another, and it is time to shift our attention from 'predicting violence to understanding its causes and preventing its (re)occurrence' (p. 38). Finally, we support the use of actuarial tests primarily as a risk baseline that will show which risk group the client most closely matches. However, for a better understanding of the clients being assessed, the use of an appropriate SPJ is suggested (e.g., Boer, 2006; Hanson & Morton-Bourgon, 2004, 2007).

References

Abbott, B. (2009). Applicability of the new Static-99 experience tables in sexually violent predator risk assessments. *Sexual Offender Treatment, 4*(1), 1–24. Retrieved from http://www .sexual-offender-treatment.org/index.php?id=73&type=123

Abbott, B. (2011). Throwing the baby out with the bath water: Is it time for clinical judgment to supplement actuarial risk assessment? *Journal of the American Academy of Psychiatry and the Law, 39*, 222–230.

Archer, R. P., Buffington-Vollum, J. K., Stredny, R. V., & Handel, R. W. (2006). A survey of psychological test use patterns among forensic psychologists. *Journal of Personality Assessment, 87*, 84–94.

Babchishin, K. M., Hanson, R. K., & Helmus, L. (2012). Even highly correlated measures can add incrementally to predicting recidivism among sex offenders. *Assessment, 19*, 442–461.

Barbaree, H. E., Langton, C. M., & Peacock, E. J. (2006a). The factor structure of static actuarial items: Its relation to prediction. *Sexual Abuse: A Journal of Research and Treatment, 18*, 207–226.

Barbaree, H. E., Langton, C. M., & Peacock, E. J. (2006b). Different actuarial risk measures produce different risk rankings for sexual offenders. *Sexual Abuse: A Journal of Research and Treatment, 18*, 423–440.

Barbaree, H. E., Seto, M. C., Langton, C. M., & Peacock, E. J. (2001). Evaluating the predictive accuracy of six risk assessment instruments for adult sex offenders. *Criminal Justice and Behavior, 28*, 490–521.

Beggs, S. M., & Grace, R. C. (2010). Assessment of dynamic risk factors: An independent validation study of the Violence Risk Scale: Sexual Offender Version. *Sexual Abuse: A Journal of Research and Treatment, 22*, 234–251.

Beggs, S. M., & Grace, R. C. (2011). Treatment gains for sexual offenders against children predicts reduced recidivism: A comparative validity study. *Journal of Consulting and Clinical Psychology, 79*, 182–192.

Belfrage, H., Strand, S., Storey, J. E., Gibas, A. L., Kropp, P. R., & Hart, S. D. (2012). Assessment and management of risk for intimate partner violence by police officers using the Spousal Assault Risk Assessment Guide. *Law and Human Behavior, 36*(1), 60–67.

Boer, D. P. (2006). Sexual offender risk assessment strategies: Is there a convergence of opinion yet? *Sexual Offender Treatment, 1*(2), 1–4. Retrieved from http://www.sexual-offender-treatment.org/index.php?id=38&type=123

Boer, D. P., & Hart, S. D. (2009). Sex offender risk assessment: Research, evaluation, 'best-practice' recommendations and future directions. In J. L. Ireland, C. A. Ireland, & P. Birch (Eds.), *Violent and sexual offenders: Assessment, treatment, and management* (pp. 27–42). Cullompton, England: Willan.

Boer, D. P., Hart, S. D., Kropp, P. R., & Webster, C. D. (1997). *Manual for the Sexual Violence Risk – 20: Professional guidelines for assessing risk of sexual violence.* Vancouver, Canada: Mental Health, Law, and Policy Institute.

Campbell, T. W. (2011). Predictive accuracy of Static-99R and Static-2002R. *Open Access Journal of Forensic Psychology, 3,* 82–106.

Campbell, T. W., & DeClue, G. (2010a). Flying blind with naked factors: Problems and pitfalls in adjusted actuarial sex offender risk assessment. *Open Access Journal of Forensic Psychology, 2,* 75–101.

Campbell, T. W., & DeClue, G. (2010b). Maximizing predictive accuracy in sexually violent predator evaluations. *Open Access Journal of Forensic Psychology, 2,* 148–232.

Campbell, D. T., & Fiske D. W. (1959). Convergent and discriminant validation by the multitrait–multimethod matrix. *Psychological Bulletin, 56,* 81–105.

Coid, J. W., Yang, M., Ullrich, S., Zhang, T., Sizmur, S., Farrington, D., & Rogers, R. (2011). Most items in structured risk assessment instruments do not predict violence. *Journal of Forensic Psychiatry & Psychology, 22*(1), 3–21.

Cooke, D. J. (2010). More prejudicial than probative? A critique of violence risk assessment of offenders using actuarial tools, due to their limitations in predicting the future behaviour of individuals. *The Journal of the Law Society of Scotland.* Retrieved from http://www .journalonline.co.uk/Magazine/55-2/1007494#.VMjzh7l0zcs

Cooke, D. J., & Michie, C. (2010). Limitations of diagnostic precision and predictive utility in the individual case: A challenge for forensic practice. *Law and Human Behavior, 34,* 259–274.

Craig, L. A., Browne, K. D., Stringer, I., & Beech, A. (2004). Limitations in actuarial risk assessment of sexual offenders: A methodological note. *British Journal of Forensic Practice, 6,* 16–32.

Dawes, R. M., Faust, D., & Meehl, P. E. (1989). Clinical versus actuarial judgement. *Science, 243,* 1668–1674.

DeClue, G. (2013). Years of predicting dangerously. *Open Access Journal of Forensic Psychology, 5,* 16–28.

de Vogel, V., de Ruiter, C., van Beek, D., & Mead, G. (2004). Predictive validity of the SVR-20 and Static-99 in a Dutch sample of treated sex offenders. *Law and Human Behavior, 28,* 235–251.

Donaldson, T. S., & Abbott, B. R. (2011). Prediction in the individual case: An explanation and application of its use with the Static-99R in sexually violent predator risk assessments. *American Journal of Forensic Psychology, 1,* 5–35.

Doren, D. M. (2002). *Evaluating sex offenders. A manual for civil commitments and beyond.* Thousand Oaks, CA: Sage.

Douglas, K. S., Hart, S. D., Webster, C. D., Belfrage, H., Guy, L. S., & Wilson, C. M. (2014). Historical–Clinical-Risk Management-20, Version 3 (HCR-20 V3): Development and overview. *International Journal of Forensic Mental Health, 13*(2), 93–108.

Douglas, K. S., & Skeem, J. (2005). Violence risk assessment: Getting specific about being dynamic. *Psychology, Public Policy, and Law, 11,* 347–383.

Dvoskin, J. A., & Heilbrun, K. (2001). Risk assessment and release decision-making: Toward resolving the great debate. *Journal of the American Academy of Psychiatry and the Law Online, 29,* 6–10.

Eher, R., Matthes, A., Schilling, F., Haubner-MacLean, T., & Rettenberger, M. (2012). Dynamic risk assessment in sexual offenders using STABLE-2000 and the STABLE-2007: An investigation of predictive and incremental validity. *Sexual Abuse: A Journal of Research and Treatment, 24,* 5–28.

Eher, R., Rettenberger , M., Schilling, F., & Pfäfflin, F. (2008). Failure of Static-99 and SORAG to predict relevant reoffense categories in relevant sexual offenders. *Sexual Offender Treatment*, *3*(1), 1–14. Retrieved from http://www.sexual-offender-treatment.org/1-2008_02.html

Falzer, P. R. (2013). Valuing structured professional judgment: Predictive validity, decision-making, and the clinical–actuarial Conflict. *Behavioral Sciences & the Law*, *31*(1), 40–54.

Fazel, S., Singh, J. P., Doll, H., & Grann, M. (2012). Use of risk assessment instruments to predict violence and antisocial behaviour in 73 samples involving 24 827 people: Systematic review and meta-analysis. *BMJ*, *345*, e4692.

Garb, H. N. (2003). Incremental validity and the assessment of psychopathology in adults. *Psychological Assessment*, *15*, 508–520.

Grove, W. M., & Meehl, P. E. (1996). Comparative efficiency of informal (subjective, impressionistic) and formal (mechanical, algorithmic) prediction procedures: The clinical–statistical controversy. *Psychology, Public Policy, & Law*, *2*, 293–323.

Grove, W. M., Zald, D. H., Lebow, B. S., Snitz, B. E., & Nelson, C. (2000). Clinical versus mechanical prediction: A meta-analysis. *Psychological Assessment*, *12*, 19–30.

Guy, L. S., Packer, I. K., & Warnken, W. (2012). Assessing risk of violence using structured professional judgment guidelines. *Journal of Forensic Psychology Practice*, *12*, 270–283.

Hansen, K., Gerbasi, M., Todorov, A., Kruse, E., & Pronin, E. (2014). People claim objectivity after knowingly using biased strategies. *Personality and Social Psychology Bulletin*, *40*, 691–699.

Hanson, R. K., Bourgon, G., Helmus, L., & Hodgson, S. (2009). The principles of effective correctional treatment also apply to sexual offenders: A meta-analysis. *Criminal Justice and Behavior*, *36*, 865–891.

Hanson, R. K., Harris, A. J. R., Scott, T., & Helmus, L. (2007). *Assessing the risk of sexual offenders on community supervision: The Dynamic Supervision Project* (User Report 2007-05). Ottawa, Canada: Public Safety Canada.

Hanson, R. K., & Morton-Bourgon, K. (2004). *Predictors of sexual recidivism: An updated meta-analysis* (Corrections User Report 2004-02). Ottawa, Canada: Public Safety and Emergency Preparedness Canada, Corrections Research.

Hanson, R. K., & Morton-Bourgon, K. (2007). *The accuracy of recidivism risk assessments for sexual offenders: A meta-analysis* (Corrections User Report 2007-01). Ottawa, Canada: Public Safety and Emergency Preparedness Canada, Corrections Research.

Hanson, R. K., & Morton-Bourgon, K. (2009). The accuracy of recidivism risk assessments for sexual offenders: A meta-analysis of 118 prediction studies. *Psychological Assessment*, *21*, 1–21.

Hanson, R. K., & Thornton, D. (1999). *Static 99: Improving actuarial risk assessments for sex offenders* (User Report 1999-02). Ottawa, Canada: Department of the Solicitor General of Canada.

Hanson, R. K., Thornton, D., Helmus, L.-M., & Babchishin, K. M. (2015). What sexual recidivism rates are associated with Static-99R and Static-2002R scores? *Sexual Abuse: A Journal of Research and Treatment*. Published online 25 March 2015. doi:10.1177/1079063215574710

Haque, Q., & Webster, C. D. (2013). Structured professional judgement and sequential redirections. *Criminal Behaviour and Mental Health*, *23*, 241–251.

Hare, R. D. (2003). *Manual for the Psychopathy Checklist – Revised* (2nd ed.). Toronto, Canada: Multi-Health Systems.

Harris, A. J. R., & Hanson, R. K. (2010). Clinical, actuarial, and dynamic risk assessment of sexual offenders: Why do things keep changing? *Journal of Sexual Aggression*, *16*, 296–310.

Harris, G. T., Rice, M. E., & Quinsey, V. L. (1993). Violent recidivism of mentally disordered offenders: The development of a statistical prediction instrument. *Criminal Justice and Behavior*, *20*, 315–335.

Hart, S. D. (2008). Preventing violence: The role of risk assessment and management. In A. C. B. F. W. Winkel (Ed.), *Intimate partner violence prevention and intervention: The risk assessment and management approach* (pp. 7–18). Hauppauge, NY: Nova Science.

Hart, S. D., & Boer, D. P. (2009). Structured professional judgement guidelines for sexual violence risk assessment: The Sexual Violence Risk-20 (SVR-20) and Risk for Sexual Violence Protocol (RSVP). In R. K. Otto & K. S. Douglas (Eds.), *Handbook of violence risk assessment* (pp. 269–294). Abingdon, England: Routledge.

Hart, S. D., & Cooke, D. J. (2013). Another look at the (im-)precision of individual risk estimates made using actuarial risk assessment instruments. *Behavioral Sciences & the Law*, *31*(1), 81–102.

Hart, S. D., Michie, C., & Cooke, D. J. (2007). Precision of actuarial risk assessment instruments: Evaluating the 'margins of error' of group v. individual predictions of violence. *British Journal of Psychiatry*, *190*, 60–65.

Haynes, S. N., & Lench, H. C. (2003). Incremental validity of new clinical assessment measures. *Psychological Assessment*, *15*, 456–466.

Helmus, L., Hanson, R. K., & Thornton, D. (2009). Reporting Static-99 in light of new research on recidivism norms. *ATSA Forum*, *21*(1), 38–45.

Helmus, L., Thornton, D., Hanson, R. K., & Babchishin, K. M. (2012). Improving the predictive accuracy of Static-99 and Static-2002 with older sex offenders: Revised age weights. *Sexual Abuse: A Journal of Research and Treatment*, *24*, 64–101.

Hilton, N. Z., Carter, A. M., Harris, G. T., & Sharpe, A. J. B. (2008). Does using nonnumerical terms to describe risk aid violence risk communication? Clinician agreement and decision making. *Journal of Interpersonal Violence*, *23*, 171–188.

Hunsley, J. (2003). Introduction to the special section on incremental validity and utility in clinical assessment. *Psychological Assessment*, *15*, 443–445.

Hunsley, J., & Meyer, G. J. (2003). The incremental validity of psychological testing and assessment: Conceptual, methodological, and statistical issues. *Psychological Assessment*, *15*, 446–455.

Janus, E. S., & Meehl, P. E. (1997). Assessing the legal standard for predictions of dangerousness in sex offender commitment proceedings. *Psychology, Public Policy, and Law*, *3*(1), 33–64.

Janus, E. S., & Prentky, R. A. (2003). Forensic use of actuarial risk assessment with sex offenders: Accuracy, admissibility, and accountability. *American Criminal Law Review*, *40*, 1–59.

Kahneman, D. (2003). A perspective on judgment and choice: Mapping bounded rationality. *American Psychologist*, *58*, 697–720.

Kahneman, D. (2011). *Thinking, fast and slow*. New York, NY: Farrar, Straus and Giroux.

Kahneman, D., & Tversky, A. (1973). On the psychology of prediction. *Psychological Review*, *80*, 237–251.

Kahneman, D., & Tversky, A. (1984). Choices, values and frames. *American Psychologist*, *39*, 341–350.

Kahneman, D., & Tversky, A. (1996). On the reality of cognitive illusions. *Psychological Review*, *103*, 582–591.

Knight, R. A., & Thornton, D. (2007). *Evaluating and improving risk assessment schemes for sexual recidivism: A long-term follow-up of convicted sexual offenders* (Final Report: US Department of Justice, Award No. 2003-WG-BX-1002). Retrieved from http://www.ncjrs.gov/pdffiles1/nij/grants/217618.pdf

Kroner, D. G, Mills, J. F., & Reddon, J. R. (2005). A coffee can, factor analysis, and prediction of antisocial behavior: The structure of criminal risk. *International Journal of Law and Psychiatry*, *28*, 360–374.

Kropp, P. R., & Hart, S. D. (2000). The Spousal Assault Risk Assessment (SARA) guide: Reliability and validity in adult male offenders. *Law and Human Behavior*, *24*(1), 101–118.

Kuran, T., & Sunstein, C. R. (1999). Availability cascades and risk regulation (University of Chicago, Public Law Working Paper No. 181; University of Chicago Law & Economics, Olin Working Paper No. 384). *Stanford Law Review*, *51*(4), 683–768. Retrieved from http://ssrn.com/abstract=138144.

Langton, C. M., Barbaree, H. E., Seto, M. C., Peacock, E. J., Harkins, L., & Hansen, K. T. (2007). Actuarial assessment of risk for reoffense among adult sexual offenders: Evaluating the predictive accuracy of the Static-2002 and five other instruments. *Criminal Justice and Behavior*, *34*(1), 37–59.

Lanyon, R. I. (2001). Psychological assessment procedures in sex offending. *Professional Psychology: Research and Practice*, *32*, 252–260.

Lehmann, R. J. B., Hanson, R. K., Babchishin, K. M., Gallasch-Nemitz, F., Biedermann, J., & Dahle, K.-P. (2013). Interpreting multiple risk scales for sex offenders: Evidence for averaging. *Psychological Assessment*, *25*, 1019–1024.

Lewandowsky, S., Ecker, U. K. H., Seifert, C. M., Schwarz, N., & Cook, J. (2012). Misinformation and its correction: Continued influence and successful debiasing. *Psychological Science in the Public Interest*, *13*(3), 106–131.

Lieberman, J. D., Krauss, D. A., & Kyger, M. (2007). Determining dangerousness in sexually violent predator evaluations: Cognitive-experiential self-theory and juror judgments of expert testimony. *Behavioral Sciences & the Law*, *25*, 507–526.

Lussier, P., & Davies, G. (2011). A person-oriented perspective on sexual offenders, offending trajectories, and risk of recidivism: A new challenge for policymakers, risk assessors, and actuarial prediction? *Psychology, Public Policy, and Law*, *17*, 530–561.

Mann, R. E., Hanson, R. K., & Thornton, D. (2010). Assessing risk for sexual recidivism: Some proposals on the nature of psychologically meaningful risk factors. *Sexual Abuse: A Journal of Research and Treatment*, *22*, 191–217.

McNeil, D. E., & Binder, R. L. (1994). Screening for risk of inpatient violence: Validation of an actuarial tool. *Law and Human Behavior*, *18*, 579–586.

Meehl, P. E. (1954). *Clinical versus statistical prediction: A theoretical analysis and a review of the evidence*. Minneapolis, MN: University of Minnesota Press.

Meehl, P. E. (1986). Causes and effects of my disturbing little book. *Journal of Personality Assessment*, *50*, 370–375.

Moffitt, T. E. (1993). Adolescence-limited and life-course-persistent antisocial behavior: A developmental taxonomy. *Psychological Review*, *100*, 1–28.

Mokros, A., Stadtland, C., Osterheider, M., & Nedopil, N. (2010). Assessment of risk for violent recidivism through multivariate Bayesian classification. *Psychology, Public Policy, and Law*, *16*, 418–450.

Monahan, J. (1981). *Predicting violent behavior: An assessment of clinical techniques*. Beverly Hills, CA: Sage.

Monahan, J. (1984). The prediction of violent behavior: Toward a second generation of theory and policy. *American Journal of Psychiatry*, *141*, 10–15.

Monahan, J., & Steadman, H. J. (1994). *Violence and mental disorder: Developments in risk assessment*. Chicago, IL: University of Chicago Press.

Monahan, J., & Steadman, H. J. (1996). Violent storms and violent people: How meteorology can inform risk communication in mental health law. *American Psychologist*, *51*, 931–938.

Mossman, D. (2006). Another look at interpreting risk categories. *Sexual Abuse: A Journal of Research and Treatment*, *18*, 41–63.

Mossman, D. (2008). Analyzing the performance of risk assessment instruments: A response to Vrieze and Grove (2007). *Law and Human Behavior*, *32*, 279–291.

Mossman, D., & Sellke, T. (2007). Avoiding errors about 'margins of error'. *British Journal of Psychiatry*, *191*, 561.

Neal, T. M. S., & Grisso, T. (2014). The cognitive underpinnings of bias in forensic mental health evaluations. *Psychology, Public Policy, and Law*, *20*, 200–211.

Olver, M. E., Nicholaichuk, T. P., Kingston, D. A., & Wong, S. C. P. (2014). A multisite examination of sexual violence risk and therapeutic change. *Journal of Consulting and Clinical Psychology*, *82*, 312–324.

Olver, M. E., Wong, S. C. P., Nicholaichuk, T., & Gordon, A. (2007). The validity and reliability of the Violence Risk Scale – Sexual Offender version: Assessing sex offender risk and evaluating therapeutic change. *Psychological Assessment*, *19*, 318–329.

Otto, R. K. (1992). Prediction of dangerous behavior: A review and analysis of 'second generation' research. *Forensic Reports*, *5*, 103–133.

Pedersen, L., Rasmussen, K., & Elsass, P. (2010). Risk assessment: The value of structured professional judgments. *International Journal of Forensic Mental Health*, *9*, 74–81.

Petrila, J., & Otto, R. K. (2001). Admissibility of expert testimony in sexually violent predator proceedings. In A. Schlank (Ed.), *The sexual predator: Legal issues, clinical issues, special populations* (Vol. II, pp. 3–7). Kingston, NJ: Civic Research Institute.

Phenix, A., Helmus, L., & Hanson, R. K. (2015). *STATIC-99R & STATIC-2002R evaluators' workbook*. Retrieved from http://www.static99.org/pdfdocs/Static-99RandStatic-2002R_EvaluatorsWorkbook-Jan2015.pdf

Prentky, R. A., Janus, E., Barbaree, H., Schwartz, B., & Kafka, M. (2006). Sexually violent predators in the courtroom: Science on trial. *Psychology, Public Policy, and Law*, *12*, 357–393.

Quinsey, V. L., Harris, G. T., Rice, M. E., & Cormier, C. A. (1998). *Violent offenders: Appraising and managing risk*. Washington, DC: American Psychological Association.

Quinsey, V. L., Rice, M. E., & Harris, G. T. (1995). Actuarial prediction of sexual recidivism. *Journal of Interpersonal Violence*, *10*, 85–105.

Rettenberger, M., Boer, D. P., & Eher, R. (2011). The predictive accuracy of risk factors in the Sexual Violence Risk-20 (SVR-20). *Criminal Justice and Behavior*, *38*, 1009–1027.

Rettenberger, M., Briken, P., Turner, D., & Eher, R. (2015). Sexual offender recidivism among a population-based prison sample. *International Journal of Offender Therapy and Comparative Criminology*, *59*, 424–444.

Rettenberger, M., & Eher, R. (2013). Actuarial risk assessment in sexually motivated intimate-partner violence. *Law and Human Behavior*, *37*, 75–86.

Rettenberger, M., Haubner-MacLean, T., & Eher, R. (2013). The contribution of age to the Static-99 risk assessment in a population-based prison sample of sexual offenders. *Criminal Justice and Behavior*, *40*, 1413–1433.

Rettenberger, M., Matthes, A., Boer, D. P., & Eher, R. (2010). Actuarial recidivism risk assessment and sexual delinquency: A comparison of five risk assessment tools in different sexual offender subtypes. *International Journal of Offender Therapy and Comparative Criminology*, *54*, 169–186.

Rice, M. E., Harris, G. T., & Lang, C. (2013). Validation of and revision to the VRAG and SORAG: The Violence Risk Appraisal Guide-Revised (VRAG-R). *Psychological Assessment*, *25*, 951–965.

Ross, L. (1977). The intuitive psychologist and his shortcomings: Distortions in the attribution process. In L. Berkowitz (Ed.), *Advances in experimental social psychology* (Vol. 10, pp. 173–220). New York, NY: Academic Press.

Sampson, R. J., & Laub, J. H. (2005). A life-course view of the development of crime. *The Annals of the American Academy of Political and Social Science*, *602*, 12–45.

Sandler J. C., Freeman, N., & Socia, K. M. (2008). Does a watched pot boil?: A time-series analysis of New York State's sex offender registration and notification law. *Psychology, Public Policy, and Law*, *14*, 284–302.

Seto, M. C. (2005). Is more better? Combining actuarial risk scales to predict recidivism among adult sex offenders. *Psychological Assessment*, *17*, 156–167.

Singer, J. C., Boer, D. P., & Rettenberger, M. (2013). A convergent approach to sex offender risk assessment. In K. Harrison & B. Rainey (Eds.), *Legal and ethical aspects of sex offender treatment and management* (pp. 341–355). Chichester, England: John Wiley & Sons, Ltd.

Singh, J. P., Grann, M., & Fazel, S. (2011). A comparative study of violence risk assessment tools: A systematic review and metaregression analysis of 68 studies involving 25,980 participants. *Clinical Psychology Review*, *31*, 499–513.

Sjöstedt, G., & Grann, M. (2002). Risk assessment: What is being predicted by actuarial prediction instruments? *International Journal of Forensic Mental Health*, *1*(2), 179–183.

Skeem, J. L., & Monahan, J. (2011). Current directions in violence risk assessment. *Current Directions in Psychological Science*, *20*, 38–42.

Smid, W. J., Kamphuis, J. H., Wever, E. C., & Van Beek, D. J. (2014). A comparison of the predictive properties of nine sex offender risk assessment instruments. *Psychological Assessment*, *26*, 691–703.

Storey, J. E., Watt, K. A., Jackson, K. J., & Hart, S. D. (2012). Utilization and implications of the Static-99 in practice. *Sexual Abuse: A Journal of Research and Treatment*, *24*, 289–302.

Tully, R. J., Browne, K. D., & Craig, L. A. (2015). An examination of the predictive validity of the structured assessment of risk and need–treatment needs analysis (SARN-TNA) in England and Wales. *Criminal Justice and Behavior*, *42*, 509–528.

Tully, R. J., Chou, S., & Browne, K. D. (2013). A systematic review on the effectiveness of sex offender risk assessment tools in predicting sexual recidivism of adult male sex offenders. *Clinical Psychology Review*, *33*, 287–316.

Tversky, A., & Kahneman, D. (1974). Judgment under uncertainty: Heuristics and biases. *Science*, *185*, 1124–1131.

Tversky, A., & Kahneman, D. (1983). Extensional versus intuitive reasoning: The conjunction fallacy in probability judgment. *Psychological Review*, *90*, 293–315.

Vrieze, S. L., & Grove, W. M. (2008). Predicting sex offender recidivism. I. Correcting for item overselection and accuracy overestimation in scale development. II. Sampling error-induced attenuation of predictive validity over base rate information. *Law and Human Behavior*, *32*, 266–278.

Vrieze, S. L., & Grove, W. M. (2009). Survey on the use of clinical and mechanical prediction methods in clinical psychology. *Professional Psychology: Research and Practice*, *40*, 525–531.

Vrieze, S. L. & Grove, W. M. (2010). Multidimensional assessment of criminal recidivism: Problems, pitfalls, and proposed solutions. *Psychological Assessment*, *22*, 382–395.

Waggoner, J., Wollert, R., & Cramer, E. (2008). A re-specification of Hanson's 2006 Static-99 experience table that controls for the effects of age in a sample of 552 young sex offenders. *Law, Probability, and Risk*, *7*, 305–312.

Wollert, R. (2006). Low base rates limit expert certainty when current actuarials are used to identify sexually violent predators: An application of Bayes' theorem. *Psychology, Public Policy, and Law, 12,* 56–85.

Wollert, R. (2007). Poor diagnostic reliability, the Null-Bayes logic model, and their implications for sexually violent predator evaluations. *Psychology, Public Policy, & Law, 13,* 167–203.

Wollert, R., & Waggoner, J. (2009). Bayesian computations protect sexually violent predator evaluations from the degrading effects of confirmatory bias and illusions of certainty: A reply to Doren and Levenson. *Sexual Offender Treatment, 4*(1), 1–23. Retrieved from http://www.sexual-offender-treatment.org/index.php?id=74&type=123

Wong, S. C. P., Olver, M. E., Nicholaichuk, T. P., & Gordon, A. (2003). *The Violence Risk Scale: Sexual Offender version (VRS-SO).* Saskatoon, Canada: Regional Psychiatric Centre and University of Saskatchewan.

Yang, M., Wong, S. C. P., & Coid, J. (2010). The efficacy of violence prediction: A meta-analytic comparison of nine risk assessment tools. *Psychological Bulletin, 136,* 740–767.

Section III
Assessing Treatment Need

33

Risk Assessment and Treatment Planning

Jayson Ware and Danielle Matsuo

Corrective Services New South Wales, Australia

Introduction

The assessment of a sexual offender's risk of recidivism is an essential task that influences all aspects of their management. Risk assessments inform decisions with respect to sentencing, community registration or notification, release from prison or a hospital, release conditions, and levels of supervision and monitoring. The results of a comprehensive risk assessment will also provide information as to *who* should be treated, *how much* treatment they might require, *what* treatment should seek to change, and *when* risk might be reduced as a consequence of treatment. As noted by Collie, Ward, and Vess (2008), 'without accurate [risk] assessment it is impossible to determine the suitability and focus of treatment, nor whether treatment has had any positive impact' (p. 65).

In completing a risk assessment that will be used to assist in treatment planning, professionals typically will use information based on both static or historical (largely non-changeable) factors and dynamic (changeable) factors. Most commonly they will use a combination of actuarial risk assessment measures and structured professional judgement protocols (Craig, Beech, & Harkins, 2009).

In this chapter, we explore how the information gained from a comprehensive risk assessment can be used in treatment planning. We examine in turn the usefulness of information from risk assessments that focus on static or historical and dynamic risk factors. Specific to static and historical risk factors, we examine how these can be used to determine who should complete treatment, how much treatment is required, and how these historical factors may actually serve as potential markers of treatment targets. We briefly consider the limitations of these measures, if used in isolation, for treatment planning. We then examine the relative importance of dynamic risk factors, arguing

The Wiley Handbook on the Theories, Assessment, and Treatment of Sexual Offending.
Edited by Douglas P. Boer. Volume II: Assessment, edited by Leam A. Craig and Martin Rettenberger.
© 2017 John Wiley & Sons, Ltd. Published 2017 by John Wiley & Sons, Ltd.

that individualized formulations of each sex offender's risk is essential to treatment and that the sharing of the risk assessment results with sex offenders is an important treatment (planning) opportunity. We discuss the types of dynamic risk measures and their usefulness for treatment planning and then point out the differences in dynamic risk measures in terms of what risk factors they measure. Then, we discuss the use of dynamic risk measures to assess treatment changes (and subsequent risk reduction) before finally reflecting on whether treatment programmes are, in fact, adequately using the results of risk assessments in their treatment planning.

We note at this point that there remain limitations in administering the majority of established static or historical and dynamic risk assessment measures with unique groups of sexual offenders, including females, those who offended using the Internet, individuals who are cognitively impaired, and juveniles. Although the broad uses of risk assessment for treatment planning that we will outline can, in many instances, be applied to these groups, practitioners should be informed by the literature on the most appropriate risk assessment measures to identify risk factors for these unique populations (see Craig & Beech, 2010).

Risk Assessments Focusing on Static or Historical Factors

Irrespective of the reason for a risk assessment, whether it be for the courts for sentencing or a treatment provider to plan treatment, actuarial risk assessments focusing on static or historical (unchangeable) factors are the most commonly used approach (Kingston et al., 2008). The assessment of static or historical risk factors is best done by using one of the many actuarial risk measures developed for that specific purpose. These measures consist of a number of empirically derived items (individual risk factors) that are scored as present or not and in some instances are weighted. The sum scores of these items are then translated into a level of risk (e.g., low, medium, high). Essentially, the individual offender, on the basis of his sum score, is compared with a group of sex offenders with similar sum scores. The reconviction rates of the offenders from the validation sample group are then used to describe what percentage of similar offenders can be expected to reoffend over particular time periods.

The reliability and validity of this approach have been well established (Craig et al., 2009) and actuarial risk measures consistently outperform empirically guided clinical judgement (e.g., Hanson & Morton-Bourgon, 2007). Examples of actuarial measures with established predictive validity include the Static-99 (Hanson & Thornton, 2000), Static-2002 (Hanson & Thornton, 2003), Rapid Risk Assessment of Sexual Offence Recidivism (RRASOR) (Hanson, 1997), Sex Offender Risk Appraisal Guide (SORAG) (Quinsey, Harris, Rice, & Cormier, 1998), Risk Matrix 2000 (Thornton et al., 2003), and the Minnesota Sex Offender Screening Tool – Revised (MnSOST-R) (Epperson, Kaul, & Hesselton, 1998). The value of these measures is that they are relatively quick to administer based on file information alone, they are cost-effective, have a large evidence base, and provide a baseline measure of risk of sexual recidivism for an individual compared with a group.

Usefulness of Static or Historical Risk Measures for Treatment Planning

The widely adopted context for the incorporation of assessment of risk in treatment planning for offenders is the Risk–Needs–Responsivity (RNR) model (Andrews & Bonta, 2010). The RNR model operates at the broad level of programme or treatment design. It tells us that treatment should focus on offenders who pose the highest risk and should vary in dose according to risk (*risk principle*), should target the issues that caused the offending or correlate with recidivism (*needs*), and should be delivered in a way to which offenders will respond (*responsivity*). Treatment for offenders that adheres to these principles is more effective at reducing reoffending than treatment that does not (Andrews & Bonta, 2010; Hanson, Bourgon, Helmus, & Hodgson, 2009). Hanson et al. (2009) specifically conducted a review of 23 sex offender treatment programme evaluations to examine whether these RNR principles applied to sex offenders. Treatment programmes adhering to RNR principles had lower recidivism rates (10.9%) than programmes that did not (19.2%). Similarly, general (non-sexual) recidivism rates were also lower in these programmes (31.8% versus 48.3%). Clearly, it is important to use risk assessment results in order to adhere to the RNR principles. Actuarial risk measures, based upon static or historical factors, represent the clearest cut and most cost-efficient approach to determining who needs treatment and how much treatment is required. They may also provide clear markers of long-standing psychological and behavioural issues that require change.

Static or Historical Factors Can Serve as Markers of Treatment Targets

There are a number of static or historical factors that are consistently associated with sexual recidivism, including prior criminality, diagnosis of psychopathy or antisocial personality disorder, previous sexual offences, sexual preoccupation, relationship to the victim, gender of victim, and relationship history (Hanson & Morton-Bourgon, 2004). Meta-analyses of risk factors for sex offenders demonstrate that there are two dimensions predicting recidivism for sex offenders: (1) sexual deviance and repeat sexual offences and (2) criminality/antisociality (Hanson & Morton-Bourgon, 2005; Parent, Guay, & Knight, 2011). It makes some intuitive sense that an individual with an enduring interest in deviant sexual activity who also displays a willingness to disregard the rights of others will be assessed as higher risk.

From a treatment planning perspective, the presence of criminality/antisociality is an important consideration. Treatment refusal, a lack of treatment engagement, and treatment non-completion are all more likely in sex offenders who have characteristics related to antisocial personality disorder or certain features of antisocial personality disorder (Olver & Wong, 2009). Nunes and Cortoni (2008), for example, found that it was higher general criminality and not sexual deviance that predicted treatment attrition. Non-completion is an important issue for sex offender treatment programmes. Sex offenders who commence but do not complete treatment have higher recidivism rates than those who do not commence treatment (Hanson et al., 2002).

Static or historical factors may also point to other areas of treatment need. Beech and Ward (2004) argued that historical or static risk factors reflect 'markers' of long-standing or important psychological problems. They posited that static factors (items within actuarial risk measures) will therefore reflect psychological vulnerabilities or dispositional behaviours and that these can be grouped across four domains: sexual interests/sexual self-regulation, attitudes supportive of sexual assault, interpersonal functioning, and impulsive/emotional lability problems. These domains largely reflect dynamic risk factors and, indeed, Mann, Hanson, and Thornton (2010) suggested that if 'this conceptualization is adopted; the conceptual distinction between static and dynamic factors loses meaning' (p. 194). According to Beech and Ward (2004), the Static-99 (Hanson & Thornton, 2000), as an example, would measure sexual self-regulation through the items assessing non-contact offences and prior sex offences. A marker of long-standing difficulties with impulsive/emotional lability problems would be items assessing index non-sexual violence and prior non-sexual violence. The SORAG (Quinsey et al., 1998) would measure sexual self-regulation through the evidence of deviant sexual preferences and previous sexual convictions items, and difficulties with impulsive/emotional lability through violent criminality, non-violent criminality, evidence of psychopathy, and failure on conditional release.

The assessment of static and historical risk factors therefore provides important opportunities for those planning treatment that are not, at first sight, so obvious. If, as Beech and Ward (2004) surmised, these factors are reflective of long-standing psychological issues causing sex offending, then the presence of these factors may alert those planning treatment to areas of particular focus (see also Olver, Wong, Nicholaichuk, & Gordon, 2007).

Determining Who Needs Treatment and How Much Treatment Is Required

The risk principle suggests that treatment will be most effective when intensive services are reserved for the higher risk offenders and that these offenders will require a higher intensity of treatment. Very few treatment programmes or private practitioners have the resources to treat all sex offenders even when all are seeking and volunteering for treatment. Prioritizing those sex offenders assessed as high risk into treatment is therefore important. The treatment provided for these high-risk offenders must, however, be of adequate intensity. A sex offender assessed as high risk using static or historical factors alone will, in most instances, require more treatment than a low-risk sex offender. These offenders may have a longer history of sexual offences and a greater level of sexual deviancy and criminality/antisociality. They are therefore assumed to have a greater number or severity of criminogenic needs and will require extensive treatment in order to change entrenched and long-standing attitudes, beliefs, and behaviours, and that this will take considerably increased effort and time. Allocating sex offenders to the most appropriate level of treatment is therefore a critical issue in treatment planning and one that often occurs at a programme or referral level (Hanson et al., 2009; Mann, Ware, & Fernandez, 2011).

There is now increasing research evidence indicating that treatment providers should focus their attention on the higher risk sex offenders, including those assessed with an actuarial risk measure as low risk but who might have a high number or severity of dynamic risk factors (see the next main section, on dynamic risk). In a large meta-analysis of treatment effectiveness and the importance of the RNR principles, Hanson et al. (2009) found that there were stronger treatment effects for the higher risk offenders. They concluded that 'treatment providers should be cognizant that notice-able reductions in recidivism are not to be expected among the lowest risk offenders' (p. 886) (see also Lowenkamp, Latessa, & Holsinger, 2006).

Importantly, contrary to public opinion, recidivism rates for sexual offenders, par-ticularly for those assessed as low risk, are comparatively low, even without treatment. This raises the question of whether lower risk sex offenders even require treatment and, if so, how much. Many correctional jurisdictions will still provide some form of treat-ment to low-risk sex offenders owing to the political concerns of ignoring this group. Clearly, private practitioners will provide treatment irrespective of risk, particularly if the offender himself is seeking it.

Mailloux et al. (2003) examined this issue concluding that, in their study, low-risk sex offenders may have received too much treatment and that this 'over-treating' could lead to increased recidivism rates. Lowenkamp and Latessa (2002) reported that a half-way house residential treatment programme that treated low-, medium-, and high-risk sex offenders was not found to be effective overall. When risk was controlled for, the high-risk offenders had a 7% reduction in recidivism, whereas there was a 9% increase in recidivism for low-risk offenders. The inference is that the low-risk sex offenders received too much treatment, which may have disrupted their life circumstances, or were adversely affected by being placed in the vicinity of high-risk offenders with their antisocial or sexually deviant beliefs and behaviours (see also Lovins, Lowenkamp, & Latessa, 2009).

There is very little research evidence to date examining *how much* treatment is required for higher and lower risk sex offenders (Ware, 2011). Beech, Fisher, and Beckett (1999) examined the benefits of different doses of treatment for sexual offenders. They categorized offenders in terms of deviancy and denial rather than dividing their sample into different risk groups. As noted by Wakeling, Mann, and Carter (2012), these 'high-deviancy' offenders had more sexual offence victims, were more likely to have a previous conviction for a sexual offence, and were more likely to have committed non-familial offences, hence it is reasonable to assume that the deviancy classification broadly approximates risk groups. Beech et al. found that, for low-deviancy (low-risk) sex offenders, there was no difference in terms of improvement in pro-offending attitudes and overall change on psychometric measures between an 80- and a 160-hour programme. Higher deviancy offenders (higher risk) showed significantly more progress in the longer 160-hour programme.

Friendship, Mann, and Beech (2003), in a large-scale evaluation of a 160-hour treatment programme in the United Kingdom, found that treatment was effective (in terms of reduction of recidivism) for medium-low- and medium-high-risk sexual offenders (using the Static-99) but was *not* effective for offenders assessed as low or high risk. Noting that the follow-up period was only 2 years, they suggested that the reoffending rates for untreated low-risk sex offenders were so low that no statistical difference between groups was expected. With respect to the high-risk sex offenders, they concluded that this was sufficient evidence that they required a higher 'dose' of treatment.

Until further research is conducted to clarify the issue of how much treatment is required – including the issue of individual (not group-based) treatment – treatment planners need broadly to follow the RNR principle of risk, based on the outcomes of an actuarial risk measure examining historical or static factors, and then use professional judgement to decide what constitutes an appropriate treatment dose to enable a client to make and sustain change. Ideally, this suggested that treatment dosage then should serve as a guide only as certain offenders will make progress more quickly than others. Individual treatment and open-ended groups, where offenders complete the treatment only when their treatment needs have been satisfactorily addressed, will allow for this flexibility (Marshall, Marshall, Serran, & O'Brien, 2011; Ware & Bright, 2008; Ware, Mann, & Wakeling, 2009). Professional judgements relating to treatment dosage and progress should be based on an examination of changes in dynamic risk factors (see later).

Limitations of Static or Historical Risk Measures for Treatment Planning

There are a number of limitations of static or historical risk measures for treatment planning, particularly if they are used in isolation (see Craig et al., 2009). Generally, the most important limitation is that actuarial risk measures can only ever relate the individual to a group of similar individuals. If, say, 49% of the validation sample who scored a particular score reoffended over a particular time period, this does not suggest that an individual whom has just been scored with the same total score has a 49% chance of reoffending or that the individual will be one of the 49% who might be expected to reoffend.

Actuarial risk measures may under- or overestimate the risk of certain groups of sex offenders. Parent et al. (2011) studied the predictive validity of nine risk assessment instruments, including actuarial measures (e.g., MnSOST-R, RM2000, RRASOR, SORAG, Static-99, Static-2002, VRAG), and found that these instruments were more effective at predicting the sexual recidivism of child molesters and the violent and general recidivism of rapists. Bartosh, Garby, Lewis, and Gray (2003) found the RRA-SOR, Static 99, and SORAG predicted sexual, violent, and general recidivism with intrafamilial child sex offenders but had less predictive validity with rapists and were not significantly valid for non-contact offenders. Rettenberger, Matthes, Boer, and Eher (2010) also found differences between instruments (Static 99, SORAG, RRA-SOR, SVR-20, and PCL) in predicting reoffending in offender subgroups such as child molesters, rapists, and 'hands-off' sexual offenders. Although they were unable to provide further analysis on the rapist subgroup owing to very low rates of recidivism, they found the RRASOR failed to predict reoffence of any kind for child molesters. The Static-99 and SORAG failed to predict violent reoffences in intra-familial child molesters.

A treatment plan based solely upon historical or static risk factors may also be of limited use in the case of first-time or young offenders who have not had the chance to 'build' a sexual and non-sexual criminal history despite the fact that they have committed many instances of sexual offending initially (Craig, Browne, Stringer, & Beech,

2005). Notwithstanding these limitations, static or historical risk factors are critical to treatment planning.

Risk Assessments Focusing on Dynamic Factors

Although static and historical risk factors provide a useful method for predicting long-term risk of recidivism and therefore who may need treatment and of what intensity, they can only serve as 'markers' of what needs to change to decrease an individual offender's risk. A detailed examination of dynamic or changeable factors is also included within comprehensive risk assessments. These are characteristics of the individual that have a demonstrated empirical relationship with sexual offending behaviour and that, when reduced, may lead to reductions in recidivism (Hanson, 2006). These factors were assessed to be present at the time of offending and therefore may have directly precipitated or caused the offending, can change over time or with intervention, and are therefore arguably amenable to treatment. Hanson and Harris (2000) usefully distinguished between stable and acute risk factors. Stable dynamic risk factors were defined as relatively enduring characteristics related to risk. Acute dynamic risk factors are rapidly changing situations or context or expression of stable dynamic risk factors that are useful in identifying when, or in what circumstances, an offender is most at risk of sexual offending.

Clearly, these are fundamentally important to treatment planning. A number of treatment-related terms are used to describe these dynamic risk factors. They have been variously labelled criminogenic needs (Andrews & Bonta, 2010), causal psychological risk factors (Beech & Ward, 2004), or psychologically meaningful risk factors (Mann et al., 2010). Craissati and Beech (2003) reviewed the role of dynamic risk factors in risk prediction and outlined five core domains of dynamic risk: intimacy deficits/social competencies, social influences, pro-offending attitudes, sexual self-regulation, and general self-regulation. These factors provide an overview of treatment targets relevant to the offender. For example, individuals who show patterns of deviant arousal may require sex offender-specific treatment (e.g., fantasy or arousal modification), whereas others may require intervention in other areas (e.g., impulsivity, aggression/anger management, community support) (Wong, Olver, & Stockdale, 2009).

A number of risk measures have been developed that assess dynamic factors. Examples include Sexual-Violence-Risk Management 20 (SVR-20) (Boer, Hart, Kropp, & Webster, 1997), Risk of Sexual Violence Protocol (RSVP) (Hart et al., 2003), Structured Risk Assessment (SRA) (Thornton, 2002), the Sex Offender Treatment Intervention and Progress Scale (SOTIPS) (McGrath, Lasher, & Cumming, 2012), the Violence Risk Scale: Sex Offender Version (VRS:SO) (Olver et al., 2007), and Stable-2007 and Acute-2007 (Hanson, Harris, Scott, & Helmus, 2007). These dynamic risk measures show similar levels of predictive validity to the actuarial risk measures using static or historical factors and, indeed, appear to strengthen their predictive validity when used in combination (Beech, Friendship, Erikson, & Hanson, 2002; Beggs & Grace, 2011; Hanson et al., 2007; Knight & Thornton, 2007; Olver et al., 2007).

Usefulness of Dynamic Measures for Treatment Planning

Relative Importance of Dynamic Risk Factors

The risk measures developed to assess dynamic factors invariably assess for the relevance or existence of a large number of these factors. These are not necessarily weighted by the risk measure and consequently may be treated equally by a treatment provider when, in fact, the risk factors with the strongest evidence should be emphasized in treatment.

In their review of sex offender dynamic risk factors (which they called 'psychologically meaningful' risk factors), Mann et al. (2010) categorized risk factors into four groups, on the basis of their predictive validity: empirically supported risk factors, promising risk factors, risk factors that are unsupported overall, but with interesting exceptions, and factors with little or no relationship to sexual recidivism.

Risk factors that are empirically supported (defined as at least three studies suggesting significant predictive value) and therefore should be prioritized in treatment include sexual preoccupation, any deviant sexual interest, offence-supportive attitudes, emotional congruence with children, lack of emotionally intimate relationships with adults, lifestyle impulsivity, poor cognitive problem solving, resistance to rules and supervision, grievance/hostility, and negative social influences.

Promising risk factors with at least one study demonstrating significant predictive value for sexual recidivism, and where there are other kinds of relevant supportive evidence, included hostile beliefs about women, Machiavellianism, lack of concern for others, and dysfunctional, sexualized, or externalized coping. These should also be prioritized in treatment if relevant to the individual.

Mann et al. (2010) listed depression, poor social skills, poor victim empathy, and lack of motivation for treatment at intake as having little or no relationship with recidivism and therefore should not be considered risk factors. In the strictest sense, these should not be treatment targets. They also noted that certain factors, such as mental illness and denial, may be a risk factor for some but not for others. In their view, denial might represent a dynamic risk factor 'when it is motivated by the crass desire to avoid punishment or by a failure to recognize their transgression as sexual crimes' (p. 206). However, for others they noted that 'it is likely that some aspects of denial are genuinely protective'. Ware and Mann (2012) examined this issue in more detail, arguing that, given the lack of relationship with reoffending, for the most part denial represents a normal human reluctance to admit one's errors rather than pathology of sexual offending. They highlighted the fact that denial occurs after the offending and is not causal and, in fact, is likely to be used as an understandable strategy by the offender to minimize negative consequences (rather than explicitly to continue offending) in certain situations or contexts. They recommended that denial should not necessarily be an explicit treatment target.

Importantly, in the opinion of Mann et al. (2010), none of the risk factors alone had an overly strong relationship to sexual offending. This has important treatment implications, specifically that treatment providers should not be over-influenced by the presence of any single risk factor and that treatment, therefore, needs to be comprehensive, targeting multiple risk factors (Marshall et al., 2011). Second, many treatment providers or programmes should examine the content of their treatment to see if there is sufficient focus on empirically supported risk factors and not an over-emphasis on too few risk factors (at the expense of others) or an over-emphasis on risk factors that do not appear to be valid (such as victim empathy). Third, the presence of factors such as denial needs to be understood by the treatment provider in order to understand its relevance to risk of recidivism (and therefore treatment goals). This requires a clear individualized case formulation.

Individualized Formulations for Dynamic Risk Factors

An assessment of dynamic risk should include a detailed functional analysis of an individual's offending behaviour and an individualized case formulation that provides a meaningful framework for understanding risk for the individual sex offender (Boer, Thakker, & Ward, 2009; Collie et al., 2008). Mann et al. (2010) usefully proposed the individual risk factors as 'propensities' in order to emphasize that these risk factors will be present only in certain environmental contexts. As Doren (2002) noted, no sex offender will be at risk of harming everyone all the time or, indeed, even children or vulnerable adults unless the context is right.

This is important to treatment planning. Conveying the message to a sex offender, as an example, that they are sexually deviant all the time is, in almost all contexts, simply not true. Maruna and Mann (2006) argued that what treatment providers should be emphasizing is a sense of personal agency and an ability to control their propensities in similar circumstances in the future (see also Ware & Mann, 2012). Treatment planning therefore should consider the contextual aspects in any dynamic risk assessment and needs to be individualized to the offender's personal circumstances in order to maximize his or her engagement and treatment benefit. We describe the differences in how dynamic risk measures construe risk in a later section.

Collaboration in Dynamic Risk Assessment and Treatment Planning

Shingler and Mann (2006) argued for risk assessments to be completed collaboratively, or at least their details shared, with offenders. The result of this collaborative process is a much stronger connection for the offender between risk assessment and his treatment. Shingler and Mann (2006) recommended informing the offenders about the risk assessment process and explaining how it can benefit the offender, including planning for how best to assist him through treatment. In their view, the results of all static and dynamic risk measures should be shared openly with the offender and the scoring explained. The offender should be encouraged to draw his own conclusions as to his risk. From a treatment planning perspective, instances where an offender disagrees that a particular dynamic risk factor is relevant to him is important information to be used in motivational and engagement strategies prior to and during treatment.

Differences in How Dynamic Risk Measures Assess Risk Factors

Dynamic risk measures provide the assessor with an opportunity to consider a more individualized picture of an offender's behaviour, but these measures vary in their purpose and the way in which they are scored and interpreted. They also differ in terms of the number and type of dynamic risk factors included. The majority, if not all, of the most commonly used dynamic risk measures listed above have a range of risk items that can be categorized into four domains: intimacy deficits/social competencies, social influences, sexual self-regulation, and general self-regulation. The extent to which each dynamic risk measure focuses on these domains differs. Similarly, as illustrated in Table 33.1, there are distinct differences in the number and descriptions of risk items. Certain dynamic risk measures include risk items that sit outside the domains and that have no empirical relationship to recidivism. Those tasked with planning treatment must understand these differences and the limitations of particular measures.

Dynamic risk measures are either actuarial tools or structured professional judgements (SPJs). Measures that employ an actuarial approach to dynamic risk, such as the Stable-2007 and Acute-2007 (Hanson et al., 2007), include only those risk factors that have been empirically linked to sexual recidivism. A structured professional judgement approach to dynamic risk, such as the RSVP, includes most of these factors shown to be related to sexual recidivism and also others that may seem more intuitively relevant but have little to no empirical relationship to sexual recidivism based on current findings. There are strengths and limitations with these approaches that are considered in turn.

There are very clear advantages to actuarial dynamic risk measures. The risk factors included in the Stable-2007 and Acute-2007 (Hanson et al., 2007), for example, have a moderately strong statistical relationship with sexual recidivism. The Stable-2007 and Acute-2007 are also able to be combined with the Static-99 score (Hanson & Thornton, 2000), which provides an actuarially adjusted estimate of overall risk. This estimate has a slightly greater predictive validity than the Static-99 alone (Hanson et al., 2002). Matrices have been developed that combine these measures to assist treatment planners. As an example, a sex offender who is assessed as moderate–low risk on the Static-99 but high risk on the Stable-2007 will require intensive treatment. These measures have clear scoring rules and are validated on large normative groups from which risk probabilities are derived.

Actuarial risk measures do have limitations. Factors that did not predict recidivism in the original research samples are excluded even when other research has consistently demonstrated their relationship to recidivism. This has implications for those planning treatment. The Stable-2007, for example, does not include 'offence-supportive attitudes' as a risk factor. A recent large-scale meta-analysis by Helmus, Hanson, Babchishin, and Mann (2013) found that attitudes supportive of sexual offending had a small but consistent relationship with sexual recidivism. Mann et al. (2010) also identified offence-supportive attitudes as a psychologically meaningful risk factor. Interestingly, the original version of the Stable (Stable-2000) did include three items relating to offence-supportive attitudes (sexual entitlement, rape attitudes, and child molester attitudes), but these were omitted in the Stable-2007 as they were no longer found statistically to predict recidivism (in the newer samples of sex offenders). Because of the strict algorithmic application of actuarial dynamic risk measures, they also do not necessarily allow for the inclusion of unique factors that may be relevant in the prediction of an individual's future offending (see the previous section on

Table 33.1 Five core dynamic risk domains measured on selected risk assessment instruments

Core domain	Stable-2007	Acute-2007	SVR-20	RSVP	VRS:SO
Intimacy deficits/social competencies	Capacity for relationship stability Emotional identification with children Hostility towards women General social rejection Lack of concern for others	–	Intimate relationship problems	Intimate relationship problems	Intimacy deficits
Social influences	Significant social influences	Collapse of social support	–	Non-intimate relationship problems	Community support
Pro-offending attitudes	–	–	Attitudes that support or condone sex offences	Attitudes that support or condone sex offences	Cognitive distortions
Sexual self-regulation	Sex drive/preoccupation Sex as coping Deviant sexual preference	Sexual preoccupation Victim access	Sexual deviance High-density sex offences Multiple sex offence types Physical harm to victims Use of weapons or threats of death Escalation in frequency or severity of sex offences	Sexual deviance Chronicity of sex offences Diversity of sex offending Physical coercion Psychological coercion Escalation in frequency or severity of sex offences	Sexually deviant lifestyle Sexual compulsivity Offence planning Sexual offending cycle Deviant sexual preference

(continued overleaf)

Table 33.1 (*Continued*)

Core domain	Stable-2007	Acute-2007	SVR-20	RSVP	VRS:SO
General self-regulation	Impulsive Poor problem-solving skills Negative emotionality Cooperation with supervision	Emotional collapse Hostility Substance abuse Rejection of supervision	Substance use problems Employment problems Past non-sexual violence Past non-violent offences Prior supervision failure Lacks realistic plans Negative attitude towards intervention	Substance use problems Employment problems Problems with stress or coping Non-sexual criminality Problems with planning Problems with treatment Problems with supervision	Interpersonal aggression Emotional control Substance abuse Impulsivity Compliance with community supervision Treatment compliance
Items that sit outside the five core domains	–	–	*Extreme minimization or denial* *Victim of child sexual abuse* *Psychopathy* *Major mental illness* *Suicidal or homicidal ideation*	*Extreme minimization or denial* *Victim of child sexual abuse* *Psychopathy* *Major mental illness* *Suicidal or homicidal ideation* *Problems with self-awareness*	*Criminal personality* *Insight*
Allows for inclusion of 'other' unique factors	*No*	*No*	*Yes – suggested inclusions: psychological coercion; non-intimate relationship problems; self-awareness; stress/coping*	*Yes*	*No*

the relative importance of risk factors). These approaches may not identify all of an individual's risk factors or treatment needs.

Actuarial dynamic risk measures also do not explicitly require a detailed formulation of an individual's risk (Collie et al., 2008). Parent et al. (2011) argued that applying an actuarial model may not account for context or differences in aetiology of offending pathways. Although they refer primarily to actuarial instruments using static or historical factors, the same argument may apply to the actuarial approach to dynamic risk assessment. We have seen in practice that assessors can score a Static-99 and a Stable-2007 by following the explicit scoring rules, have a sense of what should be targeted in treatment, but still cannot conceptualize why and how the individual offended and consequently what situations may present the greatest risk for the individual upon release and what his treatment needs actually are.

The use of SPJ measures as a part of a convergent risk assessment (using an actuarial or static assessment as a baseline measure) has gained increasing support in the field (Rettenberger & Hucker, 2011). Although there is currently less empirical evidence supporting SPJ measures, in practice they provide the ability to make a distinctly individualized formulation or treatment plan because they directly consider the context of the offending. Most of these assessments consider historical factors or 'psychological vulnerabilities' (e.g., the psychological adjustment factors and the nature of the previous sexual offences in the same context with the meaningful or causal psychological dynamic risk factors (Boer & Hart, 2009). The SPJ approach encourages (even forces) the practitioner to think critically about the individual they are assessing in a more holistic way rather than rely on a formula or algorithm. The risk assessment is therefore contextualized and specific to the individual. However, treatment planners must be mindful that many of the SPJ measures include a number of items that do not have an empirical relationship to sexual recidivism. Denial and being a victim of child abuse are two clear examples. Further, it is often difficult in practice to rate the items and subsequently interrater reliability can be problematic. Another issue that we have observed in practice is the potential for an assessor to focus on particular risk items and to rate them heavily (without explicit instruction or guidance to do so).

There are, however, many aspects of SPJ measures that are attractive to those planning treatment. SPJ measures such as the RSVP (Hart et al., 2003) and SVR-20 scale (Boer et al., 1997) ask the evaluator to consider historical, dispositional, contextual, and clinical factors related to recidivism. The individual offender's risk factors can be divided into motivators, disinhibitors, and destabilizers in order to make comments on the nature, severity, imminence, frequency, duration, and likelihood of future sexual violence presented as 'risk scenarios'. These scenarios are based on the individual's offending history, the risk factors identified as present and relevant, and future situational or protective factors, such as where the person will be living (Hart & Logan, 2011). These scenarios may then directly inform treatment and management (and case prioritization) and assist in informing the evaluator's overall judgement of the individual as low, moderate, or high risk. These broad descriptors of risk that can be applied may be considered somewhat unscientific and open to bias or subjectivity, hence the necessity to use an actuarial measure to provide a baseline assessment of risk (Rettenberger & Hucker, 2011). If the practitioner anchors their judgement to an actuarial assessment and is provided with supervision or case team discussion to avoid 'drift', this approach has many strengths for individual treatment planning.

Other measures have more specific purposes, such as examining change after treatment. For example, the VRS:SO (Wong, Olver, Nicholaichuk, & Gordon, 2003) is a 'conceptual actuarial' measure. It provides an estimate of probability of reoffence (compared with a normative group) based on both static and dynamic risk factors, but was also developed with the intention of directly informing individual treatment planning and measuring change (Wong et al., 2009). Because of its actuarial nature, it does not allow for inclusion of additional unique risk factors, but it does include numerous factors that are not considered by, for example, the Stable-2007. It has been found to measure reliably post-treatment change on the included dynamic risk factors, leading Olver, Lewis, and Wong (2013) to suggest that this is evidence that these risk factors must be causally related to sexual offending. Measuring change after treatment is discussed later.

Dynamic Risk Assessment and Measuring Treatment Changes

Treatment planning is an ongoing process. Dynamic risk measures, by virtue of their ability to measure change, are essential as post-treatment measures. How otherwise can one assess whether treatment has reduced the risk of reoffending or if further treatment needs to be planned? A number of studies have now demonstrated that the measurement of dynamic risk factors pre- and post-treatment adds incremental predictive validity to static risk factor measures.

Olver et al. (2007) used the VRS:SO (Wong et al., 2003) to assess change in dynamic risk factors after treatment. Using a sample of 321 sexual offenders who completed a 6–8-month treatment programme followed up for an average of 10 years post-release, they found that change on the dynamic scales of the VRS:SO was negatively related to sexual recidivism and increased predictive validity over the scales measures static or historical factors. Positive changes, therefore, were significantly related to reduction in recidivism. When their sample was divided into low- and high-risk groups, these positive changes were only predictive in reductions in recidivism amongst the high-risk offenders. Olver and Wong (2009) also found that changes in the VRS:SO dynamic scales were associated with reductions in sexual and violent recidivism for psychopathic high-risk offenders.

To strengthen this research approach, Beggs and Grace (2011) compared three methods for assessing treatment change with a sample of 218 lower risk child molesters treated in prison and followed up for an average of 12 years. They used pre- and post-treatment change scores from a battery of psychometric self-report instruments, the VRS:SO, and post-treatment ratings on the Standard Goal Attainment Scaling for sex offenders (SGAS) (Hogue, 1994). They found that, in particular, the changes in the self-reported psychometric instruments significantly predicted reductions in sexual recidivism. Interestingly, the VRS:SO results were similarly predictive but non-significant. An important finding from this study is that changes in dynamic risk factors can be assessed using common psychometrics and not just specific dynamic risk measures.

Olver and Wong (2011) also found that the predictive validity of static risk assessments (Static-99) decreased with treatment improvements as measured by the VRS:SO. This would make intuitive sense, as static risk factors are not amendable to change and may therefore effectively 'penalize' those offenders who have made the most treatment gains. Although they interpreted their findings with caution, they suggested that the use of static instruments alone post-treatment may actually be overestimating risk in instances where the offender has made significant changes in treatment.

Do Treatment Programmes Adequately Target Risk Factors?

The extent to which treatment planning informs treatment programmes is clearly important. The assumption is that treatment programmes or an individual clinician will focus a large part of their treatment efforts on those risk factors assessed as most relevant for each offender. Mann et al. (2010) argued that treatment programmes should focus the majority of their efforts on sexual preoccupation and sexual deviance, sexual preference for pre-pubescent or pubescent children, sexualized violence, offence-supportive attitudes (which is distinct from denial and minimizations; see Marshall, Marshall, & Ware, 2009), emotional congruence with children, lack of emotionally intimate relationships with adults, lifestyle impulsiveness, poor problem solving, resistance to rules and supervision, grievance/hostility, and negative social influences.

It appears, however, that many treatment programmes place an emphasis on treatment targets that are not empirically established risk factors (Mann et al., 2011). McGrath, Cumming, Burchard, Zeoli, and Ellerby (2010) completed a large-scale survey of North American and Canadian sex offender treatment programmes for juveniles and adults in community and residential settings. They found that offence responsibility and victim awareness/empathy were the two most common treatment targets in spite of a lack of evidence indicating that addressing these treatment targets results in reduced reoffending rates. In contrast, they noted that a comparatively small percentage of treatment programmes reported targeting offence-supportive attitudes and problems controlling their arousal (e.g., sexual preoccupation and deviant sexual interests) within their programmes. Ware and Mann (2012) suggested that therapists can fall victim to 'correctional quackery' (Gendreau, Smith, & Theriault, 2009), where they can prioritize personal experience, values, and anecdotal evidence, or the pressure from non-therapists involved in sex offender management or even the general public, above evidence resulting from rigorous, large-scale research efforts into risk factors. McGrath et al. (2010), however, also noted that some treatment targets, such as self-esteem or lack of motivation, may not be related directly to the reduction of risk factors but may be necessary for treatment engagement purposes.

Conclusions

Mann and Marshall (2009) argued that there is 'little excuse for providing treatment that is not preceded by careful risk and need assessment'. This risk assessment ought to be based on a careful examination of both static or historical and dynamic risk factors, through the use of any of a number of validated risk measures. Static or historical risk factors will provide a valid predictor of long-term risk that assists the treatment provider to plan for how much treatment will be required and who should be prioritized into treatment when resources are scarce. Static or historical risk factors may also serve as useful markers of long-term psychological issues that have caused sex offending. Treatment providers also require information relating to dynamic or changeable risk factors. These are essentially the targets of treatment. Treatment providers should ensure that they have completed an individualized formulation of the sexual offending and understand the context around the offender's future risk. This should be conveyed to the offender. Treatment providers should also ensure that they are aware of, and targeting, the dynamic risk factors with the strongest empirical relationship to sexual recidivism. It appears that this is not always the case. Sexual deviance, if present, must be targeted in treatment. In contrast, denial, if present, may not be so important to target. Treatment providers need to understand the differences in dynamic risk measures – what these will tell them that is relevant to treatment, and what they will not. Finally, treatment providers should use dynamic risk assessments to evaluate treatment outcomes. Risk assessment therefore is essential to treatment planning both prior to, and at the conclusion of, treatment.

References

Andrews, D. A., & Bonta, J. (2010). *The psychology of criminal conduct* (4th ed.). Cincinnati, OH: Anderson.

Bartosh, D. L., Garby, T., Lewis, D., & Gray, S. (2003). Differences in the predictive validity of actuarial risk assessments in relation to sex offender type. *International Journal of Offender Therapy and Comparative Criminology, 47*, 422–438.

Beech, A., Fisher, D., & Beckett, R. C. (1999). *Step 3: An evaluation of the prison sex offender treatment programme* (UK Home Office Occasional Report). London, England: HMSO.

Beech, A. R., Friendship, C., Erikson, M., & Hanson, R. K. (2002). The relationship between static and dynamic risk factors and reconviction in a sample of UK childabusers. *Sexual Abuse: A Journal of Research and Treatment, 14*, 155–167.

Beech, A. R., & Ward, T. (2004). The integration of etiology and risk in sexual offenders: A theoretical framework. *Aggression and Violent Behaviour, 10*, 31–63.

Beggs, S. M., & Grace, R.C. (2011). Treatment gain for sexual offenders against children predicts reduced recidivism: A comparative validity study. *Journal of Consulting and Clinical Psychology, 79*, 182–192.

Boer, D. P., & Hart, S. D. (2009). Sex offender risk assessment: Research, evaluation, 'best-practice' recommendations and future directions. In J. Ireland, C. Ireland, & P. Birch (Eds.), *Violent and sexual offenders* (pp. 27–42). Cullompton, England: Willan.

Boer, D. P., Hart, S. D., Kropp, P. R., & Webster, C. D. (1997). *Manual for the Sexual Violence Risk – 20: Professional guidelines for assessing risk of sexual violence*. Vancouver, Canada: British Columbia Institute Against Family Violence.

Boer, D. P., Thakker, J., & Ward, T. (2009). Sex offender risk-based case formulation. In A. R. Beech, L. A. Craig, & K. D. Browne (Eds.), *Assessment and treatment of sex offenders: A handbook* (pp. 77–87). Chichester, England: John Wiley & Sons, Ltd.

Collie, R., Ward, T., & Vess, J. (2008). Assessment and case conceptualization in sex offender treatment. *Journal of Behavioral Analysis of Offender and Victim Treatment and Prevention, 1,* 65–81.

Craig, L. A., & Beech, A. R. (2010). Towards a guide to best practice in conducting actuarial risk assessments with sex offenders. *Aggression & Violent Behavior, 15,* 278–293.

Craig, L. A., Beech, A. R., & Harkins, L. (2009). The predictive accuracy of risk factors and frameworks. In A. R. Beech, L. A. Craig, & K. D. Browne (Eds.), *Assessment and treatment of sex offenders: A handbook* (pp. 53–72). Chichester, England: John Wiley & Sons, Ltd.

Craig, L. A., Brown, K. D., Stringer, I., & Beech, A. R. (2005). Sexual recidivism: A review of static, dynamic, and actuarial predictors. *Journal of Sexual Aggression, 11,* 65–84.

Craissati, J., & Beech, A. (2003). A review of dynamic variables and their relationship to risk prediction in sex offenders. *Journal of Sexual Aggression, 9,* 41–55.

Doren, D. (2002). *Evaluating sex offenders: A manual for civil commitments and beyond.* London, England: Sage.

Epperson, D. L., Kaul, J. D., & Hesselton, D. (1998, October). *Final report on the development of the Minnesota Sex Offender Screening Tool – Revised (MnSOST-R).* Paper presented at the 17th Annual Conference of the Association for the Treatment of Sexual Abusers, Vancouver, Canada.

Friendship, C., Mann, R. E., & Beech, A. R. (2003). Evaluation of a national prison based treatment program for sexual offenders in England and Wales. *Journal of Interpersonal Violence, 18,* 744–759.

Gendreau, P., Smith, P., & Theriault, Y. L. (2009). Chaos theory and correctional treatment: Common sense, correctional quackery and the law of fartcatchers. *Journal of Contemporary Criminal Justice, 25,* 384–396.

Hanson, R. K. (1997). *The development of a brief actuarial risk scale for sexual offense recidivism* (User Report 1997-04). Ottawa, Canada: Department of the Solicitor General of Canada.

Hanson, R. K. (2006). Stability and changes: Dynamic risk factors for sexual offenders. In W. L. Marshall, Y. M. Fernandez, L. E. Marshall, & G. A. Serran (Eds.), *Sexual offender treatment: Controversial issues* (pp. 17–31). Chichester, England: John Wiley & Sons, Ltd.

Hanson, R. K., Bourgon, G., Helmus, L., & Hodgson, S. (2009). The principles of effective correctional treatment also apply to sexual offenders: A meta-analysis. *Criminal Justice and Behavior, 36,* 865–891.

Hanson, R. K., Gordon, A., Harris, A. J. R., Marques, J. K., Murphy, W. D., Quinsey, V. L., & Seto, M. C. (2002). First report of the collaborative outcome data project on the effectiveness of psychological treatment of sex offenders. *Sexual Abuse: A Journal of Research and Treatment, 14,* 169–195.

Hanson, R. K., & Harris, A. (2000). Where should we intervene: Dynamic predictors of sexual offence recidivism. *Criminal Justice and Behavior, 27,* 6–35.

Hanson, R. K., Harris, A. J. R., Scott, T.-L., & Helmus, L. (2007). *Assessing the risk of sexual offenders on community supervision: The Dynamic Supervision Project* (Corrections Research User Report 2007-05). Ottawa, Canada: Public Safety Canada.

Hanson, R. K., & Morton-Bourgon, K. (2004). *Predictors of sexual recidivism: An updated meta-analysis* (User Report 2004-02). Ottawa, ON: Public Safety and Emergency Preparedness Canada.

Hanson, R. K., & Morton-Bourgon, K. E. (2005). The characteristics of persistent sexual offenders: A meta-analysis of recidivism studies. *Journal of Consulting and Clinical Psychology, 73,* 1154–1163.

Hanson, R. K., & Morton-Bourgon, K. (2007). *The accuracy of recidivism risk assessment for sexual offenders: A meta-analysis* (Corrections Research User Report 2007-01). Ottawa,

Canada: Public Safety Canada. Retrieved from https://www.ccoso.org/sites/default/files/import/accuracy-of-risk-assessments.pdf

Hanson, R. K., & Thornton, D. (2000). Improving risk assessment for sex offenders: A comparison of three actuarial scales. *Law and Human Behavior, 24,* 119–136.

Hanson, R. K., & Thornton, D. (2003). *Notes on the development of Static-2002* (Corrections Research User Report 2003-01). Ottawa, Canada: Department of the Solicitor General of Canada. Retrieved from http://www.publicsafety.gc.ca/cnt/rsrcs/pblctns/nts-dvlpmnt-sttc/nts-dvlpmnt-sttc-eng.pdf

Hart, S. D., Kropp, P. R., Laws, D. R., Klaver, J., Logan, C., & Watt, K. A. (2003). *The Risk for Sexual Violence Protocol (RSVP) – Structured professional guidelines for assessing risk of sexual violence.* Burnaby, Canada: Mental Health, Law, and Policy Institute, Simon Fraser University.

Hart, S. D., & Logan, C. (2011). Formulation of violence risk using evidence based assessments: The structured professional judgment approach. In P. Sturmey & M. McMurran (Eds.), *Forensic case formulation.* Chichester, England: John Wiley & Sons, Ltd.

Helmus, L., Hanson, R. K., Babchishin, K. M., & Mann, R. E. (2013). Attitudes supportive of sexual offending predict recidivism: A meta-analysis. *Trauma, Violence, and Abuse, 14,* 34–53.

Hogue, T. E. (1994). Goal attainment scaling: A measure of clinical impact and risk assessment. *Issues in Criminological & Legal Psychology, 21,* 96–102.

Kingston, D., Yates, P. M., Firestone, P., Babchishin, K. M., & Bradford, J. M. (2008). Long term predictive validity of the Risk Matrix 2000: A comparison with the Static-99 and the Sex Offender Risk Appraisal Guide. *Sexual Abuse: A Journal of Research and Treatment, 20,* 466–484.

Knight, R. A., & Thornton, D. (2007). Evaluating and improving risk assessment schemes for sexual recidivism: A long-term follow-up of convicted sexual offenders (Final Report: US Department of Justice, Award No. 2003-WG-BX-1002). Retrieved from http://www.ncjrs.gov/pdffiles1/nij/grants/217618.pdf

Lovins, B., Lowenkamp, C. T., & Latessa, E. J. (2009). Applying the risk principle to sex offenders. Can treatment make some sex offenders worse? *The Prison Journal, 89,* 344–357.

Lowenkamp, C., & Latessa, E. (2002). *Evaluation of Ohio's community based correctional facilities and halfway house programs.* Unpublished manuscript, Division of Criminal Justice, University of Cincinnati, OH.

Lowenkamp, C., Latessa, E., & Holsinger, A. (2006). The risk principle in action: What have we learned from 13,676 offenders and 97 correctional programs? *Crime and Delinquency, 52,* 77–93.

Mailloux, D. L., Abracen, J., Serin, R., Cousineau, C., Malcolm, B., & Looman, J. (2003). Dosage of treatment to sexual offenders: Are we overprescribing? *International Journal of Offender Therapy and Comparative Criminology, 47,* 171–184.

Mann, R. E., Hanson, R. K., & Thornton, D. (2010). Assessing risk for sexual recidivism: Some proposals on the nature of psychologically meaningful risk factors. *Sexual Abuse: A Journal of Research and Treatment, 22,* 191–217.

Mann, R. E., & Marshall, W. L. (2009). Advances in the treatment of adult incarcerated sex offenders. In A. R. Beech, L. A. Craig, & K. D. Browne (Eds.), *Assessment and treatment of sex offenders* (pp. 329–348). Chichester, England: John Wiley & Sons, Ltd.

Mann, R. E., Ware, J., & Fernandez, Y. M. (2011). Managing sex offender treatment programs. In D. P. Boer, R. Eher, L. A. Craig, M. H. Miner, & F. Pfäfflin (Eds.), *International perspectives on the assessment and treatment of sexual offenders. Theory, practice and research* (pp. 331–354). Chichester, England: John Wiley & Sons, Ltd.

Marshall, W. L., Marshall, L. E., Serran, G. A., & O'Brien, M. D. (2011). *The rehabilitation of sexual offenders: Strengths-based approach*. Washington, DC: American Psychological Association.

Marshall, W. L., Marshall, L. E., & Ware, J. (2009). Cognitive distortions in sexual offenders: Should they all be treatment targets? *Sexual Abuse in Australia and New Zealand, 2*, 21–33.

Maruna, S., & Mann, R. E. (2006). A fundamental attribution error? Rethinking cognitive distortions. *Legal and Criminological Psychology, 11*, 155–177.

McGrath, R. J., Cumming, G. F., Burchard, B., Zeoli, S., & Ellerby, L. (2010). *Current practices and emerging trends in sexual abuser management: The Safer Society 2009 North American Survey*. Brandon, VT: Safer Society Press.

McGrath, R. J., Lasher, M. P., & Cumming, G. F. (2012). The Sex Offender Treatment Intervention and Progress Scale (SOTIPS): Psychometric properties and incremental predictive validity with Static-99R. *Sexual Abuse: A Journal of Research and Treatment, 24*, 431–458.

Nunes, K. L., & Cortoni, F. (2008). Dropout from sex-offender treatment and dimensions of risk of sexual recidivism. *Criminal Justice and Behavior, 35*, 24–33.

Olver, M. E., Lewis, K., & Wong, S. C. P. (2013). Risk reduction treatment of high-risk psychopathic offenders: The relationship of psychopathy and treatment change to violent recidivism. *Personality Disorder: Theory, Research and Treatment, 4*, 160–167.

Olver, M. E., & Wong, S. C. P. (2009). Therapeutic responses of psychopathic sexual offenders: Treatment attrition, therapeutic change, and long-term recidivism. *Journal of Consulting and Clinical Psychology, 77*, 328–336.

Olver, M. E., & Wong, S. C. P. (2011). A comparison of static and dynamic assessment of sexual offender risk and need in a treatment context. *Criminal Justice and Behaviour, 38*, 113–126.

Olver, M. E., Wong, S. C. P., Nicholaichuk, T., & Gordon, A. (2007). The validity and reliability of the Violence Risk Scale – Sexual Offender Version: Assessing sex offender risk and evaluating therapeutic change. *Psychological Assessment, 19*, 318–329.

Parent, G., Guay, J. P., & Knight, R. (2011). An assessment of long-term risk of recidivism by adult sex offenders: One size doesn't fit all. *Criminal Justice and Behavior, 38*, 188–209.

Quinsey, V. L., Harris, G. T., Rice, M. E., & Cormier, C. A. (1998). *Violent offenders: Appraising and managing risk*. Washington, DC: American Psychological Association.

Rettenberger, M., & Hucker, S. J. (2011). Structured professional guidelines: International applications. In D. P. Boer, R. Eher, L. A. Craig, M. H. Miner, & F. Pfäfflin (Eds.), *International perspectives on the assessment and treatment of sexual offenders. Theory, practice and research* (pp. 85–110). Chichester, England: John Wiley & Sons, Ltd.

Rettenberger, M., Matthes, A., Boer, D. P., & Eher, R. (2010). Actuarial recidivism risk assessment and sexual delinquency: A comparison of five risk assessment tools in different sexual offender subtypes. *International Journal of Offender Therapy and Comparative Criminology, 54*, 169–186.

Shingler, J., & Mann, R. E. (2006). Collaboration in clinical work with sexual offenders: Treatment and risk assessment. In W. L. Marshall, Y. M. Fernandez, L. E. Marshall, & D. A. Serran (Eds.), *Sexual offender treatment: Controversial issues* (pp. 25–240). Chichester, England: John Wiley & Sons, Ltd.

Thornton, D. (2002). Constructing and testing a framework for dynamic risk assessment. *Sexual Abuse: A Journal of Research and Treatment, 14*, 137–151.

Thornton, D., Mann, R., Webster, S., Blud, L., Travers, R., Friendship, C., & Erikson, M. (2003). Distinguishing and combining risks for sexual and violent recidivism. *Annals of the New York Academy of Sciences, 989*, 225–235.

Wakeling, H. C., Mann, R. E., & Carter, A. J. (2012). Do low risk sexual offenders need treatment? *The Howard Journal of Criminal Justice, 51*, 286–299.

Ware, J. (2011). The importance of contextual issues within sexual offender treatment. In D. P. Boer, R. Eher, L. A. Craig, M. H. Miner, & F. Pfäfflin (Eds.), *International perspectives on the assessment and treatment of sexual offenders. Theory, practice and research* (pp. 299–312). Chichester, England: John Wiley & Sons, Ltd.

Ware, J., & Bright, D. A. (2008). Evolution of a treatment program: Recent changes to NSW Custody Based Intensive Treatment (CUBIT). *Psychiatry, Psychology, and Law, 15*, 340–349.

Ware, J., & Mann, R. E. (2012). How should 'acceptance of responsibility' be addressed in sexual offending treatment programs? *Aggression and Violent Behavior, 17*, 279–288.

Ware, J., Mann, R. E., & Wakeling, H.C. (2009). Group vs. individual treatment: What is the best modality for treating sex offenders? *Sexual Abuse in Australia and New Zealand, 2*, 2–13.

Wong, S. C. P., Olver, M. E., Nicholaichuk, T. P., & Gordon, A. E. (2003). *The Violence Risk Scale: Sexual Offender version (VRS:SO)*. Saskatoon, Canada: Department of Psychology and Research. Regional Psychiatric Centre.

Wong, S. C. P., Olver, M. E., & Stockdale, K. C. (2009). The utility of dynamic and static actors in risk assessment, prediction, and treatment. In J. T. Andrade (Ed.), *Handbook of violence risk assessment and treatment: New approaches for mental health professionals* (pp. 83–120). New York: Springer.

34

Case Formulation

Jo Thakker

University of Waikato, New Zealand

Introduction

The chapter begins with a general discussion about case formulation that includes sections on the meaning of the term and the methods that may be used in developing a formulation. There is then a brief section on case formulation in the field of forensic psychology, which examines the idea that a formulation is essentially a theory. The remainder of the chapter looks at case formulation in the sexual offending field, including theories of sexual offending, the formulation of risk, the formulation of protective factors, and the issue of formulation-based versus manual-based treatment. The approach taken is inclusive; each topic is discussed briefly, usually with a concise overview and one or two examples. The chapter concludes with a brief summary and suggestions for further research.

What Is Case Formulation?

Case formulation is fundamental to the work of most contemporary psychologists and psychotherapists (Pain, Chadwick, & Abba, 2008). How could it be otherwise? Given that all it really means is making sense of the client and understanding his or her difficulties, it must necessarily be central to clinical practice. As stated by Restifo (2010), 'case formulation represents the bridge between assessment and treatment' (p. 210). If a good assessment is conducted, then it should be possible to diagnose accurately the client's presenting problem or problems and identify the various factors that have led to its development. Furthermore, a formulation should be evidence based, that is, it should be based on accepted and established theory and practices (Hart, Sturmey, Logan, & McMurran, 2011). It should, in other words, be consistent with the scientist practitioner model, which requires that clinicians are up to date with best-practice approaches. In fact, the origins of the practice of case

The Wiley Handbook on the Theories, Assessment, and Treatment of Sexual Offending.
Edited by Douglas P. Boer. Volume II: Assessment, edited by Leam A. Craig and Martin Rettenberger.
© 2017 John Wiley & Sons, Ltd. Published 2017 by John Wiley & Sons, Ltd.

formulation have been traced to the 1950s and the emergence then of the scientist practitioner model (British Psychological Society, 2011).

A case formulation is in essence a hypothesis, which should serve to explain the client's presentation and lead to effective treatment (Persons, Beckner, & Tompkins, 2013). It is a theory generated to explain what it going on and therefore to assist the clinician in identifying the best treatment for the client. As explained by Persons et al., within the mental health field the development of a hypothesis is often carried out in collaboration with the client. The clinician may first come up with a hypothesis but will typically discuss it with the client before it is finalized, to see if the client believes that it fits with their own conceptualization of their difficulties. For example, a formulation has been described as a 'shared narrative', which must have some meaning and relevance to the client (British Psychological Society, 2011). Thus, as further explained by the British Psychological Society, it is unlike a medical diagnosis, which is typically an 'expert pronouncement' that does not usually take into account the views of the patient.

Approaches to Case Formulation

There are a variety of approaches to case formulation. One approach commonly discussed in the literature is the 'Five Ps' method, where, as explained by Macneil, Hasty, Conus, and Berk (2012), the Five Ps stand for presenting problem, predisposing factors, precipitating factors, perpetuating factors, and protective/positive factors. Arguably, one of the advantages of the Five Ps approach is the inherent structure in the model, which serves to remind the writer of the key areas that need to be covered. Another approach, introduced by Vertue and Haig (2008) is the abductive method, is founded on the idea that clinical reasoning and psychological formulation are more suited to an abductive reasoning approach rather than a hypothetico-deductive model as is commonly used in medicine. As outlined by Vertue and Haig, the abductive method involves considering a range of explanations for the client's presentation, and then choosing the explanation that explains more of the psychological phenomena that are being observed. Further, they argue that it is important that formulations are based on well-accepted theories of psychological disorders so that they are consistent with the research. Vertue and Haig proposed that this sort of approach has the advantage of being better equipped to deal with the complexities of human psychological phenomena.

Although referring to psychiatric rather than psychological formulation, Fernando, Cohen, and Henskens (2012) made a similar point. For example, they explain that hypotheses may be drawn from 'an array of elaborated psychological theories' (p. 122), which will typically cover a variety of contributing factors, including biological (including genetic), cognitive, behavioural, and familial. Further, they state that a formulation 'involves the ability to link salient information gathered from the patient with those theoretical models that have the most explanatory power, with the aim of achieving a seamless integration of the linked components' (p. 122). As explained by the authors, formulations based on different underlying theoretical perspectives are not necessarily mutually exclusive. Rather, they can each contribute something unique to the understanding of the client's presentation. Thus, the clinician does not necessarily have to choose a particular underlying theory, but may rather consider how different theoretical bases may change the formulation. In this way, it is suggested that the unique complexities of the clients are more likely to be fully understood by the clinician.

It has been proposed (e.g., Persons, Roberts, Zalecki, & Brechwald, 2006) that treatment that is founded on a good case formulation has a number of advantages over more standardized treatment approaches. For example, treatment can be tailored to the needs of the specific individual, which may result in a multipronged approach. Furthermore, as case formulations are constantly re-evaluated, if a treatment method is not working then changes can be made to the nature of the intervention. In discussing the role of case formulation in emotion-focused therapy, Watson (2010) proposed that therapists need to be highly responsive to their clients and should continually modify their treatment approach based on the emergence of new information and, accordingly, new conceptualizations of their clients.

There appears to be a dearth of research on the efficacy of case formulation in clinical psychology and psychiatry. However, a study by Persons et al. (2006) on the use of case formulation in the application of cognitive–behavioural therapy in the treatment of clients with anxiety and depression found that the treatment led to statistically significant improvements in clients' symptoms. In further work, Persons et al. (2013) used a case study approach to illustrate the process of case formulation and to highlight its benefits. Using two case examples, they described how the clinicians involved used a case formulation approach. They stated, 'Both clinicians worked with their clients to develop a case formulation or hypothesis, about psychological mechanisms causing and maintaining the patient's symptoms, to collect data to test the formulation by monitoring changes in those mechanisms, and to evaluate the effectiveness of the treatment plan based on the formulation by monitoring symptom change' (p. 9). Used in this way, the case formulation creates a framework for testing hypotheses and making important changes to treatment along the way.

Case Formulation in the Field of Forensic Psychology

In their paper on case formulation in the forensic field, Hart et al. (2011) outlined a number of criteria that should be used to evaluate a formulation:

- External coherence – This is the extent to which the formulation is consistent with established and accepted theory and research.
- Factual foundation – This refers to the degree to which the formulation is based on sufficient data about the case; the more data the better.
- Internal coherence – This relates to the idea that the formulation should be internally consistent; that is, each aspect should be consistent with every other aspect.
- Explanatory breadth – This refers to the extent to which the formulation accounts for all of the data. A better formulation is one that explains more of the available information.

- Diachronicity – This is essentially a sub-aspect of explanatory breadth; it relates to the degree to which a formulation can account for past, present, and future details.
- Simplicity – Sometimes referred to as parsimony, this refers to the idea that a formulation should involve the least complex explanation possible to explain the data. The formulation should not be unnecessarily complex or obscure.
- Reliability – This is the degree to which the formulation is consistent with the formulations or explanations provided by other health professionals who have also been involved in the case.
- Generativity – Sometimes referred to as fertility, this relates to the degree to which the formulation is both testable and applicable, that is, it should be able to be tested (for example, by the efficacy of treatment) and it should have practical application. As detailed by Hart et al., in a forensic context a formulation should lead to strategies for managing risk.
- Accuracy – Sometimes referred to as predictive validity, this refers to the idea that any predictions generated by the formulation are accurate.
- Acceptability – This relates to the extent that the formulation is considered to be useful by the individual client and all those who are involved with the client (such as others involved in the client's rehabilitation or the Parole Board).

These criteria are similar to those outlined by Thagard (1978), a philosopher who provided a list of criteria for determining whether a theory is scientifically sound. Although Thagard listed fewer criteria than those outlined above, all of those above could be subsumed by Thagard's criteria, as his are simply broader. Although it may be argued that the above list is impractical as a checklist for a formulation owing to its length, it is nonetheless important as it provides a format for evaluating one's general approach to formulation. Furthermore, it is helpful to have a reminder of what an ideal formulation might look like.

In presenting a case study of homicide by an 'older adult offender', Arsuffi (2010) outlined the importance of a thorough formulation in terms of developing an understanding of the crime and of the offender's treatment needs. For example, in identifying the role of 'negative automatic thoughts' (NATs) over a several-month period leading up to the homicide, the clinician then had some clear treatment targets. Also, in bringing to bear the diasthesis stress model as a way of explaining the connection between vulnerability and the offender's recent circumstances, the clinician was able to consider the role that stress had played in the offender's actions, and this was useful for treatment planning. This provides a useful illustration of how a formulation can draw on broad psychological theories in explaining offending behaviour.

Case Formulation and Sexual Offending

So far, the discussion has focused on case formulation in general; now the focus turns to some of the particular issues and areas that are especially relevant in the area of sexual offending. Although, of course, the above topics are relevant to case formulation in the sex offender field, they are not specific to the field. Along with these more general issues, given the nature of this book, it is important to consider the sorts of issues that are particularly important in the assessment and treatment of sexual offenders.

What Is Being Explained?

To begin with, one needs to ask the question of what the case formulation is trying to explain. In the area of mental health, the case formulation is typically used to identify the presenting problem and explain the various factors that have contributed to its development. Further, one often wants to explain how the problem is maintained over time. Within the correctional field, the focus is usually on the development of the offending behaviour, as psychologists working in this area are typically tasked with assisting the offender to cease offending. The predominant view is that if the underlying causal factors can be identified, then these can be addressed in treatment, thereby leading to a reduction in future risk. Furthermore, risk itself is often the focus of the formulation; in other words, the clinician needs to develop a clear understanding of the nature and level of risk that the offender may pose to the community in the future. For instance, if the offender is released, what are the chances that he or she will reoffend? And what sort of offence is he or she most likely to commit?

Similarly, in working with sexual offenders, the clinician usually aims to determine the underlying vulnerability factors along with the more proximal factors in order to develop an explanation of how the offending came about. This then contributes to the development of an individualized treatment plan. Or, if treatment is manualized (for example, in a group treatment setting), then a formulation should still play a role in tailoring the intervention, as outlined by Ward, Nathan, Drake, Lee, and Pathé (2000). Also, as with general offending, risk assessment is an important aspect of the assessment and treatment of sexual offenders. Only a small proportion of sexual offenders go on to commit further sexual offences (Cortoni, Hanson, & Coache, 2010), so it is important to be able to identify those who are most at risk for this.

Another reason why a sound understanding of risk is important is that the nature and level of risk are often used to determine the type and intensity (or amount) of treatment (Andrews & Bonta, 2003). Andrews and Bonta's well-established Risk–Need–Responsivity (RNR) model highlights the importance of a good formulation of risk based on the idea that the nature and level of risk will allow for more appropriate and efficient allocation of treatment resources. Thus, according to the RNR model, a high-risk sex offender should receive more in-depth and extensive treatment, while a low-risk offender may not require treatment.

Theories Informing Formulations of Sexual Offending Behaviour

As mentioned above, in order for any case formulation to be consistent with the scientist practitioner approach, it needs to be consistent with known and accepted science. Hence it needs to be based on accepted and established theories. Accordingly, this section provides a brief overview of two key theories, one of which is an example of a theory of child sexual offending and the other an example of a theory of sexual offending against adult women. For a fuller explanation and critique of these theories, see Thakker (2012).

In their Quadripartite Model, Hall and Hirschman (1991) outlined four key factors that they suggested may lead to sexual offending against women: offence-related sexual arousal, pro-rape cognitions, affective dyscontrol, and 'developmentally related personality problems'. Hall and Hirschman proposed that sexual arousal is a necessary feature of sexual offending, but they argued that in the case of rape, it is not necessarily deviant. On elaboration, they referred to research (e.g., Malamuth, Check, & Briere, 1986) that found that sexual arousal to 'rape stimuli' was exhibited by both rapists and non-rapists. Furthermore, in the case of sexual aggression towards adult females, there is no problem with the type of stimuli that arouses such men; rather, the problem lies in the way in which they attempt to meet their sexual needs. Hall and Hirschman therefore concluded that sexual arousal is a necessary but not sufficient condition for sexual offending against women.

The second aspect of the model – pro-rape cognitions – refers to the pro-rape attitudes and beliefs that the offender may have about women. The model suggests that while the offender is feeling sexually aroused he cognitively appraises the situation and, in doing so, brings to bear his women-related attitudes and beliefs, which then influence his choice of action from that point. The next component of the model – affective dyscontrol – refers to problems with the management of negative emotion. Hall and Hirschman proposed that anger and hostility are especially significant in a man's motivation to rape. They stated that 'sexually aggressive behaviour occurs when these affective states become so compelling and powerful that they overcome inhibitions' (p. 664). The fourth aspect of the model – developmentally related personality problems – refers to antisocial personality traits that are believed to result from aversive early life experiences. For instance, Hall and Hirschman noted that most rapists have been exposed to neglect and various forms of abuse during their childhoods. They also noted that such individuals often struggle through the school system (with little success) and have a history of conduct problems from a reasonably young age.

The Quadripartite Model also acknowledges the role of environmental variables in the commission of a sexual offence. For example, the model proposes that the presence of a victim may increase the likelihood that an offence will occur. Alternatively, if the perpetrator is intoxicated with alcohol then he will be more likely to commit a rape owing to increased disinhibition. Thus, essentially, the Quadripartite Model presupposes that a sexual offence arises out of the presence of the four individual factors along with a variety of environmental variables.

In contrast to the above-outlined model, Finkelhor's Precondition Model focuses on sexual offending against children (Finkelhor, 1984). This model proposes that there are four primary factors that lead to these sorts of sexual offences. First, Finkelhor suggested that 'emotional congruence with children' is an important factor. This factor refers to the notion that child sexual offenders use children to meet their emotional needs because they struggle to meet such needs through interaction with adults. The second factor in the model is sexual arousal, which simply refers to the idea that child sexual offenders see children as sexual objects and find them to be sexually arousing. The third factor in the model is titled 'blockage', which pertains to the proposition that these sorts of offenders have a number of significant psychological problems that impede their ability to meet their emotional and sexual needs in the context of appropriate intimate relationships with adults. The final aspect of Finkelhor's model is 'disinhibition', which is conceptualized fairly broadly and may include a variety of underlying factors that may lead the offender to act in a disinhibited manner. For example, the offender may be intoxicated with alcohol or may have general problems with impulse control. Finkelhor theorized that these four factors are the primary contributors to child sexual offending.

There are many other models that have been put forward to explain sexual offending, such as Marshall and Barbaree's Integrated Theory (1990) and Knight and Sims-Knight's Three Paths Model (2004). However, the point here is not to provide an in-depth review of such models, but rather to show how they might be utilized in a formulation. This is an important aspect of the formulation process as it is crucial that a formulation – both in this field and across all fields – is grounded in theory and research. Of course, it is not necessary to follow just one theoretical approach in putting together a formulation; rather, a formulation may include ideas from a range of diverse theories. However, causal factors that appear in many different theories may be seen to carry more weight, on the basis that various theoreticians have agreed on their significance. For example, most theories of sexual offending agree that sexual arousal plays an important role.

Formulation of Risk

The assessment of risk is not typically fundamental to the formulation of an individual's offending; the formulation usually focuses on explaining the past rather than predicting the future. However, there is an important link between the formulation and the risk assessment. For example, causal factors that are identified in the formulation may be relevant to the understanding of future risk. Conversely, risk factors that are identified may provide additional information in formulating the case. Hence the formulation and the risk assessment are likely to be closely connected and interdependent. It is for this reason that risk assessment is included in this chapter.

Obviously there are many aspects of the assessment and formulation of risk of sexual offending that could be discussed here. For example, there are many different assessment tools (for a useful list and description, see Studer, Aylwin, Sribney, & Reddon, 2011), ongoing discussions about the accuracy of risk assessments (for a review, see Hanson & Morton-Bourgon, 2009), and discussions about problems with relying purely on clinical judgement (e.g., Kennington, 2008). However, for the sake of brevity, the focus in this section is on the role of static and dynamic factors, and one well-established measure for each of these types of factors is described. The purpose of this is to show how these factors and measures fit within the various steps to formulation that are listed in Table 34.1.

Static factors are historical variables that are unchangeable (Boer, Thakker, & Ward, 2009). Therefore, regardless of what the offender does now and in the future, static factors will remain the same. Measures that assess static factors typically include variables such as the age of the offender and the number and nature of previous convictions. The Static-99 is a 10-item measure for assessing an adult male's risk for further sexual offending based on static factors (Hanson & Thornton, 2000). A full description of the measure and information on the revised version (Static-99R) can be found

Table 34.1 Summary of key steps in formulation for sexual offending

Step	Description	Examples	Other considerations
1.	Choose recognized approach to formulation	Five Ps model Abductive method	You may use one particular approach or a combination of approaches
2.	Following thorough assessment, formulate case based on established theories of sexual offending	Marshall and Barbaree's integrated theory	Of course, you may use multiple models in this process. The key is to ensure that the contributing factors that you identify are known to act as contributing factors. Also, other psychological theories will be relevant here, for example, attachment theory
3.	Include positive and protective factors in formulation	Good Lives model can provide structure here	A more general strengths-based approach may also be useful here
4.	Reflect on the formulation in relation to the criteria for a good theory	Internal coherence Explanatory breadth	It may be helpful to focus on a few key criteria rather than address each one
5.	Formulate risk based on established measures of stable and dynamic factors	Static-99 STABLE-2007	Evidence suggests that assessing both static and dynamic factors leads to a better risk assessment
5.	Discuss formulation with client and modify if necessary		Clients may be resistant to aspects of the formulation, especially if they deny their offending. Hence it may be necessary to agree to disagree
6.	Continue to reflect on formulation throughout the process of treatment		The formulation may change based on new information or the client's response to treatment

on the Static-99 website (www.static99.org). The following items/areas are included in the Static-99R: age at release, previous long-term intimate relationships, index violent and general convictions, previous violent and general convictions, prior sexual offences, previous sentencing dates, previous non-contact sexual offences, unrelated victims, stranger victims, and male victims.

Note that some items are weighted more heavily than others; for example, prior sexual offences are subdivided into charges and convictions and a total score of three is possible, while other items, such as those pertaining to victim types, can only receive a maximum score of one. Once the scores for each item are added up, the offender is given a total score which will place him in one of four categories, ranging from low to high. The Static-99 was developed following research that was carried out in Canada and the United Kingdom and it is intended to be scored based purely on information that is available in corrections services files (Helmus, Hanson & Morton-Bourgon, 2011).

In their review of the Static-99, Helmus et al. (2011) concluded that the measure 'showed moderate accuracy in predicting relative risk for sexual, violent, and any recidivism' (p. 73), although there was some variation in accuracy across countries. The main advantage of static measures such as the Static-99 is that they do not require any sort of judgement or opinion by the clinician, hence they allow for a more objective assessment of risk.

In contrast, the assessment of dynamic factors is usually more complicated and generally requires more input from the clinician. Dynamic factors are variables that are changeable; they may change in relation to aspects of a situation and they may respond to treatment, hence they are often treatment targets. In their approach to assessing dynamic risk factors for sexual reoffending, Hanson and Harris (2000a, 2000b) separated dynamic factors into stable and acute risk factors. They developed the STABLE-2000 and ACUTE-2000, where the STABLE was designed to assess factors that are changeable but reasonably stable, whereas the ACUTE was designed to assess factors that are more likely to change suddenly and in response to an individual's current situation.

The five general domains that are covered in the STABLE are significant social influences, intimacy deficits, general self-regulation, sexual self-regulation, and cooperation with supervision. The factors that are included in the ACUTE section of the measure (which are meant to be assessed in relation to current or very recent circumstances) are victim access, hostility, sexual preoccupation, rejection of supervision, emotional collapse, collapse of social supports, and substance abuse. Note that Hanson, Harris, Scott, and Helmus (2007) revised the original version of the STABLE in 2007; in particular, they made changes to the way in which some of the factors were coded. More recent research (Eher, Matthes, Schilling, Haubner-MacLean, & Rettenberger, 2012) compared the predictive accuracy of the 2000 and 2007 versions of the STABLE and found that the latter version was superior in predicting sexual recidivism. Furthermore, Eher et al. concluded that using the STABLE-2007 alongside the Static-99 was especially helpful in predicting sexual reoffending. Therefore, they suggested that a combination of static and dynamic measures may be superior in risk prediction for sexual offending.

As noted in Table 34.1, these are two of the tools that may be useful in formulating the nature and level of risk that a sexual offender may pose to the community. Further to this, as mentioned above, the information that is uncovered during the process of risk assessment may be useful in formulating the case. For example, the STABLE-2007 interview guide requires detailed questioning in relation to an offender's sexual functioning, and this can be very useful in understanding the role of sexual arousal in the individual's offending. Also, it requires a thorough assessment of the individual's functioning in intimate relationships, which is obviously crucial in developing an appreciation of the offender's current relationship status and his relationship history.

Formulation of Positive and Protective Factors

Over the last decade or so, there has been an increasing focus on positive and protective factors in both the mental health and corrections fields (see Wong, 2006, for an example of the former and Maruna, 2001, for an example of the latter). Also, according to the Five Ps method of formulation outlined above (Macneil et al., 2012), protective factors should be included in all case formulations. A focus on such factors is important for a number of reasons. First, it is always useful and constructive to be able to provide the client with positive feedback. This is especially important in a correctional setting, as usually the client's offending is a central focus of the assessment and intervention. Second, examining positive and protective factors can provide important ideas and strategies for treatment; for example, the therapist can assist the client to build on aspects of his or her life that are already working. Lastly, a positive focus may assist the client in feeling more optimistic and hopeful about the future.

Ward and colleagues' (e.g., Ward & Stewart, 2003) Good Lives model (GLM), which has become prominent in the field since its emergence over a decade ago, provides a useful format for considering positive and protective factors. As explained by Ward (with various colleagues over the years), the GLM is based on the idea that most human activity arises from a desire to fulfil fundamental human needs or 'goods'. For example, maintaining a healthy lifestyle would contribute to the basic good of physical well-being, and playing a musical instrument may fulfil the basic good of creativity. According to the GLM, when these sorts of goods are present in a person's life, then it may be said that he or she has a 'good' life. Furthermore, the model proposes that all human beings are driven to achieve basic goods by virtue of their inherent nature. For example, Ward, Collie, and Bourke (2009) stated that 'both sexual and non-sexual offenders are naturally disposed to seek a range of primary human goods that if secured will result in greater self-fulfilment and sense of purpose' (p. 304).

Ward and Stewart (2003) proposed that there are at least 10 primary human goods, namely 'Life (including healthy living and functioning), knowledge, excellence in play and work (including mastery experiences), excellence in agency (i.e., autonomy and self-directedness), inner peace (i.e., freedom from emotional turmoil and stress), friendship (including intimate, romantic and family relationships), community, spirituality (in the broad sense of finding meaning and purpose in life), happiness, and creativity' (p. 356). Note that the GLM also includes reference to secondary goods, which are essentially the various activities and means used to attain primary goods; however, a detailed description this aspect of the model is beyond the scope of this chapter. The GLM assumes that, as with all human beings, offenders strive to attain and maintain primary goods in their lives, but they do so in problematic and antisocial ways. For example, in attempting to attain the good of 'friendship', a sexual offender may engage in sexual activity with a child or rape an adult female.

As described by Ward and colleagues, the use of the GLM in offender treatment involves a comprehensive assessment of the relationship between the nature of the offending and the goods that the offender is seeking via the offending. Following this, a Good Lives plan is developed, which involves the identification of goals that could lead to the fulfilment of these goods in a prosocial manner. Thus, although the offender's needs are acknowledged as valid, their ways of achieving these are challenged and they are encouraged to find ways of meeting their needs that are both prosocial and lawful. The GLM assumes that if basic needs or goods can be met in this way, then the risk for reoffending will be reduced.

As indicated in Table 34.1, the GLM can provide a useful means of framing positive and protective factors that are outlined in the formulation. Traditionally, such factors are outlined at the conclusion of the formulation, which has the advantage of finishing formulation on a positive note. The idea here is that the 10 primary goods can be used as a checklist for the identification of the positive and protective aspects in a person's life. Thus, all aspects of an individual's life can be considered. For instance, in the case of a child sexual offender, although there will be problems in the way in which the individual has attempted to fulfil the good of friendship, the individual may have strengths in the goods of agency (such as stable employment) and creativity (such as artistic painting). These aspects of the person's life that are sound and strong are important, as they provide opportunities for strengths-based treatment.

Formulation-Based Treatment Versus Manual-Based Treatment

In their article on the role of formulation in the treatment of sexual offenders, Ward et al. (2000) argued that individual factors and the formulation of these are often neglected in sex offender treatment. Furthermore, they suggested that there is a lack of clarity around the issue. For example, they stated (p. 252):

> ... it is not clear whether the treatment of sexual offenders should be guided by an understanding of needs, problems, and their hypothesized causal relationships, or whether it should proceed on the basis of a diagnostic strategy.

On elaboration, the authors explained that often there is a focus on classifying a sex offender as a particular subtype according to the nature of the offending and this is then used to determine the type of treatment than an offender receives. However, this can be problematic as it can lead to the more unique aspects of the individual and his or her offending being overlooked (Palermo, 2002). Ward et al. proposed that this approach can be problematic as it can lead to a lack of attention to the formulation of the underlying factors that led to the offending.

As explained by Ward and colleagues, the diagnostic approach is fundamental in the use of manual-based treatments. In a manual-based approach, offenders are assigned to a standardized treatment approach that is usually run in a group setting. This sort of treatment is usually delivered by one or two facilitators in groups of 8–10 persons (Marshall, 2001). As explained by Marshall, sex offender group treatment has been found to be both effective and economical. Furthermore, he suggested that clinicians are less likely to collude with offenders in such contexts. Hence it appears that group treatment has a number of important advantages.

A number of researchers have argued that group-based treatment and individual formulation-based treatment are not necessarily incompatible. For instance, Marx,

Miranda, and Meyerson (1999) proposed that group facilitators should tailor their approach to each individual in order to take account of his or her unique personality traits and learning styles. Thus, even in a group setting, it is still possible to respond to individual needs. However, of course, the extent to which this would be effective would depend on the quality of the assessment and formulation. In other words, individualized approaches within the context of group treatment would require reflection on how well the formulation fits and then possibly rethinking if the formulation is not contributing to treatment efficacy. Arguably, in any setting, a formulation should not be considered to be *the last word* on the client because, as treatment progresses, it is likely that new information will emerge.

It appears that many group-based treatment programmes around the globe have managed to incorporate some individualized components. For example, the Te Piriti Special Treatment Programme is a New Zealand prison-based programme that provides group-based treatment to child sexual offenders. Importantly, it uses a treatment approach that combines traditional cognitive behavioural methods and Māori tikanga (which refers to customs and traditions based on a Māori world view). A comprehensive evaluation of the programme by Nathan, Wilson, and Hillman (2003) reported that the programme was successful in combining these two different world views. What is most relevant to this discussion, however, is that the Te Piriti Special Treatment Programme also offers individual sessions along with the group treatment approach when such sessions are considered to be appropriate. Such sessions allow the facilitators to gain further understanding of the client and to offer more individualized treatment if needed. This example highlights the importance that is placed on responding to unique individual factors in treatment and, accordingly, the importance of formulation.

Conclusion

This chapter has covered a range of topics that are relevant to case formulation in the sexual offending field, summarized in Table 34.1. This table offers a framework for the conceptualization of the various dimensions of case formulation in the sexual offending field. As indicated by the table, there are many different facets of literature that are pertinent to the practice of case formulation in this field. Although the steps are presented in numerical order, there is no reason why they have to remain in that order. The way in which the steps are presented is simply a result of a consideration of the most logical order; however, the order is not particularly important.

Given the breadth of literature either covered here, or at least alluded to, there are numerous possibilities for further research. For example, it would be useful for the utility of various theories to be tested. Although most key theories have been tested via discussion and argument, they have not been tested empirically. In other words, we do not know to what extent various theories lead to useful formulation and effective treatment. Also, in terms of approaches to formulation, it remains unclear whether one particular model is superior to the others. Further, in terms of the GLM, although there is some emerging literature on its efficacy, it is too early to assess whether its inclusion in formulation and treatment leads to long-term changes in offending behaviour.

Although this chapter has provided only a brief discussion of this very important aspect of clinical work with sexual offenders, it is hoped that it will serve as a useful summary of relevant factors and a prompt for further discussion and research.

References

Andrews, D. A., & Bonta, J. (2003). *The psychology of criminal conduct* (3rd ed.). Cincinatti, OH: Anderson.

Arsuffi, L. (2010). Homicide by an older adult offender: Assessment, formulation, and treatment. *British Journal of Forensic Practice, 12,* 45–53. doi:10.5042/bjfp.2010.0425

Boer, D., Thakker, J., & Ward, T. (2009). Sex offender risk-based case formulation. In A. R. Beech, L. A. Craig, & K. D. Browne (Eds.), *Assessment and treatment of sex-offenders: A handbook* (pp. 77–87). Chichester, England: John Wiley & Sons, Ltd. doi:10.1002/9780470714362.ch5

British Psychological Society (2011). *Good practice guidelines on the use of psychological formulation.* Leicester, England: British Psychological Society.

Cortoni, F., Hanson, R. K., & Coache, M.-E. (2010). The recidivism rates of female sexual offenders are low: A meta-analysis. *Sexual Abuse: A Journal of Research and Treatment, 22,* 387–401. doi:10.1177/1079063210372142

Eher, R., Matthes, A., Schilling, F., Haubner-MacLean, T., & Rettenberger, M. (2012). Dynamic risk assessment in sexual offenders using STABLE-2000 and the STABLE-2007. An investigation of predictive and incremental validity. *Sexual Abuse: A Journal of Research and Treatment, 24,* 5–28. doi:10.1177/1079063211403164

Fernando, I., Cohen, M., & Henskens, F. (2012). Pattern-based formulation: A methodology for psychiatric case formulation. *Australasian Psychiatry, 20,* 121–126. doi:10.1177/1039856212437255.

Finkelhor, D. (1984). *Child sexual abuse: New theory and research.* New York, NY: The Free Press.

Hall, G. C., & Hirschman, R. (1991). Toward a theory of sexual aggression: A quadripartite model. *Journal of Consulting and Clinical Psychology, 59,* 662–669. doi:10.1037/0022-006X.59.5.662

Hanson, R. K., & Harris, A. J. R. (2000a). *STABLE-2000.* Unpublished manuscript. Department of the Solicitor General Canada. Available from the authors: andrew.harris@psepc-sppcc.gc.ca

Hanson, R. K., & Harris, A. J. R. (2000b). Where should we intervene? Dynamic predictors of sex offense recidivism. *Criminal Justice and Behavior, 27,* 6–35.

Hanson, R. K., Harris, A. J., Scott, T., & Helmus, L. (2007). *Assessing the risk for sexual offenders on community supervision: The Dynamic Supervision Project* (Corrections Research User Report 2007-05). Ottawa, Canada: Public Safety and Emergency Preparedness Canada. Retrieved from http://www.publicsafety.gc.ca/cnt/rsrcs/pblctns/ssssng-rsk-sxl-ffndrs/index-eng.aspx

Hanson, R. K., & Morton-Bourgon, K. E. (2009). The accuracy of recidivism risk assessments for sexual offenders: A meta-analysis of 118 prediction studies. *Psychological Assessment, 21*(1), 1–21. doi:10.1037/a0014421

Hanson, R. K., & Thornton, D. (2000). Improving risk assessments for sex offenders: A comparison of three actuarial scales. *Law and Human Behavior, 24,* 119–136. doi:10.1023/A:1005482921333

Hart, S., Sturmey, P., Logan, C., & McMurran, M. (2011). Forensic case formulation. *International Journal of Forensic Mental Health*, *10*, 118–126. doi:10.1080/
14999013.2011.57717

Helmus, L., Hanson, R. K., & Morton-Bourgon, K. E. (2011). International comparisons of
the validity of actuarial risk tools for sexual offenders, with a focus on Static-99. In D. P.
Boer, R. Eher, L. A. Craig, & F. Pfäfflin (Eds.), *International perspectives on the assessment
and treatment of sexual offenders: Theory, Practice and Research* (pp. 57–83). Chichester,
England: John Wiley and Sons, Ltd. doi:10.1002/9781119990420.ch4

Kennington, R. (2008). Risk assessment in adult sex offenders. In M. C. Calder (Ed.), *Risk
assessment in safeguarding children* (pp. 232–239). Lyme Regis, England: Russell House.

Knight, R. A., & Sims-Knight, J. E. (2004). Testing an etiological model for male juvenile
sexual offending against females. In R. Geffner, K. C. Franey, T. G. Arnold, & R. Falconer
(Eds.), *Identifying and treating youth who sexually offend: Current approaches, techniques,
and research* (pp. 33–55). New York, NY: Haworth Press.

Macneil, C. A., Hasty, M. K., Conus, P., & Berk, M. (2012). Is diagnosis enough to guide
interventions in mental health? Using case formulation in clinical practice. *BMC Medicine*,
10, 111. doi:10.1186/1741-7015-10-111

Malamuth, N. M., Check, J. V. R., & Briere, J. (1986). Sexual arousal in response to aggression:
Ideological, aggressive, and sexual correlates. *Journal of Personality and Social Psychology*,
50, 330–340. doi:10.1037/0022-3514.50.2.330

Marshall, W. L. (2001). Adult sexual offenders against women. In C. R. Holin (Ed.), *The handbook of offender assessment and treatment* (pp. 333–348). Chichester, England: John Wiley
& Sons, Ltd.

Marshall, W. L., & Barbaree, H. E. (1990). An integrated theory of the etiology of sexual
offending. In W. L. Marshall, D. R. Laws, & H. E. Barbaree (Eds.), *Handbook of sexual assault: Issues, theories, and treatment of the offender* (pp. 257–275). New York, NY:
Plenum.

Maruna, S. (2001). *Making good: How ex-convicts reform and rebuild their lives*. Washington,
DC: American Psychological Association.

Marx, B. P., Miranda, R., & Meyerson, L. A. (1999). Cognitive–behavioral treatment for
rapists: Can we do better? *Clinical Psychology Review*, *19*, 875–894. doi.org/10.1016/
S0272-7358

Nathan, L., Wilson, N. J., & Hillman, D. (2003). *Te Whakakotahitanga: An evaluation of the
Te Piriti Special Treatment Programme for child sex offenders in New Zealand*. Wellington,
New Zealand: Department of Corrections Psychological Service.

Pain, C. M., Chadwick, P., & Abba, N. (2008). Clients' experience of case formulation in cognitive behavior therapy for psychosis. *British Journal of Clinical Psychology*, *47*, 127–138.
doi:10.1348/014466507X235962

Palermo, G. (2002). A dynamic formulation of sex offender behavior and its therapeutic relevance. *Journal of Forensic Psychology Practice*, *2*, 25–51. doi: 10.1300/J158v02n02_02

Persons, J. B., Beckner, V. L., & Tompkins, M. A. (2013). Testing case formulation hypotheses
in psychotherapy: Two case examples. *Cognitive and Behavioral Practice*, *20*, 399–409.
doi:10.1016/j.cbpra.2013.03.004

Persons, J. B., Roberts, N. A., Zalecki, C. A., & Brechwald, W. A. G. (2006).
Naturalistic outcome of case formulation-driven cognitive–behavior therapy for
anxious depressed outpatients. *Behavior Research and Therapy*, *44*, 1041–1051.
doi:10.1016/j.brat.2005.08.005

Restifo, S. (2010). An empirical categorization of psychosocial factors for clinical case formulation and treatment planning. *Australasian Psychiatry*, *18*, 210–213. doi:10.3109/
10398561003681335

Studer, L. H., Aylwin, A. S., Sribney, C., & Reddon, J. R. (2011). Uses, misuses, and abuses of risk assessment with sexual offenders. In D. P. Boer, R. Eher, L. A. Craig, M. H. Miner, & F. Pfäfflin (Eds.), *International perspectives on the assessment and treatment of sexual offenders: Theory, practice, and research* (pp. 193–212). Chichester, England: John Wiley and Sons, Ltd. doi:10.1002/9781119990420.ch9

Thagard, P. (1978). The best explanation: Criteria for theory choice. *The Journal of Philosophy*, *75*, 76–92.

Thakker, J. (2012). An integrated theory of sexual recidivism. *Sexual Abuse in Australia and New Zealand*, *4*, 41–52.

Vertue, F. M., & Haig, B. D. (2008). An abductive perspective on clinical reasoning and case formulation. *Journal of Clinical Psychology*, *64*, 1046–1068. doi:10.1002/jclp.20504

Ward, T., Collie, R. M., & Bourke, P. (2009). Models of offender rehabilitation: The Good Lives Model and the Risk–Need–Responsivity Model. In A. R. Beech, L. A. Craig, & K. D. Browne (Eds.), *Assessment and treatment of sex offenders: A handbook* (pp. 293–310). Chichester, England: John Wiley & Sons, Ltd.

Ward, T., Nathan, P., Drake, C. R., Lee, J. K. P., & Pathé, M. (2000). The role of formulation-based treatment for sexual offenders. *Behavior Change*, *17*, 251–264. doi:10.1375/bech.17.4.251

Ward, T., & Stewart, C. A. (2003). The treatment of sexual offenders: Risk management and good lives. *Professional Psychology: Research and Practice*, *34*, 353–360. doi:10.1037/0735-7028.34.4.353

Watson, J. C (2010). Case formulation in emotion focused therapy (EFT). *Journal of Psychotherapy Integration*, *20*, 89–100. doi:10.1037/a0018890

Wong, Y. J. (2006). Strength-centred therapy: A social constructionist, virtues-based psychotherapy. *Psychotherapy: Theory, Research, Practice, Training*, *2*, 133–146. doi:10.1037/0033-3204.43.2.133

35

Neurobiological Implications in Assessing Treatment Need in Sexual Offenders

Andreas Mokros

University Hospital of Psychiatry Zurich, Switzerland; University of Regensburg, Germany

Benedikt Habermeyer

University Hospital of Psychiatry Zurich, Switzerland

Elmar Habermeyer

University Hospital of Psychiatry Zurich, Switzerland

Introduction

Based on general neurophysiological findings on the sexual arousal response, this chapter reviews studies on brain functioning and structure associated with deviant sexual interest, arousal, and behaviour. More specifically, electrophysiological and neuroimaging studies are considered, in addition to findings from neuropsychology and neuroendocrinology.

Sexual Arousal and the Brain

At the neural level, sexual arousal is associated with changes of blood flow in cortical and limbic structures. More specifically, the cortical areas involved comprise the occipital (i.e., visual) and the orbitofrontal area and also the anterior cingulate gyrus, whereas the pertinent limbic structures include the amygdala, the hippocampus, parts of the thalamus, and the hypothalamus (Stoléru, Fonteille, Cornélis, Joyal, & Moulier, 2012; Sylva et al., 2013). These limbic structures project to the nucleus accumbens

The Wiley Handbook on the Theories, Assessment, and Treatment of Sexual Offending.
Edited by Douglas P. Boer. Volume II: Assessment, edited by Leam A. Craig and Martin Rettenberger.
© 2017 John Wiley & Sons, Ltd. Published 2017 by John Wiley & Sons, Ltd.

(Sylva et al., 2013) as part of the mesolimbic dopaminergic reward system that, if activated, induces a state of reward seeking (Alcaro, Huber, & Panksepp, 2007).

Both the anatomy of brain structures and the temporal sequence of activation as highlighted in functional neuroimaging studies (Arnow et al., 2002; Ferretti et al., 2005; Karama et al., 2002; Stoléru et al., 1999) are concomitant with stepwise information-processing models of the sexual arousal response (Janssen, Everaerd, Spiering, & Janssen, 2000; Redouté et al., 2000; Singer, 1984; Stoléru et al., 1999). Basically, these information-processing models of the sexual arousal response differentiate between (1) a cognitive appraisal stage with the preattentive recognition of pertinent stimuli as sexual, (2) an emotional evaluation stage in which the content of sexual stimuli triggers an affective response, and (3) a physiological/locomotor stage in which both vegetative reactions (such as the release of hormones) and movement are affected (Janssen et al., 2000; Singer, 1984; Stoléru et al., 1999).

According to Kühn and Gallinat (2011), who reviewed pertinent studies on cue-induced sexual arousal in men, the parietal cortex, the anterior cingulate cortex, the thalamus, and the insula are primarily involved at the early cognitive appraisal stage of the sexual arousal response, whereas the amygdala and the insula are associated with the second stage of attaching emotional significance to stimuli. Next, the precentral gyrus and the parietal cortex would be linked to motivational processes. Finally, according to Kühn and Gallinat, the hypothalamus, thalamus, and insula are involved in the physiological response. A recent meta-analysis by Poeppl, Langguth, Laird, and Eickhoff (2014) further differentiated the brain circuits involved in sexual interest on the one hand and sexual arousal on the other. Apparently, sexual arousal can be differentiated from other emotional valences objectively. In one neuroimaging study, Walter et al. (2008) found that the anterior cingulate cortex in addition to the hypothalamus and the nucleus accumbens were specifically linked to sexual arousal, whereas the dorsomedial prefrontal cortex, the thalamus, and the amygdala were associated with emotional processing more generally. A deep-brain stimulation/probe electrode in a single patient indicated increased delta waves in the amygdala during orgasm (Heath, 1972). Recordings of event-related brain potentials (ERPs) seem to indicate a selective brain response towards sexual stimuli compared with non-erotic content (Anokhin et al., 2006; Feng, Wang, Wang, Gu, & Luo, 2012).

The brain responses toward sexual stimuli differ between men and women (Canli & Gabrieli, 2004; Sylva et al., 2013) and between individuals with either homo- or heterosexual orientation (Hu et al., 2008; Kagerer et al., 2011; Paul et al., 2008; Savic & Lindström, 2008; Swaab, 2008). In men, hypothalamus activation seems to modulate the elicitation of sexual arousal only if stimuli of the corresponding sexual orientation are presented (such as videoclips showing male-to-female sexual intercourse for heterosexual men; Paul et al., 2008).

Concerning the differences in brain activation patterns associated with sexual arousal in men and women, Canli and Gabrieli (2004) noted a stronger response of both the hypothalamus and the amygdala – and thus likely a more intense reaction sexually and emotionally, respectively (according to the results of Walter et al., 2008) – in men than in women. Similarly, Karama et al. (2002) found both stronger self-reported sexual arousal and stronger activation of the hypothalamus in men than in women when watching erotic videoclips. Moreover, an unobtrusive study of sex-related queries and the use of erotic paysites on the Internet – albeit not peer reviewed – seems to corroborate the point that visual sexual stimuli are more interesting and possibly more gratifying for men than for women (Ogas & Gaddam, 2012).

Furthermore, the observation of Canli and Gabrieli (2004) is in accordance with the result that women tend to be less discriminating for visual sexual stimuli (Chivers, Rieger, Latty, & Bailey, 2004). The lack of stimulus specificity in the female sexual arousal response even extends to non-human primates (e.g., videoclips showing sexual activity of bonobos, or pygmy chimpanzees): women showed significantly greater genital arousal towards the sexual clips depicting great apes than to neutral stimuli, yet their genital arousal toward clips showing human couples in sexual interactions (male–female, female–female, or male–male) was highest (Chivers & Bailey, 2005). Men, in contrast, showed a graded pattern of genital sexual arousal in the same study (i.e., no arousal towards non-human stimuli, intermediate arousal towards male–male sex scenes, and strongest arousal towards videoclips showing male–female and female–female sexual activity). A recent study showed that women likely show specific sexual arousal patterns based on preferences for sexual activity rather than gender, however (Chivers, Roy, Grimbos, Cantor, & Seto, 2014).

Sexual Arousal and the Risk of Sexual Offending

Barbaree and Marshall (1991) discussed six theoretical models that could account for male sexual arousal as a risk factor for sexual coercion. Barbaree and Marshall divided these models into stimulus control and response control models. The latter (i.e., response control models) would either entail an inability to suppress sexual arousal in the presence of coercion or violence; alternatively, the exertion of force and sexual arousal could be conceptualized as mutually non-exclusive responses in men at risk of sexual offending. That is, these men would lack an inhibitory mechanism present in others. The former (i.e., stimulus control models) either would involve an excitatory effect of deviant sexual cues (such as images of children or displays of sexual violence) caused by an innate preference for such stimuli, or, alternatively, non-sexual arousal could become augmented by sexual cues, thereby attenuating and ultimately overriding any inhibition caused by other features (such as the physique of a child or the physical resistance of a woman).

In fact, an experimental study by Ariely and Loewenstein (2006) showed that participants would become less discriminating in their decision-making if they were sexually aroused. Furthermore, sexual offenders may be at a particular risk of compensating aversive emotional states by indulging in sexual fantasy (Lussier, Proulx, & McKibben, 2001; Proulx, McKibben, & Lusignan 1996), thereby possibly enforcing preference for deviant sexual stimuli.

The theory that a preference for deviant sexual stimuli, fuelled by corresponding sexual fantasies, would be at the core of sexual offending (McGuire, Carlisle, & Young, 1965) has been very influential and received support from the finding that sexual deviance is the single most important predictor of sexual recidivism in convicted sexual offenders (Hanson & Morton-Bourgon, 2005), even though the magnitude of the effect of sexual deviance on sexual recidivism was small, with a Cohen's d coefficient of 0.30 in the meta-analysis by Hanson and Morton-Bourgon. On the other hand, as Leitenberg and Henning (1995) wrote in a review on sexual fantasy, 'Even if sexual fantasies have an impact on sex offenders' behavior, however, no studies have assessed the relative importance of fantasy in comparison with all other contributing factors in rapists, child molesters, or exhibitionists. Moreover, and most important, there is no evidence that sexual fantasies, by themselves, are either a sufficient or a necessary condition for committing a sexual offense. For example, as reviewed earlier in this article, many men who have never committed a sexual assault have fantasies of forcing sex on someone' (p. 488). Phallometric assessments indicate a stronger sexual arousal, as measured by penile tumescence, in a sizable proportion of child molesters, whereas the results are less clear for exhibitionists, rapists, or putative sexual sadists (Marshall, 2014; see also Chapters 38 and 39).

Therefore, different modes of influence of sexual arousal may be at play in different sexual offenders (Barbaree & Marshall, 1991), along with other situational factors (e.g., Murray, 2001). If focusing on risk factors present in the person of the perpetrator, the meta-analysis by Hanson and Morton-Bourgon (2005) on sexual recidivism offers valuable guidance. Among the dynamic risk factors linked with sexual recidivism, Hanson and Morton-Bourgon reported a sexual preoccupation, general self-regulation problems, deviant sexual interest, psychopathy, antisocial personality disorder, and hostility (in descending order of magnitude) as relevant. In the following, we review the findings of neurobiological studies pertaining to two of these risk factors, namely sexual preoccupation and deviant sexual interest. Second, the corresponding types of assessment recommended for single-case diagnostics (medical, neurophysiological, and neuropsychological) are highlighted. The findings are ordered according to the type of research strategy used: (1) event-related brain potentials, (2) neurological case studies, (3) neuroimaging, (4) psychometric assessment, and (5) neuroendocrinology. Table 35.1 provides a summary of neurological case studies and of structural and functional brain-imaging findings on paraphilias (mostly paedophilia). The majority of studies listed in Table 35.1 included samples of sexual offenders most of whom were sexual abusers of children.

Event-Related Brain Potentials

Event-related brain potentials (ERPs) register changes in the electroencephalogram (EEG) of the brain in response to stimuli administered by the experimenter. The advantage of ERPs over modern techniques of neuroimaging is the greater temporal resolution that they offer. The downside is that ERPs are limited to cortical areas of the brain and have a relative lack of spatial resolution. Nevertheless, ERP studies possibly allow finding out whether sexual offenders respond differently to sexual cues within a short time of the stimulus onset. The notion that EEG activity could be indicative of sexual preference goes back to Costell, Lunde, Kopell, and Wittner (1972).

Electrophysiological research with regard to sexual deviance is scarce. To the best of our knowledge, Emrich (1978, 1979) was the first to apply ERP recording to a mixed

Table 35.1 Summary of brain imaging studies with paraphilic individuals (mostly paedophiles)

Studies	Localization of brain lesions	Task	Imaging technique	Main finding	Study group (n)/ control group (n)	First author	Year
Lesion and clinical studies	rFL		PE	Tumour leading to paedophilic behaviour	Case report	Lesniak	1972
				Tumour, anoxic encephalopathy leading to paedophilic behaviour	Case series (4)	Regestein	1978
	FL, DE, LS		CT, EEG, NP	Tumour, ischaemia, aneurysma, post-encephalitic, L-Dopa in Parkinson disease, all leading to hypersexuality or changes of sexual preference	Case series (6 males, 2 females)	Miller	1986
	rTL		PET	Degeneration leading to paedophilic behaviour	Case series (2)	Mendez	2000
	rFL		MRI	Tumour leading to paedophilic behaviour	Case report	Burns	2003
	rTL		MRI, EEG	Lobectomy leading to paedophilic behaviour	Case report	Devinsky	2010
	Fl, TL, BG		MRI, PET	Degeneration leading to paedophilic behaviour	Case series (8)	Mendez	2011
	FL		CT, MRI, SPECT	Degeneration leading to paedophilic behaviour	Case report	Rainero	2011

(continued overleaf)

Table 35.1 (*Continued*)

Studies	Localization of brain lesions	Task	Imaging technique	Main finding	Study group (n)/control group (n)	First author	Year
Structural imaging studies	FL, TL		CT, CBF, NP	50% decreased density measures, reduced blood flow and impaired performance on NP	Sexual offenders (6)/normal controls	Graber	1982
	rTL		CT, NP	Right-sided temporal horn dilatation more often in sadists than in the non-sadistic assaulters and controls, on neuropsychological tests non-sadists showed more global impairment than the other two groups	Sexual offenders (51; 22 sadists)/normal controls (36)	Hucker	1988
	lTL, PL		CT, NP	Left temporoparietal pathology was noted more often for paedophiles	Paedophilias (39)/non-violent non-sexual offenders (14)	Hucker	1986
	Not specified		CT, CBF	Less dense skulls, lower CBF in child molesters	Sexual offenders against children (16)/normal controls	Hendricks	1988
	TL		CT, NP	1/4 incest perpetrators show TL lobe abnormality, lower IQ, 1/8 pathological NP	Incest offenders (91)/non-violent non-sexual offenders (36)	Langevin	1988
	None		CT; NP	No difference	Exhibitionist (15)/non-violent non-sexual offenders (36)	Langevin	1989a

None	CT, NP	No difference	Child abusers (160), incest perpetrators (123), sexual offenders against adult females (108)/non-violent non-sexual offenders (36)	Langevin	1989b
ITL, IFL	CT	66.7% paedophiles, 53.1% sex offenders had asymmetric brains, on average smaller left hemisphere in paedophilia, smaller left TL and FL in sex offenders	Paedophiles (18), incest offenders (12), sex offenders against adult females (34)/non-violent non-sexual offenders (12)	Wright	1990
	MRI	44% with structural brain abnormality	Sexual offenders (38)	Eher	2000
TL, FL, INS, PU, LS	MRI	Reduced GM in bilateral orbitofrontal cortex, the bilateral insula, the bilateral ventral striatum (putamen), and some limbic gyri (cingulate and parahippocampal)	Homo- (9) and heterosexual (9) paedophiles/homo- (12) and heterosexual (12) controls	Schiffer	2007
rAG, hyothalami, substatia innominata, BNST	MRI	Reduced GM in right amygdala, bilateral hyothalamus, septal regions, substantia innominata and bed nucleus of striae terminalis	Paedophiles (15)/controls (15)	Schiltz	2007
White matter tracts	MRI	Reduced WM in right fronto-occipital fasciculus and arcuate fasciculus	Paedophiles (44)/teleophilic sexual offenders (21)/controls (53)	Cantor	2008

(continued overleaf)

Table 35.1 (*Continued*)

Studies	Localization of brain lesions	Task	Imaging technique	Main finding	Study group (*n*)/control group (*n*)	First author	Year
	rAG		MRI	Reduced GM in right amygdala; correlations of GM volume in left insula, parietal operculum, and dorsolateral PFC with record-based index of paedophilic sexual interest; correlation of age of youngest victim with GM in OFC and with GM in left and right angular gyrus	Paedophiles (9)/non-sexual offender controls (11)	Poeppl	2013
Functional imaging studies	TL	auditory	PET	Stronger bilateral activation for target and control stimulus than in controls which showed mostly a right TL activation	Sadist (1)/controls (2)	Garnett	1988
	rTL, rFL	auditory	PET	Lower glucose metabolism in rTL and rFL in the neutral condition	Heterosexual non-exclusive paedophiles (7)/controls (7)	Cohen	2002
	rOFC, BS, BG, CG, PFC	visual	MRI	Pictures of boys led to a significant activation of the attention network and the right orbitofrontal cortex in the paedophilic offender	Homosexual paedophile (1)/heterosexual controls (2)	Dressing	2001

Region	Stimulus	Method	Findings	Groups	Author	Year
Hypothalamus, lat PFC	visual	MRI	Reduced activation in hypothalamus and lateral PFC	Paedophiles (13)/controls (14)	Walter	2007
Thalamus, GP, ST	visual	MRI	Sexual stimuli activated the thalamus, globus pallidus and striatum in paedophiles, but not in control subjects	Homosexual paedophiles (11)/homosexual controls (12)	Schiffer	2008a
FL	visual	MRI	Similar activation in both groups, but in paedophilia activation in PFC and not in OFC as in controls	Heterosexual paedophiles (8)/controls (12)	Schiffer	2008b
AG	visual	MRI	Controls showed less amygdala activation to pictures of children compared with adults, the activation profile was reversed in subjects with paedophilia	Homosexual paedophiles (10)/heterosexual controls (10)	Sartorius	2008
CG, INS	visual	MRI	Differential effects found in the cingulate gyrus and insular region	Paedophiles (9)/non-sexual offender controls (11)	Poeppl	2011
AG, INS	visual	MRI	Sadists showed greater amygdala activation when viewing pain pictures and showed a positive correlation between pain severity ratings and activity in the anterior insula	Sadistic sexual offenders (8)/non-sadistic sexual offenders (7)	Harenski	2012

(continued overleaf)

Table 35.1 *(Continued)*

Studies	Localization of brain lesions	Task	Imaging technique	Main finding	Study group (n)/ control group (n)	First author	Year
	Pattern classification	visual	MRI	Response patterns allow the identification of paedophiles with 95% accuracy (100% specificity, 88% sensitivity)	Hetero- (11) and homosexual (13) admitting paedophiles/ hetero- (18) and homosexual (14) controls	Ponseti	2012
	rOFC	visual	MRI	In paedophilic subjects, erotic pictures activate a brain region attributed to reward and punishment, and to the suppression of erotic response and deception	Heterosexual paedophiles (8)/ controls (8)	Habermeyer	2013a

Abbreviations: r, right; l, left; FL, frontal lobe; DE, diencephalon; LS, limbic structures; TL, temporal lobe; BG, basal ganglia; INS, insula; PU, putamen; AG, amygdala; PFC, prefrontal cortex; BNST, bed nucleus of striae terminalis; OFC, orbitofrontal cortex; BS, brain stem; GP, globus pallidus; ST, striatum; CG, cingulate gyrus; PE, pneumoencephalography; MRI, magnetic resonance imaging; EEG, electroencephalography; CT, computed tomography; PET, positron emission tomography; SPECT, single photon emission computed tomography; CBF, cerebral blood flow; NP, neuropsychological tests; GM, grey matter; WM, white matter.

sample of 20 adult male sexual offenders. Stimuli were black-and-white images of landscapes (neutral condition) or depicting offence-related content (emotional condition). The stimuli were presented in random order for 2.5 s at a very dim brightness, precluding the participants from recognizing the stimuli consciously. At a frontal electrode on the subjects' non-dominant hemisphere, about half of the participants showed larger summed potentials for emotional than for neutral stimuli. Even though the subliminal processing of sexual stimuli may appear surprising, other experimental paradigms such as priming (Kamphuis, De Ruiter, Janssen, & Spiering, 2005) or binocular rivalry (Jiang, Costello, Fang, Huang, & He, 2006) also attest to its feasibility.

A study by Howard, Longmore, Mason, and Martin (1994) (cf. Howard, 2002) addressed the reactions of presumably paedophilic men to pictures of children in a match/mismatch paradigm using ERP recording. Howard et al. (1994) observed stronger expectancy waves (so-called *contingent negative variation*, CNV) for only four out of eight paedophilic child molesters with regard to child stimuli. Non-paedophilic participants, in contrast, on average showed a more pronounced CNV towards images of nude adult females compared with images depicting nude girls. Waismann, Fenwick, Wilson, Hewett, and Lumsden (2003) noted a heightened P600 response (P600 denotes a positive peak in an ERP recording that has a latency of approximately 600 ms after the onset of the stimulus) for paraphilic stimuli among men sampled from the community with self-reported interest in such stimuli. More generally, recent experimental work with student participants, who presumably did not suffer from any sexual preference disorder, corroborated the significance of late positive potentials (comparable to the P600 described by Waismann et al., 2003), but also an early positivity component (P2) appearing within 150–250 ms after stimulus onset (van Hooff, Crawford, & van Vugt, 2011). Interestingly, Emrich (1979) had already noted late-onset positive signals in sexual offenders; Emrich attributed these to the low brightness of the stimulus presentation, however. Moreover, ERP recording was truncated at 500 ms in Emrich's study.

Furthermore, Schupp, Junghöfer, Weike, and Hamm (2003) showed that an early ERP component – a negative potential associated with selective attention, the early posterior negativity – was more pronounced for sexual stimuli than for other pleasant emotional stimuli in 15 student participants, eight of whom were female (see also Anokhin et al., 2006, and Feng et al., 2012, for ERP studies on the putative selectivity of a brain response in processing erotic stimuli). Roye, Höfel, and Jacobsen (2008) reported on differences in the time window and polarity of potentials associated with the evaluation of male or female faces as beautiful. Roye et al. did not test this effect separately for the male and female participants of their experiment, however. Hence no gender-specific results are available from the study by Roye et al.

As a tentative conclusion of the current literature on the electrophysiology of the sexual arousal response, studies with community (mostly student) volunteers indicate that sexual stimuli are processed differently from other (non-sexual) emotional stimuli (Roye et al., 2008; Schupp et al., 2003; van Hooff et al., 2011), entailing a pronounced early negativity component indicative of selective attention (Schupp et al., 2003). Unfortunately, some of these studies (Feng et al., 2012; Roye et al., 2008; Schupp et al., 2003) did not report the results separately for the two genders of participants, even though the ERP response of females to sexual stimuli was shown to vary with the menstrual cycle (Krug, Plihal, Fehm, & Born, 2000). Van Hooff et al. (2011) did not observe early-onset negativity but pronounced early and late positivity to pleasant rather than unpleasant faces of the opposite sex, with late positivity becoming apparent in male participants in particular. In contrast to the study by Schupp and colleagues (2003), van Hooff et al. did not use sexually explicit stimuli. A study with paraphilic men (Waismann et al., 2003) highlighted a positive potential setting in about 600 ms after stimulus onset (i.e., P600) as the most pronounced difference between paraphilic men and controls. The controls clearly differed in their P600 responses to conventional sexual and paraphilic stimuli, whereas paraphilic participants displayed a relatively indifferent pattern with similar activations for both types of stimuli (conventional sexual and paraphilic). The most pronounced group difference for paraphilic stimuli was found at an electrode above the left (dominant) hemisphere (larger amplitude for paraphilics than for controls), whereas the clearest differences for conventional sexual stimuli was observed at an electrode placed above the parietal region of the right hemisphere (larger amplitude for controls than for paraphilic individuals). Similarly to the results of Waismann et al. (2003), Howard et al. (1994) also observed a non-specific ERP pattern in 34 child molesters towards images of persons of either gender across three age groups (children, pubescents, and adults). Out of the subgroup of clearly paedophilic participants in the study by Howard et al. ($n = 8$), only four showed a distinctive pattern (i.e., larger contingent negative variation towards child than towards adult stimuli). If the ERP wave in question is really indicative of sexual desire, as argued by Howard (2002), the lack of a differential pattern across stimulus categories in paraphilic men compared with healthy controls (as observed by both Howard et al., 1994, and Waismann et al., 2003) may be reflective of the subdued pattern noted in similar subjects in viewing time and related studies of sexual interest (Banse, Schmidt, & Clarbour, 2010; Mokros, Dombert, Osterheider, Zappalà, & Santtila, 2010).

Flor-Henry, Lang, Koles, and Frenzel (1991) examined the EEGs of 52 paedophilic and 46 control participants. They noted increased levels of slow waves (alpha, delta, and theta activity) among the paedophilic subjects compared with the controls as registered at frontal electrodes. The most pronounced group differences were observed for delta (< 4 Hz) and theta activity (4–7 Hz) at small to moderate effect sizes under cognitive engagement. Similarly, Cassens, Ford, Lothstein, and Gallenstein (1988) observed peculiarities in the EEGs of five paedophilic men in the left frontotemporal area. Contrary to the findings of Flor-Henry et al. (1991), Cassens et al. (1988) observed a decrease in the amplitude of delta waves. Further EEG studies with sexual offenders diagnosed with paraphilia were conducted with exhibitionists (Flor-Henry, 1987; Flor-Henry, Lang, Koles, & Frenzel, 1988) and with a mixed sample of sexual offenders diagnosed with paraphilias (Kirenskaya-Berus & Tkachenko, 2003).

In sum, a distinct EEG or ERP peculiarity of, say, paedophilic sexual offenders has not yet been demonstrated. Therefore, electrophysiological assessment currently plays a minor role in assessing sexual offenders. The exception is sexual offenders suffering from seizures or from other organic defects affecting the brain (such as brain tumours or encephalitis). In these cases, a detailed neurological assessment including EEG recording is routinely conducted to assess the type and scope of the disorder and also to monitor treatment success. Future research in the area should focus on early ERP components that likely tap into attentional processes of stimulus appraisal (Janssen et al., 2000), such as early posterior negativity (Schupp et al., 2003) or a positive shift at about 250 ms after stimulus onset (i.e., P2) (Anokhin et al., 2006; Feng et al., 2012; van Hooff et al., 2011).

Brain Damage

There are several case studies of late-onset paraphilia and/or sexual offending due to neoplastic disease (Burns & Swerdlow, 2003; Lesniak, Szymusik, & Chrzanowski, 1972; Miller, Cummings, McIntyre, Ebers, & Grode, 1986; Regestein & Reich, 1978), dementia and other neurological disorders (Devinsky, Sacks, & Devinsky, 2010; Mendez, Chow, Ringman, Twitchell, & Hinkin, 2000; Mendez & Shapira, 2011; Rainero et al., 2011). In sexual offences against children, the development of corresponding sexual fantasies and urges in old-age perpetrators is not a rare phenomenon and has been labelled 'old-age paedophilia' (Schorsch, 1971). Most likely, the occurrence of such paedophilic fantasies, urges, and behaviours in later life can be attributed to the subtle onset of cerebral involution. Consequently, neurological testing may not yield any immediate results (Prahlada Rao, Chand, & Murthy, 2007).

Despite earlier assumptions to the contrary, a population-based study in Sweden (Fazel, Lichtenstein, Grann, & Långström, 2011) did not find a significant link between epilepsy and violent offending once the family background was controlled for (i.e., the rate of violent offences on behalf of unaffected siblings). Epilepsy in general seems to be associated with sexual hypo-rather than hyperarousal for both partial (Shukla, Srivastava, & Katiyar, 1979) and generalized seizures (Hamed, Mohamed, El-Taher, Hamed, & Omar, 2006). If epilepsy is associated with deviant sexual interests, then it will more frequently be complex partial epilepsy and thus concern the temporal lobes (Ellison, 1982; Kolářský, Freund, Machek, & Polák, 1967). Fazel et al. (2011) did find a significantly increased association with violent offending, however, among individuals with *traumatic* brain injury.

In a community-based cohort of patients with traumatic brain injury ($n = 507$), Simpson, Sabaz, and Daher (2013) noted a comparatively high reporting rate of inappropriate sexual behaviours. The behaviours in question mostly concerned sexual talk, but also touching and – less frequently – exhibitionistic acts or public masturbation. Sexual disinhibition likely affects a minority of patients with traumatic brain injury only: compared with 142 controls, patients with traumatic brain injury ($n = 865$) on average reported a reduction in sex drive and sexual activity (Downing, Stolwyk, & Ponsford, 2013).

Other studies looked at sexual or violent offenders as a frame of reference, testing whether there was a larger than expected rate of individuals with a history of traumatic brain injury. In smaller clinical samples, DelBello et al. (1999) and Rosenbaum and Hoge (1989) noted a higher prevalence of traumatic head injury among sexual offenders with co-morbid bipolar disorder or among males with a history of spousal assault, respectively. More cogently, Blanchard et al. (2002) found more than twice the rate of severe head injuries in childhood – assessed retrospectively – in paedophilic offenders

(42 out of 412 individuals, or 10.2%) compared with non-paedophilic offenders (35 out of 791 individuals, or 4.4%).

In sum, there is some evidence that particular forms of brain lesion due to injury or disease may heighten the risk of sexual offending. Furthermore, two studies indicated that indirect indicators of cerebral dysfunction or damage (such as learning disorder, low IQ, being placed in special education, or a history of head injuries involving unconsciousness) are weakly, yet significantly, associated with violent and sexual offence recidivism (Harris, Rice, & Lalumière, 2001; Langevin & Curnoe, 2011). The incremental contribution of these signs of cerebral dysfunction or damage was weak, however, compared with the proportion of variance explained by psychopathy and antisociality.

There is no clear-cut association indicating that certain brain lesions would necessarily lead to paraphilia and/or sexual offending, nor is sexual offending in itself a risk marker for cerebral disease or trauma. If a person admitted for assessment reports on sustained head injury (especially if this event led to unconsciousness) or encephalitis or if sexual symptoms (such as hypersexuality) or sexual offence behaviour represent a marked change in comparison with that person's biography, a detailed neurological assessment is warranted. The assessment should include brain-imaging techniques and also detailed neuropsychological testing (see below). It should be clear that the more sexual offending is determined by a medical condition acquired later in life, the more difficult it will be to influence the corresponding fantasies, urges, and propensities by psychological treatment. Consequently, curative medical treatment takes the lead in such cases.

The localization of brain lesions in the case studies of late-onset paraphilia mentioned above suggests a preponderance of frontal and temporal sites. This outcome accords with the notion of a dual-deficit model comprising both frontal and temporal dysfunction as risk factors for sexual offending: The latter purportedly relate to abnormality in sexual arousability and the appraisal of cues as sexually interesting, the former is considered as increasing sexual desire while reducing the capacity for behavioural inhibition (Cohen et al., 2002).

Neuroimaging

Structural Brain Imaging

Earlier studies on the integrity of the architecture of the brain in sexual offenders mostly utilized computed tomography (CT), whereas more recent studies relied on variants of magnetic resonance imaging (MRI), such as voxel-based morphometry. CT scans in a mixed sample of sexual offenders indicated on average a decreased density of brain matter compared with a control group (Graber, Hartmann, Coffman, Huey, & Golden, 1982). Hucker et al. (1986, 1988), Hendricks et al. (1988), and Langevin et al. (1988, 1989a, 1989b) used CT scanning to compare sadistic, paedophilic, exhibitionistic, or incest offenders with controls (see also Langevin, 1990). Overall, the results were relatively unspecific in terms of the exact brain regions involved, even though the temporal lobe seemed to be primarily affected. According to the CT studies, brain abnormality was more common in sadistic (Hucker et al., 1988) and paedophilic offenders (Hendricks et al., 1988; Hucker et al., 1986) than in controls, even though the latter result was not unequivocal (Langevin et al., 1989b; Wright, Nobrega, Langevin, & Wortzman, 1990). There were no significant group differences, however, for either exhibitionists (Langevin et al., 1989a) or incest offenders (Langevin et al., 1988) compared with controls.

To our knowledge, the first study that utilized MRI was conducted by Eher, Aigner, Fruehwald, Frottier, and Gruenhut (2000), who observed structural brain abnormality in nearly half (44.7%, $n = 17$) of 38 sexual offenders in a mixed sample of child molesters ($n = 15$) and rapists ($n = 23$). The study did not include a control group of non-sexual offenders or community volunteers. Among those with some form of brain lesion, violent offences were more prevalent (13 out of 17 individuals) than among those without any lesion (10 out of 21 individuals) – an outcome approaching statistical significance ($p = 0.10$, two-sided, according to a Fisher exact test).

The most recent relevant studies utilizing MRI all concerned paedophilic offenders (Cantor et al., 2008; Poeppl et al., 2013; Schiffer et al., 2007; Schiltz et al., 2007; see also Cantor & Blanchard, 2012). In all four studies, various forms of structural abnormality were observed. It is impossible, however, to provide a common denominator as the studies implicated different areas of the brain. More specifically, the studies reported decreases in grey matter in the orbitofrontal region and the striatum (Schiffer et al., 2007), in dorsolateral areas (Poeppl et al., 2013) or volume reductions of the right amygdala (Poeppl et al., 2013; Schiltz et al., 2007), whereas Cantor and colleagues (Cantor et al., 2008; cf., Cantor & Blanchard, 2012) did not find any reductions at all in grey matter but a decrease in white matter.

The differences between structural MRI studies of paedophiles are likely due to a lack of representativeness of paedophilic samples, differences in sexual orientation between the paedophiles surveyed, varying control groups such as non-sexual offenders versus healthy controls (Cantor et al., 2008), or a combination of these factors. In any case, it would be premature to postulate any particular type of brain lesion as indicative of paedophilia. Lesions in prefrontal areas of the brain, in particular, may be associated with lack of impulse control in violent offenders rather than with paedophilia (Blanchard, Cantor, & Robichaud, 2006; cf., Habermeyer et al., 2013b). Consequently, structural MRI cannot be recommended as a routine method of assessment in child molesters or other sexual offenders. Structural MRI scans should be obtained, however, if there is evidence for sustained concussion or head trauma.

Functional Brain Imaging

Functional brain-imaging methods give an indication of the dynamics of the metabolism of the brain. Positron emission tomography (PET) scanning necessitates the use of weakly radioactive isotopes. The dispersion of the radioactive tracing substance under cognitive engagement is registered. In a mixed sample of six sexual offenders, Graber et al. (1982) observed abnormality in blood flow among three individuals. The finding of a somewhat lower average cerebral blood flow was replicated in a sample of 16 child molesters by Hendricks et al. (1988). Cohen et al. (2002) used PET scanning with seven paedophilic individuals. Compared with seven control participants and in a neutral experimental trial only, the glucose metabolism on average was lower among the paedophilic than among the control subjects in two areas of the brain, the right inferior temporal cortex and the superior ventral frontal gyrus. Garnett, Nahmias, Wortzman, Langevin, and Dickey (1988) used PET scanning to compare the brain activation of a sadist with activation of two controls. Relative to the controls, stronger bilateral activation during exposure with both target and neutral stimuli was recorded for the sadist, whereas the controls predominantly showed an activation of the right hemisphere.

Most of the pertinent studies, however, relied on functional magnetic resonance imaging (fMRI). In fMRI, the blood oxygen level-dependent (BOLD) response is registered within a strong magnetic field. Increases in the BOLD signal are indicative of an increase in regional blood flow and hence of stronger activation of the corresponding areas of the brain. In comparison with EEG or ERP methods, fMRI offers higher spatial resolution.

In fMRI studies, paedophilic men on average showed stronger BOLD signals upon visual engagement with pictures of children in cortical areas such as the anterior cingulate cortex, the ventromedial prefrontal cortex (Schiffer et al., 2008a, 2008b), the lateral orbitofrontal cortex (Habermeyer et al., 2013a), the fusiform gyrus (Dressing et al., 2001; Schiffer et al., 2008b), and the insula (Poeppl et al., 2011; Ponseti et al., 2012). Moreover, paedophilic men displayed stronger activations upon congruent visual stimulation with child images in limbic areas, including the hippocampus and the thalamus (Schiffer et al., 2008b), and also the amygdala (Sartorius et al., 2008). Upon stimulation with incongruent images (i.e., pictures showing adults), paedophilic individuals showed weaker BOLD signals than controls in the hypothalamus, the right occipital cortex, and the left insula (Walter et al., 2007; cf., Wiebking, Witzel, Walter, Gubka, & Northoff, 2006). Wiebking and Northoff (2013) provided a review of the pertinent findings. Polisois-Keating and Joyal (2013) integrated these findings in a meta-analysis. Chapter 43 contains a detailed overview of fMRI methods and results in the assessment of sexual offenders.

In an fMRI study with eight sexual offenders diagnosed with sadism and seven controls, Harenski, Thornton, Harenski, Decety, and Kiehl (2012) observed stronger activation of the left amygdala towards pictures showing painful scenes among the sadists. Furthermore, ratings of pain severity were positively correlated with the incremental change of activity in the anterior insula in both hemispheres among the sadists but not in the controls. Beyond the association of the amygdala with sexual arousal in general (e.g., Walter et al., 2008), Harenski et al. (2012) speculated that 'the increased amygdala activity in sadists represents a more general positive emotion than sexual arousal, such as excitement' (p. 288). According to Harenski et al., this interpretation receives support from a recent study showing increased levels of sexual arousal towards cues of violence or injury among self-identified sadists sampled from the community (Seto, Lalumière, Harris, & Chivers, 2012; see also Chapter 39).

Seto (2008) and Schiffer et al. (2008b) tentatively concluded that there may not be a distinct brain response of paedophiles towards child-related stimuli given the overlap in active regions with those involved in sexual arousal in general. This interpretation was corroborated by the meta-analytic results of Polisois-Keating and Joyal (2013). On comparing paedophilic and non-paedophilic groups of participants under fMRI conditions with visual engagement by sexual stimuli of the preferred kind, they noted that 'the pattern of activation did not seem to differ significantly between the groups. All activated brain regions associated with sexual arousal in the non-pedophilic group were also found in the pedophilic group and no significant differences emerged between the groups; however, the number of significant foci was higher in the pedophilic group' (p. 1112).

So far, it is unclear whether the overlap in brain regions between normal and paedophilic sexual arousal will extend to other forms of sexual preference disorders. If true, the outcome would be in accordance with the stimulus-control models of sexual arousal described by Barbaree and Marshall (1991). That is, paraphilic individuals would not have a pathological brain response but rather a regular response to an inappropriate target. Still, using visual stimuli congruent with the sexual preference disorder, in the long run fMRI may become useful as a diagnostic tool, as highlighted by Ponseti et al. (2012), for example.

Psychometric Testing

General Cognitive Ability

As a group, sexual offenders on average have lower IQs than non-sexual offender controls or the population mean, according to a meta-analysis by Cantor, Blanchard, Robichaud, and Christensen (2005). In that study, the lowest IQ average was reported for sexual offenders against children, whereas sexual offenders against adults took an intermediate position compared with the population mean. Judging from Figure 2 in the paper by Cantor et al. (2005, p. 560), the weighted and adjusted full-scale IQs were about 93.3 and 94.5 for child molesters and for sexual offenders against adults, respectively. The results reported by Cantor et al. also point to a significant correlation between an offender's IQ and victim age, at least judging from sample IQs and the upper limit of the victims' age range in the corresponding studies ($r = 0.64$, $p < 0.001$). The lower the age cut-off for the corresponding definition of child victims was, the lower the average IQ of child molesters seemed to be. These results tie in with earlier findings from the same working group, according to which weak signs of neurodevelopmental disturbance such as non-righthandedness were more prevalent among paedophilic sexual offenders than among non-paedophilic sexual offenders (Cantor et al., 2004). Finally, Rice, Harris, Lang, and Chaplin (2008) found a higher prevalence of paedophiles in a sample of 69 mentally retarded sexual offenders compared with 69 sexual offenders who had average or above-average IQ levels. It should be noted, however, that intellectual disability in itself apparently is no risk factor for sexual offending. Langevin and Curnoe (2008) did not observe a significant preponderance of intellectually disabled individuals in a mixed sample of 2286 male sex offenders; they did, however, find a proportion of individuals with specific learning disabilities among the sexual offenders that was larger than expected.

Generally, a psychometric assessment of a sexual offender's IQ is warranted, also with risk assessment (Phenix & Sreenivasan, 2009) and treatment planning in mind. The assessment of the cognitive abilities of sexual offenders should provide an estimate of (1) *fluid intelligence* or cognitive problem-solving skill, involving inductive and deductive reasoning, and also information on (2a) general intelligence and (2b) its components such as working memory, attention span, processing speed, visuospatial reasoning, and language comprehension. In this way, the assessment would follow the rationale implied by Carroll's (1993) hierarchical factor model of cognitive ability. Furthermore, the use of such a comprehensive assessment of cognitive ability is more robust against artefacts that otherwise may occur with screening tests which may be confounded with covariates such as motor speed or dexterity. For the assessment of the treatment needs of sexual offenders with intellectual disabilities, see Chapter 48.

Neuropsychology

A recent meta-analysis by Joyal, Beaulieu-Plante, and de Chantérac (2014) provides a summary of extant findings on neuropsychological peculiarities of sexual offenders. The meta-analysis was based on 23 individual studies and 1756 subjects. The neuropsychological tests used in sufficient studies to facilitate comparison were the Stroop interference test, trail-making B task, Wisconsin Card Sorting Test (WCST), Halstead–Reitan Category Task, Raven's Standard Progressive Matrices (SPM), Control Oral Word Association Test (COWAT), and the logical memory subtest, in addition to the visual reproduction subtest of the Wechsler Memory Scale (WMS). According to Joyal et al., the tests in question referred to cognitive capabilities such as reasoning/fluid intelligence (WCST, Halstead–Reitan Category Task, SPM), cognitive inhibition (Stroop test), task switching/cognitive flexibility (WCST), verbal fluency (COWAT), and memory (subtests of the WMS).

Joyal et al. (2014) noted a medium-sized performance deficit in sexual offenders in general ($d = 0.59$) compared with the general population when all neuropsychological tests were combined based on 14 individual studies. This global performance deficit was more pronounced in sexual offenders against adults ($d = 0.98$; five studies) than in child molesters ($d = 0.42$; nine studies). Between-group comparisons of sexual offenders against adults with child molesters could only be carried out for some neuropsychological tests (COWAT, Stroop test, trail-making B task, and WCST) as there were too few studies for the remaining tests. According to these comparisons for individual tests, sexual offenders against adults on average performed better on the WCST ($d = 0.23$), whereas the child molesters on average obtained higher scores on the COWAT ($d = 0.52$) and the Stroop test ($d = 0.52$). Consequently, the mean differences between sexual offender subgroups equalled weak to moderate effect sizes. There was no significant mean difference between sexual offenders against adults and child molesters on the trail-making B task in terms of processing speed.

Joyal et al. (2014) made it clear that the results of the meta-analysis are heterogeneous even after separating sexual offenders against adults from child molesters. They interpreted this outcome as indicating that further meaningful distinctions between subgroups of sexual offenders would be relevant in terms of neuropsychological performance. Relevant criteria for subgroups could be the presence of a paraphilia (and its type) and also opportunistic versus premeditated offending. In this regard, typologies of sexual offenders such as the classification schemes for rapists and for child molesters developed by Knight and Prentky (1990) may prove fruitful if applied in conjunction with neuropsychological tests in future research.

As far as the choice of suitable neuropsychological tests is concerned, one should distinguish between lower and higher order executive functions: capabilities such as behavioural inhibition or selective attention would be examples of the former, whereas reasoning, fluid intelligence, planning competency, or cognitive flexibility would be aspects of the latter (Joyal et al., 2014). Therefore, basic cognitive exercises that address inhibition (as evidenced by go/no-go tasks or the Stroop test), performance speed, and selective attention should be combined with cognitive flexibility (as measured by the WCST), fluid intelligence, memory, and planning (as measured by the Tower of London test, for instance) if one wished to administer a comprehensive testing battery. Such a testing battery would resemble the choice of measures recommended for assessing competency to stand trial (Denney, 2005).

It should be acknowledged, however, that the results described above with reference to the meta-analysis of Joyal et al. (2014) represent general trends. Sexual offenders do not show a unique and specific pattern of scores on the aforementioned neuropsychological tests, nor are these tests in themselves specific for particular types of disorder. Therefore, Joyal et al. opined that future research in the area would likely benefit from using neuropsychological tests that tap into more circumscribed mental abilities in order to disentangle motor impulsivity from behavioural disinhibition or risk taking.

Second, it should be acknowledged that data from an extensive neuropsychological testing battery must be interpreted with caution: the more tests being used, the more likely it is that at least one of them will show a putatively abnormal result (Larrabee, 2005a). Conversely, grossly abnormal scores could be due to malingering rather than to cognitive deficits (Larrabee, 2005b).

Nevertheless, a careful neuropsychological examination can help to establish whether a sexual offender is suffering from particular cognitive performance deficits. The exact type and scope of such deficits, in turn, can help to inform strategies for treatment and risk management. A highly impulsive individual may profit from medication more than from cognitive therapy. A memory-impaired offender may need smaller increments and more repetitions of the content provided in psychological treatment. Methods to determine if individual scores deviate from the population norm in a significant way have been developed by Crawford and colleagues (Crawford & Garthwaite, 2005, 2007; Crawford, Howell, & Garthwaite, 1998). The resemblance between an individual profile from a testing battery and a reference profile can be determined using the Mahalanobis distance (for alternative methods for comparing single-case and group profiles, see Huber, 1973).

Again, it should be acknowledged that the findings summarized above refer to *samples* of sexual offenders – they do not necessarily pertain to an individual case. Furthermore, it should be acknowledged that many studies referred to above did not discriminate between, say, paedophilic and non-paedophilic child molesters, thus treating these individuals as a homogeneous group despite evidence to the contrary (Schiffer & Vonlaufen, 2011).

Genetics, Chromosomal Aberrations, and Neuroendocrinology

Genetics

It has been surmised that genetic factors may be involved in the aetiology of sexual preference disorders, particularly paedophilia (Comings, 1994; Seto, 2008; Tost et al., 2004; cf., Langevin, 1993). Two family studies (Gaffney, Lurie, & Berlin, 1984; Labelle, Bourget, Bradford, Alda, & Tessier, 2012) showed an accumulation of paedophilic individuals in the families of paedophilic patients. Although this outcome may be indicative of genetic effects, it does not rule out the possibility of social factors within the families that may have caused the accumulation of paedophilic cases. The first behavioural genetic study so far that involved twin modelling (Alanko, Salo, Mokros, & Santtila, 2013) yielded support for weak but significant non-additive genetic effects but addressed interest in sex with underage persons, not paedophilia proper. For the sample of 3987 Finnish men (twins and siblings) surveyed in this study, the heritability sexual interest in underage children and youth was estimated at 15% (20% with respect to corresponding masturbation fantasies).

Consequently, there is no evidence to date that would show unequivocally that paraphilias or sexual offending were associated with the genetic makeup. More generally, there is a more comprehensive body of literature addressing antisociality and psychopathy at the genetic level. The interested reader should consult the papers by Viding and McCrory (2012) and Viding, Larsson, and Jones (2008) (see also Waldman & Rhee, 2006).

Connatal Disorders and Chromosomal Aberrations

In a nationwide register-based study in Denmark, data from all men from the cohort aged 15–70 years between 1960 and 2006 for whom karyotyping had been conducted were analysed with respect to criminal convictions (Stochholm, Bojesen, Skakkebæk Jensen, Juul, & Højbjerg Gravholt, 2012). Compared with age-matched controls from the general population, the risk of criminal convictions for sexual offences was significantly increased both for men with Klinefelter's syndrome (47, XXY; $n = 934$) and for men with the 47, XYY karyotype ($n = 161$), with adjusted hazard rates of 2.74 and 3.66, respectively. This outcome was corroborated by a study by Briken, Habermann, Berner, and Hill (2006), who analysed the mental health reports on 166 sexual murderers that had been prepared as part of expert evidence in court. At 3 out of 166 cases with an XYY karyotype (1.8%), the relative rate appeared elevated according to Briken et al. in comparison with estimates for this particular type of chromosome trisomy based on population-based samples (~0.01%) and in prisoner samples (<1%). Therefore, cytogenetic analyses have to be commissioned if the outward appearance of a patient or information obtained during the interview makes it seem likely that the individual in question belongs to either of the two chromosome trisomies mentioned above (i.e., the 47, XXY karyotype, or Klinefelter's syndrome, or the 47, XYY karyotype).

Neuroendocrinology

According to a review by Briken, Hill, and Berner (2006), the analysis of potential peculiarities of sexual offenders in terms of hormones focused on testosterone, luteinizing hormone-releasing hormone (LHRH), and prolactin (PRL). For testosterone, a causal role can be assumed both for sexual drive/appetence in general (Jordan, Fromberger, Stolpmann, & Müller, 2011a) and for sexual aggression in particular (Jordan, Fromberger, Stolpmann, & Müller, 2011b). Nevertheless, only some studies that measured testosterone levels found significantly higher levels in sexual offenders than in controls (Dabbs, Carr, Frady, & Riad, 1995; Giotakos, Markianos, Vaidakis, & Christodoulou, 2003, 2004; Studer, Aylwin, & Reddon, 2005) whereas others did not (e.g., Aromäki, Lindman, Eriksson, 2002; Bain et al., 1988; Kingston et al., 2012; Lang, Flor-Henry, & Frenzel, 1990; Langevin et al., 1985; Rada, Laws, & Kellner, 1976). If any differences were observed, they concerned rapists rather than child molesters.

In a study with 501 adult male sex offenders, Studer et al. (2005) observed a significant correlation between testosterone levels and offence severity (rated from 1 = non-contact to 6 = severe violence). Furthermore, the authors noted a significant correlation between testosterone levels and sexual offence recidivism among those offenders who had not completed a treatment programme. Both effect sizes were small, at $r = 0.19$ and $r = 0.17$, respectively. This study was subsequently replicated irrespective of treatment status (Kingston et al., 2012): testosterone levels were unrelated to either violent or sexual recidivism, whereas the levels of luteinizing hormone (LH) were associated with both at a medium effect size.

Some studies noted elevated mean LH levels in rapists (Giotakos et al., 2003) and – albeit to a non-significant degree – in child molesters (Giotakos et al., 2004). Finally, PRL levels were observed to be higher among sexual offenders than among controls in some studies (Lang et al., 1990; Studer & Aylwin, 2006; but see Maes, van West, et al., 2001).

In summary, it does not seem too surprising that the results of studies looking for higher average levels of testosterone and other hormones in sexual offenders remained somewhat inconclusive. Testosterone levels, in particular, are subject to changes across the life span and show considerable interindividual variation. Consequently, the notion of sexual offenders as high-testosterone individuals is reminiscent of the simplistic assumption that sexual offenders would have a particularly strong sex drive. Rather than having a different hormone level compared with non-offender controls, the endocrine *response* of some sexual offenders may differ (cf., Lieverse, Assies, & Gooren, 2000). Provocation tests of paedophilic subjects with *meta*-chlorophenylpiperazine (Maes, van West, et al., 2001; Maes, De Vos, et al., 2001) or LHRH injection (Gaffney & Berlin, 1984; Lang et al., 1990) led to increased secretion of cortisol (Maes, van West, et al., 2001), catecholamines, particularly epinephrine (Maes, De Vos, et al., 2001), and LH (Gaffney & Berlin, 1984; Lang et al., 1990). In a mixed sample of 10 sexual offenders, no differential endocrine response was observed, however, during sexual stimulation or after orgasm (Haake et al., 2003).

Nevertheless, surgical and pharmacological castration of sexual offenders is commonly regarded as an effective intervention to reduce the risk of reoffending in sexual offenders, even though methodologically sound studies using a randomized controlled design are lacking (Rice & Harris, 2011). Given the serious side-effects of androgen deprivation therapy such as gynaecomastia or osteoporosis, the method should be limited to those high-risk offenders who are suffering from the sexual preoccupations that were identified as the strongest dynamic risk factor of sexual offence recidivism in a meta-analysis by Hanson and Morton-Bourgon (2005).

Medroxyprogesterone acetate blocks the androgen receptors, thereby intercepting the effects of testosterone peripherally; cyproterone acetate also has a secondary effect of attenuating the LHRH secretion in the hypophysis (Hill, Briken, Lietz, & Berner, 2005). LHRH agonists directly affect LHRH receptors in the pituitary gland. The LHRH analogues first lead to an increase in LHRH secretion until the continuous stimulation of the receptors leads to their desensitization and ultimately downregulation of LH, thus reducing the secretion of testosterone to virtually nil. Three case studies utilizing fMRI demonstrated pre–post effects in the BOLD signal in response to sexual stimuli after treatment of paedophilic patients with LHRH agonists (Habermeyer et al., 2012; Moulier et al., 2012; Schiffer, Gizewski, & Krueger, 2009).

If pharmacological androgen deprivation therapy is being used, clinical monitoring of hormonal status is essential, also to detect possible countermeasures on behalf of the patient such as testosterone substitution (Hansen & Lykke-Olesen, 1997). Otherwise, screening the hormonal status of sexual offenders seems dispensable unless there are indications of endocrinological dysfunction such as reports of delayed or premature onset of puberty, or of anatomical abnormalities of the testes (cf., Rettenberger, Hill, Dekker, Berner, & Briken, 2013).

Surgical castration, in contrast, does not lead to low levels of testosterone as does pharmacological androgen deprivation therapy, because a small amount of testosterone is produced in the adrenal cortex. Surgical castration has been shown to reduce the recidivism rate of sexual offenders very considerably (Lösel & Schmucker, 2005; Wille & Beier, 1989, 1997). This result remains controversial, however, because castration likely was used as a 'last resort' (Wille & Beier, 1989, p. 130) with patients who were presumably older and had already undergone several other forms of treatment. The design of studies on surgical castration was methodologically weak (Lösel & Schmucker, 2005; Rice & Harris, 2011). Second, and more decisively, surgical castration as such seems to represent a form of the talion principle ('an eye for an eye … ') rather than curative care (Pfäfflin, 2008), especially in light of the grave side-effects. Surgical castration has remained in place in the Czech Republic and Germany, for instance, where the method was criticized by the European Committee for the Prevention of Torture and Inhuman or Degrading Treatment or Punishment (Anti-Folter-Komitee, 2012; Pfäfflin, 2010). Attempts at surgical castration at the cerebral level by stereotactic brain surgery in Germany during the 1970s (e.g., Dieckmann & Hassler, 1975; Müller, Röder, & Orthner, 1973) were discontinued after critical appraisal of the method and its ethical implications (Fülgraff & Barbey, 1978; Schorsch & Schmidt, 1979).

Conclusion

As sexual offending is a legally defined variety of behaviours that belongs to the social and environmental domain, it is evident that there cannot be a single neurobiological explanation for its occurrence (Mokros, in press). One also should be cautious not to overinterpret neuroimaging data as necessarily implying defect, disturbance, or disorder. The cerebral blood flow responses of, say, paedophilic individuals may differ from those of controls because the paedophiles are in fact responding to pictures of children with immediate sexual interest and arousal. Alternatively, the paedophilic individuals may simply be more guarded and therefore more engaged in self-monitoring than controls (cf., Habermeyer et al., 2013b). Finally, aggregate data on the association of particular genetic, chromosomal, or endocrine variants with sexual offending do not necessarily translate to the individual case. The relations described above are *probabilistic*, not deterministic.

Hence the findings summarized above should be taken as an aide-mémoire for neurobiological substrates of dispositions that may increase the risk for sexual or violent reoffending in a given case. Depending on a thorough psychiatric examination and psychological interview, the additional tests suggested above can be administered or commissioned. The decision for or against additional tests or screenings should heed the risk of false-positive outcomes, however, that increase with the number of tests employed (Ingraham & Aiken, 1996). Hence tests for neural abnormality should be applied according to the specifics of a given case, not as routine measures.

References

Alanko, K., Salo, B., Mokros, A., & Santtila, P. (2013). Evidence for heritability of adult men's sexual interest in youth under age 16 from a population-based extended twin design. *Journal of Sexual Medicine, 10*, 1090–1099. doi:10.1111/jsm.12067

Alcaro, A., Huber, R., & Panksepp, J. (2007). Behavioral functions of the mesolimbic dopaminergic system: An affective neuroethological perspective. *Brain Research Reviews, 56*, 283–321. doi:10.1016/j.brainresrev.2007.07.014

Anokhin, A. P., Golosheykin, S., Sirevaag, E., Kristjansson, S., Rohrbaugh, J. W., & Heath, A. C. (2006). Rapid discrimination of visual scene content in the human brain. *Brain Research, 1093*, 167–177. doi:10.1016/j.brainres.2006.03.108

Anti-Folter-Komitee (2012). *Europarat rügt chirurgische Kastration von Sextätern* [Council of Europe admonished surgical castration of sex offenders]. SPIEGEL ONLINE, 22 February 2012. Retrieved from http://www.spiegel.de/panorama/anti-folter-komitee-europarat-ruegt-chirurgische-kastration-von-sextaetern-a-816781.html

Ariely, D., & Loewenstein, G. (2006). The heat of the moment: The effect of sexual arousal on sexual decision making. *Journal of Behavioral Decision Making, 19*, 87–98. doi:10.1002/bdm.501

Arnow, B. A., Desmond, J. E., Banner, L. L., Glover, G. H., Solomon, A., Polan, M. L., … Atlas, S. W. (2002). Brain activation and sexual arousal in healthy, heterosexual males. *Brain, 125*, 1014–1023. doi:10.1093/brain/awf108

Aromäki, A. S., Lindman, R. E., & Eriksson, C. J. (2002). Testosterone, sexuality and antisocial personality disorder: A pilot study. *Psychiatry Research, 110*, 239–247. doi:10.1016/S0165-1781(02)00109-9

Bain, J., Langevin, R., Hucker, S., Dickey, R., Wright, P., & Schonberg, C. (1988). Sex hormones in pedophiles: I baseline values of six hormones; II the gonadotropin releasing hormone test. *Annals of Sex Research, 1*, 443–454. doi:10.1007/BF00878108

Banse, R., Schmidt, A. F., & Clarbour, J. (2010). Indirect measures of sexual interest in child sex offenders: A multimethod approach. *Criminal Justice and Behavior, 37*, 319–335. doi:10.1177/0093854809357598

Barbaree, H. E., & Marshall, W. L. (1991). The role of male sexual arousal in rape: Six models. *Journal of Consulting and Clinical Psychology, 59*, 621–630. doi:10.1037/0022-006X.59.5.621

Blanchard, R., Cantor, J. M., & Robichaud, L. K. (2006). Biological factors in the development of sexual deviance and aggression in males. In H. E. Barbaree & W. L. Marshall (Eds.), *The juvenile sex offender* (pp. 77–104). New York, NY: Guilford Press.

Blanchard, R., Christensen, B. K., Strong, S. M., Cantor, J. M., Kuban, M. E., Klassen, P., ... Blak, T. (2002). Retrospective self-reports of childhood accidents causing unconsciousness in phallometrically diagnosed pedophiles. *Archives of Sexual Behavior, 31*, 511–526. doi:10.1023/A:1020659331965

Briken, P., Habermann, N., Berner, W., & Hill, A. (2006). XYY chromosome abnormality in sexual homicide perpetrators. *American Journal of Medical Genetics Part B – Neuropsychiatric Genetics, 141*, 198–200. doi:10.1002/ajmg.b.30279

Briken, P., Hill, A., & Berner, W. (2006). Paraphilien und Sexualdelinquenz: Neurobiologische und neuropsychologische Aspekte [Paraphilias and sexual delinquency: Neurobiological and neuropsychological aspects]. *Zeitschrift für Sexualforschung, 19*, 295–333. doi:10.1055/s-2006-955198

Burns, J. M., & Swerdlow, R. H. (2003). Right orbitofrontal tumor with pedophilia symptom and constructional apraxia sign. *Archives of Neurology, 60*, 437–440. doi:10.1001/archneur.60.3.437

Canli, T., & Gabrieli, J. D. E. (2004). Imaging gender differences in sexual arousal. *Nature Neuroscience, 7*, 325–326. doi:10.1038/nn0404-325

Cantor, J. M., & Blanchard, R. (2012). White matter volumes in pedophiles, hebephiles, and teleiophiles. *Archives of Sexual Behavior, 41*, 749–752. doi:10.1007/s10508-012-9954-2

Cantor, J. M., Blanchard, R., Christensen, B. K., Dickey, R., Klassen, P. E., Beckstead, A. L., ... Kuban, M. E. (2004). Intelligence, memory, and handedness in pedophilia. *Neuropsychology, 18*, 3–14. doi:10.1037/0894-4105.18.1.3

Cantor, J. M., Blanchard, R., Robichaud, L. K., & Christensen, B. K. (2005). Quantitative reanalysis of aggregate data on IQ in sexual offenders. *Psychological Bulletin, 131*, 555–568. doi:10.1037/0033-2909.131.4.555

Cantor, J. M., Kabani, N., Christensen, B. K., Zipursky, R. B., Barbaree, H. E., Dickey, R., ... Blanchard, R. (2008). Cerebral white matter deficiencies in pedophilic men. *Journal of Psychiatric Research, 42*, 167–183. doi:10.1016/j.jpsychires.2007.10.013

Carroll, J. B. (1993). *Human cognitive abilities: A survey of factor-analytic studies*. Cambridge, England: Cambridge University Press.

Cassens, G., Ford, M., Lothstein, L., & Gallenstein, T. (1988). Neuropsychological dysfunction and brain-imaging studies in paraphiles: Preliminary studies [Abstract]. *Journal of Clinical and Experimental Neuropsychology, 10*, 73.

Chivers, M. L., & Bailey, J. M. (2005). A sex difference in features that elicit genital response. *Biological Psychology, 70*, 115–120. doi:10.1016/j.biopsycho.2004.12.002

Chivers, M. L., Rieger, G., Latty, E., & Bailey, J. M. (2004). A sex difference in the specificity of sexual arousal. *Psychological Science, 15*, 736–744. doi:10.1111/j.0956-7976.2004.00750.x

Chivers, M. L., Roy, C., Grimbos, T., Cantor, J. M., & Seto, M. C. (2014). Specificity of sexual arousal for sexual activities in men and women with conventional and masochistic sexual interests. *Archives of Sexual Behavior*, *43*, 931–940. doi:10.1007/s10508-013-0174-1

Cohen, L. J., Nikiforov, K., Gans, S., Poznansky, O., McGeoch, P., Weaver, C., ... Galynker, I. (2002). Heterosexual male perpetrators of childhood sexual abuse: A preliminary neuropsychiatric model. *Psychiatric Quarterly*, *74*, 313–336. doi:10.1023/A:1020416101092

Comings, D. E. (1994). Role of genetic factors in human sexual behavior based on studies of Tourette syndrome and ADHD probands and their relatives. *American Journal of Medical Genetics*, *54*, 227–241. doi:10.1002/ajmg.1320540309

Costell, R. M., Lunde, D. T., Kopell, B. S., & Wittner, W. K. (1972). Contingent negative variation as an indicator of sexual preference. *Science*, *172*, 718–720. doi:10.1126/science.177.4050.718

Crawford, J. R., & Garthwaite, P. H. (2005). Testing for suspected impairments and dissociations in single-case studies in neuropsychology: Evaluation of alternatives using Monte Carlo simulations and revised tests for dissociations. *Neuropsychology*, *19*, 318–331. doi:10.1037/0894-4105.19.5.664

Crawford, J. R., & Garthwaite, P. H. (2007). Comparison of a single case to a control or normative sample in neuropsychology: Development of a Bayesian approach. *Cognitive Neuropsychology*, *24*, 343–372. doi:10.1080/02643290701290146

Crawford, J. R., Howell, D. C., & Garthwaite, P. H. (1998). Payne and Jones revisited: Estimating the abnormality of test score differences using a modified paired samples *t*-test. *Journal of Clinical and Experimental Neuropsychology*, *20*, 898–905. doi:10.1076/jcen.20.6.898.1112

Dabbs, J. M., Carr, T. S., Frady, R. L., & Riad, J. K. (1995). Testosterone, crime, and misbehavior among 692 prison inmates. *Personality and Individual Differences*, *18*, 627–633. doi:10.1016/0191-8869(94)00177-T

DelBello, M. P., Soutullo, C. A., Zimmerman, M. E., Sax, K. W., Williams, J. R., McElroy, S. L., & Strakowski, S. M. (1999). Traumatic brain injury in individuals convicted of sexual offenses with and without bipolar disorder. *Psychiatry Research*, *89*, 281–286. doi:10.1016/S0165-1781(99)00112-2

Denney, R. L. (2005). Criminal forensic neuropsychology and assessment of competency. In G. L. Larrabee (Ed.), *Forensic neuropsychology: A scientific approach* (pp. 378–424). New York, NY: Oxford University Press.

Devinsky, J., Sacks, O., & Devinsky, O. (2010). Klüver–Bucy syndrome, hypersexuality, and the law. *Neurocase*, *16*, 140–145. doi:10.1080/13554790903329182

Dieckmann, G., & Hassler, R. (1975). Unilateral hypothalamotomy in sexual delinquents: Report on six cases. *Confinia Neurologica*, *37*, 177–186. doi:10.1159/000102736

Downing, M. G., Stolwyk, R., & Ponsford, J. L. (2013). Sexual changes in individuals with traumatic brain injury: A control comparison. *Journal of Head Trauma Rehabilitation*, *28*, 171–178. doi:10.1097/HTR.0b013e31828b4f63

Dressing, H., Obergriesser, T., Tost, H., Kaumeier, S., Ruf, M., & Braus, D. F. (2001). Homosexuelle Pädophilie und funktionelle Netzwerke – fMRI-Fallstudie [Homosexual pedophilia and functional networks – an fMRI case report and literature review]. *Fortschritte der Neurologie-Psychiatrie*, *69*, 539–544. doi:10.1055/s-2001-18380

Eher, R., Aigner, M., Fruehwald, S., Frottier, P., & Gruenhut, C. (2000). Social information processed self-perceived aggression in relation to brain abnormalities in a sample of incarcerated sexual offenders. *Journal of Psychology & Human Sexuality*, *11*(3), 37–47. doi:10.1300/J056v11n03_04

Ellison, J. M. (1982). Alterations of sexual behavior in temporal lobe epilepsy. *Psychosomatics*, *23*, 499–500, 505–509. doi:10.1016/S0033-3182(82)73382-1

Emrich, H. (1978). Psychophysiologische Parameter der Sexualdelinquenz: Pulsverlauf und evozierte Summenpotentiale bei Darbietung deliktspezifischer Bilder [Psychophysiological parameters of sexual delinquency: Heart rate and event related sum potentials upon presentation of offence-specific pictures]. In G. Nass (Ed.), *Kriminalpädagogik als Kriminalpolitik: Beiträge aus der Grundlagenforschung zur Kriminologie* (6. Folge, pp. 7–29). Kassel, Germany: Gesellschaft für vorbeugende Verbrechensbekämpfung.

Emrich, H. (1979). Psychophysiologie des Nicht-bewußten [Psychophysiology of the non-conscious]. In G. Nass (Ed.), *Kriminalpädagogik als Kriminalpolitik: Beiträge aus der Grundlagenforschung zur Kriminologie* (8. Folge, pp. 101–116). Kassel, Germany: Gesellschaft für vorbeugende Verbrechensbekämpfung.

Fazel, S., Lichtenstein, P., Grann, M., & Långström, N. (2011). Risk of violent crime in individuals with epilepsy and traumatic brain injury: A 35-year Swedish population study. *PLoS Medicine*, *8*(12), e1001150. doi:10.1371/journal.pmed.1001150

Feng, C., Wang, L., Wang, N., Gu, R., & Luo, Y. (2012). The time course of implicit processing of erotic pictures: An event-related potential study. *Brain Research*, *1489*, 48–55. doi:10.1016/j.brainres.2012.10.019

Ferretti, A., Caulo, M., Del Gratta, C., Di Matteo, R., Merla, A., Montorsi, F., … Romani, G. L. (2005). Dynamics of male sexual arousal: Distinct components of brain activation revealed by fMRI. *NeuroImage*, *26*, 1086–1096. doi:10.1016/j.neuroimage.2005.03.02

Flor-Henry, P. (1987). Cerebral aspects of sexual deviation. In G. D. Wilson (Ed.), *Variant sexuality: Research and theory* (pp. 49–83). Beckenham, England: Croom Helm.

Flor-Henry, P., Lang, R. A., Koles, Z. J., & Frenzel, R. R. (1988). Quantitative EEG investigations of genital exhibitionism. *Annals of Sex Research*, *1*, 49–62. doi:10.1007/BF00852882

Flor-Henry, P., Lang, R. A., Koles, Z. J., & Frenzel, R. (1991). Quantitative EEG studies of pedophilia. *International Journal of Psychophysiology*, *10*, 253–258.

Fülgraff, G., & Barbey, J. (1978). *Stereotaktische Hirnoperationen bei abweichendem Sexualverhalten: Abschlussbericht der Kommission beim Bundesgesundheitsamt [Stereotactic brain surgery for deviant sexual behavior: Final report of the Commission at the Federal Office of Health]*. Berlin, Germany: Reimer.

Gaffney, G. R., & Berlin, F. S. (1984). Is there hypothalamic-pituitary–gonadal dysfunction in paedophilia? *British Journal of Psychiatry*, *145*, 657–660. doi:10.1192/bjp.145.6.657

Gaffney, G. R., Lurie, S. F., & Berlin, F. S. (1984). Is there familial transmission of pedophilia? *Journal of Nervous and Mental Disease*, *172*, 546–548. doi:10.1097/00005053-198409000-00006

Garnett, S., Nahmias, C., Wortzman, G., Langevin, R., & Dickey, R. (1988). Positron emission tomography and sexual arousal in a sadist and two controls. *Annals of Sex Research*, *1*, 387–399. doi:10.1007/BF00878105

Giotakos, O., Markianos, M., Vaidakis, N., & Christodoulou, G. N. (2003). Aggression, impulsivity, plasma sex hormones, and biogenic amine turnover in a forensic population of rapists. *Journal of Sex & Marital Therapy*, *39*, 215–225. doi:10.1080/00926230390155113

Giotakos, O., Markianos, M., Vaidakis, N., & Christodoulou, G. N. (2004). Sex hormones and biogenic amine turnover of sex offenders in relation to their temperament and character dimensions. *Psychiatry Research*, *127*, 185–193. doi:10.1016/j.psychres.2003.06.003

Graber, B., Hartmann, K., Coffman, J. A., Huey, C. J., & Golden, C. I. (1982). Brain damage among mentally disordered sex offenders. *Journal of Forensic Science*, *27*, 125–134.

Haake, P., Schedlowski, M., Exton, M. S., Giepen, C., Hartmann, U., Osterheider, M., … Krüger, T. H. C. (2003). Acute neuroendocrine response to sexual stimulation in sexual offenders. *Canadian Journal of Psychiatry, 48*, 265–271.

Habermeyer, B., Esposito, F., Händel, N., Lemoine, P., Klarhöfer, M., Mager, R., … Graf, M. (2013a). Immediate processing of erotic stimuli in paedophilia and controls: A case–control study. *BMC Psychiatry, 13*, 88. doi:10.1186/1471-244X-13-88

Habermeyer, B., Esposito, F., Händel, N., Lemoine, P., Kuhl, H. C., Klarhöfer, M., … Graf, M. (2013b). Response inhibition in pedophilia: An fMRI pilot study. *Neuropsychobiology, 68*, 228–237. doi:10.1159/000355295

Habermeyer, B., Händel, N., Lemoine, P., Klarhöfer, M., Seifritz, E., Dittmann, V., & Graf, M. (2012). LH–RH agonists modulate amygdala response to visual sexual stimulation: A single case fMRI study in pedophilia. *Neurocase, 18*, 489–495. doi:10.1080/13554794.2011.627346

Hamed, S., Mohamed, K., El-Taher, A., Hamed, E., & Omar, H. (2006). The sexual and reproductive health in men with generalized epilepsy: A multidisciplinary evaluation. *International Journal of Impotence Research, 18*, 287–295. doi:10.1038/sj.ijir.3901406

Hansen, H., & Lykke-Olesen, L. (1997). Treatment of dangerous sexual offenders in Denmark. *Journal of Forensic Psychiatry, 8*, 195–199. doi:10.1080/09585189708412004

Hanson, R. K., & Morton-Bourgon, K. E. (2005). The characteristics of persistent sexual offenders: A meta-analysis of recidivism studies. *Journal of Consulting and Clinical Psychology, 73*, 1154–1163. doi:10.1037/0022-006X.73.6.1154

Harenski, C. L., Thornton, D. M., Harenski, K. A., Decety, J., & Kiehl, K. A. (2012). Increased frontotemporal activation during pain observation in sexual sadism. *Archives of General Psychiatry, 69*, 283–292. doi:10.1001/archgenpsychiatry.2011.1566

Harris, G. T., Rice, M. E., & Lalumière, M. (2001). Criminal violence: The roles of psychopathy, neurodevelopmental insults, and antisocial parenting. *Criminal Justice and Behavior, 28*, 402–426. doi:10.1177/009385480102800402

Heath, R. G. (1972). Pleasure and brain activity in man: Deep and surface electroencephalograms during orgasm. *Journal of Nervous and Mental Disease, 154*, 3–18. doi:10.1097/00005053-197201000-00002

Hendricks, S. E., Fitzpatrick, D. F., Hartmann, K., Quaife, M. A., Stratbucker, R. A., & Graber, B. (1988). Brain structure and function in sexual molesters of children and adolescents. *Journal of Clinical Psychiatry, 49*, 108–111.

Hill, A., Briken, P., Lietz, K., & Berner, W. (2005). Standards der Diagnostik, Behandlung und Prognose von Sexualstraftätern [Standards of assessment, treatment and prognosis of sexual offenders]. In D. Schläfke, F. Hässler, & J. M. Fegert (Eds.), *Sexualstraftaten: Forensische Begutachtung, Diagnostik und Therapie* (pp. 77–98). Stuttgart, Germany: Schattauer.

Howard, R. C. (2002). Brain waves, dangerousness and deviant desires. *Journal of Forensic Psychiatry, 13*, 367–384. doi:10.1080/09585180210152346

Howard, R. C., Longmore, F. J., Mason, P. A., & Martin, J. L. (1994). Contingent negative variation (CNV) and erotic preference in self-declared homosexuals and in child sex offenders. *Biological Psychology, 38*, 169–181. doi:10.1016/0301-0511(94)90037-X

Hu, S.-H., Wei, N., Wang, Q.-D., Yan, L.-Q., Wei, E.-Q., Zhang, M.-M., … Xu, Y. (2008). Patterns of brain activation during visually evoked sexual arousal differ between homosexual and heterosexual men. *American Journal of Neuroradiology, 29*, 1890–1896. doi:10.3174/ajnr.A1260

Huber, H. P. (1973). *Psychometrische Einzelfalldiagnostik [Psychometric single case assessment]*. Weinheim, Germany: Beltz.

Hucker, S. J., Langevin, R., Dickey, R., Handy, L., Chambers, J., Wright, S., … Wortzman, G. (1988). Cerebral damage and dysfunction in sexually aggressive men. *Annals of Sex Research*, *1*, 33–47. doi:10.1007/BF00852881

Hucker, S. J., Langevin, R., Wortzman, G., Bain, J., Handy, L., Chambers, J., & Wright, S. (1986). Neuropsychological impairment in pedophiles. *Canadian Journal of Behavioural Science*, *18*, 440–448. doi:10.1037/h0079965

Ingraham, L. J., & Aiken, C. B. (1996). An empirical approach to determining criteria for abnormality in test batteries with multiple measures. *Neuropsychology*, *10*, 120–124. doi:10.1037/0894-4105.10.1.120

Janssen, E., Everaerd, W., Spiering, M., & Janssen, J. (2000). Automatic processes and the appraisal of sexual stimuli: Toward an information processing model of sexual arousal. *Journal of Sex Research*, *37*, 8–23. doi:10.1080/00224490009552016

Jiang, Y., Costello, P., Fang, F., Huang, M., & He, S. (2006). A gender- and sexual orientation-dependent spatial attentional effect of invisible images. *Proceedings of the National Academy of Sciences of the United States of America*, *103*, 17048–17052. doi:10.1073/pnas.0605678103

Jordan, K., Fromberger, P., Stolpmann, G., & Müller, J. L. (2011a). The role of testosterone in sexuality and paraphilia – a neurobiological approach. Part I: Testosterone and sexuality. *Journal of Sexual Medicine*, *8*, 2993–3007. doi:10.1111/j.1743-6109.2011.02394.x

Jordan, K., Fromberger, P., Stolpmann, G., & Müller, J. L. (2011b). The role of testosterone in sexuality and paraphilia – a neurobiological approach. Part II: Testosterone and paraphilia. *Journal of Sexual Medicine*, *8*, 3008–3029. doi:10.1111/j.1743-6109.2011.02393.x

Joyal, C. C., Beaulieu-Plante, J., & de Chantérac, A. (2014). The neuropsychology of sex offenders: A meta-analysis. *Sexual Abuse: A Journal of Research and Treatment*, *26*, 149–177. doi:10.1177/1079063213482842

Kagerer, S., Klucken, T., Wehrum, S., Zimmermann, M., Schienle, A., Walter, B., … Stark, R. (2011). Neural activation toward erotic stimuli in homosexual and heterosexual males. *Journal of Sexual Medicine*, *8*, 3132–3143. doi:10.1111/j.1743-6109.2011.02449.x

Kamphuis, J. H., De Ruiter, C., Janssen, B., & Spiering, M. (2005). Preliminary evidence for an automatic link between sex and power among men who molest children. *Journal of Interpersonal Violence*, *20*, 1351–1365. doi:10.1177/0886260505278719

Karama, S., Lecours, A. R., Leroux, J.-M., Bourgouin, P., Beaudoin, G., Joubert, S., & Beauregard, M. (2002). Areas of brain activation in males and females during viewing of erotic film excerpts. *Human Brain Mapping*, *16*, 1–13. doi:10.1002/hbm.10014

Kingston, D. A., Seto, M. C., Ahmed, A. G., Fedoroff, P., Firestone, P., & Bradford, J. M. (2012). The role of central and peripheral hormones in sexual and violent recidivism in sex offenders. *Journal of the American Academy of Psychiatry and the Law*, *40*, 476–485.

Kirenskaya-Berus, A. V., & Tkachenko, A. A. (2003). Characteristic features of EEG spectral characteristics in persons with deviant sexual behavior. *Human Physiology*, *29*, 278–287. doi:10.1023/A:1023982119972

Knight, R. A., & Prentky, R. A. (1990). Classifying sexual offenders: The development and collaboration of taxonomic models. In W. L. Marshall, D. R. Laws, & H. E. Barbaree (Eds.), *Handbook of sexual assault: Issues, theories and treatment of the offenders* (pp. 23–52). New York, NY: Plenum.

Kolářský, A., Freund, K., Machek, J., & Polák, O. (1967). Male sexual deviation: Association with early temporal lobe damage. *Archives of General Psychiatry*, *17*, 735–743.

Krug, R., Plihal, W., Fehm, H. L., & Born, J. (2000). Selective influence of the menstrual cycle on perception of stimuli with reproductive significance: An event related potential study. *Psychophysiology*, *37*, 111–122. doi:10.1111/1469-8986.3710111

Kühn, S., & Gallinat, J. (2011). A quantitative meta-analysis on cue-induced male sexual arousal. *Journal of Sexual Medicine, 8*, 2269–2275. doi:10.1111/j.1743-6109. 2011.02322.x

Labelle, A., Bourget, D., Bradford, J. M. W., Alda, M., & Tessier, P. (2012). Familial paraphilia: A pilot study with the construction of genograms. *ISRN Psychiatry, 2012*, 692813. doi:10.5402/2012/692813

Lang, R. A., Flor-Henry, P., & Frenzel, R. R. (1990). Sex hormone profiles in pedophilic and incestuous men. *Annals of Sex Research, 3*, 59–74. doi:10.1007/BF00849721

Langevin, R. (1990). Sexual anomalies and the brain. In W. L. Marshall, D. R. Laws, & H. E. Barbaree (Eds.), *Handbook of sexual assault: Issues, theories, and treatment of the offender* (pp. 103–113). New York, NY: Plenum.

Langevin, R. (1993). A comparison of neuroendocrine abnormalities and genetic factors in homosexuality and in pedophilia. *Annals of Sex Research, 6*, 67–76. doi:10.1007/BF00849746

Langevin, R., Bain, J., Ben-Aron, M. H., Coulthard, R., Day, D., Handy, L., ... Wortzman, G. (1985). Sexual aggression: Constructing a predictive equation. In R. Langevin (Ed.), *Erotic preference, gender identity, and aggression in men* (pp. 39–76). Hillsdale, NJ: Erlbaum.

Langevin, R., & Curnoe, S. (2008). Are the mentally retarded and learning disordered overrepresented among sex offenders and paraphilics? *International Journal of Offender Therapy and Comparative Criminology, 52*, 201–215. doi:10.1177/0306624X07305826

Langevin, R., & Curnoe, S. (2011). Psychopathy, ADHD, and brain dysfunction as predictors of lifetime recidivism among sex offenders. *International Journal of Offender Therapy and Comparative Criminology, 55*, 5–26. doi:10.1177/0306624X09360968

Langevin, R., Lang, R. A., Wortzman, G., Frenzel, R. R., & Wright, P. (1989a). An examination of brain damage and dysfunction in genital exhibitionists. *Annals of Sex Research, 2*, 77–94. doi:10.1007/BF00850681

Langevin, R., Wortzman, G., Dickey, R., Wright, P., & Handy, L. (1988). Neuropsychological impairment in incest offenders. *Annals of Sex Research, 1*, 401–415. doi:10.1007/BF00878106

Langevin, R., Wortzman, G., Wright, P., & Handy, L. (1989b). Studies of brain damage and dysfunction in sex offenders. *Annals of Sex Research, 2*, 163–179. doi:10.1007/BF00851321

Larrabee, G. L. (2005a). A scientific approach to forensic neuropsychology. In G. L. Larrabee (Ed.), *Forensic neuropsychology: A scientific approach* (pp. 3–28). New York, NY: Oxford University Press.

Larrabee, G. L. (2005b). Assessment of malingering. In G. L. Larrabee (Ed.), *Forensic neuropsychology: A scientific approach* (pp. 115–158). New York, NY: Oxford University Press.

Leitenberg, H., & Henning, K. (1995). Sexual fantasy. *Psychological Bulletin, 117*, 469–496. doi:10.1037/0033-2909.117.3.469

Lesniak, R., Szymusik, A., & Chrzanowski, R. (1972). Multidirectional disorders of sexual drive in a case of brain tumor. *Forensic Science, 1*, 333–338. doi:10.1016/0300-9432(72)90031-3

Lieverse, R., Assies, J., & Gooren, L. J. G. (2000). The psychoneuroendocrinology of (sexual) aggression. *Journal of Psychology & Human Sexuality, 11*, 19–36. doi:10.1300/J056v11n03_03

Lösel, F., & Schmucker, M. (2005). The effectiveness of treatment for sexual offenders: A comprehensive meta-analysis. *Journal of Experimental Criminology, 1*, 117–146. doi:10.1007/s11292-004-6466-7

Lussier, P., Proulx, J., & McKibben, A. (2001). Personality characteristics and adaptive strategies to cope with negative emotional states and deviant sexual fantasies in sexual aggressors. *International Journal of Offender Therapy and Comparative Criminology, 45*, 159–170. doi:10.1077/0306624X01452003

Maes, M., De Vos, N., Van Hunsel, F., Van West, D., Westenberg, H., Cosyns, P., & Neels, H. (2001). Pedophilia is accompanied by increased plasma concentrations of catecholamines, in particular epinephrine. *Psychiatry Research, 103*, 43–49. doi:10.1016/S0165-1781(01)00268-2

Maes, M., van West, D., De Vos, N., Westenberg, D., Van Hunsel, F., Hendriks, D., … Scharpé, S. (2001). Lower baseline plasma cortisol and prolactin together with increased body temperature and higher mCPP-induced cortisol responses in men with pedophilia. *Neuropsychopharmacology, 24*, 37–46. doi:10.1016/S0893-133X(00)00177-9

Marshall, W. L. (2014). Phallometric assessments of sexual interests: An update. *Current Psychiatry Reports, 16*, 428. doi:10.1007/s11920-013-0428-6

McGuire, R. J., Carlisle, J. M., & Young, B. G. (1965). Sexual deviations as conditioned behaviour: A hypothesis. *Behavioural Research and Therapy, 2*, 185–190. doi:10.1016/0005-7967(64)90014-2

Mendez, M. F., Chow, T., Ringman, J., Twitchell, G., & Hinkin, C. H. (2000). Pedophilia and temporal lobe disturbances. *Journal of Neuropsychiatry and Clinical Neuroscience, 12*, 71–76.

Mendez, M. F., & Shapira, J. S. (2011). Pedophilic behavior from brain disease. *Journal of Sexual Medicine, 8*, 1092–1100. doi:10.1111/j.1743-6109.2010.02172.x

Miller, B. L., Cummings, J. L., McIntyre, H., Ebers, G., & Grode, M. (1986). Hypersexuality or altered sexual preference following brain injury. *Journal of Neurology, Neurosurgery, and Psychiatry, 49*, 867–873. doi:10.1136/jnnp.49.8.867

Mokros, A. (in press). Sexual offending. In A. R. Beech, A. J. Carter, R. E. Mann, & P. Rotshtein (Eds.), *The Wiley-Blackwell handbook of forensic neuroscience*. Chichester, England: John Wiley & Sons, Ltd.

Mokros, A., Dombert, B., Osterheider, M., Zappalà, A., & Santtila, P. (2010). Assessment of pedophilic sexual interest with an attentional choice reaction time task. *Archives of Sexual Behavior, 39*, 1081–1090. doi:10.1007/s10508-009-9530-6

Moulier, V., Fonteille, V., Pélégrini-Issac, M., Cordier, B., Baron-Lafôret, S., Boriasse, E., … Stoléru, S. (2012). A pilot study of the effects of gonadotropin-releasing hormone agonist therapy on brain activation pattern in a man with pedophilia. *International Journal of Offender Therapy and Comparative Criminology, 56*, 50–60. doi:10.1177/0306624X10392191

Müller, D., Röder, F., & Orthner, H. (1973). Further results of stereotaxis in the human hypothalamus in sexual deviations: First use of this operation in addiction to drugs. *Neurochirurgia, 16*, 113–126.

Murray, J. (2001). Situational factors in sexual offending. In D. P. Farrington, C. R. Hollin, & M. McMurran (Eds.), *Sex and violence: The psychology of crime and risk assessment* (pp. 175–194). London, England: Routledge.

Ogas, O., & Gaddam, S. (2012). *A billion wicked thoughts: What the internet tells us about sexual relationships*. New York, NY: Plume.

Paul, R., Schiffer, B., Zwarg, T., Krüger, T. H. C., Karama, S., Schedlowski, M., … Gizewski, E. R. (2008). Brain response to visual sexual stimuli in heterosexual and homosexual males. *Human Brain Mapping, 29*, 726–735. doi:10.1002/hbm.20435

Pfäfflin, F. (2008). Sexualstraftaten [Sexual offences]. In K. Foerster & H. Dressing (Eds.), *Venzlaff/Foerster – Psychiatrische Begutachtung* (5th ed., pp. 330–360). Munich, Germany: Urban & Fischer.

Pfäfflin, F. (2010). Die chirurgische Kastration von in Freiheitsentzug befindlichen Sexualstraftätern kommt einer erniedrigenden Behandlung gleich [The surgical castration of detained sex offenders amounts to degrading treatment]. *Recht & Psychiatrie, 28,* 179–182.

Phenix, A., & Sreenivasan, S. (2009). A practical guide for the evaluation of sexual recidivism risk in mentally retarded sex offenders. *Journal of the American Academy of Psychiatry and Law, 37,* 509–524.

Poeppl, T. B., Langguth, B., Laird, A. R., & Eickhoff, S. B. (2014). The functional neuroanatomy of male psychosexual and physiosexual arousal: A quantitative meta-analysis. *Human Brain Mapping, 35,* 1404–1421. doi:10.1002/hbm.22262

Poeppl, T. B., Nitschke, J., Dombert, B., Santtila, P., Greenlee, M. W., Osterheider, M., & Mokros, A. (2011). Functional cortical and subcortical abnormalities in pedophilia: A combined study using a choice reaction time task and fMRI. *Journal of Sexual Medicine, 8,* 1660–1674. doi:10.1111/j.1743-6109.2011.02248.x

Poeppl, T. B., Nitschke, J., Santtila, P., Schecklmann, M., Langguth, B., Greenlee, M. W., … Mokros, A. (2013). Association between brain structure and phenotypic characteristics in pedophilia. *Journal of Psychiatric Research, 47,* 678–685. doi:10.1016/j.jpsychires.2013.01.003

Polisois-Keating, A., & Joyal, C. C. (2013). Functional neuroimaging of sexual arousal: A preliminary meta-analysis comparing pedophilic to non-pedophilic men. *Archives of Sexual Behavior, 42,* 1111–1113. doi:10.1007/s10508-013-0198-6

Ponseti, J., Granert, O., Jansen, O., Wolff, S., Beier, K., Neutze, J., … Bosinski, H. A. G. (2012). Assessment of pedophilia using hemodynamic brain response to sexual stimuli. *Archives of General Psychiatry, 69,* 187–194. doi:10.1001/archgenpsychiatry.2011.130

Prahlada Rao, N., Chand, P. K., & Murthy, P. (2007). A case of late-onset pedophilia and response to sertraline. *Primary Care Companion to the Journal of Clinical Psychiatry, 9,* 235–236.

Proulx, J., McKibben, A., & Lusignan, R. (1996). Relationships between affective components and sexual behaviors in sexual aggressors. *Sexual Abuse: A Journal of Research and Treatment, 8,* 279–289. doi:10.1177/107906329600800404

Rada, R. T., Laws, D. R., & Kellner, R. (1976). Plasma testosterone levels in the rapist. *Psychosomatic Medicine, 38,* 257–268.

Rainero, I., Rubino, E., Negro, E., Gallone, S., Galimberti, D., Gentile, S., … Pinessi, L. (2011). Heterosexual pedophilia in a frontotemporal dementia patient with a mutation in the progranulin gene. *Biological Psychiatry, 70,* e43–e44. doi:10.1016/j.biopsych.2011.06.015

Redouté, J., Stoléru, S., Grégoire, M.-C., Costes, N., Cinotti, L., Lavenne, F., … Pujol, J.-F. (2000). Brain processing of visual sexual stimuli in human males. *Human Brain Mapping, 11,* 162–177. doi:10.1002/1097-0193(200011)11:3<162::AID-HBM30>3.0.CO;2-A

Regestein, Q. R., & Reich, P. (1978). Pedophilia occurring after onset of cognitive impairment. *Journal of Nervous and Mental Disease, 166,* 794–798. doi:10.1097/00005053-197811000-00007

Rettenberger, M., Hill, A., Dekker, A., Berner, W., & Briken, P. (2013). Genital abnormalities in early childhood in sexual homicide perpetrators. *Journal of Sexual Medicine, 10,* 972–980. doi:10.1111/jsm.12051

Rice, M. E., & Harris, G. T. (2011). Is androgen deprivation therapy effective in the treatment of sex offenders? *Psychology, Public Policy, and Law, 17,* 315–332. doi:10.1037/a0022318

Rice, M. E., Harris, G. T., Lang, C., & Chaplin, T. C. (2008). Sexual preferences and recidivism of sex offenders with mental retardation. *Sexual Abuse: A Journal of Research and Treatment, 20,* 409–425. doi:10.1177/1079063208324662

Rosenbaum, A., & Hoge, S. K. (1989). Head injury and marital aggression. *American Journal of Psychiatry, 146,* 1048–1051.

Roye, A., Höfel, L., & Jacobsen, T. (2008). Aesthetics of faces: Behavioral and electrophysiological indices of evaluative and descriptive judgment processes. *Journal of Psychophysiology, 22,* 41–57. doi:10.1027/0269-8803.22.1.41

Sartorius, A., Ruf, M., Kief, C., Demirakca, T., Bailer, J., Ende, G., ... Dressing, H. (2008). Abnormal amygdala activation profile in pedophilia. *European Archive of Psychiatry and Clinical Neuroscience, 258,* 271–277. doi:10.1007/s00406-008-0782-2

Savic, I., & Lindström, P. (2008). PET and MRI show differences in cerebral asymmetry and functional connectivity between homo- and heterosexual subjects. *Proceedings of the National Academy of Sciences of the United States of America, 105,* 9403–9408. doi:10.1073/pnas.0801566105

Schiffer, B., Gizewski, E., & Krueger, T. H. C. (2009). Reduced neuronal responsiveness to visual sexual stimuli in a pedophile treated with a long-acting LH–RH agonist. *Journal of Sexual Medicine, 6,* 890–895. doi:10.1111/j.1743-6109.2008.01094.x

Schiffer, B., Krueger, T. H. C., Paul, T., de Greiff, A., Forsting, M., Leygraf, N., ... Gizewski E. (2008a). Brain response to visual sexual stimuli in homosexual pedophiles. *Journal of Psychiatry and Neuroscience, 33,* 23–33.

Schiffer, B., Paul, T., Gizewski, E., Forsting, M., Leygraf, N., Schedlowski, M., & Krueger, T. H. C. (2008b). Functional brain correlates of heterosexual paedophilia. *Neuroimage, 41,* 80–91. doi:10.1016/j.neuroimage.2008.02.008

Schiffer, B., Peschel, T., Paul, T., Gizewski, E., Forsting, M., Leygraf, N., ... Krueger, T. H. C. (2007). Structural brain abnormalities in the frontostriatal system and cerebellum in pedophilia. *Journal of Psychiatric Research, 41,* 753–762. doi:10.1016/j.jpsychires.2006.06.00

Schiffer, B., & Vonlaufen, C. (2011). Executive dysfunctions in pedophilic and nonpedophilic child molesters. *Journal of Sexual Medicine, 8,* 1975–1984. doi:10.1111/j.1743-6109.2010.02140.x

Schiltz, K., Witzel, J., Northoff, G., Zierhut, K., Gubka, U., Fellmann, H., ... Bogerts, B. (2007). Brain pathology in pedophilic offenders: Evidence of volume reduction in the right amygdala and related diencephalic structures. *Archives of General Psychiatry, 64,* 737–746. doi:10.1001/archpsyc.64.6.737

Schorsch, E. (1971). *Sexualstraftäter* [Sexual offenders]. Stuttgart, Germany: Enke.

Schorsch, E., & Schmidt, G. (1979). Hypothalamotomie bei sexuellen Abweichungen: Eine Kritik aus sexualwissenschaftlicher Sicht [Hypothalamotomy in sexual deviations: A critique from the point of view of sexology]. *Nervenarzt, 50,* 689–699.

Schupp, H. T., Junghöfer, M., Weike, A. I., & Hamm, A. O. (2003). Attention and emotion: An ERP analysis of facilitated emotional stimulus processing. *Neuroreport, 14,* 1107–1110. doi:10.1097/00001756-200306110-00002

Seto, M. C. (2008). *Pedophilia and sexual offending against children: Theory, assessment, and intervention.* Washington, DC: American Psychological Association. doi:10.1037/11639-000

Seto, M. C., Lalumière, M. L., Harris, G. T., & Chivers, M. L. (2012). The sexual responses of sexual sadists. *Journal of Abnormal Psychology, 121,* 739–753. doi:10.1037/a0028714

Shukla, G. D., Srivastava, O. N., & Katiyar, B. C. (1979). Sexual disturbances in temporal lobe epilepsy: A controlled study. *British Journal of Psychiatry, 134,* 288–292. doi:10.1192/bjp.134.3.288

Simpson, G. K., Sabaz, M., & Daher, M. (2013). Prevalence, clinical features, and correlates of inappropriate sexual behavior after traumatic brain injury: A multicenter study. *Journal of Head Trauma Rehabilitation, 28,* 202–210. doi:10.1097/HTR.0b013e31828dc5ae

Singer, B. (1984). Conceptualizing sexual arousal and attraction. *Journal of Sex Research, 20*, 230–240. doi:10.1080/00224498409551222

Stochholm, K., Bojesen, A., Skakkebæk Jensen, A., Juul, S., & Højbjerg Gravholt, C. (2012). Criminality in men with Klinefelter's syndrome and XYY syndrome: A cohort study. *British Medical Journal Open, 2*, e000650. doi:10.1136/bmjopen-2011-000650

Stoléru, S., Fonteille, V., Cornélis, C., Joyal, C., & Moulier, V. (2012). Functional neuroimaging studies of sexual arousal and orgasm in healthy men and women: A review and meta-analysis. *Neuroscience and Biobehavioral Reviews, 36*, 1481–1509. doi:10.1016/j.neubiorev.2012.03.006

Stoléru, S., Grégoire, M.-C., Gérard, D., Decety, J., Lafarge, E., Cinotti, L., ... Comar, D. (1999). Neuroanatomical correlates of visually evoked sexual arousal in human males. *Archives of Sexual Behavior, 28*, 1–21. doi:10.1023/A:1018733420467

Studer, L. H., & Aylwin, A. S. (2006). Elevated prolactin levels among adult male sex offenders. *Psychological Reports, 98*, 841–848. doi:10.2466/pr0.98.3.841-848

Studer, L. H., Aylwin, A. S., & Reddon, J. R. (2005). Testosterone, sexual offense recidivism, and treatment effect among adult male sex offenders. *Sexual Abuse: A Journal of Research and Treatment, 17*, 171–181. doi:10.1007/sl 1194-005-4603-0

Swaab, D. F. (2008). Sexual orientation and its basis in brain structure and function. *Proceedings of the National Academy of Sciences of the United States of America, 105*, 10273–10274. doi:10.1073/pnas.0805542105

Sylva, D., Safron, A., Rosenthal, A. M., Reber, P. J., Parrish, T. B., & Bailey, J. M. (2013). Neural correlates of sexual arousal in heterosexual and homosexual women and men. *Hormones and Behavior, 64*, 673–684. doi:10.1016/j.yhbeh.2013.08.003

Tost, H., Vollmert, C., Brassen, S., Schmitt, A., Dressing, H., & Braus, D. F. (2004). Pedophilia: Neuropsychological evidence encouraging a brain network perspective. *Medical Hypotheses, 63*, 528–531. doi:10.1016/j.mehy.2004.03.004

van Hooff, J. C., Crawford, H., & van Vugt, M. (2011). The wandering mind of men: ERP evidence for gender differences in attention bias towards attractive opposite sex faces. *Social Cognitive and Affective Neuroscience, 6*, 477–485. doi:10.1093/scan/nsq066

Viding, E., Larsson, H., & Jones, A. P. (2008). Quantitative genetic studies of antisocial behaviour. *Philosophical Transactions of the Royal Society B, 363*, 2519–2527. doi:10.1098/rstb.2008.0037

Viding, E., & McCrory, E. J. (2012). Genetic and neurocognitive contributions to the development of psychopathy. *Development and Psychopathology, 24*, 969–983. doi:10.1017/S095457941200048X

Waismann, R., Fenwick, P. B. C., Wilson, G. D., Hewett, T. D., & Lumsden, J. (2003). EEG responses to visual erotic stimuli in men with normal and paraphilic interests. *Archives of Sexual Behavior, 32*, 135–144. doi:10.1023/A:1022448308791

Waldman, I. D., & Rhee, S. H. (2006). Genetic and environmental influences on psychopathy and antisocial behavior. In C. J. Patrick (Ed.), *Handbook of psychopathy* (pp. 205–228). New York, NY: Guilford Press.

Walter, M., Bermpohl, F., Mouras, H., Schiltz, K., Tempelmann, C., Rotte, M., ... Northoff, G. (2008). Distinguishing specific sexual and general emotional effects in fMRI – Subcortical and cortical arousal during erotic picture viewing. *NeuroImage, 40*, 1482–1494. doi:10.1016/j.neuroimage.2008.01.040

Walter, M., Witzel, J., Wiebking, C., Gubka, U., Rotte, M., Schiltz, K., ... Northoff, G. (2007). Pedophilia is linked to reduced activation in hypothalamus and lateral prefrontal cortex during visual erotic stimulation. *Biological Psychiatry, 62*, 698–701. doi:10.1016/j.biopsych.2006.10.018

Wiebking, C., & Northoff, G. (2013). Neuroimaging in pedophilia. *Current Psychiatry Reports*, *15*, 351. doi:10.1007/s11920-013-0351-x

Wiebking, C., Witzel, J., Walter, M., Gubka, U., & Northoff, G. (2006). Vergleich der emotionalen und sexuellen Prozessierung zwischen Gesunden und Patienten mit einer Pädophilie – Eine kombinierte Studie aus Neuropsychologie und fMRT [Comparison of emotional and sexual processing between healthy individuals and patients with pedophilia – A combined study of neuropsychology and fMRT]. *Forensische Psychiatrie und Psychotherapie – Werkstattschriften*, *13*, 79–93.

Wille, R., & Beier, K. M. (1989). Castration in Germany. *Annals of Sex Research*, *2*, 103–133. doi:10.1007/BF00851318

Wille, R., & Beier, K. M. (1997). Nachuntersuchungen von kastrierten Sexualstraftätern. [Catamnestic examinations of castrated sexual offenders]. *Sexuologie*, *4*, 1–26.

Wright, P., Nobrega, J., Langevin, R., & Wortzman, J. (1990). Brain density and symmetry in pedophilic and sexually aggressive offenders. *Annals of Sex Research*, *3*, 319–328. doi:10.1007/BF00849186

36

Assessing Treatment Change in Sexual Offenders

Mark E. Olver

University of Saskatchewan, Canada

Stephen C. P. Wong

University of Saskatchewan, Canada; University of Nottingham, United Kingdom

Introduction

Best practice in sexual offender assessment and intervention emphasizes the accurate identification of high-risk sexual offenders and application of intervention and risk management strategies to prevent further sexual violence. The previous 15–20 years have witnessed substantial growth in research and evidence-informed practice about when to intervene clinically with sexual offenders to achieve such aims (e.g., Hanson & Morton-Bourgon, 2009).

The principles of effective correctional intervention, or the Risk–Need–Responsivity (RNR) model (Andrews & Bonta, 1994, 2010a), posits that treatment intensity should be matched to the individual's risk level (*risk principle*), that dynamic criminogenic (crime-causing) factors be prioritized for intervention (*need principle*), and, as per the *responsivity principle*, that services be tailored to the unique characteristics and personal circumstances of the offender (e.g., motivation, cognitive ability, culture) (*specific responsivity*) delivered according to a cognitive–behavioural model (*general responsivity*). Adherence to the RNR principles has demonstrated substantive reductions in recidivism in correctional programmes in general (Andrews & Bonta, 2010b) and a meta-analysis of sex offender treatment outcome by Hanson, Bourgon, Helmus, and Hodgson (2009) demonstrated successively larger reductions in post-treatment sexual violence as programmes adhered to a greater number of principles.

The Wiley Handbook on the Theories, Assessment, and Treatment of Sexual Offending.
Edited by Douglas P. Boer. Volume II: Assessment, edited by Leam A. Craig and Martin Rettenberger.
© 2017 John Wiley & Sons, Ltd. Published 2017 by John Wiley & Sons, Ltd.

Unfortunately, not every sex offender who attends sex offender treatment completes it, or necessarily completes it well. Although some men may make large strides and significant personal gains in treatment, many will be more sporadic or inconsistent in their progress, and still others may do little more than 'warm a seat' or coast through the programme and demonstrate little or no improvement. In a meta-analysis of offender treatment attrition, Olver, Stockdale, and Wormith (2011) observed a mean 27.6% non-completion rate from sexual offender treatment programmes, and for programme non-completers there was an approximate 15% increase in rates of sexual recidivism. Among the several predictors of non-completion identified in this study, those who failed to complete sex offender treatment had also demonstrated poorer therapeutic engagement and change.

The realities of patchy progress and attrition are endemic to correctional populations, underscoring the importance of examining within-treatment change and its possible links to risk reduction. As per the RNR model, the reduction of risk is presumed to be an important therapeutic mechanism at work in treatment that will translate into reductions in recidivism. This in turn is based on a further presumption that risk itself is dynamic and amenable to change (for better or for worse) with treatment or management. These notions are particularly salient for treatment programmes that have shared goals of reducing risk to manageable levels to promote safe community reintegration and reduced sexual victimization.

This chapter presents a review and examination of issues, research, and applications in the assessment of sexual offender treatment change. We begin with an overview of some important conceptual, methodological, and statistical considerations in the evaluation of treatment change. We then proceed to review international sex offender treatment change research employing (i) psychometric batteries and (ii) structured clinical evaluations of change, with a commentary provided on each approach. We conclude with a discussion regarding the applications of sex offender treatment change information and, more specifically, how this may be incorporated into risk appraisals.

Change Methodology: Conceptual and Statistical

We argue that there are several important conceptual and statistical issues in measuring, evaluating, and analysing the information obtained from offender change assessments. We discuss some of these issues in the following section as a prelude to reviewing research and applications of sex offender treatment change information.

Psychologically Meaningful Risk Factors

One important consideration is the assessment and identification of what Mann, Hanson, and Thornton (2010) termed 'psychologically meaningful risk factors'. Akin to criminogenic needs as defined by Andrews and Bonta (1994, 2010a), psychologically meaningful risk factors are those that could serve as a plausible cause of sexual offending and that reliably predict future sexual violence. Drawing on prior meta-analytic findings and contributions from new datasets, Mann et al. (2010, p. 199) identified psychologically meaningful risk factors 'supported' by evidence for these two sets of criteria to include sexual preoccupation, any deviant sexual interest, offence-supportive attitudes, emotional congruence with children, intimacy deficits, lifestyle impulsivity, poor problem solving, poor cooperation with rules/supervision, hostility, and negative social influences. 'Promising' risk factors (owing to the small number of existing studies) included hostility towards women specifically, psychopathic personality characteristics (e.g., Machiavellianism, callousness), and dysfunctional coping. Mann et al. (2010) further identified a set of dynamic factors that were largely unsupported, except for some 'interesting exceptions' (p. 205), to be denial, low self-esteem, major mental illness, and loneliness, while factors 'unrelated' to sexual recidivism included depression, social skills deficits, lack of victim empathy, and lack of motivation for treatment at intake. When it comes to the assessment of change from treatment, if such change is to have much relationship to desired outcomes such as recidivism reduction, then the changes arguably should occur on psychologically meaningful dimensions such those identified by Mann et al. (2010), which have been shown to covary with recidivism, as per the need principle, so that the changes have risk relevance. We discuss this in the light of supporting data in further detail below.

Credible Change Agents

A second issue involves the presence of a credible change agent, such as evidence-informed treatment (e.g., as per RNR and GLM), although arguably other agents such as intensive and structured supervision or ageing (over a longer term) can promote positive changes. The meta-analytic evidence has demonstrated cognitive–behavioural and biomedical treatment approaches to be associated with reductions in sexual recidivism (Löesel & Schmucker, 2005), and an increase in the number of RNR principles adhered to is associated with larger treatment effects (Hanson et al., 2009). As such, changes occurring over the course of a risk reduction sex offender programme, whose mandate and primary objective are to prevent new sexual violence, would arguably be more closely linked to reductions in recidivism than any changes documented from a less effective programme. Kraemer et al. (1997) asserted that when changes occur on a putatively dynamic variable following exposure to a change agent and such changes are then linked to changes in the outcome (e.g., reduced recidivism), then these dynamic variables become causal variables. As per Mann et al. (2010), just as psychologically meaningful risk factors serve as plausible causes of sexual violence (i.e., they are criminogenic), so too may changes in these variables be causally linked to reductions in recidivism.

Controls for Pretreatment Score and Risk

A third issue concerns risk. It has been very well established that high-risk sex offenders, as assessed by a structured risk assessment tool, are more likely to reoffend in almost all forms than lower risk offenders (Hanson & Morton-Bourgon, 2009); unfortunately, this continues to be the case even when high-risk offenders have completed treatment (Olver & Wong, 2011). High-risk offenders by definition would have a greater number and severity of dynamic risk factors and hence greater room to change at pretreatment than lower risk offenders; hence they would be better able to demonstrate positive changes than lower risk offenders, who are likely to remain low risk following treatment regardless of any changes they may make. In addition, individuals with lower pretreatment scores simply have little room to move, a 'floor effect' so to speak, whereas high-risk individuals who have higher pretreatment scores have considerably more room to change. In short, this situation necessitates some control for the initial pretreatment score and risk level on both clinical and statistical grounds.

Some Statistical Considerations

To assess changes in risk, obviously at least two time points are required and additional time points, if attainable, are ideal (Douglas & Skeem, 2005). There are a number of possibilities regarding what to do with the 'quantity in the middle'. In this section, we provide a brief and not exhaustive review of some statistical considerations in examining sex offender risk change and its relationship to outcome, including Cox regression survival analysis, use of standardized residual change scores, and applications of logistic regression.

Cox regression survival analysis is a survival analytic technique that examines failure rate (e.g., recidivism) over time and permits the examination of unique predictor criterion relationships (e.g., change to recidivism) while controlling for important covariates (e.g., pretreatment score). As variability in follow-up time tends to be a rule rather than an exception in recidivism research, and therefore individuals will have unequal temporal opportunities to reoffend, a particularly important advantage of this technique is that it adjusts and accounts for individual differences in follow-up time. Whereas employing fixed follow-ups (e.g., as in logistic regression) can by necessity result in an exclusion of cases with shorter follow-ups, Cox regression survival analysis permits the inclusion of all cases. In recidivism change research, discussed later, continuous change and pretreatment scores are entered as predictors, and their unique relationships to recidivism over time are examined. The technique, in turn, generates an exponentiated beta coefficient (e^B) or hazard ratio, representing the predicted change in the hazard of recidivism, for every one-point change in the predictor (e.g., change score). With multiple predictors, the interpretation and application of hazard ratios would be particularly complex as the values are intertwined (e.g., a one-point increase in change score while controlling for pretreatment risk level).

Standardized residual change scores have been employed to examine the unique relationship of a change predictor to outcome after partialling out pretreatment score variance. Beggs and Grace (2011) employed this technique by regressing the change score on the pretreatment score of a measure (e.g., a measure of hostility), obtaining the residuals (i.e., actual change score minus predicted change score), which were then standardized. The result is a standardized residual change score (RCZ), which is the change score after removing variance accounted for by pretreatment score (Beggs & Grace, 2011). When the RCZ is correlated with a criterion variable such as recidivism, this is a semi-partial correlation (i.e., correlation between a partialled predictor and unpartialled criterion). As will be discussed further, Begg and Grace (2011) found the use of RCZs generated in regression analyses to be an effective way to control for risk and improved the relationship of changes on the psychometric measures they examined to changes in sexual recidivism.

Logistic regression examines the relationship between one or more predictors and a dichotomous outcome variable, such as binary recidivism. As the criterion is measured in a static way without the added dimension of time, the technique does not control for individual differences in follow-up time. Although the information generated from Cox regression is valuable, worthwhile, and important for identifying the strength and direction of effects, applying the findings in a clinically practical manner with this technique is more difficult, as discussed above. Hanson, Helmus, and Thornton (2010), for instance, used logistic regression at fixed 5- and 10-year follow-up periods to estimate sexual recidivism base rates at all possible Static-2002 scores from the magnitude of the instrument's relationship to outcome (unstandardized B) and the observed sexual recidivism rates of the sample. The use of logistic regression has certain advantages. Recidivism rates can be poorly estimated for extreme scores with a small number of cases (e.g., a score of 13 on the Static-2002), and the use of logistic regression with fixed follow-up periods can smooth out the trend line of recidivism values at different scores while eliminating large fluctuations due to sampling variability (Hanson et al., 2010). Thornton (2011) applied logistic regression modelling to estimate recidivism rates while combining multiple (i.e., static and dynamic) risk measures. Using the Static-99R to provide a measure of static risk, Thornton (2011) found that the odds of sexual recidivism increased linearly with each increment in static and dynamic score, across a range of dynamic tools using unstandardized B-values and base rate information. The use of logistic regression to generate recidivism estimates at specific scores (or clusters of scores) arguably increases the utility and practicality of risk assessment information communicated for decision-making purposes while reducing bias. Conceivably, this methodology could be extended to predictor variables with inverse relationships to outcome, such as treatment change, to obtain recidivism estimates at different risk and change score thresholds. This logistic regression application would allow an estimation of the recidivism rates and amount of reduction of risk associated with different amounts of change, and examples of this application are provided later.

Operationalizing Treatment Change

We argue that the methods for conceptualizing, assessing, and communicating risk change information should be coherent, parsimonious, and clinically useful. In this section, we discuss some methods to operationalize sex offender treatment change for analysis (as discussed above) and risk communication; near the end of this chapter, we discuss methods for incorporating change information into risk appraisals.

One means is simply to re-rate the variables pre- and post-treatment (in the case of clinical rating scales) or similarly have the patient complete a self-report measure (e.g., a measure of cognitive distortions or hostility) at multiple time points. Over a large number of patients completing similar measures, an averaged change score can be computed and a measure of effect size (e.g., Cohen's d) can be computed to examine the amount of change in standard deviation units in which values of 0.20, 0.50, and 0.80 correspond to small, medium, and large effect sizes, respectively (Cohen, 1992).

This can be done across as many time points as are available, or alternatively, time points can also be collapsed to simplify analysis. On an individual patient-by-patient basis, arguably knowing how much an individual changed in standard deviation units with respect to their own cohort or some comparative norm would also be useful. In the aggregate it is also useful, as significant and or larger effect size magnitudes directly reflect whether or not patients on average tend to benefit from the programme, and thus also indicate to some extent a programme's treatment efficacy.

A second means involves the application of behaviour change models, such as the transtheoretical model of change, also known as the Stages of Change (SOC) model (Prochaska, DiClemente, & Norcross, 1992). Originally applied to changes in health-related behaviours (e.g., smoking cessation, weight loss, exercise), the SOC posits that individuals undergo a series of cognitive, behavioural, and experiential changes in a stage-like manner as they remediate problem areas. The SOC model, in turn, involves a dynamic continuum, in which the person can progress or regress along five stages. The following is an illustration of one adaptation of the SOC model to offender populations by Wong and colleagues (Wong & Gordon, 1999–2003; Wong, Olver, Nicholaichuk, & Gordon, 2003–2009): Precontemplation (absence of insight or unwillingness to change the problem behaviour), Contemplation (awareness of problem behaviour, but no use of cognitive or behavioural skills or strategies to manage it), Preparation (use of skills and strategies, although the changes are either very recent and/or lapses are frequent), Action (sustained cognitive and behavioural change in the problem areas of interest), and Maintenance (sustained changes that have generalized to a variety contexts). Clinical applications of the SOC model have been extended to diverse offender populations, including violent offenders (Lewis, Olver, & Wong, 2013), adolescent offenders (Hemphill & Howell, 2000), domestically violent offenders (Levesque, Gelles, & Velicer, 2000), and sexual offenders (Tierny & McCabe, 2005; Olver, Wong, Nicholaichuk, & Gordon, 2007). Later, we discuss quantitative applications of the SOC model to conceptualizing sex offender treatment change, which can also be evaluated in standard deviation units (e.g., for the computation of an effect size) and also linked to outcome, or applied in terms of other models such as the reliable change index described next.

A third method discussed here involves the computation of a reliable change index (RCI) (Jacobson & Truax, 1991) to evaluate clinically significant change. The RCI is computed to generate cut-offs for clinically significant change based on the amount of pre–post change occurring as a function of the test retest reliability of the psychometric measure, the standard deviation of the pretreatment score, and a statistical adjustment for measurement error (see Wise, 2004). RCI values of ±1.64 or ±1.96 generated from this formula have been used as criteria for reliable change (depending on the study). Studies that have used the RCI, in turn, classify the men at posttreatment based on the magnitude of their scores and the amount of change they have made. Individuals who score in the pathological direction above a healthy normative cut-off are designated 'dysfunctional' in a given domain, whereas those scoring within the healthy normative range are considered 'functional'. Using the RCI language, five categories can be created: (i) men who are dysfunctional at pretreatment and who made reliable change for the worse post-treatment are considered to have 'deteriorated'; (ii) those who do not demonstrate reliable change in either direction are considered 'unchanged'; (iii) those who demonstrate reliable change in the positive direction but still score above a healthy normative cut-off (i.e., are still high risk) are 'improved'; (iv) those who demonstrate reliable change in the positive direction and score within the normative cut-off are considered 'recovered'; and (v) those who score in a non-pathological manner at pretreatment and continue to do so post-treatment are considered 'already okay' (i.e., they are low risk to begin with, and remain so at post-treatment).

There are merits and potential issues to applying this model to therapeutic change with sexual offenders. One issue is that of language. For instance, 'recovered' implies a restoration of normal or healthy functioning, which in turn implies that an individual was functioning well psychologically in these domains prior to becoming a sexual offender. The personal histories of these men are often marked by pain, abuse, dysfunctional upbringing, and inadequate functioning in the community. For many of these men, new skills, capacities, strengths, supports and resources are being nurtured and developed for the very first time; arguably, healthy functioning is being created rather than being restored to a normal level of premorbid well-being. Second, there is an inherent hierarchy of risk embedded within these schemes; thus, the categories confound risk level and treatment change as described above. Those who are 'already okay' are arguably low-risk offenders to start with, whereas those who are 'recovered' are those who manifested substantive treatment changes with a healthy score post-treatment; however, in order to be recovered, one cannot score too high at pretreatment. Conceivably, two individuals can both manifest reliable and clinically significant change; only one person achieves the healthy normative cut-off whereas the other does not. One gets to be 'recovered' whereas the latter individual is relegated to being 'improved'. The extent to which an individual can advance to one change category or another is determined in part by their pretreatment score. Individuals who are 'improved' are those who have high scores before and after treatment but who still made significant changes. Arguably, an analysis of the relationship of these categories to recidivism outcome would be strengthened through controlling for pretreatment score or some other proxy measure of risk.

We suspect that individuals who make substantive changes, regardless of the model or method invoked, may continue on a trajectory of positive change, a momentum so to speak that continues beyond the treatment programme and into the community as the individual engages supports, may complete additional programming, or follow a community safety plan to continue the trajectory of risk reduction. These caveats about applications of the RCI scheme aside, a strength of the model is the emphasis placed on attaining healthy psychological functioning. While the primary objective of sex offender treatment is ultimately to prevent new acts of sexual violence, assisting men in the restoration or initial achievement of healthy functioning in important psychological domains is a worthwhile and laudable goal, and arguably one that can have risk-related implications.

Self-Report Versus Service Provider Ratings of Change

A further consideration is whether to use client self-report and/or service provider ratings of treatment change for the basis of evaluating treatment progress, risk reduction, and incorporation into post-treatment risk appraisals. We discuss this in further detail in the next section based on extant research findings examining change as evaluated from these two sources and the extent to which such changes are linked to decreases in risk and post-treatment recidivism. We advise against simply relying on self-report indicators of change, owing to the obvious concerns of impression management and response set biases that can occur, particularly within forensic evaluation contexts. It is also debatable to what extent clients can be objective evaluators of their own change, and to what extent such personal evaluations are risk relevant (i.e., entail change on psychologically meaningful risk factors). We suggest that both sources of information are important and should be cross-checked and corroborated as much as possible.

Assessing Sex Offender Treatment Change with Psychometric Batteries

A growing body of research has used psychometric batteries, often administered in the course of routine clinical services, to assess treatment-relevant domains for sex offenders and then examined these changes over the course of sex offender treatment and possibly to post-release outcome. A very wide range of psychological constructs have been examined in this capacity, some of which fall under the rubric of a psychologically meaningful risk factor, and others which either do not or perhaps are more ambiguous. Significant pre–post changes have been observed on psychometric measures of sex offender attitudes and cognitive distortions, anger/hostility, interpersonal aggression, loneliness, intimacy deficits, deviant sexual interests, denial/minimization, motivation, anxiety, social anxiety, depressive symptoms, self-esteem, locus of control, and empathy (see Beggs & Grace, 2011; Brown, Harkins, & Beech, 2012; Jung & Guyalets, 2011; Kingston, Yates, & Olver, 2014; Mandeville-Norden, Beech, & Hayes 2008; Marshall, Champagne, Sturgeon, & Bryce, 1997; Nunes, Babchishin, & Cortoni, 2011; Olver, Kingston, Nicholaichuk, & Wong, 2014b; Olver, Nicholaichuk, & Wong, 2014a; Terry & Mitchell, 2001; Wakeling, Beech, & Freemantle, 2013; Williams, Wakeling, & Webster, 2007). Fewer studies have examined the predictive accuracy of these psychometric measures in general or the relationship of such changes to possible reductions in recidivism. These are important questions concerning the risk relevance of these tools and the constructs that they measure. Selected studies examining psychometric treatment change from international sex offender programmes are reviewed in the following.

Findings from New Zealand's Kia Marama Programme

A body of research from the Kia Marama Programme, a child molester treatment programme operated by New Zealand Department of Corrections, examining risk and treatment change from their psychometric battery, has also yielded informative results. An early study by Hudson, Wales, Bakker, and Ward (2002) on a sample of 218 treated child molesters found that most of these measures and their respective change scores did not significantly predict sexual recidivism (and some were in the opposite direction to that expected), although positive changes in empathy, trait anger, and assertiveness did. Allan, Grace, Rutherford, and Hudson (2007) subsequently conducted an exploratory factor analysis of this battery on a sample of 495 child molesters, generating four factors labelled Social Inadequacy, Sexual Interests, Anger/Hostility, and Pro-Offending Attitudes, which were consistent with Thornton's (2002, 2011) Structured Risk Assessment (SRA) model of primary sex offender risk–need domains. These four psychometric factors also each significantly predicted sexual recidivism to varying extents.

In an extended 12-year follow-up of this sample on the 218 men from Hudson et al.'s (2002) study, Beggs and Grace (2011) reanalysed change scores on these measures and the relationship of these treatment changes to recidivism outcome. Moderate to large treatment gains were noted pre- and post-treatment across most measures (significant d values ranged from 0.25 to 0.89). Standardized residual change scores were created by partialling out pretreatment scores in their respective domains as mentioned above. Prior to partialling, the change score relations to outcome were not substantively different from those of Hudson et al. (2002); however, after partialling out pretreatment scores, the change scores for all individual measures were in the expected direction in their relationship to outcome, and several of the associations were now significant. Moreover, changes in the domains of Sexual Interests, Anger/Hostility, Social Inadequacy, and a composite change index averaged across all the factors were significantly associated with reductions in sexual recidivism ($r = -0.19$ to -0.25), even after controlling for actuarial risk (Static-99 score). Interestingly, however, changes in Pro-Offending Attitudes were not significantly associated with reductions in sexual recidivism.

Sex Offender Programmes in the Correctional Service of Canada

A further body of work on psychometric treatment change has its origins in the National Sex Offender Program (NaSOP), operated by the Correctional Service of Canada (CSC), a federal correctional department which has jurisdiction over offenders serving sentences in excess of 2 years. The NaSOP is based on the RNR principles and has included three levels of treatment programme intensity corresponding to low (2–3 months), medium (4–5 months), and high (7–8 months) (CSC, 2009). A battery of well-known psychometric measures was introduced with the implementation of this programme in the early 2000s and a body of research has emerged examining treatment change with these tools. Nunes et al. (2011), in a sample of treated sex offenders ($ns = 198–262$) from the low- and moderate-intensity streams of the NaSOP examined treatment changes on psychometric measures of cognitive distortions (Rape and Molest Scales; Bumby, 1996), loneliness (Revised UCLA Loneliness Scale; Russell, Peplau, & Cutrona, 1980), and intimacy (Miller Social Intimacy Scale; Miller & Lefcourt, 1982). Significant positive pre–post changes were found in cognitive distortions and loneliness ranging from moderate to large in magnitude ($d = -0.41$ to -0.75), although no significant differences were found on measures of intimacy.

Some parallel findings were obtained by Olver et al. (2014b) (see also Kingston et al., 2014), who prospectively examined pre–post changes on the NaSOP battery in a sample of 392 sex offenders from all three intensity streams and examined their relation to recidivism outcomes over approximately 5.4 years of follow-up. The sample demonstrated similar magnitudes of change as in Nunes et al. (2011) on the same measures of cognitive distortions, loneliness, and intimacy, but also demonstrated significant pre–post differences (approximately half a standard deviation in magnitude) on child and rapist measures of empathy (Fernandez & Marshall, 2003; Fernandez, Marshall, Lightbody, & O'Sullivan, 1999), hostility (Buss & Perry, 1992), and a multidimensional measure of sex offender acceptance of responsibility (Peacock, 2000). The measures evidenced weak predictive accuracy for sexual, violent, and general recidivism, however, and changes tended not to be significantly associated with any of the recidivism outcomes. A noteworthy example, however, was measures of hostility, verbal and physical aggression, and anger from the Buss–Perry Aggression Questionnaire, on which treatment changes significantly predicted reductions in each of the recidivism outcomes to varying extents.

Additional CSC-based research examining change on psychometric batteries has included the Clearwater Sex Offender Program, a sex offender treatment programme operated by CSC located within a designated mental health facility, the Regional Psychiatric Centre, in Saskatoon, Saskatchewan, Canada. Established in the early 1980s, the Clearwater Program has historically been geared towards high-risk clientele, has followed a CBT model, and incorporated principles of evidence-informed treatment (e.g., RNR) with advances in the field over the years (Olver & Wong, 2013). Olver et al. (2014a) examined pre–post-treatment changes on a psychometric battery administered to a sample of 257 Clearwater Program participants who completed the instruments as part of routine clinical services. The men, in turn, were followed up for 18 years prospectively in the community. Significant pre–post changes that were moderate to large in magnitude (exceeding $d = 0.50$) were found in important domains of psychological functioning that included social self-esteem, hostility towards women, global hostility, rape myth acceptance, locus of control, social anxiety, and depressive symptoms. On average, the men also tended to score below the healthy psychological mean on many of these measures (e.g., social self-esteem) despite such changes. A factor analysis of the battery generated three factors consistent with the SRA domains which predicted sexual and violent recidivism to varying extents. As with Beggs and Grace (2011), standardized residual change scores were computed to examine the relationship of treatment changes to reductions in recidivism after controlling for the Static-99. Changes on an anger/hostility domain were significantly associated with reductions in violence, and standardized residual change scores on an overall need index predicted reductions in both general and sexual violence.

Prison- and Probation-Based Sex Offender Programmes in the United Kingdom

A final grouping of studies reviewed that examine psychometric assessments of change on treated sex offenders comes from work in the United Kingdom. Much of this work has featured applications of the RCI, as discussed above. This body of sex offender treatment change work has extended to community and institutional programmes for sex offenders. Mandeville-Norden et al. (2008) examined treatment change in a sample of 341 child molester probationers who had attended sex offender services in sites across England and Wales. The men completed a psychometric battery of eight measures that included measures of distortions, emotional congruence with children, victim empathy, self-esteem, loneliness, assertiveness, locus of control, and personal distress (from the Interpersonal Reactivity Index measure of empathy). At post-treatment, between 50 and 75% of the sample scored in the normative range on the measures. The men were grouped according to low, medium, and high need overall on the measures, and from our review of the data, it seemed that greater shifts in clinically significant change occurred as the need level of the offender increased. Specifically, 50–80% of high-need offenders demonstrated significant clinical change on six of the eight measures; the proportion of low-need offenders did not exceed 26% in achieving this level of change on any of the measures, and the proportion of medium-need offenders achieved this level of change for one measure.

Barnett, Wakeling, Mandeville-Norden, and Rakestrow (2013), in turn, examined psychometric treatment change and its relationship to violent recidivism in a large sample of 3402 convicted sexual offenders in the United Kingdom who had also attended probation-based sex offender treatment in the community in different sites across England and Wales. A battery of psychometric measures as described in Mandeville-Norden et al. (2008) was administered to the men pre- and post-treatment by site staff. RCI was computed for each of the measures to identify men who from the point of baseline had deteriorated, were unchanged, were improved, or had recovered based on their functioning at pretreatment. There was considerable variability in the change trajectories across each of the measures; few men actually deteriorated (most typically < 10%), roughly one-third were unchanged depending on the measure, and more than half of the men were judged as improved or even recovered in the domain assessed for seven out of nine measures. The most substantive changes were observed for measures of self-esteem, victim empathy, cognitive distortions, emotional congruence with children, and loneliness; however, these observed changes were not associated with reductions in violent (including sexual) recidivism.

In the context of institutionally based sex offender programmes, Williams et al. (2007) examined treatment change on a psychometric battery in a sample of 211 sex offenders with cognitive and social impairments who attended Her Majesty's Prison Service's Adapted Sex Offender Treatment Programme. Significant pre–post treatment changes were found on five out of six measures, with effect size magnitudes for significant effects ranging from $d = 0.29$ to 1.34 on measures of denial/minimization, pro-offence attitudes, victim empathy, relapse prevention knowledge, and self-esteem (no such changes were found on loneliness).

A subsequent large-scale investigation by Wakeling et al. (2013) examined the relationship of treatment change using the RCI classification system to recidivism in a large UK sample of 3773 treated sex offenders from 38 prisons across England and Wales. The men had attended the Core Programme (for moderate-risk sex offenders) or the Rolling Programme (for lower risk sex offenders). Compared with the community samples described above, a larger battery of measures had been administered to this sample, which included selected scales assessing sexual deviance from the Multiphasic Sex Inventory, attitudes of sexual entitlement, child molester distortions, hostility towards women, impulsivity, angry rumination, intimacy, and also locus of control, loneliness, empathy, and self-esteem. Again, very few men were judged as having deteriorated, while most (approximately half to two-thirds) were unchanged on most of the measures, and the remainder were evaluated as improved, recovered, or already okay.

Interestingly, on the individual measures, the men who were judged as already okay at pretreatment (and hence did not need to change, and by definition would seem to be low risk) on most of the measures had the lowest recidivism rates, whereas those who improved (i.e., made substantive changes but still had high scores at post-treatment) actually had the highest recidivism rates among the groups; in this regard, the results did not seem substantively different from those of Barnett et al. (2013). When the battery was broken down according to the SRA/SARN domains, men who were judged as still requiring change in the domains of Sexual Interests, Socio-affective Problems, and Self-Regulation Problems had significantly higher rates of violent reconviction than men judged as not requiring change in those areas. It is important to note, however, that the men judged as not requiring change were only those who had recovered or were already okay at post-treatment on half or more of the psychometric tests subsumed under a given domain. Given that the change scores were not analysed directly, it remains unclear if larger amounts of change were associated with reductions in recidivism. For instance, it is not clear if the 'recovered' group actually made more change than the 'improved' group or if they simply had lower and more normal post-treatment scores owing in part to also having had lower pretreatment scores to begin with. Importantly, Wakeling et al. (2013) conducted a Cox regression comparing overall change categories (changed versus unchanged) while controlling for Risk Matrix 2000 score and found that the change category trended towards significance ($p = 0.07$).

Comments and Conclusions on the Psychometric Assessment of Sex Offender Treatment Change

Several comments and conclusions can be drawn from this review and discussion of the sex offender psychometric treatment change literature. First, it seems apparent that many of the constructs assessed from the psychometric batteries in treatment programmes are not psychologically meaningful risk factors (e.g., locus of control, empathy, depression, anxiety, self-esteem). They often do not predict sexual violence (or other forms of recidivism) particularly well and changes are frequently not linked to reductions in recidivism. This does not necessarily make such variables poor candidates for treatment, although it may be debatable about whether they should be prioritized in sex offender-specific services. The changes, in turn, may signal improved psychological health (e.g., decreased anxiety, improved self-esteem) but have little impact on risk reduction. That is, such changes may have limited risk relevance, even if they do purport to measure a construct that in principle has been meaningfully linked to the causation and maintenance of sexual violence (e.g., sex offender attitudes).

Moreover, it is possible that self-report may not be the best way to measure the construct of interest, especially in a correctional treatment setting. There are two issues related to this. First, a recent meta-analysis by Helmus, Hanson, Babchishin, and Mann (2013) found offence-supportive attitudes in sex offenders to be a robust and significant predictor of sexual recidivism ($d = 0.22$) across 46 samples. Helmus et al. (2013) also found that professional ratings of sex offender attitudes (e.g., from purpose-built dynamic risk instruments) had a stronger relationship to sexual recidivism than self-report measures (at $p = 0.056$). At least in the case of sex offenders, it is possible that assessments of sex offender attitudes/cognitions may have greater criminogenic relevance when assessed by a trained clinician with an eye towards appraising risk, and this may extend to other psychological constructs. A second issue concerning the use of self-reports is understandable demand characteristics or impression management biases that offenders may demonstrate, especially when being evaluated post-treatment and/or in the context of a review for conditional release or security reclassification. The issue of whether to correct for social desirability in forensic assessment research and clinical practice is contentious (Tan & Grace, 2008). Controlling for social desirability does not necessarily improve the predictive accuracy of risk assessment (Mills & Kroner, 2006), and navigating impression management biases and verifying the accuracy of information are endemic to forensic practice.

Finally, sex offenders may still have problems in the area despite making changes and, in many studies, treated sex offenders have continued to fall well below the norm on self-esteem and above the norm on loneliness, intimacy concerns, and anxiety and depressive symptoms (Olver et al., 2014a). Although the risk relevance of some changes may be debatable, the psychological health of such issues or non-criminogenic needs is less contentious, and arguably increasing psychological health and life satisfaction are important aims of sex offender treatment, management, and reintegration (Ward, Mann, & Gannon, 2007).

Assessing Sex Offender Treatment Change with Dynamic Clinical Rating Scales

An additional line of research has examined treatment changes on sex offender risk assessment measures that contain dynamic items and, in turn, linked these changes to outcome. These are structured clinical evaluations of risk-related change that are administered by service providers instead of the clients themselves. In principle, most of the items should be psychologically meaningful risk factors targeted for treatment and with the potential to change.

Brief Review of Structured Dynamic Risk Change Measures

This section provides an overview of dynamic tools intended to capture change in offenders. As a comprehensive review of all dynamic sex offender measures is beyond the scope of this chapter, this review is intentionally brief and is limited to the following four measures that have been empirically evaluated in sex offender risk-related treatment change research: the Violence Risk Scale – Sexual Offender version (VRS-SO) (Wong et al., 2003–2009), the Stable and Acute 2000 (Hanson & Harris, 2001) and 2007 (Hanson, Harris, Scott, & Helmus, 2007), the Sex Offender Treatment Intervention and Progress Scale (SOTIPS) (McGrath, Lasher, & Cumming, 2011), and the

Treatment Readiness, Responsivity, and Gain Scale: Short Version (TRRG:SV) (Serin, Kennedy, & Mailloux, 2005).

The VRS-SO is one instrument developed specifically to link assessment and treatment and to evaluate changes in risk. It is a clinician-rated dynamic actuarial tool designed to provide pre- and post-treatment estimates of risk, comprising seven static and 17 dynamic risk variables rated on a 0–3-point scale. A structured assessment of change is made on each of the dynamic variables through a modified application of Prochaska et al.'s (1992) Stages of Change (SOC) model operationalized for each dynamic item. SOC ratings are given only for criminogenic items (i.e., score of 2 or 3) at pre- and post-treatment; 0.5 points are then deducted for each stage of improvement, while points can be added for deterioration (with the exception of progress from Precontemplation to Contemplation, in which no behavioural change, and hence risk reduction, is evident). The change ratings for each item are then summed to generate a dynamic change score, which is subtracted from the pretreatment risk rating to arrive at a post-treatment estimate of risk. In addition to providing a quantitative measure of change and, hence, risk reduction, the VRS-SO change mechanism is based on a theoretical model in which offenders progress through cognitive, behavioural, and experiential changes as they address their treatment targets. Change is on a continuum and offenders can progress for the better (advance a stage) or deteriorate for the worse (slide back a stage). A factor analysis of the VRS-SO dynamic items generated three oblique factors labelled Sexual Deviance, Criminality, and Treatment Responsivity (Olver et al., 2007).

The Stable and Acute 2000 and 2007 are dynamic risk tools designed to identify targets for intervention and to assess changes in risk. The tools were developed and normed on large samples of sex offender probationers. The Stable contains stable dynamic risk variables, that is, psychologically meaningful risk factors that are otherwise stable but have the capacity to change gradually, such as sexual preoccupation, emotional congruence with children, and poor problem solving. The Stable-2000 had 16 items whereas the most recent 2007 iteration has 13 items, each of which is rated on a 0–2-point scale. The Acute assesses fleeting, highly transient variables that may fluctuate over the course of hours or days (e.g., anger, victim access, negative affect). The Acute-2007 includes seven items organized into two domains: Approach (Victim access, Sexual preoccupation, Rejection of supervision, Hostility) and Collapse (Emotional collapse, Substance abuse, Collapse of supports) rated on a 0–3-point scale.

The SOTIPS is a 16-item clinician-administered dynamic sex offender risk assessment and treatment planning tool. Each item is scored on a 0–3-point scale in which item ratings correspond to 'minimal to no need for improvement', 'some need for improvement', 'considerable need for improvement', and 'very considerable need for improvement.' A factor analysis (McGrath, Lasher, & Cumming, 2012) of the items generated three factors labelled Sexual Deviance, Criminality, and Social Stability and Supports. Total scores range from 0 to 48 and are organized into categories of low (0–10), moderate (11–20), and high (21–48). Change is evaluated through re-rating the items at subsequent administrations and recomputing the total score.

Finally, the TRRG:SV is a clinical rating scale designed to assess an offender's readiness for correctional treatment, responsiveness to treatment, and gains made over the course of treatment. These three domains are each arranged into eight items rated on a 0–3-point scale. The Treatment Readiness and Treatment Responsivity items are rated at pre- and post-treatment and change scores on each item can range from −3 to +3; the change scores for each item are then summed across the two domains. The Gain scale is rated at post-treatment to document the offender's level of performance with their correctional programme.

Retrospective Investigations

A series of retrospective investigations have been conducted to examine sex offender risk-related treatment change and the relationship of such changes to outcome. In this paradigm, dynamic measures, as outlined above, are rated at multiple time points, most typically pre- and post-treatment, from comprehensive treatment file information on offenders who had previously attended the treatment programme from years earlier and were subsequently released into the community. The ratings are made blind to outcome and then criminal records are updated to track post-programme recidivism in the community following their earlier release. These investigations have important strengths and limitations. The most important shortcoming is that the quality of ratings is highly dependent on the level of detail available in the clinical files; unless the files are highly detailed the ratings can be compromised. On the other hand, there is a consistent body of information available for each individual assessed, and well-trained raters coding comprehensive files can generate high-quality data. The outcome data, in turn, can be immediately accessed, negating the long waits that may be involved in prospective designs.

Several archival evaluations have been conducted on the VRS-SO to examine the relationship of treatment changes to reductions in recidivism. Olver et al. (2007) examined VRS-SO on a sample of 321 Clearwater Program participants, who were rated from detailed file information on the tool pre- and post-treatment and followed up in the community for an average of 10 years post-release, 24.6% of whom were convicted for a new sexual offence. The Clearwater participants made significant pre–post changes overall, corresponding to roughly one-third of a standard deviation ($d = 0.34$). Using Cox regression survival analysis to control statistically for pretreatment risk (VRS-SO static and pretreatment total scores), VRS-SO change scores were significantly linked to reductions in sexual recidivism. With an observed hazard ratio of $e^B = 0.90$ for VRS-SO change score, this would be interpreted to be an approximate 10% predicted reduction in sexual recidivism for each one-point increase in change, after accounting for risk. Positive change scores were also significantly related to reductions in sexual recidivism among high-risk sexual offenders ($r = -0.15$) but not among low-risk sexual offenders ($r = 0.01$). Follow-up analyses performed by Olver and Wong (2011) on this sample found that actuarially high-risk sex offenders from the Clearwater Program (as assessed by Hanson & Thornton's [1999] Static-99) who scored above the mean change rating had significantly lower rates of sexual recidivism (27%) than actuarially high-risk sex offenders who scored below the mean change rating (43%); all this despite the two high-risk groups having nearly identical Static-99 scores. These results suggested that the men's levels of risk had changed, possibly owing to treatment; the changes were captured by a dynamic risk assessment tool but not reflected in a static tool.

Beggs and Grace (2011) extended the findings of Olver et al. (2007) using archival VRS-SO ratings from New Zealand's Kia Marama Programme for child molesters. The men were followed up for 12 years post-release, of whom 13.3% were convicted for a new sexual offence. Positive treatment changes were significantly associated with reductions in sexual recidivism ($r = -0.23$) and the changes also maintained significance after controlling for actuarial risk through Cox regression survival analyses; particularly strong relationships to recidivism reduction were observed for changes in the total dynamic score and on the Sexual Deviance factor. In an Australian study of 93 incest offenders who attended a residential treatment programme, Goodman-Delahunty and O'Brien (2012, 2014) examined archival ratings of the VRS-SO completed from treatment files and the performance of the tool in predicting outcome. Although the VRS-SO predicted violent and general (but not sexual) recidivism, change scores were not significantly associated with reductions in recidivism. Few details were provided regarding the nature and magnitude of the relationship of change to outcome, although it is possible that the base rates, which were low (e.g., 4.4% sexual recidivism) in comparison with previous VRS-SO studies, may have attenuated predictive accuracy.

Most recently, in an archival study on treated Clearwater patients, Sowden (2013) examined the relationship of risk, treatment readiness, and therapeutic change to recidivism in a sample of 180 men. This was a later cohort (1998–2001) of men subsequent to the Olver et al. (2007) sample, who in turn were followed up for an average of 10 years post-release, of whom 20% were convicted for a new sexual offence. Several risk and treatment change instruments were rated, including the VRS-SO, Stable-2007, and TRRG:SV. As in previous VRS-SO change investigations, Sowden (2013) found that significant pre–post changes were observed on the VRS-SO overall ($d = 0.74$); significant pre–post treatment changes approaching large in magnitude of effect size were also found for the Stable-2007 ($d = 0.77$) and TRRG:SV ($d = 0.84–0.93$). Computing semi-partial correlations, VRS-SO change scores (dynamic total) were significantly associated with reductions in violent ($r = -0.19$) but not sexual ($r = -0.12$) recidivism, whereas change scores on the TRRG:SV were associated with reductions in both outcomes ($r = -0.19$ to -0.21 and -0.15 to -0.16, respectively), and changes on the Stable-2007 were not significantly associated with any recidivism outcomes. In follow-up Cox regression survival analyses, VRS-SO change scores were significantly associated with decreases in any violence ($e^B = 0.90$) after controlling for pretreatment risk and Stable-2007 change scores trended towards significance ($e^B = 0.93$) in the prediction of this outcome after the imposition of similar controls. Change scores on the TRRG: SV were significantly associated with reductions in sexual and violent recidivism ($e^B = 0.90$ to 0.91) in the Cox regression survival analyses after controlling for the Static-99R and VRS-SO pretreatment score.

Prospective Evaluations

Fewer investigations of risk-related change in treated sex offenders have involved prospective examinations, that is, when the measure (and changes made therein) is rated in real time by service providers, and then the client is followed up in real time in the community. Prospective evaluations, as they involve real-world clinical ratings on the tool, add an important measure of ecological validity and entail examining a tool in terms of how it is actually used in service delivery contexts (e.g., sex offender treatment, community supervision). Three lines of prospective change evaluation research, examining the relationship of change to outcome, are discussed, featuring institutionally treated samples (VRS-SO), sex offender probationers on community supervision (Stable and Acute), and sex offenders attending community-based treatment services (SOTIPS).

The first line of prospective research involved federally incarcerated sex offenders who attended either hospital- or prison-based sex offender treatment through CSC's NaSOP, as mentioned above. In this body of work, Olver, Nicholaichuk, Kingston, and Wong (2014) conducted a large-scale prospective multisite evaluation of the VRS-SO across the five geographic regions of CSC. VRS-SO ratings were completed by service providers (e.g., psychiatric nurses, psychologists, programme officers) on sex offenders treated in the NaSOP programmes as part of routine service delivery. The Static-99 had also been rated as part of routine service delivery, and the Static-99R was computed from the available information. Clinical pre–post VRS-SO ratings were extracted for 572 men who were followed up for 6.3 years post-release into the community. The base rates were 5.1% for sexual recidivism, 14% for violent (including sexual) recidivism, and 33% for general (any) recidivism.

On average, the men demonstrated significant pre–post changes that ranged from small to moderate in magnitude (median $d = 0.43$), with larger changes associated with increases in programme intensity, consistent with the risk and need principles. VRS-SO change scores on the dynamic total and its three domains (Sexual Deviance, Criminality, Treatment Responsivity) were significantly associated with reductions in sexual, violent, and general recidivism after controlling for pretreatment score (significant semi-partial $rs = -0.09$ to -0.15). In Cox regression survival analyses, change ratings on the VRS-SO were associated with reductions in the recidivism outcomes to varying extents after controlling for pretreatment risk and Static-99R score: specifically, changes on Criminality were associated with reductions in sexual violence, changes on Sexual Deviance were associated with reductions in general violence, and changes on the total score and the Sexual Deviance and Treatment Responsivity factors were associated with reductions in general recidivism. Finally, the men were also found to shift in their stages of change on criminogenic variables; approximately 85% of the need areas were identified as being in the very early stages of change at pretreatment (Precontemplation or Contemplation), whereas more than two-thirds (71%) were identified as having progressed to the Preparation or Action stages at post-treatment.

A second line of prospective sex offender risk change research features Hanson et al.'s (2007) dynamic supervision project of over 900 sex offenders on community supervision. In this large-scale undertaking, Hanson et al. (2007) trained probation officers to rate the Stable-2000/2007 every 6 months on their sex offender clientele and the Acute items at each meeting. Over a median follow-up period of 41 months, rates of recidivism were 9.1% for sexual recidivism, 13.5% for violent (including sexual) recidivism, and 28% for any criminal recidivism. Significant pre–post change scores were found on a subsample of men re-rated at 6 months ($n = 292$) on the Stable-2000/2007, although these changes were not associated with changes in any recidivism outcomes. Acute-2000/2007 ratings were obtained on 744 men; although the individual factors and total score frequently predicted recidivism at each time point they were reassessed, changes in the acute factors were not associated with changes in any of the recidivism outcomes.

Babchishin (2013) subsequently examined changes on Acute-2007 ratings from the Dynamic Supervision Project with updated outcome data using hierarchical linear modelling procedures as described above to examine the rate of change over multiple time points. Babchishin collapsed the ratings across three separate time intervals (1–2, 3–4, and 5–6 months) and used HLM procedures to examine rates of change on the Acute-2007 factors to changes in recidivism outcomes on a sample of 317 offenders with complete ratings. Sexual recidivists showed significantly fewer positive changes on the Collapse dimension of the Acute-2007 ($d = 0.35$), although no significant differences were found with respect to the Approach or Acute totals, and no significant differences were found on the three sets of Acute-2007 scores for violent or general recidivism. The HLM procedure also allowed the examination of rates of change as a function of moderators such as probation officer and offender risk level. Higher risk offenders, interestingly, showed lower rates of positive change than lower risk offenders, and probation officers who demonstrated higher amounts of conscientiousness in their administration of the risk protocols also registered lower rates of change over the time intervals. Babchishin's (2013) reanalysis of these data provided evidence consistent with the notion that sex offenders can change on risk-relevant propensities and the dynamism of the Acute-2007.

A third line of sex offender risk-change outcome research featured a sample of 759 adult male sex offenders who attended community-based treatment services through the Vermont Treatment Program for Sexual Abusers. The SOTIPS was rated on treatment participants at multiple time intervals in the course of treatment service delivery. McGrath et al. (2012) examined risk and change ratings made at three time points. The recidivism rates at 3 years' fixed follow-up were 4.6% for sexual, 8.6% for violent (including sexual), and 23.1% for any criminal recidivism. The sample as a whole was broadly low to moderate risk, with a mean Static-99R score of 2.48 ($SD = 2.09$), although there was clear heterogeneity in risk level. The change analyses focused on sexual recidivism across the three time points, and whereas non-recidivists ($n = 434$) demonstrated significant amounts of change on the SOTIPS total score and the majority of its 16 items, the small collection of sexual recidivists ($n = 18$) did not. Of note, after randomly selecting 5% of non-recidivists ($n = 17$) and re-running the time point change comparisons, even with this small subsample, significant change was observed for seven of the SOTIPS items and also the total score. Although there were no direct comparisons on treatment change between recidivists and non-recidivists, the results have consistency with previous evaluations showing positive changes to be associated with reductions in recidivism.

Comments and Conclusions on Structured Clinical Assessments of Change

An increasing body of prospective and retrospective research has examined treatment changes on purpose-built dynamic sex offender risk instruments. As such instruments are designed with the intention of assessing risk and contain psychologically meaningful risk factors linked to sexual violence (e.g., sexual deviance, hostility, impulsivity, negative attitudes), it stands to reason that measured changes occurring following a credible change agent (e.g., risk reduction sex offender programme, intensive community supervision) are themselves risk relevant. The research reviewed above provides support that dynamic tools can capture changes, and that in some circumstances the changes are linked to reductions in recidivism outcomes. Specifically, on average, the hazard ratios suggest an approximately 10% reduction in the hazard of sexual and other forms of recidivism for everyone one point of risk change, after controlling for risk. Unless such changes translate into reductions in sexual or other forms of recidivism, there are arguably limits to which one can draw conclusions about the practicality and meaningfulness of such changes in relation to sexual reoffending. Importantly, there seem to have been increased research efforts recently to examine these issues, with some promising leads.

Clinical Applications of Change Information

The next challenge as we see it is continued research activity to examine risk-relevant change in sex offender populations and for emerging findings to inform applications in clinical practice. Increasingly sophisticated analytical techniques have been applied to examine sex offender risk change information; although knowledge that an effect exists may bring some comfort, how to communicate that knowledge to service providers and to apply this information in a user-friendly and clinically meaningful manner is a different issue. For instance, it may be helpful to know that a one-point change on the VRS-SO is associated with a 10% decrease in the hazard of sexual or violent recidivism while holding risk constant, but how does one 'hold risk constant' for an individual case?

One potential application of clinical change information is to report relative risk information such as percentile ranks (e.g., Hanson, Lloyd, Helmus, & Thornton, 2012). This can be helpful in reporting both risk and change information. For instance, it would be helpful to know if a sex offender applying for parole scored at the 93rd percentile relative to other sex offenders on a given tool in the normative sample. The conclusions drawn about the manageability of this level of risk in the community and the resulting release decisions may also be very different for an individual with this risk score who also scored in the 93rd percentile on risk-relevant treatment changes made in a sex offender programme versus an individual at a comparable risk level who scored at the 10th percentile on changes made in a similar programme. As we stated at the outset of the chapter, we surmise that some offenders may well continue a positive trajectory of change into the community and beyond the expiration of their sentence, such as may be the case for an individual scoring high on a tool at post-treatment, but who nevertheless made considerable risk-related gains.

Moreover, recidivism estimates can be generated based on the magnitude of treatment change on a given tool. Olver, Beggs Christofferson, Grace, and Wong (2014c), for instance, conducted an extended follow-up and examination of change data on the VRS-SO after combining the Olver et al. (2007) and Beggs and Grace

(2011) samples. Olver et al. (2014c) used logistic regression modelling based on similar applications by Hanson et al. (2010) and Thornton (2011) as described above. Five-year estimates of recidivism were then generated for low (0–20), medium–low (21–30), medium–high (31–40), and high (41–72) scores on the VRS-SO at low (< 1.5 points), medium (1.5–5 points), and high (5.5 points and above) amounts of treatment change on the tool. For instance, high-risk men who demonstrated low amounts of change had a 5-year estimate of sexual recidivism of 43.6% and of violent recidivism 62.6%. By contrast, similarly high-risk men at pretreatment who made high or large amounts of change had 5-year estimates of sexual and violent recidivism of 24.6 and 40%, respectively. The amount of risk reduction in these two scenarios is not trivial, and in accordance with the risk and need principles, the impact of treatment change on risk reduction will be more substantive for higher risk (as opposed to lower risk) sex offenders. Conceivably, the use of logistic regression modelling in this manner could be applied to other dynamic sex offender risk tools (e.g., Stable-2007) with change scores obtained between reassessments.

Obviously, obtaining measurements of risk change requires the use of a dynamic tool of some sort and repeated measurements or administrations of it. From a pure prediction standpoint, the value of incorporating dynamic tools is underscored by extant meta-analytic research showing comparable predictive accuracy for sexual violence between static and dynamic tools (Hanson & Morton-Bourgon, 2009). Additional lines of research have also demonstrated that dynamic sex offender tools have incremental validity beyond static instruments (e.g., Craig, Thornton, Beech, & Browne, 2007; Hanson et al., 2007; Olver et al., 2007; Thornton, 2002). However, given that risk is putatively dynamic, and intervention programmes and community supervision strategies exist in an effort to reduce and manage it, some research has suggested that the predictive accuracy of static tools can decrease in samples demonstrating significant amounts of risk change (Olver, Nicholaichuk, Gu, & Wong, 2013; Olver & Wong, 2011). The available evidence reviewed in this chapter provides support for the dynamism of sexual violence risk and underscores the clinical importance of incorporating dynamic tools into risk appraisals, especially for treated individuals. Regardless of the method used, we recommend a systematic approach that involves the use of static and dynamic tools, and refraining from the temptation to make unsystematic or unstructured adjustments to actuarial tools.

References

Allan, M., Grace, R. C., Rutherford, B., & Hudson, S. M. (2007). Psychometric assessment of dynamic risk factors for child molesters. *Sexual Abuse: A Journal of Research and Treatment*, *19*, 347–367. doi:10.1177/107906320701900402

Andrews, D. A., & Bonta, J. (1994). *The psychology of criminal conduct* (1st ed.). Cincinnati, OH: Anderson.

Andrews, D. A., & Bonta, J. (2010a). *The psychology of criminal conduct* (5th ed.). New Providence, NJ: LexisNexis.

Andrews, D. A., & Bonta, J. (2010b). Rehabilitating criminal justice policy and practice. *Psychology, Public Policy, and Law*, *16*, 39–55. doi:10.1037/a0018362

Babchishin, K. M. (2013). *Sex offenders do change on risk-relevant propensities: Evidence from a longitudinal study of the Acute-2007* (Unpublished doctoral dissertation). Carleton University, Ottawa, Canada.

Barnett, G. D., Wakeling, H., Mandeville-Norden, R., & Rakestrow, J. (2013). Does change in psychometric test scores tell us anything about risk of reconviction in sexual offenders? *Psychology, Crime & Law, 19,* 85–110. doi:10.1080/1068316X.2011.607820

Beggs, S. M., & Grace, R. C. (2011). Treatment gains for sexual offenders against children predicts reduced recidivism: A comparative validity study. *Journal of Consulting and Clinical Psychology, 79,* 182–192. doi:10.1037/a0022900

Brown, S., Harkins, L., & Beech, A. R. (2012). General and victim specific empathy: Associations with actuarial risk, treatment outcome, and sexual recidivism. *Sexual Abuse: A Journal of Research and Treatment, 24,* 411–430. doi:10.1177/1079063211423944

Bumby, K. M. (1996). Assessing the cognitive distortions of child molesters and rapists: Development and validation of the MOLEST and RAPE scales. *Sexual Abuse: A Journal of Research and Treatment, 8,* 37–54. doi:10.1177/107906329600800105

Buss, A. H., & Perry, M. P. (1992). The Aggression Questionnaire. *Journal of Personality and Social Psychology, 63,* 452–459. doi:10.1037/0022-3514.63.3.452

Cohen, J. (1992). A power primer. *Psychological Bulletin, 112,* 155–159.

Craig, L. A., Thornton, D., Beech, A., & Browne, K. D. (2007). The relationship of statistical and psychological risk markers to sexual reconviction in child molesters. *Criminal Justice and Behavior, 34,* 314–329. doi:10.1177/0093854806291416

CSC (2009). *Correctional programs descriptions.* Ottawa, Canada: Correctional Service of Canada. Retrieved from: http://www.csc-scc.gc.ca/text/prgrm/cor-pro-2009-eng .shtml#_Toc231830460

Douglas, K., & Skeem, J. (2005). Violence risk assessment: Getting specific about being dynamic. *Psychology, Public Policy, and Law, 11,* 347–383. doi:10.1037/1076-8971.11.3.347

Fernandez, Y. M., & Marshall, W. L. (2003). Victim empathy, social self-esteem, and psychopathy in rapists. *Sexual Abuse: A Journal of Research and Treatment, 15,* 11–26. doi:10.1177/107906320301500102

Fernandez, Y. M., Marshall, W. M., Lightbody, S., & O'Sullivan, C. (1999). The child molester empathy measure: Description and examination of its reliability and validity. *Sexual Abuse: A Journal of Research and Treatment, 11,* 17–31. doi:10.1177/107906329901100103

Goodman-Delahunty, J., & O'Brien, K. (2012). *Reoffence risk in intrafamilial child sexual offenders.* Sydney, Australia: Australian Graduate School of Policing and Security.

Goodman-Delahunty, J., & O'Brien, K. (2014). Parental sexual offending: Managing risk through diversion. *Trends & Issues in Crime and Criminal Justice, 482,* 481–500.

Hanson, R. K., Bourgon, G., Helmus, L., & Hodgson, S. (2009). The principles of effective correctional treatment also apply to sexual offenders: A meta-analysis. *Criminal Justice and Behavior, 36,* 865–891. doi:10.1177/0093854809338545

Hanson, R. K., & Harris, A. J. R. (2001). A structured approach to evaluating change among sexual offenders. *Sexual Abuse: A Journal of Research and Treatment, 13,* 105–122. doi:10.1177/107906320101300204

Hanson, R. K., Harris, A. J. R., Scott, T.-L., & Helmus, L. (2007). *Assessing the risk of sex offenders on community supervision* (User Report 2007-05). Ottawa, Canada: Public Safety and Emergency Preparedness Canada.

Hanson, R. K., Helmus, L., & Thornton, D. (2010). Predicting recidivism among sexual offenders: A multi-site study of Static-2002. *Law and Human Behavior, 34,* 198–211. doi:10.1007/s10979-009-9180-1

Hanson, R. K., Lloyd, C. D., Helmus, L., & Thornton, D. (2012). Developing non-arbitrary metrics for risk communication: Percentile ranks for the Static-99/R and Static-2002/R sexual offender risk tools. *International Journal of Forensic Mental Health*, *11*, 9–23. doi:10.1080/14999013.2012.667511

Hanson, R. K., & Morton-Bourgon, K. (2009). The accuracy of recidivism risk assessments for sexual offenders: A meta-analysis of 118 prediction studies. *Psychological Assessment*, *21*, 1–21. doi:10.1037/a0014421

Hanson, R. K., & Thornton, D. (1999). *Static 99: Improving actuarial risk assessments for sex offenders* (User Report 99-02). Ottawa, Canada: Department of the Solicitor General of Canada.

Helmus, L., Hanson, R. K., Babchishin, K. M., & Mann, R. E. (2013). Attitudes supportive of sexual offending predict recidivism: A meta-analysis. *Trauma, Violence, & Abuse*, *14*, 34–53. doi:10.1177/1524838012462244

Hemphill, J. F., & Howell, A. J. (2000). Adolescent offenders and stages of change. *Psychological Assessment*, *12*, 371–381. doi:10.1037/1040-3590.12.4.371

Hudson, S. M., Wales, D. S., Bakker, L., & Ward, T. (2002). Dynamic risk factors: The Kia Marama evaluation. *Sexual Abuse: A Journal of Research and Treatment*, *14*, 103–119. doi:10.1177/107906320201400203

Jacobson, N. S., & Truax, P. (1991). Clinical significance: A statistical approach to defining meaningful change in psychotherapy research. *Journal of Consulting and Clinical Psychology*, *59*, 12–19. doi:10.1037/0022-006X.59.1.12

Jung, S., & Guyalets, M. (2011). Using clinical variables to evaluate treatment effectiveness in programmes for sexual offenders. *Journal of Sexual Aggression*, *17*, 166–180. doi:10.1080/13552601003802238

Kingston, D. A., Yates, P. M., & Olver, M. E. (2014). The self-regulation model of sexual offending: Intermediate outcomes and post-treatment recidivism. *Sexual Abuse: A Journal of Research and Treatment*, *26*, 429–449. doi:10.1177/1079063213495896

Kraemer, H. C., Kazdin, A. E., Offord, D. R., Kessler, R. C., Jensen, P. S., & Kupfer, D. J. (1997). Coming to terms with the terms of risk. *Archives of General Psychiatry*, *54*, 337–343. doi:10.1001/archpsyc.1997.01830160065009

Levesque, D. A., Gelles, R. J., & Velicer, W. F. (2000). Development and validation of a stages of change measure for men in batterer treatment. *Cognitive Therapy and Research*, *24*, 175–199. doi:10.1023/A:1005446025201

Lewis, K., Olver, M. E., & Wong, S. C. P. (2013). The Violence Risk Scale: Predictive validity and linking treatment changes with recidivism in a sample of high risk offenders with psychopathic traits. *Assessment*, *20*, 150–164.

Löesel, F., & Schmucker, M. (2005). The effectiveness of treatment for sexual offenders: A comprehensive meta-analysis. *Journal of Experimental Criminology*, *1*, 117–146. doi:10.1007/s11292-004-6466-7

Mandeville-Norden, R., Beech, R., & Hayes E. (2008). Examining the effectiveness of a UK community-based sexual offender treatment programme for child abusers. *Psychology, Crime & Law*, *14*, 493–512. doi:10.1080/10683160801948907

Mann, R. E., Hanson, R. K., & Thornton, D. (2010). Assessing risk for sexual recidivism: Some proposals on the nature of psychologically meaningful risk factors. *Sexual Abuse: A Journal of Research and Treatment*, *22*, 191–217. doi:10.1177/1079063210366039

Marshall, W. L., Champagne, F., Sturgeon, C., & Bryce, P. (1997). Increasing the self-esteem of child molesters. *Sexual Abuse: A Journal of Research and Treatment*, *9*, 321–333. doi:10.1177/107906329700900405

McGrath, R. J., Lasher, M. P., & Cumming, G. F. (2011). *A model of static and dynamic risk assessment* (Final grant report to the National Institute of Justice, Grant Award No. 2008-DD-BX-0013). Washington, DC: United States Department of Justice.

McGrath, R. J., Lasher, M. P., & Cumming, G. F. (2012). The Sex Offender Treatment Intervention and Progress Scale (SOTIPS): Psychometric properties and incremental predictive validity with the Static-99R. *Sexual Abuse: A Journal of Research and Treatment, 24,* 431–458. doi:10.1177/1079063211432475

Miller, R. S., & Lefcourt, H. M. (1982). The assessment of social intimacy. *Journal of Personality Assessment, 46,* 514–518. doi:10.1207/s15327752jpa4605_12

Mills, J. F., & Kroner, D. G. (2006). Impression management and self-report among violent offenders. *Journal of Interpersonal Violence, 21,* 178–192. doi:10.1177/0886260505282288

Nunes, K. L., Babchishin, K. M., & Cortoni, F. (2011). Measuring treatment changes in sex offenders: Clinical and statistical significance. *Criminal Justice and Behavior, 38,* 157–173. doi:10.1177/0093854810391054

Olver, M. E., Beggs Christofferson, S. M., Grace, R. C., & Wong, S. C. P. (2014c). Incorporating change information into sexual offender risk assessments using the Violence Risk Scale – Sexual Offender version. *Sexual Abuse: A Journal of Research and Treatment, 26,* 472–499. doi:10.1177/1079063213502679

Olver, M. E., Kingston, D. A., Nicholaichuk, T. P., & Wong, S. C. P. (2014b). A psychometric examination of treatment change in a multisite sample of treated Canadian federal sexual offenders. *Law and Human Behavior, 38,* 544–559. doi:10.1037/lhb0000086

Olver, M. E., Nicholaichuk, T. P., Gu, D., & Wong, S. C. P. (2013). Sex offender treatment outcome, actuarial risk, and the aging sex offender in Canadian corrections: A long-term follow-up. *Sexual Abuse: A Journal of Research and Treatment, 25,* 396–422. doi:10.1177/1079063212464399

Olver, M. E., Nicholaichuk, T. P., Kingston, D. A., & Wong S. C. P. (2014). A multisite examination of sexual violence risk and therapeutic change. *Journal of Clinical and Consulting Psychology, 82,* 312–324. doi:10.1037/a0035340

Olver, M. E., Nicholaichuk, T. P., & Wong, S. C. P. (2014a). The predictive and convergent validity of a psychometric battery used to assess sex offenders in a treatment program: An 18-year follow-up. *Journal of Sexual Aggression, 20,* 216–239. doi:10.1080/13552600.2013.816791

Olver, M. E., Stockdale, K. C., & Wormith, J. S. (2011). A meta-analysis of predictors of offender treatment attrition and its relationship to recidivism. *Journal of Consulting and Clinical Psychology, 79,* 6–21. doi:10.1037/a0022200

Olver, M. E., & Wong, S. C. P. (2011). A comparison of static and dynamic assessment of sexual offender risk and need in a treatment context. *Criminal Justice and Behavior, 38,* 113–126. doi:10.1177/0093854810389534

Olver, M. E., & Wong, S. C. P. (2013). A description and research review of the Clearwater Sex Offender Treatment Program. *Psychology, Crime & Law, 19,* 477–492.

Olver, M. E., Wong, S. C. P., Nicholaichuk, T., & Gordon, A. (2007). The validity and reliability of the Violence Risk Scale – Sexual Offender version: Assessing sex offender risk and evaluating therapeutic change. *Psychological Assessment, 19,* 318–329. doi:10.1037/1040-3590.19.3.318

Peacock, E. J. (2000). *Sex Offender Acceptance of Responsibility Scales.* Ottawa, Canada: Warkworth Institution, Correctional Service of Canada.

Prochaska, J. O., DiClemente, C. C., & Norcross, J. C. (1992). In search of how people change: Applications to the addictive behaviors. *American Psychologist, 47,* 1102–1114.

Russell, D., Peplau, L. A., & Cutrona, C. E. (1980). The Revised UCLA Loneliness Scale: Concurrent and discriminant validity evidence. *Journal of Personality and Social Psychology*, *39*, 472–480.

Serin, R. C., Kennedy, S. M., & Mailloux, D. L. (2005). *Manual for the Treatment Readiness, Responsivity, and Gain Scale: Short Version (TRRG:SV)*. Ottawa, Canada: Carleton University.

Sowden, J. N. (2013). *Examining the relationship of risk, treatment readiness, and therapeutic change to recidivism in a sample of treated sex offenders* (Unpublished doctoral dissertation). University of Saskatchewan, Saskatoon, Canada.

Tan, L., & Grace, R. (2008). Social desirability and sexual offenders: A review. *Sexual Abuse: A Journal of Research and Treatment*, *20*, 61–87. doi:10.1177/1079063208314820

Terry, K. J., & Mitchell, E. W. (2001). Motivation and sex offender treatment efficacy: Leading a horse to water and making it drink? *International Journal of Offender Therapy and Comparative Criminology*, *45*, 663–672. doi:10.1177/0306624X01456003

Thornton, D. (2002). Constructing and testing a framework for dynamic risk assessment. *Sexual Abuse: A Journal of Research and Treatment*, *14*, 139–153. doi:10.1177/107906320201400205

Thornton, D. (2011, November). *Interpreting SRA-FV total need scores*. Paper presented at the 30th Annual Meeting of the Association for the Treatment of Sexual Abusers (ATSA), Toronto, Canada.

Tierney, D. W., & McCabe, M. P. (2005). The utility of the trans-theoretical model of behavior change in the treatment of sex offenders. *Sexual Abuse: A Journal of Research and Treatment*, *17*, 153–170. doi:10.1007/s11194-005-4602-1

Wakeling, H., Beech, A. R., & Freemantle, N. (2013). Treatment change and its relationship to recidivism in a sample of 3773 sex offenders in the UK. *Psychology, Crime, and Law*, *19*, 233–252. doi:10.1080/1068316X.2011.626413

Ward, T., Mann, R. E., & Gannon, T. A. (2007). Good lives model of offender rehabilitation: Clinical implications. *Aggression and Violent Behavior*, *12*, 87–107. doi:10.1016/j.avb.2006.03.004

Williams, F., Wakeling, H., & Webster, S. (2007). A psychometric study of six self-report measures for use with sexual offenders with cognitive and social functioning deficits. *Psychology, Crime & Law*, *13*, 505–552. doi:10.1080/10683160601060739

Wise, E. A. (2004). Methods for analyzing psychotherapy outcomes: A review of clinical significance, reliable change, and recommendations for future directions. *Journal of Personality Assessment*, *82*, 50–59. doi:10.1207/s15327752jpa8201_10

Wong, S., & Gordon, A. (1999–2003). *The Violence Risk Scale*. Saskatoon, Canada: Regional Psychiatric Centre and University of Saskatchewan.

Wong, S., Olver, M. E., Nicholaichuk, T. P., & Gordon, A. (2003–2009). *The Violence Risk Scale: Sexual Offender version (VRS-SO)*. Saskatoon, Canada: Regional Psychiatric Centre and University of Saskatchewan.

Section IV

Diagnostic Assessment and Sexual Interest

37

Clinical Assessment of Sexual Deviance

Jan Looman

Regional Treatment Centre, Kingston, Canada

Introduction

The assessment of sexual deviance is a fundamental part of risk assessment with sexual offenders, and also for treatment planning, and any assessment that overlooks this aspect of the offender is fundamentally lacking. Although psychometric measures such as the Multiphasic Sex Inventory II (MSI-II) (Nichols & Molinder, 2005), phallometric testing, and visual reaction time testing (Gray et al., 2015) are useful tools in the assessment of deviance, a clinical assessment is also required in order both to interpret the results of the latter testing and also to place the sexual behaviour within the context of the individual and develop a plan to address it.

The purpose of assessment is to develop a case conceptualization (Boer, Thakker, & Ward, 2009), in order not only to assess risk for reoffence but also to understand the overall pattern of offending in order to engage in effective treatment. In addition, whereas contemporary treatment often focuses only on factors associated with risk for reoffence (Hanson & Morton-Bourgon, 2005; Mann, Hanson, & Thornton, 2010), most offenders present with problems beyond offence-specific factors (e.g., depression, anxiety). For this reason, a complete assessment must include consideration of factors other than simply those included in actuarial risk measures.

Assessment of Criminogenic Needs

Research has indicated that certain factors are related to sexual reoffending. These factors fall into two broad groups: static and dynamic risk factors (Mann et al., 2010), the latter of which can also be seen as treatment targets or criminogenic needs (Andrews & Bonta, 2010). These dynamic factors include such factors as sexual

The Wiley Handbook on the Theories, Assessment, and Treatment of Sexual Offending.
Edited by Douglas P. Boer. Volume II: Assessment, edited by Leam A. Craig and Martin Rettenberger.
© 2017 John Wiley & Sons, Ltd. Published 2017 by John Wiley & Sons, Ltd.

interest in children, emotional identification with children, sexual preoccupation, offence-supportive attitudes, lack of emotionally intimate relationships with adults, and general self-regulation problems, among others (Mann et al., 2010). Therefore, an assessment of risk and treatment needs should include consideration of these factors.

Structure of the Assessment

Any assessment process should be based on a working model of sexual offending – that is, the assessor should have a theory regarding the offending process in mind when conducting the assessment in order to guide the process. Among models of offending currently in use is the Relapse Prevention Model (Laws, 1989), which posits that sexual offenders follow a predictable process leading up to reoffending, characterized by ineffective coping with life stressors. This model of offending was popular during the 1990s but came under criticism owing to its failure to acknowledge multiple pathways to offending (Ward, 2011).

Ward and colleagues (Ward, Hudson, & Keenan, 1998; Ward, Louden, Hudson, & Marshall, 1995) developed the Self-Regulation Model of sex offender relapse to account for this weakness. Within this model there are four 'pathways' to offending: (1) Avoidant-Passive, in which the offender wishes to avoid offending but takes none of the steps necessary; (2) Avoidant-Active, in which the offender wishes to avoid offending but uses ineffective or inappropriate coping; (3) Approach-Automatic, in which the offender desires to offend but forms no explicit plan, rather they simply fail to control their behaviour; and (4) Approach-Explicit, in which the offender desires to offend and forms explicit plans to do so. In this case, it is not the offender's self-regulatory skills that are the problem, rather it is their goals (Yates, Prescott, & Ward, 2010).

Hence an assessment should begin by exploring issues related to the type and nature of the offence. What is the client's choice of victim (male versus female; child versus adult)? Whether or not the victim is male relates to risk for reoffence (Hanson & Morton-Bourgon, 2005). Is the victim someone known to the offender, or is it a stranger? An offender who chooses victims unknown to them are higher risk than those who offend within the family (Hanson & Morton-Bourgon, 2005).

If the offences are characterized by an Approach pathway, the intervention chosen will be different from that for an offender whose offences follow an Avoidance pathway (Yates et al., 2010). For example, an Avoidant offender may require treatment focused on the development of appropriate coping skills, whereas the Approach offender may require treatment focused on issues related to personality features, attitudes, and sexual preferences. Therefore, an understanding of the offender's motives for offending and the factors leading up to the offence (i.e., his offence chain) is important.

Assessment

The clinical assessment of sexual deviance starts with a complete sexual history. The starting point for this assessment is a psychosocial history, as would be obtained when doing any clinical work: where was the person born, how many siblings they have, whether they lived with both parents growing up, and so on. The interview such as that for the Psychopathy Checklist – Revised (PCL-R) (Hare, 2003) is an appropriate psychosocial history for an offender population. However, in order to understand issues related to sexual deviance, the clinician has to delve deeper into the client's sexual development.

There are a number of sexual history interviews/guides already in existence, and there is no need to detail those here. The manuals that come with dynamic risk assessment instruments such as the Stable-2007 (Fernandez, Harris, Hanson, & Sparks, 2012), the Sexual Violence Risk-20 (SVR-20) (Boer, Hart, Kropp, & Webster, 1997), and the Risk for Sexual Violence Protocol (RSVP) (Hart et al., 2003) provide suggested questions for a sexual history related to assessing the offender's status on known dynamic risk factors. The clinician may have to add questions about early sexual experiences such as history of abuse, childhood sexual activity (masturbation, sexual play with peers, etc.); however, such guides provide an excellent structure for evaluating the necessary areas.

Relevant Areas for Evaluation

When evaluating an offender for sexual deviance, there are a number of known psychologically meaningful risk factors (Mann et al., 2010). These factors are also common across clinical assessment measures such as Structured Risk Assessment (SARN) (Thornton, 2002) and Stable-2007 (Fernandez et al., 2012). This section briefly describe these factors and provides suggested questions for assessing the area.

Sexual preoccupation. This refers to an abnormally intense interest in sex that dominates psychological functioning (Mann et al., 2010). A person who is sexually preoccupied pursues sex for its own sake, rather than as part of an emotionally intimate relationship. They may have multiple sexual partners and frequent one-night stands, use pornography frequently, employ the services of prostitutes, and so on. Questions related to frequency of orgasm (more than four orgasms per week for someone under 30 years old; Fernandez et al., 2012), pornography use, engagement in extra-marital affairs, and so on are used to assess this factor.

Indicators of deviant sexual preference. These include a sexual preference for prepubescent or pubescent children, arousal to sexualized violence, and evidence of multiple paraphilias (Mann et al., 2010). Of these, a sexual preference for prepubescent children is the strongest predictor of recidivism and has the most empirical support as a predictor. Evidence for a deviant preference can be derived from phallometric testing results, and also self-report and offence history indicators (e.g., having two or more under-aged victims; Fernandez et al., 2012). Questions related to unusual sexual practices (activities involving urine, faeces, fetishes, bondage, etc.) are useful in obtaining information related to paraphilias.

Offence-supportive attitudes. This factor includes expressed attitudes supportive of sexual activity with children and/or attitudes that condone rape (Mann et al., 2010). It is important to note that the presence of such attitudes cannot be assumed simply because the person has offences of that nature. There are multiple reasons why people engage in illegal sexual activity and attitudes are only part of the picture. Sometimes the attitudes will become apparent in the interview ('Come on, look at the way she was dressed!'; 'She was a flirty girl'), but questionnaires may also be helpful in assessing the presence of these attitudes/beliefs (e.g., The Rape and Molest Scales; Bumby, 1996). Questions during the interview directed at determining the offender's thinking about the victim(s) and their behaviour prior to the offence often elicit these attitudes, for example, 'What did you think when she said no to you?'; 'What was going on in your mind when she climbed into your lap?'.

Emotional congruence with children. This refers to the tendency for some child molesters to feel more comfortable with children than with adults, and to receive more emotional satisfaction from relationships with children (Wilson, 1999). Such offenders may report that they are in love with their victim or that, in the case of incest offenders, their victim became a substitute for their wife. This factor is relevant for child molesters, but not rapists of adult females, and is associated with sexual recidivism in the meta-analyses (Mann et al., 2010). Again, these attitudes often come out during the interview in spontaneous comments.

Lack of emotionally intimate relationships with adults. As noted by Mann et al. (2010), this factor refers both to offenders who have no intimate relationships and to those whose relationships are filled with conflict and infidelity. However, it is likely that the mechanism by which this factor acts differs between those who do not desire such a relationship and those for whom a relationship is desired but either not achieved or, if achieved, is conflictual. The associated treatment targets for such differing offenders would also be different. In terms of assessing this factor, questions related to the nature of past relationships, if any, the manner in which they met their partner(s), problems that they encountered in their relationships, and so on are helpful. If the offender reports not having relationships, queries as to why this is the case are advised – did they desire a relationship but lack the skills to form one, or do they prefer to be unattached?

Lifestyle impulsiveness. This is a risk factor associated with general criminality, but also with sexual recidivism (Hanson & Morton-Bourgon, 2004). This factor relates to Facet 3 of the PCL-R (Hare, 2003) and reflects instability in employment and housing, general irresponsibility, lack of meaningful routines, and substance use. The PCL-R interview, referred to above, taps this factor well, with questions related to substance use, employment, and housing instability, and an attraction to high-risk behaviour.

Poor problem solving. This factor involves an inability to identify problems, generate appropriate solutions, and implement those solutions (Fernandez et al., 2012). Rather than engaging in appropriate problem solving, offenders may ruminate over life difficulties and engage in ineffective problem solving, if any. Mann et al. (2010) reported that this factor is associated with both sexual and general recidivism. Questions related to this factor address areas such as what the offender does when he encounters a problem, how effective he is in addressing conflict with others, and his response when his first attempt at problem solving fails. Information from collateral sources such as prison/supervision records is also helpful. For example, information regarding whether or not the offender gets into conflicts with others on his living unit or work assignments, and the manner in which he resolves these issues, provide important information in this regard.

Resistance to rules and supervision. Mann et al. (2010) reported that rule violations, non-compliance with supervision, and violation of conditional release were consistently large predictors of sexual recidivism in meta-analyses. This factor can be assessed by looking at the offender's supervision history – do they have multiple violations, do they have a history of committing new offences while under supervision? Also, questions regarding their thoughts about the need for supervision conditions, their chances of reoffence, and their need for ongoing treatment reveal useful information related to this factor. For men who are still incarcerated, the concern becomes their compliance with institutional rules/expectations.

Grievance/hostility. This factor refers to the perception of being wrongly treated by the world, that others are responsible for their problems, and wanting to punish others as a result (Mann, et al., 2010). These offenders tend to ruminate on perceived injustices and thoughts of vengeance. In Hanson and Morton-Bourgon's (2004) meta-analysis, this factor predicted sexual recidivism. Questions asking how easily the offender is able to let go of issues and the extent to which they ruminate on perceived slights are useful for assessing this factor. More useful, however, is information from collateral sources such as previous treatment/supervision providers regarding their functioning on this factor.

Negative social influences. This factor refers to the number and quality of the influences that an offender has in his life. Who does he associate with and what sort of influence do these people have on his behaviour? The presence of negative social influences is a significant predictor of general recidivism (Andrews & Bonta, 2010) and a weaker, but still significant, predictor of sexual recidivism (Mann et al., 2010).

Additional Factors

Mann et al. (2010), in addition to the risk factors listed above, identified what they termed 'promising risk factors', that is, factors with support in one or two studies, in addition to supporting evidence of other kinds. These factors include the following.

Hostile beliefs about women. This factor relates to the view that women are malicious and deceptive in their interactions with men, that women like making fools of men, that women seldom express their true feelings directly, and that if a women appears sexually interested in a man then the expression is probably deceitful and manipulative. Men who hold these views see women as a separate class, not worthy of trust and respect. These attitudes may be assessed via questionnaires (e.g., the Hostility Toward Women questionnaire; Malamuth & Thornhill, 1994). In interviews, questions assessing the offender's relationships with women are useful. Has he had female friends, how does he get along with women in the workplace, has he ever had a female supervisor and were there problems in that relationship?

Machiavellianism. Mann et al. (2010) noted that Machiavellianism consists of (a) a tendency to view others as weak, cowardly, and easily manipulated, and (b) an interpersonal strategy in which it is viewed as sensible and appropriate to take advantage of others. It has also been found that this pattern predicted sexual offending over and above its relationship to past offending. Questionnaires exist with which to measure this trait (e.g., the Mach-IV; Christie & Geis, 1970; available online); however, questions related to tendencies to see others as potential victims or 'marks', a willingness to lie to get an advantage, and similar tendencies assess this trait.

Lack of concern for others. This factor reflects a tendency for the person to be self-centred and to engage in relationships for instrumental purposes. Such individuals are described as selfish, cynical, and willing to be cruel to meet their own needs. Lack of concern for others has been found to be related to all types of recidivism (sexual, violent, and non-violent offending) (Fernandez et al., 2012). This item is adequately assessed via Facet 2 of the PCL-R (Hare, 2003).

Dysfunctional coping. This refers to the manner in which offenders manage negative emotions such as anger, anxiety, rejection, and humiliation, which are related to their risk for sexual recidivism (Mann et al., 2010). This factor includes both using sex as a coping strategy and externalized coping (i.e., reacting in a reckless, impulsive manner when faced with problems) (Mann et al., 2010). Sexualized coping involves the tendency to use sex – such as impersonal sex, use of pornography – to manage life stressors.

Other Factors

A number of other factors are of interest when conducting assessments of sexual offenders for clinical purposes. Typically, such factors are not related to recidivism in meta-analytic research; however, they are of interest in terms of treatment planning. For example, although denial has not been found to be related to recidivism in recent meta-analyses (e.g., Mann et al., 2010; but see Marshall, Marshall, & Kingston, 2011), the extent to which an offender denies the offences is relevant from a clinical perspective, as he may be more difficult to treat. Indeed, some argue that offenders in denial should not be treated in regular sex offender treatment programmes (Blagden, Winder, Gregson, & Thorne, 2013). Marshall, Marshall, Serran, and O'Brien (2011) have designed programmes to provide treatment to offenders who deny their offences, while others chose to consider denial a treatment target to be addressed in a regular programme (e.g., Looman, 2014).

Other targets that may be considered include low self-esteem, depression, and poor social skills. Although research indicates that these are not related to recidivism (Mann et al., 2010), addressing these targets in a comprehensive programme may be important for other reasons. For example, someone who suffers from depression may have difficulty finding motivation to engage in treatment, and may have difficulty concentrating. An offender with poor social skills may lack the confidence to engage in behaviours important for managing his risk (e.g., becoming involved with prosocial peers).

Clinical Formulation

As noted earlier, in order to carry out a meaningful assessment of deviance, the clinician must situate their assessment within a working model of sexual offending. The Self-Regulation Model, discussed above, is one such model with demonstrated utility (Yates et al., 2010). Once the assessment of risk factors is complete, the assessor needs to perform a case formulation – that is, provide an explanation of the offender's behaviour in order to inform treatment (Boer et al., 2009; see Chapter 34). Although the dynamic factors/treatment needs discussed above are all related to recidivism, it is unlikely that they are all present in a given offender. The case formulation should describe how each of the enumerated factors is related to risk for reoffence for the person under consideration.

For example, referring back to the Self-Regulation Model and the four paths to offending, it may be that the Approach-Explicit child molester has never had an intimate adult relationship because it is not desired, whereas the Avoidant-Passive offender may have had a relationship but it was full of conflict and infidelity. The Approach-Explicit offender is likely to experience deviant arousal and significant distorted thinking about relationships with children, whereas the Avoidant-Active offender is likely to have problems with hostility and emotional self-regulation. These different risk factors and treatment needs will necessarily lead to different priorities and approaches to treatment.

Thus, developing a theory related to the offender's offence pattern and motivations in the form of a detailed case formulation allows the development of a treatment plan specific to each client's needs. Although the treatment of each offender should be individualized according to their needs, for most offenders addressing treatment needs in a group format is appropriate, as there is much overlap in the treatment targets addressed and individualization can occur through homework assignments and adjunctive individual sessions. In addition, during group discussions questioning can occur, which encourages individual clients to apply knowledge and skills to themselves.

Summary and Conclusions

Clinical assessment of sexual deviance is a process in which one's assessment is guided by a theory of sexual offending, in order to inform treatment or risk management. The factors addressed in the assessment are those which are associated with risk (i.e., dynamic risk factors/criminogenic need), but also those related to responsivity issues associated with treatment (e.g., denial, depression). A detailed assessment will guide the treatment process and effectively direct the attention of those managing the offender under supervision.

References

Andrews, D. A., & Bonta, J. (2010). *The psychology of criminal conduct* (5th ed.). Cincinnati, OH: Anderson.

Blagden, N., Winder, B., Gregson, M., & Thorne, K. (2013). Working with denial in convicted sexual offenders: A qualitative analysis of treatment professionals' views and experiences and their implications for practice. *International Journal of Offender Therapy and Comparative Criminology, 57,* 332–356. doi:10.1177/0306624X11432301

Boer, D. P., Hart, S. D., Kropp, P. R., & Webster, C. D. (1997). *Manual for the Sexual Violence Risk-20: Professional guidelines for assessing risk of sexual violence.* Vancouver, Canada: British Columbia Institute Against Family Violence.

Boer, D. P., Thakker, J., & Ward, T. (2009). Sex offender risk-based case formulation. In A. R. Beech, L. A. Craig, & K. D. Browne (Eds.), *Assessment and treatment of sex offenders: A handbook* (pp. 77–87). Chichester, England: John Wiley & Sons, Ltd.

Bumby, K. M. (1996). Assessing the cognitive distortions of child molesters and rapists: Development and validation of the MOLEST and RAPE scales. *Sexual Abuse: A Journal of Research and Treatment, 8,* 37–54.

Christie, R., & Geis, F. L. (1970). *Studies in Machiavellianism.* New York, NY: Academic Press.

Fernandez, Y., Harris, A. J., Hanson, R. K., & Sparks, J. (2012). *Stable-2007 Coding Manual Revised 2012.* Ottawa, Canada: Public Safety Canada.

Gray, S. R., Abel, G. G., Jordan, A., Garby, T., Wiegel, M., & Harlow, N. (2013). Visual Reaction Time™ as a predictor of sexual offense recidivism. *Sexual Abuse: A Journal of Research and Treatment, 27,* 173–188. doi:10.1177/1079063213502680

Hanson, R. K., & Morton-Bourgon, K. E. (2004). *Predictors of sexual recidivism: An updated meta-analysis (Corrections User Report 2004-02).* Ottawa, Canada: Public Safety Canada.

Hanson, R. K., & Morton-Bourgon, K. E. (2005). The characteristics of persistent sexual offenders: A meta-analysis of recidivism studies. *Journal of Consulting and Clinical Psychology, 73,* 1154–1163. doi:10.1037/0022-006X.73.6.1154.

Hare, R. (2003). *Hare Psychopathy Checklist – Revised (PCL-R): Technical manual* (2nd ed.). Toronto, Canada: Multi-Health Systems.

Hart, S. D., Kropp, P. R., Laws, D. R., Klaver, J., Logan, C., & Watt, K. A. (2003). *The Risk for Sexual Violence Protocol (RSVP): Structured professional guidelines for assessing risk of sexual violence.* Burnaby, Canada: Mental Health, Law, and Policy Institute, Simon Fraser University.

Laws, D. R. (1989). *Relapse prevention with sexual offenders.* New York, NY: Guilford Press.

Looman, J. (2014). Denial and recidivism among high-risk, treated sexual offenders. In B. Schwartz (Ed.), *The sexual predator: Legal, administrative, assessment and treatment concerns* (Vol. V, pp. 18-1–18-13). Kingston, NJ: Civic Research Institute.

Malumuth, N. M., & Thornhill, N. W. (1994). Hostile masculinity, sexual aggression, and gender-biased domineeringness in conversations. *Aggressive Behavior, 20,* 185–193.

Mann, R., Hanson, R., & Thornton, D. (2010). Assessing risk for sexual recidivism: Some proposals on the nature of psychologically meaningful risk factors. *Sexual Abuse: A Journal of Research and Treatment, 22,* 191–217. doi:10.1177/1079063210366039

Marshall, W. L., Marshall, L. E., & Kingston, D. A. (2011) Are the cognitive distortions of child molesters in need of treatment? *Sexual Aggression, 17,* 118–129.

Marshall, W. L., Marshall, L. E., Serran, G., & O'Brien, M. (2011). Rockwood Deniers' Program. In W. L. Marshall, L. E. Marshall, G. A. Serran, & M. D. O'Brien (Eds.), *Rehabilitating sexual offenders: A strength-based approach* (pp. 163–171). Washington, DC: American Psychological Association.

Nichols, H. R., & Molinder, I. (2005). *Multiphasic Sex Inventory II: Adult male form.* Tacoma, WA: Nichols & Molinder Assessments.

Thornton, D. (2002). Constructing and testing a framework for dynamic risk assessment. *Sexual Abuse: A Journal of Research and Treatment, 14*, 139–153. doi:10.1177/107906320201400205.

Ward, T. (2011). A self-regulation model of the relapse process in sexual offenders. In S. K. Schwartz (Ed.), *Handbook of sex offender treatment* (pp. 10-1–10-8). Kingston, NJ: Civic Research Institute.

Ward, T., Hudson, S. M., & Keenan, T. (1998). A self-regulation model of the sexual offense process. *Sexual Abuse: A Journal of Research and Treatment, 10*, 141–157. doi:10.1023/A:1022071516644.

Ward, T., Louden, K., Hudson, S. M., & Marshall, W. L. (1995). A descriptive model of the offense chain for child molesters. *Journal of Interpersonal Violence, 10*, 452–472. doi:10.1177/088626095010004005

Wilson, R. J. (1999). Emotional congruence in sexual offenders against children. *Sexual Abuse: A Journal of Research and Treatment, 1*, 33–47.

Yates, P. M., Prescott, D., & Ward, T. (2010). *Applying the Good Lives and Self-Regulation Models to sex offender treatment: A practical guide for clinicians.* Brandon, VT: Safer Society Press.

38

The Use of Phallometric Testing in the Diagnosis, Treatment, and Risk Management of Male Adults Who Have Sexually Offended

Robin J. Wilson

Wilson Psychological Services, United States
McMaster University, Canada

Introduction

The sexual abuse of women, children, and other vulnerable persons remains one of the most pressing issues in modern society. The increased focus of the past several decades has been fuelled partly by greater media interest leading to political attention and community concern. Accordingly, there has also been an increase in research regarding the assessment, treatment, and risk management of persons who have sexually offended. It is clear that the public is seeking answers to their fears about sexual violence; however, professionals have not been effective in helping the public understand the implications and meaning of scientific findings (Center for Sex Offender Management, 2010). Indeed, the public and even many professionals often rely more on myth than fact with respect to sexual deviance and the level of risk posed by identified offenders.

The nature and aetiology of sexual deviance continue to cause considerable controversy among the general public and professionals, but a good deal of academic unrest also exists. In the run-up to the recent release of the fifth edition of the *Diagnostic and Statistical Manual of Mental Disorders* (DSM-5) (American Psychiatric Association, 2013), bitter (and sometimes personal) debates raged as to how best to characterize the inappropriate sexual behaviours demonstrated by some persons who have sexually offended. Interestingly, DSM-5 for the first time differentiates between Paraphilias (i.e., unusual sexual interests and preferences) and Paraphilic Disorders (when experience of the unusual interests and preferences leads to problems in the paraphilic client's

The Wiley Handbook on the Theories, Assessment, and Treatment of Sexual Offending.
Edited by Douglas P. Boer. Volume II: Assessment, edited by Leam A. Craig and Martin Rettenberger.
© 2017 John Wiley & Sons, Ltd. Published 2017 by John Wiley & Sons, Ltd.

life). However, and in spite of intense scientific inquiry over the past 15–20 years (e.g., Blanchard, 2010, 2011; D'Orazio, Wilson, & Thornton, 2011), the diagnostic criteria for the various paraphilic *disorders* have not changed appreciably in nearly 20 years. This has caused some to question the contemporary relevance of DSM criteria in the diagnosis of sexual deviance, and many to urge caution in their application in high-stakes situations, such as civil commitment (Brandt, Wilson, & Prescott, 2015). Indeed, in several investigations, DSM criteria have been found to be unreliable and of little predictive validity (regarding Sexual Sadism, see Kingston, Seto, Firestone, & Bradford, 2010; Marshall, Kennedy, & Yates, 2002; Marshall, Kennedy, Yates, & Serran, 2002; regarding Pedophilia, see Kingston, Firestone, Moulden, & Bradford, 2007; Wilson, Abracen, Looman, Picheca, & Ferguson, 2011). This is in line with research on other diagnostic categories (for a specific review, see Duncan, Miller, & Sparks, 2004).

Running parallel to the focus on sexual deviance in forensic psychology and psychiatry is another line of scientific inquiry conducted by sexologists. Although the interests of these two groups may share many aspects in common, sexological research is often concerned more with the conditions and their origins and manifestations than the diagnostic methods and legal consequences associated with engaging in the behaviour. As such, sexology may be less inclined to consider psycholegal constructions in favour of collecting data on patterns in behavioural observations. In a popular US television series, *Masters of Sex*, pioneering sex researchers William Johnson and Virginia Masters are depicted conducting studies that led to their watershed publication *Human Sexual Response* (Masters & Johnson, 1966). They are far more concerned with what is 'going on' than what it might ultimately be called. The television show also depicts Masters and Johnson using specialized tools and procedures to collect their data, including such interesting inventions as vibrators with cameras. In reality, Masters and Johnson were keenly interested in the mechanics of sexual interest and arousal, and their legacy of taking risks to find the truth sets an example for sexological researchers even today.

Notwithstanding the more purely scientific approach taken by Masters and Johnson, there are clearly practical applications of sexological research when considering how best to characterize and manage sexual behaviour that puts others at risk. In this vein, devices and procedures designed to study sexuality have been pressed into service in the interests of criminal justice and social control. Possibly the most common procedure of this sort used in the assessment and risk management of persons who have sexually offended is that of psychophysiological sexual preference testing. The *phallometric* test, or penile plethysmograph (commonly known as the PPG; see Bancroft, Jones, & Pullan, 1966; Barlow, Becker, Leitenberg, & Agras, 1970; Freund, Sedlacek, & Knob, 1965), involves the measurement of changes in penile physiology (volume or circumference) during the presentation of potentially erotic audiovisual stimuli. Specifically, subjects are evaluated as to whether they show greater preference for inappropriate stimuli (e.g., children, sexual violence) than appropriate stimuli (e.g., adults, consenting sexual interactions). As one might conclude, measuring penile physiology while essentially presenting 'dirty pictures' or other sexually charged stimuli has drawn criticism from ethicists, civil libertarians, and political and religious conservatives. Despite these concerns, two highly influential meta-analyses of the predictors of sexual reoffending both identified possession of deviant sexual interests (as measured by phallometry) to be the single most robust predictor (Hanson & Bussière, 1998; Hanson & Morton-Bourgon, 2005). This predictive aspect creates a dilemma for novice clinicians and evaluators. On the one hand, the predictive validity of phallometrics is compelling. On the other, this same predictive validity cannot be used in isolation. Even with the advent of actuarial scales, it can be tempting to misinterpret these data in risk assessments.

This chapter reviews the pertinent research regarding phallometric assessment of sexual deviance, particularly as it pertains to the methodology, reliability, validity, and general utility of phallometric procedures designed to identify sexually deviant interests and preferences. We also review the use of phallometric test data in the construction of treatment and risk management plans.

A Brief History of the Objective Measurement of Sexual Arousal

The basic assumption in phallometry is that sexual preferences may be determined by measuring sexual arousal and that this arousal is best illustrated by activity in penile physiology (Masters & Johnson, 1966). Bayliss (1908) studied sexual arousal patterns in dogs and is believed to be the first person to attempt to measure sexual arousal. It was not until almost three decades later that Hynie (1934) first used penile changes in studies of human sexuality. Ohlmeyer, Brilmayer, and Hullstrung (1944) later constructed a very crude circumferential plethysmograph in their studies of nocturnal erections; however, their device was strictly an 'on–off' sensor and did not measure gradations of sexual arousal.

Czech psychiatrist Kurt Freund (1957; Freund, Diamant, & Pinkava, 1958; see history in Wilson & Freund-Mathon, 2007) is generally acknowledged as the pioneer of the modern phallometric method as used in forensic and sexological research contexts over the past 60 years. Freund devised a volumetric sensor (described in detail below; see also Figure 38.1) and originally used it as a means of discriminating between heterosexuality and homosexuality, specifically as a means to evaluate the veracity of claims of homosexuality by Czech men attempting to avoid compulsory military service. Freund quickly realized, however, that his method might be expanded to discriminations of preferences in sexually deviant behaviour patterns – what we now generally describe as paraphilias.

Following Freund's introduction of the volumetric phallometer, Fisher, Gross, and Zuch (1965) developed a circumferential device based on a mercury-in-rubber strain gauge described by Whitney (1949), and used it in the study of erectile potentials during sleep. This apparatus was modified slightly by Bancroft et al. (1966), and a Bancroft-style device is most widely used today. Another circumferential device was later devised by Barlow et al. (1970), but it has proven to be less popular.

Phallometric testing is currently used as a diagnostic, treatment planning, and risk management tool in a variety of jurisdictions. Perhaps the most active phallometric research centre in the world is the Kurt Freund Laboratory at the Centre for Addiction and Mental Health, a psychiatric teaching hospital affiliated with the University of

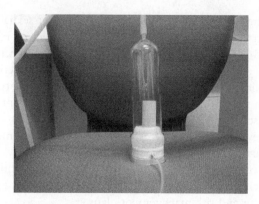

Figure 38.1   Volumetric phallometric apparatus. Source: Photograph courtesy of the Kurt Freund Laboratory, Toronto, ON, Canada.

Toronto in Canada. Nearly 20 years after his death, Freund's legacy of field-leading research in sexual preference testing continues in the laboratory named after him. Interestingly, despite the relatively widespread use of phallometric procedures, there have been only a few comprehensive critical evaluations of the method's sensitivity and specificity, and standardization remains elusive. Regarding the latter, beyond testing protocols and equipment that are available commercially, surprisingly little has been published regarding ideal stimulus sets and methods to ensure accuracy (Marshall & Fernandez, 2003).

It is important to focus precisely on these difficulties regarding standardization, accuracy, and ethics. With the aforementioned recent public focus on sexual deviations and their manifestations, it is all the more important that phallometric diagnostic clinics establish and periodically re-evaluate the psychometric properties and practical utility of the procedures that they employ. It is important to ensure that the phallometric procedure does not go the way of the lie detector test, or polygraph, which has been subject to considerable scrutiny in the recent past, largely because of a dearth of data regarding validity and reliability. In general, it is critical that persons using phallometric methods be aware of the strengths and limitations involved in administering such tests, specifically regarding false positives, false negatives, faking, and the general misuse of the method for purposes other than that for which it was originally conceived. Further, the context in which phallometric testing takes place requires considerable ethical consideration. For example, a US Appeals Court decision, *Harrington v. Almy*,[1] found that phallometric testing could not be used as a condition of employment. In other situations, ethical considerations regarding informed consent exist where an evaluation subject may face consequences (e.g., civil commitment) depending upon the results of testing. Specifically, in *US v. McLaurin*,[2] the US Court of Appeals for the Second Circuit (New York) vacated a lower court ruling compelling a sexual offender to cooperate with PPG evaluation.

---

[1] http://www.leagle.com/decision/19921014977F2d37_11009.
[2] http://www.ca2.uscourts.gov/decisions/isysquery/c1aaee69-7cdc-4326-9229-0a5edf4cc7b4/1/doc/12-3514_opn.pdf.

Two Types of Phallometer

Volumetric Method

As mentioned above, there are currently two methods for measuring changes in penile physiology during phallometric testing. The first involves measuring changes in air volume displacement in a glass cylinder that is placed over the subject's penis (Freund et al., 1965; McConaghy, 1974a). Once this apparatus is attached, penile tumescence is measured as the client is presented with a variety of audiovisual stimuli in discrete categories (some of which are normative whereas others represent anomalous interests). The means by which penile tumescence is measured, as explained and illustrated by Freund et al. (1965), is highly precise although somewhat indirect. The penis is inserted through an inflatable ring (fashioned from a prophylactic) into a small chamber – a glass cylinder. When the ring (or 'cuff' – see Figure 38.1) is inflated around the base of the penis, the air in the cylinder is sealed off from the outside atmosphere, allowing the measurement of discrete air pressure differentials within the enclosed chamber. For example, any increase in volume of the penis results in a corresponding compression of the air in the cylinder and a positive pressure difference is measured. As the stimulus trial runs, air pressure differentials are sent to a nearby transducer via a thin rubber tube. The pressure transducer senses these changes and converts them to electrical output, which is then converted using an analogue-to-digital converter. The digitized data are transferred to a computer for storage, after which they can be regenerated in analogue form and subsequently scored, plotted, edited of artefact, rescored, and finally evaluated (see detailed descriptions in Freund & Blanchard, 1989; Freund & Watson, 1991).

Circumferential Method

The second phallometric method involves the measurement of changes in penile circumference using one of two instruments devised for this purpose. The first is a simple strain gauge comprised of a length of silicone rubber tubing filled with mercury (or, more recently, indium–gallium) and fitted with an adjustable electrode at either end (Bancroft et al., 1966) (see Figure 38.2). This tubing is then fashioned into a ring through which the penis may be inserted and arranged midway along the shaft of the client's penis. Another circumferential strain gauge apparatus was devised by Barlow et al. (1970) and consists of a spring made of surgical steel. This device fits around the penis about half way along the shaft. Its diameter increases or decreases with changes in penile circumference.

Once calibrated, any changes in the diameter of the loop of the Bancroft-style gauge or increases in strain on the spring of the Barlow-style gauge cause a resultant change in current. These changes in current can be recorded via an EEG or polygraph machine and evaluations of sexual arousal made from the resultant hard output. Barlow et al. (1970) noted that their strain gauge was limited by its inability to stretch with larger changes in arousal; however, Laws (1976) found that there were no significant differences between the two strain gauges.

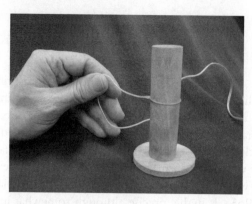

Figure 38.2 Circumferential phallometric apparatus. Source: Photograph courtesy of the Kurt Freund Laboratory, Toronto, ON, Canada.

Strengths and Weaknesses of the Methods

Each technique, volumetric or circumferential, has both good and bad points. An immediate advantage that the strain gauge has over the volumetric device is that it is simpler, less expensive in the immediate sense, and is commercially available (e.g., Behavioral Technology [Monarch 21 PPG]; Limestone Industries). Freund's volumetric method has consistently required the production of both specialized equipment and software, but is arguably more sensitive to extraneous movement artefact than circumferential methods. Further, although it has often been suggested that Freund's device is more cumbersome and awkward (Bancroft et al., 1966; Barlow et al., 1970), clinical experience has shown that although this may be initially true, the client becomes quickly accustomed to the apparatus.

When measuring penile tumescence, it appears that the volumetric method is more precise and sensitive than the strain gauge device (Clark, 1972; Freund, Langevin, & Barlow, 1974a; Kuban, Barbaree, & Blanchard, 1999; McConaghy, 1974a). This is likely because the volumetric device measures changes in three dimensions and not just circumference. It has been shown that the penis tends to elongate in the first few seconds of arousal while circumference decreases (McConaghy, 1974a). In such a case, the volumetric device would register a *positive* change in size/arousal whereas a strain gauge would actually show a *decrease* in circumference. The strain gauge appears to be good indicator of gross sexual arousal; however, this method is not as effective in the measurement of smaller levels of arousal (Freund & Blanchard, 1981; Kuban et al., 1999). Volumetric phallometry allows the accurate discrimination of exceptionally small responses to sexually explicit stimuli (Freund et al., 1974a). Indeed, upon completion of the testing procedure, some test subjects are apologetic because of their perceived lack of response, even though their output may have been sufficient to declare the test protocol valid. This sensitivity to low levels of responding is particularly powerful in combating interference with the test outcome by the subject (Freund, 1971; Freund, Watson, & Rienzo, 1988; Wilson, 1998; see also below). Overall, output measured concurrently by the two methods is highly correlated; however, the strength of the correlation increases with the amount of arousal demonstrated

(Kuban et al., 1999). Lower level responding in circumferential testing appears to have less reliability, which has led some to suggest that a minimum degree of arousal be observed before the test protocol can be declared valid (Kuban et al., 1999; see also Scoring and Interpretation, below).

Stimuli

In the almost 60 years since the inception of the phallometric method for the diagnosis of paraphilias, there have been many technical and practical refinements. Researchers using both the volumetric and circumferential techniques are now confident that the method accurately measures penile blood differentials. One of the problems that persists, however, is concerned with which type(s) of stimulus materials produce the most objective and effective results. Also, owing to the much greater intolerance and social difficulty associated with child abuse images (i.e., child pornography), jurisdictional issues may play a factor in how explicit stimuli in phallometric procedures can be used without inflaming local judicial interest. Indeed, some locations continue to use visual images that depict people in the nude; however, other jurisdictions have, for reasons of social propriety, effectively outlawed the use of phallometry.

Freund et al. (1958) originally started with the use of black and white still photographs of nude models, and this later evolved to motion picture material, also featuring nude models often shown walking toward the camera. Still photographs and motion pictures have been compared by both Freund, Langevin, and Zajac (1974b) and McConaghy (1974b). As would be expected, both studies indicated the supremacy of motion picture stimuli over still photography. This is presumably because of the more life-like qualities inherent in motion pictures, although the activities depicted could themselves provide sexual novelty and simulate elements of the courtship process. To create a standard full-figure film series for diagnosing gender and age preferences, Freund attended a naturist camp in Ontario in the early 1970s and gave a lecture on sexual health in exchange for the families agreeing to travel to the psychiatric hospital to be filmed. Each film segment consists of a model walking towards the camera in the nude, then turning and walking away – lasting approximately 28–30 s (see Freund & Blanchard, 1989). The same curtain background is used, so that the only thing that changes from segment to segment is the model. At the same time, still photographs were also taken of each model, including full-figure front and back, genital area, chest, and hands and feet – again, the backgrounds were identical, with the only thing that changed being the model.

In attempting to establish which stimulus form might be best, one must consider the variety of sexually deviant interests and preferences that the examiner may be attempting to identify. The means by which one would stimulate an age/partner preference offender (e.g., paedophilia, hebephilia – sexual interest in children or early adolescents, respectively) may be different from the way in which one would stimulate an activity preference offender (e.g., rape, sadism, courtship disorders; Freund & Watson, 1990). In the former, one might conjecture that body shape is more important, requiring the use of visual stimuli, whereas, activity preference issues may require more descriptiveness ultimately better served by audiotaped narratives.

In studies in which the author[3] participated at the Kurt Freund Laboratory in Toronto, it was found that visual stimuli work best for disorders of partner preference (e.g., paedophilia, hebephilia). As noted above, this is likely because the interests in question include a large aspect based on anatomical preference, or body shape (Freund, 1988). Although audiotaped narratives have become the stimuli of choice for many researchers (Avery-Clark & Laws, 1984; Byrne, 2001) because of their strength, they often muddle the stimuli, adding an unwanted subjective, activity-related element. Narratives have been profitably used to augment visual stimuli, thereby increasing their overall strength (see Freund & Watson, 1991); however, it is important to recognize that the greater the erotic component in the narrative, the greater is the degree of potential response and the less discriminative ability the subject will have (Malcolm, Davidson, & Marshall, 1985). Indeed, this was an issue faced in the Kurt Freund Laboratory during the 1980s, during which considerably difficulty was experienced in attempting to distinguish sexual aggressives from community controls when presenting filmed rape scenes. It appeared as if the community controls were being stimulated by the sexual elements such that we could not separate them reliably from those aroused by the strictly violent elements. In other words, some controls appeared able to overlook the violent elements and enjoy the sexual elements, thereby not distinguishing themselves from the subjects who had histories of overt sexual violence.

Overall, phallometrically derived diagnoses of deviant activity preferences, such as exhibitionism, voyeurism, or sexual dangerousness (e.g., coercion, sexual sadism), have proven difficult to achieve. This may have a lot to do with the sometimes idiosyncratic nature of sexual expression, even among offenders. For example, not all persons who are sexually aroused by coercion act out their deviant interests in the same manner. There are several dozen paraphilias that have been described (Money, 1986), and it would be virtually impossible to compose a standardized test for activity anomalies that encompasses the whole gamut of possibilities. Most clinicians or researchers do not have the time or resources to allow for tailoring test stimuli to each individual offender.

Another critical factor in the development of an adequate phallometric stimuli series is the availability of stimulus materials. The stimulus materials used for age and gender preference testing at the Kurt Freund Laboratory are likely without rival; however, many of these films (originally 16 mm) and slides were fairly old and showing signs of decay (loss of colour, breakage, etc.) before they could be digitally converted. This would not normally be a problem, as average visual stimuli can be rephotographed whenever necessary. Unfortunately, the pertinent materials here include images of children in the nude. The social climate has changed so dramatically over the past 45 years that materials relatively easily obtained in the late 1960s and early 1970s are now virtually impossible to replace. Some efforts have been made to create digital images (e.g., computer graphics; see Konopasky & Konopasky, 2000); however, the same concerns regarding child pornography might remain. Additionally, real questions exist as to whether computer-generated images can elicit sexual responding in the same way that 'real' pictures do.

---

[3] For information purposes, Robin Wilson and Robin Watson are one and the same.

A Sample Phallometric Procedure

The phallometric test of paedohebephilia typically used at the Kurt Freund Laboratory (see Blanchard, Klassen, Dickey, Kuban, & Blak, 2001; Freund & Blanchard, 1989; Freund & Watson, 1991) is administered in two sessions; however, a subject diagnosed as erotically preferring minors in Session One would not be required to undergo Session Two. In Session One, 16 mm colour filmclips of nude female and male individuals are presented, as described above, in four age categories: 5–8-year-old children, 8–11-year-old children, pubescents (11–14 years old), and physically mature persons (18+ years old). Additionally, sexually neutral filmclips (e.g., landscape scenes) are shown. This test session consists of three blocks of nine trials (27 in total), each of 28 s duration. Every trial consists of two consecutive film strips of 14 s duration showing either different individuals of the same gender–age category or landscapes. These visual stimuli are presented concurrently with a taped narrative describing involvement of the depicted persons in non-sexual activities (such as swimming). The narratives stress characteristic features of the depicted persons' body shape, and the landscape scenes have associated sexually neutral descriptions. The depictions of the eight gender–age categories and the landscapes are presented in fixed random succession with the exception that direct succession of trials of the same gender–age category is not allowed.

In Session Two, slides are presented showing nude 8–11-year-old girls and boys, physically mature persons of both genders, and landscapes. In each trial, nine slides depicting three different views of three different persons of the same gender–age category are presented such that each of three screens shows three slides – front view, rear view, and genital region – in fixed random succession. No two slides with the same type of view are shown at the same time. Each gender–age category is presented once in each of five blocks arranged in fixed random order with the exception that direct succession of two trials of the same gender–age category is not allowed. Each trial is accompanied by a narrative depicting a person of the presented gender–age category in sexual interaction with the subject.

The above example relates to what might be done in a volumetric phallometric test procedure, each session of which typically takes about 1 h. In a circumferential evaluation, the procedures are largely similar, except that the equipment and stimuli are usually commercially obtained and do not include nude models. Instead, pictures of clothed models accompany taped narratives. Similarly to the volumetric protocol, individual test sessions last approximately 1 h. In both procedures, the client is seated in a La-Z-Boy chair, reclined so as to allow free blood flow to the groin area. The test administrator is generally in the same room with the client, who is provided with a sheet to cover himself; however, there is often a partition between them and direct observations of the client are usually accomplished via closed-circuit television.

Scoring and Interpretation

Once the phallometric test has been administered and raw data are available, the administrator must then score and interpret the data to determine the subject's sexual interests and preferences. There is currently no consistent way in which phallomet-ric outcome data are either scored or interpreted; however, the research literature provides considerable guidance on both subjects (e.g., Her Majesty's Prison Service, 2007; Lalumière & Harris, 1998; Marshall & Fernandez, 2003). Ultimately, the goal is to use the subject's differential responses to the various categories of stimuli to make inferences about erotic preferences and to assess risk for recidivism. Logically, persons with sexual offence histories who demonstrate deviant interests or preferences are more likely to be both paraphilic and at risk for future illegal sexual conduct (Fre-und & Blanchard, 1989); however, it is important to remember that this is not always the case.

The sort of data collected may differ depending on the method of phallometry used – volumetric versus circumferential. In the former, penile volume changes are measured in two ways: (1) as the largest deviation from baseline occurring during the trial (known as 'D-type scores'), and (2) as the area under the plotted curve of penile volume change (known as 'A-type scores'). For each session, the subject's D-type scores are converted into standard scores, and the same operation is carried out on each subject's A-type scores. Next, these standardized D- and A-type scores are combined to yield a composite (C-type) score for each trial of a session, using z-scores according to the equation $C = (z_D + z_A)/2$. In Figure 38.3, curves A and B each show the same magnitude of overall volume change (D-type); however, the area under curve B (A-type) is greater, owing to the speed with which subject B achieved maximum deviation from the baseline. The validity of the test protocol itself is established by calculating an Output Index (see Freund & Blanchard, 1989; Freund & Watson, 1991), which is calculated as the average of the three largest D-type scores, not including responses to sexually neutral stimuli. Output indices ≥ 1.0 mL are generally considered sufficient in volumetric procedures.

In circumferential testing procedures, there are also two change scores that are typically recorded: (1) percentage of full erection (as measured prior to testing) and

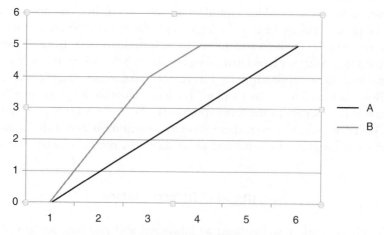

Figure 38.3 Peak responding (A) versus area under the curve (B).

Table 38.1 Sample diagnostic flow chart

Formula	Resultant z-score	Diagnosis
$z_{adults} - z_{children}$	<-0.25	Paedophilia
$z_{adults} - z_{children}$	Between limits $-0.25/+0.25$	No differentiation[a]
$z_{adults} - z_{children}$	$>+0.25$	Preference for adults

[a]Some laboratories may consider no differentiation between children and adults to be indicative of paedophilic interests.

(2) change in penile circumference (again, peak minus baseline, usually measured in millimetres). Research by Howes (2003) supports the conversion of raw responses to percentage of full arousal as the preferred method; however, this is greatly dependent on the subject's ability to achieve full erection and the administrator's confidence that 'fullness' has actually been achieved in the calibration process prior to testing. Both Marshall and Fernandez (2003) and Lalumière and Harris (1998) noted that the use of percentage of full erection can be problematic, citing issues with respect to individual differences in penis size and responsiveness. These issues are less pronounced if one uses changes in penile circumference as the indicator of arousal; however, the standard remains percentage of full erection (Lalumière & Harris, 1998). Research (see Kuban et al., 1999) has suggested that 10% of full erection, or a 2.5 mm increase in circumference, is required to declare a circumferential protocol to be valid.

No matter which method is used, volumetric or circumferential, most researchers agree that conversion of change scores to standard scores (i.e., z-scores) is the preferred procedure to facilitate interpretation (see Freund & Blanchard, 1989; Lalumière & Harris, 1998). Given that most phallometric test protocols include multiple presentations of individual stimulus categories, it is common for the z-scores for individual trials to be averaged across the category, giving a more reliable indication of level of interest or preference than a single presentation alone (see Freund & Watson, 1991; Lalumière & Quinsey, 1994). For volumetric procedures, the z-scores for peak change in volume (D-type) and z-scores for area under the curve (A-type) within any individual trial (and, ultimately, within stimulus categories) are also typically averaged.

Once the z-score transformations are completed, the differences between stimulus categories (or lack thereof) can be compared and interpreted. A preference index can then be calculated by subtracting the z-score associated with the greater mean response to either gender category of children (boys and girls) from the z-score for the greater mean response to the two categories of adults (men and women). Table 38.1 provides a sample flow chart. Typically, phallometric test constructors sacrifice a degree of sensitivity (the percentage of people with paedophilia who will test positive for paedophilia) in order to minimize difficulties in specificity (the false-positive rate in persons without the deviant interests or preference). As such, most laboratories look for a clear difference in the preference index (see Freund & Watson, 1991), hence the ±0.25 z cushion around the zero point as shown in Table 38.1.

Technological Advances

In early days, the use of phallometric methods to assess erotic preferences required considerable work on the part of the test administrator, who needed to start and stop stimuli and make many measurements by hand, thus increasing the potential for human error. With the advent of personal computers in the 1980s, phallometry could be fully automated (Barnard, Robbins, Tingle, Shaw, & Newman, 1987). Full-package phallometric kits can now be commercially obtained, with specialized training available for staff who will conduct the testing. Regarding software for scoring, Freund and Blanchard (1989; see also Freund & Watson, 1991) were among the first to implement a computerized diagnostic programme, the Phallometric Expert System (PES), which was designed to emulate Freund's clinical decision-making processes. When all test information was fed into the computer, PES could render a reliable diagnosis in offenders against children (Freund & Blanchard, 1989; Freund & Watson, 1991). Software for test administration and interpretation has continued to grow in sophistication.

Psychometric Properties

All psychometric procedures must be evaluated for their reliability and validity, among other constructs. Reliability refers to the consistency of findings – essentially, how often will the test give the same answer in the same person? Validity, on the other hand, refers to how well the procedure measures what it is intending to measure. Standardization is another important construct requiring that phallometric procedures be common and consistent, both within testing sites and from site to site. Like other tests, phallometry has its share of foibles with regard to psychometric properties.

Standardization is likely phallometry's greatest challenge at this time, despite a call by the Association for the Treatment of Sexual Abusers (2005) for standard protocols. There are individual laboratories that have standardized their procedures, in-house, but standardization across sites remains less than optimal (Marshall & Fernandez, 2003). Currently, most laboratories are likely to purchase their equipment and stimuli from one of two main companies – Behavioral Technology or Limestone Technologies – which has no doubt led to at least some greater degree of standardization. However, the general lack of standardization extends beyond simply using the same equipment and stimuli to methods of scoring and interpretation (Her Majesty's Prison Service, 2007, Marshall & Fernandez, 2003).

Reliability requires that a test be able to produce consistent findings regardless of setting and timing. When tests demonstrate problems in reliability, questions arise as to the strength that we can attribute to the findings. Overall, the phallometric method has not enjoyed strong support with regard to reliability, although reasons for this remain unclear. Adequate levels of internal consistency have been achieved by increasing the number of stimuli per category (e.g., children, pubescents, adults; see Lalumière & Quinsey, 1994) and by ensuring that extraneous influences are minimized (e.g., different backgrounds in photographs, different voices in audiotaped stimuli). Ideally, all that should change from stimulus to stimulus is the construct being measured.

Regarding test–retest reliability, evaluations of offenders against either adults or children produced only minimal levels (see Marshall & Fernandez, 2003). It has been argued that one of the principal reasons for low reliability in phallometric testing is because of its susceptibility to learning and faking (see Marshall & Fernandez, 2003; Wilson, 1998). Essentially, the more often one takes a test, the more familiar one becomes with the methods and intent. Given the high degree of social desirability associated with providing 'non-deviant' responses, it comes as no great surprise that test subjects are highly motivated (and able) to influence the outcome (Freund et al., 1988; Orne, 1962; Wilson, 1998).

Specificity refers to the method's propensity to give true-negative results, that is, how often does the test indicate non-deviant interests in someone who actually does not possess them? Freund and Watson (1991) reported a specificity rate of 97%, meaning that only three of every 100 persons without sexual interest in minors would show such interests (i.e., a 3% false-positive rate). However, in order to achieve this degree of specificity, we generated our control sample from sexual offenders against adults who professed no interest in children. When using paid community volunteers (mostly college students and job placement clients), we found that nearly 20% showed sexual interest in children, leading to the conjecture that subjects' test-taking attitudes were not equivalent to those of the child molester clients, in that they did not face the same demand situation (e.g., the tendency of persons to alter their conduct depending on perceived benefits or costs of the situation in which they find themselves; see Orne, 1962). Later, Blanchard et al. (2001) showed clearly that the degree of proof that a test subject was gynaephilic (a sexual preference for female adults, as demonstrated in Blanchard et al. (2001) by number of female adult partners) was positively correlated with increased specificity. Overall, specificity does not seem to be a major problem for the phallometric test, with most studies reporting rates in the 95% range (e.g., Barsetti, Earls, Lalumière, & Belanger, 1998; Chaplin, Rice, & Harris, 1995; Marshall, Barbaree, & Christophe, 1986).

The crux in phallometric testing is how well the test is able to detect deviant sexual interests in those who actually possess them – known as sensitivity. It is well established that not all sexual offenders have sexually deviant preferences and that not all persons with sexually deviant preferences are sexual offenders. In establishing the validity of the method, the first step is to establish how often the method gives true-positive results (sensitivity); for example, how often does the phallometric test for paedophilia identify such interests in persons who are truly paedophilic? Sensitivity levels reported in research have varied, depending on the study. Marshall et al. (1986) reported 40% sensitivity in their child molester clients, whereas Malcolm, Andrews, and Quinsey (1993) reported 41% and Barsetti et al. (1998) reported 68% for intrafamilial child molesters and 65% for extra-familial child molesters – with all these studies having demonstrated 95% specificity in their (supposedly) non-deviant control samples. Freund and Watson (1991) showed that sensitivities could vary depending on the target gender of the victims and the number of victims that the offender had had. When offenders with at least two victims were used, sensitivity was 78.2% for those who targeted girls and 88.6% for those who targeted boys. Of those offenders with only one victim, sensitivity was 44.5% for those with a female victim versus 86.7% for those with a male victim. Freund, Watson, and Dickey (1991) showed additionally that identification of paedophilic interests on phallometric testing could be predicted by both number of victims and whether victims were solicited from outside familial contexts.

Once deviant interests and preferences have been identified, the next question to be asked is how often persons with those interests and preferences go on to commit similar offences (i.e., predictive validity). It makes some logical sense that persons with such interests and who have acted on them in the past will be more likely to engage in similar behaviour in the future. In both Hanson meta-analyses of the predictors of sexual reoffending (Hanson & Bussière, 1998; Hanson & Morton-Bourgon, 2005), a paedophilia index derived from phallometric testing was the most robust predictor of recidivism. This is echoed in research by Kingston et al. (2007) and Wilson et al. (2011), each of whom found that deviant profiles on phallometric testing were predictive of future offending. Interestingly, in each of these studies, DSM-IV-TR (American Psychiatric Association, 2000) criteria were not predictive of outcome.

In the preceding paragraph, strong results were reported regarding the phallometric test's predictive validity with offenders against minors. Interestingly, the same results have not been consistently found regarding offenders against adults (e.g., rapists). Indeed, where the research has generally supported the use of the phallometric test for distinguishing age and gender preference, it has been mixed regarding sexual dangerousness (rape, coercion, sexual sadism). For instance, during nearly 8 years of exhaustive attempts in the Kurt Freund Laboratory during the 1980s to develop a reliable and valid test protocol for sexual dangerousness, Freund and the present author were only able to show group differences between offenders and community control subjects – we were never able to achieve a level of specificity that would support individual diagnosis. Others have suggested that the phallometric test can be used to diagnose sexual dangerousness reliably (e.g., Lalumière, Quinsey, Harris, Rice, & Trautrimas, 2003); however, the degree of diagnostic power remains well below that enjoyed by the phallometric protocol for age and gender preferences.

Intentional Interference, Feigning, and Other Problems with Phallometric Testing

It is easy to determine from the above discussion that techniques of measuring sexual arousal are far from foolproof. A major problem with phallometric testing (and most other psychophysiological methods) is the degree of conscious control that a subject may have on the body function being measured – in this case, penile tumescence. Faking of phallometric responses can be very perplexing for clinicians and researchers and, particularly, for those working in forensic circumstances. Not only does faking muddle the results, it makes phallometric diagnosis very difficult, which can have serious consequences in high-stakes forensic arenas such as sexual offender civil commitment.

An early report by Laws and Rubin (1969) determined that subjects were able to manipulate their sexual arousal when instructed to do so; describing various techniques of suppression such as reciting poetry, counting, etc., Laws and Rubin claimed that subjects in their research could effectively decrease their arousal by as much as 50%.

Card and Farrall (1990) noted that response suppression is easier for subjects to do than enhancement; however, others (Smith & Over, 1987; Wilson, 1998) have shown that subjects can easily increase penile arousal to non-preferred categories, usually accomplished through fantasy. In the circumferential method, it has been shown that at arousal levels of 50% of full erection or greater, attenuation of the response is fairly easy (Malcolm et al., 1985).

Freund et al. (1988) conducted research in which volunteer control subjects were instructed to fake as best they could. Responses were then categorized according to their self-reported feigning techniques. Three reliable signs of faking emerged: (1) 'pumping' – voluntary perineal muscle contractions with the intent of increasing response to a particular category (also alluded to in earlier publications by Freund, 1965; Quinsey & Bergersen, 1976); (2) highest mean responses to sexually neutral stimuli (e.g., images of landscapes) – a sign of suppression; and (3) equally high mean responses to male and female categories and of which at least one of these is an adult category – a further sign of suppression. Each of these three signs of feigning can be reliably determined upon inspection of the hard copy of the data (i.e., tracings). Further, it is thought that a low output index in volumetric testing or a lack of responding in circumferential testing (i.e., proxies of arousability) in younger men may also indicate response suppression (Freund, 1977), presumably because it is uncommon for younger men to experience difficulties in sexual arousability.

Voluntary control of sexual response can be highly dependent on the type of stimuli being used. Freund (1971) found that longer stimulus lengths gave the subject too much time during which to modify his responses. As such, shorter stimulus lengths may be preferable; however, this presents difficulties for circumferential phallometricians, because that method is not as sensitive to small changes in sexual arousal (Abel, Becker, Murphy, & Flanagan, 1981; Avery-Clark & Laws, 1984). Lalumière and Harris (1998) suggested that the minimum length should be 60 s, although they were reporting on circumferential methods. Overall, it would appear that there is some advantage to using the volumetric plethysmograph, owing to its greater ability to measure more subtle arousal. The Kurt Freund Laboratory has consistently demonstrated that 30 s is sufficient for volumetric methods.

At present, there are many ways of combating faking, none of which seems to work with 100% efficiency. Quinsey and Chaplin (1987) described a semantic tracking task in which the subject was required to listen for verbal cues in audiotaped stimuli and then press buttons appropriately. A further way of combating response faking is to increase stimulus strength in an attempt to 'flood' the subject, so that he is unable to 'escape' from the stimuli. At the Kurt Freund Laboratory, this is accomplished by presenting stimuli simultaneously on three screens arranged in an arc around the subject. Further, some sexual offender programmes require polygraph examinations after phallometric testing to help verify adherence to test expectations (see Kaine & Mersereau, 1986). Indeed, most circumferential phallometric procedures include simultaneous measurement of other psychophysiological responding, similarly to polygraphy. However, it is important to stress again that although these attempts to identify and diminish the effects of faking may help, they have not eliminated the problem.

Alternative Methods

Attempts have been made to measure sexual arousal using psychophysiological indicators of general arousal (i.e., sexual arousal is an example of 'specific' arousal). Although non-genital measures have given some promising results in research settings, in practical application it is generally believed that the genitals are the best indicators of sexual arousal (Masters & Johnson, 1966). For the accurate diagnosis of sexual preference, it is of paramount importance that the arousal being measured is very specific (Freund, 1977, 1981). One major drawback to this, however, is that unlike with the polygraph, the subject is acutely aware of from where the arousal measurement is being taken.

In the 1960s, considerable research was conducted using pupil dilation (pupillometry) as an indicator of sexual arousal (Hess & Polt, 1960; Hess, Seltzer, & Shlien, 1965; Nunnaly, Knott, Duchnowski, & Parker, 1967). It was shown that this method could reliably distinguish between homo- and heterosexual orientations in both male and female subjects. The same abilities were subsequently demonstrated using functional magnetic resonance imaging (fMRI) (Safron et al., 2007), in which gender preference was reliably distinguished in both male and female subjects. However, although neuroimaging methods have shown some promise (see Cantor et al., 2008), they are not yet at the level of precision required for individual diagnosis.

Viewing time (VT) methods are currently the major competitor to phallometry. In such procedures – best exemplified by the Abel Assessment method (Abel, Huffman, Warberg, & Holland, 1998; Abel, Jordan, Hand, Holland, & Phipps, 2001) and to a lesser extent the Affinity method (Glasgow, Osborne, & Croxen, 2003) – the person being evaluated is seated in front of a computer screen, where pictures of a variety of individuals or situations are presented and the length of time the person waits until switching to the next picture is measured. The inference is that the longer one looks at a certain type of picture, the more likely it is that this represents interest or a preference of sorts. VT methods have been widely used in US settings and elsewhere; however, criticisms have been levelled at the Abel Assessment method owing to the author's maintenance of proprietary rights to the evaluative algorithms. Further, others have noted that VT measures sexual interest and not sexual arousal, the latter of which has been more consistently shown to be the best indicator of sexual response (Masters & Johnson, 1966). Indeed, the best-known VT measure is called the Abel Assessment of Sexual *Interest* (italics added). Although both phallometric and viewing time measures involve processes that are, to some extent, beyond the subject's awareness, phallometry may be less subject to that person's cognitive response to the stimuli.

Additional research has been undertaken to identify other methods of determining sexual preferences. Screening tools consisting of card sort methods (Holland, Zolondek, Abel, Jordan, & Becker, 2000) have been used with some success, particularly with intellectually disabled clients (Wilson et al., 2007). However, owing to a high social desirability bias, these methods are often more easily faked than phallometric approaches. There can also be concerns – particularly with more vulnerable populations – that the card sort method may actually introduce new ideas for sexual acting out. For example, a questionnaire that asks to what extent the subject would like to tie someone up or be tied up may produce an iatrogenic effect in someone who has never considered this activity. Measures of implicit association have also provided some promise in identifying sexual interest in children (Nunes, Firestone, & Baldwin, 2007), but further study is needed.

Measurement of Sexual Arousal in Female Subjects

In the context of this chapter, the rationale behind measurement of sexual arousal in females is often entirely different from that of measurement in males. Genital plethysmography has a practical application in males (e.g., diagnosis of paraphilias); however, these deviant behaviour patterns appear, for the most part, to be of considerably greater concern for males. An early report by O'Connor (1987) cited UK Home Office statistics stating that of all sexually related crimes, only 0.95% are perpetrated by females. Recent literature has suggested that this is likely an underestimate, but most of the behaviour of this sort is still engaged in by males. Cortoni and colleagues (Cortoni, Hanson, & Coache, 2010; see also Gannon & Cortoni, 2010) have compellingly argued that 'female sexual offenders are different'. Specifically, many offences committed by females are for aiding and abetting a male in his sexually offensive behaviour. There is also research suggesting that female offenders against children under 16 years of age are likely to have prior psychiatric diagnoses or histories (Gannon & Cortoni, 2010), something that is not found as commonly in their male counterparts. Generally, paraphilic presentations in females are rare (Gannon & Cortoni, 2010) and sexual reoffence rates in females vary from approximately 1 to 5%, depending on the study (see Cortoni et al., 2010). Therefore, at present the measurement of female sexual arousal appears to have research implications only.

Notwithstanding the lack of a good rationale for the widespread use of psychophysiological procedures to measure female sexual arousal, there are devices that could be used. One apparatus used to measure sexual arousal in women consists of a vaginal photoplethysmograph which, when inserted about 2–3 cm into the vagina, detects differences in vaginal wall opacity, which varies with blood flow (Geer, 1980; Geer, Morokoff, & Greenwood, 1974; Hoon, Wincze, & Hoon, 1976). An earlier device, consisting of an isothermal relative blood flow meter located in the outer ring of a vaginal diaphragm, was used with limited success by Cohen and Shapiro (1971). Although Geer and Hoon's groups have claimed that measurement of female sexual arousal is extremely precise, reliable, and valid, they acknowledge that it is somewhat invasive and extremely sensitive to movement, generating reliable results only when the woman is completely immobile.

Of course, extreme care should be taken in understanding the differences between sexual arousal and interest among females of all ages. Setting aside the broader differences between male and female sexuality, some studies (e.g., Chivers, Seto, & Blanchard, 2007) have suggested that sexual arousal as measured by the photoplethysmograph may be related to protective and/or evolutionary processes. For example, it makes sense that upon seeing images of intercourse, a woman's vagina would automatically begin to prepare itself for penetration whether intercourse was desired or not. This kind of reflexive action is common in other areas of human experience (e.g., startle reflexes, adopting protective physical postures in the face of an imminent attack).

Under these circumstances, there can be very real differences between sexual interest and arousal.

Phallometry as a Measure of Treatment Effectiveness

One cannot divine guilt or innocence using the phallometric test, and phallometry should never be used for such purposes. Indeed, the guidelines of the Association for the Treatment of Sexual Abusers (2005) make it clear that test results should not be used in a way that would lead a trier of fact to conclude guilt or innocence. In an era in which the results of risk assessments can have dire consequences for sexual offenders and the community alike, it is crucial to bear in mind that the principal intent of phallometric testing is to distinguish between persons who demonstrate problematic sexual arousal and preferences and those who do not (i.e., discriminant validity). Those persons demonstrating deviant profiles on the phallometric test are likely to require somewhat different treatment interventions than those who have offended but who do not show deviant sexual interests, while the results of testing can inform risk management and safety planning (e.g., decisions around who a client can live with, and/or under what conditions). Of course, it would be foolish to base any risk management or treatment decision solely on the results of an individual test.

Phallometric assessment methods were originally designed solely as a diagnostic tool, to be used in making distinctions as to erotic preferences. However, these methods have also been co-opted for use in measuring effectiveness of treatment. For example, some practitioners have described it as a kind of biofeedback tool, in which clients see if they have developed self-regulation skills for managing sexual arousal, and use phallometry in the hope that it will provide an objective measure. Often, phallometry is used in concert with behavioural approaches that specifically target sexual arousal, such as aversive reconditioning (Earls & Castonguay, 1989; Laws & Marshall, 2003), using either mild shock or noxious smells (the latter of which may ultimately be carried into the community, for 'smelling' whenever the client feels he is being inappropriately aroused/stimulated). In other programmes, phallometry is used as one measure in assessing a person's overall level of change as a consequence of involvement in cognitive–behavioural treatment.

In the present author's opinion, the results of research establishing the method's utility in this regard are conflicting and can be misleading. MacCulloch and Feldman (1970) were among the first to question the treatment evaluation potential of phallometric methods. Of greatest concern is that with each successive test administered, the subject's ability to fake his responses successfully increases (Freund, 1977; Freund & Blanchard, 1981; Wilson, 1998). It may also be the case that the sorts of techniques that one might use to fake the test are the same as those we teach clients in treatment regarding cognitive–behavioural management of intrusive, deviant fantasies and urges (e.g., Morin & Levenson, 2002). These can include techniques such as thought-stopping or cognitive problem-solving skills such as stopping and thinking, generating options, and considering the consequences of a course of action. Likewise, many treatment programmes use mindfulness and meditation exercises as a means of regulating emotional arousal. In essence, completing treatment is akin to having taken a course in 'How-to-Fake-the-Phallometric-Test-101'. Of course, this may or may not be a positive prognostic indicator, depending on the client's motivations.

Generally, a client's phallometrically derived diagnosis is directly proportional to his level of admission of a deviant preference. Accordingly, better diagnoses are made with admitters than with non-admitters, the latter of whom have greater motivation to interfere with the test (Freund, Chan, & Coulthard, 1979) owing to their demand situation (Orne, 1962). Freund (1977) stated that a test result is more likely to be valid in a person with a history of anomalous behaviour when it contradicts a 'socially favourable' claim than when it confirms a socially favourable claim. This social desirability aspect is a significant threat to the veracity of test results showing 'changes' in sexual arousability and preferences, to the extent that inferences from such testing could be fatally flawed.

Conrad and Wincze (1976) showed that even though a large number of patients may claim that therapy has led to a change in their erotic preferences, post-treatment phallometrics have often confirmed the pretreatment preference. This is not to say that treatment is invalid and unlikely to assist clients in changing their sexual behaviour. Rather, it suggests that some paraphilic presentations may be similar to orientations (see Blanchard, 2010; Seto, 2012). In these circumstances, it is unlikely that the core *preferences* will change, but the treated client is still able to adjust his *behaviour* patterns. Indeed, while sexual interests and behaviours can change in various ways over a life span, there is very little evidence that available behavioural methods such as aversion therapy are effective in the long run. Controversies regarding so-called reparative therapy (e.g., Nicolosi, 1991; Spitzer, 2012) provide further evidence that the treatment of sexual behaviour is rarely a straightforward process. Rather, there is an emerging consensus that effective treatment for people who sexually abuse and have a sexual interest in children should focus on rebuilding one's life and preventing further abuse through the development of better understanding and sexual self-regulation.

Ultimately, phallometric testing can yield excellent information about arousal and preferences – providing a helpful window into potential reoffence processes and other situations that move a person from unwilling to willing to act on their interests. However, it is vital that phallometric measurement be understood as only one part of the interactive process of human functioning. For example, treatment targeting social skills may lead to the interpersonal competencies and successes that in turn result in reduced risk for future sexual crimes, with or without changes in phallometric testing. Further, an often-overlooked aspect of holistic treatment approaches is that sexual arousal is only one component of physiological and emotional arousal. Many people engage in behaviours as a result of diverse forms of arousal (e.g., sympathetic nervous system arousal can lead to both violence and acts of heroism; Perry, 2003).

Conclusion

The introduction of the phallometric method represented a giant leap forward in the understanding of male sexual arousal and preferences, particularly with regard to forensic applications. In spite of the difficult optics (and, perhaps, ethics) associated with measuring penile responses, the value added to treatment and risk management endeavours is clear – especially in a field dominated by risk, need, and responsivity concerns (Andrews & Bonta, 2010). Given the meta-analytic findings showing that deviant sexual preferences are robust predictors of reoffending (Hanson & Bussière, 1998) and phallometry's demonstrated ability to predict reoffending (Kingston et al., 2007; Wilson et al., 2011), there is no question that the test is of use to those who seek to prevent reoffending. However, the role of sexual preference in sexual offending is far from clear, noting that there are those with deviant preferences who do not engage in sexual offending, and there are many who engage in inappropriate sexuality seemingly without attendant deviant sexual interests or preferences (Freund et al., 1991).

As many professionals have observed, mapping the workings of the body and mind can be like observing Planet Earth at night from space: one can see the lights without fully understanding what they mean, or why they are there. Phallometric testing is largely unsurpassed in its capacity to do what it was designed for – the assessment of sexual arousal – but it is clearly not without its pitfalls. Where the method has got into trouble is with regard to its misinterpretation and misuse. This author suggests that the phallometric test was designed primarily to be used as a diagnostic tool, and that its use in the evaluation of treatment efficacy is both unsupported and unwise. This is especially true given ongoing issues regarding standardization and idiosyncratic use of the method – all of which have threatened phallometry's place in the toolbox available to risk managers.

Although this author would argue that the sexual arousal measured by phallometry is a proxy for sexual preference and, at times, maybe orientation, one must concede that this is still an unanswered question. There is no doubt that people can and do change over time, albeit often very slowly. However, are these changes in preference or behaviour? Clearly, men are capable of acting outside of their sexual 'preferences' – many gay men led heterosexual lifestyles in the earlier part of the 20th century, simply because they often had no choice but to conform. Regarding sexual offending, over-reliance on sexual arousal as a fixed indicator of willingness to abuse in the absence of other indicators can only result in poor practice and policy. There is some irony in the fact that Freund's original research, compelled as it was by the Czech government, was itself misused; not all men who have sex together during military service are homosexual, and not all homosexuals are at risk for engaging in sex with others during military service. Ultimately, phallometry's reliability and validity depend on practitioners using it with the expertise that comes only with practice and consultation, and within the limits of our existing knowledge.

Acknowledgements

The author would like to thank David Prescott for his comments on and contributions to an earlier draft of this chapter. The author is also greatly appreciative of Kurt Freund, Ray Blanchard, and Ron Langevin for their mentorship regarding the maintenance of precision and empiricism in sexual psychodiagnostics.

References

Abel, G. G., Becker, J., Murphy, W., & Flanagan, B. (1981). Identifying dangerous child molesters. In R. B. Stewart (Ed.), *Violent behavior: Social learning approaches to prediction, management, and treatment* (pp. 116–137). New York, NY: Brunner/Mazel.

Abel, G. G., Huffman, J., Warberg, B., & Holland, C. L. (1998). Visual reaction time and plethysmography as measures of sexual interest in child molesters. *Sexual Abuse: A Journal of Research & Treatment, 10,* 81–96.

Abel, G. G., Jordan, A. D., Hand, C. G., Holland, L. A., & Phipps, A. (2001). Classification models of child molesters utilizing the Abel Assessment for Sexual Interest. *Child Abuse & Neglect, 25,* 703–718.

American Psychiatric Association. (2000). *Diagnostic and statistical manual of mental disorders* (4th ed., text revision) (DSM-IV-TR). Washington, DC: Author.

American Psychiatric Association. (2013). *Diagnostic and statistical manual of mental disorders* (5th ed.) (DSM-5). Arlington, VA: American Psychiatric Publishing.

Association for the Treatment of Sexual Abusers (2005). *Practice standards and guidelines for members of the association of for the treatment of sexual abusers.* Beaverton, OR: Author.

Avery-Clark, C., & Laws, D. R. (1984). Differential erection response patterns of sexual child abusers to stimuli describing activities with children. *Behavior Therapy, 15,* 71–83.

Bancroft, J., Jones, H., & Pullan, G. (1966). A simple transducer for measuring penile erection, with comments on its use in the treatment of sexual offenders. *Behaviour Research & Therapy, 4,* 239–241.

Barlow, D., Becker, J., Leitenberg, H., & Agras, W. (1970). Technical note: A mechanical strain gauge for recording penile circumference change. *Journal of Applied Behavior Analysis, 3,* 73–76.

Barnard, G., Robbins, L., Tingle, D., Shaw, T., & Newman, G. (1987). Development of a computerized sexual assessment laboratory. *Bulletin of the American Academy of Psychiatry and the Law, 15,* 339–347.

Barsetti, I., Earls, C. M., Lalumière, M. L., & Belanger, N. (1998). The differentiation of intrafamilial and extrafamilial heterosexual child molesters. *Journal of Interpersonal Violence, 13,* 275–286.

Bayliss, W. (1908). On reciprocal innervation in vaso-motor reflexes and the action of strychnine and chloroform thereon. *Proceedings of the Royal Society of London, Series B: Biological Sciences, 80,* 339–375. Cited in K. Freund, *Assessment of sexual dysfunction and deviation.* In M. Hersen & A. Bellack (Eds.), *Behavioral assessment: A practical handbook* (2nd ed., pp. 427–455). New York, NY: Pergamon.

Blanchard, R. (2010). The DSM diagnostic criteria for Pedophilia. *Archives of Sexual Behavior, 39,* 304–316.

Blanchard, R. (2011). A brief history of field trials of the DSM diagnostic criteria for paraphilias [Letter to the Editor]. *Archives of Sexual Behavior, 40,* 861–862.

Blanchard, R., Klassen, P., Dickey, R., Kuban, M. E., & Blak, T. (2001). Sensitivity and specificity of the phallometric test for pedophilia in nonadmitting sex offenders. *Psychological Assessment, 13,* 118–126.

Brandt, J., Wilson, R. J., & Prescott, D. S. (2015). Doubts about SVP programs: A critical review of sexual offender civil commitment in the US. In B. K. Schwartz (Ed.), *The sex offender: Insights on treatment and policy development* (Vol. 8). Kingston, NJ: Civic Research Institute.

Byrne, P. (2001). *The reliability and validity of less explicit audio and 'clothed' visual penile plethysmograph stimuli with child molesters and nonoffenders* (Unpublished doctoral thesis), University of Utah.

Cantor, J. M., Kabani, N., Christensen, B. K., Zipursky, R. B., Barbaree, H. E., Dickey, R., ... Blanchard, R. (2008). Cerebral white matter deficiencies in pedophilic men. *Journal of Psychiatric Research, 42*, 167–183.

Card, R. D., & Farrall, W. R. (1990). Detecting faked responses to erotic stimuli: A comparison of stimulus conditions and response measures. *Annals of Sex Research, 3*, 381–396.

Center for Sex Offender Management (2010). *Exploring public awareness and attitudes about sex offender management: Findings from a national public opinion poll.* Washington, DC: Author.

Chaplin, T. C., Rice, M. E., & Harris, G. T. (1995). Salient victim suffering and the sexual responses of child molesters. *Journal of Consulting and Clinical Psychology, 163*, 249–255.

Chivers, M. L., Seto, M. C., & Blanchard, R. (2007). Gender and sexual orientation differences in sexual response to sexual activities versus gender of actors in sexual films. *Journal of Personality and Social Psychology, 93*, 1108–1121.

Clark, T. O. (1972). Penile volume responses, sexual orientation and conditioning performance [Letter to the Editor]. *British Journal of Psychiatry, 120*, 126.

Cohen, H. D., & Shapiro, A. (1971). A method for measuring sexual arousal in the female. *SPR Abstracts, 8*, 251–252.

Conrad, S., & Wincze, J. (1976). Orgasmic reconditioning: A controlled study of its effects upon the sexual arousal and behavior of adult male homosexuals. *Behavior Therapy, 7*, 155–166.

Cortoni, F., Hanson, R. K., & Coache, M.-E. (2010). The recidivism rates of female sexual offenders are low: A meta-analysis. *Sexual Abuse: A Journal of Research & Treatment, 22*, 387–401.

D'Orazio, D., Wilson, R. J., & Thornton, D. (2011, November). *Prevalence of pedohebephilia, paraphilic coercive disorder, and sadism diagnoses produced with the proposed DSM-5 criterion sets.* Paper presented at the 30th Annual Conference of the Association for the Treatment of Sexual Abusers, Toronto, Canada.

Duncan, B. L., Miller, S. D., & Sparks, J. A. (2004). *The heroic client: A revolutionary way to improve effectiveness through client-directed, outcome-informed therapy.* San Francisco, CA: Jossey-Bass.

Earls, C. M., & Castonguay, L. G. (1989). The evaluation of olfactory aversion for a bisexual pedophile with a single-case multiple baseline design. *Behaviour Therapy, 20*, 137–146.

Fisher, C., Gross, J., & Zuch, J. (1965). Cycle of penile erection synchronous with dreaming (REM) sleep. *Archives of General Psychiatry, 12*, 29–45.

Freund, K. (1957). Diagnostika homosexuality u muzu [Diagnosing homosexuality in men]. *Cs. Psychiatry, 53*, 382–393.

Freund, K. (1965). Diagnosing heterosexual pedophilia by means of a test for sexual interest. *Behaviour Research & Therapy, 3*, 229–234.

Freund, K. (1971). A note on the use of the phallometric method of measuring mild sexual arousal in the male. *Behavior Therapy, 2*, 223–228.

Freund, K. (1977). Psycho-physiological assessment of change in erotic preference. *Behaviour Research and Therapy, 15*, 297–301.

Freund, K. (1981). Assessment of pedophilia. In M. Cook & K. Howells (Eds.), *Adult sexual interest in children* (pp. 139–179). London, England: Academic Press.

Freund, K. (1988). *An aetiological theory of pedophilia.* Unpublished manuscript.

Freund, K., & Blanchard, R. (1981). Assessment of anomalous erotic preferences and coital dysfunctions. In M. Hersen & A. S. Bellack (Eds.), *Behavioral assessment: A practical handbook* (2nd ed., pp. 427–455). New York, NY: Pergamon.

Freund, K., & Blanchard, R. (1989). Phallometric diagnosis of pedophilia. *Journal of Consulting and Clinical Psychology, 57,* 1–6.

Freund, K., Chan, S., & Coulthard, R. (1979). Phallometric diagnosis with 'non-admitters'. *Behaviour Research and Therapy, 17,* 451–457.

Freund, K., Diamant, J., & Pinkava, V. (1958). On the validity and reliability of the phalloplethysmographic diagnosis of some sexual deviations. *Review of Czechoslovak Medicine, 4,* 145–151.

Freund, K., Langevin, R., & Barlow, D. (1974a). Comparison of two penile measures of erotic arousal. *Behaviour Research & Therapy, 12,* 355–359.

Freund, K., Langevin, R., & Zajac, Y. (1974b). A note on the erotic arousal value of moving and stationary forms. *Behaviour Research and Therapy, 12,* 117–119.

Freund, K., Sedlacek, F., & Knob, K. (1965). A simple transducer for mechanical plethysmography of the male genital. *Journal of the Experimental Analysis of Behavior, 8,* 169–170.

Freund, K., & Watson, R. (1990). Mapping the boundaries of courtship disorder. *Journal of Sex Research, 27,* 589–606.

Freund, K., & Watson, R. (1991). Assessment of the sensitivity and specificity of a phallometric test: An update of 'Phallometric diagnosis of pedophilia'. *Psychological Assessment, 3,* 254–260.

Freund, K., Watson, R., & Dickey, R. (1991). Sex offenses against female children perpetrated by men who are not pedophiles. *Journal of Sex Research, 28,* 409–423.

Freund, K., Watson, R., & Rienzo, D. (1988). Signs of feigning in the phallometric test. *Behaviour Research and Therapy, 26,* 105–112.

Gannon, T. A., & Cortoni, F. (2010). *Female sexual offenders: Theory, assessment, and treatment.* Chichester, England: John Wiley & Sons, Ltd.

Geer, J. (1980). Measurement of genital arousal in human males and females. In I. Martin & P. Venables (Eds.), *Techniques in psychophysiology* (pp. 431–458). New York, NY: John Wiley & Sons, Inc.

Geer, J., Morokoff, P., & Greenwood, P. (1974). Sexual arousal in women: The development of a measurement device for vaginal blood flow. *Archives of Sexual Behavior, 3,* 559–564.

Glasgow, D. V., Osborne, A., & Croxen, J. (2003). An assessment tool for investigating paedophile sexual interest using viewing time: An application of a single case methodology. *British Journal of Learning Disabilities, 31,* 96–102.

Hanson, R. K., & Bussière, M. T. (1998). Predicting relapse: A meta-analysis of sexual offender recidivism studies. *Journal of Consulting and Clinical Psychology, 66,* 348–362.

Hanson, R. K., & Morton-Bourgon, K. E. (2005). The characteristics of persistent sexual offenders: A meta-analysis of recidivism studies. *Journal of Consulting and Clinical Psychology, 73,* 1154–1163.

Her Majesty's Prison Service (2007). *Penile plethysmograph (PPG): Interpretation guidelines.* London, England: Author.

Hess, E., & Polt, J. (1960). Pupil size as related to interest value of visual stimuli. *Science, 132,* 349–350.

Hess, E., Seltzer, A., & Schlien, J. (1965). Pupil response to hetero- and homosexual males to pictures of men and women: A pilot study. *Journal of Abnormal Psychology, 70,* 165–168.

Holland, L. A., Zolondek, S. C., Abel, G. G., Jordan, A. D., & Becker, J. V. (2000). Psychometric analysis of the Sexual Interest Cardsort Questionnaire. *Sexual Abuse: A Journal of Research & Treatment, 12,* 107–122.

Hoon, P., Wincze, J., & Hoon, E. (1976). Physiological assessment of sexual arousal in women. *Psychophysiology, 13,* 196–204.

Howes, R. J. (2003). Circumferential change scores in phallometric assessment: Normative data. *Sexual Abuse: A Journal of Research & Treatment, 15,* 365–375.

Hynie, J. (1934). Nova objektivni metoda vysetrovani muszke sexualni potence [A new objective method of investigation of male sexual potency]. *Casopis Lekaru Ceskych, 73,* 34–39. Cited in K. Freund, Assessment of sexual dysfunction and deviation. In M. Hersen & A. Bellack (Eds.) (1981), *Behavioral assessment: A practical handbook* (2nd ed., pp. 427–455). New York, NY: Pergamon.

Kaine, A., & Mersereau, G. (1986). *Lie detection and plethysmography: Their uses and limitation in offender assessment.* Ottawa, Canada: Solicitor General Canada.

Kingston, D. A., Firestone, P., Moulden, H. M., & Bradford, J. M. (2007). The utility of the diagnosis of pedophilia. A comparison of various classification procedures. *Archives of Sexual Behavior, 36,* 423–436.

Kingston, D. A., Seto, M. C., Firestone, P., & Bradford, J. M. (2010). Comparing indicators of sexual sadism as predictors of recidivism among adult male sexual offenders. *Journal of Consulting and Clinical Psychology, 78,* 574–584.

Konopasky, R. J., & Konopasky, A. W. B. (2000). Remaking penile plethysmography. In D. Laws, S. M. Hudson, & T. Ward (Eds.), *Remaking relapse prevention with sex offenders: A sourcebook* (pp. 257–284). Thousand Oaks, CA, Sage.

Kuban, M., Barbaree, H. E., & Blanchard, R. (1999). A comparison of volume and circumference phallometry: Response magnitude and method agreement. *Archives of Sexual Behavior, 28,* 345–359.

Lalumière, M. L., & Harris, G. T. (1998). Common questions regarding the use of phallometric testing with sexual offenders. *Sexual Abuse: A Journal of Research and Treatment, 10,* 227–237.

Lalumière, M. L., & Quinsey, V. L. (1994). The discriminability of rapists from non-sex offenders using phallometric measures: A meta-analysis. *Criminal Justice and Behavior, 21,* 150–175.

Lalumière, M. L., Quinsey, V. L., Harris, G. T., Rice, M. E., & Trautrimas, C. (2003). Are rapists differentially aroused by coercive sex in phallometric assessments? In R. A. Prentky, E. Janus, & M. Seto (Eds.), *Sexual coercion: Understanding and management* (pp. 211–224). New York, NY: New York Academy of Sciences.

Laws, D. R. (1976). *A comparison of the measurement characteristics of three penile transducers.* Unpublished manuscript.

Laws, D. R., & Marshall, W. L. (2003). A brief history of behavioral and cognitive behavioral approaches to sexual offenders: Part 1. Early developments. *Sexual Abuse: A Journal of Research and Treatment, 15,* 75–92.

Laws, D. R., & Rubin, H. (1969). Instructional control of autonomic sexual response. *Journal of Applied Behavioral Analysis, 2,* 93–99.

MacCulloch, M., & Feldman, M. (1970). Comment on Bancroft's paper – 'Aversion therapy of homosexuality'. *British Journal of Psychiatry, 116,* 673–676.

Malcolm, P. B., Andrews, D. A., & Quinsey, V. L. (1993). Discriminant and predictive validity of phallometrically measured sexual age and gender preference. *Journal of Interpersonal Violence, 8,* 486–501.

Malcolm, P., Davidson, P., & Marshall, W. L. (1985). Control of penile tumescence: The effects of arousal level and stimulus content. *Behaviour Research & Therapy, 23,* 272–280.

Marshall, W. L., Barbaree, H. E., & Christophe, D. (1986). Sexual offenders against female children: Sexual preferences for age of victims and type of behaviour. *Canadian Journal of Behavioural Science, 18,* 424–439.

Marshall, W. L., & Fernandez, Y. M. (2003). *Phallometric testing with sexual offenders: Theory, research and practice*. Brandon, VT: Safer Society Press.

Marshall, W. L., Kennedy, P., & Yates, P. M. (2002). Issues concerning the reliability and validity of the diagnosis of sexual sadism applied in prison settings. *Sexual Abuse: A Journal of Research and Treatment*, 14, 310–311.

Marshall, W. L., Kennedy, P., Yates, P. M., & Serran, G. A. (2002). Diagnosing sexual sadism in sexual offenders: Reliability across diagnosticians. *International Journal of Offender Therapy and Comparative Criminology*, 46, 668–676.

Masters, W., & Johnson, V. (1966). *Human sexual response*. New York, NY: Bantam.

McConaghy, N. (1974a). Measurements of change in penile dimensions. *Archives of Sexual Behavior*, 3, 381–388.

McConaghy, N. (1974b). Penile volume responses to moving and still pictures of male and female nudes. *Archives of Sexual Behavior*, 3, 656–570.

Money, J. (1986). *Lovemaps: Clinical concepts of sexual/erotic health and pathology, paraphilia, and gender transposition in childhood, adolescence, and maturity*. New York, NY: Prometheus.

Morin, J. W., & Levenson, J. S. (2002). *The road to freedom: A comprehensive competency-based workbook for sexual offenders in treatment*. Brandon, VT: Safer Society Press.

Nicolosi, J. (1991). *Reparative therapy of male homosexuality: A new clinical approach*. Lanham, MD: Jason Aronson.

Nunes, K. L., Firestone, P., & Baldwin, M. W. (2007). Indirect assessment of cognitions of child sexual abusers with the Implicit Association Test. *Criminal Justice and Behavior*, 34, 454–475.

Nunnally, J., Knott, P., Duchnowski, A., & Parker, R. (1967). Pupillary response as a general measure of activation. *Perception & Psychophysiology*, 2, 149–155.

O'Connor, A. (1987). Female sex offenders. *British Journal of Psychiatry*, 150, 615–620.

Ohlmeyer, P., Brilmayer, H., & Hullstrung, H. (1944). Periodische vorgange im Schlaf [Periodical events in sleep]. *Pflugers Archiv*, 248, 559–560. Cited in K. Freund (1981), Assessment of sexual dysfunction and deviation. In M. Hersen & A. Bellack (Eds.), *Behavioral assessment: A practical handbook* (2nd ed., pp. 427–455). New York, NY: Pergamon.

Orne, M. (1962). On the social psychology of the psychological experiment: With particular reference to demand characteristics and their implications. *American Psychologist*, 17, 776–783.

Perry, B. C. (2003). *Effects of traumatic events on children: An introduction*. Houiston, TX: ChildTrauma Academy. Retrieved from www.childtrauma.org

Quinsey, V. L., & Bergersen, S. (1976). Instructional control of penile circumference assessments of sexual preference. *Behavior Therapy*, 7, 489–493.

Quinsey, V. L., & Chaplin, T. (1987, January). *Preventing faking in phallometric assessments of sexual preference*. Paper presented at the New York Academy of Sciences Conference on Human Sexual Aggression, New York, NY.

Safron, A., Barch, B., Bailey, J. M., Gitelman, D. R., Parrish, T. B., & Reber, P. J. (2007). Neural correlates of sexual arousal in homosexual and heterosexual men. *Behavioral Neuroscience*, 121, 237–248.

Seto, M. C. (2012). Is pedophilia a sexual orientation? *Archives of Sexual Behavior*, 41, 231–236.

Smith, D., & Over, R. (1987). Male sexual arousal as a function of the content and the vividness of erotic fantasy. *Psychophysiology*, 24, 334–339.

Spitzer, R. L. (2012). Spitzer reassesses his 2003 study of reparative therapy of homosexuality [Letter to the Editor]. *Archives of Sexual Behavior*, 41, 757.

Whitney, P. (1949). The measurement of changes in human limb volume by means of a mercury-in-rubber strain gauge. *Journal of Psychology, 109*(1–2), Proc., 5.

Wilson, R. J. (1998). Psychophysiological indicators of faking in the phallometric test. *Sexual Abuse: A Journal of Research and Treatment, 10,* 113–126.

Wilson, R. J., Abracen, J., Looman, J., Picheca, J. E., & Ferguson, M. (2011). Pedophilia: An evaluation of diagnostic and risk management methods. *Sexual Abuse: A Journal of Research & Treatment, 23,* 260–274.

Wilson, R. J., Burns, M., Tough, S., Nethercott, A., Outhwaite, C., & Repp, A. (2007, November). *Clinical conundrums: Sexuality and the developmentally-delayed.* Symposium presented at the 26th Annual Conference of the Association for the Treatment of Sexual Abusers, San Diego, CA.

Wilson, R. J., & Freund-Mathon, H. (2007). Looking backward to inform the future: Remembering Kurt Freund, 1914–1996. In D. Prescott (Ed.), *Knowledge and practice: Practical applications in the treatment and supervision of sexual abusers.* Oklahoma City, OK: Wood'n'Barnes.

39

Assessment of Sexual Sadism

William L. Marshall
Rockwood Psychological Services, Canada

Stephen J. Hucker
University of Toronto, Canada

Joachim Nitschke
Ansbach District Hospital, Germany

Andreas Mokros
University Hospital of Psychiatry Zurich, Switzerland; University of Regensburg, Germany

Introduction

The notion of sexual sadism has a long history dating back to the writings of Richard Von Krafft-Ebing in the latter decades of the 19th century. Von Krafft-Ebing (1886) adopted the term from the name of the infamous Marquis de Sade (Donatien Alphonse François de Sade), who lived in France from 1740 to 1814. Sade was imprisoned for his sexually cruel acts and during his incarceration he wrote explicit works on sexual perversions much of which involved physical and psychological suffering of another person who, at least in part, was consenting. Consistent with de Sade's practices and writings, the key features of sexual sadism embodied in the current version of the American Psychiatric Association's *Diagnostic and Statistical Manual of Mental Disorders* (DSM-5), involves the infliction of physical and psychological suffering (American Psychiatric Association, 2013). However, since there are people who willingly enjoy experiencing suffering and humiliation at the hands of others, DSM-5 distinguishes sexual sadists from those who engage in these more benign acts by requiring the victim of the sexual sadist to be non-consenting. The World Health Organization also has a diagnostic system, called the *International Classification of Diseases* (ICD-10) (World Health Organization, 1992). In the ICD-10, sadism and masochism are combined,

The Wiley Handbook on the Theories, Assessment, and Treatment of Sexual Offending.
Edited by Douglas P. Boer. Volume II: Assessment, edited by Leam A. Craig and Martin Rettenberger.
© 2017 John Wiley & Sons, Ltd. Published 2017 by John Wiley & Sons, Ltd.

where masochists are the recipients and sadists the providers of pain, humiliation, or bondage. Although a dimensional approach has significant advantages over a simple categorical classification, as exemplified by these two manuals, the majority of reported studies of sadists have employed a dichotomous approach.

Sexual sadism has been described as 'an elusive concept to define and measure' (Yates, Hucker, & Kingston, 2008, p. 13), despite the fact that there is a reasonably extensive literature that has purported to examine features of sadists (for a comprehensive review, see Marshall & Kennedy, 2003). In the various studies, different ways of identifying sadists has been common. Moreover, some studies have included in their examination of sadists other types of offenders, such as lust murderers, serial sexual murderers, and necrophiliacs, to give just a few of the problems that have led to confusion in the literature (for a discussion of this issue, see Hucker, 2008). On this point, Healey, Lussier, and Beauregard (2012) lament the incertitude in the literature, noting the absence of agreed upon conceptual and methodological frameworks to guide the study of sadism. As Proulx and Beauregard (2009) pointed out, 'there are no valid and reliable measures of sexual sadism to assist researchers (and) clinicians' (p. 403). Not surprisingly, almost all available studies have focused exclusively on male offenders, but there are also some women who, by any criteria, would be judged to be sadists (Pflugradt & Bradley, 2011).

Assessment Approaches

There have been a variety of approaches to the assessment of sexual sadism, with the four most common being (1) a diagnosis based on the criteria specified in either the ICD-10 or the DSM-5; (2) a measure of a man's erectile responses to sexual stimuli (phallometry); (3) an estimate derived from crime scene data; and (4) the creation of a measure based on the appraisal of a variety of data some of which may include one or more of the previous three approaches.

Diagnosis

As mentioned, the majority of reports in the literature on sadism have indicated a reliance on a DSM-5 diagnosis as a starting point to allocate participants to groups such as sadists or non-sadists. The DSM-5 defines sexual sadism as involving 're-current and intense sexual arousal from the physical or psychological suffering of another person, as manifested by fantasies, urges, or behaviour' (American Psychiatric Association, 2013, p. 695). Added to these criteria is the requirement that 'The individual has acted on these sexual urges with a non-consenting person, or the sexual urges or fantasies cause clinically significant distress or impairment in social, occupational, or other important areas of functioning' (American Psychiatric Association, 2013, p. 695). The essence of these criteria reflects similar notions embodied in previous versions of the DSM.

Some authors (Kingston & Yates, 2008; Marshall, 1997, 2006; O'Donohue, Regev, & Hagstrom, 2000) have challenged the DSM criteria for the various paraphilias, claiming they are too vague, and as a consequence result in unreliable interpretations.

In their review of the literature, Marshall and Kennedy (2003) found that almost all studies employed unique criteria for identifying participants as sadists; these distinctive criteria, Marshall and Kennedy noted, were rarely a match for the features described in the DSM. This review of the literature revealed that although authors typically stated in their introduction that they had used the official criteria (i.e., either DSM or ICD) to diagnose sadists, in fact in their method sections they specified a reliance on idiosyncratic features that did not always correspond to DSM or ICD criteria. Some authors saw the exercise of power and control by the offender as the critical diagnostic feature, others considered violence in the attack as crucial, while some researchers identified ritualism and pre-planning as the most important factors. Interestingly, few studies mentioned suffering and humiliation as crucial to their criteria, despite the fact that ever since von Krafft-Ebing's original work, these have been the most commonly recurring themes.

It might be expected that studies employing different criteria to classify participants as sadistic or not would generate different findings, and that appears to be the case (Marshall & Kennedy, 2003). This suggests that the reliability of the diagnosis across clinicians may not be satisfactory. As Nelson-Gray (1991) noted, establishing the reliability of a diagnosis is the first essential step in creating a valid diagnosis; the absence of reliable diagnostic criteria renders any attempt to integrate the literature as at best frustrating and at worst meaningless. Unfortunately, the reliability of the DSM diagnosis of sexual sadism appears to be poor.

In a follow-up study of their review, Marshall, Kennedy, and Yates (2002a) examined the diagnoses applied by expert forensic psychiatrists who were required to appraise a group of violent sexual offenders with a view to establishing whether or not these men met criteria for sexual sadism. Of the 59 offenders involved in these appraisals during a 10-year period, some ($n = 41$) were identified by the diagnosticians as sadists and some ($n = 18$) were not found to be sadists. These forensic psychiatrists were provided with extensive information on each of these offenders, including their life histories, previous psychiatric appraisals, extensive psychological test data, the results of phallometric appraisals, and crime scene information. These experts also conducted their own interviews with the offenders. To Marshall et al.'s (2002a) surprise, the information on which the psychiatrists relied indicated that those offenders who were deemed by the assessors to be non-sadistic displayed features that have been commonly attributed to sadists; for example, the non-sadists were more likely than the sadists to have tortured their victims and the non-sadists displayed greater deviance in their responses on the phallometric tests. In fact, the only feature among the extensive array of information provided to the psychiatrists that predicted their diagnostic decision was whether a previous clinician had, or had not, viewed the offender as a sadist.

The final report in this series (Marshall, Kennedy, Yates, & Serran, 2002b) examined the diagnostic decisions, and ratings of the importance of various criteria, by 15 internationally acknowledged experts on sexual sadism. In terms of the interdiagnostician reliability of their judgements, these experts fell well short of acceptable standards. Identifying an offender as a sadist or not has very important implications for the future of the offender. For example, depending upon the diagnostic decision, a sex offender may or may not be released from prison on parole, or he may or may not be civilly committed as a *sexually violent predator* (SVP). Of course, the release or continued confinement of an at-risk sex offender has serious implications for public safety. The level of diagnostic reliability in such cases should, therefore, be high if these critical decisions are to be sufficiently accurate; for example kappa coefficients above $\kappa = 0.8$ should be expected. The experts in Marshall et al.'s (2002b) study failed to achieve anywhere near this level of agreement ($\kappa = 0.14$). This, of course, is very disappointing and raises serious concerns about the value (i.e., validity) of the diagnosis, since validity depends on pre-established reliability (Nelson-Gray, 1991).

In her study of the reliability of diagnoses made by appraisers accredited to do assessments for SVP hearings in the state of Florida, Levenson (2004) found similarly unsatisfactory agreements in the diagnosis of sadism between pairs of these evaluators ($\kappa = 0.30$). Noting that the kappa coefficients may underestimate the true agreement between diagnosticians, Packard and Levenson (2006) applied alternative statistical analyses to Levenson's earlier data, and reported more impressive diagnostic agreement. Nevertheless, the overall data available to date on the diagnostic reliability of the status of sexual sadism are discouraging. At the very least, the reported agreement among diagnosticians varies considerably across studies (see the review by Nitschke, Mokros, Osterheider, & Marshall, 2013). It is important to note that the conditions imposed on diagnosticians conducting appraisals for SVP hearings are fairly rigorous and the diagnoses are likely to be challenged by either, or both, the state's attorney or the offender's lawyer. These conditions ought to maximize reliability, whereas under the usual circumstances of clinical work, or even apparently in research projects, diagnoses are likely to be less thoroughly scrutinized. Kingston, Firestone, Moulden, and Bradford (2007) found that among the factors they examined in sadists that might predict reoffending, a DSM diagnosis, applied carefully by experienced forensic psychiatrists, failed to predict recidivism whereas other indices (including phallometric results) did.

Given the available data, we cannot rely on a DSM diagnosis to identify sexual sadists. We will now turn to alternative methods that have been employed by some researchers.

Phallometry

The term 'phallometry' will be used in this chapter to describe assessment procedures in which the magnitude of a man's erectile response to various sexual stimuli is said to reveal his preferences or interests in particular sexual behaviours. Others use the term 'penile plethysmography' (PPG) to denote these procedures, but this term only describes (and even then somewhat inaccurately) those attempts to measure circumference changes in the penis, whereas phallometry also includes measures of penile volume, the use of which forms the basis of several studies reported in the literature. Phallometric evaluations have been seen as vital to the assessment and diagnosis of sexual sadism (Abel, 1989; Hollin, 1997; Hucker, 1997).

Given that sexual sadists are, fortunately for public safety, a very small percentage of the offenders available in any setting, there have been few phallometric studies specifically targeting these offenders. Even fewer studies have employed stimuli specifically designed to detect sadistic interests, partly, at least, because there is little agreement on what it is that is expected to produce sexual arousal in sadists. Healey et al. (2012) remarked that, 'The fantasies of sexual sadists are thought to reflect ... themes of violence, domination, and humiliation' (p. 405) due to evidence of these features in crime scene behaviours. In an attempt to evaluate the MTC:R3 (Knight & Prentky, 1990) classification domains, Barbaree, Seto, Serin, Amos, and Preston (1994) employed, among other measures, the standard phallometric protocol that they used in their clinic. This protocol allows the generation of various indices of deviance with the one used in Barbaree et al.'s study reflecting arousal to rape stimuli (some of which described a violent rape) relative to arousal to consenting sex. Although these were the standard stimuli used in their clinical appraisals over the years, they were not specifically designed to detect sadistic interests and do not reflect aspects of the motivations that are said to define sadism. Barbaree et al. found that employing these stimuli failed to reveal differences between sadistic and non-sadistic rapists, but the numbers in these two sexual groups of rapists were small (eight versus 15).

In Lalumière and Quinsey's (1994) meta-analysis of 16 studies that phallometrically assessed rapists, the stimulus set that produced the strongest discrimination between rapists and non-rapists depicted graphic images, including brutality by the perpetrator. These results suggest that rapists are maximally aroused by violence against women. However, in an earlier study, Barbaree, Marshall, and Lanthier (1979) found that rapists were not actually aroused by depictions of aggression towards women, but rather they were not inhibited by the presence of violence within a sexual context. Knight (2012) reported that rapists who employ excessive levels of aggression in their attacks do so because they are either angry at women or angry at the world. In fact, Barbaree and Marshall found that it was relatively easy to disinhibit normal males' constraints against sexual arousal to violence either by intoxicating them prior to testing (Barbaree, Marshall, Yates, & Lightfoot, 1983) or by invoking anger towards a woman (Yates, Barbaree, & Marshall, 1984). In Knight, Prentky, and Cerce's (1994) *multi-dimensional assessment of sex and aggression* (MASA), angry rapists are distinguished from sadists where the latter group are said to be aroused by the humiliation and degradation of women rather than motivated to be violent. Knight et al.'s point is that sadists are a unique subset of those men who are sexually aggressive towards women. In confirmation of his view, Knight (2012) reported phallometric evaluations revealing that rather than sadists being aroused by violence, their sexual responses were simply not inhibited by the presence of violence in the depictions.

In their attempt to identify sadistic sex offenders, Rice, Chaplin, Harris, and Coutts (1994) derived a deviance index from phallometric test results. This index reflected the differential erectile responses to consenting sex between adults and the responses to a particularly brutal rape. Contrary to expectations, the non-sadists displayed greater deviance than did the sadists. Both Langevin et al. (1985) and Seto and Kuban (1996) failed to find differences between sadistic and non-sadistic rapists using similar indices. In Seto and Kuban's study, a group of non-offending men, who admitted to having sadistic fantasies and urges, displayed arousal patterns that matched the responses of both the sadistic and the non-sadistic rapists. However, the sexual responses of these sadistic non-offenders were more deviant than was true of the non-offending community comparison group. In both Langevin et al.'s and Seto and Kuban's studies, the measurement defined deviance in terms of arousal to a particularly forcible rape, as did Barbaree et al. (1994). This is a problem because although sadists typically engage in forceful and sometimes brutal attacks, the primary criteria identified in both DSM-5 and ICD-10 for sadists include sexually arousing fantasies and behaviours involving the infliction of physical or psychological suffering of a non-consenting person.

Continuing their interest in this approach, Seto, Lalumière, Harris, and Chivers (2012) recruited additional samples of non-offending men from the community. Eighteen subjects self-identified as sadists according to the terms of a local newspaper advertisement. Despite noting the requirement for the infliction of humiliation and degradation on victims as a prerequisite for sexual sadism in both DSM and ICD definitions, Seto et al. then ignored this in their recruitment of subjects. Their advertisement defined the requirements for this group as men who were 'sexually interested in being dominant in BDSM activities' (Seto et al., 2012, p. 741), where BDSM was defined as sexual activities involving bondage and discipline in sadistic/masochistic activities. Oddly, the stimuli they employed in the phallometric test of sexual sadism did not include any reference to dominance but rather focused on the violence of the act, again without including humiliation. The sadists responded more to scenes of violence than did the two comparison groups (both also community recruits with either fewer sadistic interests or no sadistic interests). However, many studies, including several from this group, have consistently shown that non-sadistic rapists show elevated arousal to forceful or even brutal sexual assault scenarios (Lalumière & Quinsey, 1994).

In an alternative approach, Fedora et al. (1992) used still slides to depict non-sexual violence against females as their sadistic stimuli. Although this concept is in keeping with the approaches of the studies just reviewed, still images cannot capture the dynamic nature of physical or sexual assault, much less elements indicating an intent to humiliate and degrade. The proper phallometric assessments of sadists should, therefore, include clear depictions of the victim's suffering and humiliation.

In Marshall et al.'s (2002b) report, 15 international experts on sadism rated intent to humiliate and degrade a victim as one of the four critical features of sexual sadism. Two of the other features involved the exercise of power and control over a victim, and the torture of a victim, while the fourth critical feature indicated by these experts was sexual arousal induced by the other three critical features. Thus phallometric stimuli meant to assess sadistic interests should include the intentional humiliation, degradation, and torture of a victim, in addition to the exercise of power and control by the offender. Although it should not be difficult to generate such stimuli, we found that ethics committees were loathe to give approval to studies using such extreme stimuli, particularly if non-offender subjects were to be used as comparison groups.

Fortunately, there is one test reported in the literature that comes close to identifying these critical stimuli. Jean Proulx and his colleagues at the University of Montréal and the Philippe-Pinel Institute in Québec have developed what appears to be the only phallometric test that actually assesses some of the critical features of sadists. Proulx, Blais, and Beauregard (2005) employed sexually explicit audiotapes that portrayed (1) a rape that was physically violent, (2) a rape that involved humiliation of the victim, and (3) a non-sexual physically violent attack on a woman. Responses to both the humiliating rape and the violent rape distinguished sexual sadists from the non-sadistic rapists, but there were no differences in responses to the non-sexual violence. Further development of stimuli such as these should include several variations of sadistic images that tap additional aspects of the most important features identified by Marshall et al.'s (2002b) experts, for example, cruelty and mutilation. In that way, phallometric results could serve as the basis for a more accurate diagnosis and as a way to validate other types of assessments of sadists (e.g., MASA). Appropriately designed sexual stimuli would result in a phallometric test circumventing the difficulties inherent in DSM diagnoses, which require inferences about the motivation of an offender being evaluated to determine whether or not he is a sadist.

The problem, then, in phallometric assessments aimed at identifying sadistic motivation among sex offenders is to distinguish responses to violence from responses to the infliction of cruelty and the humiliation and degradation of victims. However, distinguishing cruelty from other forms of violence in phallometric depictions would be difficult and no-one has yet described stimuli that might achieve this goal.

Crime Scene Data

Several commentators and researchers (Michaud & Hazelwood, 1999; Myers, Burgess, Burgess, & Douglas, 1999; Ressler, Burgess, & Douglas, 1988; Ressler, Burgess, Douglas, Hartman, & D'Agostino, 1986) have pointed to the value of crime scene data in identifying sexual sadists. Dietz, Hazelwood, and Warren (1990), for example, identified consistent features across the crime scenes of their subjects. They found that 93% of sadists carefully planned their attacks, 87% used methods to restrain their victims, 77% engaged in bondage, 76% kidnapped or confined their victims, 40% kept trophies, and 22% forced the victims to utter degrading and humiliating phrases. Furthermore, McLawsen, Jackson, Vannoy, Galliardi, and Scalora (2008) were able to show that professionals with experience in dealing with sadists could reliably identify crime scene information as indicating either sadistic or non-sadistic motivation in the offender. These studies, with their exclusive reliance on crime scene data, have been appropriately criticized (Kingston & Yates, 2008). These critics point to the fact that the data in these studies were derived from groups that included serial and sexual murderers, not all of whom are necessarily sadistic (Grubin, 1994), and no diagnostic criteria were employed specifically to identify sadists. In addition, there were no comparison groups, thereby precluding inferences about the motivation for the behaviours.

The best work to date on sexual sadists examining data that might be present in careful crime scene analyses comes from Proulx and colleagues (Beauregard & Proulx, 2002; Proulx, Blais, & Beauregard, 2006). They compared sadistic and non-sadistic sexual aggressors with each group being identified by the MTC:R3 criteria. Knight and Prentky's (1990) description of MTC:R3 indicates that the sadism scales identify as critical the following features that could potentially be evident in crime scene data: torture of the victim, ritualized violence, post-mortem intercourse, post-mortem mutilation, marks of violence on erogenous zones, burns to the victim's body, and the insertion of objects. In Proulx et al.'s studies, sadists were shown to have more carefully planned their assaults, to have confined their victims, to have employed bondage and weapons, to have used expressive violence, to have humiliated and mutilated the victims, and to have inserted objects into the victims' orifices. Gratzer and Bradford (1995) reported somewhat similar findings. However, the international experts in

Marshall et al.'s (2002b) study did not rank all features as equally critical to the diagnosis of sexual sadism. Indeed, these experts did not regard the use of a weapon as at all relevant and they assigned low importance to the bondage of the victim and to the insertion of objects into the orifices of victims. These experts indicated that the most critical factors were (1) the exercise of power and control, (2) the humiliation or degradation of the victim, (3) the enactment of cruelty, and (4) the enactment of torture and sexual mutilation. Other potential crime scene data that were given ratings of relevance (although of less importance) by these experts included evidence of careful pre-offence planning, mutilation of non-sexual body parts, strangulation, the abduction or confinement of the victim, and the offender engaging in post-mortem sex on the victim.

A study by Healey et al. (2012) examined the value of various features derived from crime scene analyses in differentiating sexual sadists from other types of sexual offenders. They included 182 sexual aggressors (their term essentially describes rapists) and 86 sexual murderers. From their review of the literature, and their own previous work, Healey et al. identified 10 features that could be derived from crime scene records; these 10 features served as the basis for comparing sadists with non-sadistic aggressive sexual offenders. However, only four of these features (premeditated intentions, use of physical restraints, mutilation of the victim, and humiliation of the victim) differed significantly between sadists and non-sadists, and both the use of restraints and mutilation were relatively low-frequency occurrences (33.3 and 21.1% respectively). Although humiliation of the victim was frequent among the sadists (63.2%), it also occurred relatively often (36.7%) among non-sadists, an observation that recurs throughout the literature. Even premeditation was apparent in non-sadists (62%), although it was higher (89.5%) in the sadists. Most problematic was that the same crime scene evidence that provided the basis for distinguishing sadists from non-sadists in this study also importantly contributed to the diagnosis of sadism. This is a problem that bedevils many studies and it is not easy to see how it can be circumvented, particularly in studies examining the value of crime scene data.

In summary, there appears to be some degree of consistency across studies, suggesting that crime scene data may be useful in attempts to diagnose sexual sadism. However, as Marshall et al.'s (2002b) study showed, international experts, although generally agreeing that many of the features identified in crime scene studies were relevant, applied different ratings of importance across these features and they also added other features.

Rating Scales

On the basis of their observations of the results of crime scene studies and the differential ratings of the international experts, Marshall and Hucker (2006a, 2006b) designed a rating scale that was meant both to identify sadists (i.e., categorically diagnose) and to provide an index of the degree of sadism apparent in any particular individual. Each item in this scale was given a weighted value based on the rated importance by the experts in Marshall et al.'s (2002b) study. The sum of the weighted ratings both produced the overall dimensional score and also allowed a specific score to be used as a cut-off for diagnostic purposes. Marshall and Hucker noted that researchers in other clinical areas (e.g., Livesley, 2001; Widiger & Coker, 2003) had pointed to the advantages of a dimensional approach over the DSM's categorical diagnoses. These proposals suggested that dimensional scores of various aspects of any particular psychological problem would provide more valuable information to treatment providers.

In addition to providing an indication of the degree of sadism, Marshall and Hucker's (2006a, 2006b) scale would also lend itself rather better to risk assessment than would a simple diagnosis. Another advantage of Marshall and Hucker's scale is that it provides the opportunity to identify the degree of harm inherent in sexually sadistic attacks. To date, risk assessment instruments for sexual offenders have ignored the issue of harm, as have estimates of the long-term effects of treatment. On this latter issue, it is entirely possible that not only might treatment reduce subsequent recidivism rates but also, among those treated clients who do reoffend, the degree of injury may be reduced. Since harm reduction has become an important topic in various fields, including addictions (Des Jarlais, 1995; Marlatt, Larimer, Baer, & Quigley, 1993) and sexual offender treatment (Laws, 1996, 1999), measures that allow estimates of potential harm should prove useful.

Although Marshall and Hucker's scale represented a possible step forward in the assessment of sadism, it had not been subjected to rigorous evaluation, particularly of its psychometric properties including interrater agreement. Nitschke, Osterheider, and Mokros (2009) took up this task. They reviewed the files of all sexual offenders housed in a high-security psychiatric hospital in Germany. Among the 535 patients for whom data were available, 50 admitted to having repetitive sadistic sexual fantasies and had committed crimes that were distinctly sadistic. Nitschke et al. compared these sadists with 50 non-sadistic sex offenders from the same hospital. Scaling analyses using nometric item response theory methods produced a scale of 10 items derived from Marshall and Hucker's original 17 items, with the addition of an item concerning the insertion of objects (the manual for Nitschke et al.'s measure is available from dr.joachim.nitschke@bezirkskliniken-mfr.de). Nitschke et al. demonstrated that their measure fulfilled Guttman's (1950) scaling criteria (for details, see Mokken, 1997) and yielded significant coefficients of scalability ($H = 0.83$; $p < 0.001$) and reliability ($r_{tt} = 0.93$). Interrater agreement was also high ($k = 0.86$). A replication confirmed these data (Mokros, Osterheider, Schilling, Eher, & Nitschke, 2012), although both reliability and interrater agreement were slightly lower in Mokros et al.'s study. Furthermore, a probabilistic scale was a better fit for the data than a deterministic scale in this study. Pflugradt and Bradley (2011) extended these appraisals to data on female sexual offenders, including female sadists, housed in a maximum security facility in the United States, and so did Wilson, Pake, and Duffee (2011) with men in a sexually violent predator facility in the United States.

In a meta-analysis that summarized the four available studies, Nitschke et al. (2013) showed that both the sensitivity (95%) and specificity (99%) of their scale with regard to a clinical diagnosis of sadism were exceptionally high. One of the most important items in both Marshall and Hucker's scale and Nitschke et al.'s adaptation assesses the offender's sexual arousal to sadistic acts. While all the other items in both scales can be determined reasonably accurately from crime scene information or from detailed personal or criminal histories, estimates of sexual arousal may not always rest on secure grounds. In the absence of phallometric data indicating significant responses to sadis-tic stimuli, or an admission by the offender that he finds these stimuli arousing, the clinician scoring this item must make an inference based on less objective information. Again, the failure to develop an appropriate phallometric test to identify sexual interest in sadistic acts raises problems for the accurate appraisal of sadistic motivation.

Interestingly, when Nitschke et al. (2013) scrutinized the data from the three most recent studies (Mokros et al., 2012; Pflugradt & Bradley, 2011; Wilson et al., 2011), each of which examined all available sexual offenders in the various institutions, they found a prevalence rate of 6.1%. Although each of these institutions houses offenders specifically selected for the seriousness of their sexual crimes, this does provide an estimate that is meaningful for similar institutions. Furthermore, this estimate mirrors earlier prevalence rates of approximately 5% reported by both Groth (1979) and Eher, Rettenberg, and Schilling (2010). Hopefully, the prevalence rates would be lower in less secure settings, although the available data on the prevalence of sadists cover a remarkable range (see the review by Marshall & Kennedy, 2003).

Conclusions

The identification of sexually sadistic offenders is critical to a variety of important deci-sions by clinicians, courts, and parole boards. The decision as to whether a particular offender is or is not a sexual sadist has extremely important implications both for the offender and for the safety of the public. As a result, the accurate assessment of the presence or absence of sadistic features and their magnitude is vital. Not only does the accuracy of these assessments have relevance to sentencing and release decisions, such accuracy is critical to risk assessments, including estimates of potential harm, and to decisions regarding appropriate treatment targets. Furthermore, in the absence of an agreed-upon measure of sadism, findings from different studies cannot be meaning-fully integrated.

Our review suggests that a DSM diagnosis relies too heavily on insufficiently pre-cise criteria and the accuracy or otherwise of clinical inference. As a result, inter-diagnostician reliability is typically too low to serve as a satisfactory basis for important decision-making. Phallometric diagnostic tests have not yet proved to be satisfactory, primarily because the stimuli employed in almost all studies bear, at best, a tangential relationship with the purported features of sadists. While sadists may enact violence, so do other types of sexual offenders, and yet this is the most common feature of phallo-metric stimuli said to assess sadism. Although Proulx et al.'s (2005) phallometric test is a closer approximation than most to the assumed motivational features of sadists (i.e., intent to humiliate), it is incomplete since it does not include the exercise of power and control, which is seen as an essential feature of sadists. Although Proulx et al.'s inclu-sion of humiliation in the stimuli fulfils a necessary requirement, many non-sadistic rapists also indicate a desire to humiliate (Darke, 1990; Marshall & Darke, 1982). Appropriate phallometric stimuli would seem to be critical to conclusions about the sexual motivation of sadists, but an appropriate stimulus set has yet to be designed.

Reliance on crime scene data appears to have potential, but the currently available studies leave much to be desired. Most of the studies included a mixture of offenders such as sexual murderers and violent rapists, some of whom may be sadists but some may not. Nevertheless, crime scene information does offer more objective data upon which to make a diagnosis. One of the problems with such data is that personal history features (e.g., non-sexual cruelty to persons or animals, sadistic elements in consensual sex), are absent and yet these can provide critically important information.

Finally, scales for clinicians that rely on a range of mostly objective information sources appear to offer the best assessment alternatives currently available. Again, however, these have limitations dependent upon the extent and quality of the available information. In their best form, these scales allow both a categorical diagnosis and a dimensional estimate of the degree of sexual sadism. The latter would seem to have more utility for risk assessment instruments (which have yet to be developed for sadists), including estimates of potential future harm, and for decisions about specific treatment targets.

Our view is that progress is being made in the assessment of these very dangerous offenders but far more research is required, and such research needs to be more carefully designed particularly with participants being more carefully selected. We are most hopeful about clinician-rated scales such as those developed by ourselves, but those currently available (including our own) need to be evaluated across several settings before we can confidently conclude that we are really distinguishing sadists. We suggest that the real advantage of clinician-rated scales is that they allow estimates along a dimension of the degree of sadistic motivation, which we believe would contribute more valuable information and might allow treatment providers to estimate the offender's success in reducing his problems.

References

Abel, G. G. (1989). Paraphilias. In H. I. Kaplan & B. J. Sadock (Eds.), *Comprehensive textbook of psychiatry* (5th ed., Vol. 1, pp. 1069–1089). Baltimore, MD: Williams & Wilkins.

American Psychiatric Association (2013). *Diagnostic and statistical manual of mental disorders* (5th ed.) (DSM-5). Arlington, VA: American Psychiatric Publishing.

Barbaree, H. E., Marshall, W. L., & Lanthier, R. D. (1979). Deviant sexual arousal in rapists. *Behaviour Research and Therapy, 17*, 215–222.

Barbaree, H. E., Marshall, W. L., Yates, E., & Lightfoot, L. (1983). Alcohol intoxication and deviant sexual arousal in male social drinkers. *Behaviour Research and Therapy, 21*, 365–373.

Barbaree, H. E., Seto, M. C., Serin, R. C., Amos, N. L., & Preston, D. L. (1994). Comparisons between sexual and non-sexual rapist subtypes: Sexual arousal to rape, offense precursors and offense characteristics. *Criminal Justice and Behavior, 21*, 95–114.

Beauregard, E., & Proulx, J. (2002). Profiles in the offending process of non-serial sexual murderers. *International Journal of Offender Therapy and Comparative Criminology, 46*, 386–399.

Darke, J. L. (1990). Sexual aggression: Achieving power through humiliation. In W. L. Marshall, D. R. Laws, & H. E. Barbaree (Eds.), *Handbook of sexual assault: Issues, theories, and treatment of the offender* (pp. 55–72). New York, NY: Plenum.

Des Jarlais, D. C. (1995). Editorial: Harm reduction: A framework for incorporating science into drug policy. *American Journal of Public Health, 85*, 10–12.

Dietz, P. E., Hazelwood, R. R., & Warren, J. (1990). The sexually sadistic criminal and his offenses. *Bulletin of the American Academy of Psychiatry and the Law, 18*, 163–178.

Eher, R., Rettenberger, M., & Schilling, F. (2010). Psychiatrische Diagnosen von Sexual-straftätern: Eine empirische Untersuchung von 807 inhaftierten Kindermissbrauchstätern und Vergewaltigern [Psychiatric disgnoses of sexual offenders: An empirical study of 807 incarcerated sexual offenders against children and rapists]. *Zeitschrift für Sexualforschung, 23*, 23–35.

Fedora, O., Reddon, J. R., Morrison, J. W., Fedora, S. K., Pascoe, H., & Yeudall, L. T. (1992). Sadism and other paraphilias in normal controls and aggressive and nonaggressive sex offenders. *Archives of Sexual Behavior, 21*, 1–15.

Gratzer. T., & Bradford, J. M. W. (1995). Offender and offense characteristics of sexual sadists: A comparative study. *Journal of Forensic Sciences, 40*, 450–455.

Groth, N. (1979). *Men who rape: The psychology of the offender*. New York, NY: Plenum.

Grubin, D. (1994). Sexual murder. *British Journal of Psychiatry, 165*, 524–629.

Guttman, L. (1950). Problems of reliability. In S. A. Stouffer, L. Gottman, E. A. Suchman, P. F. Laserfeld, S. A. Star, & J. A. Clausen (Eds.), *Studies in social psychology in World War II: Vol. 4. Measurement and prediction* (pp. 277–311). Princeton, NJ: Princeton University Press.

Healey, J., Lussier, P., & Beauregard, E. (2012). Sexual sadism in the context of rape and sexual homicide: An examination of crime scene indicators. *International Journal of Offender Therapy and Comparative Criminology, 57*, 402–424.

Hollin, C. R. (1997). Sexual sadism: Assessment and treatment. In D. R. Laws & W. T. O'Donohue (Eds.), *Sexual deviance: Theory, assessment, and treatment* (pp. 210–224). New York, NY: Guilford Press.

Hucker, S. J. (1997). Sexual sadism: Psychopathology and theory. In D. R. Laws & W. T. O'Donohue (Eds.), *Sexual deviance: Theory, assessment, and treatment* (pp. 194–209). New York, NY: Guilford Press.

Hucker, S. J. (2008). Manifestations of sexual sadism: Sexual homicide, sadistic rape, and necrophilia. In F. M. Saleh, A. J. Grudzinska, J. M. Bradford, & D. J. Brodsky (Eds.), *Sexual offenders: Identification, risk assessments, treatment, and legal issues* (pp. 340–352). New York, NY: Oxford University Press.

Kingston, D. A., Firestone, P., Moulden, H. A., & Bradford, J. M. W. (2007). The utility of the diagnosis of pedophilia: A comparison of various classification procedures. *Archives of Sexual Behavior, 36*, 423–436.

Kingston, D. A., & Yates, P. M. (2008). Sexual sadism: Assessment and treatment. In D. R. Laws & W. T. O'Donohue (Eds.), *Sexual deviance: Theory, assessment, and treatment* (pp. 231–249). New York, NY: Guilford Press.

Knight, R. A. (2012, September). *Issues in sexual sadism*. Paper presented at the 12th Conference of the International Association for the Treatment of Sexual Offenders, Berlin, Germany.

Knight, R. A., & Prentky, R. A. (1990). Classifying sexual offenders: The development and corroboration of taxonomic models. In W. L. Marshall, D. R. Laws, & H. E. Barbaree (Eds.), *Handbook of sexual assault: Issues, theories, and treatment of the offender* (pp. 27–52). New York, NY: Plenum.

Knight, R. A., Prentky, R. A., & Cerce, D. D. (1994). The development, reliability, and validity of an inventory for the multi-dimensional assessment of sex and aggression. *Criminal Justice and Behavior, 21*, 72–94.

Lalumière, M. L., & Quinsey, V. L. (1994). The discriminability of rapists from non-sex offenders using phallometric measures: A meta-analysis. *Criminal Justice and Behavior, 21*, 150–174.

Langevin, R., Bain, J., Ben-Aron, M. H., Coulthard, R., Day, D., Handy, L., ... Wortzman, G. (1985). Sexual aggression: Constructing a predictive equation. A controlled pilot study. In R. Langevin (Ed.), *Erotic preference, gender identity, and aggression in men: New research studies* (pp. 39–76). Hillsdale, NJ: Erlbaum.

Laws, D. R. (1996). Relapse prevention or harm reduction? *Sexual Abuse: A Journal of Research and Treatment, 8*, 243–247.

Laws, D. R. (1999). Harm reduction or harm facilitation? A reply to Maletzky. *Sexual Abuse: A Journal of Research and Treatment, 11*, 233–241.

Levenson, J. S. (2004). Reliability of sexual violent predator civil commitment criteria in Florida. *Law and Human Behavior, 28*, 357–368.

Livesley, W. J. (2001). Commentary on reconceptualising personality disorder categories using trait dimensions. *Journal of Personality, 69*, 277–286.

Marlatt, G. A., Larimer, M. E., Baer, J. S., & Quigley, L. A. (1993). Harm reduction for alcohol problems: Moving beyond the controlled drinking controversy. *Behavior Therapy, 24*, 461–504.

Marshall, W. L. (1997). Pedophilia: Psychopathology and theory. In D. R. Laws & W. T. O'Donohue (Eds.), *Handbook of sexual deviance: Theory and application* (pp. 152–174). New York, NY: Guilford Press.

Marshall, W. L. (2006). Diagnostic problems with sexual offenders. In W. L. Marshall, Y. M. Fernandez, L. E. Marshall, & G. A. Serran (Eds.), *Sexual offender treatment: Controversial issues* (pp. 33–43). Chichester, England: John Wiley & Sons, Ltd.

Marshall, W. L., & Darke, J. L. (1982). Inferring humiliation as motivation in sexual offenses. *Treatment for Sexual Aggressives, 5*, 1–3.

Marshall, W. L., & Hucker, S. J. (2006a). Severe sexual sadism: Its features and treatment. In R. D. McAnulty & M. M. Burnette (Eds.), *Sex and sexuality: Sexual deviation and sexual offenses* (Vol. 3, pp. 227–250). Westport, CT: Praeger.

Marshall, W. L., & Hucker, S. J. (2006b). Issues in the diagnosis of sexual sadism. *Sexual Offender Treatment, 1*(2), 1–5.

Marshall, W. L., & Kennedy, P. (2003). Sexual sadism in sexual offenders: An elusive diagnosis. *Aggression and Violent Behavior, 8*, 1–22.

Marshall, W. L., Kennedy, P., & Yates, P. (2002a). Issues concerning the reliability and validity of the diagnosis of sexual sadism applied in prison settings. *Sexual Abuse: A Journal of Research and Treatment, 14*, 301–311.

Marshall, W. L., Kennedy, P., Yates, P., & Serran, G. A. (2002b). Diagnosing sexual sadism in sexual offenders: Reliability across diagnosticians. *International Journal of Offender Therapy and Comparative Criminology, 46*, 668–677.

McLawsen, J. E., Jackson, R. L., Vannoy, S. D., Galliardi, G. J., & Scalora, M. S. (2008). Professional perspectives on sexual sadism. *Sexual Abuse: A Journal of Research and Treatment, 20*, 272–304.

Michaud, S. G., & Hazelwood, R. R. (1999). *The evil that men do*. New York, NY: St. Martin's Press.

Mokken, R. J. (1997). Nonparametric models for dichotomous responses. In W. J. van der Linden & R. K. Hambleton (Eds.), *Handbook of modern item response theory* (pp. 351–367). New York, NY: Springer.

Mokros, A., Osterheider, M., Schilling, S., Eher, R., & Nitschke, J. (2012). The Severe Sexual Sadism Scale: Cross-validation and scale properties. *Psychological Assessment, 24*, 764–769.

Myers, W. C., Burgess, A. W., Burgess A. G., & Douglas, J. E. (1999). Serial murder and sexual homicide. In V. van Hasselt & M. Herson (Eds.), *Handbook of psychological approaches with violent offenders* (pp. 153–172). New York, NY: Kluwer/Plenum.

Nelson-Gray, R. D. (1991). DSM-IV: Empirical guidelines from psychometrics. *Journal of Abnormal Psychology, 100*, 308–315.

Nitschke, J., Mokros, A., Osterheider, M., & Marshall, W. L. (2013). Sexual sadism: Current diagnostic vagueness and the benefit of behavioral definitions. *International Journal of Offender Therapy and Comparative Criminology, 57*, 1441–1453.

Nitschke, J., Osterheider, M., & Mokros, A. (2009). A cumulative scale of severe sexual sadism. *Sexual Abuse: A Journal of Research and Treatment, 21*, 262–278.

O'Donohue, W. T., Regev, L. G., & Hagstrom, A. (2000). Problems with the DSM-IV diagnosis of pedophilia. *Sexual Abuse: A Journal of Research and Treatment, 12*, 95–105.

Packard, R. L., & Levenson, J. S. (2006). Revisiting the reliability of diagnostic decisions in sex offender civil commitment. *Sexual Offender Treatment, 1*(3), 1–15.

Pflugradt, D. M., & Bradley, P. A. (2011, November). *Evaluating female sex offenders using the cumuliative scale of severe sexual sadism*. Poster presented at the 30th Annual Conference of the Association for the Treatment of Sexual Abusers (ATSA), Toronto, Canada.

Proulx, J., & Beauregard, E. (2009). Decision making during the offending process: An assessment among subtypes of sexual aggressors of women. In A. R. Beech, L. A. Craig, & K. D. Browne (Eds.), *Assessment and treatment of sex offenders: A handbook* (pp. 181–197). Chichester, England: John Wiley & Sons, Ltd.

Proulx, J., Blais, E., & Beauregard, E. (2005). Sadistic sexual offenders. In J. Proulx, E. Beauregard, M. Cusson, & A. Nicole (Eds.), *Sexual murderers: A comparative analysis and new perspectives* (pp. 107–122). Chichester, England: John Wiley & Sons, Ltd.

Proulx, J., Blais, E., & Beauregard, E. (2006). Sadistic sexual aggressors. In W. L. Marshall, Y. M. Fernandez, L. E. Marshall, & G. A. Serran (Eds.), *Sexual offender treatment: Controversial issues* (pp. 61–77). Chichester, England: John Wiley & Sons, Ltd.

Ressler, R. K., Burgess, A. W., & Douglas, J. E. (1988). *Sexual homicide: Pattern and motives*. New York, NY: Free Press.

Ressler, R. K., Burgess, A. W., Douglas, J. Hartman, C. R., & D'Agostino, R. B. (1986). Sexual killers and their victims: Identifying patterns through crime scene analysis. *Journal of Interpersonal Violence, 1*, 273–287.

Rice, M. E., Chaplin, T. C., Harris, G. T., & Coutts, J. (1994). Empathy for the victim and sexual arousal among rapists and non-rapists. *Journal of Interpersonal Violence, 9*, 435–449.

Seto, M. C., & Kuban, M. (1996). Criterion-related validity of a phallometric test for paraphilic rape and sadism. *Behaviour Research and Therapy, 34*, 175–183.

Seto, M. C., Lalumière, M. L., Harris, G. T., & Chivers, M. L. (2012). The sexual responses of sexual sadists. *Journal of Abnormal Psychology, 121*, 739–753.

von Krafft-Ebing, R. (1886). *Psychopathia sexualis*. Philadelphia, PA: F. A. Davis.

Widiger, T. A., & Coker, L. A. (2003). Mental disorder as discrete clinical conditions: Dimensional versus categorical classification. In M. Hersen & S. M. Turner (Eds.), *Adult psychopathology and diagnosis* (4th ed., pp. 3–35). Hoboken, NJ: John Wiley & Sons, Inc.

Wilson, R. J., Pake, D. R., & Duffee, S. (2011, November). *DSM-5 Pedohebephilia, PCD, and sadism diagnoses: Reliability in Florida*. Paper presented at the 30th Annual Conference of the Association for the Treatment of Sexual Abusers (ATSA), Toronto, Canada.

World Health Organization (1992). *The ICD-10 classification of mental and behavioral disorders*. Geneva: Author.

Yates, E., Barbaree, H. E., & Marshall, W. L. (1984). Anger and deviant sexual arousal. *Behavior Therapy, 15*, 287–294.

Yates, P. M., Hucker, S. J., & Kingston, D. A. (2008). Sexual sadism: Psychopathy and theory. In D. R. Laws & W. T. O'Donohue (Eds.), *Sexual deviance: Theory, assessment, and treatment* (pp. 213–230). New York, NY: Guilford Press.

40

The Forensic Relevance of Paedophilia in the Assessment of Child Molesters

Reinhard Eher

Federal Evaluation Centre for Violent and Sexual Offenders, Austria;
University of Ulm, Germany

Diagnosing Paedophilia and Paedophilic Disorder by DSM in Child Molesters

According to the *Diagnostic and Statistical Manual of Mental Disorders*, 5th edition (DSM-5) (American Psychiatric Association, 2013), 'the diagnostic criteria for Pedophilic Disorder are intended to apply both to individuals who freely disclose this paraphilia and to individuals who deny any sexual attraction to prepubertal children' (p. 698). For the diagnosis of a paedophilic disorder, it is required (a) that the patient exhibits recurrent, intense, sexually arousing fantasies or *behaviours* involving sex with prepubescent children and (b) that he has *acted* on these urges or is at least markedly distressed and/or experiences interpersonal difficulties as a consequence of these urges or fantasies. Also, the manual further discriminates between an 'exclusive type' and a 'non-exclusive type' of paedophilia, and whether the patient is attracted to males, females, or both, and whether the offensive behaviour or the fantasies/urges are limited to incest or not. *Having not acted* on paedophilic impulses or urges, or having no feelings of guilt, shame, or anxiety or not being limited by such impulses of fantasies, however, would not justify a diagnosis of paedophilic disorder but rather a paedophilic sexual orientation.

Although the DSM-5 includes a differentiation between 'Pedophilic Disorder' and 'Pedophilic Sexual Orientation', it is obvious that – along with the usage of the DSM-5 – in forensic settings the previous DSM-IV (American Psychiatric Association, 1994) and DSM-IV-TR (American Psychiatric Association, 2000) diagnoses of 'Pedophilia' will simply be replaced by the diagnosis of a 'Pedophilic Disorder', given that acting on

The Wiley Handbook on the Theories, Assessment, and Treatment of Sexual Offending.
Edited by Douglas P. Boer. Volume II: Assessment, edited by Leam A. Craig and Martin Rettenberger.
© 2017 John Wiley & Sons, Ltd. Published 2017 by John Wiley & Sons, Ltd.

paedosexual urges includes the requirement of becoming convicted or at least charged with offences for such behaviours. In other words, those paedosexual child molesters convicted for sexual offences who have been diagnosed with paedophilia, according to the DSM-IV or DSM-IV-TR criteria, will ultimately meet the diagnostic criteria of a 'Pedophilic Disorder' according to the new DSM-5. It is hard to imagine a convicted child molester meeting only the criteria of paedophilic sexual preferences but not meeting the criteria of a paedophilic disorder, since this would mean that he has paedophilic sexual urges or fantasies, but that his motives for sexual offences against minors have nothing to do with these fantasies/urges.

As a consequence of this fact, the critique that Blanchard (2010) made previously with regard to diagnosing paedophilia in sexual offenders would also apply to the diagnosis of paedophilic disorder according to DSM-5. Basically, Blanchard (2010) criticized that paedophilia – as it may be defined according to the DSM-IV and DSM-IV-TR criteria by acts alone – would confound a distinction between sexual offending against children and a mental disorder of paedophilia.[1] First and Frances (2008) made the same critique about re-including the 'behaviours' in the criterion A of paedophilia in DSM-IV. Originally, along with the revision process in DSM-III-R (American Psychiatric Association, 1987), 'pedophilic *behavior*' was removed from criterion A and replaced with 'sexually arousing *fantasies involving sexual activity*', and instead inserted into criterion B ('the person has *acted* on these urges or is markedly distressed'). Although the statement 'sexually arousing fantasies involving sexual activity' may also have been found to be ambiguous, according to DSM-III-R sexual behaviours involving only prepubescent children were clearly not sufficient enough to reach criterion A if they would not have gone along with corresponding sexually arousing fantasies. Therefore, a child sexual abuser denying (or not having) paedosexual fantasies would not have been diagnosed as a paedophile independent of the fact of whether or not he had sexually offended against minors. As child molesters – comparable to sadists (Seto, Lalumière, Harris, & Chivers, 2012) – are frequently reluctant to disclose their deviant fantasies or might not be aware of the specific cues underlying their sexual arousal, it is obvious that a diagnostic criterion that is related to the presence or absence of fantasies of the subject may only be captured by an inferential process or by directly measuring genital response. However, a valid diagnosis of paedophilia – as in sadists – would very much depend 'on the inferential skills of the practitioner or researcher, which in turn depend on the adequacy of the available data considered' (Marshall & Kennedy, 2003, p. 15). It is not surprising, therefore, that the validity and reliability of a DSM diagnosis of paedophilia have been found to be poor, as is commonly found with diagnoses of paraphilias in general, and that the usefulness of the diagnosis of paedophilia has been questioned specifically (Marshall, 1997, 2007).

On the other hand, requiring evidence for the existence of recurrent sexual urges or fantasies involving children for diagnosing a paedophilia in DSM-III-R has made it impossible to make a diagnosis of paedophilia without further clinical evidence aside from official criminal acts. Therefore, the DSM-III-R diagnostic criteria – although

---

[1] Criterion A (DSM-IV and DSM-IV-R): 'Over a period of at least 6 months, recurrent, intense sexually arousing fantasies, sexual urges, or *behaviors* involving sexual activity with a prepubescent child.'

threatening validity and reliability because of their inherent need for an inferential process or at least the presence of further clinical evidence – might have fulfilled the requirements of a clinical diagnostic process more appropriately than the subsequent revisions of the DSM.

In the DSM-IV, however, 'sexual urges or behaviors' were again reinserted into criterion A as signs and symptoms of paedophilia. For meeting criterion A, therefore, (recurrent) *behaviours* involving sexual activity with minors alone were sufficient. In other words, having repeatedly (over a period of 6 months) sexually abused a prepubescent child – independent of its motivation – would meet criterion A as per the definition. Ultimately, along with the revision to DSM-IV-TR, criterion B was also changed (in DSM-IV: 'the fantasies, sexual urges, or behaviors cause clinically significant distress or impairment in social, occupational, or other important areas of functioning') into 'the person has *acted* on these urges or is markedly distressed by them'. According to DSM-IV criteria, it was possible that criterion A was met through recurrent and intense paedophilic behaviour, but the offender still would not have been diagnosed with paedophilia simply because he might have claimed that this behaviour would not have caused him any distress or restrictions in his important areas of life. This led to at least two unwanted consequences: first, ego-syntonic paedophiles, even if acting on their urges, could not be diagnosed with paedophilia as long as they claimed that they would not have any restriction in their life as a consequence of their urges, and second, being convicted for sexual offences was equal to fulfilling criterion B as a general inherent rule as it led to distress or impairment in important areas of life functioning as per definition. Ultimately, in those offenders, the court made the diagnosis, since a conviction complied with the required criterion B. The same offender with the same offences, on the other hand, could not have been diagnosed with paedophilia if not convicted. Of course, these conditions called for a change in diagnostic criteria.

In the DSM-IV-TR, criterion B was changed back to the definition in DSM-III-R, namely that criterion B was met if the person would have acted on his paedophilic urges or he would be markedly distressed by them. Therefore, since the publication of DSM-IV-TR, the 'behavior' criterion was an aspect of criterion A *and* of criterion B so that 'sexual *acts* simultaneously indicate that pedophilia is present and that it is causing problems' (Blanchard, 2010, p. 305) as per definition. Therefore, sexual acts with children, according to DSM-IV-TR, would not only satisfy the signs and symptoms criterion (criterion A), but also the distress and impairment criterion (criterion B) and therefore ultimately suffice for the diagnosis of paedophilia.

As a consequence, First and Francis (2008) criticized that including 'behaviors' in the criterion A 'led some forensic evaluators to conclude that sexual offenders might qualify as having a mental disorder based only on their having committed sexual offences' (p. 1240) and that this fact may have sometimes justified evaluators making diagnoses based solely on the evidence of crimes. Also, they argued that such 'a poorly worded DSM-IV criterion [also] blurs the distinction between mental disorder and ordinary criminality' (First & Frances, 2008, p. 1240). In accordance with their critique, they cautioned that a diagnosis made in this way might also trigger unwarranted indefinite civil psychiatric commitment for sexual violent offenders.

However, the objections of First and Frances (2008) – although stating that their arguments seem reasonable if not compelling – were countered by Blanchard (2010). First, he claimed that in clinical practice, the history of sexual offences would often be the only evidence for the patient's sexual disorder. Second, he noted that histories of recurrent sexual offences against prepubescent children may simply not be explained by anything else than by an underlying paedosexual preference. Third, he claimed that given the general unavailability of phallometric testing and the unreliability of self-reports in child molesters, 'repeated sexual acts involving children are practically indispensable as a diagnostic sign of pedophilia' (p. 306).

In any case, the diagnostic value of DSM-defined paedophilia remains question-able and has been criticized elsewhere (Kingston, Firestone, Moulden, & Bradford, 2007; Schmidt, Gykiere, Vanhoeck, Mann, & Banse, 2013a). As a result, the terms 'paedophiles', 'child molesters', and 'paedosexuals' have been used interchangeably. Clinicians, therefore, are led to diagnose a paedophilia solely by the evidence of blamed or convicted offences without verifying the existence of further clinical evidence by an underlying clinical concept, and judges – on the other hand – are seduced to make relevant decisions (e.g., indefinite psychiatric commitment) on the basis of possibly useless diagnoses.

Given the broad and – from a clinical conceptual point of view – non-specific def-inition of paedophilia by DSM criteria and its poor validity and reliability, one might also seriously question its usefulness for forensic assessment and management. More-over, given the risk that criminal acts alone may be equalled with a mental disorder or a mental abnormality, which is the prerequisite for civil or criminal commitment in many countries with sexual predator statutes, one might even come to the conclusion that the application of a DSM diagnosis of paedophilia (or in DSM-5: 'Pedophilic Disor-der') in sexual offenders is of little use or might even be counterproductive. Probably as a direct consequence of its unspecific nature, it is not surprising that studies using DSM-IV-TR criteria revealed high base rates of paedophilia in child molester offender samples (Eher, Rettenberger, & Schilling 2010a; Wilson, Abracen, Looman, Picheca, & Ferguson, 2011).

The Prevalence of DSM-Diagnosed Paedophilia and Its Value in Convicted Child Molesters

Generally, paedophilia is diagnosed at a prevalence of 30–70% in child sexual abuser samples. Differences in base rates obviously are due to specific sample characteristics and how a diagnosis of paedophilia is made or operationalized. Kingston et al. (2007) applied the DSM-III (American Psychiatric Association, 1980) and DSM-III-R (American Psychiatric Association, 1987) diagnostic criteria in their study on the utility of various classification systems for paedosexuals. They found 41% of men to be diagnosed as paedophilic out of a sample of $n = 206$ extra-familial child molesters convicted of hands-on sexual offences against children. However, when taking into account that they had clinical diagnoses only for $n = 164$ offenders, the base rate for paedophilia would be about 52% ($n = 85$). All of the offenders had been assessed at a Canadian university hospital between 1982 and 1992; $n = 56$ offenders had been diagnosed according to DSM-III criteria and $n = 108$ n according to DSM-III-R criteria. Whereas in the DSM-III version the behavioural aspect (sexual activity with minors) was part of criterion A and thus was sufficient for meeting the signs and symptoms of paedophilia, a DSM-III-R diagnosis of paedophilia could not simply be given by behavioural evidence, but only when suffering from deviant fantasies and/or urges, since paedophilic acts were removed from criterion A. Moulden, Firestone, Kingston, and Bradford (2009), using the same offender population from their 2007 study, stated that 'this [diagnostic criterion] change would have likely resulted in fewer men being diagnosed as pedophilic using the DSM-III-R' (p. 681). Also, it was required in criterion B that the person would have acted on these urges, or would at least be markedly distressed by them. Since the majority of offenders had been diagnosed using the DSM-III-R, the diagnosis of paedophilia was inevitably more comprehensive in comparison with studies relying on DSM-III or DSM-IV rules.

Wilson et al. (2011), using the DSM-IV-TR coding rules, reported that 70.7% of their sample of 130 men convicted of sexual offences against children met the diagnostic criteria of paedophilia. Also, all 130 offenders were phallometrically assessed according to a standard protocol. In this procedure, they calculated the 'paedophilia index' by subtracting scores of phallometrically assessed sexual arousal to children from scores of sexual arousal to adults. A score of less than zero would indicate a preference for children. For phallometrically classifying paedophilic and non-paedophilic child molesters, only those demonstrating an unambiguous deviance index of −0.25 were classified as paedophilic; 57.7% of the total sample demonstrated a so-defined deviant sexual arousal to children. Compared with rates of DSM-IV-TR paedophilia diagnoses (70.7%), phallometrically defined rates of paedophilia, therefore, were substantially lower. Moreover, in the group of DSM-IV-TR-diagnosed paedophiles, only 40.7% were diagnosed as paedophiles by phallometry, whereas in the non-paedophile group, according to DSM-IV-TR criteria, 17% were paedophiles defined by phallometry. Also, DSM-IV-TR paedophilia was not associated with deviant sexual arousal ($r = 0.04$).

Eher et al. (2010a) found a similar base rate of 72% DSM-IV-TR-diagnosed paedophiles in a representative sample of $n = 430$ incarcerated child molesters in the Austrian prison system. Since both studies (Wilson et al., 2011, and Eher et al., 2010a) used DSM-IV-TR diagnostic criteria – with sexual *behaviour* against children to meet the signs and symptoms criteria and also the stress and impairment criteria – it is not surprising that the prevalence rates are higher than in the study of Kingston et al. (2007), which used the more restrictive DSM-III and DSM-III-R criteria. Interestingly, in Eher et al. (2010a), only 17% of the child molester sample was diagnosed as 'exclusive paedophiles'. A diagnosis of exclusive paedophilia requires the fact that the patient/offender has never had adult intimate partners or at least has never had a genuine sexual interest in them. Admitting this fact might be easier for the offender than to admit sexual preferences for children. Not being sexually interested in adults, on the one hand, and having (a) criminal sanction(s) for a history of repeated sexual acts against children, on the other, make the existence of recurrent sexual urges or fantasies for sex with children conceivable. In other words, having no sexual interest in adults, but being convicted for repeated sexual crimes against children, is compelling evidence for the existence of sexual fantasies regarding and sexual urges for children.

A diagnosis of paedophilia according to DSM-IV-TR without any further differentiation, in this study, however, was shown to be unspecific, broad, and probably of little forensic value.

Kingston et al. (2007), in their study, also challenged the clinical utility of a DSM-defined paedophilia. On comparing child molesters with and without a DSM diagnosis of paedophilia, they found only a few differences on some psychological measures, also corroborating the unspecific nature of a DSM paedophilia diagnosis in child molesters. They concluded that their findings evidenced that DSM-diagnosed paedophiles and non-paedophiles were different on fewer variables than expected. Contrary to their expectations, DSM-diagnosed paedophiles and non-paedophiles were not significantly different in age, education, marital status, and number of victims (although the paedophiles had 4.2 victims on average compared with 2.5 in the non-paedophilic group) or concerning the intrusiveness of their sexual assault. Also, groups did not differ in any self-reported measure of alcohol consumption, sexual functioning, or hostility. However, the DSM-defined paedophiles were found to have applied less violence during their offences and had a higher paedophile index (calculated by dividing the participant's highest response to children by the highest response to consenting sex with adults). In the same study, the authors investigated the differences between groups, if further divided by other definitions of paedophilia – phallometry, on the one hand, and the Screening Scale for Paedophilic Interests (SSPI) (Seto & Lalumière, 2001), on the other. They again concluded by and large that there were not many relevant differences between groups. However, the most relevant differences could be observed when groups were divided by phallometric results. When so defined, paedophiles were found to be lower in their sexual functioning and exhibited higher hostility scores.

In summary, the non-specific nature of a DSM paedophilia diagnosis has been demonstrated in several studies. This lack of specificity might be at least one reason for the fact that a diagnosis of paedophilia is often ignored by clinicians (Marshall, 1997). The change from DSM-III-R to DSM-IV and DSM-IV-TR might, on the one hand, have improved its reliability by including the behaviours in criterion A, thus preventing the diagnostician from the need to infer a diagnosis from clinical evidence of fantasies and urges. On the other hand, the clinical relevance of a so-defined paedophilia diagnosis was ultimately further blurred and now seems to be non-existent.

Prevalence of Paedophilia Defined by Other Means Than by DSM

In line with apparent problems and difficulties arising from diagnosing paedophilia with the DSM, phallometric testing was revealed to offer a serious alternative for providing evidence of a paedophilic preference. Blanchard, Klassen, Dickey, Kuban, and Blak (2001) investigated the prevalence rate of paedophilia as defined by phallometric procedures with a high degree of statistical confidence. For assigning offenders to the group of paedophiles, a paedophilic index was computed (the highest phallometric response to either prepubescent or pubescent girls or boys minus the highest response to adult men or women). Patients with a paedophilic index score of greater than 0.25

were diagnosed as paedophiles. The authors found a so-defined paedophilia prevalence rate of 30% in a sample of non-admitting extra-familial child molesters with one victim, a rate of 42% in those with two victims, and 61% in the group with three or more victims (= sensitivity). Also, the paedophilic index was positively correlated with the total number of victims in the extra-familial child molester group. In the rapist group with more than five adult victims, on the other hand, only 11% had a positive paedophilic index, and for those rapists with more than 23 adult victims the specificity was 96% (which equals a positive paedophilic index in 4%).

Similarly, Seto and Lalumière (2001) found 27% of a large child molester sample ($n = 1113$) having offended against at least one child met similar criteria to be included in their paedophilic group. They applied a 90% specificity cut-off score on the phallometric paedophilic index. This cut-off score corresponded to 0.39 in the paedophilic Index. This index was slightly different to that computed by Blanchard et al. (2001), inasmuch as positive scores to pubescent children alone were not included in their calculation.

In a subsequent study, Seto, Harris, Rice, and Barbaree (2004) investigated a sample of $n = 66$ child sexual abusers (study 1) who had been convicted of at least one sexual offence against children. Offenders had been referred to a sex offender treatment programme in a penitentiary in Canada. Participants were assessed phallometrically and a paedophilic differential index was computed by subtracting the single largest response to adults from the single largest response to children. 48% of offenders had a positive paedophilic differential index, meaning that almost half of the offenders had a greater sexual arousal to depictions of children than to those of adults. In this study, however, the sample number was small and the cut-off of the paedophilic index was virtually zero, which must have been accompanied by a higher sensitivity and a lower specificity, ultimately leading to higher prevalence rates of paedophilia – at least as compared with the studies of Seto and Lalumière (2001) and Blanchard et al. (2001). In study 2, Seto et al. (2004) investigated $n = 145$ participants who had committed a sexual contact offence with a child. Most of them had been referred from a maximum security forensic psychiatric facility in Canada after being charged or convicted. Some of them had been charged for a sexual crime against adults, but had evidence in their reports about previously having sexually abused a child. Unlike in study 1, the paedophilic differential index was calculated by standardized responses within individuals (subtracting the largest average response to an adult from the largest average response to a child stimulus). A total of 68% of these offenders, however, were classified as paedophiles by the paedophilic differential index, responding more to stimuli depicting minors than to those of adults.

Kingston et al. (2007) and Moulden et al. (2009) reported on the same sample of child molesters. Although they measured sexual arousal by phallometry and calculated a paedophile index (by dividing the patient's highest sexual response to children by the highest response to consenting sex with adults) and a paedophile assault index (by dividing the highest sexual response to an assault stimulus to children by the highest response of child initiates or child mutual stimulus), unfortunately none of the authors reported prevalence rates of so-defined paedophiles. However, they described $n = 110$ of their sample ($n = 206$) to have either a positive paedophile or paedophile assault index compared with $n = 45$ who were classified as non-paedophiles according to their definition. These data would have equalled an unexpected 70% prevalence rate for phallometrically assessed paedophilia. In comparison, they found a lower base rate of DSM-diagnosed paedophiles of about 50% ($n = 85$ paedophiles versus $n = 79$ non-paedophiles) in their sample. Obviously, the authors had a substantial amount of missing data inasmuch as not all participants were assessed with both diagnostic methods. Also, a positive paedophile assault index would not necessarily indicate the existence of an absolute paedophilic preference, since it measures the relative arousal to assault in children and, therefore, might be more specific to a sexual preference for violence than to a sexual preference specific for children.

Although phallometry can be seen as an established and well-validated indirect measure of deviant interests, it is expensive, generally unavailable, and 'labor intensive as a method in everyday routine practice' (Schmidt et al., 2013, p. 110). Therefore, alternative measures of deviant sexual arousal have been developed and first data on relevant validation studies have been published. Of those, latency-based indirect measures have so far yielded acceptable validity. Mokros et al. (2013) published data for a computerized assessment tool ('Affinity') that combines self-report and viewing time. They compared a sample of ICD-10 (World Health Organization, 1992)-diagnosed paedophilic child molesters from a medium-to-high security forensic psychiatric hospital with non-paedophilic forensic controls and community controls. They found significantly longer viewing times for images with small children or prepubescent children in the paedophile sample compared with both control groups. However, only 50% of the ICD-10-diagnosed paedophiles were diagnosed as paedophiles according to the Affinity programme at the cost of 13% specificity.

Gray et al. (2015) investigated the predictive validity of the viewing time paradigm in $n = 621$ adult male sexual offenders. They found that the participants with at least one standard deviation higher than the mean had an approximately twofold increased risk for sexual reoffence.

Banse, Schmidt, and Clarbour (2010) developed a multimethod approach – Explicit and Implicit Sexual Interest Profile (EISIP) – based on different indirect measurement paradigms. The EISIP is based on self-reports on the one hand (Explicit Sexual Interest Questionnaire) and on indirect latency-based measures on the other (Viewing Time and Implicit Association Test). The EISIP has been demonstrated to differentiate between different relevant child sexual abuser subgroups and was shown to correlate with sexual fantasizing, behavioural measures of paedophilic interests, and recidivism risk (Schmidt et al., 2013a). Most recently, taxometric analyses of the EISIP identified 26.8% paedophiles in a child sexual abuser sample (Schmidt, Mokros, & Banse, 2013b).

In summarizing the results of the available data about different clinical measures that attempt to diagnose paedophilia in child sexual abusers, it is obvious that a more restrictive and comprehensive definition of paedophilia based on clinical and psychological concepts – operationalized by the presence of phallometric evidence, by latency-based results, or by the evidence of exclusive arousal to children – generates lower prevalence rates when compared with the more behaviour-oriented definitions of the DSM-IV-TR, where committing sexual offences against children alone may suffice for diagnosing paedophilia. The broad and almost unspecific definition of paedophilia in the DSM cannot be expected to have relevant utility in forensic practice (Marshall, 1997), whereas other definitions of paedophilia so far have proved to have at least some forensic relevance.

The Relevance of Paedophilia in Predicting Criminal Relapse

Child sexual abusers with deviant sexual interests are consistently reported as a sub-group of sexual offenders with a higher risk for sexually motivated reoffending compared with non-deviant child molesters (Hanson & Bussiére, 1998). These findings, on the one hand, would suggest a clinical diagnosis of paedophilia to be related to sexual reoffence risk. Given the broad definition criteria and its dubious clinical significance, a DSM diagnosis of paedophilia, on the other hand, would not be expected to have any predictive relevance. In fact, a relation between a diagnosis of paedophilia set by DSM criteria and sexual reoffence has so far failed to be shown in convicted child molesters. Moulden et al. (2009), for instance, found no differences in relapse rates between DSM-III- and DSM-III-R-diagnosed paedophiles and non-paedophiles. Moreover, in a logistic regression model including a DSM diagnosis of paedophilia, a phallometrically defined paedophilia by either a deviant paedophile or paedophile assault index, or a 'paedophilia' defined by three or more points in the SSPI, the full model reliably distinguished between recidivists and non-recidivists. However, a DSM paedophilia diagnosis in this model was actually associated with a decreased likelihood of sexual reoffence in spite of a statistically significant full model.

Comparatively, Eher, Rettenberger, Matthes, and Schilling (2010b) reported similar results. They followed up a sample of $n = 127$ incarcerated child sexual abusers for up to 6.4 years after discharge; 67% of the offenders had been diagnosed with paedophilia according to DSM-IV-TR diagnostic criteria. However, no relationship between a DSM-IV-TR-diagnosed paedophilia and sexual relapse could be found. Also, Wilson et al. (2011) could not find any significant relationship between a DSM diagnosis of paedophilia and sexual reoffence. They followed up a sample of $n = 106$ child molesters for up to 8.8 years on average. Neither a DSM-IV-TR diagnosis of paedophilia nor expert ratings of paedophilia predicted sexual reoffence significantly (in the DSM-IV-TR paedophilia group, 16.4% recidivated sexually compared with 10% in the non-paedophile group). In this study, however, phallometrically measured sexual interest in children failed to predict sexual reoffence.

Since the DSM diagnostic criteria of paedophilia have become so vague from a clinical point of view, a DSM-defined paedophilia diagnosis would not even have been expected to represent a relevant risk factor for sexual reoffence. As a consequence, it was obvious to investigate the potential influence of more coherent and clinically distinct definitions of paedophilia on sexual relapse. Following these hypotheses, Eher et al. (2010b) found the diagnosis of an exclusive paedophilia to represent a robust predictor for sexual reoffence. Exclusive paedophilia was found in 12% of their child molester sample; it correlated significantly with sexual reoffence with $r = 0.30$. In a subsequent study focusing only on DSM-IV-TR-diagnosed paedophiles ($n = 189$), Eher, Olver, Heurix, Schilling, and Rettenberger (2015) again found an exclusive paedophilia to be significantly related to sexual reoffence with $r = 0.27$ or area under the curve (AUC) = 0.67.

Also, the SSPI was related to sexual reoffence with $r = 0.29$ in child molesters. Further, the SSPI was positively correlated with deviant sexual interests in child molesters (Seto et al., 2004). The authors interpreted their findings in the way that the scores of the SSPI, a phallometrically measured deviant preference, and also a history of prior sexual offending against minors would all be uniquely relevant factors and indicators of deviant paedophilic interests and risk for reoffence. In a replication study on the construct and predictive validity of the SSPI with the offender sample of the Dynamic Supervision Project (Hanson, Harris, Scott, & Helmus, 2007), the predictive validity of the SSPI could be confirmed for sexual reoffence. However, replacing the 'deviant sexual interest' item of the Stable-2007 (a risk assessment instrument for sexual offenders based on dynamic factors with good predictive validity; Eher, Matthes, Schilling, Haubner-MacLean, & Rettenberger, 2012; Hanson et al., 2007) with the SSPI did not lead to meaningful differences in the predictive accuracy of the Stable-2007. Nonetheless, Eher et al. (2015) demonstrated good predictive validity scores for the SSPI in their study on paedophilic child molesters (AUC = 0.71). Interestingly, Eher et al. (2015) found that the Violence Risk Scale: Sexual Offender Version (VRS:SO) (Olver, Wong, Nicholaichuk, & Gordon, 2007), among several risk assessment instruments, yielded the best predictive accuracy for sexual reoffence in DSM-IV-TR-diagnosed paedophiles in their study (AUC = 0.76). Moreover, the VRS:SO total score – as the only risk assessment instrument – incrementally added to the predictive validity of the diagnosis of exclusive paedophilia.

The findings of Eher et al. (2015) on the predictive validity of the SSPI and VRS:SO are consistent with previous results. Whereas Seto et al. (2004) found low to moderate effect sizes of the SSPI in predicting sexual reoffence in two samples of child molesters (AUC = 0.62 and 0.67), the VRS:SO static items and the VRS:SO total score have been shown to yield higher predictive accuracy for sexual reoffence (AUC = 0.70 and 0.79) in a sample of $n = 218$ child molesters (Beggs & Grace, 2010). One explanation for these findings could be that the SSPI, as it was conceptualized as a screening instrument for paedophilia and risk, includes only four items, whereas the static section of the VRS:SO comprises seven items, most of them conceptually related to deviance (age items and item content pertaining to previous sexual offences). Also, the static section of the VRS:SO comprises five items clearly related to deviance. The better predictive accuracy of the VRS:SO, therefore, might reflect more item content pertaining to deviance.

Although deviant sexual interest has consistently been reported as one of the strongest risk factors for sexual recidivism in child sexual abusers (Hanson & Bussiére, 1998; Hanson & Morton-Bourgon, 2005; Mann, Hanson, & Thornton, 2010), studies demonstrating a persuasive correlation between phallometrically measured sexual preference for children and sexual reoffence are lacking. Seto et al. (2004) failed to demonstrate that the paedophile differential index adds significantly to the prediction of sexual recidivism once scores of the Psychopathy Checklist were revised (PCL-R) (Hare, 2003) or the SSPI had been entered into the model. Likewise, Wilson et al. (2011) failed to demonstrate a significant correlation between phallometrically assessed paedophilic sexual interests and sexual reoffence in child molesters.

However, they reported an evident trend of phallometrically defined paedophiles to be at higher risk for sexual reoffences compared with non-paedophiles with sexual relapse rates of 17.9% and only 8.8%, respectively. Also, the results of Moulden et al. (2009) concerning relapse rates of phallometrically defined paedophiles are somewhat ambiguous and fail to add clear answers to the question of whether or not phallometrically assessed paedophilic sexual preference is related to sexual reoffence. The only relevant predictor for sexual reoffending that they found was the paedophile assault index, but not the paedophile index. The paedophile assault index, however, can be seen to measure a sexual preference for violence rather than for a paedophilic preference per se, since the paedophile assault index captures the relative difference between sexual arousal to violent sex with children and sexual arousal to mutually consenting sex with children. The paedophile index, however, in measuring the relative sexual arousal to children compared with the arousal to adults, had no predictive relevance. Also, survival rates of paedophilic and non-paedophilic offenders (as measured by phallometry) were not significantly different for either sexual, violent, or general reoffence.

Nonetheless, some evidence exists that latency-based measurement of paedosexual preferences can contribute to risk assessment in child molesters. Gray et al. (2015) demonstrated that offenders, whose sexual interest had been measured by their increase in visual attention, had a recidivism rate of 27% when their measured sexual deviance was one standard deviation higher than the mean, which had an estimated recidivism rate of only 7%. On the other hand, of those offenders with a visual reaction time of at least one standard deviation lower than the mean, no relapse was reported.

In the light of the existing findings reviewed, it is conceivable that a broad diagnostic category such as a DSM diagnosis of paedophilia has little clinical or forensic value for the assessment or treatment of child molesters. Instead, one would assume that valid measures of deviance would generally be of more forensic relevance and also hold the greatest prognostic promise. Although the necessity for diagnosing child molesters by DSM criteria has to be acknowledged, it seems crucial for risk assessment – and also for defining a category of paedophiles representing patients with a mental illness – to incorporate additional factors relevant for diagnosis and risk assessment. A better understanding of whether or not a paedophilic preference is exclusive and/or has clinical evidence for an intense and stable paedosexual preference, be it derived from phallometry, latency-based data, or risk assessment instruments capturing factors specific for deviance, seems to be crucial for this purpose.

References

American Psychiatric Association. (1980). *Diagnostic and statistical manual of mental disorders* (3rd ed.) (DSM-III). Washington, DC: Author.

American Psychiatric Association. (1987). *Diagnostic and statistical manual of mental disorders* (3rd ed., revised) (DSM-III-R). Washington, DC: Author.

American Psychiatric Association. (1994). *Diagnostic and statistical manual of mental disorders* (4th ed.) (DSM-IV). Washington, DC: Author.

American Psychiatric Association. (2000). *Diagnostic and statistical manual of mental disorders* (4th ed., text revision) (DSM-IV-TR). *Washington, DC*: Author.

American Psychiatric Association. (2013). *Diagnostic and statistical manual of mental disorders* (5th ed.) (DSM-5). Arlington, VA: American Psychiatric Publishing.

Banse, R., Schmidt, A. F., & Clarbour, J. (2010). Indirect measures of sexual interest in child sex offenders: A multimethod approach. *Criminal Justice and Behavior, 37*, 319–335. doi:10.1177/0093854809357598

Beggs, S. M., & Grace, R. C. (2010). Assessment of dynamic risk factors: An independent validation study of the Violence Risk Scale: Sexual Offender Version. *Sexual Abuse: A Journal of Research and Treatment, 22*, 234–251. doi:10.1177/1079063210369014

Blanchard, R. (2010). The DSM diagnostic criteria for pedophilia. *Archives of Sexual Behavior, 39*, 304–316. doi:10.1007/s10508-009-9536-0

Blanchard, R., Klassen, P., Dickey, R., Kuban, M. E., & Blak, T. (2001). Sensitivity and specificity of the phallometric test for pedophilia in nonadmitting sex offenders. *Psycholological Assessment, 13*, 118–126. doi:10.1037/1040-3590.13.1.118

Eher, R., Matthes, A., Schilling, F., Haubner-MacLean, T., & Rettenberger, M. (2012). Dynamic risk assessment in sexual offenders using STABLE-2000 and the STABLE-2007: An investigation of predictive and incremental validity. *Sexual Abuse: A Journal of Research and Treatment, 24*, 5–28. doi:10.1177/1079063211403164

Eher, R., Olver, M. E., Heurix, I., Schilling, F., & Rettenberger, M. (2015). Predicting reoffense in pedophilic child molesters by clinical diagnoses and risk assessment. *Law and Human Behavior, 39*, 571–580.

Eher, R., Rettenberger, M., & Schilling, F. (2010a). Psychiatrische Diagnosen von Sexualstraftätern: Eine empirische Untersuchung von 807 inhaftierten Kindesmissbrauchstätern und Vergewaltigern [Psychiatric diagnoses of sexual offenders. An empirical study of 807 incarcerated child abuse offenders and rapists]. *Zeitschrift für Sexualforschung, 23*, 23–35. doi:10.1055/s-0030-1247274

Eher, R., Rettenberger, M., Matthes, A., & Schilling, F. (2010b). Stable dynamic risk factors in child sexual abusers: The incremental predictive power of narcissistic personality traits beyond the Static-99/Stable-2007 priority categories on sexual reoffense. *Sexual Offender Treatment, 5*(1), 1–12. Retrieved from http://www.sexual-offender-treatment.org/2-2010_02.html

First, M. B., & Frances, A. (2008). Issues for DSM-V – unintended consequences of small changes: The case of paraphilias. *American Journal of Psychiatry, 165*, 1240–1241. doi:10.1176/appi.ajp.2008.08030361

Gray, S. R., Abel, G. G., Jordan, A., Garby, T., Wiegel, M., & Harlow, N. (2015). Visual Reaction Time[TM] as a predictor of sexual offense recidivism. *Sexual Abuse: A Journal of Research and Treatment, 27*, 173–188. doi:10.1177/1079063213502680

Hanson, R. K., & Bussiere, M. T. (1998). Predicting relapse: A meta-analysis of sexual offender recidivism studies. *Journal of Consulting and Clinical Psychology, 66*, 348–362. doi:10.1037/0022-006X.66.2.348

Hanson, R. K., Harris, A. J. R, Scott, T.-L., & Helmus, L. (2007). *Assessing the risk of sexual offenders on community supervision: The Dynamic Supervision Project* (User Report 2007-05). Ottawa, Canada: Public Safety and Emergency Preparedness Canada. Retrieved from http://www.publicsafety.gc.ca/cnt/rsrcs/pblctns/ssssng-rsk-sxl-ffndrs/index-eng.aspx

Hanson, R. K., & Morton-Bourgon, K. E. (2005). The characteristics of persistent sexual offenders: A meta-analysis of recidivism studies. *Journal of Consulting and Clinical Psychology, 73*, 1154–1163. doi:10.1037/0022-006X.73.6.1154

Hare, R. D. (2003). *Hare Psychopathy Checklist – Revised* (2nd ed.). Toronto, Canada: Multi-Health Systems.

Kingston, D. A., Firestone, P., Moulden, H. M., & Bradford, J. M. (2007). The utility of the diagnosis of pedophilia: A comparison of various classification procedures. *Archives of Sexual Behavior*, 36, 423–436. doi: 10.1007/s10508-006-9091-x

Mann, R. E., Hanson, R. K., & Thornton, D. (2010). Assessing risk for sexual recidivism: Some proposals on the nature of psychologically meaningful risk factors. *Sexual Abuse: A Journal of Research and Treatment*, 22, 191–217. doi:10.1177/1079063210366039

Marshall, W. L. (1997). Pedophilia: Psychopathology and theory. In D. R. Laws & W. O'Donohue (Eds.), *Sexual deviance: Theory, assessment, and treatment* (pp. 152–174). New York, NY: Guilford Press.

Marshall, W. L. (2007). Diagnostic issues, multiple paraphilias, and comorbid disorders in sexual offenders: Their incidence and treatment. *Aggression and Violent Behavior*, 12, 16–35. doi:10.1016/j.avb.2006.03.001

Marshall, W. L., & Kennedy, P. (2003). Sexual sadism in sexual offenders: An elusive diagnosis. *Aggression and Violent Behavior*, 8, 1–22. doi:10.1016/S1359-1789(01)00052-0

Mokros, A., Gebhard, M., Heinz, V., Marschall, R. W., Nitschke, J., Glasgow, D. V., … Laws, D. R. (2013). Computerized assessment of pedophilic sexual interest through self-report and viewing time: Reliability, validity, and classification accuracy of the affinity program. *Sexual Abuse: A Journal of Research and Treatment*, 25, 230–258. doi: 10.1177/1079063212454550

Moulden, H. M., Firestone, P., Kingston, D., & Bradford, J. (2009). Recidivism in pedophiles: An investigation using different diagnostic methods. *The Journal of Forensic Psychiatry & Psychology*, 20, 680–701. doi:10.1080/14789940903174055

Olver, M. E., Wong, S. C., Nicholaichuk, T., & Gordon, A. (2007). The validity and reliability of the Violence Risk Scale – Sexual Offender version: Assessing sex offender risk and evaluating therapeutic change. *Psychological Assessment*, 19, 318–329. doi: 10.1037/1040-3590.19.3.318

Schmidt, A. F., Gykiere, K., Vanhoeck, K., Mann, R. E., & Banse, R. (2013a). Direct and indirect measures of sexual maturity preferences differentiate subtypes of child sexual abusers. *Sexual Abuse: A Journal of Research and Treatment*, 26, 107–128. doi: 10.1177/1079063213480817

Schmidt, A. F., Mokros, A., & Banse, R. (2013b). Is pedophilic sexual preference continuous? A taxometric analysis based on direct and indirect measures. *Psychological Assessment*, 25, 1146–1153. doi:10.1037/a0033326

Seto, M. C., Harris, G. T., Rice, M. E., & Barbaree, H. E. (2004). The screening scale for pedophilic interests predicts recidivism among adult sex offenders with child victims. *Archives of Sexual Behavior*, 33, 455–466. doi:10.1023/B:ASEB.0000037426.55935.9c

Seto, M. C., & Lalumière, M. L. (2001). A brief screening scale to identify pedophilic interests among child molesters. *Sexual Abuse: A Journal of Research and Treatment*, 13, 15–25. doi:10.1177/107906320101300103

Seto, M. C., Lalumière, M. L., Harris, G. T., & Chivers, M. L. (2012). The sexual responses of sexual sadists. *Journal of Abnormal Psychology*, 121, 739–753. doi:10.1037/a0028714

Wilson, R. J., Abracen, J., Looman, J., Picheca, J. E., & Ferguson, M. (2011). Pedophilia: An evaluation of diagnostic and risk prediction methods. *Sexual Abuse: A Journal of Research and Treatment*, 23, 260–274. doi:10.1177/1079063210384277

World Health Organization (1992). *International statistical classification of diseases and related health problems, 10th revision (ICD-10)*. Geneva: Author.

41

The Assessment of Paraphilic and Non-Paraphilic Rapists

Drew A. Kingston

Royal Ottawa Health Care Group, Brockville Ontario, Canada

Introduction

Rape is a widespread phenomenon that is associated with significant physical and psychological harm in victims. It has generally been accepted that between 10 and 30% of adult females have been victims of rape during their lifetime (Black et al., 2011; Russell, 1984), although prevalence estimates vary because of a number of different methodological considerations, such as the way in which data are collected and how rape is defined. Traditionally, rape has been defined as forced vaginal, oral, or anal penetration without consent, but there is substantial variability in the legal definition of rape across jurisdictions – differences have been noted with regard to gender of the perpetrator, the object and source of penetration, and the definition of consent (Gannon & Ward, 2008).

The literature on rape is sufficiently large and comprehensive reviews on aetiology, assessment, and treatment have been provided (Gannon, Collie, Ward, & Thakker, 2008; Lalumière, Harris, Quinsey, & Rice, 2005). This chapter focuses on the diagnostic and methodological issues related to the assessment of paraphilic and non-paraphilic rapists. First, a brief review of the characteristics of rapists is provided, then the common assessment methods and primary areas for assessment relevant to this type of sexual offender are discussed.

Characteristics of Rapists

Rapists are a particularly diverse offender group, with varying family and developmental experiences, psychological profiles, and criminal histories. Research has predominantly focused on incarcerated males, although some investigators have examined the

The Wiley Handbook on the Theories, Assessment, and Treatment of Sexual Offending.
Edited by Douglas P. Boer. Volume II: Assessment, edited by Leam A. Craig and Martin Rettenberger.
© 2017 John Wiley & Sons, Ltd. Published 2017 by John Wiley & Sons, Ltd.

characteristics of men (typically college students) who self-report engaging in sexual aggression but have no detected criminal history (e.g., Malamuth, 2003). Research with incarcerated and non-incarcerated sexual aggressors has largely been conducted independently, given some early findings suggesting that the latter group tends to offend against acquaintances and that these men were less antisocial than the incarcerated group (Koss, Leonard, Beezley, & Oros, 1985). However, more recent studies (Knight & Sims-Knight, 2003; Malamuth, 2003) have shown that these groups are fairly similar with regard to early developmental experiences and adult characteristics.

Rapists are generally considered to be more antisocial than other types of sexual offenders. Indeed, in most respects, rapists are more similar to non-sexually violent offenders than to child molesters. For example, in relation to child molesters, rapists are younger (Hanson, 2001), have less education (Bard et al., 1987), and are of lower socioeconomic status (Gannon & Ward, 2008). Rapists also generally commence with criminal activity at an earlier age for both general and sexual offending (Baxter, Marshall, Barbaree, Davidson, & Malcom, 1984; Lussier, 2005) and they have reported more difficulties in elementary school along with greater general adolescent antisocial behaviour (Harris, Mazerolle, & Knight, 2009) compared with child molesters. Not surprisingly, rapists evidence a more diverse criminal history than child molesters (Smallbone, Wheaton, & Hourigan, 2003) and this offence history is similar to what is evident among violent offenders (Simon, 2000).

Such diversity has been discussed within the two broad hypotheses regarding offending patterns among sexual offenders. According to the *specialization hypothesis*, sexual offenders are a distinct offender group and are categorically different from non-sexual offenders. Proponents of the specialization hypothesis suggest that rapists (and other sexual offenders) who persist with criminal activity will likely commit further sexually motivated crimes. In contrast, proponents of the *generalization hypothesis* argue that sexual offenders are not a distinct offender group and they propose that offence patterns are versatile and sexual offending is but one manifestation of a general antisocial disposition.

Lussier (2005) reviewed the extant literature pertaining to the specialization and generalization theories and found substantial support for the latter: that is, sexual offenders' criminal activity is versatile and antisocial behaviour is dependent upon the type of criminal opportunity available. An important finding is that rapists' offending characteristics are particularly versatile compared with those of child molesters (Hanson, 2002; Harris et al., 2009). Indeed, several studies have shown that sexual offending among rapists represents less than 30% of their overall criminal activity, whereas such crimes represent almost half of the offences among child molesters (Baxter et al., 1984; Lussier, LeBlanc, & Proulx, 2005). In a more recent study, Harris et al. (2009) examined the offence histories of 374 adult male sexual offenders referred for civil commitment and they utilized the specialization threshold (which is represented by more than 50% of an individual's offences) to determine offence specialization. Consistent with previous investigations, the results indicated that the majority of rapists (88%) were determined to be versatile offenders (i.e., generalists), whereas child molesters were much more likely to specialize in sexual offending.

In terms of adult characteristics and personality profile, a number of studies have examined the rates of psychopathy among rapists. Psychopathy is characterized by a distinct pattern of interpersonal and affective deficits, in addition to behavioural dis-inhibitions, which often result in antisocial behaviour (Hare, 1991). Particular traits include extreme egocentricity, a profound lack of empathy, and a limited ability to experience remorse. Several studies have shown that the rates of psychopathy are par-ticularly high among rapists (Porter et al., 2000). In a review of the literature, Knight and Guay (2006) reported that between 12 and 40% of rapists generally meet crite-ria for psychopathy and that psychopathy is relatively more prevalent in this group than what is observed in child molesters. Unpublished data on 400 rapists and child molesters collected at the Sexual Behaviours Clinic at the Royal Ottawa Health Care Group (e.g., Kingston, Yates, & Firestone, 2012) revealed that rapists obtained a higher PCL-R score (mean = 25) compared with child molesters (mean = 18).

Assessment

Psychological assessment involves a systematic process of collecting, evaluating, and integrating relevant information about a particular client; it is a fundamental com-ponent of risk management and effective rehabilitation. Several types of assessments are employed with rapists. Diagnostic assessment is intended to provide a common taxonomy to facilitate communication and categorize individuals into homogeneous groups, which is intended to convey useful information about aetiology, treatment planning, and prognosis (Meehl, 1973; Spitzer, 2001). In addition to diagnostic assessment, other types of assessments are often used that pertain to establishing an individual's risk for reoffending and in determining the predominant treatment needs (i.e., criminogenic needs) (Andrews & Bonta, 2006).

Diagnostic Assessment

Many clinicians working with sexual offenders rely on diagnoses that are based on cri-teria specified in either the *International Classification of Diseases*, 10th revision (ICD-10) (World Health Organization, 1992) or the *Diagnostic and Statistical Manual of Mental Disorders*, 5th edition (DSM-5) (American Psychiatric Association, 2013). The DSM-5 lists several diagnoses that may be relevant to individuals who sexually offend (e.g., Antisocial Personality Disorder, Substance-Use Disorders). Among these diagnoses, considerable attention has been directed toward the paraphilias (Laws & O'Donohue, 2008).

The term 'paraphilia' denotes an atypical sexual interest that is intense and persis-tent and can be based on anomalous activity preferences or anomalous target prefer-ences (American Psychiatric Association, 2013, p. 685). A number of paraphilias have been identified in the literature (Aggrawal, 2009; Money, 1999); the DSM-5 lists the diagnostic criteria for eight paraphilic disorders (Voyeuristic Disorder, Exhibitionistic Disorder, Frotteuristic Disorder, Sexual Masochism Disorder, Sexual Sadism Disor-der, Paedophilic Disorder, Fetishistic Disorder, and Transvestic Disorder). Individuals who exhibit an atypical sexual interest in an object or activity that is not adequately represented by these earlier eight categories can be subsumed within the categories Other Specified Paraphilic Disorder or Unspecified Paraphilic Disorder.

In contrast to other sexual offenders, such as child molesters and exhibitionists, there is no obvious diagnostic category that could accommodate individuals who rape, and there is considerable controversy about whether rapists suffer from a paraphilic disorder (Knight, 2009; Quinsey, 2009; Thornton, 2009). Among the listed DSM-5 paraphilic disorders, Sexual Sadism Disorder and Other Specified Paraphilic Disorder – formerly referred to as Paraphilia (NOS) in DSM-IV-TR (American Psychiatric Association, 2000) – are the most frequently applied diagnoses among rapists.

Sexual Sadism Disorder. Sexual Sadism Disorder is a paraphilia that describes an individual who derives sexual pleasure from the physical or psychological suffering of another person (American Psychiatric Association, 2013, p. 695; Kingston & Yates, 2008; Kingston, Seto, Firestone, & Bradford, 2010; see also Chapter 39). The DSM-5 specifies two diagnostic criteria for Sexual Sadism Disorder: '(A) Over a period of at least 6 months, recurrent and intense sexual arousal from the physical or psychological suffering of another person, as manifested by fantasies, urges, or behaviors; and, (B) The individual has acted on these sexual urges with a non-consenting person, or the sexual urges or fantasies cause clinically significant distress or impairment in social, occupational, or other important areas of functioning' (p. 695).

It is generally accepted that the rate of sexual sadism among sexual offenders is low, although prevalence estimates vary considerably. For example, Krueger (2009) reviewed 27 studies published between 1900 and 2008 and reported prevalence rates ranging from 0 to 80%. Such variability is undoubtedly due to differences across studies in samples and in assessment and diagnostic methodology. In a more recent study of 586 sexual offenders, Kingston et al. (2010) reported that 8% of sexual offenders met diagnostic criteria for sexual sadism; however, when this sample was restricted to rapists ($n = 86$), the rate increased to about 40%.

Problems associated with subjective judgements such as those used in making psychiatric diagnoses were identified decades ago by Meehl (1954), and different authors have identified problems in the definition, operationalization, and assessment of sexual sadism (for a review, see Kingston & Yates, 2008). For example, the terms 'recurrent' and 'intense' in Criterion A have been interpreted differently across evaluators, the motivation for behaviour involving the infliction of pain must be inferred, and whether an act is intended or experienced as humiliating is subjective (see Doren, 2002; O'Donohue, Regev, & Hagstrom, 2000).

There is accumulating evidence of specific problems with the reliability and validity of the diagnosis of sexual sadism. Marshall, Kennedy, and Yates (2002) found that sexual offenders diagnosed as sexually sadistic did not differ from those who did not receive the diagnosis on features considered important to sexual sadism (e.g., sexually violent fantasies); in fact, the nominally non-sadistic offenders scored higher on some of these variables. This study also found a lack of agreement across experienced diagnosticians on the features they considered to be important to the diagnosis of sexual sadism, in addition to inconsistency in decisions made by the same diagnostician. In another study, Marshall, Kennedy, Yates, and Serran (2002) provided forensic psychiatrists with information on random samples of offenders who were diagnosed as sadists in the previously cited study. The reliability of diagnosis among 15 respondents was low ($\kappa = 0.14$). Inadequate reliability was also reported by Levenson (2004) for sexual sadism ($\kappa = 0.30$). These findings, however, may underestimate the reliability of diagnosis as a result of the statistical procedures used (Packard & Levenson, 2006) or because of the quality of information available to the evaluators and increased scrutiny in adversarial situations (Doren & Elwood, 2009). More recently, Kingston et al. (2010) reported poor predictive utility (in terms of recidivism) for the psychiatric diagnosis of sexual sadism and they argued that more emphasis should be placed on objective criteria, such as phallometrically assessed sexual arousal to sexual violence, along with certain behavioural indicators (e.g., excessive violence evident during the offence).

Other Specified Paraphilic Disorder (Paraphilia [NOS]). Paraphilia (NOS) is a diagnostic category that was intended to account for clinical presentations that are inconsistent with current diagnostic nomenclature or for disorders that are not prevalent enough to warrant their own diagnoses (Penix, 2008). Unless a diagnosis of sexual sadism disorder is warranted, evaluators are left to use the other specified category for rapists. Doren (2002) was particularly influential in his suggestion that the most appropriate diagnosis for a rapist with an interest in non-consensual sex is Paraphilia (NOS) (along with the descriptor 'non-consent'). Zander (2008) noted that the NOS category is the second most prevalent diagnosis among men subject to sexually violent predator (SVP) civil commitment (Paedophilia is the most common diagnosis).

Marshall (2006) noted several concerns with the paraphilic diagnoses and particularly the lack of clinical utility provided by a Paraphilia (NOS) diagnosis. Levenson (2004) demonstrated that the interrater reliability of the NOS diagnosis among sexual offenders was low ($\kappa = 0.36$). Additionally, in a more recent article, the Chair and Editor of the DSM-IV-TR (Frances & First, 2011) noted that using the NOS diagnosis for rape is inaccurate and that it is based on a mistaken interpretation of the DSM-IV-TR text; they emphasized that using NOS to encompass rape is not congruent with the original intent of the paraphilia workgroup. In addition to these concerns, there is some debate about whether repeated incidents of rape should be considered paraphilic.

Paraphilic rape. A number of studies have demonstrated that rapists show greater genital response to depictions of rape than non-sexual offenders (Lalumière, Quinsey, Harris, Rice, & Trautrimas, 2003). When employing optimal testing procedures, about 60% of rapists showed greater arousal to rape than about 90% of non-rapists (Lalumière et al., 2005). Lalumière et al. (2003) summarized three explanations for the arousal patterns observed in rapists; one model was non-specific and focused on general antisociality, whereas the other two models were specific and sexual.

The first model focused on antisocial traits (e.g., psychopathy) and stipulated that such traits result in feelings of indifference towards others and thus sexual arousal is not inhibited by viewing distress as it is in men without these traits. Barbaree, Marshall, and Lanthier (1979) described a similar process, which they termed the *sexual inhibition hypothesis*. According to this model, rapists are not sexually aroused by cues of violence per se, but their sexual arousal fails to be inhibited by cues of violence and non-consent. Several empirical studies have supported this first non-specific explanation of rapists' genital response to depictions of rape. In non-offender samples, experimental data have shown that sexually coercive college males show greater sexual arousal to consensual stimuli than coercive stimuli and that the addition of coercive cues fails to produce the same degree of detumescence in these men compared with non-coercive males (Bernat, Calhoun, & Adams, 1999; Lohr, Adams, & Davis, 1997). In offender samples, support for the sexual inhibition hypothesis has come from the fact that rapists typically show similar responses to rape and mutually consenting sex (Lalumière et al., 2005).

In contrast to the above model, some studies (Earls & Proulx, 1986; Quinsey, Chaplin, & Upfold, 1984) have shown that high rape indices to coercive stimuli exceed the arousal to consensual stimuli, highlighting the importance of excitatory processes. The first explanation pertains to Sexual Sadism Disorder (described earlier) and it is based on arousal to depictions of violence and injury. The final explanation is based on an interest in non-consent-related cues.

Sexual arousal to non-consent. A number of researchers have argued for a distinct psychopathological condition that denotes a preference for coercive sex. Several terms have been used to describe this putative condition; including 'preferential rape' (Freund, Scher, Racansky, Campbell, & Heasman, 1986; Freund, Seeley, Marshall, & Glinfort, 1972), 'raptophilia' (Money, 1999), 'biastophilia' or 'biastophilia rapism' (Lalumière et al., 2003; Money, 1999), and 'paraphilic coercive disorder' (PCD) (Knight, 2009; Thornton, 2009); the term Paraphilic Coercive Disorder (PCD) will be used throughout this chapter.

PCD highlights excitatory processes in the elicitation of sexual arousal to rape cues. Such a preference for coercive sex is most often hypothesized to be less severe than sexual sadism, but a distinct category nonetheless. In the 1980s, the DSM Paraphilias sub-workgroup proposed the inclusion of this diagnosis in the DSM-III-R (American Psychiatric Association, 1987), which was ultimately rejected. These criteria were such that individuals must demonstrate recurrent and intense sexual urges and fantasies for sexual contact with a non-consenting person. Importantly, Criterion B emphasized the coercive nature of the sexual act that is sexually exciting rather than the elements attributed to sexual sadism (e.g., psychological suffering). Most recently, the paraphilias sub-workgroup for DSM-5 had once again suggested diagnostic criteria for PCD (www.dsm5.org; see Table 41.1) and, similarly to previous editions, has been ruled out as a paraphilia and also was not included in the Appendix that is used for disorders requiring further research.

An important question regarding the inclusion of PCD in future nosological systems pertains to whether PCD is truly distinct from sexual sadism. In an attempt to address this question, a number of studies have examined the relationship between arousal to rape – typically defined by a positive penile plethysmography (PPG) rape index – and sexual sadism. A significant association between rape and sexual sadism would suggest that these constructs are best viewed along a continuum, whereas an inconsistent relationship would suggest naturally occurring categories.

Results reported in previous studies have been mixed, such that some studies (e.g., Barbaree, Seto, Serin, Amos, & Preston, 1994) reported that sadists evidenced more deviant phallometric rape indices than non-sadistic rapists, whereas others (e.g., Seto & Kuban, 1996) found that sadists had lower rape indices than non-sadistic rapists.

Table 41.1 DSM-5 proposed criteria[a] for Paraphilic Coercive Disorder

---

A. Over a period of at least 6 months, an equal or greater arousal from sexual coercion than from consensual interaction, as manifested by fantasies, urges, or behaviours.

B. The individual has acted on these sexual urges with a non-consenting individual, or the sexual urges or fantasies cause marked distress or impairment in social, occupational, or other important areas of functioning.

C. The diagnosis of Paraphilic Coercive Disorder is not made if the patient meets criteria for a diagnosis of Sexual Sadism Disorder.

D. The individual is at least 18 years of age.

Specify if:

In a Controlled Environment.

In Remission (No Distress, Impairment, or Recurring Behaviour for Five Years and in an Uncontrolled Environment).

---

[a]DSM proposed criteria were rejected and do not appear in the DSM-5 text.
Source: http://www.dsm5.org.

In an attempt to explain these mixed findings, Seto, Lalumière, Harris, and Chivers (2012) hypothesized that the non-consent and violence cues contained in previous PPG stimulus sets were likely confounded and, as such, they designed a PPG stimulus set that would distinguish between cues associated with sexual sadism (e.g., violence) from cues associated with PCD (e.g., non-consent and resistance). Two parallel studies were conducted among samples of self-identified male sexual sadists, men with sub-threshold sexual sadism, and community controls (Seto et al., 2012), in addition to a small group of rapists and community controls (Harris, Lalumière, Seto, Rice, & Chaplin, 2012). The results of these two studies demonstrated that sexual sadists responded more than the other groups to the cues of violence and injury, whereas the rapists responded to indicators of non-consent rather than sadistic cues. Taken together, these results were consistent with the notion that some men exhibit an interest in coercive rape but not other kinds of sadistic activities.

Knight has argued against the disambiguation of PCD and sexual sadism and proposed the term Agonistic Continuum to denote the putative dimensional construct of sexual sadism/PCD. The Agonistic Continuum positions sexual sadism at the upper end of the continuum as an extreme form of sexual violence, whereas PCD represents the lower end of the continuum. In terms of the PPG data reported earlier, Knight, Sims-Knight, and Guay (2013) suggested that the method of defining sexual sadism is a significant moderator of this relationship, such that studies employing more reliable criteria tend to demonstrate a consistent relationship between sexual sadists and high rape indices, whereas studies based on less reliable criteria tend not to exhibit this association. Knight and colleagues reported that studies utilizing the criteria of the Massachusetts Treatment Center: Rape 3 typology (MTC:R3) (Knight & Prentky, 1990) reveal that sadists consistently evidence higher rape indices than non-sadists.

Additionally, Knight and colleagues have shown that self-report scales from the Multidimensional Inventory of Development, Sex, and Aggression (MIDSA) (Augur Enterprises, 2007) pertaining to PCD and sexual sadism are highly correlated. For example, among 529 sexual offenders, the correlation between the PCD scale and the sexual sadism fantasy scale was high, $r = 0.76$. Most recently, Knight et al. (2013) tested the validity of the Agonistic Continuum in a sample of adult male sexual offenders. Participants completed a comprehensive self-report inventory (MIDSA) and these data were subjected to three separate analytical strategies (exploratory factor analyses, item response theory analyses, and taxometrics). Both the factor analyses and the item response theory analyses indicated high covariation among items measuring paraphilic coercion and sexual sadism; the taxometric procedures also supported a dimensional structure rather than naturally occurring categories or taxa.

The reliable assessment of PCD (like most of the paraphilias) can be difficult; indeed, it is difficult to ascertain reliably the content of an individual's sexual urges and fantasies, particularly within a forensic/correctional context. Additional problems are evident when trying to disentangle an individual's interest in non-consent versus sadistic cues.

Several researchers have argued that evaluators should focus on objective, behavioural indicators associated with a particular paraphilia (Kingston et al., 2010). With regard to rape, Doren (2002) provided a list of behaviours evident during a sexual assault that demonstrates a paraphilic interest in non-consent related cues. Other researchers have adopted a similar approach and have provided a list of behaviours suggestive of a diagnosis of sexual sadism (Marshall et al., 2002; Marshall & Hucker, 2006). Table 41.2 presents some of the offence-related behaviours that have been associated with an interest in non-consent as well as sexual sadism. These behaviours are not exhaustive and there is considerable overlap between the items. Doren (2002) further suggested that an evaluator also consider behaviours that could serve as contraindications of a rape-related paraphilia. He suggested the following examples: (a) interrupting a sexual assault when the victim becomes emotionally distressed; (b) grooming that involves emotional and/or sexual seduction; (c) offender makes comments suggesting that he thought the act was consensual or was enjoyable for the victim; and, (d) the offender not being attentive to the victim's response. With regard to sexual sadism, in particular, the third column in Table 41.2 presents the list of behaviours included in the recently developed Severe Sexual Sadism Scale (Nitschke, Osterheider, & Mokros, 2009). This 11-item scale includes behaviours that are objective and it has recently been shown to be a reliable instrument that is able to discriminate sexual sadists from non-sadists.

Risk for Reoffending

Risk assessment of sexual offenders has become increasingly important to criminal justice decision-making and the number of sex offender-specific risk appraisal tools has proliferated in the past 20 years. The majority of validated measures are actuarial in nature, such that they contain a fixed number of items with specified decision-making rules for scoring. Items contained in these scales are typically based on research demonstrating an empirical link to recidivism (Hanson & Morton-Bourgon, 2005), and these items combine to provide probabilistic estimates of the likelihood of a new offence. Other risk assessment measures are structured professional guides that include risk factors that are empirically related to recidivism along with items that are considered

Table 41.2　Comparison of behavioural indicators for sexual sadism and PCD

Behaviours associated with a Paraphilia Coercive Disorder[a]	*Behaviours associated with Sexual Sadism[a]*	*Severe Sexual Sadism Scale[b]*
1. Ejaculation or other clear signs of sexual arousal during non-consensual acts	1. Mutilating the victim	1. Offender engages in gratuitous violence
2. Repetitive patterns of actions, as if scripts	2. Deliberately injuring, causing bleeding, or causing death	2. Offender exercises power/control/domination
3. Virtually all of the criminal activity is sexual in nature	3. Performing acts that are designed to terrorize the victim	3. Offender humiliates or degrades the victim
4. Raping a victim who was willing to have consensual sex	4. Repeatedly choking the victim to near death	4. Offender is sexually aroused by the act
5. Individual commits rape shortly after being released from custody	5. Slowly inflicting physical pain on the victim after the victim has been subdued	5. Offender tortures the victim or engages in cruelty
6. Raping someone in a situation with a high likelihood of being caught	6. Forcing fellatio immediately after anal intercourse	6. Evidence of ritualism
7. Having concomitant cooperative sexual partners	7. Inserting inanimate objects into victims' orifices	7. Victim is abducted or confined
8. Various victim types across sexual offences	8. Forcing one victim to have sexual contact with another person	8. Insertion of objects into orifices
9. Maintenance of a rape kit	9. Forcing one victim to watch the sexual assault of another	9. Offender mutilates the sexual parts of the body
	10. Involving prolonged periods of assault (many hours or days)	10. Offender mutilates the non-sexual parts of the body
	11. Taking 'trophies' of the experience	11. Offender keeps 'trophies' of the victim or keeps records or the offence

[a]List of behaviours from Doren (2002).
[b]The Severe Sexual Sadism Scale was developed by Nitschke, Osterheider, and Mokros (2009).

to be clinically important. Risk assessors make judgements about risk for reoffending after considering the list of factors, without probabilistic estimates.

A detailed review of all actuarial risk assessment measures and structured professional guides is beyond the scope of this chapter. Some of the more common risk assessment tools include the Static-99 and the Static-99R (Hanson & Thornton, 2000), the Static-2002 (Hanson & Thornton, 2003), the Violence Risk Appraisal Guide (VRAG) and the Sex Offender Risk Appraisal Guide (SORAG) (Quinsey et al., 2006), the Minnesota Sex Offender Screening Tool – Revised (MnSOST-R) (Epperson, Kaul, & Hesselton, 1999; Epperson, Kaul, Huot, Goldman, & Alexander, 2003), and the Sexual Violence Risk-20 (SVR-20) (Boer, Hart, Kropp, & Webster, 1997). Some of these measures are predominantly comprised of static or historical risk factors such as criminal history. As such, dynamic risk measures have been developed to account for potential changes in risk. The Stable-2007 and Acute-2007 are two measures that differentiate between stable and acute dynamic risk factors and have been shown to be predictive of recidivism (Hanson, Harris, Scott, & Helmus, 2007).

Given the variety of risk appraisal tools available, it can be difficult for clinicians to select the most appropriate one to assess risk for recidivism. Although the use of multiple measures in risk assessment is common, interpretation becomes difficult when divergent measures produce discrepant findings (Barbaree, Langton, & Peacock, 2006). Additionally, research pertaining to the incremental validity of multiple measures is mixed. For example, Seto (2005) found that the combination of multiple risk measures did not improve predictive accuracy in risk assessment with sexual offenders, whereas more recent studies have shown that actuarial instruments can add incrementally to the prediction of recidivism (Babchishin, Hanson, & Helmus, 2012; Lloyd, 2008).

Some researchers have suggested that the diversity of sexual offenders may pose a problem with regard to the predictive accuracy of risk appraisal tools. Hanson and Thornton (2000) stated that the Static-99, probably the most popular risk assessment instrument, was equally valid in the prediction of recidivism for rapists and child molesters. Subsequent studies, however, have shown that type of sexual offender may be an important moderating variable. Bartosh, Garby, Lewis, and Gray (2003) reported that the SORAG demonstrated good predictive accuracy among offenders with child victims but poor predictive accuracy among rapists. Rettenberger, Matthes, Boer, and Eher (2010) compared the predictive validity of five risk assessment instruments (Static-99, the Rapid Risk Assessment for Sexual Offense Recidivism, SORAG, SVR-20, and the Psychopathy Checklist – Revised [PCL-R]) across different types of sexual offenders. For the total sample, most instruments demonstrated moderate predictive accuracy, but the authors highlighted the importance of considering the instrument and type of offender as potential moderating factors. For example, among the rapists, the SVR-20 and the PCL-R did not predict general violent and criminal recidivism, although these instruments did predict recidivism in other offender groups. Finally, Parent, Guay, and Knight (2011) compared the predictive accuracy of nine risk assessment instruments across three types of sexual offenders. The results showed that the instruments demonstrated differential predictive utility depending on the type of sexual offender and type of recidivism. Among rapists, most of the measures investigated were better predictors of subsequent violent and non-violent recidivism than sexual recidivism.

Research and theory have shown that sexual offence risk is multidimensional in nature, with at least two distinct dimensions of risk (antisociality/general criminality and sexual deviance) (Doren, 2002) and that actuarial risk assessment instruments often produce different results on these dimensions. In some of the studies noted earlier, the antisocial/general criminality dimension seems to play a more prominent role in predicting recidivism among rapists, whereas the sexual deviance dimension is more important for recidivism prediction among child molesters.

The Offence Cycle/Process

In addition to risk for reoffending, treatment providers are often interested in clarifying the offence process and the context within which the offence was enacted. The offence process highlights the affective, behavioural, cognitive, and contextual factors that culminate in the occurrence of a sexual offence for a specific offender (Kingston, 2010; Marshall, Anderson, & Fernandez, 1999). There have been numerous attempts to describe the various elements within the offence chain (Pithers, 1990; Salter, 1995; Wolf, 1984), although the most popular with rapists and other types of sexual offenders has been the relapse prevention model (Pithers, 1990; Pithers, Marques, Gibat, & Marlatt, 1983).

The relapse prevention model was derived from social learning theory (Bandura, 1986) and was originally developed as a maintenance programme for alcoholic patients who were motivated for treatment (Marlatt, 1982); the relapse prevention model has been described in detail elsewhere (see Pithers, 1990). A major shortcoming of the relapse prevention model was that it did not address all possible pathways or processes involved in offending and reoffending, relying instead on a single offence pathway. Empirical research has confirmed the existence of additional pathways to offending and also differential self-regulation styles associated with offending (Hudson, Ward, & McCormack, 1999).

The self-regulation model (Ward & Hudson, 1998) was designed to account for the diversity of sexual offending and to describe better the offence process, particularly as shown in rapists, without the limitations inherent in the relapse prevention model (Ward, Louden, Hudson, & Marshall, 1995; Yates & Kingston, 2005). The self-regulation model was derived from self-regulation theory, a complex model of decision-making and goal-directed behaviour (Baumeister & Heatherton, 1996; Baumeister & Vohs, 2004), and describes a nine-phase model of the offence progression, from the initial event that initiates the progression through to decision-making and evaluation of behaviour following the commission of a sexual offence.

The model also delineates four pathways to offending based on whether goal-directed actions result from inhibitory goals or acquisitional or appetitive goals and the use of either passive or active strategies to achieve offence-related goals. Individuals following an *avoidant-passive pathway* are characterized by a desire to refrain from sexual offending but they lack requisite strategies to achieve this inhibitory goal (i.e., under-regulated self-regulatory style). Individuals following an *avoidant-active pathway* also desire to avoid sexual offending but they are guided by a misregulated self-regulatory style during the sexual offence progression, such that they employ ineffective strategies (e.g., alcohol) to achieve their inhibitory goal. These last two offence pathways are most similar to the relapse prevention offence process. The final two pathways are guided by approach-related goals (i.e., they desire to offend sexually); individuals following an *approach-automatic pathway* are under-regulated and, as such, are impulsive, whereas individuals following an *approach-explicit pathway* possess intact self-regulatory skills and utilize conscious and explicit planning in order to facilitate the sexual offence.

Research in support of the application of the self-regulation model to the treatment of sexual offenders continues to accumulate, with evidence supporting the major tenets of the model, such as the embedded flexibility and the ability of the model to account for diverse offender and offence characteristics. With regard to sexual offender type, Kingston and colleagues (Kingston, 2010; Kingston et al., 2012; Yates & Kingston, 2006; Yates, Kingston, & Ward, 2009) compared various types of sexual offenders with regard to their offending process. The results consistently showed that many rapists do not typically follow a relapse prevention offence process, that is, one that is guided by inhibitory offence-related goals and self-regulatory failure. Rather, rapists are particularly likely to follow an approach-automatic offence pathway, which is a behavioural progression predominantly characterized by impulsivity and general criminality.

Additional Treatment-Related Needs

In addition to actuarially assessed risk for reoffending and knowledge of the offence process, there are a variety of offender needs that may be important to consider for sexual offenders in general and rapists in particular. A detailed review of each of these domains is beyond the scope of this chapter; some of the more important domains may include emotional dysregulation (Buss & Durkee, 1957), social functioning (Miller & Lefcourt, 1982; Russell, Peplau, & Cutrona, 1980), and antisociality/psychopathy (Hare, 1991).

Among the diverse assessment areas that are of interest to clinicians, the Multidimensional Assessment of Development, Sex, and Aggression (MIDSA) (Auger Enterprises, 2007, 2011; Knight & Sims-Knight, 2003) is one of the most comprehensive instruments for sexual offending currently available. The MIDSA is a contingency-based computerized self-report inventory with a heavy emphasis on the reporting of specific life experiences in addition to subjective emotional states, fantasies, attitudes, behavioural proclivities, and cognitions. The measure includes 53 subscales and includes several content scales aimed at assessing lying, defensive responding, and poor test engagement. The MIDSA scales cover a variety of essential assessment domains, including, for example, developmental history, sexual history, antisocial history, personality traits (e.g., hostility), insight into offence precursors, and deviant sexual interests and arousal. The MIDSA also includes a Sexual Sadism scale that includes two subscales: sadistic fantasies and sadistic behaviours.

The MIDSA has undergone extensive validation since its initial version, the Multidimensional Assessment of Sexual Aggression (Knight, Prentky, & Cerce, 1994), and recent studies have continued to support the validity of the measure (for a more detailed review see, for example, Auger Enterprises, 2011; Knight & Sims-Knight, 2003, 2011; Miner et al., 2009; Schatzel-Murphy, Harris, Knight, & Milburn, 2009). Among adult sexual offenders, the internal consistency of all scales across the 14 domains exceeded 0.65 and most scales produced coefficients between 0.85 and 0.95. Similarly, studies have shown adequate test–retest reliability with coefficients exceeding 0.75 across all scales. The measure has also shown excellent concurrent validity with other scales measuring similar constructs (Auger Enterprises, 2011; Knight & Sims-Knight, 2003, 2011).

Listed below are some additional measures that tap specifically into other important assessment areas, namely attitudes and beliefs and sexual interests and behaviours.

Attitudes and Beliefs

Attitudes can be defined as overall evaluations of an object (e.g., person or behaviour) that can affect behaviour and are amenable to change. With regard to sexual offenders, 'attitudes' is a broad term and has been used to denote several cognitive processes, such as rationalizations and justifications of sexual offending, cognitive distortions (Marshall, Marshall, & Kingston, 2011), hostility towards women, and stereotypical beliefs about victims (Nunes, Hermann, & Ratcliffe, 2013). Attitudes supportive of sexual offending are considered important in multifactorial theories of sexual offending (Malamuth, 2003; Ward & Beech, 2006) and have been identified as psychologically meaningful risk factors for sexual recidivism (Mann, Hanson, & Thornton, 2010).

Recently, Helmus, Hanson, Babchishin, and Mann (2013) conducted a meta-analysis of 46 samples ($n = 13,782$ sexual offenders). The results indicated that attitudes supportive of sexual offending had a small but significant relationship with sexual recidivism. Interestingly, type of offender was a significant moderator, such that rape attitudes and child molester attitudes predicted recidivism among child molesters but the effects were not significant among rapists. However, the conclusions were based on a relatively small sample of rapists and further investigation is warranted. Some of the more common measures of attitudes and beliefs among rapists are listed below.

Rape Scale. The Rape Scale (Bumby, 1996) is a self-report measure consisting of 36 statements reflecting rape-related cognitive distortions (e.g., women often falsely accuse men of rape). Participants indicate the degree to which they agree with these statements (on a four-point Likert-type scale) and higher scores represent greater endorsement of cognitive distortions. The Rape Scale has demonstrated good reliability and validity in several previous studies (Arkowitz & Vess, 2003; Bumby, 1996; Hermann, Babchishin, Nunes, Leth-Steensen, & Cortoni, 2012; Kingston, 2010). Hermann et al. (2012) reported that the Rape Scale was multidimensional and results of an exploratory factor analysis revealed a two-factor model (excusing rape and justifying rape). Importantly, the Rape Scale has also been shown to be unrelated to socially desirable responding (Bumby, 1996; Hermann et al., 2012).

Rape Myth Acceptance Scale. The Rape Myth Acceptance Scale (RMA) (Burt, 1980) is a brief, 19-item self-report measure designed to measure respondents' attitudes and beliefs pertaining to rape. Examples of such beliefs include women enjoy being raped or that rape victims are usually promiscuous. Factor analyses have revealed three factors that include attitudes in support of sex-role stereotyping, adversarial sexual beliefs, and acceptance of violence towards women. The RMA has been used in a number of studies, particularly with non-criminal sexual aggressors (Malamuth, 1989a, 1989b). Previous research indicates that item-total correlations range from 0.27 to 0.62 and the scale has been found to be internally consistent with alpha coefficients ranging from 0.88 (Burt, 1980) to 0.92 (Marshall & Hambley, 1996) and to have adequate criterion validity (Lonsway & Fitzgerald, 1995).

Illinois Rape Myth Acceptance Scale. The Illinois Rape Myth Acceptance Scale (Payne, Lonsway, & Fitzgerald, 1999) is a 45-item measure that includes seven subscales: 'She asked for it', 'It wasn't really rape', 'He didn't mean to', 'She wanted it', 'She lied', 'Rape is a trivial event', and 'Rape is a deviant event'. Corrected correlations between each subscale and the overall score ranged from 0.54 to 0.74, indicating that the subscales are each very much related to general rape myth acceptance. The alpha coefficients of the subscales ranged from 0.74 to 0.84 and the overall alpha coefficient of the scale was reported as 0.93 (Payne et al., 1999). There is a short-form version of this scale that includes 17 items and three filler statements to reduce the likelihood of response sets. The alpha coefficient of the short version was reported to be between 0.85 (Chapleau, Oswald, & Russell, 2007) and 0.87 (Payne et al., 1999) and the correlation between the full and short-form measures was 0.97.

Hostility Toward Women Scale. The Hostility Toward Women Scale (Check, 1985) is a 30-item, true/false, self-report measure designed to assess men's level of hostility towards women (Check, Perlman, & Malamuth, 1985). Research indicates that the scale has satisfactory internal consistency, test–retest reliability, and concurrent validity (Check et al., 1985; Marshall & Hambley, 1996). Lonsway and Fitzgerald (1995) developed a 10-item modification of the Hostility Toward Women Scale. Examples of items include 'I am easily angered by women' and 'Women are responsible for most of my troubles', and respondents are asked to indicate their level of agreement on a seven-point scale from 1 (strongly disagree) to 7 (strongly agree). Responses are summed to produce a total score; higher scores indicate higher levels of hostility. The modified scale has been shown to have good internal consistency with alpha coefficients ranging from 0.78 (Forbes, Collinsworth, Jobe, Braun, & Wise, 2007) to 0.85 (Cowan & Mills, 2004).

Implicit attitudes towards rape. Many self-report measures, such as those described earlier, tap into explicit attitudes towards rape – that is, attitudes that are deliberate, intentional, and available to conscious awareness. In contrast, implicit attitudes are automatically activated, are not accessed by introspection, and are often outside conscious awareness. The Implicit Association Test (IAT) (Banse, Schmidt, & Clabour, 2010) is a popular latency-based measure that taps into implicit attitudes. More specifically, the measure examines the strength of associations between concepts – that is, how closely associated a given attitude object (e.g., rape) is with an evaluative attribute (i.e., good versus bad). The IAT requires an individual to categorize such concepts rapidly, such that faster responses are interpreted as more strongly associated in memory than slower responses.

One of the advantages of the IAT is the presumed resistance of the measure to intentional faking or socially desirable responding (Greenwald, Poehlman, Uhlmann, & Banaji, 2009). Consequently, several researchers have applied the IAT procedure to detect implicit cognitions in sexual offenders (Gray, Brown, MacCulloch, Smith, & Snowden, 2005; Mihailides, Devilly, & Ward, 2004). Recently, Nunes et al. (2013) designed an IAT to measure implicit attitudes towards rape among 86 male university students. The results supported the relationship between implicit attitudes toward rape and self-reported sexual aggression. Nunes et al. also reported that combining measures of implicit and explicit attitudes (i.e., self-report and IAT) were strongly associated with self-reported sexual aggression in a non-offender sample.

Assessment of Sexual Preferences and Behaviours

Various procedures have been developed to assess the sexual preferences and behaviours of rapists (for a review, see Kalmus & Beech, 2005). Evaluators can employ non-physiological measures of sexual interest (e.g., interview/questionnaires), measures based on attentional methodologies (e.g., viewing time, information processing measures), or physiological measures (e.g., plethysmography).

Non-physiological measures of sexual interest. Self-reported sexual interest can be obtained via a comprehensive clinical interview, whereby respondents are asked questions pertaining to their sexual thoughts, interests, and behaviours. Interviews can be informative, particularly when a respondent admits to sexually inappropriate thoughts and behaviours. However, interviews are subject to socially desirable responding and many sexual offenders deny or minimize certain aspects of their sexual histories.

One way to reduce the reluctance of individuals to disclose their sexual interests is to administer questionnaires. Although some of the more commonly used measures incorporate validity scales that detect impression management, many of these scales are somewhat transparent and are therefore vulnerable to self-reporting biases. Some of the more common measures that can be used with rapists are as follows.

Multiphasic Sex Inventory. The Multiphasic Sex Inventory (MSI) (Nichols & Molinder, 1984) is a 300-item, true/false, self-report instrument used widely with sexual offenders. The MSI generates 20 core scales that measured interest in child molestation, rape, and exhibitionism, with additional scales measuring other paraphilias (e.g., fetishism, sadomasochism). The MSI has shown good psychometric properties (Kalichman, Henderson, Shealy, & Dwyer, 1992) and the scales are able to differentiate between rapists and child molesters (Nichols & Molinder, 1984). Craig, Browne, Beech, and Stringer (2006) reported that certain subscales (Sexual Deviance Factor, Sexual Obsessions, Sexual/Social Desirability, and Sexual Dysfunction) were able to predict recidivism; however, their sample did not include rapists. Of note, the MSI has been updated and expanded (MSI-II) to include 560 true/false questions (Nichols & Molinder, 2000). There is limited research available on the validity of the revised measure, although the test developers provide some psychometric data (see www.nicholsandmolinder.com).

Sexual Experiences Survey.   The Sexual Experiences Survey (SES) (Koss & Gidycz, 1985) was a revision of an earlier scale (see Koss & Oros, 1982), and was developed to improve clarity and to maintain consistency with the legal definition of rape. The revised SES is a 10-item, true/false, self-report measure designed to assess sexual relations involving various degrees of sexual coercion, threat, or aggression. The questions are worded to depict female victimization and male aggression; the survey initially inquires about less severe instances of sexual coercion and then it taps into increasingly aggressive sexual experiences. Research indicates that reported values of Cronbach's alpha are consistently above 0.70 (Cecil & Matson, 2006; Koss, Figueredo, Bell, Tharan, & Tromp, 1996; Koss & Gidycz, 1985; Messman-Moore, Long, & Siegfried, 2000). Koss and Gidycz (1985) reported 93% item agreement between two administrations 1 week apart, indicating stable responses.

Attraction to Sexual Aggression Scale.   The Attraction to Sexual Aggression (ASA) scale (Malamuth, 1989a,b) includes nine questions (e.g., how often the respondent thinks about a behaviour) and each question is followed by a different list of behaviours (i.e., heterosexual intercourse, raping a woman, robbing a bank, etc.). The ASA scale was designed to identify men with attractions involving sexual aggression while also assessing the likelihood of engaging in various forceful behaviours indicated by self-reported responses. Respondents are required to rate their behaviour and attractions towards a range of sexual and non-sexual behaviours. The latter was included so as to reduce demand characteristics and control for response sets. In support of the reliability and validity of the ASA scale, internal consistency was measured at 0.91 and item-total correlations were reported to range from 0.46 to 0.77 (Malamuth, 1989a, 1989b). Adequate test–retest reliability has also been reported ($r = 0.76$) (Schewe & O'Donohue, 1998). Significant relationships have been reported between both attitudes supportive of rape ($r = 0.46$) and sexual arousal in response to sexually coercive stimuli ($r = 0.22 – 0.56$) (Malamuth, 1989b).

More recently, Voller, Long, and Aosved (2009) used a revised version of the scale that included three subscales (*attraction to sexual violence, attraction to criminality,* and *attraction to child sexual abuse*). The authors reported the revised scale's internal consistency at 0.94 and found the internal consistency of the three subscales also to be good: for attraction to sexual violence it was 0.90, attraction to criminality 0.89, and attraction to child sexual abuse 0.86.

Attentional measures of sexual interest.   There are several measures of sexual interest that are based on attentional processes (for a review, see Kalmus & Beech, 2005) and are far less intrusive than PPG (described below). Viewing time measures are based on the notion that viewing time is indicative of sexual interest (Abel, Lawry, Karlstrom, Osborn, & Gillespie, 1994; Rosenzweig, 1942; Ware, Brown, Amoroso, Pilkey, & Preusse, 1972), that is, individuals will inherently view attractive images longer than images they find to be unattractive or neutral. The Abel Assessment for Sexual Interest

(AASI) (Abel, Jordan, Hand, Holland, & Phipps, 2001) is an example of a viewing time measure that utilizes entirely non-nude images of children and adults. The AASI combines explicit self-report ratings of sexual interest and covert measures of viewing time. The measure assesses the time spent viewing a series of slides depicting 16 categories of children and adults in addition to six paraphilias (frotteurism, exhibitionism, fetishism, voyeurism against females, and sadomasochism against males and females). Overall, numerous problems have been noted with regard to the scale's psychometric properties, such as a lack of internal consistency, temporal stability, and predictive utility (Fischer, 2000; Fischer & Smith, 1999). However, Letourneau (2002) noted that the sadomasochism scales produced sufficient internal consistency for depictions of female victims ($\alpha = 0.91$) and male victims ($\alpha = 0.87$).

Physiological assessment. Currently, the most widely used method of assessing sexual interest of offenders is penile plethysmography (PPG) (phallometry). Phallometry involves the objective measurement of erectile changes in response to stimuli that varies on the particular dimension of interest, such as the age and gender of the individual(s) depicted or the level of coercion/violence during the sexual act. Phallometry has been subject to a number of studies evaluating both the discriminative and predictive validity and, although some researchers have pointed out some limitations and concerns (Howes, 1998; Marshall & Fernandez, 2000), evidence has generally supported the clinical and research use of phallometry in the assessment of deviant sexual preference (Hanson & Bussière, 1998; Lalumière et al., 2003; Seto, 2008).

There has been an accumulation of studies examining the extent to which relative penile responses to stimuli depicting rape versus stimuli depicting consensual sex differentiate convicted rapists from other men. Although there are some discrepancies in the literature, two meta-analyses (Hall, Shondrick, & Hirschman, 1993; Lalumière & Quinsey, 1994) demonstrated that rapists tend to respond more to scenarios describing coercive sex than other men; the overall effects in these analyses were moderate to large. In general, the effects are particularly strong when the stimuli emphasize brutality and victim suffering and when participants have not been previously assessed with phallometry.

Conclusions

Rapists are an extremely heterogeneous offender group in terms of their developmental histories and adult characteristics (Gannon et al., 2008). Despite the notion that rapists are often considered a distinct and specialized offender group, research has shown that rapists are more similar to non-sexual offenders than they are to other types of sexual offenders. This chapter has cited research that highlights the versatility of rapists' criminal histories along with studies that have shown rapists to present with various types of antisocial traits that are similar to those of offenders without any known sexual offence histories.

Such heterogeneity presents considerable challenges to evaluators, which underscores the importance of comprehensive and reliable assessment. There are a number of different assessment methods that can be employed with rapists. One method, intended to create homogeneous subgroups, is the application of nosological diagnoses. In many jurisdictions, evaluators are required to apply psychiatric diagnoses to sexual offenders being considered for civil commitment. The DSM-5 lists several diagnoses that may be relevant to rapists, although considerable attention has been devoted to the paraphilias. Despite the consistent finding that there are a subset of individuals who show a preference for non-consent sexual behaviour (Harris et al., 2012; Seto et al., 2012), there is no diagnosis for rape in the DSM-5. As such, evaluators most often apply a diagnoses of Paraphilia (NOS) (Doren, 2002; Zander, 2008). Unfortunately, this diagnosis has been criticized for its lack of reliability and validity and also its practical utility (Marshall, 2006).

This chapter has emphasized other assessment domains that are important when evaluating individuals who sexually offend against women and may be more clinically useful than considering specific DSM diagnostic categories. These include, for example, risk for reoffending, the offence chain, attitudes and beliefs, and sexual interests and behaviours. These domains provide practical information that assists in risk management and in delivering effective treatment.

Acknowledgement

The author thanks Martin Lalumière for his very helpful comments.

References

Abel, G. G., Jordan, A., Hand, C. G., Holland, L. A., & Phipps, A. (2001). Classification models of child molesters utilizing the Abel Assessment for Sexual Interest. *Child Abuse and Neglect, 25*, 703–718.

Abel, G. G., Lawry, S. S., Karlstrom, E., Osborn, C. A., & Gillespie, C. F. (1994). Screening tests for pedophilia. *Criminal Justice and Behavior, 21*(1), 115–131.

Aggrawal, A. (2009). *Forensic and medico-legal aspects of sexual crimes and unusual sexual practices*. Boca Raton, FL: CRC Press.

American Psychiatric Association. (1987). *Diagnostic and statistical manual of mental disorders* (3rd ed., revised) (DSM-III-R). Washington, DC: Author.

American Psychiatric Association. (2000). *Diagnostic and statistical manual of mental disorders* (4th ed., text revision) (DSM-IV-TR). Washington, DC: Author.

American Psychiatric Association. (2013). *Diagnostic and statistical manual of mental disorders* (5th ed.) (DSM-5). Arlington, VA: American Psychiatric Publishing.

Andrews, D. A., & Bonta, J. (2006). *The psychology of criminal conduct* (4th ed.). Newark, NJ: LexisNexis/Matthew Bender.

Arkowitz, S., & Vess, J. (2003). An evaluation of the Bumby RAPE and MOLEST scales as measures of cognitive distortions with civilly committed sexual offenders. *Sexual Abuse: A Journal of Research and Treatment, 15*(4), 237–249.

Augur Enterprises (2007). *MIDSA: Multidimensional Inventory of Development, Sex, and Aggression*. Bend, OR: Author. Retrieved from http://www.midsa.us

Augur Enterprises (2011). *MIDSA clinical manual*. Bend, OR: Author. Retrieved from http://www.midsa.us/learnmore.php

Babchishin, K. M., Hanson, R. K., & Helmus, L. (2012). Even highly correlated measures can add incrementally to predicting recidivism among sex offenders. *Assessment, 19*(4), 442–461.

Banse, R., Schmidt, A. F., & Clabour, J. (2010). Indirect measures of sexual interest in child sex offenders: A multi-method approach. *Criminal Justice and Behavior, 37*, 319–335.

Barbaree, H. E., Langton, C. M., & Peacock, E. J. (2006). Different actuarial risk measures produce different risk rankings for sexual offenders. *Sexual Abuse: A Journal of Research and Treatment, 18*(4), 423–440.

Barbaree, H. E., Marshall, W. L., & Lanthier, R. D. (1979). Deviant sexual arousal in rapists. *Behaviour Research and Therapy, 17*(3), 215–222.

Barbaree, H. E., Seto, M. C., Serin, R. C., Amos, N. L., & Preston, D. L. (1994). Comparisons between sexual and non-sexual rapist subtypes: Sexual arousal to rape, offense precursors and offense characteristics. *Criminal Justice and Behavior, 21*, 95–114.

Bard, L. A., Carter, D. L., Cerce, D. D., Knight, R. A., Rosenberg, R., & Schneider, B. (1987). A descriptive study of rapists and child molesters: Developmental, clinical, and criminal characteristics. *Behavioural Sciences and the Law, 5*, 203–220.

Bartosh, D. L., Garby, T., Lewis, D., & Gray, S. (2003). Differences in the predictive validity of actuarial risk assessments in relation to sex offender type. *International Journal of Offender Therapy and Comparative Criminology, 47*(4), 422–438.

Baumeister, R. F., & Heatherton, T. F. (1996). Self-regulation failure: An overview. *Psychological Inquiry, 7*(1), 1–15.

Baumeister, R. F., & Vohs, K. D. (2004). *Handbook of self-regulation: Research, theory, and applications*. New York, NY: Guilford Press.

Baxter, D. J., Marshall, W. L., Barbaree, H. E., Davidson, P. R., & Malcolm, P. B. (1984). Differentiating sex offenders by criminal history, psychometric measures, and sexual response. *Criminal Justice and Behavior, 11*, 477–501.

Bernat, J. A., Calhoun, K. S., & Adams, H. E. (1999). Sexually aggressive and nonaggressive men: Sexual arousal and judgments in response to date rape and consensual analogues. *Journal of Abnormal Psychology, 108*, 662–673.

Black, M. C., Basile, K. C., Breiding, M. J., Smith, S. G., Walters, M. L., Merrick, M. T., … Stevens, M. R. (2011). *The National Intimate Partner and Sexual Violence Survey (NISVS): 2010 summary report*. Atlanta, GA: National Center for Injury Prevention and Control, Centers for Disease Control and Prevention.

Boer, D. P., Hart, S. D., Kropp, P. R., & Webster, C. D. (1997). *Manual for the Sexual Violence Risk-20*. Vancouver, Canada: Mental Health, Law and Policy Institute and Simon Fraser University.

Bumby, K. M. (1996). Assessing the cognitive distortions of child molesters and rapists: Development and validation of the molest and rape scales. *Sexual Abuse: A Journal of Research and Treatment, 8*(1), 37–54.

Burt, M. R. (1980). Cultural myths and supports for rape. *Journal of Personality and Social Psychology, 38*(2), 217–230.

Buss, A. H., & Durkee, A. (1957). An inventory for assessing different types of hostility. *Journal of Consulting and Clinical Psychology, 21*, 343–349.

Cecil, H., & Matson, S. C. (2006). Sexual victimization among African American adolescent females: Examination of the reliability and validity of the sexual experiences survey. *Journal of Interpersonal Violence, 21*(1), 89–104.

Chapleau, K. M., Oswald, D. L., & Russell, B. L. (2007). How ambivalent sexism toward women and men supports rape myth acceptance. *Sex Roles, 57*(1–2), 131–136.

Check, J. V. (1985). The hostility toward women scale. *Dissertation Abstracts International, 45*(12B), 3993–3993.

Check, J. V. P., Perlman, D., & Malamuth, N. M. (1985). Loneliness and aggressive behaviour. *Journal of Social and Personal Relationships, 2*(3), 243–252.

Cowan, G., & Mills, R. D. (2004). Personal inadequacy and intimacy predictors of men's hostility toward women. *Sex Roles, 51*(1–2), 67–78.

Craig, L. A., Browne, K. D., Beech, A., & Stringer, I. (2006). Psychosexual characteristics of sexual offenders and the relationship to sexual reconviction. *Psychology, Crime & Law, 12*(3), 231–243.

Doren, D. M. (2002). *Evaluating sex offenders: A manual for civil commitments and beyond.* Thousand Oaks, CA: Sage.

Doren, D., & Elwood, R. (2009). The diagnostic reliability of sexual sadism. *Sexual Abuse: A Journal of Research and Treatment, 21*(3), 251–261.

Earls, C.M., & Proulx, J. (1986). The differentiation of francophone rapists and nonrapists using penile circumferential measures. *Criminal Justice and Behaviour, 13*(4), 419–429.

Epperson, D., Kaul, J., & Hesselton, D. (1999). *Minnesota Sex Offender Screening Tool – Revised (MnSOST-R): Development, performance, and recommended risk level cut scores.* Unpublished manuscript.

Epperson, D. L., Kaul, J. D., Huot, S., Goldman, R., & Alexander, W. (2003). *Minnesota Sex Offender Screening Tool – Revised (MnSOST-R) technical paper: Development, validation, and recommended risk level cut scores.* St. Paul, MN: Minnesota Department of Corrections.

Fischer, L. (2000). The Abel Screen: A nonintrusive alternative? In D. R. Laws, S. M. Hudson, & T. Ward (Eds.), *Remaking relapse prevention with sex offenders: A sourcebook* (pp. 303–318). Thousand Oaks, CA: Sage.

Fischer, L., & Smith, G. (1999). Statistical adequacy of the Abel Assessment for interest in paraphilias. *Sexual Abuse: A Journal of Research and Treatment, 11*(3), 195–205.

Forbes, G. B., Collinsworth, L. L., Jobe, R. L., Braun, K. D., & Wise, L. M. (2007). Sexism, hostility toward women, and endorsement of beauty ideals and practices: Are beauty ideals associated with oppressive beliefs? *Sex Roles, 56*(5–6), 265–273.

Frances, A., & First, M. B. (2011). Paraphilia NOS, nonconsent: Not ready for the courtroom. *Journal of the American Academy of Psychiatry and the Law, 39*(4), 555–561.

Freund, K., Scher, H., Racansky, I. G., Campbell, K., & Heasman, G. (1986). Males disposed to commit rape. *Archives of Sexual Behavior, 15*, 23–35.

Freund, K., Seeley, H. R., Marshall, W. E., & Glinfort, E. K. (1972). Sexual offenders needing special assessment and/or therapy. *Canadian Journal of Criminology and Criminal Justice, 14*, 345–365.

Gannon, T. A., Collie, R. M., Ward, T., & Thakker, J. (2008). Rape: Psychopathology, theory and treatment. *Clinical Psychology Review, 28*(6), 982–1008.

Gannon, T. A., & Ward, T. (2008). Rape: Psychopathology and theory. In D. R. Laws & W. T. O'Donohue (Eds.), *Sexual deviance: Theory, assessment, and treatment* (pp. 336–355). New York, NY: Guilford Press.

Gray, N. S., Brown, A. S., MacCulloch, M. J., Smith, J., & Snowden, R. J. (2005). An implicit test of the associations between children and sex in pedophiles. *Journal of Abnormal Psychology, 114*(2), 304–308.

Greenwald, A. G., Poehlman, T. A., Uhlmann, E. L., & Banaji, M. R. (2009). Understanding and using the implicit association test: III. Meta-analysis of predictive validity. *Journal of Personality and Social Psychology, 97*(1), 17–41.

Hall, G. C. N., Shondrick, D. D., & Hirschman, R. (1993). The role of sexual arousal in sexually aggressive behavior: A meta-analysis. *Journal of Consulting and Clinical Psychology, 61*(6), 1091–1095.

Hanson, R. K. (2001). *Age and sexual recidivism: A comparison of rapists and child molesters* (User Report 2001-01). Ottawa, Canada: Department of the Solicitor General of Canada.

Hanson, R. K. (2002). Recidivism and age. *Journal of Interpersonal Violence, 17,* 1046–1062.

Hanson, R. K., & Bussière, M. T. (1998). Predicting relapse: A meta-analysis of sexual offender recidivism studies. *Journal of Consulting and Clinical Psychology, 66,* 348–362.

Hanson, R. K., Harris, A. J. R., Scott, T.-L., & Helmus, L. (2007). *Assessing the risk of sexual offenders on community supervision: The Dynamic Supervision Project* (User Report 2007-05). Ottawa, Canada: Public Safety Canada.

Hanson, R. K., & Morton-Bourgon, K. E. (2005). The characteristics of persistent sexual offenders: A meta-analysis of recidivism studies. *Journal of Consulting and Clinical Psychology, 73,* 1154–1163.

Hanson, R. K., & Thornton, D. (2000). Improving risk assessments for sex offenders: A comparison of three actuarial scales. *Law and Human Behavior, 24*(1), 119–138.

Hanson, R. K., & Thornton, D. (2003). *Notes on the development of Static-2002* (Corrections Research User Report 2003-01). Ottawa, Canada: Solicitor General of Canada.

Hare, R. D. (1991). *The Hare Psychopathy Checklist – Revised.* Toronto, Canada: Multi-Health Systems.

Harris, D. A., Mazerolle, P., & Knight, R. A. (2009). Understanding male sexual offending: A comparison of general and specialist theories. *Criminal Justice and Behavior, 36*(10), 1051–1069.

Harris, G. T., Lalumière, M. L., Seto, M. C., Rice, M. E., & Chaplin, T. C. (2012). Explaining the erectile responses of rapists to rape stories: The contributions of sexual activity, nonconsent, and violence with injury. *Archives of Sexual Behavior, 41*(1), 221–229.

Helmus, L., Hanson, R. K., Babchishin, K. M., & Mann, R. E. (2013). Attitudes supportive of sexual offending predict recidivism: A meta-analysis. *Trauma, Violence, & Abuse, 14*(1), 34–53.

Hermann, C. A., Babchishin, K. M., Nunes, K. L., Leth-Steensen, C., & Cortoni, F. (2012). Factor structure of the Bumby RAPE scale: A two-factor model. *Criminal Justice and Behavior, 39*(7), 869–886.

Howes, R. J. (1998). Plethysmographic assessment of incarcerated nonsexual offenders: A comparison with rapists. *Sexual Abuse, 10,* 183–194.

Hudson, S. M., Ward, T., & McCormack, J. C. (1999). Offense pathways in sexual offenders. *Journal of Interpersonal Violence, 14*(8), 779–798.

Kalichman, S. C., Henderson, M. C., Shealy, L. S., & Dwyer, S. M. (1992). Psychometric properties of the multiphasic sex inventory in assessing sex offenders. *Criminal Justice and Behavior, 19*(4), 384–396.

Kalmus, E., & Beech, A. R. (2005). Forensic assessment of sexual interest: A review. *Aggression and Violent Behavior, 10*(2), 193–217.

Kingston, D. A. (2010). *The offense progression in sexual offenders: An examination of the self-regulation model of the offense process* (Unpublished doctoral dissertation). University of Ottawa.

Kingston, D. A., Seto, M. C., Firestone, P., & Bradford, J. M. (2010). Comparing indicators of sexual sadism as predictors of recidivism among sexual offenders. *Journal of Consulting and Clinical Psychology, 78,* 574–584.

Kingston, D. A., & Yates, P. M. (2008). Sexual sadism: Assessment and treatment. In D. R. Laws & W. T. O'Donohue (Eds.), *Sexual deviance: Theory, assessment, and treatment* (2nd ed., pp. 231–249). New York, NY: Guilford Press.

Kingston, D. A., Yates, P. M., & Firestone, P. (2012). The self-regulation model of sexual offender treatment: Relationship to risk and need. *Law and Human Behavior, 36*(3), 215–224.

Knight, R. A. (2009). Typologies for rapists: The generation of a new structural model. In A. Schlank (Ed.),*The sexual predator* (Vol. 4, Chapter 17, pp. 1–28). New York, NY: Civic Research Institute.

Knight, R. A., & Guay, J. (2006). *The role of psychopathy in sexual coercion against women.* New York, NY: Guilford Press.

Knight, R. A., & Prentky, R. A. (1990). *Classifying sexual offenders: The development and corroboration of taxonomic models.* New York, NY: Plenum.

Knight, R. A., Prentky, R. A., & Cerce, D. D. (1994). The development, reliability, and validity of an inventory for the multidimensional assessment of sex and aggression. *Criminal Justice and Behavior, 21,* 72–94.

Knight, R. A., & Sims-Knight, J. E. (2003). The developmental antecedents of sexual coercion against women: Testing alternative hypotheses with structural equation modeling. *Annals of the New York Academy of Sciences, 989,* 72–85; Discussion, 144–153.

Knight, R. A., & Sims-Knight, J. (2011). *Risk factors for sexual violence.* In J. W. White, M. P. Koss, & A. E. Kazdin (Eds.), *Violence against women and children, Volume* (Vol. 1, pp. 125–150). Washington, DC: American Psychological Association.

Knight, R. A., Sims-Knight, J. E., & Guay, J. P. (2013). Is a separate disorder category defensible for paraphilic coercion? *Journal of Criminal Justice, 41,* 90–99.

Koss, M. P., Figueredo, A. J., Bell, I., Tharan, M., & Tromp, S. (1996). Traumatic memory characteristics: A cross-validated mediational model of response to rape among employed women. *Journal of Abnormal Psychology, 105*(3), 421–432.

Koss, M. P., & Gidycz, C. A. (1985). Sexual experiences survey: Reliability and validity. *Journal of Consulting and Clinical Psychology, 53*(3), 422–423.

Koss, M. P., Leonard, K. E., Beezley, D. A., & Oros, C. J. (1985). Non-stranger sexual aggression: A discriminant analysis of psychological characteristics of nondetected offenders. *Sex Role, 12,* 981–992.

Koss, M. P., & Oros, C. J. (1982). Sexual experience survey: A research instrument investigating sexual aggression and victimization. *Journal of Consulting and Clinical Psychology, 50,* 455–457.

Krueger, R. B. (2009). The DSM diagnostic criteria for sexual sadism. *Archives of Sexual Behavior, 39*(2), 325–345.

Lalumière, M. L., Harris, G. T., Quinsey, V. L., & Rice, M. E. (2005). *The causes of rape: Understanding individual differences in male propensity for sexual aggression.* Washington, DC: American Psychological Association.

Lalumière, M. L., & Quinsey, V. L. (1994). The discriminability of rapists from non-sex offenders using phallometric measures: A meta-analysis. *Criminal Justice and Behavior, 21*(1), 150–175.

Lalumière, M. L., Quinsey, V. L., Harris, G. T., Rice, M. E., & Trautrimas, C. (2003). Are rapists differentially aroused by coercive sex in phallometric assessments? *Annals of the New York Academy of Sciences, 989,* 211–224; Discussion, 236–246.

Laws, D. R., & O'Donohue, W. T. (Eds.) (2008). *Sexual deviance: Theory, assessment, and treatment* (2nd ed.). New York, NY: Guilford Press.

Letourneau, E. J. (2002). A comparison of objective measures of sexual arousal and interest: Visual reaction time and penile plethysmography. *Sexual Abuse: A Journal of Research and Treatment, 14*(3), 207–223.

Levenson, J. S. (2004). Reliability of sexually violent predator civil commitment criteria in Florida. *Law and Human Behavior, 28*(4), 357–368.

Lloyd, M. D. (2008). Incremental validity of commonly-used risk assessment measures in predicting serious sexual recidivism. *Dissertation Abstracts International, 69*(9B), 5784–5784.

Lohr, B. A., Adams, H. E., & Davis, J. M. (1997). Sexual arousal to erotic and aggressive stimuli in sexually coercive and noncoercive men. *Journal of Abnormal Psychology, 106*(2), 230–242.

Lonsway, K. A., & Fitzgerald, L. F. (1995). Attitudinal antecedents of rape myth acceptance: A theoretical and empirical reexamination. *Journal of Personality and Social Psychology, 68*(4), 704–711.

Lussier, P. (2005). The criminal activity of sexual offenders in adulthood: Revisiting the specialization debate. *Sexual Abuse: A Journal of Research and Treatment, 17*(3), 269–292.

Lussier, P., LeBlanc, M., & Proulx, J. (2005). The generality of criminal behavior: A confirmatory factor analysis of the criminal activity of sex offenders in adulthood. *Journal of Criminal Justice, 33*(2), 177–189.

Malamuth, N. M. (1989a). The attraction to sexual aggression scale: Part one. *Journal of Sex Research, 26,* 26–49.

Malamuth, N. M. (1989b). The attraction to sexual aggression scale: Part two. *Journal of Sex Research, 26,* 324–354.

Malamuth, N. M. (2003). Criminal and noncriminal sexual aggressors: Integrating psychopathy in a hierarchical–mediational confluence model. *Annals of the New York Academy of Sciences, 989,* 33–58; Discussion, 144–153.

Mann, R. E., Hanson, R. K., & Thornton, D. (2010). Assessing risk for sexual recidivism: Some proposals on the nature of psychologically meaningful risk factors. *Sexual Abuse: A Journal of Research and Treatment, 22*(2), 191–217.

Marlatt, G. A. (1982). Relapse prevention: A self-control program for the treatment of addictive behaviours. In R. B. Stuart (Ed.), *Adherence, compliance, and generalization in behavioural medicine* (pp. 329–378). New York, NY: Brunner/Mazel.

Marshall, W. L. (2006). Diagnostic problems with sexual offenders. In W. L. Marshall, Y. M. Fernandez, L. E. Marshall, & G. A. Serran (Eds.), *Sexual offender treatment: Controversial issues* (pp. 33–43). Chichester, England: John Wiley & Sons, Ltd.

Marshall, W. L., Anderson, D., & Fernandez, Y. (1999). *Cognitive behavioural treatment of sexual offenders.* New York, NY: John Wiley & Sons, Inc.

Marshall, W. L., & Fernandez, Y. M. (2000). Phallometric testing with sexual offenders: Limits to its value. *Clinical Psychology Review, 20*(7), 807–822.

Marshall, W. L., & Hambley, L. S. (1996). Intimacy and loneliness, and their relationship to rape myth acceptance and hostility toward women among rapists. *Journal of Interpersonal Violence, 11*(4), 586–592.

Marshall, W. L., & Hucker, S. J. (2006). *Severe sexual sadism: Its features and treatment* (pp. 227–250). Westport, CT: Praeger.

Marshall, W. L., Kennedy, P., & Yates, P. (2002). Issues concerning the reliability and validity of the diagnosis of sexual sadism applied in prison settings. *Sexual Abuse: A Journal of Research and Treatment, 14*(4), 301–311.

Marshall, W. L., Kennedy, P., Yates, P., & Serran, G. (2002). Diagnosing sexual sadism in sexual offenders: Reliability across diagnosticians. *International Journal of Offender Therapy and Comparative Criminology, 46*(6), 668–677.

Marshall, W. L., Marshall, L. E., & Kingston, D. A. (2011). Are the cognitive distortions of child molesters in need of treatment? *Journal of Sexual Aggression, 17,* 118–129.

Meehl, P. E. (1954). *Clinical versus statistical prediction: A theoretical analysis and a review of the evidence.* Minneapolis, MN: University of Minnesota Press.

Meehl, P. E. (1973). *Psychodiagnosis: Selected papers.* Minneapolis, MN: University of Minnesota Press.

Messman-Moore, T., Long, P. J., & Siegfried, N. J. (2000). The revictimization of child sexual abuse survivors: An examination of the adjustment of college women with child sexual abuse, adult sexual assault, and adult physical abuse. *Child Maltreatment*, 5(1), 18–27.

Mihailides, S., Devilly, G. J., & Ward, T. (2004). Implicit cognitive distortions and sexual offending. *Sexual Abuse: A Journal of Research and Treatment*, 16(4), 333–350.

Miller, R. S., & Lefcourt, H. M. (1982). The assessment of social intimacy. *Journal of Personality Assessment*, 46(5), 514–518.

Miner, H. M., Robinson, B. E., Knight, R. A., Berg, D., Romine, R. S., & Netland, J. (2009). Understanding sexual perpetration against children: Effects of attachment style, interpersonal involvement, and hypersexuality. *A Journal of Research and Treatment*, 22(1), 58–77.

Money, J. (1999). *The lovemap guidebook: A definitive statement*. New York, NY: Continuum.

Nichols, H., & Molinder, I. (1984). *Manual for the Multiphasic Sex Inventory*. Tacoma, WA: Crime and Victim Psychology Specialists.

Nichols, H. R., & Molinder, I. (2000). *Manual for the Multiphasic Sex Inventory* (2nd ed.). Tacoma, WA: Crime and Victim Psychology Specialists. Available from Nichols & Molinder, 437 Bowes Drive, Tacoma, WA 98466-70747, USA.

Nitschke, J., Osterheider, M., & Mokros, A. (2009). A cumulative scale of severe sexual sadism. *Sexual Abuse: A Journal of Research and Treatment*, 21(3), 262–278.

Nunes, K. L., Hermann, C. A., & Ratcliffe, K. (2013). Implicit and explicit attitudes towards rape are associated with sexual aggression. *Journal of Interpersonal Violence*, 28, 2657–2675.

O'Donohue, W., Regev, L. G., & Hagstrom, A. (2000). Problems with the DSM-IV diagnosis of pedophilia. *Sexual Abuse: A Journal of Research and Treatment*, 12, 95–105.

Packard, R. L., & Levenson, J. (2006). Revisiting the reliability of diagnostic decisions in sex offender civil commitment. *Sexual Offender Treatment*, 1(3). Retrieved from http://www.sexual-offender-treatment.org/50.0.html

Parent, G., Guay, J. P., & Knight, R. A. (2011). An assessment of long-term risk of recidivism by adult sex offenders: One size doesn't fit all. *Criminal Justice and Behavior*, 38, 188–209.

Payne, D. L., Lonsway, K. A., & Fitzgerald, L. F. (1999). Rape myth acceptance: Exploration of its structure and its measurement using the Illinois Rape Myth Acceptance Scale. *Journal of Research in Personality*, 33, 27–68.

Penix, T. M. (2008). Paraphilia not otherwise specified: Assessment and treatment. In D. R. Laws, & W. T. Donohue (Eds.), *Sexual deviance: Theory, assessment, and treatment* (2nd ed., pp. 416–438). New York, NY: Guilford Press.

Pithers, W. D. (1990). Relapse prevention with sexual aggressors: A method for maintaining therapeutic change and enhancing external supervision. In W. L. Marshall, D. R. Laws, & H. E. Barbaree (Eds.), *The handbook of sexual assault: Issues, theories, and treatment of the offender* (pp. 363–385). New York, NY: Plenum.

Pithers, W. D., Marques, J. K., Gibat, C. C., & Marlatt, G. A. (1983). Relapse prevention: A self-control model of treatment and maintenance of change for sexual aggressives. In J. Greer & I. Stuart (Eds.), *The sexual aggressor: Current perspectives on treatment* (pp. 214–239). New York, NY: Van Nostrand Reinhold.

Porter, S., Fairweather, D., Drugge, J., Hervé, H., Birt, A., & Boer, D. P. (2000). Profiles of psychopathy in incarcerated sexual offenders. *Criminal Justice and Behavior*, 27(2), 216–233.

Quinsey, V. L. (2009). Coercive paraphilic disorder. *Archives of Sexual Behaviour*, 39(2), 405–410.

Quinsey, V. L., Chaplin, T. C., & Upfold, D. (1984). Sexual arousal to nonsexual violence and sadomasochistic themes among rapists and non-sex-offenders. *Journal of Consulting and Clinical Psychology, 52*(4), 651–657.

Quinsey, V. L., Harris, G. T., Rice, M. E., & Cormier, C. A. (2006). *Violent offenders: Appraising and managing risk* (2nd ed.). Washington, DC: American Psychological Association.

Rettenberger, M., Matthes, A., Boer, D. P., & Eher, R. (2010). Prospective actuarial risk assessment: A comparison of five risk assessment instruments in different sexual offender subtypes. *International Journal of Offender Therapy and Comparative Criminology, 54*(2), 169–186.

Rosenzweig, S. (1942). The photoscope as an objective device for evaluating sexual interest. *Psychosomatic Medicine, 4*, 150–158.

Russell, D. (1984). *Sexual exploitation: Rape, child sexual abuse, and workplace harassment.* Beverly Hills, CA: Sage.

Russell, D., Peplau, L. A., & Cutrona, C. A. (1980). The revised UCLA loneliness scale: Concurrent and discriminant validity evidence. *Journal of Personality and Social Psychology, 39*(3), 472–480.

Salter, A. (1995). *Transforming trauma: A guide to understanding and treating adult survivors of child sexual abuse.* Thousand Oaks, CA: Sage.

Schatzel-Murphy, E. A., Harris, D. A, Knight, R. A., & Milburn, M. (2009). Sexual coercion in men and women: Similar behaviors, different predictors. *Archives of Sexual Behavior, 38*, 974–986.

Schewe, P. A., & O'Donohue, W. (1998). Psychometrics of the rape conformity assessment and other measures: Implications for rape prevention. *Sexual Abuse: A Journal of Research and Treatment, 10*(2), 97–112.

Seto, M. C. (2005). Is more better? Combining actuarial risk scales to predict recidivism among adult sex offenders. *Psychological Assessment, 17*, 156–167.

Seto, M. C. (2008). Pedophilia: Psychopathology and theory. In D. R. Laws & W. O'Donohue (Eds.), *Sexual deviance* (2nd ed., pp. 164–182). New York, NY: Guilford Press.

Seto, M. C., & Kuban, M. (1996). Criterion-related validity of a phallometric test for paraphilic rape and sadism. *Behaviour Research and Therapy, 34*, 175–183.

Seto, M. C., Lalumière, M. L., Harris, G. T., & Chivers, M. L. (2012). The sexual responses of sexual sadists. *Journal of Abnormal Psychology, 121*(3), 739–753.

Simon, L. M. J. (2000). An examination of the assumptions of specialization, mental disorder, and dangerousness in sex offenders. *Behavioral Sciences & the Law, 18*, 275–308.

Smallbone, S. W., Wheaton, J., & Hourigan, D. (2003). Trait empathy and criminal versatility in sexual offenders. *Sexual Abuse: A Journal of Research and Treatment, 15*(1), 49–60.

Spitzer, R. L. (2001). Values and assumptions in the development of DSM-III and DSM-III-R: An insider's perspective and a belated response to Sadler, Hulgus, and Agich's 'On values in recent American psychiatric classification'. *The Journal of Nervous and Mental Disease, 189*, 351–359. Retrieved from http://journals.lww.com/jonmd/pages/default.aspx

Thornton, D. (2009). Evidence regarding the need for a diagnostic category for a coercive paraphilia. *Archives of Sexual Behavior, 39*(2), 411–418.

Voller, E. K., Long, P. J., & Aosved, A. C. (2009). Attraction to sexual violence towards women, sexual abuse of children, and non-sexual criminal behavior: Testing the specialist vs. generalist models in male college students. *Archives of Sexual Behavior, 38*(2), 235–243.

Ward, T., & Beech, A. (2006). An integrated theory of sexual offending. *Aggression and Violent Behavior, 11*(1), 44–63.

Ward, T., & Hudson, S. M. (1998). A model of the relapse process in sexual offenders. *Journal of Interpersonal Violence, 13*(6), 700–725.

Ward, T., Louden, K., Hudson, S. M., & Marshall, W. L. (1995). A descriptive model of the offense chain for child molesters. *Journal of Interpersonal Violence, 10*(4), 452–472.

Ware, E. E., Brown, M., Amoroso, D. M., Pilkey, D. W., & Pruesse, M. (1972). The semantic meaning of pornographic stimuli for college males. *Canadian Journal of Behavioural Science/Revue Canadienne des Sciences du Comportement, 4*(3), 204–209.

Wolf, S. C. (1984, November). *A multifactor model of deviant sexuality.* Paper presented at the Third International Conference on Victimology, Lisbon, Portugal.

World Health Organization (1992). *International statistical classification of diseases and related health problems, 10th revision* (ICD-10). Geneva: Author.

Yates, P. M., & Kingston, D. A. (2005). Pathways to sexual offending. In B. K. Schwartz (Ed.), *The sex offender* (Vol. 5, pp. 3-1–3-15). Kingston, NJ: Civic Research Institute.

Yates, P. M., & Kingston, D. A. (2006). The self-regulation model of sexual offending: The relationship between offense pathways and static and dynamic sexual offense risk. *Sexual Abuse: A Journal of Research and Treatment, 18*(3), 259–270.

Yates, P. M., Kingston, D. A., & Ward, T. (2009). *The self-regulation model of the offense and re-offense process: Volume III: A guide to assessment and treatment planning using the integrated good lives/self-regulation model of sexual offending.* Victoria, Canada: Pacific Psychological Assessment Corp. Retrieved from www.pacific-psych.com

Zander, T. K. (2008). Commentary: Inventing diagnosis for civil commitment of rapists. *Journal of the American Academy of Psychiatry and the Law, 36*(4), 459–469.

42

Use of the DSM-5 Paraphilias Taxonomy and Its Residual Categories in Sexually Violent Predator Evaluations

Richard Wollert

Independent Practice, United States

Allen Frances

Duke University, United States

Introduction

Evaluations including diagnostic assessments based on criteria sets from the *Diagnostic and Statistical Manual* (DSM) of the American Psychiatric Association (APA) are completed for virtually all respondents to sexually violent predator (SVP) petitions before proceedings that may result in lifelong post-prison civil confinement. We have been involved with DSM's development, or with using DSM for teaching, research, or clinical purposes, since the late 1970s, when the descriptive 'neo-Kraepelinian approach' (Compton & Guze, 1995; Decker, 2007; Klerman, 1978; Mayes & Horwitz, 2005; Rogler, 1997; Wilson, 1993; Winokur, Zimmerman, & Cadoret, 1988) of DSM-III (APA, 1980) replaced the more theoretical psychobiological and psychodynamic formulations of DSM-I (APA, 1952) and DSM-II (APA, 1968). During the last 5–15 years, we have also used DSM in SVP evaluations, testified in SVP proceedings about specified paraphilias such as 'Sexual Sadism' and 'Pedophilia' or residual categories called 'Paraphilia (Not Otherwise Specified)' (PNOS), and published several articles about psychodiagnosis (e.g., Frances, 2013; Frances & First, 2011a, 2011b; Frances & Wollert, 2012; Wollert, 2007, 2011; Wollert & Cramer, 2011).

Each modern DSM before DSM-5 (APA, 2013) has included strong cautionary statements about the potential shortcomings of applying the DSM to legal taxonomies. The importance of using caution in forensic proceedings is reflected in

The Wiley Handbook on the Theories, Assessment, and Treatment of Sexual Offending.
Edited by Douglas P. Boer. Volume II: Assessment, edited by Leam A. Craig and Martin Rettenberger.
© 2017 John Wiley & Sons, Ltd. Published 2017 by John Wiley & Sons, Ltd.

the fact that DSM-III-R (APA, 1987), DSM-IV (APA, 1994), and DSM-IV-TR (APA, 2000) each included *two* such warnings. These warnings have stressed three points. First, DSM is a psychiatric taxonomy, or system for the classification of mental disorders, for clinicians and researchers. Second, the DSM taxonomy is not isomorphic with any legislatively defined taxonomy for adjudication. Third, DSM is susceptible to misuse in forensic settings due to this 'disjunction' (First & Halon, 2008, p. 444).

The text of DSM-5 suggests that APA may now have a less cautious stance. Whereas the three previous DSMs emphasized the risks that 'diagnostic information will be misused in court settings were "significant"' (APA, 1994, pp. xxxii–xxxiii), the latest version (APA, 2013, p. 25) reads:

> Although the DSM-5 diagnostic criteria and text are primarily designed to assist clinicians … DSM-5 is also used as a reference for the courts and attorneys in assessing the forensic consequences of mental disorders. As a result, it is important to note that the definition of mental disorder included in DSM-5 was developed to meet the needs of clinicians, public health professionals, and research professionals rather than all of the technical needs of the courts and legal professionals.

All DSMs since DSM-III-R have suggested that a DSM diagnosis might enhance forensic determinations, but none has differentiated between the DSM's applicability to the legal taxonomy for mental health civil commitments and its applicability to the legal taxonomy for SVP civil commitments. This is a serious oversight for two reasons. The first is that APA worked diligently with state legislatures to apply psychiatric symptomatology to achieve a workable and close alignment with the former taxonomy (Zander, 2005; Zonana, Bonnie, & Hoge, 2003). It explicitly rejected such an alignment with the SVP taxonomy. The APA Task Force on Dangerous Sex Offenders, for example, concluded that 'Sexual predator commitment laws represent a serious assault on the integrity of psychiatry, particularly with regard to defining mental illness and the clinical conditions for compulsory treatment' (APA, 1999, p. 173).

Another unambiguous example of organized medicine's rejection of the SVP taxonomy occurred in 2012, when the DSM-5 Paraphilias sub-workgroup proposed adding paraphilic coercive disorder (rape), hebephilia, and hypersexuality as specified paraphilias. These terms had frequently been construed as residual subclasses by State experts in SVP trials. APA strongly rejected all of the proposals on the basis of numerous objective criteria summarized by DSM-5 forensic reviewer Paul Appelbaum (2014, p. 137). The depth of negative opinion about these terms was further reflected in decisions to ban each of them from a DSM-5 Appendix for disorders needing research (Frances, 2012).

The second reason why APA should differentiate between using DSM-5 in mental health versus SVP commitments is that the paraphilias taxonomy is too weak to sustain a valid extension to the SVP taxonomy. There are many issues with using the paraphilias taxonomy to identify a person's location in the SVP taxonomy. Experts who claim that the DSM taxonomy is highly accurate for SVP determinations without disclosing its limitations may face ethical sanctions.

This chapter discusses these problems in relation to theoretical, historical, and contemporary contexts. The first section lays out a theoretical context by reviewing some basic principles of taxonomic classification. The second and third sections provide historical context by describing SVP laws and discussing events leading to the adoption of the paraphilias taxonomy as a vehicle for pursuing SVP convictions. Contemporary context is presented in the fourth section by discussing changes in DSM-5 that are relevant for evaluations of paraphilia. The fifth section draws on the earlier sections to summarize practice issues with using residual labels in SVP evaluations. It also considers how these limitations apply to some specified paraphilias because PNOS categories complement the specified paraphilias. Another reason for including the specified paraphilias in our analysis is that a PNOS category might become a specified paraphilia (e.g., Frotteurism in 1987) or a specified paraphilia might become a PNOS category (Zoophilia in 1987). The Conclusion section makes a number of recommendations for APA and evaluators.

Taxonometric Classification

Taxonometric classification is the process by which a specified set of target objects from the natural world is divided into a pre-existing and non-arbitrary set of classes and subclasses on the basis of shared characteristics (Hempel, 1961; Millon, 1991). The framework is a *taxonomy*, or a *nosology* when mental disorders are the classes, and the set of names for the divisions in a taxonomy is a *nomenclature*. Each subclass, or *taxon*, is ideally defined by whatever conditions a relevant object must have to belong to that particular subclass.

A taxonomy therefore sorts out a specified set of objects into different *taxa* by applying a set of classificatory concepts *and* terms of definition to these objects. The concepts and terms that are used in a field of science are called its *vocabulary of science* (Hempel, 1961, p. 6). *Diagnosis* is the process of identifying the state of a mental disorder concept in relation to a patient.

The value of a system for classifying human characteristics depends on how adequately it addresses two scientific challenges. The first is to formulate concepts that allow different observers to sort target objects reliably into distinct categories; vague criteria that elicit subjective judgements undermine reliability. Later, validity evidence needs to be collected indicating that the taxa are linked to other important concepts. Eventually, results derived from theory building rather than observation are expected.

A diagnosis that meets the test of reliability may not meet the second test, that of validity. When Philosopher of Science Carl Hempel addressed APA members in the DSM-I era, he pointed out (Hempel, 1961, p. 14) that 'characteristics of the elements which serve as criteria of membership in a given class' from a scientifically fruitful classification 'are associated … with … extensive clusters of other characteristics … a classification of this sort should be viewed as somehow having objective existence in nature' due to its capacity for 'carving nature at the joints'. He also distinguished such taxonomies from more '"artificial classifications", in which the defining characteristics have few … connections with other traits'.

The SVP Taxonomy

In early 1990, the Washington State Legislature found 'a small but extremely dangerous group of sexually violent predators exists' and passed the first statute in the United States for the post-prison civil commitment of those meeting the legal criteria as SVPs (APA, 1999). According to Section 71.09.020 (16) of the Revised Code of Washington, an SVP is defined as 'any person who has been convicted of or charged with a crime of sexual violence and who suffers from a mental abnormality or personality disorder which makes the person likely to engage in predatory acts of sexual violence'.

Although the meaning of a personality disorder was not codified when the law was passed, a mental abnormality, per Section 71.09.020 (8), has always been 'a congenital or acquired condition affecting the emotional or volitional capacity which predisposes the person to the commission of criminal sexual acts'. At trials, the burden of proof is on the state to show that an accused SVP, or 'respondent', meets these criteria: Section 71.09.060 states that 'the court shall determine whether, beyond a reasonable doubt, the person is a sexually violent predator.'

About 20 states and the federal government followed Washington in adopting SVP or sexually dangerous person (SDP) statutes. There are wording differences in different laws (Jackson & Richards, 2008, pp. 185–189), but SVP and SDP laws are conceptually similar.

The US Supreme Court has ruled that SVP laws do not violate the Constitution. In *Kansas v. Hendricks* (1997), it considered a case where the Kansas Supreme Court had 'invalidated the (Kansas) Act, holding that … "mental abnormality" did not satisfy … the "substantive" due process requirement that … commitment must be predicated on a finding of "mental illness"'. The majority observed 'we have never required State legislatures to adopt any particular nomenclature'. They also indicated that Kansas's law satisfied due process because it 'coupled proof of dangerousness with … a … "mental abnormality"' in such a way as 'to limit … civil confinement to those who suffer from a volitional impairment … that makes it difficult … for the person to control his dangerous behavior'.

In *Kansas v. Crane* (2002), it considered another case where the Kansas Court reversed a trial court's SVP finding because the court did not make a finding on whether the defendant could 'control his dangerous behavior'. This time the trial court's verdict was upheld on the logic that a 'lack-of-control determination' was necessary, but all that was required was a showing that the respondent had 'serious difficulty in controlling behavior' (p. 5) and met the other SVP criteria. The *Crane* court did not further clarify what it meant by serious difficulty. It instead decided that a 'contextual' and 'case-specific' approach should be followed because 'States retain considerable leeway in defining the mental abnormalities' and 'the science of psychiatry, which informs … legal determinations, is an ever-advancing science …' (pp. 5–6).

This decision equated the concept of serious difficulty controlling behavior with a volitional impairment but did not define the meaning of either.

The Paraphilias Taxonomy, PNOS, and SVP Evaluations

Paraphilias must meet the DSM criteria for Mental Disorder listed in the left-hand column of Table 42.1 if they are to be included in the DSM. The right-hand column of Table 42.1 shows that the DSM paraphilia criteria have been substantially revised since DSM-I, when sexual deviates were described as 'ill … in terms of … conformity with the prevailing cultural milieu'. This characterization was firmly discarded in DSM-III, which pointed out that mental disorders involved dysfunctions that were 'more than a conflict with societal values'. DSM-III also clarified that a mental disorder required the presence of a 'syndrome' of symptoms and clinically significant syndromatic consequences such as 'distress or disability'. The former requirement has since been referred to as the 'essential features' or 'A criterion' whereas the latter is the 'clinical threshold' or 'B criterion'. The right-hand column of Table 42.1 reflects the use of this convention in that items preceded by an 'A' indicate characteristics referenced as 'essential features' in one of the modern DSMs whereas items preceded by a 'B' indicate 'clinical threshold' conditions. The capital letters in the left-hand column, in contrast, stand for different elements of the mental disorder definition and therefore do not necessarily refer to essential features or clinical thresholds.

In *Crane*, the Supreme Court endorsed a case-specific approach and left derivation of mental abnormality definitions in the hands of states with SVP laws. The states, in turn, relied on the case-by-case opinions of experts retained by the prosecution.

An example from Washington provides a plausible theory of how mental abnormalities have generally come to be defined within the context of this case-specific and expert-centred approach. Psychologist Robert Wheeler, retained extensively by state prosecutors, explained his reasoning on this issue in 1992. He observed that DSM-III-R was 'the … accepted source … for cataloguing … diagnostic terms' and that some of the paraphilias overlapped the mental abnormality concept in being associated with 'compulsive sexual urges' (Wheeler, 1992, p. 2). He therefore considered specific paraphilias such as Pedophilia and Sexual Sadism to be mental abnormalities.

Wheeler was reticent about using PNOS diagnoses. For example, he cautioned colleagues about overusing PNOS because this was 'not strictly adhering to the DSM-III-R' (p. 3).

Some of Wheeler's colleagues were less hesitant. As early as 1991, different experts in different cases had 'diagnosed "rape as paraphilia," within the category of "paraphilia not otherwise specified"' (APA, 1999, p. 21; *In re Young*, 1993).

Vance Cunningham and Andre Young, respondents committed on PNOS (Rape) diagnoses, appealed their convictions in part on the grounds that PNOS (Rape) was too broadly drawn to differentiate sex offenders with a mental abnormality from sex offenders without one (*In re Young*, 1993). The Washington State Supreme Court suggested that a rape paraphilia would eventually be added to the DSM and indicated that the legislature's adoption of an inclusive non-psychiatric taxonomy was within its discretion. The Court's citation of the following passage indicated that it envisioned a broad diagnostic perspective (Brooks, 1992, p. 733):

> In using the concept of mental abnormality, the legislature has invoked a more generalized terminology that can cover a much larger variety of disorders. Some, such as the paraphilias,

Table 42.1 Definitions and descriptions of 'mental disorder' and 'paraphilia' in each DSM

Mental disorder	Paraphilia
DSM-I: Mental disorder was not defined. A comprehensive system of 'concepts of modern psychiatry and neurology' that facilitated communication and research was envisioned (pp. v–vi; Section IIA, p. 9)	(Section IIB, pp. 38–39). All 'sexual deviations' were listed in the Psychopathic Personality Disturbance chapter. Class members were described as 'ill … in terms of … conformity with the prevailing cultural milieu'. The diagnosis was 'for deviant sexuality which is not symptomatic of … schizophrenic and obsessional reactions … (it) will specify the … behavior: homosexuality, transvestism, pedophilia, fetishism, and sexual sadism'
DSM-II: Mental disorder was not defined, but it was discussed in the same way as in DSM-I	(Section 3, p. 44). All sexual deviations were listed as Personality Disorders. The diagnosis was for those 'whose sexual interests are … toward objects other than people of the opposite sex, toward sexual acts not … associated with coitus, or toward coitus … under bizarre circumstances.' Eight specific labels were listed without explanation: Homosexuality, Fetishism, Pedophilia, Transvestitism, Exhibitionism, Voyeurism, Sadism, and Masochism
DSM-III (p. 6). **A**[a]: Each mental disorder is a clinically significant behavioural or psychological syndrome that is **B**: typically related to either distress (a painful symptom) or disability (impairment in one or more important areas of functioning). **C**: There is an inference that it is a behavioral, psychological, or biological dysfunction in the person **D**: that is more than a conflict with societal values	(pp. 266–267). **A**:[b] The essential feature is that unusual or bizarre imagery or acts are necessary for sexual excitement. **A1**: They tend to be insistently and involuntarily repetitive, and **A2**: Generally involve nonhuman objects, pain or humiliation, or nonconsenting partners. **A3**: Previous classifications call these Sexual Deviations. **A4**: The term Paraphilia better clarifies the deviation (para) is in that to which one is attracted (philia). **A5**: Paraphilias in this manual have traditionally been identified by previous classifications. **A6**: Paraphiliacs are usually seen by mental health professionals when their behavior has brought them into conflict with society

Table 42.1   (*Continued*)

Mental disorder	Paraphilia
DSM-III-R (p. xxii). **A**: DSM-III A, above. **B**: DSM-III B, but 'typically' is omitted and 'present' precedes 'distress.' **C**: or with a significantly increased risk of suffering, pain, disability or an important loss of freedom. **D**: DSM-III C, except 'currently' follows the first 'is'. **E**: The syndrome is not a typical response to an event like death of a loved one. **F**: Sexually deviant behavior is not a disorder unless it results from a dysfunction in the person	(pp. 279–280). **A** (replaced DSM-III A and A1, above): The essential feature is recurrent intense sexual urges and sexually arousing fantasies. **A1** (changes DSM-III A2): Generally involving (1) nonhuman objects, (2) suffering or humiliation of oneself or one's partner, (3) children or other nonconsenting persons. **B**:*c* A diagnosis is made only if the person has acted on these urges, or is markedly distressed by them. **B1**: DSM-III A3. **B2**: DSM-III A4. **B3** (added): Paraphilic preferences are episodic in some cases. **B4**: DSM-III A5, except 'traditionally' is removed. **B5**: DSM-III A6, except 'sexual partners or' is added after 'with'
DSM-IV (pp. xxi–xxii). **A**: DSM-III A. **B–F**: DSM-III-R B–F	(pp. 522–523). **A**: (replaced DSM-III-R A, important changes are in italics): *Over 6 months* the essential feature is recurrent, intense sexually arousing fantasies, sexual urges, *or behaviors.* **A1**: DSM-III-R A1. **B**: (replaces DSM-III-R B): The behavior, sexual urges, or fantasies cause clinically significant distress or impairment in social, occupational, or other important areas of functioning. **B1**: DSM-III-R B3. **B2**: DSM-III-R B4. **B3**: DSM-III-R B5
DSM-IV-TR (p. xxxi). **A–F**: DSM-IV A–F	(p. 566). **A–A1**: DSM-IV A–A1. **B** (replaces DSM-IV B): For Pedophilia, Voyeurism, Exhibitionism, and Frotteurism, the diagnosis is made if the person has acted on these urges or the urges or sexual fantasies cause marked distress or interpersonal difficulty. For Sexual Sadism, the diagnosis is made if the person has acted on these urges with a nonconsenting person or the urges, sexual fantasies, or behaviors cause marked distress or interpersonal difficulty. For the remaining Paraphilias, the diagnosis is made if the behavior, sexual urges, or fantasies cause clinically significant distress or impairment in social, occupational, or other important areas of functioning (Criterion B). **B1**: DSM-III-R B3. **B2**: DSM-III-R B4. **B3**: DSM-III-R B5

Table 42.1 (*Continued*)

Mental disorder	Paraphilia
DSM-5 (A–E from p. 20; F from p. 22). **A**: A syndrome characterized by clinically significant disturbance in an individual's cognition, emotion regulation, or behavior that **B**: reflects a dysfunction in the psychological, biological, or developmental processes underlying mental functioning. **C**: DSM-III B, so that 'usually' precedes 'related' and DSM-III-R C has been removed. **D**: DSM-III-R E. **E**: DSM-III-R F. **F**: A diagnosis is usually applied to the individual's current presentation	(pp. 685–686). **A**: The term *paraphilia* refers to any sexual interest that is qualitatively 'greater than or equal to normophilic sexual interests' (p. 685). To meet the criterion for the presence of a paraphilia, a person must go through a 6-month period having non-normophilic 'recurrent and intense arousal' that is 'manifested by fantasies, urges, or behavior'. **B**: A *paraphilic disorder* is a paraphilia that is currently causing distress or impairment to the person or a paraphilia whose satisfaction has entailed personal harm, or risk of harm, to others. **B1**: Only those who meet both **A** and **B** should be diagnosed with a paraphilic disorder. **B2**: Others may be said to have a paraphilia but not a paraphilic disorder. **B3**: DSM-III A5, with the explanation that there are eight specific paraphilias because they are relatively common and some are crimes.

[a]Capital letters in the left-hand column stand for different elements of the mental disorder definition.
[b]Items preceded by '**A**' stand for the 'essential features' criterion that defines a paraphilia. '**A1**' elaborates on the 'A criterion', and so on.
[c]Items preceded by '**B**' stand for the 'clinical threshold' criterion for a paraphilia. '**B1**' elaborates on the 'B criterion', and so on.

are covered in DSM-III-R; others are not. The fact that pathologically-driven rape, for example, is not yet in DSM-III-R does not invalidate such a diagnosis … What is critical … is that … clinicians who testify in good faith as to mental abnormality are able to identify sexual pathologies that are as real and meaningful as other pathologies … in the DSM.

Psychologist Dennis Doren (2002) attempted to effect an unauthorized alignment of the paraphilias taxonomy with the SVP taxonomy that state evaluators could use for diagnosing SVP respondents with PNOS. He presented a five-level argument. *Conceptually*, he cited a DSM-IV passage (APA, 1994, pp. 522–523), also in Table 42.1, to claim (Doren, 2002, p. 56) that a paraphilia was defined as (A) 'recurrent, intense sexually arousing fantasies, sexual urges, or behaviors generally involving (1) nonhuman objects; (2) the suffering or humiliation of oneself or one's partner, or (3) children or other nonconsenting persons that occur over a period of 6 months', and (B) 'the behavior, sexual urges, or fantasies cause clinically significant distress or impairment in social occupational, or other important areas of functioning'. *Interpretively*, he took the term 'nonconsenting' under item (A)(3) to mean any non-consenting person who was sexually assaulted and the term 'children' to mean pubescent minors.

Definitionally, he consistently equated the 'B' criterion of impairment with incarceration for being convicted of a sex crime. *Pragmatically*, he concluded that 'examiners … need to rely on documentation of the subjects' behaviors alone' (p. 66) because examiners 'do not typically enjoy the benefit of a fully honest disclosure of the subject's sexual fantasies and urges'. Finally, at a *social acceptance* level, he assured readers that a PNOS diagnosis was 'considered just as meaningful by the writers of the DSM-IV as … any of the individually listed diagnoses' on the *condition* that it included a qualifier that produced a 'differentiation of this specific type of paraphilia from others listed as NOS' (p. 67).

A criminal history that included charges for sexual abuse of an adolescent or rape on different occasions therefore included all that Doren's formulation needed for a viable PNOS diagnosis: recurrence, sexual behaviour against non-consenting adults or adolescent minors, and impairment via incarceration. The addition of behavioural qualifiers per Doren's last proposition produced 'PNOS (nonconsent)' and 'PNOS (hebephilia)'.

Doren's (2002) book was widely circulated. Many state experts accepted his two labels. They also had the ring of science in court. In reality, however, Doren's attempt to extend the paraphilias taxonomy to the SVP taxonomy was a rogue action that did not have APA's approval.

Observing that 'there has been a great deal of struggle concerning what the concept of 'affecting … "volitional capacity" means', Doren's book also acknowledged that 'describing the relevant impairment … can be tricky' (p. 15). In a three-page section on this challenge (pp. 14–17), he proposed that evaluators might deal with it by claiming that evaluees who repeated criminal behaviours in spite of their consequences had volitional impairments (Zander, 2005).

Doren did not explicitly advise evaluators to ignore the issue of volitional control but he did not encourage them to get too close to it either. In a 'Sample Precommitment Evaluation Report', he suggested that experts might conclude their reports with the following text that dispositively alludes to an impairment's presence without describing it (pp. 223–224):

> Mr. T. was found to suffer from three psychiatric conditions, two of which qualify as a mental abnormality … Specifically, this examiner came to the opinion … that Mr. T. suffers from Pedophilia, and Antisocial Personality Disorder, each of which, for Mr. T., is an acquired or congenital condition affecting his emotional or volitional capacity that predisposes him to commit sexually violent acts …

Bernard Thorell was found to be an SVP in 1998. He appealed his conviction on the grounds that a mental abnormality determination required a separate finding of volitional impairment. In 2003, the Washington Supreme Court ruled that a serious difficulty test was required by *Crane*, but that this 'lack of control determination may be included in the finding of a mental abnormality' (*In re Thorell*, 2003, p. 376). Thereafter, a mere diagnostic label was accepted as meeting a fact finder's legal needs for making a mental abnormality determination (Jackson & Richards, 2008, p. 193).

We have used anecdotal and formal methods to evaluate the possibility that SVP laws, decisions such as *Young* and *Thorell*, and Doren's book produced an increased rate of

PNOS diagnoses among sex offenders. In one anecdotal approach, we reviewed a few reports for confined offenders who were evaluated on at least one occasion before RCW 71.09 and as possible SVPs on at least one occasion after 71.09. A striking difference in these reports was that specified diagnoses stood out in the earlier evaluations whereas PNOS diagnoses were evident in later ones. In another, a small group of providers who treated sex offenders prior to the SVP laws told us that the level of professional interest in PNOS diagnoses during that era was virtually nil.

More formally, we were able to identify two studies reporting data on the prevalence of PNOS among sex offenders. The first, by psychiatrist Gene Abel and colleagues (Abel, Becker, Cunningham-Rathner, Mittelman, & Rouleau, 1988), assessed 561 US sex offenders in the '1977 to 1985' (p. 154) pre-SVP period. By our calculation, the maximum estimate of the PNOS prevalence rate in Abel et al.'s cohort approximated 10% (57/561 = 10.2%).

In the second study, psychiatrist Reinhard Eher and colleagues (Eher, Rettenberger, Matthes, & Schilling, 2010) administered routine assessments between 2002 and 2005 to 119 incarcerated child molesters in Austria, which does not have an SVP law. About 7.6% of the offenders were classified as meeting PNOS criteria at some time during their lives.

In contrast to these findings, data on 1362 SVPs from five states (Jumper, Babula, & Casbon, 2012) show that 47.3% ($n = 645$) were assigned a PNOS diagnosis (Jumper et al., 2012). PNOS ranked alongside Pedophilia as the most widely assigned diagnosis in SVP evaluations by state-retained psychiatrists and psychologists.

This history points to three conclusions. First, decisions such as *Hendricks, Crane, Young,* and *Thorell* have lowered the legal bar for classifying offenders as SVPs. Second, the practice of assigning PNOS diagnoses to SVP respondents has exploded since the adoption of SVP laws. Third, SVP convictions can be obtained with controversial diagnoses that do not require additional proof of impairment.

Such developments affect the attitudes of experts towards their own behaviour. Some have even reached the point of claiming they do not have to assign *any* type of authorized diagnosis to make an SVP determination. Dismissing the SVP significance of any paraphilias in DSM-5, psychiatrist Douglas Tucker and attorney Samuel Brakel (2012, p. 533) echoed language from *Young* to argue that 'the various courts … are all in agreement that … it does not matter what the mental abnormality is called … the critical point … is that … clinicians who testify in good faith as to a mental abnormality are able to identify sexual pathologies that are conceptually and empirically meaningful, regardless of whether they are listed in the DSM'.

Tucker and Brakel's opinions reflect the extent to which SVP proceedings came to be marked by subjective rather than scientific judgement prior to the publication of DSM-5.

DSM-5 and the Paraphilias Taxonomy

Four important changes in wording outside the Paraphilic Disorders Chapter (PDC) have been made to DSM-5 that hold implications for diagnosing the paraphilias. The most straightforward one, in the 'Elements of a Diagnosis' section of the DSM-5

Introduction states that 'a DSM-5 diagnosis is usually applied to the individual's *current presentation*' (p. 22, our emphasis).

A more subtle change to the mental disorder definition, also included in Table 42.1, is that the evidence for a 'dysfunction' necessary to identify a mental disorder is characterized as a 'reflection' in DSM-5 rather than as the 'inference' that was needed in DSM-III, DSM-IV, and DSM-IV-TR. In science, a reflection is a response that returns from a target when a source observes it or sends it a signal. The *reflection requirement* reinforces the *current presentation requirement* by emphasizing the importance of recent data as evidence for a dysfunction.

The third important general change stems from a step the DSM-5 Task Force took to address a 'growing inability to integrate DSM disorders with the results of genetic studies and other scientific findings' (p. 10). To address this dilemma, the Task Force decided 'to enhance diagnostic specificity' (p. 15) by replacing 'the previous NOS designation with two options for clinical use: other specified disorder and unspecified disorder'. This was not meant to imply that clinicians can use residual diagnoses willy-nilly, as a modifying passage indicated that 'In an emergency department setting, it may be possible to identify only the most prominent symptom expressions associated with a particular (disorder) chapter – so that an "unspecified" disorder in that category is identified until a fuller differential diagnosis is possible' (pp. 19–20).

Regarding the last of the general changes, Table 42.1 indicates that all modern DSMs have included the concept of disability, equated with an 'impairment', as a clinical significance criterion for making a DSM diagnosis. They also all shared the problem of not providing a definition for impairment. DSM-5 addresses this oversight in two ways. One is that it discusses the impairment concept in a new section in its Introduction on the 'Criterion for Clinical Significance' (p. 21). The other is that it includes a number of psychosocial assessment instruments for measuring disability and impairment in a new 'Assessment Measures' section (pp. 733–748). These measures clarify that a DSM impairment is a difficulty in adjustive functioning that has been present within one or more of the past 4 weeks due to mental disorder.

The significance of this clarification is reinforced by wording in the PDC Introduction. The last sentence in the next to last paragraph (p. 686), for example, begins with the declaration that 'the distress and impairment stipulated in Criterion B are ... the ... *result of the paraphilia*' (our emphasis). It closes by pointing out that distress and impairment 'may be quantified with multipurpose measures of psychosocial functioning or quality of life'. The only measures meeting this description are in the DSM-5 Assessment Measures section and no other measures for this purpose are recommended. Evaluators who claim to use DSM-5 for diagnostic purposes therefore need to use the DSM-5 Assessment Measures section for the impairment assessment required for the assignment of a diagnosis.

This clarification also refutes Doren's *definitional assumption* that a restriction of liberty due to incarceration is a psychiatric impairment.

The PDC includes five other noteworthy features. One is that its first sentence states the term 'nonconsenting' applies only to 'frotteuristic disorder' and the term 'children' applies only to 'pedophilic disorder' (p. 685). This refutes Doren's (2002) *interpretive assumptions* about the meaning of 'nonconsent' and 'children.'

The second noteworthy PDC change is that the *paraphilia* concept has been modified by introducing a *paraphilic disorder* concept. In previous DSMs, a paraphilia referred to an authorized diagnosis. A paraphilia is now defined as any sexual interest that is 'greater than or equal to normophilic sexual interests' (p. 685). To meet this A criterion, a person must have non-normophilic 'recurrent and intense arousal' that is 'manifested by fantasies, urges, or behavior' for a 6-month period.

A *paraphilic disorder*, in contrast, is 'a paraphilia that is currently causing distress or impairment to the individual or a paraphilia whose satisfaction has entailed personal harm, or risk of harm, to others' (pp. 685–686). These negative consequences satisfy the B criterion. Only those who meet both criteria A and B can be diagnosed with a paraphilic disorder.

Regarding the third, the 'Highlights of Changes from DSM-IV to DSM-5' section (p. 816) states that 'an overarching change for DSM-IV is the addition of *in remission*' as a course specifier 'for all the paraphilic disorders' (p. 816). The most general definition of *in remission*, included in all the criteria sets for disorders that often result in incarceration except Pedophilia, is that 'the individual has not acted on the urges (from the A criterion) with a nonconsenting person, and there has been no distress or impairment ... for at least 5 years while in an uncontrolled environment'. This change rules out the assignment of a paraphilic disorder to a person who has lived in the community for 5 years without further problems. The wording of the 'Highlights' section also indicates that the *remission* rule applies to Pedophilia. Its omission is thus an editorial error. A member of the DSM-5 Paraphilias sub-workgroup has verified this (R. Krueger, personal communication, 10 January 2014).

Regarding the fourth, psychiatrists Michael First and Allen Frances explained (First & Francis, 2008) that an editorial mistake was made when – as DSM-IV Text Editor and Task Force Chair – they moved the behavioural 'has acted on urges' passage from the DSM-III-R B criterion (see Table 42.1) into the A criterion. The B criterion consequently stated that 'the disturbance causes clinically significant distress or impairment ...' (p. 1240) while the A criterion stated the essential feature of a paraphilia was 'recurrent, intense sexually arousing fantasies, sexual urges, *or behaviors*' (our emphasis). Focusing on the proposed B criterion change, some religious groups voiced concern that DSM-IV did 'not recognize Pedophilia as a mental disorder unless it caused distress'. First reinstated the DSM-III-R B criterion in DSM-IV-TR to settle this dispute but overlooked deleting 'or behaviors' from the A criterion (First & Halon, 2008). An unintended consequence of this inclusionary mistake was that Doren and others used the DSM-IV-TR A criterion 'to justify making a paraphilia diagnosis based solely on a history of repeated acts of sexual violence' and then argued that their diagnosis met the 'statutory mandate for ... a "mental abnormality"' (Frances & First, 2011a, p. 1250).

Although First and Frances (2008) advised that it would be 'important to ... restore Criterion A to its DSM-III-R wording', DSM-5 did not include this correction. The A criterion and the B criterion for all of the specified paraphilias in DSM-5 could therefore still be satisfied by behaviour alone if the *current presentation, reflection*, and *impairment assessment* requirements had not been added to DSM-5.

Table 42.2   Definitions and descriptions of residual paraphilia categories in each DSM

DSM-I (pp. 38–39): Five sexual deviations (homosexuality, transvestism, pedophilia, fetishism, and sexual sadism) were specified but not defined. A residual category was not included

DSM-II (p. 44): **Other Sexual Deviation** and **Unspecified Sexual Deviation** were inserted at the end of an enumerated list that referenced the DSM-I deviations plus three additions (exhibitionism, voyeurism, and masochism). No information about any of the 10 terms was provided

DSM-III (p. 275): **Atypical Paraphilia**. 'This is a residual category for individuals with Paraphilias that cannot be classified in any of the other categories. Such conditions include: Coprophilia (feces); Frotteurism (rubbing); Klismaphilia (enema); Mysophilia (filth); Necrophilia (corpse); Telephone Scatologia (lewdness); and Urophilia (urine)'

DSM-III-R (p. 290): **Paraphilia Not Otherwise Specified (PNOS)**. 'Paraphilias that do not meet criteria for any of the specific categories. Examples: Telephone scatalogia … Necrophilia … Partialism (exclusive focus on part of body) … Zoophilia (animals) … Coprophilia … Klismaphilia … Urophilia'

DSM-IV (p. 532): **PNOS**. 'Is for coding Paraphilias that do not meet the criteria for any of the specific categories. Examples include, but are not limited to, telephone scatalogia … necrophilia … partialism … zoophilia … coprophilia … klismaphilia … and urophilia.'

DSM-IV-TR (p. 576): **PNOS**. Same as DSM-IV

DSM-5 (p. 705): **Other Specified Paraphilic Disorder (OSPD)**. 'Applies to presentations in which symptoms characteristic of a Paraphilic disorder that cause clinically significant distress or impairment in social, occupational, or other important areas of functioning predominate but do not meet the full criteria for any of the disorders in the … class. OSPD is used in situations in which the clinician chooses to communicate the specific reason that the presentation does not meet the criteria for any specific … disorder. This is done by recording "other specified Paraphilic disorder" followed by the specific reason (e.g., "zoophilia")' Examples of presentations that can be specified using the 'OSPD' designation include, but are not limited to, recurrent and intense sexual arousal involving telephone scatologia … necrophilia … zoophilia … coprophilia … klismaphilia … or urophilia … that has been present for at least six months and causes marked distress or impairment in social, occupational, or other important areas of functioning. Other specified Paraphilic disorder can be specified as in remission and/or as occurring in a controlled environment'

DSM-5 (p. 705): **Unspecified Paraphilic Disorder (UPD)**. '[first sentence the same as OSPD] … The UPD category is used in situations in which the clinician chooses *not* to specify the reason that the criteria are not met for a specific Paraphilic disorder, and includes presentation in which there is insufficient information to make a more specific diagnosis'

Regarding the last important feature, the residual PNOS category from the three previous DSMs has been replaced by two residual categories. One is 'Other Specified Paraphilic Disorder' (OSPD) and the other is 'Unspecified Paraphilic Disorder' (UPD). This is a potentially significant change because each previous DSM confined its discussion of PNOS to a comment in the Paraphilias Chapter Introduction that PNOS was uncommon and included a two-sentence description at the chapter's end that did not include any criteria sets. The PNOS descriptions for all DSMs are presented in Table 42.2.

DSM-5 departs from this minimalist tradition in that the last three sentences of the PDC Introduction extol the potential significance of OSPD and UPD by stating (p. 685) that

> The eight listed (specified) disorders do not exhaust the list of … paraphilic disorders. Many dozens … have been … named, and almost any of them could … rise to the level of a paraphilic disorder. The diagnoses of the other specified and unspecified paraphilic disorders are therefore indispensable …

The complete definitions for OSPD and UPD, which are much more extensive than the PNOS definitions in previous DSMs, are included in the bottom row of Table 42.2.

Issues in Using the DSM-5 Paraphilias Taxonomy and Residual Categories

We believe that SVP evaluators should refer to the following issues in their evaluations and testimony when relevant.

Normophilia Does Not Adequately Conceptualize the Paraphilias

The PDC defines normophilia as 'sexual interest in genital stimulation or preparatory fondling with phenotypically normal, consenting adult partners'. A person with any intense and persistent interest other than this for a 6-month period has a paraphilia. Psychologist Ray Blanchard, who chaired the Paraphilias sub-workgroup, referred to this as a 'definition by exclusion' (Blanchard, 2009). Table 42.1 shows that DSM-II and DSM-III also attempted to capture the paraphilias with exclusionary language, using terms such as 'bizarre' rather than normophilic (Hinderliter, 2010). These terms were discarded in DSM-III-R because psychiatrist and Task Force Chair Robert Spitzer had concerns about their 'subjectivity and unreliability' (Frances & First, 2011b, p. 79). The same taxonomic criticisms apply to normophilia. Normophilia is also susceptible to a high false-positive rate because of its cultural relativity: any sexual behavior that conflicts with US norms may qualify as a paraphilia.

Evaluators should alert the courts to this weakness.

The Residual Diagnoses Are Unreliable

Frances and First assumed that residual paraphilias have poor reliability coefficients because 'NOS categories do not have criteria sets' (Frances & First, 2011a, p. 558). Their 'poor reliability theory' was first addressed by Human Services Professor Jill Levenson (2004), who collected dual-rater data on the diagnostic status of 277 offenders evaluated for civil commitment. She calculated kappa coefficients (Cohen, 1960) to estimate the reliability for various criteria sets. Her kappa value for PNOS was 0.36, which she considered inadequate.

Psychologist Richard Wollert (2007, p. 179) calculated another reliability measure for PNOS, the likelihood ratio (LR), from Levenson's data. His LR for PNOS, obtained by dividing a sensitivity of 0.47 by the complement of a specificity of 0.56, was 1.07. This value did not differ from chance (i.e., where the LR equals 1.0), was smaller than the LRs for all seven of Levenson's alternatives with specified criteria sets, and did not meet the taxonomic standard that 'reliable diagnostic grouping requires … (favorable) specificity and sensitivity' levels (Greenberg, Shuman, & Meyer, 2004, p. 3; Karson, 2010).

Residual Diagnoses Are Associated with Great Diagnostic Certainty

The LR for PNOS does not differ from 1.0. The level of certainty for making a diagnosis equals the disorder's prevalence rate when its LR is 1.0 (Wollert, 2007, 2011; Wollert & Waggoner, 2009). The prevalence rate of PNOS does not exceed 10% in studies that have controlled for the inflationary effects of SVP laws (Abel et al., 1988; Eher et al., 2010). The level of uncertainty for a PNOS diagnosis thus equals 90%. The PDC's insinuation that forensic evaluators are able to assign the residual diagnoses with high levels of diagnostic certainty (p. 685) is mathematically false.

Two Residual Diagnoses Are Unnecessary and Counterproductive

One DSM-5 section indicated that all DSM-IV-TR chapters included a residual category but a second was added 'to enhance diagnostic specificity' (p. 15). Another section suggested that this was done to accommodate advances in studying the 'major and mild neurocognitive disorders' because 'biological markers' were discovered that separated them 'into specific subtypes' (DSM-5, pp. xii–xiii).

This rationale does not apply to OSPD or UPD because neither has biological validators.

Time constraints may make it necessary to assign residual diagnoses temporarily to neurology patients seen in emergency rooms (APA, 2013, pp. 19–20). These conditions do not apply to SVP respondents who are in custody. The addition of another residual option with poor reliability to the PDC is also likely to consolidate further the inadequate reliability of the residual paraphilias and invite time-wasting courtroom argumentation.

The Residual Paraphilias Have Not Been Empirically Validated

A simple and informative approach to determining whether a taxon is associated with Hempel's 'extensive cluster of characteristics' is to assess simultaneously the taxon and a battery of characteristics with which it should be correlated (Campbell & Fiske, 1959). No-one, to our knowledge, has undertaken such a study of the residual paraphilias in general. Examining rapists and sexual sadists, psychologist Ray Knight (2010) and his colleagues were unable to differentiate a group who might meet the criteria for a PNOS-non-consent taxon.

Validational research has challenged even the specified paraphilias. Award-winning research by psychologist Evelyn Hooker (1957) found that 'male overt homosexuals' and heterosexual males were equally well adjusted. Such research and subsequent protests by gay rights activists (Bayer, 1987; Silverstein, 2009) led to the removal of homosexuality from the DSM (Hinderliter, 2010; Mayes & Horwitz, 2005; Rogler, 1997).

Many psychiatrists and others have since suggested that the entire PDC should be eliminated from DSM because it either pathologizes cultural and preferential variations in sexual behaviour among non-clinical populations or medicalizes criminal behaviour (Green, 2002; Hinderliter, 2010; Keenan, 2013; Milner, Dopke, & Crouch, 2008; Moser & Kleinplatz, 2005; Silverstein, 2009; Tallent, 1977).

It is also the case that empirical studies have not provided compelling evidence for the validity of even the specified paraphilias. Research on Pedophilia, for example, has 'indicated … few significant differences between pedophilic and non-pedophilic molesters' (Kingston, Firestone, Moulden, & Bradford, 2007) and non-significant correlations – from −0.02 to 0.08 – with sexual recidivism (Eher et al., 2010; Wilson, Abracen, Looman, Picheca, & Ferguson, 2011). Four long-term studies have also reported non-significant correlations – from 0 to 0.12 – between sexual sadism and sexual recidivism (Berner, Berger, & Hill, 2003; Eher et al., 2010; Hill, Habermann, Klusmann, Berner, & Briken, 2007; Kingston, Seto, Firestone, & Bradford, 2010).

Pre-DSM-5 Arguments for Assigning PNOS Diagnoses in SVP Cases Have Been Refuted

First and Frances (2011a, p. 556) refuted Doren's *conceptual assumption*, explaining that 'the … DSM-IV Paraphilia section was written long before the issue of SVP commitment arose … it was never anticipated that the opening sentence … would be considered a forensic definition of paraphilia … it was meant … as … a simple table of contents'.

Doren's *definitional assumption* equating impairment with incarceration has been refuted by the PDC's declaration (p. 686) that 'the distress and impairment stipulated in Criterion B are … the … *result of the paraphilia*'.

First and Frances (2008, p. 1240) disputed Doren's *pragmatic assumption* by claiming he capitalized on a DSM-IV-TR wording error – where 'or' rather than 'and' was used in Criterion A – to conclude a PNOS diagnosis could be made solely from past behavior. DSM-5's definition of mental disorder also precludes the assignment of a diagnosis solely from past behaviour.

In the following statement, Frances and First (2011a, pp. 557–558), who *were* primarily responsible for writing DSM-IV, forcefully disagreed with Doren's *social acceptance assumption* that PNOS diagnoses are 'considered just as meaningful by the writers of the DSM-IV as … individually listed diagnoses':

> DSM-IV includes 46 NOS categories to … code patients who do not fit well into any of the official categories … The NOS categories are provided because psychiatric presentations are so … idiosyncratic … NOS diagnoses are meant to be no more than residual wastebaskets provided by DSM-IV to encourage research and for the convenience of clinicians … The problem is that PNOS has been widely misapplied in SVP hearings to criminals who have no mental disorder by evaluators who have misinterpreted DSM-IV. Psychiatric diagnoses … are generally considered admissible in court because they are accepted by the field …

By virtue of their residual and idiosyncratic nature, cases given the label of NOS are by definition outside of what is generally accepted … as … reliable and valid … Furthermore, the NOS categories do not have criteria sets and therefore can never be diagnosed reliably … The use by evaluators of the PNOS diagnosis fails to satisfy the standards … for expert testimony.

Evaluators who assign PNOS or equivalent labels to offenders in the future should inform the court about the total inadequacy of Doren's (2002) assumptions and explain why they believe these diagnoses are authorized for use in SVP proceedings.

Conclusion

Evaluators have used the taxonomy for the paraphilias and PNOS for around 20 years for making mental abnormality determinations. The courts have recognized that legal nomenclatures and taxonomies differ from psychiatric taxonomies and the DSM developers have made the same point.

The value of a source taxonomy for determining a person's location in a target taxonomy depends on the quality of the alignment between the taxonomies and the reliability and validity of the source taxonomy. The psychiatric symptomatology in the DSM, by common consensus, has been of great value for determining the mental health status of respondents to mental health civil commitment petitions. The value of the paraphilias taxonomy for sex offender civil commitment, in contrast, has been fiercely contested since the first law was adopted.

Some aspects of this controversy have to do with psychometric findings and differences of interpretation. Other aspects almost certainly have to do with the ongoing conflict between the state and organized medicine over this issue. The state's power to restrict the liberty of US citizens via civil commitment or public health policies is greatly legitimized by inputs from organized medicine. This is illustrated in quarantine laws and the mental health civil commitment laws. Organized psychiatry has, however, strongly opposed sex offender civil commitments for many years and is likely to continue to do so. There is a good chance that SVP laws will eventually come to be viewed as nothing more than an exercise of the state's police power. This could result in an increased perception of the SVP laws as unconstitutional because civil confinement or quarantine requires not just dangerousness, but dangerousness due to illness (*Foucha v. Louisiana*, 1992). Residual diagnoses that are used to "shoehorn" respondents inappropriately into the mental abnormality criterion may be also be rejected by the courts. In the first test of the admissibility of OSPD (non-consent) under the 'Frye' (*Frye v. U.S.*, 1923) criteria, for example, a New York trial court ruled that such a diagnosis was inadmissible because the state was unable to identify a generally accepted set of criteria that defined it and distinguished it from other psychiatric conditions (*State of New York v. Jason C.*, 2016).

Although a second Frye hearing on OSPD (non-consent) has been ordered in California (*People v. LaBlanc*, 2015), it is unlikely that the question of the admissibility of residual diagnoses in SVP proceedings will be resolved by the courts in the near future. Meanwhile, many courts may continue to accept all paraphilic diagnoses as proxies for mental abnormalities. This possibility raises questions about how the APA and evaluators might conceptualize and respond to the challenge of SVP laws.

Regarding the APA, we believe the additions of the 'Assessment Measures' section and the *current presentation, reflection,* and *remission* rules provide needed quality controls to SVP evaluations. APA's plans for ongoing revisions to DSM-5 (p. 13) could also be valuable for correcting errors in wording, disseminating statements on the use of the DSM for mental health civil commitment evaluations versus SVP civil commitment evaluations, and generating other DSM-related policies that impact the SVP adjudication process.

With respect to evaluations, we recommend that evaluators consider incorporating the concepts discussed in the section DSM-5 and the Paraphilias Taxonomy in their evaluation procedures and adopting a proactive stance towards discussing in court and in their reports the limitations of the paraphilias taxonomy and the residual paraphilias – cited in the section Issues in Using the DSM-5 Paraphilias Taxonomy and Residual Categories – for mental abnormality determinations. We advise against assigning the equivalent of a PNOS diagnosis in SVP cases for the reasons stated in the latter section.

We also advise against making any SVP determinations on the basis of unauthorized diagnoses because they have no connection with a vocabulary of science or accepted scientific methods of conceptualization, hypothesis testing, determination of reliability and error rates, peer review, and professional acceptance. The likelihood of identifying a 'meaningful' sexual pathology in the isolated context of an idiosyncratic diagnosis is minimal.

Our last piece of advice to evaluators is to keep the major events in the compilation of DSM-5 and the previous DSMs in perspective. Each new DSM introduces some revisions and retains some errors. Trying to explain these details in court is tempting but fruitless. It is much more important to concentrate on the big picture of the APA's basic position on the paraphilias and the residual paraphilias. This position is unmistakably obvious in the decisions that the APA has made on proposals for expanding the list of specified paraphilias. From this vantage point, three facts should guide all SVP evaluations. The first is that 'paraphilic rapism (has) been considered and ruled out' (Frances, 2011; Frances & First, 2011a, p. 557) of DSM-III, DSM-III-R, and DSM-IV. The second is that Hebephilia, Hypersexuality, and the latest iteration of paraphilic rapism known as Paraphilic Coercive Disorder – all ideas grounded in an expansion of the PNOS concept – were excluded from DSM-5 (Appelbaum, 2014). The third is that the proposed paraphilias were even rejected as concepts 'in need of further research' (Frances, 2012).

The consistency of these decisions over time speaks much louder than any change in wording that is susceptible to multiple parsings by different sides in an SVP case. Taken together, they indicate clear support for a reliance on authorized diagnoses. This, more than any other diagnostic principle, should be conveyed to the court.

References

Abel, G. G., Becker, J., Cunningham-Rathner, J., Mittelman, M., & Rouleau, J. (1988). Multiple paraphilic diagnoses among sex offenders. *Bulletin of the American Academy of Psychiatry and the Law, 16*(2), 153–168.

APA. (1952). *Diagnostic and statistical manual of mental disorders* (1st ed.) (DSM-I). Washington, DC: Author.

APA. (1968). *Diagnostic and statistical manual of mental disorders* (2nd ed.) (DSM-II). Washington, DC: Author.

APA. (1980). *Diagnostic and statistical manual of mental disorders* (3rd ed.) (DSM-III). Washington, DC: Author.

APA. (1987). *Diagnostic and statistical manual of mental disorders* (3rd ed., revised) (DSM-III-R). Washington, DC: Author.

APA. (1994). *Diagnostic and statistical manual of mental disorders* (4th ed.) (DSM-IV). Washington, DC: Author.

APA. (1999). *Dangerous sex offenders: A Task Force report*. Washington, DC: Author.

APA. (2000). *Diagnostic and statistical manual of mental disorders* (4th ed., text revision) (DSM-IV-TR). Washington, DC: Author.

APA. (2013). *Diagnostic and statistical manual of mental disorders* (5th ed.) (DSM-5). Arlington, VA: American Psychiatric Publishing.

Appelbaum, P. (2014). Commentary: DSM-5 and forensic psychiatry. *Journal of the American Academy of Psychiatry and the Law, 42*, 136–140.

Bayer, R. (1987). *Homosexuality and American psychiatry: The politics of diagnosis*. Princeton, NJ: Princeton University Press.

Berner, W., Berger, P., & Hill, A. (2003). Sexual sadism. *International Journal of Offender Therapy and Comparative Criminology, 47*, 383–395. doi:10.1177/0306624X08327305

Blanchard, R. (2009, April). *Paraphilias vs. Paraphilic disorders, pedophilia vs. pedo- and hebephilia, and autogynephilic vs. fetishistic transvestism*. Paper presented at the Annual Meeting of the Society for Sex Therapy and Research, Arlington, VA.

Brooks, A. D. (1992). The constitutionality and morality of civilly committing violent sexual predators. *University of Puget Sound Law Review, 15*, 709–754.

Campbell, D. T., & Fiske, D. (1959). Convergent and discriminant validation by the multitrait–multimethod matrix. *Psychological Bulletin, 56*, 81–105.

Cohen, J. (1960). A coefficient of agreement for nominal scales. *Educational and Psychological Measurement, 20*, 37–46.

Compton, W. M., & Guze, S. (1995). The neo-Kraeplinian revolution in psychiatric diagnosis. *European Archives of Psychiatry and Clinical Neuroscience, 245*, 196–201.

Decker, H. S. (2007). How Kraepelinian was Kraepelin? How Kraepelinian are the neo-Kraepelinians? – from Emil Kraepelin to DSM-III. *History of Psychiatry, 18*(3), 337–360.

Doren, D. (2002). *Evaluating sex offenders*. Thousand Oaks, CA: Sage.

Eher, R., Rettenberger, M., Matthes, A., & Schilling, F. (2010). Stable dynamic risk factors in child sexual abuse. *Sex Offender Treatment, 5*(1), 1–12.

First, M. B., & Frances, A. (2008). Issues for DSM-5: Unintended consequences of small changes: The case of paraphilias. *American Journal of Psychiatry, 165*, 1240–1241.

First, M. B., & Halon, R. (2008). Use of DSM paraphilia diagnoses in sexually violent predator commitment cases. *The Journal of the American Academy of Psychiatry and the Law, 36*, 443–454.

Foucha v. Louisiana, 504 U.S. 71 (1992).

Frances, A. (2011). The rejection of Paraphilia Rape in DSM-III: A first-hand historical narrative. Retrieved from http://www.psychologytoday.com

Frances, A. (2012). DSM 5 is guide not bible – Ignore its ten worst changes. Retrieved from http://www.psychologytoday.com

Frances, A. (2013). *Saving normal*. New York, NY: HarperCollins.

Frances, A., & First, M. (2011a). Paraphilia NOS, Nonconsent: Not ready for the courtroom. *The Journal of the American Academy of Psychiatry and the Law, 39*, 555–561.

Frances, A., & First, M. (2011b). Hebephilia is not a mental disorder in DSM-IV-TR and should not become one in DSM-5. *The Journal of the American Academy of Psychiatry and the Law, 39*, 78–85.

Frances, A., & Wollert, R. (2012). Sexual Sadism: Avoiding its misuse in sexually violent predator evaluations. *Journal of the American Academy of Psychiatry and the Law, 40*, 409–416.

Frye v. United States, 293 F 1013, 54 App DC 46 (DC Cir) (1923).

Green, R. (2002). Is pedophilia a mental disorder? *Archives of Sexual Behavior, 31*, 467–471.

Greenberg, S. A., Shuman, D., & Meyer, R. (2004). Unmasking forensic diagnosis. *International Journal of Law and Psychiatry, 27*, 1–15.

Hempel, C. G. (1961). Introduction to problems of taxonomy. In J. Zubin (Ed.), *Field studies in the mental disorders* (pp. 3–22). New York, NY: Grune & Stratton.

Hill, N., Habermann, N., Klusmann, D., Berner, W., & Briken, P. (2007). Criminal recidivism in sexual homicide perpetrators. *International Journal of Offender Therapy and Comparative Criminology, 52*, 638–648. doi:10.1177/0306624X07307450

Hinderliter, A. C. (2010). Defining paraphilia: Excluding exclusion. *Open Access Journal of Forensic Psychology, 2*, 241–272.

Hooker, E. (1957). The adjustment of the male overt homosexual. *Journal of Projective Techniques, 21*, 18–31.

In re Thorell, 149 Wn.2d 724, 72 P3d 708 (S. Ct. WA 2003).

In re Young, 857 P2d 998 (Wash 1993) 64, at 1002.

Jackson, R. L., & Richards, H. (2008). Evaluations for the civil commitment of sexual offenders. In R. Jackson (Ed.), *Learning forensic assessment* (pp. 183–209). New York, NY: Routledge.

Jumper, S., Babula, M., & Casbon, T. (2012). Diagnostic profiles of civilly committed sexual offenders in Illinois and other reporting jurisdictions. *International Journal of Offender Therapy and Comparative Criminology, 56*, 838–855. doi:10.1177/0306624X11415509

Kansas v. Crane, 534 U.S. 407 (2002).

Kansas v. Hendricks, 521 U.S. 346 (1997).

Karson, M. (2010, June). Bayes' theorem and the DSM: Is it a book of definitions or a book of tests. *WebPsychEmpiricist*. Retrieved from http://wpe.in/papers_table.html

Keenan, J. (2013, March). We're kinky, not crazy: Including 'paraphilic disorders' in the DSM V is redundant, unscientific, and stigmatizing. Retrieved from http://www.slate.com

Kingston, D. A., Firestone, P., Moulden, H., & Bradford, J. (2007). The utility of the diagnosis of Pedophilia: A comparison of various classification procedures. *Archives of Sexual Behavior, 36*, 423–436. doi:10.1007/s105080069091-x

Kingston, D. A., Seto, M. Firestone, P., & Bradford, J. (2010). Comparing indicators of sexual sadism as predictors of recidivism among adult male sexual offenders. *Journal of Consulting and Clinical Psychology, 78*, 574–584. doi:10.1007/s10508-006-9091-x

Klerman, G. L. (1978). The evolution of the scientific nosology. In J. D. Shershow (Ed.), *Schizophrenia: Science and practice.* (pp. 99–121). Cambridge, MA: Harvard University Press.

Knight, R. A. (2010). Is a diagnostic category for Paraphilic Coercive Disorder defensible? *Archives of Sexual Behavior, 39*, 419–426.

Levenson, J. (2004). Sexual predator civil commitment: A comparison of selected and released groups. *International Journal of Offender Therapy and Comparative Criminology, 48*, 638–648. doi:10.1177/0306624X004265089

Mayes, R., & Horwitz, A. W. (2005). DSM-III and the revolution in the classification of mental illness. *Journal of the History of the Behavioral Sciences, 41*, 249–267.

Millon, T. (1991). Classification in psychopathology: Rationale, alternatives, and standards. *Journal of Abnormal Psychology, 100*, 245–261.

Milner, J. S., Dopke, C., & Crouch, J. (2008). Paraphilia Not Otherwise Specified: Psychopathology and theory. In D. R. Laws & W. T. O'Donohue (Eds.), *Sexual deviance: Theory, assessment and treatment* (pp. 384–418). New York, NY: Guilford Press.

Moser, C., & Kleinplatz, P. (2005). DSM-IV-TR and the paraphilias: An argument for removal. *Journal of Psychology and Human Sexuality, 17*, 91–109.

New York v. Jason C. N.Y. Misc. Lexis 197; 2016 NY Slip Op 26018 (January 22, 2016).

People v. LaBlanc. 238 Cal App 4th 1059, 189 Cal. Rptr 3d 886, 2015 Cal App Lexis 646 (July 22, 2015).

Rogler, L. H. (1997). Making sense of historical changes in the Diagnostic and Statistical Manual of Mental Disorder: Five propositions. *Journal of Health and Social Behavior, 38*, 9–20.

Silverstein, C. (2009). The implications of removing homosexuality from the *DSM* as a mental disorder [Letter to the editor]. *Archives of Sexual Behavior, 38*, 161–163.

Tallent, N. (1977). Sexual deviation as a diagnostic entity: A confused and sinister concept. *Bulletin of the Menninger Clinic, 41*, 40–60.

Tucker, D., & Brakel, A. (2012). DSM-5 paraphilic diagnoses and SVP law [Letter to the editor]. *Archives of Sexual Behavior, 41*, 533.

Wheeler, J. R. (1992, October). *Applying the sexually violent predator statute.* Paper presented at the Annual Convention of the Association for the Treatment of Sexual Abusers, Salt Lake City, UT.

Wilson, M. (1993). DSM-III and the transformation of American psychiatry: A history. *The American Journal of Psychiatry, 150*, 399–410.

Wilson, R., Abracen, J., Looman, J., Picheca, J., & Ferguson, M. (2011). Pedophilia: An evaluation of diagnostic and risk prediction methods. *Sexual Abuse: A Journal of Research and Treatment, 23*, 260–274. doi:10.1177/1079063210384277

Winokur, G., Zimmerman, M., & Cadoret, R. (1988). Cause the Bible tells me so. *Archives of General Psychiatry, 45*, 683–684.

Wollert, R. (2007). Poor diagnostic reliability, the Null–Bayes Logic Model, and their implications for sexually violent predator evaluations. *Psychology, Public Policy, and Law, 13*(3), 167–203.

Wollert, R. (2011). Paraphilic Coercive Disorder does not belong in DSM-5 for statistical, historical, conceptual, and practical reasons [Letter to the editor]. *Archives of Sexual Behavior, 40*, 1097–1098. doi:10.1007/s10508-011-9814-5

Wollert, R., & Cramer, E. (2011). Sampling extreme groups invalidates research on the paraphilias: Implications for DSM-5 and sex offender risk assessments. *Behavioral Sciences and the Law, 29*, 554–565.

Wollert, R., & Waggoner, J. (2009). Bayesian computations protect sexually violent predator evaluations from the degrading effects of confirmatory bias and illusions of certainty. *Sexual Offender Treatment, 4*, 1–23.

Zander, T. K. (2005). Civil commitment without psychosis: The law's reliance on the weakest links in psychodiagnosis. *Journal of Sexual Offender Civil Commitment and the Law, 1*, 17–82.

Zonana, H., Bonnie, R., & Hoge, S. (2003). In the wake of Hendricks: The treatment and restraint of sexually dangerous offenders viewed from the perspective of American psychiatry. In B. J. Winick & J. Q. La Fond (Eds.), *Protecting society from sexually dangerous offenders: Law, justice, and therapy* (pp. 131–145). Washington, DC: American Psychological Association.

43

Structural and Functional Magnetic Resonance Imaging in Assessing Sexual Preference

Kirsten Jordan, Peter Fromberger, and Jürgen L. Müller

Georg-August-University, Germany

Introduction

At first glance, the assessment of sexual preference seems not to be a very difficult task: one can simply interview the person and in most cases a sufficient answer will be given. Sexual preference can be seen where a person feels sexually attracted by another person and/or an object (Schmidt, Mokros, & Banse, 2013; Seto, 2012).

However, the assessment of sexual preference becomes a very complex task in cases where respondents are unwilling to expose their sexual preference and attempt to conceal it. The forensic sector and broader legal settings where deviant sexual preference plays a major role in particular are confronted with this issue. On the one hand, self-reports suffer from insufficient validity and reliability owing to participants' tendency to answer in a socially desirable manner (O'Donohue, Regev, & Hagstrom, 2000). On the other hand, deviant sexual preference is said to be one of the strongest (single) predictors of sexual offence recidivism (Hanson & Morton-Bourgon, 2005), which highlights the importance of and necessity for a valid and reliable assessment tool to measure deviant sexual preference, beneficial not only for risk assessment but also for diagnostic purposes and planning of paraphilia treatment.

As for the detection of sexual preference, penile plethysmography (PPG) seems to provide an adequate solution to this problem. Developed by Freund, Diamant, and Pinkava (1958) nearly 60 years ago, PPG is still the gold standard in assessing deviant sexual preference in North America. It is based on good classification accuracy, demonstrated in a multitude of studies (e.g., Blanchard, Klassen, Dickey, Kuban, & Blak, 2001; Freund & Blanchard, 1989). Nevertheless, PPG is not a universal

The Wiley Handbook on the Theories, Assessment, and Treatment of Sexual Offending.
Edited by Douglas P. Boer. Volume II: Assessment, edited by Leam A. Craig and Martin Rettenberger.
© 2017 John Wiley & Sons, Ltd. Published 2017 by John Wiley & Sons, Ltd.

method, primarily because of the intrusiveness of the method, the high proportion of non-responders, and inconsistent results regarding discriminant validity and selectivity (Freund & Watson, 1991; Howes, 1995; Kalmus & Beech, 2005; Marshall & Fernandez, 2000; Seto, 2008). In addition to PPG, a broad range of assessment methods exist that focus on cognitive processes for the indirect assessment of sexual interests (Thornton & Laws, 2009). The most prominent method is the viewing time (VT) approach. The VT approach is based on the finding that people show longer viewing times in response to stimuli to which they feel sexually attracted (in accordance with their sexual preference) than to stimuli not in accordance with their sexual preference. However, VT should be used with caution in clinical settings owing to its questionable reliability and validity (Glasgow, 2009; Sachsenmaier & Gress, 2009). Other indirect methods have demonstrated promising results, but mostly in fewer studies and with smaller sample sizes, such as the implicit association task (IAT) (Brown, Gray, & Snowden, 2009), the eye tracking method (Fromberger et al., 2012, 2013), the choice–reaction–time task (CRT) (Mokros, Dombert, Osterheider, Zappala, & Santtila, 2010), the rapid serial visual presentation test (RSVP) (Beech et al., 2008), and an adaptation of the emotional Stroop task for sexual offenders (Smith & Waterman, 2004).

All of the above-mentioned methods target psychophysiological or cognitive mechanisms applying well-known methods to measure these processes. Interestingly, neurobiological processes and modern brain imaging techniques, such as functional magnetic resonance imaging (fMRI) and positron emission tomography (PET) as clinical assessment tools, have not been a major focus of research. With the increasing interest in the neurobiological area in the last two decades and the growing accessibility of brain imaging techniques, this is unexpected given the putative advantages of measuring neurofunctional processes, e.g., the possible lower susceptibility to manipulations of brain activation and the non-intrusiveness of the method (Ponseti et al., 2012). The results of imaging studies in basic science, that is, measuring sexual arousal and sexual preference in order to elucidate the underlying neurofunctional processes of human sexuality, demonstrated that our knowledge concerning the neurofunctional patterns associated with deviant sexual preference – in contrast to normophilic sexual preference – is far from showing a clear picture.

So far there has been one approach using brain imaging techniques as a clinical tool to assess deviant sexual preference. Ponseti et al. (2012) applied an automatic pattern classification method to differentiate between brain activation patterns of a group of paedophilic patients and a group of healthy subjects. They analysed brain activation patterns in response to the presentation of visual sexually explicit stimuli. The combination of the eye tracking method and fMRI could provide another approach to assess deviant sexual preference. Our group has shown that eye movements, which represent automatic attentional processes, demonstrated high diagnostic accuracy in assessing deviant sexual interest (Fromberger et al., 2012).

Combining this method with functional imaging could give a more detailed insight into neurofunctional mechanisms of deviant sexual interest and also increase the diagnostic accuracy (Fromberger, 2010). As promising as such approaches seem at first glance, several replications using larger sample sizes will be needed in order for fMRI to become a reliable clinical assessment tool. Furthermore, knowledge about the neurobiological basis of (deviant) sexual interests seems to be essential in order to be able to assess these interests validly.

In the following sections, the basics of modern brain imaging techniques are briefly explained. The neurobiological methods, findings, and theories regarding sexual arousal and sexual preferences in healthy subjects and paraphilic patients are critically summarized and the consequences for the further development of new assessment instruments based on brain imaging techniques are highlighted. Finally, the potential and the limitations of the assessment of sexual preference using fMRI are discussed. Since most of our knowledge about the underlying neurobiological processes of deviant sexual interest evolved from studies with paedophiles, the focus of this chapter is directed mainly towards this special field of paraphilia.

Short Introduction to Brain Imaging Techniques and Experimental Approaches to Measuring Sexual Arousal and Sexual Preference

Brain Imaging Techniques

Neuroimaging techniques allow the investigation of structural and functional aspects of the brain in vivo. One of the first brain imaging methods to be used was positron emission tomography (PET). Tomography is an imaging approach that involves the reconstruction of a dataset into three-dimensional (3D) images. PET uses cameras to detect photons emitted by the radioactive decay of unstable isotopes to create functional images. Contrast agents apply these isotopes to the human body by binding to molecules that carry the radioactive isotopes to their targets in the body. Simple molecules normally used by the body, such as glucose, water, and ammonia, and also more complex molecules such as a substrate for the dopamine transporter can be used as radioligands. In this way, PET allows the metabolism of the brain to be visualized with relatively high temporal resolution (Rushing, Pryma, & Langleben, 2012). A common application, for example, is to measure the rate of consumption of glucose or blood flow in different parts of the brain in studies to understand strokes and dementia. Chemical neurotransmitters such as dopamine can also be tracked (Berger, 2003). An important limitation, compared with magnetic resonance imaging in particular, is the relatively low spatial resolution of about 2 mm (Rushing et al., 2012).

Magnetic resonance (MR) images are representations of the intensities of electromagnetic signals emerging from hydrogen nuclei. The MR signal is the result of a resonance interaction between hydrogen nuclei and externally applied magnetic fields. The most important components of MRI are the protons, an external magnetic field, the interaction of the protons with the magnetic field and excitation of the protons by radiofrequency (RF) pulses (Bigler, Allen, & Stimac, 2012). At present, fMRI is the most prominent and popular imaging method for mapping brain functions. As early as the 1890s, the underlying physiological principles were described, predicated on the close connection between neural activity and energy metabolism (Roy & Sherrington, 1890; Wiebking & Northoff, 2013). Neural activity in a certain brain area, induced for example by the presentation of a sexually preferred stimulus, leads to an increase in metabolic activity, i.e., increased oxygen consumption in the area in question. The increased demand for oxygen leads to a local increase in blood flow in the predetermined region, with a higher concentration of oxyhaemoglobin than deoxyhaemoglobin. These two molecules differ in their magnetic properties: the oxygen-rich oxyhaemoglobin is diamagnetic and has no impact on the MR signal, whereas deoxyhaemoglobin is a paramagnetic molecule and modulates the MR signal. The increase in the ratio of oxyhaemoglobin and deoxyhaemoglobin concentrations leads to a higher MR signal as a consequence of the above-mentioned neural activity. This effect, peaking at about 2 s after demand onset and the postponed decline, provides the biological basis for fMRI. It is called the blood oxygenation level-dependent (BOLD) contrast, first described by Ogawa et al. (1992). In contrast to PET, the MRI technique is non-invasive (i.e., participants do not need contrast agents and no radiotracer has to be injected) and has a much higher resolution, despite the lower temporal resolution (Bigler et al., 2012; Wiebking & Northoff, 2013).

Experimental Approaches to Measuring Sexual Arousal and Sexual Preference

Numerous studies examining the underlying neurobiological basis of sexual arousal in healthy subjects have been reported, but only a few studies have presented data on sexual preference in paedophilic patients. Despite the very interesting and important results, which will be discussed in later sections, great methodological variability has been shown. Owing to the well-known fact that the use of different experimental methods is one important reason for different results being obtained, in the following the most commonly used experimental designs and methods for measuring sexual arousal and sexual preference are discussed.

Experimental designs can vary owing to the use of different parameters. The most common experimental design for measuring sexual arousal is the presentation of short video sequences or photographs depicting hetero- or homosexual sexual intercourse to subjects who passively watch the stimuli. For example, the majority of the 73 studies that were included in a comprehensive review by Stoléru, Fonteille, Cornélis, Joyal, and Moulier (2012) used short video sequences and photographs depicting male–female intercourse. Other studies have used audio presentation of sexual scripts, photographs of nude males or females, or smelling of a sexually attractive pheromone. The exact definition of the type of stimuli and the response elicited are essential. For instance, video sequences and photographs displaying explicit sexual activity will elicit different responses to photographs of nude persons in a non-explicit sexual position. The first kind of stimulation elicits a stronger sexual arousal than the latter, also to be seen in brain activation.

Control conditions vary between neutral or humorous material, sport video sequences, non-sexual male–female interactions, and photographs. The selection of an adequate control condition is one of the most important methodological aspects in functional brain imaging studies. Owing to the classical subtraction approach, differences are usually calculated between the experimental and the control condition. Different control conditions lead to variable differential activation patterns and thus lead to wide variability between studies. This can be seen in the activation differences between a sexually explicit condition (e.g., pornographic picture, intercourse) and a neutral condition such as sports or humour, where the differences will be greater than between sexually preferred (pornographic picture of a woman) and sexually non-preferred pictures (pornographic picture of a man). Furthermore, in a meta-analysis Poeppl, Langguth, Laird, and Eickhoff (2014), distinguished their studies according to the type of analysis of sexual arousal (see also the section Neurobiology of Sexuality and the Measurement of Sexual Arousal in Healthy Subjects). The analysed brain activation caused by visual sexual stimuli differed from brain activation patterns associated with penile erection.

Likewise, different presentation times can modulate the activity of certain brain regions that are involved in the development of sexual arousal. In an fMRI study by Sundaram et al. (2010), for example, erotic video clips showing sexual interactions for 3 min were presented to heterosexual men. Analysing the first, second, and third minutes separately, significant increases and decreases in various brain regions were found, which in turn were involved in different stages of sexual arousal. For instance, haemodynamic responses in the thalamus decreased from the first to the third minute, whereas haemodynamic responses in the amygdala, the inferior frontal gyrus, the insula, and midbrain structures increased. Sundaram et al. (2010) suggested that the first minute may represent an early stage of sexual arousal comprising cognitive, emotional, and motivational component. The 'late' stage of sexual arousal, e.g., the third minute, may illustrate the fully developed sexual arousal with a higher level of genital response and cognitive processing of the stimuli. Kagerer et al. (2011) also discussed that a short presentation time of about 4 s will cover only the very early stage of sexual arousal, most likely reflecting initial autonomic responses, hedonic feelings, and attention, in contrast to longer presentation times of up to minutes.

Summary

We have explained briefly the most typical brain imaging techniques, PET and fMRI, with their pros and cons, and have described the most common experimental designs in imaging studies in order to assess sexual arousal and sexual preference. We sought to point out the variations among studies due to their methodological characteristics. It is noteworthy that despite these acknowledged discrepancies, studies have not been explicitly distinguished according to their methodological characteristics, which might occasionally be responsible for the high inter-study variability. Therefore, where appropriate, in the following sections we briefly mention the applied stimulation design and the type of analysis in a particular study.

Neurobiology of Sexuality and the Measurement of Sexual Arousal and Sexual Preference in Healthy Subjects

Human Sexuality – Theories

According to Bancroft, human sexuality can be seen as a 'human condition which is manifested as sexual desire or appetite, associated physiological response patterns, and behavior which leads to orgasm, or at least pleasurable arousal, often between two people, but not infrequently by an individual alone' (Bancroft, 2009, p. 18).

For more than 100 years theoretical models have been put forward in attempts to explain human sexual behaviour. In contrast to historical approaches, seeing sexuality as a primary drive, recent models consider sexuality in the context of theories outlining emotion and motivation. Rosen and Beck (1988) postulated that the male sexual reaction is comparable to emotions, which can be seen as a complex of physiological, psychological, and behavioural components. The dual-control model describes the interaction between sexual excitatory and sexual inhibitory processes at a cognitive and behavioural level (Bancroft, Graham, Janssen, & Sanders, 2009; Bancroft & Janssen, 2000).

Sexual arousal as one aspect of human sexual response has attracted most attention in empirical psychological and neuroscientific research. Subjective sexual arousal can be defined as an emotional experience including the awareness of autonomic arousal, expectations of reward, and motivated desire (Everaerd, 1988). Spiering and Everaerd (2007) proposed a model in which they assume an interaction of automatic and controlled cognitive processes, and an incremental influence of attentional processes on subjective experience and the physiological aspects of sexual arousal.

In the context of forensic psychiatry and psychology, the assessment of sexual preference is of special interest. Sexual preference can be seen as if a person feels sexually attracted by another person or an object (Schmidt et al., 2013; Seto, 2012). According to current theories, a sexually interesting stimulus can automatically attract attention, which leads to an automatic and controlled processing of the stimulus and the development of sexual desire, arousal, and, if appropriate, a full sexual response (Spiering & Everaerd, 2007).

Neurobiology of Sexuality and the Measurement of Sexual Arousal in Healthy Subjects

Most studies concerned with the underlying neurobiological processes of sexuality in healthy subjects examined sexual arousal mostly in heterosexual, healthy, male volunteers. Based on the above-mentioned theoretical models and results of a functional brain imaging study, Stoléru et al. (1999) proposed a neurobiological model of sexual arousal, the so-called four-component model. Similarly to the dual-control model, excitatory and inhibitory processes in the development of sexual arousal are proposed. Excitatory processes comprise cognitive, emotional, motivational, and autonomic components, which are assumed to be closely coordinated. Based on 73 functional brain imaging studies Stoléru et al. (2012) adapted their four-component neurophenomenological model (see Figure 43.1).

According to their model, the cognitive component embodies a process through which a stimulus is perceived, categorized as a sexual incentive, and quantitatively evaluated (Stoléru et al., 2012). First, sensory processes take place in the primary and secondary visual sensory lateral occipital and temporal cortices. Lateral occipital brain regions, which are not explicitly involved in the model, are proposed not to be involved only in the processing of lower level features such as luminance, colour, or shape; the processing of the general emotional salience and the specific sexually

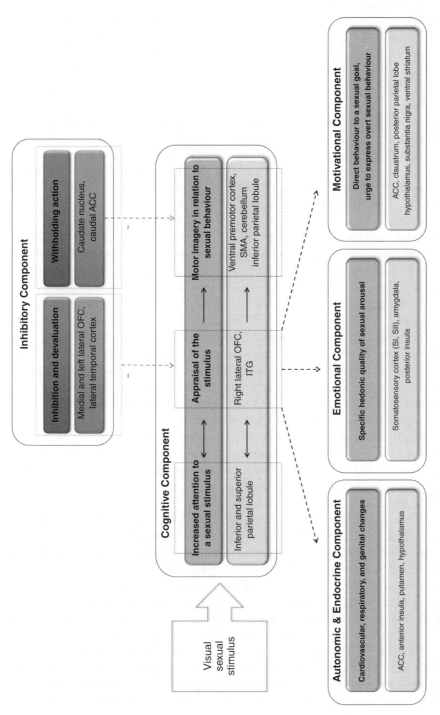

Figure 43.1 The four-component model of sexual arousal (Stoléru et al., 2012). Source: modified and translated with permission from Jordan, Fromberger, and Müller (2013).

arousing character of the stimulus are assumed also to be the source of the activation of these brain regions. The following appraisal of the sexual stimuli is considered to be the earliest one, linked to the right lateral orbitofrontal cortex (OFC) and the inferior temporal cortex. Subsequently, increased attentional processes in reaction to the sexual stimuli have been associated with activity in the inferior and superior parietal lobule (IPL, SPL), whereas motor imagery in relation to sexual behaviour should be linked to the ventral premotor cortex, the supplementary motor area (SMA), the cerebellum, and the IPL.

The specific hedonic quality of sexual behaviour, e.g., the experienced pleasure associated with rising arousal and the perception of bodily changes such as penile tumescence that characterize the emotional component, seems to be associated with activity in the amygdala, in the somatosensoric cortex (SI, SII), and in the posterior insula. The thalamus, which is not included in the model but discussed in the review, is considered to be interconnected to the general emotional arousal that accompanies sexual arousal and at the same time the perception of erection (Stoléru et al., 2012).

The motivational component comprises the processes that direct the behaviour to a sexual goal, including the perceived urge to express overt sexual behaviour (Stoléru et al., 2012). Brain regions such as the anterior cingulum (ACC), the claustrum, the hypothalamus, the substantia nigra, and the ventral striatum are assumed to be associated with the motivational component. Additionally, the activation of the posterior parietal lobule, as mentioned in some studies, might be related to its role in motor imagery processes, e.g., the imagination of overt sexual behaviour in particular.

Cardiovascular, respiratory, and genital responses constitute the autonomic and endocrinological component. They incite the subject to a state of physiological readiness for sexual behaviour (Stoléru et al., 2012). The anterior cingulum, the anterior insula, the hypothalamus, and the putamen are structures that are associated with the autonomic and endocrinological component.

According to the model, inhibitory processes comprise (i) the inhibition and devaluation of sexual arousal and (ii) the inhibition of overt behavioural expression. The left lateral and medial OFC and the lateral temporal cortex are assumed to be involved in the former processes, whereas the caudate nucleus and the caudal part of the ACC seem to be involved in the latter processes.

An interesting region in this context is the frontal lobe, which has been discussed by Stoléru et al. (2012) but was not explicitly included in the model. Activations are mainly described in the inferior but also in the middle and superior frontal and the prefrontal gyrus. The inferior frontal regions, especially BA 44/45 (BA = Brodman area) are known to be part of the mirror-neuron system. Mirror neurons fire in the case when an action is performed, or a similar or identical action is passively observed, and also in situations of imitation (Molenberghs, Cunnington, & Mattingley, 2012; Rizzolatti & Craighero, 2004). Hence it is possible that subjects imagined sexual activity with the displayed sexually preferred person. The dorsolateral prefrontal cortex is known for its role in modulating executive cognitive functions of goal-directed behaviours, including attention, self-regulation, planning, inhibition, and control of impulsive behaviour. This region has many reciprocal connections with cortical and subcortical regions (Wood & Grafman, 2003). This leads to the assumption that the inferior frontal regions should be linked to the cognitive and inhibitory components of sexual arousal.

Summing up, the four-component model illustrates that several brain regions are in involved in the development and control of sexual arousal. Nevertheless, it should be pointed out that none of these brain regions is specifically and exclusively associated with the processing of sexual stimuli, rather they are involved in many other non-sexual functions. Additionally, not all of the studies included in the review of Stoléru et al. (2012) found an activation of all the brain regions of the four-component model. Furthermore, it appears that several structures that play an important role in the processing of sexual stimuli and are discussed in the review are not included in the model, e.g., the occipital cortex, the thalamus, and frontal regions. One of the conceivable reasons could lie in the different methodological designs and control conditions used in the studies as described briefly in the previous section (for details, see Jordan, Fromberger, Stolpmann, & Müller, 2011a; Stoléru et al., 2012).

Recently Poeppl et al. (2014) proposed to distinguish between the so-called psychosexual arousal and physiosexual arousal. Psychosexual arousal was defined as the core mental operations during the processing of sexual stimuli, including early automatic appraisal and attentional phenomena, which may eventually 'lead to subjective experience of sexual arousal and genital response' (Janssen, Everaerd, Spiering, & Janssen, 2000; Poeppl et al., 2014). Physiosexual arousal was associated with penile tumescence and turgidity, as it seems to be the most valid indicator of male sexual arousal (Freund & Blanchard, 1989). Poeppl et al. (2014) performed a meta-analysis between brain imaging studies (i) analysing brain activation in relation to visual sexual stimulation (e.g., psychosexual arousal) and (ii) analysing brain activation in association with penile erection (e.g., physiosexual arousal). Most of the 20 included studies were also involved in the review by Stoléru et al. (2012) and used sexually explicit stimuli depicting female–male intercourse. Brain networks, which showed stronger activation during psychosexual compared with physiosexual arousal, comprised the inferior lateral occipital cortex, the superior and inferior parietal lobule, the caudate nucleus, the inferior frontal gyrus, the hippocampus, and the amygdala. In contrast, the insula and parts of the opercular cortex and of the middle and anterior cingulate cortex showed stronger activations during physiosexual arousal compared with psychosexual arousal (Poeppl et al., 2014). Considering the above-discussed four-component model of Stoléru et al. (2012), psychosexual arousal (associated with visual sexual stimulation) can be allocated to all four components, whereas physiosexual arousal (associated with penile erection) seems mainly to be related to the autonomic component.

Despite this crucial differentiation between psychosexual and physiosexual arousal, the study of Poeppl et al. (2014) places emphasis on the issue of the variability between the imaging studies examining sexual arousal. According to them, the variability of results depends on the diverse ways of data analysis.

Measurement of Sexual Preference in Healthy Subjects

The above-discussed models focused on the neurobiological underpinnings of sexual arousal. Only a few functional imaging studies were concerned with the neural networks associated with sexual preference, especially with hetero- and homosexual sexual preferences in healthy subjects. These studies are very important considering the challenge in forensic psychiatry and psychology to differentiate between normophilic and paraphilic sexual preference instead of measuring sexual arousal. Compared with the studies examining sexual arousal, these studies presented sexually explicit stimuli (e.g., sexual activity, sexually aroused genitals) but some of them also used sexually non-explicit stimuli (e.g., nude males & females, faces).

According to a study with 53 hetero- and homosexual men and women, the ventral striatum, the centromedian thalamus, and the premotor cortex, but also posterior parietal areas, respond specifically to a sexually preferred stimulus compared with a non-preferred stimulus (Ponseti et al., 2006). Comparing the haemodynamic responses to a sexually preferred stimulus (female and male sexually aroused genitals) with haemodynamic responses to a sexually non-preferred stimulus (male and female aroused genitals), Ponseti et al. (2006) found a similar activation pattern in all four groups. They concluded that sexual core stimuli are sufficient in triggering neural responses in the mesiocentral structures of the human reward system. Interestingly, comparing both sexually preferred and non-preferred stimuli with non-sexual control stimuli – non-sexual stimuli of the International Affective Picture System (IAPS) (Lang, Bradley, & Cuthbert, 2001) – an increase in the left lateral occipital cortex, bilateral parietal areas, the ACC, the ventral striatum, the centromedian thalamus, and the OFC, and at a weaker statistical threshold in the amygdala, was detected. As mentioned above, only some of these regions responded specifically more strongly to the sexually preferred stimulus (Ponseti et al., 2006).

The presentation of sexually explicit videos, depicting heterosexual or homosexual intercourse, elicited similar haemodynamic responses associated with the four components of sexual arousal in heterosexual and homosexual men while watching a videoclip corresponding to their sexual orientation compared with a sexually neutral film clip (Paul et al., 2008). Interestingly, film excerpts opposite to the sexual orientation of the subjects evoked haemodynamic responses in brain regions associated with intense (aversive) autonomic and emotional response (e.g., bilateral insula, amygdala), except in the hypothalamus. Thereby, the hypothalamus was more strongly activated when haemodynamic responses to heterosexual intercourse videos in the heterosexual group were compared with the haemodynamic responses to heterosexual intercourse videos in the homosexual group, and vice versa (Paul et al., 2008). This indicates that the hypothalamus seems to function as a key structure regarding sexual preference, mainly associated with the autonomic and motivational component of sexual arousal. Similarly, Kagerer et al. (2011) did not find group differences between hetero- and homosexual men regarding the brain activation patterns in response to the preferred sexually explicit videos compared with neutral and aversive stimuli.

Not only sexually explicit stimuli but also faces seem to evoke activation patterns resembling the individual sexual preference (Kranz & Ishai, 2006). In a group of 40 hetero- and homosexual men and women, the thalamus and the medial orbitofrontal cortex responded most strongly to the sexually preferred face compared with the sexually non-preferred face (Kranz & Ishai, 2006).

In summary, it seems that independent of the specific stimulus, subjects respond in a similar manner to their sexually preferred stimulus. The thalamus and the hypothalamus seem to be brain structures particularly sensitive and responsive to sexually preferred stimuli, regions that are connected to the autonomic and motivational aspects of sexual arousal. Other structures that have sometimes been found to respond specifically to sexually preferred stimuli are the posterior parietal areas, the orbitofrontal cortex, the premotor cortex, and the ventral striatum. According to the four-component model, these structures are assumed to be mainly associated with the cognitive component. Despite these interesting results, the intervening methodological differences such as the type of stimulation, the specific stimuli, and the control condition, should not be neglected. It is still questionable if brain structures exist that respond in a specific manner depending on the individual sexual orientation.

Summary

In this section, we discussed theoretical and neurobiological models of sexuality. Among these models, the four-component model of sexual arousal was introduced. This model includes a cognitive, emotional, motivational, and an autonomic excitatory component and also an inhibitory component, each interacting with one another. This approach has received empirical support from other studies focusing on healthy heterosexual male subjects where a complex pattern of responsive brain areas was found (see Figure 43.1). A few studies placed emphasis on the question of the impact of sexual preference on these activation patterns. Despite the fact that the presentation of sexually preferred stimuli evoked similar reaction patterns in both hetero- and homosexual subjects, some brain areas did respond more specifically to the preferred sexual stimulus in comparison with the non-preferred stimulus.

In the following section, we focus on paraphilia. Before discussing studies examining sexual (deviant) interest in paraphilic patients, we describe the most recent knowledge about neurobiological models of paraphilia, especially paedophilia, and discuss structural abnormalities in this disorder. Structural changes in the brain could lead to alterations of sexual interest and behaviour and, from a more methodological point of view, could alter the functional processes.

Neurobiological Models of Paraphilia

The Integrated Theory of Sexual Offending (ITSO) provides a framework to explain the onset, development, and maintenance of sexual offending (Ward & Beech, 2006). It incorporates factors that affect brain development, such as evolution, genetic variations, and neurobiology, and also ecological factors, such as social and cultural environment, personal circumstances, and physical environment, and their impact upon neuropsychological functions. In relation to the neurobiological factors, deficits in three interlocking neuropsychological systems are proposed: the motivational and emotional system, the action selection and control system, and the perception and memory system (Pennington, 2002; Ward & Beech, 2006). The ITSO provides for the first time a theoretical framework for sexual offending considering neurofunctional factors. From our present state of knowledge, the hypotheses regarding the neurobiological basis of sexual offending remain untested.

Other theories have tried to describe the neurobiological basis of paraphilia based on recent findings of neuroimaging studies, most prominent in paedophilia (Jordan,

Fromberger, Stolpmann, & Müller, 2011b). So far, three neurobiological theories for paedophilia have been proposed (Cantor et al., 2008). The frontal-dysexecutive theory was put forward by Graber, Hartmann, Coffman, Huey, and Golden (1982) and assumes that structural and functional damage to the frontal lobe might lead to behavioural disinhibition, which favours paedophilic behaviour. Support for this theory comes from Burns and Swerdlow (2003) in a case study of a man who developed paedophilic behaviour due to an orbitofrontal tumour. Structural and functional imaging data obtained by Schiffer and colleagues provide support for this theory (see also the following two main sections; Schiffer et al., 2007; Schiffer, Krüger, et al., 2008; Schiffer, Paul, et al., 2008). The critical point in this theory is the lack of specificity: frontal disturbances and the consequent disinhibition are associated with impulsive–aggressive behaviour, sexually disinhibited behaviour, and the loss of moral concepts (Fromberger, Stolpmann, Jordan, & Müller, 2009). The temporal-limbic theory posits that the temporal and limbic brain regions play a major role in sexual functions. Especially lesions of the temporal lobe are associated with hypersexual behaviour (Kaplan & Krueger, 2010). Some functional imaging studies revealed changes of activation in the limbic regions in paedophilic patients, thus also supporting this hypothesis (see the section Measuring Sexual Preference in Paraphilic Patients – Current Results of fMRI Studies; Walter et al., 2007; Wiebking, Witzel, Walter, Gubka, & Northoff, 2006). The dual-dysfunctional theory connects the former theories, assuming dysfunctions in both temporal and frontal brain areas. According to the latter theory, hypersexual behaviour caused by temporal deficits – together with behavioural disinhibition caused by frontal deficits – leads to paedophilic behaviour. Structural imaging studies (Cantor et al., 2008; Cohen et al., 2002) and neuropsychological studies (Joyal, Black, & Dassylva, 2007) support this hypothesis.

Summary

Despite the comprehensive ITSO, only three other theories have tried to describe the underlying neurobiological basis of paraphilia predicated on the most recent findings of brain imaging studies and within the realm of paraphilia: the frontal-dysexecutive theory, the temporal-limbic theory, and the dual-dysfunctional theory. In the following section, structural abnormalities in paraphilic patients, partially supporting the above-mentioned theories, are discussed.

Structural Brain Abnormalities in Paraphilic Patients

So far, we have no thorough understanding of the neurobiology of paraphilia (see also Jordan et al., 2011b). Case studies of hypersexual and paraphilic behaviour in neurological and psychiatric disorders have demonstrated that paedophilic and paraphilic behaviour is predominantly related to dysfunctions in the frontal and/or temporal lobe (e.g., Burns & Swerdlow, 2003; Mendez, Chow, Ringman, Twitchell, & Hinkin, 2000; Mendez & Shapira, 2011, 2013; Müller, 2011). Most structural imaging studies on brain abnormalities in paraphilia stem from studies with paedophilic patients (Cantor et al., 2008; Schiffer et al., 2007; Schiltz et al., 2007; Schiltz, Witzel, & Bogerts, 2006). A comprehensive discussion of the potential of and especially the methodological issues with these four studies was published by Fromberger, Krippl, Stolpmann, and Müller (2007) and Fromberger et al. (2009).

In the first structural study, Schiltz et al. (2006) found an enlargement of the anterior temporal horn of the lateral ventricle in four paedophilic patients. In the second study, they found a decrease in grey matter in the right amygdala, the hypothalamus, the substantia innominata, and the stria terminalis in 15 paedophilic patients compared with 15 control persons (Schiltz et al., 2007). Schiffer et al. (2007) found a volume reduction of grey matter in 18 paedophilic patients, compared with 24 healthy controls, in the following structures: orbitofrontal cortex, insula, ventral striatum, cerebellum, and some limbic gyri (cingulate gyrus, parahippocampal gyrus). With a weaker statistical threshold, volume reduction was also detected in the parietal cortex (precuneus) and in the middle and superior temporal gyri. Cantor et al. (2008) examined a group of 65 paedophilic patients and compared them with 62 non-paedophilic offenders. The paedophilic patients showed a volume reduction in white matter in the arcuate fasciculus and the superior fronto-occipital fasciculus compared with non-paedophilic offenders. More recently, Cantor and Blanchard (2012) reanalysed these data, searching for differences between paedophilic and hebephilic patients, i.e., patients with a sexual preference for early pubertal children. They found that the neuroanatomy of hebephiles resembles that of paedophiles more precisely than that of teleiophiles, i.e., persons with a sexual interest in adults (Cantor & Blanchard, 2012). Poeppl et al. (2013) were interested in the association between brain structures and phenotypic characteristics. They examined nine male paedophilic patients and 11 male non-sexual offenders. Similarly to Schiltz et al. (2007), they found a volume reduction of the right amygdala in paedophiles compared with the non-sexual offenders. Within this small group of paedophilic patients, paedosexual interest and sexual recidivism was correlated with a decrease in grey matter in the left dorsolateral cortex and the insular cortex. Lower age of victims was strongly associated with grey matter reductions in the orbitofrontal cortex and angular gyri bilaterally (Poeppl et al., 2013).

Summary

As outlined above, structural brain imaging studies with paedophilic patients indicated primarily a volume reduction in those patients compared with a control group, albeit with a high variability caused by the changes in different brain regions. However, these structural changes are not specific for paedophilia, since they can also be found in other mental disorders. Yet it seems evident that paedophilia is associated with disturbances in brain regions that are involved in sexual functions, e.g., regions in the frontal, temporal, and parietal cortex, the limbic system, and subcortical structures, such as the hypothalamus and the striatum, partially supporting the above-mentioned theories. Moreover, considering the results of the study by Poeppl et al. (2013), these structural changes could be associated with phenotypic characteristics in paedophiles. Certainly, it is evident that a sample of nine patients is insufficient to generalize the results towards a broader view of the associations between structural brain abnormalities in paedophiles and, for instance, the dimension of deviant sexual interest or recidivism.

Functional MRI in Paraphilic Patients Measuring Sexual Preference

Experimental Methods to Measure Sexual Preference in Paedophiles

As most fMRI studies examining deviant sexual preference have been performed with paedophilic patients, the following discussion is focused on this special field of paraphilia. So far, 10 studies have been published examining sexual preference in paedophiles, with new and interesting but also conflicting results (Cohen et al., 2002; Dressing et al., 2001; Habermeyer et al., 2013; Poeppl et al., 2011; Ponseti et al., 2012; Sartorius et al., 2008; Schiffer, Krüger, et al., 2008; Schiffer, Paul, et al., 2008; Walter et al., 2007; Wiebking et al., 2006). As already mentioned, many different experimental methods have been applied to measure sexual arousal and sexual preference in healthy subjects, and the same is true for the 10 published studies examining a deviant sexual interest in paedophilic patients.

Table 43.1 illustrates the methodological details for these studies. In addition to the large variation in the number of subjects, ranging from one to 56, approximately 10 subjects were included per group. Most but not all studies defined the sexual preference with regard to gender and compared only subjects with the same sexual orientation. Typically, paedophilic patients were compared with healthy controls. One study included a forensic control group (non-sexual offenders) (Poeppl et al., 2011). This is important since a forensic control group is much more comparable to paedophile patients than a healthy control group regarding, for example, their intelligence, co-morbidity, criminality, hospitalization, etc. (Fromberger et al., 2012; Krüger & Schiffer, 2011). In most cases, one person per trial is presented, mostly nude persons or persons clothed in swimsuits in sexually non-explicit positions, also meeting ethical concerns. One common commercially available stimulus set is the Not-Real-People picture set, which does not display images of real people and meets contemporary legal and ethical requirements. The pictures are not pornographic, depicting solely non-explicit sexual poses or sexual activities in different Tanner stages (Laws & Gress, 2004; Mokros et al., 2011; Pacific Psychological Assessment Corporation, 2004; Tanner, 1973). The use of non-explicit sexual stimuli is in contrast to the above-discussed studies in healthy subjects, examining sexual arousal by presenting sexually explicit videos or photographs depicting sexual interaction (see the sections Experimental Approaches to Measuring Sexual Arousal and Sexual Preference, and Neurobiology of Sexuality and the Measurement of Sexual Arousal in Healthy Subjects). These differences in stimulation paradigms have to be considered when comparing brain activation patterns between the studies with paedophiles and the studies of sexual arousal in healthy subjects.

The control stimuli are of great importance in brain imaging studies. The haemodynamic responses to these stimuli normally have to be compared with the haemodynamic responses to the experimental stimuli in order to extract only those regions linked to sexual interest or sexual arousal (see also the section Experimental Approaches to Measuring Sexual Arousal and Sexual Preference). As can be seen from Table 43.1, these control stimuli varied between studies, often due to different functions of the control condition. Some studies, for instance, wanted to control

Table 43.1 Brain imaging studies examining paedophilic interest – Experimental designs

Study	Method	Experimental group (EG) Sexual orientation	Control group (CG) Sexual orientation	Modality	Stimuli E: Experimental condition C: Control condition	Presentation time (one stimulus)	Experimental design
Dressing et al. (2001)	fMRI	Paedophile (n = 1) Homosexual	Healthy (n = 2) Heterosexual	Visual Block-design	E: One person in underwear/swimsuit (common mail order catalogue): boy, woman C: Abstract picture with similar colour intensity and complexity	19.2 s	Passive viewing
Cohen et al. (2002)	PET	Paedophiles (n = 7) Heterosexual	Healthy (n = 7) Heterosexual	Auditive Block-design	E: Sexual script describing sexual interaction: girl–man, woman–man C: Non-sexual words	30 min	Passive listening
Wiebking et al. (2006)	fMRI	Paedophiles (n = 13) n/a	Healthy (n = 14) n/a	Visual Block-design	E: One adult person – erotic condition (IAPS) C: One adult person – emotional, neutral condition (IAPS)	N/A	Passive viewing
Walter et al. (2007)	fMRI	Paedophiles (n = 13) n/a	Healthy (n = 14) n/a	Visual Block-design	E: One adult person – erotic position (IAPS) C: One adult person - emotional, neutral position (IAPS)	5 s	Passive viewing (button press)

(continued overleaf)

Table 43.1 (*Continued*)

Study	Method	Experimental group (EG) Sexual orientation	Control group (CG) Sexual orientation	Modality	Stimuli E: Experimental condition C: Control condition	Presentation time (one stimulus)	Experimental design
Sartorius et al. (2008)	fMRI	Paedophiles (*n* = 10) Homosexual	Healthy (*n* = 10) Heterosexual	Visual Block-design	E: One person in swimsuit (common mail order catalogue): girl, boy, woman, man C: Geometric figures (target, coloured circles; non-target, coloured squares)	1 s	Passive viewing (button press) and active task Oddball paradigm
Schiffer et al. (2008a)	fMRI	Paedophiles (*n* = 8) Heterosexual	Healthy (*n* = 12) Heterosexual	Visual Block-design	E: One nude person (EG, Internet, mail order art catalogues; CG, IAPS): girl, woman C: Dressed persons (EG, Internet, mail order art catalogues; CG, IAPS): girl, woman	38.5 s	Passive viewing
Schiffer et al. (2008b)	fMRI	Paedophiles (*n* = 11) Homosexual	Healthy (*n* = 12) Homosexual	Visual Block-design	E: One nude person (EG, Internet, mail order art catalogues; CG, IAPS): boy, man C: Dressed persons (EG, Internet, mail order art catalogues; CG, IAPS): boy, man	38.5 s	Passive viewing

Study	Method	EG	CG	Design	Stimuli	Duration	Task
Poeppl et al. (2011)	fMRI	Paedophiles (n = 9) Heterosexual (n = 2) Homosexual (n = 7)	Non-sexual offenders (n = 11) Heterosexual	Visual Block-design	E: One nude person (NRP set) Prepubescent, pubescent, adult (male and female) C: One scrambled NRP picture with similar colour intensity and complexity	4 s	Active task: Choice Reaction Time Task (CRTT)
Ponseti et al. (2012)	fMRI	Paedophiles (n = 24) Heterosexual (n = 11) Homosexual (n = 13)	Healthy (n = 32) Heterosexual (n = 18) Homosexual (n = 14)	Visual Event-related design	E: One nude person or genitals only: Girl, boy, woman, man C: Non-sexual picture (IAPS)	1 s	Passive viewing and active task Oddball stimulus
Habermeyer et al. (2013)	fMRI	Paedophiles (n = 8) Heterosexual	Healthy (n = 8) Heterosexual	Visual Event-related design	E: One Person in erotic condition: Girl, boy, woman, man C: One neutral object	750 ms	Passive viewing

Only men were included in all studies.

EG, experimental group; CG, control group; E, experimental condition; C, control condition; N/A, not applicable; IAPS set, International Affective Picture System (Lang et al.; 2001); NRP set, Not Real People stimuli set for the assessment of sexual interest (Pacific Psychological Assessment Corporation, 2004).

the low-level features of the experimental stimuli, e.g. the colour, shape, or contrast. Therefore, simple abstract stimuli were used (e.g., Dressing et al., 2001; Poeppl et al., 2011). Other researchers were mainly interested in the differences between the processing of erotic and emotional stimuli (Walter et al., 2007; Wiebking et al., 2006). Therefore, the latter served as a control stimulus. Some studies additionally compared the haemodynamic differences between preferred and non-preferred stimuli in order to distinguish the specific pattern of sexual preference (e.g., Habermeyer et al., 2013; Poeppl et al., 2011; Schiffer, Paul, et al., 2008).

As shown in Table 43.1, presentation times for stimuli varied between 750 ms and 30 min. As already discussed in the section Experimental Approaches to Measuring Sexual Arousal and Sexual Preference, different presentation times can lead to different stages of development of sexual arousal and thus to different activation patterns, which in turn are associated with different stages of processing of sexual stimuli. Most studies used passive paradigms, e.g., the passive viewing of sexual stimuli with the subjects being asked to let the arousal occur. Some researchers ask the subjects to press a button if the stimulus appears, in order to control subject's vigilance in the scanner. However, a passive task has some disadvantages, e.g., it cannot be controlled if subjects really watch the stimuli and let the arousal occur, and they are susceptible to manipulations. For this reasons, two studies chose active tasks in order to capture the attention of the subjects while presenting the visual sexual stimuli (Poeppl et al., 2011; Sartorius et al., 2008).

Despite interesting and new results, these methodological differences might partially cause the great variability of the results. A detailed overview of seven of the 10 studies with a critical discussion of their potential and especially their methodological problems can also be found in two of our papers (Fromberger et al., 2007, 2009). In the following section, the results of these 10 studies are explained in more detail. Considering the above-mentioned methodological variability, we mainly compare studies with similar designs or contrasts, or point out the differences between them.

Measuring Sexual Preference in Paraphilic Patients – Current Results of fMRI Studies

The results of the 10 functional imaging studies examining sexual interest in paedophilic subjects are summarized in Tables 43.2–43.4. The activated brain regions are arranged according to the four-component model of sexual arousal (see the section Experimental Approaches to Measuring Sexual Arousal and Sexual Preference). Considering that some studies reported more activated regions than those associated with the four-component model, these additional brain areas are also listed in the tables.

The first interesting question is whether paedophilic subjects exhibit similar or different brain activation patterns to healthy subjects, when viewing their preferred sexual stimulus compared with a neutral (non-sexual) stimulus (see Table 43.2). Six out of the 10 studies determined that kind of contrast. Five out of these six studies found haemodynamic responses in brain regions associated with at least three of the four excitatory components for sexual arousal, as well as in brain areas associated with the inhibitory component. Additionally, activations were mainly found in the frontal lobe,

Table 43.2 Results of brain imaging studies examining paedophilic interest for the comparison of the sexually preferred stimuli and the neutral stimuli in paedophile subjects. The activated brain regions are arranged according to the four-component model of Stoléru et al. (2012) (see the section Neurobiology of Sexuality and the Measurement of Sexual Arousal in Healthy Subjects)

Study	Four-component model					Inhibitory component	Additional brain regions not assigned to the four-component model
	Component:	Cognitive	Emotional	Motivational	Autonomic		
	Brain region:	Attention: IPL, SPL Appraisal: *right lateral OFC, ITG* Motor imagery: *vPM, SMA, CB, IPL*	*Somatosensory cortex (SI, SII), amygdala, posterior insula*	*ACC, claustrum, posterior parietal cortex, hypothalamus, substantia nigra, ventral striatum*	ACC, anterior insula, putamen, hypothalamus	Inhibition and devaluation: *medial and left lateral OFC, lateral temporal cortex* Inhibition of motor reaction: *caudate nucleus, cACC*	
	Comparison						
Dressing et al. (2001) Boy vs neutral		Right OFC, fusiform gyrus (ITG)		ACC (basal ganglia)	ACC		Occipital cortex, brain stem, right prefrontal cortex
Cohen et al. (2002) Girl		ITG		Cingulate gyrus	Cingulate gyrus	Medial OFC, caudate nucleus. inferior temporal cortex	Thalamus, ventral superior frontal gyrus

(*continued overleaf*)

Table 43.2 (*Continued*)

Study	Four-component model						Inhibitory component	Additional brain regions not assigned to the four-component model
	Component:	Cognitive	\<Excitatory components\> Emotional	Motivational	Autonomic			
	Brain region:	Attention: IPL, SPL Appraisal: *right lateral OFC, ITG* Motor imagery: *vPM, SMA, CB, IPL*	Somatosensory cortex (SI, SII), amygdala, posterior insula	ACC, claustrum, posterior parietal cortex, hypothalamus, substantia nigra, ventral striatum	ACC, anterior insula, putamen, hypothalamus		Inhibition and devaluation: medial and left lateral OFC, lateral temporal cortex Inhibition of motor reaction: caudate nucleus, cACC	
	Comparison							
Wiebking et al. (2006)	No such contrast							
Walter et al. (2007)	No such contrast							
Sartorius et al. (2008)	Children vs neutral		Amygdala					

Schiffer et al. (2008a)	Nude girl vs dressed girl	Precentral gyrus, fusiform gyrus, ITG, IPL, SPL	Insula, amygdala	ACC, substantia nigra, SPL	ACC, insula	Caudate body, middle temporal gyrus	Frontal lobe (VLPFC, DLPFC, FPPFC), thalamus, hippocampus, parahippocampal gyrus, middle, inferior occipital gyrus, precuneus
Schiffer et al. (2008b)	Nude boy vs dressed boy	Fusiform gyrus, ITG, SPL	Postcentral gyrus	ACC, substantia nigra, SPL	ACC, putamen	Caudate head, middle, superior temporal gyrus	Inferior, middle superior frontal gyrus, globus pallidus, precuneus, middle occipital gyrus
Poeppl et al. (2011)	Children vs neutral	ITG/fusiform gyrus, precentral gyrus, SPL	Hippocampus–amygdala complex, postcentral gyrus	SPL		Superior temporal gyrus	Middle frontal gyrus, posterior cingulate gyrus, calcarine gyrus, parahippocampal gyrus/hippocampus, middle occipital gyrus

(continued overleaf)

Table 43.2 (*Continued*)

Study	Four-component model				Inhibitory component	Additional brain regions not assigned to the four-component model
	Excitatory components		Motivational	Autonomic		
Component:	*Cognitive*	*Emotional*	*Motivational*	*Autonomic*		
Brain region:	Attention: IPL, SPL Appraisal: *right lateral OFC, ITG* Motor imagery: *vPM, SMA, CB, IPL*	*Somatosensory cortex (SI, SII), amygdala, posterior insula*	*ACC, claustrum, posterior parietal cortex, hypothalamus, substantia nigra, ventral striatum*	*ACC, anterior insula, putamen, hypothalamus*	Inhibition and devaluation: *medial and left lateral OFC, lateral temporal cortex* Inhibition of motor reaction: *caudate nucleus, cACC*	

Comparison

Ponseti et al. (2012) No such contrast
Habermeyer et al. (2013) No such contrast

AM, amygdala; ACC, anterior cingulate cortex; CB, cerebellum; IPL, inferior parietal lobule; OFC, orbitofrontal cortex; SMA, supplementary motor area; SPL, superior parietal lobule; TC, temporal cortex; vPM, ventral premotor cortex; VLPFC, ventral lateral prefrontal cortex; DLPFC, dorsal lateral prefrontal cortex; FPPFC, frontopolar prefrontal cortex.

Table 43.3 Results of the brain imaging studies examining paedophilic interest for the comparison between paedophile subjects and a control group. The specific contrast per study is given. The activated brain regions are arranged according to the four-component model of Stoléru et al. (2012) (see the section Neurobiology of Sexuality and the Measurement of Sexual Arousal in Healthy Subjects)

Study	Four-component model					Additional brain regions not assigned to the four-component model
	Excitatory components				Inhibitory component	
	Cognitive	Emotional	Motivational	Autonomic		
Component:	*Attention:* IPL, SPL *Appraisal: right lateral* OFC, ITG *Motor imagery:* vPM, SMA, CB, IPL	*Somatosensory cortex (SI, SII), amygdala, posterior insula*	*ACC, claustrum, posterior parietal cortex, hypothalamus, substantia nigra, ventral striatum*	*ACC, anterior insula, putamen, hypothalamus*	Inhibition and devaluation: *medial and left lateral OFC, lateral temporal cortex* Inhibition of motor reaction: *caudate nucleus, cACC*	
Brain region:						
Comparison						
Dressing et al. (2001)	No such contrast					
Cohen et al. (2002)	EG > CG for: girl n.s.	n.s.	n.s.	n.s.	n.s.	
Wiebking et al. (2006)	EG < CG: erotic vs emotional[a] Lateral parietal cortex	Insula	Lateral parietal cortex	Hypothalamus, insula		Periaqueductal grey

(*continued overleaf*)

Table 43.3 (Continued)

Study	Four-component model					Inhibitory component	Additional brain regions not assigned to the four-component model
	Component:	Cognitive	Emotional	Motivational	Autonomic		
		Excitatory components					
	Brain region:	*Attention:* IPL, SPL *Appraisal: right lateral OFC, ITG Motor imagery: vPM, SMA, CB, IPL*	*Somatosensory cortex (SI, SII), amygdala, posterior insula*	*ACC, claustrum, posterior parietal cortex, hypothalamus, substantia nigra, ventral striatum*	*ACC, anterior insula, putamen, hypothalamus*	Inhibition and devaluation: *medial and left lateral OFC, lateral temporal cortex* Inhibition of motor reaction: *caudate nucleus, cACC*	
Comparison							
Walter et al. (2007)	EG < CG: erotic vs emotional[a]	Lateral parietal cortex	Insula	Lateral parietal cortex	Hypothalamus, insula		Dorsolateral prefrontal cortex, occipital cortex
Sartorius et al. (2008)	EG > CG for: child > adult		Amygdala				
Schiffer et al. (2008a)	EG > CG for: girl	Fusiform gyrus					Hippocampus, thalamus, pulvinar

	EG > CG for: preferred > neutral					ACC		frontal lobe: DLPFC
Schiffer et al. (2008b)	EG > CG for: boy[b]			ACC				Ventromedial prefrontal cortex DLPFC
	EG > CG for: preferred > neutral[b]	Fusiform gyrus						
Poeppl et al. (2011)	EG > CG for: child > neutral	Cerebellum	Medial temporal lobe (insula)				Middle temporal gyrus	Posterior cingulate gyrus, thalamus, medial frontal lobe, hippocampus
	EG > CG for: preferred > neutral	IPL	Postcentral gyrus, insula		Anterior midcingulate gyrus, IPL	Anterior midcingulate gyrus, insula	Middle temporal gyrus	
Ponseti et al. (2012)	EG > CG for: boy > man	Cerebellum, fusiform gyrus, ITG, angular gyrus						Lingual gyrus, anterior thalamus, hippocampus, occipital lobe
	EG > CG for: girl > woman	SPL, ITG, fusiform gyrus, cerebellum	Amygdala, insula		Cingulate gyrus	Cingulate gyrus, insula	Caudate nucleus	Occipital lobe, inferior frontal gyrus, thalamus

(continued overleaf)

Table 43.3 (*Continued*)

Study	Four-component model						Additional brain regions not assigned to the four-component model
	Component:	Cognitive	Emotional	Motivational	Autonomic	Inhibitory component	
		Excitatory components					
	Brain region:	Attention: *IPL, SPL* Appraisal: *right lateral OFC, ITG* Motor imagery: *vPM, SMA, CB, IPL*	Somatosensory cortex (SI, SII), amygdala, posterior insula	ACC, claustrum, posterior parietal cortex; hypothalamus, substantia nigra, ventral striatum	ACC, anterior insula, putamen, hypothalamus	Inhibition and devaluation: *medial and left lateral OFC, lateral temporal cortex* Inhibition of motor reaction: *caudate nucleus, cACC*	
	Comparison						
Habermeyer et al. (2013)	EG > CG for: girl > woman	Right lateral OFC					

AM, amygdala; ACC, anterior cingulate cortex; CB, cerebellum; IPL, inferior parietal lobule; OFC, orbitofrontal cortex; SMA, supplementary motor area; SPL, superior parietal lobule; TC, temporal cortex; vPM, ventral premotor cortex; VLPFC, ventral lateral prefrontal cortex; DLPFC; dorsal lateral prefrontal cortex; FPPFC, frontopolar prefrontal cortex; CG, control group; EG, experimental group.

Note by Schiffer et al.:

[a]Wiebking et al. (2006) and Walter et al. (2006) analysed *decreased* activation patterns in paedophilic patients (EG) *vs* healthy controls (CG) for the contrast erotic pictures *vs* emotional pictures.

[b]Comparisons need to be interpreted carefully because the control subjects generally showed weaker activations.

Table 43.4 Results of brain imaging studies examining paedophilic interest for the comparison of the sexually preferred stimuli and the non-preferred stimuli in the paedophile subjects (or similar appropriate comparisons). The activated brain regions are arranged according to the four-component model of Stoléru et al. (2012) (see the section Neurobiology of Sexuality and the Measurement of Sexual Arousal in Healthy Subjects)

Study	Four-component model					Additional brain regions not assigned to the four-component model
	Excitatory components				Inhibitory component	
Component:	Cognitive	Emotional	Motivational	Autonomic		
Brain region:	Attention: IPL, SPL Appraisal: *right lateral OFC, ITG* Motor imagery: *vPM, SMA, CB, IPL*	Somatosensory cortex (SI, SII), amygdala, posterior insula	ACC, claustrum, posterior parietal cortex, hypothalamus, substantia nigra, ventral striatum	ACC, anterior insula, putamen, hypothalamus	Inhibition and devaluation: *medial and left lateral OFC, lateral temporal cortex* Inhibition of motor reaction: *caudate nucleus, cACC*	
Comparison						
Dressing et al. (2001) Boy vs woman	Right OFC, fusiform gyrus (ITG)		ACC (basal ganglia)	ACC		Occipital cortex, brain stem, prefrontal cortex
Cohen et al. (2002) No such contrast						
Wiebking et al. (2006) No such contrast						

(continued overleaf)

Table 43.4 (Continued)

Study	Four-component model						Additional brain regions not assigned to the four-component model
	Component:	Cognitive	Emotional	Motivational	Autonomic	Inhibitory component	
			Excitatory components				
	Brain region:	Attention: IPL, SPL Appraisal: right lateral OFC, ITG Motor imagery: vPM, SMA, CB, IPL	Somatosensory cortex (SI, SII), amygdala, posterior insula	ACC, claustrum, posterior parietal cortex, hypothalamus, substantia nigra, ventral striatum	ACC, anterior insula, putamen, hypothalamus	Inhibition and devaluation: medial and left lateral OFC, lateral temporal cortex Inhibition of motor reaction: caudate nucleus, cACC	
	Comparison						
Walter et al. (2007)	No such contrast						
Sartorius et al. (2008)	Children vs adults		Amygdala				
Schiffer et al. (2008a)	Girl vs woman	Insula	Insula		Insula		Frontal lobe: DLPFC, thalamus, hippocampus, inferior, middle occipital gyrus

Schiffer et al. (2008b)	Boy vs man	Inferior temporal gyrus	Insula, amygdala	Insula		Inferior and middle frontal gyrus, parahippocampal gyrus, precuneus, middle temporal gyrus, middle occipital gyrus
Poeppl et al. (2011)	Children vs adult	Fusiform gyrus, cerebellum, inferior frontal gyrus (orbital)	Insula	Insula, putamen	Superior, middle temporal gyrus, inferior frontal gyrus (orbital)	Inferior, middle, medial frontal gyrus, hippocampus, parahippocampal gyrus, precuneus, thalamus, midbrain, cuneus, middle, inferior occipital gyrus
Ponseti et al. (2012)	No such contrast					
Habermeyer et al. (2013)	Girl vs woman	Right lateral OFC				

AM, amygdala; ACC, anterior cingulate cortex; CB, cerebellum; IPL, inferior parietal lobule; OFC, orbitofrontal cortex; SMA, supplementary motor area; SPL, superior parietal lobule; TC, temporal cortex; vPM, ventral premotor cortex; VLPFC, ventral lateral prefrontal cortex; DLPFC, dorsal lateral prefrontal cortex; FPPFC, frontopolar prefrontal cortex; CG, control group; EG, experimental group.

thalamus, hippocampus, and occipital regions. Interestingly, Stoléru et al. (2012) discussed most of these brain regions in their review, with the finding that many studies with healthy subjects also reported activations in those regions. Nevertheless, they did not include these brain regions in the four-component model. In the section Neurobiology of Sexuality and the Measurement of Sexual Arousal in Healthy Subjects, the involvement of these brain regions in sexual arousal and preference was discussed. Additionally, the hippocampal/parahippocampal regions, parts of the limbic system, were described as being activated in two studies. The processing of emotional aspects but also memory processes might be associated with activations in those regions.

Hence, despite some inconsistencies, we can conclude that the four-component model of sexual arousal and the additionally described brain regions, proposed on basis of studies with healthy subjects, may also be valid for paedophilic subjects when viewing their preferred stimuli. It should be pointed out that not all studies reported activations in each of the four components. One possible reason for the difference in activations might lie in the use of the specific type of stimuli: studies with healthy subjects used explicit sexual stimuli, whereas studies with paedophiles used non-explicit sexual stimuli.

The second relevant question is whether there are differences between haemodynamic responses of paedophiles and healthy subjects while viewing sexual stimuli. The differentiation between a normophilic and a paedophilic preference is probably the most interesting question with regard to the clinical application of fMRI as an assessment tool for deviant sexual preference. Table 43.3 shows selected results from the 10 studies, presenting different comparisons between the two groups. These group comparisons comprise the analysis of child stimuli, differences between child and adult stimuli, and differences between preferred and non-preferred stimuli. Despite this large variability of the analysed comparisons, one can conclude that paedophilic subjects exhibit stronger haemodynamic responses to child stimuli than healthy subjects in various brain regions associated with sexual arousal. These stronger haemodynamic responses affect the fusiform gyrus, parietal areas, the amygdala, insula, and ACC, but also prefrontal, hippocampal, and thalamic activations. Some studies pointed out that paedophiles show stronger activations than healthy subjects while watching their preferred stimulus (children in the case of paedophiles, adults in the case of healthy subjects) (Poeppl et al., 2011; Ponseti et al., 2012). The involved brain regions embody all four excitatory components of sexual arousal, and also memory and control functions. Only two studies considered the inhibitory component (Poeppl et al., 2011; Ponseti et al., 2012). Four of the 10 studies reported also the opposite comparison, i.e., the extent to which control subjects showed stronger haemodynamic responses to adult stimuli than paedophiles. However, the results are inconsistent, varying from no group differences (Sartorius et al., 2008), small and focal subcortical stronger activations (Poeppl et al., 2011; Ponseti et al., 2012), to widespread stronger activations in healthy subjects compared with paedophiles when viewing adult stimuli (Schiffer, Krüger et al., 2008; Schiffer, Paul, et al., 2008). The variable stimulus presentation time, varying from 1 to 35 s (see Table 43.1), could provide one possible reason for these inconsistent results. Thus, so far it is not clear whether paedophiles show generally stronger brain activation to their preferred sexual stimuli (child) in relation to the responses of healthy subjects to their preferred stimuli (adult).

The important question from a clinical point of view is whether or not there is an adequate method to differentiate between normophilic and paedophilic subjects. In our opinion, the comparison between the two groups according to the question of whether or not they show stronger activations to child versus adult stimuli (or vice versa) could form an adequate method. Sartorius et al. (2008) and Ponseti et al. (2012) reported the outcomes of these comparisons, but with different results. In the study of Sartorius et al. (2008), the amygdala was the only region that was more strongly activated in the paedophilic group than in the control group, whereas Ponseti et al. (2012) found a widespread stronger activation in the paedophilic group compared with the healthy subjects. Ponseti et al. (2012) provided a new classification approach to differentiate between the two groups, which is discussed in the next section.

Another important question regarding the measurement of sexual preference in paedophilic subjects is whether they respond differentially to their preferred sexual stimulus compared with their non-preferred sexual stimulus. From a scientific point of view, this comparison allows the exploration of the specific neurofunctional basis of a paedophilic preference. From a more clinical point of view, this contrast could allow the differentiation between the exclusive type of paedophilia and the non-exclusive type. Some imaging studies examined this question by analysing the haemodynamic responses to children compared with adults within the group of paedophiles (see Table 43.4). As can be seen from Table 43.4, the results of the studies show great variability regarding the reported brain regions. Taking these results together, a stronger activation in reaction to children compared with adults has been found in the OFC, the fusiform gyrus, the inferior temporal and inferior frontal gyrus, the amygdala, insula, and the ACC, but also in hippocampal and thalamic regions. These results partially match the results of those studies with healthy subjects, which examined differential haemodynamic responses regarding the hetero- or homosexual orientation (see the section Measurement of Sexual Preference in Healthy Subjects). In healthy hetero- and homosexual subjects, the hypothalamus, posterior parietal areas, premotor cortex, and ventral striatum respond differentially to the preferred stimulus. These brain structures are linked to the cognitive, motivational, and autonomic component. In paedophiles, several brain regions, which are mainly linked with the cognitive, emotional, and autonomic component of sexual arousal, seem to respond differently to child and adult stimuli (see Table 43.4).

At the same time, it is questionable whether it is plausible to compare these activation patterns in paedophiles with the results of studies examining sexual preference in healthy subjects. Studies with healthy subjects mostly ask for differences regarding the gender of the stimuli, e.g., the preference for women or men. In contrast, studies examining paedophilic sexual preference are interested in differences with respect to the age of the presented stimulus, e.g., child or adult. In general, each stimulus can serve as a sexually preferred stimulus. One approach to distinguish between the two effects was presented by Habermeyer et al. (2013) (see Table 43.1). In this study, an analysis of variance was applied with the factors age and gender of the stimulus. According to the results, the gender factor explained the variance in various brain structures, whereas the age factor only explained the variance in the superior frontal gyrus. Considering the ongoing debate on defining paedophilia as a sexual orientation (e.g., Seto, 2012), both factors (gender and age of the presented stimuli) should be considered and analysed in imaging studies.

fMRI as an Assessment Tool for Sexual Preferences

So far, we do not have a convenient clinical tool for assessing sexual preference using brain imaging methods. A first approach to establishing such a tool was reported by Ponseti et al. (2012), who used a new automatic classification approach to differentiate between normophilic and paedophilic subjects (Soriano-Mas et al., 2007). This study is discussed below in more detail, pointing out both the potential and the limitations.

In this fMRI study, Ponseti et al. (2012) examined 24 paedophilic outpatients and 32 healthy male controls. Each paedophilic patient openly admitted to paedophilia. According to the self-report questionnaire, seven out of the 24 paedophilic subjects belonged to the non-exclusive type. Groups were matched in terms of age and intelligence. The task required the subjects to watch passively images of entire persons or genitals, which were compared with a set of non-sexual stimuli (see Table 43.1). In addition to the already described analyses (see Tables 43.2–43.4), an individual expression value was calculated for the subjects in order to determine the classification accuracy. This individual expression value represented the difference between the individual differential functional imaging maps (e.g., haemodynamic responses for the comparison boys versus men; girls versus women) and the group mean for the same contrasts. These individual expression values were subjected to two different classification analyses. The Fisher's linear discriminant classification analyses revealed the best classification results for the four classes, the hetero- and homosexual healthy subjects and the hetero- and homosexual paedophilic subjects. Only three participants were misclassified (as false negative). Of the three misclassified paedophiles, two were heterosexual and one was homosexual. All of them belonged to the non-exclusive type. For this classification analysis, a specificity of 100% and a sensitivity of 88% were reached.

Hence, by using these individual expression values, Ponseti et al. (2012) were able to classify normophilic subjects and paedophilic patients correctly according to their individual sexual preference. This approach is of great interest, because it not only shows group differences but could also be able to differentiate between normophilic and paedophilic sexual preference on the basis of the individual brain activation patterns of the subject. Nevertheless, several issues have to be considered, mostly the need for further validation studies with other subjects, e.g., denying their paedophilic preference. Another crucial limitation is the inclusion of exclusive and non-exclusive paedophiles in one group, as shown in the misclassification of three non-exclusive paedophilic subjects. Intelligence was matched up using only one subtest of the most common IQ test, which could be problematic because of the well-known fact that paedophiles often show lower intelligence scores than healthy subjects. Furthermore, it is not clear if the presentation of child genitals leads to the sexual arousal patterns as described in the sections above, or might also cause feelings of disgust, shame, or even psychological strain.

Summary

In this section, the methods used in the 10 brain imaging studies to assess sexual preference in paedophiles were introduced. In Table 43.1, the experimental details are summarized. Studies differ in the number of included subjects, the presented experimental and control stimuli, the presentation time, and also the applied experimental design. Despite interesting and new results, these methodological differences might partially cause the great variability of the results.

In general, the results of these 10 studies demonstrate that paedophilic subjects show similar brain activations to healthy subjects while watching their preferred sexual stimulus. Hence the four-component model of sexual arousal can also be applied to paedophiles. But it is still not clear if paedophiles generally respond more strongly or more weakly to their preferred stimulus compared with normophilic subjects. Within the group of paedophiles, the detected activation patterns regarding the difference between the haemodynamic responses to the preferred sexual stimulus compared with the non-preferred sexual stimulus did not reveal a clear picture. Probably the cognitive, autonomic, and emotional component of sexual arousal plays a role regarding this specific question.

We also discussed a first approach to the use of fMRI as a clinical tool for the assessment of sexual (deviant) preference. This automatic classification approach seems to be a promising objective clinical tool for assessing sexual deviant preference, but further research is needed.

Potential and Limitations of the Assessment of Sexual Preference Using fMRI – Suggestions for Future Development

The application of structural and functional brain imaging methods has significantly enhanced our knowledge of the neural correlates of sexual arousal and sexual preference. The results of functional brain imaging methods measuring sexual arousal and sexual preference deliver a new and complex picture about the neural basis of these functions in healthy subjects and paraphilic patients. In contrast to clinical interviews or questionnaires, the application of functional neuroimaging methods is a promising step towards a reliable tool for assessing sexual preference without any conscious subjective response of the patient. However, only one study demonstrated this approach using an automatic classification algorithm. Therefore, further research is needed before functional imaging can be used as a clinical tool.

Recently, four case studies showed that fMRI can also detect changes in brain activation patterns in response to visual sexual stimuli probably evoked by antiandrogen treatment (Habermeyer et al., 2012; Jordan, Fromberger, Laubinger, Dechent, & Müller, 2014; Moulier et al., 2012; Schiffer, Gizewski, & Krüger, 2009). This approach demonstrates the potential of neuroimaging methods in evaluating therapeutic effects in forensic psychiatry and psychology. Up to now, this has only been demonstrated for antiandrogen therapy based on these few case studies. However, it also seems possible to depict psychotherapeutic changes as has already been done with regard to other psychiatric disorders (e.g., Hoflich, Baldinger, Savli, Lanzenberger, & Kasper, 2012).

Combining the eye tracking method with simultaneous functional imaging could also give a more detailed insight into the underlying neurofunctional processes of deviant sexual interest and at the same time increase the diagnostic accuracy. However, so far no such study has been published. In summary, functional neuroimaging techniques provide much more potential for a reliable clinical application regarding paraphilia than has been shown until now.

In addition to the development of the recently introduced approaches to assessing sexual preference, we propose the improvement of the experimental designs. In our view, it is essential to include a forensic control group in order to accomplish better group matching. Furthermore, an active task capturing the subject's attention could contribute to lower individual variability between subjects. Another stimulation design useful for avoiding possible manipulations by the subjects seems to be the subliminal presentation of visual sexual stimuli. Subliminal stimuli are shown with a presentation time of 50 ms at the most. The threshold of 50 ms ensures that the stimuli are in most instances not consciously perceivable by the subjects, which decreases the possibility of manipulation of the subjective reaction. It has been shown that the subliminal presentation of visual sexual stimuli can elicit haemodynamic responses in brain areas that are linked with the four components of sexual arousal (e.g., Gillath & Canterberry, 2012; Jordan et al., 2014). Owing to ethical concerns, we recommend the use of non-explicit sexual stimuli. As demonstrated in this chapter, similarly to explicit sexual stimuli, non-explicit sexual stimuli could evoke haemodynamic responses in brain regions that are equally linked to the four components of sexual arousal. If the technical adjustment is possible, additional psychophysiological measures, e.g., skin conductance or PPG, could enhance the information on the processing of sexual stimuli.

Even though we are convinced that in the future the application of functional brain imaging can be a useful tool for assessing sexual preference, it should always be used in combination with other diagnostic instruments, i.e., clinical interviews, questionnaires, and direct or indirect psychophysiological methods. A potential fMRI tool could reveal additional information about the sexual preference of the subject, which is more or less independent of the subjective answers of the subject. The combination of the different methods could enhance the diagnostic accuracy.

Acknowledgement

We thank Sarah Jung for careful linguistic revision of the text.

References

Bancroft, J. (2009). Models of human sexuality: The role of theory. In J. Bancroft (Ed.), *Human sexuality and its problems* (3rd ed., pp. 5–19). Edinburgh, Scotland: Churchill Livingstone.

Bancroft, J., Graham, C. A., Janssen, E., & Sanders, S. A. (2009). The dual control model: Current status and future directions. *Journal of Sex Research, 46*(2), 121–142.

Bancroft, J., & Janssen, E. (2000). The dual control model of male sexual response: A theoretical approach to centrally mediated erectile dysfunction. *Neuroscience and Biobehavioral Reviews*, 24(5), 571–579.

Beech, A. R., Kalmus, E., Tipper, S. P., Baudouin, J. Y., Flak, V., & Humphreys, G. W. (2008). Children induce an enhanced attentional blink in child molesters. *Psychological Assessment*, 20(4), 397–402. doi:10.1037/a0013587

Berger, A. (2003). Positron emission tomography. *British Medical Journal*, 326(7404), 1449. doi:10.1136/bmj.326.7404.1449

Bigler, E. D., Allen, M., & Stimac, G. K. (2012). MRI and functional MRI. In J. R. Simpson (Ed.), *Neuroimaging in forensic psychiatry* (pp. 27–40). Chichester, England: John Wiley & Sons, Ltd.

Blanchard, R., Klassen, P., Dickey, R., Kuban, M. E., & Blak, T. (2001). Sensitivity and specificity of the phallometric test for pedophilia in nonadmitting sex offenders. *Psychological Assessment*, 13(1), 118–126.

Brown, A. S., Gray, N. S., & Snowden, R. J. (2009). Implicit measurement of sexual associations in child sex abusers. *Sexual Abuse: A Journal of Research and Treatment*, 21(2), 166–180.

Burns, J. M., & Swerdlow, R. H. (2003). Right orbitofrontal tumor with pedophilia symptom and constructional apraxia sign. *Archives of Neurology*, 60(3), 437–440.

Cantor, J., & Blanchard, R. (2012). White matter volumes in pedophiles, hebephiles, and teleiophiles. *Archives of Sexual Behavior*, 41(4), 749–752. doi:10.1007/s10508-012-9954-2

Cantor, J. M., Kabani, N., Christensen, B. K., Zipursky, R. B., Barbaree, H. E., Dickey, R., ... Blanchard, R. (2008). Cerebral white matter deficiencies in pedophilic men. *Journal of Psychiatric Research*, 42(3), 167–183.

Cohen, L. J., Nikiforov, K., Gans, S., Poznansky, O., McGeoch, P., Weaver, C., ... Galynker, I. (2002). Heterosexual male perpetrators of childhood sexual abuse: A preliminary neuropsychiatric model. *Psychiatric Quarterly*, 73(4), 313–336.

Dressing, H., Obergriesser, T., Tost, H., Kaumeier, S., Ruf, M., & Braus, D. F. (2001). Homosexuelle Pädophilie und funktionelle Netzwerke – eine fMRI-Fallstudie. [Homosexual paedophilia and functional networks – An fMRI case report and literature review]. *Fortschritte der Neurologie-Psychiatrie*, 69(11), 539–544.

Everaerd, W. (1988). Commentary on sex research: Sex as an emotion. *Journal of Psychology & Human Sexuality*, 1(2), 3–15.

Freund, K., & Blanchard, R. (1989). Phallometric diagnosis of pedophilia. *Journal of Consulting and Clinical Psychology*, 57(1), 100–105.

Freund, K., Diamant, J., & Pinkava, V. (1958). On the validity and reliability of the phalloplethysmographic (Php) diagnosis of some sexual deviations. *Review of Czechoslovak Medicine*, 4(2), 145–151.

Freund, K., & Watson, R. J. (1991). Assessment of the sensitivity and specificity of a phallometric test: An update of phallometric diagnosis of pedophilia. *Psychological Assessment*, 3, 254–260.

Fromberger, P. (2010). Funktionelle Magnetresonanztomographie und Blickregistrierung bei sexueller Erregung: Neue Perspektiven für die Grundlagenforschung bei pädosexuellen Straftätern? In J. L. Müller (Ed.), *Neurobiologie forensisch-relevanter Störungen* (pp. 440–452). Stuttgart, Germany: Kohlhammer.

Fromberger, P., Jordan, K., Steinkrauss, H., von Herder, J., Stolpmann, G., Kröner-Herwig, B., & Müller, J. L. (2013). Eye movements in pedophiles: Automatic and controlled attentional processes while viewing prepubescent stimuli. *Journal of Abnormal Psychology*, 122(2), 587–599. doi:10.1037/a0030659

Fromberger, P., Jordan, K., Steinkrauss, H., von Herder, J., Witzel, J., Stolpmann, G., ... Müller, J. L. (2012). Diagnostic accuracy of eye movements in assessing pedophilia. *Journal of Sexual Medicine, 9*(7), 1868–1882. doi:10.1111/j.1743-6109.2012.02754.x

Fromberger, P., Krippl, M., Stolpmann, G., & Müller, J. (2007). Neurobiologie der pädophilen Störung – eine methodenkritische Darstellung bisheriger Forschungsergebnisse [Neurobiology of pedophilia – a critical review of present findings and paradigms]. *Forensische Psychiatrie, Psychologie, Kriminologie, 1*(4), 249–258.

Fromberger, P., Stolpmann, G., Jordan, K., & Müller, J. L. (2009). Neurobiologische Forschung bei Pädophilie – Ergebnisse und deren Konsequenzen für die Diagnostik pädosexueller Straftäter [Neurobiological research on pedophilia – results and their consequences for the assessment of pedophilic offenders]. *Zeitschrift für Neuropsychologie, 20*(3), 193–205.

Gillath, O., & Canterberry, M. (2012). Neural correlates of exposure to subliminal and supraliminal sexual cues. *Social Cognitive and Affective Neuroscience, 7*(8), 924–936. doi:10.1093/scan/nsr065

Glasgow, D. V. (2009). Affinity: The development of a self-report assessment of paedophile sexual interest incorporating a viewing time validity measure. In D. Thornton & D. R. Laws (Eds.), *Cognitive approaches to the assessment of sexual interest in sexual offenders* (pp. 59–84). Chichester, England: John Wiley & Sons, Ltd.

Graber, B., Hartmann, K., Coffman, J. A., Huey, C. J., & Golden, C. J. (1982). Brain damage among mentally disordered sex offenders. *Journal of Forensic Sciences, 27*(1), 125–134.

Habermeyer, B., Esposito, F., Handel, N., Lemoine, P., Klarhofer, M., Mager, R., ... Graf, M. (2013). Immediate processing of erotic stimuli in paedophilia and controls: A case control study. *BMC Psychiatry, 13*(1), 88.

Habermeyer, B., Händel, N., Lemoine, P., Klarhöfer, M., Seifritz, E., Dittmann, V., & Graf, M. (2012). LH–RH agonists modulate amygdala response to visual sexual stimulation: A single case fMRI study in pedophilia. *Neurocase, 18*(6), 489–495. doi:10.1080/13554794.2011.627346

Hanson, R. K., & Morton-Bourgon, K. E. (2005). The characteristics of persistent sexual offenders: A meta-analysis of recidivism studies. *Journal of Consulting and Clinical Psychology, 73*(6), 1154–1163.

Hoflich, A., Baldinger, P., Savli, M., Lanzenberger, R., & Kasper, S. (2012). Imaging treatment effects in depression. *Reviews in the Neurosciences, 23*(3), 227–252. doi:10.1515/revneuro-2012-0038

Howes, R. J. (1995). A survey of plethysmographic assessment in North America. *Sexual Abuse: A Journal of Research and Treatment, 7*(1), 9–24. doi:10.1177/107906329500700104

Janssen, E., Everaerd, W., Spiering, M., & Janssen, J. (2000). Automatic processes and the appraisal of sexual stimuli: Toward an information processing model of sexual arousal. *Journal of Sex Research, 37*(1), 8–23.

Jordan, K., Fromberger, P., Laubinger, H., Dechent, P., & Müller, J. L. (2014). Changed processing of visual sexual stimuli under GnRH-therapy – a single case study in pedophilia using eye tracking and fMRI. *BMC Psychiatry, 14*(1), 142.

Jordan, K., Fromberger, P., & Müller, J. L. (2013). Neurobiologie der Sexualität und sexueller Störungen. In P. Briken & M. Berner (Eds.), *Praxisbuch Sexuelle Störungen*. Stuttgart, Germany: Thieme.

Jordan, K., Fromberger, P., Stolpmann, G., & Müller, J. L. (2011a). The role of testosterone in sexuality and paraphilia – a neurobiological approach. Part I: Testosterone and sexuality. *Journal of Sexual Medicine, 8*(11), 2993–3007. doi:10.1111/j.1743-6109.2011.02394.x

Jordan, K., Fromberger, P., Stolpmann, G., & Müller, J. L. (2011b). The role of testosterone in sexuality and paraphilia – a neurobiological approach. Part II: Testosterone and paraphilia. *Journal of Sexual Medicine, 8*(11), 3008–3029. doi:10.1111/j.1743-6109.2011.02393.x

Joyal, C. C., Black, D. N., & Dassylva, B. (2007). The neuropsychology and neurology of sexual deviance: A review and pilot study. *Sexual Abuse: A Journal of Research and Treatment, 19*(2), 155–173.

Kagerer, S., Klucken, T., Wehrum, S., Zimmermann, M., Schienle, A., Walter, B., … Stark, R. (2011). Neural activation toward erotic stimuli in homosexual and heterosexual males. *Journal of Sexual Medicine, 8*(11), 3132–3143. doi:10.1111/j.1743-6109.2011.02449.x

Kalmus, E., & Beech, A. R. (2005). Forensic assessment of sexual interest: A review. *Aggression and Violent Behavior, 10*(2), 193–217.

Kaplan, M. S., & Krueger, R. B. (2010). Diagnosis, assessment, and treatment of hypersexuality. *Journal of Sex Research, 47*(2), 181–198.

Kranz, F., & Ishai, A. (2006). Face perception is modulated by sexual preference. *Current Biology, 16*(1), 63–68.

Krüger, T. H. C., & Schiffer, B. (2011). Neurocognitive and personality factors in homo- and heterosexual pedophiles and controls. *Journal of Sexual Medicine, 8*(6), 1650–1659.

Lang, P. J., Bradley, M. B., & Cuthbert, B. N. (2001). *International Affective Picture System.* Gainesville, FL: NIMH Center for the Study of Emotion and Attention, University of Florida.

Laws, D. R., & Gress, C. L. Z. (2004). Seeing things differently: The viewing time alternative to penile plethysmography. *Legal and Criminological Psychology, 9*(2), 183–196.

Marshall, W. L., & Fernandez, Y. M. (2000). Phallometric testing with sexual offenders: Limits to its value. *Clinical Psychology Review, 20*(7), 807–822.

Mendez, M. F., Chow, T., Ringman, J., Twitchell, G., & Hinkin, C. H. (2000). Pedophilia and temporal lobe disturbances. *The Journal of Neuropsychiatry and Clinical Neurosciences, 12*(1), 71–76.

Mendez, M. F., & Shapira, J. S. (2011). Pedophilic behavior from brain disease. *Journal of Sexual Medicine, 8*(4), 1092–1100.

Mendez, M. F., & Shapira, J. S. (2013). Hypersexual behavior in frontotemporal dementia: A comparison with early-onset Alzheimer's disease. *Archives of Sexual Behavior, 42*(3), 501–509. doi:10.1007/s10508-012-0042-4

Mokros, A., Butz, M., Dombert, B., Santtila, P., Bäuml, K.-H., & Osterheider, M. (2011). Judgment of age and attractiveness in a paired comparison task: Testing a picture set developed for diagnosing paedophilia. *Legal and Criminological Psychology, 16*(2), 323–334. doi:10.1348/135532510x514104

Mokros, A., Dombert, B., Osterheider, M., Zappala, A., & Santtila, P. (2010). Assessment of pedophilic sexual interest with an attentional choice reaction time task. *Archives of Sexual Behavior, 39*(5), 1081–1090.

Molenberghs, P., Cunnington, R., & Mattingley, J. B. (2012). Brain regions with mirror properties: A meta-analysis of 125 human fMRI studies. *Neuroscience and Biobehavioral Reviews, 36*(1), 341–349. doi:10.1016/j.neubiorev.2011.07.004

Moulier, V., Fonteille, V., Pélégrini-Issac, M., Cordier, B., Baron-Laforêt, S., Boriasse, E., … Stoléru, S. (2012). A pilot study of the effects of gonadotropin-releasing hormone agonist therapy on brain activation pattern in a man with pedophilia. *International Journal of Offender Therapy and Comparative Criminology, 56*(1), 50–60. doi:10.1177/0306624X10392191

Müller, J. L. (2011). Are sadomasochism and hypersexuality in autism linked to amygdalohippocampal lesion? *Journal of Sexual Medicine, 8*(11), 3241–3249. doi:10.1111/j.1743-6109.2009.01485.x

O'Donohue, W., Regev, L. G., & Hagstrom, A. (2000). Problems with the DSM-IV diagnosis of pedophilia. *Sexual Abuse: A Journal of Research and Treatment, 12*(2), 95–105.

Ogawa, S., Tank, D. W., Menon, R., Ellermann, J. M., Kim, S. G., Merkle, H., & Ugurbil, K. (1992). Intrinsic signal changes accompanying sensory stimulation: Functional brain mapping with magnetic resonance imaging. *Proceedings of the National Academy of Sciences of the United States of America, 89*(13), 5951–5955.

Pacific Psychological Assessment Corporation. (2004). *The NRP (Not Real People) stimulus set for the assessment of sexual interest*. Victoria, Canada: Pacific Psychological Assessment Corporation.

Paul, T., Schiffer, B., Zwarg, T., Krüger, T. H., Karama, S., Schedlowski, M., ... Gizewski, E. R. (2008). Brain response to visual sexual stimuli in heterosexual and homosexual males. *Human Brain Mapping, 29*(6), 726–735.

Pennington, B. F. (2002). *The development of psychopathology: Nature and nurture*. New York, NY: Guilford Press.

Poeppl, T. B., Langguth, B., Laird, A. R., & Eickhoff, S. B. (2014). The functional neuroanatomy of male psychosexual and physiosexual arousal: A quantitative meta-analysis. *Human Brain Mapping, 35*(4), 1404–1421. doi:10.1002/hbm.22262

Poeppl, T. B., Nitschke, J., Dombert, B., Santtila, P., Greenlee, M. W., Osterheider, M., & Mokros, A. (2011). Functional cortical and subcortical abnormalities in pedophilia: A combined study using a choice reaction time task and fMRI. *Journal of Sexual Medicine, 8*(6), 1660–1674.

Poeppl, T. B., Nitschke, J., Santtila, P., Schecklmann, M., Langguth, B., Greenlee, M. W., ... Mokros, A. (2013). Association between brain structure and phenotypic characteristics in pedophilia. *Journal of Psychiatric Research, 47*(5), 678–685. doi:http://dx.doi.org/10.1016/j.jpsychires.2013.01.003

Ponseti, J., Bosinski, H. A., Wolff, S., Peller, M., Jansen, O., Mehdorn, H. M., ... Siebner, H. R. (2006). A functional endophenotype for sexual orientation in humans. *NeuroImage, 33*(3), 825–833.

Ponseti, J., Granert, O., Jansen, O., Wolff, S., Beier, K., Neutze, J., ... Bosinski, H. (2012). Assessment of pedophilia using hemodynamic brain response to sexual stimuli. *Archives of General Psychiatry, 69*(2), 187–194. doi:10.1001/archgenpsychiatry.2011.130

Rizzolatti, G., & Craighero, L. (2004). The mirror-neuron system. *Annual Review of Neuroscience, 27*(1), 169–192.

Rosen, R. C., & Beck, J. G. (1988). *Patterns of sexual arousal: Psychophysiological processes and clinical applications*. New York, NY: Guilford Press.

Roy, C. S., & Sherrington, C. S. (1890). On the regulation of the blood-supply of the brain. *The Journal of Physiology, 11*(1–2), 85–158.

Rushing, S. E., Pryma, D. A., & Langleben, D. D. (2012). PET and SPECT. In J. R. Simpson (Ed.), *Neuroimaging in forensic psychiatry* (pp. 3–25). Chichester, England: John Wiley & Sons, Ltd.

Sachsenmaier, S. J., & Gress, C. L. Z. (2009). The Abel assessment for sexual interests – 2: A critical review. In D. Thornton & D. R. Laws (Eds.), *Cognitive approaches to the assessment of sexual interest in sexual offenders* (pp. 31–57). Chichester, England: John Wiley & Sons, Ltd.

Sartorius, A., Ruf, M., Kief, C., Demirakca, T., Bailer, J., Ende, G., ... Dressing, H. (2008). Abnormal amygdala activation profile in pedophilia. *European Archives of Psychiatry and Clinical Neuroscience, 258*(5), 271–277.

Schiffer, B., Gizewski, E., & Krüger, T. (2009). Reduced neuronal responsiveness to visual sexual stimuli in a pedophile treated with a long-acting LH–RH agonist. *Journal of Sexual Medicine, 6*(3), 892–894.

Schiffer, B., Krüger, T., Paul, T., de Greiff, A., Forsting, M., Leygraf, N., ... Gizewski, E. (2008). Brain response to visual sexual stimuli in homosexual pedophiles. *Journal of Psychiatry & Neuroscience, 33*(1), 23–33.

Schiffer, B., Paul, T., Gizewski, E., Forsting, M., Leygraf, N., Schedlowski, M., & Krüger, T. H. C. (2008). Functional brain correlates of heterosexual paedophilia. *NeuroImage, 41*(1), 80–91.

Schiffer, B., Peschel, T., Paul, T., Gizewski, E., Forsting, M., Leygraf, N., ... Krüger, T. H. (2007). Structural brain abnormalities in the frontostriatal system and cerebellum in pedophilia. *Journal of Psychiatric Research, 41*(9), 753–762.

Schiltz, K., Witzel, J. G., & Bogerts, B. (2006). Hirnstrukturelle Auffälligkeiten bei pädophilen Probanden im Maßregelvollzug. *Forensische Psychiatrie und Psychotherapie – Werkstattschriften, 13,* 59–77.

Schiltz, K., Witzel, J., Northoff, G., Zierhut, K., Gubka, U., Fellmann, H., ... Bogerts, B. (2007). Brain pathology in pedophilic offenders: Evidence of volume reduction in the right amygdala and related diencephalic structures. *Archives of General Psychiatry, 64*(6), 737–746.

Schmidt, A. F., Mokros, A., & Banse, R. (2013). Is pedophilic sexual preference continuous? A taxometric analysis based on direct and indirect measures. *Psychological Assessment.* doi:10.1037/a0033326

Seto, M. C. (2008). *Pedophilia and sexual offending against children: Theory, assessment, and intervention* (Vol. 1). Washington, DC: American Psychological Association.

Seto, M. C. (2012). Is pedophilia a sexual orientation? *Archives of Sexual Behavior, 41*(1), 231–236. doi:10.1007/s10508-011-9882-6

Smith, P., & Waterman, M. (2004). Processing bias for sexual material: The emotional Stroop and sexual offenders. *Sexual Abuse: A Journal of Research and Treatment, 16*(2), 163–171.

Soriano-Mas, C., Pujol, J., Alonso, P., Cardoner, N., Menchón, J. M., Harrison, B. J., ... Gaser, C. (2007). Identifying patients with obsessive–compulsive disorder using whole-brain anatomy. *NeuroImage, 35*(3), 1028–1037.

Spiering, M., & Everaerd, W. (2007). The sexual unconscious. In E. Janssen (Ed.), *The psychophysiology of sex* (pp. 166–183). Bloomington, IN: Indiana University Press.

Stoléru, S., Fonteille, V., Cornélis, C., Joyal, C., & Moulier, V. (2012). Functional neuroimaging studies of sexual arousal and orgasm in healthy men and women: A review and meta-analysis. *Neuroscience and Biobehavioral Reviews, 36*(6), 1481–1509. doi:10.1016/j.neubiorev.2012.03.006

Stoléru, S., Gregoire, M. C., Gerard, D., Decety, J., Lafarge, E., Cinotti, L., ... Comar, D. (1999). Neuroanatomical correlates of visually evoked sexual arousal in human males. *Archives of Sexual Behavior, 28*(1), 1–21.

Sundaram, T., Jeong, G. W., Kim, T. H., Kim, G. W., Baek, H. S., & Kang, H. K. (2010). Time-course analysis of the neuroanatomical correlates of sexual arousal evoked by erotic video stimuli in healthy males. *Korean Journal of Radiology, 11*(3), 278–285. doi:10.3348/kjr.2010.11.3.278

Tanner, J. M. (1973). Growing up. *Scientific American, 229*(3), 34–43.

Thornton, D., & Laws, D. R. (2009). *Cognitive approaches to the assessment of sexual interest in sexual offenders.* Chichester, England: John Wiley & Sons, Ltd.

Walter, M., Witzel, J., Wiebking, C., Gubka, U., Rotte, M., Schiltz, K., ... Northoff, G. (2007). Pedophilia is linked to reduced activation in hypothalamus and lateral prefrontal cortex during visual erotic stimulation. *Biological Psychiatry, 62*(6), 698–701.

Ward, T., & Beech, A. (2006). An integrated theory of sexual offending. *Aggression and Violent Behavior, 11*(1), 44–63.

Wiebking, C., & Northoff, G. (2013). Neuroimaging in pedophilia. *Current Psychiatry Reports*, *15*(4), 351. doi:10.1007/s11920-013-0351-x

Wiebking, C., Witzel, J., Walter, M., Gubka, U., & Northoff, G. (2006). Vergleich der emotionalen und sexuellen Prozessierung zwischen Gesunden und Patienten mit einer Pädophilie – eine kombinierte Studie aus Neuropsychologie und fMRT. *Forensische Psychiatrie und Psychotherapie – Werkstattschriften*, *13*, 79–93.

Wood, J. N., & Grafman, J. (2003). Human prefrontal cortex: Processing and representational perspectives. *Nature Reviews Neuroscience*, *4*(2), 139–147.

44

Indirect Measures of Deviant Sexual Interest

Ross M. Bartels
University of Lincoln, United Kingdom

Nicola S. Gray
Pastoral Healthcare and Swansea University, United Kingdom

Robert J. Snowden
Cardiff University, United Kingdom

Introduction

Deviant sexual interest (DSI) is a major risk factor for the onset and recurrence of sexual offending (Hanson & Morton-Bourgon, 2005). As a result, addressing DSI is typically a core part of sex offender treatment programmes, hence it is paramount that clinicians (and researchers) have access to a reliable and valid tool for assessing DSI. Historically, DSI has been assessed using self-report, case file information, and penile plethysmography (PPG). However, there are numerous issues with these methods (Kalmus & Beech, 2005). For example, self-report can be easily faked and PPG is expensive, invasive, and also open to faking (Gress & Laws, 2009). As a result, researchers have turned to adapting sociocognitive methods of assessment as they are thought to be less affected by these issues (Thornton & Laws, 2009). These cognitive measures are often interchangeably referred to as 'implicit measures' and 'indirect measures'. However, the two are distinct (De Houwer, 2006). An implicit measure refers to the functional properties of a measurement outcome, such as being 'automatic' in some manner (e.g., lacking voluntary control over the outcome). On the other hand, an indirect measure refers to the nature of the measurement procedure, that is, inferring a construct from a participant's behaviour other than direct expression (e.g., reaction times on a categorization task). Hence, indirect measures can be used to assess both implicit and explicit outcomes.

The Wiley Handbook on the Theories, Assessment, and Treatment of Sexual Offending.
Edited by Douglas P. Boer. Volume II: Assessment, edited by Leam A. Craig and Martin Rettenberger.
© 2017 John Wiley & Sons, Ltd. Published 2017 by John Wiley & Sons, Ltd.

A collection of measures have been adapted for the indirect assessment of DSI. Some authors refer to these as 'attention-based measures' (Gress & Laws, 2009), whereas others prefer the term 'latency-based indirect measures' because the processes underlying each measure are still under investigation (Schmidt, Banse, & Imhoff, 2015). However, not all measures are based on latencies but rather response accuracy (e.g., the Rapid Serial Visual Presentation). Therefore, 'latency/accuracy-based indirect measures' may be a more encompassing term. In this chapter, we will use the term 'indirect measure' review the empirical literature on the most widely researched indirect measures of DSI. For each measure, the procedural details are described followed by a discussion of the available validity and reliability data (Table 44.1 also summarizes this information). Effect sizes are typically used to determine the discriminative ability of a measure. Within the studies reviewed here, the most commonly reported effect sizes are the 'area under the curve' (AUC) statistic (derived from a Receiver Operating Characteristic [ROC]) analysis] and Cohen's d. An AUC of 0.50 can be produced by chance alone and thus suggests that a measure has no discriminatory value; an AUC of 0.75 is the midpoint between worthlessness and perfection, and 0.80 is regarded as good (Santtila et al., 2009). Concerning Cohen's d, a d of 0.2 is regarded as a small effect size, 0.5 is regarded as medium, and 0.8 is large (Cohen, 1988). In addition to their psychometric properties, assumptions about the processes underlying each measure are also discussed. Suggestions for future research are also provided throughout.

Viewing Time

Viewing Time (VT) procedures involve presenting participants with images of target individuals (e.g., adults, children) or scenes (e.g., violence). During each presentation, the individual must rate their level of attractiveness towards the image, while the response-latency is unobtrusively recorded. VT is based on the premise that people spend more time viewing images that they find sexually appealing relative to images that they find sexually unappealing (Rosenzweig, 1942). Research indicates that VT tasks can reliably differentiate between non-offending heterosexual and homosexual males (Bourke & Gormley, 2012; Imhoff et al., 2010; Israel & Strassberg, 2009; Zamansky, 1956). Also, bisexual men and women tend to show non-preferential VTs (Ebsworth & Lalumière, 2012). Given the robustness of the VT effect, researchers have investigated whether it can index DSI.

Harris, Rice, Quinsey, and Chaplin (1996) found that child abusers could be discriminated from non-offenders using a VT deviance index ($d = 1.0$). Other researchers have found similar results between child abusers and non-offending controls (Glasgow, 2009; Mokros et al., 2013; ds from 0.43 to 1.15), and also between a mixed group of sexual offenders and non-offender controls (Gress, Anderson, & Laws, 2013; ds from 0.91 to 1.66). Studies have also shown that VT can discriminate child abusers from various offender control groups, such as non-sexual offenders (Babchishin, Nunes, & Kessous, 2014; Mokros et al., 2013; ds from 0.57 to 1.15) and rapists (Gress, 2005; $d = 1.08$), and also samples comprised of both non-offending and offending controls (Banse, Schmidt, & Clarbour, 2010; Fromberger et al., 2012b; 2013; ds from 0.76 to 0.82). Gress et al. (2013) also found that a mixed group of sexual offenders could

Table 44.1 Summary of the psychometric data from each study that used an indirect measure to assess deviant sexual interest

Measure	Study	Categories	Reliability	Target group (n)	Control group (n)	Reported effect size	Cohen's d equivalent
VT	Harris, Rice, Quinsey, & Chaplin (1996)	Adult–child	n/a	CSO (26)	NOC (25)	$d = 1.00$**	1.00
	Abel, Huffman, Warberg, & Holland (1998)	Adult male	$\alpha = 0.88$	CSO (exact ns not specified)	n/a	$r = 0.60$***	1.50
		Adolescent male	$\alpha = 0.89$			n/a	n/a
		Young male	$\alpha = 0.87$				
		Adult female	$\alpha = 0.86$				
		Adolescent female	$\alpha = 0.84$				
		Young female	$\alpha = 0.90$				
	Letourneau (2002)	Male child (2–4 yrs)	$\alpha = 0.60$				
		Male child (8–10 yrs)	$\alpha = 0.75$				
		Male adolescents	$\alpha = 0.90$				
		Male adults	$\alpha = 0.90$				
		Male children (0–10 yrs)	n/a	CSO with boy victims (10)	SO (47)	$r = 0.69$**	2.51
		Female child (2–4 yrs)	$\alpha = 0.87$				
		Female child (8–10 yrs)	$\alpha = 0.86$				
		Female adolescents	$\alpha = 0.85$				
		Female adults	$\alpha = 0.80$				
		Female children (0–10 yrs)	n/a	CSO with girl victims (34)	SO (23)	$r = 0.08$	0.16

Table 44.1 (Continued)

Measure	Study	Categories	Reliability	Target group (n)	Control group (n)	Reported effect size	Cohen's d equivalent
	Abel et al. (2004)	Children–adults	n/a	Adolescent CSO (1170)	Adolescent NOC (534)	AUC = 0.64[snr]	0.51
	Gress (2005)	Children–adults	n/a	CSO (19)	Rapists (7)	Frequency table	1.08*
	Gray & Plaud (2005)	Not explicitly specified	n/a	Reflexive CSO (28)	Dissimulating CSO (11)	Frequency table	-2.13*
	Worling (2006)	Pre-/post-pubescent[b]	n/a	Adolescent CSO (52)	Adolescent SOC (26)	AUC[b] = 0.61	0.40
		Male toddlers	$\alpha = 0.82$				
		Male preadolescents	$\alpha = 0.79$	CSO with 2+ victims;	SOC (26)	AUC = 0.60	0.36
		Male adolescents	$\alpha = 0.62$				
		Male adults	$\alpha = 0.72$	CSO with any male victims;	SOC (26)	AUC= 0.69**	0.70
		Female toddlers	$\alpha = 0.73$				
		Female preadolescents	$\alpha = 0.82$	CSO with only male victims;	SOC (26)	AUC = 0.73**	0.87
		Female adolescents	$\alpha = 0.77$	CSO with any female victims;	SOC (26)	AUC = 0.42	-0.29
		Female adults	$\alpha = 0.77$	CSO with only female victims	SOC (26)	AUC = 0.43	-0.25
	Glasgow (2009)	Male child	$\alpha = 0.93$				
		Male preadolescent	$\alpha = 0.8$				
		Male adolescent	$\alpha = 0.9$				
		Male adult	$\alpha = 0.89$				
		Female child	$\alpha = 0.92$				

Study	Subgroup	α				
	Female preadolescent	α = 0.87				
	Female adolescent	α = 0.89				
	Female adult	α = 0.93				
	Adult–child	n/a	CSO (31)	NOC (31)	AUC = 0.87[snr]	1.59
Banse, Schmidt, & Clarbour (2010)	Prepubescent males	α = 0.85	CSO (38)	NSOC (37) and NOC (38)	AUC = 0.80*	1.19
	Prepubescent females	α = 0.77			AUC = 0.76*	1.00
	Adult males	α = 0.85			AUC = 0.82*	1.29
	Adult females	α = 0.86			AUC = 0.56	0.21
	Children–adults	n/a			AUC = 0.51	0.04
Fromberger et al. (2012b, 2013)	Children–adults	n/a	Paedophilic CSO (19)	SOC (7) and NOC (48)	AUC = 0.76***	0.99
Babchishin, Nunes, & Kessous (2014)	Child–adult	n/a	CSO (35)	NSOC (21)	d = 1.15*	1.15
			Admitting CSO (20)	NSOC (20)	d = 1.32*	1.32
			Denying CSO (12)	NSOC (20)	d = 1.22*	1.22
Gress, Anderson, & Laws (2013)	Female child	α = 0.94	SO (22)	YNSOC (44)	AUC = 0.66[snr]	0.58
	Male child	α = 0.92			AUC = 0.72[snr]	0.82
	Female mature	α = 0.89			AUC = 0.73[snr]	0.86
	Male mature	α = 0.9			AUC = 0.79[snr]	1.14
	Female child		SO (22)	NOC (59)	AUC = 0.74[snr]	0.91
	Male child				AUC = 0.88[snr]	1.66
	Female mature				AUC = 0.87[snr]	1.59
	Male mature				AUC = 0.84[snr]	1.41

(continued overleaf)

Table 44.1 (Continued)

Measure	Study	Categories	Reliability	Target group (n)	Control group (n)	Reported effect size	Cohen's d equivalent
	Mokros et al. (2013)	Female small child	α = 0.88				
		Female prejuvenile	α = 0.85				
		Female juvenile	α = 0.79				
		Female adult	α = 0.86				
		Male small child	α = 0.82				
		Male prejuvenile	α = 0.83				
		Male juvenile	α = 0.89				
		Male adult	α = 0.83				
		Small children	n/a	CSO (42)	NOC (95)	d = 0.86***	0.86
		Prejuvenile	n/a			d = 0.82***	0.82
		Juvenile	n/a			d = 0.77***	0.77
		Adult	n/a			n/a	n/a
		Adult–child	n/a			AUC = 0.62*	0.43
		Small children	n/a	CSO (42)	NSOC (27)	d = 0.57*	0.57
		Prejuvenile	n/a			d = 0.67**	0.67
		Juvenile	n/a			n/a	n/a
		Adult	n/a			n/a	n/a
		Adult–child	n/a			n/a	n/a
	Gray et al. (2015)	Children images	n/a	Sexual recidivists (22)	Non- (sexual) recidivists (599)	d = 0.71**	0.71
	Schmidt, Gykiere, Vanhoeck, Mann, & Banse (2014)	Prepubescent males	α = 0.95	CSO with male or mixed victims (18)	CSO with female victims (36)	r = 0.47*	1.13

			α	Community BDSM group (134)	Community non-BDSM group (72)		
		Prepubescent females				$r = 0.00$	0.00
		Adult males				$r = 0.47**$	1.13
		Adult females				$r = -0.37**$	0.84
		Children–adults	n/a			$r = 0.42**$	0.98
	Larue et al. (2014)	Non-violent images	$\alpha = 0.96^m$			$d = 0.06$	0.06
			$\alpha = 0.95^f$				
		Violent images	$\alpha = 0.96^m$			$d = -0.95**$	-0.95
			$\alpha = 0.96^f$				
		Violence–non-violence	$\alpha = 0.82^m$			$d = -0.14**$	-0.14
			$\alpha = 0.87^f$				
IAT	Gray, Brown, MacCulloch, Smith, & Snowden (2005)	Children–adults/ Sex–non-sex	n/a	CSO (18)	SOC and NSOC (60)	$d = 0.84*$	0.84
	Nunes, Firestone, & Baldwin (2007)	Children–adults/ Sexy–not sexy	n/a	CSO (24)	NOC (29)	$r = 0.33*$	0.70
	Steffens, Yundina, & Panning (2008)	Erotic–not erotic/ Child–woman	$\alpha = 0.83$	Excl. CSO (17)	Non-excl. CSO (30)	$R_p{}^2 = 0.06*$	0.53
		Erotic–not erotic/ Humiliation–harmony	$\alpha = 0.82$	All SO (46)	NOC (47)	Not reported	n/a
				Unclear	Unclear	n/a	n/a

(continued overleaf)

Table 44.1 (*Continued*)

Measure	Study	Categories	Reliability	Target group (*n*)	Control group (*n*)	Reported effect size	Cohen's *d* equivalent
	Brown, Gray, & Snowden (2009)	Children–adults/ Sex–non-sex	α = 0.80	CSO with victims <12 yrs (54)	CSO with victims >12 yrs (21)	*d* = 0.77**	0.77
			r = 0.63	CSO (54)	NSOC (49)	*d* = 0.92***	0.92
				Admitters (20)	NSOC (49)	*d* = 0.75*	0.75
				Deniers (55)	NSOC (49)	*d* = 1.01**	1.01
				Admitters (20)	Deniers (55)	*d* = 0.27	0.27
	Banse, Schmidt, & Clarbour (2010)	1. Boys–men/ Sexually exciting–sexually unexciting	α = 0.65	CSO (38)	NSOC (37) and NOC (38)	AUC = 0.62*	0.43
		2. Girls–women/ Sexually exciting–sexually unexciting	α = 0.79				AUC = 0.72*	0.82
		3. Children–adults/ Sexually exciting–sexually unexciting	n/a				AUC = 0.71*	0.78
		1		CSO with only boy victims (14)	NSOC (37)	AUC = 0.60	0.36
		2				AUC = 0.67	0.62
		3				AUC = 0.71*	0.78

Study	Measure / Construct	Reliability	Group 1	Group 2	Statistic	Effect
	1		CSO with only girl victims (16)	NSOC (37)	AUC = 0.57	0.25
	2				AUC = 0.56	0.21
	3				AUC = 0.60	0.36
van Leeuwen et al. (2013)	Children–adult/Sexual–neutral	n/a	Self-identified community CSO (20)	NOC (20)	AUC = 0.89^snr	1.73
Babchishin, Nunes, Hermann, & Malcom (2015)	Adult–child/Sexy–not sexy	n/a	CSO (29)	NSOC (28)	$d = 0.32$	0.32
	Woman–girl/Sexy–not sexy	n/a			$d = 0.31$	0.31
	Man–boy/Sexy–not sexy	n/a			$d = 0.27$	0.27
Schmidt, Gykiere, Vanhoeck, Mann, & Banse (2014)	Boys–men/Sexually exciting–sexually unexciting	$\alpha = 0.61$	CSO with male or mixed victims (18)	CSO with only girl victims (36)	$r = 0.29*$	0.64
	Girls–women/Sexually exciting–sexually unexciting	$\alpha = 0.82$			$r = 0.23$	0.50
	Children–adults/Sexually exciting–sexually unexciting	n/a			$r = 0.32*$	0.72
Babchishin, Nunes, & Kessous (2014)	Children–adults/Sexy–not sexy	n/a	CSO (35)	NSOC (21)	$d = 0.44$	0.44
			Admitters (22)	NSOC (21)	$d = 0.35$	0.35
			Deniers (13)	NSOC (21)	$d = 0.51$	0.51

(continued overleaf)

Table 44.1 (*Continued*)

Measure	Study	Categories	Reliability	Target group (n)	Control group (n)	Reported effect size	Cohen's d equivalent
	Larue et al. (2014)	Violence–non-violence/Sexually exciting–sexually unexciting	$\alpha = 0.84^f$ $\alpha = 0.88^m$	Community BDSM group (134)	Community non-BDSM group (72)	$d = -0.73$***	-0.73
Stroop variants	Johnston, Hudson, & Ward (1997) (Emotional Stroop using cards)	Sexual–related	n/a	Preferential CSO (n/a)	Situational CSOs (n/a)	n/a	n/a
					NSOC (n/a)	n/a	n/a
		Child–related	n/a	Preferential CSO (n/a)	Situational CSOs (n/a)	n/a	n/a
					NSOC (n/a)	n/a	n/a
	Smith & Waterman (2004) (Emotional Stroop)	Sexual–neutral	n/a	CSO (5)	Rapists (5)	$t = 0.831$	0.53
	Price & Hanson (2007) (Emotional Stroop)	Sexual–neutral	n/a	CSO (15)	Rapists (15)	n/a	-0.45

Study	Stimuli		Group 1	Group 2		
	Child molesting–neutral	n/a	CSO (15)	VNSOC (15)	n/a	-0.03
			CSO (15)	NVNSOC (15)	n/a	0.14
			CSO (15)	NOC (15)	n/a	0.82 *
			CSO (15)	Rapists (15)	n/a	-0.28
	Rape–neutral	n/a	CSO (15)	VNSOC (15)	n/a	0.26
			CSO (15)	NVNSOC (15)	n/a	0.07
			CSO (15)	NOC (15)	n/a	0.58
			CSO (15)	Rapists (15)	n/a	0.19
Ó Ciardha & Gormley (2012) (Pictorial Stroop)	Children–adults	n/a	CSO (24)	NOC (24)	AUC = 0.56	0.21
van Leeuwen et al. (2013) (Picture–Word Stroop)	Children–adults	n/a	Highly deviant CSO (15)	NOC (24)	AUC = 0.59	0.32
			Self-identified community CSO (20)	NOC (20)	AUC = 0.84^{snr}	1.41
Price, Beech, Mitchell, & Humphreys (2013) (Emotional Stroop)	Sexual–neutral	n/a	SO (27)	NSOC (21)	n/a	0.37
				NOC (36)	r = 0.32*	0.68

(continued overleaf)

Table 44.1 (Continued)

Measure	Study	Categories	Reliability	Target group (n)	Control group (n)	Reported effect size	Cohen's d equivalent
		Aggression–neutral	n/a	SO (27)	NSOC (21)	n/a	−0.06
					NSOC (36)	n/a	0.32
		Personality descriptors–matched controls	n/a	SO (27)	NSOC (21)	n/a	0.22
					NOC (36)	r = 0.29*	0.61
		Physical descriptors–matched controls	n/a	SO (27)	NSOC (21)	n/a	−0.35
					NOC (36)	n/a	−0.29
		Sexual actions–matched controls	n/a	SO (27)	NSOC (21)	n/a	0.27
					NOC (36)	n/a	0.01
	Price, Beech, Mitchell, & Humphreys (2014) (Emotional Stroop)	Sexual–neutral	n/a	ASO (23)	ANSOC (21)	n/a	0.55
					ANOC (20)	n/a	0.67
		Aggression–neutral	n/a	ASO (23)	ANSOC (21)	n/a	0.03
					ANOC (20)	n/a	0.38
		Personality descriptors–matched controls	n/a	ASO (23)	ANSOC (21)	n/a	0.14
					ANOC (21)	n/a	−0.01

Study	Group					
	Physical descriptors–matched controls	n/a	ASO (23)	ANSOC (21)	n/a	0.04
	Sexual actions–matched controls	n/a	ASO (23)	ANOC (21)	n/a	0.01
				ANSOC (21)	n/a	0.03
CRT	Giotakos (2005)	Children–adults	n/a	CSO (27)	ANOC (21)	n/a	0.14
				Rapist (31), NOC (53), and FNOC (24)	n/a	n/a
	Mokros, Dombert, Osterheider, Zappala, & Santtila (2010)	Children–adults	n/a	CSO (21)	NSOC (21)	AUC = 0.84***	1.41
	Poeppl et al. (2011)	Children–adults	n/a	CSO (9)	NSOC (11)	d = 0.99*	0.99
	Gress, Anderson, & Laws (2013)	Female child	α = 0.98	SO (22)	YNSOC (44)	n/a	n/a
		Male child	α = 0.98			n/a	n/a
		Female mature	α = 0.97			n/a	n/a
		Male mature	α = 0.97			n/a	n/a
		Female child		SO (22)	NOC (59)	n/a	n/a
		Male child				n/a	n/a
		Female mature				n/a	n/a
		Male mature				n/a	n/a

(continued overleaf)

Table 44.1 (*Continued*)

Measure	Study	Categories	Reliability	Target group (n)	Control group (n)	Reported effect size	Cohen's d equivalent
RSVP	Beech et al. (2008)	T1 child–T1 animal	n/a	Intrafamilial CSO (16)	NSOC (17)	$r = 0.45$**	1.00
				Extrafamilial CSO (18)	NSOC (17)	$r = 0.54$***	1.28
	Crooks, Rostill-Brookes, Beech, & Bickley (2009)	T1 child–T1 animal	n/a	ACSO (20)	Adolescent NSOC (26)	n/a	n/a
Eye-tracking	Fromberger et al. (2012b)	Children–adults (initial fixation)	n/a	CSO (19)	Rapists (7) & NOC (48)	AUC = 0.90***	1.81
		Children–adults (relative fixation time)	n/a		Rapists (8) & NOC (48)	AUC = 0.83***	1.35

CSO = child sexual offender; NSOC = non-sexual offender control; NOC = non-offender control; SO = sexual offender; ACSO = adolescent child sexual offender; ASO = adolescent sexual offender; ANSOC = adolescent non-sexual offender control; ANOC = adolescent non-offender control; YNSOC = youth non-sexual offender control; AUC = area under the curve; n/a = not available; [m] = male participants only; [f] = female participants only; [b] = All comparisons/effect sizes reported in Worling (2006) are based on the 'Prepubescent/Postpubescent Deviance Index'; [snr] = significance not reported.
*$p < 0.05$; **$p < 0.01$; ***$p < 0.001$.

be discriminated from non-sexual youth offenders (*d*s from 0.58 to 1.14). Abel et al. (2004) found that adolescent child abusers could be distinguished from non-offending adolescents (*d* = 0.51). Similarly, Worling (2006) found that adolescent child abusers with any male/male-only victims (*n* = 52) could be distinguished from adolescent sexual offenders with peer and/or adult victims (*n* = 26, five of whom victimized a male) (*d* = 0.70 and 0.87, respectively).

Assuming that the child abusers had a DSI in children, the above findings indicate that VT has good known-group validity; a form of construct validity (Cronbach & Meehl, 1955). However, not all child abusers harbour a DSI in children (Seto, 2008). Hence, the construct validity of VT can be further examined by comparing subtypes of child abusers. For example, Schmidt, Gykiere, Vanhoeck, Mann, and Banse (2014) found that child abusers with any male/male-only victims viewed child images for longer than child abusers with female-only victims (*d*s from 0.84 to 1.13). Since child abusers with male victims demonstrate stronger paedophilic interests than those without (Seto & Lalumière, 2001), this finding corroborates VT as a measure of DSI in children. Also, Larue et al. (2014) found that a community sample of BDSM participants viewed images of violence (i.e., men being violent towards women) longer than non-BDSM participants (*d* = 0.95) (BDSM is an overlapping abbreviation for 'Bondage and Discipline, Dominance and Submission, Sadism and Masochism; affiliates of BDSM are interested in 'sexual activities that involve explicit consensual sexualized violence' [Larue et al., 2014, p. 1173]). This suggests that VT can index distinct paraphilic interests.

The construct validity of child-related VTs can also be inferred by examining convergent validity. In relation to self-report measures, Babchishin et al. (2014) found that paedophilia scores on the Sexual Interest Profiling Scale (SIPS) (Laws, 1986) correlated with the VT deviance index (*r* = 0.28). In relation to file-based measures of paedophilia, Schmidt et al. (2014) demonstrated that the Screening Scale for Paedophilic Interests (SSPI) (Seto & Lalumière, 2001) correlated with VT for boys (*r* = 0.38) and VT Deviance Index (*r* = 0.48). However, these relationships were not found by Banse et al. (2010) or Babchishin et al. (2014), both of whom found that VT correlates with another indirect measure of DSI, the Implicit Association Test (*r* = 0.33 and 0.26, respectively). Finally, Letourneau (2002) and Stinson and Becker (2008) found that VT converges with paedophilic DSI measured by PPG, with *r*s ranging from 0.20 to 0.61. However, Babchishin et al. (2014) found that VT and PPG indices were negatively associated (e.g., *r* = −0.48). Therefore, although VT shows some convergence with known measures of DSI, the inconsistent findings (i.e., in relation to SIPS and PPG) prevent any solid conclusions from being drawn. The findings may suggest that VT procedures measure a related but distinct construct from those indexed by file-based and PPG measures (Snowden, Craig, & Gray, 2011).

As shown in Table 44.1, internal consistencies (i.e., Cronbach's alpha) across stimulus categories generally range from good (0.72) to excellent (0.95). Mokros et al. (2013) tested the split-half reliability of a child-related VT procedure and found that the coefficients (r_{tt}) ranged from 0.81 to 0.91. There are currently no published test–retest reliability data for VT.

Imhoff et al. (2010) stated that VT effects are often attributed to three underlying processes. One is a deliberate delay driven by an individual's desire to view a sexually attractive stimulus for longer. This is plausible as the non-restricted nature of VT procedures allows for subjective conscious experiences (Ó Ciardha, 2011). However, using non-offenders, Imhoff et al. (2010) showed that VT effects occurred even when (1) stimuli were removed after a fixed time period and (2) the response window was restricted to 1000 ms. This finding rules out the deliberate delay account. It also rules out the idea that VT effects are caused by an attentional adhesion that interferes with participants' performance on the rating task. The third explanation is that a 'sexual content-induced delay' (SCID) (Geer & Bellard, 1996) occurs. SCIDs are thought to occur when a *sexual* stimulus interferes with one's performance on a secondary task. However, Imhoff et al. (2010) found prolonged response latencies for stimuli that had all sexual characteristics removed (i.e., they presented only the heads of target individuals).

The fact that prolonged latencies were found under time-restricted conditions has implications for forensic populations (Imhoff et al., 2010). That is, a speeded variant would turn the procedure into a performance task that measures automatic processes and reduces the ability for offenders to 'fake it'. This is important because, although VT appears to work with denying child abusers who are not told about faking strategies (Babchishin et al., 2014), the task may be open to faking once offenders know that their viewing time is being recorded to assess DSI (Babchishin et al., 2014). Imhoff, Schmidt, Weis, Young, and Banse (2012) also found that VT effects were mainly a function of task-specific effects (e.g., having to judge whether a stimulus possesses attractive features) rather than of stimulus-specific effects (e.g., schematic processes cued by sexual stimuli). They argued that this poses a problem to the diagnostic validity of the VT. Hence, a speeded VT variant could help eliminate these task-specific effects (Imhoff et al., 2012).

In summary, VT tasks show great value as a measure of DSI. The robustness of VT effects has resulted in the development of commercially available procedures, such as the *Abel Assessment for Sexual Interest*™ (AASI) (Abel et al., 2004) and *Affinity*™ (Glasgow, Osborne, & Croxen, 2003). Abel and colleagues have published extensively on the AASI, although the work has been criticized on the grounds that important data and methodological details have not been published (see Sachsenmaier & Gress, 2009). Less research has been conducted using Affinity, although Mokros et al. (2013) found that it had sufficient reliability and validity for research purposes, rather than as a diagnostic tool for single cases. The authors emphasized that Affinity should be used as part of a more comprehensive assessment of sexual interests (as originally intended by the creator). Future research should aim to establish whether VT effects are stable over time and whether they have any predictive validity (Sachsenmaier & Gress, 2009). Also, researchers should investigate whether task-specific effects (Imhoff et al., 2012) influence prolonged latencies in sex offender populations and, if so, whether a speeded VT variant can reduce them.

Implicit Association Test

The Implicit Association Test (IAT) (Greenwald, McGhee, & Schwartz, 1998) is designed to index how strongly an individual associates two target concepts (e.g.,

Flowers and *Insects*) with a particular attribute (e.g., *Pleasant*). The task involves randomly presenting stimuli that represent two target concepts (e.g., images of flowers and insects) and two attribute terms (e.g., pleasant and unpleasant words). Participants must quickly categorize the stimuli into their correct category. The IAT has two 'critical blocks', one where congruent target and attribute categories (i.e., *Flowers* and *Pleasant*) share the same key and one where two incongruent categories (i.e., *Insects* and *Pleasant*) share the same key. It is presumed that if participants associate a target concept with a certain attribute, their response latencies will be faster when those two categories share the same key. Since the IAT requires rapid responding, it is thought to be less affected by deliberative thought (Nosek, Greenwald, & Banaji, 2007) and less prone to faking (Steffens, 2004). Given these properties, the IAT has been adapted to assess sexual interests. For example, on an IAT measuring men–sex and women–sex associations, heterosexual and homosexual men (and also homosexual women) showed response latencies consistent with their sexual orientation (Snowden & Gray, 2013). Moreover, IAT preference indices have shown a strong ability to discriminate heterosexual and homosexual males (Ó Ciardha & Gormley, 2013; Snowden, Wichter, & Gray, 2008; $d = 2.75$ and 1.85, respectively). Hence, the IAT may be useful for assessing DSI.

Indeed, Gray, Brown, MacCulloch, Smith, and Snowden (2005) found that child abusers exhibited stronger child–sex associations than adult–sex associations, relative to sexual and non-sexual offender controls ($d = 0.84$). A similar result was also found between child abusers and non-sexual offenders in a follow-up study using a pictorial IAT with just the two critical blocks (Brown, Gray, & Snowden, 2009; $d = 0.92$). Nunes, Firestone, and Baldwin (2007) created an IAT measuring child–sexy associations and found that it could discriminate child abusers from non-offenders ($d = 0.92$). However, pictorial child–sexy IATs have been unsuccessful in discriminating child abusers from non-sexual offenders (Babchishin et al., 2014; Babchishin, Nunes, Hermann, & Malcolm, 2015). Steffens, Yundina, and Panning (2008) found that an IAT measuring child–erotic associations could discriminate exclusive child abusers from non-exclusive child abusers ($d = 0.53$). Finally, Banse et al. (2010) developed two IATs, one to measure associations between *boy* and *sexually exciting* and the other to measure associations between *girl* and *sexually exciting*. They found that both could discriminate child abusers from a sample of non-sexual offenders and non-offenders ($d = 0.43$ and 0.82, respectively). However, Babchishin et al. (2015) found that neither a boy–sexy or girl–sexy IAT could discriminate child abusers from non-sexual offenders.

Although there are some inconsistencies, research generally indicates that child–sex IATs can discriminate child abusers from non-child abusers. This conclusion is supported by a recent meta-analysis (Babchishin et al., 2013) (M-weighted $d = 0.63$). The inconsistent findings may be due to methodological differences. For example, Babchishin et al. (2015) found that IATs using 'sex' and 'not sex' as attribute categories showed the greatest discriminatory ability. This may, in part, account for the null findings in studies that use 'sexy' and 'not sexy' as attributes (Babchishin et al., 2014, 2015). The inconsistent findings may also be a result of sample characteristics. For example, Babchishin et al. (2013) noted that most IAT studies primarily tested less paedophilic abusers (e.g., those with related or female victims only). This would decrease group differences.

However, some researchers have compared child abuser subgroups. For example, Brown et al. (2009) differentiated child abusers with victims aged < 12 years old from abusers with victims aged 12+ years old ($d = 0.77$). Schmidt et al. (2014) found that child abusers with any/only male victims could be discriminated from those with only female victims using a boy–sexually exciting IAT and an IAT deviance index (i.e., the difference between scores on the boy IAT and girl IAT) ($d = 0.64$ and 0.72, respectively). In addition, van Leeuwen et al. (2013) found that a non-incarcerated sample of self-identified paedophiles could be discriminated from non-offender controls ($d = 1.73$). These findings suggest that child–sex IATs may be able to discriminate sexually deviant individuals from less deviant individuals, providing good known-groups validity.

Researchers have found that child–sex IATs correlate with other measures of DSI (rs ranging from 0.33 to 0.48), including self-report (i.e., SIPS) (Babchishin et al., 2014), interview-based (i.e., STABLE-2007) (Babchishin et al., 2014), file-based (i.e., SSPI) (Schmidt et al., 2014), VT (Babchishin et al., 2014), and PPG measures (Babchishin et al., 2015). However, these moderate correlations do not provide conclusive evidence that child–sex IATs measure paedophilic interest. Perhaps child–sex IATs index a related but separate construct to what is indexed by other DSI measures (Babchishin et al., 2013). Indeed, a children–sexual IAT was used to index the implicit theory that children are sexual beings (Mihailides, Devilly, & Ward, 2004). Given this, Ó Ciardha (2011) suggested that child–sex IATs may measure schematic associations underlying both DSI and distorted implicit theories.

The reliability of child–sex IATs is generally good, with Cronbach's alpha ranging from 0.65 to 0.83. However, Banse et al. (2010) and Schmidt et al. (2014) found lower alpha values for boy-specific IATs (0.61 and 0.65, respectively) relative to girl-specific IATs (0.79 and 0.82, respectively). Retest stability was examined by Brown et al. (2009) and was found to be good for a latency-based measure ($r_{tt} = 0.63$).

One core limitation of the IAT is that it does not provide an absolute index of association strength (Snowden et al., 2011). Therefore, it is difficult to ascertain whether child abusers hold strong child–sex associations or weak adult–sex associations. This is certainly an issue that requires further examination. Research also indicates that low and high IAT scores can be faked (Röhner, Schröder-Abé, & Schütz, 2013), particularly if participants have prior experience with the task or are instructed on how to fake it (Fiedler & Bluemke, 2005).

In summary, the IAT shows promise as a measure of DSI given its ability to distinguish child abusers (and sexually deviant individuals) from controls. Future researchers should investigate whether scores on the child–sex IAT decrease as a function of treatment participation (particularly treatment targeting DSI). This may be the case, as Babchishin et al. (2013) found larger differences between untreated child abusers and controls on child–sex IATs, but weaker differences between treated child abusers and controls. However, this observation may simply be a result of sampling biases (Schmidt et al., 2015). Also, more research on whether the IAT can measure other types of sexual deviance is needed. Steffens et al. (2008) were unsuccessful at indexing sadistic interests using a humiliation–erotic IAT, while

Larue et al. (2014) found that non-offending BDSM affiliates showed stronger 'violence–sexually exciting' associations than non-BDSM participants ($d = -0.73$).

Emotional Stroop

Stroop (1935) found that naming the colour in which a word is written is more difficult (i.e., takes longer) than simply reading the actual word. The interference in colour naming caused by the semantic meaning of the word is known as the 'Stroop effect'. The Emotional Stroop (E-Stroop) is a variation of the traditional Stroop task. It involves naming the colour in which an emotion-inducing word is written. Here, a further source of interference is introduced, caused by the emotional content of the word (Price, Beech, Mitchell, & Humphreys, 2012). Hence, if colour-naming latencies are longer for words representing a particular emotional category, relative to neutral words, it may indicate an attentional bias towards that category (Ó Ciardha & Gormley, 2012). This paradigm has been used with sexual offenders to assess DSI.

Johnston, Hudson, and Ward (1997) asked preferential child abusers (i.e., those who sexually prefer children over adults), situational child abusers (i.e., those who do not have sexual preference for children but offend due to other factors), and non-offenders either to think out loud while suppressing sexual thoughts or to think out loud with no further instructions. All participants then completed a non-computerized E-Stroop. The preferential abusers who had previously suppressed sexual thoughts were slowest at colour naming sexual and child-related words. According to Johnston et al. (1997), the preferential abusers' sexual and child-related thoughts had become activated and, thus, more accessible as a result of the suppression task. This is in accordance with the view that delays experienced on word-based E-Stroops are caused by the activation of schemas underlying a sexual interest (Ó Ciardha, 2011).

Smith and Waterman (2004) found that sexual offenders were slower at colour naming sexual words than non-offenders. Price and Hanson (2007) replicated this finding ($d = 0.82$), as did Price, Beech, Mitchell, and Humphreys (2013) using a group of mixed sexual offenders ($d = 0.68$). Price et al. (2013) also found that their mixed sample showed a Stroop bias for emotional personality descriptors of potential victims (e.g., *innocent*) more slowly than non-offenders ($d = 0.61$). However, using the same stimuli sets, Price, Beech, Mitchell, and Humphreys (2014) found no differences between adolescent sexual offenders and adolescent offender and non-offender controls.

These results suggest that E-Stroops using sexual words are able to discriminate adult sexual offenders from non-offender controls. Although this may indicate that the E-Stroop is effective at measuring sexual preoccupation (Price et al., 2013), Ó Ciardha (2011) warned that the context in which the words have become salient needs to be considered (e.g., early sexual abuse). The E-Stroop was also able to differentiate sexual offenders from controls using words that describe emotional personality characteristics of potential victims. Given that these words were derived from offenders' accounts about who is most at risk from them, Price et al. (2013) argued that they may reflect what sexual offenders find sexually attractive. However, this is difficult to determine as a heterogeneous sample was used and no convergence data were provided.

Price et al. (2012) noted that the E-Stroop is limited by the lack of standardized word sets that are able to distinguish between offender types. However, identifying words where each reflects a sexual interest seems a difficult feat. Hence, E-Stroops that use more salient sexual stimuli may provide better group discrimination. This was investigated by Ó Ciardha and Gormley (2012) using a pictorial variant of the E-Stroop, where pictures of children and adults were re-coloured and participants had to identify the colour of the image. Drawing upon the E-Stroop literature, Ó Ciardha and Gormley proposed that interference on the pictorial E-Stroop is driven by 'slow effects', whereby increased attention by one stimulus is carried over to the next. However, child abusers and non-offenders were found not to differ. van Leeuwen et al. (2013) developed an E-Stroop variant where sexual and neutral words were superimposed on images of children and adults. They found that community paedophiles classified the sexual words superimposed on children faster than non-offenders ($d = 1.41$). Therefore, rather than an interference effect, this E-Stroop is based upon a facilitatory effect caused by the presumed association between children and sex.

In summary, research using the E-Stroop has produced mixed findings. Future research should address the various methodological issues, establish more psychometric properties, and determine which variant is most effective. Also, the fakeability of the E-Stroop should be investigated.

Choice Reaction Time

The Choice Reaction Time (CRT) task involves detecting a target (e.g., a dot) superimposed on sexually preferred and sexually non-preferred images. Non-offenders tend to be slower at detecting dots superimposed upon sexually preferred images (Santtila et al., 2009; Wright & Adams, 1994; but see Ó Ciardha & Gormley, 2013). Given these results, the CRT has been used to assess DSI in child abusers. Giotakos (2005) found that extra-familial abusers took longer to detect a dot that was superimposed on images of prepubescent females, whereas intra-familial abusers (and female non-offenders) took longer when the dot was superimposed on images of adolescent females. Rapists and male non-offenders took longest when the dot was superimposed on images of adult females. Mokros, Dombert, Osterheider, Zappala, and Santtila (2010) found that child abusers were slower at detecting dots superimposed upon images of children, whereas offender controls were slower when dots were superimposed on images of adults. In addition, they found that a 'preference index' discriminated child abusers from controls ($d = 1.41$). Similarly, Poeppl et al. (2011) found that a CRT 'preference index' could discriminate child abusers from offender controls ($d = 0.99$). Gress et al. (2013) were less successful at discriminating a mixed group of sexual offenders from non-sexual youth offenders or non-offenders (although a 'preference index' was not examined). This null result may have been due to sample heterogeneity, as only half of the sample were child abusers.

Mokros et al. found that, for child abusers, the CRT preference index correlated significantly with the sum score from the SSPI ($r = 0.43$). In terms of reliability, Gress et al. (2013) reported good to excellent internal consistencies (α values ranging from 0.77 to 0.99). The CRT effect is thought to be driven by a SCID. This is supported by researching showing that target detection is longer for explicit sexual images than non-explicit images, for both offenders (Mokros et al., 2010) and non-offenders (Santtila et al., 2009). Ó Ciardha and Gormley (2013) also added that, whereas the E-Stroop may tap slow effects (as mentioned earlier), CRTs may be tapping 'fast effects' (i.e., the immediate capture of attention).

In summary, the CRT shows some value as a measure of DSI. However, given the small number of studies, more research is needed. Researchers should aim to establish the psychometric properties of the CRT, and whether it is resilient to faking. Future research should also investigate habituation effects further. Santtila et al. (2009) found evidence for a habituation effect in non-offenders, but Mokros et al. (2010) found no evidence despite using more trials. Also, Conaglen (2004) found that non-offenders with lower levels of sexual desire respond more slowly to sexual stimuli. These individuals appraised sexual words as less acceptable and familiar, suggesting that the negative valence of sexual stimuli was responsible for their slower responding (Conaglen, 2004). Hence, if the CRT is driven by SCID, the moderating effects of low sexual desire should be explored.

Rapid Serial Visual Presentation

In the Rapid Serial Visual Presentation task (RSVP), a series of stimuli are rapidly presented, and participants are required to identify two stimuli (T1 and T2) among the series. However, when T2 is presented <500 ms after T1, participants' identification of T2 tends to be poor (Broadbent & Broadbent, 1987). This effect is known as the 'attentional blink' (AB) (Raymond, Shapiro, & Arnell, 1992). The AB tends to be more pronounced when T1 has more emotional value; an effect termed 'emotion-induced blindness' (Most, Chun, Widders, & Zald, 2005). Hence, researchers have hypothesized that the AB (measured by the RSVP) may be useful for indirectly indexing sexual interest. Recently, Zappalà and colleagues (2013a, 2013b) developed an RSVP that only uses human images for T1 and T2. Zappalà et al. (2013b) found that non-offending homosexual men made more errors for T2 when T1 was a nude male as opposed to a clothed female. Also, to a lesser extent, heterosexual men made more errors for T2 when T1 was a nude female relative to a clothed male. This supports the idea that an AB occurs when T1 is a sexually preferred stimulus.

Beech et al. (2008) found that, relative to offender controls, extra- and intra-familial child abusers were less accurate at detecting T2 (i.e., images of trains and chairs) when T1 was an image of a child as opposed to an animal ($d = 1.28$ and 1.00, respectively). This effect was also found when participants only had to detect T2. However, extra-familial abusers (who are known to be more sexually deviant) did not differ from intra-familial abusers. Using the same RSVP task, Crooks, Rostill-Brookes, Beech, and Bickley (2009) found no group differences between adolescent child abusers and adolescent non-sexual offenders. Paradoxically, both groups displayed an AB for T2 when T1 was an animal. To explain this result, the authors referred to a number of issues related to the animal stimuli.

An AB is thought to occur because T1 captures individuals' attention, impairing their ability to detect T2. The numerous explanations for this impairment are generally linked to the depletion of resources required to process T2 and/or to the interference caused by the delay in disengaging one's attention away from T1 (Flak, Beech, & Humphreys, 2009). Drawing upon these accounts, Zappalà et al. (2013b) asked straight non-offending males to fake their responses on the RSVP. It was theorized that the 'faking task' would increase cognitive load, reducing the resources required to process T1. Thus, detection of T2 was predicted to be greater for fakers relative to non-fakers. This hypothesis was confirmed, suggesting the RSVP is moderately resilient to faking.

Zappalà et al. (2013a) also found that homosexual and heterosexual males were better at detecting T1 images depicting adolescent/adult males and females, respectively. They conceptualized this preattentive bias as a 'pop-out' effect, whereby emotionally salient stimuli are located effortlessly amongst distractors. They also found that a 'combined preference index' (based on pop-out indices for T1 and T2 images depicting adolescents/adults) was able to strongly differentiate the two groups ($d = 1.47$). Thus, this RSVP task produces two effects that can be used to index sexual interest. This may prove useful for assessing DSI in sexual offenders.

Other Promising Measures

Preliminary research suggests there are other methods that can indirectly assess DSI. These include Nosek and Banaji's (2001) 'Go/No-Go Association Task' (Bartels, Beech, Harkins, & Thornton, 2015a), Bar-Anan, Nosek, and Vianello's (2009) 'Sorting Paired Features' task (Bartels, Harkins, Beech, & Thornton, 2015b), Barnes-Holmes et al.'s (2006) 'Implicit Relational Assessment Procedure' (Dawson, Barnes-Holmes, Gresswell, Hart, & Gore (2009), and Imhoff, Schmidt, Bernhardt, Dierksmeier, and Banse's (2011) 'Semantic Misattribution Procedure' (Larue et al., 2014). A notable method that is gaining attention is 'eye-tracking'. Researchers using this method have found that non-offending males show faster initial fixations (i.e., an immediate attentional bias) and longer fixation times for sexually preferred images (Fromberger et al. 2012a; Hall, Hogue, & Guo, 2011; Trottier, Rouleau, Renaud, & Goyette, 2014). Moreover, Fromberger et al. (2012b, 2013) found that child abusers show faster initial fixations for child images than adult images. However, Fromberger et al. (2013) found that child abusers showed greater relative fixation times for adult images. They suggested that, since this is a controlled attentional process, the abusers may have been responding in a socially desirable manner. Hence, the initial fixation latency may be a better indicator of DSI. Indeed, Fromberger et al. (2102b) found that this variable discriminated child abusers from controls to a greater extent than relative fixation time ($d = 1.83$ and 1.34, respectively).

Conclusion

A number of different indirect measures have been adapted for assessing DSI, with VT and the IAT receiving the most empirical attention. In general, the VT and IAT show a good ability to discriminate sexual offenders from controls, and also an ability to differentiate sexual offender subtypes. The other measures (E-Stroop, CRT, and

RSVP) have attracted less empirical attention. The CRT and RSVP appear to be useful measures of DSI, although more psychometric data are needed. The E-Stroop has been less successful in distinguishing sexual abusers from controls, which seems to be related to limitations associated with the stimuli. However, a 'word–picture' E-Stroop variant shows promise as a measure of DSI (van Leeuwen et al. 2013).

It should be emphasized that no one measure will provide a clear-cut indication of DSI, because individual differences and contextual factors can affect task performance. Also, each method possesses distinct properties that account for discrepant results across methods. For example, the IAT is impervious to stimulus type and the number of items, whereas VT depends crucially on the nature of the items. Hence, these factors can reduce the validity of one's interpretation regarding the measurement outcome (Babchishin et al., 2014). Arguably, then, the assessment of DSI is likely to be more accurate if a multimethod approach is adopted. Models of the human sexual response provide good grounds for a multimethod approach. For example, Singer (1984) proposed that sexual arousal is based on three sequential stages: (1) an aesthetic response that orients attention to an attractive stimulus; (2) an approach response; and (3) a genital response. Sexual interest can, therefore, be inferred from a number of sources (i.e., implicit and explicit cognition, physiological responses). Moreover, what one automatically attends to or physiologically responds to may not always reflect their subjective (explicit) experience of sexual arousal (Spiering & Everaerd, 2007). Therefore, from a conceptual standpoint, a multimethod approach will help clinicians formulate a more complete picture of an individual's DSI profile.

Babchishin et al. (2014) found that a composite score based on two indirect measures (IAT and VT) and a self-report measure (SIPS) explained 47% of the variance and was able to discriminate child abusers from offender controls ($d = 1.66$). Banse et al. (2010) developed the 'Explicit and Implicit Sexual Interest Profile' (EISIP), a multimethod approach that involves various VT and IAT tasks along with self-report measures of sexual interest. Banse et al. (2010) found the EISIP to be very effective at discriminating child abusers from a mix of offender and non-offender controls ($d = 2.33$), and it explained 75% of the variance. Schmidt et al. (2014) found that the EISIP was also able to differentiate extra-familial abusers from intra-familial abusers ($d = 0.84$) and child pornography offenders ($d = 0.17$). These results empirically support the use of a multimethod approach to assessing DSI. Therefore, future researchers should aim to validate the EISIP further and also examine other combinations of measures.

In summary, indirect measures appear to be a valuable addition to the arsenal of tools designed to assess DSI. However, more research is needed to understand, refine, and standardize those that have a larger empirical base (e.g., VT, IAT), and develop those still in their infancy (e.g., RSVP, eye-tracking). Therefore, researchers and clinicians are encouraged to pursue these exciting lines of research further.

References

Abel, G. G., Huffman, J., Warberg, B., & Holland, C. L. (1998). Visual reaction time and plethysmography as measures of sexual interest in child molesters. *Sexual Abuse: A Journal of Research and Treatment, 10*, 81–95. doi: 10.1023/A:1022063214826

Abel, G. G., Jordan, A., Rouleau, J. L., Emerick, R., Barboza-Whitehead, S., & Osborn, C. (2004). Use of visual reaction time to assess male adolescents who molest children. *Sexual Abuse: A Journal of Research and Treatment, 16*, 255–265. doi:10.1177/107906320401600306

Babchishin, K. M., Nunes, K. L., & Hermann, C. A. (2013). The validity of Implicit Association Test (IAT) measures of sexual attraction to children: A meta-analysis. *Archives of Sexual Behavior, 42*, 487–499. doi:10.1007/s10508-012-0022-8

Babchishin, K. M., Nunes, K. L., Hermann, C. A., & Malcom, J. R. (2015). Implicit sexual interest in children: Does separating gender influence discrimination when using the Implicit Association Test? *Journal of Sexual Aggression, 21*, 194–208. doi:10.1080/13552600.2013.836575

Babchishin, K. M., Nunes, K., & Kessous, N. (2014). A multimodal examination of sexual interest in children: A comparison of sex offenders and non-sex offenders. *Sexual Abuse: A Journal of Research and Treatment, 26*, 343–374. doi:10.1177/1079063213492343

Banse, R., Schmidt, A. F., & Clarbour, J. (2010). Indirect measures of sexual interest in child sex offenders: A multi-method approach. *Criminal Justice and Behavior, 37*, 319–335. doi:10.1177/0093854809357598

Bar-Anan, Y., Nosek, B. A., & Vianello, M. (2009). The sorting paired features task: A measure of association strengths. *Experimental Psychology, 56*, 329–343. doi:10.1027/1618-3169.56.5.329

Barnes-Holmes, D., Barnes-Holmes, Y., Power, P., Hayden, E., Milne, R., & Stewart, I. (2006). Do you really know what you believe? Developing the Implicit Relational Assessment Procedure (IRAP) as a direct measure of implicit beliefs. *The Irish Psychologist, 32*, 169–177.

Bartels, R. M., Beech, A. R., Harkins, L., & Thornton, D. (2015a). *Assessing child abusers' sexual interest in children using the Go/No-Go Association Test*. Manuscript submitted for publication.

Bartels, R. M, Harkins, L., Beech, A. R., & Thornton, D. (2015b). *Applying the Sorting Paired Features task to the investigation of child abuser' cognition*. Manuscript submitted for publication.

Beech, A. R., Kalmus, E., Tipper, S. P., Baudouin, J. Y., Flak, V., & Humphreys, G. W. (2008). Children induce an enhanced attentional blink in child molesters. *Psychological Assessment, 20*, 397–402. doi:10.1037/a0013587

Bourke, A. B., & Gormley, M. J. (2012). Comparing a pictorial Stroop task to viewing time measures of sexual interest. *Sexual Abuse: A Journal of Research and Treatment, 24*, 479–500. doi:1079063212438922.10.1177/1079063212438922

Broadbent, D. E., & Broadbent, M. H. P. (1987). From detection to identification: Response to multiple targets in rapid serial visual presentation. *Perception & Psychophysics, 42*, 105–113. doi:10.3758/BF03210498

Brown, A. S., Gray, N. S., & Snowden, R. J. (2009). Implicit measurement of sexual associations in child sex abusers: Role of victim type and denial. *Sexual Abuse: A Journal of Research and Treatment, 21*, 166–180. doi:10.1177/1079063209332234

Cohen, J. (1988). *Statistical power analysis for the behavioral sciences* (2nd ed.). Hillsdale, NJ: Erlbaum.

Conaglen, H. M. (2004). Sexual content induced delay: A re-examination investigating relation to sexual desire. *Archives of Sexual Behavior, 33*, 359–367. doi:10.1023/B:ASEB.0000028889.63425.fb

Cronbach, L. J., & Meehl, P. E. (1955). Construct validity in psychological tests. *Psychological Bulletin, 52*, 281–302. doi:10.1037/h0040957

Crooks, V. L., Rostill-Brookes, H., Beech, A. R., & Bickley, J. A. (2009). Applying Rapid Serial Visual Presentation to adolescent sexual offenders attentional bias as a measure of deviant sexual interest? *Sexual Abuse: A Journal of Research and Treatment, 21*, 135–148. doi: 10.1177/1079063208328677

Dawson, D. L., Barnes-Holmes, D., Gresswell, D. M., Hart, A. J. P., & Gore, N. J. (2009). Assessing the implicit beliefs of sexual offenders using the Implicit Relational Assessment Procedure: A first study. *Sexual Abuse: A Journal of Research and Treatment, 21*, 57–75. doi:10.1177/1079063208326928

De Houwer, J. (2006). What are implicit measures and why are we using them? In R. W. Wiers & A. W. Stacy (Eds.), *The handbook of implicit cognition and addiction* (pp. 11–28). Thousand Oaks, CA: Sage.

Ebsworth, M., & Lalumière, M. L. (2012). Viewing time as a measure of bisexual sexual interest. *Archives of Sexual Behavior, 41*(1), 161–172. doi:10.1007/s10508-012-9923-9

Fiedler, K., & Bluemke, M. (2005). Faking the IAT: Aided and unaided response control on the Implicit Association Tests. *Basic and Applied Social Psychology, 27*, 307–316. doi:10.1207/s15324834basp2704_3

Flak, V. E., Beech, A. R., & Humphreys, G. W. (2009). The rapid serial visual presentation test of sexual interest in child molesters. In D. Thornton & D. R. Laws (Eds.), *Cognitive approaches to the assessment of sexual interest in sexual offenders* (pp. 145–158). Chichester, England: John Wiley & Sons, Ltd.

Fromberger, P., Jordan, K., Steinkrauss, H., von Herder, J., Stolpmann, G., Kröner-Herwig, B., & Müller, J. L. (2013). Eye movements in pedophiles: Automatic and controlled attentional processes while viewing prepubescent stimuli. *Journal of Abnormal Psychology, 122*, 587–599. doi:10.1037/a0030659

Fromberger, P., Jordan, K., Steinkrauss, H., von Herder, J., Witzel, J., Stolpmann, G., ... Müller, J. L. (2012b). Diagnostic accuracy of eye movements in assessing pedophilia. *The Journal of Sexual Medicine, 9*, 1868–1882. doi:10.1111/j.1743-6109.2012.02754.x

Fromberger, P., Jordan, K., von Herder, J., Steinkrauss, H., Nemetschek, R., Stolpmann, G., & Müller, J. L. (2012a). Initial orienting towards sexually relevant stimuli: Preliminary evidence from eye movement measures. *Archives of Sexual Behavior, 41*, 919–928. doi:10.1007/s10508-011-9816-3

Geer, J. H., & Bellard, H. S. (1996). Sexual content induced delays in unprimed lexical decisions: Gender and context effects. *Archives of Sexual Behavior, 25*, 91–107. doi:10.1007/BF02437581

Giotakos, O. (2005). A combination of viewing reaction time and incidental learning task in child molesters, rapists, and control males and females. *European Journal of Sexology, Sexologies, 54*, 13–22.

Glasgow, D. V. (2009). Affinity: The development of a self-report assessement of paedophile sexual interest incorporating a viewing time validity measure. In D. Thornton & D. R. Laws (Eds.), *Cognitive approaches to the assessment of sexual interest in sexual offenders* (pp. 59–84). Chichester, England: John Wiley & Sons, Ltd. doi:10.1002/9780470747551.ch3

Glasgow, D. V., Osborne, A., & Croxen, J. (2003). An assessment tool for investigating paedophile sexual interest using viewing time: An application of single case methodology. *British Journal of Learning Disabilities, 31*, 96–102. doi:10.1046/j.1468-3156.2003.00180.x

Gray, S. R., Abel, G. G., Jordan, A., Garby, T., Wiegel, M., & Harlow, N. (2015). Visual Reaction Time™ as a predictor of sexual offense recidivism. *Sexual Abuse: A Journal of Research and Treatment, 27*, 173–188. doi: 1079063213502680

Gray, N. S., Brown, A. S., MacCulloch, M. J., Smith, J., & Snowden, R. J. (2005). An implicit test of the associations between children and sex in pedophiles. *Journal of Abnormal Psychology, 114*, 304–308. doi:10.1037/0021-843X.114.2.304

Gray, S. R., & Plaud, J. J. (2005). A comparison of the Abel Assessment for Sexual Interest and penile plethysmography in an outpatient sample of sexual offenders. *Journal of Sexual Offender Commitment: Science and the Law, 1*, 1–10. Retrieved from http://www.soccjournal.org/

Greenwald, A. G., McGhee, D. E., & Schwartz, J. L. K. (1998). Measuring individual differences in implicit cognition: The Implicit Association Test. *Journal of Personality and Social Psychology, 74*, 1464–1480. doi:10.1037//0022-3514.74.6.1464

Gress, C. L. Z. (2005). Viewing time measures and sexual interest: Another piece of the puzzle. *Journal of Sexual Aggression, 11*, 117–125. doi:10.1080/13552600500063666

Gress, C. L. Z., Anderson, J. O., & Laws, D. R. (2013). Delays in attentional processing when viewing sexual imagery: The development and comparison of two measures. *Legal and Criminological Psychology, 18*, 66–82. doi:10.1111/j.2044-8333.2011.02032.x

Gress, C. L. Z., & Laws, R. D. (2009). Measuring sexual deviance: Attention-based measures. In A. R. Beech, L. A. Craig, & K. D. Browne (Eds.), *Assessment and treatment of sex offenders: A handbook* (pp. 109–128). Chichester, England: John Wiley & Sons, Ltd.

Hall, C., Hogue, T., & Guo, K. (2011). Differential gaze behavior towards sexually preferred and non-preferred human figures. *The Journal of Sex Research, 48*, 461–469. doi:10.1080/00224499.2010.521899

Hanson, R. K., & Morton-Bourgon, K. E. (2005). The characteristics of persistent sexual offenders: A meta-analysis of recidivism studies. *Journal of Consulting and Clinical Psychology, 73*, 1154–1163. doi:10.1037/0022-006X.73.6.1154

Harris, G. T., Rice, M. E., Quinsey, V. L., & Chaplin, T. C. (1996). Viewing time as a measure of sexual interest among child molesters and normal heterosexual men. *Behaviour Research and Therapy, 34*, 389–394. doi:10.1016/0005-7967(95)00070-4

Imhoff, R., Schmidt, A. F., Bernhardt, J., Dierksmeier, A., & Banse, R. (2011). An inkblot for sexual preference: A semantic variant of the Affect Misattribution Procedure. *Cognition and Emotion, 25*(4), 676–690. doi:10.1080/02699931.2010.508260

Imhoff, R., Schmidt, A. F., Nordsiek, U., Luzar, C., Young, A. W., & Banse, R. (2010). Viewing time effects revisited: Prolonged response latencies for sexually attractive targets under restricted task conditions. *Archives of Sexual Behavior, 39*, 1275–1288. doi:10.1007/s10508-009-9595-2

Imhoff, R., Schmidt, A. F., Weis, S., Young, A. W., & Banse, R. (2012). Vicarious Viewing Time: Prolonged response latencies for sexually attractive targets as a function of task- or stimulus-specific processing. *Archives of Sexual Behavior, 41*, 1389–1401. doi:10.1007/s10508-011-9879-1

Israel, E., & Strassberg, D. S. (2009). Viewing time as an objective measure of sexual interest in heterosexual men and women. *Archives of Sexual Behavior, 38*(4), 551–558. doi:10.1007/s10508-007-9246-4

Johnston, L., Hudson, S. M., & Ward, T. (1997). The suppression of sexual thoughts by child molesters: A preliminary investigation. *Sexual Abuse: A Journal of Research and Treatment, 9*, 303–319. doi: 10.1007/BF02674855

Kalmus, E., & Beech, A. R. (2005). Forensic assessment of sexual interest: A review. *Aggression and Violent Behavior, 10*, 193–218. doi:10.1016/j.avb.2003.12.002

Larue, D., Schmidt, A. F., Imhoff, R., Eggers, K., Schönbrodt, F. D., Banse, R. (2014). Validation of direct and indirect measures of preference for sexual violence. *Psychological Assessment, 26*, 1173–1183.

Laws, D. R. (1986). *Sexual deviance card sort*. Unpublished manuscript.

Letourneau, E. J. (2002). A comparison of objective measures of sexual arousal and interest: Visual reaction time and penile plethysmography. *Sexual Abuse: A Journal of Research and Treatment, 14*, 207–223. doi:10.1177/107906320201400302

Mihailides, S., Devilly, G. J., & Ward, T. (2004). Implicit cognitive distortions and sexual offending. *Sexual Abuse: A Journal of Research and Treatment*, 16, 333–350. doi:10.1177/107906320401600406

Mokros, A., Dombert, B., Osterheider, M., Zappala, A., & Santtila, P. (2010). Assessment of pedophilic sexual interest with an attentional choice reaction time task. *Archives of Sexual Behavior*, 39, 1081–1090. doi:10.1007/s10508-009-9530-6

Mokros, A., Gebhard, M., Heinz, V., Marschall, R. W., Nitschke, J., Glasgow, D. V., ... Laws, D. R. (2013). Computerized assessment of pedophilic sexual interest through self-report and viewing time: Reliability, validity, and classification accuracy of the affinity program. *Sexual Abuse: A Journal of Research and Treatment*, 25, 230–258. doi:10.1177/1079063212454550.

Most, S. B., Chun, M. M., Widders, D. M., & Zald, D. H. (2005). Attentional rubbernecking: Cognitive control and personality in emotion-induced blindness. *Psychonomic Bulletin & Review*, 12, 654–661. doi:10.3758/BF03196754

Nosek, B. A., & Banaji, M. R. (2001). The go/no-go association task. *Social Cognition*, 19, 625–666. doi:10.1521/soco.19.6.625.20886

Nosek, B. A., Greenwald, A. G., & Banaji, M. R. (2007). The Implicit Association Test at age 7: A methodological and conceptual review. In J. A. Bargh (Ed.), *Automatic processes in social thinking and behavior* (pp. 265–292). New York, NY: Psychology Press.

Nunes, K. L., Firestone, P., & Baldwin, M. W. (2007). Indirect assessment of cognitions of child sexual abusers with the Implicit Association Test. *Criminal Justice and Behavior*, 34, 454–475. doi:10.1177/0093854806291703

Ó Ciardha, C. (2011). A theoretical framework for understanding deviant sexual interest and cognitive distortions as overlapping constructs contributing to sexual offending against children. *Aggression and Violent Behavior*, 16, 493–502. doi:10.1016/j.avb.2011.05.001

Ó Ciardha, C., & Gormley, M. (2012). Using a pictorial-modified Stroop task to explore the sexual interests of sexual offenders against children. *Sexual Abuse: A Journal of Research and Treatment*, 24, 175–197. doi:10.1177/1079063211407079

Ó Ciardha, C., & Gormley, M. (2013). Measuring sexual interest using a pictorial modified Stroop task, a pictorial Implicit Association Test and a Choice Reaction Time task. *Journal of Sexual Aggression*, 19, 158–170. doi:10.1080/13552600.2012.677486

Poeppl, T. A., Nitschke, J., Dombert, B., Santtila, P., Greenlee, M. W., Osterheider, M., & Mokros, A. (2011). Functional cortical and subcortical abnormalities in pedophilia: A combined study using a choice reaction time task and fMRI. *Journal of Sexual Medicine*, 8, 1660–1674. doi:10.1111/j.1743-6109.2011.02248.x

Price, S. A., Beech, A. R., Mitchell, I. J., & Humphreys, G. W. (2012). The promises and perils of the emotional Stroop task: A general review and considerations for use with forensic samples. *Journal of Sexual Aggression*, 18, 253–268. doi:10.1080/13552600.2010.545149

Price, S. A., Beech, A. R., Mitchell, I., & Humphreys, G. W. (2013). Measuring deviant sexual interest using the emotional Stroop task. *Criminal Justice and Behavior*, 40, 970–987. doi:10.1177/0093854813476264

Price, S. A., Beech, A., Mitchell, I. J., & Humphreys, G. W. (2014). Measuring deviant sexual interest in adolescents using the emotional Stroop task. *Sexual Abuse: A Journal of Research and Treatment*, 26, 450–471. doi:10.1177/1079063213495897

Price, S. A., & Hanson, R. K. (2007). A modified Stroop task with sexual offenders: Replication of a study. *Journal of Sexual Aggression*, 13, 203–216. doi:10.1080/13552600701785505

Raymond, J. E., Shapiro, K. L., & Arnell, K. A. (1992). Temporary suppression of visual processing in an RSVP task: An attentional blink? *Journal of Experimental Psychology: Human Perception and Performance, 18*, 849–860. doi:10.1037//0096-1523.18.3.849

Röhner, J., Schröder-Abé, M., & Schütz, A. (2013). What do fakers actually do to fake the IAT? An investigation of faking strategies under different faking conditions. *Journal of Research in Personality, 47*, 330–338. doi:10.1016/j.jrp.2013.02.009.

Rosenzweig, S. (1942). The photoscope as an objective device for evaluating sexual interest. *Psychosomatic Medicine, 4*, 150–157.

Sachsenmaier, S. J., & Gress, C. L. Z. (2009). The Abel Assessment for Sexual Interests – 2: A critical review. In D. Thornton & D. R. Laws (Eds.), *Cognitive approaches to the assessment of sexual interest in sexual offenders* (pp. 31–57). Chichester, England: John Wiley & Sons, Ltd. doi:10.1002/9780470747551.ch2

Santtila, P., Mokros, A., Viljanen, K., Koivisto, M., Sandnabba, N. K., Zappala, A., & Osterheider, M. (2009). Assessment of sexual interest using a choice reaction time task and priming: A feasibility study. *Legal and Criminological Psychology, 14*, 65–82. doi:10.1348/135532507X267040

Schmidt, A. F., Banse, R., & Imhoff, R. (2015). Indirect measures in forensic contexts. In T. M. Ortner & F. J. R. van de Vijver (Eds.), *Behavior-based assessment: Going beyond self-report in the personality, affective, motivation, and social domains* (pp. 173–194). Göttingen, Germany: Hogrefe.

Schmidt, A. F., Gykiere, K., Vanhoeck, K., Mann, R. E., & Banse, R. (2014). Direct and indirect measures of sexual maturity preferences differentiate subtypes of child sexual abusers. *Sexual Abuse: A Journal of Research and Treatment, 26*, 107–128. doi:10.1177/1079063213480817

Seto, M. C. (2008). *Pedophilia and sexual offending against children: Theory, assessment and intervention.* Washington, DC: American Psychiatric Association. doi:10.1037/11639-000

Seto, M. C., & Lalumiere, M. L. (2001). A brief screening scale to identify pedophilic interests among child molesters. *Sexual Abuse: A Journal of Research and Treatment, 13*, 15–25. doi:10.1177/107906320101300103

Singer, B. (1984). Conceptualizing sexual arousal and attraction. *Journal of Sex Research, 20*, 230–240. doi:10.1080/00224498409551222

Smith, P., & Waterman, M. (2004). Processing bias for sexual material: The Emotional Stroop and sexual offenders. *Sexual Abuse: A Journal of Research and Treatment, 16*, 163–171. doi:10.1177/107906320401600206

Snowden, R. J., Craig, R. L., & Gray, N. S. (2011). Indirect behavioral measures of cognition among sexual offenders. *The Journal of Sex Research, 48*, 192–217. doi:10.1080/00224499.2011.557750.

Snowden, R. J., & Gray, N. S. (2013). Implicit sexual associations in heterosexual and homosexual women and men. *Archives of Sexual Behavior, 42*, 475–485. doi:10.1007/s10508-012-9920-z

Snowden, R. J., Wichter, J., & Gray, N. S. (2008). Implicit and explicit measurements of sexual preference in gay and heterosexual men: A comparison of priming techniques and the implicit association task. *Archives of Sexual Behavior, 37*, 558–565. doi:10.1007/s10508-006-9138-z

Spiering, M., & Everaerd, W. (2007). The sexual unconscious. In E. Janssen (Ed.), *The psychophysiology of sex* (pp. 166–184). Bloomington, IN: Indiana University Press.

Steffens, M. C. (2004). Is the implicit association test immune to faking? *Experimental Psychology, 51*, 165–179. doi:10.1027/1618-3169.51.3.165

Steffens, M. C., Yundina, E., & Panning, M. (2008). Automatic associations with 'erotic' in child sex offenders: Identifying those in danger of re-offence. *Sexual Offender Treatment*, *3*, 1–9.

Stinson, J. D., & Becker, J. V. (2008). Assessing sexual deviance: A comparison of physiological, historical, and self-report measures. *Journal of Psychiatric Practice*, *14*, 379–388. doi:10.1097/01.pra.0000341892.51124.85

Stroop, J. R. (1935). Studies of interference in serial verbal reactions. *Journal of Experimental Psychology*, *18*, 643–662. doi:10.1037/h0054651

Thornton, D., & Laws, D. R. (2009). *Cognitive approaches to the assessment of sexual interest in sexual offenders*. Chichester, England: John Wiley & Sons, Ltd. doi:10.1002/9780470747551

Trottier, D., Rouleau, J. L., Renaud, P., & Goyette, M. (2014). Using eye tracking to identify faking attempts during penile plethysmography assessment. *The Journal of Sex Research*, *51*, 946–955. doi:10.1080/00224499.2013.832133

van Leeuwen, M. L., van Baaren, R. B., Chakhssi, F., Loonen, M. G., Lippman, M., & Dijksterhuis, A. (2013). Assessment of implicit sexual associations in non-incarcerated pedophiles. *Archives of Sexual Behavior*, *42*, 1501–1507. doi:10.1007/s10508-013-0094-0

Worling, J. R. (2006). Assessing sexual arousal with adolescent males who have offended sexually: Self-report and unobtrusively measured viewing time. *Sexual Abuse: A Journal of Research and Treatment*, *18*, 383–400. doi:10.1177/107906320601800406

Wright, L. W., & Adams, H. E. (1994). Assessment of sexual preference using a choice reaction time task. *Journal of Psychopathology and Behavioral Assessment*, *16*, 221–231. doi:10.1007/BF02229209

Zamansky, H. S. (1956). A technique for measuring homosexual tendencies. *Journal of Personality*, *24*, 436–448. doi:10.1111/j.1467-6494.1956.tb01280.x

Zappalà, A., Antfolk, J., Bäckström, A., Dombert, B., Mokros, A., & Santtila, P. (2013a). Differentiating sexual preference in men: Using dual task rapid serial visual presentation task. *Scandinavian Journal of Psychology*, *54*, 320–327. doi:10.1111/sjop.12050

Zappalà, A., Antfolk, J., Bäckström, A., Dombert, B., Mokros, A., & Santtila, P. (2013b). Using a dual-target Rapid Serial Visual Presentation Task (RSVP) as an attention-based measurement procedure of sexual preference: Is it possible to fake? *Psychiatry, Psychology and Law*, *20*, 73–90. doi:10.1080/13218719.2011.619642

45

Eye-Tracking and Assessing Sexual Interest in Forensic Contexts

Todd E. Hogue and Charlotte Wesson
University of Lincoln, United Kingdom

Derek Perkins
Royal Holloway University of London, United Kingdom

What Is Eye-Tracking and Why Is It Important?

Eye-trackers are used to estimate an individual's gaze direction (Weigle & Banks, 2008). They are important because eye movements are the most frequently made human movement (Richardson & Spivey, 2004), and therefore could potentially provide insight into human perception, action, and cognition. Eye-tracking has a variety of applications (Duchowski, 2002), from understanding low-level vision and cognition to a range of applied applications such as driving (e.g., Mackenzie & Harris, 2014) and marketing (van der Laan, Hooge, de Ridder, Viergever, & Smeets, 2015). Furthermore, although eye-trackers have become increasingly popular and used to address a range of different questions over the past 50 years, there now seems to be a consensus on in its importance and usage (Jacob & Karn, 2003).

How Is Eye-Tracking Used?

Eye-tracking has been implemented in a wide variety of diverse settings. For instance, it has been used to assist text entry to a computer by using the eyes and is essential for communication purposes for those who are severely disabled, and otherwise could not communicate effectively (Majaranta & Räihä, 2007). Similarly, eye-tracking has been used to rehabilitate children with conditions such as cerebral visual impairment,

The Wiley Handbook on the Theories, Assessment, and Treatment of Sexual Offending.
Edited by Douglas P. Boer. Volume II: Assessment, edited by Leam A. Craig and Martin Rettenberger.
© 2017 John Wiley & Sons, Ltd. Published 2017 by John Wiley & Sons, Ltd.

which involves damage to areas of the brain linked to visual processing, using the medium of a game (Linehan, Waddington, Hodgson, Hicks & Banks, 2014). Lastly, eye-tracking has been used for research purposes, on which this chapter is mainly focused, in disciplines such as psychology and marketing.

The History of Eye-Tracking

Dodge and Cline have been credited as being the first individuals to create an unobtrusive measurement of eye-gaze in 1901 (Drewes, 2010). They did this by using a photographic plate, whereby a vertical line of light was refracted off the cornea and then projected through a horizontal slit, behind which the photographic plate was situated (Richardson & Spivey, 2004). In order to measure the horizontal eye position, the photographic plate moved vertically and recorded time and horizontal motion as the variables, thereby allowing Dodge and Cline to estimate eye-gaze (Richardson & Spivey, 2004). This was the first precise and non-invasive eye-tracking technique that actually used light reflected from the cornea to measure gaze (Jacob & Karn, 2003).

Although this unobtrusive measure of eye-tracking was evidently revolutionary, the major innovation in eye-tracking research was the invention of the head-mounted eye-tracker, which is still widely used today (Mohamed, Perreira da Silva, & Courboulay, 2007). This invention was conceptualized in 1948 by Hartridge and Thompson (1948), and thus eliminated the need for head-restriction and allowed free movement (Lupu & Ungureanu, 2013). However, the most recent developments stem from the 1980s, when video-based eye-trackers became popular (Drewes, 2010). As advances in eye-gaze sensing technology have improved, the systems have become more precise, less intrusive, and more portable (Mohamed et al., 2007), making the current video-based eye-trackers so popular today.

How Does an Eye-Tracker Work?

The type of eye-tracking discussed here is video-based eye-tracking, which is currently the most common method. The aim of video-based eye-tracking is to calculate the direction of the participant's gaze from a video image of the participant's face (Drewes, 2010). There are two main systems for video-based eye-tracking: head-mounted and non-intrusive (Mohamed et al., 2007). The head-mounted system typically consists of between one and three cameras and a diode to provide light, and uses the analysis of Purkinje images, which are 'reflections of objects from the structure of the eye' (Mohamed et al., 2007, p. 7). The purpose of most of these systems is to compare the corneal pupil images with the retinal images. Head-mounted eye-trackers are wearable and allow free mobility and interaction with the real-world environment; however, this typically requires a laptop to be with the participant in order to record such data (Drewes, 2010). Conversely, stationary eye-tracker systems often involve a desktop computer with integrated eye-tracker and compatible software. Some systems utilize a chin rest to keep the participant's head stationary.

Recently, a range of eye-trackers have been developed that do not need a chin rest and therefore allow free, naturalistic head movements. These stationary, non-intrusive eye-trackers have traditionally been seen as superior for numerous reasons, such as their performance with various eye shapes and their compatibility with contact lenses and spectacles, in addition to being portable and operating in 'real time' (Mohamed et al., 2007).

Visual Information-Inferring Processing

One of the main issues, apart from actually measuring eye movements, is mapping the movement coordinates onto the real world to infer where participants are looking. A calibration procedure used to achieve this (Feng, 2011) locates the movement of the pupil for each individual participant and maps this onto the corresponding visual image (Weigle & Banks, 2008). The feature of the eye used for eye-tracking in these systems is the pupil–iris boundary and iris–sclera boundary. Infrared light is used to induce a 'bright pupil' effect, which is a reflection from the retina that makes the pupil appear white (Drewes, 2010). This is better than a 'dark pupil' effect, which locates the position of the black pupil in the images; however, the contrast between a dark-coloured iris and a black pupil is low, making this problematic (Drewes, 2010). The solution to using the contrast between pupil and iris is to use corneal reflections, also known as 'the glint' or 'gleam' (Feng, 2011). As the cornea is almost a perfect sphere, the 'glint' remains in the same location for any direction of gaze (Drewes, 2010). This is achieved by tracking the pupil position and a spot of light reflected from the cornea, and then calculating the angle of the visual axis and location of the fixation point on the display surface. This method has greatly reduced the need for bite bars, chin rests, and other head restraints (Mohamed et al., 2007).

By utilizing knowledge of where someone is looking, it is possible to infer underlying cognitive processes. Where individuals fixate on the scene, the duration for which they look at different identified areas of interest and the saccades that they make between different fixation points all become an essential part of inferring underlying interests and cognitive processes (Salvucci & Goldberg, 2000). This can be done with individuals who cannot communicate verbally, such as infants, and also non-humans, such as dogs and monkeys. Eye-tracking therefore allows us to infer cognition from the individuals' gaze patterns and can give us insight into their thoughts, feelings, behaviours and cognitive processes.

Studies with primates have been a major focus of eye-tracking studies to infer cognitive processes. Akin to humans, non-human primates rely primarily on vision to retrieve information from the outside world (Kano & Tomonaga, 2013). We know, for example, that face perception is crucial to primate social communication (Guo, Robertson, Mahmoodi, Tadmor, & Young, 2003). Guo et al. (2003) found that eyes were the most salient feature in both human and non-human faces, with the likelihood of the eyes becoming more salient increasing when the face was less familiar. Guo et al. (2003) suggested that this may be linked to a sophisticated visual communication system between conspecifics, which may have gone unexplored without eye-tracking technology.

Kano and Call (2014) further used eye-tracking with non-human primates in order to assess proactive goal-directed eye movements, as non-human primates have been shown to make predictions about actions. They found that the eye movements of great apes were proactive when viewing the reaches of another individual, whereas they were reactive when viewing the reaches of a non-human object (a claw). They looked towards the object that had already been reached-for in the familiarization trial, even when it had moved position on the screen (Kano & Call, 2014).

Eye-tracking is useful not only for inferring cognition with non-humans, but also for studying pre-vocal infants. Tenenbaum, Shah, Sobel, Malle, and Morgan (2013) investigated face-scanning behaviours in infants aged 6, 9, and 12 months, with the aim of exploring how attention to faces changes as a function of age. When the woman on the videoclip stimulus was speaking, the mouth attracted more attention than when the stimulus was smiling, with attention to the eyes decreasing correspondingly, under-lining the importance of the mouth for infants. Tenenbaum et al. (2013) suggested that this eye-tracking was relevant as patterns of face scanning may indicate future pat-terns of child development. Importantly, the methodology is used extensively to infer cognitive processes that otherwise would be inaccessible to study.

Clinical Populations

Eye-tracking has been used to investigate a number of clinical problems that it may not have been posible to study otherwise. For instance, Pinhas et al. (2014) investigated body image in individuals with anorexia nervosa using eye-tracking, predicting that sufferers would spend more time viewing 'thin' or 'fat' body shapes than their typical counterparts. They found exactly what they predicted, with individuals diagnosed with anorexia spending more time looking at 'fat' or 'thin' body shapes versus controls. Pinhas et al. (2014) suggested that these biases were associated with early stages of anorexia, thus implicating eye-tracking as a possible detection method for anorexia.

Greenberg, Reuman, Hartmann, Kasarskis, and Wilhelm (2014) studied body dys-morphic disorder. They found that individuals with a preoccupation with their appear-ance were more likely to dwell on negative features of their own face, developing a negative attention bias. They concluded that if this negative bias is associated with both the development and maintenance of body dysmorphic disorder, then training could be put in place to broaden attention away from negative stimuli (Greenberg et al., 2014). This highlights the utility of eye-tracking in a clinical setting, particularly to aid understanding, improve diagnosis, and develop treatments for such cognitive-based disorders.

As eye-tracking has become progressively less intrusive and offers a direct measure of social attention (Guillon, Hadjikhani, Baduel, & Rogé, 2014), it has increasingly been used to study social interactions in autism studies. For example, Chawarska, Macari, and Shic (2013) played videoclips of an actress participating in various different social activities. They found that even at 6 months old, infants who later will be diagnosed with autism demonstrated decreased attention to social scenes. Likewise, two studies by Klin, Lin, Gorrindo, Ramsay, and Jones (2009) and Falck-Ytter, Rehnberg, and Bölte (2013) found that 24- and 40-month-old children, respectively, with autism, compared with those without the condition, do not look preferentially towards videos showing biological motion. These studies illustrate that eye-tracking can be used in order to understand and investigate concepts that are perhaps not understood or necessarily explained by the individual.

Eye-tracking also extends beyond understanding individual differences into other areas, such as marketing. Reutskaja, Nagel, Camerer, and Rangel (2011) used an eye-tracking paradigm in order to study consumers' decision-making and computational processes under time pressure. When presented with images of groups of snack items and asked to make a time-restricted decision, participants responded to more pressure (being presented with a greater number of items) by shortening the fixation time and lengthening the search time in order to optimize their gaze behaviour. They also found that individuals were more likely to look at items that were placed in the centre region of the display. Both aspects have implications for how items are marketed in order to increase consumer purchasing.

The use of eye-tracking to measure, understand, and infer cognitive processes with such a diverse range of populations where direct communication is difficult demonstrates how eye-tracking can use viewing time (VT) in order to infer cognition and prediction in a situation where this otherwise would not have been possible. Within the context of understanding sexual interest, and particularly offence-related sexual interest, eye-tracking may therefore act as a particularly useful methodology.

Challenges of Sex Offender Assessment

The use of eye-tracking methodology has increasingly taken a crucial place in research, enabling us to infer cognitive processes and develop methods of diagnosis and treatment just based on an individual's eye gaze. Within the sexual offending area, it is critical to develop a clear understanding of offence-related cognitions and cognitive processes.

A review by Snowden, Craig, and Gray (2011) highlighted the weaknesses of using different types of assessment methodologies with sexual offenders. In particular, they identified the need to utilize assessment methodologies that do not rely on or assume that the participant is being honest about or has a good understanding of their problem. This is particularly a problem when assessing sexual interest, where there may be strong demand characteristics to encourage misreporting

Snowden et al. (2011) identified that self-report methods are flawed for use with sex offenders, and in general sexuality research, for many reasons. First, they assume that the information that is being asked to be provided is available to report (i.e., it is in the participant's conscious awareness). Likewise, it is difficult for individuals to have insight into their own behaviours, with sexual offenders being particularly prone to denial, and this has an impact on their response to self-report assessments (Nunes & Jung, 2012). Perhaps most importantly, self-reporting relies on the individual being honest, yet sex offenders have a strong motivation to distort the truth (Cooper, 2005). Such subjective measures are often dismissed as there are legal pressures for these individuals to deny such deviancy (Laws, Hanson, Osborn, & Greenbaum, 2000).

Hence the validity of self-report measures is jeopardized owing to impression management by the individual being assessed (Banse, Schmidt, & Clarbour, 2010), and relying on such explicit measures may be inaccurate (Snowden, Wichter, & Gray, 2008). Card sorts are another self-report measure used in order to assess deviant sexual preference. These require participants to rate how arousing or attractive they find the stimulus, and have been found to be useful when individuals admit to these paraphilias (Laws et al., 2000), yet it is more difficult when they do not (Akerman & Beech, 2012).

The most notable objective measure used in sex offender research is penile plethysmography (PPG). PPG is often used to investigate sexual deviance and involves having a measurement device fitted around the penis, with penile tumescence (equated to sexual arousal) being measured in response to explicit stimuli (Mackaronis, Byrne, & Strassberg, 2016). Although the most common measure of male sexuality (Worling, 2006) and the current 'gold standard' of sexuality research (Fromberger et al., 2012a), this methodology does have a variety of issues. Janssen, McBride, Yarber, Hill, and Butler (2008) found that their participants elicited many indicators of sexual arousal, including behavioural and psychological signs, suggesting that the purely physiological response of an erection is not sufficient to determine arousal. Moreover, the procedure is very invasive, which is a deterrent for participants, and is unavailable in many countries because of 'ethical concerns' (Babchishin, Nunes, & Hermann, 2013), in addition to having weak test–retest reliability (Renaud et al., 2010). There is also a lack of standardization concerning stimuli and procedures, highlighting a problem with consistency (Laws, 2009). Most worryingly, PPG is susceptible to faking behaviours (Trottier, Rouleau, Renaud, & Goyette, 2014). Renaud et al. (2009) found that, when asked, 80% of participants were able to exert voluntary control over their erectile responses. Also, Stinson and Becker (2008) could not identify rapists as having a preference for coerced sex, hence PPG may not be valid for use with this type of sex offender. Therefore, although PPG currently remains the most robust and valid method of assessing sexual arousal, it comes with a number of practical difficulties (Dean & Perkins, 2008), including the following:

1. The challenge of achieving offender engagement with the procedure (PPGs can be seen as intrusive, embarrassing, or anxiety provoking).
2. It is time consuming (generally taking about 2 h for briefing, carrying out the assessment, and debriefing).
3. It is complex to administer, owing to the specific and demanding requirements of the laboratory procedure.

PPG assessment is therefore suboptimal in terms of its wide-scale application and ease of administration within criminal justice and forensic mental health services.

Indirect Measures

Another set of objective measures used to assess sexual interest are called 'indirect measures', where the participant is not asked to self-assess an attribute directly, yet this attribute is implied based on another response (De Houwer & Moors, 2010). Snowden et al. (2011) published a useful review of indirect measures used to assess sexual interest with sexual offenders.

An example of such an indirect assessment of interest is the Choice Reaction Time (CRT), which uses 'sexual content-induced delay' (SCID), an attentional bias that occurs in the presence of salient and sexually arousing stimuli that interferes with the processing of target stimuli, to assess sexual interest (Snowden et al., 2011). Wright and Adams (1994) demonstrated the use of CRT to measure sexual preference, and found that longer reaction times were exhibited for preferred sexual partners compared with non-preferred sexual partners, indicating that sexual arousal does interfere with cognitive processing. More recently, Santtila et al. (2009) validated the use of CRT methods in hetero- and homosexual men, with participants demonstrating longer reaction times to sexually explicit, compared with non-explicit, pictures of their preferred gender, due to SCID.

CRT studies have demonstrated strong internal reliability in terms of their potential as an indirect measure of sexual interest (Snowden et al., 2011); however, as only a relatively small number of studies have been published, it is difficult to suggest whether or not CRT studies are entirely predictive of sexuality (Snowden et al., 2011). Furthermore, only a very limited number of studies used CRT, or a CRT-like measure, with sex offenders. Mokros, Dombert, Osterheider, Zappalà, and Santtila (2010) are considered to be the first to report a study that used CRT and specifically gave the age of the victims, i.e., children. Child-sex offenders had longer reaction times for stimuli from the 'non-adult' category, as opposed to the 'adult' category, with this expected interaction indicating a relatively strong effect, thus showing promise for the use of CRT with respect to deviant sexual interest. However, Gress, Anderson, and Laws (2013) endeavoured to create two attention-based response latency instruments that were based on both CRT and VT, and they found that, with regard to CRT, no significant differences were found between adult sex offenders and the non-sexually offending group. This demonstrates that CRT perhaps is not suitable for sex offender assessment.

Similarly, an Implicit Association Test (IAT) works on the premise that individuals' response times will be faster for internal beliefs, with participants associating two concepts with the same predetermined key, e.g., 'Child' and 'Adult' ascribed to keys 'A' and 'B', respectively, and then 'Sexy' and 'Not Sexy' also associated with the same two keys (Snowden et al., 2011). Related concepts are said to produce faster reaction times than non-related concepts, giving insight into an individual's beliefs. Although the IAT has precisely identified sexuality (Snowden et al., 2008), it has been reported to be prone to 'faking behaviours' (Gray & Snowden, 2009). Also, an association between children and sex cannot be said to be definitive proof of an abnormal sex interest in children (Snowden et al., 2011), thus questioning the validity of the method.

VT and IAT procedures have been used successfully in the assessment of child sexual offenders and have, for example, been successfully integrated, along with self-reports of sexual fantasies and behaviours, within the 'Explicit and Implicit Sexual Interest Profile' (EISIP) method (Banse et al., 2010). The EISIP assessment procedure takes

20–30 min to complete and can be administered in most interview and clinic settings. This multifaceted, computer-administered procedure, however, is currently able to assess only relative age and gender sexual interests, and its use is therefore confined to child sexual offender assessment. There are currently no similarly effective procedures for assessing sexual arousal/interests in adult sexual violence.

These are just a few examples of the available ways of assessing deviant sexual interest, often with indirect measures of association. Akerman and Beech (2012) and Snowden et al. (2011) presented comprehensive reviews of the multitude of ways in which deviant sexual interest can be assessed, with no clearly preferred method being identified. Given the possibility of inferring underlying cognitive processes from eye-fixations and movements, this remains a possibility for use within forensic contexts.

Eye-Tracking Use with Sex Interest and Orientation

It has been said that gender differences to visual, sexual stimuli have been widely acknowledged, but this area is still poorly documented (Rupp & Wallen, 2008). Gaze patterns of individuals have been said to indicate their sexual interest, with men and women responding markedly differently to different sexual stimuli (Tsujimura et al., 2008). As there are apparent gender differences in viewing visual sexual stimuli and what evokes a sexual response, it is important to evaluate this visual attention (Tsujimura et al., 2008). Thus, as eye-tracking measures such visual attention, it is evident that this method can inform about what individuals attend to when they are exposed to erotic visual situations (Lykins, Meana, & Kambe, 2006). Eye-tracking is suitable for the study of human sex interest not only because it is a reliable and valid measure of attention (Tsujimura et al., 2008), but also because it assesses such visual attention that is not under conscious control and therefore unable to be consciously manipulated by individuals (Akhter, 2011).

Lykins et al. (2006) were one of the pioneers in investigating sex differences in visual processing to sexual stimuli (Akhter, 2011). They used colour images of individual men and women, which were erotic and non-erotic, to investigate gaze behaviour. They found that different body regions attracted greater or lesser attention, with participants attending more to the body area of the image in the erotic compared with the non-erotic condition (Lykins et al., 2006). They speculated from their results that it is possible that women's visual attention may be more dramatically altered by erotic content (Lykins et al., 2006). This led Lykins et al. (2006) to conclude that sexually salient stimuli are processed in a wholly different manner to non-erotic stimuli and that eye-tracking is a valid measure to capture the differences in the processing of both erotic and non-erotic stimuli at a visual level.

Jiang, Costello, Fang, Huang, and He (2006) provided further support for this conclusion by investigating whether interocularly suppressed, 'invisible' erotic pictures were able to direct the distribution of visual spatial attention. Both heterosexual males and females demonstrated an attentional benefit towards their preferred gender (female nude pictures and male nude pictures, respectively). Jiang et al. (2006)

concluded that, even when salient images are masked, the emotional system processes these images in a specific fashion, supporting the claim that erotic content is processed differently to non-erotic content.

Lykins, Meana, and Strauss (2008) went on to carry out a study that was similar to that of Lykins et al. (2006), but also investigated gender differences. They used pictures of couples performing various foreplay acts and matched non-erotic pictures to investigate the gaze patterns of men and women. Again, similarly to Lykins et al. (2006), they found that the bodies of the stimuli were attended to preferentially, whether it was non-erotic or erotic; however, they suggested that this may have been because the body was the largest region of interest, and thus naturally was allocated more attention (Lykins et al., 2008). With regard to gender differences, they found that men attended to their preferred gender, regardless of whether the image was erotic or non-erotic, whereas women divided their attention more equally between genders, suggesting non-specificity for female sexual arousal (Lykins et al., 2008).

Hall, Hogue, and Guo (2011) conducted an eye-tracking study to investigate the extent to which gaze behaviours were related to high-level mental processes, such as attractiveness judgements. Using 50 greyscale images from five age groups, they discovered that men's viewing patterns with respect to human figures was linked to their sexual preference in that they had a distinctive gaze pattern when viewing same-aged, 20-year-old female images, with more fixations and attention being directed towards body areas essential for signalling fertility (e.g., waist–hip ratio [WHR]). Nummenmaa, Hietanen, Santtila, and Hyönä (2012) found that nude images attracted more fixations than clothed images, suggesting, similarly to aforementioned studies, that erotic content is processed differently to non-erotic content.

Fromberger et al. (2012b) conducted a pioneering study into the exploration of attentional engagement when presented with two sexual stimuli that differed only in their sexual relevance to the subject (i.e., whether they were their preferred gender or not). They used the Not-Real-People picture set at Tanner stages 1, 2, 4, and 5, and found that men fixated on their sexually preferred gender more than their non-preferred gender, giving further support that sexual stimuli attract more attention. This study showed for the first time using eye-tracking attentional biases to sexually relevant stimuli when presented simultaneously with sexually irrelevant pictures (Fromberger et al., 2012b).

Thus far, all of the studies mentioned used only still images as stimuli. Tsujimura et al. (2009) were the first investigators to use videos in order to assess sexuality using eye-tracking methodology, with the view that they would find more detailed sex differences when moving images were used. They used sexually explicit videos in which the actors did or did not touch the genitals. They found that there is a clear difference as to which regions men and women pay attention to when presented with the same sexual stimuli, with men viewing the opposite-sex actor longer and women viewing the same-sex actor longer.

Eye-tracking has been useful in understanding general sexuality research; however, it seems ambiguous how this is applicable to real life. One area in which it has applications is in evolutionary research, specifically around what individuals find attractive in a mate. Suschinsky, Elias, and Krupp (2007) investigated whether attention is allocated to reproductively relevant parts of the stimuli. They found that more attention was allocated to reproductively relevant regions of interest, with more attention being devoted to, and higher ratings being given to, lower WHR which signals fertility.

Further research has been conducted in this particular field by Dixson, Grimshaw, Linklater, and Dixson (2011). They wanted to investigate the relationship between breast size and WHR, as these are both linked to the sexual attractiveness of women. Using digitally manipulated images and an Eyelink 1000 Tower Mount head-supported system, they found that men spent the most time looking at the breast region, with more attention allocated in general to the more 'upper body' regions, including the face and breasts. However, WHR mainly influenced attraction ratings, with a ratio of 0.7 being rated as consistently more attractive regardless of breast size (Dixson et al., 2011).

Dixson, Grimshaw, Ormsby, and Dixson (2014) also carried out a comparative study on what body types women find attractive in men, with the view that 'mesomorphs' would draw more attention. Using back-posed, nude, black-and-white photographs of the three male somatotypes, they found that somatotype accounted for 90% variance in the attractiveness ratings, with ratings increasing as muscularity increased (Dixson et al., 2014).

In the general sexuality research area, it can be seen that eye-tracking can be used to indicate sexual interest and informs about human sexual interactions. Although eye-tracking can be informative about human sex interest and its application to evolutionary psychology, one of the main, and perhaps most important, applications is to deviant sex interest. Inappropriate sexual preference is one of the strongest predictors of future sexual recidivism (Hanson & Morton-Bourgon, 2005). The development of an objective assessment method such as eye-tracking may have implications for the measurement of risk and assessment of treatment effectiveness with sex offenders.

Eye-Tracking Use with Offenders

Given the use of eye-tracking in typical sexuality research, it seems appropriate to apply eye-tracking technology to the assessment of deviant sex interest. There are many reasons why it seems appropraite to use eye-tracking with sexual offenders. For instance, initial eye movements are automatic, and therefore difficult to control and alter completely (Hall, Hogue, & Guo, 2012). As sex offenders are known to attempt, sometimes successfully, to inhibit their sexual responses to stimuli (Trottier et al., 2014), eye-tracking would be a both helpful and plausible methodology to distinguish the actual sexual preferences of the individual.

Furthermore, eye-tracking can be implicated in the understanding and allocation of the correct treatment for sex offenders. Jordan, Fromberger, Laubinger, Dechent, and Müller (2014) undertook a case study using eye-tracking to explore the impact of testosterone suppression via antiandrogen medication on automatic and controlled attentional processes. They found that this medication did not affect initial orienting to stimuli, with lower fixation latencies (akin to automatic attentional processes) for 'girl' (versus 'woman') stimuli both before and after treatment. Although this was only a case study, it demonstrates that the treatment that had been chosen for this individual had in fact no impact on his paedophilic preference, leading the authors to suggest that it may be the case that the medication allowed the individual to avoid deviant sexual stimuli consciously, which is why it affected the relative fixation time (equated to controllable attentional processes).

Lastly, eye-tracking can be used to validate new measures for the investigation into deviant sex interest. Renaud and colleagues (Renaud et al., 2012, 2014) used eye-tracking to validate virtual reality in assessing sexual preference, with the view that this may be more useful than current techniques as it is both immersive and interactive (Renaud, Rouleau, Granger, Barsetti, & Bouchard, 2002). Not only can it be used in the creation of *new* methods, but also in the exploration of *old* methods. Trottier et al. (2014) used eye-tracking methodology to identify faking attempts in PPG. Although PPG is the most widely used method of assessment for sex offenders, many individuals exert voluntary control over their responses in order to gain a non-deviant sexual profile (Trottier et al., 2014), which then questions the validity and reliability of such methods and the responses that are produced. They found that, even during inhibition, the fixation duration to the individual's preferred sexual stimuli remained constant, suggesting that individuals are able to 'fake' their responses. This also provides a case for using eye-tracking more frequently in sex offender research if it is able to prevail where other, more popular and long-standing methods cannot.

Only a handful of studies have actually used primarily eye-tracking to assess deviant sexual interest. Fromberger et al. (2012a) carried out one of the first studies to look at eye movements in assessing paedophilia. They predicted that the relative fixation time for stimuli that were sexually relevant would be significantly longer than for the same stimuli used with non-paedophiles, and fixation latency would be shorter than in non-paedophiles. They found that automatic attentional processes differentiated paedophiles from non-paedophiles better than controlled processes (Fromberger et al., 2012a), perhaps reflective of individuals trying to suppress their true feelings in a socially desirable way. They concluded that age preference based on fixation latency was more appropriate for diagnosing paedophilia, with VT correctly classifying individuals at levels between 65.6 and 96% (Fromberger et al., 2012a). They also argued that eye-tracking had an accuracy comparable to, or even better than, those of methods already in existence.

Fromberger and colleagues then extended their research into gaze behaviour in paedophiles by exploring controlled and automatic processing (Fromberger et al., 2013). They used the Not-Real-People picture set at Tanner stages 1, 2, 4, and 5 to present pictures of a child and an adult simultaneously. They found that paedophiles had a significantly shorter average entry time for the child pictures, compared with the adult pictures, when contrasted with non-paedophiles. However, they also found that paedophiles demonstrated longer relative fixation times for adult than for child pictures. Fromberger et al. (2013) suggested that this may be a product of individuals trying to act in a socially desirable manner, similarly to their earlier study (Fromberger et al., 2012a, 2012b). Hence their study demonstrates that eye-tracking is useful in sex offender research as it is possible to look at automatic processes that are harder to control and thus manipulate, which is one of the pitfalls of many other methods in this area (Akerman & Beech, 2012).

Hall, Hogue, and Guo (2015) highlighted that the extent to which eye gaze may infer a deviant sexual interest is severely lacking at present, despite the inumerable benefits over other methods. They investigated whether naturalistic gaze patterns could be used to differentiate between offenders and non-offenders when viewing clothed adult and child stimuli. They found that child-sex offenders demonstrate significantly more fixations to the upper body of 10-year-old girls, yet post hoc revealed no significant differences in these viewing patterns between offenders and non-offenders. However, offenders showed a significantly greater difference in their viewing patterns of child males and females, whereas non-offenders could only be differentiated when viewing adult figures (Hall et al., 2015), suggesting that they were viewing these as a function of their preference. Hall et al. (2015) concluded that their results add to the research proposing that eye-tracking is a viable method of assessing deviant sexual interest.

To date, very little work has investigated forced sex utilizing eye-tracking. Süssenbach, Bohner, and Eyssel (2012) use eye-tracking to examine the impact of Rape-Myth Acceptance (RMA) on viewing behaviour. RMA is the tendency to perceive the victim of a sexual assault as responsible owing to their behaviour or situational clues. They presented participants with pictures including RMA-consistent clues that were 'expected' (an alcoholic beverage) or 'unexpected' (a poster depicting a nude male torso). They found that individuals with a higher RMA fixated on an expected clue earlier and for less time, insinuating hypervigilance. The authors suggested that eye-tracking is ideal for looking at underlying perceptual processes and to further knowledge about RMA and indeed about the underlying motivations behind rape.

Eye-Tracking Use in Applied Practice

In order to provide the most effective treatment and risk management for sexual and sexually violent offenders, it is essential that empirically determined risk factors for their offending are able to be validly and reliably assessed. These factors therefore need to be accurately monitored over time and incorporated into offence formulations that permit the provision of relevant treatments and risk management plans. Mentally disordered offenders, managed through the high-, medium-, and low-security forensic mental health services, present with a range of risks to the public and to themselves. Those in high-security services have typically offended with extreme physical and sexual violence, including violent and sexual offending against children, sexually motivated violence against adults (usually women), and homicides (of adults or children), within which the role of sexual motivation may be unclear.

Eye-tracking appears to have some potential value within a forensic context for assessing sex offenders and assisting in forensic case formulation (Sturmey & McMurran, 2011). Eye-tracking technology has also been shown to have clinical utility running alongside PPG assessments, to understand faking attempts (Trottier et al., 2014). Recently, eye-tracking has been paired clinically with PPG to try and ensure (or at least appraise) subject compliance with the PPG procedure (i.e., ensuring that subjects are viewing the stimulus screen), and in analysing precisely where subjects are looking during the assessment (which can then be cross-referenced with peaks and troughs in the subject's PPG profile during the assessment) (Perkins & Hogue, 2014).

In the assessment of offence-related sexual interests with offenders whose sexual violence is directed towards adults (mainly rape and homicide), eye-tracking is potentially able to examine eye movements across the various types of visual stimuli used within PPG assessments of such offenders. These stimuli typically comprise moving images depicting consenting adult sexual activity (C), coercive sexual activity (rape; R), and non-sexual violence (V), known as the CRV assessment (Perkins & Hogue, 2013). The PPG procedure when using these types of stimuli, as mentioned above, normally takes about 2 h to complete.

Perkins and Hogue (2013) reported preliminary findings from measuring eye movements across the CRV moving stimuli with non-offender subjects and a small sample of sexual offenders against women. There are two challenges to this work: first, selecting an appropriate range of moving imagery that will be effective in differentiating between (a) offenders and non-offenders and (b) different typologies of sexual aggressors (e.g., compensatory versus sadistic rapists), and in so doing ultimately contributing to assessments of future offending risk and treatment need.

The eye-tracker procedure is able to record precisely where subjects (offenders or controls) are looking, the directions of travel of these eye movements, and for how long specific stimulus sections are fixated, while the subjects' penile responses are monitored. Figure 45.1 illustrates variations between a series of subjects in the extent to

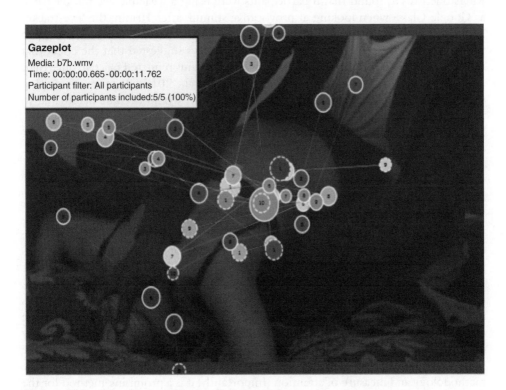

Figure 45.1   Use of eye-tracking in clinical assessment.

which their eye-tracking covers the field of vision as well as (not shown in the figure) the directions of travel of the eye movements and lengths of fixation.

Limitations

The eye-tracking methodology is not without its limitations. First, stationary eye-trackers in particular are often not easily portable devices, meaning that it has to be set up in a specific way in a laboratory setting, which may be inconvenient, especially if trying to reach an offender population. Historically, eye-tracking equipment has been costly, which meant that they are often not readily available and are expensive if they break (Kumar, 2006). Lastly, and potentially most importantly, participants can be hyper-aware of the fact that their eye gaze is being tracked, and may attempt to bias the results by responding in a way that portrays them in a favourable light, which is already an issue for sex offenders. For instance, Risko and Kingstone (2011) found that wearing an eye-tracker, which was an implied social presence, led typical individuals to avoid looking at provocative stimuli.

This poses an issue for eye-tracking methodologies and suggests that there is an 'eye-tracker awareness', with participants being particularly sensitive to having their eye gaze monitored, and are thus willing and able to adjust their gaze behaviour accordingly (Risko & Kingstone, 2011). Similarly, Nasiopoulos, Risko, Foulsham, and Kingstone (2015) found that if participants were using a wearable eye-tracker (such as Google Glass) when looking at provocative stimuli, after 10 min, the 'eye-tracker awareness' was abolished. Only if the participants had their attention drawn back to the eye-tracker was the effect reactivated. The authors suggested that the effect that the eye-tracker had on individuals was transient, and thus rendered inactive once their attention was shifted away from it (Nasiopoulos et al., 2015). Hence free-viewing stimuli may not be as much of an issue as participants would become habituated to the eye-tracker after a period of time; however, if they had to respond to the stimuli, this may reactivate the 'eye-tracker awareness'. All of these issues need further study, especially as they apply to assessments undertaken in clinical practice.

Conclusions

The accurate identification of sexual interest and motivation remains a critical feature of understanding sexual offending behaviour. A range of newly developed methods for assessing sexual interest and deviant sexual interest show promise (Akerman & Beech, 2012; Snowden et al., 2011), although all have some inherent weakness. Eye-tracking technology has increasingly been used to infer intent and cognitive process in a range of different situations and populations. There is an increasing literature on the use of eye-tracking to understand sexual behaviour and increasingly sexually inappropriate and sexually aggressive behaviour. Future studies and forensic practice should take advantage of the eye-tracking methodology as it can act as a non-intrusive methodology and measure of attention. Importantly, it is a promising method for the assessment of deviant sexual interest and offence-related cognitions.

References

Akerman, G., & Beech, A. (2012). A systematic review of measures of deviant sexual interest and arousal. *Psychiatry, Psychology and Law, 19*(1), 118–143. doi:10.1080/13218719.2010.547161

Akhter, S. (2011). *Visual attention to erotic stimuli in androphilic male-to-female transsexuals.* (Doctoral thesis, University of Nevada, Las Vegas, NV).

Babchishin, K., Nunes, K., & Hermann, C. (2013). The validity of Implicit Association Test (IAT) measures of sexual attraction to children: A meta-analysis. *Archives of Sexual Behavior, 42*, 487–499. doi:10.1007/s10508-012-0022-8

Banse, R., Schmidt, A., & Clarbour, J. (2010). Indirect measures of sexual interest in child sex offenders: A multimethod approach. *Criminal Justice and Behavior, 37*(3), 319–335. doi:10.1177/0093854809357598

Chawarska, K., Macari, S., & Shic, F. (2013). Decreased spontaneous attention to social scenes in 6-month-old infants later diagnosed with Autism Spectrum Disorders. *Biological Psychiatry, 74*, 195–203. doi:10.1016/j.biopsych.2012.11.022

Cooper, S. (2005). Understanding, treating, and managing sex offenders who deny their offense. *Journal of Sexual Aggression, 11*, 85–94.

De Houwer, J., & Moors, A. (2010). Implicit measures: Similarities and differences. In B. Gawronski & K. B. Payne (Eds.), *Handbook of implicit social cognition: Measurement, theory, and applications.* New York, NY: Guilford Press.

Dean, C., & Perkins, D. (2008). Penile plethysmography. *Prison Service Journal, 178*, 20–25.

Dixson, B., Grimshaw, G., Linklater, W., & Dixson, A. (2011). Eye-tracking of men's references for waist-to-hip ratio and breast size of women. *Archives of Sexual Behavior, 40*, 43–50. doi:10.1007/s10508-009-9523-5

Dixson, B., Grimshaw, G., Ormsby, D., & Dixson, A. (2014). Eye-tracking women's preferences or men's somatotypes. *Evolution and Human Behavior, 35*, 73–79. doi:10.1016/j.evolhumbehav.2013.10.003

Drewes, H. (2010). *Eye gaze tracking for human computer interaction.* (Doctoral dissertation, Ludwig-Maximilians-Universität, Munich, Germany).

Duchowski, A., (2002). A breadth-first survey of eye tracking applications. *Behavior Research Methods, Instruments, and Computers, 34*(4), 455–470. doi:10.3758/BF03195475

Falck-Ytter, T., Rehnberg, E., & Bölte, S. (2013). Lack of visual orienting to biological motion in 3-year-olds with autism. *PLoS ONE, 8*(7), e68816. doi:10.1371/journal.pone.0068816

Feng, G. (2011). Eye tracking: A brief guide for developmental researchers. *Journal of Cognition and Development, 12*(1), 1–11. doi:10.1080/15248372.2011.547447

Fromberger, P., Jordan, K., Steinkrauss, H., von Herder, J., Stolpmann, G., Kröner-Herwig, B., & Müller, J. (2013). Eye movements in pedophiles: Automatic and controlled attentional processes while viewing prepubescent stimuli. *Journal of Abnormal Psychology, 122*(2), 587–599. doi:10.1037/a0030659

Fromberger, P., Jordan, K., Steinkrauss, H., von Herder, J., Witzel, J., Stolpmann, G., ... Müller, J. (2012a). Diagnostic accuracy of eye movements in assessing pedophilia. *The Journal of Sexual Medicine, 9*, 1868–1882. doi:10.1111/j.1743-6109.2012.02754.x

Fromberger, P., Jordan, K., von Herder, J., Steinkrauss, H., Nemetschek, R., Stolpmann, G., & Müller, J. (2012b). Initial orienting towards sexually relevant stimuli: Preliminary evidence from eye movements measures. *Archives of Sexual Behavior, 41*, 919–928. doi:10.1007/s10508-011-9816-3

Gray, N., & Snowden, R. (2009). The Implicit Association Test as a measure of sexual interest. In D. Thornton & D. R. Laws (Eds.), *Cognitive approaches to the assessment of sexual interest in sexual offenders* (pp. 101–125). Chichester, England: John Wiley & Sons, Ltd.

Greenberg, J., Reuman, L., Hartmann, A., Kasarskis, I., & Wilhelm, S. (2014). Visual hot spots: An eye tracking study of attention bias in body dysmorphic disorder. *Journal of Psychiatric Research, 57*, 125–132. doi:10.1016/j.jpsychires.2014.06.015

Gress, C., Anderson, J., & Laws, R. (2013). Delays in attentional processing when viewing sexual imagery: The development and comparison of two measures. *Legal and Criminological Psychology, 18*(1), 66–82. doi:10.1111/j.2044-8333.2011.02032.x

Guillon, Q., Hadjikhani, N., Baduel, S., & Rogé, B. (2014). Visual social attention in autism spectrum disorder: Insights from eye tracking studies. *Neuroscience and BiobehavioralReviews, 42*, 279–297. doi:10.1016/j.neubiorev.2014.03.013

Guo, K., Robertson, R., Mahmoodi, S., Tadmor, Y., & Young, M. (2003). How do monkeys view faces? – A study of eye movements. *Experimental Brain Research, 150*, 363–374. doi:10.1007/s00221-003-1429-1

Hall, C., Hogue, T., & Guo, K. (2011). Differential gaze behavior towards sexually preferred and non-preferred human figures. *Journal of Sex Research, 48*(5), 461–469. doi:10.1080/00224499.2010.521899

Hall, C., Hogue, T., & Guo, K. (2012). Sexual cognition guides viewing strategies to human figures. *Journal of Sex Research, 51*(2), 184–196. doi:10.1080/00224499.2012.716872

Hall, C., Hogue, T., & Guo, K. (2015). Gaze patterns to child figures reflect deviant sexual preference in child sex offenders – A first glance. *Journal of Sexual Aggression, 21*(3), 303–317. DOI:

Hanson, R., & Morton-Bourgon, K. (2005). The characteristics of persistent sexual offenders: A meta-analysis of recidivism studies. *Journal of Consulting and Clinical Psychology, 73*(6), 1154–1163. doi:10.1037/0022-006X.73.6.1154

Hartridge, H., & Thomson, L. (1948). Methods of investigating eye movements. *British Journal of Ophthalmology, 32*, 581–591. doi:10.1136/bjo.32.9.581

Jacob, R., & Karn, K., (2003). Eye tracking in human–computer interaction and usability research: Ready to deliver the promises. *Mind, 2*(3), 4.

Janssen, E., McBride, K., Yarber, W., Hill, B., & Butler, S. (2008). Factors that influence sexual arousal in men: A focus group study. *Archives of Sexual Behavior, 37*, 252–265. doi:10.1007/s10508-007-9245-5

Jiang, Y., Costello, P., Fang, F., Huang, M., & He, S. (2006). A gender- and sexual orientation-dependent spatial attentional effect of invisible images. *Proceedings of the National Academy of Sciences of the United States of America, 101*(45), 17048–17052. doi:10.1073/pnas.0605678103

Jordan, K., Fromberger, P., Laubinger, H., Dechent, P., & Müller, J. (2014). Changed processing of visual sexual stimuli under GnRH-therapy – A single case study in pedophilia using eye tracking and fMRI. *BMC Psychiatry, 14*, 142 –155. doi:10.1186/1471-244X-14-142

Kano, F., & Call, J. (2014). Great apes generate goal-based action predictions: An eye-tracking study. *Psychological Science, 25*(9), 1691–1698. doi:10.1177/0956797614536402

Kano, F., & Tomonaga, M. (2013). Head-mounted eye tracking of a chimpanzee under naturalistic conditions. *PLoS ONE, 8*(3), e5978. doi:10.1371/journal.pone.0059785

Klin, A., Lin, D., Gorrindo, P., Ramsay, G., & Jones, W. (2009). Two-year-olds with autism orient to non-social contingencies rather than biological motion. *Nature, 459*, 257–263. doi:10.1038/nature07868

Kumar, M. (2006). *Reducing the cost of eye tracking systems* (Technical Report CSTR 2006-08, Stanford University). Retrieved from http://hci.stanford.edu/cstr/reports/2006-08.pdf

Laws, D. R. (2009). Penile plethysmography: Strengths, limitations, innovations. In D. Thornton and D. R. Laws (Eds.), *Cognitive approaches to the assessment of sexual interest in sexual offenders* (pp. 7–29). Chichester, England: John Wiley & Sons, Ltd.

Laws, D., Hanson, R., Osborn, C., & Greenbaum, P. (2000). Classification of child molesters by plethysmographic assessment of sexual arousal and a self-report measure of sexual preference. *Journal of Interpersonal Violence, 15*(12), 1297–1312. doi: 10.1177/088626000015012004

Linehan, C., Waddington, J., Hodgson, T., Hicks, K., & Banks, R. (2014). Designing games for the rehabilitation of functional vision for children with cerebral visual impairment. In *Proceedings of ACM CHI EA '14 Conference on Human Factors in Computing Systems (CHI 2014), Canada* (pp. 1207–1212). New York, NY: ACM Press. doi:10.1145/2559206.2581219

Lupu, R., & Ungureanu, F. (2013). A survey of eye tracking methods and applications. *Buletinul Institutului Politehnic din Iaşi*, 71–86.

Lykins, A., Meana, M., & Kambe, G. (2006). Detection of differential viewing patterns to erotic and non-erotic stimuli using eye-tracking methodology. *Archives of Sexual Behavior, 35*, 569–575.

Lykins, A., Meana, M., & Strauss, G. (2008). Sex differences in visual attention to erotic and non-erotic stimuli. *Archives of Sexual Behavior, 37*(2), 219–228.

Mackaronis, J. E., Byrne, P. M., & Strassberg, D. S. (2016). Assessing Sexual Interest in Adolescents Who Have Sexually Offended. *Sexual Abuse: A Journal of Research and Treatment, 28*(2), 96–115. doi:10.1177/1079063214535818

Mackenzie, A. K., & Harris, J. M. (2014). Characterizing visual attention during driving and non-driving hazard perception tasks. In *Proceedings of the 2014 Symposium on Eye Tracking Research and Applications* (pp. 127–130). New York, NY: ACM Press. doi:10.1145/2578153.2578171

Majaranta, P., & Räihä, K. (2007). Text entry by daze: Utilizing eye-tracking. In I. MacKenzie and K. Tanaka-Ishii (Eds.), *Text Entry Systems* (pp. 175–187). San Francisco, CA: Morgan Kaufmann.

Mohamed, A. O., Perreira da Silva, M., & Courboulay, V. (2007). *A history of eye gaze tracking*, Rapport Interne, hal-00215967. Retrieved from https://hal.archives-ouvertes.fr/hal-00215967/document.

Mokros, A., Dombert, B., Osterheider, M., Zappala, A., & Santtila, P. (2010). Assessment of pedophilic sexual interest with an attentional Choice Reaction Time task. *Archives of Sexual Behavior, 39*(5), 1081–1090.

Nasiopoulos, E., Risko, E. F., Foulsham, T., & Kingstone, A. (2015). Wearable computing: Will it make people prosocial? *British Journal of Psychology, 106*, 209–216. doi:10.1111/bjop.12080

Nummenmaa, L., Hietanen, J., Santtila, P., & Hyönä, J. (2012). Gender and visibility of sexual cues influence eye movements while viewing faces and bodies. *Archives of Sexual Behavior, 41*, 1439–1451. doi:10.1007/s10508-012-9911-0

Nunes, K. L., & Jung, S. (2012). Are cognitive distortions associated with denial and minimization among sex offenders? *Sexual Abuse, 20*(10), 1–23. doi:10.1177/1079063212453941

Perkins, D., & Hogue, T. (2013, October/November). *Development of an eye-tracker assessment of sexual interest for sexual violence towards women.* Paper presented at the 32nd Annual Conference of the Association for the Treatment of Sexual Abusers, Chicago, IL.

Perkins, D., & Hogue, T. E. (2014, September). *Assessing offense-related sexual interest in perpetrators of adult sexual violence.* Paper presented at the National Organisation for the Treatment of Abusers (NOTA) Annual Conference, York.

Pinhas, L., Fok, K., Chen, A., Lam, E., Schachter, R., Eizenman, O., Grupp, L., & Eizenman, M. (2014). Attentional biases to body shape images in adolescents with anorexia nervosa: An exploratory eye-tracking study. *Psychiatry Research, 220*, 519–526. doi:10.1016/j.psychres.2014.08.006

Renaud, P., Chartier, S., Rouleau, J., Proulx, J., Decarie, J., Trottier, D., ... Bouchard, S. (2009). Gaze behavior nonlinear dynamics assessed in virtual immersion as a diagnostic index of sexual deviancy: Preliminary results. *Journal of Virtual Reality and Broadcasting, 6*(3).

Renaud, P., Goyette, M., Chartier, S., Zhornitski, S., Trottier, D., Rouleau, J., ... Bouchard, S. (2010). Sexual affordances, perceptual-motor invariance extraction and intentional nonlinear dynamics: Sexually deviant and non-deviant patterns in male subjects. *Nonlinear Dynamics, Psychology, and Life Sciences, 14*(4), 463–489.

Renaud, P., Nolet, K., Chartier, S., Trottier, D., Goyette, M., Rouleau, J.-L., & Bouchard, S. (2012). Sexual presence and intentional dynamics: Deviant and non-deviant sexual self-regulation from the first person stance. *Journal of Eye-Tracking, Visual Cognition and Emotions, 2*(1), 82–96.

Renaud, P., Rouleau, J., Granger, L., Barsetti, I., & Bouchard, S. (2002). Measuring sexual preference in virtual reality: A pilot study. *Cyberpsychology & Behavior, 5*(1), 1–9.

Renaud, P., Trottier, D., Nolet, K., Rouleau, J. L., Goyette, M., & Bouchard, S. (2014). Sexual self-regulation and cognitive absorption as factors of sexual response toward virtual characters. *Cyberpsychology, Behavior, and Social Networking, 17*(4), 241–247. doi:10.1089/cyber.2013.0165

Reutskaja, E., Nagel, R., Camerer, C., & Rangel, A.(2011). Search dynamics in consumer choice under time pressure: An eye-tracking study. *American Economic Review, 101*(2), 900–926. doi:10.1257/aer.101.2.900

Richardson, D. C., & Spivey, M. J. (2004). Eye tracking: Characteristics and methods. *Encyclopedia of biomaterials and biomedical engineering, 3*, 1028–1042.

Risko, E., & Kingstone, A. (2011). Eyes wide shut: Implied social presence, eye tracking and attention. *Attention, Perception and Psychophysics, 73*, 291–296. doi:10.3758/s13414-010-0042-1

Rupp, H., & Wallen, K. (2008). Sex differences in response to visual sexual stimuli: A review. *Archives of Sexual Behavior, 37*(2), 206–218. doi:10.1007/s10508-007-9217-9

Salvucci, D. D., & Goldberg, J. H. (2000, November). Identifying fixations and saccades in eye-tracking protocols. In *Proceedings of the 2000 Symposium on Eye Tracking Research and Applications* (pp. 71–78). New York, NY: ACM Press.

Santtila, P., Mokros, A., Viljanen, K., Koivisto, M., Sandnabba, K., Zappala, A., & Osterheider, M. (2009). Assessment of sexual interest using a Choice Reaction Time task and priming: A feasibility study. *Legal and Criminological Psychology, 14*(1), 65–82. doi:10.1348/135532507X267040

Snowden, R., Craig, R., & Gray, N. (2011). Indirect behavioral measures of cognition among sexual offenders. *Journal of Sex Research, 48*(2–3), 192–217. doi:10.1080/00224499.2011.557750

Snowden, R., Wichter, J., & Gray, N. (2008). Implicit and explicit measurements of sexual preference in gay and heterosexual men: A comparison of priming techniques and the Implicit Association Task. *Archives of Sexual Behavior, 37*, 558–565. doi:10.1007/s10508-006-9138-z ,

Sturmey, P., & McMurran, M. (2011). *Forensic case formulation*. Chichester, England: John Wiley & Sons, Ltd.

Stinson, J. D., & Becker, J. V. (2008). Assessing sexual deviance: A comparison of physiological, historical, and self-report measures. *Journal of Psychiatric Practice, 14*, 379–388.

Suschinsky, K. D., Elias, L. J., & Krupp, D. B. (2007). Looking for Ms. Right: Allocating attention to facilitate mate choice decisions. *Evolutionary Psychology, 5*(2), 428–441.

Süssenbach, P., Bohner, G., & Eyssel, F. (2012). Schematic influences of rape myth acceptance on visual information processing: An eye-tracking approach. *Journal of Experimental Social Psychology, 48*, 660–668.

Tenenbaum, E., Shah, R., Sobel., D., Malle., B., & Morgan, J. (2013). Increased focus on the mouth among infants in the first year of life: A longitudinal eye-tracking study. *Infancy, 18*(4), 534–553. doi:10.1111/j.1532-7078.2012.00135.x

Trottier, D., Rouleau, J., Renaud, P., & Goyette, M. (2014). Using eye tracking to identify faking attempts during penile plethysmography assessment. *Journal of Sex Research, 51*(8), 946–955. doi:10.1080/00224499.2013.832133

Tsujimura, A., Miyagawa, Y., Takada, S., Matsuoka, Y., Takao, T., Hirai, T., … Okuyama, A. (2008). Sex differences in visual attention to sexually explicit videos: A preliminary study. *The Journal of Sexual Medicine, 6*, 1011–1017. doi:10.1111/j.1743-6109.2008.01031.x

van der Laan, L. N., Hooge, I., de Ridder, D., Viergever, M., & Smeets, P. (2015). Do you like what you see? The role of first fixation and total fixation duration in consumer choice. *Food Quality & Preference, 39*, 46–55. doi:10.1016/j.foodqual.2014.06.015

Weigle, C., & Banks, D. C. (2008). Analysis of eye-tracking experiments performed on a Tobii T60. *Proceeding ofs SPIE, 6809*, 680903.

Worling, J. (2006). Assessing sexual arousal with adolescent males who have offended sexually: Self-report and unobtrusively measured viewing time. *Sex Abuse, 18*, 383–400. doi:10.1007/s11194-006-9024-1

Wright, L., & Adams, H. (1994). Assessment of sexual preference using a Choice Reaction Time Task. *Journal of Psychopathology and Behavioral Assessment, 16*(3), 221–231.

Section V
Special Populations

46

The Assessment of Female Sexual Offenders

Franca Cortoni

Université de Montréal, Canada

Theresa A. Gannon

University of Kent, United Kingdom

Introduction

Just as with male sexual offenders, the assessment of women who have committed sexual offences is predominantly driven by the need to establish the likelihood of future sexual offending behaviour, identify problematic issues related to their offending, and outline interventions that would reduce their risk of recidivism. Women are also subjected to the same sanctions as males in the criminal justice system, including social control policies (e.g., Sexually Violent Predator laws in the United States). Hence it is crucial that the assessment of their risk and treatment needs be based on empirically validated approaches. Owing to the dearth of information on female sexual offenders' risk of sexual recidivism and related treatment needs, the assessment of these women has traditionally been conducted using male-based risk assessment procedures. Basically, the idea was that (1) crime is neutral, and (2) male-based tools are better than nothing. In more recent years, however, these two premises have been refuted. First, research has now established that gender matters in criminal behaviour. In other words, there exist gender-specific issues that need to be taken into account when assessing women. Second, research shows that female sexual offenders differ greatly from their male counterparts in terms of recidivism rates. Hence risk assessment tools validated for males would over-evaluate risk of recidivism in females. Because of these issues, the assessment of risk and treatment needs of female sexual offenders remains a difficult endeavour. The low prevalence of female sexual offending, and their low rates of recidivism, render the development of women-specific empirically validated risk assessment tools and practices difficult. Despite these difficulties, there

The Wiley Handbook on the Theories, Assessment, and Treatment of Sexual Offending.
Edited by Douglas P. Boer. Volume II: Assessment, edited by Leam A. Craig and Martin Rettenberger.
© 2017 John Wiley & Sons, Ltd. Published 2017 by John Wiley & Sons, Ltd.

is now a growing empirical foundation on which evaluators can draw to improve the validity of their assessment of female sexual offenders. This chapter reviews this empirical foundation and provides guidelines for the evaluation of female sexual offenders' risk and treatment needs.

Assessing Risk of Recidivism

Professionals tasked with the evaluation of risk of recidivism of female sexual offenders should be thoroughly familiar with the general principles of assessment for risk of recidivism. A brief review of these principles may be useful here to place into context the difficulties that currently underlie the assessment of risk of sexual recidivism in women. Within the context of criminal justice, the assessment of risk of recidivism is a process that evaluates and attempts to limit the probability that a new crime will reoccur. Integral to the risk assessment are the determination of the type of event being predicted (general offence; criminal violent behaviour; sexual recidivism), its likelihood of reoccurrence (low, moderate, high), the conditions under which it may occur (dynamic risk factors and related situational factors, e.g., ongoing relationship with co-offender), whether these conditions are present (e.g., have these dynamic risk factors been resolved?), and which interventions (therapeutic or otherwise) might prevent these conditions from occurring. Consequently, a comprehensive assessment of risk of recidivism contains many pieces of information that, when integrated together, provide a full portrait of the individual that informs decision-makers and case managers on the case (for a review of these steps, see Douglas, Blanchard, & Hendry, 2013; see also Chapters 28, 29, and 30).

The first step in risk assessment is therefore to identify the likelihood that once an individual has been detected and sanctioned for a criminal act, he or she will do it again. Fundamental to this task is empirical knowledge about (a) base rates of recidivism and (b) static and dynamic risk factors. Base rates are the proportion of the population that demonstrates the phenomenon of interest. In the present case, this means the proportion of female sexual offenders who reoffend with a new sexual crime. Risk factors are individual characteristics of the offender that increase or decrease the probability of recidivism. Static risk factors are aspects in the offender's history that cannot be changed through an intervention. Dynamic risk factors are those aspects of the offender that are amenable to change. These are the issues addressed in therapeutic and related interventions (e.g., education) designed to reduce and manage an offender's risk of recidivism.

Recidivism Rates of Female Sexual Offenders

Research shows that the base rates of sexual recidivism of female sexual offenders are very low. Cortoni, Hanson, and Coache (2010) conducted a meta-analysis of 10 studies examining the recidivism rates of female sexual offenders. The number of women in the sample was 2490 and the average follow-up time was 6.5 years. Cumulative sexual, violent, and any recidivism were examined separately. The results showed recidivism rates of 20% for any new type of recidivism and 6% for new violent (including sexual) offences. The rate of recidivism for new sexual offences, however, was 1.5%.

Since the Cortoni et al. (2010) meta-analysis, another large-scale study has calculated the recidivism rates of female sexual offenders. Wijkman and Bijleveld (2013) examined the recidivism rates of all adult females ($n = 261$) over the age of 18 years convicted for at least one contact sexual offence in The Netherlands between 1993 and 2011. The average follow-up time was 13.2 years. The sexual recidivism rate of 1.1% and the violent recidivism rate of 7.3% are consistent with meta-analytical findings. The rate for any recidivism, however, was slightly higher: 27.6% of the women had committed a new crime.

In addition to understanding differences between recidivism and lifetime offending patterns, recent findings indicate that attention must also be paid to the varying patterns of recidivism among various subgroups of women that all bear the label of sexual offenders. The accumulating evidence indicates that female sexual offenders represent a diverse group of individuals with differing motivational and offending patterns, and also differing recidivism rates (e.g., Gannon, Rose, & Ward, 2008; Gannon et al., 2014; Mathews, Matthews, & Speltz, 1989; Sandler & Freeman, 2007; Vandiver & Kercher, 2004). For example, in Vandiver and Kercher's (2004) category of homosexual criminals, none of the women had a conviction for a contact sexual offence. Instead, they had all been convicted of offences such as indecency or compelling the victim into prostitution. Sandler and Freeman (2009) demonstrated that this subgroup of women have very different rates of sexual recidivism to traditional contact offenders. Their study of 1466 female sexual offenders in New York State included a subgroup of 79 women who only had promoting prostitution of a minor as a sexual offence. Whereas the traditional (i.e., contact/child pornography) offenders had a 1.59% rate of rearrest for new sexual offences (22 out of 1387), the prostitution-only group had much higher rates of rearrest for new sexual offences: 10 out of the 79 women (12.66%) were rearrested for new prostitution-related offences. Further, Cortoni, Sandler, and Freeman (2015) demonstrated that women with only prostitution-related offences have criminal histories more consistent with general criminality and exhibit more general antisocial features than women convicted of traditional sexual offences (e.g., rape, sexual assault). These results suggest that evaluators should distinguish between women with traditional sexual offences and those who commit only prostitution-related offences; the latter group presents very different criminogenic features and recidivism rates than the former.

Static Risk Factors

Broadly, it could be argued that there are two classes of static risk factors that differentially predict recidivism: those related to general recidivism and those related to sexual recidivism. For example, among male sexual offenders, static risk factors for general and violent (non-sexual) recidivism include being at a younger age, being single, and having a history of lifestyle instability, rule violations, and prior criminal history (Andrews & Bonta, 2010; Hanson & Morton-Bourgon, 2005). Static factors specifically related to sexual recidivism include prior sexual offences and having male, stranger, and/or unrelated victims (Hanson & Thornton, 2000). Among female sexual offenders, the evidence indicates the same general distinction of factors related to different types of recidivism.

There is sufficient empirical evidence to suggest that the static risk factors for *general* recidivism in women are similar to those of males. Specifically, the number of prior convictions for any type of offence (misdemeanours, drugs, violence) was related to non-sexual general or violent recidivism (Sandler & Freeman, 2009; Vandiver, 2007; Wijkman & Bijleveld, 2013). In addition, a younger age (less than 30 years old) was related to non-sexual recidivism. The finding that prior criminal history is related to future non-sexual recidivism among female sexual offenders is not surprising. It is indicative of an antisocial orientation and is common to all types of offenders, whether males or females (Andrews & Bonta, 2010; Blanchette & Brown, 2006).

The evidence, however, is different when sexual recidivism is examined. Although she had a large sample ($n = 471$) and a high base rate of sexual offending among women (11%), Vandiver (2007) could not establish any static factor specifically related to the commission of a new sexual offence. Sandler and Freeman (2009) did find a relationship between age and sexual recidivism. In contrast to findings for males, however, being older was linearly related to sexual recidivism among females, but only for those women convicted of prostitution-related offences. For females convicted of contact sexual offences, age was not related to sexual recidivism.

Finally, despite the low base rates of sexual recidivism, Sandler and Freeman (2009) found that the presence of a prior child abuse offence of any type was specifically and only related to sexual recidivism. This finding provides the first evidence that static risk factors related to sexual recidivism among women are gender specific: research has never identified general patterns of child abuse to be related to sexual recidivism among male sexual offenders. The significance of this factor remains unclear. Perhaps because women tend to be the primary caregivers, they are more likely than men to come to the attention of the criminal justice system for non-sexual abuse of children. Alternatively, it may be that the sexual abuse of children, for these women, is part of a broader generalized pattern of abuse against children. Further research is needed.

Dynamic Risk Factors

The dynamic risk factors related to sexual recidivism in women are unknown. This is not surprising given the extremely low base rates of sexual recidivism in this group. Here again, evaluators need to be aware that a simple transfer of knowledge from the male sexual offender literature to females is simply not appropriate. The accumulating evidence indicates that although women appear to share some characteristics with men, these characteristics manifest themselves in different ways for women (Cortoni & Gannon, 2016). Further, given their very low base rates of sexual recidivism, it is currently impossible to determine what the relationship might be between these characteristics and a woman's likelihood that she will commit a new sexual offence. For example, although a woman may present with cognitions that support sex with her victim, there is no evidence to date to suggest that these cognitions augment her risk of committing a sexual offence against a new victim.

On the basis of available evidence, denial or minimization of the offending behaviour, distorted cognitions about the sexual offending and sexual abuse in general, problematic relationship and intimacy deficits, and the use of sex to fulfil intimacy needs have all been found in women (Gannon et al., 2008; Nathan & Ward, 2002; Saradjian & Hanks, 1996; see also our later discussion of treatment needs). Sexual gratification, a desire for intimacy (with either a victim or a co-defendant), or instrumental goals such as revenge or humiliation are also associated with female sexual offending (Gannon et al., 2008; Saradjian & Hanks, 1996). An examination of these issues will inform on the woman's personal circumstances and elements that have likely contributed to the offending behaviour, including whether a co-offender played a role (Cortoni, 2010). It is reiterated, however, that although these areas may be problematic and in need of intervention, their relationship with sexual recidivism among women is unknown.

Given the similarities in static risk factors for general recidivism among sexual and non-sexual female offenders, Cortoni (2013) hypothesized that both groups of women share the same dynamic risk factors but only for violent (non-sexual) and general recidivism. These dynamic risk factors likely include cognitions supportive of criminal behaviour, relationships with antisocial associates, poor familial relationships and general community functioning, and substance abuse problems (for an in-depth review of this research, see Blanchette & Brown, 2006). It is noted here that some of these factors manifest themselves in gender-specific ways. Benda (2005) found that family factors such as prosocial family support and the presence of children are a predictor of positive community reintegration for female but not male offenders. Andrews et al. (2012) found a stronger relationship between substance abuse and recidivism for women than for men. Among female sexual offenders, Wijkman and Bijleveld (2013) found that substance abuse and antisocial personality predicted general and violent recidivism.

Implications for Risk Assessment

There are a number of ways in which risk for recidivism may be assessed, but a large body of research indicates that empirically based actuarial-type methods of risk assessment have the best predictive validity with all types of male offenders, including sexual offenders (e.g., Craig & Beech, 2010). Currently, however, there exists no actuarial or structured professional judgement risk assessment instrument validated for the assessment of risk of sexual recidivism among women.

The reason for this lack of instrument is simple. The evidence indicates that the large majority (i.e., ~98%) of female sexual offenders, once they have been detected and sanctioned for sexual offences, will not commit a new one. This low rate of sexual recidivism, combined with the low prevalence of female sexual offending (about 5% of adult sexual offenders – see Cortoni, Hanson, & Coache, 2009), means that much larger samples than are currently available will be needed to identify empirically the factors that distinguish the female sexual recidivist from the non-recidivist, and develop a risk assessment tool. At this time, therefore, evaluators can only rely on their professional judgement, structured by the empirically established risk factors described above, to assess risk of sexual recidivism among women.

Within this context, it is imperative for evaluators to remember that the likelihood of a false-positive prediction of recidivism among women will be very high. False-positive prediction (i.e., the false alarm rate; for a review, see Craig & Beech, 2010) is the prediction that an individual will reoffend but does not. Because of their low risk of sexual recidivism, female sexual offenders would virtually never be considered to pose a high risk for sexual recidivism. To reduce the possibility of a high false-alarm rate, the recidivism risk factors clinically judged to be relevant in a given case must be sufficiently present – in fact, quite blatant (e.g., she tells you she will do it again; see Cortoni et al., 2010) – in order to make a determination of high risk for sexual recidivism among women (for a discussion of issues related to the assessment of women for civil commitment, see Vess, 2011).

The lack of risk assessment tools for female sexual offenders has led some evaluators to utilize male-based tools when assessing a woman for her risk of sexual recidivism. Because tools for male sexual offenders have not been validated for women, however, using these tools is not acceptable for the following reasons. First, these tools provide estimates of risk of recidivism that are predicated on the base rate of recidivism among adult male sexual offenders. Given the significantly lower rates of sexual recidivism of female sexual offenders, tools validated for males would statistically grossly overestimate risk among women. Second, the items in these risk assessment tools were selected based on their established empirical relationship with recidivism. For example, factors such as prior sexual offences, and having male, stranger, and/or unrelated victims, have a well-established relationship to sexual recidivism among *male* offenders (Hanson & Thornton, 2000). Among female offenders, as was seen earlier, none of these factors has ever demonstrated an empirical relationship with sexual recidivism. Hence, not only will risk assessment tools validated only for males overestimate risk among female sexual offenders, they will do so on the basis of items that have no demonstrated links to sexual recidivism among women (Cortoni, 2010).

Although no tool exists to assess risk of sexual recidivism among women, the picture is not so bleak for the assessment of risk of general recidivism among female sexual offenders. Attempts to develop a women-specific instrument specifically to assess risk for violent recidivism have yielded interesting promising results, but only for the prediction of violence within an inpatient context (de Vogel & de Vries Robbé, 2013). These research findings, however, are very preliminary; the sample size is small ($n = 46$) and the research only examined inpatient behaviour. The utility of the tool to assess risk of criminal violent reoffending after release has not yet been examined.

To date, the Level of Supervision Inventory (LSI; and revised, LSI-R) (Andrews & Bonta, 1995) is the only instrument that has demonstrated good predictive validity for the assessment of risk for *general* (i.e., non-sexual) criminal recidivism among women (Smith, Cullen, & Latessa, 2009). Further research, however, indicates the LSI does overestimate risk in some women. Women assessed as high risk on the LSI had actual recidivism rates similar to those of their high-risk male counterparts. Women in the lower risk ranges, however, had significantly lower actual rates of recidivism than the males in the equivalent risk categories (Andrews et al., 2012). These findings confirm that even the use of general risk assessment tools to assess risk among female sexual offenders requires an understanding of the research on risk factors and recidivism among female offenders in general (e.g., Blanchette & Brown, 2006; Folsom & Atkinson, 2007; Holtfreter & Cupp, 2007; Manchak, Skeem, Douglas, & Siranosian, 2009).

Assessing Treatment Needs

The dynamic risk factors associated with male sexual offenders' risk of sexual offending are well established as being *inappropriate sexual interests, offence-supportive cognition, intimacy and social functioning deficits,* and *self-regulation* issues (Beech, Fisher, & Thornton, 2003; Hanson & Morton-Bourgon, 2005; Marshall, Marshall, Serran, & O'Brien, 2011). As noted above, although knowledge concerning female sexual offending is beginning to increase, the dynamic risk factors associated with female sexual offending are still unknown. Because of this, professionals working with female sexual offenders can generally expect the assessment and treatment of female sexual offenders to be a challenging task. Fortunately, however, there is some research *suggestive* of the underlying dynamic risk factors associated with female sexual offending (Cortoni, 2010; Gannon, Rose, & Cortoni, 2010). Consequently, it is possible to assess for factors that have been associated with female sexual offenders and their behaviour in order to formulate the likely treatment needs of female sexual offenders. However, given the limited knowledge base underpinning the treatment needs of female sexual offenders, there is a distinct lack of female-specific assessments available, necessitating an almost complete reliance on skilled clinical interview.

Available research evidence suggests that female sexual offenders are likely to share some basic treatment needs in common with their male sexual offending counterparts. Importantly, however, these basic treatment needs appear to manifest differently in females, seemingly as a result of key physiological and socialization-related gender differences (Gannon, Hoare, Rose, & Parrett, 2012; Rousseau & Cortoni, 2010). Further, on the basis of gender, female sexual offenders appear to hold a suite of unique treatment needs that are not generally shared by their male counterparts. In the following sections, we outline the key literature relating to the probable treatment needs of female sexual offenders. Because of the lack of research knowledge in relation to specific dynamic risk factors related to female sexual offending, we take a necessarily broad view of the likely range of factors that assessors should consider.

A good number of treatment needs that should be considered for female sexual offenders represent, at least at surface level, some of the key treatment needs identified in male sexual offenders (i.e., inappropriate sexual interests, offence-supportive cognition, intimacy and social functioning deficits, and self-regulation issues). We evaluate the research evidence pertaining to each of these particular needs – taking care to highlight key gender differences and pertinent assessment issues – before examining treatment needs and associated assessment issues that appear most unique to female sexual offenders.

Inappropriate Sexual Interests and Sexual Regulation

Given the relative importance of inappropriate sexual interests in sexual offending behaviour among males (Hanson & Morton-Bourgon, 2005), this area is surprisingly meagre in the female sexual offender research. Studies conducted have tended to be case study based or obtained from clinical practice self-report data (Cooper, Swaminath, Baxter, & Poulin, 1990; Saradjian & Hanks, 1996). In general, the research literature suggests that, compared with males, a relatively small proportion of females appear to hold inappropriate sexual interests of some extent (Green & Kaplan, 1994; Nathan & Ward, 2002; Saradjian & Hanks, 1996). Certainly, there appears to be a much lower prevalence of paedophilia and associated paraphilia diagnoses in women compared with their male counterparts (Abel & Osborn, 2000; Davin, Hislop, & Dunbar, 1999; Federoff, Fishell, & Federoff, 1999). A particularly useful perspective on women's sexual arousal in relation to gender differences has been established by Chivers and colleagues (Chivers, Rieger, Latty, & Bailey, 2004; Suschinsky, Lalumière, & Chivers, 2009). They found that sexual arousal in women functions rather differently than in men since it is less revealing of stable sexual interests. This creates issues for the instrumental measurement of sexual arousal in women and for conclusions regarding sexual interests.

A key task for assessors, then, relates to determining what (if any) level of inappropriate sexual interest exists, and the role of any inappropriate sexual interest in the woman's sexually abusive behaviour. *Wilson's Sex Fantasy Questionnaire* (Wilson, 1978) may be utilized with women and may represent a useful tool with which to explore relevant possibilities (i.e., what types of sexual behaviours have been engaged in and which are thought about frequently). However, the presence and extent of inappropriate sexual interests are likely to become most apparent from a skilled analysis of the offending behaviour gleaned across numerous sources and explored with the woman in question.

Finally, the development and history of sexual behaviour are another important area to assess. This includes the meaning and role of sex in the woman's life. Her beliefs about sexual activity and, by extension, sexual abuse may be linked to her beliefs about gender roles, sense of entitlement, or refusal to acknowledge the harm caused by the abuse. Within this context, the role that sex in general plays in the woman's life should be examined to establish its potential motivational role in the offending behaviour. Among male sexual offenders, *sexual coping* has been established as a commonly utilized coping mechanism (Cortoni & Marshall, 2001). In other words, males appear to use both appropriate and inappropriate sexual activity as part of an established coping repertoire. In the light of this, we suggest that assessors should also explore any possible use of sexual coping for the woman. Evaluators should be mindful, however, that whether or not female sexual offenders engage in such coping has not been tested within the research literature. Professional confidence and reassurance to the client that women experience various sexual interests, behaviours, and fantasies are likely to be crucial for building a rapport that will permit a frank discussion of these issues.

Offence-Supportive Cognitions

This area is perhaps one of the better researched areas, with female sexual offenders having been subjected to both quantitative and qualitative investigations in recent years (e.g., Beech, Parrett, Ward, & Fisher, 2009; Elliott, Eldridge, Ashfield, & Beech, 2010; Gannon et al., 2012; Gannon & Rose, 2009; Kubik & Hecker, 2005; Strickland, 2008; for a systematic review, see Gannon & Alleyne, 2013). Some research has suggested that female sexual offenders share very similar offence-supportive beliefs, schemas, or implicit theories to those of their male counterparts (Beech et al., 2009; Elliott et al., 2010; Kubik & Hecker, 2005). Other research, however, has suggested that although there might be some general similarities in the belief structures of male and female sexual offenders, there are also key differences attributable to gender (Gannon et al., 2012; Gannon & Rose, 2009). Key differences that have been highlighted regarding offence-supportive cognition appear to revolve around female sexual offenders' appraisals of males in relation to females. For example, the male sexual offender literature suggests that males view sexual abuse as a form of *entitlement*, and as relatively *harmless*, in addition to viewing males and females as *threatening and dangerous*, and children as *sexually interested* (Ward & Keenan, 1999). In comparison, female sexual offenders appear to view sexual abuse as an entitlement *for males* (rather than themselves as females) and relatively harmless *when perpetrated by a female*, in addition to viewing *males* (rather than females) as threatening and dangerous, and their own victim (rather than children generally) as sexually interested (Gannon et al., 2012; Gannon & Rose, 2009).

Gannon et al. (2012) suggested that female sexual offenders' offence-supportive implicit schemas may reflect a severe form of gender-role stereotyping in which males are viewed as *powerful* and women are viewed as *powerless*. Such cognitions might be especially relevant for females who abuse with a co-perpetrating male. A key challenge for assessors, then, relates to determining what (if any) level of offence-supportive cognition exists, how exactly this cognition differs from that of males, and the role of this cognition in the woman's sexually abusive behaviour, particularly if the female has abused alongside a co-perpetrating male. In the absence of any female-specific measure dedicated to the measurement of these issues, we suggest that assessors appraise not only the woman's personal reflection on the offence situation and the factors that facilitated it (e.g., a belief that female abuse was relatively harmless), but also her long-standing beliefs and perceptions of male and female roles and entitlements.

Intimacy and Social Functioning Deficits

Unfortunately, intimacy and social functioning deficits have not yet been researched specifically in relation to female sexual offending. Nevertheless, a number of reviews and studies refer to probable issues in this area. For example, female sexual offenders generally report their developmental experiences to be characterized by adversarial relationships with caregivers and/or characterized by physical, sexual, or emotionally abusive experiences (Allen, 1991; Gannon, Rose, & Ward, 2008, 2010; Saradjian & Hanks, 1996). Problematic developmental attachment experiences are likely to affect an individual's ability to form effective relationships in adulthood (Bartholomew, 1990; Bowlby, 1969, 1973). It is therefore not surprising that female sexual offenders tend to demonstrate important social inadequacies and problematic adult relationships (Gannon et al., 2008, 2010; Strickland, 2008).

A key motivation associated with female-perpetrated sexual abuse appears to be intimacy. Researchers have found that female sexual offenders sexually offend against children to obtain intimacy either with their child victim or with a male co-perpetrator (Gannon et al., 2008; Saradjian & Hanks, 1996). This desire to obtain intimacy may be as a result of poor social skills and/or contextual factors that foster isolation and emotional loneliness. Research does indicate that female sexual offenders appear to be socially isolated around the time of their offence and lacking any clear support structure (Gannon et al., 2008; Saradjian & Hanks, 1996). Such experiences – in the presence of other vulnerabilities such as sexual victimization histories – are likely to facilitate inappropriate manifestations of intimacy seeking, and may also leave a woman vulnerable to male sexual offenders who may target them as a co-perpetrator.

A key difference amongst women relative to their male offending counterparts appears to reside in this manifestation of intimacy difficulties. Female sexual offenders appear to experience extensive levels of relationship abuse (Gannon et al., 2008; Wijkman & Bijleveld, 2008) and appear to present with passive traits and also extreme dependency in relation to men or male intimate partners (Eldridge & Saradjian, 2000; Grayston & De Luca, 1999). These findings suggest that in assessing female sexual offenders, key aspects of exploration are likely to revolve around the presence and quality of social support in addition to an in-depth exploration of their current and past intimate relationship dynamics. Clearly, this issue will be especially pertinent in terms of the presence of any co-perpetrating male (see co-perpetrating males described below). Again, multiple sources of input will be useful here in addition to standard clinical interview.

Self-Regulation Issues

Although scant, existing research available in this area suggests that, like males, female sexual offenders experience problems in their abilities to cope with stressful life events and regulate negative affect (Gannon et al., 2008; Saradjian & Hanks, 1996). Research examining female sexual offenders' personal offence narratives shows that they self-report particularly chaotic and stressful life experiences immediately preceding their offence(s) (Gannon et al., 2008, 2010). A key difference between female and male offenders appears to reside in the *source* of these stressful experiences. Female sexual offenders report experiencing extreme stress, turbulence, and highly negative affect as a result of multiple caregiver responsibilities (e.g., looking after children in addition to ageing or ill parents) and emotionally or physically abusive relationships. It appears that in the face of such stressful life circumstances, female sexual offenders feel inadequately equipped to cope and have very little social support (Gannon et al., 2008). These findings suggest that any assessment of female sexual offenders should explore not only their life circumstances and difficulties around the time of the offending, but also the exact deficits associated with any emotional regulation problems. For example, limited brain functioning in the form of intellectual disability may lead to self-regulation problems and associated offending behaviour (Frey, 2010; Gannon et al., 2010).

Some female sexual offenders may not exhibit problems with poor regulation and instead may exhibit strong values, morals, or faulty cognitions that underpin and drive offending via intact self-regulation skills. For example, a woman may be motivated to offend against their victim due to experiences of anger (e.g., perceiving the victim to have 'wronged' them or broken a sacred moral code). As a result, this woman may experience strong positive affect in relation to her offence (e.g., anticipatory excitement or post-offence pride) and plan the offence almost as a military exercise. Here, exploring the motivation underpinning the explicit planning of such offences is likely to be especially critical.

Previous Victimization

As noted previously, a high prevalence of developmental and adult victimization experiences has been associated with female sexual offenders (Allen, 1991; Gannon et al., 2008; Green & Kaplan, 1994; Lewis & Stanley, 2000). Most notably, research findings suggest that female sexual offenders, in relation to male sexual offenders, experience victimization that is unique in frequency and severity (Allen, 1991; Miccio-Fonseca, 2000; Pothast & Allen, 1994). To illustrate, Allen (1991) found that female sexual offenders were significantly more likely to report experiences of physical abuse such as being slapped or hit by their parents. Research conducted by Wijkman and Bijleveld (2008) has also shown that victimization experiences (e.g., relationship violence, school bullying, and childhood physical abuse) were associated with an increased number of sexual offences committed by women.

Establishing the nature and extent of any previous victimization should be a primary task for any assessing professional. There is evidence accumulating in the wider research literature to suggest that unresolved trauma (i.e., *Post Traumatic Stress Disorder* [PTSD] according to DSM-5; American Psychiatric Association, 2013) is associated with neuropsychological impairments that are not only personally distressing for the individual but may also severely inhibit that individual's ability to process and appropriately assimilate information discussed during talking therapies such as cognitive–behavioural therapy (Beech & Fisher, 2011; Clark, Tyler, Gannon, & Kingham, 2014; Gray et al., 2003). Consequently, the extent and nature of trauma presentation should be explored thoroughly at an early stage using established measures designed for this purpose (e.g., *The Impact of Events Scale – Revised* (Weiss & Marmar, 1997) or the *Clinician-Administered PTSD Scale* (Blake et al., 1995)). When trauma is clearly present, the assessing professional should additionally clinically determine whether the trauma should be addressed prior to, concurrently with, or after the offence-specific work. Finally, assessors should remain open-minded regarding the underpinning sources of trauma since trauma might also be experienced as a *result* of offending behaviour itself (Clark et al., 2014; Gray et al., 2003).

Male Coercion and Dependency

A further key difference between female sexual offenders and their male counterparts revolves around the issue of male coercion. Research suggests that up to half of women who sexually offend have co-offended with a male (Wijkman, Bijleveld, & Hendriks, 2011). Most critical, perhaps, in terms of assessment, is when a female identifies her co-perpetrating male partner as having *coerced* her into the sexually offending behaviour. It is critical within the assessment to determine whether or not the male co-perpetrator has played any coercive role in the abuse or whether the female has acted of her own volition and is simply accompanied by the male (Ford, 2010). The former is likely to indicate that the woman has important treatment needs revolving around excessive dependency and associated concepts such as low self-esteem, shame, and passive coping and communication styles.

The issue of genuine coercion can be difficult to ascertain, especially when relying on self-reports from the woman herself. Research suggests that assessors should be particularly thorough in their assessment of this issue (Heil, Simons, & Burton, 2010; Saradjian & Hanks, 1996). For example, Heil et al. (2010) found that women who had been officially recorded as male coerced ($n = 3$) all admitted during a polygraph examination to having offended independently prior to having offended in the company of a male. In their clinical self-report study, Saradjian and Hanks (1996) found that a small number of male-coerced women ($n = 4$) reported masturbating to fantasies about children. None of these women, however, reported engaging in child molestation or masturbation to child-related fantasies *prior* to having been coerced into the offending behaviour. It is noteworthy, however, that these four women later went on to offend of their own volition. Taken as a whole, these pieces of research suggest that a deep exploration of the concept of coercion is warranted during assessment. Assessors should use multiple sources to form an opinion in this area (e.g., police and witness reports, court reports, psychiatrist reports) and then should remain open to the possibility that, even in a case in which coercion appears wholly evident, a female may develop interests, fantasies, and/or behaviours that result in later non-coerced offending. The motivators underlying any later non-coerced offending should be explored in detail since they may reflect a variety of goals (e.g., to gratify a previously coercive male or to fulfil one's own sexual desires and fantasies).

Other Potential Treatment Needs

In addition to the potential treatment needs noted above, evaluators should ensure that they examine as part of their assessment the more generic dynamic risk factors or treatment needs empirically associated with general female criminal behaviour. Thus, asking questions and collating evidence concerning general offence-supportive attitudes and antisocial sentiments and associates will be important, as will enquiries regarding substance abuse (Blanchette & Brown, 2006; Wijkman & Bijleveld, 2013). Given that child sexual abuse perpetrated by women might reflect a more general pattern of abuse or neglect of children (Sandler & Freeman, 2009), assessors should be mindful of exploring any underlying attitudes or norms driving general child abuse (if it is present) and also mental health factors and unresolved trauma, both of which have been associated with female perpetrated abuse and neglect (Conron, Beardslee, Koenen, Buka, & Gortmaker, 2009; Mapp, 2006). These issues may have played a central role in the woman's commission of sexual abuse or its passive acceptance at the hand of a co-offender.

Mental health is a particularly important area to be addressed as part of standard assessment. Women in prison appear to hold needs in this area that exceed those of incarcerated men or women living in the community (Blanchette & Brown, 2006; Ogloff & Tye, 2007). Research examining the mental health characteristics of female sexual offenders appears partly divided. Some researchers have suggested that female sexual offenders are highly likely to exhibit problems in this area and that levels of mental health issues are likely to be higher than those of other female offenders (Green & Kaplan, 1994). However, Swedish research conducted by Fazel, Sjöstedt, Grann, and Langström (2008) has shown that although female sexual offenders ($n = 93$) exhibit higher levels of psychosis than females in the community, no substantial differences appear to exist between female sexual offenders and female violent offenders in terms of mental health.

Conducting the Assessment

In conducting an assessment to examine the potential treatment needs of any woman who has sexually offended, it is vital to obtain information from varied sources regarding the offence behaviour(s). A full clinical interview should then be conducted with the woman herself in order to ascertain her own perspective on the circumstances, motivators, and affective and cognitive experiences associated with the offending behaviour. Conducting a sound clinical interview with a female sexual offender should, like any forensic assessment, begin with the assessor explaining the reasons underlying the assessment and of the limits to confidentiality. The clinical interview should then proceed via a general 'timeline' structure in which the assessor begins with questions concerning the woman's developmental history. Not only will this structure allow the woman being assessed to develop more of a rapport with the interviewer prior to speaking about her offending behaviour, but it also allows the assessor to establish key areas that may require exploration later in the interview. For example, a woman who discloses frequent childhood sexual and physical abuse at the hands of men might experience PTSD as a result of this, and/or experience men as being ultimately powerful; both of which may have played a facilitatory role in the sexual offence.

A comprehensive assessment should cover historical factors (attachment history, key developmental experiences/trauma, and notable childhood behaviours associated with mental health issues or criminal behaviour), personality factors (e.g., passive or dependent personality styles; personality disorder), sexual development and history, relationship history (particularly in relation to domestic abuse and/or a co-perpetrating male), contextual and individual factors leading up to, during, and after the offence period (i.e., factors such as social supports, relationships with co-offender(s), relationship status, sexual functioning and fantasy, employment, education and caregiving responsibilities, coping style, offence-related cognition and affect, planning, mental health issues, and substance misuse). Being aware of the female sexual offending literature and thus sensitive to possible gender nuances is central to any thorough assessment of treatment needs of women who have engaged in sexually offending behaviour.

Exploring in depth the woman's history and how this history might link to her offending behaviour is a core assessment activity to develop an adequate clinical formulation of the offence behaviour and attendant treatment needs. Within this context, it may be helpful for evaluators to establish the likely pathway that led to the woman's offending behaviour (Gannon et al., 2008, 2010). A pathway refers to the style with which an offender undertakes their sexual offending; it also includes associated offence-supportive cognitions and affect (Ward, Louden, Hudson, & Marshall, 1995). Gannon and colleagues' research examining female sexual offenders' offence narratives has suggested that there are likely to be three pathways characterizing female sexual abuse: explicit-approach, directed-avoidant, and implicit-disorganized. *Explicit-approach* refers to women who explicitly plan their offending for various reasons (e.g., sexual gratification, intimacy, revenge). These women present as effective regulators who tend to experience positive affect (e.g., excitement) and associated cognitions prior to, at the time of, and post-offence. Women who follow this pathway to their offending may work alongside a male but an exploration of their offending is likely to highlight the female's autonomous role in the offence. *Directed-avoidant* refers to women who have been clearly emotionally or physically coerced into their offending by a co-perpetrating male. Generally, these women tend to have been involved in an abusive relationship with the co-perpetrating male or targeted and groomed by him. Such women are characterized by a distinct lack of autonomy and planning in relation to their offence, an excessive dependence on men, and a general subjugation of their own needs. These women are likely to offend due to fear of their co-perpetrator or in order to gain acceptance and intimacy from him. Their regulatory processes are generally overridden by the co-perpetrating male and they typically report having experienced negative affect and associated cognitions in relation to their offence (e.g., 'I have to do this or he will kill me'). *Implicit-disorganized* refers to women who do not appear to be driven by any explicit desire to offend, but who appear to experience significant self-regulatory failure immediately prior to their sexual offence. Such women tend to report 'finding' themselves in situations that increase the chances of them sexually offending; they do not explicitly plan their offending. Often, however, an exploration of the factors leading up to the offence reveals decisions on the part of the woman that appear to have implicitly increased the likelihood of sexual offending (i.e., implicit planning). These women tend to describe their offending as impulsive, a snap decision associated with either positive or negative affect.

Each of these three pathways likely holds distinct treatment needs. A preliminary checklist has been developed in order to aid clinicians in their identification of these pathways (Gannon et al., 2014). It is highly important for assessors to keep in mind, however, that offence pathways do not represent static typological descriptors. In other words, if a woman has committed multiple sexual offences, she may shift pathways. Because of this, it is important that assessors consider all instances of sexual offending when conceptualizing a woman's pathway to offending. It is very possible, for example, for a woman to shift from a directed-coerced to an explicit-approach pathway (Heil et al., 2010). Under such circumstances, the assessor's task becomes complex: the treatment needs analysis must take into account the factors that have led to the initial sexual offence, and the additional factors that have led to the autonomous offending.

In terms of treatment needs, explicit-approach women, as they tend not to hold deficient self-regulatory processes, would likely require treatment that focuses on the goals and values underpinning their offending (e.g., inappropriate sexual arousal) in addition to the associated cognition and affect. Directed-avoidant women, on the other hand, are likely to require work examining intimacy and attachment, personality styles, and cognitions in relation to men (i.e., dependent and passive traits), in addition to their problem-solving and assertiveness skills. A particularly important aspect of treatment might also include education regarding the detection of male grooming and protection of children. Finally, implicit-disorganized women are those most likely to benefit from treatment related to self-regulation since these women appear to lose control over their impulses in the context of strong positive or negative affect (e.g., wanting to satisfy sexual needs or gain revenge). In such cases, women are likely to benefit from work designed to heighten their sensitivity to factors likely to trigger relapse and their ability to cope with signs of regulatory failure as it unfolds.

Conclusion

Evaluators now have much more research available to them than they had a decade ago to guide their assessment of female sexual offenders. In terms of risk for sexual recidivism, the data show that women, once detected and sanctioned for contact sexual offences, are unlikely to commit new ones. The data also reveal, however, that attention must be paid to the sub-type of offender under evaluation: women convicted for prostitution-related offences demonstrate very different patterns of recidivism than women convicted for contact sexual offences. Furthermore, research shows that non-sexual offences are also committed by female sexual offenders. Although there are no instruments that have been validated to assess risk of sexual recidivism in women, there are validated approaches and tools to assess their risk of general (i.e., non-sexual) recidivism that can be utilized with confidence. Evaluators, however, should always carefully frame their evaluation of risk of recidivism of female sexual offenders within the context of the existing research; the danger of an overestimation of risk of sexual recidivism in females is real.

There is now also a research base that suggests a number of likely treatment needs among women. Further, research that examined pathways to offending is available in order to guide the evaluation of treatment needs among female sexual offenders. These needs include, but are not limited to, offence-supportive cognitions, relationship factors (e.g., dependency, intimacy issues), emotional regulation and coping deficits, sexual regulation patterns, and inappropriate sexual interests. Particular goals underlying the sexual offence (e.g., to gain revenge or to humiliate others) are also likely to represent pertinent treatment needs. Despite these advances, still very clearly absent at present are psychometric tests designed specifically for use with female sexual offenders. In the light of this, we remind evaluators not to be tempted to use those tests designed and validated only for male offenders; the accumulating evidence is showing that factors related to sexually offending behaviour have gender-specific manifestations. Evaluators should always explore and evaluate the treatment need of female sexual offenders within a comprehensive and gender-informed clinical interview.

References

Abel, G. G., & Osborn, C. (2000). The paraphilias. In M. C. Gelder, J. J. Lopez-Ibor, & N. C. Andreasen (Eds.), *New Oxford textbook of psychiatry* (pp. 897–913). Oxford, England: Oxford University Press.

Allen, C. M. (1991). *Women and men who sexually abuse children: A comparative analysis.* Orwell, VT: Safer Society Press.

American Psychiatric Association. (2013). *Diagnostic and statistical manual of mental disorders* (5th ed.) (DSM-5). Arlington, VA: American Psychiatric Publishing.

Andrews, D. A., & Bonta, J. (1995). *Level of Service Inventory – Revised*. Toronto, Canada: Multi-Health Systems.

Andrews, D. A., & Bonta J. (2010) *The psychology of criminal conduct* (5th ed.). Cincinnati, OH: Anderson.

Andrews, D. A., Guzzo, L., Raynor, P., Rowe, R. C., Rettinger, J., Brews, A., & Wormith, S. (2012). Are the major risk/need factors predictive of both female and male reoffending?: A test with the eight domains of the level of service/case management inventory. *International Journal of Offender Therapy and Comparative Criminology, 56*, 113–133.

Bartholomew, K. (1990). Avoidance of intimacy: An attachment perspective. *Journal of Social and Personal Relationships, 7*, 147–178.

Beech, A. R., & Fisher, D. (2011, October). *The way forward in sex offender treatment*. Paper presented at New Directions in Sex Offender Practice Conference and Workshop, University of Birmingham, England.

Beech, A. R., Fisher, D., & Thornton, D. (2003). Risk assessment of sex offenders. *Professional Psychology: Research and Practice, 34*, 339–352.

Beech, A. R., Parrett, N., Ward, T., & Fisher, D. (2009). Assessing female sexual offenders' motivations and cognitions: An exploratory study. *Psychology, Crime, and Law, 15*, 201–216. doi:10.1080/10683160802190921

Benda, B. B. (2005). Gender differences in life-course theory of recidivism: A survival analysis. *International Journal of Offender Therapy and Comparative Criminology, 49*, 325–342.

Blake, D. D., Weathers, F. W., Nagy, L. M., Kaloupek, D. G., Gusman, F. D., Charney, D. S., & Keane, T. M. (1995). The development of a clinician-administered PTSD scale. *Journal of Traumatic Stress, 8*, 75–90.

Blanchette, K., & Brown, S. L. (2006). *The assessment and treatment of women offenders: An integrated perspective*. Chichester, England: John Wiley & Sons, Ltd.

Bowlby, J. (1969). *Attachment and loss, Volume 1: Attachment*. New York, NY: Basic Books.

Bowlby, J (1973). *Attachment and loss, Volume 2: Separation*. New York, NY: Basic Books.

Chivers, M. L., Rieger, G., Latty, E., & Bailey, J. M. (2004). A sex difference in the specificity of sexual arousal. *Psychological Science, 15*, 736–744.

Clark, L., Tyler, N., Gannon, T. A., & Kingham, M. (2014). Eye movement desensitisation and reprocessing for offence-related trauma in a mentally disordered sexual offender. *Journal of Sexual Aggression, 20*, 240–249.

Conron, K. J., Beardslee, W., Koenen, K. C., Buka, S. L., & Gortmaker, S. L. (2009). A longitudinal study of maternal depression and child maltreatment in a national sample of families investigated by child protective services. *Archives of Pediatrics and Adolescent Medicine, 163*, 922–930.

Cooper, A. J., Swaminath, S., Baxter, D., & Poulin, C. (1990). A female sex offender with multiple paraphilias: A psychologic, physiologic (laboratory sexual arousal) and endocrine case study. *Canadian Journal of Psychiatry, 35*, 334–337.

Cortoni, F. (2010). The assessment of female sexual offenders. In T. A. Gannon & F. Cortoni (Eds.), *Female sexual offenders: Theory, assessment, and treatment* (pp. 87–100). Chichester, England: John Wiley & Sons, Ltd.

Cortoni, F., (2013, October). *Criminal features of female sexual offenders: Implications for risk assessment*. Paper presented at the 32nd Annual Research and Treatment Conference of the Association for the Treatment of Sexual Abusers, Chicago, IL.

Cortoni, F., & Gannon, T. A. (2011). Female sexual offenders. In D. P. Boer, R. Eher, L. A. Craig, M. Miner, & F. Phafflin (Eds.), *International perspectives on the assessment and treatment of sex offenders: Theory, practice and research* (pp. 35–54). Chichester, England: John Wiley & Sons, Ltd.

Cortoni, F., & Gannon, T. A. (2016). Understanding female sexual offenders. In T. Ward & A. R. Beech (Eds.), *Theories of Sexual Offending.* (pp. 453–471). Chichester, England: Wiley-Blackwell.

Cortoni, F., Hanson, R. K., & Coache, M. E. (2009). Les délinquantes sexuelles: Prévalence et récidive [Female sexual offenders: Prevalence and recidivism]. *Revue Internationale de Criminologie et de Police Technique et Scientifique, 62*, 319–336.

Cortoni, F., Hanson, R. K., & Coache, M. E. (2010). The recidivism rates of female sexual offenders are low: A meta-analysis. *Sexual Abuse: A Journal of Research and Treatment, 22*, 387–401.

Cortoni, F., Sandler, J. C., & Freeman, N. J. (2015). Are females convicted of promoting prostitution of a minor like females convicted of traditional sexual offenses? A brief research report. *Sexual Abuse: A Journal of Research & Treatment, 27*, 324–334.

Cortoni, F., & Marshall, W. L. (2001). Sex as a coping strategy and its relationship to juvenile sexual history and intimacy in sexual offenders. *Sexual Abuse: A Journal of Research and Treatment, 13*, 27–43.

Craig, L. A., & Beech, A. R. (2010). Towards a best practice in conducting actuarial risk assessments with adult sexual offenders. *Aggression and Violet Behavior, 15*, 278–293.

Davin, P. A., Hislop, J. C. R., & Dunbar, T. (Eds.). (1999). *The female sexual abuser: Three views.* Brandon, VT: Safer Society Press.

de Vogel, V., & de Vries Robbé, M. (2013). Working with women: Towards a more gender-sensitive violence risk assessment. In C. Logan & L. Johnstone (Eds.), *Managing clinical risk: A guide to effective practice* (pp. 224–241). New York, NY: Routledge.

Douglas, K. S., Blanchard, A. J. E., & Hendry, M. C. (2013). Violence risk assessment and management: Putting structured professional judgment in practice. In C. Logan & L. Johnstone (Eds.), *Managing clinical risk: A guide to effective practice* (pp. 29–55). New York, NY: Routledge.

Eldridge, H., & Saradjian, J. (2000). Replacing the function of abusive behaviors for the offender: Remaking relapse prevention in working with women who sexually abuse children. In D. Laws, S. Hudson, & T. Ward (Eds.), *Remaking relapse prevention with sex offenders: A sourcebook.* (pp. 402–427). Thousand Oaks, CA: Sage.

Elliott, I. A., Eldridge, H. J., Ashfield, S., & Beech, A. R. (2010). Exploring risk: Potential static, dynamic, protective and treatment factors in the clinical histories of female sex offenders. *Journal of Family Violence, 25*, 595–602.

Fazel, S., Sjöstedt, G., Grann, M., & Langström, N. (2008). Sexual offending in women and psychiatric disorder: A national case–control study. *Archives of Sexual Behavior, 39*, 161–167.

Federoff, J. P., Fishell, A., & Federoff, B. (1999). A case series of women evaluated for paraphilic disorders. *The Canadian Journal of Human Sexuality, 8*, 127–140.

Folsom, J., & Atkinson, J. L. (2007). The generalizability of the LSI-R and the CAT to the prediction of recidivism in female offenders. *Criminal Justice and Behavior, 34*, 1044–1056.

Ford, H. (2010). The treatment needs of female sexual offenders. In T. A. Gannon & F. Cortoni (Eds.), *Female sexual offenders: Theory, assessment, and treatment* (pp. 101–118). Chichester, England: John Wiley & Sons, Ltd.

Frey, L. L. (2010). The juvenile female sexual offender: Characteristics, treatment, and research. In T. A. Gannon & F. Cortoni (Eds.), *Female sexual offenders: Theory, assessment, and treatment* (pp. 53–72). Chichester, England: John Wiley & Sons, Ltd.

Gannon, T. A., & Alleyne, E. K. A. (2013). Female sexual abusers' cognition. *Trauma, Violence, and Abuse, 14*, 67–79. doi:10.1177/1524838012462245

Gannon, T. A., Hoare, J., Rose, M. R., & Parrett, N. (2012). A re-examination of female child molesters' implicit theories: Evidence of female specificity? *Psychology, Crime and Law, 8,* 209–224. doi:10.1080/10683161003752303

Gannon, T. A., & Rose, M. R. (2009). Offense-related interpretative bias in female child molesters: A preliminary study. *Sexual Abuse: A Journal of Research and Treatment, 21,* 194–207.

Gannon, T. A., Rose, M. R., & Cortoni, F. (2010). Developments in female sexual offending and considerations for future research and treatment. In T. A. Gannon & F. Cortoni (Eds.), *Female sexual offenders: Theory, assessment, and treatment* (pp. 181–198). Chichester, England: John Wiley & Sons, Ltd.

Gannon, T. A., Rose, M. R., & Ward, T. (2008). A descriptive model of the offense process for female sexual offenders. *Sexual Abuse: A Journal of Research & Treatment, 20,* 352–374.

Gannon, T. A., Rose, M. R., & Ward, T. (2012). A descriptive offense process model of female sexual offending. In B. Schwartz (Ed.), *The sex offender* (Vol. 7, pp. 16.1–16.19). Kingston, NJ: Civic Research.

Gannon, T. A., Waugh, G., Taylor, K., Blanchette, K., O'Connor, A., Blake, E., & Ó Ciardha, C. (2014). Women who sexually offend display three main offense styles: A reexamination of the descriptive model of female sexual offending. *Sexual Abuse: A Journal of Research and Treatment, 26,* 207–224. doi:10.1177/1079063213486835

Gray, N. S., Carmen, N. G., Rogers, P., MacCulloch, M. J., Hayward, P., & Snowden, R. J. (2003). Post-traumatic stress disorder caused in mentally disordered offender by the committing of a serious violent or sexual assault. *Journal of Forensic Psychiatry and Psychology, 14,* 27–43.

Grayston, A. D., & De Luca, R. V. (1999). Female perpetrators of child sexual abuse: A review of the clinical and empirical literature. *Aggression and Violent Behavior, 4,* 93–106.

Green, A. H., & Kaplan, M. S. (1994). Psychiatric impairment and childhood victimization experiences in female child molesters. *Journal of the American Academy of Child and Adolescent Psychiatry, 33,* 954–961.

Hanson, R. K., & Morton-Bourgon, K. E. (2005). The characteristics of persistent sexual offenders: A meta-analysis of recidivism studies. *Journal of Consulting and Clinical Psychology, 73,* 1154–1163.

Hanson, R. K., & Thornton, D. (2000). Improving risk assessments for sex offenders: A comparison of three actuarial scales. *Law and Human Behavior, 24,* 119–136.

Heil, P., Simons, D., & Burton, D. (2010). Using the polygraph with female sexual offenders. In T. A. Gannon & F. Cortoni (Eds.), *Female sexual offenders: Theory, assessment, and treatment* (pp. 143–160). Chichester, England: John Wiley & Sons, Ltd.

Holtfreter, K., & Cupp, R. (2007). Gender and risk assessment: The empirical status of the LSI-R for women. *Journal of Contemporary Criminal Justice, 23,* 363–382.

Kubik, E. K., & Hecker, J. E. (2005). Cognitive distortions about sex and sexual offending: A comparison of sex offending girls, delinquent girls, and girls from the community. *Journal of Child Sexual Abuse, 11,* 63–83.

Lewis, C. F., & Stanley, C. R. (2000). Women accused of sexual offenses. *Behavioral Sciences and the Law, 18,* 73–81.

Manchak, M. A., Skeem, J. L., Douglas, K. S., & Siranosian, M. (2009). Does gender moderate the predictive utility of the Level of Service Inventory – Revised (LSI-R) for serious violent offenders? *Criminal Justice and Behavior, 36,* 425–442.

Mapp, S. C. (2006). The effects of sexual abuse as a child on the risk of mothers physically abusing their children: A path analysis using systems theory. *Child Abuse and Neglect, 30,* 1293–1310.

Marshall, W. L., Marshall, L. E., Serran, G. A., & O'Brien, M. D. (2011). *Rehabilitating sexual offenders: A strengths-based approach*. London, England: APA Books.

Mathews, R., Matthews, J. K., & Speltz, K. (1989). *Female sexual offenders: An exploratory study*. Orwell, VT: Safer Society Press.

Miccio-Fonseca, L. C. (2000). Adult and adolescent female sex offenders: Experiences compared to other female and male sex offenders. *Journal of Psychology & Human Sexuality*, *11*, 75–88. doi:10.1300/J056v11n03_08

Nathan, P., & Ward, T. (2002). Female sex offenders: Clinical and demographic features. *The Journal of Sexual Aggression*, *8*(1), 5–21.

Ogloff, J., & Tye, C. (2007). Responding to mental health needs of women offenders. In R. Sheehan, G. McIvor, & C. Trotter (Eds.), *What works with women offenders*. Cullompton, England: Willan.

Pothast, H. L., & Allen, C. M. (1994). Masculinity and femininity in male and female perpetrators of child sexual abuse. *Child Abuse & Neglect*, *18*, 763–767.

Rousseau, M. M., & Cortoni, F. (2010). The mental health needs of female sexual offenders. In T. A. Gannon & F. Cortoni (Eds.), *Female sexual offenders: Theory, Assessment, and treatment* (pp. 73–86). Chichester, England: John Wiley & Sons, Ltd.

Sandler, J. C., & Freeman, N. J. (2007). Typology of female sex offenders: A test of Vandiver and Kercher. *Sexual Abuse: A Journal of Research and Treatment*, *19*, 73–89.

Sandler, J. C., & Freeman, N. J. (2009). Female sex offender recidivism: A large-scale empirical analysis. *Sexual Abuse: A Journal of Research and Treatment*, *21*, 455–473.

Saradjian, J., & Hanks, H. (1996). *Women who sexually abuse children: From research to clinical practice*. Chichester, England: John Wiley & Sons, Ltd.

Smith, P., Cullen, F. T., & Latessa, E. J. (2009). Can 14,737 women be wrong? A meta-analysis of the LSI-R and recidivism for female offenders. *Criminology & Public Policy*, *8*, 183–208.

Strickland, S. M. (2008). Female sex offenders: Exploring issues of personality, trauma, and cognitive distortions. *Journal of Interpersonal Violence*, *23*, 474–489. doi:10.1177/0886260507312944

Suschinsky, K. D., Lalumière, M. L., & Chivers, M. L. (2009). Sex differences in patterns of genital sexual arousal: Measurement artifacts or true phenomena? *Archives of Sexual Behavior*, *38*, 559–573.

Vandiver, D. (2007, March). *An examination of re-arrest rates of 942 male and 471 female registered sex offenders*. Seattle, WA: Academy of the Criminal Justice Sciences, Feature Panel on Sex Offenders.

Vandiver, D. M., & Kercher, G. (2004). Offender and victim characteristics of registered sexual offenders in Texas: A proposed typology of female sexual offenders. *Sexual Abuse: A Journal of Research and Treatment*, *16*, 121–137.

Vess, J. (2011). Risk assessment with female sex offenders: Can women meet the criteria of community protection laws? *Journal of Sexual Aggression*, *17*, 77–91.

Ward, T., & Keenan, T. (1999). Child molesters' implicit theories. *Journal of Interpersonal Violence*, *14*, 821–838.

Ward, T., Louden, K., Hudson, S. M., & Marshall, W. L. (1995). A description of the offense chain for child molesters. *Journal of Interpersonal Violence*, *10*, 452–472.

Weiss, D. S., & Marmar, C. R. (1997). The Impact of Event Scale – Revised. In J. P. Wilson & T. M. Keane (Eds.), *Assessing psychological trauma and PTSD: A practitioner's handbook*. (2nd ed., pp. 168–189). New York, NY: Guilford Press.

Wijkman, M., & Bijleveld, C. (2008, September). *Female sex offenders: Recidivism and criminal careers*. Paper presented at the 8th Annual Conference of the European Society of Criminology, Edinburgh, Scotland.

Wijkman, M., & Bijleveld, C. (2013, October). *Criminal career features of female sex offenders: Preliminairy results*. Paper presented at the 32nd Annual Research and Treatment Conference of the Association for the Treatment of Sexual Abusers, Chicago, IL.

Wijkman, M., Bijleveld, C., & Hendriks, J. (2011). Female sex offenders: Specialists, generalists and once-only offenders. *Journal of Sexual Aggression, 17,* 34–45.

Wilson, G. (1978). *The secrets of sexual fantasy*. London, England: J. M. Dent.

47

Internet Offenders

Typologies and Risk

Ethel Quayle

University of Edinburgh, United Kingdom

Introduction

The International Telecommunication Union (ITU) (2013) estimated that by the end of 2013, 6.8 billion mobile/cellular phone subscriptions were likely to exist, which represents almost as many people as there are on the planet, with as many as 2.7 billion people using the Internet worldwide. The ITU noted that for more than two decades there has been discussion on the emergence of a global population of young people who were born into this digital era and who are growing up using information and communication technologies (ICTs) in their everyday lives. Such networked digital young people are often referred to as 'digital natives' and although as yet there is no consensus on the impacts that ICTs have on young people, it is acknowledged that digital media change our social landscape, influence the way in which we learn, and affect how we participate in civic involvement. We are also starting to see research comparing ICTs across two generations of digital natives and noting the ubiquitous and pervasive nature of this technology in everyday lives (Joiner et al., 2013).

That such large numbers of people, and in particular young people, are using ICTs is accompanied by anxieties about the risk of technology-facilitated child abuse and exploitation (Altobelli, 2010; Jewkes & Wykes, 2012) and fears that the rate of technological change is outpacing parents' technological knowledge, young people's understanding of the impact of their activities (Ostrager, 2010; Sorbring, 2014), and law enforcement's expertise and resources. As with other cybercrimes, ICTs enable criminals to collaborate more easily, across jurisdictions and borders, and to teach themselves how to evade detection (Kirwan & Power, 2013). Meanwhile, law enforcement practitioners often do not have sufficient time or resources to keep up with new innovations and surmount jurisdictional limitations (Yar, 2013). Furthermore, the use of forensic tools to collect and document digital evidence efficiently often requires high

The Wiley Handbook on the Theories, Assessment, and Treatment of Sexual Offending.
Edited by Douglas P. Boer. Volume II: Assessment, edited by Leam A. Craig and Martin Rettenberger.
© 2017 John Wiley & Sons, Ltd. Published 2017 by John Wiley & Sons, Ltd.

levels of training and expertise (Rashid, Greenwood, Walkerdine, Baron, & Rayson, 2012). Online offenders can create and adapt new technological strategies whereas the process of changing legislation requires consensus. In 2013, the UK Prime Minister, David Cameron, pledged to tackle the problems of online child abuse images through policing the 'dark net', a general term for areas of the Internet not accessible through search engines (Hern, 2013). However, within an international context, higher levels of cultural variations and legal structures are likely to complicate the process (Gillespie, 2013).

Internet Sex Offenders

Internet sex offenders clearly use the Internet, via a computer, mobile device, games console, smart TV, and so on, to commit a crime and, as previously mentioned, can be seen in this way as similar to other cybercriminals such as those involved in identity theft or phishing (Hunton, 2011). A variety of terms are used to describe the producers and users of materials depicting the sexual abuse or exploitation of children: paedophiles (Holt, Blevins, & Berkert, 2010; Seto, 2010); online sex offenders (Babchishin, Hanson, & Hermann, 2011; Bourke & Hernandez, 2009); Internet sexual offenders (Elliott, Beech, Mandeville-Norden, & Hayes, 2009); and Internet-based sexual offenders (Henry, Mandeville-Norden, Hayes, & Egan, 2010). The generic term 'Internet offenders' is often used to describe people whose index crime is possession of child abuse images, also called indecent images of children (IIOC) or child pornography; however, the range of sexual crimes against children that take place on the Internet includes the production of abusive images, their distribution, and online solicitation or grooming of children. All of these are relatively new crimes and, in the United Kingdom, now include prohibited images of children (PIOC). Antoniou (2013) discussed the creation of legislation to tackle the demand for non-photographic images of child sexual abuse. The rationale for criminalizing these images in part is a response to concerns that they legitimize the sexual abuse and exploitation of children (Bausbaum, 2010). It was already illegal to publish or distribute (but not to possess) such images in the United Kingdom under the Obscene Publications Act 1959. This law makes reference to computer-generated child sexual abuse images, and also manga images, private cartoons, and drawings depicting children being sexually abused.

The debate that dominates research on Internet offenders is whether they are similar, or different to, existing offender groups. It is apparent that some of those who commit Internet-related offences will also have committed, or will go on to commit, non-Internet-related contact offences against children. In many studies, the former are often called mixed offenders (Elliott, Beech, & Mandeville-Norden, 2013; Neutze, Grundmann, Scherner, & Beier, 2012) or generalist sexual offenders (Wakeling, Howard, & Barnett, 2011). However, an attempt to distinguish between these groups of online and offline offenders largely depends on whether someone has a known conviction for an additional contact offence, or a known disclosure, and it would seem that there are differences between the two. For example, Seto, Hanson, and Babchishin (2011), in a meta-analysis of studies examining histories of contact offending by online offenders, found that approximately one in eight had an officially known contact offence sexual history, but in the six studies that used self-report data, one in two offenders admitted to a contact offence (which had not previously been disclosed). However, there are challenges in making sense of this analysis given the variety of methodologies, offence definitions, populations, and time frames for the included studies. For many practitioners, particularly when trying to establish the level of risk of future offending, this poses considerable challenges and has led to the suggestion that the use of polygraphs may have utility for work with Internet offenders and result in the disclosure of previously unknown contact offences or risk factors for reoffending (Robilotta, Mercardo, & De Gue, 2008). In studies that have used the polygraph (e.g., Bourke & Hernandez, 2009; Buschman, Wilcox, Krapohl, Oelrich, & Hackett, 2010), there were differences between the self-reported and polygraph-confirmed elicited disclosure concerning grooming behaviours and contact behaviours towards children in men whose index offence was possession of IIOC. In addition to possible under-reporting, the Buschman et al. (2010) study also indicated that these offenders tended to overestimate the ages of the children in the images collected (suggesting that they were older than they were) and underestimate the level of sexual victimization within the images (saying, for example, that they were posed sexual pictures rather than ones that depicted specific sexual acts).

To date, the majority of research studies have used samples of convicted contact offenders (with no known history of offences related to IIOC) or mixed offenders as comparison groups in relation to risk, recidivism, or across a number of largely self-reported variables. One exception to this is a study by Neutze et al. (2012), who sampled self-referred paedophiles and hebephiles recruited from the community, all of whom met DSM-IV-TR criteria (American Psychiatric Association, 2000) and reported lifetime sexual offending against pubescent and/or pubescent children. More recently, comparisons have been made between Internet offenders who have been convicted of the possession of IIOC and those convicted of online grooming or solicitation. This is examined further later in the chapter. There are additional challenges in comparing the results across studies in that it is difficult for the reader always to know whether the mixed offender group committed crimes that related to the production of IIOC, which had been uploaded to the Internet or distributed through other means such as a mobile phone. For example, the production of IIOC, outside of commercial sexual exploitation, is likely to involve photographs taken by the offender while abusing a child. Where this has happened, it might be argued that these are also Internet offences as image production may have been in the service of the commission of further Internet crimes (Taylor & Quayle, 2003).

Differences between Internet and contact offenders have also been examined in relation to other characteristics such as age, level of education, and measures of intelligence (Eke, Seto, & Williams, 2011), and also psychological variables such as cognitive distortions, emotional dysregulation, empathy, and impression management (Bates & Metcalf, 2007; Howitt & Sheldon, 2007; Middleton, Elliott, Mandeville-Norden, & Beech, 2006). Babchishin et al. (2011), in a meta-analysis of 27 samples, found that online offenders tended to be Caucasian males younger than the general population, who, although they did not differ in terms of education, were more likely to be unemployed. Both online and offline offenders were more likely to have experienced physical and sexual abuse than the general population. In comparison with offline offenders, online offenders had greater victim empathy, greater sexual deviancy, and lower impression management. The authors concluded that youth and unemployment are risk factors for online sexual offending and that this was consistent with typical crime patterns. More recently, Faust, Bikart, Renaud, and Camp (2015) compared groups of Internet offenders and contact offenders in relation to group demographics and criminal histories. Rates of recidivism were also examined using survival curves and Cox proportional hazard regression models. The results of this study showed significant differences on demographic and criminal history variables. Internet image offenders demonstrated a lower frequency of prior criminal offending and substance abuse, and higher rates of pre-incarceration employment and level of education. In addition, the rates of recidivism were significantly different between the two groups, with Internet offenders showing lower rates of reoffence for most measures of recidivism.

Elliott et al. (2013) examined the psychological profiles of Internet, contact, and mixed Internet–contact sex offenders using self-report measures. These included the assessment of offence supportive beliefs, socioaffective functioning, emotional management, and socially desirable responding. Their multivariate general linear model indicated a mixed offender profile that was more similar to the Internet offender group than the contact offender sample. The contact offender group demonstrated lower victim empathy, greater pro-offending attitudes, an externalized locus of control, more assertiveness, a diminished ability to relate to fictional characters, and greater impulsivity. The mixed offender group showed higher levels of empathic concern for victims. They also demonstrated increased personal distress and perspective-taking ability than the Internet offender group. However, the main factor that distinguished the groups related to offence-supportive attitudes and identification with fictional characters. The second factor identified included higher levels of empathic concern and poorer self-management. These results are similar to earlier findings by Webb, Craissati, and Keen (2007), where Internet offenders exhibited lower levels of psychopathy, more control over their behaviour, relatively higher levels of victim empathy, and fewer cognitive distortions. Similarly, Henry et al. (2010), using a standard psychometric screening battery, were able to group their sample of Internet offenders into apparently normal, inadequate, and deviant. The inadequate group had clear socioaffective deficits and was not high in pro-offending measures. The deviant group was characterized by poor victim empathy.

A further study by Marshall, O'Brien, Marshall, Booth, and Davis (2012) reported data from a preliminary study comparing Internet offenders with contact offenders on measures of social anxiety, loneliness, and obsessive–compulsive tendencies. They found support for obsessive–compulsive disorder and loneliness as features that differentiate these offenders. Although interesting, the sample size in this study was relatively small and the authors noted that in addition the Internet offenders scored above the cut-off for social anxiety on the Social Phobia Inventory (SPIN) (Connor et al., 2000), and that a larger dataset that includes responses from a non-offending sample may show that these offenders are in fact experiencing high levels of social anxiety. Similarly, Prat, Bertsch, and Jonas (2013), using data from forensic assessments of people who possessed sexual images of minors, found that one-third expressed a sense of loneliness, which was significantly different from offline offenders.

Not all comparisons have been made solely with contact offenders. Graf and Dittman (2011) noted that there may be a variety of differential diagnoses for Internet offenders, which includes voyeurism. Jung, Ennis, Choy, and Hook (2013) commented that it is plausible that some of the social and relational deficits observed in Internet offenders may have an influence on the indirect way in which they offend, similar to what is observed in voyeurs and exhibitionists. They suggested that Internet offenders may be sexually excited by the voyeuristic nature of viewing pornography and masturbating to fantasies while at home, and engaging in maladaptive beliefs that they are not physically hurting a child. Their study compared 50 Internet offenders whose offences related to image possession, 45 exhibitionists or voyeurs, and 101 contact offenders. The results suggested that the three groups were largely similar in terms of personality traits, psychiatric history, intimate relationships, and sexual and cultural history. However, differences were found between the groups in terms of academic achievement and elementary-school behaviour. All three groups were likely to have been in cohabiting relationships but the Internet offenders had fewer biological children and more often were single at the time when the offence was committed. This may indicate that low rates of contact abuse by Internet offenders could be related to lack of access to children. They also suggested that the Internet offenders showed less interpersonal warmth, which may not be because of a dislike of interpersonal relationships but be due to a lack of social skills that make these relationships uncomfortable and anxiety provoking.

However, there have been criticisms of comparisons of Internet offenders with other sex-offender subgroups. Magaletta, Faust, Bikart, and McLearan (2014) noted that these studies may have limited generalizability and examined primarily treated or treatment samples and did not compare them with non-treated community samples. Their study used multiple comparison groups to examine mean score differences on the Personality Assessment Inventory (PAI), and used the normative data for the PAI to compare with men convicted of possession of IIOC and those convicted of contact offences. These were admission cohorts and were not recruited from treatment groups. Their results indicated that interpersonal deficits and depression were predominant features in the profiles of the image-related offenders, who also obtained lower scores on aggression and dominance compared with the child molesters and the male normative sample.

Typologies

The typologies that have been described in relation to Internet offenders predominantly focus on offending behaviour related to IIOC, although some (e.g., Krone, 2004) include grooming activities which may include an offline contact offence. Kloess, Beech, and Harkins (2014) suggested that these typologies could be considered along a broad and diverse spectrum of individuals who engage in problematic Internet use. One of the earliest typologies related to IIOC was that of Hartmann, Burgess, and Lanning (1984) that predated the Internet but still has relevance today. They described four categories of offenders, which related to their behaviour: closet, isolated, cottage, and commercial. Closet offenders were secretive, and not interested in molesting children. Isolated offenders were people actively molesting children and collecting images. Cottage offenders shared their collection and sexual activities with others, and commercial offenders recognized the monetary value of their collection which was shared with others. Lanning (2001) built on this typology in relation to Internet sex offenders and described: preferential offenders, situational offenders, and miscellaneous offenders. The last type included media reporters, pranksters, older 'boyfriends', and overzealous civilians. A behavioural typology was also suggested by Durkin (1997), who described four offender groups who used the Internet: traders, networkers, groomers, and travellers. This typology included grooming behaviour and is similar to that presented by Alexy, Burgess, and Baker (2005) and McLaughlin (2000). Probably the most cited typology of offenders is that of Krone (2004), which considered the seriousness of the offence in relation to behavioural properties. This typology included browsers, private fantasizers, traders, non-secure collectors, secure collectors, groomers, physical abusers, producers, and distributors.

The typologies developed by Cooper, Scherer, Boies, and Gordon (1999), and then Sullivan and Beech (2004), focused instead on motivation. The latter described three types of offenders. In Type 1, collecting images was seen as part of a larger pattern of sexual offending, Type 2 engaged in collecting to feed a developing sexual interest in children, and Type 3 accessed IIOC out of curiosity. In many ways, this is similar to a later typology (Beech, Elliott, Birgden, & Findlater, 2008) that included four categories. In the first, images were accessed sporadically/impulsively and/or out of curiosity; the second related to images being accessed to fuel a sexual interest in children; in the third, images were seen as part of a pattern of online contact offending; and the fourth category related to images being collected for non-sexual reasons, such as profit. Elliott and Beech (2009) integrated previous typologies into a four-category Internet offender typology. These were described as periodically prurient offenders, fantasy-only offenders, direct victimization offenders, and commercial exploitation offenders.

What increasingly becomes apparent is the attempt to distinguish Internet offenders on the basis of whether their offences relate to fantasy or are contact driven, and this will also be apparent in the later section on online grooming. A recent study by Merdian, Curtis, Thakker, Wilson, and Boer (2013) examined three different subgroups of IIOC offenders according to three dimensions. Dimension 1 dichotomizes types of offending into fantasy driven versus contact driven. Dimension 2 considers motivation according to whether it is paedophilic, general deviant sexual interest, financial motivation, or 'other'. The final dimension considers the social component of the offending and the role of the offender's social network. The authors concluded that, 'An individual's pathway is defined by the function of child pornography in his offending process, the underlying motivation and the social networking in his offending behaviour' (p. 10). Lanning (2012) revisited his earlier typology where he distinguished between situational- and preferential-type sexual offenders according to a motivation continuum that is based on associated behaviour patterns that are needs driven. In this revised typology, he differentiates between three groups: paedophilias (and hebephiles), diverse offenders, and latent offenders. Diverse offenders are described as not having a strong interest in children and adolescents but rather displaying a variety of sexual interests, whereas latent offenders have more recently begun to act on what was previously only a sexual interest. In the latter case, inhibitions are weakened after arousal patterns are both fuelled and validated through online social activity (communication). As can be seen, there are similarities between the typologies presented by Lanning (2012) and Merdian et al. (2013).

Online Grooming

Internet solicitation, and grooming of children for sexual purposes, have attracted less attention than the production, distribution, or downloading of IIOC (Whittle, Hamilton-Giachristis, Beech, & Collings, 2013). Grooming has been described as a process by which an individual prepares a child and their environment for sexual abuse to take place, including gaining access to the child, creating compliance and trust, and ensuring secrecy to avoid detection (Craven, Brown, & Gilchrist, 2007).

It is apparent that accounts of sexual grooming predate the Internet (e.g., Lang & Frenzel, 1988), and also are seen in contemporaneous accounts such as recent concerns over group localized grooming (GLG) in the United Kingdom (Mooney & Ost, 2013). These cases involved groups convicted of targeting, sexually abusing, and exploiting adolescents in UK cities and towns, including Derby, Rochdale, and Oxford. However, in 2001 Lanning had described grooming activities in relation to the Internet, where individuals attempted to sexually exploit children by gradually enticing their targets through the use of attention, affection, kindness, and gifts. We need to remember that in 2001 the majority of ordinary people did not have the Internet and those who did were likely to use dial-up connections. Wolak, Finkelhor, and Mitchell (2009) compared survey data obtained from US law enforcement agencies in 2000 and 2006 that showed a 21% increase in online predators. In these surveys, unwanted sexual solicitations were defined as requests to engage in sexual activities or sexual talk or to give personal sexual information that was unwanted or made by an individual ≥5 years older than the young person, whether the young person wanted this or not. There was also a subgroup of aggressive sexual solicitations, in which offenders attempted or made offline contact with young people through surface mail, by telephone, or in person (Jones, Mitchell, & Finkelhor, 2012). In 2006, of those who were arrested for online solicitation, 87% had actually targeted online under-cover investigators. This in itself is of interest, as more recent work by Lincoln and Coyle (2013) involved a deception condition study in which pairs of subjects engaged in computer-mediated interaction and were then asked to evaluate the age and gen-der of their interlocutors. Contrary to expectations, they were successful in this and seemed to base their judgements on the content of online situations. However, unlike in online solicitation or grooming cases, it is unlikely that participants were in a state of sexual arousal during the task, and this may be a factor in successful deception.

Earlier work in this area described a model of online grooming that emphasized process, where the offender, in looking for a potential target, focuses on accessibil-ity, opportunity, and vulnerability (O'Connell, 2003). These online observation data, using the researcher as a 'decoy', described seven stages that form the grooming pro-cess. These stages were sequential and included friendship and relationship forming, risk assessment, exclusivity, sexual, fantasy re-enactment, and damage limitation. More recently, two studies examined this process model of grooming using open-source data from the Perverted Justice website (Gupta, Kumaraguru, & Sureka, 2012; Williams, Elliott, & Beech, 2013). The latter study identified three 'themes' that reflected rapport building, sexual content, and assessment. However, across the transcripts analysed, these themes did not appear in any consistent order. This research does suggest that there are discrete stages in relation to online grooming but that they do not conform to any one sequence, nor are all of these stages evident across all offenders.

A qualitative study by Malesky (2007) of 31 male prisoners, convicted of sexual offences against minors whom they met and communicated with online, analysed data from questionnaires to examine comments on what attracted them to a child. Nearly half of these offenders viewed the online profiles of potential victims. Three central themes were identified: a minor mentioning sex in any fashion online; targeting a child who appeared 'needy' or 'submissive'; and using information from screen names, especially if they indicated youth. It might be argued that the Internet provides a platform supporting the rationalization of such activities. Malesky and Ennis (2004), using data from an Internet message board for men with a sexual interest in children, created a checklist of distorted cognitions. They found that cognitive distortions were relatively uncommon, but respondents did romanticize their relationships with children and romanticized minors. In another qualitative analysis of web forums, Holt et al. (2010) found that paedophile subcultures place significant value on sexuality seen through a notional lens of love and care for children. Such online forums appear to offer important support from like-minded individuals that may promote pro-offending beliefs in people who might otherwise feel marginalized (O'Halloran & Quayle, 2010).

Grooming Typologies

Over the years there have been several attempts to develop typologies of grooming behaviour (Krone, 2004). Webster et al. (2012), from a qualitative analysis of interviews with 36 men convicted of offences in the United Kingdom, identified three types of offenders: intimacy seeking, adaptable, and hyper-sexual. These were differentiated by their motivation to offend, their use of deception and indecent images of children, and their bid to meet their victim offline. An exploratory study by Briggs, Simon, and Simonsen (2011) of 51 people convicted of an Internet sex offence in the United States suggested two subgroups of offenders: a contact-driven group who were motivated to engage in offline sexual behaviour, and a fantasy-driven group motivated to engage in cybersex, but without an express wish to meet young people offline. The study's clinical and behavioural data were taken from the offender's offence-specific evaluation and from chatroom transcripts, and 90% of participants were apprehended through proactive police operations. As noted previously, a similar typology was described by Merdian et al. (2013) in relation to 'child pornography offenders' who were defined by the function of child pornography (fantasy driven or contact driven) in the offending process, the underlying motivation, and the social networking in the offending behaviour. Gallagher (2007) examined data in relation to one category of Internet offenders: Internet-initiated incitement and conspiracy to commit child sexual abuse. In his review of case data, he examined offenders' modus operandi from which a typology was generated. This four-level typology included: an individual offering a specific child for sexual abuse, an individual seeking a child for sexual abuse, one individual inciting another to sexually abuse an unspecified child, and two or more individuals conspiring to sexually abuse a child.

A further Canadian study (Seto, Wood, Babchishin, & Flynn, 2012) compared 38 contact offenders, 38 child pornography offenders, and 70 online solicitation offenders. Compared with child pornography offenders, online solicitation offenders had a lower capacity for relationship stability and lower levels of sex drive or preoccupation and deviant sexual preference. Compared with contact offenders, they were more likely to have viewed child pornography, to report hebephilic sexual interests (in pubescent young people), to have problems in their capacity for relationship stability, to be better educated, and to be more likely to have unrelated and stranger victims.

However, recent research (Wolak & Finkelhor, 2013) has challenged the view that online predators are distinctly dangerous sex offenders and that there is a need to develop specific programmes to protect young people from online predation. They collected data from a national sample of law enforcement agencies about arrests in 2009 for Internet-related sexual crimes. They presented a subset of online cases (143) and 139 people known in person. 'Online-meeting offenders first met victims on the Internet or through a cell phone (talking or text messaging). Know-in-person/online offenders were family members or acquaintances of victims and knew them offline before the crime' (p. 3). The authors concluded that the majority of cases across the samples involved non-forcible illegal sexual activity with young people (statutory rape), or non-contact offences such as child pornography possession or online solicitation. The recommendation that followed from this research was that online/offline crimes should not be treated as different and that rather we should have comprehensive programmes that address statutory rape.

Internet Properties

As yet there is little consensus about whether there are inherent properties of the Internet that encourage the commission of these offences or whether the use of technology has simply made them easier to detect (Jung, Ennis, & Malesky, 2012; Yewkes, 2010). Parallel research has focused on victim surveys (Finkelhor, Mitchell, & Wolak, 2000; Wolak, Mitchell, & Finkelhor, 2006), which indicated that the stereotype of the Internet child molester who uses trickery and violence to assault children is largely inaccurate (Wolak, Finkelhor, Mitchell, & Ybarra, 2008) and suggested that most Internet-initiated sex crimes involve adult men who use the Internet to meet and seduce underage adolescents into sexual encounters, and that in the majority of cases victims are aware that they are conversing online with adults. In the first N-JOV study, the authors found that only 5% pretended to be teens when they met potential victims online, and that offenders rarely deceived young people about their sexual interests (Wolak et al., 2008). The deceptions that did occur related to offers of love and romance, where clearly the motive was sexual.

However, rather than dispute whether we should focus on this group of offenders or the vulnerabilities of children online, it does seem relevant to explore what it is about technology that makes these crimes possible, given the role that ICTs play in our lives. For young people in particular, use of the Internet is embedded in their everyday lives and mediates important social relationships in addition to mundane routine activities (Livingstone, Haddon, Görzig, & Ólafsson, 2011).

Risk Assessment

So far there have been few studies that have examined recidivism of Internet offenders over a long period of time and the most substantial data come from Canada. Research by Eke et al. (2011) on the offence histories of Internet offenders and the likelihood of future offending suggests that with a longer period post-offence more offenders are detected for new offences, with recidivism for contact sexual offences predicted by criminal history, and in particular violent offence history and the age of the offender at the time of their first conviction. What is important is that this study also examined failures on conditional release, in particular where offenders put themselves in 'risky' situations, such as being alone with children. The finding that one-quarter of the extended sample was charged with failures was consistent with the findings from other sex offender groups. Such failures included breaches of conditions about being alone with children, accessing the Internet, contacting children, and downloading child abuse material, in addition to other violations that were non-sexual or indicated non-compliance. This is of interest because while 34% of offenders had a charge for any type of further offence, only 4% were charged with any new contact sexual offence and 7% were charged with new child pornography-related offences.

Elliott, Beech, Mandeville-Norden, and Hayes (2009) compared 505 Internet sex offenders and 526 contact offenders on a range of psychological measures relating to offence-supportive beliefs, empathic concern, interpersonal functioning, and emotional management. Contact offending was predicted by increases in scores of scales of locus of control, perspective taking, empathic concern, over-assertiveness, victim empathy distortions, cognitive distortions, and cognitive impulsivity. Increases in scores on scales of fantasy, under-assertiveness, and motor impulsivity were predictive of an Internet offence type. Eke et al. (2011) also reported on an unpublished study by Faust, Bickart, and Renaud (2009), who examined potential risk factors in a sample of 870 child pornography offenders. They identified five variables as being significant predictors of rearrest for a sexual crime: lower education, being single, having non-Internet child pornography, prior sexual offender treatment, and not having pictures of 'adolescent minors'. It is unclear whether this might suggest an older group of offenders, but it does link with concerns about whether we should distinguish men who access images of prepubescent children from those who access images of pubescent or sexually mature young people (Seto, 2010). This also touches upon some of the challenges regarding how 'child' is operationalized in national and supranational law (Gillespie, 2010).

Whereas analyses of images by law enforcement agencies suggest that the typical child depicted is a prepubescent girl (e.g., Baartz, 2008; Wolak, Finkelhor, & Mitchell,

2005, 2009), an analysis of a sample of seized images within one UK law enforcement database suggests that the odds of the abuse images being of females versus males were about 4:1, and the odds of the images being of white children versus non-white children were about 10:1. Of those white female children, approximately 48% were pubescent (Quayle & Jones, 2011). It may be that in many instances we can at best approximate the content of image collections, given the potential volume of images collected and the limited forensic resources of most specialist police units, and Glasgow (2010) suggested that the volume, complexity, and inaccessibility of digital evidence have deterred a systematic analysis of the relationship between downloaded material and potential risk.

Apart from the Internet Behaviours and Attitudes Questionnaire (IBAQ), developed by O'Brien and Webster (2007), and the Children and Sexual Activities (C&SA) Scale (Howitt & Sheldon, 2007), there are no measures that have been developed specific to an Internet-offending population, with authors such as Tomak, Weschler, Ghahramanlou-Holloway, Virden, and Nademin (2009) suggesting that personality scales such as the MMPI-2 have limited utility in differentiating between these different subtypes of sex offenders. However, Magaletta et al. (2014), using the PAI, did find differences between Internet offenders, contact offenders, and a normative sample from the PAI. Their results indicated that interpersonal deficits and depression featured most prominently in the profiles of Internet offenders, who also obtained lower scores on aggression and dominance than contact offenders or the normative sample (Quayle & Hayes, 2014).

At present there are no specific risk assessment tools in relation to Internet offenders, and this has raised issues about the utility of existing measures. Wakeling et al. (2011) compared the validity of a modified version of the Risk Matrix 2000 (RM2000) (Thornton, 2007) with the Offender Group Reconviction Scale 3 (OGRS3) (Howard, Francis, Soothill, & Humphreys, 2009) on a sample of adult males convicted of an offence of possession, manufacturing, or sharing IIOC, with the majority having at least 1-year proven reoffending follow-up data. The sample was made up of two groups: 304 generalist sex offenders and 690 'Internet specialists'. The results indicated that those in the very high-risk category sexually reoffended at a greater rate than the rest of the sample, but there was little difference between the rates in the other three risk categories. Internet specialists seemed less criminal than the generalist group and had lower general reoffending and sexual reoffending risk. For the Internet specialists, almost all sexual reoffending was Internet related, whereas for the generalists, two-thirds of all the sexual reoffending was Internet related but one-third was non-Internet related. This preliminary work suggests that modified actuarial measures may have some predictive utility, although low reoffending rates made comparisons challenging. Webb et al. (2007), using the RM2000 and Stable-2000 (Hanson & Harris, 2001), also noted this to be problematic. Osborn, Elliott, Middleton, and Beech (2010) used the Static-99, RM2000, and a revised RM2000. This last version was changed in relation to Internet offenders and removed factors relating to 'stranger victims' and 'non-contact offences'. In their study, none of the offenders was convicted for a new offence in the follow-up period (1.5–4 years), so it was not possible to look at predictive accuracy, but the authors did examine risk categorizations using the original two scales and felt that both overestimated the risk for Internet offenders. Similarly, Endrass et al. (2009), in a study of 231 men charged with child pornography offences, examined recidivism 6 years after the index offence. In this study, 4.8% of the sample had prior convictions for sexual or violent offences and 1% for a contact offence against a child. Using a broad definition of recidivism, 3% recidivated with a violent or sexual offence, 3.9% with a non-contact sexual offence, and 0.8% with a contact offence, leading these authors to conclude that downloading child pornography alone is not a risk factor for the commission of a contact offence.

One final area that is worthy of consideration is the role of forensic evidence and how this might inform assessment and intervention with Internet offenders. An important aspect of this offending, not previously seen in quite the same way in contact offences against children, is that these offences leave behind a permanent product: images or text that relate to the offence. Glasgow (2010) argued that such digital evidence provides insights into the preferred material that is used to generate augmented sexual and interpersonal fantasies, which may evolve over time and change the types of images sought. The pattern of images accessed and viewed over time may reflect evolving sexual interests, an escalation of instrumental behaviour, and indications of growing compulsivity. The images also provide an accurate record of what the offender was accessing, which can be compared with self-reports.

The only tool that has been developed to rate the content of images systematically is the COPINE Scale (Taylor, Holland, & Quayle, 2001), which was adapted by the UK Sentencing Advisory Panel (SAP) to provide a five-point scale giving an objective estimation of the level of victimization in the images collected. This was used as a 'multiplier' in relation to other aspects of the offence to determine possible sentencing. The content of the images, as measured by the SAP guidelines, was also used by Long, Alison, and McManus (2013) to examine the relationship between IIOC possession and contact offending. Their original sample included 30 dual offenders and 30 non-contact offenders examined in relation to the quantity and types of images collected and their relationship with offending behaviour. It was possible to discriminate between groups according to previous conviction, access to children, and the number, proportion, and type of IIOC viewed. Within the dual offenders, there was a close match between the type of offence (sexual touching, penetrative abuse, and sadism) and the content of the images in their possession. The implications of this research are important in that it addresses the activity of these offenders in the context of both online and offline activity and may result in a risk appraisal tool that will permit prioritization of risk.

Conclusions

The last decade has seen an increase in research studies focused on sexual offending committed through the Internet or mobile devices. What has been generally concluded is that the subjects represent a heterogeneous population who share some common characteristics with people who commit sexual offences offline, but also with some differences, which may in part relate to a generation growing up with technology embedded in their everyday lives. Although there are indications that the risk of future (or past) offending posed by these individuals is low, this is likely to be challenged by further polygraph studies which suggest that these people are essentially good at avoiding detection. There are also tensions within the research and practitioner community as to whether we are placing undue emphasis on the importance of this offending group and, as a consequence, diverting resources away from a core group of offenders and their victims. However, what we do need to consider is not whether they represent a larger threat but, given the way in which technology mediates much of our lives (and is likely to become more pervasive), how technology enables these crimes to proliferate and what solutions might also be technologically afforded.

References

Alexy, E. M., Burgess, A. W., & Baker, T. (2005). Internet offenders: Traders, travelers, and combination trader–travelers. *Journal of Interpersonal Violence, 20*, 804–812. doi:10.1177/08862605052 76091

Altobelli, T. (2010). Cyber-abuse – a new worldwide threat to children's rights. *Family Court, 48*(3), 459–481.

American Psychiatric Association (2000). *Diagnostic and statistical manual of mental disorders* (4th ed., text revision) (DSM-IV-TR). Washington, DC: Author.

Antoniou, A. (2013). Possession of prohibited images of children: Three years on. *The Journal of Criminal Law, 77*, 337–353.

Baartz, D. (2008). *Australians, the Internet and technology-enabled child sex abuse: A statistical profile*. Canberra, Australia: Australian Federal Police.

Babchishin, K. M., Hanson, R. K., & Hermann, C. A. (2011). The characteristics of online sex offenders: A meta-analysis. *Sexual Abuse: A Journal of Research and Treatment, 23*(1), 92–123.

Bates, A., & Metcalf, C. (2007). A psychometric comparison of Internet and non-Internet sex offenders from a community treatment sample. *Journal of Sexual Aggression, 13*, 11–20.

Bausbaum, J. P. (2010). Inequitable sentencing for possession of child pornography: A failure to distinguish voyeurs from pederasts. *Hastings Law Journal, 61*(5), 1281–1305.

Beech, A. R., Elliott, I. A., Birgden, A., & Findlater, D. (2008). The Internet and child sexual offending: A criminological review. *Aggression and Violent Behavior, 13*, 216–228.

Bourke, M., & Hernandez, L. (2009). The 'Butner Study' Redux: A Report of the Incidence of Hands-on Child Victimization by Child Pornography Offenders. *Journal of Family Violence, 24*(3), 183–191.

Briggs, P., Simon, W. T., & Simonsen, S. (2011). An exploratory study of Internet initiated sexual offenses and the chat room sex offender: Has the Internet enabled a new typology of sex offender? *Sexual Abuse: A Journal of Research and Treatment, 23*(1), 72–91.

Buschman, J., Wilcox, D., Krapohl, D., Oelrich, M., & Hackett, S. (2010). Cybersex offender risk assessment. An explorative study. *Journal of Sexual Aggression, 16*(2), 197–209.

Connor, K. M., Davidson, J. R. T., Churchill, L. E., Sherwood, A., Weisler, R. H., & Foa, E. (2000). Psychometric properties of the Social Phobia Inventory (SPIN): New self-rating scale. *British Journal of Psychiatry, 176*, 379–386.

Cooper, A., Scherer, C. R., Boies, S. C., & Gordon, B. L. (1999). Sexuality on the Internet: From sexual exploration to pathological expression. *Professional Psychology: Research and Practice, 30*(2), 154–164.

Craven, S., Brown, S., & Gilchrist, E. (2007). Current responses to sexual grooming: Implication for prevention. *Howard Journal of Criminal Justice, 46*, 60–71. doi:10.1111/j.1468-2311.2007.00454.x

Durkin, K. (1997). Misuse of the Internet by pedophiles: Implications for law enforcement and probation practice. *Federal Probation, 61*(3), 14–18.

Eke, A. W., Seto, M. C., & Williams, J. (2011). Examining the criminal history and future offending of child pornography offenders: An extended prospective follow-up study. *Law and Human Behavior, 35*(6), 466–478.

Elliott, I., & Beech, A. (2009). Understanding online child pornography use: Applying sexual offense theory to Internet offenders. *Aggression & Violent Behavior, 14*(3), 180–193.

Elliott, I. A., Beech, A. R., & Mandeville-Norden, R. (2013). The psychological profiles of Internet, contact, and mixed Internet/contact sex offenders. *Sexual Abuse: A Journal of Research and Treatment, 25*(1), 3–20.

Elliott, I. A., Beech, A. R., Mandeville-Norden, R., & Hayes, E. (2009). Psychological profiles of Internet sexual offenders. *Sexual Abuse: A Journal of Research and Treatment, 23*, 76–92. doi:10.1177/1079063208326929

Endrass, J., Urbaniok, F., Hammermeister, L., Benz, C., Elbert, T., Laubacher, A., & Rossegger, A. (2009). The consumption of Internet child pornography and violent and sex offending. *BMC Psychiatry, 9*, 43.

Faust, E., Bickart, W., & Renaud, C. (2009, October). *Predictors of re-offense among a sample of federally convicted child pornography offenders.* Paper presented at the 28th Annual Conference of the Association for the Treatment of Sexual Abusers. Dallas, TX.

Faust, E., Bickart, W., Renaud, C., & Camp, S. (2015). Child pornography possessors and child contact sex offenders: A multilevel comparison of demographic characteristics and rates of recidivism. *Sexual Abuse: A Journal of Research and Treatment. Date of Electronic Publication: 2015, 27*(5), 460–478.

Finkelhor, D., Mitchell, K. J., & Wolak, J. (2000). *Online victimization: A report on the nation's youth.* Alexandria, VA: National Center for Missing & Exploited Children. Retrieved from http://www.unh.edu/ccrc/pdf/Victimization_Online_Survey.pdf

Gallagher, B. (2007). Internet-initiated incitement and conspiracy to commit child sexual abuse (CSA): The typology, extent and nature of known cases. *Journal of Sexual Aggression, 13*(2), 101–119.

Gillespie, A. (2010). Legal definitions of child pornography. *Journal of Sexual Aggression, 16*(1), 19–31.

Gillespie, A. (2013). Jurisdictional issues concerning online child pornography. *International Journal of Law and Information Technology, 20*(3), 151–177.

Glasgow, D. (2010). The potential of digital evidence to contribute to risk assessment of internet offenders. *Journal of Sexual Aggression, 16*(1), 87–106.

Graf, M., & Dittmann, V. (2011). Forensic–psychiatric treatment for Internet sex offenders. In: D. P. Boer, R. Eher, L. A. Craig, M. H. Miner, & F. Pfäfflin (Eds.), *International perspectives on the assessment and treatment of sexual offenders: Theory, practice, and research.* Chichester, England: John Wiley & Sons, Ltd.

Gupta, A., Kumaraguru, P., & Sureka, A. (2012) Characterizing pedophile conversations on the Internet using online grooming. In *Proceedings of CoRR Conference, 2012.*

Hanson, K., & Harris, A. J. R. (2001). A structured approach to evaluating change among sexual offenders. *Sexual Abuse: A Journal of Research and Treatment, 13*, 105–122.

Hartman, C. R., Burgess, A. W., & Lanning, K. V. (1984). Typology of collectors. In A. W Burgess (Ed.), *Child pornography and sex rings* (pp. 93–109). Lanham, MD: Lexington Books.

Henry, O., Mandeville-Norden, R., Hayes, E., & Egan, V. (2010). Do Internet-based sexual offenders reduce to normal, inadequate and deviant groups? *Journal of Sexual Aggression*, *16*(1), 33–46.

Hern, A. (2013, November 18). David Cameron: GCHQ will be brought in to tackle child abuse images. *The Guardian*. Retrieved from http://www.theguardian.com/technology/2013/nov/18/david-cameron-gchq-child-abuse-images

Holt, T. J., Blevins, K. B., & Berkert, N. (2010). Considering the pedophile subculture online. *Sexual Abuse: A Journal of Research and Treatment*, *22*(1), 3–24.

Howard, P., Francis, B., Soothill, K., & Humphreys, L. (2009). *OGRS 3: The revised Offender Group Reconviction Scale* (Ministry of Justice Research Summary 7/09). London, England: Ministry of Justice. Retrieved from https://core.ac.uk/download/files/59/1556521.pdf

Howitt, D., & Sheldon, K. (2007). The role of cognitive distortions in pedophilic offending: Internet and contact offenders compared. *Psychology, Crime & Law*, *13*(5), 469–486.

Hunton, P. (2011). A rigorous approach to formalising the technical investigation stages of cybercrime and criminality within a UK law enforcement environment. *Digital Investigation*, *7*, 105–113.

ITU (2013) *Measuring the information society*. Retrieved from https://www.itu.int/en/ITU-D/Statistics/Documents/publications/mis2013/MIS2013_without_Annex_4.pdf

Jewkes, Y., & Wykes, M. (2012). Reconstructing the sexual abuse of children: 'Cyber-paeds', panic and power. *Sexualities*, *15*(8), 934–952.

Joiner, R., Gavin, J., Brosnan, M., Cromby, J., Gregory, H., Guiller, J., Maras, P., & Moon, A. (2013). Comparing first and second generation digital natives' Internet use, Internet anxiety, and Internet identification. *Cyberpsychology, Behavior, and Social Networking*, *16*(7), 549–552.

Jones, L. M., Mitchell, K. J., & Finkelhor, D. (2012). Trends in youth Internet victimization: Findings from three youth Internet safety surveys 2000–2010. *Journal of Adolescent Health*, *50*(2), 179–186.

Jung, S., Ennis, L., Choy, A. L., & Hook, T. (2013). Child pornography possessors: Comparisons and contrasts with contact and non-contact offenders. *Journal of Sexual Aggression*, *19*(3), 295–310.

Jung, S., Ennis, L., & Malesky, L. A. Jr. (2012). Child pornography offending seen through three theoretical lenses. *Deviant Behavior*, *33*(8), 655–673.

Kirwan, G., & Power, A. (2013). *Cybercrime: The psychology of online offenders*. Cambridge, England: Cambridge University Press.

Kloess, J. A., Beech, A. R., & Harkins, L. (2014). Online child sexual exploitation: Prevalence, process, and offender characteristics. *Trauma, Violence & Abuse*, *15*(2), 126–139.

Krone, T. (2004). A typology of online child pornography offending. *Trends and Issues in Crime and Criminal Justice*, (*279*), 1–6.

Lang, R. A., & Frenzel, R. R. (1988). How sex offenders lure children. *Annals of Sex Research*, *1*(2), 303–317.

Lanning, K. V. (2001). *Child molesters: A behavioral analysis*. Alexandria, VA: National Center for Missing and Exploited Children.

Lanning, K. V. (2012). Cyber 'pedophiles': A behavioral perspective. In K. Borgeson & K. Kuehnle (Eds.), *Serial offenders: Theory and practice* (pp. 71–87). Sudbury, MA: Jones & Bartlett Learning.

Lincoln, R., & Coyle, I. R. (2013). No-one knows you're a dog on the Internet: Implications for proactive police investigation of sexual offenders. *Psychiatry, Psychology and Law*, *20*(2), 294–300.

Livingstone, S., Haddon, L., Görzig, A., & Ólafsson, K. (2011). *Risks and safety on the Internet. Perspective of European children. Full findings and policy implications from EU Kids Online survey of 9–16 year olds and their parents in 25 countries.* Retrieved from www.eukidsonline .net

Long, M. L., Alison, L. A., &. McManus, M. A. (2013). Child pornography and likelihood of contact abuse: A comparison between contact child sexual offenders and noncontact offenders. *Sexual Abuse: A Journal of Research and Treatment, 25*(4), 370–395.

Magaletta, P., Faust, E., Bickart, W., & McLearen, A. (2014). Exploring clinical and personality characteristics of adult male Internet-only child pornography offenders. *International Journal of Offender Therapy and Comparative Criminology, 58*(2), 137–153.

Malesky, L. A. (2007). Predatory online behavior: Modus operandi of convicted sex offenders in identifying potential victims and contacting minors over the Internet. *Journal of Child Sexual Abuse, 16*(2), 23–32.

Malesky, L. A., & Ennis, L. (2004). Supportive distortions: An analysis of posts on a pedophile Internet message board. *Journal of Addictions and Offender Counseling, 24*, 92–100.

Marshall, L. E., O'Brien, M. D., Marshall, W. L., Booth, B., & Davis, A. (2012). Obsessive compulsive disorder, social phobia, and loneliness in incarcerated Internet child pornography offenders. *Sexual Addiction & Compulsivity: The Journal of Treatment & Prevention, 19*(1–2), 41–52.

McLaughlin, J. F. (2000). Cyber child sex offender typology. *Knight Stick: Publication of the New Hampshire Police Association, 55*, 39–42. Retrieved from http://eprints.lincoln.ac .uk/4843/1/ReviewISO2009.pdf

Merdian, H. L., Curtis, C., Thakker, J., Wilson, N., & Boer, D. P. (2013). The three dimensions of online child pornography offending, *Journal of Sexual Aggression, 19*(1), 121–132.

Middleton, D., Elliott, I. A., Mandeville-Norden, R., & Beech, A. R. (2006). An investigation into the applicability of the Ward and Siegert Pathways Model of child sexual abuse with Internet offenders. *Psychology, Crime and Law, 12*(6), 589–603.

Mooney, J.-L., & Ost, S. (2013). Group localised grooming: What is it and what challenges does it pose for society and law? *Child & Family Law Quarterly, 25*(4), 425–450.

Neutze, J., Grundmann, D., Scherner, G., & Beier, K. M. (2012). Undetected and detected child sexual abuse and child pornography offenders. *International Journal of Law and Psychiatry, 35*, 168–175.

O'Brien, M., & Webster, D. (2007). The construction and preliminary validation of the Internet Behaviours and Attitudes Questionnaire (IBAQ). *Sexual Abuse: A Journal of Research and Treatment, 19*(3), 237–256.

O'Connell, R. (2003). *A typology of child cybersexploitation and online grooming practices.* Preston, England: Cyberspace Research Unit, University of Central Lancashire. Retrieved from http://image.guardian.co.uk/sys-files/Society/documents/2003/07/ 17/Groomingreport.pdf

O'Halloran, E., & Quayle, E. (2010). A content analysis of a 'Boy Love' support forum: Revisiting Durkin & Bryant. *Journal of Sexual Aggression, 16*(1), 71–85.

Osborn, J., Elliott, I. A., Middleton, D., & Beech, A. R. (2010). The use of actuarial risk assessment measures with UK Internet child pornography offenders. *Journal of Aggression, Conflict and Peace Research, 2*(3), 16–24.

Ostrager, B. (2010). SMS.OMG! TTYL: Translating the law to accommodate today's teens and the evolution from texting to sexting. *Family Court Review, 48*(4), 712–726.

Prat, S., Bertsch, I., & Jonas, C. (2013). Child pornographers: Clinical features of a virtual assault. *European Psychiatry, 28*(Suppl. 1), 1.

Quayle, E., & Hayes, E. (2014). Interventions with an Internet sexual offender. In D. T. Wilcox, T. Garrett, & L. Harkins (Eds.), *Case studies in sex offender treatment* (pp. 163–180). Chichester, England: John Wiley & Sons, Ltd.

Quayle, E., & Jones, T. (2011). Sexualized images of children on the Internet. *Sexual Abuse: A Journal of Research and Treatment, 23*(1), 7–21.

Rashid, A., Greenwood, P., Walkerdine, J., Baron, A., & Rayson, P. (2012). Technological solutions to offending. In E. Quayle & K. Ribsil (Eds.), *Internet child pornography: Understanding and preventing on-line child abuse.* London, England: Routledge.

Robilotta, S. A., Mercado, C. C., & De Gue, S. (2008). Application of the polygraph examination in the assessment and treatment of Internet sex offenders. *Journal of Forensic Psychiatry Practice, 8*(4), 383–393.

Seto, M. (2010). Child pornography use and Internet solicitation in the diagnosis of pedophilia. *Archives of Sexual Behavior, 39*, 591–593.

Seto, M. C., Hanson, R. K., & Babchishin, K. M. (2011). Contact sexual offending by men with online sexual offenses. *Sexual Abuse: A Journal of Research and Treatment, 23*, 124–145.

Seto, M. C., Wood, J. M., Babchishin, K. M., & Flynn, S. (2012). Online solicitation offenders are different from child pornography offenders and lower risk contact sexual offenders. *Law and Human Behavior, 36*(4), 320–330.

Sorbring, E. (2014). Parents' concerns about their teenage children's Internet use. *Journal of Family Issues, 35*(1), 75–96.

Sullivan, J., & Beech, A. R. (2004). Assessing Internet sex offenders. In M. C. Calder (Ed.), *Child sexual abuse and the Internet: Tackling the new frontier* (pp. 69–83). Lyme Regis, England: Russell House.

Taylor, M., Holland, G., & Quayle, E. (2001). Typology of paedophile picture collections. *The Police Journal, 2001, 74*(2), 97–107.

Taylor, M., & Quayle, E. (2003). *Child pornography: An Internet crime.* Hove, England: Routledge.

Thornton, D. (2007). *Scoring guide for the Risk Matrix 2000.9/SVC: February 2007 version.* Retrieved from http://www.cfcp.bham.ac.uk/Extras/SCORING%20GUIDE%20FOR%20RISK%20MATRIX%202000.9-%20SVC%20-%20%28ver.%20Feb%202007%29.pdf

Tomak, S., Weschler, F. S., Ghahramanlou-Holloway, M., Virden, T., & Nademin, M. E. (2009). An empirical study of the personality characteristics of Internet sex offenders. *Journal of Sexual Aggression, 15*(2), 139–148.

Wakeling, H. C., Howard, P., & Barnett, G. (2011). Comparing the validity of the RM2000 Scales and OGRS3 for predicting recidivism by Internet sexual offenders. *Sexual Abuse: A Journal of Research and Treatment, 23*(1), 146–168.

Webb, L., Craissati, J., & Keen, S. (2007). Characteristics of Internet child pornography: A comparison with child molesters. *Sexual Abuse: A Journal of Research and Treatment, 19*, 449–465.

Webster, S., Davidson, J., Bifulco, A., Gottschalk, P., Caretti, V., Pham, T., … Craparo, G. (2012). *Final report. European Online Grooming Project.* Retrieved from http://www.europeanonlinegroomingproject.com/media/2076/european-online-grooming-project-final-report.pdf

Whittle, H., Hamilton-Giachritsis, C., Beech, A., & Collings, G. (2013). A review of online grooming: Characteristics and concerns. *Aggression and Violent Behavior, 18*, 62–70.

Williams, R., Elliott, I. A., & Beech, A. R. (2013). Identifying sexual grooming themes used by Internet sex offenders, *Deviant Behavior, 34*(2), 135–152.

Wolak, J., & Finkelhor, D. (2013). Are crimes by online predators different from crimes by sex offenders who know youth in-person? *Journal of Adolescent Health, 53*(6), 736–741.

Wolak, J., Finkelhor, D., & Mitchell, K. J. (2005). *Child pornography possessors and the Internet: A national study*. Arlington, VA: National Center for Missing & Exploited Children.

Wolak, J., Finkelhor, D., & Mitchell, K. J. (2009). *Trends in arrests of 'online predators'*. Durham, NH: Crimes Against Children Research Center, University of New Hampshire. Retrieved from www.unh.edu/ccrc

Wolak, J., Finkelhor, D., Mitchell, K. J., & Ybarra, M. L. (2008). Online 'predators' and their victims: Myths, realities, and implications for prevention and treatment. *The American Psychologist, 63*(2), 111–128.

Wolak, J., Mitchell, K., & Finkelhor, D. (2006). *Online victimization: 5 years later (NCMEC 07-06-025)*. Alexandria, VA: National Center for Missing & Exploited Children.

Yar, M. (2013). The policing of Internet sex offenses: Pluralised governance versus hierarchies of standing. *Policing and Society: An International Journal of Research and Policy, 23*(4), 482–497.

Yewkes, Y. (2010). Much ado about nothing? Representations and realities of online soliciting of children. *Journal of Sexual Aggression, 16*(1), 5–18.

48

Offence-Related Issues, Quality of Life, and Risk in Sex Offenders with Intellectual Disability

William R. Lindsay

Danshell Healthcare and University of the West of Scotland, United Kingdom

Introduction

One of the first issues that the assessor must address when considering an individual who might fall into this category of offender is the presence or absence of intellectual disability itself. Although this point might seem trite, it is an essential starting point and professionals can make the mistake of an erroneous assumption. Once intellectual disability has been established (or discounted), the extent and nature of the disability are crucial in determining the type of approach, management, and treatment that might be required. For example, several researchers have demonstrated that if one defines intellectual disability (ID) as having an IQ of less than 80, the number of individuals who fall into the category of offenders with ID can increase. Hayes (1991) found that 2% of offenders had a formal IQ below 70, in the ID range. However, a further 10% were identified in the range of borderline intelligence (IQ 70–80), and these individuals are often included in considerations of offenders with intellectual limitations (Farrington et al., 2006; Hayes, 1991). Therefore, an intellectual assessment is important when reviewing individual requirements for offence-related assessment and treatment.

Having made this point, there are other texts that deal with cognitive assessment in great detail (e.g., Kaufman & Lichtenberger, 1999) and the specific relevance to offenders with intellectual and developmental disabilities (IDD) is less than in other areas of assessment. This chapter reviews risk assessment, assessment of offence-related issues, and assessment related to quality of life (QoL) and the Good Lives Model (GLM).

The Wiley Handbook on the Theories, Assessment, and Treatment of Sexual Offending.
Edited by Douglas P. Boer. Volume II: Assessment, edited by Leam A. Craig and Martin Rettenberger.
© 2017 John Wiley & Sons, Ltd. Published 2017 by John Wiley & Sons, Ltd.

Quality of Life (QoL), Good Lives Model (GLM), and Relationships

Although we tend to consider the sex offence first, contemporary theories of offending and sexual offending emphasize the importance of life experiences, good QoL and relationships in the development of offenders. Hirschi (1969) noted poor community identification in the development of an offending lifestyle and several authors have researched and written on the relationships between childhood adversity and offending careers (Farrington et al., 2006; Sampson & Laub, 2005). With reference to sexual offenders, Ward and colleagues (Ward & Stewart 2003; Ward & Gannon 2006) developed the Good Lives Model (GLM), which postulates a series of mechanisms whereby sex offenders can achieve human goods through better relationships and life experiences rather than inappropriate sexuality.

In the field of IDD, QoL has been a cornerstone of services for the last 35 years and Lindsay (2009) outlined obvious parallels between GLM and QoL for sex offenders with IDD. Emerson and Halpin (2013) have shown that childhood adversity is associated strongly with antisocial and offending behaviour in teenagers with ID. In the NCAP study (O'Brien et al., 2010, Lindsay et al., 2010), involving 477 offenders with IDD, it was found that fewer than 20% had a significant relationship and 40% lacked any meaningful daytime activity. However, this study was set up to investigate pathways into offender services rather than employ control groups of non-offenders.

With reference to assessment and treatment, several authors have stressed the importance of promoting social contact, interpersonal relationships, and community identification in sex offenders with IDD, from both practical and theoretical standpoints (Keeling & Rose, 2012; Lindsay, 2009). Such increased social inclusion allows others to monitor the individual offender and ensures that their views and attitudes are constantly being adjusted, reviewed, and even challenged by ordinary social contact. Social isolation and loneliness have been shown to be important aspects in the development of the cycle leading up to a sexual offence in mainstream offenders. Steptoe et al. (2006) compared a cohort of 28 sex offenders with IDD and 28 control participants with IDD. They were reviewing QoL as measured by the Life Experience Checklist (LEC) (Ager, 1990) and relationships as measured by the Significant Others Scale (SOS) (Power, Champion, & Aris, 1988). They found that the two groups did not differ on the home, opportunities, and freedom domains of the LEC but that although they had similar opportunities to establish relationships, the sex offender cohort showed significantly lower scores on the relationships domain. On the SOS, the sex offenders showed poorer relationships than the control participants but, interestingly, there was no difference in their satisfaction regarding relationships. Therefore, although the sex offender cohort had more impoverished relationships than control participants, they reported being quite happy with this more restricted range. This underlines the importance of both improving the relationships of sex offenders with IDD and letting them experience the human fulfilment that can be achieved from good relationships. Wheeler, Clare, and Holland (2013) recently replicated this finding, showing that a mixed group of offenders had significantly poorer relationships than non-offender controls and that a simple measure of quality of relationships predicted offending. This led to the conclusion that the promotion of appropriate relationships, contact with the community, and prosocial influences are an important area for assessment and treatment. Therefore, it is important to incorporate assessment of QoL and relationships into both assessment and treatment in working with sex offenders with IDD. Furthermore, dynamic risk assessment (discussed later) employs current relationships and relationship style extensively in the prediction of future incidents with sex offenders with ID.

Risk Assessment

Static Factors

The last 10 years have seen a considerable increase in research on the relevance of static, historical variables in the assessment of sex offenders with IDD. There had been a burgeoning of clinical and research work on the predictive value of historical variables in mainstream offenders (Barbaree, Seto, Langton, & Peacock, 2001; Hanson, 1997; Hanson & Thornton, 1999; Harris, Rice, & Quinsey, 1993; Quinsey, Harris, Rice, & Cornier, 1998). These various projects produced standardized risk assessment protocols for the prediction of violence (Quinsey et al., 1998) and for the prediction of sexual offences (Hanson & Thornton, 1999). A number of research projects found that the protocols predicted future incidents at a rate better than chance and, more importantly, considerably better than clinical judgement, which had previously been severely criticized as unreliable (Litwack, 2001). Of particular relevance was the Static-99 (Hanson & Thornton, 1999), which was specifically designed for the prediction of recidivism in sex offenders. The Static-99 was based on the Rapid Risk Assessment for Sex Offender Recidivism (RRASOR) (Hanson, 1997), which is a simple item checklist including previous sexual offences, age of the perpetrator, relationship to the victim, and gender of the victim. Hanson and Thornton (2000) found that the RRASOR predicted those who would commit a further sexual offence and those who did not with a medium effect size (receiver operator characteristic [ROC], area under the curve [AUC] = 0.68). Risk assessment research employs ROCs as the predictive statistical choice. This provides an AUC value between 0 and 1; the higher the value of the AUC, the better is the prediction of those individuals who go on to, and those individuals who did not, perpetrate an incident. Rice and Harris (2005) suggested that for AUCs, a small effect size is around 0.56, a medium effect size is greater than 0.65, and a large effect size is greater than 0.72 (for a more detailed description of ROCs, see McMillan, Hastings, & Coldwell, 2004).

The Static-99 has become standard in sex offender risk assessment. It includes variables related to the sexual offence but also variables related to general antisociality (e.g., prior non-sexual offences) and a general attachment variable (ever cohabited with a partner for at least 2 years). As research on risk assessment developed, several groups compared the predictive accuracy of different risk assessments on a range of databases. For example, Kingston, Yates, Firestone, Babchishin, and Bradford, (2008) followed up a sample of 351 sexual offenders over an average period of 11.4 years. They compared three standardized risk assessments for sexual offender recidivism: the Static-99, the Risk Matrix 2000: Sexual (RM 2000S) (Thornton et al., 2003), and the

Sex Offender Risk Appraisal Guide (SORAG) (Quinsey et al., 1998, 2006) for accuracy of prediction. They found that the Static-99 and the SORAG were the best predictors of future incidents, with AUCs of 0.76 and 0.77, respectively. The RM 2000S was less accurate but still significantly better than chance (AUC = 0.65). In a large meta-analysis based on 147 studies with mainstream sex offenders, Hanson and Morton-Bourgon (2009) calculated the effect sizes for a range of actuarial instruments, structured clinical judgement assessments (see later), and unstructured professional judgements on the prediction of sex offender recidivism. They found that actuarial instruments were the best predictors with medium to large effect sizes, structured professional judgement assessments predicted with medium effect sizes, and professional judgement alone also predicted with a medium effect size. The Static-99 calculations were based on by far the largest number of studies and the effect size was medium to large. Therefore, in mainstream research on sex offenders, static/actuarial assessments have been shown to be more accurate predictors of recidivism than other methods.

There is now a growing body of research on risk prediction in offenders with ID. Several authors have reviewed the effectiveness of the Static-99. Lindsay et al. (2008a) conducted a comparison of actuarial assessments on 212 violent and sexual offenders with IDD followed up for 1 year. They found that the Static-99 predicted future sexual incidents with a medium to large effect size (AUC = 0.71), and the RM 2000S predicted with a small effect size (AUC = 0.62). Wilcox, Beech, Markall, and Blacker (2009) compared the Static-99 with the RM 2000S and the RRASOR with 27 sex offenders with IDD and found that the Static-99 was the best predictor with a small to medium effect size (AUC = 0.64) whereas the RM 2000S had a small effect size (AUC = 0.58) and the RRASOR was a very poor predictor (AUC = 0.42). Lofthouse et al. (2013) used the Static-99 to predict recidivism in 64 sex offenders with IDD followed up for 6 years and found an AUC = 0.75 (large effect size). Hanson, Sheahan, and VanZuylen (2013) recently analysed six published and unpublished studies that had evaluated risk assessments for sex offenders with IDD. The Static-99 was the best predictor with a moderate effect size, but the authors cautioned that there were insufficient data in all the studies combined to afford firm conclusions. They then conducted their own study on a database of 52 sex offenders with IDD. The assessment of IDD was not systematic, again suggesting cautious interpretation. They found that all the assessments used (i.e., RRASOR and four versions of the Static) predicted recidivism with large effect sizes. Therefore, it would seem that the Static-99 has predictive utility in sex offenders with IDD similar to that found in mainstream work on sex offenders.

Static risk seems as predictive with this client group as it is with mainstream sex offenders. The importance of static risk assessment is that it provides a broad framework for considering individuals. If a client is assessed with high static risk, this contextualizes any further work on dynamic risk assessment and management. On the other hand, a low-risk offender should be considered very differently in terms of dynamic factors and management.

Structured Clinical Judgement

Contiguous with the development of actuarial risk assessments, risk assessments based on structured clinical judgement (SCJ) were also being developed. These assessments incorporate static/historical items that cannot be changed but also include items related to current clinical presentation. The first and most widely used was the Historical Clinical Risk – 20 Items (HCR 20) developed by Webster, Douglas, Eaves, and Hart (1997). Studies have found that the HCR 20 may predict future violent incidents for offenders with IDD as well as or better than in studies on mainstream offenders (Gray, Fitzgerald, Taylor, MacCulloch, & Snowden, 2007; Lindsay et al., 2008a). The sexual equivalent of the HCR 20 is the Sexual Violence Risk – 20 Items (SVR 20) (Boer, Hart, Kropp, & Webster, 1997). The SVR 20 includes 11 psychosocial adjustment items, seven sexual offence items, and two items on future plans. Blacker, Beech, Wilcox, and Boer (2011) reported on the predictive validity of the SVR 20 with 44 participants with special needs, including 10 individuals with IDD. For the special-needs group as a whole, the SVR 20 was a poor predictor of sexual incidents (AUC = 0.45), but for the small group of sex offenders with IDD, it had a large effect size (AUC = 0.75). This suggests that there are some preliminary data supporting its use in the management of sex offenders with IDD. It should be remembered, as a caution, that Hanson and Morton-Bourgon (2009), in the comparison of actuarial assessments and structured clinical judgement, noted that 'the clinical adjustments (structured clinical judgement) deceased the predictive accuracy over that observed for the pure actuarial measures' (p. 9).

Dynamic Factors

Dynamic risk assessment contrasts with static risk assessment in that the variables can be changed through treatment and management of the individual. In this respect, SCJ includes some aspects of dynamic risk assessment in that attention is paid to current clinical presentation, management arrangements, and the way in which the individual responds to these management arrangements. As has been mentioned already, this involves consideration of relationships of several kinds. Dynamic risk assessment can be incorporated into effective risk management plans for sex offenders with IDD. Studies investigating the predictive value of dynamic variables in relation to recidivism have suggested that they are as good as static variables in predicting future offences for this client group. Three early studies suggested the importance of clinical and dynamic indicators. Lindsay, Elliot, and Astell (2004a) investigated a number of static and dynamic variables in relation to sex offence recidivism. They studied 52 male sex offenders with IDD (average IQ = 64) with a mean follow-up period of 3.3 years. They included 15 static variables and 35 proximal variables, all of which had either been identified in previous research or added on the basis of clinical experience. The significant variables to emerge from the regression models included familiar static items such as attachment problems, juvenile crime, previous violence, and experience of sexual abuse. However, a number of dynamic variables emerged with equivalent predictive value, including antisocial attitudes, poor response to treatment, low treatment motivation, poor compliance with management, and allowances made by staff. In fact, the dynamic predictors had a relationship with reoffending status that was as strong as or stronger than static predictors. In retrospect, this was one of the first indications that dynamic factors might be as or more important in this client group.

Quinsey et al. (2004) and McMillan et al. (2004) reported similar findings with groups of offenders with IDD that included sexual and non-sexual offenders.

Boer, Tough, and Haaven (2004) developed a dynamic assessment and management system (the ARMIDILO) specifically for sex offenders with IDD. This includes a number of items in four sections: stable dynamic client items, acute dynamic client items, stable dynamic staff and environment items, and acute dynamic staff and environment items. The predictive value of the ARMIDILO was assessed by Blacker et al. (2011) in a study comparing 44 special-needs sex offenders with 44 mainstream sex offenders. With special-needs offenders, the ARMIDILO predicted incidents with AUCs between 0.73 and 0.76 and with a small subgroup of 10 sex offenders with ID it predicted with AUCs between 0.75 and 0.86. Lofthouse et al. (2013) studied 64 sex offenders with IDD with a follow-up period of 6 years. They found that the predictive values of different sections of the ARMIDILO ranged between AUC 0.79 and 0.90, with an AUC of 0.92 for total score. These values are extremely high, suggesting that the population studied by Lofthouse et al. (2013) is very homogeneous. In a final study, Sindall and Murphy (n.d.) followed up 16 sex offenders with IDD over a period of 1–6 months. The rate for further incidents of inappropriate sexual behaviour (ISB) was high at 32%, and the ARMIDILO showed good predictive accuracy with an overall AUC of 0.83, which again is a large effect size. Therefore, three studies of sex offenders with IDD using the ARMIDILO have all found large effect sizes in the prediction of future incidents.

Because there seemed to be an emerging powerful relationship between dynamic risk factors and future incidents for this client group, Lofthouse, Lindsay, Totsika, and Hastings (2012) reanalysed the risk assessment data published by Lindsay et al. (2008a), where they had found that both recognized static and dynamic risk assessments for future violent incidents had equivalent risk predictive values of AUC 0.71 and 0.72, respectively. They used a statistical model to investigate the functional relationships between risk factors, enabling the investigator to determine whether the risk factors are overlapping, independent, mediating, moderating, or acting as a proxy (Kraemer, Stice, Kazdin, & Kupfer, 2001). They found that the dynamic variables acted as a proxy for the static variables. They concluded that since these risk factors captured elements of the same underlying risk associated with violence, and since dynamic variables are more accessible and contribute towards risk management regimes, dynamic assessments could provide immediate information more relevant to intervention planning and the reduction of presenting risk.

These developments may have significant implications for the assessment and management of risk for sexual incidents in offenders with IDD. Three studies have shown that large effect sizes on the ARMIDILO and dynamic risk variables are more accessible and relevant to current circumstances. This could have a significant impact on helping sex offenders with IDD to access better services. It is a familiar experience for those of us working with sex offenders with IDD that assessment of individuals using static variables only places them in a permanent category of high or very high risk, despite significant response to treatment and management. With the advent of these new, powerful technologies, this position may gradually become eroded, allowing more sensitive and person-centred management. The crucial aspect in this work is to encourage more research to validate previous studies.

Assessment of Offence-Related Issues

Thornton (2002) developed a framework for dynamic risk factors in sex offenders that includes issues that would be considered for offence-related interventions. He set out four domains: socioaffective functioning, distorted attitudes and beliefs, self-management/self regulation, and offence-related sexual preference, which was split into sexual drive and deviant sexual preference. Although this categorization was proposed for dynamic risk factors, it includes a number of factors that are offence-related issues.

Socioaffective Functioning

Most of the information on the assessment of socioaffective functioning is gained through self-report questionnaires; this is true for the whole field of psychological assessment of affective functioning. The normal process is that participants fill out questionnaires and return them. At the outset, it is important to understand that none of this is true for any groups of participants, including offenders, with IDD. Because of the literacy deficits involved in the population, all assessments will be read out to participants in a structured setting. However, the very nature of this process means that all assessments are conducted under conditions of structured interview rather than self-report. The assessor not only has the participant's verbal response to the question but will also be able to observe their behavioural and emotional response to the questions. This is a considerable strength in such assessments with individuals with IDD, but it also means that even a 20-item assessment is likely to take up to an hour to administer. This lengthy process is a considerable strength in that the assessor has an increased amount of time in direct contact with the participant and, as has been mentioned, the assessor has behavioural observations or reactions to assessment questions. Therefore, one can observe the enthusiasm and conviction for certain items, indifference to questions, reluctance to engage with items, and, crucially, any lack of understanding that a client may be having with questions or issues. However, it also means that all processes including assessment and treatment take much longer.

In the field of ID, hostility and anger have attracted a large amount of research compared with other dynamic risk factors. Research on aggressive behaviour has suggested that it also presents a serious risk for staff in IDD services (Taylor, 2002). Lindsay et al. (2013) found, in a comparison of 156 male sex offenders and 126 male non-sexual offenders referred to a forensic IDD service, that 31% of the sex offenders were assessed as having problems with anger and aggression (although very few committed violent offences). In the NCAP study, the number of sex offenders with recorded problems with aggression was similar at 24%, but significantly lower than non-sexual offenders (Lindsay et al, 2012). Notwithstanding, it is a significantly frequent problem in all offenders.

Novaco and Taylor (2004) sought to evaluate the reliability and validity of anger assessment procedures with 129 male inpatients with ID, most of whom had forensic histories. In this study, specially modified self-report measures of anger disposition (Novaco Anger Scale [NAS], Novaco, 2003; Spielberger State–Trait Anger

Expression Inventory [STAXI], Spielberger, 1996; anger reactivity – NAS Provocation Inventory [NAS-PI], Novaco, 2003; and informant-rated anger attributes – Ward Anger Rating Scale [WARS], Novaco, 1994) were investigated. The STAXI and NAS showed substantial intercorrelations, providing evidence for concurrent validity for these instruments. WARS staff ratings for patient anger, based on ward observations, were found to have high internal consistency and to correlate significantly with patient anger self-reports. Anger, self-reported by the participants, was significantly related to their record of assaultive behaviour in hospital. Predictive validity was assessed retrospectively, examining patient assault behaviour in the hospital as predicted by patient-rated anger in a hierarchical regression analysis. Controlling for age, length of stay, IQ, violent offence and personality measures, the NAS total score was found to be significantly predictive of whether the patient physically assaulted others in the hospital and the total number of physical assaults. This is a particularly important finding since it demonstrates that a dispositional assessment (NAS total score) has predictive validity in terms of assaultive behaviour of offenders.

Alder and Lindsay (2007) reported on a provocation inventory that was shorter than the NAS and easily accessible. The Dundee Provocation Inventory (DPI) was developed within the context of Novaco's (1975) analysis of the functions of anger. The DPI is a self-report measure specifically developed for use with individuals with IDD. It covers a range of social situations that could produce an anger reaction depending on the individual's appraisal of events and construction of threat. There were high correlations between the DPI and the NAS ($r = 0.57$) and the DPI and the NAS-PI ($r = 0.75$). In a further factor analysis, they found that the most easily interpreted structure was a five-factor solution of threat to self-esteem, locus of control, resentment, frustration, and rejection. These factors can be considered as basic self-schemas about the world that offenders may hold. Actions arising from such schemas may give rise to aggressive responses. Threat to self-esteem is consistent with findings on anger that have emerged from several studies (Beech, Friendship, Erikson, & Hanson, 2002; Jahoda, Trower, Pert, & Finn, 2001; Payne & Jahoda, 2004).

Two studies have evaluated the psychometric properties of several assessments with sex offenders with IDD. Four assessment instruments were adapted and tested on a small cohort of sexual offenders with special needs by Keeling, Rose, and Beech (2007). They recruited 16 sexual offenders with special needs and 53 mainstream sexual offenders to investigate the psychometric properties of the Social Intimacy Scale (SIS) (Miller & Lefcourt, 1982), the Relationship Scales Questionnaire (RSQ) (Griffin & Bartholomew, 1994), the Criminal Sentiments Scale (CSS) (Gendreau, Grant, Leipcieger, & Collins, 1979), and the Victim Empathy Distortion Scale (VES) (Beckett & Fisher, 1994). One of the difficulties with their study was that 'special needs' was not synonymous with IDD and included participants with organic deficits in the range of average IQ. They found that the adapted versions of the SIS and VES were psychometrically consistent with and correlated highly with the originals. The RSQ and CSS showed poorer psychometric properties with inadequate internal consistency and poor convergence with other similar scales.

In a study conducted in the context of the English prison service sex offender programme, Williams, Wakeling, and Webster (2007) investigated the psychometric properties of six adapted measures with 211 men who had undertaken the treatment programme and had low intellectual functioning. The mean IQ for the sample was 71.9 with a range from 56 to 80, which is higher than for other samples in the field. It indicates that many of the sample members were functioning outside the range of IDD. The Sex Offender Self Appraisal Scale (SOSAS) was a measure of cognitive distortions related to sex offences; the Sex Offender Opinion Test (SOOT) and Victim Empathy Consequences Task (VECT) evaluated attitudes to victims; the Self Esteem Questionnaire (SEQ) and Emotional Loneliness Scale (ELS) assessed personal variables, and the Relapse Prevention Interview (RPI) reviewed risk factors. They found that three tests had good internal consistency with alpha values over 0.8 (the SOOT, the RPI, and the ELS) and three had adequate internal consistency with alpha values over 0.75 (the SOSAS, the VECT and the SEQ). Factor analyses of the tests found logical underlying structures but each of the analyses accounted for less than 40% of the total variance. The authors also found that all the assessments except the ELS reflected improvements after completion of the programme.

There are now a range of assessments that have been developed and adapted for sex offenders with ID and that allow an assessor to gather reliable and valid information from this client group. These assessments include the NAS, the BAI, the BDI, the SOS, the LEC, the DPI, and the IPT and the range of assessments employed by Keeling et al. (2007) and Williams et al. (2007). These tests allow us to augment interview material and historical background information with valid psychometric data. In this way, we can begin to make a very structured assessment of socioaffective functioning.

Assessment of Attitudes, Cognitions, and Beliefs

With this client group, it is important not only to review cognitive distortions but also to consider the level of sexual knowledge that an individual may have. One of the first hypotheses put forward to account for inappropriate sexual behaviour (ISB) in this group was that lack of sexual knowledge may lead the individual to attempt inappropriate sexual contact precisely because they are unaware of the means to establish appropriate interpersonal and sexual relationships. This hypothesis was entitled 'counterfeit deviance' and was first mentioned and recently updated by Griffiths and colleagues (Hingsburger, Griffiths, & Quinsey, 1991; Griffiths, Hingsburger, Hoath, & Ioannou, 2013). The term refers to behaviour that is undoubtedly deviant but may be precipitated by factors such as lack of knowledge, limited opportunities to establish sexual relationships, sexual naïvety, and poor social and heterosexual skills rather than a preference or sexual drive towards inappropriate objects. Therefore, remediation should focus on educational issues and developmental maturation rather than inappropriate sexuality. Counterfeit deviance would suggest that some men with IDD commit sexual offences because they have poorer social–sexual knowledge, do not understand the rules and morals of society, and are unaware of taboos relating to sexuality. Therefore, men with IDD who have committed sexual offences should have poorer sexual knowledge than those who do not.

A number of studies have appeared that tested this hypothesis directly. Talbot and Langdon (2006) assessed the sexual knowledge of 11 sex offenders with IDD who had been in treatment, 13 who had not been in treatment, and 26 control participants (non-offenders) with IDD. There were no significant differences between the untreated sex offenders and the non-offenders and the authors' conclusion was 'limited sexual knowledge may not be a factor that sufficiently places men with IDD at risk of committing sexual offences' (p. 529). Lambrick and Glaser (2004), in a review of sex offenders with IDD, reported from their service that a number of offenders had excellent social skills and a good understanding of the issues related to sexuality. Lockhart, Guerin, Shanahan, and Coyle (2010) also found that sex offenders with IDD had better sexual knowledge than controls. They concluded that poor sexual knowledge was unlikely to be a primary reason for the perpetration of sexual offences in these individuals.

Michie, Lindsay, Martin, and Grieve (2006) also found that there were significant differences between groups of sex offenders with IDD and controls with IDD and in each case the sex offenders showed higher levels of sexual knowledge. They then found a significant positive correlation between IQ and SSKAT total score for the control group ($r = 0.71$) but no significant relationship between IQ and sexual knowledge scores for the sex offender cohort ($r = 0.17$). They reasoned that, by definition, all the sex offender cohort have some experience of sexual interaction. It is unlikely that these experiences of sexual interaction are random and one might therefore conclude that these sex offenders have given some thought and attention to sexuality at least in the period prior to the perpetration of the inappropriate sexual behaviour or sexual abuse. Therefore, we can be sure that they have at least one experience of sexual activity, which is not the case for the control participants. Second, these individuals may have a developmental history of increased sexual arousal. This in turn may have led to selective attention and interest in sexual information gained from informal sources. Such persistence of attention would lead to a greater retention of information through rehearsal and perhaps to a greater level of associated appropriate sexual activity such as masturbation. These behavioural and informal educational experiences would lead to a higher level of sexual knowledge. In this latter hypothesis, sexual arousal and sexual preference are hypothesized to have an interactive effect with knowledge acquisition and, perhaps, attitudes and beliefs. However, once again, these authors showed that sex offenders did not have a poorer level of sexual knowledge than non-sexual offenders.

Lunsky, Frijters, Griffiths, Watson, and Williston (2007) conducted a more sensitive analysis of this issue in a comparison of 48 men with ID who had committed sexual offences and 48 men with IDD who had no known sexual offence history. They administered the Socio-Sexual Knowledge and Attitudes Assessment Tool – Revised (SSKAAT-R) (Griffiths & Lunsky, 2003) and split the sexual offenders into a group of 27 participants who had committed repeated or forced offences and 16 participants who had committed inappropriate sexual behaviour such as public masturbation or inappropriate touching. In this more subtle analysis, they found that the forceful offenders had a greater level of knowledge and more liberal attitudes than the inappropriate offenders who had similar attitudes to the control group. This was a significant finding, suggesting that the counterfeit deviance hypothesis may continue to pertain to inappropriate offenders rather than persistent deviant offenders.

It is generally recognized that cognitive distortions that justify, minimize, or mitigate sexual offences are crucial in the offending cycle of perpetrators. A number of assessments have been developed to assess these cognitive distortions and these developments have spread to the field of ID. Kolton, Boer, and Boer (2001) employed the Abel and Becker Cognitions Scale (ABCS) (Abel et al., 1989) with 89 sex offenders with IDD. They found that the response options of the test needed to be changed to a dichotomous assessment to reduce extremity bias and the revised assessment preserved the psychometric integrity of the original test. As mentioned, Keeling, Rose, and Beech (2007) revised the Victim Empathy Distortion Scale (VES) (Beckett & Fisher, 1994) for use with special-needs sexual offenders. An adapted VES was also used in an evaluation of sex offender pathways by Langdon, Maxted, and Murphy (2007), who found that it did not differentiate between different types of sexual offenders with IDD.

The most widely reported assessment of attitudes and beliefs associated with sexual offending is the Questionnaire on Attitudes Consistent with Sexual Offending (QACSO) (Lindsay et al., 2004c). The QACSO consists of seven scales assessing attitudes that could be considered permissive of or consistent with seven different types of sexual offences. The types of attitudes assessed are those which minimize the harm to the victim, mitigate the offender's responsibility, shift responsibility for the offence onto the victim, and other attitudes that might excuse the actions of the offender for various reasons. The scales cover attitudes related to rape and women, dating abuse, voyeurism, exhibitionism, stalking, sexual offences against children, and sexual offences against men. It also contains a social desirability scale.

Broxholme and Lindsay (2003) completed a pilot project on the QACSO that assessed six of these seven scales and found that the scales discriminated significantly between groups of sexual offenders with IDD and a group of non-sexual offenders with IDD. A further, more extensive, study was completed by Lindsay, Whitefield, and Carson (2007). They found that items were reliable, the scales showed internal cohesion, and they discriminated successfully between groups. The QACSO has been used by four groups in addition to the original authors. Rose, Jenkins, O'Conner, Jones, and Felce (2002) and Rose, Rose, Hawkins, and Anderson (2012) used the instrument to assess outcome in a sex offender treatment group for men with IDD. They reported large effect sizes with statistical significance related to improvements. Langdon and Talbot (2006) also used the QACSO to assess levels of cognitive distortions in sex offenders and found that this cohort had significantly higher scores on the QACSO than non-offenders. Murphy et al. (2010) and Heaton and Murphy (2013) reported significant improvements with large effect sizes and significant improvements in a large treatment study at both post-treatment and follow-up assessments. Craig, Stringer, and Sanders (2012) reported similar significant improvements on the QACSO following treatment.

In addition to demonstrating differences between sexual offenders, non-sexual offenders, and non-offenders, Lindsay et al. (2006) found that offenders against women had higher scores than the other cohorts on the rape and attitudes to women scale whereas the offenders against children had higher scores on the child scale than the other cohorts. Therefore, there were some indications of specificity in cognitive distortions between offenders against women and offenders against children. There were no significant differences between groups on the scales related to non-contact offences. Lindsay and Smith (1998) found that sex offenders with IDD treated for 2 years showed significantly greater improvements on the QACSO than men treated for

1 year. Therefore, these authors found that the QACSO has utility in demonstrating the effects of treatment and may also have some utility in discriminating between offenders against adults and offenders against children.

Self-Management and Self-Regulation

Self-regulation has become a fundamental concept in the assessment and treatment of sex offenders since the publication of the Ward and Hudson (1998, 2000) model of self-regulation pathways in the perpetration of sexual offences and recidivism. Ward and Hudson (1998) proposed four basic pathways for offending into which sex offenders can be categorized. These four pathways were split into two with approach goals and two with avoidant goals. The nature of the pathway within each goal (approach or avoidant) is determined by whether the self-regulation style is active or passive. The first is the approach/explicit pathway, in which the individual has a clear wish to offend sexually and uses explicit plans and procedures to carry out the act. The approach/automatic pathway involves the individual engaging in over-learned behavioural scripts which are consistent with sexual offending. Their behaviour may be poorly planned and somewhat impulsive within the context of these behavioural scripts. The third pathway is avoidant/active, where the individual attempts to control their thoughts and behaviour that might lead towards sexual offending. However, their strategies are ineffective and counterproductive, leading to an increased risk of sexual offending. The fourth pathway is avoidant/passive, where the individual may wish to avoid sexual offending or abusive incidents but lacks coping skills to prevent it from happening.

Several authors have reported empirical support for this model (Bickley & Beech, 2002; Webster, 2005; Yates & Kingston, 2006). In their application of the sex offending pathways model to offenders with ID, Keeling and Rose (2005) referred to research that found that offenders with ID were characterized as having low self-esteem, low self-worth, and unassertiveness. They also drew on research that suggested that insight was required to understand the consequences of one's actions and, without insight, it seemed unlikely that sex offenders with ID would engage in conscious explicit planning. Therefore, they would be more likely to be aligned with avoidant/passive or approach/automatic pathways. They concluded that 'What does seem clear from the literature is that intellectually disabled sex offenders seemed to have very little in common with the offender who relapses via the approach/explicit pathway' (p. 81).

In a pilot evaluation of these hypotheses, Keeling, Rose, and Beech (2006) conducted a study of 16 sex offenders with special needs and found that these individuals could be assigned reliably to one of the four sex offender pathways. However, against the predictions of Keeling and Rose (2005), all but one participant was assigned to the active pathways. In another study, Langdon et al. (2007) classified 34 sex offenders with IDD and borderline intelligence using the four pathways model. They reported that six (18%) fell into the avoidant pathways and 28 (82%) fell into the active pathways, with almost half (16, 47%) in the approach/explicit pathway. In addition, Langdon et al. (2007) found that offenders with IDD with a passive strategy had lower levels of general intellectual functioning than offenders with an active strategy. There were no differences between offenders falling into different pathways on number of known offences, victim empathy, socio/sexual knowledge, or victim type. Ford, Rose, and Thrift (2009) found that of 28 participants with IDD, all but three were allocated to approach goal pathways, and that those with an active self-regulation style had a significantly higher average IQ than those with a passive self-regulation style. Lindsay, Steptoe, and Beech (2008b) used the Offense Pathway Checklist developed by Bickley and Beech (2002) to allocate 62 sexual offenders with IDD to one of the four self-regulation pathways. They found that the overwhelming majority (95.1%) of participants were allocated to approach pathways. This reinforced the previous findings of Keeling et al. (2006) and Langdon et al. (2007). With so few participants assigned to the avoidant pathways, all subsequent analyses were confined to categories of self-regulation style rather than approach or avoidant goals. Explicit/active offenders had a higher rate of contact offences, a lower rate of non-contact offences, and a lower reoffend rate at 3 years' follow-up. They also found, similarly to Langdon et al. (2007) and Ford et al. (2009), that the automatic/passive offenders had a significantly lower mean IQ.

The first point to emerge from these studies is that offence pathways can be reliably allocated in sex offenders with IDD, thus influencing treatment considerations. It is interesting that these studies also consistently allocated the majority of sexual offenders with IDD to categories of approach goals. The available literature suggests some preliminary explanations for these findings. It has already been noted that some studies have found that sex offenders with IDD show lower levels of emotional disregulation than other client groups. Impulsivity is a personal characteristic that is often cited in relation to sex offenders in general and also sex offenders with IDD. Ward and Hudson (1998), in their elucidation of the offence pathways of mainstream sex offenders, mentioned impulsivity in relation to a number of subtypes. Not all pathways rely on impulsive reactions from the sex offender. The approach/explicit pathway does not invoke impulsivity at all and the extent to which it is incorporated into other pathways is variable.

Several authors (Cohen et al., 2002; Nussbaum et al., 2002) have conducted studies in which it appeared that sex offenders were less impulsive than other types of offenders when these personality traits were measured systematically. Both Parry and Lindsay (2003) and Snoyman and Aicken (2011) found that sex offenders with IDD have lower rates of impulsiveness than other groups of offenders with IDD. Although these findings may appear counterintuitive, colleagues who work in the field of offenders with IDD have been unsurprised by this result. When they work with sex offenders and other types of offenders, they have noticed that the sex offender group are quieter, less demonstrative, and more self-contained. It may be that we are overly influenced by the very high-risk individuals who are extremely disinhibited and take up a great deal of staff time, attention, and concern. Poor impulse control is a clearer concept than impulsivity. Carers may remark to me, 'he is so impulsive, as soon as you turn your back he will do something'. The important point is that he employed some self-restraint until staff reduced their level of vigilance. Here they seem to be referring to a lack of longer term self-restraint and the willingness to engage in something that is viewed as impulsive behaviour, to take advantage of any opportunity even if short-term consequences are likely. Therefore, poor impulse control, opportunism, and a low perceived level of threat combine to provide a setting that promotes sex offending and reoffending. However, when one of these factors is altered, such as a raising of the threat threshold through treatment, then lower rates of reoffending are recorded.

Sexual Preference and Sexual Drive

In mainstream sex offender work, inappropriate sexual preference and sexual drive have been considered as primary motivation by several authors (Blanchard et al., 1999; Harris et al., 2003). Although some of this work is beginning to extend to men with lower intellectual functioning, there have been no studies that specifically assess sexual drive and sexual preference in sex offenders with IDD. One can draw inferences from other studies that reviewed the persistence of offending and investigated the relationship between sexual preference and IQ. Some of the main inferences have been drawn from studies that have noted previous sexual offending and patterns of offending and cohorts of referred clients. Day (1994), in a study of 31 sexual offenders with IDD referred to his clinic, reported that all of them had previous recorded incidents of inappropriate sexual behaviour or sexual offences. This suggests that there is considerable persistence in the sexual behaviour of these men rather than the incident being isolated. Lindsay et al. (2004b) found that for 62% of referrals, there was either a previous conviction for a sexual offence or clear documented evidence of sexual abuse having been perpetrated by the individual. If one considers the social context of an individual with IDD, any incident of sexual abuse is typically met with a great deal of criticism towards the offending individual on the part of his victim's family or his caregivers. This would be a considerable disincentive to the further commission of additional sexual offences and one must conclude that sexual drive and sexual preference may be significant factors in the persistence of this behaviour in the face of such criticism. Therefore, there is some oblique evidence that suggests that sex offenders with IDD show some persistence in their sexual behaviour.

However, other pieces of evidence, although not directly testing sexual drive, suggest a more complicated picture. Lindsay, Steptoe, and Beech (2008b) found that approach/explicit offenders had significantly lower rates of reoffending. This ran counter to the hypothesis (Hudson & Ward 2000) that approach/explicit offenders would have higher rates of reoffending. Revisiting the 'counterfeit deviance' hypothesis, Lindsay et al. (2008b) felt that although sex offenders with IDD had a greater level of sexual knowledge, they may retain a poor understanding of the extent to which society condemns inappropriate sexual behaviour and may not have developed appropriate self-regulation mechanisms with regard to sex. In addition, some individuals with IDD may have a general difficulty in developing self-restraint strategies and this generalized difficulty is reflected in sexual self-restraint. All of the individuals in their study received extended treatment that focused on challenging cognitive distortions and promoting self-regulation. Given that these approach/explicit offenders had a lower rate of reoffending, rather than the higher rate hypothesized, these individuals may have indeed lacked appropriate strategies to regulate sexuality.

Treatment may have served to reinforce strongly the understanding that such sexual activity is socially taboo and also help to promote the effective self-restraint strategies that a normally able individual might develop through maturation experiences. These individuals were better able to develop self-regulation strategies, which countermands the notion of a pervasive persistence in sexual behaviour. In fact, it suggests that treatment may be particularly effective in promoting self-regulation strategies for sexual drive in this classification of sexual offenders with IDD.

Blanchard et al. (1999, 2007) investigated patterns of sexual offending in large groups of participants. They found that lower functioning sex offenders were significantly more likely to commit offences against younger children and male children. Cantor, Blanchard, Robichaud, and Christensen (2005) published a meta-analytic study of previous reports that had included reliable data on IQ and sexual offending. In a reanalysis of data on 25,146 sex offenders and controls, they found a robust relationship between lower IQ and sexual offending, but specifically lower IQ and paedophilia. They hypothesized that 'a third variable – a perturbation of prenatal or childhood brain development – produces both paedophilia and low IQ' (p. 565). They went on to accept that psychosocial influences are likely to be important but incomplete in explaining paedophilia, emphasizing the value of investigating the range of hypotheses presented for the genesis of sexual offending. Blanchard et al. (2007) compared referrals from a number of different sources in order to test the hypothesis that ascertainment bias would increase the number of offenders with IDD who had assaulted children. They found little difference between the referral sources. Rice, Harris, Lang, and Chaplin (2008) found that sex offenders with IDD had more male victims, more younger victims, and a greater phalometric response to pictures of younger victims than control sex offenders without IDD. On the other hand, Langevin and Curnoe (2008) reported on 2286 male sex offenders referred to a university hospital and private clinic over a period of 39 years. Over half had a full intellectual assessment using a version of the WAIS and all participants had further assessments of learning disability as defined earlier. Across this population, there was no increase in the level of IDD (2.4%) or borderline intelligence (7.2%) compared with the proportion expected in the general population, and the group with IDD had a pattern of offending no different from the rest of the cohort. Summarizing this research, Blanchard et al. (2007) noted the small effect sizes and wrote, 'the statistical relations of IQ … to paedophilia, although valuable as potential clues to the etiology of this disorder, are far too small to permit these variables to be used as diagnostic indicators' (p. 308). This emphasizes the importance of broad-based assessment in this field.

Conclusions

Although there is less research, this chapter started with the assessment of QoL and relationships, since it has consistently been shown to be the most potent factor in the development of offending careers. In addition, it has been cited as crucial in the development of socially appropriate forms of human need and fulfilment in treatment (Lindsay, 2009; Ward & Gannon, 2006). Although as clinicians we do speak of the importance of these factors, most effort is aimed at assessment and treatment of criminogenic risk factors and establishment of sex offender programmes. However, the chapter has also dealt in some depth with risk assessment and the assessment of other socioaffective factors. Dynamic risk assessment seems to be emerging as extremely important with this client group and there are some promising appropriate assessment schedules that can be used with clients and staff groups. Research on static risk has continued and these instruments seem important in establishing a framework for the individual, their dynamic risk assessment, appropriate treatment, and least restrictive management.

References

Abel, G. G., Gore, D. K., Holland, C. L., Camp, N., Becker, J. V., & Rathner, J. (1989). The measurement of the cognitive distortions of child molesters. *Annals of Sex Research, 3,* 135–153.

Ager, A. (1990). *The Life Experience Checklist*. Kidderminster, England: British Institute of Learning Disabilities.

Alder, L., & Lindsay, W. R. (2007). Exploratory factor analysis and convergent validity of the Dundee Provocation Inventory. *Journal of Intellectual & Developmental Disabilities, 32,* 179–188.

Barbaree, H. E., Seto, M. C., Langton, C. M., & Peacock, E. J. (2001). Evaluating the predictive accuracy of six risk assessment instruments for adult sex offenders. *Criminal Justice & Behaviour, 28,* 490–521.

Beckett, R., Fisher, D. (1994). Victim Empathy Measure. In R. Beckett, A. Beech, D. Fisher, & A. S. Fordham (Eds.), *Community based treatment for sex offenders: An evaluation of seven treatment programmes*. London, England: Home Office.

Beech, A., Friendship, C., Erikson, M., & Hanson, R. K. (2002). The relationship between static and dynamic risk factors and reconviction in a sample of UK child abusers. *Sexual Abuse: A Journal of Research & Treatment, 14,* 155–167.

Bickley, J. A., & Beech, A. R. (2002). An investigation of the Ward and Hudson pathways model of the sexual offence process with child abusers. *Journal of Interpersonal Violence, 17,* 371–393.

Blacker, J., Beech, A. R., Wilcox, D. T., & Boer, D. P. (2011). The assessment of dynamic risk and recidivism in a sample of special needs sexual offenders. *Psychology, Crime & Law, 17,* 75–92.

Blanchard, R., Kella, N. J., Cantor, J. M., Classen, P. E., Dickey, R., Kuban, M. E., & Black, T. (2007). IQ, handedness and paedophilia in adult male patients stratified by referral source. *Sexual Abuse: A Journal of Research & Treatment, 19,* 285–309.

Blanchard, R., Watson, M., Choy, A., Dickey, R., Klassen, P., Kuban, N., & Feren, D. J. (1999). Paedophiles: Mental retardation, mental age and sexual orientation. *Archives of Sexual Behaviour, 28,* 111–127.

Boer, D. P., Hart, S. D., Kropp, P. R., & Webster, C. D. (1997). *Manual for the Sexual Violence Risk – 20: Professional guidelines for assessing risk of sexual violence*. Vancouver, Canada: British Columbia Institute on Family Violence and Mental Health, Law and Policy Institute, Simon Fraser University.

Boer, D. P., Tough, S., & Haaven, J. (2004). Assessment of risk manageability of developmentally disabled sex offenders. *Journal of Applied Research in Intellectual Disabilities, 17,* 275–284.

Broxholme, S., & Lindsay, W. R. (2003). Development and preliminary evaluation of a questionnaire on cognitions related to sex offending for use with individuals who have mild intellectual disability. *Journal of Intellectual Disability Research, 47,* 472–482.

Cantor, J. M., Blanchard, R., Robichaud, L. K., & Christensen, B. K. (2005). Quantitative reanalysis of aggregate data on IQ in sexual offenders. *Psychological Bulletin, 131,* 555–568.

Cohen, L. J., Gans, S. W., McGeoch, P. G., Bozansky, O., Itskovich, Y., Murphy, S., … Galynker, I. (2002). Impulsive personality traits in male paedophiles versus healthy controls: Is paedophilia an impulsive–aggressive disorder? *Comprehensive Psychology, 43,* 127–134.

Craig, L. A., Stringer, I., & Sanders, C. E. (2012). Treating sex offenders with intellectual limitations in the community. *The British Journal of Forensic Practice, 14,* 5–20.

Day, K. (1994). Male mentally handicapped sex offenders. *British Journal of Psychiatry, 165,* 630–639.

Emerson, E., & Halpin, S. (2013). Antisocial behaviour and police contact among 13–15 year English adolescents with and without mild/moderate intellectual disability. *Journal of Applied Research in Intellectual Disabilities, 26,* 362–369.

Farrington, D. P., Coid, J. W., Harnett, L. M., Jolliffe, D., Soteriou, N., Turner, R. E., & West, D. J. (2006). *Criminal careers up to age 50 and life success up to age 48: New findings from the Cambridge Study in Delinquent Development* (2nd ed.). London, UK: Home Office Research, Development and Statistics Directorate.

Ford, H. J., Rose, J. L., & Thrift, S. (2009). An evaluation of the applicability of the self-regulation model to sexual offenders with intellectual disabilities. *Journal of Forensic Psychiatry and Psychology, 20,* 440–457.

Gendreau, P., Grant, B. A., Leipcieger, M., & Collins, S. (1979). Norms and recidivism rates for the MMPI and selected environmental scales on a Canadian delinquent sample. *Canadian Journal of Behavioural Science, 11,* 21–31.

Gray, N. S., Fitzgerald, S., Taylor, J., MacCulloch, M. J., & Snowden, R. J. (2007). Predicting future reconviction in offenders with intellectual disabilities: The predictive efficacy of VRAG, PCL-SV and the HCR-20. *Psychological Assessment, 19,* 474–479.

Griffin, D. W., & Bartholomew, K. (1994). The metaphysics of measurement: The case of adult attachment. In K. Bartholomew & D. Perlman (Eds.), *Attachment process in adulthood* (pp. 17–52). London, England: Jessica Kingsley.

Griffiths, D., Hingsburger, D., Hoath, J., & Ioannou, S. (2013). 'Counterfeit deviance' revisited. *Journal of Applied Research in Intellectual Disabilities, 26,* 471–480.

Griffiths, D., & Lunsky, Y. (2003). *Sociosexual Knowledge and Attitudes Assessment Tool (SSKAAT-R).* Wood Dale, IL: Stoelting.

Hanson, R. K. (1997). *The development of a brief actuarial risk scale for sexual offence recidivism* (User Report 1997-04). Ottawa, Canada: Department of the Solicitor General of Canada.

Hanson, R. K., & Morton-Bourgon, K. E. (2009). The accuracy of recidivism risk assessments for sexual offenders: A meta-analysis of 118 prediction studies. *Psychological Assessment, 21*(1), 1–21. doi:10.1037/a0014421

Hanson, K., Sheahan, C., & VanZuylen, H. (2013). STATIC-99 and RRASOR predict recidivism among developmentally delayed sexual offenders: A cumulative meta-analysis. *Sexual Offender Treatment, 8*(1). Retrieved from www.sexual-offender-treatment.org./119.html

Hanson, R. K., & Thornton, D. (1999). *Static-99: Improving actuarial risk assessments for sex offenders* (User Report 1999-02). Ottawa, Canada: Department of the Solicitor General of Canada.

Hanson, R. K., & Thornton, D. (2000). Improving risk assessments for sexual offenders: A comparison of three actuarial scales. *Law & Human Behaviour, 24,* 119–136.

Harris, G. T., Rice, M. E., & Quinsey, V. L. (1993). Violent recidivism of mentally disordered offenders: The development of a statistical prediction instrument. *Criminal Justice & Behaviour, 20*, 315–335.

Harris, G. T., Rice, M. E., Quinsey, V. L., Lalumière, M. L., Boer, D., & Lang, C. (2003). A multi-site comparison of actuarial risk instruments for sex offenders. *Psychological Assessment, 15*, 413–425.

Hayes, S. (1991). Sex offenders. *Australia & New Zealand Journal of Developmental Disabilities (Journal of Intellectual & Developmental Disabilities), 17*, 220–227.

Heaton, K., & Murphy, G. (2013). Men with intellectual disabilities who have attended sex offender treatment groups: A follow up. *Journal of Applied Research in Intellectual Disabilities, 26*, 489–500.

Hingsburger, D., Griffiths, D., & Quinsey, V. (1991). Detecting counterfeit deviance: Differentiating sexual deviance from sexual inappropriateness. *Habilitation Mental Health Care Newsletter, 10*, 51–54.

Hirschi, T. (1969). *Causes of delinquency*. Berkeley, CA: University of California Press.

Hudson, S. M., & Ward, T. (2000). Relapse prevention: Assessment and treatment implications. In D. R. Laws, S. M. Hudson, & T. Ward (Eds.), *Remaking relapse prevention with sex offenders: A source book* (pp. 102–122). Thousand Oaks, CA: Sage.

Jahoda, A., Trower, P., Pert, C., & Finn, D. (2001). Contingent reinforcement or defending the self? A review of evolving models of aggression in people with mild learning disabilities. *British Journal of Medical Psychology, 74*, 305–321.

Kaufman, A. S., & Leichtenberger, E. O. (1999). *Essentials of WAIS-III assessment*. Chichester, England: John Wiley & Sons, Ltd.

Keeling, J. A., & Rose, J. L. (2005). Relapse prevention with intellectually disabled sex offenders. *Sexual Abuse: A Journal of Research & Treatment, 17*, 407–423.

Keeling, J. A., & Rose, J. L. (2012). Implications of the self regulation model for treatment with sexual offenders with intellectual disability. *The British Journal of Forensic Practice, 14*, 29–39.

Keeling, J. A., Rose, J. L., & Beech, A. R. (2006). A comparison of the application of the self-regulation model of the relapse process for mainstream and special needs offenders. *Sexual Abuse: A Journal of Research & Treatment, 18*, 373–382.

Keeling, J. A., Rose, J. L., & Beech, A. R. (2007). A preliminary evaluation of the adaptation of four assessments for offenders with special needs. *Journal of Intellectual & Developmental Disability, 32*, 62–73.

Kingston, D. A., Yates, P. M., Firestone, P., Babchishin, K., & Bradford, J. M. (2008). Long-term predictive validity of the Risk Matrix-2000. *Sexual Abuse: A Journal of Research and Treatment, 20*, 466–484.

Kolton, D. J. C., Boer, A., & Boer, D. P. (2001). A revision of the Abel and Becker Cognition Scale for intellectually disabled sexual offenders. *Sexual Abuse: A Journal of Research & Treatment, 13*, 217–219.

Kraemer, H. C., Stice, E., Kazdin, A., & Kupfer, D. (2001). How do risk factors work together to produce an outcome? Mediators, moderators, independent, overlapping and proxy risk factors. *American Journal of Psychiatry, 258*, 848–856.

Lambrick, F., & Glaser, W. (2004). Sex offenders with an intellectual disability. *Sexual Abuse: A Journal of Research & Treatment, 16*, 381–392.

Langdon, P. E., Maxted, H., & Murphy, G. H. (2007). An exploratory evaluation of the Ward and Hudson Offending Pathways Model with sex offenders who have intellectual disabilities. *Journal of Intellectual & Developmental Disabilities, 32*, 94–105.

Langdon, P. E., & Talbot, T. J. (2006). Locus of control and sex offenders with an intellectual disability. *International Journal of Offender Therapy & Comparative Criminology, 50,* 391–401.

Langevin, R., & Curnoe, S. (2008). Are the mentally retarded and learning disordered overrepresented among sex offenders and paraphilics? *International Journal of Offender Therapy and Comparative Criminology, 52,* 401–415.

Lindsay, W. R. (2009). *The treatment of sex offenders with developmental disabilities. A practice workbook.* Chichester, England: John Wiley & Sons, Ltd.

Lindsay, W. R., Carson, D., Holland, A. J., Michie, A., Taylor, J., Bambrick, M., ... Steptoe, L. (2012). A comparison of sexual offenders and other types of offenders referred to intellectual disability forensic services. *Psychiatry, Psychology and Law, 19,* 556–576.

Lindsay, W. R., Elliot, S. F., & Astell, A. (2004a). Predictors of sexual offence recidivism in offenders with intellectual disabilities. *Journal of Applied Research in Intellectual Disabilities, 17,* 299–305.

Lindsay, W. R., Hogue, T. E., Taylor, J. L., Steptoe, L., Mooney, P., O'Brien, G., ... Smith, A. H. W. (2008a). Risk assessment in offenders with intellectual disability. *International Journal of Offender Therapy and Comparative Criminology, 52,* 90–111.

Lindsay, W. R., Michie, A. M., Whitefield, E., Martin, V., Grieve, A., & Carson, D. (2006). Response patterns on the Questionnaire on Attitudes Consistent with Sexual Offending in groups of sexual offenders with intellectual disability. *Journal of Applied Research in Intellectual Disabilities, 19,* 47–54.

Lindsay, W. R., O'Brien, G., Carson, D. R., Holland, A. J., Taylor, J. L., Wheeler, J. R., ... Johnston, S. (2010). Pathways into services for offenders with intellectual disabilities: Childhood experiences, diagnostic information and offence related variables. *Criminal Justice & Behaviour, 37,* 678–694.

Lindsay, W. R., & Smith, A. H. W. (1998). Responses to treatment for sexual offenders with intellectual disability: A comparison of men with 1 and 2 year probation sentences. *Journal of Intellectual Disability Research, 42,* 346–353.

Lindsay, W. R., Smith, A. H. W., Law, J., Quinn, K., Anderson, A., Smith, A., & Allan, R. (2004b). Sexual and non-sexual offenders with intellectual and learning disabilities: A comparison of characteristics, referral patterns and outcome. *Journal of Interpersonal Violence, 19,* 875–890.

Lindsay, W. R., Steptoe, L., & Beech, A. R. (2008b). The Ward and Hudson Pathways model of the sexual offence process applied to offenders with intellectual disability. *Sexual Abuse: a Journal of Research and Treatment, 20,* 379–392.

Lindsay, W. R., Steptoe, L., Wallace, L., Haut, F., & Brewster, E. (2013). An evaluation and 20 year follow up of recidivism in a community intellectual disability service. *Criminal Behaviour and Mental Health, 23,* 138–149.

Lindsay, W. R., Whitfield, E., & Carson, D. (2007). An assessment for attitudes consistent with sexual offending for use with offenders with intellectual disability. *Legal & Criminological Psychology, 12,* 55–68.

Lindsay, W. R., Whitefield, E., Carson, D., & Steptoe, L. (2004c). *The Questionnaire on Attitudes Consistent with Sexual Offending.* Unpublished manuscript.

Litwack, T. R. (2001). Actuarial versus clinical assessments of dangerousness. *Psychology, Public Policy & Law, 7,* 409–443.

Lockhart, K., Guerin, S., Shanahan, S., & Coyle, K. (2010). Expanding the test of counterfeit deviance: Are sexual knowledge, experience, and needs a factor in the sexualised challenging behaviour of adults with intellectual disability? *Research in Developmental Disabilities, 31,* 117–130.

Lofthouse, R., Lindsay, W., Totsika, V., & Hastings, R. (2012). How do static and dynamic risk factors work together to predict reoffending amongst offenders with ID? *Journal of Intellectual Disability Research, 56*(7–8), 683.

Lofthouse, R. E., Lindsay, W. R., Totsika, V., Hastings, R. P., Boer, D. P., & Haaven, J. L. (2013). Prospective dynamic assessment of risk of sexual reoffending in individuals with an intellectual disability and a history of sexual offending behaviour. *Journal of Applied Research in Intellectual Disabilities, 26*(5), 394–403.

Lunsky, Y., Frijters, J., Griffiths, D. M., Watson, S. L., & Williston, S. (2007). Sexual knowledge and attitudes of men with intellectual disabilities who sexually offend. *Journal of Intellectual & Developmental Disability, 32*, 74–81.

McMillan, D., Hastings, R., & Coldwell, J. (2004). Clinical and actuarial prediction of physical violence in a forensic intellectual disability hospital: A longitudinal study. *Journal of Applied Research in Intellectual Disabilities, 17*, 255–266.

Michie, A. M., Lindsay, W. R., Martin, V., & Grieve, A. (2006). A test of counterfeit deviance: A comparison of sexual knowledge in groups of sex offenders with intellectual disability and controls. *Sexual Abuse: A Journal of Research & Treatment, 18*, 271–279.

Miller, R. S., & Lefcourt, H. M. (1982). The assessment of social intimacy. *Journal of Personality Assessment, 46*, 514–518.

Murphy, G. H., Sinclair, N., Hays, S.-J., Heaton, K., Powell, S., Langdon, P., … Craig, L. (SOTSEC-ID). (2010). Effectiveness of group cognitive–behavioural treatment for men with intellectual disabilities at risk of sexual offending. *Journal of Applied Research in Intellectual Disabilities, 26*, 537–551.

Novaco, R. W. (1975). *Anger control: The development and evaluation of an experimental treatment*. Lexington, MA: D. C. Heath.

Novaco, R. W. (1994). Anger as a risk factor for violence among the mentally disordered. In J. Monahan & H. J. Steadman (Eds.), *Violence in mental disorder: Developments in risk assessment*. Chicago, IL: University of Chicago Press.

Novaco, R. W. (2003). *The Novaco Anger Scale and Provocation Inventory Manual (NAS-PI)*. Los Angeles, CA: Western Psychological Services.

Novaco, R. W., & Taylor, J. L. (2004). Assessment of anger and aggression in offenders with developmental disabilities. *Psychological Assessment, 16*, 42–50.

Nussbaum, D., Collins, M., Cutler, J., Zimmerman, W., Farguson, B., & Jacques, I. (2002). Crime type and specific personality indices: Cloninger's TCI impulsivity, empathy and attachment subscales in non-violent, violent and sexual offenders. *American Journal of Forensic Psychology, 20*, 23–56.

O'Brien, G., Taylor, J. L., Lindsay, W., Carson, D. R., Holland, A. J., Wheeler, J. R., … Steptoe, L. (2010). Multicentre study of adults with learning disabilities referred to services for antisocial offending behaviour: Demographic, individual, offending and service characteristics. *Journal of Learning Disabilities and Offending Behaviour, 1*(2), 5–15.

Parry, C., & Lindsay, W. R. (2003). Impulsiveness as a factor in sexual offending by people with mild intellectual disability. *Journal of Intellectual Disability Research, 47*, 483–487.

Payne, R., & Jahoda, A. (2004). The Glasgow Social Self-Efficacy Scale – A new scale for measuring social self-efficacy in people with intellectual disability. *Clinical Psychology & Psychotherapy, 11*, 265–274.

Power, M., Champion, L., & Aris, S. J. (1988). The development of a measure of social support: The Significant Others Scale (SOS). *British Journal of Clinical Psychology, 27*, 349–358.

Quinsey, V. L., Book, A., & Skilling, T. A. (2004). A follow-up of deinstitutionalised men with intellectual disabilities and histories of antisocial behaviour. *Journal of Applied Research in Intellectual Disabilities, 17*, 243–254.

Quinsey, V. L., Harris, G. T., Rice, M. E., & Cormier, C. A. (1998). *Violent offenders: Appraising and managing risk* (1st ed.). Washington, DC: American Psychological Association.

Quinsey, V. L., Harris, G. T., Rice, M. E., & Cormier, C. A. (2006). *Violent offenders: Appraising and managing risk* (2nd ed.). Washington, DC: American Psychological Association.

Rice, M. E., & Harris, G. T. (2005). Comparing effect sizes in follow-up studies: ROC area, Cohen's *d*, and *r*. *Law and Human Behaviour, 29*, 615–620.

Rice, M. E., Harris, G. T., Lang, C., & Chaplin, T. (2008). Sexual preferences and recidivism of sex offenders with mental retardation. *Sexual Abuse: A Journal of Research and Treatment, 20*, 409–425.

Rose, J., Jenkins, R., O'Conner, C., Jones, C., & Felce, D. (2002). A group treatment for men with intellectual disabilities who sexually offend or abuse. *Journal of Applied Research in Intellectual Disabilities, 15*, 138–150.

Rose, J., Rose, D., Hawkins, C., & Anderson, C. (2012). Sex offender treatment group for men with intellectual disabilities in community settings. *Journal of Forensic Practice, 14*, 21–28.

Sampson, R. J., & Laub, J. H. (2005). A life-course view of the development of crime. *The Annals of the American Academy of Political and Social Science, 602*, 12–45.

Sindall, O., & Murphy, G. (n.d.) *An exploratory validation study of a dynamic risk assessment tool for male intellectually disabled sex offenders.* Unpublished manuscript, Tizard Centre, University of Kent, Canterbury, England.

Snoyman, P., & Aicken, B. (2011). Self-reported impulsivity in male offenders with low cognitive ability in New South Wales prisons. *Psychology, Crime and Law, 17*, 149–162.

Spielberger, C. D. (1996). *State–Trait Anger Expression Inventory Professional Manual.* Lutz: FL: Psychological Assessment Resources.

Steptoe, L., Lindsay, W. R., Forrest, D., & Power, M. (2006). Quality of life and relationships in sexual offenders with intellectual disability. *Journal of Intellectual and Developmental Disabilities, 31*, 13–19.

Talbot, T. J., & Langdon, P. E. (2006). A revised sexual knowledge assessment tool for people with intellectual disabilities. *Journal of Intellectual Disability Research, 50*, 523–531.

Taylor, J. L. (2002). A review of the assessment and treatment of anger and aggression in offenders with intellectual disability. *Journal of Intellectual Disability Research, 46*(Suppl. 1), 57–73.

Thornton, D. (2002). Constructing and testing a framework for dynamic risk assessment. *Sexual Abuse: A Journal of Research & Treatment, 14*, 139–153.

Thornton, D., Mann, R., Webster, S., Blud, L., Travers, R., Friendship, C., & Erikson, M. (2003). Distinguishing and combining risks for sexual and violent recidivism. *Annals of the New York Academy of Sciences, 989*, 225–235.

Ward, T., & Gannon, T.A. (2006). Rehabilitation, etiology and self-regulation: The comprehensive Good Lives Model of treatment for sexual offenders. *Aggression & Violent Behaviour, 11*, 214–223.

Ward, T., & Hudson, S. M. (1998). A model of the relapse process in sexual offenders. *Journal of Interpersonal Violence, 13*, 700–725.

Ward, T., & Hudson, S. M. (2000). A self-regulation model of the relapse prevention process. In D. R. Laws, S. M. Hudson, & T. Ward (Eds.), *Remaking relapse prevention with sex offenders: A source book* (pp. 79–101). Thousand Oaks, CA: Sage.

Ward, T., & Stewart, C. A. (2003). The treatment of sex offenders: Risk management and good lives. *Professional Psychology, Research and Practice, 34*, 353–360.

Webster, S. D. (2005). Pathways to sexual offence recidivism following treatment: An examination of the Ward and Hudson Self-Regulation Model of Relapse. *Journal of Interpersonal Violence, 20*, 1175–1196.

Webster, C. D., Douglas, K. S., Eaves, D., & Hart, S. D. (1997). *HCR-20: Assessing the Risk for Violence (Version 2)*. Vancouver, Canada: Mental Health, Law, and Policy Institute, Simon Fraser University.

Wheeler, J., Clare, I., & Holland, A. T. (2013). Offending by people with intellectual disabilities in community settings: A preliminary examination of contextual factors. *Journal of Applied Research in Intellectual Disabilities, 26*, 370–383.

Wilcox, D., Beech, A., Markall, H. F., & Blacker, J. (2009). Actuarial risk assessment and recidivism in a sample of UK intellectually disabled sexual offenders. *Journal of Sexual Aggression, 15*(1), 97–106.

Williams, F., Wakeling, H., and Webster, S. (2007). A psychometric study of six self report measures for use with sexual offenders with cognitive and social functioning deficits. *Psychology, Crime and Law, 13*, 505–522.

Yates, P. M., & Kingston, D. A. (2006). The self regulation model of sex offending. The relationship between offence pathways and static and dynamic sexual offence risk. *Sexual Abuse: A Journal of Research and Treatment, 18*, 259–270.

49

Mentally Ill Sex Offenders

Johann Brink

University of British Columbia, Canada

Karen Chu

British Columbia Mental Health and Substance Use Services, Canada

Introduction

The identification, assessment, treatment, and community management of two distinct, but overlapping, criminal justice populations have mustered over the past two decades the increased interest of clinicians, researchers, philosophers, policy-makers, and politicians: those with major mental illness in conflict with the law and their increasing penetration of the criminal justice system, and those who have committed a sexual offence and are perceived as continuing to present a public safety risk. Although a robust academic literature attests to the higher prevalence of major mental illness (schizophrenia spectrum and bipolar disorder, major depression) in criminal justice settings compared with the general population, and much is known about the clinical characteristics and best management of sex offenders, a body of research has only relatively recently evolved that addresses the clinical, legal, and policy-related aspects regarding mentally ill sex offenders. This chapter examines the scientific literature on the co-occurrence and assessment of major mental illness and sexual offending, identifies knowledge gaps, and provides recommendations for the assessment of persons with mental illness who have committed a sexual offence.

Definition of Mental Disorder

Several diagnostic approaches are available for the identification of mental illness and mental disorder; for example, the American Psychiatric Association (APA) *Diagnostic and Statistical Manual of Mental Disorders*, 5th edition (DSM-5), defines mental disorder as 'a syndrome characterized by clinically significant disturbance in an

The Wiley Handbook on the Theories, Assessment, and Treatment of Sexual Offending.
Edited by Douglas P. Boer. Volume II: Assessment, edited by Leam A. Craig and Martin Rettenberger.
© 2017 John Wiley & Sons, Ltd. Published 2017 by John Wiley & Sons, Ltd.

individual's cognition, emotion regulation, or behaviour that reflects a dysfunction in the psychological, biological, or developmental processes underlying mental functioning' (APA, 2013).

The 10th revision of the *International Classification of Diseases* (ICD-10) defines mental disorder as 'a clinically recognisable set of symptoms or behaviours associated in most cases with distress and with interference with personal functions' (World Health Organization, 2008). Certain scholars have argued that such clinical definitions are social constructs of convenience (Szasz, 1960) or simplistic tautologies, representing an anachronistic, reductionist, and dualistic mind–body dichotomy (Kendell, 2001).

Legal definitions of mental disorder, similarly, may be regarded as socially convenient inventions. For example, the Canadian Criminal Code defines 'disease of the mind' as 'any illness, disorder or abnormal condition which impairs the human mind and its functioning, excluding however, self-induced states such as by drugs or alcohol, and transitory states such as hysteria or concussion' (Criminal Code of Canada, 1985). Although such exclusionary provisions are not unique to Canada, they nevertheless remove certain accused persons, such as those with chronic, severe psychosis as the result of long-standing crystal methamphetamine use, from consideration for the insanity defence.

For sex offenders in Canada, a sexual offence committed, for example, in a state of severe bipolar mania or psychosis could qualify the accused for an insanity defence, resulting in treatment in hospital rather than incarceration in a correctional facility, whereas substance-induced mania or psychosis would not. In the former, the person would be referred to as a mentally ill accused person under the jurisdiction of the Criminal Code Review Board, whereas the latter would be a 'sex offender'.

The term 'mental illness' typically refers to major psychiatric illnesses such as schizophrenia, schizoaffective disorder, delusional disorder, bipolar disorder, dementia, and major depression. Increasingly, autism and post-traumatic stress disorder, especially in severe form, have been recognized as major mental disorders, requiring intensive resources for proper assessment, treatment, and management. Until the publication of the fifth edition in 2013 (APA, 2013), the DSM nosology employed a multiaxial format that reserved for inclusion on Axis I psychotic, mood, anxiety, cognitive, substance use, sleep, eating, and other disorders, including sexual disorders. Axis II was reserved for personality and cognitive delay disorders, with physical conditions related to the psychiatric presentation listed on Axis III. The DSM-5 does not use a multiaxial format, and clinicians now simply list the appropriate diagnoses. It is anticipated that the extinction of clear separation in the DSM-5 between Axis I and II disorders and the introduction of new diagnostic criteria will advance clinical practice by encouraging recognition that some symptom domains that involve multiple diagnostic categories may reflect common underlying vulnerabilities while extending the boundaries of some single disorders. This development may stimulate new clinical perspectives, including in sex offender populations, where the contribution of co-occurring mental illness to offending behaviour may go unrecognized or be minimized, resulting in missed opportunities for treatment. The contribution to risk for sexual reoffending by untreated mental illness such as psychotic, mood, anxiety, and substance use disorders is well recognized, as is the need for therapeutic intervention for behavioural control deficits and procriminal attitudes stemming from personality disturbance. Similarly, the assessment of the nature and risk of problematic sexual behaviours in the context of developmental delay disorders, including autism spectrum disorder (ASD) and also traumatic brain injury, requires specific expertise.

Despite advances in our understanding of these correlations and dynamic interactions, sexual offending is still at times conceptualized in a reductionist manner as moral failure, with resultant missed opportunities for treatment and other recovery focused interventions.

Prevalence of Mental Illness in Sex Offenders

Sex-related offences committed by persons with major mental disorders can occur in situations characterized by distortions of reality due to an altered level of consciousness, such as in a state of intoxication, mania, depression, delusional preoccupation, hallucinations, obsessions, and compulsions (Berlin, Saleh, & Malin, 2009). However, there is a relative dearth of research on the prevalence, assessment, and treatment of sex offenders with major mental disorders. Much of the research on this population focuses on acts of sexual violence committed in the context of paraphilic and/or personality disorders. Paraphilia was included in the technical revisions of the fourth edition of the DSM (DSM-IV-TR) (APA, 2000) as an Axis I disorder and, thus, formally identified as a distinct psychiatric illness. The clear delineation between mental illnesses and other mental disorders as distinctly separate afflictions in DSM-IV-TR has been eroded in DSM-5 (APA, 2013) in order to facilitate enhanced awareness of the mutual contributions to the clinical presentations and functional impairments of persons with co-occurring afflictions. While research attention has focused less on sex offending in persons with major mental illnesses such as schizophrenia spectrum and other psychotic disorders (including schizophrenia, schizophreniform disorder, schizoaffective and delusional disorder, and schizotypal disorder), and bipolar and other major mood disorders, the DSM-5 format may result in greater scientific attention on this issue.

In general, schizophrenia spectrum disorders and other psychotic illnesses in sex offending populations are not a common occurrence, with rates reported as ranging from 0.7 to 16% (Cochrane, Grisso, & Frederick, 2001; Fazel, Hope, O'Donnell, & Jacoby, 2002; Fazel, Sjöstedt, Grann, & Långström, 2010; Fazel, Sjöstedt, Långström, & Grann, 2007; Kafka & Hennen, 2002; Långström, Sjöstedt, & Grann, 2004; Vess, Murphy, & Arkowitz, 2004).

The rates of mental illness in forensic sex offender populations however, appear to be significantly higher, ranging from 48 to 100% (Alish et al., 2007; Novak, McDermott, Scott, & Guillory, 2007; Stinson & Becker, 2011). Research findings also report significant co-morbidity of mental illness with paraphilias, personality disorders, and substance use disorders in offenders who commit sexual-related crimes (Aboud, 2008; Alden, Brennan, Hodgins, & Mednick, 2007; Harsch, Bergk, Steinert, Keller, & Jockusch, 2006; Laws & O'Donohoue, 2008; Marshall, 2007; Novak et al., 2007). Dunseith et al. (2004) examined 113 consecutive male sex offenders referred from prison, jail, or probation to a residential treatment facility for DSM-IV-TR

Axis I and II disorders, including sexual disorders. Participants displayed high rates of lifetime Axis I and Axis II disorders: 85% had a substance use disorder; 74% were diagnosed with a paraphilia; 58% had a mood disorder; 35% a bipolar disorder and 24% a depressive disorder; 38% an impulse control disorder; 23% an anxiety disorder; 9% an eating disorder; and 56% were assessed with antisocial personality disorder. Interestingly, no psychotic disorders were identified. The presence of a paraphilia correlated positively with the presence of any mood disorder (e.g., major depression, bipolar I disorder), any anxiety disorder, any impulse control disorder, and avoidant personality disorder (Dunseith et al., 2004).

A review of the literature by Marshall (2007) highlighted diverse rates of mental illness in sex offenders. The prevalence of mood disorders ranged from 3 to 95% (Cochrane et al., 2001; Eher et al., 2001; Fazel et al., 2002; Kafka & Prentky, 1992; Raymond, Coleman, Ohlerking, Christenson, & Miner, 1999; Seghorn, Prentky, & Boucher, 1987; Stinson & Becker, 2011), from 2.9 to 38.6% for anxiety disorders (Eher et al., 2001; Firestone, Bradford, Greenberg, Larose, & Curry, 1998; Kafka & Hennen, 2002; Stinson & Becker, 2011), and up to 60% for co-morbid substance use-related problems (Eher et al., 2001; Långström et al., 2004; Raymond et al., 1999; Stinson & Becker, 2011).

In a Canadian study, Moulden, Chaimowitz, Mamak, and Hawes (2014) reported higher rates of severe mental illness in forensic or psychiatrically based sex offenders than in the correctional population. In this study, sex offenders in a forensic psychiatric facility, compared with a correctional sample of sex offenders with mental illness, were characterized by more frequent hospitalizations and higher rates of major mental illness. The correctional group was characterized by a history of physical and sexual abuse, family history of addictions, more intrusive sexual offences, and higher rates of offending. These results highlight different profiles for sexual offenders in forensic mental health and correctional settings, indicating the need for context-specific considerations for the assessment, treatment, and risk management of mentally ill sex offenders.

In a careful and well-designed epidemiological study, Fazel et al. (2007) examined the prevalence of psychiatric admissions among 8495 males convicted of a sexual offence in comparison with a random male sample ($n = 19,925$), by controlling for sociodemographic variables such as employment, income level, and marital status. Only 5% of the male control group had a history of psychiatric hospitalization, compared with 24% of the convicted sex offending group. Psychiatric diagnoses in the sex offending group included schizophrenia and other psychotic disorders, bipolar disorder, and mood, anxiety, and adjustment disorders.

In a study of a Danish population cohort of 358,180 individuals, Alden et al. (2007) found that the presence of a co-morbid personality disorder or substance use disorder appeared to moderate the relationship between schizophrenia and aggressive sex offending in those who had been hospitalized for psychiatric reasons. Males with schizophrenia who did not have co-morbid personality disorder or substance use difficulties were not at increased risk of any sexual offence, whereas men with schizophrenia and co-morbid personality and substance use disorders were five times more likely than non-hospitalized men to be arrested (Alden et al., 2007).

Prevalence studies utilizing male sex offenders referred to outpatient and residential sex offender treatment programmes have found particularly high rates of DSM-IV-TR Axis I disorders. Between 74 and 93% of referred men are reported to meet lifetime diagnostic criteria for a mental disorder, other than a paraphilia (Dunseith et al., 2004; Kafka & Hennen, 2002; Raymond et al., 1999). Anxiety disorders ranged between 23 and 64%, and more than 50% had previous diagnoses for mood disorder (Watt & Withington, 2011).

Relationship between Mental Illness and Sexual Offending

Available evidence indicates that a minority of persons with schizophrenia commit offences of a sexual nature as a direct result of psychotic impulses such as specific delusions or command hallucinations. Phillips, Heads, Taylor, and Hill (1999) reported that although many sex offenders with schizophrenia experienced delusions and hallucinations at the time of the index sex offence, the content of their symptoms was unrelated to their offending behaviour. Other researchers (Novak et al., 2007) have commented on the methodological challenges in discerning accurate diagnoses from archival records, thus limiting the extent to which such finding can be generalized. In contrast, Smith and Taylor (1999) and Smith (2000) reviewed 80 men with a diagnosis of schizophrenia who were psychotic at the time of their sexual offences, of whom 25% reported aggressive sexual fantasies preceding their sex offence, and 16% reported a direct relation between sadistic fantasies and their index offence. Although not directly driving their offending behaviour, approximately 25% of the men reported that delusions and/or perceptual disturbances with sexual content preceded their offences (Smith, 2000). Given the sparse and conflicting evidence from the scientific literature, it is therefore important that clinicians attempt to untangle the psychotic symptomatology and the motivational dynamics that underpin sexual aggression.

Smith (2000) applied a recognized and validated sex offender classification model (Massachusetts Treatment Center Rapist Typology Version 3 – MTC: R3) to a sample comprising of 80 male inpatients with schizophrenia who committed a contact sex offence against a woman whilst psychotic and were convicted of the offence. The MTC: R3 typology allows the classification of sex offenders across nine categories (e.g., opportunistic, pervasively angry, vindictive, sadistic and non-sadistic sexual). According to this classification, these mentally ill sex offenders were sexual (54%), opportunistic (29%), vindictive (11%), and pervasively angry (6%). The sexual, non-sadistic motivational type was significantly over-represented amongst the 18 men who had specific delusional or hallucinatory impulses at the time of their index offences, compared with the 62 men who had no such dynamic drivers. Smith (2000) also reported that the interactions between psychotic symptoms and enduring behavioural profiles used to classify the different motivational types appeared to be complex, and deserving of closer examination. This study appears to be the first application of a formal classification frame to a sample of mentally ill sex offenders. As such, in addition to an accurate assessment of psychotic symptoms, the author proposed that an examination of motivational types such as in the MTC: R3 be considered to inform clinical opinion about the relevance of illness-related behavioural and contextual factors to sexual violence. Craig and Giotakos (2011) proposed that persons with severe forms of mental illness, such as schizophrenia, who engage in sexual offensive behaviours be classified as members of one of four groups: (1) those with pre-existing paraphilia, (2) those where aberrant sexuality is a manifestation of antisocial personality, (3) those whose deviant sexuality arises in the context of illness, and (4) those whose sexual offending behaviour is the result of substance use.

Sex offenders with mental illness and co-occurring mental disorders often present in a complex manner that renders difficult the task of distinguishing the respective contributions to offending behaviour. It is nevertheless necessary that this task be undertaken in a thoughtful and diligent manner so as to inform treatment planning and recovery.

Although uncommon, persons with major mental illness may commit offences of a sexual nature, driven directly by the symptoms of their ailment. The three case studies below serve as an illustration.

Case 1: A 30-year-old single, unemployed man with first-episode schizophrenia, living with his parents and sister, and who was subsequently found not criminally responsible by reason of mental illness, developed delusions of grandeur, believing that he was of royal and at times divine identity, a station in life that tasked him with the responsibility of serving the sexual educational needs of his sister, whom he believed to be a subject in his realm. Underpinned by a narcissistic personality structure and stemming from a family where male interests are prioritized ahead of those of family female members, expert opinion to the court required careful separation of delusional content from the personality, family, and cultural aspects of his presentation.

Case 2: A 28-year-old man with a history of treatment-responsive schizophrenia and difficulties with emotional regulation, and who has been compliant with medication and psychiatric follow-up, becomes frustrated and angry when his amorous advances are rebuffed by a woman he has known for several months. When she again rejects his request for sexual intimacy, he becomes enraged and rapes her. A defence of insanity is accepted by the court, based largely on psychiatric expert opinion that emphasized the role of schizophrenic illness while neglecting reference to anger dynamics and its central contribution to the index offence.

Case 3: A 34-year-old man with paranoid schizophrenia and an extensive history of addictions and criminal offending was admitted to a forensic psychiatric hospital after being found criminally not responsible for the sexual assault of a prepubescent girl. His illness was characterized by the delusional belief that he was about to be kidnapped, tortured, and murdered by officers of the state as punishment for sins committed in a previous life. He had developed the psychotic belief that the only way to placate the authorities was through the sexual molestation of a young girl. Subsequently released from hospital by a review tribunal, he relapsed into substance use, became non-compliant with psychiatric medication, and, after several months of experiencing similar delusions and fearing for his safety, he again sexually assaulted an under-age girl and was again found not criminally responsible. It is understandable that in cases such as this, public confidence in the criminal justice system is eroded and the quality of diagnostic acumen in separating paedophilic interests from psychosis is brought to the fore and subjected to scrutiny.

These cases illustrate the importance of accurate assessment of the nature and severity of the mental illness and co-occurring disorders, and the relationship to the offending behaviour.

Assessment of Mental Illness, Paraphilia, and Sexual Offending

The evaluation of sex offenders with or without mental illness typically includes review of records and documents, gathering and review of collateral information, and conducting clinical interviews. The assessment may also include a range of psychometric testing, such as personality measures, assessments of sexually related cognitive distortions, physiological measures, including phallometric assessment and visual reaction time, and polygraph testing. Clinical assessment should, and typically does, include an evaluation of the individual's family, personal, educational, occupational, military, legal, substance use, trauma, medical, and psychiatric history. In addition, a detailed sexual history includes sexual development, sexual abuse and sexual offence history, history of interpersonal and intimate relationships, sexual dysfunction, and sexual preferences and practices. For those with prior hospitalizations or incarceration, the assessment contains a more detailed review of diagnostic, medication, and treatment response history so as to inform the clinical, treatment, and rehabilitation needs of the patient.

The DSM-5 includes paraphilia and paraphilic disorder as separate entities within a general nosology of mental disorders. A *paraphilia* is defined as 'any intense and persistent sexual interest other than sexual interest in genital stimulation or preparatory fondling with phenotypically normal, mature, consenting human partners' (APA, 2013, p. 685). Some paraphilias have as primary concern the person's erotic activities (e.g., spanking, binding, strangulating another person), and others the individual's erotic targets (e.g., children, corpses, non-human animals, inanimate objects).

A *paraphilic disorder* is a paraphilia that is currently causing distress or impairment, or has resulted in harm or risk of harm to others. Eight main paraphilic disorders are listed in the DSM-5 (voyeuristic, exhibitionistic, frotteuristic, masochistic, sadistic, paedophilic, fetishistic, and transvestic disorder), with many more described in the literature.

The assessment, treatment, and management of paraphilia and paraphilic disorders are addressed in detail elsewhere in this volume; however, it is evident that, at least guided by the understanding of the DSM formulation of sexual deviance, paraphilia is a necessary but insufficient condition for a diagnosis of paraphilic disorder. The presence of paraphilia without impairment or causing harm to others may not require clinical intervention, and would not suffice for engagement with the criminal justice system. It is essential, therefore, for diagnostic, legal, and treatment need purposes that psychiatrists and psychologists address in their assessment the extent to which the paraphilia has resulted in impairment or harm. For example, a middle-aged man with a shoe fetish who lives alone and indulges his erotic behaviour in private without impacting others does not need therapeutic intervention; however, does the diagnosis become one of paraphilic disorder should such a man be married and his erotic appetite become known publicly, resulting in embarrassment and financial harm to his wife and him? A person with paedophilic paraphilia who accesses child pornography, but does not have contact with children, does not qualify for a diagnosis of paedophilic disorder. However, he presumably would if evidence existed of attempts by that person to access child Internet chat rooms, as such behaviour could be deemed attempts at luring and thus potentially placing vulnerable young persons at risk (for further discussion, see Berlin, 2014).

Societal norms and levels of tolerance dictate the bounds of normal, tolerable, reprehensible, and illegal behaviour. For example, genital exposure is normal when it occurs during a medical examination, is deemed objectionable by some but largely tolerated if done as a prank (e.g., 'mooning'), reprehensible but not necessarily illegal (e.g., public urination by a child), but invoking harm to others and subject to legal sanction if in the form of public masturbation or deliberate exposure. Berlin et al. (2009) stated that the notion of a paraphilia requires a phenomenological component, whereby sexual gratification is attained through engaging in sexual fantasy as a 'condition precedent'. It is important, therefore, that clinical and medico-legal reports to the court and review tribunals articulate clearly the criteria and process for diagnostic formulation so as to minimize stigma and challenge misconceptions regarding afflictions of a paraphilic nature. The term 'paraphilia' has attracted an increasingly pejorative connotation, frequently conflated in the public view with 'paedophilia', 'child molester', and 'sex offender', and often regarded as moral failure rather than mental illness. In this regard, the clinical professions are not beyond prejudice either. It is worth noting, for example, that although our professional language has evolved over the past several decades from the use of 'schizophrenics' to 'persons living with schizophrenia', it has not yet matured to a point where the referential term 'persons living with paedophilia' or 'those struggling with psychopathy' would be deemed appropriate.

Paraphilic sex offenders who also have co-occurring psychiatric illness face additional challenges from being doubly stigmatized as members of subgroups generally alienated by society. In addition, they present clinical challenges and concerns that may frustrate their pathways to recovery. The establishment of effective, working, clinical relationships with this clinical population can be challenging and may result in therapeutic alliances that are uneven, inconsistent, and at times perilous. Persons with psychotic illness may be poor historians, have significant cognitive deficits, have co-morbid mood, anxiety, and substance use challenges, have fluctuating symptoms, and may decompensate psychiatrically as a result of detailed assessment or therapeutic interventions. Also, as Guidry and Fabian (2004) correctly pointed out, incomplete, contradictory, or biased information sources pose additional challenges that can serve to confound efforts to elucidate the nexus between psychiatric illness and sexual offending behaviour, thus frustrating, and potentially impairing, a wholesome appraisal of treatment needs and the formulation of strategies for effective treatment and supervision.

The prevalence of psychosis and severe mental illness among persons with paraphilic disorder who have offended sexually appears to be relatively low (Ahlmeyer, Kleinsasser, Stoner, & Retzlaff, 2003; Kafka & Hennen, 2002). However, this small population poses considerable treatment and management challenges, providing additional levels of clinical complexity that call for comprehensive and individualized assessment in conjunction with risk management and treatment strategies tailored to individual needs and strengths.

Without a comprehensive appraisal that includes the clinical, legal, and public safety aspects of the person's presentation, therapeutic settings may focus too narrowly on the treatment of the psychiatric illness, with inadvertent neglect of the public harm done through the sexual offending. Some mentally ill sex offenders may thus be shielded from appropriate accountability for their sexual behaviours. Paraphilic sex offenders with psychiatric illness who are in criminal justice settings, on the other hand, may be enrolled in sex offender treatment programmes that place untenable demands on their fragile mental status, risking decompensation and resulting in failed opportunity for treatment. As such, a recovery pathway perceptive to their double alienation and characterized by a balanced compassion and accountability perspective may prove both most effective in engaging such persons in treatment and instilling the requisite skill sets for safe community reintegration (Guidry & Fabian, 2004).

Sex offences may occur in the context of behaviour seemingly uninhibited by the usual social and personal constraints. In such cases, it is crucial that the assessment seeks to clarify the nature and source of the behavioural intemperance. Persons who are psychiatrically acutely unwell may appear to be disinhibited but instead are disorganized in thought and behaviour, and may commit a sexual offence as a result. Treatment targets would include antipsychotic medication and opportunities for enhanced illness awareness, and also the development of symptom and medication management skills. This scenario is similar in delusionally driven sexual aggression, and where treatment needs to target distorted beliefs (Marshall, Marshall, Serran, & O'Brien, 2009). However, mentally ill persons who have offended sexually often have their offences in indiscriminate manner ascribed to, or minimized as, the result of 'disinhibition', with suboptimal exploration of the motivational dynamics of the offending behaviour. Relevant here is the importance of an assessment of positive and negative symptoms of schizophrenic illness, and the respective contributions to clinical presentation and treatment need (Craig & Giotakos, 2011). Such neglect may contribute to missed opportunities to address and treat an underlying paraphilic disorder.

Autism Spectrum Disorder and Sexual Offending

Although not typically regarded as a mental illness per se, persons with ASD who are in conflict with the law increasingly have come to the attention of professional disciplines charged with the assessment of the clinical, risk, and treatment needs of this population.

The literature on ASD reports the increased prevalence over the past two decades of people diagnosed with ASD from 0.05% in the 1990s to 0.62% in recent studies (Fombonne, 2003; Søndenaa et al., 2014). Public concern regarding the possible link between ASD and violent behaviour has increased following media reporting of high-profile cases. However, the scientific evidence of a causal relationship between ASD and violence remains tenuous. For example, in a meta-analysis of 147 studies, Bjørkly (2009) found that when strict diagnostic criteria were applied, only 11 studies supported a link. Regarding the nexus with sexual offending specifically, the field is further hampered by a dearth of research. Sevlever, Roth, and Gillis (2013) found in their review of published findings that studies were characterized by uneven methodological rigour, with only one study having targeted ASD specifically. Available evidence does seem to indicate that the rate of sexual offending in the ASD population is lower than that for violent offending.

Persons with ASD often suffer from severe deficits in social communication and interaction, and core skill deficits in social reciprocity that may manifest as, or result in, sexually inappropriate behaviours (Fabian, 2011; Sevlever et al., 2013). Similarly to persons with cognitive deficits across the broad spectrum of developmental delay, those with ASD are burdened by impulsivity, impaired judgement, and empathy and social skills deficits, and can display a lack of social understanding, often being unaware of the impact that their inappropriate advances or actions has on others. Furthermore, misguided perceptions of socially acceptable sexual behaviours may lead to deficits in developing and maintaining long-term interpersonal relationships. This inability to maintain intimate relationships may increase sexual frustration and the likelihood of engaging in sexually inappropriate behaviour. The putative nexus between sexual related offences and ASD can further be elucidated by the presence of recurrent thoughts and behavioural repetitive tendencies that are sexual in nature or can be perceived as such. For this complex population, these obsessive and compulsive preoccupations may be of sufficient persistence and intensity to meet criteria for a diagnosis of paraphilia or paraphilic disorder, such as fetishism, paedophilia, and exhibitionism (Fabian, 2011; Sevlever et al., 2013). Furthermore, deficits in social reciprocity may result in alienation from others, acting aggressively because of frustration, resulting in criminal justice system engagement and removal from society (Fabian, 2011; Griffiths & Fedoroff, 2009; Sevlever et al., 2013).

The assessment of persons with ASD who have committed a sexual offence should include an appraisal of social and emotional functioning, and also the level of adaptive functioning (Fabian, 2011). Evaluation of social functioning needs to encompass social abilities and interactions with others, including social presentation, quality of attachment to meaningful others such as family members, peer relationships, friendships and social networks; degree of insight into social difficulties; theory of mind (the ability for awareness and understanding of the emotional world and reactions of others); social reciprocity deficits and awareness of social norms; and the degree of empathy and responsiveness to social cues.

Assessment of emotional functioning includes ability for verbal and non-verbal expression of emotions, and the person's response to novelty, rejection, frustration, guidance, and reassurance. The evaluation of adaptive functioning addresses deficits in compensatory and coping deficits, with specific measures to assist in such appraisal being available (for details, see Fabian, 2006, 2011).

In a small ($n = 33$) Norwegian sample of persons with ASD with violent or sexual convictions, Søndenaa et al. (2014) reported that co-morbidities were common. More than one-quarter (27%) had a psychotic disorder, 24% had an affective disorder, 21% had a personality disorder, 36% had an intellectual disability, and 42% had other developmental disorders. Several participants had more than one mental health disorder, with up to four concurrent diagnoses reported (Søndenaa et al., 2014).

As with other forms of pervasive developmental disorders, it is important to explore the presence of other conditions often identified as co-morbid conditions; included here are attention deficit disorder and attendant behavioural impulsivity, and also Tourette disorder.

The assessment, however, should have a broader focus and also include the evaluation of strength factors that could potentially be protective. This includes the degree of guidance, support, and supervision the person has or could have, as strengthening those could inform a recovery and risk management plan. Murrie, Warren, Kristiansson, and Dietz (2002) suggested that persons with ASD with higher levels of adaptive functioning tend to be rule governed and 'scrupulously law abiding', thus acting as a deterrent from sexual offending.

Traumatic Brain Injury and Sexual Offending

Despite advances in the past several decades (Archer, 2004; Archer & Coyne, 2005; Habermeyer et al., 2013a, 2013b; Simpson, Blaszczynski, & Hodgkinson, 1999), there remains a limited understanding of the neurological basis of sexual behaviour generally and hence also regarding the organic basis of sexual disturbance after traumatic brain injury (TBI). Available data indicate that lesions to the frontal and frontotemporal areas and the limbic system are evident in those people who offend, and the correlation between temporal lobe seizure disorder and sexually abnormal behaviour has been well documented in the scientific literature (see Simpson et al., 1999). In a study evaluating 88 therapists' clinical ratings of 507 adults with severe TBI (median time after injury 2.2 years), Simpson, Sabaz, and Daher (2013) found a point prevalence of inappropriate sexual behaviours at 9%. The problematic behaviours that occurred most frequently were inappropriate sexual talk (58%), non-genital touching (26%), self-exposure (9%), and genital touching (3.5%). Having a more severe initial injury (based on the post-traumatic amnesia duration), a younger age, a lower level of social participation, and greater neuropsychiatric problems increased the risk for displaying inappropriate sexual behaviours (Simpson et al., 2013).

In another study assessing the clinical correlates of inappropriate sexual behaviours after brain injury, James and Young (2013) reported that only a history of prior brain injury before the actual TBI significantly increased the risk for inappropriate verbal or physical sexual behaviours, whereas a psychiatric history, prior aggression, a drug and alcohol history, current use of psychotropic medication and IQ were not associated with inappropriate sexual behaviours. In contrast with previous research findings, sexual impropriety appeared to be independent of aggressive behaviours, and the authors suggested that problematic sexual behaviours in this population should be viewed as a distinct phenomenon of multifactorial aetiology (James & Young, 2013).

Disinhibition may lead to sexually aberrant behaviour and has been theorized as linked to frontal lobe injury, whereas hypersexuality is more closely associated with bilateral temporal lobe lesions. Relatively little is known about the mechanisms of hypersexuality and disinhibition as causal agents of sexually abnormal behaviour, but a more detailed exploration of the issue is beyond the scope of this chapter.

Clinical assessment of the contribution of TBI to sexual offending should encompass not only the nature and location of organic damage, but also premorbid personality, social, and behavioural variables. Behavioural disturbances after TBI may be conceptualized as the product of the person's social interactions and personality variables, the sequelae of the brain injury itself before the cerebral insult, and the social environment within which the person is located after injury.

Case reports have documented the onset of aberrant sexual appetites and behaviours in organic brain disorders, including prefrontal brain tumours, temporal lobe lesions, right hemisphere intracerebral haemorrhage, and multiple sclerosis. As Berlin et al. (2009) observed, these cases offer tantalizing, albeit partial, insights into the biological underpinnings of human sexuality.

Scientific enquiry into sexually aberrant behaviour, especially in residential, correctional, or hospital settings, is complicated by the lack of consensus in delineating the boundaries and definitions of such behaviours (Simpson et al., 1999). Despite advances in nosology as proposed in the DSM-5 (APA, 2013), some definitions used in research studies are over-inclusive, identifying sexually inappropriate behaviours as any explicit sexual behaviour causing physical, mental, or emotional harm to either the victim or the perpetrator, resulting in unclear definitions, and rendering accurate measurement difficult (Zencius, Wesolowski, Burke, & Hough, 1990).

Assessment of Treatment Needs in Mentally Ill Sex Offenders

The assessment of treatment needs requires identification and careful elucidation of psychiatric symptoms that could be indicative of a major mental illness (schizophrenia spectrum disorders, bipolar disorder, major depression), co-occurring mental disorders (anxiety, other mood disorders, autism spectrum and attention deficit disorders), or organic brain conditions (traumatic brain injury, seizure disorders). The recent and sudden onset of unusual and out-of-character sexual appetites should alert the clinician to a possible frontal lobe space-occupying lesion or other neurodegenerative disorders such as dementing illnesses, Huntington disease, and multiple sclerosis. It is imperative that conditions of common co-morbidity such as substance use disorders be identified or excluded. Similarly, the contributions to offending behaviour by co-morbid personality disorders require careful elucidation as the various subtypes (e.g., dependent, avoidant, versus disruptive personality constellations) require specialized, type-specific interventions. For those persons who are acutely unwell, comprehensive identification and appraisal of additional personality disturbance may need to be deferred until improvement in the acute stages of psychosis or bipolar mania has been attained. The astute clinician will be careful not to attribute grandiose posturing simply to narcissistic disturbance without having considered bipolar disorder or substance-induced euphoria as the cause. Similarly, an ornery, irritable, and hostile demeanour is not to be dismissed merely as the result of oppositional, antisocial personality traits without careful assessment for untreated bipolar disorder or chronic depression. Those with frontal, and especially bilateral prefrontal, traumatic brain injury often present with emotional dysregulation, impulsive and disinhibited behaviour, and a seeming unwillingness to benefit from rebuke, at times evoke in others a punitive response that may delay timely diagnosis and the implementation of appropriate pharmacological and behavioural treatment strategies.

An assessment of personality should be attempted as soon as the person's mental status has stabilized sufficiently. In some cases, resolution of acute psychosis uncovers an underlying personality disturbance that requires additional therapeutic intervention to enhance recovery and facilitate safe community reintegration. Such individuals may benefit from cognitive–behavioural therapy (CBT) based anger management and emotional control programmes, and interventions to address cognitive distortions.

Furthermore, the aloof, socially awkward, and seemingly remorseless presentation of a person with ASD may be dismissed as the result of psychopathic personality disturbance, especially where the sexual offence was of a brutal nature.

As noted previously, the presence and nature of paraphilia and paraphilic disorder require careful exploration, especially to determine whether the sexual offending behaviour stemmed primarily from a psychotic or manic mental illness, or from aberrant sexual arousal patterns. Suitability for biological treatments including selective serotonin reuptake inhibitors (SSRIs), cyproterone acetate, medroxyprogesterone acetate, and leuprolide should be assessed as these have proven efficacy in this population (Kafka & Prentky, 1992; Saleh, 2009). Persons with severe mental illness who were acutely disorganized or manic at the time of the offence may, however, not be able to articulate reliably the nature of their thoughts or motivations at the time of the offence. Regardless, it is important that the clinician attempts to clarify the chronology of onset of the co-occurring conditions, as deviant sexual arousal that preceded the onset of mental illness is more likely to have been the dynamic driver of the offending behaviour than psychiatric illness, and would inform treatment strategies accordingly.

The high rates of traumatic experiences reported by forensic psychiatric and correctional populations (Brackenridge & Morrissey, 2010; Driessen, Schroeder, Widmann, von Schonfeld, & Schneider, 2006; Dudeck et al., 2011; Mandelli, Carli, Roy, Serretti, & Sarchiapone, 2011; Messina, Grella, Burdon, & Prendergast, 2007; Moloney, van den Bergh, & Moller, 2009; Papanastassiou, Waldron, Boyle, & Chesterman, 2004; Sarchiapone, Carli, Cuomo, Marchetti, & Roy, 2008; Spitzer, Chevalier, Gillner, Freyberger, & Barnow, 2007; Spitzer et al., 2001) indicate the need for careful elucidation of the impact that trauma may have had on emotional and behavioural patterns, and the importance of trauma-informed therapeutic approaches in this population.

As Guidry and Fabian (2004) noted, the high rates of psychopathology reported among sex offenders may limit positive treatment outcomes. Treatment effects may be improved when standard methods are guided by the relevant clinical factors and special issues raised by identified subgroups, and are targeted in treatment. Importantly, psychiatrically disordered paraphilic sex offenders often present with a complex range of clinical, social, cultural, legal, and systemic issues that require a focused yet person-centred response. For most patients, stabilizing the psychiatric condition is a necessary but usually not sufficient requirement for successful intervention. Importantly, failure to recognize and address the relationship between the person's mental disorder, the paraphilic disorder, and sex offending behaviour ignores a critical issue central to treatment success.

Assessment of Risk in Mentally Ill Sex Offenders

The clinical risk management of this complex population requires a wholesome appraisal not only of the person's psychiatric and legal history, current level of functioning, and anticipated challenges if released, but also of specific strengths and supports in the community. However, although treatment progress is normally regarded as a crucial dynamic risk factor, there has been little research on evaluating the factors that either contribute to or hinder treatment progress in the seriously mentally ill sex offender population (Stinson & Becker, 2011).

Several researchers have reported increased odds ratios (OR ranging from 2.7 to 6) for persons with severe mental illness committing a sexual offence (Fazel et al., 2007, 2010; Wallace et al., 1998). Fazel et al. (2007), using case–control methodology, reported that after adjusting for demographic and socioeconomic confounders, sexual offenders were six times more likely to have a history of psychiatric hospitalization compared with the general population (OR = 6.3, 95% confidence interval [CI] = 3.4–6.7), other psychoses (OR = 5.2, 95% CI = 3.9–6.8), or bipolar affective disorder (OR = 3.4, 95% CI = 1.8–6.4). The proportion of all sexual crimes committed by hospitalized psychiatric patients (the population attributable risk fraction) was 21.0%. These findings are not aligned with the prevailing expert opinion and indicate that clinical and public policies regarding the assessment, management, and treatment of sexual offenders may warrant review (Fazel et al., 2007).

As discussed elsewhere in this volume, several risk assessment measures are available to determine the probability of sexual recidivism. Some of these instruments are of limited utility in mentally ill sex offenders as they were developed and normed utilizing historical, static risk factors from largely correctional samples without severe mental illness (e.g., Static-99; Hanson & Thornton, 1999), or were developed from a forensic psychiatric sample, e.g., Sex Offender Risk Appraisal Guide (SORAG) (Quinsey, Harris, Rice, & Cormier, 1998). The identified variables utilized in those measures may be significant determinants of risk for such offenders but may differ from those most relevant to seriously mentally ill sexual offenders (Stinson & Becker, 2011). For example, the so-called 'actuarial' instruments utilize inflexible, algorithmic models, rely on static and historical factors related to arrest, conviction, and incarceration for sexual and violent offences, and permit a likelihood of reoffending to be expressed as a percentage only, with no opportunity for consideration of the fluctuating nature of mental illness, degree of insight, treatment compliance, or specific strengths and supports. In response to those identified gaps in clinical risk appraisal, Hanson and colleagues developed the STABLE-2000 and ACUTE-2007 (Hanson, Harris, Scott, & Helmus, 2007).

These and other challenges for, and progress in, the field have been well documented (Barbaree, Langton, Blanchard, & Boer, 2008; Barbaree, Langton, & Peacock, 2006; Boer & Hart, 2009; Craig, Browne, & Beech, 2008; Craig, Browne, Beech, & Stringer, 2006; Craig, Browne, Hogue, & Stringer, 2004; Hanson & Bussière, 1998; Hart, 2003); see also Section II of this volume.

The primary goal of risk assessment in this population is to provide an opinion using probabilistic terminology of the likelihood of violent and sexual recidivism. Although these are important goals, other factors also require consideration. For example, the level of risk posed by any one individual is not a static condition, and recent research has identified risk status and risk state as important considerations (Douglas & Skeem, 2005). A person's risk status, based on static variables or constants, may not be as informative as one's risk state, as indicated by immediate, fluid, and dynamic variables. These may include psychiatric instability, substance use, medication non-compliance, or environmental stressors including financial peril, loss of accommodation, or the loss of support from family or partner. Hence for those with severe mental illness, the complex and dynamic factors that impact offence behaviours are also those which should be considered in the evaluation of risk probabilities (Stinson & Becker, 2011). These risk state variables may be critical for estimating the fluid risk, intervention, and supervision needs of this population and an exclusive focus on violent and sexual recidivism should be resisted.

For sex offenders who are also afflicted with mental illness, continuing difficulties with illness management, substance use, residential stability, employment, and adaptive relationships should be identified through regular, structured assessments, and treatment targets adjusted accordingly. Risk measures, such as the Short-Term Assessment of Risk and Treatability (START) (Webster, Martin, Brink, Nicholls, & Desmarais, 2009), facilitate an integrated appraisal in mentally disordered forensic and correctional populations of specific strengths and historical, current, and future anticipated risk variables. The clinician is guided towards an evidence-based opinion regarding risk across seven, often co-occurring, risk domains (violence, suicide, self-harm, self-neglect, substance use, supervision failure, and being victimized).

Public Policy Issues

Public policy and legislative responses in recent years suggest a greater emphasis by society on punitive and controlling interventions for those who reoffend sexually or target vulnerable persons such as children. In the United States, Megan's Law requires public authorities to have a community notification system for convicted sex offenders who pose a risk to the public (Harris, Fisher, Veysey, Ragusa, & Lurigio, 2010). The provisions enshrined in that statute have been strengthened since their introduction in the mid-1990s, despite concerns from psychiatric experts regarding insufficient scientific evidence to support this policy direction (Zonana, 1997).

Similarly, scholars have commented that although the statutory framework in the United States concerning sexually violent predators that allows for the indefinite detention of sexual offenders upon sentence expiry includes a role for psychiatric opinion, this role may, however, serve the criminal justice system rather than the treatment and rehabilitation of mentally ill offenders (Fazel et al., 2007; Janus, 2004).

In their review of legislative shifts in the North American context over the past several decades, Harris et al. (2010) described the public policy response to two groups of marginalized persons – those with mental illness in conflict with criminal justice and those who have committed a sex offence. First, the agency-based innovations of the 1990s established 'a basic framework for addressing the problem of criminal justice-involved persons with major mental illness', and the federal initiatives that have promoted the diffusion of these strategies to every 'intercept point' in the criminal justice process. The intercept model includes 'first responder' initiatives to improve interventions and streamline processes for access of mentally ill persons in crisis to emergency departments, pre-arraignment and pretrial diversion programmes in partnership with community mental health providers and community and mental health courts designed to leverage the criminal justice system in achieving therapeutic goals. Policy-driven initiatives include enhanced correctional mental health treatment and reintegration models responsive to individual needs, and community, team-based assertive support services to integrate elements of traditional probation and parole supervision (Harris et al., 2010).

In contrast, the evolution of public policy regarding sex offenders has led to the increased marginalization of this population, and the availability of indeterminate incarceration, with less emphasis on improving access to treatment and integration of services after release. Clinicians who are tasked with the assessment of sex offenders need to be cognizant of the missed treatment opportunities if mental illness is undetected, and the likelihood of such persons being diverted to correctional settings. Similarly, as noted above, assessments should endeavour to clarify as far as is possible the respective contributions to sex offending behaviour of psychiatric symptoms and procriminal or misogynistic attitudinal styles, in order that the appropriate mix of psychiatric and psychosocial treatment needs may be identified and provided.

Recommendations for Assessment

The following recovery-oriented treatment targets may be considered in the assessment of treatment needs for sex offenders with mental illness (see also Brink & Tomita, 2015).

1. Psychiatric diagnoses should be assessed using standardized protocols, such as the DSM-5 (APA, 2013) or ICD-10 (World Health Organization, 2008).
2. Psychopharmacological treatment needs are assessed, as medication is essential in the treatment of major psychiatric illnesses such as psychotic, mood, and anxiety disorders. Prescribing practice should adhere to published Clinical Practice Guidelines.
3. Sex offenders with paraphilic disorder require assessment for suitability of pharmacological treatments, including SSRIs, cyproterone acetate, medroxyprogesterone and leuprolide. It is essential that appropriate consent is obtained and recorded before commencement of biological treatments.
4. As for all psychiatric patients, the need for non-pharmacological treatments such as electroconvulsive treatment (ECT) should be assessed and made available for all sex offenders with resistant psychosis, mania, or depression, if assessed as required, and should be administered by qualified clinicians.

5.   Psychiatric and psychosocial treatment should focus on identified, specific (e.g., positive and negative psychotic symptoms or mood dysregulation, criminogenic risk markers, medication non-compliance, substance use disorders) and general (vocational, educational) treatment needs.

6.   Professional judgement measures are available for the assessment of risk, strengths, and treatment needs and should be included in the initial and regular assessment of this population. For example, for an integrated appraisal of risk across several domains, strengths, and treatment needs, see the Short-Term Assessment of Risk and Treatability (START) (Webster et al., 2009), and for an assessment of strengths and protective factors see the Structured Assessment of Protective Factors for Violence Risk (SAPROF) (de Vogel, de Ruiter, Bouman, & de Vries Robbé, 2009).

7.   An assessment of risks and needs should permit a decision regarding the intensity and of treatment required and the best format for treatment delivery. Certain mentally ill sex offenders will require specialized assessments, including neuropsychological assessment for those with traumatic brain injury and certain forms of developmental delay such as fetal alcohol spectrum disorder. Disorder-specific assessment protocols may be required for certain populations, e.g., ASD.

8.   Assessments should include the identification of traumatic events and the extent to which trauma scripts have influenced emotional and behavioural patterns. For those individuals, treatment approaches must be trauma informed.

9.   Similarly, it is important to identify and incorporate into treatment planning the presence, degree, and impact of the double stigma that persons may experience as members of a marginalized group burdened by the stigma of mental illness in addition to paraphilic sex offending. The results of an appraisal of internalized stigma and shame-based feelings may assist in creating a supportive, therapeutic milieu.

10. Programmes should incorporate empirically informed CBT-based skills development (e.g., cognitive skills development, social learning, behavioural modification); however, as noted above, treatment modalities need to be responsive to individual needs. The identification of specific strengths and supports is important as they can inform the treatment plan and be utilized as therapeutic levers towards recovery.

11. Standard sex offender treatment typically is provided in group settings; however, many psychiatric conditions may be assessed as not amenable to such an approach. For those individuals, small groups with individual sessions may be required.

12. The assessment typically will unveil a limited understanding by the mentally ill sex offender of the illness, the emotional and behavioural cycles, and the impact on themselves and others. Providing psychoeducational opportunities for paraphilic sex offenders with co-morbid mental illness on symptom and medication management may assist individuals gain better control over their illness and sustain psychiatric stability more successfully. This type of approach also may enhance the person's degree of insight into the nature and impact of their affliction on themselves and others.

Conclusions

This chapter has reviewed the literature on sexual offending in the context of mental illness, conceptualized here as broader than major psychotic and mood disorders and including autism spectrum and traumatic brain disorders. As other chapters in this volume attest, the assessment of sex offenders requires consideration of multiple, and often overlapping, aspects of deviant sexuality. Considered in this chapter are legal and conceptual issues, prevalence rates, the importance of identifying the respective contributions to offending behaviour of psychotic and mood symptomatology, paraphilia, substance use, ASD, cerebral insults, and personality disorder, and the importance of careful assessment for treatment planning. The value of classification frames, such as the one proposed by Craig and Giotakos (2011), is discussed. Finally, clinicians need to be cognizant of the evolution of public policy regarding sex offenders and the necessity for careful assessment so as to avoid potential for missed treatment opportunities.

References

Aboud, A. M. (2008). *Mental disorder and sexual offending*. London, England: Jessica Kingsley.

Ahlmeyer, S., Kleinsasser, D., Stoner, J., & Retzlaff, P. (2003). Psychopathology of incarcerated sex offenders. *Journal of Personality Disorders, 17*(4), 306–318.

Alden, A., Brennan, P., Hodgins, S., & Mednick, S. (2007). Psychotic disorders and sex offending in a Danish birth cohort. *Archives of General Psychiatry, 64*(11), 1251–1258.

Alish, Y., Birger, M., Manor, N., Kertzman, S., Zerzion, M., Kotler, M., & Strous, R. D. (2007). Schizophrenia sex offenders: A clinical and epidemiological comparison study. *International Journal of Law and Psychiatry, 30*(6), 459–466.

APA. (2000). *Diagnostic and statistical manual of mental disorders* (4th ed., text revision) (DSM-IV-TR). Washington, DC: Author.

APA. (2013). *Diagnostic and statistical manual of mental disorders* (5th ed.) (DSM-5). Arlington, VA: American Psychiatric Publishing.

Archer, J. (2004). Sex differences in aggression in real world settings: A meta-analytic review. *Review of General Psychology, 8,* 291–322.

Archer, J., & Coyne, S. M. (2005). An integrated review of indirect, relational, and social aggression. *Personality and Social Psychology Review, 9,* 212–230.

Barbaree, H. E., Langton, C. M., Blanchard, R., & Boer, D. P. (2008). Predicting recidivism in sex offenders using the SVR-20: The contribution of age-at-release. *International Journal of Forensic Mental Health, 7,* 47–64.

Barbaree, H. E., Langton, C. M., & Peacock, E. J. (2006). Differential actuarial risk measures produce different risk rankings for sexual offenders. *Sexual Abuse: A Journal of Research and Treatment, 18,* 423–440.

Berlin, F. S. (2014). Pedophilia and DSM-5: The importance of clearly defining the nature of a pedophilic disorder. *Journal of American Academy of Psychiatry & Law, 42*(4), 404–407.

Berlin, F. S., Saleh, F. M., & Malin, H. M. (2009). Mental illness and sex offending. In F. M. Saleh, A. J. Grudzinskas, Jr., J. M. Bradford, & D. J. Brodsky (Eds.), *Sex offenders: Identification, risk assessment, treatment, and legal issues*. New York, NY: Oxford University Press.

Bjørkly, S. (2009). Risk and dynamics of violence in Asperger's syndrome: A systematic review of the literature. *Aggression and Violent Behavior, 14*(5), 306–312.

Boer, D. P., & Hart, S. D. (2009). Sex offender risk assessment: Research, evaluation, 'best-practice' recommendations and future directions. In J. L. Ireland, C. A. Ireland, & P. Birch (Eds.), *Violent and sexual offenders: Assessment, treatment, and management* (pp. 27–42). Cullompton, England: Willan.

Brackenridge, I., & Morrissey, C. (2010). Trauma and post-traumatic stress disorder (PTSD) in a high secure forensic learning disability population: Future directions for practice. *Advances in Mental Health and Intellectual Disabilities, 4*(3), 49–56.

Brink, J., & Tomita, T. (2015). Psychotic disorders. In R. L. Trestman, K. L. Appelbaum, & J. L. Metzner (Eds.), *Oxford textbook of correctional psychiatry* (pp. 178–183). New York, NY: Oxford University Press.

Cochrane, R. E., Grisso, T., & Frederick, R. I. (2001). The relationship between criminal charges, diagnoses and psycholegal opinions among federal pretrial defendants. *Behavioral Sciences and the Law, 19*, 565–582.

Craig, L. A., Browne, K. D., Beech, A., & Stringer, I. (2006). Differences in personality and risk characteristics in sex, violent, and general offenders. *Criminal Behaviour and Mental Health, 16*, 183–194.

Craig, L. A., Browne, K. D., & Beech, A. R. (2008). *Assessing risk in sex offenders: A practitioner's guide*. Chichester, England: John Wiley & Sons, Ltd.

Craig, L. A., Browne, K. D., Hogue, T. E., & Stringer, I. (2004). New directions in assessing risk for sexual offenders. In G. Macpherson & L. Jones (Eds.), *Issues in forensic psychology: Risk assessment and risk management*. Leicester, England: British Psychological Society, Division of Forensic Psychology.

Craig, L. A., & Giotakos, O. (2011). Sexual offending in psychotic patients. In D. P. Boer, R. Eher, L. A. Craig, M. H. Miner, & F. Pfäffin (Eds.), *International perspectives on the assessment and treatment of sexual offenders: Theory, practice, and research* (pp. 463–478). Chichester, England: John Wiley & Sons, Ltd.

Criminal Code of Canada, RSC, c. C-46 (1985).

de Vogel, V., de Ruiter, C., Bouman, Y., & de Vries Robbé, M. (2009). *SAPROF. Guidelines for the assessment of protective factors for violence risk. English version*. Urecht, The Netherlands: Forum Educatief.

Douglas, K. S., & Skeem, J. L. (2005). Violence risk assessment: Getting specific about being dynamic. *Psychology, Public Policy, and Law, 11*, 347–383.

Driessen, M., Schroeder, T., Widmann, B., von Schonfeld, C.-E., & Schneider, F. (2006). Childhood trauma, psychiatric disorders, and criminal behavior in prisoners in Germany: A comparative study in incarcerated women and men. *Journal of Clinical Psychiatry, 67*(10), 1486–1492.

Dudeck, M., Drenkhahn, K., Spitzer, C., Barnow, S., Kopp, D., Kuwert, P., ... Dunkel, F. (2011). Traumatization and mental distress in long-term prisoners in Europe. *Punishment & Society, 13*(4), 403–423.

Dunseith, N. W., Nelson, E. B., Brusman-Lovins, L. A., Holcomb, J. L., Beckman, D., Weldge, J. A., ... McElroy, S. L. (2004). Psychiatric and legal features of 113 men convicted of sexual offenses. *Journal of Clinical Psychiatry, 65*(3), 293–300.

Eher, R., Grunehut, C., Fruehwald, S., Frottier, P., Hobl, B., & Aigner, M. (2001). A comparison between exclusively male target and female/both sexes target child molesters on psychometric variables, DSM-IV diagnoses and MTC:CM3 typology. In M. H. Miner & E. Coleman (Eds.), *Sex offender treatment: Accomplishments, challenges, and future directions* (pp. 89–102). New York, NY: Haworth Press.

Fabian, J. M. (2006). A literature review of the utility of selected violence and sexual violence risk assessment instruments. *Journal of Psychiatry & Law, 34*(3), 307–350.

Fabian, J. M. (2011). Assessing the sex offender with Asperger's disorder: A forensic psychological and neuropsychological perspective. *Sex Offender Law Report, 12*(5), 65–80.

Fazel, S., Hope, T., O'Donnell, I., & Jacoby, R. (2002). Psychiatric, demographic and personality characteristics of elderly sex offenders. *Psychological Medicine, 32*(2), 219–226.

Fazel, S., Sjöstedt, G., Grann, M., & Långström, N. (2010). Sexual offending in women and psychiatric disorder: A national case–control study. *Archives of Sexual Behavior, 39*, 161–167.

Fazel, S., Sjöstedt, G., Långström, N., & Grann, M. (2007). Severe mental illness and risk of sexual offending in men: A case–control study based on Swedish national registers. *Journal of Clinical Psychiatry, 68*(4), 588–596.

Firestone, P., Bradford, J. M., Greenberg, D. M., Larose, M. R., & Curry, S. (1998). Homicidal and nonhomicidal child molesters: Psychological, phallometric, and criminal features. *Sexual Abuse: A Journal of Research and Treatment, 10*, 305–323.

Fombonne, E. (2003). Epidemiological surveys of autism and other pervasive developmental disorders: An update. *Journal of Autism and Developmental Disorders, 33*(4), 365–382.

Griffiths, D., & Fedoroff, J. P. (2009). Persons with intellectual disabilities who sexually offend. In F. Saleh, A. J. Grudzinskas, & J. M. Bradford (Eds.), *Sex offenders: Identification, risk assessment, treatment, and legal issues* (pp. 353–375). New York, NY: Oxford University Press.

Guidry, L. L., & Fabian, S. (2004). Clinical considerations of paraphilic sex offenders with comorbid psychiatric conditions. *Sexual Addiction & Compulsivity: The Journal of Treatment & Prevention, 11*(1–2), 21–34.

Habermeyer, B., Esposito, F., Händel, N., Lemoine, P., Klarhöfer, M., Mager, R., ... Graf, M. (2013a). Immediate processing of erotic stimuli in paedophilia and controls: A case control study. *BMC Psychiatry, 13*(1), 88–96.

Habermeyer, B., Esposito, F., Händel, N., Lemoine, P., Klarhöfer, M., Mokros, A., ... Graf, M. (2013b). Response inhibition in pedophilia: An fMRI pilot study. *Neuropsychobiology, 68*, 228–237.

Hanson, R. K., & Bussière, M. T. (1998). Predicting relapse: A meta-analysis of sexual offender recidivism studies. *Journal of Consulting and Clinical Psychology, 66*, 348–362.

Hanson, R. K., Harris, A. J., Scott, T. L., & Helmus, L. (2007). *Assessing the risk of sexual offenders on community supervision: The Dynamic Supervision Project*. Ottawa, Canada: Public Safety Canada.

Hanson, R. K., & Thornton, D. (1999). *STATIC-99: Improving actuarial risk assessments for sex offenders*. Ottawa, Canada: Department of the Solicitor General of Canada.

Harris, A. J., Fisher, W., Veysey, B. M., Ragusa, L. M., & Lurigio, A. J. (2010). Sex offending and serious mental illness: Directions for policy and research. *Criminal Justice and Behavior, 37*(5), 596–612. doi:10.1177/0093854810363773

Harsch, S., Bergk, J. E., Steinert, T., Keller, F., & Jockusch, U. (2006). Prevalence of mental disorders among sexual offenders in forensic psychiatry and prison. *International Journal of Law and Psychiatry, 29*, 443–449.

Hart, S. D. (2003). Actuarial risk assessment: Commentary on Berlin et al. *Sexual Abuse: A Journal of Research and Treatment, 15*(4), 383–388.

James, A., & Young, A. (2013). Clinical correlates of verbal aggression, physical aggression and inappropriate sexual behaviour after brain injury. *Brain Injury, 27*(10), 1162–1172.

Janus, E. S. (2004). Sexually violent predator laws: Psychiatry in service to a morally dubious enterprise. *The Lancet, 364*(Suppl. 1), 50–51.

Kafka, M. P., & Hennen, J. (2002). A DSM-IV Axis I comorbidity study of males ($n = 120$) with paraphilias and paraphilia-related disordes. *Sexual Abuse: A Journal of Research and Treatment, 14*, 349–366.

Kafka, M. P., & Prentky, R. A. (1992). Fluoxetine treatment of nonparaphilic sexual addictions and paraphilias in men. *Journal of Clinical Psychiatry, 52*, 351–358.

Kendell, R. (2001). The distinction between mental and physicial illness. *British Journal of Psychiatry, 178*, 490–493.

Långström, N., Sjöstedt, G., & Grann, M. (2004). Psychiatric disorders and recidivism in sexual offenders. *Sexual Abuse: A Journal of Research and Treatment, 16*(2), 139–150.

Laws, D. R., & O'Donohoue, W. T. (2008). *Sexual deviance: Theory, assessment and treatment* (2nd ed.). New York, NY: Guilford Press.

Mandelli, L., Carli, V., Roy, A., Serretti, A., & Sarchiapone, M. (2011). The influence of childhood trauma on the onset and repetition of suicidal behavior: An investigation in a high risk sample of male prisoners. *Journal of Psychiatric Research, 45*(6), 742–747.

Marshall, W. L. (2007). Diagnostic issues, multiple paraphilias, and comorbid disorders in sex offenders: Their incidence and treatment. *Aggression & Violent Behavior, 12*(1), 16–35.

Marshall, W. L., Marshall, L. E., Serran, G. A., & O'Brien, M. D. (2009). Psychological treatment of sexual offenders. In F. M. Saleh, A. J. Grudzinskas, J. M. Bradford, & D. J. Brodsky (Eds.), *Sex offenders: Identification, risk assessment, treatment, and legal issues*. New York, NY: Oxford University Press.

Messina, N., Grella, C., Burdon, W., & Prendergast, M. (2007). Childhood adverse events and current traumatic distress: A comparison of men and women drug-dependent prisoners. *Criminal Justice and Behavior, 34*(11), 1385–1401.

Moloney, K. P., van den Bergh, B. J., & Moller, L. F. (2009). Women in prison: The central issues of gender characteristics and trauma history. *Public Health, 123*(6), 426–430.

Moulden, H. M., Chaimowitz, G., Mamak, M., & Hawes, J. (2014). Understanding how sexual offenders compare across psychiatric and correctional settings: Examination of Canadian mentally ill sexual offenders. *Journal of Sexual Aggression: An International, Interdisciplinary Forum for Research, Theory and Practice, 20*(2), 172–181. doi:10.1080/13552600.2013.794903

Murrie, D. C., Warren, J. I., Kristiansson, M., & Dietz, P. E. (2002). Asperger's syndrome in forensic settings. *International Journal of Forensic Mental Health, 1*(1), 59–70.

Novak, B., McDermott, B. E., Scott, C. L., & Guillory, S. (2007). Sex offenders and insanity: An examination of 42 individuals found not guilty by reason of insanity. *Journal of the American Academy of Psychiatry and the Law, 35*(4), 444–450.

Papanastassiou, M., Waldron, G., Boyle, J., & Chesterman, L. P. (2004). Post-traumatic stress disorder in mentally ill perpetrators of homicide. *Journal of Forensic Psychiatry & Psychology, 15*(1), 66–75.

Phillips, S. L., Heads, T. C., Taylor, P. J., & Hill, G. M. (1999). Sexual offending and antisocial sexual behaviour among patients with schizophrenia. *Journal of Clinical Psychiatry, 60*, 170–175.

Quinsey, V. L., Harris, G. T., Rice, M. E., & Cormier, C. A. (1998). *Violent offenders: Appraising and managing risk*. Washington, DC: American Psychological Association.

Raymond, N. C., Coleman, E., Ohlerking, F., Christenson, G. A., & Miner, M. (1999). Psychiatric comorbidity in pedophilic sex offenders. *American Journal of Psychiatry, 156*, 786–788.

Saleh, F. (2009). Pharmacotherapy of paraphilic sex offenders. In F. M. Saleh, A. J. Grudzinskas, & J. M. Bradford (Eds.), *Sex offenders: Identification, risk assessment, treatment and legal issues* (pp. 189–207). New York, NY: Oxford University Press.

Sarchiapone, M., Carli, V., Cuomo, C., Marchetti, M., & Roy, A. (2008). Association between childhood trauma and aggression in male prisoners. *Psychiatry Research, 165*(1–2), 187–192.

Seghorn, T. K., Prentky, R. A., & Boucher, R. A. (1987). Childhood sexual abuse in the lives of sexual offenders. *Journal of the American Academy of Child and Adolescent Psychiatry, 26*, 262–267.

Sevlever, M., Roth, M. E., & Gillis, J. M. (2013). Sexual abuse and offending in autism spectrum disorders. *Sexuality and Disability, 31*, 189–200.

Simpson, G., Blaszczynski, A., & Hodgkinson, A. (1999). Sex offending as a psychosocial sequelea of traumatic brain injury. *Journal of Head Trauma Rehabilitation, 14*(6), 567–580.

Simpson, G., Sabaz, M., & Daher, M. (2013). Prevalence, clinical features, and correlates of inappropriate sexual behavior after traumatic brain injury: A multicenter study. *Journal of Head Trauma Rehabilitation, 28*, 202–210.

Smith, A. D. (2000). Motivation and psychosis in schizophrenic men who sexually assault women. *Journal of Forensic Psychiatry, 11*(1), 62–73.

Smith, A. D., & Taylor, P. J. (1999). Serious sex offending against women by men with schizophrenia: Relationship of illness and psychotic symptoms to offending. *British Journal of Psychiatry, 174*, 233–237.

Søndenaa, E., Helverschou, S. B., Steindal, K., Rasmussen, K., Nilson, B., & Nøttestad, J. A. (2014). Violence and sexual offending behavior in people with autism spectrum disorder who have undergone a psychiatric forensic examination. *Psychological Reports, 115*(1), 32–43.

Spitzer, C., Chevalier, C., Gillner, M., Freyberger, H. J., & Barnow, S. (2007). Complex posttraumatic stress disorder and child maltreatment in forensic inpatients. *Journal of Forensic Psychiatry & Psychology, 17*(2), 204–216.

Spitzer, C., Dudeck, M., Liss, H., Orlob, S., Gillner, M., & Freyberger, H. J. (2001). Posttraumatic stress disorder in forensic inpatients. *Journal of Forensic Psychiatry, 12*(1), 63–77.

Stinson, J. D., & Becker, J. V. (2011). Sexual offenders with serious mental illness: Prevention, risk, and clinical concerns. *International Journal of Law and Psychiatry, 34*(3), 239–245.

Szasz, T. S. (1960). The myth of mental illness. *American Psychologist, 15*, 113–118.

Vess, J., Murphy, C., & Arkowitz, S. (2004). Clinical and demographic differences between sexually violent predators and other commitment types in a state forensic hospital. *Journal of Forensic Psychiatry & Psychology, 15*(4), 669–681.

Wallace, C., Mullen, P., Burgess, P., Palmer, S., Ruschena, D., & Browne, C. (1998). Serious criminal offending and mental disorder: Case linkage study. *British Journal of Psychiatry, 172*, 477–484.

Watt, B. D., & Withington, T. (2011). Axis I mental health disorders and sexual offending. In D. P. Boer, R. Eher, L. A. Craig, M. H. Miner, & F. Pfäfflin (Eds.), *International perspectives on the assessment and treatment of sexual offenders: Theory, practice, and research* (pp. 449–462). Chichester, England: John Wiley & Sons, Ltd.

Webster, C. D., Martin, M. L., Brink, J., Nicholls, T. L., & Desmarais, S. L. (2009). *Short-Term Assessment of Risk and Treatability (START)*. Coquitlam, Canada: BC Mental Health and Substance Use Services and St. Joseph's Healthcare Hamilton.

World Health Organization. (2008). *International statistical classification of diseases and related health problems (10th revision) (ICD-10)*. Geneva: Author.

Zencius, A., Wesolowski, M., Burke, W., & Hough, S. (1990). Managing hypersexual disorders in brain-injured clients. *Brain Injury, 4*(2), 175–181.

Zonana, H. (1997). The civil commitment of sex offenders. *Science, 278*(5341), 1248–1249.

50

Assessment of Adolescents Who Have Sexually Offended

James R. Worling

Private Practice, Toronto, Canada; University of Toronto, Canada

Calvin M. Langton

University of Windsor and University of Toronto, Canada

Introduction

For many years, it has been assumed that adolescents who commit sexual crimes share a set of characteristics and needs. For example, it has been argued that they can be described by social skills deficits (e.g., Hunter, 2011), distorted values and beliefs (e.g., Underwood, Robinson, Mosholder, & Warren, 2008), deceitful responding (e.g., Perry & Orchard, 1992), and sexual deviance (e.g., Goocher, 1994). It is not surprising, therefore, that many early treatment programmes were predicated on the assumption that all adolescents who offended sexually required treatment that addressed their supposed social skills deficits, deceit, and deviant sexual interests and attitudes. Sexual offending is not a disorder or a diagnosis, however, and adolescents who offend sexually are heterogeneous (Worling, 1995). Indeed, there is no profile of an adolescent who has chosen to engage in criminal sexual behaviour (Association for the Treatment of Sexual Abusers [ATSA], 2003).

Given that there is no such thing as a profile of an adolescent who has offended sexually, it is essential that assessments are comprehensive (ATSA, 2003; Miner et al., 2006), as it is otherwise impossible to determine what specialized treatment, if any, is necessary for each adolescent. It may be tempting for professionals to focus the assessment on issues related specifically to the sexual offending that has resulted in the referral, such as past sexual behaviours and current sexual interests and attitudes. However, a comprehensive picture of the adolescent will provide more complete information regarding each individual's unique strengths, risks, and needs. Domains assessed should include developmental history and current competencies, family history and current functioning, social history and current functioning; educational history and current cognitive functioning, personality, mental health, biological and neurological vulnerabilities, sexual interests, experiences, and arousal, offence history, specific risks and assets in the adolescent, the family, and school/community setting, and amenability to intervention on the part of the adolescent and of the parents (see, for example, Leversee, 2010; National Task Force on Juvenile Sexual Offending, 1993; Rich, 2009).

The importance of a comprehensive assessment is reflected in Andrews and Bonta's (1994) Risk–Need–Responsivity model and its main principles, which meta-analyses clearly demonstrate underpin effective treatment of individuals in the criminal justice system (e.g., Andrews, Bonta, & Hoge, 1990; Hanson, Bourgon, Helmus, & Hodgson, 2009). The first of these, the *risk principle*, relates to the finding that treatment is most effective when it is proportional to the level of risk posed by the individual. As such, the most intensive treatment efforts should be reserved for those adolescents who present the greatest risk of reoffending. The *need principle* is based on the finding that treatment is most effective if criminogenic risk factors are specifically targeted in treatment. If an adolescent who has offended sexually is demonstrating difficulties with dynamic risk factors such as impulsivity, social isolation, deviant sexual interests, sexual preoccupation, and a high-stress family environment (Worling & Långström, 2006), for example, then treatment is going to reduce the likelihood of recidivism if these issues are addressed specifically. Lastly, the *responsivity principle* is predicated on the observation that for treatment to be effective it should be tailored for each client with respect to their unique strengths and any social, personal, or cultural factors that could impact/enhance treatment delivery.

Distinctions can be drawn between assessments conducted at different stages of an adolescent's involvement in the youth justice system. Each stage can be seen to have particular referral questions and purposes, which determine the scope of the assessment (Leversee, 2010; National Task Force on Juvenile Sexual Offending, 1993), although there is often considerable overlap in the content of a comprehensive assessment, particularly when contact with a clinician specially trained to conduct such an assessment is not possible or practical at multiple stages. Following an initial pre-trial stage (about which we say more shortly), stages (and referral questions) include pre-sentence (concerned principally with risk of reoffence and appropriate placement, whether in the community with or apart from the family or in a more restrictive setting), post-adjudication (focused on treatment planning, including targets as well as modalities, duration, and intensity), pre-release/treatment conclusion (covering treatment progress, updated risk of reoffence, family reunification, transition planning, community supports, and safety), and finally monitoring/follow-up, each of which require consideration of issues specific to the youth's context and setting (Worling & Langton, 2012). The practical implications of assessments in each of these stages can be profound for the youth and for the youth's family, not least because assessment results and recommendations can be (mis)used to inform decisions years after their likely (or intended) period of validity. It is incumbent on the clinician to be explicit about the time-limited nature of the findings and to include caveats and cautions to prevent misunderstandings or misapplications of the results.

Once clear about the stage and purpose of the assessment, the clinician still faces a number of significant challenges that need to be addressed before beginning the assessment process.

Challenges to Assessment

Pressure to Participate

We are most often placed in the position of assessing a young person who is being pressured to participate to some extent. Most adolescents who have offended sexually have been sent for an assessment by the courts, child protection, parents, and/or school personnel. As such, the motivation to participate in an assessment process is often not the same as it may be for self-referred clients. Even though adolescents in a number of jurisdictions certainly have the legal freedom to choose whether or not to participate in an assessment, the pressure to consent to participate is often considerable. Therefore, we argue that it is incumbent on the clinician to strive to ensure that the adolescent is aware of the risks and benefits of proceeding, and alternatives to participating, and is able, as far as possible, to make an informed choice. Of course, when the motivation to participate is very low, this can impact significantly on the quality of information that is obtained in an assessment (Lambie & McCarthy, 2004). It is true that a reluctance to participate in an assessment is not unique to youth who have offended sexually; however, the sexual nature of their criminal behaviour is often such that the degree of reluctance is very likely heightened.

Secrecy

The second factor that impacts the assessment process for an adolescent with a history of sexual offending is that we are often inquiring about issues that people would naturally rather keep private. Masturbatory fantasies and past and present exposure to sexualized media, for example, are not typically issues that most adolescents freely share with others, particularly adult strangers. Asking a client about things that are typically kept secret requires that questions be framed in an appropriate manner (Prescott, 2006; Rich, 2009; Worling, 2001), about which we say more when we discuss interviewing below. Clients are also understandably very concerned about how their personal information is going to be stored and how the resultant findings are going to be distributed. Concerns of this nature are naturally going to impact the willingness to disclose but can be directly addressed and at least partially offset by engaging the youth in a fully informed consent process, about which we also elaborate in a later section.

Shame

A closely related issue is that many adolescents who have offended are likely ashamed of their past sexual behaviours and/or current sexual interests (Worling, Josefowitz, & Maltar, 2011). Unlike guilt, which is an emotion that occurs when one evaluates one's behaviour negatively, shame involves a negative evaluation of the whole self (Tangney & Dearing, 2002). Although feelings of guilt can propel people to acknowledge past transgressions and seek reparation, shame is often accompanied by intense discomfort, a desire to avoid further exposure, and a feeling of being inadequate and unworthy (Blum, 2008). Furthermore, given that shame is fuelled by real or imagined negative appraisals by others, shame motivates individuals to deny, avoid, and withdraw (Tangney & Dearing, 2002), and this would obviously impact negatively on an interview process. Indeed, shame following sexual offending is frequently associated with victim blaming, retaliatory anger, decreases in self-esteem, reduced victim empathy (Bumby, Marshall, & Langton, 1999), minimization and denial, and self-harming behaviours (Jenkins, 2005). We suggest that clinicians anticipate such responses from the adolescent and adopt a motivational approach that is respectful and clear about both the challenges and the potential gains of engagement in the assessment in order to make the inducement of further shame less likely.

Lack of Research Regarding Adolescent Sexuality

A fourth challenge is that there is little empirical guidance regarding a number of the issues that we are assessing, which makes it difficult to determine the salience of the youth's responses. For example, when asking about masturbatory behaviours, what are we to make of a situation when a 13-year-old male informs us that he engages in this behaviour three times per day? How typical/atypical is this for a 13-year-old male? Would we consider this healthy development or evidence of sexual preoccupation? Would this have the same salience if the client was a 13-year-old female? Much of the research on adolescent sexual behaviour is focused on preventing teen pregnancy and the transmission of sexually transmitted infections (e.g., Homma, Wang, Saewyc, & Kishor, 2012). In addition to having a firm grasp of the extant empirical literature (i.e., what is known *and* what is not known about normative sexual development and psychopathology), we recommend that clinicians attend to the function of focal behaviours for the adolescent (particularly what needs appear to be met by the behaviours and how the adolescent understands and views them) rather than attempt to appraise the typicality or otherwise of such behaviours.

Impact on the Assessor

A fifth challenge for the assessment process is the potential negative impact that the information can have on the assessor. Although it is certainly true that clinicians will hear upsetting and distressing information when working with youth referred for other reasons, repeatedly listening to details regarding sexual offending can result in vicarious trauma symptomology for some clinicians (Edmunds, 1997). In their review of the literature on this issue, Moulden and Firestone (2007) suggested that vicarious trauma may be particularly more problematic for those clinicians who are new to the field, are employed in correctional settings, or have not yet developed positive coping strategies such as engaging in physical exercise or spiritual practices or seeking support and consultation. The potential for a cumulative, negative impact may be particularly problematic for people whose practice is focused on assessment rather than treatment as, in addition to being exposed to multiple offending histories, they would not have the benefit of witnessing positive therapeutic changes. We suggest that clinicians actively attend to their own self-care regime, consciously monitoring both their responses during and after clinical contacts and also the range and adequacy of their coping strategies.

Ideal Preconditions for the Assessment

Before starting the assessment process with an adolescent who has offended sexually, there are two conditions that should be met, whenever possible. First, we would argue that it is ideal that any police investigation has been completed, and there is no outstanding court date regarding questions of guilt or innocence for criminal sexual behaviour. Although there are some practitioners who conduct assessments prior to a determination of guilt or innocence, there are a number of potential problems associated with such an assessment (Letourneau, 2003). For example, although there may be laws in some jurisdictions restricting the admissibility of information garnered during such an assessment, a youth is likely to be worried about the likelihood that pre-trial information may be used against them. Indeed, how free can the youth be to participate openly in the assessment process if they perceive that the weight of the legal system rests on the outcome of the assessment? This may also impact on the accuracy of information collected from parents or caregivers. Professional standards, such as those forwarded by ATSA (2003), prohibit evaluators from providing evidence during the guilt phase of a trial.

Another problem with pre-adjudication assessments is that, in many cases, it will be necessary to re-evaluate an adolescent following the conclusion of the legal process. Take, for example, the youth who was told by his or her lawyer and/or caregivers not to say anything about sexual issues, including the sexual offending. It is very difficult for an assessor to comment on strengths, risks, and needs specific to sexual offending under such conditions. Although some information from the original assessment may be useful to the treatment planning process, it would be necessary to reassess the youth in some capacity. Of course, in addition to having to put the youth and family through a new assessment process, this is a potential waste of valuable assessment resources.

Second, we would recommend that, during the course of the assessment, the adolescent is living in a residence in which there are no individuals whom they sexually abused and, ideally, no other vulnerable individuals. It is very difficult to assess a youth when they are residing with a person whom they sexually assaulted, and there are a number of ethical concerns when proceeding in such a situation. For example, if the youth is residing with a person whom they sexually victimized, they may be fearful that information disclosed could trigger a decision to remove them from the home. This factor would be diminished if the youth is temporarily removed prior to the assessment. Also, if the adolescent is living with the person(s) against whom they offended sexually, then there may be a risk of continued sexual victimization, particularly given that the assessment process may trigger thoughts or feelings that could lead to further sexual abuse.

Informed Consent

Informed consent is a process – it is not simply a form that is filled out prior to the assessment. Although it is certainly prudent to have a youth sign a consent form prior to engaging in an assessment, the signature on the form establishes only that the youth has signed the form; it does not demonstrate that the youth has heard about the assessment process and has been given opportunities to have their questions and concerns addressed. Evans (2004) noted that informed consent requires that individuals receive full disclosure of all relevant information for a procedure, that they understand the information, and that consent is then given without deception, coercion, duress, or fraud.

There a number of issues that should be covered during the informed consent process. First, the youth should understand just what is entailed in the assessment, such as interviews with the youth, document review, interviews with adult caregivers, and any psychological and/or physiological testing that is to be carried out. Second, it is important to inform the youth about the nature of the questions that are going to be asked during the assessment. Although it may seem obvious to the assessor that questions will sometimes be focused on sexual issues, including masturbatory thoughts and behaviours, it would be best to ensure that the youth is aware of the issues that are going to be addressed in the assessment. It is also ideal to inform the youth that assessments are comprehensive and, as such, the questions will be focused on many different aspects of their life, including family relationships, social relationships, feelings, community involvement, school, etc. Without adequate description of the domains and issues to be covered, the youth's consent to the assessment is arguably not fully informed. From a process perspective, if the youth is surprised by a line of questioning their level of engagement may be adversely influenced.

It is also critical to point to policies/procedures regarding the safeguarding of information. Youth are naturally going to be concerned about the storage and distribution of their personal information because of the nature of the information that is being collected for the assessment. Given that we are inquiring about issues such as past criminal behaviours and potentially traumatic experiences, it is also essential to ensure that the youth is aware of the limits of confidentiality. Of course, outlining the limits to confidentiality is a cornerstone of the informed consent process for all clients (Pope & Vasquez, 1991). With adolescents involved in the youth justice system, discussion of these limits can pose particular challenges and requires considerable care and effort on the part of the clinician in order to ensure understanding without adversely influencing engagement and disclosure (Leschied & Wormith, 2004). In addition to limits that are broadly applicable (Josefowitz, 2004) and also those specific to assessments with court-involved youth (Leschied & Wormith, 2004), there can be others that require careful discussion with youth undergoing assessments in secure settings (Worling & Langton, 2012) and also when these subjects are being recruited as participants in research (Langton & Barbaree, 2004). In all cases, our preference is to explain the legal and ethical limits and then ask the adolescent to repeat back as many limits as they can recall in their own words. We then review the limits that they were unable to recall, correct any misinterpretations, and then summarize this conversation in the file.

Risks, Benefits, and Alternatives

Naturally, the informed consent process requires that we outline some of the anticipated potential risks and benefits of proceeding with an assessment (Evans, 2004). One potential risk is that the youth may disclose information that would trigger a report to authorities, resulting in potential investigations and, perhaps, significant legal, familial, and social consequences for someone – including the youth. Another possible risk is that it may be concluded that the youth presents a high level of risk to her-/himself or to others, and this could result in restrictions being placed on the youth. We also believe that it is important to warn youth that they may become upset and/or embarrassed during the process given the focus of many of the questions in the assessment, and there is also the possibility that they may become sexually aroused during some of the discussions. In some jurisdictions, an additional risk is that the youth may be placed on a registry for a lengthy period because of the conclusions and/or findings within an assessment (Rich, 2009), and registration/community notification could lead to irreparable harm (Human Rights Watch, 2013).

Of course, there are also a number of potential benefits to the assessment process. Most importantly, the adolescent may end up with an accurate, comprehensive picture of their strengths, risks, and needs. This could then be utilized to tailor treatment accordingly and inform decisions regarding community access and supervision. We also point out that the assessment process often leads to important insights for the youth, and it is also a way to begin making reparation for their sexually abusive behaviour.

Informed consent also requires that we provide youth with information regarding alternatives to proceeding with the assessment. One possibility would be for the youth to refuse the assessment and manage the repercussions. It is important that we do not frighten the adolescent to the point that we are coercing participation; however, it is essential to outline some of the consequences of refusal. Depending on the resources available, another alternative may be to obtain an assessment elsewhere, or with another clinician.

In addition to ensuring that the adolescent has all of the information necessary to make a decision regarding participation, this detailed informed-consent process also forms the genesis of the therapeutic alliance for the assessment. In contexts or settings where the clinician is not expected to be part of the treatment process that may follow, the assessment represents an important opportunity to provide the adolescent with an experience that is professional without being aloof or rejecting of the individual and respectful without condoning or minimizing the behaviours. Such early contacts with clinicians may increase the adolescent's willingness to engage with service providers later. The process of outlining the fact that one will be discussing potentially embarrassing topics, including masturbation, sexual thoughts and feelings, etc., sends a message to the youth that they are with a person who is comfortable talking about these issues, they are at a workplace where these assessments are common, and that they are in a safe place to share potentially embarrassing information. Through this careful process of obtaining informed consent, the adolescent is also learning that they are going to be interacting with a professional who is concerned about their rights and the protection of personal health information. The development of a positive therapeutic alliance is critical for adolescents to be maximally forthcoming (Lambie & McCarthy, 2004; Powell, 2011).

Sources of Information

Comprehensive assessments entail the collection and synthesis of information from a variety of sources, including interviews with the youth, interviews with parents/caregivers, document review, and the use of a variety of assessment tools. Indeed, the validity of the conclusions formulated in an assessment is enhanced when there is agreement between multiple sources of information. For example, although one may observe positive interpersonal boundaries during an interview with the youth, a conclusion regarding this strength would be bolstered with corollary information.

Interviewing the Youth

Some practitioners used to suggest that working with people who had offended sexually required a confrontational approach – presumably because this would somehow lead to honesty and positive changes. For example, Salter (1988) commented that 'the process of treating child sex offenders is heavily weighted in the direction of confrontation. Treatment requires continual confrontation' (p. 93). In their advice to those working with adolescents who offend sexually, Ross and Loss (1988) said that 'the offender's anxiety can facilitate disclosure by catching the offender "off guard" … The task of the interviewer is not to make the offender feel comfortable with material that is anxiety provoking to discuss' (pp. 3–4). In their review of the literature, however, Marshall et al. (2003) underscored the fact that aggressive confrontation is certainly not an empirically supported approach to eliciting client involvement or achieving change, and Powell (2011) stressed that a positive and supportive relationship with the adolescent will assist them to talk more openly about their sexually abusive behaviours.

Given the potential shame and embarrassment connected to many of the points that need to be covered during a comprehensive assessment, there are several interview strategies that may prove useful when speaking with an adolescent who has offended sexually (Worling, 2001). For example, it is important to be aware of your comfort level when discussing various topics, such as masturbation or sexual contact with animals, as the interviewer's discomfort can negatively impact the interview process. An interviewer's discomfort could also send the message that the youth's behaviour is particularly deviant or that the interviewer is unsure how to address the issue at hand.

Another critical interviewing strategy pertains to the way in which questions are framed during the assessment. First, many authors talk about the importance of asking open-ended questions (e.g., Calder et al., 2001; Rich, 2009), and there is no doubt that closed-ended questions can be quite leading. For example, when inquiring about potentially embarrassing behaviours, closed-ended questions that begin with 'Have you ever … ?', 'Did you … ?', 'Can you remember a time when … ?', or 'Do you … ?'

will often result in a negative response. If we wish to know about any additional victimized individuals, for example, it is doubtful that an adolescent will acknowledge additional offences if they are asked, 'Have you offended against anyone else?', or 'Are there any other children that you have sexually abused?' An alternative is to frame the question around the assumption that there were, indeed, more individuals involved (Worling, 2001). One way to ask, then, would be, 'How many other children did you touch sexually?'. The adolescent could simply say that there were 'none', but, if there were in fact more children, it might be easier to acknowledge this if the questions were asked in this presumptive manner. Similarly, if we would like to inquire about alcohol use, we may not get very far with the question, 'Do you ever drink alcohol?'. Some alternatives would be, 'How many days a week do you drink alcohol?' and 'How old were you the first time that you tried alcohol?'.

Another interviewing strategy is to use a variety of visual aids, such as timelines, family trees, floor plans, or outline drawings of the human body. Using paper and markers, or an electronic tablet, the adolescent can be engaged in conversation regarding many different topics. Such aids can reduce demands on the youth's receptive and expressive verbal skills while constituting activities that invite collaboration, build rapport, and provide the adolescent with a clear sense of what is being recorded. Furthermore, the use of these exercises can help create an atmosphere of enquiry rather than interrogation, and provide a point of shared focus that does not require direct eye contact when an adolescent is struggling to engage.

Interviewing Parents/Caregivers

It is important to collect information from parents and other adult caregivers, wherever possible (Calder, Hanks, & Epps, 1997; Lambie & McCarthy, 2004; Prescott, 2006). First, parents and caregivers will be able to provide a wealth of information regarding the youth's past and present functioning. Second, given the importance of later involving these adults in the youth's treatment (Rich, 2003), information regarding parent–child relationships and general family functioning is essential.

Calder et al. (2001) and Lambie and McCarthy (2004) pointed out that assessors need to be sensitive to the possibility that strong, negative emotional responses are likely to be present for parents of adolescents who have offended sexually. For example, they may be experiencing shock and disbelief regarding the fact that sexual offending has occurred, anger with their child and/or the systems' response to the offending behaviour, and despair regarding their child's future. Rich (2009) also stressed that it is important not to assume that the parents have somehow contributed to their child's decision to offend sexually, as this can lead to a non-supportive and potentially conflictual interviewing style. Whether or not an assessment requires the informed consent of parents or caregivers, working through the same issues with them can provide a means to engage them in the process through invitations to ask questions and to express their concerns about the assessment itself. More broadly, we have found that sharing findings from the research literature, for example about the positive impact of family involvement on treatment outcomes, can be a powerful way to allay concerns and build motivation to appropriately support their child's involvement in services, starting with the assessment.

It is important to be mindful when collecting information from parents that their child is the identified client for the assessment. Although parents or other adult caregivers may disclose detailed personal information, assessors should be careful only to include information in the assessment report that is germane to the assessment of their children.

Document Review

Prescott (2006) and Rich (2009) have stressed that assessors should read the available file documentation prior to assessing the adolescent. Ideally, it is best if one has access to all of the available documentation from police and/or child welfare regarding the sexual offending that occurred. Without some documentation about past sexual offending, it is difficult to evaluate the veracity of the youth's description. It also means that the assessor will be in a position of having to report information to authorities, as there would be no guidance as to whether or not the information represents a new disclosure. Of course, this would also be the case with respect to disclosures that the youth might make regarding their own history of victimization. In addition to police and/or child welfare notes or summaries, it is helpful to obtain previous assessments, school reports, and information regarding any previous interventions. Information from these sources can provide important details regarding not only past sexual offending behaviours but also past and current individual, familial, and social functioning.

Psychological Testing

Standardized psychological tests can be used to collect valuable assessment data for youth involved in the criminal justice system (Borum & Verhaagen, 2006; Hoge & Andrews, 1996). Important data regarding issues such as mood, affect regulation, personality, family relationships, intellectual functioning, and social relationships can be garnered using psychological tests and surveys, although many do not have psychometric properties established for youth who have sexually harmed others and even fewer are normed with this population. In addition, there are few psychological tests that have been developed specifically for adolescents who have offended sexually (Frey, 2010; Hunter, 2011). Many of the measures that are available in the field are experimental, and there is also a lack of independent data regarding their psychometric properties. Although these measures can provide useful information for an assessment, it is critical to be mindful of the significant limitations resulting from their use and the need to combine psychological test data with other sources of information (Rich, 2009).

Physiological Testing

Polygraph. The polygraph is currently used in approximately 50% of treatment programmes in the United States for adolescents who have sexually offended (McGrath, Cumming, Burchard, Zeoli, & Ellerby, 2010); this represents a dramatic increase from

1996, when only 22% of US treatment programmes for adolescents used this technology. Chaffin (2011) pointed out that the polygraph is rarely used with youth in the United States who commit non-sexual crimes and that there are very few countries outside the United States where the polygraph is utilized with adolescents at all. This may be because there is a lack of evidence regarding the reliability and validity of the polygraph (e.g., Fanniff & Becker, 2006; National Research Council of the National Academies, 2003; Rosky, 2013).

Proponents of the polygraph suggest that one significant benefit of the tool is that its use can lead to the discovery of previously unidentified individuals who have been sexually abused. To date, there have been only two published investigations regarding the use of the polygraph with adolescents who have offended sexually. In the first study, Emerick and Dutton (1993) found that adolescents who had offended sexually disclosed an average of almost one ($M = 0.98$) new victimized individual because of the polygraph examination. Van Arsdale, Shaw, Miller, and Parent (2012) similarly reported that adolescents disclosed an average of almost one ($M = 0.73$) new survivor of sexual abuse as a result of a polygraph examination. Although some might argue that these data support the use of the polygraph with adolescents who commit sexual crimes, this result should be contrasted with research supporting the fact that adolescents are more likely to disclose information regarding additional victimized individuals within the context of a trusting therapeutic relationship. For example, Baker, Tabacoff, Tornusciolo, and Eisenstadt (2001) found that adolescents disclosed an average of 3.3 new victimized individuals during the course of specialized treatment. Prescott (2012) also pointed out that survivors of sexual abuse may not wish to be identified via the results of a polygraph examination of the person who abused them, and it may indeed be disempowering to remove their choice of how and when to disclose.

In addition to the lack of empirical support, there are also several ethical concerns regarding the use of the polygraph with adolescents who have offended sexually. Chaffin (2011) succinctly pointed out that 'the polygraph is fundamentally a coercive interrogation tool for extracting involuntary information' (p. 320). He stressed that we should be particularly mindful of the potential harm to adolescents given their developmental vulnerabilities. Prescott (2012) explained that the coercive nature of the polygraph emulates an abusive adult–child experience for the adolescent, it can lead to the fabrication of new crimes in order to 'pass' the polygraph, and the fear and anxiety caused by the experience is counter to the formation of a strong therapeutic alliance. It should also be pointed out that there is no evidence to support the notion that adolescents must acknowledge all details of all previous sexual crimes in order to reduce their risk of recidivism. Most clinicians would likely agree that an adolescent should acknowledge that they have offended sexually and that it is ideal for clients to be open regarding the identity of the people whom they have abused and take responsibility for how they have harmed others. However, there are currently no scientific grounds for coercing youth to confess all of the details of all of their sexual crimes.

This focus on extracting a confession may be based, in part, on the assumption that denial is somehow predictive of future risk. Although this has been forwarded by some authors (e.g., Prentky & Righthand, 2003; Ross & Loss, 1988), there is no research with adolescents who have sexually offended to support this premise (Worling

& Långström, 2006). Indeed, some researchers have found that those adolescents who offend sexually and who categorically deny past offences may actually be at a reduced risk of reoffending sexually (Kahn & Chambers, 1991; Långström & Grann, 2000; Worling, 2002). Given the many scientific and ethical concerns, it is not surprising that several authors have cautioned against using the polygraph with adolescents who have sexually offended (e.g., Chaffin, 2011; Fanniff & Becker, 2006; Prescott, 2012).

Penile plethysmography. The penile plethysmograph (PPG) was originally developed to assess the sexual interests of adult males by measuring changes in penile circumference or volume (Freund, 1991). Although some authors argue that the PPG yields important data regarding men's sexual interests (e.g., Seto, 2001), concerns have been raised regarding the reliability and validity of this procedure (e.g., Marshall, 2006). According to the developer of the PPG, one of the most serious threats to the validity of this procedure is that some individuals are easily able to falsify results by suppressing arousal (Freund, 1991). It is also critical to underscore the fact that there is a significant degree of variation from one laboratory to the next with respect to test stimuli, assessment procedures, measurement equipment, and data interpretation, which makes it difficult to generalize results (Howes, 1995).

According to the most recent survey of treatment programmes in the United States for adolescent males who have offended sexually, 90% of programmes do not use the PPG. This may be attributable, in part, to the significant questions regarding the reliability and validity of this assessment technique for adolescent males. For example, deviance indices for adolescents based on PPG data are significantly impacted by age (Kaemingk, Koselka, Becker, & Kaplan, 1995), racial background (Murphy, DiLillo, Haynes, & Steere, 2001), and history of physical and sexual abuse (Becker, Hunter, Stein, & Kaplan, 1989; Becker, Kaplan, & Tenke, 1992b). Additionally, variables correlated with deviant sexual arousal in adult males, such as the number of victims, degree of force, and sexual recidivism, are not reliably correlated with pretreatment measures of deviant arousal in adolescent populations (Becker, Kaplan, & Kavoussi, 1988; Gretton, McBride, Hare, O'Shaughnessy, & Kumka, 2001; Gretton et al., 2005; Hunter, Goodwin, & Becker, 1994). There is also evidence to suggest that the utility of PPG data for adolescents is somewhat dependent on whether or not the adolescent has ever sexually abused a male (Clift, Rajlic, & Gretton, 2009; Hunter et al., 1994; Seto, Lalumière, & Blanchard, 2000). Becker et al. (1992b) also found that 58% of a sample of adolescents who denied their sexual offences provided invalid PPG data. Finally, in addition to the questions regarding validity, the only empirical support regarding the test–retest reliability of the PPG with this age group is a solitary study from 1992 where it was found that the temporal stability of the PPG ranged from excellent to poor across the various stimulus categories (Becker, Hunter, Goodwin, Kaplan, & Martinez, 1992a).

In addition to these significant scientific concerns, many authors have raised important ethical concerns regarding the use of the PPG with adolescents (e.g., Becker & Harris, 2004; Hunter & Lexier, 1998; Shaw, 1999; Worling, 1998). In particular, given that adolescents are developing their sexual identities and preferences (Bancroft, 2006), is there not a danger in exposing these youth to auditory and/or visual sexualized imagery of prepubescent children and sexual violence? Most adolescents would likely find that the PPG is a fairly intrusive procedure, and there is no evidence to suggest that the impact of this procedure is negligible. There would be particular concerns for those youth who have a history of childhood sexual victimization, as elements of the PPG procedure may trigger traumatic distress. In their review, Fanniff and Becker (2006) argued that the ethical and scientific concerns with the PPG are such that it should not be used routinely with adolescents.

Unobtrusively measured viewing time. An alternative to the PPG for measuring sexual interests is unobtrusively measured viewing time, a procedure that is used by approximately 30% of treatment programmes in the United States for adolescents who have offended sexually (McGrath et al., 2010). With this assessment paradigm, the client is asked to rate the sexual attractiveness of photographs of people in various age groups. The computer records not only the client's self-report attractiveness ratings for each photograph, but the software also unobtrusively records the amount of time that the participant viewed the photograph before entering their rating. The assumption behind this measurement approach is that, when asked to rate the sexual attractiveness of a photograph, people will look longer at images that they find attractive. It should be noted that the people depicted in the photographs of the more commonly used viewing-time systems are clothed and are not depicted in sexualized positions. As such, the concern regarding exposing adolescents to sexualized imagery of younger children is typically not present.

In research with adult males who have offended sexually, there is emerging research to support the claim that viewing time can provide useful information regarding sexual interests, typically with moderate effect sizes (e.g., Abel, Huffman, Warbert, & Holland, 1998; Banse, Schmidt, & Clarbour, 2010; Gray & Plaud, 2005; Harris, Rice, Quinsey, & Chaplin, 1996; Letourneau, 2002; Mokros et al., 2013). To date, there have been very few studies of this assessment approach with adolescents, however, and the results are mixed. For example, Smith and Fischer (1999) used the Abel Assessment for Sexual Interest (revised as the AASI-2) (Abel 2007), and they concluded that there were marked questions regarding reliability and validity. On the other hand, the developers of the AASI-2 reported moderate predictive accuracy with respect to the identification of youth who had offended sexually against younger children (Abel et al., 2004). Using the Affinity assessment software (revised as Affinity 2.5) (Glasgow, 2007), Worling (2006) found that unobtrusively measured viewing time was moderately predictive, but only for those male youth with male child victims and/or those with two or more child victims. It was also noted in that investigation that sexual deviance indices based on viewing time were not correlated with the participants' age or abuse history.

There are a number of obvious advantages to viewing time measures relative to the PPG. For example, with viewing time, one requires only a laptop and a quiet room, adolescents are not exposed to sexualized images of young children, and there is no need to put a device on the client's genitalia. Viewing time measures can also be used with both males and females, and the available procedures are relatively expedient. Despite these advantages, however, there are many questions regarding the psychometric properties of this approach. In particular, there is very little research regarding the temporal stability of viewing time measures, and the current research support for the discriminative validity with adolescents is questionable. There are also questions regarding the ability to detect response biases with viewing time paradigms. At this point, therefore, it appears that, although unobtrusively measured viewing time holds some promise, more research is needed before it can be considered a valid measure of sexual interest for adolescents.

Alternative cognitive-processing measures. A number of alternative cognitive-processing measures have been used in an effort to assess sexual interests; however, most of this research has been carried out with adults who have offended sexually. For example, some researchers have examined the implicit association test. In this paradigm, the individual categorizes concepts (e.g., 'child', 'adult') and attributes (e.g., 'sexy', 'not sexy'), and the response latency is assumed to reflect the strength of the implicit associations in memory. There is emerging research to suggest that this approach can differentiate adult males who offended sexually against children from a comparison group (e.g., Banse et al., 2010; Gray & Snowden, 2009; Nunes, Firestone, & Baldwin, 2007). Another experimental, cognitive-processing measure is the 'attentional blink' (Raymond, Shapiro, & Arnell, 1992), which is a measure of the delay that occurs when the identification of a specific stimulus within a group of distracters is influenced by a previously presented stimulus. For example, if an individual is sexually interested in young children, then it will presumably take them longer to identify a specific stimulus if an image of a young child immediately preceded the task. Although there is some research to suggest that this paradigm could provide useful information regarding the sexual interests of adult males who have offended sexually (Beech et al., 2008), Crooks, Rostill-Brookes, Beech, and Bickley (2009) found that this assessment methodology was not useful with adolescents who had offended sexually. As in the case of unobtrusively measured viewing time, there is certainly a need for further empirical work before a reliable and valid cognitive-processing measure of sexual interest is available for adolescents.

Risk Assessment

There are a number of possible risks that might be present when we are assessing a youth who has committed a sexual crime, and it is important to ensure that we are not myopically focused on the risk of a sexual reoffence. Although the referral source may be particularly interested in risk information solely with respect to sexual recidivism, other important risks to consider include the risk of self-harm and the risk of future involvement with the criminal justice system. Depending on the circumstances, one may also wish to consider the risk of substance abuse, placement breakdown, and the youth's risk of being victimized by others, for example.

Prior to 2003, most treatment programmes in the United States and Canada relied on assessments of risk of sexual recidivism undertaken without the aid of structured risk assessment tools (McGrath et al., 2010), despite the absence of evidence to support such an approach. Fortunately, a number of tools designed to assess adolescents' risk of sexually reoffending have been developed in the past decade or so and, although few have been subjected to independent empirical scrutiny, there is a growing evidence base for some (Viljoen, Mordell, & Beneteau, 2012). According to McGrath et al. (2010), the two most widely used risk assessment instruments regarding sexual recidivism in North America are the Juvenile Sex Offender Assessment Protocol – II (J-SOAP-II) (Prentky & Righthand, 2003) and the Estimate of Risk of Adolescent Sexual Offense Recidivism (ERASOR) (Worling & Curwen, 2001).

The J-SOAP-II was developed to predict both sexual and non-sexual criminal recidivism, and it is intended for males aged 12–18 years who have engaged in contact sexual crimes. The J-SOAP-II was originally designed as an actuarial tool (Prentky, Harris, Frizzell, & Righthand, 2000); however, the authors stressed that there are as yet no norms or cut-off scores. At this point, therefore, the J-SOAP-II serves as an 'empirically informed guide for the systematic review and assessment of a uniform set of items that may reflect increased risk to reoffend' (Prentky & Righthand, 2003, p. 8).

The 28 items on J-SOAP-II are divided into four scales: Sexual Drive/Preoccupation (eight items), Impulsive, Antisocial Behaviour (eight items); Intervention (seven items); and Community Stability/Adjustment (five items). All items on the J-SOAP-II are scored on a three-point scale, reflecting differing degrees of each factor, and there is a detailed coding manual that outlines rules for scoring each factor. The first 16 items on the J-SOAP-II (Sexual Drive/Preoccupation and Impulsive, Antisocial Behaviour) are static, or historical, and the remaining 12 items are dynamic, or potentially changeable, risk factors. Users are instructed to summarize J-SOAP-II results by commenting on the proportion of risk factors that are present for each of the four scales. Interrater agreement for the J-SOAP-II has generally been acceptable (Fanniff & Letourneau, 2012), particularly for the first three scales. With respect to predictive validity, Viljoen et al. (2012) conducted a meta-analysis focused on risk assessment tools for adolescent sexual recidivism, and they reported that, with a sample of nine studies, the total score from the J-SOAP-II was moderately predictive of both sexual (area under the curve [AUC_w] = 0.67; 95% confidence interval [CI] = 0.59–0.75) and non-sexual reoffending (AUC_w = 0.67; 95% CI = 0.59–0.75).

The ERASOR (Worling & Curwen, 2001) was designed to assist evaluators to estimate the short-term risk of sexual recidivism for males and females, aged 12–18 years, who offended sexually. The ERASOR was designed as a single-scale instrument, and the 25 risk factors that are evaluated fall under five headings: Sexual Interests, Attitudes, and Behaviours, Historical Sexual Assaults, Psychosocial Functioning, Family/Environmental Functioning, and Treatment. All risk factors are coded as either Present, Possibly/Partially Present, Not Present, or Unknown, and the coding manual outlines the specific coding criteria – in addition to the research/clinical support – for each factor. The nine Historical Sexual Assaults risk factors are static risk factors, whereas the remaining 16 risk factors are dynamic. Some authors (e.g., Prescott, 2006) have suggested that this makes the ERASOR useful for measuring treatment-related changes.

The ERASOR was designed in a similar fashion to other tools based on the structured professional judgement model, such as the Structured Assessment of Violence Risk in Youth (SAVRY) (Borum, Bartel, & Forth, 2006). As such, there are no norms, and evaluators make a professional judgement of risk (i.e., low, moderate, or high) based on the number and combination of risk factors that are present for the youth.

As in the case of the J-SOAP-II, researchers have found significant levels of interrater agreement using the ERASOR (Worling, 2014). In the meta-analysis of predictive accuracy by Viljoen et al. (2012), both the number of risk factors rated present (AUC_w = 0.66; 95% CI = 0.61–0.72) and the clinical judgement rating from the ERASOR (AUC_w = 0.66; 95% CI = 0.60–0.71) were equally and moderately predictive of sexual recidivism. Viljoen et al. (2012) found that there was no significant difference between the ERASOR (clinical judgement or total score) and the J-SOAP-II (total score) with respect to the predictive accuracy for sexual reoffending. They also pointed out that risk assessments with tools designed specifically for assessing the risk of sexual reoffending amongst youth are more accurate than more general risk assessment tools.

It is important to underscore the fact that the moderate degree of predictive accuracy observed for both the J-SOAP-II and ERASOR is similar to that found with tools designed to assess risk of sexual recidivism for adults (Hanson & Morton-Bourgon, 2009) and tools to assess the risk of general criminal recidivism for adolescents (Schwalbe, 2007).

Strengths and Protective Factors

It is stressed in best practice guidelines that evaluators should also focus on strengths and protective factors when assessing adolescents who have offended sexually (ATSA, 2003; Miner et al., 2006). A focus on strengths is also found in the Risk–Needs–Responsivity model (Andrews, Bonta, & Wormith, 2011). However, until recently, research in the area of violence risk assessment has been focused almost exclusively on the identification of risk factors that predict recidivism rather than on the identification of factors that predict desistance from reoffending (Rogers, 2000). This concentration on risk-only factors with risk assessment tools has likely resulted in inaccurate and biased judgements by assessors (e.g., Miller, 2006), and the accuracy of violence risk assessments should be enhanced with the inclusion of factors that predict desistance (Farrington, 2007).

Unfortunately, there have not yet been any investigations identifying protective factors for adolescent sexual recidivism. Bremer (1998) developed the Protective Factors Scale to guide placement decisions; however, this tool has yet to be subjected to empirical scrutiny. There has also been some initial work regarding the identification of protective factors for general youth violence. Preliminary, multisite research from the US Centers for Disease Control and Prevention (Hall, Simon, Lee, & Mercy, 2012) suggests that academic achievement, prosocial peer relationships, positive family management, and attachment to school may reduce the onset of youth violence. These authors stress, however, that firm conclusions regarding protective factors cannot be drawn at this time, given the current state of research. Furthermore, this research was focused on the onset of youth violence, not on recidivism. Although there are likely some risk factors that operate to increase the risk of both onset and continuance of youth violence, there are likely some factors that are uniquely related to desistence.

Unlike most of the available risk assessment tools for youth, which contain only risk factors, the SAVRY (Borum et al., 2006) contains six protective factors. There is some evidence to suggest that these protective factors are related to desistence in general criminal recidivism (Rennie & Dolan, 2010) and violent recidivism for adolescents (Lodewijks, de Ruiter, & Doreleijers, 2010). However, the available evidence indicates that the SAVRY protective factors are *not* related to desistence of sexual recidivism (Schmidt, Campbell, & Houlding, 2011; Spice, Viljoen, Latzman, Scalora, & Ullman, 2012). This suggests that there may be unique protective factors that are predictive of desistence for adolescent sexual reoffending.

The DASH-13 (Desistence for Adolescents who Sexually Harm) (Worling 2013) is an experimental checklist of 13 factors that may be related to the desistence of adolescent sexual offending. Seven of the factors are related specifically to future sexual health (prosocial sexual arousal, prosocial sexual attitudes, hope for a healthy sexual future, successful completion of sexual offence-specific treatment, awareness of consequences of sexual reoffending, environmental controls that match risk to reoffend sexually), whereas the remaining six items pertain to more general, prosocial functioning, and they are based on the limited available research described above (compassion for others, positive problem-solving skills, positive affect-regulation skills, close relationship with supportive adult, emotional intimacy with peers, and prosocial peer activity). It is hoped that research with this new instrument will identify possible protective factors for adolescent sexual recidivism and enhance the predictive accuracy of existing risk assessment tools. As Powell (2011) aptly noted, if we want adolescents to refrain from reoffending sexually, we need to teach them what to do to achieve healthy sexual futures; not simply teach them what not to do.

Conclusion

We have outlined the importance of conducting a comprehensive evaluation of each adolescent's unique strengths, risks, and needs, given that adolescents who have offended sexually are heterogeneous. We have also stressed the significance of being mindful of the particular purpose of the assessment, and a number of suggestions have been offered to address some of the more common challenges to completing such comprehensive assessments. Wherever possible, information should be gathered from multiple sources, and interviews with the adolescent require an approach that is invitational and sensitive to the nature of the questions being presented. Although several physiological assessment tools have been utilized in the assessment of adolescents who have offended sexually, such as the PPG, polygraph, and unobtrusively measured viewing time, there is clearly a need for more research before it can be established that these tools are reliable, valid, and reasonably innocuous. Similarly, although there have been recent scientific advances in the development of structured risk assessment tools, additional research is clearly needed to enhance our ability to comment more accurately on the likely sexual future for adolescents who have offended sexually.

References

Abel, G. G. (2007). *The Abel Assessment for Sexual Interest-2*™ Retrieved from http://abelscreening.com/products/evaluation-treatment-planning/aasi-2/

Abel, G. G., Huffman, J., Warberg, B., & Holland, C. L. (1998). Visual reaction time and plethysmography as measures of sexual interest in child molesters. *Sexual Abuse: A Journal of Research and Treatment*, *10*, 81–95. doi:10.1177/107906329801000202

Abel, G. G., Jordan, A., Rouleau, J. L., Emerick, R., Barboza-Whitehead, S., & Osborn, C. (2004). Use of visual reaction time to assess male adolescents who molest children. *Sexual Abuse: A Journal of Research and Treatment*, *16*, 255–265. doi:10.1177/107906320401600306

Andrews, D. A., & Bonta, J. (1994). *The psychology of criminal conduct*. Cincinnati, OH: Anderson.

Andrews, D. A., Bonta, J., & Hoge, R. D. (1990). Classification for effective rehabilitation: Rediscovering psychology. *Criminal Justice and Behavior*, *17*, 19–52. doi:10.1177/0093854890017001004

Andrews, D. A., Bonta, J., & Wormith, J. S. (2011). The Risk–Need–Responsivity (RNR) Model: Does adding the Good Lives Model contribute to effective crime prevention? *Criminal Justice and Behavior*, *38*, 735–755. doi:10.1177/0093854811406356

ATSA (2003). *Practice standards and guidelines for members of the Association for the Treatment of Sexual Abusers*. Beaverton, OR: Author.

Baker, A. J. L., Tabacoff, R., Tornusciolo, G., & Eisenstadt, M. (2001). Calculating number of offenses and victims of juvenile sexual offending: The role of posttreatment disclosures. *Sexual Abuse: A Journal of Research and Treatment*, *13*, 79–90. doi:10.1023/A:1026696103580

Bancroft, J. (2006). Normal sexual development. In H. E. Barbaree & W. L. Marshall (Eds.), *The juvenile sex offender* (2nd ed., pp. 19–57). New York, NY: Guilford Press.

Banse, R., Schmidt, A. F., & Clarbour, J. (2010). Indirect measures of sexual interest in child sex offenders: A multimethod approach. *Criminal Justice and Behavior*, *37*, 319–335. doi:10.1177/0093854809357598

Becker, J. V., & Harris, C. (2004). The psychophysiological assessment of juvenile offenders. In G. O'Reilly, W. L. Marshall, A. Carr, & R. C. Beckett (Eds.), *The handbook of clinical intervention with young people who sexually abuse* (pp. 191–202). Hove, England: Brunner-Routledge.

Becker, J. V., Hunter, J. A., Goodwin, D., Kaplan, M. S., & Martinez, D. (1992). Test–retest reliability of audio-taped phallometric stimuli with adolescent sex offenders. *Annals of Sex Research*, *5*, 45–51. doi:10.1177/107906329200500103

Becker, J. V., Hunter, J., Stein, R., & Kaplan, M. S. (1989). Factors associated with erectile response in adolescent sex offenders. *Journal of Psychopathology and Behavioral Assessment*, *11*, 353–362. doi:10.1007/BF00961533

Becker, J. V., Kaplan, M. S., & Kavoussi, R. (1988). Measuring the effectiveness of treatment for the aggressive adolescent sexual offender. *Annals of the New York Academy of Sciences*, *528*, 215–222. doi: 10.1111/j.1749-6632.1988.tb50865.x

Becker, J. V., Kaplan, M. S., & Tenke, C. E. (1992). The relationship of abuse history, denial and erectile response: Profiles of adolescent sexual perpetrators. *Behavior Therapy*, *23*, 87–97. doi:10.1016/S0005-7894(05)80310-7

Beech, A. R., Kalmus, E., Tipper, S. P., Baudouin, J., Flak, V., & Humphreys, G. W. (2008). Children induce an enhanced attentional blink in child molesters. *Psychological Assessment*, *20*, 397–402. doi:10.1037/a0013587

Blum, A. (2008). Shame and guilt, misconceptions and controversies: A critical review of the literature. *Traumatology*, *14*, 91–102. doi:10.1177/1534765608321070

Borum, R., Bartel, P., & Forth, A. (2006). *Structured assessment for violence risk in youth (SAVRY)*. Tampa, FL: Mental Health Institute, University of South Florida.

Borum, R., & Verhaagen, D. (2006). *Assessing and managing violence risk in juveniles.* New York, NY: Guilford Press.

Bremer, J. F. (1998). Challenges in the assessment and treatment of sexually abusive adolescents. *The Irish Journal of Psychology, 19,* 82–92. doi:10.1080/03033910.1998.10558172

Bumby, K. M., Marshall, W. L., & Langton, C. M. (1999). A theoretical model of the influences of shame and guilt on sexual offending. In B. Schwartz & H. Cellini (Eds.), *The sex offender* (Vol. 3, pp. 5–12). Kingston, NJ: Civic Research Institute.

Calder, M. C., Hanks, H. G., & Epps, K. J. (1997). *Juveniles and children who sexually abuse: A guide to risk assessment.* Lyme Regis, England: Russell House.

Calder, M. C., Hanks, H. G., Epps, K. J., Print, B., Morrison, T., & Henniker, J. (2001). *Juveniles and children who sexually abuse: Frameworks for assessment* (2nd ed.). Lyme Regis, England: Russell House.

Chaffin, M. (2011). The case of juvenile polygraphy as a clinical ethics dilemma. *Sexual Abuse: A Journal of Research and Treatment, 23,* 314–328. doi:10.1177/1079063210382046

Clift, R. J. W., Rajlic, G., & Gretton, H. M. (2009). Discriminative and predictive validity of the penile plethysmograph in adolescent sex offenders. *Sexual Abuse: A Journal of Research and Treatment, 21,* 335–362. doi:10.1177/1079063209338491

Crooks, V. L., Rostill-Brookes, H., Beech, A. R., & Bickley, J. A. (2009). Applying rapid serial visual presentation to adolescent sexual offenders: Attentional bias as a measure of deviant sexual interest? *Sexual Abuse: A Journal of Research and Treatment, 21,* 135–148. doi:10.1177/1079063208328677

Edmunds, S. B. (1997). *Impact: Working with sexual abusers.* Brandon, VT: Safer Society Press.

Emerick, R. L., & Dutton, W. A. (1993). The effect of polygraphy on the self-report of adolescent sex offenders: Implications for risk assessment. *Annals of Sex Research, 6,* 83–103. doi:10.1007/BF00849301

Evans, D. R. (2004). Informed consent. In D. R. Evans (Ed.), *The law, standards, and ethics in the practice of psychology* (pp. 147–183). Toronto, Canada: Edmond Montgomery.

Fanniff, A. M., & Becker, J. V. (2006). Specialized assessment and treatment of adolescent sex offenders. *Aggression and Violent Behavior, 11,* 265–282. doi:10.1016/j.avb.2005.08.003

Fanniff, A. M., & Letourneau, E. J. (2012). Another piece of the puzzle: Psychometric properties of the J-SOAP-II. *Sexual Abuse: A Journal of Research and Treatment, 24*(4), 378–408. doi:10.1177/1079063211431842

Farrington, D. P. (2007). Advancing knowledge about desistance. *Journal of Contemporary Criminal Justice, 23,* 125–134. doi:10.1177/1043986206298954

Freund, K. (1991). Reflections on the development of the phallometric method of assessing erotic preferences. *Annals of Sex Research, 4,* 221–228. doi:10.1007/BF00850054

Frey, L. L. (2010). The juvenile female sexual offender: Characteristics, treatment and research. In T. A. Gannon & F. Cortoni (Eds.), *Female sexual offender: Theory, assessment, and Treatment* (pp. 53–71). Chichester, England: John Wiley & Sons, Ltd.

Glasgow, D. V. (2007). *Introduction to Affinity.* Unpublished document.

Goocher, B. E. (1994). Some comments on the residential treatment of juvenile sex offenders. *Child & Youth Care Forum, 23,* 243–250. doi:10.1007/BF02209088

Gray, S. R., & Plaud, J. J. (2005). A comparison of the Abel Assessment for Sexual Interest and penile plethysmography in an outpatient sample of sexual offenders. *Journal of Sexual Offender Civil Commitment: Science and the Law, 1,* 1–10. Retrieved from www.soccjournal.org/index.cfm?page=http%3A//www.soccjournal.org/jsocc_home.cfm

Gray, N. S., & Snowden, R. J. (2009). The Implicit Association Test as a measure of sexual interest. In D. Thornton & D. R. Laws (Eds.), *Cognitive approaches to the assessment of sexual interest in sexual offenders* (pp. 101–123). Chichester, England: John Wiley & Sons, Ltd.

Gretton, H. M., Catchpole, R. E. H., McBride, M., Hare, R. D., O'Shaughnessy, R., & Regan, K. V. (2005). The relationship between psychopathy, treatment completion and criminal outcome over ten years: A study of adolescent sex offenders. In M. C. Calder (Ed.), *Children and young people who sexually abuse: New theory, research and practice developments* (pp. 19–31). Lyme Regis, England: Russell House.

Gretton, H. M., McBride, M., Hare, R. D., O'Shaughnessy, R., & Kumka, G. (2001). Psychopathy and recidivism in adolescent sex offenders. *Criminal Justice and Behavior, 28,* 427–449. doi:10.1177/009385480102800403

Hall, J. H., Simon, T. R., Lee, R. D., & Mercy, J. (2012). Implications of direct protective factors for public health research and prevention strategies to reduce youth violence. *American Journal of Prevention Medicine, 43*(2S1): S76–S83. doi:10.1016/j.amepre.2012.04.019

Hanson, R. K., Bourgon, G., Helmus, L., & Hodgson, L. (2009). The principles of effective correctional treatment also apply to sexual offenders: A metaanalysis. *Criminal Justice and Behavior, 36,* 865–891. doi:10.1177/0093854809338545

Hanson, R. K., & Morton-Bourgon, K. E. (2009). The accuracy of recidivism risk assessments for sexual offenders: A meta-analysis of 118 prediction studies. *Psychological Assessment, 21,* 1–21. doi:10.1037/a0014421

Harris, G. T., Rice, M. E., Quinsey, V. L., & Chaplin, T. C. (1996). Viewing time as a measure of sexual interest among child molesters and normal heterosexual men. *Behavior Research and Therapy, 34,* 389–394. doi:10.1016/0005-7967(95)00070-4

Hoge, R. D., & Andrews, D. A. (1996). *Assessing the youthful offender: Issues and techniques.* New York, NY: Plenum.

Homma, Y., Wang, N., Saewyc, E., & Kishor, N. (2012). The relationship between sexual abuse and risky sexual behavior among adolescent boys: A meta-analysis. *Journal of Adolescent Health, 51,* 18–24. doi:10.1016/j.jadohealth.2011.12.032

Howes, R. J. (1995). A survey of plethysmographic assessment in North America. *Sexual Abuse: A Journal of Research and Treatment, 7,* 9–24. doi:10.1177/107906329500700104

Human Rights Watch (2013). *Raised on the registry: The irreparable harm of placing children on sex offenders registries in the US.* New York, NY: Author.

Hunter, J. A. (2011). *Help for adolescent males with sexual behavior problems: A cognitive–behavioral treatment program: Therapist guide.* New York, NY: Oxford University Press.

Hunter, J. A., Goodwin, D. W., & Becker, J. V. (1994). The relationship between phallometrically measured deviant sexual arousal and clinical characteristics in juvenile sexual offenders. *Behaviour Research and Therapy, 32,* 533–538. doi:10.1016/0005-7967(94)90142-2

Hunter, J. A., & Lexier, L. J. (1998). Ethical and legal issues in the assessment and treatment of juvenile sex offenders. *Child Maltreatment, 3,* 339–348. doi:10.1177/1077559598003004006

Jenkins, A. (2005). Knocking on shame's door: Facing shame without shaming disadvantaged young people who have abused. In M. C. Calder (Ed.), *Children and young people who sexually abuse: New theory, research and practice developments* (pp. 114–127). Lyme Regis, England: Russell House.

Josefowitz, N. (2004). Confidentiality. In D. R. Evans (Ed.), *The law, standards, and ethics in the practice of psychology* (pp. 185–214). Toronto, Canada: Edmond Montgomery.

Kaemingk, K. L., Koselka, M., Becker, J. V., & Kaplan, M. S. (1995). Age and adolescent sexual offender arousal. *Sexual Abuse: A Journal of Research and Treatment*, *7*, 249–257. doi:10.1177/107906329500700402

Kahn, T. J., & Chambers, H. J. (1991). Assessing reoffense risk with juvenile sexual offenders. *Child Welfare*, *70*, 333–345.

Lambie, I., & McCarthy, J. (2004). Interviewing strategies with sexually abusive youth. *Journal of Child Sexual Abuse*, *13*, 107–123. doi:10.1300/J070v13n03_06

Långström, N., & Grann, M. (2000). Risk for criminal recidivism among young sex offenders. *Journal of Interpersonal Violence*, *15*, 855–871. doi:10.1177/088626000015008005

Langton, C. M., & Barbaree, H. E. (2004). Ethical and methodological issues in evaluation research with juvenile sexual abusers. In G. O'Reilly, W. L. Marshall, A. Carr, & R. C. Beckett (Eds.), *The handbook of clinical interventions with young people who sexually abuse* (pp. 419–441). Hove, England: Brunner-Routledge.

Leschied, A. D. W., & Wormith, J. S. (2004). Practice with young offenders and adult correctional clients. In D. R. Evans (Ed.), *The law, standards, and ethics in the practice of psychology* (pp. 321–356). Toronto, Canada: Edmond Montgomery.

Letourneau, E. J. (2002). A comparison of objective measures of sexual arousal and interest: Visual reaction time and penile plethysmography. *Sexual Abuse: A Journal of Research and Treatment*, *14*, 207–223. doi:10.1023/A:1015366324325

Letourneau, E. J. (2003). Ethics: Guilt-phase assessments and the ATSA Standards. *The Forum*, *15*(3). Retrieved from http://www.atsa.com/theForum/volumeXV/summer/page2.php

Leversee, T. (2010). Comprehensive and individualized evaluation and ongoing assessment. In G. Ryan, T. Leversee, & S. Lane (Eds.), *Juvenile sexual offending* (3rd ed., pp. 201–223). Hoboken, NJ: John Wiley & Sons, Inc.

Lodewijks, H. P. B., de Ruiter, C., & Doreleijers, T. A. H. (2010). The impact of protective factors in desistance from violent reoffending: A study in three samples of adolescent offenders. *Journal of Interpersonal Violence*, *25*, 568–587. doi:10.1177/0886260509334403

Marshall, W. L. (2006). Clinical and research limitations in the use of phallometry with sexual offenders. *Sexual Offender Treatment*, *1*(1), 1–18. Retrieved from http://www.sexual-offender-treatment.org/marshall.0.html

Marshall, W. L., Fernandez, Y. M., Serran, G. A., Mulloy, R., Thornton, D., Mann, R. E., & Anderson, D. (2003). Process variables in the treatment of sexual offenders: A review of the relevant literature. *Aggression and Violent Behavior*, *8*, 205–234. doi:10.1016/S1359-1789(01)00065-9

McGrath, R. J., Cumming, G. F., Burchard, B. L., Zeoli, S., & Ellerby, L. (2010). *Current practices and emerging trends in sexual abuser management: The Safer Society 2009 North American Survey*. Brandon, VT: Safer Society Press.

Miller, H. A. (2006). A dynamic assessment of offender risk, needs, and strengths in a sample of general offenders. *Behavioral Sciences and the Law*, *24*, 767–782. doi:10.1002/bsl.728

Miner, M., Borduin, C., Prescott, D., Bovensmann, H., Schepker, R., Du Bois, R., ... Pfäfflin, F. (2006). Standards of care for juvenile sexual offenders of the International Association for the Treatment of Sexual Offenders. *Sexual Offender Treatment*, *1*(3), 1–7. Retrieved from http://www.sexual-offender-treatment.org/index.php?id=49&type=123

Mokros, A., Gebhard, M., Heinz, V., Marschall, R. W., Nitschke, J., Glasgow, D. V., ... Laws, D. R. (2013). Computerized assessment of pedophilic sexual interest through self-report and viewing time: Reliability, validity, and classification accuracy of the Affinity program. *Sexual Abuse: A Journal of Research and Treatment*, *25*, 230–258. doi:10.1177/1079063212454550

Moulden, H. M., & Firestone, P. (2007). Vicarious traumatization: The impact on therapists who work with sexual offenders. *Trauma, Violence, & Abuse, 8*, 67–83. doi:10.1177/1524838006297729

Murphy, W. D., DiLillo, D., Haynes, M. R., & Steere, E. (2001). An exploration of factors related to deviant sexual arousal among juvenile sex offenders. *Sexual Abuse: A Journal of Research and Treatment, 13*, 91–103. doi:10.1023/A:1026648220419

National Research Council of the National Academies (2003). *The polygraph and lie detection.* Washington, DC: National Academies Press.

National Task Force on Juvenile Sexual Offending (1993). The revised report from the National Task Force on Juvenile Sexual Offending. *Juvenile and Family Court Journal, 44*, 1–120.

Nunes, K. L., Firestone, P., & Baldwin, M. W. (2007). Indirect assessment of cognitions of child sexual abusers with the implicit association test. *Criminal Justice and Behavior, 34*, 454–475. doi:10.1177/0093854806291703

Perry, G. P., & Orchard, J. (1992). *Assessment and treatment of adolescent sex offenders.* Sarasota, FL: Professional Resource Press.

Pope, K. S., & Vasquez, M. J. T. (1991). *Ethics in psychotherapy and counseling: A practical guide for psychologists.* San Francisco, CA: Jossey-Bass.

Powell, K. M. (2011). Working effectively with at-risk youth: A strengths-based approach. In M. C. Calder (Ed.), *Contemporary practice with young people who sexually abuse: Evidence-based developments* (pp. 69–91). Lyme Regis, England: Russell House.

Prentky, R., Harris, B., Frizzell, K., & Righthand, S. (2000). An actuarial procedure for assessing risk with juvenile sex offenders. *Sexual Abuse: A Journal of Research and Treatment, 12*, 71–93. doi:10.1023/A:1009568006487

Prentky, R., & Righthand, S. (2003). *Juvenile Sex Offender Assessment Protocol – II (J-SOAP-II): Manual.* Unpublished document. Retrieved from www.csom.org.

Prescott, D. S. (2006). *Risk assessment of youth who have sexually abused: Theory, controversy, and emerging strategies.* Hoboken, NJ: Safer Society Press.

Prescott, D. S. (2012). What do young people learn from coercion? Polygraph examinations with youth who have sexually abused. *ATSA Forum, 24*(2), 1–11.

Raymond, J. E., Shapiro, K. L., & Arnell, K. M. (1992). Temporary suppression of visual processing in an RSVP task: An attentional blink? *Journal of Experimental Psychology: Human Perception and Performance, 18*, 849–860. doi:10.1037/0096-1523.18.3.849

Rennie, C. E., & Dolan, M. C. (2010). The significance of protective factors in the assessment of risk. *Criminal Behaviour and Mental Health, 20*, 8–22. doi:10.1002/cbm.750

Rich, P. (2003). *Understanding, assessing, and rehabilitating juvenile sexual offenders.* Hoboken, NJ: John Wiley & Sons, Inc.

Rich, P. (2009). *Juvenile sexual offenders: A comprehensive guide to risk evaluation.* Hoboken, NJ: John Wiley & Sons, Inc.

Rogers, R. (2000). The uncritical acceptance of risk assessment in forensic practice. *Law and Human Behavior, 24*, 595–605. doi:10.1023/A:1005575113507

Rosky, J. W. (2013). The utility of post-conviction polygraph testing. *Sexual Abuse: A Journal of Research and Treatment, 25*(3), 259–281. doi:10.1177/1079063212455668

Ross, J. E., & Loss, P. (1988). *Risk assessment/interviewing protocol for adolescent sex offenders.* Mystic, CT: Authors.

Salter, A. C. (1988). *Treating child sex offenders and victims: A practical guide.* Newbury Park, CA: Sage.

Schmidt, F., Campbell, M. A., & Houlding, C. (2011). Comparative analyses of the YLS/CMI, SAVRY, and PCL:YV in adolescent offenders: A 10-year follow-up into adulthood. *Youth Violence and Juvenile Justice, 9*, 23–42. doi:10.1177/1541204010371793

Schwalbe, C. S. (2007). Risk assessment for juvenile justice: A meta-analysis. *Law and Human Behavior, 31,* 449–462. doi:10.1007/s10979-006-9071-7

Seto, M. C. (2001). The value of phallometry in the assessment of male sex offenders. *Journal of Forensic Psychology Practice, 1,* 65–75. doi:10.1300/J158v01n02_05

Seto, M. C., Lalumière, M. L., & Blanchard, R. (2000). The discriminative validity of a phallometric test for pedophilic interests among adolescent sex offenders against children. *Psychological Assessment, 12,* 319–327. doi:10.1037/1040-3590.12.3.319

Shaw, J. A. (1999). Practice parameters for the assessment and treatment of children and adolescents who are sexually abusive of others. *Journal of the American Academy of Child and Adolescent Psychiatry, 38,* 55S–76S. doi:10.1097/00004583-199912001-00004

Smith, G., & Fischer, L. (1999). Assessment of juvenile sexual offenders: Reliability and validity of the Abel assessment for interest in paraphilias. *Sexual Abuse: A Journal of Research and Treatment, 11,* 207–216. doi:10.1023/A:1021360208193

Spice, A., Viljoen, J. L., Latzman, N. E., Scalora, M. J., & Ullman, D. (2012). Risk and protective factors for recidivism among juveniles who have offended sexually. *Sexual Abuse: A Journal of Research and Treatment, 25,* 347–369. doi:10.1177/1079063212459086

Tangney, J. P., & Dearing, R. L. (2002). *Shame and guilt.* New York, NY: Guilford Press.

Underwood, L. A., Robinson, S. B., Mosholder, E., & Warren, K. M. (2008). Sex offender care for adolescents in secure care: Critical factors and counseling strategies. *Clinical Psychology Review, 28,* 917–932. doi:10.1016/j.cpr.2008.01.004

Van Arsdale, A., Shaw, T., Miller, P., & Parent, M. C. (2012). Polygraph testing for juveniles in treatment for sexual behavior problems: An exploratory study. *Journal of Juvenile Justice, 1,* 68–79.

Viljoen, J. L., Mordell, S., & Beneteau, J. L. (2012). Prediction of adolescent sexual reoffending: A meta-analysis of the J-SOAP-II, ERASOR, J-SORRAT-II, and Static-99. *Law and Human Behavior, 36,* 423–438. doi:10.1037/h0093938

Worling, J. R. (1995). Sexual abuse histories of adolescent male sex offenders: Differences based on the age and gender of their victims. *Journal of Abnormal Psychology, 104,* 610–613. doi:10.1037/0021-843X.104.4.610

Worling, J. R. (1998). Adolescent sexual offender treatment at the SAFE-T Program. In W. L. Marshall, Y. M. Fernandez, S. M. Hudson, & T. Ward (Eds.), *Sourcebook of treatment programs for sexual offenders* (pp. 353–365). New York, NY: Plenum.

Worling, J. R. (2001, November). *Comprehensive assessment of adolescent sexual offenders – Focus on risk assessment and the development of holistic treatment plans.* Paper presented at the 20th Annual Research and Training Conference of the Association for the Treatment of Sexual Abusers (ATSA), San Antonio, TX.

Worling, J. R. (2002). Assessing risk of sexual assault recidivism with adolescent sexual offenders. In M. C. Calder (Ed.), *Young people who sexually abuse: Building the evidence base for your practice* (pp. 365–375). Lyme Regis, England: Russell House.

Worling, J. R. (2004). The Estimate of Risk of Adolescent Sexual Offense Recidivism (ERASOR): Preliminary psychometric data. *Sexual Abuse: A Journal of Research and Treatment, 16,* 235–254. doi:10.1079-0632/04/0700-0235/0

Worling, J. R. (2006). Assessing sexual arousal for adolescents who have offended sexually: Self-report and unobtrusively measured viewing time. *Sexual Abuse: A Journal of Research and Treatment, 18,* 383–400. doi:10.1007/s11194-006-9024-1

Worling, J. R. (2013). *Desistence for Adolescents who Sexually Harm (DASH-13).* Unpublished document.

Worling, J. R. (2014). *The Estimate of Risk of Adolescent Sexual Offense Recidivism (ERASOR): Research support.* Retrieved from www.erasor.org

Worling, J. R., & Curwen, T. (2001). Estimate of Risk of Adolescent Sexual Offense Recidivism (ERASOR; Version 2.0). In M. C. Calder (Ed.), *Juveniles and children who sexually abuse: Frameworks for assessment* (pp. 372–397). Lyme Regis, England: Russell House.

Worling, J. R., Josefowitz, N., & Maltar, M. (2011). Addressing shame with adolescents who have offended sexually using cognitive-behavioral therapy. In M. C. Calder (Ed.), *Contemporary practice with young people who sexually abuse: Evidence-based developments* (pp. 320–334). Lyme Regis, England: Russell House.

Worling, J. R., & Långström, N. (2006). Assessing risk of sexual reoffending. In H. E. Barbaree & W. L. Marshall (Eds.), *The juvenile sex offender* (2nd ed., pp. 219–247). New York, NY: Plenum.

Worling, J. R., & Langton, C. M. (2012). Assessment and treatment of adolescents who sexually offend: Clinical issues and implications for secure settings. *Criminal Justice and Behavior*, *39*(6), 814–841. doi:10.1177/0093854812439378

51

Assessing Unicorns

Do Incest Offenders Warrant Special Assessment Considerations?

A. Scott Aylwin

Covenant Health, Canada

John R. Reddon

University of Alberta, Canada

Introduction

In common usage today, the term 'taboo' is used to denote an abhorrence and concomitant deterrence or prohibition of anything from the seemingly banal to the clearly significant. At a dinner party, a sommelier might note that pairing red wine with fish is tantamount to taboo. Later in conversation at the same dinner party, someone may discuss the Muslim taboo of allowing the Koran to touch the ground. The English word taboo comes from the Polynesian word *Tabu* (current usage is *Tapu*) and means forbidden and usually but not necessarily sacred (Michael Evans, University of British Columbia, Okanagan Campus, personal communication, 24 September 2013). It was adopted into Western usage in the late 1700s after James Cook's visit to Tonga and Polynesia in the 1770s. The taboo against touching the head of a Polynesian chief was so strong that to violate the taboo was thought to put the entire group at risk. Even touching the chief's shadow was considered a violation of the taboo. Thus, a cultural taboo represents something much more serious than a run of the mill prohibition or discouragement of some act or behaviour. Cultural taboos are mechanisms that promote health, place boundaries on our behaviour, engender group cohesion, and create order in society (Meyer-Rochow, 2009). According to Freud (1913/2001, p. 22), Wundt 'describes taboo as the oldest human code of laws. It is generally supposed that taboo is older than the gods and dates back to a period before any kind of religion existed'.

The Wiley Handbook on the Theories, Assessment, and Treatment of Sexual Offending.
Edited by Douglas P. Boer. Volume II: Assessment, edited by Leam A. Craig and Martin Rettenberger.
© 2017 John Wiley & Sons, Ltd. Published 2017 by John Wiley & Sons, Ltd.

There are very few behaviours that are considered universally taboo. The taboo against incest (sexual activity with related family members) is repeatedly upheld as one of the few universal taboos that crosses all of humanity throughout recorded history. One of the oft-cited reasons as to why this is apparently so is an evolutionary explanation (dismissed by Cohen, 1978). By definition, 'An individual is considered to be inbred if its parents are genetically related to each other' (Hall, Mercer, Phillips, Shaw, & Anderson, 2012, p. 151). Offspring of close blood-related parents will, owing to the disadvantages of inbreeding (known as inbreeding depression), have reduced heterozygosity and, therefore, reduced adaptive potential (especially in new or changing environments), have increased risk of birth anomaly and defects, have increased susceptibility to disease, and have reduced fecundity (Bischof, 1972; Lewin, 1989; Parker, 1976; Patterson, 2005). The manifestation of the biological consequences of inbreeding will generally require a number of generations, and under certain circumstances there may actually be some benefits, at least in the short run (Ralls, Ballou, & Templeton, 1988), that is, genetic load (i.e., deleterious recessive genes) can be reduced through inbreeding in small groups (Pekkala, Knott, Kotiaho, & Puurtinen, 2012; Zhou, Zhou, & Pannell, 2010). Nevertheless, the costs of inbreeding generally outweigh the benefits (Ralls et al., 1988); that is, having an intimate sexual relationship within one's own family would be subject to negative selection in that a fertile female involved with her father, for example, is not available for procreation with other suitable partners who would expand rather than limit the reach of her genetic code. Interestingly (Adam R. Reddon, McGill University, personal communication, 15 October 2013), 'Inbreeding has opportunity costs because tying up maternal resources in suboptimal inbred offspring will necessarily reduce the number of more viable offspring and competitive outbred offspring that can be produced. This is not necessarily so for males in that with limited parental investment there is essentially no opportunity cost to inbreeding for males. Therefore we would expect that males would be much less averse to inbreeding than would females.' There is also a phenomenon known as outbreeding depression, where genes are diluted and become less adaptive or where coadaptive gene combinations are lost (Hoben, Buunk, Fincher, Thornhill, & Schaller, 2010; Hufford, Krauss, & Veneklaas, 2012, p. 2263). In summary, inbreeding may not be that deleterious in unchanging environments and in the short run, and outbreeding may actually have deleterious consequences in some cases. There is, therefore, likely an optimal outbreeding distance that minimizes both inbreeding and outbreeding depression (Hufford et al., 2012). The prevalent propensity to mate with similar phenotypes (i.e., mating is typically not random), termed positive assortative mating (Burley, 1983), is a mechanism whereby outbreeding distance is constrained. Finally, earlier in human evolutionary history when life expectancy was short and sexual maturity in the human female was delayed relative to the present, father–daughter incest would be precluded because of the death of the father prior to the onset of sexual maturity of his daughter (Wallis & Slater, cited in Cohen, 1978). Cohen also made the point that breastfeeding and high rates of infant mortality would have made the age differential between siblings about 8 years, which would have precluded sibling incest. In the light of the foregoing, the evolutionary explanation of incest avoidance is, therefore, putative at best.

Examination of cultures and societies across time and space (i.e., Murdock's evaluation of 250 societies of all stages, cited in Bischof, 1972) reveals exceptions to the universality of the incest taboo. It is apparent, therefore, that culture, environment, and socialization are important forces in governing incest in addition to biology and evolutionary forces (e.g., Thornhill, 1991).

Some of the earliest discussions of incest are in Greek mythology (Coleman, 2011). Zeus, thought to be leader of the Olympians, married his sister Hera and raped his mother Rhea. Oedipus is another example: he was abandoned by his father as an infant and later killed his father not knowing that he *was* his father. He was also ignorant that his wife was his mother. When he discovered that was the case, Oedipus burnt his own eyes out. Thyestes raped his daughter Pelopeia, who then married her uncle Atreus. Examples of incest are also available in the Roman poet Ovid's *Metamorphoses* (completed AD 8, trans. Martin, 2004). Myrrha was sexually involved with her father Theias, after which she was turned into a tree. Nyctimene was also sexually involved with her father Epopeus, after which she was turned into an owl. Byblis was in love with her twin sister Caunis.

Classic depictions of incest in the erotica genre include the 1799 French book about father–daughter incest by Marquis de Sade entitled *Incest* (trans. Brown, 1799/2013) and stepfather–stepdaughter incest in the book *Lolita* (Nabokov, 1955). Incest can be found in Shakespeare's plays *Hamlet* and *Prince of Tyre*. In fiction, incest appears in Richard Condon's 1959 *Manchurian Candidate*, F. Scott Fitzgerald's 1934 *Tender is the Night*, Harper Lee's 1960 *To Kill a Mockingbird*, John Sanford's 2010 *Bad Blood*, and Sylvia Day's 2012 *Bared to You*. Popular films in various genres which include incest include *Cruel Intentions* in 1999, *Gladiator* in 2000, *Precious* in 2009, *The Butterfly Effect* in 2004, and *The Color Purple* in 1985. Numerous other instances in film or television can be found by searching for incest in the Internet Movie Data Base (www.imdb.com) in keywords or plots. In the international English-language popular press from 24 countries in the period 2007–2011, a recent report summarizes 44 cases of parent–child incest extending into adulthood (Middleton, 2013b). Forty-four cases may not seem very many, but these are only a subset of cases given that these 44 cases extended from childhood into adulthood and were sensational enough to reach the popular press. Few cases would be reported in the media because there would generally be a publication ban for cases in which the incest victims were not adults at the time of adjudication and because only a subset of incest cases actually come to the attention of authorities (e.g., Donalek, 2001). Sacco (cited in Middleton, 2013a) found, particularly during the 19th century, more than 500 cases of father–daughter incest in 900 US newspaper articles.

One might wonder what relevance incest in mythology, poetry, plays, fiction, film, and the popular press has for our understanding of this topic. It is important because the prevalence of incest in these media, from the earliest times until the present, indicates that incest is an issue of considerable importance to humanity. It is also important because the media are both a significant influence on and a reflection of language, ideology, culture, and civilization. Regarding the earliest depictions of incest in mythology, we note that mythology has had an impact on humanity since antiquity and continues to have an impact on the present. For instance, generations of physicians have recited and continue to recite the Hippocratic oath, which opens with

'I swear by Apollo Physician and Asclepius and Hygieia and Panaceia and all the gods and goddesses, making them my witnesses, that I will fulfil according to my ability and judgment this oath and this covenant' (Bloch, Chodoff, & Green, 1999, p. 511).

In the recent scientific literature on incest, Middleton (2013a) summarizes cases of 10 adult women whom he treated in Australia where father–daughter incest began in childhood and extended into adulthood. All 10 had also been sexually abused by others and all 10 reported that their mothers witnessed the abuse by their father. Threats by the father of death or going to Hell were received by all 10. Eight fathers were reported to be cruel to animals. All fathers were gainfully employed and half were active in their church. Nine of the women felt that their father had had a dysfunctional upbringing. Seven of the fathers told their daughters that they enjoyed sex with them more than with their mothers. This clinical report, although based on a small number of cases, does make it apparent that incest offenders can have substantial interpersonal dysfunction despite an outward appearance of normalcy in the community.

Our criminal codes outline the behaviours that we collectively deem to be criminal and worthy of punishment, but we deem none of these transgressions of social rules to be taboo. Although there are prohibitions against theft and assault in virtually all societies, there is no collective acknowledgement of the 'theft taboo' or the 'assault taboo'. Why, then, do we perpetuate the notion of an incest taboo? For something to be deemed a universal social taboo, one would assume that the incidence of its occurrence would be exceedingly low and the consequence for transgressing this boundary to be among the most harshly punished. However, when we look at present-day Western society, we see ample evidence that neither of these is the case. In fact, there is evidence to suggest that as societies evolve towards greater technological and social complexity, the incest taboo becomes reduced in scope and transgressions are construed as less severe (Leavitt, 1989). Cohen (see also Cohen, 1969) viewed the incest taboo as necessary for establishing relations with other groups and particularly with respect to trade. As societies become technically and socially more complex, the family, as the mechanism of exchange of goods between groups, is supplanted by institutions. Leavitt employed 121 societies to evaluate Cohen's (1978) hypotheses about the evolution of society and the incest taboo. A distinction was made about rules regarding sexual interaction amongst members of the nuclear family and rules of exogamy regarding sexual relations with kin. Leavitt's support for Cohen's hypotheses was in terms of sexual relations with relatives outside the nuclear family.

For a behaviour that carries with it the stigma of a universal taboo, it occurs with alarming regularity. Given that the prevalence estimates for incest are about 30% of child sexual abuse prevalence estimates (Bolen, 2002), division by three is required to obtain incest prevalence estimates from the prevalence of child sexual abuse. A recent meta-analysis on the prevalence of childhood sexual abuse by Barth, Bermetz, Helm, Trelle, and Tonia (2013) of 55 studies that were published between 2002 and 2009 with samples ranging from 106 to 127,097 participants under 18 years of age from 24 countries reported the results in terms of non-contact abuse (sexual solicitation, indecent exposure), contact abuse (touching/fondling, kissing), forced intercourse (oral, vaginal, or attempted), and mixed (when different types of abuse were combined in the studies). On average, for forced intercourse 9% of girls and 3% of boys were victims, for the mixed category 15% of girls and 8% of boys were victims, for the contact category

13% of girls and 6% of boys were victims, and for the non-contact category 31% of girls and 17% of boys were victims. Prevalence estimates for males were unrelated to region or development as indexed by the United Nations Human Development Index (HDI), a composite of life expectancy, literacy, education, standard of living, and quality of life. For girls, low prevalence was obtained with moderate HDI and the highest prevalences were for low and high HDI. In general, prevalence estimates were comparable to those obtained in two previous meta-analyses (Pereda, Guilera, Forns, & Gómez-Benito, 2009; Stoltenborgh, van Ijzendoorn, Euser, & Bakermans-Kraneburg, 2011). These rates, even after dividing by three to obtain the incest prevalence estimates, are non-trivial and, as discussed below, they are likely significant underestimates.

Confining our discussion of molestation to where the relationship between perpetrator and victim is intergenerational (i.e., excluding cases of sibling incest; cf., Carlson, Maciol, & Schneider, 2006; Rudd & Herzberger, 1999; Stroebel et al., 2013a, 2013b; Tidefors, Arvidsson, Ingevaldson, & Larsson, 2010), we find few published reports of incest prevalence rates, but these clearly indicate that the event is not rare. Among a sample of ninth-grade girls in a situation where disclosure would be very unlikely (girls still residing with perpetrators and responding to a written survey administered in the school setting), Sariola and Uutela (1996) still found that 0.5% of girls reported being sexual victims of their fathers or stepfathers. Stroebel et al. (2012) obtained a sample of 1521 females who participated in an anonymous computerized survey about the effects of childhood sexual experiences on adult sexual attitudes and adjustment. They found that 82.9% of adult women respondents reported no sexual abuse history, 15.8% reported having been sexually molested by someone other than a father figure, and 1.2% reported being sexually abused at the hands of their fathers.

Among populations that come to the attention of professionals and caregivers, the frequency with which incest occurs does not appear to be taboo at all; rather, it appears to be tragically mundane. Social response to incest at both macro and micro levels does not support the notion of the universal taboo either. When incest perpetrators are brought to the attention of authorities, one would think that a crime considered taboo would carry the greatest sanctions. Sentencing practices, however, often do not reflect this. In Canada for example, a conviction of Incest under Section 155 of the Criminal Code of Canada ('Everyone commits incest who, knowing that another person is by blood relationship his of her parent, child, brother, sister, grandparent or grandchild, as the case may be, has sexual intercourse with that person'; Canada Law Book, 2010, p. 302) carries a maximum penalty of 14 years in prison, and the more commonly used Section 151, Sexual Interference ('Every person who, for a sexual purpose, touches, directly or indirectly, with a part of the body or with an object, any part of the body under the age of 16 years'; p. 296), carries a 10 year maximum. Numerous other criminal offences carry the same or greater maximum prison terms as sentencing options, so clearly incest is considered no more heinous than many other crimes. In Canada, certainly, maximum sentences are virtually never applied in cases of intra-familial sexual abuse. There is evidence that offenders in cases of extra-familial child sexual abuse routinely receive more severe sentences than those found guilty of intra-familial child sexual abuse. Indeed, all US states have had criminal statutes for child sexual abuse since 1986, but a number of states also have incest statutes with much less severe punishments (Adams, 2009).

Sentencing in criminal matters is complicated because there are at least six considerations to reflect upon when deciding on an appropriate sentence: denunciation of unlawful conduct, general and specific deterrence, protection of the public/separation of offenders, rehabilitation, making reparations for harm done to victims, and promoting responsibility within the offender (Canada Law Book, 2010, Section 718, pp. 1397–1398). Therefore, it is admittedly an oversimplification to compare the typical sentence for incest with the typical sentence for some other crime, but the point still remains. All things considered, incest does not appear to be dealt with by the courts in the way that one would expect a universal taboo to be sanctioned.

The official actions of the state represent one level of response to incest, but there is also the unofficial response that occurs within families when incest is occurring. This is likely more powerful than any official mechanism in declaring the true degree of abhorrence or acceptance with which incestuous activity is actually viewed. Here again, we see that incestuous behaviour is very often not met with the level of objection one would expect given the standing of a universally held taboo. Abu-Baker (2013) analysed therapy records of 35 Arab–Palestinian clients and 27 Israeli clients. Reaction to child sexual abuse was better predicted by relatedness of the perpetrator to the family than by functional versus dysfunctional family status. It was found that the closer the relationship was between victim and perpetrator, the more motivated families were to keep the abuse silent. While abuse from outside the family was met with hostility and active efforts to prevent further access, disclosure of intra-familial abuse in their sample was strongly discouraged owing to the dishonour thought to befall the family (i.e., *fadiha*, a scandal impacting their reputation, and *Sharaf*, the harmfulness of extramarital relations). Therapists in Western society can anecdotally share that the influence of relationship between victim and perpetrator on the family's attitude is far from unique to Arabic families.

Studies have repeatedly found that child sexual abuse is significantly underreported (e.g., McElvaney, Greene, & Hogan, 2012; Steed & Templer, 2010). The reasons for this are many, but include such things as age of the child, normalizing the abuse, projection of blame, rewarding the victim for silence, and unwillingness or inability of the victim to report the abuser out of fear, intimidation, or threats (Donalek, 2001; Middleton, 2013a). Victims are often explicitly told or implicitly conclude that if they tell, dire consequences will befall the abuser such as imprisonment or ostracization. In many cases, reporting the abuse would impact the economic viability of the family (Kardam & Bademci, 2013). Situations of incest magnify these threats as victims sometimes conclude that the very fabric of the family is at risk should they disclose. On logical grounds, we can assume that if child sexual abuse is underreported, as many reports indicate (McElvaney et al.; Steed & Templer), incest situations must be underreported to an even greater extent.

Atwood (2007) reported that biological father–daughter incest was the most common form of intra-familial sexual abuse reported in her sample of 833 girls who reported experiencing sexual abuse within the home. In this self-selected sample, 38% reported that they were molested by their biological fathers and a large majority of those (73%) reported that the abuse began prior to the age of 10 years. An additional 11% reported a stepfather–stepdaughter relationship and 7.5% reported being molested by their grandfathers.

So, when instances of incest come to light, are they typically treated as if a universal taboo has been violated? Far from it. Sexual abuse is often the great family secret that goes unaddressed, sometimes for generations. At points in history, disclosures of incest have even been ignored or belittled. Freud (see Argentieri, 2005, p. 24) was of the view that childhood seduction by a parent was rare whereas the fantasy of seduction was ubiquitous. He did, however, view the pathogenic consequences of incest as equivalent, whether real or imagined. Consider, for example, Freud's patient Dora, where the patient accused her father of sexual abuse and the father denied any sexual involvement. Interestingly, Cournut-Janin (2005) revealed that one of Freud's brothers and one of his sisters were sexually abused by their father. Tesone (2005) remarked that incest fantasies are much less impactful than the actual experience of incest and, therefore, for the latter advocated using the term 'incestuous sexual violence'. Looking back, one should hardly be surprised that once patients had the freedom and encouragement to share their personal experiences, via the talking cure, disclosures of abuse would follow.

Not until the work of Kinsey, Pomeroy, and Martin (1948) and Kinsey, Pomeroy, Martin, and Gebhard (1953) did the topic of incestuous experiences in the general population receive any systematic examination. By the mid-1960s, a major publication based on interviews with 1500 male sex offenders was produced by the Kinsey Institute, in which three chapters were devoted to incest and a number of other chapters were devoted to extra-familial offenders (Gebhard, Gagnon, Pomeroy, & Christenson, 1965). Although these Kinsey reports were very influential in establishing sexology and deviant sexuality as legitimate fields of inquiry, the research methods, findings, and Kinsey, himself, have been extensively criticized and consequently largely dismissed (Cochran, Mosteller, & Tukey, 1953; Goode, 2011; see also the *Journal of the American Statistical Association* symposium with Kinsey et al., 1955, contributing to the evaluation of Kinsey's work).

Incest, unfortunately, occurs with sad regularity. Society via the courts does not respond to incest as if it were a most heinous behaviour, and society at the familial level similarly does not treat incest as if it actually is taboo. Atwood (2007) asserted that a universal taboo against incest implies that incest is actually a universal behaviour. Similarly, Argentieri (2005, p. 22) asserted that 'the taboo on incest is universal, as is the violation of this prohibition'. In the words of Atwood (p. 288), 'The incest itself is universal, not the absence of it'. Mohl (2010) also viewed the incest taboo as nothing less than pure myth. A point made by Freud (1913/2001, p. 143) in *Totem and Taboo*, quoting Frazer, is that 'The law only forbids men to do what their instincts incline them to do; what nature itself prohibits and punishes, it would be superfluous for the law to prohibit and punish. Accordingly we may always safely assume that crimes forbidden by law are crimes which many men have a natural propensity to commit.'

Incest is, as is all sexual behaviour, driven to some extent by the desire to propagate, which is arguably the essence of existence for all living things. In humans, in particular, immediate gratification and pleasure within the context of language, ideology, and culture provide motivation and reward for engaging in a multitude of sexual behaviours. In most species, dispersal will preclude incest but where dispersal is constrained, such as in a closed environment, inbreeding will occur. Take, for example, an aquarium containing an adult male and female *Neolamprologus pulcher*, a cooperatively breeding cichlid fish indigenous to Lake Tanganyika. When the adults produce offspring, if one parent is removed the other will mate with one of their offspring at maturity (around 1 year). If both parents are removed, the siblings will breed but the number of breeding pairs formed will be limited by the size of the tank (Adam R. Reddon, McGill University, personal communication, 18 September 2013). Consistent with this example, in humans, Bagley (cited in Cohen, 1978) views isolation (i.e., localism) of the nuclear family as a major contributory factor to incest.

The Specificity Question

Classification is concerned with organizing information in our environment. Classification is of such fundamental importance that it appears phylogenetically with the emergence of sense perception in organisms (Sokal, 1974). Typologies exist to organize processes, objects, or concepts into meaningful and discrete groups. With regard to sex offenders, it has traditionally been useful to organize this population based on behavioural characteristics involving victim and/or offence types. As a result, distinctions are made on the basis of age (offenders who assault adult women, i.e., rapists; those who assault children, i.e., child molesters and paedophiles; and those who assault older victims, i.e., gerontophiles), gender (homosexual versus heterosexual), intrafamilial versus extra-familial offenders, exhibitionists, and so on. The value of any typology is that assignment to any one of the respective categories contained within it should have some utility. Any particular offender type might share a common aetiology, perhaps a uniform response to a treatment approach, but at the very least the descriptive label should capture the essence of that group and be explanatory to a significant extent for members of the group. The group will undoubtedly have significant variability, so the best exemplar of the group is generally the average or group centroid. It was Quetelet in 1831 who introduced the concept of the average man as protypical for a group in his work *l'Homme Moyen* (Stigler, 1999, Chapter 2).

The veridicality of pure or ideal types in sex offender taxonomy can be assessed by evaluating crossover. Abel, Becker, Cunningham-Rathner, Mittelman, and Rouleau (1988) found, using self-reports from 561 sex offenders, that many had experiences with as many as 10 different types of deviant sexual behaviour with respect to gender, age, and relationship to the victim. In a heterogeneous sample of 1345 serious sex offenders (i.e., with a sentence of 4 years or more) reported by Cann, Friendship, and Gozna (2007), 24.5% of these offenders exhibited crossover. Crossover with respect to age (children versus adults) was 8%, and it was 9% for gender and 14% for relationship (intra-familial versus extra-familial). With a sample of 789 incarcerated sex offenders, Kleban, Chesin, Jeglic, and Mercado (2012) evaluated crossover in the 279 with multiple victims for the index offence (208 had prior victims). For the index offence, 13% had victims of both genders, 14% had victims of different age categories (child, adolescent, adult), and 13% had multiple relationships (family member, acquaintance, stranger). In terms of prior convictions, 20% exhibited crossover with respect to gender, 40% crossover with respect to age, and 48% had varying relationships with respect to relationship. It is currently common practice to advocate that treatment for sex offenders be individualized and specific in content because it makes logical sense that limited resources should be targeted in the most efficient and effective manner. Crossover, however, challenges our ability to provide unique approaches for seemingly distinct but heterogeneous offender groups.

Regarding incest offenders, current wisdom in the sex offender field dictates that incest offenders have a lesser likelihood of reoffending than extra-familial offenders. Reoffence rates even for untreated offenders who choose victims from within the family are typically in the 1–10% range. Rettenberger, Matthes, Boer, and Eher (2010), with 92 extra-familial offenders and 108 incest offenders and a follow-up period ranging from 18.4 to 66.6 months, obtained sexual recidivism rates of 12.0 and 0.9%, respectively. Firestone et al. (1999), with a sample of incest offenders (biological, stepchild, grandchild, or sibling victim) with no offences against adults or unrelated children and without intensive treatment, obtained a sexual recidivism rate of 6.4% with an average of 6.5 years follow-up (range 2.5–12 years). Greenberg, Bradford, Firestone, and Curry (2000), with 84 biological fathers and 59 stepfathers who abused their daughters and a mean follow-up of 12.7 years, obtained sexual offence recidivism rates of 9.5 and 6.8%, respectively.

Cascading from reports such as these are further assumptions that intra-familial offenders are less dangerous than extra-familial offenders and do not require intensive treatment, if they even require any treatment at all (Studer & Aylwin, 2006). Langevin and Curnoe (2012), in an update to a previous 25-year follow-up study published by Langevin et al. (2004) using a sample of 2190 sex offenders seen from 1966 to 2009, reported recidivism results for 704 incest offenders (559 against girls, 95 against boys, and 50 against both boys and girls) and 649 child sexual abusers (279 against boys, 297 against girls, and 73 against both boys and girls). Charges, convictions, and court appearances were reported separately. Using convictions, the recidivism rates for intra-familial and extra-familial offenders, respectively, were 47.4 versus 67.6% for offenders against boys, 44.9 versus 60.7% for offenders against girls, and 72.0 versus 69.9% for offenders against both boys and girls. In other words, extra-familial offenders recidivated at a rate that was approximately 25% greater, with the exception of offenders against both boys and girls, for whom the recidivism rates were equivalent. Langevin and Curnoe, however, did not address crossover with their sexual recidivism data.

The putative value of distinguishing between intra-familial and extra-familial offenders has received some scrutiny (e.g., Abel et al., 1988; Barsetti, Earls, Lalumière, & Belanger, 1998; Seto, Lalumière, & Kaban, 1999; Studer & Aylwin, 2006; Studer, Aylwin, Clelland, Reddon, & Frenzel, 2002; Studer, Clelland, Aylwin, Reddon, & Monro, 2000). Conte (1991) argued that there is little rationale for viewing the sexual behaviour of intra-familial and extra-familial child molesters as distinctly different from each other, and Wilson (2004) agreed that all children (i.e., not just those within the family) ought to be considered at some risk from the intra-familial offender.

The incest offender designation by definition should clarify which offenders are intra-familial and which are not. However, the label actually contributes little in this regard. A number of studies now have demonstrated substantial victim category crossover (cf., Cossins, 2011). Among a sample of 128 child molesters, Sim and Proeve (2010) stratified the group by the age of the victim. They used the categories of '5 years or less', '6–12 years', and '13 years or more', and found that age crossover was very common; 48% of their sample molested children in more than one age category. The relationship to the victim (intra-familial versus extra-familial) was a category crossed by 25.8% of the sample, and 22% of the sample assaulted victims of each gender. The overall rate of crossover in at least one of the three categories was 63%. The number of victims ranged from 2 to 15 (mean 3.2) and interestingly was significantly related to crossover for age and relationship to victim but not gender of victim. Studer et al. (2000) reported that among a sample of 150 men with incestuous convictions, 22% had assaulted additional victims where the relationship was also incestuous, and 58% had assaulted other victims outside the family. In fact, only a minority of the group (33%) did not have other victims.

A study of 102 incestuous families receiving outpatient treatment revealed that sexual abuse of more than one child in the family was not uncommon (Phelan, 1986). Approximately one-third of the incestuous fathers had multiple victims within the same family. Among a subset of 46 biological fathers, half of the subgroup had multiple victims within the family. Gathering data from the victim's perspective, Herman and Hirschman (1981) studied 40 female victims of incest. In this sample, 28% knew of siblings who were also being molested, and another 25% had unconfirmed suspicions that other children in the family were also being sexually assaulted. These two studies do not specifically refute the incest offender typology, but certainly run counter to findings that incest offenders pose little risk to others apart from their known victim.

Deviant sexual arousal is another characteristic thought to differentiate intra-familial and extra-familial offenders. Conventional wisdom in this area of offender assessment indicates that extra-familial offenders display greater arousal to paedophilic stimuli than intra-familial offenders. This seems to support the notion that extra-familial offenders are more deviant, but the idea of offenders being more or less deviant based on erotic preference testing is a somewhat dubious concept. There are now a number of studies that have reported on the limitations of erotic preference testing (e.g., Marshall, 2006) and the inability of erotic preference testing to discriminate intra-familial from extra-familial molesters. In a sample of 19 intra-familial and 20 extra-familial molesters, Barsetti et al. (1998) found that both groups responded differently (more deviant) than a group of normal controls. However, the groups were virtually indistinguishable from each other in terms of arousal response to paedophilic stimuli. Studer et al. (2002) examined differences in erotic preference testing results among 103 incestuous and 114 non-incestuous child molesters. For the 103 incestuous offenders, 12.6, 40.7, 36.9, and 9.7% responded as primarily sexually preferential to prepubescent, pubescent/hebephilic, adult, and pangynaephilic stimuli, respectively. For the 114 non-incestuous offenders, 29.8, 43.0, 19.3, and 7.9%, were prepubescent, pubescent/hebephilic, adult, and pangynaephilic in primary erotic preference, respectively. For both groups, the primary erotic category was pubescent/hebephilic and the proportions did not differ by group membership. The overall chi-squared for the two groups and the four erotic preference categories obtained statistical significance, but for the individual categories only the prepubescent and adult categories differed between groups. There was a greater propensity for non-incestuous offenders than the incestuous offenders to be in the prepubescent category (29.8 versus 12.6%) and a greater propensity for the incestuous offenders than the non-incestuous offenders to be in the adult category

(36.9 versus 19.3%). Although there is some statistical differentiation between incestuous and non-incestuous child molesters in terms of primary erotic preference, there is substantial overlap. Incest offenders were subdivided into those who had committed only incest offences ($n = 60$) versus those with non-incestuous offences also ($n = 43$); the overall chi-squared was statistically significant but only the adult category differed significantly between groups (46.6% for incestuous only versus 23.3% for non-incestuous ever). That is, there was no difference between these groups in terms of the prepubescent, pubescent/hebephilic, and pangynaephilic categories. Consequently, comparing incest-only offenders with incest offenders with other child victims there was equivalence in all erotic preference categories except adult. Finally, the incestuous offenders were also subdivided into those who were biologically related to their victim ($n = 44$) versus a non-biological relationship ($n = 59$). The overall chi-squared was not statistically significant and none of the comparisons between the four categories of primary erotic preference reached statistical significance.

Seto et al. (1999) reasoned that inbreeding avoidance for biological fathers ought to be overturned by paedophilic interest as assessed through penile plethysmography. They restricted their attention to female victims and, contrary to expectation, found that biological father offenders did not differ in terms of paedophilic interest from extended family member offenders or stepfather offenders. This study also failed to show differences related to a gradient of biological relatedness. Similarly, Greenberg, Firestone, Nunes, Bradford, and Curry (2005) assessed 84 biological fathers and 59 stepfathers. In addition to phallometric testing, demographic, offence-related features, the measures Cognition (distortion) Scale, Michigan Alcohol Screening Test, Derogatis Sexual Functioning Inventory, Buss–Durkee Hostility Scale, and Psychopathy Checklist were used. Recidivism was based on both unadjudicated charges and convictions and was categorized into sexual, violent, and any. No differences were found between groups on the demographic, offence-related features, psychometric measures, or recidivism. For the eight phallometric indices computed, only the paedophile index differed between groups (higher in stepfathers). The authors posited that because so many hypothesis tests were conducted, the one significant finding might potentially be artifactual (i.e., a Type I error). The overall finding was that biological fathers and stepfathers in this sample were equivalent.

Blanchard et al. (2006) used phallometric testing with 291 offenders who denied having an erotic preference for children. The six groups included were 30 biological fathers, 33 stepfathers, 29 non-paternal incest offenders (e.g., uncle), 60 unrelated molesters, 50 offenders against women, and 89 non-offenders. All child victims were 12 years of age or younger and only one victim was known for all offender groups (i.e., maximum was one victim). A measure of paedophilic interest was constructed using principal components analysis and was the sum of the response to prepubescent girls, prepubescent boys, pubescent girls, and pubescent boys minus the response to adult females and adult men. Non-offenders and offenders against women were equivalent and had the lowest index scores. Biological fathers and stepfathers were equivalent and intermediate between the first two groups and non-paternal incest offenders and unrelated molesters. These last two groups were equivalent.

Blanchard and Barbaree (2005) evaluated strength of sexual arousal in relation to age (range 13–79 years) with phallometric testing. Maximum plethysmographic response was the gold standard for classification and resulted in 264 men classified as paedophiles, 721 as hebephiles, and 1029 as teleophiles. Fourteen men responded equally to two of the three categories. No group differences or differences in relation to age were found. That is, phallometric testing as a putative index of sex drive and arousal showed no differences between the three groups formed based on primary erotic preference to age of victim in stimuli (i.e., paedophile, hebephile, and teleophile). The correlation between arousal and the inverse of age was approximately 0.5 in all three groups and also overall. As a consequence, sexual arousal declines uniformly with age across these sex offender groups and does not differ between these groups.

Using visual erotic heterosexual and homosexual stimuli, 12 adult homosexuals and 12 adult heterosexuals were assessed with a magnetic resonance scanner (Paul et al., 2008). When viewing materials relevant to their own orientation, both groups showed activation particularly in the hypothalamus, but the homosexual men had a lower magnitude of hypothalamic response than the heterosexual men. When viewing materials opposite to their orientation, both groups showed no arousal and if anything an aversive autonomic response. Apparently, there are unitary forces in nature that are not only manifested in terms of sexual arousal being uniform with respect to age across different sexual offender groups but are also manifested in the same brain mechanisms underlying sexual arousal for homosexual and heterosexual men.

Specifics of Assessment

In surveying the literature to ascertain what has already been written on the topic of assessing incest offenders, one quickly realizes that very little research has specifically addressed this particular group of offenders. This may be because of the prominent perspective that incest offenders are among the least dangerous sex offenders and that reoffence by this group is lower than that by other groups of sex offenders. After all, if this group is not in need of treatment, then why would we invest resources into developing assessment methodology specific to this subgroup? We offer a different perspective to consider. We suggest that no incest offender specific assessment protocols exist because incest offenders differ very little from other child molesters – so little that the distinctions are almost impossible to make and ultimately matter little. Furthermore, a recent meta-analysis of 89 studies (85 articles) published between 1990 and 2003 of child sexual abuse considered family factors, externalizing behaviours, internalizing behaviours, social deficits, sexual problems, and attitudes/beliefs and concluded that sexual offenders against children compared with sexual offenders against adults were equivalent except that sexual offenders against adults had higher levels of externalizing behaviours (Whitaker et al., 2008).

Why do incest offenders differ so little? Clinicians in this field realize that offending behaviour is multidetermined. The personal histories of offenders share definite themes but these are not strongly correlated with later victim characteristics. We suggest that the commonalities between offenders provide the most fertile ground on which therapists can understand how their patients have come to use sexual offending to meet their interpersonal deficits. Although we certainly support (and in fact participate in) ongoing research to understand better the differences between offender subtypes, our state of knowledge so far does not suggest that assessment and treatment efforts should differ significantly between intra-familial and extra-familial sex offenders. Additionally, the work of Whitaker et al. (2008) suggests that assessment and treatment efforts for offenders with adult victims ought to be similar to those for offenders with child victims.

As most therapists would agree that psychopathology, including sexual offending, is multidetermined, it follows that the treatment should also have multiple foci (e.g., Tharp et al., 2012). It is well established that outcome from psychotherapeutic interventions is not attributable to a single event, technique, or procedure. Rather, it is now clear that outcome for patients is multidetermined (Miller, Duncan, & Hubble, 1997; Wampold, 2001), and this is as true for sex offenders as it is for any other forensic or psychiatric patient population.

Assessment Recommendations

The Risk–Need–Responsivity (RNR) model of offender assessment and treatment (Andrews, Bonta, & Hoge, 1990) now also includes a number of other elements (Andrews & Dowden, 2007, pp. 444–445). The basic RNR elements include Risk, which entails providing more intensive treatment to higher risk individuals, Need, which involves targeting criminogenic needs, and Responsivity, which involves employing behavioural, social learning, and cognitive-behavioural treatment in response to learning styles and individual differences. Using the RNR model, programmes were found by Andrews and Dowden (2005) to be enhanced through improvements in programme integrity. Similarly, Dowden and Andrews (2004) found that staff practice improvements enhanced the effects of programmes. Dowden and Andrews (1999) also found that the RNR model was relevant for reducing recidivism in female offenders. Criticisms of the model underlying RNR have been provided (Polaschek, 2012; Ward, Melser, & Yates, 2007) and extensions for including the Good Lives Model have been discussed (Andrews, Bonta, & Wormith, 2011; Ward, Yates, & Willis, 2012). Of particular relevance is work examining the applicability of the RNR model to sex offenders (Harkins & Beech, 2007). Harkins and Beech view Risk as the static risk of the individual, view Need as the dynamic risk factors of the individual, and argue that in addition to Responsivity, process issues (i.e., group processes/cohesion/environment, group composition/environment, and therapist characteristics) are also essential.

In working with patients in a psychological or psychiatric capacity, it is fundamental to begin with a thorough assessment. However, busy clinicians sometimes adopt a routine assessment battery and forget to clarify exactly what they are assessing for and to what end the results will be used. An initial assessment conducted for the court during some part of the trial process will often elicit little from the patient that is not already known information. Given the potential negative consequences of being forthright with an assessor during this part of the judicial process, it may be important simply to determine if the patient is willing to acknowledge known facts of the offence.

If we can expect to find relatively little 'new' information, what then can we learn from the patient's presentation? If an offender tends towards blaming the victim, what can we conclude? If the patient glosses over the details of their offence(s), what use can we make of this in an assessment? Unfortunately, these are the kinds of points where we often make assumptions that are grounded only in our own personal biases. Sometimes clinicians conclude that a patient is 'not ready' for treatment if they tend to blame the victim, or they are denying responsibility if they minimize the details or the impact of their crime(s). We suggest that very little should be made of how patients present in the early stages of the assessment/treatment process.

As a rule, sex offenders do not suddenly conclude one day that they should commit a sexual assault. More commonly, there is a process of rationalization and erosion of boundaries that occurs over some period of time making a sexual offence increasingly 'reasonable' or 'justified' to the patient. We suggest that this process is especially true of intra-familial offenders. For those assessing for the purpose of providing treatment, it should be an assumption that all sex offenders rationalize and justify their behaviour – the only question is to what extent and under what circumstances. Therefore, our practice has been to accept virtually any offender into treatment provided they acknowledge that they were in fact present when the offence took place, and that they express some willingness to participate in treatment.

Sexual fantasies and masturbation figure prominently in the lives of many sex offenders. However, during an assessment period, patients are unlikely to be candid about these aspects of their sexuality (cf., Maletzky, 1991). Clinicians are most likely to be provided with adamant denial of fantasy and of masturbation, or some approximation of what patients think clinicians want to hear. A third presentation that is sometimes observed is when patients over-endorse their sexual fantasies for shock value or to test the therapist's level of comfort.

Here again, we need to reflect on the meanings we would make of the information provided by the offender. If they reported on assessment that they had many deviant fantasies, what would this really tell us and how would this direct their treatment? Studies have reported that some offenders have many deviant sexual fantasies, whereas others do not (e.g., Langevin, Lang, & Curnoe, 1998). Intuitively, we would think that having more deviant fantasies will make an offender more dangerous, but that connection has not been demonstrated. In fact, a study of adolescent sex offenders in residential treatment found that patients often reported very high frequencies of deviant fantasies and masturbation, but no members of the sample were known to have committed another offence during the study period despite residing in an open custody setting (Aylwin, Reddon, & Burke, 2005). Hence a high frequency of deviant fantasies apparently does not make sex offenders imminently dangerous. It *may* be a necessary condition, but not a sufficient one to cause offending.

In criminal populations, and for sex offenders also, the general finding is that measures of general intelligence are roughly half a standard deviation below the mean. Another well-known result is that most offenders have non-verbal abilities that are superior to their verbal abilities (e.g., Marceau, Meghani, & Reddon, 2008; Studer & Reddon, 1998). Relative to acute psychiatric patients and normal controls, Marceau et al. found that a heterogeneous sample of offenders were intermediate on intelligence and also a number of other neuropsychological measures. In addition, it is often the case that offenders have not done well in school, a finding that epitomizes difficulties with their general life adjustment (such as marital and vocational issues; e.g., Langevin & Curnoe, 2011; Reddon, Takacs, & Hogan, 2013). If there is any question in the mind of the assessor about the patient's cognitive capabilities, an IQ assessment and possibly a neuropsychological assessment should be conducted. It is far less relevant if the patient has an IQ in the upper end of the normal range or above (i.e., greater than the mean), and much more relevant if he has deficits that might present unique challenges to treatment. However, accurately discerning which individuals are above average intelligence based on presentation and history is difficult. A diagnosed learning disability is common in sex offenders (Langevin & Curnoe) and would highlight ways in which treatment delivery may need to be modified. It might also point to aspects in the offender's life (e.g., school) that might have been especially difficult or frustrating.

Finally, some assessment of risk of reoffending may be undertaken (for various instruments and some issues, see Studer, Aylwin, Sribney, & Reddon, 2011; for some comparisons and derivation of four dimensions to consider, namely criminal history, persistent criminal lifestyle, antisocial personality, and alcohol/mental health issues, see Kroner, Mills, & Reddon, 2005; for how risk can change with treatment, see Studer, Aylwin, & Reddon, 2005 and Studer & Reddon, 1998). Langevin and Curnoe (2011) did not find that the Psychopathy Checklist-R (PCL-R) predicted sex offender recidivism except that the historical items did predict general recidivism, a finding consistent with the work of Kennedy, Skeem, and Walters (2010) on violence prediction with the PCL-R. It would be worthwhile to have an assessment of criminal history, lifestyle, antisocial personality, and alcohol/substance abuse in addition to mental health issues. A more inclusive detailed social history would be desirable, in addition to a basic medical assessment and history. Finally, in addition to a multidimensional assessment of psychopathology/psychosocial adjustment (e.g., Jackson's Basic Personality Inventory, Livesely's Dimensional Assessment of Personality and Psychopathology, or Morey's Personality Assessment Inventory), it would be desirable to have a personality assessment of the motivational system (i.e., Murray's needs; e.g., Jackson's Personality Research Form-E) and an assessment of dimensions of social psychological constructs (i.e., values and attitudes; e.g., Jackson Personality Inventory – Revised).

Discussion

The evidence reviewed in this chapter has significant implications for the assessment and treatment of incest offenders. First and foremost is that clinicians should put only limited emphasis on the fact that a patient presents as an incest offender. It is very likely that the patient will have, in fact, committed other sexual offences against other victims that may or may not be known to authorities. Because of the extent of victim crossover, general recidivism risk for incest offenders may be underestimated with current algorithms.

Second, erotic preference testing should be regarded as a crude clinical indicator at best. This is for two reasons. There has been significant variation reported in the literature with regard to its predictive validity and general reliability (Marshall & Fernandez,

2000). If erotic preference testing were a reliable assessment method, one would expect more consistency in the literature. More vexing, however, is the meanings that can or should be made of the results of a patient's testing. The field has adopted jargon such as more or less deviant, which in turn has been associated with more or less dangerous. In the absence of other data, these crude distinctions may have some utility, but they ignore a fundamental truth about offending behaviour. By virtue of the fact that an offender has sexually assaulted at least one victim, their history demonstrates that future assaultive behaviour is a potential outcome given the collision of specific life events, stressors, and circumstances (i.e., stress–vulnerability interplay). Assessment, therefore, is best focused on what all those factors are for any given offender. Whether they assaulted within the family or outside the family may have everything to do with what they could rationalize away, what they felt they could get away with, or the opportunities they were able to create, and almost nothing to do with unique preferences for a victim type.

Third, one should cast the net far and wide and make the offer of treatment to as many patients as possible. Most patients have never been exposed to a therapeutic experience and many have long-standing interpersonal difficulties originating in the family of origin and extending into adulthood. Many offenders (and indeed many non-offenders who enter treatment) only come to see the merit of therapy once they have witnessed the positive results displayed by other group members (cf., Reddon, Payne, & Starzyk, 1999; Yalom & Leszcz, 2005). Our clinical observation in working with many hundreds of sex offenders is that some patients who initially seem unlikely to progress well in treatment will actually do very well. Alternatively, some patients who initially present as being cooperative and self-reflective end up demonstrating that they are extremely rigid and not receptive to ideas put forward by the therapist or the group. Therefore, let us not be lulled into over-confidence or over-interpret what we find in our assessments of the offenders with whom we work. The reality is that we likely have more to learn from them than we have to teach them.

References

Abel, G. G., Becker, J. V., Cunningham-Rathner, J., Mittelman, M., & Rouleau, J.-L. (1988). Multiple paraphilic diagnoses among sex offenders. *Bulletin of the American Academy of Psychiatry and Law, 16*, 153–168.

Abu-Baker, K. (2013). Arab parents' reactions to child sexual abuse: A review of clinical records. *Journal of Child Sexual Abuse, 22*, 52–71. doi:10.1080/10538712.2013.744378

Adams, A. (2009). Seen but not heard: Child sexual abuse, incest, and the law in the United States. *Utah Law Review, 2009*, 11, 591–598.

Andrews, D. A., Bonta, J., & Hoge, R. D. (1990). Classification for effective rehabilitation: Rediscovering psychology. *Criminal Justice and Behavior, 17*, 19–52. doi:10.1177/0093854890017001004

Andrews, D. A., Bonta, J., & Wormith, S. J. (2011). The Risk–Need–Responsivity (RNR) model: Does adding the Good Lives Model contribute to effective crime prevention? *Criminal Justice and Behavior, 38*, 735–755. doi:10.1177/0093854811406356

Andrews, D. A., & Dowden, C. (2005). Managing correctional treatment for reduced recidivism: A meta-analytic review of programme integrity. *Legal and Criminological Psychology, 10*, 173–187. doi:10.1348/135532505X36723

Andrews, D. A., & Dowden, C. (2007). The Risk–Need–Responsivity model of assessment and human service in prevention and corrections: Crime-prevention jurisprudence. *Canadian Journal of Criminology, 49*, 439–464. doi:10.3138/cjccj.49.4.439

Argentieri, S. (2005). Incest yesterday and today: From conflict to ambiguity. In G. Ambrosio (Ed.), *On incest: Psychoanalytic perspectives* (pp. 17–49). Exeter, England: International Psychoanalytic Association.

Atwood, J. D. (2007). When love hurts: Preadolescent girls' reports of incest. *American Journal of Family Therapy, 35*, 287–313. doi:10.1080/01926180701389644

Aylwin, A. S., Reddon, J. R., & Burke, A. (2005). Sexual fantasies of adolescent male sex offenders in residential treatment: A descriptive study. *Archives of Sexual Behavior, 34*, 231–239. doi:10.1007/s10508-005-1800-3

Barsetti, I., Earls, C. M., Lalumière, M. L., & Belanger, N. (1998). The differentiation of intrafamilial and extrafamilial heterosexual child molesters. *Journal of Interpersonal Violence, 13*, 275–286. doi:10.1177/088626098013002007

Barth, J., Bermetz, L., Helm, E., Trelle, S., & Tonia, T. (2013). The current prevalence of child sexual abuse worldwide: A systematic review a meta-analysis. *International Journal of Public Health, 58*, 469–483. doi:10.1007/s00038-012-0426-1

Bischof, N. (1972). The biological foundations of the incest taboo. *Social Science and Information, 11*, 7–36. doi:10.1177/053901847201100601

Blanchard, R., & Barbaree, H. E. (2005). The strength of sexual arousal as a function of the age of the sex offender: Comparisons among pedophiles, hebephiles, and teleophiles. *Sexual Abuse: A Journal of Research and Treatment, 17*, 441–456. doi:10.1177/107906320501700407

Blanchard, R., Kuban, M. E., Blak, T., Cantor, J. M., Klassen, P., & Dickey, R. (2006). Phallometric comparison of pedophilic interest in nonadmitting sexual offenders against stepdaughters, biological daughters, other biologically related girls, and unrelated girls. *Sexual Abuse: A Journal of Research and Treatment, 18*, 1–14. doi:10.1177/107906320601800101

Bloch, S., Chodoff, P., & Green, S. A. (1999). *Psychiatric ethics.* New York, NY: Oxford University Press.

Bolen, R. M. (2002). *Child sexual abuse: Its scope and our failure.* New York, NY: Kluwer.

Brown, A. (2013). *Marquis de Sade's Incest (completed 1799 in French in prison with the title Eugénie de Franval).* Richmond, England: Alma Classics.

Burley, N. (1983). The meaning of assortative mating. *Ethology and Sociobiology, 4*, 191–203. doi:10.1016/0162-3095(83)90009-2

Canada Law Book. (2010). *Martin's annual criminal code 2011.* Aurora, Canada: Author.

Cann, J., Friendship, C., & Gozna, L. (2007). Assessing crossover in a sample of sexual offenders with multiple victims. *Legal and Criminological Psychology, 12*, 149–163. doi:10.1348/135532506X112439

Carlson, B. E., Maciol, K., & Schneider, J. (2006). Sibling incest: Reports from forty-one survivors. *Journal of Child Sexual Abuse, 15*, 19–33. doi:10.1300/J070v15n04_02

Cochran, W. G., Mosteller, F., & Tukey, J. W. (1953). Statistical problems of the Kinsey report. *Journal of the American Statistical Association, 48*, 673–716.

Cohen, Y. (1969). Ends and means in political control: State organization and the punishment of adultery, incest, and violation of celibacy. *American Anthropologist, 71*, 658–687.

Cohen, Y. (1978). The disappearance of the incest taboo. *Human Nature, 1*, 72–78.

Coleman, J. A. (2011). *The dictionary of mythology.* London, England: Arcturus.

Conte, J. R. (1991). The nature of sexual offenses against children. In C. R. Hollin & K. Howells (Eds.), *Clinical approaches to sex offenders and their victims* (pp. 11–34). Chichester, England: John Wiley & Sons, Ltd.

Cossins, A. (2011). The behavior of serial child sex offenders: Implications for the prosecution of child sex offences in joint trials. *Melbourne University Law Review, 35*, 821–864.

Cournut-Janin, M. (2005). Incest: The crushed fantasy. In G. Ambrosio (Ed.), *On incest: Psychoanalytic perspectives* (pp. 65–80). Exeter, England: International Psychoanalytic Association.

Donalek, J. G. (2001). First incest disclosure. *Issues in Mental Health Nursing, 22*, 573–591. doi:10.1080/016128401750364129

Dowden, C., & Andrews, D. A. (1999). What works for female offenders: A meta-analytic review. *Crime and Delinquency, 45*, 438–452. doi:10.1177/0011128799045004002

Dowden, C., & Andrews, D. A. (2004). The importance of staff practice in delivering effective correctional treatment: A meta-analytic review of core correctional practice. *International Journal of Offender Therapy and Comparative Criminology, 48*, 203–214. doi:10.1177/0306624X03257765

Firestone, P., Bradford, J. M., McCoy, M., Greenberg, D. M., Larose, M. R., & Curry, S. (1999). Prediction of recidivism in incest offenders. *Journal of Interpersonal Violence, 14*, 511–531. doi:10.1177/088626099014005004

Freud, S. (2001). *Totem and taboo: Some points of agreement between the mental lives of savages and neurotics.* (Original work published 1913). London, England: Routledge.

Gebhard, P. H., Gagnon, J. H., Pomeroy, W. B., & Christenson, C. V. (1965). *Sex offenders: An analysis of types.* New York, NY: Harper & Row.

Goode, S. D. (2011). *Paedophiles in society: Reflecting on sexuality, abuse and hope.* Basingstoke, England: Palgrave Macmillan.

Greenberg, D., Bradford, J., Firestone, P., & Curry, S. (2000). Recidivism of child molesters: A study of victim relationship with the perpetrator. *Child Abuse & Neglect, 24*, 1485–1494. doi:10.1016/S0145-2134(00)00197-6

Greenberg, D. M., Firestone, P., Nunes, K. L., Bradford, J. M., & Curry, S. (2005). Biological fathers and stepfathers who molest their daughters: Psychological, phallometric, and criminal features. *Sexual Abuse: A Journal of Research and Treatment, 17*, 39–46. doi:10.1177/107906320501700105

Hall, N., Mercer, L., Phillips, D., Shaw, J., & Anderson, A. D. (2012). Maximum likelihood estimation of individual inbreeding coefficients and null allele frequencies. *Genetics Research, 94*, 151–161. doi:10.1017/S0016672312000341

Harkins, L., & Beech, A. R. (2007). A review of the factors that can influence the effectiveness of sexual offender treatment: Risk, need, responsivity, and process issues. *Aggression and Violent Behavior, 12*, 615–627. doi:10.1016/j.avb.2006.10.006

Herman, J., & Hirschman, L. (1981). Families at risk for father–daughter incest. *American Journal of Psychiatry, 138*, 967–970. doi:10.1007/978-1-4684-4754-5_17

Hoben, A. D., Buunk, A. P., Fincher, C. L., Thornhill, R., & Schaller, M. (2010). On the adaptive origins and maladaptive consequences of human inbreeding: Parasite prevalence, immune functioning, and consanguineous marriage. *Evolutionary Psychology, 8*, 658–676.

Hufford, K. M., Krauss, S. L., & Veneklaas, E. J. (2012). Inbreeding and outbreeding depression in *Stylidium hipsidum*: Implications for mixing seed sources for ecological restoration. *Ecology and Evolution, 2*, 2262–2273. doi:10.1002/ece3.302

Kardam, F., & Bademci, E. (2013). Mothers in cases of incest in Turkey: Views and experiences of professionals. *Journal of Family Violence, 28*, 253–263. doi:10.1007/s10896-013-9495-z

Kennedy, P. J., Skeem, J. L., & Walters, G. D. (2010). Do core interpersonal and affective traits of PCL-R psychopathy interact with antisocial behavior and disinhibition to predict violence? *Psychological Assessment, 22,* 569–580. doi:10.1037/a0019618

Kinsey, A. C., Hyman, H., Sheatsley, P. B., Hobbs, A. H., Lambert, R. D., Pastore, N., ... Tukey, J. W. (1955). The Cochran–Mosteller–Tukey report on the Kinsey study: A symposium. *Journal of the American Statistical Association, 50,* 811–829.

Kinsey, A. C., Pomeroy, W. B., & Martin, C. E. (1948). *Sexual behavior in the human male.* Philadelphia, PA: Saunders.

Kinsey, A. C., Pomeroy, W. B., Martin, C. E., & Gebhard, P. H. (1953). *Sexual behavior in the human female.* Philadelphia, PA: Saunders.

Kleban, H., Chesin, M. S., Jeglic, E. L., & Mercado, C. C. (2012). An exploration of crossover sexual offending. *Sexual Abuse: A Journal of Research and Treatment, 25,* 427–443. doi:10.1177/1079063212464397

Kroner, D. G., Mills, J. F., & Reddon, J. R. (2005). A coffee can, factor analysis, and prediction of antisocial behavior: The structure of criminal risk. *International Journal of Law and Psychiatry, 28,* 360–374. doi:10.1016/j.ijlp.2004.01.011

Langevin, R., & Curnoe, S. (2011). Psychopathy, ADHD, and brain dysfunction as predictors of lifetime recidivism among sex offenders. *International Journal of Offender Therapy and Comparative Criminology, 55,* 5–26. doi:10.1177/0306624X09360968

Langevin, R., & Curnoe, S. (2012). Lifetime criminal history of sex offenders seen for psychological assessment in five decades. *International Journal of Offender Therapy and Comparative Criminology, 56,* 997–1021. doi:10.1177/0306624X11420084

Langevin, R., Curnoe, S., Fedoroff, P., Bennett, R., Langevin, M., Peever, C., ... Sandhu, S. (2004). Lifetime sex offender recidivism: A 25-year follow-up study. *Canadian Journal of Criminology and Criminal Justice, 46,* 531–552. doi:10.3138/cjccj.46.5.531

Langevin, R., Lang, R. A., & Curnoe, S. (1998). The prevalence of sex offenders with deviant fantasies. *Journal of Interpersonal Violence, 13,* 315–327. doi:10.1177/088626098013003001

Leavitt, G. C. (1989). Disappearance of the incest taboo: A cross-cultural test of general evolutionary hypotheses. *American Anthropologist, 91,* 116–131. doi:10.1525/aa.1989.91.1.02a00070

Lewin, R. (1989). Inbreeding costs swamp benefits. *Science, 243,* 482. doi:10.1126/science.2911755

Maletzky, B. M. (1991). *Treating the sexual offender.* Newbury Park, CA: Sage.

Marceau, R., Meghani, R., & Reddon, J. R. (2008). Neuropsychological assessment of adult offenders. *Journal of Offender Rehabilitation, 47*(1/2), 41–73. doi:10.1080/10509670801940409

Marshall, W. L. (2006). Clinical and research limitations in the use of phallometric testing with sexual offenders. *Sexual Offender Treatment, 1,* 1–18.

Marshall, W. L., & Fernandez, Y. M. (2000). Phallometric testing with sexual offenders: Limits to its value. *Clinical Psychology Review, 20,* 807–822. doi:10.1016/S0272-7358(99)00013-6

Martin, C. (2004). *Ovid metamorphoses (completed in Latin, AD 8).* New York, NY: Norton.

McElvaney, R., Greene, S., & Hogan, D. (2012). Containing the secret of child sexual abuse. *Journal of Interpersonal Violence, 27,* 1155–1175. doi:10.1177/0886260511424503

Meyer-Rochow, V. B. (2009). Food taboos: Their origins and purposes. *Journal of Ethnobiology and Ethnomedicine, 5,* 18. doi:10.1186/1746-4269-5-18

Middleton, W. (2013a). Ongoing incestuous abuse during adulthood. *Journal of Trauma & Dissociation, 14,* 251–272. doi:10.1080/15299732.2012.736932

Middleton, W. (2013b). Parent–child incest that extends into adulthood: A survey of international press reports, 2007–2011. *Journal of Trauma & Dissociation*, *14*, 184–197. doi:10.1080/15299732.2013.724341

Miller, S. D., Duncan, B. L., & Hubble, M. A. (1997). *Escape from Babel*. New York, NY: Norton.

Mohl, A. (2010). Sexual abuse of the child: A treatment model for the incestuous family. *The Journal of Psychohistory*, *38*, 168–181.

Nabokov, V. (1955). *Lolita (completed in prison)*. New York, NY: Vintage.

Parker, S. (1976). The precultural basis of the incest taboo: Toward a biosocial theory. *American Anthropologist*, *78*, 285–305. doi:10.1525/aa.1976.78.2.02a00030

Patterson, M. (2005). Coming too close, going too far: Theoretical and cross-cultural approaches to incest and its prohibition. *Australian Journal of Anthropology*, *16*, 95–115. doi:10.1111/j.1835-9310.2005.tb00112.x

Paul, T., Schiffer, B., Zwarg, T., Krüger, T. H. C., Karama, S., Schedlowski, M., … Gizewski, E. R. (2008). Brain response to visual stimuli in heterosexual and homosexual males. *Human Brain Mapping*, *29*, 726–735. doi:10.1002/hbm.20435

Pekkala, N., Knott, K. E., Kotiaho, J. S., & Puurtinen, M. (2012). Inbreeding rate modifies the dynamics of genetic load in small populations. *Ecology and Evolution*, *2*, 1791–1804. doi:10.1002/ece3.293

Pereda, N., Guilera, G., Forns, M., & Gómez-Benito, J. (2009). The prevalence of child sexual abuse in community and student samples: A meta-analysis. *Clinical Psychology Review*, *29*, 328–338. doi:10.1016/j-cpr.2009.02.007

Phelan, P. (1986). The process of incest: Biologic father and stepfather families. *Child Abuse and Neglect*, *10*, 531–539. doi:10.1016/0145-2134(86)90058-X

Polaschek, D. L. L. (2012). An appraisal of the Risk–Need–Responsivity (RNR) model of offender rehabilitation and its application to correctional treatment. *Legal and Criminological Psychology*, *17*, 1–17. doi:10.1111/j.2044-8333.2011.2038.x

Ralls, K., Ballou, J. D., & Templeton, A. (1988). Estimates of lethal equivalents and the cost of inbreeding in mammals. *Conseveration Biology*, *2*, 185–193. doi:10.1111/j.1523-1739.1988.tb00169.x

Reddon, J. R., Payne, L. R., & Starzyk, K. B. (1999). Therapeutic factors in group treatment evaluated by sex offenders: A consumers' report. *Journal of Offender Rehabilitation*, *28*(3/4), 91–101. doi:10.1300/J076v28n03_06

Reddon, J. R., Takacs, S., & Hogan, S. (2013). Sex Offender Situational Competency Test (SOSCT) pretreatment and posttreatment effects for inpatient sex offenders in hypothetical high-risk situations. *Journal of Offender Rehabilitation*, *52*, 16–18. doi:10.1080/10509674.2012.720958

Rettenberger, M., Matthes, A., Boer, D. P., & Eher, R. (2010). Prospective actuarial risk assessment: A comparison of five risk assessment instruments in different sexual offender subtypes. *International Journal of Offender Therapy and Comparative Criminology*, *54*, 169–186. doi:10.1177/0306624X08328755

Rudd, J. M., & Herzberger, S. D. (1999). Brother–sister incest – father–daughter incest: A comparison of characteristics and consequences. *Child Abuse & Neglect*, *23*, 915–928. doi:10.1016/S0145-2134(99)00058-7

Sariola, H., & Uutela, A. (1996). The prevalence and context of incest abuse in Finland. *Child Abuse & Neglect*, *20*, 843–850. doi:10.1016/0145-2134(96)00072-5

Seto, M. C., Lalumière, M. L., & Kaban, M. (1999). The sexual preferences of incest offenders. *Journal of Abnormal Psychology*, *108*, 267–272. doi:10.1037//0021-843X.108.2.267

Sim, D. J., & Proeve, M. (2010). Crossover and stability of victim type in child molesters. *Legal and Criminological Psychology*, *15*, 401–413. doi:10.1348/135532509X473869

Sokal, R. R. (1974). Classification: Purposes, principles, progress, prospects. *Science, 185*, 1115–1123. doi:10.1126/science.185.4157.1115

Steed, J. J., & Templer, D. I. (2010). Gay men and lesbian women with molestation history: Impact on sexual orientation and experience of pleasure. *Open Psychology Journal, 3*, 36–41. doi:10.2174/1874350101003010036

Stigler, S. M. (1999). *Statistics on the table: The history of statistical concepts and methods*. Cambrige, MA: Harvard University Press.

Stoltenborgh, M., van Ijzendoorn, M. H., Euser, E. M., & Bakermans-Kraneburg, M. J. (2011). A global perspective on child sexual abuse: A meta-analysis of prevalence around the world. *Child Maltreatment, 16*, 79–101. doi:10.1177/1077559511403920

Stroebel, S. S., O'Keefe, S. L., Beard, K. W., Kou, S.-Y., Swindell, S. V. S., & Kommor, M. J. (2012). Father–daughter incest: Data from an anonymous computerized survey. *Journal of Child Sexual Abuse, 21*, 176–199. doi:10.1080/10538712.2012.654007

Stroebel, S. S., O'Keefe, S., Beard, K. W., Kuo, S.-Y., Swindell, S., & Stroupe, W. (2013a). Brother–sister incest: Data from anonymous computer-assisted self interviews. *Journal of Child Sexual Abuse, 22*, 255–276. doi:10.1080/10538712.2013.743952

Stroebel, S. S., O'Keefe, S. L., Griffee, K., Kuo, S.-Y., Beard, K. W., & Kommor, M. J. (2013b). Sister–sister incest: Data from an anonymous computerized survey. *Journal of Child Sexual Abuse, 22*, 695–719. doi:10.1080/10538712.2013.811140

Studer, L. H., & Aylwin, A. S. (2006). Pedophilia: The problem with diagnosis and limitations of CBT in treatment. *Medical Hypotheses, 67*, 774–781. doi:10.1016/j.mehy.2006.04.030

Studer, L. H., Aylwin, A. S., Clelland, S. R., Reddon, J. R., & Frenzel, R. R. (2002). Primary erotic preference in a group of child molesters. *International Journal of Law and Psychiatry, 25*, 173–180. doi:10.1016/S0160-2527(01)00111-X

Studer, L. H., Aylwin, A. S., & Reddon, J. R. (2005). Testosterone, sexual offense recidivism, and treatment effect among adult male sex offenders. *Sexual Abuse: A Journal of Research and Treatment, 17*, 171–181. doi:10.1007/s11194--005-4603-0

Studer, L. H., Aylwin, A. S., Sribney, C., & Reddon, J. R. (2011). Uses, misuses, and abuses of risk assessment with sexual offenders. In D. P. Boer, R. Eher, L. A. Craig, M. H. Miner, & F. Pfäfflin (Eds.), *International perspectives on the assessment and treatment of sexual offenders: Theory, practice, and research* (pp. 193–212). Chichester, England: John Wiley & Sons, Ltd.

Studer, L. H., Clelland, S. R., Aylwin, A. S., Reddon, J. R., & Monro, A. (2000). Rethinking risk assessment for incest offenders. *International Journal of Law and Psychiatry, 23*, 15–22. doi:10.1016/S0160-2527(99)00002-3

Studer, L. H., & Reddon, J. R. (1998). Treatment may change risk prediction for sexual offenders. *Sexual Abuse: A Journal of Research and Treatment, 10*, 175–181. doi:10.1177/107906329801000302

Tesone, J. E. (2005). Incest(s) and the negation of otherness. In G. Ambrosio (Ed.), *On incest: Psychoanalytic perspectives* (pp. 51–64). Exeter, England: International Psychoanalytic Association.

Tharp, A. T., DeGue, S., Valle, L. A., Brookmeyer, K. A., Massetti, G. M., & Matjasko, J. L. (2012). A systematic qualitative review of risk and protective factors for sexual violence perpetration. *Trauma, Violence, & Abuse, 14*, 133–167. doi:10.1177/1524838012470031

Thornhill, N. W. (1991). An evolutionary analysis of rules regulating human inbreeding and marriage. *Behavioral and Brain Sciences, 14*, 247–260. doi:10.1017/S0140525X00066449

Tidefors, I., Arvidsson, H., Ingevaldson, S., & Larsson, M. (2010). Sibling incest: A review of the literature and a clinical study. *Journal of Sexual Aggression*, *16*, 347–360. doi:10.1080/13552600903511667

Wampold, B. E. (2001). *The great psychotherapy debate: Models, methods, and findings*. Mahwah, NJ: Erlbaum.

Ward, T., Melser, J., & Yates, P. M. (2007). Reconstructing the Risk–Need–Responsivity model: A theoretical elaboration and evaluation. *Aggression and Violent Behavior*, *12*, 208–228. doi:10.1016/j.avb.2006.07.001

Ward, T., Yates, P. M., & Willis, G. M. (2012). The Good Lives Model and the Risk Need Responsivity Model: A critical response to Andrews, Bonta, and Wormith (2011). *Criminal Justice and Behavior*, *39*, 94–110. doi:10.1177/0093854811426085

Whitaker, D. J., Le, B., Hanson, R. K., Baker, C. K., McMahon, P. M., Ryan, G., ... Rice, D. D. (2008). Risk factors for the perpetration of child sexual abuse: A review and meta-analysis. *Child Abuse & Neglect*, *32*, 529–548. doi:10.1016/j.chiabu.2007.08.005

Wilson, R. F. (2004). Recognizing the threat posed by an incestuous parent to the victim's siblings: Part I: Appraising the risk. *Journal of Child and Family Studies*, *13*, 143–162. doi:10.1023/B:JCFS.0000015704.40389.56

Yalom, I. D., & Leszcz, M. (2005). *The theory and practice of group psychotherapy* (5th ed.). New York, NY: Basic Books.

Zhou, S., Zhou, C., & Pannell, J. R. (2010). Genetic load, inbreeding depression and heterosis in an age-structured metapopulation. *Journal of Evolutionary Biology*, *22*, 2324–2332. doi:10.1111/j.1420-9101.2010.02091.x

52

Assessment of Sexual Homicide Offenders

Kevin J. Kerr

Ashworth Hospital, United Kingdom

Anthony R. Beech

University of Birmingham, United Kingdom

Introduction

Compared with other areas of sexual offending, the study of sexually motivated, lethal violence is an underresearched field. Empirical investigation into the offence tends to be problematic because of methodological and practical obstacles, such as crime-incidence problems and scarce, incomplete, or inaccurate information due to legal restrictions or personal motives to lie, exaggerate, and distort (Maniglio, 2010; Schlesinger, 2007). The crime has also been notoriously difficult to define (Kerr, Beech, & Murphy, 2013). Most authors appear to agree, however, that for a homicide to be considered 'sexual', evidence of sexual activity of some kind by the perpetrator must be present. Sexual activity might occur before, during, or after the killing, or indeed throughout the event (e.g., Porter, Woodworth, Earle, Drugge, & Boer, 2003) and could range from masturbation to actual penetration of the victim (oral, anal, or vaginal) with a variety of objects, animate or inanimate. For some authors, however, a homicide need not contain any evidence of sexual activity at all to be labelled 'sexual', since the brutal act itself may be a substitute for the sexual act (Revitch, 1965; Schlesinger, 2004, 2007). In such cases, unless the offender is completely open about his motive for the attack, the sexual element may go unnoticed.

With all the difficulties inherent in defining the term, estimating the prevalence of sexual homicide is difficult. Thankfully, however, most authors would agree that cases are rare, perhaps representing between 0.2 and 3.7% of all homicides committed annually in the United Kingdom (Francis & Soothill, 2000), Canada (Porter et al., 2003), the United States (US Department of Justice, Federal Bureau of Investigation, Criminal Justice Information Services Division, 2012), and Finland

The Wiley Handbook on the Theories, Assessment, and Treatment of Sexual Offending.
Edited by Douglas P. Boer. Volume II: Assessment, edited by Leam A. Craig and Martin Rettenberger.
© 2017 John Wiley & Sons, Ltd. Published 2017 by John Wiley & Sons, Ltd.

(Häkkänen-Nyholm, Repo-Tiihonen, Lindberg, Salenius, & Weizmann-Henelius, 2009). Most offenders are males who kill adult women, and most do not fall into the category of serial killer (Campus & Cusson, 2007; Kerr et al., 2013). In addition to using different definitions, researchers have also used different terms to account for sexual homicide, and these are often used interchangeably. From lust murder to sexual murder and even erotophonophilia, many have been employed but they do not necessarily mean the same thing.

Because it makes no assumption about the motivation of the offender, the term 'sexual homicide' will be used for the purposes of this chapter. Although lagging behind other areas of forensic practice, there has been a growth of interest in this area over the past 15 years or so. Our aim here is to cover some of that research in respect of assessing such clients with a view to developing a thorough psychological understanding of their offence, potential for repetition, and possible means of treatment. The chapter begins by looking at the assessment process and the need to gather as much information as possible. We then go on to discuss common features that might be associated with the psychosocial development of incarcerated sexual homicide offenders (SHOs). We subsequently explore the potential contributions of various forms of psychopathology, anger, cognition, genetics, and neurology, and also situational factors and disinhibitors when formulating an offence. We focus our attention on adult male perpetrators who target adult women because this is where almost all of the research lies. We occasionally refer to offenders with multiple victims, but owing to their rarity we concentrate mainly on the literature exploring non-serial offenders.

The Assessment Process

The assessment of SHOs or of those charged with or convicted of a homicide with a suspected sexual element needs to be comprehensive and should include the use of collateral information, different modalities of assessment, and the testing of hypotheses throughout (Perkins, 2007). The literature is replete with cases of sexual homicide in which the perpetrator has tried just about anything to rid them of responsibility. The American serial killer Kenneth Bianchi, for example, managed to fool several experienced clinicians into believing that he had a split personality before he was eventually caught out; and another serial offender, John Wayne Gacy, deflected his guilt for years after apprehension by blaming other people for his crimes, despite irrefutable evidence, right up to his execution. Once a sexual element has been established in a case, the long process of formulating how significant that element was in terms of understanding risk and treatment, and also other factors that might contribute to the offence, can progress. We do not advocate any one definition of the offence over another, but strongly advise against using definitions based upon motive. Motivation can only be established through an interactive process of assessment using multiple sources of evidence (Kerr et al., 2013; Perkins, 2007). However, the criteria first formulated by the FBI to assist law enforcement officers in their identification of suspected sexual homicides in the 1980s are a useful place to start (see Box 52.1).

Box 52.1 FBI criteria for the identification of sexual homicides

1. The victim is found totally or partially naked
2. The genitals are exposed
3. The body is found in a sexually explicit position
4. An object has been inserted into a body cavity (anus, vagina, or mouth)
5. There is evidence of sexual contact
6. There is evidence of substitute sexual activity (e.g., masturbation and ejaculation at the crime scene) or of sadistic sexual fantasies (e.g., genital mutilation)

Source: Ressler et al. (1988).

For the most part, SHOs do not differ significantly from sexual aggressors of women who do not kill their victims (Beech, Oliver, Fisher & Beckett, 2005b; Chéné & Cusson, 2007). However, when assessing such offenders, actuarial risk assessment approaches are of limited utility, given the rarity of such cases in development samples (Hill et al., 2012; Kingston & Yates, 2008). Structured professional judgement tools such as the Risk of Sexual Violence Protocol (Hart et al., 2003) help to create a useful structure. We now explore in detail some of the key areas that are important in the assessment of SHOs. In order to reach a comprehensive, detailed, and useful formulation of the offence, it is of course important to consider how each factor may link with others. We do not focus on the process of formulation in this chapter.

Psychosocial Development

There is evidence to suggest that many SHOs grow up in chaotic family environments and thus demonstrate abnormal, often antisocial, behaviour in childhood and adolescence (Burgess, Hartman, Ressler, Douglas, & McCormack, 1986; Chéné & Cusson, 2007). FBI profilers in the United States were among the first group of researchers to study the social antecedents of sexual homicide (Ressler, Burgess, & Douglas, 1988). They produced a motivational model of the offence, which was later extended by Hickey (1997) and Arrigo and Purcell (2001). Ressler et al. found that a majority of offenders came from family backgrounds containing physical and/or sexual abuse, inadequate attachment, inadequate interpersonal relationships, and criminality. An early retreat into fantasy may compensate for the absence of real-life control and then later, as the child develops, negative personality traits, such as rebelliousness, hostility, and feelings of entitlement emerge and are translated into behaviours such as habitual lying, cruelty towards animals, juvenile delinquency, adult criminality, and ultimately sexual homicide.

Contemporary research studies support these findings and some have also investigated whether the developmental histories of SHOs differ from those of sexual aggressors who do not kill their victims. In a study by Nicole and Proulx (2007), it was found that SHOs were significantly more likely than sexual aggressors to have been the victim of both incest and physical violence prior to the age of 18 years. Milsom, Beech, and Webster (2003) also reported a higher frequency of self-disclosed physical abuse in childhood among SHOs than a comparison sample of rapists. In terms of problematic behaviour during childhood and adolescence, Nicole and Proulx (2007) found significantly higher levels of habitual lying, low self-esteem, phobias, and reckless behaviour among their sexual homicide sample. Problem behaviours were also reported by Langevin, Ben-Aron, Wright, Marchese, and Handy (1988), who found high levels of fire-setting, cruelty towards animals, and behavioural problems in school, as did Briken, Habermann, Kafka, Berner, and Hill (2006b) (e.g., fist fights, stealing, and suspensions).

The available literature suggests that SHOs and sexual aggressors of women (rapists) do not present diametrically opposed developmental trajectories, but may be distinguished from one another on the basis of the degree of their developmental disturbance (Beech et al., 2005b; Nicole & Proulx, 2007). A word of caution is warranted, however: not all SHOs experience abuse and/or disruption in childhood and most childhood victims of sexual abuse do not grow up to be delinquents or criminals, let alone perpetrators of sexual homicide (Widom & Maxfield, 2001). There was very little in the history of, for example, US serial killer Jeffrey Dahmer to account for his killing of 17 young men in the state of Wisconsin in the 1970s and 1980s. There was no reported abuse and no trauma, yet Dahmer killed, dissected, and even cannibalized a number of innocent people many times over. Because many SHOs have a tendency to lie or withhold key details that they feel might incriminate them, it is essential that other sources of information are sought (e.g., information from school reports, work colleagues, friends, relatives, and victim statements).

Social Isolation

A key psychosocial factor prevalent in SHOs, significantly more so than in sexual aggressors of women, who do not kill their victims, is social isolation (Grubin, 1994; McKenzie, 1995; Milson et al., 2003). Social isolation was a key theme identified by Kerr and Beech (2015) in the offence narratives of eight SHOs detained in a maximum security hospital. We prefer the term 'emotional loneliness' because offenders talked of feeling a lack of emotional connectedness to those around them, even if they were in an intimate relationship at the time of their offence. Participants described feeling 'alone' and 'shut off from the rest of society'. According to Grubin (1994), social isolation in SHOs can be understood either as an indicator of abnormal personality, which both causes the isolation and allows the individual to cross the boundary between sexual attack and murder, or as an indicator of abnormal affect, whereby these men are unable to empathize normally with other people, either unable to experience emotional suffering of victims or, if they do, they experience it as pleasurable and arousing. According to Marshall (1989), social isolation can, of itself, be seen as a form of psychological suffering that can lead to violence. As the child submerges into a world of solitude, he may come to rely heavily on fantasy-based methods of coping that may fuse with aggression in adolescence. Social isolation is included in all three motivational models of sexual homicide and has a growing evidence base to support its inclusion in assessment and formulation from childhood to the time that an offence is committed.

Psychopathology

Mental Illness

Mental illness (e.g., schizophrenia, anxiety, mood, and dissociative disorders) does not appear to be very common in SHOs. In a study by Firestone, Bradford, Greenberg, and Larose (1998), 48 SHOs were assessed over a 10-year period in a medium-secure psychiatric facility from 1982 to 1992 on a number of commonly used psychological inventories, criminal histories, and clinical diagnoses according to DSM-IV (American Psychiatric Association [APA], 1994). Only seven (15%) of the sample had a diagnosis of a psychotic disorder, only one (2%) had a diagnosis of a mood disorder, and only one (2%) had an anxiety disorder. In another study, Proulx and Sauvêtre (2007) investigated the prevalence of psychopathology in 30 SHOs detained in a Canadian penitentiary. Only 7% had a diagnosis of a psychotic disorder and none was diagnosed with a mood, anxiety, or dissociative disorder, according to DSM-IV criteria. In a third study of 166 psychiatric court reports of SHOs, 36 of whom had killed more than one victim, by Hill, Habermann, Berner, and Briken (2007), it was found that only 3% met formal DSM-IV criteria for schizophrenia or another psychotic disorder. Only 10% met criteria for a mood disorder and only 5% were diagnosed with an anxiety disorder.

Although mental illness appears relatively rare in cases of sexual homicide, one of the authors of this chapter has worked for many years with cases in secure psychiatric services, and believes that more research is needed in such settings. When psychosis is present at the time of an offence, it is difficult to say what impact it might have had on an individual's motivation and the sequence of events that led him to kill. Each case is unique and will likely depend on the nature of the individual's symptoms. In the author's experience, however, it is extremely rare for a psychotic individual to kill within a sexual context in response to command hallucinations (i.e., voices instructing the individual to kill and perhaps mutilate a victim's sexual organs). It is far more likely that an episode of psychosis serves only to contort and twist what is already present within the individual's mind. In this way, psychosis is more likely to act as a disinhibitor rather than a driver of aggression.

Personality Disorder

The clinical picture is different when personality disorders are considered. Firestone et al. (1998) reported a prevalence of 51% in their sample, and Hill et al. (2007) reported a prevalence of 78%. There is some confusion within the literature as to which personality disorders are more common. Studies that use a clinician-diagnosed assessment suggest that disorders in DSM-5's cluster B (APA, 2013) are more common (e.g., Antisocial, Narcissistic, Borderline) whereas studies that use self-report (e.g., Millon Clinical Multi-Axial Inventory III [MCMI III]; Millon, 1994) suggest that cluster C disorders are more prevalent (e.g., Avoidant, Dependent, Obsessive) (Oliver, Beech, Fisher, & Beckett, 2007; Proulx & Sauvêtre, 2007). According to Proulx and Sauvêtre (2007), the contradiction in findings is possibly due to the fact that self-report tools such as the MCMI III assess the person, whereas clinicians are more likely to include features of the client's offence to make a diagnosis of personality disorder. If Proulx and Sauvêtre's (2007) suggestion is correct, then it does provide some support for Brittain's (1970) personality profile of the SHO as an anxiety-ridden, shy, and reserved character.

In our experience, there is likely to be a mix of dysfunctional personality traits that may not correspond to any formal diagnosis but nevertheless are important for understanding the offence. Features of narcissism, for example, may lead an individual to the belief that he is entitled to have sex whenever and with whomever he chooses, whereas features of a more schizoid/avoidant presentation may make the individual less able to approach women and thus find a suitable partner. Self-report assessments such as the Millon Clinical Multi-Axial Inventory (Millon, Millon, Davis, & Grossman, 2009) are useful for this purpose. More research is needed with larger samples, but the current state of the literature suggests that the majority of SHOs do experience some sort of personality dysfunction.

Psychopathy

A few studies have explored the prevalence of psychopathy in SHOs using the Hare (2003) Psychopathy Checklist – Revised (PCL-R) (Hare, 1991, 2003). A North American study reported mean PCL-R ratings of 26.5 in prison-based samples (Porter et al., 2003) and 26.6 in secure psychiatric settings (Firestone et al., 1998). Estimates are somewhat lower in Europe. In the Hill et al. (2007) study, single SHOs had a mean PCL-R rating of 16.5 and serial offenders 20.2, although only 6% of their 166 cases were found to reach the North American cut-off score to classify an individual as a 'psychopath' (PCL-R total score ≥ 30). There appears to be a difference in the crime scenes of psychopaths who commit sexual homicide compared with non-psychopaths. In the former, evidence of sadism and gratuitous forms of violence are encountered far more often, possibly as a reflection of the profound lack of empathy combined with a thrill-seeking propensity (Porter et al., 2003). However, as the research suggests, although some psychopathic traits are common in SHOs, elevations that are consistent with a 'diagnosis' are rare.

Paraphilic Disorders and Paraphilia-Related Disorders

In DSM-5, a paraphilic disorder is an atypical sexual interest that causes personal distress in the individual, not merely resulting from society's disapproval, or sexual behaviour that results in psychological distress, injury, or death to another or unwilling persons or persons unable to give legal consent (APA, 2013). Eight categories are listed in DSM-5: voyeuristic disorder (spying on others in private activities), exhibitionistic disorder (exposing the genitals), frotteuristic disorder (touching or rubbing against a non-consenting individual), sexual masochism disorder (undergoing humiliation, bondage, or suffering), sexual sadism disorder (inflicting humiliation, bondage, or suffering), paedophilic disorder (sexual focus on children), fetishistic disorder (using non-living objects for sexual stimulation), and transvestic disorder (engaging in sexually arousing cross-dressing).

The above eight disorders do not exhaust the possible list of paraphilic disorders, but were selected above others on the basis that they are the most common, and most of them, because of their noxiousness or potential harm to others, are classed as criminal offences (DSM-5, p. 685). It is perhaps not surprising to note that they are fairly common in SHOs. In the Firestone et al. (1998) study, 79% of participants were diagnosed with at least one paraphilia and in the Hill et al. (2007) study 51% were found to meet criteria for at least one paraphilia. The most frequently diagnosed disorders among studies include fetishism, exhibitionism, voyeurism, and, in particular, sexual sadism (James & Proulx, 2014).

According to DSM-5, sexual sadism is defined as 'recurrent and intense sexual arousal from the physical or psychological suffering of another person, as manifested by fantasies, urges, or behaviours'. Furthermore, the individual must have 'acted on these sexual urges with a non-consenting person, or the sexual urges or fantasies cause clinically significant distress in social, occupational, or other important areas of functioning' (p. 695). Other researchers (e.g., Ressler et al., 1988) believe that the essence of sadism lies in the offender's quest for control and domination rather than pure physical or emotional suffering.

Although the diagnosis of sexual sadism continues to be controversial (Briken, Bourget, & Dufour, 2014), the sadist is often considered the prototypical SHO (Burgess et al., 1986; Douglas, Burgess, Burgess, & Ressler, 1992; James & Proulx, 2014; Ressler et al., 1988). In reality, however, only a small number of sexual homicides contain evidence of sadism (Schlesinger, 2004, 2007). Although a small number of sadists may kill directly in response to fantasy involving murder (i.e., erotophonophilia), the majority of offenders seem to kill for multiple reasons and may not derive any extra pleasure from taking another person's life (Keppel & Walter, 1999; Kerr et al., 2013). Therefore, the actual killing of a victim may not result from an extension of a sadistic drive, but rather serve an instrumental purpose to eliminate the only witness. As Keppel and Walter (1999) wrote, 'the luxury of sadism is found in the art and process of killing, not the death' (p. 431).

In addition to paraphilic disorders, paraphilia-related disorders (PRDs) have also been researched in SHOs. PRDs include behaviours such as compulsive masturbation, telephone sex addiction, and sexual promiscuity, and they appear to be fairly common in SHOs. Briken et al. (2006b) assessed for these in their sample of 161 SHOs, and 79% of their sample evidenced at least one PRD. They appear to be important in the assessment of SHOs, because those who evidenced at least one PRD in addition to at least one paraphilic disorder had the most developmental problems, the highest number of previous sexual offences, more sexual sadism, and the highest lifetime prevalence of sexual impulsivity disorders.

Fantasy

Because fantasy is so important in the crimes committed by sadistic sexual offenders, understanding the client's fantasy system is crucial if the assessor is to understand why the offence was committed in the first place. Prentky et al. (1989) defined fantasy as 'an elaborate set of cognitions (thoughts) characterized by preoccupation (or rehearsal), anchored in emotion, and originating in daydreams' (p. 889). Brittain (1970) wrote that the sadistic SHO is 'typically a day-dreamer with a very rich, active fantasy life … he imagines sadistic scenes and these he acts out in his killings' (p. 199). Because crimes can never completely mirror their fantasies, sadistic SHOs obtain only partial satisfaction of their sexually deviant desires (James & Proulx, 2014) and, because of this, they have a very high chance of repeating their crimes (Schlesinger, 2004, 2007). Serial SHOs are extremely rare, however. According to Chéné and Cusson (2007), only 2.0% of convicted SHOs will meet FBI criteria for 'serial killer' (defined as killing three or more victims with a significant cooling off period between each murder).

As a risk factor, fantasy is often extremely difficult to assess. According to Meloy (2000), the assessor should look for classical pairing of sexual arousal and extreme violence towards women, especially during the child's formative years; Meloy (2000) suggested from latency age to post-pubescence (6–14 years of age). However, unless the interviewer has a sound rapport with the client, such deeply personal experiences are unlikely to be shared. If the client is willing and engaged, a useful framework to assess fantasy is that developed by Hazelwood and Warren (1995). They postulated five components that are often present: relational, paraphilic, situational, self-perceptual, and demographic. For example, the offender may imagine that a 15-year-old girl (demographic) becomes his sex slave (relational), and he is able to rape her orally and anally at his whim (paraphilic) in his isolated mountain cabin (situational), thus enhancing his sense of omnipotence and gratifying himself sadistically (self-perception). Meloy (1988) described fantasy, particularly the relational and demographic components, as shaping the SHO's search for a suitable victim who achieves a 'goodness of fit' with his fantasy. This is not unlike the normal human mating strategies in which (usually) the male searches for a female who matches his 'template' (Money, 1986).

The mechanism by which fantasy is translated into reality is an important question that has not been fully answered in the academic literature. According to Maniglio (2010), deviant sexual fantasies can promote sexual homicide when combined with early traumatic experiences, especially childhood sexual abuse, social withdrawal, and/or sexual difficulties. Equally, however, it is well documented that most people who experience deviant sexual fantasies, in addition to the majority of abuse victims, do not engage in sexual offending (Leitenberg & Henning, 1995; Maniglio, 2010). According to Revitch and Schlesinger (1981), people who act out their sadistic fantasies do so because of a compulsion. In many cases, the compulsion is so strong that any attempt to resist it results in anxiety and somatic manifestations. Schlesinger (2004, 2007) acknowledged in later work that a compulsion to act out a fantasy is a difficult phenomenon to describe. However, other studies support such a finding. In a recent thematic analysis of the motivation to commit sexual homicide in offenders with mental disorder (Kerr & Beech, 2015), one offender commented, 'I had to kill

... there was a horrible feeling that would rise in me every so often and the only thing that got rid of it was killing ... I felt a sense of relief afterwards'.

Although some offenders may experience very detailed and elaborate fantasies, they are unlikely to make an effort to act them out in their entirety in their very first attempt. It is more likely the case that they will engage in a series of what MacCulloch, Snowden, Wood, and Mills (1983) referred to as 'behavioural tryouts'. Sections of the fantasy may be acted out first, and as the offender grows in confidence and determination, try-outs become more detailed and favourite elements may become part of a ritual. This is not to say that non-ritualistic offenders do not operate in accordance with fantasy. Many do, but remain largely unaware that sexual fantasy underlies their criminal behaviour (Hazelwood & Warren, 1995). This should be kept in mind when assessing offenders who are less articulate in their speech.

Self-report questionnaires such as the Multiphasic Sex Inventory (Nichols & Molinder, 1984) and the Wilson Fantasy Questionnaire (Wilson, 1978) can be useful in the assessment of deviant sexual interests, but they rely on the offender's honesty. The Severe Sexual Sadism Scale (Marshall, Kennedy, Yates, & Serran, 2002) is a file-based observer rating of pertinent crime-scene behaviours used as a screening tool for the assessment of sexual sadism in forensic cases. Reliability and criterion validity estimates for the clinical diagnosis of sexual sadism are reported to be good (Mokros, Schilling, Eher, & Nitschke, 2012).

Since the early 1970s, the psychophysiological method penile plethysmography (PPG) has been used to assess sexual interest. PPG involves the subject listening to or viewing material relevant to his offending behaviour (deviant stimuli) and comparison material depicting legal alternatives while his penile responses are monitored (Perkins, 2007). Research indicates that PPG data are currently the most valid indication of an individual's potential to be sexually aroused by various types of stimuli and are moderately robust against attempts at faking (Kalmus & Beech, 2005; Perkins, 2007). However, the procedure is expensive, invasive, and labour intensive, and requires a motivated and responsive subject (Laws, 2003).

There are two alternative attention-based methods of assessment currently available to clinicians: the Abel Assessment for Sexual Interest and Affinity 2.5. These measures are based on viewing time using a number of images (deviant versus non-deviant), and are based on the premise that offenders have different attentional triggers to non-offenders. An offender interested in aggressive forms of sex, for example, may take longer to view images of cruelty and torture than non-offenders. Several other measures have been used in research, with promising results (Gress & Laws, 2009). However, none have been investigated in samples of SHOs.

Anger

There is much evidence in the literature to suggest that anger is an important antecedent in the crimes of many sexual offenders (e.g., Howells, Day, & Wright, 2004; Ward & Hudson, 2000). Inherent in anger is the action tendency to hurt or cause harm (Frijda, 1986, 1987), and when this is channelled into a sexually aggressive response it becomes a very powerful weapon, capable of inflicting maximum distress in the victim (Howells et al., 2004). Anger is a feature of many sexual homicide offences, but how this translates into the actual killing of a victim is complex.

In our experience, anger may be important for understanding the offence in two different ways. In some cases, anger is expressed overtly and directed at a particular victim or group of victims who have 'wronged' the individual in some way. The drive to kill can sometimes be traced back to a negative encounter with a female. In one of our clients, a young man resorted to serial murder after a prostitute had mocked him in front of his work colleagues for the apparent small size of his penis. Although he did not kill the prostitute who ridiculed him, he targeted others in the red light district and defiled their genitalia, possibly in an attempt to 'ridicule' them. Alternatively, anger may be directed inwards to the point where the perpetrator is not fully aware of the problem or the potential destruction it may cause. This can lead to shame and self-hatred in an otherwise over-controlled individual. Another of our clients described feeling 'jinxed' because he could not perform sexually with any of his girlfriends. This led to a tremendous sense of inferiority in the client that impacted upon his sense of being a 'real man'. The client ended up stabbing a young woman over 50 times during a forced sexual encounter after he failed in his attempt to have sex with her. It is perhaps no coincidence that the violence was unleashed after the victim told him to 'hurry up and get it over with'.

The psychodynamic concept of catathymia is used fairly regularly in the field of sexual homicide research to account for such a process. The term literally means 'according to emotions or temper' and some researchers have used it to describe a certain type of sexual killing where emotionally charged complexes, such as inferiority or inadequacy, extend to the individual's sense of sexual identity. Schlesinger (2004, 2007) differentiated two types of catathymic homicide: one very sudden, unplanned and explosive form often triggered by comments made by the victim, and the other a more protracted form where the killing is planned, not in an attempt to avoid capture, but in a haphazard and disorganized manner because killing is viewed as the only solution to rid the individual of emotional turmoil. The two types have much in common: the victim is viewed in symbolic terms, conflicts often centre on strong feelings of inadequacy, the homicide has the effect of releasing emotional tension, and following the homicide, relief or flattening of emotions (or both) is common (Schlesinger, 2004, p. 138). Meloy (1988, 1992) observed that such offenders typically meet diagnostic criteria for borderline personality disorder, lack an integrated sense of identity, have problems with reality testing, and may use primitive psychological defence mechanisms, such as projective identification and splitting.

Having an over-controlled temper may be more of a feature of SHOs than rapists who do not go on to kill. Grubin (1994) found this in a study of 21 homicidal and 121 non-homicidal sex offenders detained in a UK prison. A sudden release of pent-up aggression at the time of the homicide might explain why many offences are characteristic of the term 'over-kill'. Such victims might be subject to multiple stab wounds, for example, far in excess of what would usually be considered fatal. Interestingly, there is recent evidence to suggest that the more stab wounds are inflicted upon a victim, the more likely it is that a sexual motive existed for the killing (Radojević et al., 2013).

Other research suggests that anger may have a more fundamental connection to sexual arousal. Zilmann (1989), for example, argued that anger arousal can facilitate sexual arousal since the two forms of experience are linked at various levels. They are linked at the endocrine level, at the autonomic nervous level, and in the central nervous system through the amygdala and septal structures. Excitation transfer theory suggests that residual excitation from one state (e.g., anger) can persist and intensify other states (e.g., sexual arousal).

Thus, the relationship between anger and sexual arousal is indeed a complex one that can be understood from a number of approaches (e.g., biological, psychological, and psychodynamic). The research is also clear that anger is an important antecedent to many sexual homicides and needs to be considered carefully in assessment. Several self-report assessment tools to measure anger are available, such as the Novaco Anger Scales, and the State Trait Anger Expression Inventory II (Spielberger, 1999), which is especially useful because it contains a number of subscales relating to over-control in addition to under-control of anger.

Implicit Theories

Given that the underlying motive for an individual committing a particular offence is best formulated by accessing the offender's beliefs and attitudes about themselves, the world in general, and their offending behaviour, it is important to find ways of assessing these beliefs (Fisher & Beech, 2007). There is a growing body of research that has investigated the implicit theories of sex offenders. Implicit theories are 'causal theories, interacting with personal and interpersonal experiences to form coherent structures that explain and predict our own and others' behaviour' (Ward, Polaschek, & Beech, 2006, p. 123). They likely develop early in childhood in response to specific experiences and lie outside an individual's awareness. As Ward et al. (2006) put it, 'individuals are generally not aware that they think in this way and others may not'.

Using reconstructions of psychometric scales of cognitive distortions, Ward and Keenan (1999) and Polaschek and Ward (2002) proposed five specific offence-related implicit theories for child molesters and rapists, respectively. In effect, these under-lying beliefs generate the offence-supportive attitudes and cognitive distortions that are measured at the surface level (Ward, Hudson, Johnston, & Marshall, 1997). A similar set of belief systems were found to exist in a sample of SHOs by Beech, Fisher, and Ward (2005a). They examined transcripts of interviews from 28 SHOs of adult women victims detained in a number of prisons in the United Kingdom. Offenders were asked to give an account of how they saw their offending and what led up to their offence.

The five implicit theories identified in the sample, in order of their prevalence, were as follows: (1) Dangerous world: the offender sees the world as a dangerous place and people are likely to behave in an abusive and threatening manner in order to promote their own interests; therefore, it is necessary to fight back and achieve dominance and control over other people. (2) Male sex drive is uncontrollable: sexual energy is difficult to control, and women play a key role in the loss of that control. The cause of offending is attributed to external factors, either in the victim or in a feature of the environment (e.g., alcohol). (3) Entitlement: a core idea that some people are superior to others and because of their status they have a right to assert their needs above anyone else's and expect that this will be agreed upon and accepted by those judged to be less important. (4) Women are sex objects: their main purpose is to meet the sexual needs of men, and they should always be receptive and available to meet such needs. (5) Women are unknowable: viewed as deliberately misleading, causing men to feel inadequate and rejected.

Implicit theories are important to assess in SHOs. They can help provide an understanding of why an offence came to unfold, and although resistant to change, they represent key targets for treatment. Thorough interviewing of the client with an exploration of his account of his offending will likely elicit such beliefs. In the Beech et al. (2005a) study, an interrater reliability estimate of 0.77 was observed for the labelling of implicit theories, suggesting that the assessment of such beliefs is reliable.

Neurology

A number of authors have suggested that damage to the frontal lobes would lead to sexual assaults, whereas damage to the temporal lobes would more directly (although rarely) be associated with genuine sexual deviance or a shift in sexual orientation (e.g., Langevin, 1990; Miller, Cummings, McIntyre, Ebers, & Grode, 1986; Raine, 1993). Brain damage rarely induces genuine deviance limited to sexual behaviour (Joyal, Black, & Dassylva, 2007). Instances of true paraphilias following a brain injury are extremely rare and they are usually accompanied by several manifestations of a broader disinhibition deficit such as aggressiveness, talkativeness, poor judgement, and low social abilities (Mendez, Chow, Ringman, Twitchell, & Hinkin, 2000). However, frontotemporal dysfunctions are sporadically reported among sexual offenders.

Briken, Habermann, Berner, and Hill (2005) investigated the influence of brain abnormalities on psychosocial development, criminal history, and paraphilias in their large sample of 166 SHOs. Using psychiatric court reports, they found evidence of brain abnormality in 50 cases. In a regression analysis, five predictor variables were notably more evident in the offenders with brain abnormalities. These included transvestic fetishism and paraphilias not otherwise specified, insertion of foreign objects into the victim's vagina, having victims 6 years of age or younger, and the absence of alcohol or drug addiction. More research is needed in this area, but what little guidance there is suggests that the neurological functioning of SHOs may be an important area of assessment in terms of understanding their crimes.

Sex Chromosome Abnormality

There is some support for a link between sex chromosome abnormalities and sexual homicide. As part of their retrospective analysis of court reports of 166 SHOs, Briken, Habermann, Berner, and Hill (2006a) noted that chromosomal analysis had been carried out in 13 of their cases. Three out of the 13 subjects (8%) were found to have XYY chromosome abnormality. Two were multiple murderers, having killed more than three victims; all had suffered physical abuse, had difficulties at school, and were diagnosed as sexually sadistic.

Lauerma (2001) reported on a case of a 36-year-old male with Klinefelter syndrome (karyotype XXY) who had committed a sexual homicide against a 50-year-old woman. The offender admitted to experiencing violent fantasies from a young age that centred on the mutilation of female genitalia. Although the offender claimed that his fantasies caused him much distress, this did not prevent him from enacting them upon a victim, with four large wounds being inflicted in her vagina before death from strangulation. However, although possessing the karyotype XXY was probably a contributory factor in the sexual homicide committed by this individual, it was not causative as other potentiating factors were found and included a violent childhood and hatred towards his mother. More research is needed in this area, but the above studies suggest that the inclusion of chromosome analysis in cases of sexual homicide could be significant in understanding motive.

Prior Offence Record

It appears to be the case that the majority of SHOs are, for the most part, polymorphic when it comes to their offending. Nicole, Proulx, and Cusson (2001) reported in their sample that 72% of offenders had committed at least one crime against property, and over half (62%) had committed non-sexual crimes against the person. Hence it is important to investigate prior criminal history, as there may be a pattern of escalation in the client's offending leading them to murder, for example, in the form of progressive behavioural try-outs of a fantasy.

Intellectual Functioning

Analysis of intellectual functioning is important in the assessment of SHOs, particularly in those whose offences have gone undetected for many years (Schlesinger, 2004). Clients with higher levels of intelligence may well be able to maintain complicated false accounts of events in ways not possible for less able clients, and some may be boastful of their performance during assessment (Perkins, 2007). Achieving an understanding of an offender's level of functioning is also important because this may impact on his ability to articulate any fantasies that may have been implicated in the offences, and also to grasp concepts and hypotheses put to him by the assessor. Formal tests such as the Wechsler Adult Intelligence Scales IV (Wechsler, 2008) are recommended for this purpose.

Offending Pathways

Using a number of different approaches (e.g., clinical, statistical, theory-led, and demographics), a number of studies have attempted to classify SHOs. Research has consistently found three main types: (1) those motivated by anger, hate, or revenge; (2) those motivated by a need to satisfy a sadistic sexual drive; and (3) those motivated by a need to have sex whatever the cost to the victim (Beauregard & Proulx, 2007; Beech et al., 2005a; Clarke & Carter, 1999; Schlesinger, 2004, 2007). These categories are also found in non-homicidal rapists, and despite variations in the terminologies used to describe each type, all three present with a number of consistent characteristics. The sadistic killer's behaviour can be considered ritualistic and interference with the victim's body after death often occurs (Schlesinger, 2004, 2007). He is likely to be highly intelligent, although socially isolated with multiple paraphilias. Crime scenes are likely to be organized with evidence of sadistic, gratuitous violence, and fantasy enactment (e.g., bizarre rituals carried out over the course of the killing) (Beech et al., 2005a). Strangulation is often used as the preferred method of killing and the victim is not usually known to the killer beforehand. All classification studies that we know of support the contention that this type of offender is the most likely of the three to repeat his offence.

The angry offender is likely to have average intelligence, show a pattern of impulsive actions, exhibit borderline personality functioning, and be in a relationship at the time of the homicide. Their crime scenes are likely to be disorganized with evidence of vengeance displaced to a specific victim or a victim who holds some symbolic significance to the source of anger (Schlesinger, 2004, 2007). The so-called catathymic type of offender who kills his victim out of a conflict connected with his sexuality is less likely to repeat his offences if the conflict can be addressed in therapy (Schlesinger, 2004, 2007). However, those who specifically target groups of individuals out of grievance or revenge have a strong likelihood of repeating their crimes.

The sexually motivated killer is less seen in SHO typologies, but frequently included in classifications on sexual aggressors of women. He is likely to have stereotypical views about the sexes; including those relating to a man's entitlement. However, he is less likely to be impulsive than offenders in other categories and is less driven by grievance, anger, or revenge (Beech et al., 2005a; Fisher & Beech, 2007). If he ends up killing his victim it is usually through instrumental reasons, for example, to silence the only witness to a sexual assault or through unnecessary force applied in his restraint of the victim. There is not much suggestion in the literature of such offences becoming serial in nature, but individuals who are prepared to kill in order to silence a victim present a particular concern for repetition, especially if they are psychopathic. Although most perpetrators of sexual homicide will conform to one type more than another, it is dangerous to conclude that offenders will fit neatly into one particular category. In this respect, the typology literature is limited, but it can provide a useful framework in which to gather data and formulate hypotheses.

Assessment of Motive

Crucial in the assessment of the SHO is to establish the motive for the killing. This is important because it has implications for risk and also for future treatment needs. However, the motive for the killing is rarely obvious and the client may be unwilling or unable to assist, either because of a genuine dissociative reaction at the time of the killing or because of a deep-seated conflict of which he is unaware. He may also lie in his attempt to deflect responsibility or lie in an attempt to hide a fantasy component that was present at the time. When clients are reluctant or unable to provide information, it may be useful to present them with a number of possible scenarios for their offending with the aim of helping them to remember and explain (Perkins, 2007). Key questions that the assessor might ask him- or herself include: (a) was the killing due to a mistake of applying too much force to the victim in response to her resistance?; (b) was the killing designed to silence the only witness to the offender's sexual assault?; or (c) was the killing used to serve a specific psychological need in the form of a grievance towards women or to satisfy a sadistic sexual drive?

Crime scene photographs can be helpful in determining the function of a killing by investigating the location of stab wounds, for example, in a victim killed with a knife. Many stab wounds inflicted in a frenzied manner about the victim's body before, during, or after sex likely indicate an anger-driven motive. Knife wounds inflicted more purposefully and located around the genital region of a victim might indicate a sexual motive connected with sadism. If there are more bizarre elements, for example, with the victim posed in an unusual position or body parts having been dissected, it could be evidence of a psychotic process.

Situational Factors and Disinhibitors

In our experience, SHOs rarely set out with a motive to kill, although some do, and a few may actually derive pleasure from the kill itself. However, by all accounts, situational factors at the time of the offence can provide vital clues as to why a victim ends up being killed. Research by Chéné and Cusson (2007) suggests that factors such as the presence of a weapon and especially verbal or physical resistance from a victim are useful in predicting the outcome in a sexually violent crime. If such variables are present, then homicide is more likely. An exploration of the interaction between perpetrator and victim immediately before the homicide can be extremely useful in most cases. Specific comments made by the victim to the offender that appear seemingly innocuous at first may provide clues of a repressed conflict of which the client is hardly aware. Alternatively, something may have happened to the offender in the days leading up to the homicide that might explain his actions during the offence. This is particularly significant in sadistic offenders. Brittain (1970) wrote, 'The sadist who has been laughed at by a woman or mocked by his acquaintances, particularly in his sexual contacts, or who has been demoted or discharged from his employment is likely to be at his most dangerous' (p. 199). It is also important to consider factors that may reduce an offender's inhibition in the pre-crime phase of the offence. Heavy alcohol and illicit substance misuse is fairly common in cases of sexual homicide. Pornography depicting violence is another common disinhibitor (Hill et al., 2007; Firestone et al., 1998).

Conclusions

In this chapter, efforts have been made to identify common characteristics of SHOs who target adult women. The review is not an exhaustive account of all characteristics, but we hope that it provides the clinician with a platform from which to approach their assessment. In reality, cases of sexual homicide are extremely complex, but rare. For the most part, SHOs are not unlike sexual aggressors of women who do not kill their victim. However, it is often very difficult to discern why a victim ends up being killed in such circumstances and the offender's account may not be very accurate for a variety of reasons. There is also often a lot of media interest in such cases, particularly in those with more than one victim, and this can attract stigma and poor motivation to engage. Given the seriousness of the offence, potential for repetition in some cases, and the need to recruit information from multiple sources, the process of assessment is likely to be a lengthy one.

Acknowledgement

The authors of this chapter wish to thank Dr Victoria Wilkes (Forensic Psychologist) for her helpful comments on an earlier draft of this work.

References

APA. (1994). *Diagnostic and statistical manual of mental disorders* (4th ed.) (DSM-IV). Washington, DC: Author.

APA. (2013). *Diagnostic and statistical manual of mental disorders* (5th ed.) (DSM-5). Arlington, VA: American Psychiatric Publishing.

Arrigo, B. A., & Purcell, C. E. (2001). Explaining paraphilias and lust murder: Toward an integrated model. *International Journal of Offender Therapy and Comparative Criminology*, *45*, 6–31.

Beauregard, E., & Proulx, J. (2007). A classification of sexual homicide against men. *International Journal of Offender Therapy and Comparative Criminology*, *51*, 420–432.

Beech, A. R., Fisher, D., & Ward, T. (2005a). Sexual murderers' implicit theories. *Journal of Interpersonal Violence*, *20*, 1336–1389.

Beech, A. R., Oliver, C. J., Fisher, D., & Beckett, R. C. (2005b). *STEP 4: the sex offender treatment programme in prison: addressing the offending behaviour of rapists and sexual murderers*. Birmingham, England: University of Birmingham.

Briken, P., Bourget, D., & Dufour, M. (2014). Sexual sadism in sexual offenders and sexually motivated homicide. *Psychiatric Clinics of North America*, *37*, 215–230.

Briken, P., Habermann, N. M. P., Berner, W., & Hill, A. (2005). The influence of brain abnormalities on psychosocial development, criminal history and paraphilias in sexual murderers. *Journal of Forensic Sciences*, *50*, 1–5.

Briken, P., Habermann, N. M. P., Berner, W., & Hill, A. (2006). XYY chromosome abnormality in sexual homicide perpetrators. Brief research communication. *American Journal of Medical Genetics. Part B, Neuropsychiatric Genetics*, *141B*, 198–200.

Briken, P., Habermann, N., Kafka, M. P., Berner, W., & Hill, A. (2006). The paraphilia-related disorders: An investigation of the relevance of the concept in sexual murderers. *Journal of Forensic Science*, *51*, 683–688.

Brittain, R. P. (1970). The sadistic murderer. *Medicine, Science and the Law*, *10*, 198–207.

Burgess, A. W., Hartman, C. R., Ressler, R. K., Douglas, J. E., & McCormack, A. (1986). Sexual homicide: A motivational model. *Journal of Interpersonal Violence*, *1*, 251–272.

Campus, E., & Cusson, M. (2007). Serial killers and sexual murderers. In J. Proulx, E. Beauregard, M. Cusson, & A. Nicole (Eds.), *Sexual murderers: A comparative analysis and new perspectives* (pp. 99–105). Chichester, England: John Wiley & Sons, Ltd.

Chéné, S., & Cusson, M. (2007). Sexual murderers and sexual aggressors: Intention and situation. In J. Proulx, E. Beauregard, M. Cusson, & A. Nicole (Eds.), *Sexual murderers: A comparative analysis and new perspectives* (pp. 70–86). Chichester, England: John Wiley & Sons, Ltd.

Clark, J., & Carter, A. (1999). *Sexual murderers: Their assessment and treatment.* Paper presented at the 18th Annual Research and Treatment Conference, ATSA, Lake Buena Vista, FL.

Douglas, J. E., Burgess, A. W., Burgess, A. C., & Ressler, R. K. (1992). *Crime classification manual.* Lexington, KY: Lexington Books.

Firestone, P., Bradford, J. M., Greenberg, D. M., & Larose, M. R. (1998). Homicidal sex offenders: Psychological, phallometric and diagnostic features. *Journal of the American Academy of Psychiatry and Law, 26,* 537–552.

Fisher, D., & Beech, A. R. (2007). Identification of motivations for sexual murder. In J. Proulx, E. Beauregard, M. Cusson, & A. Nicole (Eds.), *Sexual murderers: A comparative analysis and new perspectives* (pp. 175–190). Chichester, England: John Wiley & Sons, Ltd.

Francis, B., & Soothill, K. (2000). Does sex offending lead to homicide? *The Journal of Forensic Psychiatry, 11,* 49–61.

Frijda, N. H. (1986). *The emotions.* Cambridge, England: Cambridge University Press.

Frijda, N. H. (1987). Emotion, cognitive structure and action tendency. *Cognition and Emotion, 1,* 115–143.

Gress, C. L. Z., & Laws, D. R. (2009). Measuring sexual deviance: Attention-based measures. In A. R. Beech, L. A. Craig, & K. D. Browne (Eds.), *Assessment and treatment of sex offenders: A handbook* (pp. 109–128). Chichester, England: John Wiley & Sons, Ltd.

Grubin, D. (1994). Sexual murder. *British Journal of Psychiatry, 165,* 624–629.

Häkkänen-Nyholm, H., Repo-Tiihonen, E., Lindberg, N., Salenius, S., & Weizmann-Henelius, G. (2009). Finnish sexual homicides: Offence and offender characteristics. *Forensic Science International, 188,* 125–130.

Hare, R. D. (1991). *The Hare Psychopathy Checklist—Revised.* North Tonawanda, NY: Multi-Health Systems.

Hare, R. D. (2003). *Hare PCL-R: Technical Manual.* Toronto, Canada: MHS.

Hart, S. D., Kropp, R., Laws, D. R., Klaver, J., Logan, C., & Watt, K. A. (2003). *The Risk for Sexual Violence Protocol (RSVP) – Structured professional guideline for assessing risk of sexual violence.* Burnaby, Canada: Simon Fraser University, Mental Health, Law and Policy Institute.

Hazelwood, R. R., & Warren, J. I. (1995). The relevance of fantasy in serial sexual crime investigation. In R. Hazelwood & A. W. Burgess (Eds.), *Practical aspects of rape investigation* (pp. 127–138). Boca Raton: FL: CRC Press.

Hickey, E.W. (1997). *Serial murderers and their victims* (2nd ed.). Belmont, CA: Wadsworth.

Hill, A., Habermann, N., Berner, W., & Briken, P. (2007). Psychiatric disorders in single and multiple sexual murderers. *Psychopathology, 40,* 22–28.

Hill, A., Rettenberger, M., Habermann, N., Berner, W., Eher, R., & Briken, P. (2012). The utility of risk assessment instruments for the prediction of recidivism in sexual homicide perpetrators. *Journal of Interpersonal Violence, 27,* 3553–3578.

Howells, K., Day, A., & Wright, S. (2004). Affect, emotions and sex offending. *Psychology, Crime and Law, 10,* 179–195.

James, J., & Proulx, J. (2014). A psychological and developmental profile of sexual murderers: A systematic review. *Aggression and Violent Behaviour, 19,* 592–607.

Joyal, C. C., Black, D. N., & Dassylva, B. (2007). The neuropsychology and neurology of sexual deviance: A review and pilot study. *Sexual Abuse: A Journal of Research and Treatment*, *19*, 155–173.

Kalmus, E., & Beech, A. R. (2005). Forensic assessment of sexual interest: A review. *Aggression and Violent Behaviour*, *10*, 193–217.

Keppel, R. D., & Walter, R. (1999). Profiling killers: A revised classification model for understanding sexual murder. *International Journal of Offender Therapy and Comparative Criminology*, *43*, 417–37.

Kerr, K. J., & Beech, A. R. (2015). A thematic analysis of the motivation behind sexual homicide from the perspective of the killer. *Journal of Interpersonal Violence. Advance online publication*. doi: 10.1177/0886260515585529

Kerr, K. J., Beech, A. R., & Murphy, D. (2013). Sexual homicide: Definition, motivation, and comparison with other forms of sexual offending. *Aggression and Violent Behaviour*, *18*, 1–10.

Kingston, D. A., & Yates, P. M. (2008). Sexual sadism: Assessment and treatment. In R. Laws & W. T. O'Donohue (Eds.), *Sexual deviance: Theory, assessment, and treatment* (2nd ed., pp. 231–243). New York, NY: Guilford Press.

Langevin, R. (1990). Sexual anomalies and the brain. In W. L. Marshall, D. R. Laws, & H. E. Barbaree (Eds.), *Handbook of sexual assaults*. New York, NY: Plenum.

Langevin, R., Ben-Aron, M. H., Wright, P., Marchese, V., & Handy, L. (1988). The sex killer. *Annals of Sex Research*, *1*, 263–302.

Lauerma, H. (2001). Klinefelter's syndrome and sexual homicide. *The Journal of Forensic Psychiatry*, *12*, 151–157.

Laws, D. R. (2003). Penile plethysmography: Will we ever get it right? In T. Ward, D. R. Laws, & S. M. Hudson (Eds.), *Sexual deviance: Issues and controversies*. Thousand Oaks, CA: Sage.

Leitenberg, H., & Henning, K. (1995). Sexual fantasy. *Psychological Bulletin*, *117*, 469–491.

MacCulloch, M. J., Snowden, P. R., Wood, P. J. W., & Mills, H. E. (1983). Sadistic fantasy, sadistic behaviour and offending. *British Journal of Psychiatry*, *143*, 20–29.

Maniglio, R. (2010). The role of deviant sexual fantasy in the etiopathogenesis of sexual homicide: A systematic review. *Aggression and Violent Behaviour*, *15*, 294–302.

Marshall, W. L. (1989). Intimacy, loneliness and sexual offenders. *Behaviour, Research and Therapy*, *27*, 491–503.

Marshall, W. L., Kennedy, P., Yates, P., & Serran, G. A. (2002). Diagnosing sexual sadism in sexual offenders: Reliability across diagnosticians. *International Journal of Offender Therapy and Comparative Criminology*, *46*, 668–677.

McKenzie, C. (1995). A study of serial murder. *International Journal of Offender Therapy and Comparative Criminology*, *35*, 328–350.

Meloy, J. R. (1988). *The psychopathic mind: Origins, dynamics and treatment*. Northvale, NJ: Jason Aronson.

Meloy, J. R. (1992). *Violent attachments*. Northvale, NJ: Jason Aronson.

Meloy, J. R. (2000). The nature and dynamics of sexual homicide. *Aggression and Violent Behaviour*, *5*, 1–22.

Mendez, M. F., Chow, T., Ringman, J., Twitchell, G., & Hinkin, C. H. (2000). Paedophilia and temporal lobe disturbances. *Journal of Neuropsychiatry and Clinical Neurosciences*, *12*, 71–76.

Miller, B. L., Cummings, J. L., McIntyre, H., Ebers, G., & Grode, M. (1986). Hyper-sexuality or altered sexual preference following brain injury. *Journal of Neurology, Neurosurgery and Psychiatry*, *49*, 867–873.

Millon, T. (1994). *Millon Clinical Multi-Axial Inventory III manual*. Minneapolis, MN: National Computer Systems.

Millon, T., Millon, C., Davis, R., & Grossman, S. (2009). *MCMI-III* (4th ed.). Minneapolis, MN: NCS Pearson.

Milsom, J., Beech, A. R., & Webster, S. D. (2003). Emotional loneliness in sexual murderers: A qualitative analysis. *Sexual Abuse: A Journal of Research and Treatment, 15*, 285–296.

Mokros, A., Schilling, F., Eher, R., & Nitschke, K. (2012). The severe sexual sadism scale: Cross validation and scale properties. *Psychological Assessment, 24*, 764–769.

Money, J. (1986). *Lovemaps*. New York, NY: Irvington.

Nichols, H. R., & Molinder, I. (1984). *Manual for the Multiphasic Sex Inventory*. Tacoma, WA: Crime and Victim Psychology Specialists.

Nicole, A., Proulx, J., & Cusson, M. (2001, July). *Du viol au meurtre sexuel: Appréhension du dévéloppement personnel et de la trajectoire criminelle*. Paper presented at the XXVIth International Congress on Law and Mental Health, Montréal, Canada.

Nicole, A., & Proulx, J. (2007). Sexual murderers and sexual aggressors: Developmental paths and criminal history. In J. Proulx, E. Beauregard, M. Cusson, & A. Nicole (Eds.), *Sexual murderers: A comparative analysis and new perspectives* (pp. 29–50). Chichester, England: John Wiley & Sons, Ltd.

Oliver, C. J., Beech, A. R., Fisher, D., & Beckett, R. C. (2007). A comparison of rapists and sexual murderers on demographic and selected psychometric measures. In J. Proulx, E. Beauregard, M. Cusson, & A. Nicole (Eds.), *Sexual murderers: A comparative analysis and new perspectives* (pp. 159–173). Chichester, England: John Wiley & Sons, Ltd.

Perkins, D. (2007). *Diagnosis, assessment and identification of severe paraphilic disorders*. Sexual Homicide and Paraphilia: The Correctional Service of Canada's Experts Forum. Retrieved from http://www.csc-scc.gc.ca/text/rsrch/special_reports/shp2007/paraphil02-eng.shtml

Polaschek, D. L. L., & Ward, T. (2002). The implicit theories of potential rapists: What our questionnaires tell us. *Aggression and Violent Behaviour, 7*, 385–406.

Porter, S., Woodworth, M., Earle, J., Drugge, J., & Boer, D. (2003). Characteristics of sexual homicides committed by psychopathic and non-psychopathic offenders. *Law and Human Behaviour, 27*, 459–469.

Prentky, R. A., Burgess, A. W., Rokous, F., Lee, A., Hartmann, C., Ressler, R., & Douglas, J. (1989). The presumptive role of fantasy in serial sexual homicide. *American Journal of Psychiatry, 146*, 887–891.

Proulx, J., & Sauvêtre, N. (2007). Sexual murderers and sexual aggressors: Psychopathological considerations. In J. Proulx, E. Beauregard, M. Cusson, & A. Nicole (Eds.), *Sexual murderers: A comparative analysis and new perspectives* (pp. 51–69). Chichester, England: John Wiley & Sons, Ltd.

Radojević, N., Radnić, B., Petković, S., Miljen, M., Čurović, I., Čukić, D., … Savić, S. (2013). Multiple stabbing in sex-related homicides. *Journal of Forensic and Legal Medicine, 20*, 502–507.

Raine, A (1993). *The psychopathology of crime: Criminal behaviour as a clinical disorder*. New York, NY: Academic Press.

Ressler, R. K., Burgess, A. W., & Douglas, J. E. (1988). *Sexual homicide: Patterns and motives*. New York, NY: Free Press.

Revitch, E. (1965). Sex murder and the potential sex murderer. *Diseases of the Nervous System, 26*, 640–648.

Revitch, E., & Schlesinger, L. (1981). *The psychopathology of homicide*. Springfield, IL: Charles C. Thomas

Schlesinger, L. B. (2004). *Sexual murder: Catathymic and compulsive homicides.* Boca Raton, FL: CRC Press.

Schlesinger, L. B. (2007). Sexual homicide: Differentiating catathymic and compulsive murders. *Aggression and Violent Behaviour, 12,* 242–256.

Spielberger, C. D. (1999). *State trait anger expression inventory* (2nd ed.). Odessa, FL: Psychological Assessment Resources.

US Department of Justice, Federal Bureau of Investigation, Criminal Justice Information Services Division (2012). *Uniform Crime Report: Crime in the United States 2012.* Retrieved from https://www.fbi.gov/about-us/cjis/ucr/crime-in-the-u.s/2012/crime-in-the-u.s.-2012

Ward, T., & Hudson, S. (2000). A self-regulation model of relapse prevention. In D. R. Laws, S. M. Hudson, & T. Ward (Eds.), *Remaking relapse prevention with sex offenders: A sourcebook* (pp. 79–101). Thousand Oaks, CA: Sage.

Ward, S. M., Hudson, L., Johnston, W. L., & Marshall, T. (1997). Cognitive distortions in sex offenders: An integrative review. *Clinical Psychology Review, 17,* 479–507.

Ward, T., & Keenan, T. (1999). Child molesters' implicit theories. *Journal of Interpersonal Violence, 14,* 821–838.

Ward, T., Polaschek, D. L. L., & Beech, A. R. (2006). *Theories of sexual offending.* Chichester, England: John Wiley & Sons, Ltd.

Wechsler, D. (2008). *The Wechsler Adult Intelligence Scales* (4th ed.). San Antonio, TX: Psychological Corporation.

Widom, C. S., & Maxfield, M. G. (2001). *An update in the 'cycle' of violence: Technical report* (National Institute of Justice Research Brief). Washington, DC: National Institute of Justice.

Wilson, G. D. (1978). *The secrets of sexual fantasy.* London, England: Dent.

Zillmann, D. (1989). Aggression and sex: Independent and joint operations. In H. Wagner & A. Manstead (Eds.), *Handbook of social psychophysiology* (pp. 229–260). Chichester, England: John Wiley & Sons, Ltd.

Section VI
Ethics and Rights

53

Rights and Risk Assessment in Sex Offenders

Tony Ward

Victoria University of Wellington, New Zealand

Astrid Birgden

Deakin University, Australia

Introduction

Ethical issues in forensic and correctional practice arise from practitioners' obligations to consider the interests of offenders in addition to those of members of the community. In particular, ethical flashpoints occur when it comes to the matter of deciding how best to balance the apparent competing interests between offenders and others, and ascertaining which (and how) interests should be prioritized. The term *interests* is a prudential concept and as such is concerned with individual well-being and personal fulfilment. The ethical implications generated by the subject of human interests centre on access to goods and services that protect individual well-being, and minimize any possible harms (i.e., setbacks to human interests). The kinds of questions raised in these contexts typically revolve around issues of entitlements (e.g., should the state provide offenders with access to employment training?) and duties (e.g., following a period of punishment, do offenders still owe a debt to society?). The ethical backdrop to discussions over offender entitlements and obligations includes assumptions concerning the nature and limits of punishment and the moral status of individuals within the community. Background assumptions are important in moral thinking as they frame situations in ways that can result in ethical conflicts and dilemmas. For example, a key debate in the correctional and forensic domain concerns the topic of human rights and the extent of their applicability to individuals who have committed serious crimes. In our experience, forensic practitioners rarely articulate background assumptions, although they are frequently at the centre of role disputes and their associated ethical problems (Ward & Salmon, 2009). In the case of sex offenders, the degree of social disapproval is considerable and therefore there is an even greater need

The Wiley Handbook on the Theories, Assessment, and Treatment of Sexual Offending.
Edited by Douglas P. Boer. Volume II: Assessment, edited by Leam A. Craig and Martin Rettenberger.
© 2017 John Wiley & Sons, Ltd. Published 2017 by John Wiley & Sons, Ltd.

to examine critically the moral obligations of practitioners and how best to approach the many ethical problems associated with treatment and assessment. Risk assessment, by virtue of its primary focus on the need to protect other people from the possibility of further victimization, increases the salience of these concerns. In our view, risk assessment procedures and outcomes are especially likely to trigger background moral assumptions and, if not critically evaluated, may lead to unethical practice.

In essence, risk assessment is the process of using risk factors (i.e., any variable that is measurable and predictive) to estimate the likelihood of a hazard occurring to a person or persons in the future (Cook & Michie, 2013). The process of risk assessment may vary in terms of its degree of structure and reliance on professional judgement and/or a set of explicit rules (typically actuarial; Douglas, Blanchard, & Hendry, 2013). According to Monahan (2014, p. 63) such risks factors are

> (a) any variable that statistically correlates with the outcome; and (b) precedes the outcome in time. There is no implication in this definition that the risk factor in any sense 'causes' the occurrence of the outcome.

The nature of risk factors used in research and clinical assessment varies in a number of ways, including their degree of changeability (static versus dynamic), duration (stable versus acute), content (e.g., relational style, attitudes, biological marker, form) (risk versus protective), and function (causal, contributing, or contextual). The typical outcome from a risk assessment process is that an offender's score is translated into a risk band (e.g., low, medium, or high risk) and their probability of committing a further sexual/non-sexual offence within a specific time period is estimated (Helmus, Hanson, Thornton, Babchishin, & Harris, 2012). The assessed level of risk of individuals is taken into account when decisions are made concerning their treatment needs and the degree of monitoring on release from prison or while on probation, and, on occasions, to justify further periods of confinement in civil detention centres.

In this chapter, we explore a number of ethical problems and dilemmas that frequently arise in the context of sex offender risk assessment and risk management. We decided to consider at least briefly risk management alongside risk assessment because in contemporary sex offender treatment programmes the two are closely aligned. In brief, *risk management* is the application of interventions to eliminate, modify, or curtail the influence of dynamic risk factors on individuals, thereby reducing their risk of recidivism. Our treatment of this topic is fairly general and we do not discuss risk assessment in detail. First, we discuss the concepts of moral and human rights and outline their relevance for sex offender risk assessment. Second, we address ethical issues that arise *directly* from the concept of dynamic risk factors and risk assessment and management. Third, we examine ethical problems that are *indirectly* linked to risk assessment and management. These ethical concerns are created by background assumptions rather than risk assessment itself. In this section on ethical concern, we consider the question of offenders' moral status and to what extent punishment by the state is justified. This issue has important ramifications for the way in which risk assessment is conducted and the nature of the limits that should be placed on it. We also review the dual relationship problem and analyse its impact on forensic practice. During our discussion, the value-laden nature of risk assessment is highlighted and the way in which normative judgements penetrate to its core is pointed out. Finally, we conclude by considering a few important practice implications of our examination of ethical problems posed by risk assessment of sex offenders.

Human and Moral Rights

Individuals' moral rights spell out their legitimate ethical claims against other people and the corresponding duties others have to them. The claims in question arise from people's moral status or worth and are typically based on attributes such as autonomy (i.e., the capacity to be self-governing) and liberty (i.e., freedom from undue interference from others). For example, each member of the community is entitled to basic respect from others and can reasonably anticipate that their views on important issues will be taken into account when decisions concerning community services and goods are made. Individuals can justifiably claim that other persons should listen to what they have to say, consider it as much as they do their own opinions, and when making decisions give everyone's interests equal weighting. If legitimate claims are disregarded, then those responsible have failed to live up to their obligations.

Moral rights and their respective claims can be viewed as the ethical canvas against which members of the community seek to live their lives and work cooperatively to advance their own and others' interests. Moral rights are wide ranging and concerned with issues that go beyond the protection of core interests or basic human needs. Entitlements to fair consideration in work-related matters, the right to be loved and to love in return, and the right to be treated with respect all involve moral rights in some form or another. What is needed in moral decision-making in addition to moral rights are rights that protect the empowerment and well-being requirements that comprise dignity. The notion of human dignity is a fundamental moral concept that signifies the intrinsic value and universal moral equality of human beings. Owing to their inherent dignity, all human beings are presumed to have the same degree of moral standing when it comes to considering the social and political arrangements that directly affect their core interests and subsequent well-being. Rights that seek to protect dignity will guarantee each person access to services and goods that enable them to function as purposeful agents able to pursue their own conception of a good life without unjustified interference from others. Such rights are what have been termed *human rights* (Gewirth, 1981; Griffin, 2008; Nickel, 2007; Orend, 2002).

The concept of human rights is a moral (and legal) one that can fulfil this role by virtue of its ability to safeguard the provision of the social, economic, environmental, and psychological goods necessary for a dignified human life. The relationship between values and human rights is nicely captured by Freeden (1991, p. 7):

> a human right is a conceptual device, expressed in linguistic form, that assigns priority to certain human or social attributes regarded as essential to the adequate functioning of a human being; that is intended to serve as a protective capsule for those attributes; and that appeal for deliberate action to ensure such protection.

Human rights are typically cast in a universal form, and it is assumed that they apply to all human beings by virtue of their underlying common needs based on the fact of embodiment, environmental conditions, and related interests (Gewirth, 1981; Griffin, 2008; Orend, 2002). Nickel (2007) identified a number of key human rights features. According to Nickel, human rights:

- are universal and extend to all peoples of the world;
- are moral norms that provide strong reasons for granting individual significant benefits;
- have normative force through both national and international institutions;
- are evident in both specific lists of rights and at the level of abstract values;
- set minimum standards of living rather than depicting an ideal.

From a human rights perspective, offenders are simultaneously *rights holders* (with a right to non-interference in personal affairs unless they infringe upon the rights of others), *duty bearers* (in that they are able to pursue goals as long as they do not infringe upon the rights of others), and *rights violators* (when they infringe upon the rights of others through offending behaviour) (Ward & Birgden, 2007; Ward, Gannon, & Birgden, 2007). Sex offender programmes based on a human rights model would treat sex offenders as rights holders (addressing histories of neglect, abuse, and inadequate socialization that require support to achieve goals in socially acceptable ways) and also duty bearers (providing learning experiences and resources to develop due regard for the rights of others through increasing empathy skills, problem-solving capacity, supportive social networks, and intimacy skills or appropriate alternatives). The threat to sex offenders' moral and human rights as a consequence of risk assessment revolves around the way in which this assessment is undertaken, and the implications for their future release plans and management. We will return to these issues in the discussion below.

Ethical Issues Directly Raised by Risk Assessment and Management

The Nature of Risk

The identification of dynamic risk factors such as deviant sexual preferences, emotional congruence with children, offence-supportive attitudes, self and emotional dysregulation, and lack of adult intimate relationships is particularly important from a clinical perspective as they are viewed as preferential treatment targets. That is, the assumption is that if dynamic risk factors are eliminated or effectively managed, sexual reoffending rates will drop (Mann, Hanson, & Thornton, 2010; Thornton, 2013). Although researchers are careful to point out that risk estimates refer to groups and not individuals, the reality is that it is individuals who are assessed and managed according to the score. Therefore, it is likely that the results of an assessment will be interpreted as referring to an individual's likelihood of reoffending, and the psychological dispositions that underpin this offence-related likelihood (Cook & Michie, 2013).

The assumption that dispositions are relevant to, and generate, risk of further reoffending is causal in nature. The difficulty is that the structure and function of dynamic risk factors and their relationship to the aetiology of offending have been neglected by sex offender researchers and theorists. We simply do not know how dynamic risk factors cause offending, either singly or in combination (which is more likely). We only know that they are correlated. In a recent paper, Ward and Beech (2015) argue that the current conceptualization of dynamic risk factors is incoherent, vague, and essentially flawed. They argue that a risk factor such as intimacy deficits points to both 'symptom' or surface problems (e.g., social isolation) and nascent underlying causal mechanisms (e.g., dysfunctional core beliefs). Furthermore, they assert that there is conceptual disconnection between theory and research on risk factors and therefore the aetiology of sexual offending. Thus, according to Ward and Beech (2015), there are significant conceptual weaknesses in the formulation of dynamic risk factors that are transferred to risk assessment and management. These knowledge-related problems are rarely acknowledged by researchers and practitioners and, therefore, there is a danger that impoverished research practice will carry over into misdirected, and arguably unethical, treatment.

So what are the ethical implications of the above conceptual problems in the representation of risk and risk factors? In our view, there are two main difficulties. First, the lack of clarity concerning the nature of risk factors means that any conclusions concerning individuals' offence-related dispositions will be flawed. Therefore, risk-informed planning for treatment will inherit these flaws and result in treatment that is weakly justified and poorly directed. Second, the lack of theoretical attention to the structure and function of dynamic risk factors has resulted in a lack of models explicating the risk–aetiology relationship. This means that clinicians are unable to consult relatively robust theories when they assess individual sex offenders and instead are forced to rely on their own, possibly ad hoc, formulations to account for the list of factors apparent in offenders and what this means in terms of the possibility of future sexual offending. The ethical problem is that knowledge is assumed to exist (i.e., that dynamic risk factors play a causal role) when it does not. This is a serious issue, as risk assessment of offenders has a significant impact on their future lives and may result in severe restrictions on liberty, relationships, and the exercise of personal agency. If the assumptions that underpin decisions resulting in adverse consequence are not adequately justified, this is an ethical violation. In fact, it arguably constitutes a violation of human rights norms (Ward & Birgden, 2007). There is a failure to appreciate that sex offenders are human rights holders as well as transgressors and to be responsive to their entitlements as opposed to their duties to other members of the community.

Terminological Vagueness

A second cluster of ethical problems associated with the conceptualization of risk reflects a lack of clarity concerning terminology. For example, there is an important distinction between *risk assessment* and *risk management*, which if not kept in mind can lead to ethical violations on behalf of the practitioners. On the one hand, risk assessment is essentially a set of procedures that produces an estimation of sex offenders' likelihood of harming others or themselves. Risk assessment culminates in a prediction used to help criminal justice decision-makers in the determination of sentences, setting of treatment and parole conditions, and, on occasions, the imposition of civil detention on individuals who have completed their sentences. On the other hand, risk management concerns the way in which individual risk factors are handled during the intervention phase and follows on from the allocation of an offender to a risk band. In contemporary sex offender programmes, risk management techniques and strategies arguably constitute the heart of what is also called (less commonly now) treatment or therapy. It is risk management that poses the greatest ethical problem if not done well. In order to develop an intervention plan, as noted above, the causal role of dynamic risk factors has to be thought through and a case formulation (a case formulation is a clinical explanation of the origin, development, and interrelationship of an offender's problems) constructed to guide the risk management process. The identification of predisposing, precipitating, and perpetuating factors in a case formulation that revolves around risk management is likely to help practitioners decide what the intervention targets ought to be and, relatedly, any conditions that should be imposed on sex offenders during and after treatment. Care needs to be taken (as noted in the above material on causal factors) that the two tasks of risk assessment and risk management are delineated and any risk management plan is systematically constructed and draws from aetiological models in addition to information on dynamic risk factors.

Science of Risk Assessment

A third set of ethical practice issues arising from the conceptualization and definition of risk concern the science or technology of risk assessment. It is accepted that even the best risk instruments only modestly predict reoffending, and that a considerable number of individuals expected to reoffend will not and some of those who are viewed as low risk will subsequently commit another sexual offence (Cook & Michie, 2013). The concern is that individuals may be subject to severe constraints on their freedom, access to human goods and service, and so on because they were assessed as high risk. The imposition of civil detention orders, restrictions on freedom of movement, or freedom of association, or being placed on a sex offender register or subject to community notification, are potential threats to basic human rights. By way of contrast, failure to detect false negatives may result in the violation of the moral and human rights of future victims. The onus is on clinicians to be reflective in their practice and careful about the way in which risk assessment and decisions about offenders' risk status are reached.

Value-Laden Nature of Risk Assessment

A final set of ethical challenges concerns the value-laden nature of risk assessment. Categorizing risk is a policy decision, not a scientific one, based on the resources available to manage risk. Decisions about where the thresholds (i.e., where particular cut-off points are in the various measures) between the different risk bands are set and how factors are balanced (minimize risk rather than balance harms and goods) reflect prior value judgements. The kinds of questions that precede (a) the selection of cut-off points, and (b) the interpretation of the meaning of the risk bands are necessarily value judgements. Communities will need to have thought through what degree of risk is acceptable to them and have decided how best to balance the interests of the offender with those of other people. Relatedly, the practice interpretation of risk bands for risk management purposes is also in part an ethical judgement. Should all individuals with a medium risk score and above be subject to restrictions or just those who are assessed as medium–high or high risk? A worry is that there may be a lack of balance when thinking about the interests of the community and those of offenders, and the equation will always favour the community. As Ward and Birgden (2007) argued, while some offenders' human rights may be curtailed (only with a strong justification), they can never be, and should be not regarded as, forfeited. Although it may be tempting for practitioners to focus on the science of risk assessment and management, there is always a strong ethical or moral dimension also be considered. Risk assessment and risk management (or treatment) are comprised of factual and normative judgements that should both be reflected on by ethical practitioners.

Ethical Issues Indirectly Associated with Risk Assessment and Management

In this section, we discuss two clusters of background moral assumptions and values that can indirectly create problematic ethical issues for forensic and correctional practitioners, namely punishment and how best to resolve the problem of conflicting professional roles (i.e., a dual relationship problem).

Punishment – the Moral Status of Offenders

An important set of ethical issues that are indirectly related to risk assessment concern the moral status of offenders. Offenders by virtue of being members of the moral community (and hence justifiably punished) possess equal moral status to non-offenders (Ward & Salmon, 2009). This equal standing gives each person the authority to make certain claims of members of the moral community, and in turn to acknowledge his or her own obligations to respect the legitimate claims of other people. As stated earlier, preventive schemes such as civil detention restrict the liberty of serious sex offenders who *may* reoffend in the future and, as a consequence, subjects them to coerced treatment and management. Restricting liberty on the basis of what an individual may do undermines legal principles and core rights such as the presumption of innocence, finality of sentencing, the principle of proportionality, and the principle against double punishment (Doyle, Ogloff, & Thomas, 2011). However, perhaps the greatest threat to the human rights of offenders springs from the problem of punishment.

The problem of punishment arises from the need to justify ethically intentionally harming another human being, when normally such actions are deemed unacceptable. It is not enough to state that criminal actions are deserved, or that punishment is likely to result in a reduction in crime or the reformation of an offender's character. What are also required are reasons for permitting the infliction of harm on others. Hence it is necessary to provide an argument to justify the state acting in ways that impose harms on those who break the law. In addition to the suffering experienced by offenders and their families, there is the question of the financial cost to the state of building and running prisons rather than putting resources to alternative uses such as creating better healthcare services or providing free high-quality education and vocational training for everyone.

State-inflicted punishment in the criminal justice system involves the intentional imposition of pain (sanction, burden) on an individual following his or her violation of important social norms that are intended to protect significant common interests of members of the political community (Bennett, 2008). It is accepted by philosophers and theorists of law that the criminal justice institution of punishment has at least six essential elements (Boonin, 2008). In brief, the actions constituting punishment follow an offence against legal rules; are imposed and implemented by individuals authorized by the state; are intentional (directed towards a particular end or action outcome); are reprobative (express disapproval or censure); are retributive (follow an actual wrongful act committed by the offender); and are harmful (result in suffering, a burden, or deprivation to the offender).

At least three theories of the justification of punishment are evident in the literature: retributive, consequential, and communicative/restorative (Boonin, 2008; Ward & Salmon, 2009). According to the *retributive theory*, the primary aim of punishment is to hold offenders accountable for crimes by inflicting burdens that are roughly equal in harm to those inflicted on their victims. It is a question of restoring moral balance. *Consequential* theorists assert that punishment is more likely than other types of crime reduction practices to produce an overall aggregate effect of crime reduction and that this is what justifies them. The claim is that punishment functions to deter, incapacitate, or reform offenders and that these effects in turn reduce the overall crime rate. Finally, for *communicative/restorative* theorists, the aim of punishment is to repair or restore offenders' relationships with victims (if possible) and the broader community. For example, Duff (2001) argued that there are three aims integral to the institution of punishment: secular repentance, reform, and reconciliation through the imposition of sanctions.

Ward and Salmon (2009) assert that retributive and communicative theories of punishment explicitly endorse the *equal status* of all members of the moral community, whereas the consequential theory is more ambivalent, stressing as it does the overriding importance of the *consequences* of punishment. Thus, if the overall good of the community is served by the imposition of severe restrictions on offenders' freedom and access to social goods, then it is ethically justifiable. This chapter does not have the space to examine the cogency of the three theories of punishment and their implications for correctional practitioners in detail (but see Ward & Salmon, 2009). However, because of its conceptual links with utilitarianism, the consequential theory of punishment has an uneasy relationship with the concept of human rights and, arguably, struggles to find space for this important moral concept.

The relationship between punishment theories and risk assessment is complex but significant. Ward and Salmon (2009, p. 242) state that:

> the types of interventions logically implied by consequential theories of punishment resemble those promoted by the current treatment paradigm dominating correctional jurisdictions throughout the western world, the Risk–Need–Responsivity model.

The RNR model of offender rehabilitation is closely aligned with the current emphasis of sex offender practitioners on risk assessment and risk management, and in this respect, the latter inherits the ethical challenges facing consequentialist models. The concern is that sex offenders are treated as a means to the ends of other people (i.e., goals, needs) and are not treated as ends in themselves (i.e., as persons of equal value and dignity). Offenders' interests, commitments, and wishes may be too easily overridden in the perceived interests of community protection. While we appreciate the social and clinical need to identify potentially dangerous individuals and to take reasonable steps to prevent them from harming other people, it is important to take a balanced perspective when making decisions that are likely to curtail someone's rights. What is being suggested is that one of the background ethical assumptions inherent in risk management approaches to sex offender treatment (and thus is relevant for risk assessment) is the endorsement of a consequentialist theory of punishment. It is not that punishment is necessarily treatment (as cogently argued by Glaser, 2003) but rather, because sex offenders are typically undergoing or face the possibility of punishment, practitioners should confront the ethical issues that arise from this consequence. More specifically, they ought to examine critically the practices they are engaged in themselves and note any ethically problematic features of their practice or the institutions for which they work. There is a danger that risk assessment and risk management can be underpinned by a consequential defence of punishment, and thus make it easy for practitioners to justify the interests of the community rather than those of the offender. That is, there could be a lack of moral balance. For example, there may be a failure to consider the possibility of potential harm to the offenders when creating risk management treatment plans (following a risk assessment) through the imposition of unnecessarily severe restrictions and depriving them of the opportunity to make important life decisions for themselves. In addition, the weakening of core relationships and social connection to other people may cause significant damage to a sex offender, frustrating as it does basic human needs for connectedness and intimacy. Of course, it may be that a consequential justification will satisfy practitioners, but given its perceived lack of alignment with human rights norms, it makes sense to be cautious. We encourage practitioners to use the human rights distinction between entitlements and duties when formulating risk assessment reports and plans. Keeping offenders' entitlements to services and goods firmly in mind, alongside the need to protect the public from further harm, will hopefully culminate in plans that attempt to enhance offenders' functioning while also reducing their reoffending risk (Ward & Maruna, 2007).

Moral Repair

An ethical issue concerned with offenders' moral status and its implication for risk assessment revolves around the concept of moral repair. Walker (2006) stated that moral repair is 'restoring or creating trust and hope in a shared sense of value and responsibility' (p. 28) following the experience of intentional and unjustified harm at the hands of another person or persons. Sex offenders who have been physically, emotionally, or sexually abused in the past have rights to be treated accordingly. According to Walker, there are six core tasks encompassed by moral repair: (1) placing responsibility on the offender, (2) acknowledging and addressing the harm suffered by the victim, (3) asserting the authority of the norms violated by the offender and the community's commitment to them, (4) restoring or creating trust among the victims in the relevant norms and the practices that express them, (5) creating hope that the norms and the individuals responsible for supporting them are worthy of trust, and (6) re-establishing or establishing adequate moral relationships between victims, wrongdoers, and the community. It is clear that a core task is acknowledging the harm experienced by the person concerned and responding appropriately to this fact.

What are the ethical implications for practitioners engaged in risk assessment and risk management? Sexual offenders who have been victimized possess a dual status from a moral repair viewpoint: they are legitimately subject to censure and also have a right to an acknowledgement of the harm they have experienced and genuine efforts to repair the damage inflicted on them. A concern is that practitioners who are engaged in risk assessment and a risk-informed case formulation of offenders who have been victims of violence in the past might overlook their entitlements to some type of restoration. Rather, they could concentrate on the task of identifying risk levels and associated dynamic risk factors (Douglas et al., 2013). The concept of human rights can help practitioners to avoid this ethical mistake by virtue of its stress on offenders' entitlements to a range of services and goods *and* their obligations to others. The subsequent formulation of risk and a risk management plan should reflect this dual awareness and arguably seek to ensure that any subsequent interventions enhance their capabilities (and hence repair the damage inflicted) alongside reducing their risk of recidivism. A reliance on a simple risk assessment and reduction model without a strong human rights lens may result in an overly narrow and ethically problematic set of recommendations.

Dual Relationship Problem

The dual relationship problem in the correctional and forensic domains emerges from the overlap and subsequent experience of role conflict between two sets of ethical norms: those associated with community protection and justice versus norms related to individual well-being and autonomy (Ward, 2013). The problem occurs because many, if not all, forensic practitioners have their professional roots in mental health or social disciplines such as psychiatry, clinical psychology, social work, or law, and as such may struggle to justify ethically aspects of forensic and/or correctional work. The value conflict is between norms that seek to increase the well-being of individuals with whom practitioners work via the enhancement of well-being and reduction of suffering. The specific ethical codes formulated to guide practice in the domains of forensic/correctional and mental health have been designed to accomplish distinct aims and inevitably conflict in certain arenas of performance. A good example occurs in risk assessment where the aim is to arrive at a likelihood that the offender will commit another offence and there is virtually no attention paid to what is in his or her best interest, or even thinking about how best to balance offenders' interests in living 'good' lives against the desires of members of the community to feel safe, and to experience reduced rates of predation. The conflict between the two sets of codes or norm clusters may make it difficult for practitioners to decide on a course of action when assessing or treating offenders, and once this has been accomplished, make it harder to justify their intended actions. According to Ward (2013, p. 94):

> The problem of dual relationships is a manifestation of the wider underlying ethical issue of *value pluralism*. Value pluralism occurs when a number of distinct ethical codes (or if you prefer, sets of norms) exist within a society or community, none of which can be established as ethically superior by a rational, impartial observer … The clash between the various ethical codes may be a *horizontal* one between codes at the same level of abstraction (e.g., a professional ethical code versus a criminal justice employee code) or *vertical*, where professional norms conflicts with more abstract principles (e.g., human rights norms might clash with those regulating staff conduct at a high security prison).

Ward (2013) argues that all of the attempted solutions to the dual relationship problem fail because of its source in value pluralism. He argues for the application of a procedural approach based on the concept of moral acquaintances, where individuals experiencing role or value conflict (within themselves or with others) attempt to create risk management treatment plans based on shared moral commitments and beliefs. In order to have a chance at creating mutually agreed upon plans that respect individuals' varying values and beliefs, it is necessary to engage in dialogues that are open and intent on incorporating varying viewpoints. In other words, ethical focus should be on the quality of relationships in addition to principles and norms such as rights and duties.

In risk assessment (and subsequent risk management), the priority is to estimate the potential of individuals to harm others rather than to identify each individual's needs, rights, and obligations. This can create problems of balance and partialism. The ethical risks arising from the dual relationship problem for practitioners involved in risk assessment and risk management are that they (a) fail to acknowledge there is a problem or (b) dismiss its significance. The former possibility means that practitioners will suffer from *ethical blindness*, where real and pressing moral issues are simply not noticed because of a lack of knowledge and/or normative sensitivity. Human rights theory, with its insistence on the equal value of all members of the moral community, and requirement that everyone's core interest should be attended to, can help to overcome this limitation. Because there is an explicit effort to factor in actively everyone's interests and viewpoints, there is a reduced danger of privileging some group or persons at the expense of others. The latter possibility arises from failure to accept that there are multiple and at times conflicting values in play during a risk assessment process (and subsequent risk management), which cannot be easily rationally resolved. Hence all persons implicated in the assessment process should have their perspectives and personal priorities noted and taken into consideration. Adopting a human rights and moral rights framework can facilitate this task and make it much easier to ensure that the risk assessment procedure and outcome are ethically justifiable.

Conclusions

We have identified a number of ethical issues that are directly or indirectly associated with sex offender risk assessment and risk management. In our view, the concepts of moral rights and human rights can be helpful in avoiding some of the ethical pitfalls that are pervasive in the field. Ultimately, there are no easy solutions because at the very heart of risk assessment is the problem of value pluralism and the incommensurability of values such as community protection and offender freedom and well-being. By this we mean that they are genuinely independent values that cannot be subsumed within each other or definitively ranked in terms of their objective superiority across every situation. However, it is possible to reach an agreement between the parties involved in the particular situation in question or at least make a genuine effort to do so. One of the advantages of adopting a human rights framework when working with offenders is that practitioners learn to think automatically about the overall balance of interests at stake in specific assessment situations, and to take note of each person's obligations and entitlements. Reflecting on rights in a risk assessment and management context is likely to create greater knowledge of the ethical complexities of practice with sex offenders and ultimately will increase ethical responsiveness and sensitivity. There are always multiple stakeholders directly involved in a concrete risk assessment situation and therefore varying perspectives and rights (& duties) to take into account in any decisions and subsequent risk management intervention plan. In our view, we all have a responsibility to be both carers and protectors, and if we sacrifice one role for the other the likely result is ethically impoverished practice, and broader social injustice.

References

Bennett, C. (2008). *The apology ritual: A philosophical theory of punishment*. Cambridge, England: Cambridge University Press.

Boonin, D. (2008). *The problem of punishment*. New York, NY: Cambridge University Press.

Cooke, D. J., & Michie, C. (2013). Violence risk assessment: From prediction to understanding – or from what? To why? In C. Logan & L. Johnstone (Eds.), *Managing clinical risk: A guide to effective practice* (pp. 3–25). Abingdon, England: Routledge.

Douglas, K. S., Blanchard, A. J. E., & Hendry, M. C. (2013). Violence risk assessment and management: Putting structured professional judgment into practice. In C. Logan & L. Johnstone (Eds.), *Managing clinical risk: A guide to effective practice* (pp. 29–55). Abingdon, England: Routledge.

Doyle, D. J., Ogloff, J., & Thomas, S. (2011). Designated as dangerous: Characteristics of sex offenders subject to post-sentence orders in Australia. *Australian Psychologist, 46*, 41–48.

Duff, R. A. (2001). *Punishment, communication, and community*. New York, NY: Oxford University Press.

Freeden, M. (1991). *Rights*. Minneapolis, MN: University of Minnesota Press.

Gewirth, A. (1981). *Reason and morality*. Chicago, IL: University of Chicago Press.

Glaser, B. (2003). Therapeutic jurisprudence: An ethical paradigm for therapists in sex offender treatment programs. *Western Criminology Review, 4*, 143–154.

Griffin, J. (2008). *On human rights* . Oxford, England: Oxford University Press.

Helmus, L., Hanson, R. K., Thornton, D., Babchishin, K. M., & Harris, A. J. R (2012). Absolute recidivism rates predicted by Static-99R and Static-2002R sex offender risk assessment tools vary across samples: A meta-analysis. *Criminal Justice and Behavior, 39,* 1148–1171. doi:10.1177/0093854812443648

Mann, R. E., Hanson, R. K., & Thornton, D. (2010). Assessing risk for sexual recidivism: Some proposals on the nature of psychologically meaningful risk factors. *Sexual Abuse: A Journal of Research and Treatment, 22,* 191–217. doi:10.1177/1079063210366039

Monahan, J. (2014). The inclusion of biological risk factors in violence risk assessments. In I. Singh, W. Sinnott-Armstrong, & J. Savulesc (Eds.), *Bioprediction, biomarkers, and bad behavior: Scientific, legal, and ethical challenges* (pp. 57–76). New York, NY: Oxford University Press.

Nickel, J. W. (2007). *Making sense of human rights* (2nd ed.). Malden, MA: Blackwell Publishing.

Orend, B. (2002). *Human rights: Concept and context.* Peterborough, Canada: Broadview Press.

Thornton, D. (2013). Implications of our developing understanding of risk and protective factors in the treatment of adult male sexual offenders. *International Journal of Behavioral Consultation and Therapy, 8,* 62–65.

Walker, M. U. (2006). *Moral repair: Reconstructing moral relations after wrongdoings.* New York, NY: Cambridge University Press.

Ward, T. (2013). Addressing the dual relationship problem in forensic and correctional practice. *Aggression and Violent Behavior, 18,* 92–100. doi:10.1016/j.avb.2012.10.006

Ward, T., & Beech, A. (2015). Dynamic risk factors: A theoretical dead-end? *Psychology, Crime, & Law, 21,* 100–113.

Ward, T., & Birgden, A. (2007). Human rights and clinical correctional practice. *Aggression and Violent Behavior, 12,* 628–643. doi:10.1016/j.avb.2007.05.001

Ward, T., Gannon, T. E., & Birgden, A. (2007). Human rights and the treatment of sex offenders. *Sexual Abuse: A Journal of Research and Treatment, 19,* 195–204. doi:10.1007/s11194-007-9053-4

Ward, T., & Maruna, S. (2007). *Rehabilitation: Beyond the risk paradigm.* Abingdon, England: Routledge.

Ward, T., Polaschek, D., & Beech, A. R. (2006). *Theories of sexual offending.* Chichester, England: John Wiley & Sons, Ltd.

Ward, T., & Salmon, K. (2009). The ethics of punishment: Correctional practice implications. *Aggression and Violent Behavior, 14,* 239–247.

54

Risk Assessment and Culture
Issues for Research and Practice

Armon J. Tamatea

University of Waikato, New Zealand

Douglas P. Boer

University of Canberra, Australia

The existence of such practices were found when a focus group participant told the group that her sister's nine-year- old daughter became HIV positive when she was given to her uncle to 'cleanse' himself from HIV and STDs. (Meursing et al., 1995, p. 1697)

Sexual offending against children is an international social problem that is limited neither to a particular geographical location nor a period in time (Stermac, Segal, & Gillis, 1989). Although typically defined in legal terms, sexual offending behaviour occurs in a cultural context that is both informed by, and a violation of, shared social meanings that otherwise influence an individual's perception of their behaviour and the impact it has on others. Indeed, prohibitions against specific sexual acts are commonplace, suggesting a universal understanding of the harms that can occur as a result of this behaviour. Furthermore, as individuals travel across borders, societies have become more pluralistic with the consequence that mental health and criminal justice professionals will engage with increasingly diverse populations.

In Western industrialized societies, offending behaviour is an aspect of life that is quasi-medicalized, and seen through a lens that shapes our perception and experience of criminal justice concerns in psychological ways. In this regard, risk assessment, perhaps more than any other form of psychological encounter, reflects a significant power relationship between an individual 'offender' and a practitioner owing to its stated purpose of providing the basis for informing case management decisions, the consequences of which will have a long-standing impact for offenders, particularly perceptions of the usefulness of psychological engagement. The purpose

The Wiley Handbook on the Theories, Assessment, and Treatment of Sexual Offending.
Edited by Douglas P. Boer. Volume II: Assessment, edited by Leam A. Craig and Martin Rettenberger.
© 2017 John Wiley & Sons, Ltd. Published 2017 by John Wiley & Sons, Ltd.

of this chapter is to explore the issues involved at the interface of culture and risk assessment in the context of sexual offending against children. At a time when treatment programmes for sex offenders were still too new and unstandardized to generate sufficient outcome data to yield robust treatment effects with an already low base-rate behaviour, Marshall, Fernandez, Hudson, and Ward (1998) issued a challenge to modify practice with different populations. This chapter aims to discuss risk assessment by exploring broad cultural assumptions and issues with current practice with a view to offering some directions for future research and development of culturally responsive practices.

'You Don't Know What You Can't Assess': Cultural Assumptions of Risk Assessment

The psychological assessment of individuals across a spectrum of ethnic and cultural groups involves a variety of challenges. This section discusses the broad cultural assumptions of the practice of risk assessment and considers issues relating to power and representations of 'reality' that are reflected in and reinforced in current practice.

Risk Assessments and Power

Although discussed more fully elsewhere in this volume, the assessment of recidivism risk is broadly considered here to be a formal process of information gathering and synthesizing that is concerned with two primary outcomes: (1) how accurately criminal behaviour can be predicted in an individual case and (2) classification of a given offender into subgroups in order to assign them to particular interventions (Andrews & Bonta, 2010; Mills, Kroner, & Morgan, 2011). In other words, risk assessments inform decision-making for large volumes of offenders where resources are limited or scarce with a view towards reducing recidivism and, in turn, promoting safer communities.

Historically, the development of risk assessment measures has been the privilege of the test designers – who in some cases may also be service providers and have an inherent belief in the 'goodness' of the assessment process – rather than end users who consume the outcomes such as Parole Boards, the offenders themselves, or even the broader community, most of whom are likely to be generally untrained and uninitiated in the specialty of test design and construction. Consequently, risk measures are practitioner-oriented where they are administered, scored, and interpreted by practitioners and not the individual who is the subject of the assessment. Such a developmental process risks promoting a mythic ideal, where a belief exists in a single best and 'right way' of doing things. Such an ideal is often couched in terms of being 'best practice'. However, this notion reinforces a perception that there is only one way that risk assessments should be practised and also more readily dismisses alternative viewpoints, thus reducing the relevancy of risk assessments with culturally different individuals, especially those who hold a holistic worldview that permits greater degrees of ambiguity.

Risk Assessments and 'Reality'

In addition to information gathering, risk assessment is understood to be a *process* that involves (1) determining a given individual's level of risk of an offence-related outcome – typically expressed as a probability or stratified categories (e.g., 'high', 'moderate', 'low'), (2) identifying salient factors that contribute to that estimation of risk – these factors are derived from the literature and based on group data (e.g., sexual self-regulation, intimacy deficits), (3) identifying risk management strategies and considerations to address that risk (e.g., intensive group-based cognitive–behavioural therapy), and (4) communicating the significance of that risk to decision-makers (Mills et al., 2011). A function of this process is to reduce uncertainty of future danger by simplifying the complexity of a wide array of data. This is largely achievable when large data sets yield measurable variables that can be subjected to statistical analyses. However, such prescriptive approaches risk minimizing or neglecting *cultural* differences, which are not as amenable to statistical measurement and inference – and hence overlook 'realities' that are different from that of the practitioner.

Risk Assessments and Social Agendas

Risk assessment procedures are a form of cultural practice that has its roots in Western empirical traditions, and like other cultural practices, is constantly shaped by a number of factors. First, a sexual offence is a matter for the state to respond. This means that the definition and threshold for what is considered to be a sexual offence are typically defined in legislation and are therefore linked with controlled vocabularies and classification schemes that impose a special interpretive system in order to frame discussions about risk (e.g., 'dangerous', 'sexual predator', 'public protection').

Second, in Western countries, sexual offending is presumed to have a psychosocial cause. Indeed, current best practice emphasizes that a robust and judicious risk assessment of offender responsibility and prediction of future offences should be based on a multimodal, multi-informant approach (Bonta, 2002). However, there exists a dominant discourse in some jurisdictions, such as the Risk–Need–Responsivity (RNR) model (Andrews & Bonta, 1998, 2010), and psychologists are presumed to have expertise and privileged knowledge of it. For instance, commonly used analytical procedures such as receiver operator characteristic (ROC), survival curve analysis, and structural equation modelling reflect the value of predictive accuracy but also rely on a detached language of risk that is not particularly accessible to a relatively unsophisticated public who stand to benefit from this knowledge or, indeed, be sufficiently informed to respond to its limitations.

In addition, the practitioner has to approach the offending behaviour simultaneously from (1) the offender's personal and social situation (i.e., if criminogenic factors were present in the offence situation, how did they impact on the occurrence of the offence?), (2) a statistical–clinical framework (i.e., when compared with group data, what is the likelihood that a given individual will reoffend compared with other individuals with similar characteristics?), and (3) a motivational framework (e.g., to what was the offender responding?). These tasks assume an atomistic understanding of offenders that considers an individual as a totality in themselves, placing primacy on individual agency. However, such a view decontextualizes persons in relation to their communities and culture.

Third, the state (as an agency of control) imposes limits on the manner in which practitioners and psychologists are forced to define a complex and multifaceted problem in an overly simplistic way. Consequences of such political influence include the following:

1. *Privileging knowledge.* For instance, Western scientific approaches are more likely to be valued as evidenced by state-sponsored research and development than are other 'exotic' ideas that are not derived from an empirical basis. This bias against the development of indigenous or minority-led research may reflect what Sue (1999) referred to as selective reinforcement of scientific principles and can be reflected in poor research opportunities for indigenous-led research or lack of an unambiguous outcome with non-dominant research methodologies.
2. *Valuing specific outcomes.* The reduction of recidivism is a near-universal outcome that is valued across jurisdictions. However, 'improving well-being', although not unrelated, is also a goal sought by indigenous communities that does not necessarily superimpose neatly onto mainstream risk management frameworks.
3. *Prioritizing practices.* Actuarial tools are now the *sine qua non* of risk assessment practice and reflect a conclusion made by Quinsey, Harris, Rice, and Cormier (1998) that actuarial methods are 'too good and clinical judgement too poor to risk contaminating the former with the latter' (p. 171). Indeed, actuarial methods assume an atheoretical, objective (and presumably impersonal and culture-neutral) basis that relies on 'factual' information such as that derived from official criminal records rather than data derived from subjective and less rigorous approaches. However, despite the impressive predictive accuracy of some of these measures, it is noted that the data itself are decontextualized – revealing some important 'trees' but no 'forest'. Culture, on the other hand, is context specific and incongruent with pure actuarial approaches because culture is meaningless in the absence of context.

Why Culture Matters in Risk Assessment

In recent years, the sex offender assessment literature has been largely silent on the issue of culture. For the purposes of this chapter, *race* – a somewhat outmoded term with sociopolitical dimensions – represents an imposed classification based on phenotypy (e.g., genetically determined characteristics such as skin colour), whereas *ethnicity* includes race in addition to a broader range of characteristics such as shared ancestry and history (e.g., African American, Chinese) (Atkinson, Morten, & Sue, 1998). Both race and ethnicity are organizing principles and provide a convenient demarcation strategy to describe a sample. *Culture*, by contrast, is a less exact term and reflects the interaction between the social world and people's ideas about it (López & Guarnaccia, 2000), and this confluence would evolve over time, perhaps over generations. Broadly, culture is something that is learned and shared amongst a group of people and includes intangible ideas by which an individual codes and interprets their environment and events, recognizes and decides what is valued and ideal, and also what activities should be enacted or avoided (Evans, 2005), in addition to processes of problem definition and problem solving (Kleinman, 1988). In this regard, culture is best appreciated in a context of time-dependent relationships to be recognized rather than as a 'thing' to be reified and measured. Culture also suggests a totality, and only by understanding the complex of relationships and placing them back into the field from which they were abstracted can we hope to avoid misleading inferences and increase our share of understanding (Sobo, 2009). Sex offences, then, are likely to be more fully understood when the offender's cultural context is more fully considered.

The importance of culture in risk assessment is conspicuously manifest in (1) duty of care, (2) informing decision-making, and (3) illuminating complexity, and is discussed as follows.

Ethical duty. Professional psychological associations in English-speaking countries have recognized and affirmed respect for diversity as an ethical responsibility. For instance, ethical codes for psychologists in major Western jurisdictions comment that those who perform risk assessments with populations that are not only ethnically different, but also culturally complex, need to acknowledge the limitations of any standard risk assessment instrument as applied to a particular population – in particular, ethical principles of respect and dignity for people and persons (Société canadienne de psychologie, 2000; Australian Psychological Society, 2007; New Zealand Psychological Society, 2002), self-determination (Ethics Committee of the British Psychological Society, 2009), and interpreting assessment results (American Psychological Association, 2010).

Culture is informative. An uncritical application of risk assessment practices risks an over-reliance on formal tools that criminalize extraordinary experience and deny the meaning-oriented subjectivity of offending (and suffering) in favour of classifying by risk band (e.g., 'high', 'low') that lacks personal and collective significance. Culture shapes *what* behaviours one expresses and *how* they are expressed, and also influences the *meaning* that an individual attributes to their offending behaviour and also how one interacts with the criminal justice system (e.g., mistrust, suspicion; Sue & Sue, 1990). Culture also influences what a community regards as appropriate or inappropriate behaviour and what forms of social influence and control can effectively exert a powerful impact on an individual's likelihood of future sexually offensive behaviour. Culturally informed beliefs, attitudes, and behaviours vary from group to group, with some communities reflecting greater tolerance for sexually deviant behaviour. For instance, Stermac et al. (1989) emphasized the role of social attitudes and beliefs as a source of cultural variability with sex offenders, particularly communities that have a different view of, or even a relatively high tolerance for, sexually harmful behaviour. On the other hand, there are ample examples of communities and countries becoming more punitive following egregious examples of offending. For instance, many states in the United States have enacted Sexually Violent Predator statutes following terrible crimes against children (see Janus, 2006), and these statutes are reflective of a cultural shift away from therapeutic approaches to sex offenders to a more punitive approach.

Culture is complex. Every aspect of experience is touched by culture. By virtue of its very complexity, culture risks obscuring more than it reveals, which can be problematic in current risk assessment practice – a field that utilizes and values rule-governed assessment procedures and reliance on simplified and reductionistic understandings of group data. A typical risk assessment is likely to draw upon a variety of sources that are culturally informed, such as an individual's historical context, psychiatric and medical condition, developmental history, current social context, substance use, family history, and socioeconomic status. Furthermore, individuals can (and often do) identify with more than one culture. For example, offenders from communities that have experienced oppression and assimilation from the dominant group may express an affinity for both their traditional people in addition to the imposed norms of the dominant culture. To omit cultural information is to provide a superficial treatment of an individual's reality.

A primary challenge, then, of any psychological assessment is to *understand individuals in their context.* To take steps to appreciate the perspective of individuals who are culturally different is to attempt to understand an alternative and collective worldview and, by implication, a communal history (Rack, 1982; Sobo, 2009; Sue & Sue, 2013). The impact of an individual's cultural heritage and sociopolitical legacy can inform the perpetration (and victimization) of sexual abuse amongst specific communities. For instance, Ellerby (1994) described aboriginal sex offenders in Canada as being more likely than non-aboriginal sex offenders to exhibit issues associated with displacement, abandonment, and racism; personal identity confusion; history of maltreatment; poverty and death due to illness, suicide, and violence; deficits in education, employment skills, financial position, and social supports; and histories of more aggressive sexual behaviours, suggesting a range of pervasive stressors that can impact on attitudes and interactions towards others that can be manifest across a population.

In sum, risk assessment is a cultural practice that typically reflects and privileges an individualized Western cultural perspective over the realities of peoples from indigenous and minority communities. Engaging culture, then, is important in risk assessment because it offers insights into (1) *relevance* – defining meaningful outcomes for offenders and communities, (2) *rehabilitation* – determining the suitability and effectiveness of interventions, and (3) *reintegration* – informing how control in a given social group, especially one that is presumed to exert an influence on an offender, is defined and exercised.

Research Issues: 'You Can't Assess What You Don't Know'

> Simply recruiting and including ethnic minorities in a research sample would … not necessarily lead to new knowledge about ethnic minority populations. (Hall, 2001, p. 503)

The increase in the development and use of risk assessment tools is a global phenomenon that highlights the importance of cross-cultural perspectives and the development of culturally valid approaches to assessing for sexual offence risk. The ability for a measure to predict recidivism accurately has significant value for communities as a means of informing public safety and justifying resource allocation to individuals considered to possess a heightened probability of dangerousness. The array of tools that have emerged over the last two decades, such as the Rapid Risk Assessment of Sexual Offence Recidivism (RRASOR) (Hanson, 1997), the Static-99 (Hanson & Thornton, 1999) and its revision, the Static-99R (Helmus, Babchishin, Hanson, & Thornton, 2009), the Sexual Offender Risk Appraisal Guide (SORAG) (Quinsey et al., 1998), the Sex Offender Needs Assessment Rating (SONAR) (Hanson & Harris, 2001) and its derivatives the STABLE-2007 and ACUTE-2007 (Hanson, Harris, Scott, & Helmus, 2007), and the Violence Risk Scale: Sex Offender version (VRS:SO) (Wong, Olver, Nicholaichuk, & Gordon, 2003), has demonstrated utility in yielding risk estimates that justify resource allocation and increased public confidence (Singh, Desmarais, & Van Dorn, 2013; Singh & Fazel, 2010). Despite the benefits offered by these tools, the appropriate use of these measures with diverse populations is still an open question (e.g., Långström, 2004). In this section, research issues such as cross-cultural generalizability, scope of extant research, and methodological problems are discussed.

Generalizability and Cultural Validity

The spread of risk assessment measures across international jurisdictions reflects the value that such tools have in facilitating offender management solutions. Indeed, measures such as the Static-99 have enjoyed routine use beyond their country of development and have surfaced in such distant countries as Australia (Smallbone & Rallings, 2013) and New Zealand (Skelton, Riley, Wales, & Vess, 2006). However, although a measure may have been found to have a respectable level of validity during construction, it does not necessarily follow that the measure will also be valid for a specific individual in a specific situation (Groth-Marnat, 2009). Although this is an empirical question, practitioners are cautioned about the wholesale adoption of risk assessment tools that are used in jurisdictions where these measures were not developed (Hanson & Morton-Bourgon, 2008; Rogers, 2000).

Bonta (2002) argued that useful and effective risk assessment measures are quantitative, structured, and empirically linked to a relevant criterion as expressed by discrete events such as recidivism or parole failure. The benefits are fairly obvious. Quantitative methodologies serve to reduce the complexity of data and increase empirical rigour, structured protocols reduce human error (and presumably bias) by means of strict scoring rules and systematic data-collection strategies, and specific criteria reduce the range and type of outcomes of concern. Together, these aspects of risk assessment tool development reflect an increased focus on risk management as defined by specified results, but may also occlude related but competing interests that concern communities such as improving well-being or eliciting offender redemption narratives (Ward & Marshall, 2007).

'Race' as a Proxy for 'Culture'

Validation studies (e.g., Långström, 2004) and meta-analyses (e.g., Singh & Fazel, 2010) typically include 'ethnicity' as a variable; however, it becomes apparent that authors are essentially discussing 'race' as there is little or no acknowledgement, discussion, or exploration of variation within these categories, but rather a blunt categorization of groups within a sample. For instance, validation studies of Canadian-developed measures such as the Static-99 and RRASOR in Germany (Rettenberger & Eher, 2006) and the Static-99-R in Australia (Smallbone & Rallings, 2013) reveal comparable findings to the extant literature. However, the role of cultural factors that contributes to unique variance poses problems with regard to representativeness of the sample and, in turn, generalizability of the findings to others in the ethnic group. Such research risks emphasizing a *universalist* perspective, where racial, ethnic, and cultural differences are seen to have a minimal or insignificant impact on assessment and treatment outcomes – a view that is predicated on an assumption of commonality, where all human beings share the same fundamental characteristics (Tyler, Brome, & Williams, 1991). Although such a view emphasizes common offender factors (e.g., poor sexual self-regulation, prior sex offences), it also underestimates the role that culture plays in shaping and forming views and beliefs that promote or inhibit offending behaviour.

Extant research on risk assessment tools in relation to culture is typically uneven or treats the subject of ethnicity and culture in such a broad manner as to render the data meaningless, and hence compromise the generalizability of these tools. Consequently, descriptive cross-national comparative research has tended to underestimate the impact of cultural differences. Hanson and Morton-Bourgon's (2009) meta-analysis of 118 prediction studies of sex offender risk assessment tools indicated that empirically derived measures were more accurate than unstructured professional judgement. They also cautioned that prediction reflects an imperfect science and that predictive validity in one setting does not necessarily translate into another, adding that the 'extent to which the differences in predictive accuracy are due to missing records or socio-cultural differences remains to be explored' (p. 9). They further commented that all countries should conduct local validity studies prior to routine implementation of measures developed in other jurisdictions. Bonta, LaPrairie, and Wallace-Capretta (1997) commented that the design of instruments and treatment programmes among some (subgroups of aboriginal offenders) should at least be identified because some accommodation may be required. For instance, Olver et al. (2013) commented that social adversities commonly faced by indigenous peoples, such as unemployment, low education, and social marginalization, have their origins in colonization and should be given due consideration in assessments and service delivery.

Robustness of Research

Gutierrez, Wilson, Rugge, and Bonta's (2013) meta-analysis of recidivism prediction with indigenous Canadian offenders revealed that common (i.e., 'central eight'[1]; Andrews & Bonta, 2010) risk factors were predictive for indigenous offenders for

---

[1] These major risk factors concern (1) history of antisocial behaviour, (2) antisocial personality pattern, (3) antisocial cognitions, attitudes, and beliefs, (4) antisocial associates, (5) family/marital, (6) school/work, (7) leisure/recreation, and (8) substance abuse.

general and non-sexual violent offending, but that between-study variability revealed wide confidence intervals calling for the need for further research, and suggested that ethnic/cultural variations may be indicative of *relative* importance of risk/need factors. They also commented that risk assessment research with indigenous peoples has been hampered by an insufficient number of studies, small sample sizes, promising but modest statistical significance, and a likely publication bias towards inclusion of statistically significant findings.

Shaw and Hannah-Moffatt's (2000) critique of the generalizability of risk assessment measures to women and minority offenders noted that (1) these measures do not take into account sociopolitical factors such as gender, ethnicity, or social disadvantage; (2) the narrow scope of the measures reflects a limited view of offending rather than as viewing offending problems holistically; (3) the restriction of information to apparently objective 'facts' does not take into account the context of events or situations; and (4) prescriptive approaches frame decision-making with respect to descriptive representations of risk (e.g., 'high', 'moderate', 'low'), and questioned whether these representations are adequate.

Used incautiously, current risk assessment tools threaten to influence practitioners to decontextualize offence data and delegitimize the offender's experience of offending. Indeed, assessment procedures that do not cue practitioners to these broader factors may contribute to a reduced sensitivity to racism, oppression, and other impediments to social justice.

Recommendations for Research

Current mainstream risk assessment tools are developed in cultural contexts that are inherently culturally biased and generalize findings to populations with questionable relevance. Culture is difficult to 'measure' beyond race and ethnicity and hence difficult to *research* in the same way as risk assessment tools. However, in order to encourage greater transparency and inclusiveness in discussing the place of risk assessment research, the following considerations are proposed:

1. *Clarify hypotheses.* The assumptions underlying the inclusion of ethnicity should be made explicit. In general, assessment research should include fuller discussions of the sample and methodology (Okazaki & Sue, 1995). For instance, is ethnicity being referred to simply to organize a dataset, or are inferences about qualitative cultural differences being made? And if so, on what basis?

2. *Encourage open dialogue with stakeholder communities.* Fantuzzo, McWayne, and Childs (2006) identified disconnection and disengagement from services (and researchers) as the reality of vulnerable communities who have experienced poor access to services and socioeconomic disadvantage. Researchers and instrument developers should include members of the relevant ethnic or cultural communities (e.g., consultants) to discuss culturally specific factors that may contribute to risk but are not captured by risk assessment approaches. This may well be easier said than done, as there is no guarantee that such mandated representation exists or would even be interested in a knowledge-generation partnership if the community does not see the role of risk assessment as speaking to the interests of

their community. Two relevant approaches that have emerged as the result of dialogue between indigenous communities and researchers are the development of
an indigenous tool for indigenous Australian violent offenders (Allan & Dawson,
2002) and the Yókw'tól[2] – a set of guidelines for the assessment of risk manageability with aboriginal (Canada) offenders (Boer, Couture, Geddes, & Ritchie,
2003). This tool was developed over the course of conversations between the
authors and community Elders with the emerging document being approved by
the community.

3. *Encourage exploratory research.* All measures have shortcomings – and most likely
    culturally situated ones. A given measure may become a part of routine practice
    and enjoy relatively continued use by practitioners in an uncritical way because
    it has face validity and other jurisdictions may well endorse the same measure.
    Furthermore, practitioners or services may adopt the use of given tools because
    they have adopted an ideology that asserts that a particular methodology is supe-
    rior to others and emphasizes some phenomena as being central and rejecting
    others (supporting some forms of evidence while dismissing others). Empirically
    based methods are valued in many services, and this may be based in part on their
    transparency. Conversely, alternative approaches that derive from indigenous or
    minority communities may be viewed as 'exotic' and less reliable. Researchers
    need to learn about new methods to avoid the risk of becoming restricted to a
    single paradigm and the requisite type of measures through sheer repetitive use at
    the expense of overseeing vital opportunities for culturally proactive service deliv-
    ery. Research that addresses cultural concerns over and above ethnicity and race as
    categorical variables offers to create opportunities to examine what accommoda-
    tions in scoring, modifications to the tools, or even the creation of new measures
    may be needed.

The 'Risks' of Risk Assessment: Towards Culturally Responsive Practice

> It is a fundamental, and dangerous, error to assume that a risk assessment procedure devel-
> oped in Canada or the United States will function the same way in Spain, Sweden, or
> Scotland. (Cooke & Michie, 2002, p. 241)

When assessing persons from other cultures, the question arises as to whether there
are factors that are likely to affect rapport, communication, problem definition,
understanding of the offending behaviour, and treatment goals (Asahina, 2010;
Gopaul-McNicol, 1997; Illovsky, 2003).

A comprehensive risk assessment is greatly informed by observing cultural processes
that serve to promote a fair process and also develop opportunities for constructive
dialogue. Inferential errors as a result of poor sensitivity to cultural encounters can

---

[2] *Yókw'tól* is a Hal'gèmeylen (the Sto:lo language) term that refers to 'the understanding of one is complete'
(Boer et al., 2003, p. 6).

result in poorly informed assessments that, in turn, can lead to inappropriate interventions and ultimately poor outcomes. In this respect, 'errors' may be a consequence of clinician bias that may manifest in dismissive attitudes towards the values, beliefs, socialization practices, ways of knowing, or social role expectations of the offender. Such errors risk ignoring multiple cultural factors rather than understanding them as elements in a matrix of meaning (Sundararajan, Misra, & Marsella, 2013). Poor outcomes may include overestimating deviancy and criminality across a given group, overlooking potentially powerful social supports, undermining the individual's coping style by way of inducing passivity from individuals whose interactions with authorities have resulted in deferential behaviour in the interview. Alternatively, reactance to the practitioner – 'resistance' – may develop due to a perception of coercion for individuals who are wary of discrimination and oppression, and who may feel that the information offered in the assessment may be misused to increase their experience of stigmatization (Korbin, 2002; Patel & Lord, 2001). Indeed, risk assessments typically occur in coercive contexts. Although an offender has the right to withdraw consent, the consequences for doing so may be costly (e.g., declined parole) and may even be interpreted as resistance. Furthermore, risk assessments, like other kinds of psychological assessments, are also interpretive processes and involve some subjectivity on the part of the practitioner. In this section, emphasis is given to creating space for exploring and understanding the context and realities of culturally different offenders, and the development of culturally responsive practices.

Understand the Issues for Offenders and Their Communities

An understanding of offending begins with an understanding of the offender and their context. A practitioner needs to learn about the communities from which an offender originates as part of a clinical and cultural formulation of that offender. Indigenous and migrant peoples are likely to have a heritage of dislocation, migration, diverse spiritual and religious beliefs, cultural conceptions of cause of offending behaviour, and manifestations of trauma. For instance, dislocation or separation from place and community is inherently stressful, and can incur loss of meaningful role identity, introduction of downward social mobility (e.g., unemployment), and the erosion of family structures and community sanctions and attitudes – particularly around sexual behaviour. Fontes, Cruz, and Tabachnick's (2001) exploratory study of sexual abuse with Latino participants ascribed sexually abusive behaviour to changes in traditional family structures, particularly loss of family connections, culture, and community as a result of immigration, resulting in a breakdown in cultural taboos, such as *verguenza* ('lack of shame'). To not be informed risks biasing professional practices and reinforces barriers to accurate assessment (Roysircar, 2005).

To understand diversity also requires an understanding of systems and injunctions that inform the individual's (1) role(s) within a given community – in relation to elders, to the opposite sex, to children, as a provider, etc.; and (2) codes of conduct – identifying behaviour that is reinforced and which is extinguished or punished, identifying behaviour that is considered normative and acceptable within the community and behaviour that is considered abnormal and prohibited, in addition to the mechanisms for managing behaviour in the interests of the community (e.g.,

ostracism, physical punishment, imprisonment). Ultimately, the challenge for the practitioner is to understand the *meaning* of specific behaviour (e.g., offending) under
these conditions. Some challenging assessment issues include the following.

Language. Unless practitioners are fluent in multilingual communication, language
can present an obvious barrier not only to effective communication, but also to the
fidelity of the assessment – especially if there are no equivalent offence-related terms
in the offender's language. For instance, Gahir and Garrett's (1999) study of Asian
sex offenders in treatment revealed no word for 'rape' in Punjabi, despite the existence
of the act.

Sexual entitlement. This may present with offenders who observe a strong patriarchi-
cal outlook – a culture that stigmatizes (female) victims indicates a diminished social
barrier for offending and suggests a social climate that tolerates perpetrator behaviour
and disadvantages victims. Although speculative, Lalor's (2004) review of child sexual
abuse in sub-Saharan Africa proposed three culturally specific explanations for the supposed recent increase in sexual abuse in this region and included the impact of rapid
social change resulting from disintegration of clan authority, an HIV/AIDS avoidance strategy, and a consequence of patriarchal traditions (i.e., male sexual relief of
'uncontrollable' sexual urges) of those communities. Similar observations were made
by Nhundu and Shumba (2001), where teacher-perpetrated sexual offending against
pupils was considered to be reflective of a highly patriarchal society. Similarly, Meursing et al. (1995) suggested that child sexual offenders in Zimbabwe were reflective
of broader cultural beliefs of male dominance in society, men's professed inability to
control sexual desire, and magical beliefs.[3]

Attitudes towards victims. Gahir and Garrett (1999) described a scenario where a
perpetrator perceived a victim as sexually promiscuous on the grounds that they had
entered a sexual relationship outside of marriage thus encouraging the offender to rape
them. How children are located within a community and a family offers insights into
how an offender may invoke a cultural justification for their behaviour. For instance,
Hispanic cultural norms reflect that children will always obey adults, by extension
indicating likely compliance with an adult's sexual advances with the expectation that
the victim will maintain silence if adult has forbidden disclosure (Kenny & McEachern,
2000).

Disclosures. Describing and discussing sexual offending behaviour can be con-
fronting for some offenders whose culture holds a strong taboo against discussing
sex. Sanctions and disapproval against open conversations about sexual behaviour
may reflect low vigilance of boundaries or dismissive attitudes towards victims who
disclose. Puerto Rican families emphasize the value of virginity at marriage, and so
victim disclosure is inhibited and abuse is concealed. Furthermore, male victims fear
perception of homosexuality if the abuser is male, and this may affect disclosure
(Kenny & McEachern, 2000).

Shame and loss of face. Those who are interdependent tend to be concerned about
negative evaluations from others than those who are independent. Deviant behaviour
may result in loss of face or threat of loss of one's social integrity (Hall, Sue,

---

[3]See the quotation at the beginning of this chapter.

Harang, & Lilly, 2000). Cull and Wehner (1998) describe shame as being deeply experienced by many indigenous Australian men who have sexually offended.

Identifying cultural norms. Discriminating clinical (i.e., deviant) from cultural (normative) data is another significant challenge for risk assessors. Ahn and Gilbert's (1992) study of sexualized behaviour in Asian American homes reported that a significant proportion of Vietnamese, Korean, and Cambodian participants (mothers) considered it permissible for a grandfather to touch his 3-year-old grandson's genitals with pride, suggesting that normative boundaries for parent–child relations have to take into account diverse patterns of acceptable behaviour in the life of some communities. Knowledge of norms assists in the task of discriminating sexual deviance from cultural process. Furthermore, cultural data can also inform protective factors. For instance, Ferrante's (2013) study of the relationship between indigenous Australians and police arrests found that 'cultural strength' (i.e., native speaker, identification with clan, tribe, or language group, recognition of home lands, and involvement in cultural events) appeared to be related to reduced involvement in legal attention.

One approach for assessing multiple domains in an individual's context is the ADDRESSING framework (Hays, 2001) and includes Age (and generational influences), Developmental and acquired Disabilities, Religion and spiritual orientation, Ethnicity, Socioeconomic status, Sexual orientation, Indigenous heritage, National origin and Gender. An advantage of this framework is making explicit contextual factors that are not typically cued by risk assessment tools that are designed to capture offence-related data (e.g., gender of victim) or offence-relevant attributes of the individual (e.g., low intimacy).

Develop Culturally Responsive Practices

Cultural problems can emerge when communication is poor and a lack of practitioner awareness or responsiveness to cultural issues is evident in the form of stereotyping (Patel & Lord, 2001) or unintended (or unconscious) cultural projections onto the offender (i.e., 'cultural countertransference'; Stampley & Slaght, 2004). The following suggestions are made with a view to promoting a practice environment that is culturally supportive and safe and can include strategies to raise awareness and debias unhelpful practitioner perceptions and behaviours, build capacity through knowledge generation, and encourage the development of skills.

Increasing awareness/decreasing bias. Bias amongst practitioners is often inadvertent, denied, and typically beyond immediate awareness (Dana, 2005). Furthermore, the careless use of tools that require inference in order to interpret (e.g., the Psychopathy Checklist – Revised [PCL-R]; Hare, 2003) create opportunities for the expression of bias that may promote negative stereotypes and caricatures that serve both to dehumanize and to over-pathologize the individual. Common ethnocentric biases can be (1) *confirmatory* – where the practitioner searches for information and evidence that supports a hypothesis/model in addition to ignoring data that are inconsistent (e.g., personality traits); (2) *misattribution* – where the practitioner holds a different perspective of the problem behaviour to that of the offender (e.g., the offender may favour a sociocultural explanatory model, whereas a psychologist is likely to favour the personal characteristics of the offender as explanatory); and (3) *judgement heuristics*, or quick decision rules that save time when approaching data, but also short-circuit our ability to engage in self-correction (Smith, 2005; Sue & Sue, 1990). Approaches to address these biases include the following:

- Identifying and addressing stereotypical beliefs via professional supervision, self-evaluation, education, and reflective practice. Trying new ways of engagement and seeking feedback and support from individuals who have sufficient cultural capital and expertise to guide observations and considerations for engagement can facilitate effective interpersonal behaviours (Smith, 2005).
- Similarly, addressing polarized understanding of ethnic and cultural issues (Kelly, 2003). Learning to tolerate ambiguity is an important attribute when working with individuals whose model of the world and how they interact with it may be distinct or somewhat at odds with the practitioner's own cultural outlook and values.
- Engagement in educational experiences that are culturally informative and promote learning and experience with other ways of perceiving and knowing. This may mean looking beyond the agency into allied institutions with existing cultural capacity (e.g., mental health or child advocacy).
- Treating cultural issues as a routine aspect of clinical engagements in general and assessing risk in particular (Tamatea, Webb, & Boer, 2011). It is a grim reality that many indigenous and minority groups are overrepresented in prisons generally, so the likelihood is great in many jurisdictions that practitioners will encounter offenders from other ethnic groups and cultural backgrounds. Adopting an attitude that cultural difference is normative[4] and to be expected implies an openness to diversity that would offer a precondition for intercultural communication.

Knowledge generation/capacity building. Training and supervision that include experiences and an appreciation of cultural diversity are recommended to promote practitioner self-development and also cue dialogue about the role of cultural constructs in risk assessment practice. Suggested approaches include the following:

- Understanding and enhancing support structures in the offender's community with a view to seeking the involvement of others in decision-making (if appropriate). An example of a collaborative approach to this end is a *whanau hui,*[5] a process that is commonly conducted in New Zealand correctional settings as a way for an offender and their family and supporters and also the practitioner (and any other professional support) to meet and engage in dialogue about the offender's offence needs, treatment gains, and ongoing support.
- Developing agency capacity for brokering sound cultural supervision with individuals who have good standing in their particular community in addition to

---

[4]This is not to imply (or endorse) the view that ethnic minorities and indigenous peoples in prison are normative.

[5]Generally, 'whanau' is a Māori term that refers to broad notions of kindred relationships and affiliations, and 'hui' is an assembly or, more casually, a meeting.

institutional or industry knowledge of the field of risk assessment and offender management can be of immeasurable value in educating practitioners on the histories, beliefs, and practices of their people and also supporting new behaviours in the risk assessment situation.

- Conducting case conference meetings with other practitioners and cultural advisors can serve as a formative process of enriching cultural knowledge and enhancing confidence in practice. Such meetings may involve highlighting and discussing a critical incident (e.g., non-disclosure), failure to engage, or how to work with the offender's support in an efficacious way – especially if there is distrust or animosity towards practitioners.

Skill development. Cultural responsiveness involves the development of specific and nuanced understandings of cultural expectations and boundaries. Preparation for risk assessment, like other forms of clinical assessment, will involve the tripartite challenge described by Ridley, Li, and Hill (1998) of (1) identifying cultural data, (2) interpreting that information, and (3) incorporating findings into a conceptualization that is accurate and comprehensive in communicating risk and risk management issues and also meaningful to the offender. Critical in-session processes and skills to consider in enhancing effectiveness with culturally different offenders include the following:

- *Aim to achieve credibility and trust with the individual* (Comas-Díaz, 2012). This can be a considerable challenge where there is distrust, hostility, or marginalization (Rodriguez, McNeal, & Cauce, 2007). Furthermore, practitioners should be mindful that developing this understanding with offenders can take time, especially for peoples who place great value on relationships and connectedness.
- *Explore the person's explanatory model of their offending behaviour.* An individual's explanation of their offending behaviour may be discrepant from empirical notions of risk (and also file information). However, their perspectives can offer important insights into what they believe to be the causal factors (e.g., spiritual or sociopolitical factors), how controllable (and by extension, how *treatable*) they believe their offending behaviour to be, and who else should be involved in making decisions. By learning more about culturally different populations, practices and procedures can be developed that are appropriate to those peoples (Yessine & Bonta, 2009).
- *Pay attention to etiquette.* Mundane behaviours can carry social significance and communicate respect across cultural space. Kapitanoff, Lutzker, and Bigelow (2000) identified a range of situations that practitioners need to observe and consider in the course of assessment with culturally different offenders that include: (1) use of the native language (with correct pronunciation), (2) knowing proper terms to use regarding traditional cultural beliefs, attitudes, and practices, (3) knowing what subjects may be considered inappropriate to discuss with strangers, (4) use of correct greetings, (5) use (or avoidance) of eye contact or physical touch, (6) customs regarding the sharing of food, and (7) understanding the importance of spending time to get to know each other and create a trusting working alliance before assessment procedures are started.

Postscript: The Challenge of Cultural Responsiveness

It is undeniable that working cross-culturally is a demanding endeavour. Practitioners are forced to confront challenges to their sense of competence in an area where there are few clear-cut indicators of success. It is argued here that working with cultural difference is as much an attitude as it is a set of skills and involves an acceptance of the importance of the role that culture plays in the lives of both professional practitioners and offenders. In this sense, cultural issues should be treated as 'business as usual', rather than as being too difficult, irrelevant, or otherwise novel information. Ongoing recognition of cultural issues should also create opportunities for reflective spaces to develop sensitive, safe, and just practices in the workplace to enhance effectiveness in conducting assessments where cultural issues are salient. Such practices might range from refining interpersonal skills in interview contexts to larger systemic change with regard to developing safe practices and encouraging diversity at an agency level. In conclusion, we posit the following challenge to all practitioners: no-one is without bias – we are immersed in a cultural context, surrounded by other individuals and peoples with their own biases and beliefs – it is impossible to be unaffected. How does your cultural sense of identity affect your practice?

References

Ahn, H. N., & Gilbert, N. (1992). Cultural diversity and sexual abuse prevention. *Social Service Review, 66*(3), 410–427.

Allan, A., & Dawson, D. (2002). *Developing a unique risk of violence tool for Australian indigenous offenders (CRC 6/00-01) Canberra*, Australia: Criminology Research Council.

American Psychological Association (2010). *Ethical principles of psychologists and code of conduct*. Washington, DC: Author.

Andrews, D. A., & Bonta J. (1998). *The psychology of criminal conduct* (2nd ed.). Cincinatti, OH: Anderson.

Andrews, D. A., & Bonta, J. (2010). *The psychology of criminal conduct* (5th ed.). New Providence, NJ: Lexis Nexis.

Asahina, M. (2010). Japanese sexual offenders: A descriptive study. *International Journal of Comparative and Applied Criminal Justice, 34*(2), 351–365.

Atkinson, D. R., Morten, G., & Sue, D. W. (1998). *Counseling American minorities*. Boston, MA: McGraw-Hill.

Australian Psychological Society (2007). *Code of ethics*. Melbourne, Australia: Author.

Boer, D. P., Couture, J., Geddes, C., & Ritchie, A. (2003). *Yókw'tól: Risk management guide for aboriginal offenders*. Harrison Mills, Canada: Correctional Service of Canada (Aboriginal Initiatives Branch).

Bonta, J. (2002). Offender risk assessment: Guidelines for selection and use. *Criminal Justice & Behavior, 29*(4), 355–379.

Bonta, J., LaPrairie, C., & Wallace-Capretta, S. (1997). Risk prediction and re-offending: Aboriginal and non-aboriginal offenders. *Revue Canadienne de Criminologie, 39*(2), 127–144.

Comas-Díaz, L. (2012). *Multicultural care: A clinician's guide to cultural competence*. Washington, DC: American Psychological Association.

Cooke, D. J., & Michie, C. (2002). Towards valid cross-cultural measures of risk. In R. R. Corrado, R. Roesch, S. D. Hart, & J. K. Gierowski (Eds.), *Multi-problem youth: A foundation for comparative research on needs, interventions and outcomes* (pp. 241–250). Amsterdam, The Netherlands: IOS.

Cull, D. M., & Wehner, D. M. (1998). Australian aborigines: Cultural factors pertaining to the assessment and treatment of Australian Aboriginal sexual offenders. In W. L. Marshall, Y. M. Fernandez, S. M. Hudson, & T. Ward (Eds.), *Sourcebook of treatment programs for sexual offenders* (pp. 431–444). New York, NY: Plenum.

Dana, R. H. (2005). *Multicultural assessment: Principles, applications, and examples*. Mahwah, NJ: Erlbaum.

Ellerby, L. (1994). Community-based treatment of aboriginal sexual offenders: Facing realities and exploring possibilities. *Forum on Corrections Research, 6*, 23–25.

Ethics Committee of the British Psychological Society (2009). *Code of ethics and conduct*. Leicester, England: British Psychological Society.

Evans, I. M. (2005). Behavior therapy: Regulation by self, by others, and by the physical world. In C. R. O'Donnell & L. A. Yamauchi (Eds.), *Culture & context in human behavior change: Theory, research, and applications* (pp. 13–39). New York, NY: Peter Lang.

Fantuzzo, J., McWayne, C., & Childs, S. (2006). Scientist–community collaborations: A dynamic tension between rights and responsibilities. In J. E. Trimble & C. B. Fisher (Eds.), *Handbook of ethical research with ethnocultural populations and communities* (pp. 27–50). Thousand Oaks, CA: Sage.

Ferrante, A. M. (2013). Assessing the influence of 'standard' and 'culturally specific' risk factors on the prevalence and frequency of offending: The case of indigenous Australians. *Race & Justice, 3*(1), 58–82.

Fontes, L., Cruz, M., & Tabachnick, J. (2001). Views of child sexual abuse in two cultural communities: An exploratory study among African Americans and Latinos. *Child Maltreatment, 6*(2), 103–117.

Gahir, M., & Garrett, T. (1999). Issues in the treatment of Asian sexual offenders. *Journal of Sexual Aggression, 4*(2), 94–104.

Gopaul-McNicol, S. (1997). *A multicultural/multimodal/multisystems approach to working with culturally different families*. Westport, CT: Greenwood-Praeger.

Groth-Marnat, G. (2009). *Handbook of psychological assessment* (5th ed.). Hoboken, NJ: John Wiley & Sons, Inc.

Gutierrez, L., Wilson, H. A., Rugge, T., & Bonta, J. (2013). The prediction of recidivism with Aboriginal offenders: A theoretically informed meta-analysis. *Canadian Journal of Criminology & Criminal Justice, 55*(1), 55–99.

Hall, G. C. N. (2001). Psychotherapy research with ethnic minorities: Empirical, ethical, and conceptual issues. *Journal of Consulting & Clinical Psychology, 69*(3), 502–510.

Hall, G. C. N., Sue, S., Narang, D. S., & Lilly, R. S. (2000). Culture-specific models of men's sexual aggression: Intra- and interpersonal determinants. *Cultural Diversity & Ethnic Minority Psychology, 6*(3), 252–267.

Hanson, R. K. (1997). *The development of a brief actuarial scale for sexual offense recidivism*. (User Report 1997-04). Ottawa, Canada: Department of the Solicitor General of Canada.

Hanson, R. K., & Harris, A. J. R. (2001). A structured approach to evaluating change among sexual offenders. *Sexual Abuse: A Journal of Research and Treatment, 13*(2), 105–122.

Hanson, R. K., Harris, A. J. R., Scott, T., & Helmus, L. (2007). *Assessing the risk of sexual offenders on community supervision: The Dynamic Supervision Project* (Corrections Research User Report 2007-05). Ottawa, Canada: Public Safety Canada.

Hanson, R. K., & Morton-Bourgon, K. (2009). The accuracy of recidivism risk assessments for sexual offenders: A meta-analysis of 118 prediction studies. *Psychological Assessment*, *21*(1), 1–21.

Hanson, R. K., & Thornton, D. (1999). *Static-99: Improving actuarial risk assessments for sex offenders* (User Report 99-02). Ottawa, Canada: Department of the Solicitor General of Canada.

Hare, R. D. (2003). *The Hare Psychopathy Checklist – Revised (PCL-R)* (2nd ed.). Toronto, Canada: Multi-Health Systems.

Hays, P. A. (2001). *Addressing cultural complexities in practice: A framework for clinicians and counsellors*. Washington, DC: American Psychological Association.

Helmus, L., Babchishin, K. M., Hanson, R. K., & Thornton, D. (2009). Static-99R: Revised age weights. Retrieved from http://www.static99.org

Illovsky, M. E. (2003). *Mental health professionals, minorities, and the poor*. New York, NY: Brunner-Routledge.

Janus, E. (2006). *Failure to protect: America's sexual predator laws and the risk of the preventive state*. Ithaca, NY: Cornell University Press.

Kapitanoff, S. H., Lutzker, J. R., & Bigelow, K. M. (2000). Cultural issues in the relation between child disabilities and child abuse. *Aggression & Violent Behavior*, *5*(3), 227–244.

Kelly, S. (2003). African-American couples: Their importance to the stability of African-American families and their mental health issues. In J. S. Mio & G. Y. Iwamasa (Eds.), *Culturally diverse mental health* (pp. 141–157). New York, NY: Brunner-Routledge.

Kenny, M. C., & McEachern, A. C. (2000). Racial, ethnic, and cultural factors of childhood sexual abuse: A selected review of the literature. *Clinical Psychology Review*, *20*(7), 905–922.

Kleinman, A. (1988). *Rethinking psychiatry: From cultural category to personal experience*. New York, NY: Free Press.

Korbin, J. E. (2002). Culture and child maltreatment: Cultural competence and beyond. *Child Abuse & Neglect*, *26*(6–7), 637–644.

Lalor, K. (2004). Child sexual abuse in sub-Saharan Africa: A literature review. *Child Abuse & Neglect*, *28*(4), 439–460.

Långström, N. (2004). Accuracy of actuarial procedures for assessment of sexual offender recidivism risk may vary across ethnicity. *Sexual Abuse: A Journal of Research and Treatment*, *16*(2), 107–120.

López, S. R., & Guarnaccia, P. J. (2000). Cultural psychopathology: Uncovering the social world of mental illness. *Annual Review of Psychology*, *51*(1), 571–598.

Marshall, W. L., Fernandez, Y. M., Hudson, S. M., & Ward, T. (1998). Preface. In W. L. Marshall, Y. M. Fernandez, S. M. Hudson, & T. Ward (Eds.), *Sourcebook of treatment programs for sexual offenders* (pp. xi–xiii). New York, NY: Plenum.

Meursing, K., Vos, T., Coutinho, O., Moyo, M., Mpofu, S., Oneko, O., … Sibindi, F. (1995). Child sexual abuse in Matabeleland, Zimbabwe. *Social Science Medicine*, *41*(12), 1693–1704.

Mills, J. F., Kroner, D. G., & Morgan, R. D. (2011). *Clinician's guide to violence risk assessment*. New York, NY: Guilford.

New Zealand Psychological Society/Te Roopu Matai Hinengaro o Aotearoa. (2002). *Code of ethics for psychologists working in Aotearoa/New Zealand*. Wellington, NZ: Author.

Nhundu, T. J., & Shumba, A. (2001). The nature and frequency of reported cases of teacher perpetrated child sexual abuse in rural primary schools in Zimbabwe. *Child Abuse & Neglect*, *25*(11), 1517–1534.

Okazaki, S., & Sue, S. (1995). Methodological issues in assessment research with ethnic minorities. *Psychological Assessment*, *7*(3), 367–375.

Olver, M. E., Neumann, C. S., Wong, S. C. P., & Hare, R. D. (2013). The structural and predictive properties of the Psychopathy Checklist – Revised in Canadian Aboriginal and non-Aboriginal offenders. *Psychological Assessment*, 25(1), 167–179.

Patel, K., & Lord, A. (2001). Ethnic minority sex offenders' experiences of treatment. *Journal of Sexual Aggression*, 7(1), 40–50.

Quinsey, V. L., Harris, G. T., Rice, M. E., & Cormier, C. A. (1998). *Violent offenders: Appraising and managing risk*. Washington, DC: American Psychological Association.

Rack, P. (1982). *Culture, race, and mental disorder*. London, England: Tavistock.

Rettenberger, M., & Eher, R. (2006). Actuarial assessment of sex offender recidivism risk: A validation of the German version of the Static-99. *Sexual Offender Treatment*, 1(3), 1–11.

Ridley, C. R., Li, L. C., & Hill, C. L. (1998). Multicultural assessment: Re-examination, reconceptualization, and practical application. *Counseling Psychologist*, 26(6), 827–910.

Rodriguez, M. M., McNeal, C. T., & Cauce, A. M. (2007). Counseling with the marginalised. In P. B. Pedersen, J. G. Draguns, W. J. Lonner, & J. E. Trimble (Eds.), *Counseling across cultures* (6th ed., pp. 223–238). Thousand Oaks, CA: Sage.

Rogers, R. (2000). The uncritical acceptance of risk assessment in forensic practice. *Law and Human Behavior*, 24(5), 595–605.

Roysircar, G. (2005). Culturally sensitive assessment, diagnosis, and guidelines. In M. G. Constantine & D. W. Sue (Eds.), *Strategies for building multicultural competence in mental health and educational settings* (pp. 19–38). Hoboken, NJ: John Wiley & Sons, Inc.

Shaw, M., & Hannah-Moffat, K. (2000). Gender, diversity and risk assessment in Canadian corrections. *Probation Journal*, 47(3), 163–172.

Singh, J. P., Desmarais, S., & Van Dorn, R. (2013). Measurement of predictive validity in violence risk assessment studies: A second-order systematic review. *Behavioral Sciences & the Law*, 31(1), 55–73.

Singh, J. P., & Fazel, S. (2010). Forensic risk assessment: A metareview. *Criminal Justice & Behavior*, 37(9), 965–988.

Skelton, A., Riley, D., Wales, D., & Vess, J. (2006). Assessing risk for sexual offenders in New Zealand: Development and validation of a computer-scored risk measure. *Journal of Sexual Aggression*, 12(3), 277–286.

Smallbone, S., & Rallings, M. (2013). Short-term predictive validity of the Static-99 and Static-99-R for indigenous and non-indigenous Australian sexual offenders. *Sexual Abuse*, 25(3), 302–316.

Smith, T. B. (2005). A contextual approach to assessment. In T. B. Smith (Ed.), *Practicing multiculturalism: Affirming diversity in counseling and psychotherapy* (pp. 97–119). Boston, MA: Pearson.

Sobo, E. J. (2009). *Culture and meaning in health services research: A practical field guide*. Walnut Creek, CA: Left Coast Press.

Société canadienne de psychologie (2000). *Canadian code of ethics for psychologists*. Ottawa, Canada: Canadian Psychological Society.

Stampley, C., & Slaght, E. (2004). Cultural transference as a clinical obstacle. *Smith College Studies in Social Work*, 74(2), 333–347.

Stermac, L. E., Segal, Z. V., & Gillis, R. (1989). Social and cultural factors in sexual assault. In W. L. Marshall, D. R. Laws, & H. E. Barbaree (Eds.), *Handbook of sexual assault: Issues, theories, and treatment of the offender* (pp. 143–159). New York, NY: Plenum.

Sue, D. W., & Sue, D. (1990). *Counseling the culturally different: Theory and practice* (2nd ed.). New York, NY: John Wiley & Sons, Inc.

Sue, D. W., & Sue, D. (2013). *Counseling the culturally diverse: Theory and practice* (6th ed.). Hoboken, NJ: John Wiley & Sons, Inc.

Sue, S. (1999). Science, ethnicity, and bias: Where have we gone wrong? *American Psychologist*, *54*(12), 1070–1077.

Sundararajan, L., Misra, G., & Marsella, A. J. (2013). Indigenous approaches to assessment, diagnosis, and treatment of mental disorders. In F. Paniagua & A. Yamada (Eds.), *Handbook of multicultural mental health: Assessment and treatment of diverse populations* (2nd ed., pp. 69–87). New York, NY: Academic Press.

Tamatea, A. J., Webb, M., & Boer, D. P. (2011). The role of culture in sexual offender rehabilitation: A New Zealand perspective. In D. Boer, R. Eher, L. Craig, M. Miner, & F. Pfäfflin (Eds.), *International perspectives on the assessment and treatment of sex offenders: Theory, practice, and research* (pp. 313–330). Chichester, England: John Wiley & Sons, Ltd.

Tyler, F. B., Brome, D. R., & Williams, J. E. (1991). *Ethnic validity, ecology, and psychotherapy: A psychosocial competence model*. New York, NY: Plenum.

Ward, T., & Marshall, W. L. (2007). Narrative identity and offender rehabilitation. *International Journal of Offender Therapy & Comparative Criminology*, *51*(3), 279–297.

Wong, S. C. P., Olver, M. E., Nicholaichuk, T. P., & Gordon, A. (2003). *The Violence Risk Scale – Sexual Offender version (VRS:SO)*. Saskatoon, Canada: Regional Psychiatric Centre and University of Saskatchewan.

Yessine, A., & Bonta, J. (2009). The offending trajectories of youthful aboriginal offenders. *Revue Canadienne de Criminologie et de Justice Pénale*, *51*(4), 435–472.

Section VII
Conclusions

55

Risk Assessment for Sexual Offenders

Where to from Here?

Leam A. Craig

Forensic Psychology Practice Ltd, University of Birmingham, and
Birmingham City University, United Kingdom

Martin Rettenberger

Centre for Criminology (Kriminologische Zentralstelle - KrimZ),
Wiesbaden, and Johannes Gutenberg University Mainz (JGU), Germany

Introduction

Throughout this volume, we have seen how static and dynamic factors can, together and independently, contribute to the assessment of sexual recidivism risk in sexual offenders. It has been recognized for some time that static factors are good for long-term predictions of sexual recidivism risk whereas dynamic factors have been used to assess for treatment need and identify areas of intervention as part of structured treatment programmes. For some time, researchers and practitioners have assumed an orthogonal relationship between the two concepts; however, emerging research draws parallels between static and dynamic factors, suggesting that the two concepts are functionally linked (Beech & Craig, 2012). In this chapter, we consider developments in the assessment of risk of sexual recidivism and the assessment of treatment need in sexual offenders, and explore the functional relationship between static and dynamic factors. We then consider how incorporating static and dynamic factors can add incrementally to sexual recidivism risk prediction, before expanding on how aetiological models of risk assessment help us in our understanding of the functional links between static and dynamic factors.

The Wiley Handbook on the Theories, Assessment, and Treatment of Sexual Offending.
Edited by Douglas P. Boer. Volume II: Assessment, edited by Leam A. Craig and Martin Rettenberger.
© 2017 John Wiley & Sons, Ltd. Published 2017 by John Wiley & Sons, Ltd.

Assessment of Risk

The assessment of risk of sexual recidivism in sexual offenders has been dominated by the combined use of static actuarial risk assessment instruments (ARAIs) and structured dynamic frameworks, often referred to as Structured Professional Judgement (SPJ) scales. Static risk measures are useful for evaluating long-term risk, but say little of treatment need and changes in levels of risk over time. In contrast, dynamic factors are enduring factors linked to the likelihood of offending that can nevertheless be changed following intervention. Dynamic factors can be subdivided into *stable* and *acute* factors. Stable dynamic risk factors are those which are relatively persistent characteristics of the offender, which are subject to change such as levels of responsibility, cognitive distortions, and sexual arousal. Acute dynamic factors are rapidly changing factors such as substance misuse, isolation, and negative emotional states, the presence of which increases risk (Hanson & Harris, 1998). Hanson and Morton-Bourgon (2005) identified a number of promising dynamic risk factors as areas for intervention, including sexual deviancy (any deviant sexual interest, sexual preoccupations), antisocial personality (antisocial personality disorder and psychopathy as measured by the Psychopathy Checklist – Revised [PCL-R] (Hare, 2003)), and antisocial traits (general self-regulation problems, employment instability, hostility).

Static Risk Factors

Probably the best known ARAIs include Risk Matrix 2000/Sexual (RM2000/S) (Thornton et al., 2003), which is extensively used in the United Kingdom, and Static-99 (Hanson & Thornton, 2000; a description of Static-99 can also be found at www.static99.org), Static-99R (Helmus, Thornton, Hanson, & Babshichin, 2012), Static-2002R (Hanson & Thornton, 2003; Helmus et al., 2012; Phenix, Doren, Helmus, Hanson, & Thornton, 2008), and the Sex Offender Risk Appraisal Guide (SORAG) (Quinsey, Harris, Rice, & Cornier, 2006), which are more widely used in other European countries and throughout North America (for more details, see Chapter 29). These scales take into account the antisocial and sexual deviance domains to predict both non-sexual violence and sexual recidivism in sexual offenders. These scales provide superior predictive utility to unstructured clinical judgement based on traditional models of psychopathology or clinical experience (Hanson & Bussière, 1998; Hanson & Morton-Bourgon, 2009; Quinsey et al., 2006).

Actuarial instruments share a number of characteristics. Each includes 'predictor' items that were selected because they were found to be highly correlated with sexual recidivism. A sum of the risk items produces an overall *risk score*, which translates into a *risk category* (e.g., low, medium, high, or very high). Although some items may be weighted more heavily than others (such as the age risk item), individuals who are positive for many items usually obtain scores placing them in a high-risk group whereas individuals who are positive for only a few obtain low-risk scores. In most cases, the scale developers have compiled *Experience Tables* (Ohlin, 1951) from retrospective (often meta-analytical) studies of released sex offenders that show the percentage of offenders in each risk category who have recidivated. Hence a value might be extracted of 45% for an individual of high risk over a 10-year period, which means that 45 out of 100 such individuals are predicted to recidivate within this period, or conversely, he is one of the 55 out of 100 who do not.

Validation studies have consistently demonstrated predictive accuracy for these measures across samples and countries, including Australia (Allan, Dawson, & Allan, 2006), Austria (Rettenberger, Matthes, Boer, & Eher, 2010), Belgium (Ducro & Pham, 2006), Brazil (Baltieri & de Andrade, 2008), Canada (Kingston, Yates, Firestone, Babchishin, & Bradford, 2008), Denmark (Bengtson, 2008), Germany (Stadtland et al., 2005), New Zealand (Skelton, Riley, Wales, & Vess, 2006), and the United Kingdom (Craig, Beech, & Browne, 2006a). Such is the dominance of the use of ARAIs that Cortoni, Craig, and Beech (2010) noted that the use of the actuarial approach has permeated the entire criminal justice system in the United States, Canada and the United Kingdom.

The ARAI approach, typically using static risk factors, standardizes the assessment procedure, reduces clinical error, and provides a defensible and transparent decision-making process. However, this approach means that it is open to misinterpretation and misuse (Craig & Beech, 2010). In addition, although the actuarial approach is designed to limit the unreliability of clinical errors, clinical judgement is still required in choosing which measure to use. Finally, static risk factors constitute only part of the risk assessment of sexual offenders. Any estimation of an individual's risk potential should be multifactorial, including their response to treatment and community risk management items. These are the domains best explained by dynamic risk factors.

Dynamic Frameworks

Unlike the actuarial field, the development of structured clinical guidelines for assessment of risk in sexual offenders has been slow, with only a few SPJ instruments of note, namely the *Sexual Violence Risk-20* (SVR-20) (Boer, Hart, Kropp, & Webster, 1997) and the *Risk for Sexual Violence Protocol* (RSVP) (Hart, Laws, & Kropp, 2003).

The SVR-20 (Boer et al., 1997), developed more as a set of guidelines, assesses the risk of sexual violence by selecting 20 factors, from an extensive list, that could be comprehensively divided into three main sections to formulate sexual violence risk. Factors include (a) *Psychological Adjustment* – sexual deviation, victim of child abuse, cognitive impairment, suicidal/homicidal ideation, relationship/employment problems, previous offence history (non-sexual violent, non-violent), psychopathy, substance use problems, and past supervision failure; (b) *Sexual Offending* – such as high-density offences, multiple offences, physical harm to victims, use of weapon, escalation, and cognitive distortions; and (c) *Future Plans* – whether the offender lacks realistic plans and has negative attitudes towards instruction. The area under the curve (AUC) indices for the SVR-20 in predicting sexual reconviction are mixed. Craig and colleagues (Craig et al., 2006a; Craig, Browne, Beech, & Stringer, 2006b) and Sjöstedt and Långström (2002) found that the SVR-20 was a better predictor of violent reconviction than of sexual reconviction. Barbaree, Langton, Blanchard, and

Boer (2008) reported an AUC[1] of 0.63 in a sample of 468 Canadian sexual offenders whereas Rettenberger et al. (2010) reported an AUC of 0.71 in a sample of 394 Austrian sexual offenders. In a Dutch study using a sample of 122 sexual offenders admitted to a forensic psychiatric unit, de Vogel, de Ruiter, van Beek, and Mead (2004) found the SVR-20 final risk judgement to be a better predictor for sexual recidivism than Static-99. In this study, the SVR-20 obtained higher AUC scores for total score (AUC = 0.08) and final risk judgement (AUC = 0.83) than comparable results for Static-99, AUC = 0.71 and 0.66, respectively.

Rettenberger, Boer, and Eher (2011) examined the predictive accuracy and psychometric properties of the SVR-20 in a sample 493 male sexual offenders assessed between 2001 and 2007 at the Federal Evaluation Centre for Violent and Sexual Offenders (FECVSO) in the Austrian Prison System. Sexual reconviction data were examined over 3- and 5-year periods. In measuring predictive accuracy of the scale, Rettenberger et al. (2011) reported encouraging results for the total sample (AUC = 0.72) and also for the rapist subgroup ($n = 221$, AUC = 0.71) and the child molester subsample ($n = 249$, AUC = 0.77). Of the three subscales, the Psychosocial Adjustment scale produced the most promising results, significantly predicting general sexual recidivism (AUC = 0.67) for the entire sample. However, when the sample were grouped by offence category, rapist or child molester, the accuracy of this subscale in predicting sexual recidivism in the rapist-only sample (AUC = 0.63) performed less well compared with the child molester sample (AUC = 0.72). In contrast, the Sexual Offences subscale performed better in the rapist sample (AUC = 0.77) than the child molester sample (AUC = 0.65) in predicting general sexual recidivism.

Adaptations to the SVR-20 have been made in order to make the scale more relevant to sexual offenders with intellectual disabilities (Boer, Frixe, Pappas, Morrissey, & Lindsay, 2010), although these have yet to be empirically validated.

The SVR-20 is currently under revision (Boer, 2011). The revised SVR-20 (second edition) follows a clear multidimensional focus, all items having both dynamic and static features and all items having variable components (i.e., a continuum exists within items and issues within items interact to produce the complexities that we see in the individual case – with some examples within and between items). A convergent approach is recommended – using an appropriate actuarial baseline to provide an anchor for structured clinical evaluation. Many of the original 20 items remain, although some items have changed or been replaced, allowing for the inclusion of new items. As Boer (2011) noted, given the existing research base for the original SVR-20, to change the scale beyond recognition would invalidate much of the research base. In the Psychosocial Adjustment section, new items 'sexual health problems' and 'past non-sexual offending' have been included, the latter replacing 'past non-sexual violent' and 'past non-violent offences'. The item 'past supervision failure' has been

---

[1] The area under the curve (AUC) of the receiver operating characteristic (ROC) analysis is a comparison of the sensitivity (true positive divided by the sum of the true positive and false negative) with specificity (true negative divided by the sum of the false positive and false negative), i.e., hit rate against the false alarm rate. Referring to Cohen (1992), Rice and Harris (2005) formulated the following interpretation criteria for AUC values: Results of 0.71 or above are classified as 'good' and values between 0.64 and 0.71 are classified as 'moderate'. Significant AUC values that are below the value of 0.64 are classified as 'small'.

moved to the Future Plans section and renamed. In describing the changes to the Psychosocial Adjustment section, Boer (2011) argued that it is common for 'sexual health problems' to decrease risk, and it is also common that sexual desire and ability decrease with age. Hence this item measures *normal* decreases in risk with ageing for all individuals. There are also some individuals who have sexual health disorders that increase their risk if a sexual assault occurs, e.g., HIV. HIV-positive persons are not at any greater risk for offending than anyone else, but if an HIV-positive person does sexually offend, the victim may be lethally affected. Boer (2011) argued there are some unique cases in which older individuals offend in non-sexual ways owing to impotence, and there are some individuals who actually do not start offending until they are much older. Within the Sexual Offences section, a new item 'diversity of sexual offending' replaces 'multiple offence types', 'actual or threatened physical harm to victim' replaces 'physical harm to victim(s)', and 'psychological coercion in sexual offences' replaces 'use of weapons or threats of death.' It is argued that persons who have committed multiple types (as determined by differing victim characteristics and varying in nature) of sexual offences are at increased risk for sexual recidivism. This is a risk factor that likely reflects the presence of sexual deviation and attitudes that support or condone sexual violence. Psychological coercion refers to coercive tactics ranging from grooming of victims through the use of gifts or additional privileges for a victim to threats of family separation or abandonment – all of which serve to provide the offender with victim access while protecting the offender's behaviour from discovery. Boer (2011) noted that this item is supported more by the clinical treatment literature than from the meta-analyses per se. This is a risk factor that likely reflects the presence of sexual deviation (e.g., sadism) and attitudes that support or condone sexual violence. The Future Plans section includes three items (instead of two in the 1997 version). In addition to continuing to have 'realistic future plans' and 'negative attitudes towards intervention', a new item, 'negative attitudes towards supervision', has been added. It is argued that non-compliance with supervision is related to recidivism of a general, violent, and sexually violent nature, and persons who reject or do not comply with supervision are at increased risk for criminality and violence. Such attitudes may be related to future sexual violence by resulting in inadequate professional support, leading to increasing sexual deviance, increased distress, or increased risk for exposure to destabilizing influences such as drugs, alcohol, or potential victims. The scoring system has also altered to reflect changes (reductions, no change, or increases) in a risk-relevant item over a specified period of time.

The RSVP (Hart et al., 2003) can be seen as a variation and evolution of earlier SPJ scales. Like the Historical Clinical Risk-20 (HCR-20) (Webster, Douglas, Eaves, & Hart, 1997) and SVR-20, the RSVP does not employ actuarial or statistical methods to support decision-making about risk. Rather, it offers a set of guidelines for collecting relevant information and making structured risk formulations. The RSVP protocol is an evolved form of the SVR-20 and is based on a rejection of actuarial approaches to the assessment of risk of sexual violence. Similarly to the SVR-20, the RSVP identifies the potential risk factors (presence) and makes a determination of their importance to future offending (relevance). However, in addition to the SVR-20, the RSVP provides explicit guidelines for risk formulation, such as risk scenarios and management strategies.

The RSVP assumes that risk must be defined in the context in which it occurs and regards the primary risk decision as preventive, and considers steps that are required to minimize any risks posed by the individual. The RSVP is a 22-item protocol divided into five domains: sexual violence history, psychological adjustment, mental disorder, social adjustment, and manageability. The RSVP should not be used to determine whether someone committed an act(s) of sexual violence in the past, and it does not provide an estimate of specific likelihood or probability that someone will commit acts of sexual violence in the future. The test authors suggest that the RSVP is designed to highlight information relating to clinical problems rather than producing an overall risk score. Information is structured in a number of steps: case information, presence of risk factors, relevance of risk factors, risk scenarios (possible futures), risk management strategies, and summary judgements. There has been little cross-validated research reporting on the predictive accuracy or psychometric properties of the RSVP.

A criticism of 'mainstream' ARAIs and SPJ protocols is that these can only be used with individuals who share characteristics consistent with the scale development sample (Craig, Browne, Stringer, & Beech, 2004), which limits their usefulness with female sexual offenders, online sexual offenders, and sexual offenders with intellectual disabilities (Cortoni et al., 2010; Craig, 2010).

Assessment of Treatment Need

Risk of reoffending fluctuates according to the psychological functioning of the offender. A number of dynamic assessment frameworks have been developed; the most widely known include the Structured Risk Assessment (SRA) (Thornton, 2002), which has evolved into the Structured Assessment of Risk and Need: Treatment Needs Analysis (SARN:TNA) (Webster et al., 2006), the Beech Deviancy Classification (Beech, 1998; Beech, Erikson, Friendship, & Hanson, 2002), and the STABLE-2007/ACUTE-2007 (Hanson, Harris, Scott, & Helmus, 2007).

SARN/SARNR

The SRA, more widely known as the Structured Assessment of Risk and Need: Treatment Needs Analysis (SARN:TNA), is now used within what is called the SARN framework. This framework represents a research-guided multi-step framework for assessing the risk presented by a sex offender and provides a systematic way of going beyond static risk classification.

The SARN:TNA framework is widely used within National Offender Management Service (NOMS) in England and Wales. The SARN:TNA is an 'empirically guided' process for identifying factors related to risk, that is, it directs the assessor to consider only factors that are known to affect the likelihood of further offending. The framework consists of the actuarial RM2000 (Thornton et al., 2003) assessment and SARN:TNA. The SARN:TNA is used routinely alongside sex offender treatment in order to identify treatment needs through completion of the SARN:TNA. Typically, a TNA grid is 'opened' before the treatment programme and is based on a structured interview and collateral information in order to identify deficits in the offenders'

Table 55.1 SARN:TNA deviancy domains and dynamic risk factors

	Deviancy domain		
Sexual interests	*Offence-supportive attitudes*	*Relationships*	*Self-management*
Preoccupied with sex	Believing men should dominate women	Feeling inadequate	Impulsive, unstable lifestyle
Sexual preference for children	Believing you have a right to sex	Feeling more comfortable with children than adults	Not knowing how to solve life's problems
Preferring sex to include violence and humiliation	Child abuse-supportive beliefs	Suspicious, angry, and vengeful towards other people	Out-of-control emotions and urges
Other offence-related sexual interest	Believing that women cannot be trusted	Not having emotionally intimate relationships with adults	

generality (which refers to the existence of the factor in contexts other than offending) and *offence chain* (which refers to the sequence of situations, thoughts, feelings, and behaviours leading to offences, including lifestyle features that made the chain more likely to start).

The SARN:TNA comprises 15 dynamic risk factors organized into four TNA domains: *sexual interests, offence-supportive attitudes, relationships,* and *self-management.* The extent to which each potential risk factor was present in the proximal lead-up to the offence ('*offence chain*') and in the offenders' lives in general ('*generality*') is assessed and scored on a three-point scale of 0, 1, or 2. Table 55.1 briefly describes each dynamic risk factor by SARN:TNA domain. An Initial Deviancy Assessment (IDA) is calculated from the SARN:TNA and organized into three levels of deviance: *Low* deviance – when no dynamic marked risk factors are apparent (i.e., no risk factor within any SARN:TNA domain scores a 2 in both generality *and* offence chain); *Moderate* deviance – where only one domain contains a risk factor/risk factors scoring a 2 in both generality and offence chain; and *High* deviance – where there are two or more domains containing a risk factor with a score of 2 for both generality and offence chain. This is translated to *low, medium,* or *high* dynamic risk/treatment need. Assessors are trained in applying the framework and have to pass a competency test and are checked for interrater reliability. Webster et al. (2006) found a good level of interrater agreement between experienced assessors, with a mean percentage agreement of 84.3% across four cases. In assessing the SARN:TNA dynamic risk factors, psychometric evidence is considered; however, many other sources of information (official records of the offences, prison or probation files, treatment logs and reports, prison wing records) and offender interviews are also considered (Tully, Browne, & Craig (2015)). Following the completion of the treatment programme, a SARN report is produced that is designed to review the extent to which the identified treatment targets have been addressed (as identified in the SARN:TNA) and what, if any, outstanding areas of intervention remain.

Despite its wide use within NOMS, research into the SRA and adapted SARN framework as a risk assessment tool is limited. Thornton's (2002) original paper described the construction of the tool and also a test of the tool post-construction. In one of the two studies described in this paper, Thornton (2002) compared offenders with previous convictions for child molestation (Repeat) against offenders who had been convicted for child sexual offences for the first time (Current Only). Thornton measured three of the four SRA domains, *distorted attitudes, socioaffective functioning* (now termed '*relationships*' in the SARN:TNA), and *self-management*, using various psychometric measures. He found that the indicators from the three domains effectively discriminated between 'repeat' offenders and 'current only' offenders. The repeat offenders demonstrated more distorted attitudes, more socioaffective dysfunction, and poorer self-management. In a second study, he combined the number of dysfunctional domains into an overall deviance classification for 117 adult male sexual offenders and an AUC value of 0.78.

In a follow-up study using a similar methodology, Thornton and Beech (2002) found that the number of dysfunctional domains made a statistically significant contribution to prediction over and above the Static-99 risk category. Craig, Thornton, Beech, and Browne (2007) conducted similar research into psychometrically assessed deviant domains in a sample of 119 sexual offenders and found that the SRA deviancy index predicted sexual reconviction independent of the Static-99 (SRA AUC = 0.69), supporting the use of integrating statistical and psychological risk factors to predict sexual reconviction. Craig et al. (2007) calculated a Psychological Deviance Index (PDI) by standardizing each of these scale scores for a domain. A domain was counted as dysfunctional if its average standard score was greater than zero. This means that the number of dysfunctional domains index could be calculated running from 0 to 4. In measuring the risk assessment properties of the four dynamic risk domains, the *Sexual Interests* domain obtained a large effect in predicting sexual reconviction over 2-year (AUC = 0.86), and 5-year (AUC = 0.72) follow-up periods. The *Self Management* factor obtained moderate results (AUC = 0.71) in predicting sexual reconviction at 2 years. In comparison, Static-99 obtained moderate accuracy in predicting sexual reconviction at 2 years (AUC = 0.66) and 5 years (AUC = 0.60). When the rates of sexual recidivism were compared with the PDI, it was found that the increase in rates of sexual recidivism mirrored the increase in the degree of PDI. As the PDI increased from zero to one, two, three, and four, the rates of reconviction were 3, 10, 8, 14, and 26%, respectively. However, when the PDI was grouped into Low (0), Moderate (1–2), and High (3+) categories, it was found the degree of PDI and rates of reconviction were linear at 3, 18, and 40%, respectively. When the PDI and Static-99 were entered into a logistic regression analysis, it was found that the PDI made a statistically significant contribution to the prediction of sexual reconviction independent of Static-99 at the 5-year follow-up.

Common across the three SRA studies is the use of psychometric measures to assess sexual deviancy. However, in practice, the SARN framework relies heavily on collateral information and a structured interview when scoring the individual items rather than using psychometric data to identify treatment need, the methodology used in the original development study. To address this, Tully, Browne, and Craig (2015) examined the predictive accuracy of the SARN framework based on clinician ratings in a sample of 496 male sexual offenders of whom 304 had been 'at risk' for at least 2 years (i.e., had 2-year follow-up data) and 161 had been 'at risk' for 4 years. The overall rate of proven sexual reoffending increased from 5.6% at year 2 to 16.8% at year 4. The AUC for proven sexual reoffending for the SARN at 2- and 4-year follow-ups was low, i.e., 0.59 and 0.57, respectively. However, in both cases the 95% confidence interval (CI) passed through AUC 0.50, indicating non-significance. The RM2000/Sexual did not perform any better at AUC 0.53 at 2- and 4-year follow-ups, again with 95% CI passing through AUC 0.50. This research raises questions regarding the use of clinical assessments in estimating deficits in risk factors thought to be relevant in sexual offending behaviour.

Wakeling, Beech, and Freemantle (2013) examined the relationship between psychometric changes in treatment and recidivism in a sample of 3773 sex offenders based on the SARN:TNA deviancy domains framework. They reported a 2-year sexual reconviction rate of 1.7%, with a sexual and violent reconviction rate combined of 4.4%. Clinically significant changes were calculated for the psychometrics and for the overarching psychological problems. Analyses indicated that those whose scores were in the 'normal range' before and after treatment were reconvicted at a significantly lower rate than those whose scores were not in the 'normal range' after treatment on selected psychometric scales. Additionally, participants who were deemed 'changed' overall on three of the four risk domains were reconvicted at a lower rate than those who were deemed not to have changed on these domains. Psychometric variables found to be predictive of recidivism included pre-treatment self-esteem, pre- and post-treatment rumination, pre- and post-treatment impulsivity, pre-treatment entitlement to sex, pre-treatment loneliness, and pre- and post-treatment locus of control. Consistent with Craig et al. (2007), psychometric measures of sexual obsession and paraphilia obtained the highest AUC values of 0.71 and 0.62 on average in predicting sexual and violent reconviction, respectively.

When Wakeling et al. (2013) examined child molesters and rapists separately, they found that for child molesters, the socioaffective and self-regulation problem domain categories had significant associations with recidivism; those in the 'change still required' group had greater recidivism rates than offenders in the 'change not required' group. However, this association was not present for rapists, suggesting that the dynamic risk factors present among child molesters may have stronger relationships with recidivism than those present for rapists.

As part of a review and revision of the SARN framework, NOMS is incorporating protective factors into its dynamic assessment for sexual offenders, making more explicit issues of responsivity in addition to factors of desistance (see Laws & Ward, 2010). Based on the emerging literature, NOMS has developed a new needs analysis tool to help guide treatment planning, – Risk and Success Factors Analysis (RSFA) – and a new Risk Assessment Report format to bring all the evidence together – Structured Assessment of Risk, Need, and Responsivity (SARNR). The framework continues to be centred on core domains: Sexual Interests, Thoughts that make offending o.k., Relationships, and Struggling with life's problems, together with an additional item – Purpose aimed at being a responsible member of society, sticking to the rules, and getting on with the people who are supporting me (good citizenship). The assessment methodology adopts a triangulation of evidence to identify an individual's risk factors based on interview data, observation, file review, treatment programme products, and psychometric measures.

This revision explicitly incorporates ideas of Quality of Life (QoL) (see Chapter 48) and the Good Lives Model (GML) (Ward, 2002; Ward & Maruna, 2007), emphasizing the importance of life experiences. Ward and Beech (2015) and Lindsay (Chapter 48) highlight that sex offender groups often display impoverished human relationships, which underlines the importance of improving the relationships of sex offenders, letting them experience the human fulfilment that can be achieved from good relationships. Incorporating a measure of Purpose in the SARNR promotes appropriate relationships, contact with the community, and pro-social influences, which are often considered important areas for assessment and treatment intervention.

Beech Deviancy Classification

The *Deviancy Classification construct* was developed by Beech (1998). He reported that child abusers could be divided into two main groups, 'High Deviancy' and 'Low Deviancy', on the basis of their *deviation* on psychometric measures from non-offending norms. To assess this deviation, a number of scales that measure pro-offending attitudes, socioaffective problems, and deviant sexual interest were employed (see Beech, 1998, for more details of this system).

STABLE-2007/ACUTE-2007

Hanson and Harris (2000) developed a system with both stable and acute risk factors. Originally entitled SONAR (Sex Offender Need Assessment Rating), the system was renamed in two parts STABLE-2000 and ACUTE-2000, now updated to STABLE-2007 and ACUTE-2007 (Hanson et al., 2007). The STABLE-2007 consisted of 13 items divided into five subsections: significant social influences (one item), intimacy deficits (five items: capacity for relationship stability, emotional identification with children, hostility towards women, general social rejection, and lack of concern for others), sexual self-regulation (three items: sex drive/sex preoccupation, sex as coping, and deviant sexual preference), general self-regulation (three items: impulsive acts, poor problem-solving skills, and negative emotionality), and cooperation with supervision (one item). The STABLE-2007 factors are broadly consistent with the IDA and the Beech Deviancy Classification. The scale has been evaluated in prospective studies in Canada called the Dynamic Supervision Project (reported by Harris & Hanson, 2003; Hanson, 2005), and in Austria (Eher, Matthes, Schilling, Haubner-MacLean, & Rettenberger, 2012). The Canadian study, running between 2001 and 2006, followed over 1000 subjects under community supervision who had sexually offended against children or adults in all Canadian provinces, all three Canadian territories, and the Correctional Service of Canada, Alaska, and Iowa. The interrater reliability of STABLE-2000 was reported by Hanson (2005) as very good (ICC = 0.90), and the predictive accuracy being reasonably good (AUC = 0.76), for a sexual offence, and slightly better (AUC = 0.77) for any sexual offence/breach. Eher et al. (2012) reported for the STABLE-2000 and the STABLE-2007 moderate to good predictive accuracy (AUC = 0.62–0.71) after an average follow-up period of 6.4 years. In both prospective studies (Eher et al., 2012; Hanson et al., 2007), the STABLE-2007 was substantially better in predicting recidivism than its predecessor.

The ACUTE-2007 covers the following acute risk factors: victim access; emotional collapse (i.e., evidence of severe emotional disturbance/emotional crisis); collapse of social supports; hostility; substance abuse; sexual preoccupations; and rejection of supervision. The ACUTE-2007 contains two separate risk assessment dimensions: one dimension consists of acute risk factors relevant specifically for the prediction of violent and sexual recidivism (victim access, hostility, sexual preoccupation, and rejection of supervision) and the other dimension is conceptualized as a general criminality factor which contains all seven of the above-mentioned specified risk factors. The option of an eighth unspecified unique risk factor was dropped in the revised ACUTE-2007 version because this option was only rarely used and it had no relationship with recidivism (Harris & Hanson, 2010).

Identifying Areas of Intervention from Dynamic Risk Assessments

Consistent with Harkins and Beech (2007) (see Table 55.1), common across the various dynamic frameworks are four broad categories of problems: (1) (deviant) sexual interests and sexual preoccupation, (2) distorted cognitions supportive of sexual offending, (3) problematic socioaffective functioning, and (4) self-regulatory problems. These domains are consistent with the newly developed SARNR framework.

Deviant Sexual Interests

Sexual interest refers to a preference for, or strong interest in, sex with children or sexualized violence. Such interests are assessed, where possible, by physiological assessment, using penile plethysmography (PPG), official offence history, and/or self-report assessment (Craig & Beech, 2009). The extent to which an offender is generally preoccupied with sex is also related to sexual reoffending (Craig et al., 2006b; Mann, Hanson, & Thornton, 2010). Sexual offenders tend to give sex an exaggerated importance in their lives, and this importance dominates their psychological functioning (Mann et al., 2010). Sexual preoccupation is evidenced by a high frequency of impersonal sex and general sexual dissatisfaction (Mann et al., 2010). Furthermore, sexual offenders utilize both consenting and deviant sex to cope with life's difficulties and manage negative emotional states (Cortoni & Marshall, 2000), and this tendency is strongly related to sexual recidivism (Hanson et al., 2007). The presence of multiple paraphilias (deviant sexual interests) provides another indication of sexual preoccupation (Knight & Thornton, 2007).

Distorted Cognitions Supportive of Sexual Offending

This domain describes the styles of thinking that support sexual offending and are related to sexually offending behaviour (Mann et al., 2010). Sexual offenders typically hold views that support sexual offending. They also hold stereotypical, hostile, or distorted views of women, children, and sex. Offenders additionally have core beliefs about themselves and the world that predispose them to interpret ambiguous or threatening information in a hostile fashion. This predisposition, in turn, interacts with other factors such as deviant arousal or impulsivity to lead to sexual offending (Mann & Beech, 2003). Distorted cognitions can be assessed by self-reports (e.g., Bumby, 1996), or during an interview (Beech, Fisher & Ward, 2005; Beech, Ward, & Fisher, 2006; Hanson & Harris, 2001). Areas to be assessed include attitudes that generally excuse sexual offending, attitudes that indicate a sense of entitlement to sex, maladaptive beliefs about relationships, gender roles, and sexualized attitudes towards children (Thornton, 2002).

Socioaffective Difficulties (Relationships and Intimacy Deficits)

This domain relates to interpersonal difficulties, particularly characterized by a lack of emotional intimacy in relationships. Either a lack of intimate partners or the presence of conflicts within an existing relationship is predictive of sexual reoffending (Hanson & Morton-Bourgon, 2005). For rapists, difficulties in intimate relationships may be related to their experiences of adversarial or impersonal relationships with family and peers or to a general lack of concern for others (Mann et al., 2010). For men who sexually abuse children, the presence of emotional over-identification (emotional congruence) with children interferes with their ability to establish healthy adult relationships (Wilson, 1999) and is a powerful predictor of sexual recidivism (Hanson et al., 2007).

Poor Self-Regulation

This domain has two separate, but related, aspects. The first aspect refers to low self-control, impulsive lifestyle, and poor problem-solving abilities, characteristics predictive of recidivism among all offenders (Thornton, 2002). Higher risk offenders tend to exhibit chronic instability in employment and housing and have difficulties managing their daily lives. The second aspect refers to rule violations and a lack of cooperation with supervision. Offenders most at risk of recidivism tend to break their conditions of community supervision and fail to meet other commitments such as work or treatment demands. They also minimize their risk, and fail to engage in self-management strategies, including dropping out of treatment (Hanson & Morton-Bourgon, 2005).

Risk assessment involving either static or dynamic factors, or their combination, has generally come about without the benefit of substantial theoretical foundations, and the application of actuarial scales in particular has been criticized for being atheoretical. One reason why dynamic factors have yet to be fully integrated with actuarial measures may lie in the definitional problems.

Functional Links Between Static and Dynamic Factors

As the research by Wakeling et al. (2013) and Craig et al. (2007) has suggested, the relationship between static and dynamic risk factors is not clear, and it is possible that static risk items are historic markers of dynamic risk factors. It could be that the psychometric (dynamic) markers and static risk factors are so highly correlated that the psychometric measures are unlikely to be able to add any predictive power to static risk items. As Beech and Craig (2012) noted, traditionally the assumption has been that static and dynamic are treated separately, assuming an orthogonal relationship between the two concepts. Orthogonal data are usually considered to be mutually exclusive, the features of which can be used without thinking about how that usage will affect other features. This assumes independence between two data sets or concepts of risk assessment. Where a relationship is said to exist, the data cannot be assumed to be orthogonal but dependent in some way. This makes an important difference to our statistical modelling because, in orthogonal designs, the variation that is attributable to a given factor is constant, and does not depend upon the order in which factors are removed from the model. In relation to sexual offender risk assessment, if static and dynamic factors can be shown to be dependent factors, then orthogonal assumptions are questioned. There is a growing body of research drawing parallels between static and dynamic factors suggesting that the two concepts are functionally linked.

Primary/Trait Factors and Sexual Interests/Socioaffective Functioning

Beech and Ward (2004) attempted to integrate risk factors conceptually with more aetiological factors, mapping the causal relationships between risk factors (static and dynamic) and the clinical problems identified in sexual offenders. Their aetiological risk model encourages practitioners to view static factors as proxies to psychological vulnerabilities, which are changeable and become targets for intervention. Under these circumstances, 'static risk' misrepresents these primary/trait risk factors such as history (persistence) of sexual offending, intimacy deficits, and self-regulatory problems (e.g., impulsivity), which later become treatment targets. Indeed, there is some evidence to indicate actuarial (static) risk factors are artefacts of sexual preference/antisocial traits (Roberts, Doren, & Thornton, 2002), which are potentially changeable, demonstrating reductions in deviancy domains following treatment.

Primary/Trait Factors and Distorted Cognitions

Beech and Craig (2012) have tried to make more explicit the commonalities between actuarial (static) risk and dynamic frameworks (Table 55.2). The argument can be most clearly made by mapping of static risk factors, described in some of the better known risk schedules, onto the four risk domains described above. Table 55.2 clearly indicates that Static-99/2002, SORAG, SVR-20, and the RM2000/S contain items that are risk markers of *sexual interests, intimacy (socioaffective) deficits,* and *self-regulatory*. Beech and Ward (2004) suggested these are proxy measures of the level of these problems in and offender's history. Table 55.2 also clearly indicates that these schedules, with the exception of the SVR-20, do not contain any items

Table 55.2 Mapping static and dynamic risk factors onto deviancy domains

Stable dynamic factors	ARAIs		SPJ		Dynamic frameworks		
	Static-99/2002 (Hanson & Thornton, 2000)	SORAG (Quinsey et al., 1998)	Risk Matrix 2000/S (Thornton et al., 2003)	SVR-20 (Boer et al., 1997)	Beech Deviancy Classification (Beech, 1998; Beech et al., 2002)	STABLE-2007 (Hanson et al., 2007)	SRA/SARN (Thornton, 2002; Webster et al., 2006)
Sexual interests (obsession/ preoccupation)	Non-contact sexual offence Unrelated victim Stranger victim Prior sexual offence Sentencing occasions Male victim	Deviant sexual preference Prior sexual convictions	Sexual appearances Sexual offences against a male Non-contact sexual offences Stranger victim	Deviant sexual preference High-frequency sexual offences Multiple sexual offences Escalation of sexual offences	Sexually obsessed Sex deviance patterns (child molestation) marked	Sexual preoccupation/ sex drive Sex as a coping strategy Deviant sexual interests	Sexual preoccupation (obsession) Sexual preference for children Sexualized violence Other offence-related sexual interests (fetish)
Attitudes supportive of sexual offence				Pro-offending attitudes (extreme minimization and denial)	Distorted attitudes about children and children's sexuality Distorted attitudes about own victims Justifications for sexual deviance	Sexual entitlement Pro-rape attitudes Child molester attitudes	Adversarial sexual attitudes Sexual entitlement Child abuse-supportive beliefs Belief women are deceitful

Domain							
Relationships (intimacy deficits)	No relationships	Never married	Single (never been married)	Relationship problems; Employment problems	Emotional identification with children; Low self-esteem; Emotional loneliness; Under-assertiveness; Personal distress; Locus of control	Lack of lovers/intimate partners; Emotional identification with children; Hostility towards women; General social rejection/loneliness; Lack of concern for others	Personal inadequacy; Emotional congruence with children; Grievance stance; Emotional loneliness (lack of intimate relationships)
Self-regulation	Index non-sex violence; Prior non-sex violence; Age (18–24.9 years)	Violent criminality; Non-violent criminality; Psychopathy; Failure of conditional release	Age (18–34 years); Criminal appearances	Violent non-sex offences; General criminality; Psychopathy; Impulsivity		Impulsive acts; Poor cognitive problem-solving skills; Negative emotionality/hostility	Lifestyle impulsiveness – Impulsive, unstable lifestyle; Poor problem-solving ability; Poor emotional control

Source: adapted from Beech & Craig (2012).

measuring distorted attitudes. This is unsurprising, as there would not appear to be many historical items that could actually do this. The relationship between cognitive distortions (distorted attitudes) and sexual recidivism risk has yet to be made strongly (e.g., Hanson & Bussière, 1998; Hanson & Morton-Bourgon, 2005; Wakeling, Freemantle, Beech, & Elliott, 2011).

Marshall and Marshall (2010) raised concern that traditional 'cognitive–behavioural' intervention programmes target features that have been shown not to predict re-offending (i.e., denial and various other so-called 'distorted cognitions'; Marshall, Marshall, & Kingston, 2011; Marshall, Marshall, & Ware, 2009). Indeed, Marshall et al. (2009) noted that issues such as offence disclosures, denial, failing to take responsibility, and victim empathy are unrelated to sexual recidivism and are therefore not legitimate treatment targets. Marshall et al. (2009) suggested that low self-esteem and shame lead sexual offenders to generate distortions about their crimes and to adopt beliefs and attitudes that justify their offences. They argued that when a sexual offender denies he has caused any harm, he can hardly be expected to express empathy towards his victim even though he may otherwise be an empathic person.

In exploring the relationship between programme-identified treatment targets (including denial), Kingston (2010) examined the scores of 275 sexual offenders on three risk assessment instruments. Among the treatment targets identified, denial was found to be *negatively* related to scores on three risk instruments: the Static-99, the STABLE-2000, and the Violence Risk Scale: Sexual Offender Version (VRS:SO) (Olver, Wong, Nicholaichuk, & Gordon, 2007). Marshall et al. (2011) suggested that denial actually predicts a lowered chance of reoffending; in this view, denial and the other features showing an inverse relationship with risk assessment scores appear to serve as protective factors. Indeed, Hood, Shute, Feilzer, and Wilcox (2002) found that 2.1% of deniers were reconvicted of a new sexual offence compared with 17% of admitters. More recently, Harkins, Beech, and Goodwill (2010) examined denial in terms of denial of index offence, denial of risk, and absolute denial in a sample of 180 male sexual offenders. They reported a sexual recidivism rate of 15% over a 10-year follow-up. They found that high denial was significantly associated with lower sexual reconviction than for those low in denial. Absolute deniers did not differ from admitters in rates of sexual recidivism and the odds of sexual reoffending were significantly lower for those who denied future risk than those who admitted future risk. Harkins et al. (2010) also looked at levels of motivation to engage in treatment and found that those considered to be high motivators for treatment had a significantly higher risk for reoffending than low motivators. More recently, Harkins, Howard, Barnett, Wakeling, and Miles (2015) examined the relationship between denial, static risk, and sexual recidivism among different sexual offender types ($n = 6471$). The overall 2-year proven sexual reoffending rate was 3.2%. The sexual recidivism rates differed for offender types. For contact offenders with adult victims, it was 2.6%; for those with a contact offence against an intra-familial child victim, it was 1.1% compared with 3.6% for extra-familial offenders; for those with a contact offence against a child and whose relationship to the child victim was unknown, the 2-year proven sexual reoffending rate was 2.2 %; for those with non-contact offences relating to indecent images of children, the 2-year proven sexual reoffending rate was 2.7%; and for those with any other type of non-contact offence, the rate was 10.1%.

Denial was measured using a dichotomous item from the Offender Assessment System (OASys), 'Does the offender accept responsibility for the current offence(s)?'. The OASys is a structured clinical risk/needs assessment and management tool. It is used throughout NOMS in England and Wales with offenders aged 18 years and over who were convicted awaiting sentence, serving custodial sentences of at least 12 months, or serving probation sentences involving supervision. Some significant differences between deniers and admitters emerged, with deniers being older and having more criminal convictions or cautions than those who accepted responsibility for their current sexual offence. However, when sexual recidivism rates were examined, there were no significant differences between 2-year rates of proven sexual reoffending between those who accepted responsibility and those who denied responsibility for any of these offender types. Denial of responsibility predicted sexual recidivism independent of static risk measured by the modified RM2000/S, with those who denied responsibility being associated with decreased sexual recidivism. There was a moderate but non-significant difference in 2-year proven sexual reoffending rates between those who accepted responsibility (3.5%) and those who denied responsibility (2.7%). Together with earlier research, these findings do not indicate that denial is related to increased risk of sexual recidivism.

Primary/Trait Factors and Self-Regulation

From Table 55.2, self-regulatory factors include age (immaturity), violent propensity, impulsivity, negative emotionality/hostility, and poor problem-solving ability, many of which map onto ARAIs. The effect of age on sexual recidivism risk has been investigated, with a consensus that there is an inverse relationship between age and sexual reconviction (Barbaree, Blanchard, & Langton, 2003; Fazel, Sjöstedt, Långström, & Grann, 2006; Hanson, 2002, 2006; Lussier & Healey, 2009; Skelton & Vess, 2008). However, some more recent studies have reported contradictory results (Harris & Rice, 2007; Langan, Schmitt, & Durose, 2003; Prentky & Lee, 2007; Rettenberger, Briken, Turner, & Eher, 2015; Rettenberger, Haubner-MacLean, & Eher, 2013) with respect to the previously held conventional wisdom that age is inversely related to risk of sexual reconviction (for a review of the literature, see Craig, 2008). Nevertheless, consistently younger aged sexual offenders (<24 years old) are more often categorized as high risk (even when controlling for age as a risk factor), and as a predictor of sexual reconviction, the risk factor '<24 years' produced the most promising results (AUC = 0.61) compared with older age groups (Craig, 2011).

Turning to psychological factors such as violent propensity, impulsivity, negative emotionality/hostility, and poor problem-solving ability, Craig et al. (2007) considered the effectiveness of psychometric markers of risk. Of the sample of 119 sex offenders, 7 (6%), 14 (12%), and 17 (14%) were reconvicted of a sexual offences over the 2-, 5-, and 10-year follow-up periods, respectively. Although not significant, the trend was for the recidivists to obtain higher scores on measures of hostility, depression, and psychopathic deviate (violent propensity). Wakeling et al. (2013) found that measures of impulsivity have demonstrated reasonable indices of predictive accuracy, with AUC = 0.63 at 2-year follow-up.

Redefining Dynamic Risk Factors

From what we have discussed thus far, the relationship between static and dynamic risk factors is less blurred. There is some evidence that static items act as historic markers of dynamic risk factors, which are manifestations of psychological vulnerabilities. However, as Ward and Beech (2015) argue, to refer to dynamic risk factors without considering the various 'symptoms' or cluster of symptoms which make up dynamic domains is insufficient.

Ward and Beech (2015) argue that relatively little attention has been paid to theoretical issues related to risk and its conceptualization and they suggest alternative ways of understanding dynamic risk factors and their utility in theory construction and case formulation. They argue that the structure and function of dynamic risk factors is not clearly understood and has been neglected in theoretical development. They suggest that dynamic risk factors are complex clinical constructs with multiple, sometimes contradictory, conceptual strands and one should separate out the symptom-like or descriptive aspects of dynamic risk factors from their causal components, and use the nascent causal strands of dynamic risk factors to construct explanatory theories – in essence, developing a clinical theoretical understanding of the symptoms, or cluster of symptoms, which manifest in psychological vulnerabilities, which have until now been vaguely referred to as dynamic risk factors.

Ward and Beech (2015) suggest that dynamic factors should be viewed in clinical terms. For example, clusters of problems such as distorted thinking, social difficulties and intimacy problems, problems with controlling mood, negative mood, inappropriate sexual thoughts and fantasies, substance use problems, and difficulty problem solving and goal setting can be discerned in sexual offenders. They argue that all of these 'symptoms' can be conceptually linked to dynamic risk factors, but there has been no attempt to conceive them in terms of psychologically meaningful causes. They suggest that for all practical purposes, the language when referring to dynamic risk factors in clinical practice will remain largely unchanged. However, researchers should adopt a different conceptual structure where dynamic risk factors are viewed as hybrid concepts containing 'symptom' or phenomena aspects and aetiological aspects, introducing a separate explanatory phase of research that concentrates on developing causal explanations of the exemplar (i.e., symptoms, psychological problems) and its associated phenomena (Ward & Beech, 2015).

Conclusions

There have been great advances in the assessment of risk and the assessment of treatment need in sexual offenders, and the literature has witnessed a proliferation of risk scales, structured professional protocols, and psychometric measures designed to identify individuals who pose the greatest risk and treatment need. What appears consistent throughout the research is that objective and structured assessment protocols, incorporating those criminogenic factors considered to be relevant to sexual offending behaviour, produce the most promising results in differentiating levels of risk and treatment deficits in sexual offenders.

Developments in structured assessments of dynamic risk and treatment need empha-size the inclusion of protective factors making more explicit issues of responsivity in addition to factors of desistance as part of a more balanced assessment framework. Traditional assessments of risk are balanced with success factors focusing on good citizenship and adhering to supervision requirements. This is in keeping with the emerging desistance literature and ideas of Quality of Life (QoL) and the Good Lives Model (GML).

Aligned with this is our current understanding of static and dynamic risk factors with emerging evidence which suggests that these factors may be functionally linked and represent manifestations of the same behaviour measured and presented in different forms. A promising area of development is viewing dynamic factors as symptoms as part of a clinical theoretical understanding of behaviour that manifest in the form of psychological vulnerabilities. Future research into the assessment of risk and treatment need may look to redefine our understanding of traditional concepts such as static and dynamic risk factors as part of a more theoretically coherent approach to understanding the 'symptoms' (psychological problems) associated with sexual offending behaviour.

References

Allan, A., Dawson, D., & Allan, M. M. (2006). Prediction of the risk of male sexual reoffending in Australia. *Australian Psychologist*, *41*, 60–68.

Baltieri, D. A., & de Andrade, A. G. (2008). Comparing serial and non-serial sexual offenders: Alcohol and street drug consumption, impulsiveness and history of sexual abuse. *Revista Brasileira de Psiquiatria*, *30*, 25–31.

Barbaree, H. E., Blanchard, R., & Langton, C. M. (2003). The development of sexual aggres-sion through the lifespan: The effect of age on sexual arousal and recidivism among sex offenders. *Annals of the New York Academy of Sciences*, *989*, 59–71.

Barbaree, H. E., Langton, C. M., Blanchard, R., & Boer, D. P. (2008). Predicting recidivism in sex offenders using the SVR-20: The contribution of age-at-release. *International Journal of Forensic Mental Health*, *7*, 47–64.

Beech, A. R. (1998). A psychometric typology of child abusers. *International Journal of Offender Therapy and Comparative Criminology*, *42*, 319–339.

Beech, A. R., & Craig, L. A. (2012). The current status of static and dynamic factors in sex-ual offender risk assessment. *Journal of Aggression, Conflict and Peace Research*, *4*(12), 169–185.

Beech, A. R., Erikson, M., Friendship, C., & Hanson, R. K. (2002). Static and dynamic predic-tors of reconviction. *Sexual Abuse: A Journal of Research and Treatment*, *14*, 153–165.

Beech, A., Fisher, D., & Ward, T. (2005). Sexual murderers' implicit theories. *Journal of Inter-personal Violence*, *20*, 1366–1389.

Beech, A.R., & Ward, T. (2004). The integration of etiology and risk in sex offenders: A theo-retical model. *Aggression and Violent Behavior*, *10*, 31–63.

Beech, A. R., Ward, T., & Fisher, D. (2006). The identification of sexual and violent motivations in men who assault women: Implications for treatment. *Journal of Interpersonal Violence*, *21*, 1635–1653.

Bengtson, S. (2008). Is newer better? A cross-validation of the Static-2002 and the Risk Matrix 2000 in a Danish sample of sexual offenders. *Psychology, Crime and Law*, *14*, 85–106.

Boer, D. P. (2011, October). *SVR-20 2nd edition updates*. Presented at the Workshop at the New Directions in Sex Offender Practice Conference, Birmingham, England.

Boer, D. P., Frixe, M., Pappas, R., Morrissey, C., & Lindsay, W. R. (2010). In L. A. Craig., W. R. Lindsay, & K. D. Browne (Eds.), *Assessment and treatment of sexual offenders with intellectual disabilities: A handbook* (pp. 193–209). Chichester, England: John Wiley & Sons, Ltd.

Boer, D. P., Hart, S. D., Kropp, P. R., & Webster, C. D. (1997). *Manual for the Sexual Violence Risk-20: Professional guidelines for assessing risk of sexual violence*. Vancouver, Canada: Mental Health, Law, and Policy Institute, Simon Frazer University.

Bumby, K. (1996). Assessing the cognitive distortions of child molesters and rapists: Development and validation of the RAPE and MOLEST scales. *Sexual Abuse: A Journal of Research and Treatment, 8,* 37–54.

Cohen, J. (1992). A power primer. *Psychological Bulletin, 112,* 155–159. doi:10.1037/0033-2909.112.1.155

Cortoni, F., Craig, L. A., & Beech, A. R. (2010). Risk assessment of sexual offenders. In M. Herzog-Evans (Ed.), *Transnational criminology* (Vol. 3, pp. 503–527). Nijmegen, The Netherlands: Wolf Legal Publishers.

Cortoni, F., & Marshall, W. L. (2000). Sex a coping mechanism in sex offenders. *Sexual Abuse: A Journal of Research and Treatment, 12,* 27–44.

Craig, L. A. (2008). How should we understand the effect of age on sexual reconviction? *Journal of Sexual Aggression, 14,* 185–198.

Craig, L. A. (2010). Controversies in assessing risk and deviancy in sex offenders with intellectual disabilities. *Psychology, Crime & Law, 16*(1–2), 75–101.

Craig, L. A. (2011). The effect of age on sexual and violent reconviction. *International Journal of Offender Therapy and Comparative Criminology, 55*(1), 75–97.

Craig, L. A., & Beech, A. R. (2009). Psychometric assessment of sexual deviance. In A. R. Beech, L. A. Craig, & K. D. Browne, *Assessment and treatment of sex offenders: A handbook* (pp. 89–107). Chichester, England: John Wiley & Sons, Ltd.

Craig, L. A., & Beech, A. R. (2010). Towards a guide to best practice in conducting actuarial risk assessments with sex offenders. *Aggression and Violent Behavior, 15,* 278–293.

Craig, L. A., Beech, A. R., & Browne, K. D. (2006a). A cross-validation of Risk Matrix 2000 Sexual and Violent scales. *Journal of Interpersonal Violence, 21,* 612–633.

Craig, L. A., Browne, K. D., Beech, A., & Stringer, I. (2006b). Psychosexual characteristics of sexual offenders and the relationship to reconviction. *Psychology, Crime and Law, 12,* 231–243.

Craig, L. A., Browne, K. D., Stringer, I., & Beech, A. (2004). Limitations in actuarial risk assessment of sexual offenders: A methodological note. *The British Journal of Forensic Practice, 6,* 16–32.

Craig, L. A., Thornton, D., Beech, A. R., & Browne, K. D. (2007). The relationship of statistical and psychological risk markers to sexual reconviction. *Criminal Justice and Behavior, 34,* 314–329.

de Vogel, V., de Ruiter, C., van Beek, D., & Mead, G. (2004). Predictive validity of the SVR-20 and Static-99 in a Dutch sample of treated sex offenders. *Law and Human Behavior, 28,* 235–251.

Ducro, C., & Pham, T. (2006). Evaluation of the SORAG and the Static-99 in Belgian sex offenders committed to a forensic facility. *Sexual Abuse: A Journal of Research and Treatment, 18,* 15–26.

Eher, R., Matthes, A., Schilling, F. Haubner-MacLean, T., & Rettenberger, M. (2012). Dynamic risk assessment in sexual offenders using STABLE-2000 and the STABLE-2007: An investigation of predictive and incremental validity. *Sexual Abuse: A Journal of Research and Treatment, 24,* 5–28.

Fazel, S., Sjöstedt, G., Långström, N., & Grann, M. (2006). Risk factors for criminal recidivism in older sexual offenders. *Sexual Abuse: A Journal of Research and Treatment*, *18*, 159–167.

Hanson, R. K. (2002). Recidivism and age: Follow-up data from 4,673 sexual offenders. *Journal of Interpersonal Violence*, *17*, 1046–1062.

Hanson, R. K. (2005). Twenty years of progress in violence risk assessment. *Journal of Interpersonal Violence*, *2*, 212–217.

Hanson, R. K. (2006). Does Static-99 predict recidivism among older sexual offenders? *Sexual Abuse: A Journal of Research and Treatment*, *18*, 343–356.

Hanson, R. K., & Bussière, M. T. (1998). Predicting relapse: A meta-analysis of sexual offender recidivisim studies. *Journal of Consulting and Clinical Psychology*, *66*, 348–362.

Hanson. R. K., & Harris. A. (1998). *Dynamic predictors of sexual recidivism* (User Report 1998-01). Ottawa, Canada: Corrections Research Ottawa, Department of the Solicitor General Canada. Retrieved from www.static99.org/pdfdocs/hansonandharris1998.pdf

Hanson, R. K., & Harris, A. J. R. (2000). Where should we intervene? Dynamic predictors of sexual offense recidivism. *Criminal Justice and Behavior*, *27*, 6–35.

Hanson, R. K., & Harris, A. (2001). *The Sex Offender Need Assessment Rating (SONAR): A method for measuring change in risk levels*. Retrieved from https://www.publicsafety.gc.ca/cnt/rsrcs/pblctns/sx-ffndr-nd/index-en.aspx [note that this is an older version of SONAR and should not be used].

Hanson, R. K., Harris, A. J. R., Scott, T.-L., & Helmus, L. (2007). *Assessing the risk of sexual offenders on community supervision: The Dynamic Supervision Project* (User Report 2007-05). Ottawa, Canada: Public Safety Canada. Retrieved from http://www.static99.org/pdfdocs/hansonharrisscottandhelmus2007.pdf

Hanson, R. K., & Morton-Bourgon, K. (2005). *Predictors of sexual recidivism: An updated meta-analysis*. Ottawa, Canada: Corrections Research, Public Safety and Emergency Preparedness Canada. Retrieved from https://www.publicsafety.gc.ca/cnt/rsrcs/pblctns/2004-02-prdctrs-sxl-rcdvsm-pdtd/index-en.aspx

Hanson, R. K., & Morton-Bourgon, K. (2009). The accuracy of recidivism risk assessments for sexual offenders: A meta-analysis of 118 prediction studies. *Psychological Assessment*, *21*, 1–21.

Hanson, R. K., & Thornton, D. (2000). Improving risk assessments for sex offenders: A comparison of three actuarial scales. *Law and Human Behavior*, *24*(1), 119–136.

Hanson, R. K., & Thornton, D. (2003). *Notes on the development of Static-2002*. Retrieved from http://www.publicsafety.gc.ca/cnt/rsrcs/pblctns/nts-dvlpmnt-sttc/nts-dvlpmnt-sttc-eng.pdf

Hare, R. D. (2003). *The Hare Psychopathy Checklist – Revised* (2nd ed.). Toronto, Canada: Multi-Health Systems.

Harkins, L., & Beech, A.R. (2007). A review of the factors that can influence the effectiveness of sexual offender treatment: Risk, need, responsivity, and process issues. *Aggression and Violent Behavior*, *12*, 615–627.

Harkins, L., Beech, A. R., & Goodwill, A. M. (2010). Examining the influence of denial, motivation, and risk in sexual offenders. *Sexual Abuse: A Journal of Research and Treatment*, *22*, 78–94.

Harkins, L., Howard, P., Barnett, G., Wakeling, H., & Miles, C. (2015). Relationships between denial, risk, and recidivism in sexual offenders. *Archives of Sexual Behavior*, *44*, 157–166.

Harris, A. J. R., & Hanson, R. K. (2003). The Dynamic Supervision Project: Improving the community supervision of sex offenders. *Corrections Today*, *65*(5), 60–64.

Harris, A. J. R., & Hanson, R. K. (2010). Clinical, actuarial, and dynamic risk assessment of sexual offenders: Why do things keep changing? *Journal of Sexual Aggression*, *16*, 296–310.

Harris, G. T., & Rice, M. E. (2007). Adjusting actuarial violence risk assessments based on aging or the passage of time. *Criminal Justice and Behavior, 34*, 267–313.

Hart, S., Laws, D. R., & Kropp, P. R. (2003). The promise and the peril of sex offender risk assessment. In T. Ward., D. R. Laws, & S. M. Hudson (Eds.), *Sexual deviance: Issues and controversies* (pp. 207–225). Thousand Oaks, CA: Sage.

Helmus, L., Thornton, D., Hanson, R. K., & Babchishin, K. M. (2012). Improving the predictive accuracy of Static-99 and Static-2002 with older sex offenders: Revised age weights. *Sexual Abuse: A Journal of Research and Treatment, 24*(1), 64–101.

Hood, R., Shute, S., Feilzer, M., & Wilcox, A. (2002). Sex offenders emerging from long-term imprisonment: A study of their long-term reconviction rates and of parole board members' judgements of their risk. *British Journal of Criminology, 42*(2), 371–394.

Kingston, D. A. (2010). *The offense progression in sexual offenders: An examination of the self-regulation model of the offense process* (Unpublished doctoral dissertation). University of Ottawa, Ottawa, Canada.

Kingston, D. A., Yates, P. M., Firestone, P., Babchishin, K., & Bradford, J. (2008). Long term predictive validity of the Risk Matrix 2000: A comparison with the Static-99 and the Sex Offender Risk Appraisal Guide. *Sexual Abuse: A Journal of Research and Treatment, 20*, 466–484.

Knight, R. A., & Thornton, D. (2007). *Evaluating and improving risk assessment schemes for sexual recidivism: A long-term follow-up of convicted sexual offenders.* Retrieved from http://www.ncjrs.gov/pdffiles1/nij/grants/217618.pdf

Lanagan, P. A., Schmitt, E. L., & Durose, M. R. (2003). *Recidivism of sex offenders released from prison in 1994.* Washington, DC: US Department of Justice, Office of Justice Programs, Bureau of Justice Statistics.

Laws, D. R., & Ward, T. (2010). *Desistance from sex offending: Alternatives to throwing away the keys.* New York, NY: Guilford Press.

Lussier, P., & Healey, J. (2009). Rediscovering Quetelet, again: The 'aging' offender and the prediction of reoffending in a sample of adult sex offenders. *Justice Quarterly, 26*, 827–856.

Mann, R. E., & Beech, A. R. (2003). Cognitive distortions, schemas and implicit theories. In T. Ward, D. R. Laws, & S. M. Hudson (Eds.), *Theoretical issues and controversies in sexual deviance* (pp. 135–153). London, England: Sage.

Mann, R. E., Hanson, R. K., & Thornton, D. (2010). Assessing risk for sexual recidivism: Some proposals on the nature of psychologically meaningful risk factors. *Sexual Abuse: A Journal of Research and Treatment, 22*, 191–217.

Marshall, W. L., & Marshall, L. E. (2010). Can treatment be effective with sexual offenders or does it do harm? A response to Hanson (2010) and Rice (2010). *Sexual Offender Treatment, 5*(2), 1–8. Retrieved from http://www.sexual-offender-treatment.org/87.html

Marshall, W. L., Marshall, L. E., & Kingston, D. A. (2011) Are the cognitive distortions of child molesters in need of treatment? *Sexual Aggression, 17*, 118–129.

Marshall, W. L., Marshall, L. E., & Ware, J. (2009). Cognitive distortions in sexual offenders: Should they all be treatment targets? *Sexual Abuse in Australia and New Zealand, 2*, 70–78.

Ohlin, L. E. (1951). *Selection for parole: A manual for parole prediction.* New York, NY: Russell Sage Foundation.

Olver, M. E., Wong, S. C. P., Nicholaichuk, T., & Gordon, A. (2007). The validity and reliability of the Violence Risk Scale – Sexual Offender version: Assessing sex offender risk and evaluating therapeutic change. *Psychological Assessment, 19*, 318–329.

Phenix, A., Doren, D., Helmus, L., Hanson, R. K., & Thornton, D. (2008). *Coding rules for Static-2002.* Retrieved from www.static99.org/pdfdocs/static2002codingrules.pdf

Prentky, R. A., & Lee, A. F. S. (2007). Effect of age-at-release on long-term sexual re-offense rates in civilly committed sexual offenders. *Sexual Abuse: A Journal of Research and Treatment*, *119*, 43–59.

Quinsey, V. L., Harris, G. T., Rice, M. E., & Cormier, C. (1998). *Violent offenders: Appraising and managing risk* (1st ed.). Washington, DC: American Psychological Association.

Quinsey, V. L., Harris, G. T., Rice, M. E., & Cormier, C. (2006). *Violent offenders: Appraising and managing risk* (2nd ed.). Washington, DC: American Psychological Association.

Rettenberger, M., Boer, D. P., & Eher, R. (2011). The predictive accuracy of risk factors in the Sexual Violence Risk-20 (SVR-20). *Criminal Justice and Behavior*, *38*, 1009–1027.

Rettenberger, M., Briken, P., Turner, D., & Eher, R. (2015). Sexual offender recidivism among a population-based prison sample. *International Journal of Offender Therapy and Comparative Criminology*, *59*, 424–444.

Rettenberger, M., Haubner-MacLean, T. & Eher, R. (2013). The contribution of age to the Static-99 risk assessment in a population-based prison sample of sexual offenders. *Criminal Justice and Behavior*, *40*, 1413–1433.

Rettenberger, M., Matthes, A., Boer, D. P., & Eher, R. (2010). Actuarial recidivism risk assessment and sexual delinquency: A comparison of five risk assessment tools in different sexual offender subtypes. *International Journal of Offender Therapy and Comparative Criminology*, *54*, 169–186.

Rice, M. E., & Harris, G. T. (2005). Comparing effect sizes in follow-up studies: ROC, Cohen's *d* and *r*. *Law and Human Behavior*, *29*, 615–620. doi:10.1007/s10979-005-6832-7

Roberts, C. F., Doren, D. M., & Thornton, D. (2002). Dimensions associated with assessments of sex offender recidivism risk. *Criminal Justice and Behavior*, *29*, 569–589.

Sjöstedt, G., & Långström, N. (2002). Assessment of risk for criminal recidivism among rapists: A comparison of four different measures. *Psychology, Crime and Law*, *8*, 25–40.

Skelton, A., Riley, D., Wales, D., & Vess, J. (2006). Assessing risk for sexual offenders in New Zealand: Development and validation of a computer-scored risk measure. *Journal of Sexual Aggression*, *12*, 277–286.

Skelton, A., & Vess, J. (2008). Risk of sexual recidivism as a function of age and actuarial risk. *Journal of Sexual Aggression*, *14*, 199–209.

Stadtland, C., Hollweg, M., Kleindienst, N., Dietl, J., Reich, U., & Nedopil, N. (2005). Risk assessment and prediction of violent and sexual recidivism in sex offenders: Long-term predictive validity of four risk assessment instruments. *Journal of Forensic Psychiatry and Psychology*, *16*, 92–108.

Thornton, D. (2002). Constructing and testing a framework for dynamic risk assessment. *Sexual Abuse: A Journal of Research and Treatment*, *14*, 139–154.

Thornton, D., & Beech, A. R. (2002, October). *Integrating statistical and psychological factors through the structured risk assessment model*. Paper presented at the 21st Annual Research and Treatment Conference, Association of the Treatment of Sexual Abusers, Montreal, Canada.

Thornton, D., Mann, R., Webster, S., Blud, L., Travers, R., Friendship, C., & Erikson, M. (2003). Distinguishing and combining risks for sexual and violent recidivism. *Annals of the New York Academy of Sciences*, *989*, 225–235.

Tully, R., Browne, K. D., & Craig, L. A. (2015). An examination of the predictive validity of the Structured Assessment of Risk and Need Treatment Needs Analysis (SARN TNA) in England and Wales. *Criminal Justice and Behavior*, *42*, 509–528.

Wakeling, H., Beech, A. R., & Freemantle, N. (2013). Investigating treatment change and its relationship to recidivism in a sample of 3773 sex offenders in the UK. *Psychology, Crime and Law*, *19*(3), 233–252.

Wakeling, H., Freemantle, N., Beech, A. R., & Elliott, I. A. (2011). Identifying predictors of recidivism in a large sample of UK sexual offenders: A prognostic model. *Psychological Services*, *8*, 307–318.

Ward, T. (2002). Good lives and the rehabilitation of offenders: Promises and problems. *Aggression and Violent Behavior*, *7*, 513–528.

Ward, T., & Beech, A. R. (2015). Dynamic risk factors: A theoretical dead-end? *Psychology, Crime and Law*, *21*, 100–113.

Ward, T., & Maruna, S. (2007). *Rehabilitation: Beyond the risk assessment paradigm*. London, England: Routledge.

Webster, C. D., Douglas, K. S., Eaves, D., & Hart, S. D. (1997). *Historical Clinical Risk-20: Assessing risk for violence, version 2*. Burnaby, Canada: Simon Fraser University.

Webster, S. D., Mann, R. E., Carter, A. J., Long, J., Milner, R. J., O'Brien, M. D., ... Ray, N. L. (2006). Interrater reliability of dynamic risk assessment with sexual offenders. *Psychology, Crime and Law*, *12*, 439–452.

Wilson, R. J. (1999). Emotional congruence in sexual offenders against children. *Sexual Abuse: A Journal of Research and Treatment*, *11*, 33–47.